IFRS EDITION

INTERMEDIATE ACCOUNTING, VOLUME 2

IFRS EDITION

INTERMEDIATE ACCOUNTING, VOLUME 2

DONALD E. KIESO PH.D., C.P.A.
Northern Illinois University
DeKalb, Illinois

JERRY J. WEYGANDT PH.D., C.P.A.
University of Wisconsin
Madison, Wisconsin

TERRY D. WARFIELD PH.D.
University of Wisconsin
Madison, Wisconsin

WILEY

JOHN WILEY & SONS

Dedicated to our wives, Donna, Enid, and Mary, for their love, support, and encouragement

VICE PRESIDENT AND PUBLISHER	George Hoffman
ASSOCIATE PUBLISHER	Christopher DeJohn
SENIOR ACQUISITIONS EDITOR	Michael McDonald
PROJECT EDITOR	Brian Kamins
PROJECT EDITOR	Ed Brislin
DEVELOPMENT EDITOR	Terry Ann Tatro
ASSOCIATE DIRECTOR OF MARKETING	Amy Scholz
EXECUTIVE MEDIA EDITOR	Allison Morris
MEDIA EDITOR	Greg Chaput
CREATIVE DIRECTOR	Harold Nolan
SENIOR DESIGNER	Kevin Murphy
PRODUCTION MANAGER	Dorothy Sinclair
SENIOR PRODUCTION EDITOR	Trish McFadden
SENIOR PHOTO EDITOR	Elle Wagner
EDITORIAL ASSISTANT	Jacqueline Kepping
MARKETING ASSISTANT	Laura Finley
ASSISTANT MARKETING MANAGER	Diane Mars
PRODUCTION MANAGEMENT SERVICES	Ingrao Associates
COVER DESIGN	Michael Boland
COVER PHOTO	Earth Imaging/Stone/Getty Images
COVER CREDIT	Stone/Getty Images, Inc
CHAPTER OPENER PHOTO CREDIT	Pixtal/Superstock

This book was set in 10/12 Palatino by Aptara®, Inc. and printed and bound by Quad/Graphics. The cover was printed by Quad/Graphics.

This book is printed on acid free paper. ∞

The financial statements and accompanying notes reprinted from the 2008 Annual Report of Marks and Spencer plc are courtesy of Marks and Spencer plc, copyright @ 2008, all rights reserved.

ISBN-13 978-0470-61631-4

Printed in the United States of America

10 9 8 7 6 5 4 3 2 1

Donald E. Kieso, Ph.D., C.P.A., received his bachelor's degree from Aurora University and his doctorate in accounting from the University of Illinois. He has served as chairman of the Department of Accountancy and is currently the KPMG Emeritus Professor of Accountancy at Northern Illinois University. He has public accounting experience with Price Waterhouse & Co. (San Francisco and Chicago) and Arthur Andersen & Co. (Chicago) and research experience with the Research Division of the American Institute of Certified Public Accountants (New York). He has done postdoctorate work as a Visiting Scholar at the University of California at Berkeley and is a recipient of NIU's Teaching Excellence Award and four Golden Apple Teaching Awards. Professor Kieso is the author of other accounting and business books and is a member of the American Accounting Association, the American Institute of Certified Public Accountants, and the Illinois CPA Society. He has served as a member of the Board of Directors of the Illinois CPA Society, the AACSB's Accounting Accreditation Committees, the State of Illinois Comptroller's Commission, as Secretary-Treasurer of the Federation of Schools of Accountancy, and as Secretary-Treasurer of the American Accounting Association. Professor Kieso is currently serving on the Board of Trustees and Executive Committee of Aurora University, as a member of the Board of Directors of Kishwaukee Community Hospital, and as Treasurer and Director of Valley West Community Hospital. From 1989 to 1993 he served as a charter member of the national Accounting Education Change Commission. He is the recipient of the Outstanding Accounting Educator Award from the Illinois CPA Society, the FSA's Joseph A. Silvoso Award of Merit, the NIU Foundation's Humanitarian Award for Service to Higher Education, a Distinguished Service Award from the Illinois CPA Society, and in 2003 an honorary doctorate from Aurora University.

Jerry J. Weygandt, Ph.D., C.P.A., is Arthur Andersen Alumni Emeritus Professor of Accounting at the University of Wisconsin—Madison. He holds a Ph.D. in accounting from the University of Illinois. Articles by Professor Weygandt have appeared in the *Accounting Review, Journal of Accounting Research, Accounting Horizons, Journal of Accountancy*, and other academic and professional journals. These articles have examined such financial reporting issues as accounting for price-level adjustments, pensions, convertible securities, stock option contracts, and interim reports. Professor Weygandt is author of other accounting and financial reporting books and is a member of the American Accounting Association, the American Institute of Certified Public Accountants, and the Wisconsin Society of Certified Public Accountants. He has served on numerous committees of the American Accounting Association and as a member of the editorial board of the *Accounting Review;* he also has served as President and Secretary-Treasurer of the American Accounting Association. In addition, he has been actively involved with the American Institute of Certified Public Accountants and has been a member of the Accounting Standards Executive Committee (AcSEC) of that organization. He has served on the FASB task force that examined the reporting issues related to accounting for income taxes and served as a trustee of the Financial Accounting Foundation. Professor Weygandt has received the Chancellor's Award for Excellence in Teaching and the Beta Gamma Sigma Dean's Teaching Award. He is on the board of directors of M & I Bank of Southern Wisconsin. He is the recipient of the Wisconsin Institute of CPA's Outstanding Educator's Award and the Lifetime Achievement Award. In 2001 he received the American Accounting Association's Outstanding Accounting Educator Award.

Terry D. Warfield, Ph.D., is the Robert and Monica Beyer Professor of Accounting at the University of Wisconsin—Madison. He received a B.S. and M.B.A. from Indiana University and a Ph.D. in accounting from the University of Iowa. Professor Warfield's area of expertise is financial reporting, and prior to his academic career, he worked for five years in the banking industry. He served as the Academic Accounting Fellow in the Office of the Chief Accountant at the U.S. Securities and Exchange Commission in Washington, D.C. from 1995–1996. Professor Warfield's primary research interests concern financial accounting standards and disclosure policies. He has published scholarly articles in *The Accounting Review, Journal of Accounting and Economics, Research in Accounting Regulation*, and *Accounting Horizons*, and he has served on the editorial boards of *The Accounting Review, Accounting Horizons*, and *Issues in Accounting Education*. He has served as president of the Financial Accounting and Reporting Section, the Financial Accounting Standards Committee of the American Accounting Association (Chair 1995–1996), and on the AAA-FASB Research Conference Committee. He currently serves on the Financial Accounting Standards Advisory Council of the Financial Accounting Standards Board. Professor Warfield has received teaching awards at both the University of Iowa and the University of Wisconsin, and he was named to the Teaching Academy at the University of Wisconsin in 1995. Professor Warfield has developed and published several case studies based on his research for use in accounting classes. These cases have been selected for the AICPA Professor-Practitioner Case Development Program and have been published in *Issues in Accounting Education*.

Globalization is occurring rapidly. As economic and other interactions increase among countries, capital markets must provide high-quality financial information. A need therefore exists for high-quality financial reporting standards that meet this objective. Fortunately, **International Financial Reporting Standards (IFRS)** has broad international acceptance, being used in some form by more than 100 countries around the world. One securities regulator noted that IFRS is best positioned to serve as the single set of high-quality standards.

Change Is the Only Constant

Most countries want rapid action related to the acceptance of IFRS. In 2011, a number of countries will switch from their own version of accounting standards to IFRS. Students and instructors need educational materials related to IFRS in order to meet this new challenge. Our objective in writing *Intermediate Accounting*, IFRS Edition, was therefore to provide the tools needed to understand what IFRS is and how it is applied in practice. The emphasis on fair value, the proper accounting for financial instruments, and the new developments related to leasing, revenue recognition, and financial statement presentation are examined in light of current practice. In addition, given the rapid changes taking place, we provide and discuss the new conceptual framework to understand how these issues will likely be resolved in the future.

> "If this book helps teachers instill in their students an appreciation for the challenges, worth, and limitations of financial reporting, if it encourages students to evaluate critically and understand financial accounting concepts and practice, and if it prepares students for advanced study, professional examinations, and the successful and ethical pursuit of their careers in accounting or business in a global economy, then we will have attained our objectives."

IFRS—Not a Rule Book

IFRS attempts to provide a principles-based approach to the development of financial reporting standards. We therefore provide explanations of the conceptual basis used to determine standards and their related application in practice. Wherever possible, the explanations and discussions are supported and illustrated by examples from practice and from authoritative pronouncements.

A Look at U.S. GAAP

While IFRS has achieved broad acceptance, not all countries have adopted it. For example, U.S. companies still follow U.S. generally accepted accounting principles (GAAP) in preparing their financial statements. In fact, the differences between IFRS and GAAP may provide certain companies with a competitive advantage, so understanding these differences may be important in judging competing companies. In addition, the IASB and the FASB are working together to converge their standards as appropriate. Accordingly, we have included a **Convergence Corner** summary at the end of selected chapters, to highlight the important differences that remain between IFRS and GAAP, as well as the ongoing joint convergence efforts to resolve them. As a result, students truly gain a global accounting education by studying this text.

Intermediate Accounting Works

Intermediate Accounting, Thirteenth Edition (based on GAAP) is the market-leading textbook in providing the tools needed to understand what GAAP is and how it is applied in practice. With this IFRS Edition, we strive to provide the material needed to understand this subject area using IFRS. The book is comprehensive and up-to-date, and provides the instructor with flexibility in the topics to cover. We also include proven pedagogical tools, designed to help students learn more effectively and to answer the changing needs of this course. Pages vi–viii describes all of the learning tools of the textbook in detail.

We are excited about *Intermediate Accounting*, IFRS Edition. We believe it meets an important objective of providing useful information to educators and students interested in learning about IFRS. Suggestions and comments from users of this book will be appreciated. Please feel free to e-mail any one of us at *AccountingAuthors@yahoo.com*.

Donald E. Kieso
DeKalb, Illinois

Jerry J. Weygandt
Madison, Wisconsin

Terry D. Warfield
Madison, Wisconsin

FEATURES OF THE IFRS EDITION

We have developed a number of pedagogical features, designed both to help students learn more effectively and to answer the changing needs of the course.

**I
F
R
S**

Authoritative Literature

We provide references to the Authoritative Literature throughout the text. The complete citations and correspondence are presented in the Authoritative Literature section at the end of the chapter.

Underlying Concepts

Underlying Concepts

These marginal notes relate topics covered within each chapter back to the conceptual principles introduced in the beginning of the book. This continual reinforcement of the essential concepts and principles illustrates how the concepts are applied in practice and helps students understand the *why*, as well as the *how.*

Convergence Corner

Each chapter contains a single-page discussion, called the Convergence Corner, of the IFRS and GAAP accounting issues related to the chapter topics. Each Convergence Corner consists of four sections: (1) An introduction, which typically summarizes the relevant accounting issues; (2) "Relevant Facts," which explains similarities and differences of IFRS and GAAP; (3) "About the Numbers," which generally provides an example of application of GAAP (in many cases, using real companies); and (4) "On the Horizon," which discusses convergence progress and plans related to that topic. Each chapter also has assignment material related to this page.

Real-World Emphasis

One of the goals of the intermediate accounting course is to orient students to the application of accounting principles and techniques in practice. Accordingly, we provide numerous examples from real companies throughout the text. The names of these real companies are highlighted in red. Illustrations and exhibits marked by the icon shown here in the margin are excerpts from actual financial statements of real firms.

*What do the
numbers mean?*

At the start of each chapter, we provide chapter opening vignettes to provide an even better real-world context that helps motivate student interest in the chapter topic. Also, throughout the chapters, the "What Do the Numbers Mean?" boxed inserts also provide real-world extensions of the material presented in the text.

In addition, Appendix 5B contains the 2008 annual report of **Marks and Spencer plc (M&S)**. Problems in the *Using Your Judgment* section involve study of the M&S annual report or comparison of the annual reports of real companies.

Currency and Accuracy

Accounting continually changes as its environment changes; an up-to-date book is therefore a necessity. We have strived to make this IFRS Edition the most up-to-date and accurate textbook available. For the IFRS Edition, we performed three rounds of accuracy checking.

Using Your Judgment Section

The *Using Your Judgment* section at the end of each chapter includes the following elements:

- A Financial Reporting Problem, featuring **Marks and Spencer plc**.
- A Comparative Analysis Case, featuring **Cadbury** and **Nestlé**, that asks students to compare and contrast the financial reporting for these two companies.
- Financial Statement Analysis Cases that ask students to use the information in published accounting reports to conduct financial analysis.
- International Reporting Cases that explore differences in reporting by international companies.
- An Accounting, Analysis, and Principles review exercise, to help reinforce these three important elements of each chapter.
- A Professional Research case that gives students practice conducting authoritative research.
- A Professional Simulation, which provides students with an integrative context in which to apply the concepts learned in the chapter.

The *Using Your Judgment* assignments are designed to help develop students' critical thinking, analytical, and research skills.

END-OF-CHAPTER ASSIGNMENT MATERIAL

At the end of each chapter, we have provided a comprehensive set of review and home-work material. This section consists of Questions, Brief Exercises, Exercises, Problems, and short Concepts for Analysis exercises. These materials are followed by the Using Your Judgment section, described above. All of the assignment materials have been class-tested and/or triple-checked for accuracy and clarity.

The Questions are designed primarily for review, self-testing, and classroom dis-cussion purposes, as well as for homework assignments. Typically a Brief Exercise covers one topic, and an Exercise covers one or two topics. The Problems are designed to develop a professional level of achievement and are more challenging and time-consuming to solve than the Exercises. The Brief Exercises, Exercises, and Problems are classified by learning objective number. All Brief Exercises and Exercises and se-lected Problems are available in WileyPLUS with automatic grading capability. The Concepts for Analysis generally require discussion, as opposed to quantitative solu-tions. They are intended to confront the student with situations calling for concep-tual analysis and the exercise of judgment in identifying issues and problems and in evaluating alternatives.

Separate icons next to Exercises, Problems, and Concepts for Analysis indicate homework materials that offer more than just a quantitative challenge. Homework ma-terials that are especially suited for group assignments, for example, are identified by the icon shown here in the margin. Homework materials suitable as writing assign-ments are marked with the pencil icon shown here in the margin. Items that address ethics issues are identified by the scale (balance) icon. Homework materials that can be solved using the Excel Problems supplement are identified by the spreadsheet icon shown at right.

Probably no more than one-fourth of the total Exercise, Problem, and Concepts for Analysis material must be used to cover the subject matter adequately. Consequently, problem assignments may be varied from year to year without repetition.

WileyPlus

WileyPLUS is a suite of resources that contains online homework, with access to an online version of the text. WileyPLUS gives you the technology to create an environment where students reach their full potential and experience academic success. Instructor resources include a wealth of presentation and preparation tools, easy-to-navigate assignment and assessment tools, and a complete system to administer and manage your course exactly as you wish.

WileyPLUS is built around the activities you regularly perform:

- **Prepare and present class presentations** using relevant Wiley resources such as PowerPoint™ slides, image galleries, animations, and other materials. You can also upload your own resources or web pages to use in conjunction with Wiley materials.

- **Create assignments** by choosing from end-of-chapter exercises, selected problems, and test bank questions organized by chapter, study objective, level of difficulty, and source—or add your own questions. WileyPLUS automatically grades students' homework and quizzes, and records the results in your gradebook.

- **Offer context-sensitive help to students, 24/7.** When you assign homework or quizzes, you decide if and when students get access to hints, solutions, or answers where appropriate. Or they can be linked to relevant sections of their complete, online text for additional help whenever and wherever they need it most.

- **Track student progress.** You can analyze students' results and assess their level of understanding on an individual and class level using the WileyPLUS gradebook, and you can export data to your own personal gradebook.

- Seamlessly integrate all of the rich WileyPLUS content and resources with the power and convenience of your **WebCT** or **Blackboard** course—with a single sign-on.

SUPPLEMENTARY MATERIALS

Accompanying this textbook is a complete package of student learning aids and instructor teaching aids. The book companion site portal at *www.wiley.com/college/kiesoifrs* provides various tools for students and instructors. In addition, as described earlier, WileyPLUS offers resources to help you prepare class presentations, create assignments, offer help to students, and track student progress.

Other teaching and learning aids to supplement the textbook are described below.

Instructor Teaching Aids

The following teaching aids are available to support instructors using the IFRS Edition.

Solutions Manual, Vols. 1 and 2. The *Solutions Manual* provides answers to all end-of-chapter questions, brief exercises, exercises, problems, and case materials. Classification tables categorize solutions by topic, and the new solutions manual also categorizes solutions by textbook learning objective. The estimated time to complete exercises, problems, and cases is provided.

Test Bank: Vols. 1 and 2. The IFRS Edition Test Bank contains *over 500 testing questions.* Exercises, problems, true/false, multiple choice, and conceptual short-answer questions help instructors test students' knowledge and communication skills.

Instructor's Manual, Vols. 1 and 2. The *Instructor's Manual* contains lecture outlines, chapter reviews, sample syllabi, and much more.

PowerPoint™ Presentations. The PowerPoint™ presentations are designed to enhance classroom presentation of chapter topics and examples.

Course Management Resources. Course content cartridges are available from both WebCT and Blackboard.

Student Learning Aids

Student Study Guide, Vols. 1 and 2. Each chapter of the Study Guide contains a chapter review, chapter outline, and a glossary of key terms. Demonstration problems, multiple-choice, true/false, matching, and other exercises are included.

Working Papers, Vols. 1 and 2. The working papers are printed templates that can help students correctly format their textbook accounting solutions. Working paper templates are available for all end-of-chapter brief exercises, exercises, problems, and cases.

ACKNOWLEDGMENTS

We thank the many users of our first 13 U.S. GAAP editions, who contributed to this IFRS Edition through their comments and instructive criticism. Special thanks are extended to the focus group participants and the primary reviewers of and contributors to our IFRS Edition manuscript.

We also thank other colleagues who provided helpful criticism and made valuable suggestions as members of focus groups, survey participants, or as adopters and reviewers of previous editions.

John C. Borke
University of Wisconsin—Platteville

Larry R. Falcetto
Emporia State University

Paul D. Kimmel
University of Wisconsin—Milwaukee

Mark Kohlbeck
Florida Atlantic University

Ann O'Brien
University of Wisconsin—Madison

Juan Rivera
University of Notre Dame

Tom Tierney
University of Wisconsin—Madison

Patricia Walters
Fordham University

Dick Wasson
Southwestern College, San Diego State University

Steve Zeff
Rice University

WileyPLUS Developers and Reviewers

Jan Mardon

James Mraz

Melanie Yon

Practicing Accountants and Business Executives
From the fields of corporate and public accounting, we owe thanks to the following practitioners for their technical advice and for consenting to interviews.

John Gribble
PricewaterhouseCoopers

Tom Linsmeier
FASB

Lynn Turner
Former SEC Chief Accountant

Special thanks to Stephen A. Zeff, *Rice University*, for his comments on international accounting. In addition, we thank the following colleagues who contributed to several of the unique features of this edition.

Gateway to the Profession Portal

Michelle Ephraim
Worcester Polytechnic Institute

Courtney Meyer
Madison, Wisconsin

Matt Tutaj
Deloitte LLP, Chicago

"Working in Teams" Material

Edward Wertheim
Northeastern University

Ancillary Authors, Contributors, Proofers, and Accuracy Checkers

LuAnn Bean
Florida Institute of Technology

Mary Ann Benson

John C. Borke
University of Wisconsin—Platteville

Jack Cathey
University of North Carolina—Charlotte

Betty Connor
University of Colorado at Denver

Robert Derstine
Villanova University

Gregory Dold
Southwestern College

Jan Duffy
Iowa State University

Jim Emig
Villanova University

Larry Falcetto
Emporia State University

Tom Forehand
State University of New York—New Paltz

Rosemary Fullerton
Utah State University

Coby Harmon
University of California, Santa Barbara

Debra R. Hopkins
Northern Illinois University

Marilyn F. Hunt

Douglas W. Kieso
Aurora University

Mark Kohlbeck
Florida Atlantic University

Maureen Mascha
Marquette University

Ann Martin
University of Colorado at Denver

Barbara Muller
Arizona State University

Lynn Stallworth
Appalachian State University

Dick Wasson
Southwestern College, San Diego State University

In addition, we appreciate the exemplary support and professional commitment given us by the development, marketing, production, and editorial staffs of John Wiley & Sons, including the following: Susan Elbe, Chris DeJohn, Mike McDonald, Brian Kamins, Amy Scholz, Alison Stanley, Ed Brislin, Allie Morris, George Hoffman, Kara Taylor, Trish McFadden, Harry Nolan, Kevin Murphy, Anna Melhorn, and Lenore Belton. Thanks, too, to Suzanne Ingrao for her production work, to the management and staff at Aptara®, Inc. for their work on the textbook, to Cyndy Taylor, and to Danielle Urban and the management and staff at Elm Street Publishing Services for their work on the solutions manual.

Special thanks to development editor Terry Ann Tatro for her contributions to *Intermediate Accounting*, IFRS Edition.

BRIEF CONTENTS

CONTENTS

CHAPTER 23 **Statement of Cash Flows** 1240
Don't Take Cash Flows for Granted 1240

INTERMEDIATE ACCOUNTING, VOLUME 2

CHAPTER 15

EQUITY

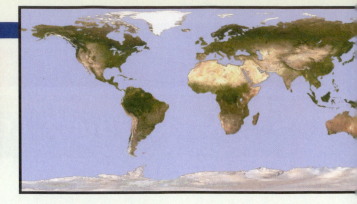

LEARNING OBJECTIVES

After studying this chapter, you should be able to:

•1 Discuss the characteristics of the corporate form of organization.

•2 Identify the key components of equity.

•3 Explain the accounting procedures for issuing shares.

•4 Describe the accounting for treasury shares.

•5 Explain the accounting for and reporting of preference shares.

•6 Describe the policies used in distributing dividends.

•7 Identify the various forms of dividend distributions.

•8 Explain the accounting for small and large share dividends, and for share splits.

•9 Indicate how to present and analyze equity.

IT'S A GLOBAL MARKET

As discussed in earlier chapters, we are moving rapidly toward one set of global financial reporting standards and one "common language" for financial information. This change will probably lead to more consolidation of our capital markets. To understand how quickly the global financial world is changing, let's examine a few trends occurring on securities exchanges around the world.

In 2007, the New York Stock Exchange (NYSE) merged with Paris-based Eurotext, creating the world's first transatlantic securities exchange. NYSE Eurotext is the world's largest exchange group, with 4,000 listed issuers representing over $29 trillion in market value. Similarly, NASDAQ, the world's largest electronic securities market, merged with OMX, the Nordic market operator. This electronic exchange will operate in 29 countries, on six continents, and will have 4,000 listed issuers, with a market value of approximately $5.5 trillion.

Another reason behind the strong impetus for international financial reporting standards can be found in recent initial public offerings (IPOs). The emerging markets are driving the global IPO market, as shown in the following table.

Top 10 IPOs by amount of capital raised, January–March 2008

Ranking	Issue Date	Issuer Name	Industry Description	Proceeds (US$m)	Primary Exchange
1	3/18/08	**Visa Inc** (USA)	Financials	19,650	NYSE
2	3/10/08	**China Railway Construction Corp** (CHN)	Industrials	5,709	Shanghai, HKEx
3	1/21/08	**Reliance Power Ltd** (IND)	Energy and power	2,964	Bombay
4	2/22/08	**Mobile Telecommunications Company Saudi Arabia** (SAU)	Telecommunications	1,867	Riyadh
5	1/5/08	**Rabigh Refining & Petrochemical Company** (SAU)	Materials	1,228	Riyadh
6	3/26/08	**Want Want China Holdings** (CHN)	Consumer staples	1,046	Hong Kong
7	2/21/08	**Seven Bank Ltd** (JPN)	Financials	486	JASDAQ
8	3/14/08	**TGK-7 (Volzhskaya TGK)** (RUS)	Energy and power	464	RTS
9	2/25/08	**Rural Electrification Corp** (IND)	Energy and power	417	Bombay
10	3/7/08	**Honghua Group Ltd** (CHN)	Energy and power	409	Hong Kong

As another example, Brazil, Russia, India, and China—often referred to as the *BRIC countries*—generated 41 percent of total IPO proceeds in 2007, compared with just 14 percent for the BRIC countries in 2004.

Finally, consider the international sales of some large corporations: **Bombardier** (CAN) now has 96 percent of its sales overseas, **Boeing** (USA) in a recent year sold more planes overseas than in the United States, and **Hyundai**'s (KOR) vehicle revenues are over 88 percent in overseas markets.

Source: **Ernst and Young,** *Growth During Economic Uncertainty: Global IPO Trends Report* (2008).

PREVIEW OF CHAPTER 15

As our opening story indicates, the growth of global equity capital markets indicates that investors around the world need useful information. In this chapter, we explain the accounting issues related to the equity of a corporation. The content and organization of the chapter are as follows.

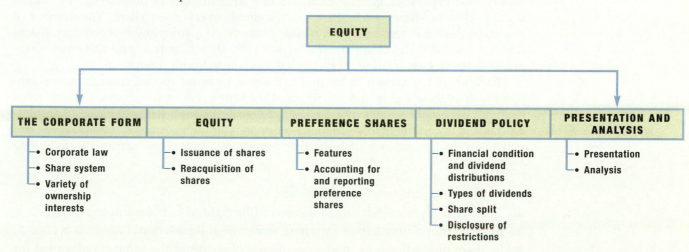

THE CORPORATE FORM OF ORGANIZATION

Objective•1

Discuss the characteristics of the corporate form of organization.

Of the three **primary forms of business organization**—the proprietorship, the partnership, and the corporation—the corporate form dominates. The corporation is by far the leader in terms of the aggregate amount of resources controlled, goods and services produced, and people employed. Although the corporate form has a number of advantages (as well as disadvantages) over the other two forms, its principal advantage is its facility for attracting and accumulating large amounts of capital.

The special characteristics of the corporate form that affect accounting include:

1. Influence of corporate law.
2. Use of the share system.
3. Development of a variety of ownership interests.

Corporate Law

Anyone who wishes to establish a corporation must generally submit **articles of incorporation** to the appropriate governmental agency for the country in which incorporation is desired. After fulfilling requirements, the governmental agency issues a corporation charter, thereby recognizing the company as a legal entity. Regardless of the number of countries in which a corporation has operating divisions, it is incorporated in only one country. It is to the company's advantage to incorporate where laws favor the corporate form of business organization.

Many governments have their own business incorporation act. The accounting for equity follows the provisions of these acts. In many cases, the laws are complex and vary both in their provisions and in their definitions of certain terms. Some laws fail to define technical terms. As a result, terms often mean one thing in one country and another thing in a different country. These problems may be further compounded because legal authorities often interpret the effects and restrictions of the laws differently.

Share System

Equity in a corporation generally consists of a large number of units or shares. Within a given class of shares, each share exactly equals every other share. The number of shares possessed determines each owner's interest. If a company has ordinary shares divided into 1,000 shares, a person who owns 500 shares controls one-half of the ownership interest. One holding 10 shares has a one-hundredth interest.

Each share has certain rights and privileges. Only by special contract can a company restrict these rights and privileges at the time it issues the shares. Owners must examine the articles of incorporation, share certificates, and the provisions of applicable laws to ascertain such restrictions on or variations from the standard rights and privileges. In the absence of restrictive provisions, each share carries the following rights:

1. To share proportionately in profits and losses.
2. To share proportionately in management (the right to vote for directors).
3. To share proportionately in corporate assets upon liquidation.
4. To share proportionately in any new issues of shares of the same class—called the **preemptive right**.[1]

---

[1]This privilege is referred to as a **share right** or **warrant**. The warrants issued in these situations are of short duration, unlike the warrants issued with other securities.

The first three rights are self-explanatory. The last right is used to protect each share-holder's proportional interest in the company. **The preemptive right protects an existing shareholder from involuntary dilution of ownership interest.** Without this right, shareholders might find their interest reduced by the issuance of additional shares without their knowledge, and at prices unfavorable to them. However, many corporations have eliminated the preemptive right. Why? Because this right makes it inconvenient for corporations to issue large amounts of additional shares, as they frequently do in acquiring other companies.

The share system easily allows one individual to transfer an interest in a company to another investor. For example, individuals owning shares in **Páo de Acucar** (BRA) **may sell them to others at any time and at any price without obtaining the consent of the company or other shareholders.** Each share is personal property of the owner, who may dispose of it at will. Páo de Acucar simply maintains a list or subsidiary ledger of shareholders as a guide to dividend payments, issuance of share rights, voting proxies, and the like. Because owners freely and frequently transfer shares, Páo de Acucar must revise the subsidiary ledger of shareholders periodically, generally in advance of every dividend payment or shareholders' meeting.

In addition, the major securities exchanges require ownership controls that the typical corporation finds uneconomic to provide. Thus, corporations often use **registrars and transfer agents** who specialize in providing services for recording and transferring shares.

Variety of Ownership Interests

In every corporation, one class of shares must represent the basic ownership interest. That class of shares is called ordinary. **Ordinary shares** represent the residual corporate interest that bears the ultimate risks of loss and receives the benefits of success. They are guaranteed neither dividends nor assets upon dissolution. But ordinary shareholders generally control the management of the corporation and tend to profit most if the company is successful. In the event that a corporation has only one authorized issue of shares, that issue is by definition ordinary shares, whether so designated in the charter or not.

In an effort to broaden investor appeal, corporations may offer two or more classes of shares, each with different rights or privileges. In the preceding section, we pointed out that each share of a given issue has the same four inherent rights as other shares of the same issue. By special contracts between the corporation and its shareholders, however, the shareholder may sacrifice certain of these rights in return for other special rights or privileges. Thus special classes of shares, usually called **preference shares**, are created. In return for any special preference, the preference shareholder always sacrifices some of the inherent rights of ordinary shareholders.

A common type of preference is to give preference shareholders a prior claim on earnings. The corporation thus assures them a dividend, usually at a stated rate, before it distributes any amount to the ordinary shareholders. In return for this preference, the preference shareholders may sacrifice their right to a voice in management or their right to share in profits beyond the stated rate.

A CLASS (B) ACT

Some companies grant preferences to different shareholders by issuing different classes of ordinary shares. Share bids put the spotlight on dual-class share structures. For example, ownership of **Dow Jones & Co.** (USA), publisher of the *Wall Street Journal*, was controlled by family members who owned Class B shares, which carry super voting powers. The same is true for the Ford family's control of **Ford Motor Co.** (USA). Class B shares are often criticized for protecting owners' interest at the expense of shareholder return. These shares often can determine if a takeover deal gets done, or not. However, the B shareholders at **Vodafone** (GBR) only get a vote if the company is to be dissolved.

What do the numbers mean?

**What do the
numbers mean?**

(continued)

Here are some notable companies with two-tiered shares.

Company	Votes Controlled by Class B Shareholders	Company	Votes Controlled by Class B Shareholders
Vodafone	0%	Google	78%
Ford	40%	Estée Lauder	88%
New York Times	70%	Polo Ralph Lauren	88%
Meredith	71%	Martha Stewart Living	91%
Cablevision Systems	73%	1-800-Flowers	93%

Data: Bloomberg Financial Markets, *BusinessWeek*, company documents.

For most retail investors, voting rights are not that important. But for family-controlled companies, issuing newer classes of lower or non-voting shares effectively creates currency for acquisitions, increases liquidity, or puts a public value on the company without diluting the family's voting control. Thus, investors must carefully compare the apparent bargain prices for some classes of shares—they may end up as second-class citizens with no voting rights.

Source: Adapted from Andy Serwer, "Dual-Listed Companies Aren't Fair or Balanced," *Fortune* (September 20, 2004), p. 83; and Alex Halperin, "A Class (B) Act," *BusinessWeek* (May 28, 2007), p. 12.

EQUITY

Objective·2

Identify the key components of equity.

**I
F
R
S**

See the Authoritative Literature section (page 801).

Equity is the residual interest in the assets of the company after deducting all liabilities. [1] Equity is often referred to as shareholders' equity, stockholders' equity, or corporate capital. Equity is often subclassified on the statement of financial position into the following categories (as discussed in Chapter 5).

1. Share capital.

2. Share premium.

3. Retained earnings.

4. Accumulated other comprehensive income.

5. Treasury shares.

6. Non-controlling interest (minority interest).

Such classifications help financial statement users to better understand the legal or other restrictions related to the ability of the company to pay dividends or otherwise use its equity for certain defined purposes.

Companies often make a distinction between contributed capital (paid-in capital) and earned capital. **Contributed capital (paid-in capital)** is the total amount paid in on capital shares—the amount provided by shareholders to the corporation for use in the business. Contributed capital includes items such as the par value of all outstanding shares and premiums less discounts on issuance. **Earned capital** is the capital that develops from profitable operations. It consists of all undistributed income that remains invested in the company. **Retained earnings** represents the earned capital of the company.

As indicated above, equity is a **residual interest** and therefore its value is derived from the amount of the corporations' assets and liabilities. Only in unusual cases will a company's equity equal the total fair value of its shares. For example, **BMW** (DEU) recently had total equity of €20,265 million and a market capitalization of €21,160 million. BMW's equity represents the net contributions from shareholders (from both majority and minority shareholders) plus retained earnings and accumulated other comprehensive income. As a residual interest, its equity has no existence apart from the assets and liabilities of BMW—equity equals net assets. Equity is not a claim to specific assets but a claim against a portion of the total assets. Its amount is not specified or fixed; it depends on BMW's profitability. Equity grows if it is profitable. It shrinks, or may disappear entirely, if BMW loses money.

Issuance of Shares

In issuing shares, companies follow these procedures: First, the applicable governmental agency must authorize the shares, generally in a certificate of incorporation or charter. Next, the corporation offers shares for sale, entering into contracts to sell these shares. Then, after receiving amounts for the shares, the corporation issues the shares. The corporation generally makes no entry in the general ledger accounts when it receives its share authorization from the jurisdiction of incorporation.

> **Objective·3**
> Explain the accounting procedures for issuing shares.

We discuss the accounting problems involved in the issuance of shares under the following topics.

1. Accounting for par value shares.

2. Accounting for no-par shares.

3. Accounting for shares issued in combination with other securities (lump-sum sales).

4. Accounting for shares issued in non-cash transactions.

5. Accounting for costs of issuing shares.

Par Value Shares

The par value of a share has no relationship to its fair value. At present, the par value associated with most ordinary share issuances is very low. For example, **PepsiCo**'s (USA) par value is 1⅔¢, **China Railway Construction Corporation**'s (CHN) is ¥1.00, and **Nestlé S.A.**'s (CHE) is CHF1. Such values contrast dramatically with the situation in the early 1900s, when practically all shares issued had a par value of $100. Low par values help companies avoid the contingent liability associated with shares sold below par.[2]

To show the required information for issuance of par value shares, corporations maintain accounts for each class of shares as follows.

1. *Preference Shares or Ordinary Shares.* Together, these two share accounts reflect the par value of the corporation's issued shares. The company credits these accounts when it originally issues the shares. It makes no additional entries in these accounts unless it issues additional shares or retires them.

2. *Share Premium.* The **Share Premium** account indicates any excess over par value paid in by shareholders in return for the shares issued to them. Once paid in, the excess over par becomes a part of the corporation's share premium. The individual shareholder has no greater claim on the excess paid in than all other holders of the same class of shares.

No-Par Shares

Many countries permit the issuance of shares without par value, called **no-par shares**. The reasons for issuance of no-par shares are twofold: First, issuance of no-par shares **avoids the contingent liability** (see footnote 2) that might occur if the corporation issued par value shares at a discount. Second, some confusion exists over the relationship

---

[2]Companies rarely, if ever, issue shares at a value below par value. The reason: The corporation may call on the original purchaser or the current holder of the shares issued below par to pay in the amount of the discount to prevent creditors from sustaining a loss upon liquidation of the corporation.

(or rather the absence of a relationship) between the par value and fair value. If shares have no par value, **the questionable treatment of using par value as a basis for fair value never arises**. This is particularly advantageous whenever issuing shares for property items such as tangible or intangible fixed assets.

A major disadvantage of no-par shares is that some countries levy a high tax on these issues. In addition, in some countries the total issue price for no-par shares may be considered legal capital, which could reduce the flexibility in paying dividends.

Corporations sell no-par shares, like par value shares, for whatever price they will bring. However, unlike par value shares, corporations issue them without a premium or a discount. The exact amount received represents the credit to ordinary or preference shares. For example, Video Electronics Corporation is organized with 10,000 ordinary shares authorized without par value. Video Electronics makes only a memorandum entry for the authorization, inasmuch as no amount is involved. If Video Electronics then issues 500 shares for cash at €10 per share, it makes the following entry:

Cash	5,000	
Share Capital—Ordinary		5,000

If it issues another 500 shares for €11 per share, Video Electronics makes this entry:

Cash	5,500	
Share Capital—Ordinary		5,500

True no-par shares should be carried in the accounts at issue price without any share premium reported. But some countries require that no-par shares have a **stated value**. The stated value is a minimum value below which a company cannot issue it. Thus, instead of being no-par shares, such stated-value shares become, in effect, shares with a very low par value. It thus is open to all the criticism and abuses that first encouraged the development of no-par shares.

If no-par shares have a stated value of €5 per share but sell for €11, all such amounts in excess of €5 are recorded as share premium, which in many jurisdictions is fully or partially available for dividends. Thus, no-par value shares, with a low stated value, permit a new corporation to commence its operations with share premium that may exceed its stated capital. For example, if a company issued 1,000 of the shares with a €5 stated value at €15 per share for cash, it makes the following entry.

Cash	15,000	
Share Capital—Ordinary		5,000
Share Premium—Ordinary		10,000

Most corporations account for no-par shares with a stated value as if they were par value shares with par equal to the stated value.

Shares Issued with Other Securities (Lump-Sum Sales)

Generally, corporations sell classes of shares separately from one another. The reason to do so is to track the proceeds relative to each class, as well as relative to each lot. Occasionally, a corporation issues two or more classes of securities for a single payment or lump sum, in the acquisition of another company. The accounting problem in such **lump-sum sales** is how to allocate the proceeds among the several classes of securities. Companies use one of two methods of allocation: (1) the proportional method and (2) the incremental method.

Proportional Method. If the fair value or other sound basis for determining relative value is available for each class of security, **the company allocates the lump sum received among the classes of securities on a proportional basis**. For instance, assume a company issues 1,000 shares of $10 stated value ordinary shares having a fair value of $20 a share, and 1,000 shares of $10 par value preference shares having a fair value of $12 a share, for a lump sum of $30,000. Illustration 15-1 shows how the company allocates the $30,000 to the two classes of shares.

Fair value of ordinary (1,000 × $20)   = $20,000
Fair value of preference (1,000 × $12) =   12,000

Aggregate fair value $32,000

Allocated to ordinary: $\dfrac{\$20,000}{\$32,000} \times \$30,000 = \$18,750$

Allocated to preference: $\dfrac{\$12,000}{\$32,000} \times \$30,000 =   11,250$

Total allocation $30,000

Incremental Method. In instances where a company cannot determine the fair value of all classes of securities, it may use the incremental method. It uses the fair value of the securities as a basis for those classes that it knows, and allocates the remainder of the lump sum to the class for which it does not know the fair value. For instance, if a company issues 1,000 shares of $10 stated value ordinary shares having a fair value of $20, and 1,000 shares of $10 par value preference shares having no established fair value, for a lump sum of $30,000, it allocates the $30,000 to the two classes as shown in Illustration 15-2.

Lump-sum receipt	$30,000
Allocated to ordinary (1,000 × $20)	(20,000)
Balance allocated to preference	$10,000

If a company cannot determine fair value for any of the classes of shares involved in a lump-sum exchange, it may need to use other approaches. It may rely on an expert's appraisal. Or, if the company knows that one or more of the classes of securities issued will have a determinable fair value in the near future, it may use a best estimate basis with the intent to adjust later, upon establishment of the future fair value.

Shares Issued in Non-Cash Transactions

Accounting for the issuance of shares for property or services involves an issue of valuation. **The general rule is: Companies should record shares issued for services or property other than cash at the fair value of the goods or services received, unless that fair value cannot be measured reliably. If the fair value of the goods or services cannot be measured reliably, use the fair value of the shares issued. [2]**

If a company can readily determine both, and the transaction results from an arm's-length exchange, there will probably be little difference in their fair values. In such cases, the basis for valuing the exchange should not matter.

If a company cannot readily determine either the fair value of the shares it issues or the property or services it receives, it should employ an appropriate valuation technique. Depending on available data, the valuation may be based on market transactions involving comparable assets or the use of discounted expected future cash flows. Companies should avoid the use of the book, par, or stated values as a basis of valuation for these transactions.

A company may exchange unissued shares or treasury shares (issued shares that it has reacquired but not retired) for property or services. If it uses treasury shares and the fair value of the property or services cannot be reliably estimated, the cost of the treasury shares should not be considered the decisive factor in establishing the fair value of the property or services. Instead, it should use the fair value of the treasury shares to value the property or services.

The following series of transactions illustrates the procedure for recording the issuance of 10,000 shares of $10 par value ordinary shares for a patent for Marlowe Company, in various circumstances.

1. Marlowe cannot readily determine the fair value of the patent, but it knows the fair value of the shares is $140,000.

Patent	140,000	
Share Capital—Ordinary (10,000 shares × $10 per share)		100,000
Share Premium—Ordinary		40,000

2. Marlowe cannot readily determine the fair value of the shares, but it determines the fair value of the patent is $150,000.

Patent	150,000	
Share Capital—Ordinary (10,000 shares × $10 per share)		100,000
Share Premium—Ordinary		50,000

3. Marlowe cannot readily determine the fair value of the shares nor the fair value of the patent. An independent consultant values the patent at $125,000 based on discounted expected cash flows.

Patent	125,000	
Share Capital—Ordinary (10,000 shares × $10 per share)		100,000
Share Premium—Ordinary		25,000

Generally, the board of directors has the power to set the value of non-cash transactions. However, boards sometimes abuse this power. The issuance of shares for property or services has resulted in cases of overstated corporate capital through intentional overvaluation of the property or services received. The overvaluation of equity resulting from inflated asset values creates **watered shares**. The corporation should eliminate the "water" by simply writing down the overvalued assets.

If, as a result of the issuance of shares for property or services, a corporation undervalues the recorded assets, it creates **secret reserves**. An understated corporate structure (secret reserve) may also result from other methods: excessive depreciation or amortization charges, expensing capital expenditures, excessive write-downs of inventories or receivables, or any other understatement of assets or overstatement of liabilities. An example of a liability overstatement is an excessive provision for estimated product warranties that ultimately results in an understatement of equity, thereby creating a secret reserve.

Costs of Issuing Shares

When a company like **Wesfarmers** (AUS) issues shares, it should report direct costs incurred to sell shares, such as underwriting costs, accounting and legal fees, printing costs, and taxes, as a reduction of the amounts paid in. Wesfarmers therefore debits issue costs to Share Premium because they are unrelated to corporate operations. In effect, **issue costs are a cost of financing**. As such, issue costs should reduce the proceeds received from the sale of the shares.

Wesfarmers should expense management salaries and other indirect costs related to the share issue because it is difficult to establish a relationship between these costs and the sale proceeds. In addition, Wesfarmers expenses recurring costs, primarily registrar and transfer agents' fees, as incurred.

THE CASE OF THE DISAPPEARING RECEIVABLE

What do the numbers mean?

Sometimes companies issue shares but may not receive cash in return. As a result, a company records a receivable.

Controversy existed regarding the presentation of this receivable on the statement of financial position. Some argued that the company should report the receivable as an asset similar to other receivables. Others argued that the company should report the receivable as a deduction from equity (similar to the treatment of treasury shares). In general, companies are required to use the contra-equity approach because the risk of collection in this type of transaction is often very high.

This accounting issue surfaced in **Enron**'s (USA) accounting. Starting in early 2000, Enron issued shares of its ordinary shares to four "special-purpose entities," in exchange for which it received a note receivable. Enron then increased its assets (by recording a receivable) and equity, a move the company called an accounting error. As a result of this accounting treatment, Enron overstated assets and equity by $172 million in its 2000 audited financial statements and by $828 million in its unaudited 2001 statements. This $1 billion overstatement was 8.5 percent of Enron's previously reported equity at that time.

As Lynn Turner, a noted accounting authority, stated, "It is a basic accounting principle that you don't record equity until you get cash, and a note doesn't count as cash." Situations like this led investors, creditors, and suppliers to lose faith in the credibility of Enron, which eventually caused its bankruptcy.

Source: Adapted from Jonathan Weil, "Basic Accounting Tripped Up Enron—Financial Statements Didn't Add Up—Auditors Overlook a Simple Rule," *Wall Street Journal* (November 11, 2001), p. C1.

Reacquisition of Shares

Companies often buy back their own shares. Corporations purchase their outstanding shares for several reasons:

Objective·4
Describe the accounting for treasury shares.

1. *To provide tax-efficient distributions of excess cash to shareholders.* Tax rates on sales of shares to the company by the shareholders are often much lower than the ordinary tax rate for many investors.

2. *To increase earnings per share and return on equity.* Reducing both shares outstanding and equity often enhances certain performance ratios. However, strategies to hype performance measures might increase performance in the short-run, but these tactics add no real long-term value.

3. *To provide shares for employee compensation contracts or to meet potential merger needs.* **Honeywell Inc.** (USA) reported that it would use part of its purchase of one million ordinary shares for employee share option contracts. Other companies acquire shares to have them available for business acquisitions.

4. *To thwart takeover attempts or to reduce the number of shareholders.* By reducing the number of shares held by the public, existing owners and managements bar "outsiders" from gaining control or significant influence.

5. *To make a market in the shares.* As one company executive noted, "Our company is trying to establish a floor for its shares." Purchasing shares in the marketplace creates a demand. This may stabilize the share price or, in fact, increase it.

Some publicly held corporations have chosen to "go private," that is, to eliminate public (outside) ownership entirely by purchasing all of their outstanding shares. Companies often accomplish such a procedure through a **leveraged buyout (LBO),** in which the company borrows money to finance the share repurchases.

After reacquiring shares, a company may either retire them or hold them in the treasury for reissue. If not retired, such shares are referred to as **treasury shares**.

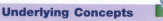

Underlying Concepts

As we indicated in Chapter 2, an asset should have probable future economic benefits. Treasury shares simply reduce ordinary shares outstanding.

Technically, treasury shares are a corporation's own shares, reacquired after having been issued and fully paid.

Treasury shares are not an asset. When a company purchases treasury shares, a reduction occurs in both assets and equity. It is inappropriate to imply that a corporation can own a part of itself. A corporation may sell treasury shares to obtain funds, but that does not make treasury shares a statement of financial position asset. When a corporation buys back some of its own outstanding shares, it has not acquired an asset; it reduces net assets.

The possession of treasury shares does not give the corporation the right to vote, to exercise preemptive rights as a shareholder, to receive cash dividends, or to receive assets upon corporate liquidation. **Treasury shares are essentially the same as unissued ordinary shares.** No one advocates classifying unissued ordinary shares as an asset in the statement of financial position.[3]

What do the numbers mean?

SIGNALS TO BUY?

The volume of share buybacks by companies on the FTSE 100 leapt 40 percent during recent market turmoil as shares fell and managers seized the opportunity to spend more than £750 million buying them on the cheap. For example, FTSE 100 companies spent £764.3 million to buy 4.7 percent of their own shares in a single week, with major companies such as **BP** (GBR), **Royal Dutch Shell** (NLD and GBR), and **Burberry** (GBR) making some of the bigger repurchases. Executives at some of the companies said the buying showed confidence that the current crisis would subside. The buys also showed that cash reserves were healthy enough for companies to believe they not only had enough cash to cover their day-to-day functions but also enough to spare to allow for generous buybacks.

In response to these signals, market analysts often look to share buybacks as a buy signal. That strategy is not that surprising if you look at the performance of companies that did buybacks. For example, in one study, buyback companies outperformed similar companies without buybacks by an average of 23 percent. In a recent three-year period, companies followed by **Buybackletter.com** (USA) were up 16.4 percent, while the S&P 500 Index was up just 7.1 percent in that period. Why the premium? Well, the conventional wisdom is that companies who buy back shares believe their shares are undervalued. Thus, analysts view the buyback announcement as an important piece of inside information about future company prospects.

Source: "FTSE 100 Buy-Backs Leap 40%," *www.marketwatch.com* (August 22, 2007).

Purchase of Treasury Shares

Companies use two general methods of handling treasury shares in the accounts: the cost method and the par value method. Both methods are generally acceptable.

- The **cost method** results in debiting the Treasury Shares account for the reacquisition cost and in reporting this account as a deduction from equity on the statement of financial position.
- The **par** or **stated value method** records all transactions in treasury shares at their par value and reports the treasury shares as a deduction from share capital only.

No matter which method a company uses, most jurisdictions consider the cost of the treasury shares acquired as a restriction on retained earnings.

Companies generally use the cost method to account for treasury shares. This method derives its name from the fact that a company maintains the Treasury Shares

---

[3]The possible justification for classifying these shares as assets is that the company will use them to liquidate a specific liability that appears on the statement of financial position.

account at the cost of the shares purchased.[4] Under the cost method, the company debits the Treasury Shares account for the cost of the shares acquired. Upon reissuance of the shares, it credits the account for this same cost. The original price received for the shares does not affect the entries to record the acquisition and reissuance of the treasury shares.

To illustrate, assume that Pacific Company issued 100,000 shares of $1 par value ordinary shares at a price of $10 per share. In addition, it has retained earnings of $300,000. Illustration 15-3 shows the equity section on December 31, 2010, before purchase of treasury shares.

<table>
<tr><td colspan="2">Equity</td></tr>
<tr><td>Share capital—ordinary, $1 par, 100,000 shares
    issued and outstanding</td><td>$ 100,000</td></tr>
<tr><td>Share premium—ordinary</td><td>900,000</td></tr>
<tr><td>Retained earnings</td><td>300,000</td></tr>
<tr><td>Total equity</td><td>$1,300,000</td></tr>
</table>

ILLUSTRATION 15-3
Equity with No Treasury Shares

On January 20, 2011, Pacific acquires 10,000 of its shares at $11 per share. Pacific records the reacquisition as follows.

January 20, 2011

Treasury Shares	110,000	
Cash		110,000

Note that Pacific debited Treasury Shares for the cost of the shares purchased. The original account, Share Capital—Ordinary, is not affected because the number of issued shares does not change. The same is true for the Share Premium—Ordinary account. Pacific then deducts treasury shares to determine total equity.

Illustration 15-4 shows the equity section for Pacific after purchase of the treasury shares.

<table>
<tr><td colspan="2">Equity</td></tr>
<tr><td>Share capital—ordinary, $1 par value, 100,000 shares
    issued and 90,000 outstanding</td><td>$ 100,000</td></tr>
<tr><td>Share premium—ordinary</td><td>900,000</td></tr>
<tr><td>Retained earnings</td><td>300,000</td></tr>
<tr><td>Less: Cost of treasury shares (10,000 shares)</td><td>110,000</td></tr>
<tr><td>Total equity</td><td>$1,190,000</td></tr>
</table>

ILLUSTRATION 15-4
Equity with Treasury Shares

Pacific subtracts the cost of the treasury shares from the total of ordinary shares, share premium—ordinary, and retained earnings. It therefore reduces equity. Many jurisdictions require a corporation to restrict retained earnings for the cost of treasury shares purchased. The restriction keeps intact the corporation's capital. When the corporation sells the treasury shares, it lifts the restriction.

Pacific discloses both the number of shares issued (100,000) and the number in the treasury (10,000). The difference is the number of shares outstanding (90,000). The term **outstanding shares** means the number of issued shares that shareholders own.

Sale of Treasury Shares

Companies usually reissue or retire treasury shares. When selling treasury shares, the accounting for the sale depends on the price. If the selling price of the treasury

---

[4]If making numerous acquisitions of blocks of treasury shares at different prices, a company may use inventory costing methods—such as specific identification, average cost, or FIFO—to identify the cost at date of reissuance.

shares equals its cost, the company records the sale of the shares by debiting Cash and crediting Treasury Shares. In cases where the selling price of the treasury shares is not equal to cost, then accounting for treasury shares sold **above cost** differs from the accounting for treasury shares sold **below cost**. However, the sale of treasury shares either above or below cost increases both total assets and equity.

Sale of Treasury Shares above Cost. When the selling price of the treasury shares exceeds its cost, a company credits the difference to Share Premium—Treasury. To illustrate, assume that Pacific acquired 10,000 treasury shares at $11 per share. It now sells 1,000 shares at $15 per share on March 10. Pacific records the entry as follows.

March 10, 2011

Cash	15,000	
Treasury Shares		11,000
Share Premium—Treasury		4,000

There are two reasons why Pacific does not credit $4,000 to Gain on Sale of Treasury Shares: (1) Gains on sales occur when selling **assets**; treasury shares are not an asset. (2) A gain or loss should not be recognized from share transactions with its own shareholders. Thus, Pacific should not include share premium arising from the sale of treasury shares in the measurement of net income. Instead, it lists share premium from treasury shares separately on the statement of financial position.

Sale of Treasury Shares below Cost. When a corporation sells treasury shares below its cost, it usually debits the excess of the cost over selling price to Share Premium—Treasury. Thus, if Pacific sells an additional 1,000 treasury shares on March 21 at $8 per share, it records the sale as follows.

March 21, 2011

Cash	8,000	
Share Premium—Treasury	3,000	
Treasury Shares		11,000

We can make several observations based on the two sale entries (sale above cost and sale below cost): (1) Pacific credits Treasury Shares at cost in each entry. (2) Pacific uses Share Premium—Treasury for the difference between the cost and the resale price of the shares. (3) Neither entry affects Share Capital—Ordinary.

After eliminating the credit balance in Share Premium—Treasury, the corporation debits any additional excess of cost over selling price to Retained Earnings. To illustrate, assume that Pacific sells an additional 1,000 shares at $8 per share on April 10. Illustration 15-5 shows the balance in the Share Premium—Treasury account (before the April 10 purchase).

ILLUSTRATION 15-5
Treasury Share Transactions in Share Premium—Treasury Account

Share Premium—Treasury			
Mar. 21	3,000	Mar. 10	4,000
		Balance	1,000

In this case, Pacific debits $1,000 of the excess to Share Premium—Treasury. It debits the remainder to Retained Earnings. The entry is:

April 10, 2011

Cash	8,000	
Share Premium—Treasury	1,000	
Retained Earnings	2,000	
Treasury Shares		11,000

Retiring Treasury Shares

The board of directors may approve the retirement of treasury shares. This decision results in cancellation of the treasury shares and a reduction in the number of issued shares. Retired treasury shares have the status of authorized and unissued shares. The accounting effects are similar to the sale of treasury shares except that corporations debit **applicable equity accounts related to the retired shares** instead of cash. For example, if a corporation originally sells the shares at par, it debits Share Capital—Ordinary for the par value per share. If it originally sells the shares at $3 above par value, it also debits Share Premium—Ordinary for $3 per share at retirement.

NOT SO GOOD ANYMORE

What do the numbers mean?

Volatility in the markets can lead to wide swings in share repurchase activity. For example, share buybacks—following a long run of high buyback activity—tumbled 66 percent in a recent quarter from a year earlier among companies in the S&P 500 Index. Specifically, buybacks fell 42 percent in all of 2008 from the record $589.1 billion members spent on buybacks in 2007. Why the pullback in buybacks? One experienced analyst reasoned that many companies have eliminated buybacks in a bid to boost liquidity and preserve cash in the face of tight credit markets and as many incur huge losses or have debt coming due that they are unable to refinance. Indeed, cash levels recently hit a record among index members as they cut spending in a host of areas. The reluctance of U.S. companies to spend money on share repurchases reflects what another analyst called a "storm-center mentality." Financial officers, watching companies teeter because of arid credit conditions and slowing business, have prioritized cash preservation above all else. And share repurchases are considered more "discretionary" than quarterly dividends from a corporate perspective.

Source: K. Grace and R. Curran, "Stock Buybacks Plummet," *Wall Street Journal* (March 27, 2009), p. C9.

PREFERENCE SHARES

As noted earlier, **preference shares** are a special class of shares that possess certain preferences or features not possessed by ordinary shares. The following features are those most often associated with preference share issues.

> **Objective·5**
> Explain the accounting for and reporting of preference shares.

1. Preference as to dividends.
2. Preference as to assets in the event of liquidation.
3. Convertible into ordinary shares.
4. Callable at the option of the corporation.
5. Non-voting.

The features that distinguish preference from ordinary shares may be of a more restrictive and negative nature than preferences. For example, the preference shares may be non-voting, non-cumulative, and non-participating.

Companies usually issue preference shares with a par value, expressing the dividend preference as a **percentage of the par value**. Thus, holders of 8 percent preference shares with a $100 par value are entitled to an annual dividend of $8 per share ($100 × 8%). This share is commonly referred to as an 8 percent preference share. In the case of no-par preference shares, a corporation expresses a dividend preference as a **specific dollar amount** per share, for example, $7 per share. This share is commonly referred to as a $7 preference share.

A preference as to dividends does not assure the payment of dividends. It merely assures that the corporation must pay the stated dividend rate or amount applicable to the preference shares before paying any dividends on the ordinary shares.

A company often issues preference shares (instead of debt) because of a high debt-to-equity ratio. In other instances, it issues preference shares through private placements with other corporations at a lower-than-market dividend rate because the acquiring corporation often receives largely tax-free dividends in certain countries.

Features of Preference Shares

A corporation may attach whatever preferences or restrictions, in whatever combination it desires, to a preference share issue, as long as it does not specifically violate its country's incorporation law. Also, it may issue more than one class of preference shares. We discuss the most common features attributed to preference shares below.

Cumulative Preference Shares

Cumulative preference shares require that if a corporation fails to pay a dividend in any year, it must make it up in a later year before paying any dividends to ordinary shareholders. If the directors fail to declare a dividend at the normal date for dividend action, the dividend is said to have been "passed." Any passed dividend on cumulative preference shares constitutes a dividend in arrears. Because no liability exists until the board of directors declares a dividend, a corporation does not record a dividend in arrears as a liability but discloses it in a note to the financial statements. A corporation seldom issues non-cumulative preference shares because a passed dividend is lost forever to the preference shareholder. As a result, this type of share issue would be less marketable.

Participating Preference Shares

Holders of participating preference shares share ratably with the ordinary shareholders in any profit distributions beyond the prescribed rate. That is, 5 percent preference shares, if fully participating, will receive not only its 5 percent return, but also dividends at the same rates as those paid to ordinary shareholders if paying amounts in excess of 5 percent of par or stated value to ordinary shareholders. Note that participating preference shares may be only partially participating.

Convertible Preference Shares

Convertible preference shares allow shareholders, at their option, to exchange preference shares for ordinary shares at a predetermined ratio. The convertible preference shareholder not only enjoys a preference claim on dividends but also has the option of converting into an ordinary shareholder with unlimited participation in earnings.

Callable Preference Shares

Callable preference shares permit the corporation at its option to call or redeem the outstanding preference shares at specified future dates and at stipulated prices. Many preference issues are callable. The corporation usually sets the call or redemption price slightly above the original issuance price and commonly states it in terms related to the par value. The callable feature permits the corporation to use the capital obtained through the issuance of such shares until the need has passed or it is no longer advantageous.

The existence of a call price or prices tends to set a ceiling on the market price of the preference shares unless they are convertible into ordinary shares. When a corporation redeems preference shares, it must pay any dividends in arrears.

Redeemable Preference Shares

Recently, more and more issuances of preference shares have features that make the securities more like debt (legal obligation to pay) than an equity instrument. For example, redeemable preference shares have a mandatory redemption period or a redemption feature that the issuer cannot control.

Previously, public companies were not permitted to report these debt-like preference share issues in equity, but they were not required to report them as a liability either. There were concerns about classification of these debt-like securities, which may have been reported as equity or in the "mezzanine" section of statements of financial position between equity and debt. There also was diversity in practice as to how dividends on these securities were reported. IFRS requires debt-like securities, like redeemable preference shares, to be classified as liabilities and be measured and accounted for similar to liabilities. **[3]**

Accounting for and Reporting Preference Shares

The accounting for preference shares at issuance is similar to that for ordinary shares. A corporation allocates proceeds between the par value of the preference shares and share premium. To illustrate, assume that Bishop Co. issues 10,000 shares of £10 par value preference shares for £12 cash per share. Bishop records the issuance as follows:

Cash	120,000	
Share Capital—Preference		100,000
Share Premium—Preference		20,000

Thus, Bishop maintains separate accounts for these different classes of shares.

Corporations consider convertible preference shares as a part of equity. In addition, when exercising convertible preference shares, there is no theoretical justification for recognition of a gain or loss. A company recognizes no gain or loss when dealing with shareholders in their capacity as business owners. Instead, the company **employs the book value method**: debit Share Capital—Preference, along with any related Share Premium—Preference; credit Share Capital—Ordinary and Share Premium—Ordinary (if an excess exists).

Preference shares generally have no maturity date. Therefore, no legal obligation exists to pay the preference shareholder. As a result, companies classify preference shares as part of equity. Companies generally report preference shares at par value as the first item in the equity section. They report any excess over par value as part of share premium. They also consider dividends on preference shares as a distribution of income and not an expense. Companies must disclose the pertinent rights of the preference shares outstanding. **[4]**

DIVIDEND POLICY

Determining the proper amount of dividends to pay is a difficult financial management decision. Companies that are paying dividends are extremely reluctant to reduce or eliminate their dividend. They fear that the securities market might view this action negatively. As a consequence, companies that have been paying cash dividends will make every effort to continue to do so. In addition, the type of shareholder the company has (taxable or non-taxable, retail investor or institutional investor) plays a large role in determining dividend policy.[5]

> **Objective·6**
> Describe the policies used in distributing dividends.

Very few companies pay dividends in amounts equal to their legally available retained earnings. The major reasons are as follows.

1. To maintain agreements (bond covenants) with specific creditors, to retain all or a portion of the earnings, in the form of assets, to build up additional protection against possible loss.

---

[5]Jeff Opdyke, "Tax Cut, Shareholder Pressure Stoke Surge in Dividends," *Wall Street Journal Online* (January 18, 2005). From January 1972 through July 2007, shares paying dividends had an average price increase of 10.2 percent a year, versus 2.4 percent for non-dividend-paying shares, as indicated in a recent study (A. Blackman, "How Well Do You Know . . . Dividends?" *Wall Street Journal* (September 10, 2007), p. R5).

2. To meet corporation requirements, that earnings equivalent to the cost of treasury shares purchased be restricted against dividend declarations.

3. To retain assets that would otherwise be paid out as dividends, to finance growth or expansion. This is sometimes called internal financing, reinvesting earnings, or "plowing" the profits back into the business.

4. To smooth out dividend payments from year to year by accumulating earnings in good years and using such accumulated earnings as a basis for dividends in bad years.

5. To build up a cushion or buffer against possible losses or errors in the calculation of profits.

The reasons above are self-explanatory except for the second. The laws of some jurisdictions require that the corporation restrict its contributed capital from distribution to shareholders, to protect against loss for creditors.[6] The applicable law determines the legality of a dividend.

Financial Condition and Dividend Distributions

Effective management of a company requires attention to more than the legality of dividend distributions. Management must also consider economic conditions, most importantly, liquidity. Assume an extreme situation as shown in Illustration 15-6.

ILLUSTRATION 15-6
Statement of Financial
Position, Showing a
Lack of Liquidity

STATEMENT OF FINANCIAL POSITION			
Plant assets	$500,000	Share capital	$400,000
	$500,000	Retained earnings	100,000
			$500,000

The depicted company has a retained earnings credit balance. Unless restricted, it can declare a dividend of $100,000. But because all its assets are plant assets used in operations, payment of a cash dividend of $100,000 would require the sale of plant assets or borrowing.

Even if a statement of financial position shows current assets, as in Illustration 15-7, the question remains as to whether the company needs those cash assets for other purposes.

ILLUSTRATION 15-7
Statement of Financial
Position, Showing Cash
but Minimal Working
Capital

STATEMENT OF FINANCIAL POSITION				
Plant assets	$460,000	Share capital	$400,000	
Cash	100,000	Retained earnings	100,000	$500,000
	$560,000	Current liabilities		60,000
				$560,000

The existence of current liabilities strongly implies that the company needs some of the cash to meet current debts as they mature. In addition, day-to-day cash requirements for payrolls and other expenditures not included in current liabilities also require cash.

Thus, before declaring a dividend, management must consider **availability of funds to pay the dividend**. A company should not pay a dividend unless both the present and future financial position warrant the distribution.

---

[6]If the corporation buys its own outstanding shares, it reduces its contributed capital and distributes assets to shareholders. If permitted, the corporation could, by purchasing treasury shares at any price desired, return to the shareholders their investments and leave creditors with little or no protection against loss.

Types of Dividends

Companies generally base dividend distributions either on accumulated profits (that is, retained earnings) or on some other equity item such as share premium. Dividends are of the following types.

> **Objective·7**
> Identify the various forms of dividend distributions.

1. Cash dividends.
2. Property dividends.
3. Liquidating dividends.
4. Share dividends.

Although commonly paid in cash, companies occasionally pay dividends in shares or some other asset. **All dividends, except for share dividends, reduce the total equity in the corporation.** When declaring a share dividend, the corporation does not pay out assets or incur a liability. It issues additional shares to each shareholder and nothing more.

The natural expectation of any shareholder who receives a dividend is that the corporation has operated successfully. As a result, he or she is receiving a share of its profits. A company should disclose a **liquidating dividend**—that is, a dividend not based on retained earnings—to the shareholders so that they will not misunderstand its source.

Cash Dividends

The board of directors votes on the declaration of **cash dividends**. Upon approval of the resolution, the board declares a dividend. Before paying it, however, the company must prepare a current list of shareholders. For this reason, there is usually a time lag between declaration and payment. For example, the board of directors might approve a resolution at the January 10 (**date of declaration**) meeting, and declare it payable February 5 (**date of payment**) to all shareholders of record January 25 (**date of record**).[7] In this example, the period from January 10 to January 25 gives time for the company to complete and register any transfers in process. The time from January 25 to February 5 provides an opportunity for the transfer agent or accounting department, depending on who does this work, to prepare a list of shareholders as of January 25 and to prepare and mail dividend checks.

A declared cash dividend is a liability. Because payment is generally required very soon, it is usually a current liability. Companies use the following entries to record the declaration and payment of an ordinary dividend payable in cash. For example, Roadway Freight Corp. on June 10 declared a cash dividend of 50 cents a share on 1.8 million shares payable July 16 to all shareholders of record June 24.

At date of declaration (June 10)

Retained Earnings (Cash Dividends Declared)	900,000	
Dividends Payable		900,000

At date of record (June 24)

No entry

At date of payment (July 16)

Dividends Payable	900,000	
Cash		900,000

To set up a ledger account that shows the amount of dividends declared during the year, Roadway Freight might debit Cash Dividends Declared instead of Retained

---

[7]Theoretically, the ex-dividend date is the day after the date of record. However, to allow time for transfer of the shares, the securities exchanges generally advance the ex-dividend date two to four days. Therefore, the party who owns the shares on the day prior to the expressed ex-dividend date receives the dividends. The party who buys the shares on and after the ex-dividend date does not receive the dividend. Between the declaration date and the ex-dividend date, the market price of the shares includes the dividend.

Earnings at the time of declaration. It then closes this account to Retained Earnings at year-end.

A company may declare dividends either as a certain percent of par, such as a 6 percent dividend on preference shares, or as an amount per share, such as 60 cents per share on no-par ordinary shares. In the first case, the rate multiplied by the par value of outstanding shares equals the total dividend. In the second, the dividend equals the amount per share multiplied by the number of shares outstanding. **Companies do not declare or pay cash dividends on treasury shares.**

Dividend policies vary among corporations. Some companies take pride in a long, unbroken string of quarterly dividend payments. They would lower or pass the dividend only if forced to do so by a sustained decline in earnings or a critical shortage of cash.

"Growth" companies, on the other hand, pay little or no cash dividends because their policy is to expand as rapidly as internal and external financing permit. For example, **Questcor Pharmaceuticals Inc.** (USA) has never paid cash dividends to its ordinary shareholders. These investors hope that the price of their shares will appreciate in value. The investors will then realize a profit when they sell their shares. Many companies focus more on increasing share price, share repurchase programs, and corporate earnings than on dividend payout.

Property Dividends

Dividends payable in assets of the corporation other than cash are called **property dividends** or **dividends in kind**. Property dividends may be merchandise, real estate, or investments, or whatever form the board of directors designates. **Ranchers Exploration and Development Corp.** (USA) reported one year that it would pay a fourth-quarter dividend in gold bars instead of cash. Because of the obvious difficulties of divisibility of units and delivery to shareholders, the usual property dividend is in the form of securities of other companies that the distributing corporation holds as an investment.

For example, after ruling that **DuPont**'s (USA) 23 percent share interest in **General Motors (GM)** (USA) violated antitrust laws, the U.S. Supreme Court ordered DuPont to divest itself of the GM shares within 10 years (which represented 63 million shares of GM's 281 million shares then outstanding). DuPont could not sell the shares in one block of 63 million. Further, it could not sell 6 million shares annually for the next 10 years without severely depressing the value of the GM shares. DuPont solved its problem by declaring a property dividend and distributing the GM shares as a dividend to its own shareholders.

When declaring a property dividend, the corporation should **restate at fair value the property it will distribute, recognizing any gain or loss** as the difference between the property's fair value and carrying value at date of declaration. The corporation may then record the declared dividend as a debit to Retained Earnings (or Property Dividends Declared) and a credit to Property Dividends Payable, at an amount equal to the fair value of the distributed property. Upon distribution of the dividend, the corporation debits Property Dividends Payable and credits the account containing the distributed asset (restated at fair value).

For example, Trendler, Inc. transferred to shareholders some of its investments (held-for-trading) in securities costing $1,250,000 by declaring a property dividend on December 28, 2010, to be distributed on January 30, 2011, to shareholders of record on January 15, 2011. At the date of declaration the securities have a fair value of $2,000,000. Trendler makes the following entries.

At date of declaration (December 28, 2010)

Equity Investments	750,000	
Unrealized Holding Gain or Loss—Income		750,000
Retained Earnings (Property Dividends Declared)	2,000,000	
Property Dividends Payable		2,000,000

At date of distribution (January 30, 2011)

Property Dividends Payable	2,000,000	
Equity Investments		2,000,000

Liquidating Dividends

Some corporations use amounts paid in by shareholders as a basis for dividends. Without proper disclosure of this fact, shareholders may erroneously believe the corporation has been operating at a profit. To avoid this type of deception, intentional or unintentional, a clear statement of the source of every dividend should accompany the dividend check.

Dividends based on other than retained earnings are sometimes described as **liquidating dividends**. This term implies that such dividends are a return of the shareholder's investment rather than of profits. In other words, **any dividend not based on earnings reduces amounts paid-in by shareholders and to that extent, it is a liquidating dividend**. Companies in the extractive industries may pay dividends equal to the total of accumulated income and depletion. The portion of these dividends in excess of accumulated income represents a return of part of the shareholder's investment.

For example, McChesney Mines Inc. issued a "dividend" to its ordinary shareholders of $1,200,000. The cash dividend announcement noted that shareholders should consider $900,000 as income and the remainder a return of capital. McChesney Mines records the dividend as follows.

At date of declaration

Retained Earnings	900,000	
Share Premium—Ordinary	300,000	
Dividends Payable		1,200,000

At date of payment

Dividends Payable	1,200,000	
Cash		1,200,000

In some cases, management simply decides to cease business and declares a liquidating dividend. In these cases, liquidation may take place over a number of years to ensure an orderly and fair sale of assets. For example, when **Overseas National Airways** (USA) dissolved, it agreed to pay a liquidating dividend to its shareholders over a period of years equivalent to $8.60 per share. Each liquidating dividend payment in such cases reduces the amount paid-in by shareholders.

Share Dividends

Companies sometimes issue a share dividend. In this case, **the company distributes no assets**. Each shareholder maintains exactly the same proportionate interest in the corporation and the same total book value after the company issues the share dividend. Of course, the book value per share is lower because each shareholder holds more shares.

A **share dividend** therefore is the issuance by a corporation of its own shares to its shareholders on a pro rata basis, without receiving any consideration. In recording a share dividend, some believe that the company should transfer the **par value of the shares issued** as a dividend from retained earnings to share capital. Others believe that it should transfer the **fair value of the shares issued**— its fair value at the declaration date—from retained earnings to share capital and share premium.

The fair value position was adopted, at least in part, in order to influence the share dividend policies of corporations. Evidently at one time, many in the accounting profession regarded periodic share dividends as objectionable. They believed that the term dividend when used with a distribution of additional shares was misleading because investors' net assets did not increase as a result of this "dividend." As a result, these groups decided to make it more difficult for corporations to sustain a series of such share dividends out of their accumulated earnings, by requiring the use of fair value when it substantially exceeded book value.[8]

> **Objective•8**
> Explain the accounting for small and large share dividends, and for share splits.

> **Underlying Concepts**
> By requiring fair value, the intent was to punish companies that used share dividends. This approach violates the neutrality concept (that is, that standards-setting should be even-handed).

[8]This was perhaps the earliest instance of "economic consequences" affecting an accounting pronouncement. The Committee on Accounting Procedure described its action as required by "proper accounting and corporate policy." See Stephen A. Zeff, "The Rise of 'Economic Consequences,'" *The Journal of Accountancy* (December 1978), pp. 53–66.

When the share dividend is less than 20–25 percent of the ordinary shares outstanding at the time of the dividend declaration, the company is therefore required to transfer the **fair value** of the shares issued from retained earnings. Share dividends of less than 20–25 percent are often referred to as small (ordinary) share dividends. This method of handling share dividends is justified on the grounds that "many recipients of share dividends look upon them as distributions of corporate earnings and usually in an amount equivalent to the fair value of the additional shares received." We consider this argument unconvincing. It is generally agreed that share dividends are not income to the recipients. Therefore, sound accounting should not recommend procedures simply because some recipients think they are income.[9]

To illustrate a small share dividend, assume that Vine Corporation has outstanding 1,000 shares of £100 par value ordinary shares and retained earnings of £50,000. If Vine declares a 10 percent share dividend, it issues 100 additional shares to current shareholders. If the fair value of the shares at the time of the share dividend is £130 per share, the entry is:

At date of declaration

Retained Earnings (Share Dividend Declared)	13,000	
Ordinary Share Dividend Distributable		10,000
Share Premium—Ordinary		3,000

Note that the share dividend does not affect any asset or liability. The entry merely reflects a reclassification of equity. If Vine prepares a statement of financial position between the dates of declaration and distribution, it should show the ordinary share dividend distributable in the equity section as an addition to share capital—ordinary (whereas it shows cash or property dividends payable as current liabilities).

When issuing the shares, the entry is:

At date of distribution

Ordinary Share Dividend Distributable	10,000	
Share Capital—Ordinary		10,000

No matter what the fair value is at the time of the share dividend, each shareholder retains the same proportionate interest in the corporation.

Some applicable laws specifically prohibit the issuance of share dividends on treasury shares. In those jurisdictions that permit treasury shares to participate in the distribution accompanying a share dividend or share split, the planned use of the treasury shares influences corporate practice. For example, if a corporation issues treasury shares in connection with employee share options, the treasury shares may participate in the distribution because the corporation usually adjusts the number of shares under option for any share dividends or splits. But no useful purpose is served by issuing additional shares to the treasury shares without a specific purpose, since they are essentially equivalent to authorized but unissued shares.

To continue with our example of the effect of the small share dividend, note in Illustration 15-8 that the share dividend does not change the total equity. Also note that it does not change the proportion of the total shares outstanding held by each shareholder.

Share Split

If a company has undistributed earnings over several years, and accumulates a sizable balance in retained earnings, the market value of its outstanding shares likely increases.

---

[9]One study concluded that *small* share dividends do not always produce significant amounts of extra value on the date after issuance (ex date) and that *large* share dividends almost always fail to generate extra value on the ex-dividend date. Taylor W. Foster III and Don Vickrey, "The Information Content of Stock Dividend Announcements," *The Accounting Review,* Vol. LIII, No. 2 (April 1978), pp. 360–370.

ILLUSTRATION 15-8
Effects of a Small (10%)
Share Dividend

Before dividend	
Share capital—ordinary, 1,000 shares of £100 par	£100,000
Retained earnings	50,000
Total equity	£150,000
Shareholders' interests:	
A. 400 shares, 40% interest, book value	£ 60,000
B. 500 shares, 50% interest, book value	75,000
C. 100 shares, 10% interest, book value	15,000
	£150,000

After declaration but before distribution of 10% share dividend	
If fair value (£130) is used as basis for entry:	
Share capital—ordinary, 1,000 shares at £100 par	£100,000
Ordinary share dividend distributable, 100 shares at £100 par	10,000
Share premium—ordinary	3,000
Retained earnings (£50,000 − £13,000)	37,000
Total equity	£150,000

After declaration and distribution of 10% share dividend	
If fair value (£130) is used as basis for entry:	
Share capital—ordinary, 1,100 shares at £100 par	£110,000
Share premium—ordinary	3,000
Retained earnings (£50,000 − £13,000)	37,000
Total equity	£150,000
Shareholders' interest:	
A. 440 shares, 40% interest, book value	£ 60,000
B. 550 shares, 50% interest, book value	75,000
C. 110 shares, 10% interest, book value	15,000
	£150,000

Shares issued at prices less than £50 a share can easily attain a market price in excess of £200 a share. The higher the market price of a share, however, the less readily some investors can purchase it.

The managements of many corporations believe that better public relations depend on wider ownership of the corporation shares. They therefore target a market price sufficiently low to be within range of the majority of potential investors. To reduce the market price of each share, they use the common device of a **share split**. For example, after its share price increased by 25-fold, **Qualcomm Inc.** (USA) split its shares 4-for-1. Qualcomm's shares had risen above $500 per share, raising concerns that Qualcomm could not meet an analyst target of $1,000 per share. The split reduced the analysts' target to $250, which it could better meet with wider distribution of shares at lower trading prices.

From an accounting standpoint, Qualcomm **records no entry for a share split**. However, it enters a memorandum note to indicate the changed par value of the shares and the increased number of shares. Illustration 15-9 shows the lack of change in equity for a 2-for-1 share split on 1,000 shares of $100 par value shares with the par being halved upon issuance of the additional shares.

ILLUSTRATION 15-9
Effects of a Share Split

Equity before 2-for-1 Split		Equity after 2-for-1 Split	
Share capital—ordinary, 1,000 shares		Share capital—ordinary, 2,000 shares	
at $100 par	$100,000	at $50 par	$100,000
Retained earnings	50,000	Retained earnings	50,000
	$150,000		$150,000

Share Split and Share Dividend Differentiated

From a legal standpoint, a share split differs from a share dividend. How? A share split increases the number of shares outstanding and decreases the par or stated value per share. **A share dividend, although it increases the number of shares outstanding, does not decrease the par value; thus it increases the total par value of outstanding shares.**

The reasons for issuing a share dividend are numerous and varied. Share dividends can be primarily a publicity gesture, **because many consider share dividends as dividends.** Another reason is that the corporation may simply wish to retain profits in the business by capitalizing a part of retained earnings. In such a situation, it makes a transfer on declaration of a share dividend from earned capital to contributed capital.

A corporation may also use a share dividend, like a share split, to increase the marketability of the shares, although marketability is often a secondary consideration. If the share dividend is large, it has the same effect on market price as a share split. **Whenever corporations issue additional shares for the purpose of reducing the unit market price, then the distribution more closely resembles a share split than a share dividend. This effect usually results only if the number of shares issued is more than 20–25 percent of the number of shares previously outstanding.** A share dividend of more than 20–25 percent of the number of shares previously outstanding is called a large share dividend.[10] Such a distribution should not be called a share dividend but instead "a split-up effected in the form of a dividend" or "share split."

Also, since a split-up effected in the form of a dividend does not alter the par value per share, companies generally are required to transfer the par value amount from retained earnings. In other words, companies transfer from retained earnings to share capital **the par value of the shares issued**, as opposed to a transfer of the market price of the shares issued as in the case of a small share dividend.[11] For example, **Brown Group, Inc.** (USA) at one time authorized a 2-for-1 split, effected in the form of a share dividend. As a result of this authorization, it distributed approximately 10.5 million shares, and transferred more than $39 million representing the par value of the shares issued from Retained Earnings to the Share Capital—Ordinary account.

To illustrate a large share dividend (share split-up effected in the form of a dividend), Rockland Steel, Inc. declared a 30 percent share dividend on November 20, payable December 29 to shareholders of record December 12. At the date of declaration, 1,000,000 shares, par value $10, are outstanding and with a fair value of $200 per share. The entries are:

At date of declaration (November 20)

Retained Earnings	3,000,000	
Ordinary Share Dividend Distributable		3,000,000

Computation: 1,000,000 shares	300,000 Additional shares
× 30%	× $10 Par value
300,000	$3,000,000

At date of distribution (December 29)

Ordinary Share Dividend Distributable	3,000,000	
Share Capital—Ordinary		3,000,000

---

[10]The U.S. SEC has added more precision to the 20–25 percent rule. Specifically, the SEC indicates that companies should consider distributions of 25 percent or more as a "split-up effected in the form of a dividend." Companies should account for distributions of less than 25 percent as a share dividend.

[11]Often, a company records a split-up effected in the form of a dividend as a debit to Share Premium instead of Retained Earnings to indicate that this transaction should affect only contributed capital accounts. No reduction of retained earnings is required except as indicated by legal requirements. *For homework purposes, assume that the debit is to Retained Earnings.* See, for example, Taylor W. Foster III and Edmund Scribner, "Accounting for Stock Dividends and Stock Splits: Corrections to Textbook Coverage," *Issues in Accounting Education* (February 1998).

Illustration 15-10 summarizes and compares the effects in the statement of financial position and related items of various types of dividends and share splits.

			Declaration and Distribution of		
	Declaration of Cash	Payment of Cash	Small Share	Large Share	Share
Effect on:	Dividend	Dividend	Dividend	Dividend	Split
Retained earnings	Decrease	–0–	Decrease[a]	Decrease[b]	–0–
Share capital	–0–	–0–	Increase[b]	Increase[b]	–0–
Share premium	–0–	–0–	Increase[c]	–0–	–0–
Total equity	Decrease	–0–	–0–	–0–	–0–
Working capital	Decrease	–0–	–0–	–0–	–0–
Total assets	–0–	Decrease	–0–	–0–	–0–
Number of shares outstanding	–0–	–0–	Increase	Increase	Increase

[a]Market price of shares. [b]Par or stated value of shares. [c]Excess of market price over par.

Disclosure of Restrictions on Retained Earnings

Many corporations restrict retained earnings or dividends, without any formal journal entries. Such restrictions are **best disclosed by note**. Parenthetical notations are sometimes used, but restrictions imposed by bond indentures and loan agreements commonly require an extended explanation. Notes provide a medium for more complete explanations and free the financial statements from abbreviated notations. The note disclosure should reveal the source of the restriction, pertinent provisions, and the amount of retained earnings subject to restriction, or the amount not restricted.

Restrictions may be based on the retention of a certain retained earnings balance, the ability to maintain certain working capital requirements, additional borrowing, and other considerations. The example from the annual report of **Samsung** (KOR) in Illustration 15-11 shows a note disclosing potential restrictions on retained earnings and dividends.

Samsung

21. RETAINED EARNINGS
Retained earnings as of December 31, 2008 and 2007, consist of the following:

(in millions of Korean won)	2008	2007
Appropriated		
Legal reserve:		
Earned surplus reserve[1]	₩ 450,789	₩ 450,789
Discretionary reserve:		
Reserve for improvement of financial structure	204,815	204,815
Reserve for business rationalization	9,512,101	8,512,101
Reserve for overseas market development	510,750	510,750
Reserve for overseas investment losses	164,962	164,982
Reserve for research and human resource development	26,936,458	22,936,458
Reserve for export losses	167,749	167,749
Reserve for loss on disposal of treasury stock	3,100,000	2,550,000
Reserve for capital expenditure	8,816,905	8,216,439
	49,864,549	**43,711,083**
Unappropriated	5,555,022	7,351,091
Total	**₩55,419,571**	**₩51,065,174**

[1]The Commercial Code of the Republic of Korea requires the Company to appropriate as a legal reserve, an amount equal to a minimum of 10% of annual cash dividends declared, until the reserve equals 50% of its issued capital stock. The reserve is not available for the payment of cash dividends, but may be transferred to capital stock through a resolution of the Board of Directors or used to reduce accumulated deficit, if any, with the ratification of the shareholders.

What do the numbers mean?

DIVIDENDS DOWN, DIVIDENDS UP?

Recently, the number of companies paying dividends is down—really down. As indicated in the chart below, for the first time in at least half a century, companies announced more dividend cuts than increases in 2009. But by the end of the year, positive actions were beginning to predominate.

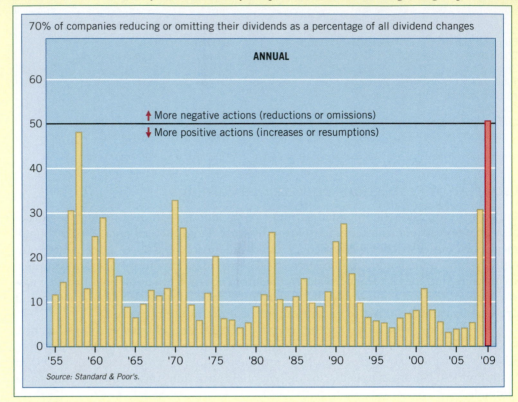

70% of companies reducing or omitting their dividends as a percentage of all dividend changes

ANNUAL

↑ More negative actions (reductions or omissions)
↓ More positive actions (increases or resumptions)

Source: Standard & Poor's.

In a normal year, companies announce 10 to 20 times more favorable than unfavorable dividend changes, but the last two years have been anything but normal. Why? Well, it appears the financial crisis forced many financial companies to cut or suspend payments, and the credit crisis and recession led many other companies to cut back wherever they could. Thus, this has not been a good time to be an investor hoping to get a return on your shares through dividends.

However, just as dividends can go down, they can recover. Indeed, by the end of the year, there were indications that the recession was over and the number of negative dividend decisions began to decline. As one analyst noted, "the fourth quarter was in no way a good period for dividends, but compared to recent history it marks a significant improvement, and when added to the stabilization in increases, the worst may be over."

In fact, the sheer rapidity of the plunge could provide an indication that the dividend recovery will be fast. It is possible that some companies made cuts fearing much worse conditions than actually arrived and will therefore be able to raise payouts even without much improvement in business.

Source: F. Norris, "As Dividends Have Fallen, So May They Rise," *New York Times* (January 9, 2010).

PRESENTATION AND ANALYSIS OF EQUITY

Presentation of Equity

Objective•9

Indicate how to present and analyze equity.

Statement of Financial Position

Illustration 15-12 shows a comprehensive equity section from the statement of financial position of Frost Company that includes the equity items we discussed in this chapter.

Frost should disclose the pertinent rights and privileges of the various securities outstanding. For example, companies must disclose all of the following: dividend and

ILLUSTRATION 15-12
Comprehensive Equity
Presentation

FROST COMPANY EQUITY DECEMBER 31, 2011			
Share capital—preference, €100 par value, 7% cumulative,			
100,000 shares authorized, 30,000 shares issued and outstanding	€3,000,000		
Share capital—ordinary, no par, stated value €10 per share,			
500,000 shares authorized, 400,000 shares issued	4,000,000		
Ordinary share dividend distributable	200,000	€ 7,200,000	
Share premium—preference	150,000		
Share premium—ordinary	840,000	990,000	
Retained earnings		4,360,000	
Treasury shares (2,000 ordinary shares)		(190,000)	
Accumulated other comprehensive loss[12]		(360,000)	
Total equity		€12,000,000	

liquidation preferences, participation rights, call prices and dates, conversion or exercise prices and pertinent dates, sinking fund requirements, unusual voting rights, and significant terms of contracts to issue additional shares. Liquidation preferences should be disclosed in the equity section of the statement of financial position, rather than in the notes to the financial statements, to emphasize the possible effect of this restriction on future cash flows.

Presentation of Statement of Changes in Equity

Companies are also required to present a **statement of changes in equity**. The statement of changes in equity includes the following.

1. Total comprehensive income for the period, showing separately the total amounts attributable to owners of the parent and to non-controlling interests.

2. For each component of equity, the effects of retrospective application or retrospective restatement.

3. For each component of equity, a reconciliation between the carrying amount at the beginning and the end of the period, separately disclosing changes resulting from:
   (a) Profit or loss;
   (b) Each item of other comprehensive income; and
   (c) Transactions with owners in their capacity as owners, showing separately contributions by and distributions to owners and changes in ownership interests in subsidiaries that do not result in a loss of control.

A statement of changes in equity for Park Company is presented in Illustration 15-13.

	Share Capital	Retained Earnings	Unrealized Holding Gain (Loss) on Non-Trading Equity Investments	Unrealized Holding Gain (Loss) on Property, Plant, and Equipment	Total
Balance—December 31, 2010	$600,000	$120,000	$22,000	$15,000	$ 757,000
Issue of Ordinary Shares	200,000				200,000
Total Comprehensive Income		70,000	11,000	8,000	89,000
Dividends		(20,000)			(20,000)
Balance—December 31, 2011	$800,000	$170,000	$33,000	$23,000	$1,026,000

ILLUSTRATION 15-13
Statement of Changes
in Equity

[12]Companies may include a number of items in the "Accumulated other comprehensive loss" or "Accumulated other comprehensive income." Among these items are "Foreign currency translation adjustments" (covered in advanced accounting), "Unrealized holding gains and losses for non-trading equity investments" (covered in Chapter 17), and "Unrealized holding gains or losses on property, plant, and equipment" (covered in Chapter 11), often referred to as revaluation surplus.

In addition, Park is required to present, either in the statement of changes in equity or in the notes, the amount of dividends recognized as distributions to owners during the period and the related amount per share. [5]

Analysis

Analysts use equity ratios to evaluate a company's profitability and long-term solvency. We discuss and illustrate the following three ratios below.

1. Rate of return on ordinary share equity.
2. Payout ratio.
3. Book value per share.

Rate of Return on Ordinary Share Equity

The **rate of return on ordinary share equity** (or return on equity) measures profitability from the ordinary shareholders' viewpoint. This ratio shows how many dollars of net income the company earned for each dollar invested by the owners. Return on equity (ROE) also helps investors judge the worthiness of a share when the overall market is not doing well.

Return on equity equals net income less preference dividends, divided by average ordinary shareholders' equity. For example, assume that Gerber's Inc. had net income of $360,000, declared and paid preference dividends of $54,000, and average ordinary shareholders' equity of $2,550,000. Illustration 15-14 shows how to compute Gerber's ratio.

ILLUSTRATION 15-14
Computation of Rate of Return on Ordinary Share Equity

$$\text{Rate of Return on Ordinary Share Equity} = \frac{\text{Net income} - \text{Preference dividends}}{\text{Average ordinary shareholders' equity}}$$

$$= \frac{\$360,000 - \$54,000}{\$2,550,000}$$

$$= 12\%$$

As shown in Illustration 15-14, when preference shares are present, income available to ordinary shareholders equals net income less preference dividends.

A company can improve its return on ordinary share equity through the prudent use of debt or preference share financing. **Trading on the equity** describes the practice of using borrowed money or issuing preference shares in hopes of obtaining a higher rate of return on the money used. Ordinary shareholders win if return on the assets is higher than the cost of financing these assets. When this happens, the rate of return on ordinary share equity will exceed the rate of return on total assets. In short, the company is "trading on the equity at a gain." In this situation, the money obtained from bondholders or preference shareholders earns enough to pay the interest or preference dividends and leaves a profit for the ordinary shareholders. On the other hand, if the cost of the financing is higher than the rate earned on the assets, the company is trading on equity at a loss and shareholders lose.

Payout Ratio

Another ratio of interest to investors, the **payout ratio**, is the ratio of cash dividends to net income. If preference shares are outstanding, this ratio equals cash dividends paid to ordinary shareholders, divided by net income available to ordinary shareholders. For example, assume that Troy Co. has cash dividends of $100,000 and net income of

$500,000, and no preference shares outstanding. Illustration 15-15 shows the payout ratio computation.

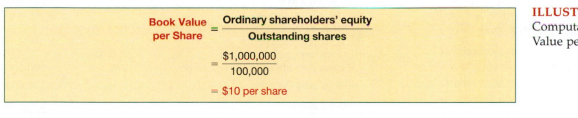

ILLUSTRATION 15-15
Computation of Payout
Ratio

Recently, the payout ratio has plummeted. In 1982, more than half of earnings were converted to dividends. In the second quarter of 2007, just 29 percent of the earnings of the S&P 500 was distributed via dividends.[13]

Book Value per Share

Another basis for evaluating net worth is found in the book value or equity value per share. **Book value per share** is the amount each share would receive if the company were liquidated **on the basis of amounts reported on the statement of financial position**. However, the figure loses much of its relevance if the valuations on the statement of financial position fail to approximate fair value of the assets. Book value per share equals ordinary shareholders' equity divided by outstanding ordinary shares. Assume that Chen Corporation's ordinary shareholders' equity is $1,000,000 and it has 100,000 shares of ordinary shares outstanding. Illustration 15-16 shows its book value per share computation.

ILLUSTRATION 15-16
Computation of Book
Value per Share

You will want to read the
**CONVERGENCE
CORNER** on page 796

For discussion of how international convergence efforts relate to equity.

---

[13]Andrew Blackman, "How Well Do You Know . . . Dividends?" *Wall Street Journal* (September 10, 2007), p. R5.

CONVERGENCE CORNER

EQUITY

The accounting for transactions related to equity, such as issuance of shares, purchase of treasury shares, and declaration and payment of dividends, are similar under both IFRS and U.S. GAAP. Major differences relate to terminology used and presentation of equity information.

RELEVANT FACTS

• Many countries have different investor groups than the United States. For example, in Germany, financial institutions like banks are not only the major creditors but often are the largest shareholders as well. In the United States and the United Kingdom, many companies rely on substantial investment from private investors.

• The accounting for treasury share retirements differs between IFRS and U.S. GAAP. Under U.S. GAAP, a company has three options: (1) charge the excess of the cost of treasury shares over par value to retained earnings, (2) allocate the difference between paid-in capital and retained earnings, or (3) charge the entire amount to paid-in capital. Under IFRS, the excess may have to be charged to paid-in capital, depending on the original transaction related to the issuance of the shares.

• The statement of changes in equity is usually referred to as the statement of stockholders' equity (or shareholders' equity) under U.S. GAAP.

• Both IFRS and U.S. GAAP use the term retained earnings. However, IFRS relies on the term "reserve" as a dumping ground for other types of equity transactions, such as other comprehensive income items as well as various types of unusual transactions related to convertible debt and share option contracts. U.S. GAAP relies on the account Accumulated Other Comprehensive Income (Loss). We also use this account in the chapter as it appears this account is gaining prominence within the IFRS literature.

• Under IFRS, it is common to report "Revaluation Surplus" related to increases or decreases in items such as property, plant, and equipment; mineral resources; and intangible assets. The term surplus is generally not used in U.S. GAAP. In addition, unrealized gains on the above items are not reported in the financial statements under U.S. GAAP.

ABOUT THE NUMBERS

As indicated, numerous differences in terminology exist in comparing equity under IFRS and U.S. GAAP. The following excerpt from a U.S. statement of financial position (balance sheet) illustrates these distinctions (you might compare the presentation here to that in Illustration 15-12 on page 793 under IFRS).

FROST COMPANY STOCKHOLDERS' EQUITY DECEMBER 31, 2011		
Capital stock		
Preferred stock, $100 par value, 7% cumulative, 100,000 shares authorized, 30,000 shares issued and outstanding		$ 3,000,000
Common stock, no par, stated value $10 per share, 500,000 shares authorized, 400,000 shares issued		4,000,000
Common stock dividend distributable, 20,000 shares		200,000
Total capital stock		7,200,000
Additional paid-in capital		
Excess over par—preferred	$150,000	
Excess over stated value—common	840,000	990,000
Total paid-in capital		8,190,000
Retained earnings		4,360,000
Total paid-in capital and retained earnings		12,550,000
Less: Cost of treasury stock (2,000 shares, common)		(190,000)
Accumulated other comprehensive loss		(360,000)
Total stockholders' equity		$12,000,000

ON THE HORIZON

As indicated in earlier discussions, the IASB and the FASB are currently working on a project related to financial statement presentation. An important part of this study is to determine whether certain line items, subtotals, and totals should be clearly defined and required to be displayed in the financial statements. For example, it is likely that the statement of changes in equity and its presentation will be examined closely. In addition, the options of how to present other comprehensive income under U.S. GAAP will change in any converged standard.

SUMMARY OF LEARNING OBJECTIVES

[1] **Discuss the characteristics of the corporate form of organization.** Among the specific characteristics of the corporate form that affect accounting are the: (1) influence of corporate law, (2) use of the share system, and (3) development of a variety of ownership interests. In the absence of restrictive provisions, each ordinary share carries the right to share proportionately in: (1) profits and losses, (2) management (the right to vote for directors), (3) corporate assets upon liquidation, and (4) any new issues of shares of the same class (called the preemptive right).

[2] **Identify the key components of equity.** Equity is classified into two categories: contributed capital and earned capital. Contributed capital (paid-in capital) describes the total amount paid in as share capital. Put another way, it is the amount that shareholders advance to the corporation for use in the business. Contributed capital includes items such as the par value of all outstanding shares and premiums less any discounts on issuance. Earned capital is the capital that develops if the business operates profitably; it consists of all undistributed income that remains invested in the company.

[3] **Explain the accounting procedures for issuing shares.** Accounts are kept for the following different types of shares: *Par value shares:* (a) Share Capital—Preference or Share Capital—Ordinary, (b) Share Premium—Preference and Share Premium—Ordinary. *No-par shares:* Share Capital—Ordinary or Share Capital—Ordinary and Share Premium—Ordinary if stated value used. Shares issued in combination with other securities (lump-sum sales): The two methods of allocation available are (a) the proportional method, and (b) the incremental method. Shares issued in non-cash transactions: When issuing shares for services or property other than cash, the company should record the exchange at the fair value of the property or services received unless that fair value cannot be reliably measured. Otherwise, use the fair value of the shares issued.

[4] **Describe the accounting for treasury shares.** The cost method is generally used in accounting for treasury shares. This method derives its name from the fact that a company maintains the Treasury Shares account at the cost of the shares purchased. Under the cost method, a company debits the Treasury Shares account for the cost of the shares acquired and credits it for this same cost upon reissuance. The price received for the shares when originally issued does not affect the entries to record the acquisition and reissuance of the treasury shares.

[5] **Explain the accounting for and reporting of preference shares.** Preference shares are a special class of shares that possess certain preferences or features not possessed by the ordinary shares. The features that are most often associated with preference share issues are: (1) preference as to dividends, (2) preference as to assets in the event of liquidation, (3) convertible into ordinary shares, (4) callable at the option of the corporation, and (5) non-voting. At issuance, the accounting for preference shares is similar to that for ordinary shares. When convertible preference shares are converted, a company uses the book value method: It debits Share Capital—Preference, along with any related Share Premium—Preference, and credits Share Capital—Ordinary and Share Premium—Ordinary (if an excess exists).

[6] **Describe the policies used in distributing dividends.** The incorporation laws normally provide information concerning the legal restrictions related to the payment of dividends. Corporations rarely pay dividends in an amount equal to the legal limit. This is due, in part, to the fact that companies use assets represented by undistributed earnings to finance future operations of the business. If a company is considering declaring a dividend, it must ask two preliminary questions: (1) Is the condition of the

KEY TERMS

book value per share, *795*
callable preference shares *782*
cash dividends, *785*
contributed (paid-in) capital, *772*
convertible preference shares, *782*
cost method, *778*
cumulative preference shares *782*
dividend in arrears, *782*
earned capital, *772*
equity, *772*
large share dividend, *790*
leveraged buyout (LBO), *777*
liquidating dividends, *785, 787*
lump-sum sales, *774*
no-par shares, *773*
ordinary shares, *771*
par (stated) value method, *778*
participating preference shares, *782*
payout ratio, *794*
preemptive right, *770*
preference shares, *771, 781*
property dividends, *786*
rate of return on ordinary share equity, *794*
redeemable preference shares, *782*
residual interest, *772*
retained earnings, *772*
share dividends, *787*
share premium, *773*
share split, *789*
small (ordinary) share dividends, *788*
stated value, *774*
statement of changes in equity, *793*
trading on the equity, *794*
treasury shares, *777*

corporation such that the dividend is **legally permissible**? (2) Is the condition of the corporation such that a dividend is **economically sound**?

•7 **Identify the various forms of dividend distributions.** Dividends are of the following types: (1) cash dividends, (2) property dividends, (3) liquidating dividends (dividends based on other than retained earnings), and (4) share dividends (the issuance by a corporation of its own shares to its shareholders on a pro rata basis, but without receiving consideration).

•8 **Explain the accounting for small and large share dividends, and for share splits.** Accounting for small share dividends (less than 20–25 percent) relies on the fair value of the shares issued. When declaring a share dividend, a company debits Retained Earnings at the fair value of the shares it distributes. The entry includes a credit to Ordinary Share Dividend Distributable at par value times the number of shares, with any excess credited to Share Premium—Ordinary. If the number of shares issued exceeds 20–25 percent of the shares outstanding (large share dividend), it debits Retained Earnings at par value and credits Ordinary Share Dividend Distributable— there is no share premium.

A share dividend is a capitalization of retained earnings that reduces retained earnings. The par value per share and total equity remain unchanged with a share dividend, and all shareholders retain their same proportionate share of ownership. A share split results in an increase or decrease in the number of shares outstanding, with a corresponding decrease or increase in the par or stated value per share. No accounting entry is required for a share split.

•9 **Indicate how to present and analyze equity.** The equity section of a statement of financial position includes share capital, share premium, and retained earnings. A company may also have additional items such as treasury shares, accumulated other comprehensive income (loss), and minority interest. Companies are required to present a statement of changes in equity. Ratios that use equity amounts are rate of return on ordinary share equity, payout ratio, and book value per share.

APPENDIX 15A | **DIVIDEND PREFERENCES AND BOOK VALUE PER SHARE**

DIVIDEND PREFERENCES

Objective•10

Explain the different types of preference share dividends and their effect on book value per share.

Illustrations 15A-1 to 15A-4 indicate the **effects of** various **dividend preferences** on dividend distributions to ordinary and preference shareholders. Assume that in 2011, Mason Company is to distribute $50,000 as cash dividends, its outstanding ordinary shares have a par value of $400,000, and its 6 percent preference shares have a par value of $100,000. Mason would distribute dividends to each class, employing the assumptions given, as follows.

1. If the preference shares are non-cumulative and non-participating:

ILLUSTRATION 15A-1
Dividend Distribution, Non-Cumulative and Non-Participating Preference

	Preference	Ordinary	Total
6% of $100,000	$6,000		$ 6,000
The remainder to ordinary		$44,000	44,000
Totals	$6,000	$44,000	$50,000

2. If the preference shares are cumulative and non-participating, and Mason Company did not pay dividends on the preference shares in the preceding two years:

	Preference	Ordinary	Total
Dividends in arrears, 6% of $100,000 for 2 years	$12,000		$12,000
Current year's dividend, 6% of $100,000	6,000		6,000
The remainder to ordinary		$32,000	32,000
Totals	$18,000	$32,000	$50,000

ILLUSTRATION 15A-2
Dividend Distribution, Cumulative and Non-Participating Preference Shares, with Dividends in Arrears

3. If the preference shares are non-cumulative and are fully participating:[14]

	Preference	Ordinary	Total
Current year's dividend, 6%	$ 6,000	$24,000	$30,000
Participating dividend of 4%	4,000	16,000	20,000
Totals	$10,000	$40,000	$50,000

The participating dividend was determined as follows:

Current year's dividend:		
Preference, 6% of $100,000 = $ 6,000		
Ordinary, 6% of $400,000 = 24,000	$30,000	
Amount available for participation ($50,000 − $30,000)	$20,000	
Par value of shares that are to participate ($100,000 + $400,000)	$500,000	
Rate of participation ($20,000 ÷ $500,000)	4%	
Participating dividend:		
Preference, 4% of $100,000	$ 4,000	
Ordinary, 4% of $400,000	16,000	
	$20,000	

ILLUSTRATION 15A-3
Dividend Distribution, Non-Cumulative and Fully Participating Preference Shares

4. If the preference shares are cumulative and are fully participating, and Mason Company did not pay dividends on the preference shares in the preceding two years:

	Preference	Ordinary	Total
Dividends in arrears, 6% of $100,000 for 2 years	$12,000		$12,000
Current year's dividend, 6%	6,000	$24,000	30,000
Participating dividend, 1.6% ($8,000 ÷ $500,000)	1,600	6,400	8,000
Totals	$19,600	$30,400	$50,000

ILLUSTRATION 15A-4
Dividend Distribution, Cumulative and Fully Participating Preference Shares, with Dividends in Arrears

BOOK VALUE PER SHARE

Book value per share in its simplest form is computed as net assets divided by outstanding shares at the end of the year. The computation of book value per share becomes more complicated if a company has preference shares in its capital structure. For

[14]When preference shares are participating, there may be different agreements as to how the participation feature is to be executed. However, in the absence of any specific agreement the following procedure is recommended:

    a. After the preference shares are assigned its current year's dividend, the ordinary shares will receive a "like" percentage of par value outstanding. In example (3), this amounts to 6 percent of $400,000.

    b. In example (3), shown in Illustration 15A-3, the remainder of the declared dividend is $20,000. We divide this amount by total par value ($500,000) to find the rate of participation to be applied to each class of shares. In this case, the rate of participation is 4% ($20,000 ÷ $500,000), which we then multiply by the par value of each class of shares to determine the amount of participation.

example, if preference dividends are in arrears, if the preference shares are participating, or if preference shares have a redemption or liquidating value higher than its carrying amount, the company must allocate retained earnings between the preference and ordinary shareholders in computing book value.

To illustrate, assume that the following situation exists.

ILLUSTRATION 15A-5
Computation of Book Value per Share—No Dividends in Arrears

Equity	Preference	Ordinary
Preference shares, 5%	$300,000	
Ordinary shares		$400,000
Share premium—ordinary		37,500
Retained earnings		162,582
Totals	$300,000	$600,082
Shares outstanding		4,000
Book value per share		$150.02

The situation in Illustration 15A-5 assumes that no preference dividends are in arrears and that the preference shares are not participating. Now assume that the same facts exist except that the 5 percent preference shares are cumulative, participating up to 8 percent, and that dividends for three years before the current year are in arrears. Illustration 15A-6 shows how to compute the book value of the ordinary shares, assuming that no action has yet been taken concerning dividends for the current year.

ILLUSTRATION 15A-6
Computation of Book Value per Share—with Dividends in Arrears

Equity	Preference	Ordinary
Preference shares, 5%	$300,000	
Ordinary shares		$400,000
Share premium—ordinary		37,500
Retained earnings:		
Dividends in arrears (3 years at 5% a year)	45,000	
Current year requirement at 5%	15,000	20,000
Participating—additional 3%	9,000	12,000
Remainder to ordinary		61,582
Totals	$369,000	$531,082
Shares outstanding		4,000
Book value per share		$132.77

In connection with the book value computation, the analyst must know how to handle the following items: the number of authorized and unissued shares, the number of treasury shares on hand, any commitments with respect to the issuance of unissued shares or the reissuance of treasury shares, and the relative rights and privileges of the various types of shares authorized. As an example, if the liquidating value of the preference shares is higher than its carrying amount, the liquidating amount should be used in the book value computation.

SUMMARY OF LEARNING OBJECTIVE FOR APPENDIX 15A

•10 **Explain the different types of preference share dividends and their effect on book value per share.** The dividend preferences of preference shares affect the dividends paid to shareholders. Preference shares can be (1) cumulative or non-cumulative, and (2) fully participating, partially participating, or non-participating. If preference dividends are in arrears, if the preference shares are participating, or if preference shares have a redemption or liquidation value higher than its carrying amount, allocate retained earnings between preference and ordinary shareholders in computing book value per share.

AUTHORITATIVE LITERATURE

Authoritative Literature References

[1] "Framework for the Preparation and Presentation of Financial Statements" (London, U.K.: IASB, 2001), par. 49.

[2] International Financial Reporting Standard 2, *Share-Based Payment* (London, U.K.: International Accounting Standards Committee Foundation, 2004), par. 10.

[3] International Accounting Standard 32, *Financial Instruments: Presentation* (London, U.K.: International Accounting Standards Committee Foundation, 2003), paras. 18–20.

[4] International Accounting Standard 1, *Presentation of Financial Statements* (London, U.K.: International Accounting Standards Committee Foundation, 2003), par. 79.

[5] International Accounting Standard 1, *Presentation of Financial Statements* (London, U.K.: International Accounting Standards Committee Foundation, 2003), paras. 106–107.

Note: All asterisked Questions, Exercises, and Problems relate to material in the appendix to the chapter.

QUESTIONS

1. In the absence of restrictive provisions, what are the basic rights of shareholders of a corporation?

2. Why is a preemptive right important?

3. Distinguish between ordinary and preference shares.

4. Why is the distinction between contributed capital (paid-in capital) and retained earnings important?

5. Explain each of the following terms: authorized ordinary shares, unissued ordinary shares, issued ordinary shares, outstanding ordinary shares, and treasury shares.

6. What is meant by par value, and what is its significance to shareholders?

7. Describe the accounting for the issuance for cash of no-par value ordinary shares at a price in excess of the stated value of the ordinary shares.

8. Explain the difference between the proportional method and the incremental method of allocating the proceeds of lump-sum sales of share capital.

9. What are the different bases for share valuation when assets other than cash are received for issued shares?

10. Explain how underwriting costs and accounting and legal fees associated with the issuance of shares should be recorded.

11. For what reasons might a corporation purchase its own shares?

12. Discuss the propriety of showing:

    (a) Treasury shares as an asset.

    (b) "Gain" or "loss" on sale of treasury shares as additions to or deductions from income.

    (c) Dividends received on treasury shares as income.

13. What features or rights may alter the character of preference shares?

14. Kim Inc. recently noted that its 4% preference shares and 4% participating preference shares, which are both cumulative, have priority as to dividends up to 4% of their par value. Its participating preference shares participate equally with the ordinary shares in any dividends in excess of 4%. What is meant by the term participating? Cumulative?

15. Where in the financial statements are preference shares normally reported?

16. List five sources of equity.

17. BMG Inc. purchases 10,000 shares of its own previously issued €10 par ordinary shares for €290,000. Assuming the shares are held in the treasury with intent to reissue,

what effect does this transaction have on (a) net income, (b) total assets, (c) retained earnings, and (d) total equity?

18. Indicate how each of the following accounts should be classified in the equity section.

(a) Share Capital—Ordinary

(b) Retained Earnings

(c) Share Premium—Ordinary

(d) Treasury Shares

(e) Share Premium—Treasury

(f) Accumulated Other Comprehensive Income

(g) Share Capital—Preference

19. What factors influence the dividend policy of a company?

20. What are the principal considerations of a board of directors in making decisions involving dividend declarations? Discuss briefly.

21. Dividends are sometimes said to have been paid "out of retained earnings." What is the error, if any, in that statement?

22. Distinguish among cash dividends, property dividends, liquidating dividends, and share dividends.

23. Describe the accounting entry for a share dividend, if any. Describe the accounting entry for a share split, if any.

24. Share splits and share dividends may be used by a corporation to change the number of its shares outstanding.

(a) What is meant by a share split effected in the form of a dividend?

(b) From an accounting viewpoint, explain how the share split effected in the form of a dividend differs from an ordinary share dividend.

(c) How should a share dividend that has been declared but not yet issued be classified in a statement of financial position? Why?

25. The following comment appeared in the notes of Mona Corporation's annual report: "Such distributions, representing proceeds from the sale of Sarazan, Inc. were paid in the form of partial liquidating dividends and were in lieu of a portion of the Company's ordinary cash dividends." How would a partial liquidating dividend be accounted for in the financial records?

26. This comment appeared in the annual report of Christensen Inc.: "The Company could pay cash or property dividends on the Class A ordinary shares without paying cash or property dividends on the Class B ordinary shares. But if the Company pays any cash or property dividends on the Class B ordinary shares, it would be required to pay at least the same dividend on the Class A ordinary shares." How is a property dividend accounted for in the financial records?

27. For what reasons might a company restrict a portion of its retained earnings?

28. How are restrictions of retained earnings reported?

29. Mary Tokar is comparing a U.S. GAAP-based company to a company that uses IFRS. Both companies report non-trading equity investments. The IFRS company reports unrealized losses on these investments under the heading "Reserves" in its equity section. However, Mary can find no similar heading in the U.S. GAAP company financial statements. Can Mary conclude that the U.S. GAAP company has no unrealized gains or losses on its non-trading equity investments? Explain.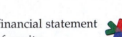

30. Briefly describe some of the similarities and differences between U.S. GAAP and IFRS with respect to the accounting for equity.

31. Briefly discuss the implications of the financial statement presentation project for the reporting of equity.

*32. Wang Corp. had $100,000 of 7%, $20 par value preference shares and 12,000 shares of $25 par value ordinary shares outstanding throughout 2011.

(a) Assuming that total dividends declared in 2011 were $64,000, and that the preference shares are not cumulative but are fully participating, ordinary shareholders should receive 2011 dividends of what amount?

(b) Assuming that total dividends declared in 2011 were $64,000, and that the preference shares are fully participating and cumulative with preference dividends in arrears for 2010, preference shareholders should receive 2011 dividends totaling what amount?

(c) Assuming that total dividends declared in 2011 were $30,000, that the preference shares are cumulative, non-participating and were issued on January 1, 2010, and that $5,000 of preference dividends were declared and paid in 2010, the ordinary shareholders should receive 2011 dividends totaling what amount?

BRIEF EXERCISES

•3 BE15-1 Kaymer Corporation issued 300 shares of €10 par value ordinary shares for €4,500. Prepare Kaymer's journal entry.

•3 BE15-2 Swarten Corporation issued 600 shares of no-par ordinary shares for €8,200. Prepare Swarten's journal entry if (a) the shares have no stated value, and (b) the shares have a stated value of €2 per share.

·4 ·9 **BE15-3** Wilco Corporation has the following account balances at December 31, 2010.

Share capital—ordinary, €5 par value	€ 510,000
Treasury shares	90,000
Retained earnings	2,340,000
Share premium—ordinary	1,320,000

Prepare Wilco's December 31, 2010, equity section.

·3 **BE15-4** Ravonette Corporation issued 300 shares of $10 par value ordinary shares and 100 shares of $50 par value preference shares for a lump sum of $13,500. The ordinary shares have a market price of $20 per share, and the preference shares have a market price of $90 per share. Prepare the journal entry to record the issuance.

·3 **BE15-5** On February 1, 2010, Gruber Corporation issued 3,000 shares of its £5 par value ordinary shares for land worth £31,000. Prepare the February 1, 2010, journal entry.

·3 **BE15-6** Moonwalker Corporation issued 2,000 shares of its $10 par value ordinary shares for $60,000. Moonwalker also incurred $1,500 of costs associated with issuing the shares. Prepare Moonwalker's journal entry to record the issuance of the company's shares.

·4 **BE15-7** Sprinkle Inc. has outstanding 10,000 shares of €10 par value ordinary shares. On July 1, 2010, Sprinkle reacquired 100 shares at €87 per share. On September 1, Sprinkle reissued 60 shares at €90 per share. On November 1, Sprinkle reissued 40 shares at €83 per share. Prepare Sprinkle's journal entries to record these transactions using the cost method.

·4 **BE15-8** Arantxa Corporation has outstanding 20,000 shares of $5 par value ordinary shares. On August 1, 2010, Arantxa reacquired 200 shares at $80 per share. On November 1, Arantxa reissued the 200 shares at $70 per share. Arantxa had no previous treasury share transactions. Prepare Arantxa's journal entries to record these transactions using the cost method.

·5 **BE15-9** Hinges Corporation issued 500 shares of €100 par value preference shares for €61,500. Prepare Hinges's journal entry.

·6 **BE15-10** Woolford Inc. declared a cash dividend of $1 per share on its 2 million outstanding shares. The dividend was declared on August 1, payable on September 9 to all shareholders of record on August 15. Prepare all journal entries necessary on those three dates.

·6 ·7 **BE15-11** Silva Inc. owns shares of Costa Corporation classified as a non-trading equity investment. At December 31, 2010, the non-trading equity investment was carried in Silva's accounting records at its cost of R$875,000, which equals its fair value. On September 21, 2011, when the fair value of the investment was R$1,200,000, Silva declared a property dividend whereby the Costa securities are to be distributed on October 23, 2011, to shareholders of record on October 8, 2011. Prepare all journal entries necessary on those three dates.

·6 ·7 **BE15-12** Zhang Mining Company declared, on April 20, a dividend of ¥500,000 payable on June 1. Of this amount, ¥125,000 is a return of capital. Prepare the April 20 and June 1 entries for Zhang.

·8 **BE15-13** Green Day Corporation has outstanding 400,000 shares of $10 par value ordinary shares. The corporation declares a 5% share dividend when the fair value is $65 per share. Prepare the journal entries for Green Day Corporation for both the date of declaration and the date of distribution.

·8 **BE15-14** Use the information from BE15-13, but assume Green Day Corporation declared a 100% share dividend rather than a 5% share dividend. Prepare the journal entries for both the date of declaration and the date of distribution.

·10 *****BE15-15** Nottebart Corporation has outstanding 10,000 shares of $100 par value, 6% preference shares and 60,000 shares of $10 par value ordinary shares. The preference shares were issued in January 2010, and no dividends were declared in 2010 or 2011. In 2012, Nottebart declares a cash dividend of $300,000. How will the dividend be shared by ordinary and preference shareholders if the preference is (a) non-cumulative and (b) cumulative?

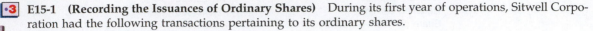

EXERCISES

·3 **E15-1** **(Recording the Issuances of Ordinary Shares)** During its first year of operations, Sitwell Corporation had the following transactions pertaining to its ordinary shares.

Jan. 10	Issued 80,000 shares for cash at €6 per share.	
Mar. 1	Issued 5,000 shares to attorneys in payment of a bill for €35,000 for services rendered in helping the company to incorporate.	
July 1	Issued 30,000 shares for cash at €8 per share.	
Sept. 1	Issued 60,000 shares for cash at €10 per share.	

Instructions

(a) Prepare the journal entries for these transactions, assuming that the ordinary shares have a par value of €3 per share.

(b) Briefly discuss how the entries in part (a) will change if the shares are no-par with a stated value of €2 per share.

·3 **E15-2** **(Recording the Issuance of Ordinary and Preference Shares)** Abernathy Corporation was organized on January 1, 2010. It is authorized to issue 10,000 shares of 8%, $50 par value preference shares, and 500,000 shares of no-par ordinary shares with a stated value of $2 per share. The following share transactions were completed during the first year.

Jan. 10	Issued 80,000 ordinary shares for cash at $5 per share.
Mar. 1	Issued 5,000 preference shares for cash at $108 per share.
Apr. 1	Issued 24,000 ordinary shares for land. The asking price of the land was $90,000; the fair value of the land was $80,000.
May 1	Issued 80,000 ordinary shares for cash at $7 per share.
Aug. 1	Issued 10,000 ordinary shares to attorneys in payment of their bill of $50,000 for services rendered in helping the company organize.
Sept. 1	Issued 10,000 ordinary shares for cash at $9 per share.
Nov. 1	Issued 1,000 preference shares for cash at $112 per share.

Instructions

Prepare the journal entries to record the above transactions.

·3 **E15-3** **(Shares Issued for Land)** Twenty-five thousand shares reacquired by Pierce Corporation for $48 per share were exchanged for undeveloped land that has an appraised value of $1,700,000. At the time of the exchange, the ordinary shares were trading at $60 per share on an organized exchange.

Instructions

(a) Prepare the journal entry to record the acquisition of land, assuming that the purchase of the shares was originally recorded using the cost method.

(b) Briefly identify the possible alternatives (including those that are totally unacceptable) for quantifying the cost of the land and briefly support your choice.

·3 **E15-4** **(Lump-Sum Sale of Shares with Bonds)** Fogelberg Corporation is a regional company, whose securities are thinly traded. Fogelberg has issued 10,000 units. Each unit consists of a $500 par, 12% subordinated debenture and 10 shares of $5 par ordinary shares. The investment banker has retained 400 units as the underwriting fee. The other 9,600 units were sold to outside investors for cash at $850 per unit. Prior to this sale, the 2-week ask price of ordinary shares was $40 per share. Twelve percent is a reasonable market yield for the debentures, and therefore the par value of the bonds is equal to the fair value.

Instructions

(a) Prepare the journal entry to record Fogelberg's transaction, under the following conditions.
 (1) Employing the incremental method.
 (2) Employing the proportional method, assuming the recent price quote on the ordinary shares reflects fair value.

(b) Briefly explain which method is, in your opinion, the better method.

·3 ·5 **E15-5** **(Lump-Sum Sales of Ordinary and Preference Shares)** Hartman Inc. issues 500 shares of €10 par value ordinary shares and 100 shares of €100 par value preference shares for a lump sum of €100,000.

Instructions

(a) Prepare the journal entry for the issuance when the fair value of the ordinary shares is €168 each and fair value of the preference shares is €210 each. (Round to nearest euro.)

(b) Prepare the journal entry for the issuance when only the fair value of the ordinary shares is known and it is €170 per share.

•3 •4 E15-6 (Share Issuances and Repurchase) Loxley Corporation is authorized to issue 50,000 shares of $10 par value ordinary shares. During 2010, Loxley took part in the following selected transactions.

1. Issued 5,000 shares at $45 per share, less costs related to the issuance of the shares totaling $7,000.
2. Issued 1,000 shares for land appraised at $50,000. The shares were actively traded on a national securities exchange at approximately $46 per share on the date of issuance.
3. Purchased 500 treasury shares at $44 per share. The treasury shares purchased were issued in 2009 at $40 per share.

Instructions

(a) Prepare the journal entry to record item 1.
(b) Prepare the journal entry to record item 2.
(c) Prepare the journal entry to record item 3 using the cost method.

•4 E15-7 (Effect of Treasury Share Transactions on Financials) Goosen Company has outstanding 40,000 shares of R5 par ordinary shares which had been issued at R30 per share. Goosen then entered into the following transactions.

1. Purchased 5,000 treasury shares at R45 per share.
2. Resold 500 of the treasury shares at R40 per share.
3. Resold 2,000 of the treasury shares at R49 per share.

Instructions

Use the following code to indicate the effect each of the three transactions has on the financial statement categories listed in the table below, assuming Goosen Company uses the cost method: I = Increase; D = Decrease; NE = No effect.

#	Assets	Liabilities	Equity	Share Premium	Retained Earnings	Net Income
1						
2						
3						

•3 •5 •10 E15-8 (Preference Share Entries and Dividends) Weisberg Corporation has 10,000 shares of $100 par value, 6%, preference shares and 50,000 ordinary shares of $10 par value outstanding at December 31, 2010.

Instructions

Answer the questions in each of the following independent situations.

(a) If the preference shares are cumulative and dividends were last paid on the preference shares on December 31, 2007, what are the dividends in arrears that should be reported on the December 31, 2010, statement of financial position? How should these dividends be reported?

(b) If the preference shares are convertible into seven shares of $10 par value ordinary shares and 3,000 shares are converted, what entry is required for the conversion, assuming the preference shares were issued at par value?

(c) If the preference shares were issued at $107 per share, how should the preference shares be reported in the equity section?

•3 •4 E15-9 (Correcting Entries for Equity Transactions) Davison Inc. recently hired a new accountant with extensive experience in accounting for partnerships. Because of the pressure of the new job, the accountant was unable to review what he had learned earlier about corporation accounting. During the first month, he made the following entries for the corporation's ordinary shares.

May 2	Cash		192,000	
	Share Capital—Ordinary			192,000
	(Issued 12,000 shares of $10 par value ordinary shares at $16 per share)			
10	Cash		600,000	
	Share Capital—Ordinary			600,000
	(Issued 10,000 shares of $30 par value preference shares at $60 per share)			
15	Share Capital—Ordinary		14,000	
	Cash			14,000
	(Purchased 1,000 ordinary shares for the treasury at $14 per share)			
31	Cash		8,500	
	Share Capital—Ordinary			5,000
	Gain on Sale of Shares			3,500
	(Sold 500 treasury shares at $17 per share)			

Instructions

On the basis of the explanation for each entry, prepare the entries that should have been made for the ordinary share transactions.

·3 ·4 **E15-10** **(Analysis of Equity Data and Equity Section Preparation)** For a recent 2-year period, the statement of financial position of Jones Company showed the following equity data at December 31 in millions.

	2011	2010
Share premium—ordinary	$ 891	$ 817
Share capital—ordinary	545	540
Retained earnings	7,167	5,226
Treasury shares	(1,428)	(918)
Total equity	$7,175	$5,665
Ordinary shares issued	218	216
Ordinary shares authorized	500	500
Treasury shares	34	27

Instructions

(a) Answer the following questions.
   (1) What is the par value of the ordinary shares?
   (2) What is the cost per treasury share at December 31, 2011, and at December 31, 2010?
(b) Prepare the equity section at December 31, 2011.

·7 ·8 **E15-11** **(Equity Items on the Statement of Financial Position)** The following are selected transactions that may affect equity.

1. Recorded accrued interest earned on a note receivable.
2. Declared and distributed a share split.
3. Declared a cash dividend.
4. Recorded a retained earnings restriction.
5. Recorded the expiration of insurance coverage that was previously recorded as prepaid insurance.
6. Paid the cash dividend declared in item 3 above.
7. Recorded accrued interest expense on a note payable.
8. Declared a share dividend.
9. Distributed the share dividend declared in item 8.

Instructions

In the following table, indicate the effect each of the nine transactions has on the financial statement elements listed. Use the following code:

| | | | I = Increase | D = Decrease | NE = No effect | |

Item	Assets	Liabilities	Equity	Share Premium	Retained Earnings	Net Income

•7 E15-12 (Cash Dividend and Liquidating Dividend) Addison Corporation has 10 million shares of ordinary shares issued and outstanding. On June 1, the board of directors voted a 60 cents per share cash dividend to shareholders of record as of June 14, payable June 30.

Instructions

(a) Prepare the journal entry for each of the dates above, assuming the dividend represents a distribution of earnings.

(b) How would the entry differ if the dividend were a liquidating dividend?

•8 E15-13 (Share Split and Share Dividend) The ordinary shares of Warner Inc. are currently selling at $110 per share. The directors wish to reduce the share price and increase share volume prior to a new issue. The per share par value is $10; book value is $70 per share. Five million shares are issued and outstanding.

Instructions

Prepare the necessary journal entries assuming the following.

(a) The board votes a 2-for-1 share split.

(b) The board votes a 100% share dividend.

(c) Briefly discuss the accounting and securities market differences between these two methods of increasing the number of shares outstanding.

•8 E15-14 (Entries for Share Dividends and Share Splits) The equity accounts of Lawrence Company have the following balances on December 31, 2010.

Share Capital—Ordinary, €10 par, 200,000 shares issued and outstanding	€2,000,000
Share Premium—Ordinary	1,200,000
Retained Earnings	5,600,000

Shares of Lawrence Company are currently selling at €37.

Instructions

Prepare the appropriate journal entries for each of the following cases.

(a) A share dividend of 5% is declared and issued.

(b) A share dividend of 100% is declared and issued.

(c) A 2-for-1 share split is declared and issued.

•7 •8 E15-15 (Dividend Entries) The following data were taken from the statement of financial position accounts of Murless Corporation on December 31, 2010.

Current Assets	R540,000
Investments	624,000
Share Capital—Ordinary (par value R10)	600,000
Share Premium—Ordinary	150,000
Retained Earnings	840,000

Instructions

Prepare the required journal entries for the following unrelated items.

(a) A 5% share dividend is declared and distributed at a time when the market price of the shares is R39 per share.

(b) The par value of the ordinary shares is reduced to R2 with a 5-for-1 share split.

(c) A dividend is declared January 5, 2011, and paid January 25, 2011, in bonds held as an investment. The bonds have a book value of R90,000 and a fair value of R125,000.

·6 ·7 ·8 E15-16 (Computation of Retained Earnings) The following information has been taken from the ledger accounts of Choi Corporation (all amounts in 000).

Total Income since Incorporation	₩287,000
Total Cash Dividends Paid	60,000
Total Value of Share Dividends Distributed	40,000
Gains on Treasury Share Transactions	18,000
Accumulated Other Comprehensive Income	32,000

Instructions

Determine the current balance of retained earnings.

·9 E15-17 (Equity Section) Teller Corporation's post-closing trial balance at December 31, 2010, was as follows.

TELLER CORPORATION POST-CLOSING TRIAL BALANCE DECEMBER 31, 2010		
	Dr.	Cr.
Accounts payable		€ 310,000
Accounts receivable	€ 480,000	
Accumulated depreciation—building and equipment		185,000
Allowance for doubtful accounts		30,000
Bonds payable		700,000
Building and equipment	1,450,000	
Cash	190,000	
Dividends payable on preference shares—cash		4,000
Inventories	560,000	
Land	400,000	
Prepaid expenses	40,000	
Retained earnings		201,000
Share capital—ordinary (€1 par value)		200,000
Share capital—preference (€50 par value)		500,000
Share premium—ordinary		1,000,000
Share premium—treasury		160,000
Treasury shares—ordinary at cost	170,000	
Totals	€3,290,000	€3,290,000

At December 31, 2010, Teller had the following number of ordinary and preference shares.

	Ordinary	Preference
Authorized	600,000	60,000
Issued	200,000	10,000
Outstanding	190,000	10,000

The dividends on preference shares are €4 cumulative. In addition, the preference shares have a preference in liquidation of €50 per share.

Instructions

Prepare the equity section of Teller's statement of financial position at December 31, 2010.

·4 ·7 ·8 E15-18 (Dividends and Equity Section) Elizabeth Company reported the following amounts in the equity section of its December 31, 2010, statement of financial position.

Share capital—preference, 8%, $100 par (10,000 shares authorized, 2,000 shares issued)	$200,000
Share capital—ordinary, $5 par (100,000 shares authorized, 20,000 shares issued)	100,000
Share premium	125,000
Retained earnings	450,000
Total	$875,000

During 2011, Elizabeth took part in the following transactions concerning equity.

1. Paid the annual 2010 $8 per share dividend on preference shares and a $2 per share dividend on ordinary shares. These dividends had been declared on December 31, 2010.
2. Purchased 2,700 shares of its own outstanding ordinary shares for $40 per share. Elizabeth uses the cost method.
3. Reissued 700 treasury shares for land valued at $30,000.
4. Issued 500 preference shares at $105 per share.
5. Declared a 10% share dividend on the outstanding ordinary shares when the shares are selling for $45 per share.
6. Issued the share dividend.
7. Declared the annual 2011 $8 per share dividend on preference shares and the $2 per share dividend on ordinary shares. These dividends are payable in 2012.

Instructions

(a) Prepare journal entries to record the transactions described above.
(b) Prepare the December 31, 2011, equity section. Assume 2011 net income was $330,000.

·9 E15-19 (Comparison of Alternative Forms of Financing) Shown below is the equity and liabilities section of the statement of financial position for Ingalls Company and Wilder Company. Each has assets totaling $4,200,000.

Ingalls Co.		Wilder Co.	
Share capital—ordinary ($20 par)	$2,000,000	Share capital—ordinary ($20 par)	$2,900,000
Retained earnings (Cash		Retained earnings (Cash	
dividends, $220,000)	700,000	dividends, $328,000)	700,000
Non-current liabilities, 10%	1,200,000	Current liabilities	600,000
Current liabilities	300,000		
	$4,200,000		$4,200,000

For the year, each company has earned the same income before interest and taxes.

	Ingalls Co.	Wilder Co.
Income from operations	$1,200,000	$1,200,000
Interest expense	120,000	–0–
Income before income tax	1,080,000	1,200,000
Income tax (40%)	432,000	480,000
Net income	$ 648,000	$ 720,000

At year-end, the market price of an Ingalls's share was $101, and Wilder's was $63.50. Assume statement of financial position amounts are representative for the entire year.

Instructions

(a) Which company is more profitable in terms of return on total assets?
(b) Which company is more profitable in terms of return on ordinary share equity?
(c) Which company has the greater net income per share? Neither company issued or reacquired shares during the year.
(d) From the point of view of net income, is it advantageous to the shareholders of Ingalls Co. to have the current liabilities outstanding? Why?
(e) What is the book value per share for each company?

·9 E15-20 (Trading on the Equity Analysis) Presented below is information from the annual report of DeVries Plastics, Inc.

Operating income	€ 532,150
Bond interest expense	135,000
Income before income tax	397,150
Income tax	183,432
Net income	€ 213,718
Bonds payable	€1,500,000
Share capital—ordinary	875,000
Retained earnings	575,000

Instructions

(a) Compute the return on ordinary share equity and the rate of interest paid on bonds. (Assume balances for debt and equity accounts approximate averages for the year.)

(b) Is DeVries Plastics, Inc. trading on the equity successfully? Explain.

•10 *E15-21 (Preference Dividends) The outstanding share capital of Pennington Corporation consists of 2,000 shares of $100 par value, 6% preference, and 5,000 shares of $50 par value ordinary.

Instructions

Assuming that the company has retained earnings of $70,000, all of which is to be paid out in dividends, and that preference dividends were not paid during the 2 years preceding the current year, determine how much each class of shares should receive under each of the following conditions.

(a) The preference shares are non-cumulative and non-participating.

(b) The preference shares are cumulative and non-participating.

(c) The preference shares are cumulative and participating. (Round dividend rate percentages to four decimal places.)

•10 *E15-22 (Preference Dividends) Martinez Company's ledger shows the following balances on December 31, 2010.

Share Capital—Preference, 5%—$10 par value, outstanding 20,000 shares	$ 200,000
Share Capital—Ordinary—$100 par value, outstanding 30,000 shares	3,000,000
Retained Earnings	630,000

Instructions

Assuming that the directors decide to declare total dividends in the amount of $266,000, determine how much each class of shares should receive under each of the conditions stated below. One year's dividends are in arrears on the preference shares.

(a) The preference shares are cumulative and fully participating.

(b) The preference shares are non-cumulative and non-participating.

(c) The preference shares are non-cumulative and are participating in distributions in excess of a 7% dividend rate on the ordinary shares.

•10 *E15-23 (Preference Share Dividends) Hagar Company has outstanding 2,500 shares of $100 par, 6% preference shares and 15,000 shares of $10 par value ordinary. The schedule below shows the amount of dividends paid out over the last 4 years.

Instructions

Allocate the dividends to each type of shares under assumptions (a) and (b). Express your answers in per-share amounts using the format shown below.

		Assumptions			
		(a) Preference, non-cumulative, and non-participating		(b) Preference, cumulative, and fully participating	
Year	Paid-out	Preference	Ordinary	Preference	Ordinary
2009	$12,000				
2010	$26,000				
2011	$52,000				
2012	$76,000				

•10 *E15-24 (Computation of Book Value per Share) Johnstone Inc. began operations in January 2009 and reported the following results for each of its 3 years of operations.

2009 $260,000 net loss   2010 $40,000 net loss   2011 $700,000 net income

At December 31, 2011, Johnstone Inc. share capital accounts were as follows.

Share Capital—Preference, 6% cumulative, par value $100; authorized, issued, and outstanding 5,000 shares	$500,000
Share Capital—Ordinary, par value $1.00; authorized 1,000,000 shares; issued and outstanding 750,000 shares	$750,000

Johnstone Inc. has never paid a cash or share dividend. There has been no change in the share capital accounts since Johnstone began operations. The country law permits dividends only from retained earnings.

Instructions

(a) Compute the book value of the ordinary shares at December 31, 2011.

(b) Compute the book value of the ordinary shares at December 31, 2011, assuming that the preference shares have a liquidating value of $106 per share.

PROBLEMS

·3 ·4 ·9 P15-1 (Equity Transactions and Statement Preparation) On January 5, 2010, Phelps Corporation received a charter granting the right to issue 5,000 shares of $100 par value, 8% cumulative and non-participating preference shares, and 50,000 shares of $10 par value ordinary shares. It then completed these transactions.

Jan. 11 Issued 20,000 ordinary shares at $16 per share.

Feb. 1 Issued to Sanchez Corp. 4,000 preference shares for the following assets: machinery with a fair value of $50,000; a factory building with a fair value of $160,000; and land with an appraised value of $270,000.

July 29 Purchased 1,800 ordinary shares at $17 per share. (Use cost method.)

Aug. 10 Sold the 1,800 treasury shares at $14 per share.

Dec. 31 Declared a $0.25 per share cash dividend on the ordinary shares and declared the preference dividend.

Dec. 31 Closed the Income Summary account. There was $175,700 net income.

Instructions

(a) Record the journal entries for the transactions listed above.

(b) Prepare the equity section of Phelps Corporation's statement of financial position as of December 31, 2010.

·4 ·9 P15-2 (Treasury Share Transactions and Presentation) Clemson Company had the following equity as of January 1, 2010.

Share capital—ordinary, €5 par value, 20,000 shares issued	€100,000
Share premium—ordinary	300,000
Retained earnings	320,000
Total equity	€720,000

During 2010, the following transactions occurred.

Feb. 1 Clemson repurchased 2,000 treasury shares at a price of €19 per share.

Mar. 1 800 shares of treasury shares repurchased above were reissued at €17 per share.

Mar. 18 500 shares of treasury shares repurchased above were reissued at €14 per share.

Apr. 22 600 shares of treasury shares repurchased above were reissued at €20 per share.

Instructions

(a) Prepare the journal entries to record the treasury share transactions in 2010, assuming Clemson uses the cost method.

(b) Prepare the equity section as of April 30, 2010. Net income for the first 4 months of 2010 was €130,000.

·3 ·4 ·7 ·8 P15-3 (Equity Transactions and Statement Preparation) Hatch Company has two classes of share capital outstanding: 8%, $20 par preference and $5 par ordinary. At December 31, 2010, the following accounts were included in equity.

Share Capital—Preference, 150,000 shares	$ 3,000,000
Share Capital—Ordinary, 2,000,000 shares	10,000,000
Share Premium—Preference	200,000
Share Premium—Ordinary	27,000,000
Retained Earnings	4,500,000

The following transactions affected equity during 2011.

Jan. 1 30,000 preference shares issued at $22 per share.

Feb. 1 50,000 ordinary shares issued at $20 per share.

June 1 2-for-1 share split (par value reduced to $2.50).

July 1 30,000 ordinary treasury shares purchased at $10 per share. Hatch uses the cost method.

Sept. 15 10,000 treasury shares reissued at $11 per share.

Dec. 31 The preference dividend is declared, and an ordinary dividend of 50¢ per share is declared.

Dec. 31 Net income is $2,100,000.

Instructions
Prepare the equity section for Hatch Company at December 31, 2010. Show all supporting computations.

·3 ·5 P15-4 (Share Transactions—Lump Sum) Seles Corporation's charter authorized issuance of 100,000 ordinary shares of €10 par value and 50,000 shares of €50 preference shares. The following transactions involving the issuance of shares were completed. Each transaction is independent of the others.

1. Issued a €10,000, 9% bond payable at par and gave as a bonus one preference share, which at that time was selling for €106 a share.
2. Issued 500 ordinary shares for machinery. The machinery had been appraised at €7,100; the seller's book value was €6,200. The most recent market price of the ordinary shares is €16 a share.
3. Issued 375 ordinary shares and 100 preference shares for a lump sum amounting to €10,800. The ordinary had been selling at €14 and the preference at €65.
4. Issued 200 shares of ordinary and 50 shares of preference for furniture and fixtures. The ordinary shares had a fair value of €16 per share; the furniture and fixtures have a fair value of €6,500.

Instructions
Record the transactions listed above in journal entry form.

·4 P15-5 (Treasury Shares—Cost Method) Before Smith Corporation engages in the treasury share transactions listed below, its general ledger reflects, among others, the following account balances (par value is £30 per share).

Share Premium—Ordinary	Share Capital—Ordinary	Retained Earnings
£99,000	£270,000	£80,000

Instructions
Record the treasury share transactions (given below) under the cost method of handling treasury shares; use the FIFO method for purchase-sale purposes.

(a) Bought 380 treasury shares at £40 per share.
(b) Bought 300 treasury shares at £45 per share.
(c) Sold 350 treasury shares at £42 per share.
(d) Sold 110 treasury shares at £38 per share.

·4 ·7 ·9 P15-6 (Treasury Shares—Cost Method—Equity Section Preparation) Washington Company has the following equity accounts at December 31, 2010.

Share Capital—Ordinary—$100 par value, authorized 8,000 shares	$480,000
Retained Earnings	294,000

Instructions
(a) Prepare entries in journal form to record the following transactions, which took place during 2011.
   (1) 280 ordinary shares were purchased at $97 per share. (These are to be accounted for using the cost method.)
   (2) A $20 per share cash dividend was declared.
   (3) The dividend declared in No. 2 above was paid.
   (4) The treasury shares purchased in No. 1 above were resold at $102 per share.
   (5) 500 shares were purchased at $105 per share.
   (6) 350 of the shares purchased in No. 5 above were resold at $96 per share.
(b) Prepare the equity section of Washington Company's statement of financial position after giving effect to these transactions, assuming that the net income for 2011 was $94,000. Country law requires restriction of retained earnings for the amount of treasury shares.

·4 ·7 P15-7 (Cash Dividend Entries) The books of Conchita Corporation carried the following account balances as of December 31, 2010.

Cash	$ 195,000
Share capital—preference, 6% cumulative, non-participating, $50 par	300,000
Share capital—ordinary, no-par value, 300,000 shares issued	1,500,000
Share premium—preference	150,000
Treasury shares (ordinary 2,800 shares at cost)	33,600
Retained earnings	105,000

The company decided not to pay any dividends in 2010.

The board of directors, at their annual meeting on December 21, 2011, declared the following: "The current year dividends shall be 6% on the preference and $.30 per share on the ordinary. The dividends in arrears shall be paid by issuing 1,500 treasury shares." At the date of declaration, the preference is selling at $80 per share, and the ordinary at $12 per share. Net income for 2011 is estimated at $77,000.

Instructions

(a) Prepare the journal entries required for the dividend declaration and payment, assuming that they occur simultaneously.

(b) Could Conchita Corporation give the preference shareholders 2 years' dividends and ordinary shareholders a 30 cents per share dividend, all in cash?

·7··8· P15-8 (Dividends and Splits) Myers Company provides you with the following condensed statement of financial position information.

Assets		Equity and Liabilities		
Equipment (net)	€250,000	Equity		
Intangibles	60,000	Share capital—ordinary (€5 par)	€ 20,000	
Investments in ABC shares		Share premium—ordinary	110,000	
(10,000 shares at cost)	70,000	Retained earnings	180,000	€310,000
Current assets	40,000	Non-current and current liabilities		100,000
Total assets	€420,000	Total equity and liabilities		€410,000

Instructions

For each transaction below, indicate the euro impact (if any) on the following five items: (1) total assets, (2) share capital—ordinary, (3) share premium—ordinary, (4) retained earnings, and (5) equity. (Each situation is independent.)

(a) Myers declares and pays a €1 per share cash dividend.

(b) Myers declares and issues a 10% share dividend when the market price is €14 per share.

(c) Myers declares and issues a 30% share dividend when the market price is €15 per share.

(d) Myers declares and distributes a property dividend. Myers gives one ABC share for every two shares held of Myers Company. ABC is selling for €10 per share on the date the property dividend is declared.

(e) Myers declares a 2-for-1 share split and issues new shares.

·3··4··7· P15-9 (Equity Section of Statement of Financial Position) The following is a summary of all relevant
·9· transactions of Vicario Corporation since it was organized in 2010.

In 2010, 15,000 shares were authorized and 7,000 ordinary shares ($50 par value) were issued at a price of $57. In 2011, 1,000 shares were issued as a share dividend when a share was selling for $60. Three hundred ordinary shares were bought in 2012 at a cost of $64 per share. These 300 shares are still in the company treasury.

In 2011, 10,000 preference shares were authorized and the company issued 5,000 of them ($100 par value) at $113. Some of the preference shares were reacquired by the company and later reissued for $4,700 more than it cost the company.

The corporation has earned a total of $610,000 in net income and paid out a total of $312,600 in cash dividends since incorporation.

Instructions

Prepare the equity section of the statement of financial position in proper form for Vicario Corporation as of December 31, 2012. Account for treasury shares using the cost method.

·8· P15-10 (Share Dividends and Share Split) Oregon Inc.'s $10 par ordinary shares are selling for $110 per share. Four million shares are currently issued and outstanding. The board of directors wishes to stimulate interest in Oregon ordinary shares before a forthcoming share issue but does not wish to distribute cash at this time. The board also believes that too many adjustments to the equity section, especially retained earnings, might discourage potential investors.

The board has considered three options for stimulating interest in the shares:

1. A 20% share dividend.
2. A 100% share dividend.
3. A 2-for-1 share split.

Instructions

Acting as financial advisor to the board, you have been asked to report briefly on each option and, considering the board's wishes, make a recommendation. Discuss the effects of each of the foregoing options.

·7··8··9· P15-11 (Share and Cash Dividends) Earnhart Corporation has outstanding 3,000,000 ordinary shares with a par value of $10 each. The balance in its retained earnings account at January 1, 2010, was

$24,000,000, and it then had Share Premium of $5,000,000. During 2010, the company's net income was $4,700,000. A cash dividend of $0.60 per share was declared on May 5, 2010, and was paid June 30, 2010, and a 6% share dividend was declared on November 30, 2010, and distributed to shareholders of record at the close of business on December 31, 2010. You have been asked to advise on the proper accounting treatment of the share dividend.

The existing shares of the company are quoted on a national securities exchange. The market price of the shares has been as follows.

October 31, 2010	$31
November 30, 2010	$34
December 31, 2010	$38

Instructions

(a) Prepare the journal entry to record the declaration and payment of the cash dividend.

(b) Prepare the journal entry to record the declaration and distribution of the share dividend.

(c) Prepare the equity section (including schedules of retained earnings and share premium) of the statement of financial position of Earnhart Corporation for the year 2010 on the basis of the foregoing information. Draft a note to the financial statements setting forth the basis of the accounting for the share dividend, and add separately appropriate comments or explanations regarding the basis chosen.

P15-12   (Analysis and Classification of Equity Transactions)   Penn Company was formed on July 1, 2008. It was authorized to issue 300,000 shares of $10 par value ordinary shares and 100,000 shares of 8% $25 par value, cumulative and non-participating preference shares. Penn Company has a July 1–June 30 fiscal year.

The following information relates to the equity accounts of Penn Company.

Ordinary Shares

Prior to the 2010–11 fiscal year, Penn Company had 110,000 ordinary shares outstanding issued as follows.

1. 85,000 shares were issued for cash on July 1, 2008, at $31 per share.
2. On July 24, 2008, 5,000 shares were exchanged for a plot of land which cost the seller $70,000 in 2002 and had an estimated fair value of $220,000 on July 24, 2008.
3. 20,000 shares were issued on March 1, 2009, for $42 per share.

During the 2010–11 fiscal year, the following transactions regarding ordinary shares took place.

November 30, 2010	Penn purchased 2,000 of its own shares on the open market at $39 per share. Penn uses the cost method for treasury shares.
December 15, 2010	Penn declared a 5% share dividend for shareholders of record on January 15, 2011, to be issued on January 31, 2011. Penn was having a liquidity problem and could not afford a cash dividend at the time. Penn's ordinary shares were selling at $52 per share on December 15, 2010.
June 20, 2011	Penn sold 500 of its own ordinary shares that it had purchased on November 30, 2010, for $21,000.

Preference Shares

Penn issued 40,000 preference shares at $44 per share on July 1, 2009.

Cash Dividends

Penn has followed a schedule of declaring cash dividends in December and June, with payment being made to shareholders of record in the following month. The cash dividends which have been declared since inception of the company through June 30, 2011, are shown below.

Declaration Date	Ordinary Shares	Preference Shares
12/15/09	$0.30 per share	$1.00 per share
6/15/10	$0.30 per share	$1.00 per share
12/15/10	—	$1.00 per share

No cash dividends were declared during June 2011 due to the company's liquidity problems.

Retained Earnings

As of June 30, 2010, Penn's retained earnings account had a balance of $690,000. For the fiscal year ending June 30, 2011, Penn reported net income of $40,000.

Instructions

Prepare the equity section of the statement of financial position, including appropriate notes, for Penn Company as of June 30, 2011, as it should appear in its annual report to the shareholders.

CONCEPTS FOR ANALYSIS

CA15-1 (Preemptive Rights and Dilution of Ownership) Wallace Computer Company is a small, closely held corporation. Eighty percent of the shares are held by Derek Wallace, president. Of the remainder, 10% is held by members of his family and 10% by Kathy Baker, a former officer who is now retired. The statement of financial position of the company at June 30, 2010, was substantially as shown below.

Assets		Equity and Liabilities	
Cash	$ 22,000	Share capital—ordinary	$250,000
Other	450,000	Retained earnings	172,000
	$472,000	Current liabilities	50,000
			$472,000

Additional authorized ordinary shares of $300,000 par value have never been issued. To strengthen the cash position of the company, Wallace issued ordinary shares with a par value of $100,000 to himself at par for cash. At the next shareholders' meeting, Baker objected and claimed that her interests had been injured.

Instructions

(a) Which shareholder's right was ignored in the issue of shares to Derek Wallace?

(b) How may the damage to Baker's interests be repaired most simply?

(c) If Derek Wallace offered Baker a personal cash settlement and they agreed to employ you as an impartial arbitrator to determine the amount, what settlement would you propose? Present your calculations with sufficient explanation to satisfy both parties.

CA15-2 (Issuance of Shares for Land) Martin Corporation is planning to issue 3,000 shares of its own $10 par value ordinary shares for two acres of land to be used as a building site.

Instructions

(a) What general rule should be applied to determine the amount at which the land should be recorded?

(b) Under what circumstances should this transaction be recorded at the fair value of the land?

(c) Under what circumstances should this transaction be recorded at the fair value of the shares issued?

(d) Assume Martin intentionally records this transaction at an amount greater than the fair value of the land and the shares. Discuss this situation.

CA15-3 (Conceptual Issues—Equity) The IASB has set forth a conceptual framework that it will use in developing standards. As part of this Framework, the IASB defines various elements of financial statements.

Instructions

Answer the following questions based on the Framework.

(a) Define and discuss the term "equity."

(b) What transactions or events change equity?

(c) What financial statement element other than equity is typically affected by owner investments?

(d) What financial statement element other than equity is typically affected by distributions to owners?

(e) What are examples of changes within equity that do not change the total amount of equity?

CA15-4 (Share Dividends and Splits) The directors of Merchant Corporation are considering the issuance of a share dividend. They have asked you to discuss the proposed action by answering the following questions.

Instructions

(a) What is a share dividend? How is a share dividend distinguished from a share split (1) from a legal standpoint, and (2) from an accounting standpoint?

(b) For what reasons does a corporation usually declare a share dividend? A share split?

(c) Discuss the amount, if any, of retained earnings to be capitalized in connection with a share dividend.

CA15-5 (Share Dividends) Yamada Inc., a client, is considering the authorization of a 10% ordinary share dividend to ordinary shareholders. The financial vice president of Yamada wishes to discuss the accounting implications of such an authorization with you before the next meeting of the board of directors.

Instructions

(a) The first topic the vice president wishes to discuss is the nature of the share dividend to the recipient. Discuss the case against considering the share dividend as income to the recipient.

(b) The other topic for discussion is the propriety of issuing the share dividend to all "shareholders of record" or to "shareholders of record exclusive of shares held in the name of the corporation as treasury shares." Discuss the case against issuing share dividends on treasury shares.

CA15-6 **(Share Dividend, Cash Dividend, and Treasury Shares)** Mask Company has 30,000 shares of €10 par value ordinary shares authorized and 20,000 shares issued and outstanding. On August 15, 2010, Mask purchased 1,000 shares of treasury shares for €18 per share. Mask uses the cost method to account for treasury shares. On September 14, 2010, Mask sold 500 shares of the treasury shares for €20 per share.

In October 2010, Mask declared and distributed 1,950 shares as a share dividend from unissued shares when the market price of the ordinary shares was €21 per share.

On December 20, 2010, Mask declared a €1 per share cash dividend, payable on January 10, 2011, to shareholders of record on December 31, 2010.

Instructions

(a) How should Mask account for the purchase and sale of the treasury shares, and how should the treasury shares be presented in the statement of financial position at December 31, 2010?

(b) How should Mask account for the share dividend, and how would it affect equity at December 31, 2010? Why?

(c) How should Mask account for the cash dividend, and how would it affect the statement of financial position at December 31, 2010? Why?

 CA15-7 **(Treasury Shares)** Lois Kenseth, president of Sycamore Corporation, is concerned about several large shareholders who have been very vocal lately in their criticisms of her leadership. She thinks they might mount a campaign to have her removed as the corporation's CEO. She decides that buying them out by purchasing their shares could eliminate them as opponents, and she is confident they would accept a "good" offer. Kenseth knows the corporation's cash position is decent, so it has the cash to complete the transaction. She also knows the purchase of these shares will increase earnings per share, which should make other investors quite happy. (Earnings per share is calculated by dividing net income available for the ordinary shareholders by the weighted-average number of shares outstanding. Therefore, if the number of shares outstanding is decreased by purchasing treasury shares, earnings per share increases.)

Instructions

Answer the following questions.

(a) Who are the stakeholders in this situation?

(b) What are the ethical issues involved?

(c) Should Kenseth authorize the transaction?

USING YOUR JUDGMENT

FINANCIAL REPORTING

Financial Reporting Problem

Marks and Spencer plc (M&S)

The financial statements of **M&S** are presented in Appendix 5B or can be accessed at the book's companion website, **www.wiley.com/college/kiesoifrs**.

Instructions

 Refer to M&S's financial statements and the accompanying notes to answer the following questions.

(a) What is the par or stated value of M&S's preference shares?

(b) What is the par or stated value of M&S's ordinary shares?

(c) What percentage of M&S's authorized ordinary shares was issued at December 31, 2008?

(d) How many ordinary shares were outstanding at December 31, 2008, and December 31, 2007?

(e) What was the pound amount effect of the cash dividends on M&S's equity?

(f) What is M&S's rate of return on ordinary share equity for 2008 and 2007?

(g) What is M&S's payout ratio for 2008 and 2007?

Comparative Analysis Case

Cadbury and Nestlé

Instructions

Go to the book's companion website and use information found there to answer the following questions related to **Cadbury** and **Nestlé**.

(a) What is the par or stated value of Cadbury's and Nestlé's ordinary shares?

(b) What percentage of authorized shares was issued by Cadbury and Nestlé at December 31, 2008?

(c) How many shares are held as treasury shares by Cadbury at December 31, 2008, and by Nestlé at December 31, 2008?

(d) How many Cadbury ordinary shares are outstanding at December 31, 2008? How many Nestlé ordinary shares are outstanding at December 29, 2007?

(e) What amounts of cash dividends per share were declared by Cadbury and Nestlé in 2008? What were the dollar amount effects of the cash dividends on each company's equity?

(f) What are Cadbury's and Nestlé's rate of return on equity for 2008 and 2007? Which company gets the higher return on the equity of its shareholders?

(g) What are Cadbury's and Nestlé's payout ratios for 2008?

Financial Statement Analysis Case

Case 1   BHP Billiton

BHP Billiton (GBR) is the world's largest diversified natural resources company. The company extracts and processes minerals, oil, and gas from its production operations located primarily in Australia, the Americas, and southern Africa. BHP Billiton sells its products globally, with sales and marketing taking place through its principal hubs of The Hague and Singapore. Presented below are some basic facts for BHP Billiton.

Billiton
(000)

	2009	2008
Sales	$50,211	$59,473
Net earnings	6,338	15,962
Total assets	78,770	76,008
Total liabilities	38,059	36,965
Share capital	2,343	2,343
Reserves	1,305	750
Retained earnings	36,831	36,831
Treasury shares	525	514
Number of shares outstanding (millions)	5,565	5,590

Instructions

(a) What are some of the reasons that management purchases its own shares?

(b) Explain how earnings per share might be affected by treasury share transactions.

(c) Calculate the ratio of debt to total assets for 2008 and 2009, and discuss the implications of the change.

Case 2   Wiebold, Incorporated

The following note related to equity was reported in **Wiebold, Inc.**'s (USA) annual report.

On February 1, the Board of Directors declared a 3-for-2 share split, distributed on February 22 to shareholders of record on February 10. Accordingly, all numbers of common (ordinary) shares, except unissued shares and treasury shares, and all per share data have been restated to reflect this share split.

On the basis of amounts declared and paid, the annualized quarterly dividends per share were $0.80 in the current year and $0.75 in the prior year.

Instructions

(a) What is the significance of the date of record and the date of distribution?

(b) Why might Weibold have declared a 3-for-2 for share split?

(c) What impact does Wiebold's share split have on (1) total equity, (2) total par value, (3) outstanding shares, and (4) book value per share?

Accounting, Analysis, and Principles

On January 1, 2010, Agassi Corporation had the following equity accounts.

Share Capital—Ordinary ($10 par value, 60,000 shares issued and outstanding)	$600,000
Share Premium—Ordinary	500,000
Retained Earnings	620,000

During 2010, the following transactions occurred.

Jan. 15	Declared and paid a $1.05 cash dividend per share to shareholders.
Apr. 15	Declared and issued a 10% share dividend. The market price of the shares was $14 per share.
May 15	Reacquired 2,000 ordinary shares at a market price of $15 per share.
Nov. 15	Reissued 1,000 shares held in treasury at a price of $18 per share.
Dec. 31	Determined that net income for the year was $370,000.

Accounting

Journalize the above transactions. (Include entries to close net income to Retained Earnings.) Determine the ending balance amounts for Share Capital—Ordinary, Retained Earnings, and Equity.

Analysis

Calculate the payout ratio and the return on equity ratio.

Principles

R. Federer is examining Agassi's financial statements and wonders whether the "gains" or "losses" on Agassi's treasury share transactions should be included in income for the year. Briefly explain whether, and the conceptual reasons why, gains or losses on treasury share transactions should be recorded in income.

I F R S | BRIDGE TO THE PROFESSION

Recall from Chapter 13 that Hincapie Co. (a specialty bike-accessory manufacturer) is expecting growth in sales of some products targeted to the low-price market. Hincapie is contemplating a preference share issue to help finance this expansion in operations. The company is leaning toward preference shares because ownership will not be diluted, but the investors will get an extra dividend if the company does well. The company management wants to be certain that its reporting of this transaction is transparent to its current shareholders and wants you to research the disclosure requirements related to its capital structure.

Instructions

Access the IFRS authoritative literature at the IASB website (*http://eifrs.iasb.org/*). When you have accessed the documents, you can use the search tool in your Internet browser to respond to the following questions. (Provide paragraph citations.)

(a) Identify the authoritative literature that addresses disclosure of information about capital structure.

(b) What information about share capital must companies disclose? Discuss how Hincapie should report the proposed preference share issue.

Professional Simulation

In this simulation, you are asked to address equations related to the accounting for equity. Prepare responses to all parts.

KWW_Professional _Simulation

| Equity | Time Remaining 4 hours 10 minutes | copy | paste | calculator | sheet | standards | help | splitter | done |

Directions | **Situation** | **Explanation** | **Analysis** | **Resources**

Presented below are the equity sections for AMR Corporation (USA), which reports under U.S. GAAP. All amounts are in millions, except number of shares and par value.

	Current Year	Prior Year
Equity (Deficit)		
Common stock (Share capital—ordinary) $1 par value, 750,000,000 shares authorized; 182,350,259 shares issued	$ 182	$ 182
Additional paid-in capital	2,521	2,605
Treasury shares at cost: current year—21,194,312; prior year—22,768,027	(1,308)	(1,405)
Accumulated other comprehensive loss	(664)	(785)
Accumulated deficit	(1,312)	(551)
	$ (581)	$ 46

Directions | **Situation** | **Explanation** | **Analysis** | **Resources**

(a) Explain why common stock is classified as part of equity.
(b) Explain why treasury shares are not classified as an asset.
(c) Explain what is meant by "Accumulated other comprehensive loss."
(d) Why is the accumulated deficit larger in the current year than in the prior year?

Directions | **Situation** | **Explanation** | **Analysis** | **Resources**

Compute book value per share for AMR for the current year.

Remember to check the book's companion website to find additional resources for this chapter.

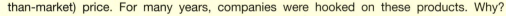

CHAPTER **16**

DILUTIVE SECURITIES AND EARNINGS PER SHARE

LEARNING OBJECTIVES

After studying this chapter, you should be able to:

•1 Describe the accounting for the issuance, conversion, and retirement of convertible securities.

•2 Explain the accounting for convertible preference shares.

•3 Contrast the accounting for share warrants and for share warrants issued with other securities.

•4 Describe the accounting for share compensation plans.

•5 Discuss the controversy involving share compensation plans.

•6 Compute earnings per share in a simple capital structure.

•7 Compute earnings per share in a complex capital structure.

KICKING THE HABIT

Some habits die hard. Take share options—called by some "the crack cocaine of incentives." Share options are a form of compensation that gives key employees the choice to purchase shares at a given (usually lower-than-market) price. For many years, companies were hooked on these products. Why? The combination of a hot equity market and favorable accounting treatment made share options the incentive of choice. They were compensation with no expense to the companies that granted them, and they were popular with key employees, so companies granted them with abandon. However, the accounting rules that took effect in 2005 required *expensing* the fair value of share options. This new treatment has made it easier for companies to kick this habit.

As shown in the chart on the left, a review of option use for the U.S. companies in the S&P 500 indicates a decline in the use of option-based compensation. Fewer companies are granting share options, following implementation of share-option expensing. As a spokesperson at one company commented, "Once you begin expensing options, the attractiveness significantly drops."

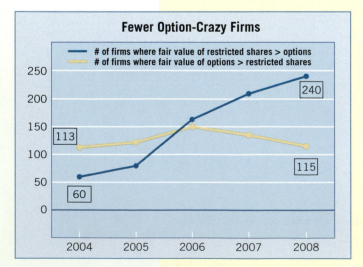

Fewer Option-Crazy Firms

— # of firms where fair value of restricted shares > options
— # of firms where fair value of options > restricted shares

In the 1990s, executives with huge option stockpiles had an almost irresistible incentive to do whatever it took to increase the share price and cash in their options. By reining in options, many companies are taking the first steps toward curbing both out-of-control executive pay and the era of corporate corruption that it spawned.

Some of the ways that companies are curbing option grants include replacing options with restricted shares. As indicated in the table on the right, which shows the fair value by industry sector of restricted shares and option grants in a recent year, restricted shares are now the plan of choice. Even if the financial sector is excluded, the value of restricted shares exceeds the value of share-option grants. And in the information technology area (where in the past, share options were heavily favored), the fair value of restricted-share plans exceeds that for share options. Some companies are simply reducing option grants, without offering a replacement, while others, like **Microsoft** (USA) and **Yahoo** (USA), have switched to restricted-share plans completely.

S&P 500: FAIR VALUES OF GRANTS BY INDUSTRY SECTOR Options vs. Restricted Shares		
($ in billions)	Restricted Shares	Options
Financials	$23.8	$3.0
Energy	2.5	1.0
Consumer discretionary	3.8	2.7
Industrials	2.5	1.7
Utilities	0.4	0.1
Telecom	0.5	0.2
Info tech	8.5	8.3
Materials	0.5	0.6
Consumer staples	1.8	2.3
Health care	3.0	4.3
Total	$47.3	$24.2
Total non-financials	$23.5	$21.2

Is this a good trend? Most believe it is; the requirement to expense share-based compensation similar to other forms of compensation has changed the focus of compensation plans to rewarding talent and performance without breaking the bank. The positive impact on corporate behavior, while hard to measure, should benefit investors in years to come.

Sources: Adapted from: Louis Lavelle, "Kicking the Stock-Options Habit," *BusinessWeekOnline* (February 16, 2005). Graphs from J. Ciesielski, "S&P 500 Stock Compensation: Who Needs Options?" *The Analyst's Accounting Observer* (July 30, 2008) and J. Ciesielski, "S&P 500 Stock Compensation: Running Out of Options," *The Analyst's Accounting Observer* (August 25, 2009).

PREVIEW OF CHAPTER 16

As the opening story indicates, companies are rethinking the use of various forms of share-based compensation. The purpose of this chapter is to discuss the proper accounting for share-based compensation. In addition, the chapter examines issues related to other types of financial instruments, such as convertible securities, warrants, and contingent shares, including their effects on reporting earnings per share. The content and organization of the chapter are as follows.

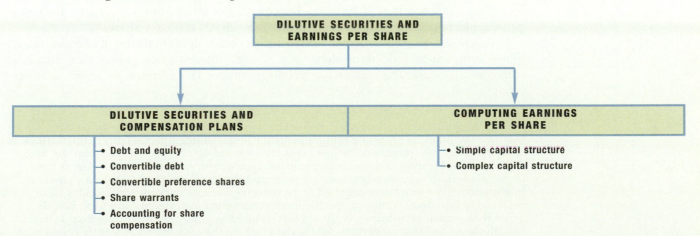

DILUTIVE SECURITIES AND EARNINGS PER SHARE

DILUTIVE SECURITIES AND COMPENSATION PLANS
- Debt and equity
- Convertible debt
- Convertible preference shares
- Share warrants
- Accounting for share compensation

COMPUTING EARNINGS PER SHARE
- Simple capital structure
- Complex capital structure

SECTION 1 • DILUTIVE SECURITIES AND COMPENSATION PLANS

DEBT AND EQUITY

Many of the controversies related to the accounting for financial instruments such as share options, convertible securities, and preference shares relate to whether companies should report these instruments as a liability or as equity. For example, companies should classify non-redeemable ordinary shares as equity because the issuer has no **obligation** to pay dividends or repurchase the shares. Declaration of dividends is at the issuer's discretion, as is the decision to repurchase the shares. Similarly, preference shares that are not redeemable do not require the issuer to pay dividends or repurchase the shares. Thus, non-redeemable ordinary or preference shares lacks an important characteristic of a liability—an obligation to pay the holder of the ordinary or preference shares at some point in the future.[1]

In this chapter, we discuss securities that have characteristics of *both* debt and equity. For example, a convertible bond has both debt and equity characteristics. Should a company classify this security as debt, as equity, or as part debt and part equity? In addition, how should a company compute earnings per share if it has convertible bonds and other convertible securities in its capital structure? Convertible securities, as well as options, warrants, and other securities, are often called **dilutive securities** because upon exercise they may reduce (dilute) earnings per share.

CONVERTIBLE DEBT

Objective•1

Describe the accounting for the issuance, conversion, and retirement of convertible securities.

Convertible bonds can be changed into other corporate securities during some specified period of time after issuance. A convertible bond combines the benefits of a bond with the privilege of exchanging it for shares at the holder's option. Investors who purchase it desire the security of a bond holding (guaranteed interest and principal) plus the added option of conversion if the value of the shares appreciates significantly.

Corporations issue convertibles for two main reasons. One is to raise equity capital without giving up more ownership control than necessary. To illustrate, assume a company wants to raise $1 million; its ordinary shares are selling at $45 a share. To raise the $1 million, the company would have to sell 22,222 shares (ignoring issue costs). By selling 1,000 bonds at $1,000 par, each convertible into 20 ordinary shares, the company could raise $1 million by committing only 20,000 ordinary shares.

A second reason to issue convertibles is to obtain debt financing at cheaper rates. Many companies could issue debt only at high interest rates unless they attach a conversion option. The conversion privilege entices the investor to accept a lower

---

[1]Presently, the IASB and the FASB are working jointly to develop a standard that will improve the financial reporting requirements for financial instruments with characteristics of equity. They recognize that the line between debt and equity is sometimes blurred, and therefore classification of these instruments is inconsistent. At this point, the Boards have identified certain securities that indicate preferred classification. For example, a perpetual instrument is one that is not required to be redeemed unless the company decides to, or is forced to liquidate. Without a specific limit to perpetual instruments' lives, the Boards agree that perpetual instruments should be classified as equity. Similarly, the Boards have tentatively agreed that convertible debt should be split into a debt and an equity component if it is exchanged for a specified number of shares. If not exchangeable for a specified number of shares, the instrument would be classified entirely as debt.

interest rate than would normally be the case on a straight debt issue. For example, **Amazon.com** (USA) at one time issued convertible bonds that pay interest at an effective yield of 4.75 percent. This rate was much lower than Amazon.com would have had to pay by issuing straight debt. For this lower interest rate, the investor receives the right to buy Amazon.com's ordinary shares at a fixed price until the bond's maturity.[2]

Accounting for Convertible Debt

Convertible debt is accounted for as a **compound instrument** because it contains both a liability and an equity component. IFRS requires that compound instruments be separated into their liability and equity components for purposes of accounting. [1] Companies use the **"with-and-without" method** to value compound instruments.

Illustration 16-1 identifies the components used in the with-and-without method.

I F R S See the Authoritative Literature section (page 861).

| Fair value of convertible debt at date of issuance **(with both debt and equity components)** | − | Fair value of liability component at date of issuance, based on present value of cash flows | = | Equity component at date of issuance **(without the debt component)** |

ILLUSTRATION 16-1
Convertible Debt Components

As indicated, the equity component is the residual amount after subtracting the liability component. IFRS does not permit companies to assign a value to the equity amount first and then determine the liability component. To do so would be inconsistent with the definition of equity, which is considered a residual amount. [2]

To implement the with-and-without approach, companies do the following:

1. First, determine the total fair value of the convertible debt *with both* the liability and equity component. **This is straightforward, as this amount is the proceeds received upon issuance.**

2. The company then determines the liability component by computing the net present value of all contractual future cash flows discounted at the market rate of interest. This market rate is the rate the company would pay on similar non-convertible debt.

3. In the final step, the company subtracts the liability component estimated in the second step from the fair value of the convertible debt (issue proceeds) to arrive at the equity component. That is, the equity component is the fair value of the convertible debt *without* the liability component.

Accounting at Time of Issuance

To illustrate the accounting for convertible debt, assume that **Roche Group** (DEU) issues 2,000 convertible bonds at the beginning of 2011. The bonds have a four-year term with a stated rate of interest of 6 percent, and are issued at par with a face value of €1,000 per bond (the total proceeds received from issuance of the bonds are €2,000,000). Interest is payable annually at December 31. Each bond is convertible into 250 ordinary shares with a par value of €1. The market rate of interest on similar non-convertible debt is 9 percent.

[2]As with any investment, a buyer has to be careful. For example, **Wherehouse Entertainment Inc.** (USA), which had 6¼ percent convertibles outstanding, was taken private in a leveraged buyout. As a result, the convertible was suddenly as risky as a junk bond of a highly leveraged company with a coupon of only 6¼ percent. As one holder of the convertibles noted, "What's even worse is that the company will be so loaded down with debt that it probably won't have enough cash flow to make its interest payments. And the convertible debt we hold is subordinated to the rest of Wherehouse's debt." These types of situations have made convertibles less attractive and have led to the introduction of takeover protection covenants in some convertible bond offerings. Or, sometimes convertibles are permitted to be called at par, and therefore the conversion premium may be lost.

The time diagram in Illustration 16-2 depicts both the interest and principal cash flows.

ILLUSTRATION 16-2
Time Diagram for
Convertible Bond

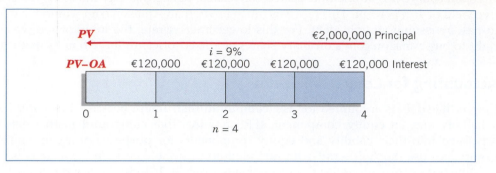

The liability component of the convertible debt is computed as shown in Illustration 16-3.

ILLUSTRATION 16-3
Fair Value of Liability
Component of Convertible
Bond

Present value of principal: €2,000,000 × .70843 (Table 6-2; $n = 4$, $i = 9\%$)	€1,416,860
Present value of the interest payments: €120,000 × 3.23972 (Table 6-4; $n = 4$, $i = 9\%$)	388,766
Present value of the liability component	€1,805,606

The equity component of Roche's convertible debt is then computed as shown in Illustration 16-4.

ILLUSTRATION 16-4
Equity Component of
Convertible Bond

Fair value of convertible debt at date of issuance	€2,000,000
Less: Fair value of liability component at date of issuance	1,805,606
Fair value of equity component at date of issuance	€ 194,394

The journal entry to record this transaction is as follows.

Cash	2,000,000	
Bonds Payable		1,805,606
Share Premium—Conversion Equity		194,394

The liability component of Roche's convertible debt issue is recorded as Bonds Payable. As shown in Chapter 14, the amount of the discount relative to the face value of the bond is amortized at each reporting period so at maturity, the Bonds Payable account is reported at €2,000,000 (face value). The equity component of the convertible bond is recorded in the Share Premium—Conversion Equity account and is reported in the equity section of the statement of financial position. Because this amount is considered part of contributed capital, it does not change over the life of the convertible.[3]

Settlement of Convertible Bonds
We illustrate four settlement situations: (1) repurchase at maturity, (2) conversion at maturity, (3) conversion before maturity, and (4) repurchase before maturity.

Repurchase at Maturity. If the bonds are not converted at maturity, Roche makes the following entry to pay off the convertible debtholders.

Bonds Payable	2,000,000	
Cash		2,000,000
(To record the purchase of bonds at maturity)		

[3]Transaction costs related to the liability and equity components are allocated in proportion to the proceeds received from the two components. *For purposes of homework, use the Share Premium—Conversion Equity account to record the equity component.* In practice, there may be considerable variance in the accounts used to record this component.

Because the carrying value of the bonds equals the face value, there is no gain or loss on repurchase at maturity. The amount originally allocated to equity of €194,384 either remains in the Share Premium—Conversion Equity account or is transferred to Share Premium—Ordinary.

Conversion of Bonds at Maturity. If the bonds are converted at maturity, Roche makes the following entry.

Share Premium—Conversion Equity	194,394	
Bonds Payable	2,000,000	
Share Capital—Ordinary		500,000
Share Premium—Ordinary		1,694,394
(To record the conversion of bonds at maturity)		

As indicated, Roche records a credit to Share Capital—Ordinary for €500,000 (2,000 bonds × 250 shares × €1 par) and the remainder to Share Premium—Ordinary for €1,694,394. There is no gain or loss on conversion at maturity. The original amount allocated to equity (€194,394) is transferred to the Share Premium—Ordinary account. As a result, Roche's equity has increased by a total of €2,194,394 through issuance and conversion of the convertible bonds. This accounting approach is often referred to as the **book value method** in that the carrying amount (book value) of the bond and related conversion equity determines the amount in the ordinary equity accounts.

Conversion of Bonds before Maturity. What happens if bonds are converted before maturity? To understand the accounting, we again use the Roche Group example. A schedule of bond amortization related to Roche's convertible bonds is shown in Illustration 16-5.

ILLUSTRATION 16-5
Convertible Bond
Amortization Schedule

SCHEDULE OF BOND AMORTIZATION
EFFECTIVE-INTEREST METHOD
6% BOND DISCOUNTED AT 9%

Date	Cash Paid	Interest Expense	Discount Amortized	Carrying Amount of Bonds
1/1/11				€1,805,606
12/31/11	€120,000	€162,505	€42,505	1,848,111
12/31/12	120,000	166,330	46,330	1,894,441
12/31/13	120,000	170,500	50,500	1,944,941
12/31/14	120,000	175,059*	55,059	2,000,000

*$14 difference due to rounding.

Assuming that Roche converts its bonds into ordinary shares on December 31, 2012, Roche debits the Bonds Payable account for its carrying value of €1,894,441 (see Illustration 16-5). In addition, Roche credits Share Capital—Ordinary for €500,000 (2,000 × 250 × €1) and credits Share Premium—Ordinary for €1,588,835. The entry to record this conversion is as follows.

Share Premium—Conversion Equity	194,394	
Bonds Payable	1,894,441	
Share Capital—Ordinary		500,000
Share Premium—Ordinary		1,588,835
(To record the conversion of bonds before maturity)		

There is no gain or loss on conversion before maturity: The original amount allocated to equity (€194,394) is transferred to the Share Premium—Ordinary account.

Repurchase before Maturity. In some cases, companies decide to repurchase the convertible debt before maturity. The approach used for allocating the amount paid upon repurchase follows the approach used when the convertible bond was originally issued. That is, Roche determines the fair value of the liability component of the convertible bonds at December 31, 2012, and then subtracts this amount from the fair value of the convertible bond issue (including the equity component) to arrive at the value for the equity. After this allocation is completed:

1. The difference between the consideration allocated to the liability component and the carrying amount of the liability is recognized as a gain or loss, and

2. The amount of consideration relating to the equity component is recognized (as a reduction) in equity. [3]

To illustrate, instead of converting the bonds on December 31, 2012, assume that Roche repurchases the convertible bonds from the bondholders. Pertinent information related to this conversion is as follows.

- Fair value of the convertible debt (including both liability and equity components), based on market prices at December 31, 2012, is €1,965,000.

- The fair value of the liability component is €1,904,900. This amount is based on computing the present value of a non-convertible bond with a two-year term (which corresponds to the shortened time to maturity of the repurchased bonds).

We first determine the gain or loss on the liability component, as computed in Illustration 16-6.

ILLUSTRATION 16-6
Gain or Loss on Debt Repurchase

Present value of liability component at December 31, 2012 (given above)	€ 1,904,900
Carrying value of liability component at December 31, 2012 (per Illustration 16-5)	(1,894,441)
Loss on repurchase	€ 10,459

Roche has a loss on this repurchase because the value of the debt extinguished is greater than its carrying amount. To determine any adjustment to the equity, we compute the value of the equity as shown in Illustration 16-7.

ILLUSTRATION 16-7
Equity Adjustment on Repurchase of Convertible Bonds

Fair value of convertible debt at December 31, 2012 (**with equity component**)	€1,965,000
Less: Fair value of liability component at December 31, 2012 (similar 2-year non-convertible debt)	1,904,900
Fair value of equity component at December 31, 2012 (**without debt component**)	€ 60,100

Roche makes the following compound journal entry to record the entire repurchase transaction.

Bonds Payable	1,894,441	
Share Premium—Conversion Equity	60,100	
Loss on Repurchase	10,459	
Cash		1,965,000
(To record the repurchase of convertible bonds)		

In summary, the repurchase results in a loss related to the liability component and a reduction in Share Premium—Conversion Equity. The remaining balance in Share Premium—Conversion Equity of €134,284 (€194,384 − €60,100) is often transferred to Share Premium—Ordinary upon the repurchase.

Induced Conversions

Sometimes, the issuer wishes to encourage prompt conversion of its convertible debt to equity securities in order to reduce interest costs or to improve its debt to equity ratio. Thus, the issuer may offer some form of additional consideration (such as cash or ordinary shares), called a "sweetener," to **induce conversion**. The issuing company reports the sweetener as an expense of the current period. Its amount is the fair value of the additional securities or other consideration given.

Assume that Helloid, Inc. has outstanding $1,000,000 par value convertible debentures convertible into 100,000 ordinary shares ($1 par value). When issued, Helloid recorded Share Premium—Conversion Equity of $15,000. Helloid wishes to reduce its annual interest cost. To do so, Helloid agrees to pay the holders of its convertible debentures an additional $80,000 if they will convert. Assuming conversion occurs, Helloid makes the following entry.

Conversion Expense	65,000	
Share Premium—Conversion Equity	15,000	
Bonds Payable	1,000,000	
Share Capital—Ordinary		100,000
Share Premium—Ordinary		900,000
Cash		80,000

Helloid records the additional $80,000 as **an expense of the current period** and not as a reduction of equity. [4]

Some argue that the cost of a conversion inducement is a cost of obtaining equity capital. As a result, they contend that companies should recognize the cost of conversion as a cost of (a reduction of) the equity capital acquired and not as an expense. However, the IASB indicated that when an issuer makes an additional payment to encourage conversion, the payment is for a service (bondholders converting at a given time) and should be reported as an expense.

CONVERTIBLE PREFERENCE SHARES

Convertible preference shares include an option for the holder to convert preference shares into a fixed number of ordinary shares. The major difference between accounting for a convertible bond and a convertible preference share is their classification. Convertible bonds are compound instruments because they have both a liability and an equity component. Convertible preference shares (unless mandatory redemption exists) are not compound instruments because they have only an equity component. As a result, convertible preference shares are reported as part of equity. When preference shares are converted or repurchased, there is no gain or loss recognized. The rationale is: A company does not recognize a gain or loss involving transactions with its existing shareholders.

> **Objective·2**
> Explain the accounting for convertible preference shares.

To illustrate, assume that Morse Company issues 1,000 convertible preference shares that have a par value of €1 per share. The shares were issued at a price of €200 per share. The journal entry to record this transaction is as follows.

Cash (1,000 × €200)	200,000	
Share Capital—Preference (1,000 × €1)		1,000
Share Premium—Conversion Equity		199,000
(To record the issuance of convertible		
preference shares)		

If we assume that each share is subsequently converted into 25 each ordinary shares (€2 par value) that have a fair value of €410,000, the journal entry to record the conversion is as follows.

Share Capital—Preference	1,000	
Share Premium—Conversion Equity	199,000	
Share Capital—Ordinary (1,000 × 25 × €2)		50,000
Share Premium—Ordinary		150,000
(To record the conversion of convertible		
preference shares)		

As indicated, Morse uses the book value method and does not recognize a gain or loss. The fair value of the ordinary shares is therefore ignored in this computation. If the convertible preference shares are repurchased instead of converted, Morse makes the following entry.

Share Capital—Preference	1,000	
Share Premium—Conversion Equity	199,000	
Retained Earnings	210,000	
Cash		410,000
(To record the repurchase of convertible preference shares)		

Morse does not report a gain or loss on the repurchase. Any excess paid above the book value of the convertible preference shares is often debited to Retained Earnings on the theory that an excess dividend is being paid to the preference shareholders to facilitate the repurchase.

HOW LOW CAN YOU GO?

What do the numbers mean?

Financial engineers are always looking for the next innovation in security design to meet the needs of both issuers and investors. Consider the convertible bonds issued by **STMicroelectronics (STM)** (USA). STM's 10-year bonds have a zero coupon and are convertible into STM ordinary shares at an exercise price of $33.43. When issued, the bonds sold at an effective yield of −0.05 percent. That's right—a negative yield.

How could this happen? When STM issued the bonds, investors thought the options to convert were so valuable that they were willing to take zero interest payments and invest an amount *in excess of* the maturity value of the bonds. In essence, the investors are paying interest to STM, and STM records interest revenue. Why would investors do this? If the share price rises, as many thought it would for STM and many tech companies at this time, these bond investors could convert and get a big gain in the shares.

Investors did get some additional protection in the deal: They can redeem the $1,000 bonds after three years and receive $975 (and after five and seven years, for lower amounts), if it looks like the bonds will never convert. In the end, STM has issued bonds with a significant equity component.

Source: STM Financial Reports. See also Floyd Norris, "Legal but Absurd: They Borrow a Billion and Report a Profit," *New York Times* (August 8, 2003), p. C1.

SHARE WARRANTS

Objective•3

Contrast the accounting for share warrants and for share warrants issued with other securities.

Warrants are certificates entitling the holder to acquire shares at a certain price within a stated period. This option is similar to the conversion privilege: Warrants, if exercised, become ordinary shares and usually have a dilutive effect (reduce earnings per share) similar to that of the conversion of convertible securities. However, a substantial difference between convertible securities and share warrants is that upon exercise of the warrants, the holder has to pay a certain amount of money to obtain the shares.

The issuance of warrants or options to buy additional shares normally arises under three situations:

1. When issuing different types of securities, such as bonds or preference shares, companies often include warrants **to make the security more attractive**—by providing an "equity kicker."

2. Upon the issuance of additional ordinary shares, existing shareholders have a **preemptive right to purchase ordinary shares** first. Companies may issue warrants to evidence that right.

3. Companies give warrants, often referred to as *share options*, **to executives and employees** as a form of **compensation**.

The problems in accounting for share warrants are complex and present many difficulties—some of which remain unresolved. The following sections address the accounting for share warrants in the three situations listed on the previous page.

Share Warrants Issued with Other Securities

Warrants issued with other securities are basically long-term options to buy ordinary shares at a fixed price. Generally, the life of warrants is five years, occasionally 10 years; very occasionally, a company may offer perpetual warrants.

A **share warrant** works like this: **Tenneco, Inc.** (USA) offered a unit comprising one ordinary share and one share warrant. In this case, Tenneco's warrants were detachable; that is, they can be detached (separated) from the ordinary shares and traded as a separate security. Companies may also issue non-detachable warrants with debt, which means the warrant cannot be separated from the debt. In either case, debt issued with warrants is considered a compound instrument for accounting purposes. The Tenneco warrant in this example is exercisable at $24.25 per share and good for five years. The unit (share plus detachable warrant) sold for 22.75 ($22.75). Since the price of the ordinary share the day before the sale was 19.88 ($19.88), the difference suggests a price of 2.87 ($2.87) for the warrant.

The investor pays for the warrant in order to receive the right to buy ordinary shares, at a fixed price of $24.25, sometime in the future. It would not be profitable at present for the purchaser to exercise the warrant and buy the share, because the price of the share was much below the exercise price. But if, for example, the price of the share rises to $30, the investor gains $2.88 ($30 − $24.25 − $2.87) on an investment of $2.87, a 100 percent increase! If the price never rises, the investor loses the full $2.87 per warrant.[4]

Debt issued with share warrants is a compound instrument that has a debt and an equity component. As a result, the company should use the with-and-without method to allocate the proceeds between the two components.

Illustration

At one time, **AT&T** (USA) issued bonds with detachable five-year warrants to buy one ordinary share (par value $5) at $25. At the time, an ordinary share of AT&T was selling for approximately $50. These warrants enabled AT&T to price its bond offering at par with an 8¾ percent yield (quite a bit lower than prevailing rates at that time). AT&T was able to sell the bonds plus the warrants for $10,200,000.

To account for the proceeds from this sale, AT&T uses the with-and-without method. Using this approach, AT&T determines the present value of the future cash flows related to the bonds, which is $9,707,852. It then subtracts this amount from $10,200,000 to determine the equity component. Determination of the equity component, using the with-and-without method, is shown in Illustration 16-8.

Fair value of bonds with warrants	$10,200,000
Less: Fair value of liability component at date of issuance	9,707,852
Equity component at date of issuance	$ 492,148

ILLUSTRATION 16-8
Equity Component of Security Issue

In this situation, the bonds sell at a discount. AT&T records the sale as follows.

Cash	9,705,882	
Bonds Payable		9,705,882

In addition, AT&T sells warrants that it credits to Share Premium—Share Warrants. It makes the following entry.

Cash	492,148	
Share Premium—Share Warrants		492,148

[4]From the illustration, it is apparent that buying warrants can be an "all or nothing" proposition.

AT&T may combine the entries if desired. Here, we show them separately, to indicate that the purchaser of the bond is buying not only a bond but also a possible future claim on ordinary shares.

Assuming investors exercise all 10,000 warrants (one warrant per one ordinary share), AT&T makes the following entry.

Cash (10,000 × $25)	250,000	
Share Premium—Share Warrants	492,148	
Share Capital—Ordinary (10,000 × $5)		50,000
Share Premium—Ordinary		692,148

What if investors fail to exercise the warrants? In that case, AT&T debits Share Premium—Share Warrants for $492,148, and credits Share Premium—Expired Share Warrants for a like amount. The Share Premium—Expired Share Warrants reverts to the former shareholders.

Summary Analysis

The IASB indicates that companies should separate the debt and equity components of securities, such as convertible debt or bonds issued with warrants. We agree with this position. In both situations (convertible debt and debt issued with warrants), the investor has made a payment to the company for an equity feature—the right to acquire an equity instrument in the future. The only real distinction between them is that the additional payment made when the equity instrument is formally acquired takes different forms. The warrant holder pays additional cash to the issuing company; the convertible debtholder pays for shares by forgoing the receipt of interest from the conversion date until maturity and by forgoing the receipt of the maturity value itself. Thus, the difference is one of method or form of payment only, rather than one of substance.

Rights to Subscribe to Additional Shares

If the directors of a corporation decide to issue new ordinary shares, the old shareholders generally have the right (**preemptive privilege**) to purchase newly issued shares in proportion to their holdings. This privilege, referred to as a **share right**, saves existing shareholders from suffering a dilution of voting rights without their consent. Also, it may allow them to purchase shares somewhat below their market value. Unlike the warrants issued with other securities, the warrants issued for share rights are of short duration.

The certificate representing the share right states the number of shares the holder of the right may purchase. Each share owned ordinarily gives the owner one share right. The certificate also states the price at which the new shares may be purchased. The price is normally less than the current market value of such shares, which gives the rights a value in themselves. From the time they are issued until they expire, holders of share rights may purchase and sell them like any other security.

Companies make only a memorandum entry when they issue rights to existing shareholders. This entry indicates the number of rights issued to existing shareholders in order to ensure that the company has additional unissued shares registered for issuance in case the rights are exercised. Companies make no formal entry at this time because they have not yet issued shares nor received cash.

If holders exercise the share rights, a cash payment of some type usually is involved. If the company receives cash equal to the par value, it makes an entry crediting Share Capital—Ordinary at par value. If the company receives cash in excess of par value, it credits Share Premium—Ordinary. If it receives cash less than par value, a debit to Share Premium—Ordinary is appropriate.

Share Compensation Plans

The third form of warrant arises in share compensation plans to pay and motivate employees. This warrant is a **share option**, which gives key employees the option to purchase ordinary shares at a given price over an extended period of time.

A consensus of opinion is that effective compensation programs are ones that do the following: (1) base compensation on employee and company performance, (2) motivate employees to high levels of performance, (3) help retain executives and allow for recruitment of new talent, (4) maximize the employee's after-tax benefit and minimize the employer's after-tax cost, and (5) use performance criteria over which the employee has control. Straight cash-compensation plans (salary and perhaps a bonus), though important, are oriented to the short run. Many companies recognize that they need a longer-term compensation plan in addition to the cash component.

Long-term compensation plans attempt to develop company loyalty among key employees by giving them "a piece of the action"—that is, an equity interest. These plans, generally referred to as **share-based compensation plans**, come in many forms. Essentially, they provide the employee with the opportunity to receive shares if the performance of the company (by whatever measure) is satisfactory. Typical performance measures focus on long-term improvements that are readily measurable and that benefit the company as a whole, such as increases in earnings per share, revenues, share price, or market share.

As indicated in our opening story, companies are changing the way they use share-based compensation. Illustration 16-9 indicates that share-option use is on the decline and that another form of share-based compensation, **restricted shares**, is on the rise. The major reasons for this change are two-fold. Critics often cited the indiscriminate use of share options as a reason why company executives manipulated accounting numbers in an attempt to achieve higher share price. As a result, many responsible companies decided to cut back on the issuance of options, both to avoid such accounting manipulations and to head off investor doubts. In addition, IFRS now results in companies recording a higher expense when share options are granted.

Fair Value of Share Compensation Grants S&P 500 ($ in billions)

Restricted shares | Options

Source: J. Ciesielski, "S&P 500 Stock Compensation: Running Out of Options?" *The Analyst's Accounting Observer* (August 25, 2009).

ILLUSTRATION 16-9
Share-Option
Compensation Expense

Illustration 16-9 reinforces the point that the design of compensation plans is changing. For example, from 2004–2008, the fair value of restricted-share grants jumped 237 percent. Share options, on the other hand, decreased 39 percent.

The Major Reporting Issue

Suppose that, as an employee for Hurdle Inc., you receive options to purchase 10,000 shares of the firm's ordinary shares as part of your compensation. The date you receive the options is referred to as the **grant date**. The options are good for 10 years. The market price and the exercise price for the shares are both $20 at the grant date. **What is the value of the compensation you just received?**

Some believe that what you have received has no value. They reason that because the difference between the market price and the exercise price is zero, no compensation results. Others argue these options do have value: If the share price goes above $20 any time in the next 10 years and you exercise the options, you may earn substantial compensation. For example, if at the end of the fourth year, the share market price is $30 and you exercise your options, you earn $100,000 [10,000 options × ($30 − $20)], ignoring income taxes.

The question for Hurdle is how to report the granting of these options. One approach measures compensation cost by the excess of the market price of the shares over their exercise price at the grant date. This approach is referred to as the **intrinsic-value method**. It measures what the holder would receive today if the option was immediately exercised. The intrinsic value **is the difference between the market price of the shares and the exercise price of the options at the grant date**. Using the intrinsic-value method, Hurdle would not recognize any compensation expense related to your options because at the grant date the market price equaled the exercise price. (In the preceding paragraph, those who answered that the options had no value were looking at the question from the intrinsic-value approach.)

The second way to look at the question of how to report the granting of these options bases the cost of employee share options on the **fair value** of the share options granted. Under this **fair value method**, companies use acceptable option-pricing models to value the options at the date of grant. These models take into account the many factors that determine an option's underlying value.[5]

The IASB guidelines require that companies recognize compensation cost using the fair value method. **[5]** The IASB position is that companies should base the accounting for the cost of employee services on the fair value of compensation paid. This amount is presumed to be a measure of the value of the services received. We will discuss more about the politics of IFRS in this area later (see "Debate over Share-Option Accounting," page 838). Let's first describe the procedures involved.

ACCOUNTING FOR SHARE COMPENSATION
Share-Option Plans

Objective•4

Describe the accounting for share compensation plans.

Share-option plans involve two main accounting issues:

1. How to determine compensation expense.
2. Over what periods to allocate compensation expense.

Determining Expense

Under the fair value method, companies compute total compensation expense based on the fair value of the options expected to vest on the date they grant the options to the employee(s) (i.e., the **grant date**).[6] Public companies estimate fair value by using an option-pricing model, with some adjustments for the unique factors of employee share options. No adjustments occur after the grant date in response to subsequent changes in the share price—either up or down.

Allocating Compensation Expense

In general, a company recognizes compensation expense in the periods in which its employees perform the service—the **service period**. Unless otherwise specified, the

---

[5]These factors include the volatility of the underlying shares, the expected life of the options, the risk-free rate during the option life, and expected dividends during the option life.

[6]"To vest" means "to earn the rights to." An employee's award becomes vested at the date that the employee's right to receive or retain shares or cash under the award is no longer contingent on remaining in the service of the employer.

service period is the vesting period—the time between the grant date and the vesting date. Thus, the company determines total compensation cost at the grant date and allocates it to the periods benefited by its employees' services.

Share Compensation Example

An example will help show the accounting for a share-option plan. Assume that on November 1, 2010, the shareholders of Chen Company approve a plan that grants the company's five executives options to purchase 2,000 shares each of the company's ¥100 par value ordinary shares. The company grants the options on January 1, 2011. The executives may exercise the options at any time within the next 10 years. The option price per share is ¥6,000, and the market price of the shares at the date of grant is ¥7,000 per share.

Under the fair value method, the company computes total compensation expense by applying an acceptable fair value option-pricing model (such as the Black-Scholes option-pricing model). To keep this illustration simple, we assume that the fair value option-pricing model determines Chen's total compensation expense to be ¥22,000,000.

Basic Entries. Under the fair value method, a company recognizes the value of the options as an expense in the periods in which the employee performs services. In the case of Chen Company, assume that the expected period of benefit is two years, starting with the grant date. Chen would record the transactions related to this option contract as follows.

At date of grant (January 1, 2011)

No entry.

To record compensation expense for 2011 (December 31, 2011)

Compensation Expense	11,000,000	
Share Premium—Share Options (¥22,000,000 ÷ 2)		11,000,000

To record compensation expense for 2012 (December 31, 2012)

Compensation Expense	11,000,000	
Share Premium—Share Options		11,000,000

As indicated, Chen allocates compensation expense evenly over the two-year service period.

Exercise. If Chen's executives exercise 2,000 of the 10,000 options (20 percent of the options) on June 1, 2014 (three years and five months after date of grant), the company records the following journal entry.

June 1, 2014

Cash (2,000 × ¥6,000)	12,000,000	
Share Premium—Share Options (20% × ¥22,000,000)	4,400,000	
Share Capital—Ordinary (2,000 × ¥100)		200,000
Share Premium—Ordinary		16,200,000

Expiration. If Chen's executives fail to exercise the remaining share options before their expiration date, the company transfers the balance in the Share Premium—Share Options account to a more properly titled share premium account, such as Share Premium—Expired Share Options. Chen records this transaction at the date of expiration as follows.

January 1, 2021 (expiration date)

Share Premium—Share Options	17,600,000	
Share Premium—Expired Share Options		17,600,000
(80% × ¥22,000,000)		

Adjustment. An unexercised share option does not nullify the need to record the costs of services received from executives and attributable to the share-option plan. Under IFRS, a company therefore does not adjust compensation expense upon expiration of the options.

Once the total compensation is measured at the date of grant, can it be changed in future periods? The answer is that it depends on whether the adjustment is caused by a service or market condition. A **service condition** requires employees to complete a specified period of service to receive the award. If a service condition exists, the company is permitted to adjust the number of share options expected to the actual number of instruments vested. **Thus, compensation can be adjusted.** The company should adjust the estimate of compensation expense recorded in the current period (as a change in estimate). A company records this change in estimate by debiting Share Premium—Share Options and crediting Compensation Expense for the amount of cumulative compensation expense recorded to date (thus decreasing compensation expense in the period of forfeiture).

A **market condition** results when vesting or exercisability of the share option depends on a performance condition, such as a rise in the market price of the company's ordinary shares. Because market conditions are reflected in the determination of fair value at the grant date, **no adjustment to compensation expense is permitted**.

Many question this accounting treatment. The practice of not reversing share-option awards due to market conditions (share price stays below exercise price) means that a company may recognize an expense for an option that is never exercised. However, if the reason the option is not exercised relates to a service condition (failure to stay as an employee and provide services), the compensation expense related to the option is adjusted. In summary, estimates of the number of share options that are expected to vest are adjusted to the actual number that do vest. Cancellations due to market conditions are not adjusted.[7]

Restricted Shares

As indicated earlier, many companies are also using restricted shares (or replacing options altogether) to compensate employees. **Restricted-share plans** transfer shares to employees, subject to an agreement that the shares cannot be sold, transferred, or pledged until vesting occurs. Similar to share options, these shares are subject to forfeiture if the conditions for vesting are not met.[8]

Major advantages of restricted-share plans are:

1. *Restricted shares never become completely worthless*. In contrast, if the share price does not exceed the exercise price for a share option, the options are worthless. The restricted shares, however, still have value.

2. *Restricted shares generally result in less dilution to existing shareholders*. Restricted-share awards are usually one-half to one-third the size of share options. For example, if a company issues share options on 1,000 shares, an equivalent restricted-share offering might be 333 to 500 shares. The reason for the difference is that at the end of the vesting period, the restricted shares will have value, whereas the share options may not. As a result, fewer shares are involved in restricted-share plans, and therefore less dilution results if the share price rises.

[7]Companies sometimes modify the terms and conditions on which the share options were granted, to reward outstanding performance or provide a morale boost for some or all employees. Modifications may reduce the exercise period, extend the term of the options, or increase the number of shares issuable upon exercise. Modifications to share-based arrangements that decrease the fair value of the grant are basically ignored. However, if the fair value of the grant increases due to a modification, then the incremental fair value of the modified grant should be accounted for as additional compensation expense over the remaining vesting period.

[8]Most companies base vesting on future service for a period of generally three to five years. Vesting may also be conditioned on some performance target such as revenue, net income, cash flows, or some combination of these three factors. The employee also collects dividends on the restricted shares, and these dividends generally must be repaid if forfeiture occurs.

3. *Restricted shares better align the employee incentives with the companies' incentives.* The holder of restricted shares is essentially a shareholder and should be more interested in the long-term objectives of the company. In contrast, the recipients of share options often have a short-run focus, which leads to taking risks to hype the share price for short-term gain to the detriment of the long-term.

The accounting for restricted shares follows the same general principles as accounting for share options at the date of grant. That is, the company determines the fair value of the restricted shares at the date of grant (usually the fair value of a share) and then expenses that amount over the service period. Subsequent changes in the fair value of the shares are ignored for purposes of computing compensation expense.

Restricted Shares Example

Assume that on January 1, 2011, Ogden Company issues 1,000 restricted shares to its CEO, Christie DeGeorge. Ogden's shares have a fair value of $20 per share on January 1, 2011. Additional information is as follows.

1. The service period related to the restricted shares is five years.
2. Vesting occurs if DeGeorge stays with the company for a five-year period.
3. The par value is $1 per share.

Ogden makes the following entry on the grant date (January 1, 2011).

Unearned Compensation	20,000	
Share Capital—Ordinary (1,000 × $1)		1,000
Share Premium—Ordinary (1,000 × $19)		19,000

The credits to Share Capital—Ordinary and Share Premium—Ordinary indicate that Ogden has issued shares. The debit to Unearned Compensation (often referred to as Deferred Compensation Expense) identifies the total compensation expense the company will recognize over the five-year period. **Unearned Compensation represents the cost of services yet to be performed, which is not an asset.** Consequently, the company reports Unearned Compensation in equity in the statement of financial position, as a contra-equity account (similar to the reporting of treasury shares at cost).

At December 31, 2011, Ogden records compensation expense of $4,000 (1,000 shares × $20 × 20%) as follows.

Compensation Expense	4,000	
Unearned Compensation		4,000

Ogden records compensation expense of $4,000 for each of the next four years (2012, 2013, 2014, and 2015).

What happens if DeGeorge leaves the company before the five years has elapsed (that is, she does not fulfill a service condition)? In this situation, DeGeorge forfeits her rights to the shares, and Ogden reverses the compensation expense already recorded.

For example, assume that DeGeorge leaves on February 3, 2013 (before any expense has been recorded during 2013). The entry to record this forfeiture is as follows.

Share Capital—Ordinary	1,000	
Share Premium—Ordinary	19,000	
Compensation Expense ($4,000 × 2)		8,000
Unearned Compensation		12,000

In this situation, Ogden reverses the compensation expense of $8,000 recorded through 2012. In addition, the company debits Share Capital—Ordinary and Share Premium—Ordinary, reflecting DeGeorge's forfeiture. It credits the balance of Unearned Compensation since none remains when DeGeorge leaves Ogden.

This accounting is similar to accounting for share options when employees do not fulfill vesting requirements. Recall that once compensation expense is recorded for share options, it is not reversed. The only exception is if the employee does not fulfill a service condition, by leaving the company early.

In Ogden's restricted-share plan, vesting never occurred because DeGeorge left the company before she met the service requirement. Because DeGeorge was never vested, she had to forfeit her shares. Therefore, the company must reverse compensation expense recorded to date.[9]

Employee Share-Purchase Plans

Employee share-purchase plans (ESPPs) generally permit all employees to purchase shares at a discounted price for a short period of time. The company often uses such plans to secure equity capital or to induce widespread ownership of its ordinary shares among employees. **These plans are considered compensatory and should be recorded as expense over the service period.**

To illustrate, assume that Masthead Company offers all its 1,000 employees the opportunity to participate in an employee share-purchase plan. Under the terms of the plan, the employees are entitled to purchase 100 ordinary shares (par value £1 per share) at a 20 percent discount. The purchase price must be paid immediately upon acceptance of the offer. In total, 800 employees accept the offer, and each employee purchases on average 80 shares. That is, the employees purchase a total of 64,000 shares. The weighted-average market price of the shares at the purchase date is £30 per share, and the weighted-average purchase price is £24 per share. The entry to record this transaction is as follows.

Cash (64,000 × £24)	1,536,000	
Compensation Expense [64,000 × (£30 − £24)]	384,000	
Share Capital—Ordinary (64,000 × £1)		64,000
Share Premium—Ordinary		1,856,000
(Issue shares in an employee share-purchase plan)		

The IASB indicates that there is no reason to treat broad-based employee share plans differently from other employee share plans. Some have argued that because these plans are used to raise capital, they should not be compensatory. However, IFRS requires recording expense for these arrangements. The Board notes that because these arrangements are available only to employees, it is sufficient to conclude that the benefits provided represent employee compensation.[10] [6]

Disclosure of Compensation Plans

Companies must fully disclose the status of their compensation plans at the end of the periods presented. To meet these objectives, companies must make extensive disclosures. Specifically, a company with one or more share-based payment arrangements must disclose information that enables users of the financial statements to understand:

1. The nature and extent of share-based payment arrangements that existed during the period.
2. How the fair value of the goods and services received, or the fair value of the equity instruments granted during the period, was determined.
3. The effect of share-based payment transactions on the company's net income (loss) during the period and on its financial position. [7]

---

[9]There are numerous variations on restricted-share plans, including restricted-share units (for which the shares are issued at the end of the vesting period) and restricted-share plans with performance targets, such as EPS or share price growth.

[10]As indicated, employee share-purchase plans offer company shares to workers through payroll deduction, often at significant discounts. Unfortunately, many employees do not avail themselves of this benefit. Hopefully, if you have the opportunity to purchase your company's shares at a significant discount, you will take advantage of the plan. By not participating, you are "leaving money on the table."

Illustration 16-10 presents the type of information disclosed for compensation plans.

ILLUSTRATION 16-10
Share-Option Plan
Disclosure

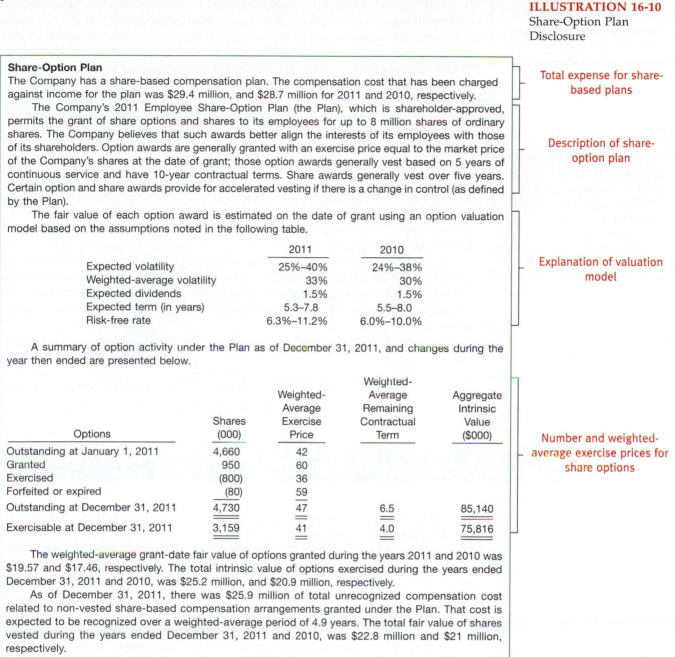

Share-Option Plan

The Company has a share-based compensation plan. The compensation cost that has been charged against income for the plan was $29.4 million, and $28.7 million for 2011 and 2010, respectively.

Total expense for share-based plans

The Company's 2011 Employee Share-Option Plan (the Plan), which is shareholder-approved, permits the grant of share options and shares to its employees for up to 8 million shares of ordinary shares. The Company believes that such awards better align the interests of its employees with those of its shareholders. Option awards are generally granted with an exercise price equal to the market price of the Company's shares at the date of grant; those option awards generally vest based on 5 years of continuous service and have 10-year contractual terms. Share awards generally vest over five years. Certain option and share awards provide for accelerated vesting if there is a change in control (as defined by the Plan).

Description of share-option plan

The fair value of each option award is estimated on the date of grant using an option valuation model based on the assumptions noted in the following table.

	2011	2010
Expected volatility	25%–40%	24%–38%
Weighted-average volatility	33%	30%
Expected dividends	1.5%	1.5%
Expected term (in years)	5.3–7.8	5.5–8.0
Risk-free rate	6.3%–11.2%	6.0%–10.0%

Explanation of valuation model

A summary of option activity under the Plan as of December 31, 2011, and changes during the year then ended are presented below.

Options	Shares (000)	Weighted-Average Exercise Price	Weighted-Average Remaining Contractual Term	Aggregate Intrinsic Value ($000)
Outstanding at January 1, 2011	4,660	42		
Granted	950	60		
Exercised	(800)	36		
Forfeited or expired	(80)	59		
Outstanding at December 31, 2011	4,730	47	6.5	85,140
Exercisable at December 31, 2011	3,159	41	4.0	75,816

Number and weighted-average exercise prices for share options

The weighted-average grant-date fair value of options granted during the years 2011 and 2010 was $19.57 and $17.46, respectively. The total intrinsic value of options exercised during the years ended December 31, 2011 and 2010, was $25.2 million, and $20.9 million, respectively.

As of December 31, 2011, there was $25.9 million of total unrecognized compensation cost related to non-vested share-based compensation arrangements granted under the Plan. That cost is expected to be recognized over a weighted-average period of 4.9 years. The total fair value of shares vested during the years ended December 31, 2011 and 2010, was $22.8 million and $21 million, respectively.

Restricted-Share Awards

The Company also has a restricted-share plan. The Plan is intended to retain and motivate the Company's Chief Executive Officer over the term of the award and to bring his total compensation package closer to median levels for Chief Executive Officers of comparable companies. The fair value of grants during the year was $1,889,000, or $35.68 per share, equivalent to 92% of the market value of a share of the Company's Ordinary Shares on the date the award was granted.

Restricted-share activity for the year ended 2011 is as follows.

	Shares	Price
Outstanding at December 31, 2010	57,990	—
Granted	149,000	$12.68
Vested	(19,330)	—
Forfeited	—	—
Outstanding at December 31, 2011	187,660	

Description of restricted-share plan

Debate over Share-Option Accounting

Objective•5
Discuss the controversy involving share compensation plans.

The IASB faced considerable opposition when it proposed the fair value method for accounting for share options. This is not surprising, given that the fair value method results in greater compensation costs relative to the intrinsic-value model.

Many small high-technology companies have been especially vocal in their opposition, arguing that only through offering share options can they attract top professional management. They contend that recognizing large amounts of compensation expense under these plans places them at a competitive disadvantage against larger companies that can withstand higher compensation charges. As one high-tech executive stated, "If your goal is to attack fat-cat executive compensation in multi-billion dollar firms, then please do so! But not at the expense of the people who are 'running lean and mean,' trying to build businesses and creating jobs in the process."

Underlying Concepts

The share-option controversy involves economic-consequence issues. The IASB believes companies should follow the neutrality concept. Others disagree, noting that factors other than accounting theory should be considered.

The share-option saga is a classic example of the difficulty the IASB faces in issuing new accounting guidance. Many powerful interests aligned against the Board. Even some who initially appeared to support the Board's actions later reversed themselves. These efforts undermine the authority of the IASB at a time when it is essential that we restore faith in our financial reporting system.

Transparent financial reporting—including recognition of share-based expense—should not be criticized because companies will report lower income. We may not like what the financial statements say, but we are always better off when the statements are representationally faithful to the underlying economic substance of transactions.

By leaving share-based compensation expense out of income, reported income is biased. Biased reporting not only raises concerns about the credibility of companies' reports, but also of financial reporting in general. Even good companies get tainted by the biased reporting of a few "bad apples." If we write standards to achieve some social, economic, or public policy goal, financial reporting loses its credibility.

SECTION 2 • COMPUTING EARNINGS PER SHARE

The financial press frequently reports earnings per share data. Further, shareholders and potential investors widely use this data in evaluating the profitability of a company. **Earnings per share** indicates the income earned by each ordinary share. Thus, **companies report earnings per share only for ordinary shares**. For example, if Oscar Co. has net income of $300,000 and a weighted average of 100,000 ordinary shares outstanding for the year, earnings per share is $3 ($300,000 ÷ 100,000). Because of the importance of earnings per share information, companies must report this information on the face of the income statement. **[8]** The exception, due to the cost constraint, is non-public companies.[11] Generally, companies report earnings per share information below net income in the income statement. Illustration 16-11 shows Oscar Co.'s income statement presentation of earnings per share.

ILLUSTRATION 16-11
Income Statement
Presentation of EPS

Net income	$300,000
Earnings per share	$3.00

[11]In general, a non-public enterprise is an enterprise whose debt or equity securities are not traded in a public market on a foreign or domestic securities exchange or in the over-the-counter market (including securities quoted locally or regionally). An enterprise is not considered a non-public enterprise when its financial statements are issued in preparation for the sale of any class of securities in a public market.

When the income statement contains discontinued operations, companies are required to report earnings per share from continuing operations and net income on the face of the income statement. The presentation in Illustration 16-12 is representative.

ILLUSTRATION 16-12
Income Statement
Presentation of EPS
Components

Earnings per share:	
Income from continuing operations	$4.00
Loss from discontinued operations, net of tax	0.60
Net income	$3.40

These disclosures enable the user of the financial statements to compare performance between different companies in the same reporting period and between different reporting periods for the same company. Even though earnings per share data have limitations because of the different accounting policies that may be used for determining "earnings," a consistently determined denominator enhances financial reporting. **[9]**

EARNINGS PER SHARE—SIMPLE CAPITAL STRUCTURE

A company's capital structure is **simple** if it consists only of ordinary shares or includes no potential ordinary shares that upon conversion or exercise could dilute earnings per ordinary share. In this case, a company reports **basic earnings per share**. A capital structure is **complex** if it includes securities (potential ordinary shares) that could have a dilutive effect on earnings per ordinary share.[12] In this situation, a company reports **diluted earnings per share**.

Objective·6
Compute earnings per share in a simple capital structure.

The computation of basic earnings per share for a simple capital structure involves two items (other than net income)—(1) preference share dividends and (2) weighted-average number of shares outstanding.

Preference Share Dividends

As we indicated earlier, earnings per share relates to earnings per ordinary share. When a company has both ordinary and preference shares outstanding, **it subtracts the current-year preference share dividend from net income to arrive at income available to ordinary shareholders**. Illustration 16-13 shows the formula for computing earnings per share.

ILLUSTRATION 16-13
Formula for Computing
Earnings per Share

$$\text{Earnings per Share} = \frac{\text{Net Income} - \text{Preference Dividends}}{\text{Weighted-Average Number of Shares Outstanding}}$$

In reporting earnings per share information, a company must calculate income available to ordinary shareholders. To do so, the company subtracts dividends on preference shares from income from continuing operations and net income. If a company declares dividends on preference shares and a net loss occurs, **the company adds the preference dividend to the loss** for purposes of computing the loss per share.

If the preference shares are cumulative and the company declares no dividend in the current year, it subtracts (or adds) **an amount equal to the dividend that it should**

---

[12]A potential ordinary share is a financial instrument or other contract that may entitle its holder to ordinary shares. Examples of potential ordinary shares are (1) convertible debt and convertible preference shares that are convertible into ordinary shares, (2) options and warrants, and (3) shares that would be issued upon the satisfaction of conditions resulting from contractual arrangements, such as the purchase of a business or other assets. These concepts are discussed later in this chapter.

have declared for the current year only from net income (or to the loss). The company should have included dividends in arrears for previous years in the previous years' computations.[13]

Weighted-Average Number of Shares Outstanding

In all computations of earnings per share, the **weighted-average number of shares outstanding** during the period constitutes the basis for the per share amounts reported. Shares issued or purchased during the period affect the amount outstanding. Companies must **weight the shares by the fraction of the period they are outstanding**. The rationale for this approach is to find the equivalent number of whole shares outstanding for the year.

To illustrate, assume that Franks Inc. has changes in its ordinary shares outstanding for the period, as shown in Illustration 16-14.

ILLUSTRATION 16-14
Shares Outstanding, Ending Balance— Franks Inc.

Date	Share Changes	Shares Outstanding
January 1	Beginning balance	90,000
April 1	Issued 30,000 shares for cash	30,000
		120,000
July 1	Purchased 39,000 shares	39,000
		81,000
November 1	Issued 60,000 shares for cash	60,000
December 31	Ending balance	141,000

Franks computes the weighted-average number of shares outstanding as follows.

ILLUSTRATION 16-15
Weighted-Average Number of Shares Outstanding

Dates Outstanding	(A) Shares Outstanding	(B) Fraction of Year	(C) Weighted Shares (A × B)
Jan. 1–Apr. 1	90,000	3/12	22,500
Apr. 1–July 1	120,000	3/12	30,000
July 1–Nov. 1	81,000	4/12	27,000
Nov. 1–Dec. 31	141,000	2/12	23,500
Weighted-average number of shares outstanding			103,000

As Illustration 16-15 shows, 90,000 shares were outstanding for three months, which translates to 22,500 whole shares for the entire year. Because Franks issued additional shares on April 1, it must weight these shares for the time outstanding. When the company purchased 39,000 shares on July 1, it reduced the shares outstanding. Therefore, from July 1 to November 1, only 81,000 shares were outstanding, which is equivalent to 27,000 shares. The issuance of 60,000 shares increases shares outstanding for the last two months of the year. Franks then makes a new computation to determine the proper weighted shares outstanding.

Share Dividends and Share Splits

When **share dividends** or **share splits** occur, companies need to restate the shares outstanding before the share dividend or split, in order to compute the weighted-average number of shares. For example, assume that Vijay Corporation had 100,000 shares outstanding on January 1 and issued a 25 percent share dividend on June 30. For purposes of computing a weighted-average for the current year, it assumes the additional 25,000

---

[13]Recall that an ordinary share is an equity instrument that is subordinate to all other classes of equity instruments. In addition, we assume that ordinary shares relate only to the controlling (majority) interest. As a result, the earnings per share computation does not include earnings related to the non-controlling (minority) interest.

shares outstanding as a result of the share dividend to be **outstanding since the beginning of the year**. Thus, the weighted-average for the year for Vijay is 125,000 shares.

Companies restate the issuance of a share dividend or share split, but not the issuance or repurchase of shares for cash. Why? Because share splits and share dividends do not increase or decrease the net assets of the company. The company merely issues additional shares. Because of the added shares, it must restate the weighted-average shares. Restating allows valid comparisons of earnings per share between periods before and after the share split or share dividend. Conversely, the issuance or purchase of shares for cash **changes the amount of net assets**. As a result, the company either earns more or less in the future as a result of this change in net assets. Stated another way, **a share dividend or split does not change the shareholders' total investment**—it only increases (unless it is a reverse share split) the number of ordinary shares representing this investment.

To illustrate how a share dividend affects the computation of the weighted-average number of shares outstanding, assume that Sabrina Company has the following changes in its ordinary shares during the year.

Date	Share Changes	Shares Outstanding
January 1	Beginning balance	100,000
March 1	Issued 20,000 shares for cash	20,000
		120,000
June 1	60,000 additional shares (50% share dividend)	60,000
		180,000
November 1	Issued 30,000 shares for cash	30,000
December 31	Ending balance	210,000

ILLUSTRATION 16-16
Shares Outstanding, Ending Balance—Sabrina Company

Sabrina computes the weighted-average number of shares outstanding as follows.

Dates Outstanding	(A) Shares Outstanding	(B) Restatement	(C) Fraction of Year	(D) Weighted Shares (A × B × C)
Jan. 1–Mar. 1	100,000	1.50	2/12	25,000
Mar. 1–June 1	120,000	1.50	3/12	45,000
June 1–Nov. 1	180,000		5/12	75,000
Nov. 1–Dec. 31	210,000		2/12	35,000
Weighted-average number of shares outstanding				180,000

ILLUSTRATION 16-17
Weighted-Average Number of Shares Outstanding—Share Issue and Share Dividend

Sabrina must restate the shares outstanding prior to the share dividend. The company adjusts the shares outstanding from January 1 to June 1 for the share dividend, so that it now states these shares on the same basis as shares issued subsequent to the share dividend. Sabrina does not restate shares issued after the share dividend because they are on the new basis. The share dividend simply restates existing shares. **The same type of treatment applies to a share split.**

If a share dividend or share split occurs after the end of the year, but before the financial statements are authorized for issuance, a company must restate the weighted-average number of shares outstanding for the year (and any other years presented in comparative form). For example, assume that Hendricks Company computes its weighted-average number of shares as 100,000 for the year ended December 31, 2011. On January 15, 2012, before authorizing the issuance of the financial statements, the company splits its shares 3 for 1. In this case, the weighted-average number of shares used in computing earnings per share for 2011 is now 300,000 shares. If providing earnings per share information for 2010 as comparative information, Hendricks must also adjust it for the share split.

Comprehensive Example

Let's study a comprehensive illustration for a simple capital structure. Darin Corporation has income from continuing operations of $580,000 and a gain on discontinued operations, net of tax, of $240,000. In addition, it has declared preference dividends of $1 per share on 100,000 shares of preference shares outstanding. Darin also has the following changes in its ordinary shares outstanding during 2011.

ILLUSTRATION 16-18
Shares Outstanding, Ending Balance—Darin Corp.

Dates	Share Changes	Shares Outstanding
January 1	Beginning balance	180,000
May 1	Purchased 30,000 treasury shares	30,000
		150,000
July 1	300,000 additional shares (3-for-1 share split)	300,000
		450,000
December 31	Issued 50,000 shares for cash	50,000
December 31	Ending balance	500,000

To compute the earnings per share information, Darin determines the weighted-average number of shares outstanding as follows.

ILLUSTRATION 16-19
Weighted-Average Number of Shares Outstanding

Dates Outstanding	(A) Shares Outstanding	(B) Restatement	(C) Fraction of Year	(D) Weighted Shares (A × B × C)
Jan. 1–May 1	180,000	3	4/12	180,000
May 1–July 1	150,000	3	2/12	75,000
July 1–Dec. 31	450,000		6/12	225,000
Weighted-average number of shares outstanding				480,000

In computing the weighted-average number of shares, the company ignores the shares sold on December 31, 2011, because they have not been outstanding during the year. Darin then divides the weighted-average number of shares into income from continuing operations and net income to determine earnings per share. It subtracts its preference dividends of $100,000 from income from continuing operations ($580,000) to arrive at income from continuing operations available to ordinary shareholders of $480,000 ($580,000 − $100,000).

Deducting the preference dividends from the income from continuing operations also reduces net income without affecting the gain on discontinued operations. The final amount is referred to as **income available to ordinary shareholders**, as shown in Illustration 16-20.

ILLUSTRATION 16-20
Computation of Income Available to Ordinary Shareholders

	(A) Income Information	(B) Weighted Shares	(C) Earnings per Share (A ÷ B)
Income from continuing operations available to ordinary shareholders	$480,000*	480,000	$1.00
Gain on discontinued operations (net of tax)	240,000	480,000	0.50
Income available to ordinary shareholders	$720,000	480,000	$1.50

*$580,000 − $100,000

Darin must disclose the per share amount for gain on discontinued operations (net of tax) either on the face of the income statement or in the notes to the financial statements.

Illustration 16-21 shows the income and per share information reported on the face of Darin's income statement.

Income from continuing operations	$580,000
Gain on discontinued operations, net of tax	240,000
Net income	$820,000
Earnings per share:	
Income from continuing operations	$1.00
Gain on discontinued operations, net of tax	0.50
Net income	$1.50

ILLUSTRATION 16-21
Earnings per Share, with Gain on Discontinued Operations

EARNINGS PER SHARE—COMPLEX CAPITAL STRUCTURE

The EPS discussion to this point applies to **basic EPS** for a simple capital structure. One problem with a **basic EPS** computation is that it fails to recognize the potential impact of a corporation's dilutive securities. As discussed at the beginning of the chapter, **dilutive securities** are securities that can be converted to ordinary shares.[14] Upon conversion or exercise by the holder, the dilutive securities reduce (dilute) earnings per share. This adverse effect on EPS can be significant and, more importantly, *unexpected* unless financial statements call attention to their potential dilutive effect.

Objective•7
Compute earnings per share in a complex capital structure.

As indicated earlier, a complex capital structure exists when a corporation has convertible securities, options, warrants, or other rights that upon conversion or exercise could dilute earnings per share. When a company has a complex capital structure, **it reports both basic and diluted earnings per share**.

Computing **diluted EPS** is similar to computing basic EPS. The difference is that diluted EPS includes the effect of all potential dilutive ordinary shares that were outstanding during the period. The formula in Illustration 16-22 shows the relationship between basic EPS and diluted EPS.

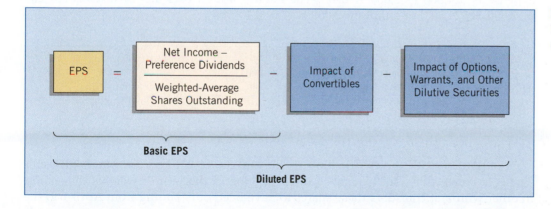

ILLUSTRATION 16-22
Relation between Basic and Diluted EPS

Some securities are antidilutive. **Antidilutive securities** are securities that upon conversion or exercise **increase** earnings per share (or reduce the loss per share). Companies with complex capital structures will not report diluted EPS if the securities in their capital structure are antidilutive. The purpose of presenting both basic and diluted EPS is to inform financial statement users of situations that will likely occur (basic EPS) and also to provide "worst case" dilutive situations (dilutive EPS). If the securities are antidilutive, the likelihood of conversion or exercise is considered remote.

---

[14]Issuance of these types of securities is typical in mergers and compensation plans.

Thus, companies that have only antidilutive securities must report only the basic EPS number. We illustrated the computation of basic EPS in the prior section. In the following sections, we address the effects of convertible and other dilutive securities on EPS calculations.

Diluted EPS—Convertible Securities

At conversion, companies exchange convertible securities for ordinary shares. Companies measure the dilutive effects of potential conversion on EPS using the **if-converted method**. This method for a convertible bond assumes: (1) the conversion of the convertible securities at the beginning of the period (or at the time of issuance of the security, if issued during the period), and (2) the elimination of related interest, net of tax. Thus, the additional shares assumed issued increase the **denominator**—the weighted-average number of shares outstanding. The amount of interest expense, net of tax associated with those potential ordinary shares, increases the **numerator**—net income.

Comprehensive Example—If-Converted Method

As an example, Mayfield Corporation has net income of $210,000 for the year and a weighted-average number of ordinary shares outstanding during the period of 100,000 shares. The basic earnings per share is therefore $2.10 ($210,000 ÷ 100,000). The company has two convertible debenture bond issues outstanding. One is a 6 percent issue sold at 100 (total $1,000,000) in a prior year and convertible into 20,000 ordinary shares. Interest expense for the current year related to the liability component of this convertible bond is $62,000. The other is a 7 percent issue sold at 100 (total $1,000,000) on April 1 of the current year and convertible into 32,000 ordinary shares. Interest expense for the current year related to the liability component of this convertible bond is $80,000.[15] The tax rate is 40 percent.

As Illustration 16-23 shows, to determine the numerator for diluted earnings per share, Mayfield adds back the interest on the if-converted securities, less the related tax effect. Because the if-converted method assumes conversion as of the beginning of the year, Mayfield assumes that it pays no interest on the convertibles during the year. The effective interest on the 6 percent convertibles is $62,000 for the year. The increased tax expense is $24,800 ($62,000 × 0.40). The interest added back net of taxes is $37,200 ($62,000 − $24,800) or simply $62,000 × (1 − 0.40).

ILLUSTRATION 16-23
Computation of Adjusted Net Income

Net income for the year	$210,000
Add: Adjustment for interest (net of tax)	
6% debentures ($62,000 × [1 −.40])	37,200
7% debentures ($80,000 × 9/12 × [1 −.40])	36,000
Adjusted net income	$283,200

Continuing with the information in Illustration 16-23, because Mayfield issues 7 percent convertibles subsequent to the beginning of the year, it weights the shares. In other words, it considers these shares to have been outstanding from April 1 to the end of the year. As a result, the interest adjustment to the numerator for these bonds reflects the interest for only nine months. Thus, the interest added back on the 7 percent convertible is $36,000 [$80,000 × 9/12 year × (1 − 0.4)]. The final item in Illustration 16-23 shows the adjusted net income. This amount becomes the numerator for Mayfield's computation of diluted earnings per share.

---

[15]The two examples assumed that Mayfield sold its bonds at face value. However, as indicated earlier, a convertible is a compound instrument that has both a liability and an equity component. As a result, the interest expense reported on the income statement will not equal the interest paid in cash during the period. Instead, the interest expense reported on the income statement is the amount of interest, net of tax, added back to net income.

Mayfield then calculates the weighted-average number of shares outstanding, as shown in Illustration 16-24. This number of shares becomes the denominator for Mayfield's computation of diluted earnings per share.

ILLUSTRATION 16-24
Computation of Weighted-Average Number of Shares

Weighted-average number of shares outstanding	100,000
Add: Shares assumed to be issued:	
6% debentures (as of beginning of year)	20,000
7% debentures (as of date of issue, April 1; 9/12 × 32,000)	24,000
Weighted-average number of shares adjusted for dilutive securities	144,000

In its income statement, Mayfield reports basic and diluted earnings per share.[16] Illustration 16-25 shows this dual presentation.

ILLUSTRATION 16-25
Earnings per Share Disclosure

Net income for the year	$210,000
Earnings per Share (Note X)	
Basic earnings per share ($210,000 ÷ 100,000)	$2.10
Diluted earnings per share ($283,200 ÷ 144,000)	$1.97

Other Factors

The conversion rate on a dilutive security may change during the period in which the security is outstanding. For the diluted EPS computation in such a situation, the **company uses the most dilutive conversion rate available.** [10] For example, assume that a company issued a convertible bond on January 1, 2009, with a conversion rate of 10 ordinary shares for each bond starting January 1, 2011. Beginning January 1, 2014, the conversion rate is 12 ordinary shares for each bond, and beginning January 1, 2018, it is 15 ordinary shares for each bond. In computing diluted EPS in 2009, the company uses the conversion rate of 15 shares to one bond.

Another issue relates to preference shares. For example, assume that Mayfield's 6 percent convertible debentures were instead 6 percent convertible *preference shares*. In that case, Mayfield considers the convertible preference shares as potential ordinary shares. Thus, it includes them in its diluted EPS calculations as shares outstanding. The company does not subtract preference dividends from net income in computing the numerator. Why not? Because for purposes of computing EPS, it assumes conversion of the convertible preference shares to outstanding ordinary shares. The company uses net income as the numerator—it computes **no tax effect** because preference dividends generally are not tax-deductible.

Diluted EPS—Options and Warrants

A company includes in diluted earnings per share all share options and warrants outstanding (whether or not presently exercisable), unless they are antidilutive. Companies use the **treasury-share method** to include options and warrants and their equivalents in EPS computations.

The treasury-share method assumes that the options or warrants are exercised at the beginning of the year (or date of issue if later), and that the company uses those proceeds to purchase ordinary shares for the treasury. If the exercise price is lower than the market price of the shares, then the proceeds from exercise are insufficient to buy back all the shares. The company then adds the incremental shares remaining to the

---

[16]Conversion of bonds is dilutive because EPS with conversion ($1.97) is less than basic EPS ($2.10). See Appendix 16B for a comprehensive evaluation of antidilution with multiple securities.

weighted-average number of shares outstanding for purposes of computing diluted earnings per share.

For example, if the exercise price of a warrant is $5 and the fair value of the shares is $15, the treasury-share method increases the shares outstanding. Exercise of the warrant results in one additional share outstanding, but the $5 received for the one share issued is insufficient to purchase one share in the market at $15. The company needs to exercise three warrants (and issue three additional shares) to produce enough money ($15) to acquire one share in the market. Thus, a net increase of two shares outstanding results.

To see this computation using larger numbers, assume 1,500 options outstanding at an exercise price of $30 for an ordinary share and a market price per ordinary share of $50. Through application of the treasury-share method, the company would have 600 incremental shares outstanding, computed as shown in Illustration 16-26.[17]

ILLUSTRATION 16-26
Computation of
Incremental Shares

Proceeds from exercise of 1,500 options (1,500 × $30)	$45,000
Shares issued upon exercise of options	1,500
Treasury shares purchasable with proceeds ($45,000 ÷ $50)	(900)
Incremental shares outstanding (potential common shares)	600

Thus, if the exercise price of the option or warrant is **lower** than the market price of the shares, dilution occurs. An exercise price of the option or warrant **higher** than the market price of the shares reduces ordinary shares. In this case, the options or warrants are **antidilutive** because their assumed exercise leads to an increase in earnings per share.

For both options and warrants, exercise is assumed only if the average market price of the share exceeds the exercise price during the reported period.[18] As a practical matter, a simple average of the weekly or monthly prices is adequate, so long as the prices do not fluctuate significantly.

Comprehensive Example—Treasury-Share Method

To illustrate application of the treasury-share method, assume that Kubitz Industries, Inc. has net income for the period of $220,000. The average number of shares outstanding for the period was 100,000 shares. Hence, basic EPS—ignoring all dilutive securities—is $2.20. The average number of shares related to options outstanding (although not exercisable at this time), at an option price of $20 per share, is 5,000 shares. The average market price of the ordinary shares during the year was $28. Illustration 16-27 shows the computation of EPS using the treasury-share method.

Contingently Issuable Shares

Contingently issuable ordinary shares are defined as ordinary shares issuable for little or no cash consideration upon satisfaction of specified conditions in a contingent share agreement. For example, in business combinations, the acquirer may agree to issue additional shares—contingently issuable shares—under certain circumstances. Companies generally issue these contingent shares based on a measure, such as attainment of

---

[17]The incremental number of shares may be more simply computed:

$$\frac{\text{Market price} - \text{Option price}}{\text{Market price}} \times \text{Number of options} = \text{Number of shares}$$

$$\frac{\$50 - \$30}{\$50} \times 1,500 \text{ options} = 600 \text{ shares}$$

[18]Options and warrants have essentially the same assumptions and computational problems, although the warrants may allow or require the tendering of some other security, such as debt, in lieu of cash upon exercise. This subject is beyond the scope of this book.

ILLUSTRATION 16-27
Computation of Earnings
per Share—Treasury-Share
Method

	Basic Earnings per Share	Diluted Earnings per Share
Average number of shares related to options outstanding:		5,000
Option price per share		× $20
Proceeds upon exercise of options		$100,000
Average market price of ordinary shares		$28
Treasury shares that could be repurchased with proceeds ($100,000 ÷ $28)		3,571
Excess of shares under option over the treasury shares that could be repurchased (5,000 − 3,571)—potential ordinary incremental shares		1,429
Average number of ordinary shares outstanding	100,000	100,000
Total average number of ordinary shares outstanding and potential ordinary shares	100,000 (A)	101,429 (C)
Net income for the year	$220,000 (B)	$220,000 (D)
Earnings per share	$2.20 (B ÷ A)	$2.17 (D ÷ C)

a certain earnings or market price level. The basic rule is that the number of contingent shares to be included in diluted earnings per share is based on the number of shares that would be issuable as if the end of the period were the end of the contingency period.[19] **[11]**

For example, assume that Watts Corporation purchased Cardoza Company in 2010 and agreed to give Cardoza's shareholders 20,000 additional shares in 2013 if Cardoza's net income in 2012 is $90,000. Here is what happened in the next two years:

1. In 2011, Cardoza's net income is $100,000. Cardoza therefore has met the net income test in 2011 and **should include** the 20,000 shares in diluted earnings per share for 2011.

2. In 2012, Cardoza's net income is $80,000. Cardoza therefore does not meet the earnings test in 2102 and **should not** include the shares in diluted earnings per share in 2012.

Because Cardoza's earnings in 2011 may change in 2012, the calculation of basic EPS does not include contingent shares until the end of the contingency period because not all conditions have been satisfied.

Antidilution Revisited

In computing diluted EPS, a company must consider the aggregate of all dilutive securities. But first it must determine which potentially dilutive securities are in fact individually dilutive and which are antidilutive. **A company should exclude any security that is antidilutive**, nor can the company use such a security to offset dilutive securities.

Recall that including antidilutive securities in earnings per share computations increases earnings per share (or reduces net loss per share). With options or warrants, whenever the exercise price exceeds the market price, the security is antidilutive. Convertible debt is antidilutive if the addition to income of the interest (net of tax) causes a greater percentage increase in income (numerator) than conversion of the bonds causes a percentage increase in ordinary and potentially dilutive shares (denominator). In other words, convertible debt is antidilutive if conversion of the security causes ordinary share earnings to increase by a greater amount per additional ordinary share than earnings per share was before the conversion.

---

[19]In addition to contingent issuances of shares, other situations that might lead to dilution are the issuance of participating securities and two-class ordinary shares. The reporting of these types of securities in EPS computations is beyond the scope of this book.

To illustrate, assume that Martin Corporation has a $1,000,000 debt issue that is convertible into 10,000 ordinary shares. Interest expense on the liability component of this convertible bond is $60,000. Net income for the year is $210,000, the weighted-average number of ordinary shares outstanding is 100,000 shares, and the tax rate is 40 percent. In this case, assumed conversion of the debt into ordinary shares at the beginning of the year requires the following adjustments of net income and the weighted-average number of shares outstanding.

ILLUSTRATION 16-28
Test for Antidilution

Net income for the year	$210,000	Average number of shares outstanding	100,000
Add: Adjustment for interest (net of tax) on bonds $60,000 \times (1 - .40)$	36,000	Add: Shares issued upon assumed conversion of debt	10,000
Adjusted net income	$246,000	Average number of ordinary and potential ordinary shares	110,000

Basic EPS = $210,000 ÷ 100,000 = $2.10
Diluted EPS = $246,000 ÷ 110,000 = $2.24 = **Antidilutive**

As a shortcut, Martin can also identify the convertible debt as antidilutive by comparing the EPS resulting from conversion, $3.60 ($36,000 additional earnings × 10,000 additional shares), with EPS before inclusion of the convertible debt, $2.10.

Companies should ignore antidilutive securities in all calculations and in computing diluted earnings per share. This approach is reasonable. The profession's intent was to inform the investor of the possible dilution that might occur in reported earnings per share and not to be concerned with securities that, if converted or exercised, would result in an increase in earnings per share. Appendix 16B to this chapter provides an extended example of how companies consider antidilution in a complex situation with multiple securities.

EPS Presentation and Disclosure

A company should present both basic and diluted EPS information as follows.

ILLUSTRATION 16-29
EPS Presentation—
Complex Capital Structure

Earnings per ordinary share	
Basic earnings per share	$3.30
Diluted earnings per share	$2.70

When the earnings of a period include discontinued operations, a company should show per share amounts for the following: income from continuing operations, discontinued operations, and net income. Companies that report a discontinued operation should present per share amounts **for those line items** either on the face of the income statement or in the notes to the financial statements. Illustration 16-30 shows a presentation reporting discontinued operations.

ILLUSTRATION 16-30
EPS Presentation, with
Discontinued Operations

Basic earnings per share	
Income from continuing operations	$3.80
Discontinued operations	0.80
Net income	$3.00
Diluted earnings per share	
Income from continuing operations	$3.35
Discontinued operations	0.65
Net income	$2.70

The following information should also be disclosed:

1. The amounts used as the numerators in calculating basic and diluted earnings per share, and a reconciliation of those amounts to net income or loss. The reconciliation should include the individual effect of each class of instruments that affects earnings per share.

2. The weighted-average number of ordinary shares used as the denominator in calculating basic and diluted earnings per share, and a reconciliation of these denominators to each other. The reconciliation shall include the individual effect of each class of instruments that affects earnings per share.

3. Instruments (including contingently issuable shares) that could potentially dilute basic earnings per share in the future but were not included in the calculation of diluted earnings per share because they are antidilutive for the period(s) presented.

4. A description of ordinary share transactions or potential ordinary share transactions that occur after the reporting period and that would have significantly changed the number of ordinary shares or potential ordinary shares outstanding at the end of the period if those transactions had occurred before the end of the reporting period.

Note that if the number of ordinary or potential ordinary shares outstanding increases as a result of a share dividend or share split, or decreases as a result of diluted EPS calculations, such changes in the number of shares shall be disclosed.

Illustration 16-31 presents the reconciliation and the related disclosure to meet the requirements of this standard. [12]

ILLUSTRATION 16-31
Reconciliation for Basic and Diluted EPS

	For the Year Ended 2011			
	Income (Numerator)	Shares (Denominator)	Per Share Amount	
Income from continued operations	$7,500,000			Numerator amounts
Less: Preference share dividends	(45,000)			
Basic EPS	7,455,000	3,991,666	$1.87	Per share calculation
Warrants		30,768		Potentially dilutive securities shares
Convertible preference shares	45,000	308,333		
Convertible bonds (net of tax)	60,000	50,000		
Diluted EPS	$7,560,000	4,380,767	$1.73	Reconciliation schedule

Share options to purchase 1,000,000 shares of ordinary shares at $85 per share were outstanding during the second half of 2010 but were not included in the computation of diluted EPS because the options' exercise price was greater than the average market price of the ordinary shares. The options were still outstanding at the end of year 2010 and expire on June 30, 2020.

Summary of EPS Computation

As you can see, computation of earnings per share is a complex issue. It is a controversial area because many securities, although technically not ordinary shares, have many of its basic characteristics. Indeed, some companies have issued these other securities rather than ordinary shares in order to avoid an adverse dilutive effect on earnings per share. Illustrations 16-32 and 16-33 (on page 850) display the elementary points of calculating earnings per share in a simple capital structure and in a complex capital structure.

ILLUSTRATION 16-32
Calculating EPS, Simple
Capital Structure

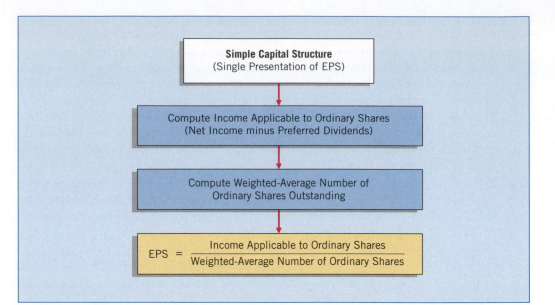

ILLUSTRATION 16-33
Calculating EPS, Complex
Capital Structure

You will want to read the
**CONVERGENCE
CORNER** on page 851

For discussion of how in-
ternational convergence
efforts relate to dilutive
securities and earnings
per share.

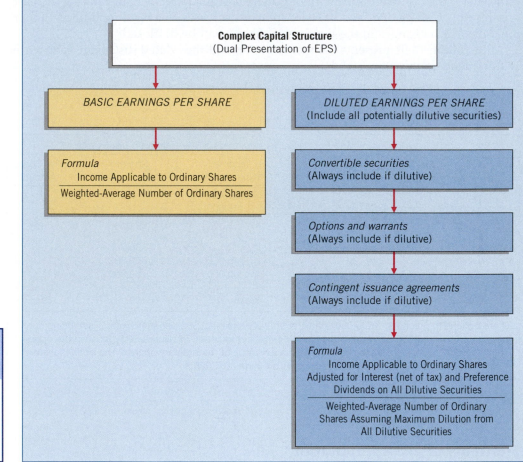

CONVERGENCE CORNER

DILUTIVE SECURITIES AND EARNINGS PER SHARE

Both the IASB and the FASB are working on a standard related to the distinction between liabilities and equity. The IASB approach to account for certain dilutive securities, such as convertible debt and debt issued with share warrants, is different than U.S. GAAP. The accounting and disclosure requirements for accounting for share options and EPS computations are similar between IFRS and U.S. GAAP.

RELEVANT FACTS

• A significant difference between U.S. GAAP and IFRS is the accounting for securities with characteristics of debt and equity, such as convertible debt. Under U.S. GAAP, all of the proceeds of convertible debt are recorded as long-term debt unless settlement is in cash. Under IFRS, convertible bonds are "split"—separated into the equity component (the value of the conversion option) of the bond issue and the debt component.

• Both U.S. GAAP and IFRS follow the same model for recognizing share-based compensation: The fair value of shares and options awarded to employees is recognized over the period to which the employees' services relate.

• Although the calculation of basic and diluted earnings per share is similar between U.S. GAAP and IFRS, the Boards are working to resolve the few minor differences in EPS reporting. One proposal in the FASB project concerns contracts that can be settled in either cash or shares. IFRS requires that share settlement must be used, while U.S. GAAP gives companies a choice. The FASB project proposes adopting the IFRS approach, thus converging U.S. GAAP and IFRS in this regard.

• Related to employee share-purchase plans, under IFRS all employee purchase plans are deemed to be compensatory; that is, compensation expense is recorded for the amount of the discount. Under U.S. GAAP, these plans are often considered non-compensatory and therefore no compensation is recorded. Certain conditions must exist before a plan can be considered non-compensatory—the most important being that the discount generally cannot exceed 5%.

• Modification of a share option results in the recognition of any incremental fair value under both IFRS and U.S. GAAP. However, if the modification leads to a reduction, IFRS does not permit the reduction but U.S. GAAP does.

ABOUT THE NUMBERS

As indicated, a significant difference in U.S. GAAP and IFRS is the accounting for convertible debt. To illustrate, assume **PepsiCo** (USA) issued, at par, $10 million of 10-year convertible bonds with a coupon rate of 4.75%. Assuming the conversion is settled in shares, PepsiCo makes the following entry to record the issuance under U.S. GAAP.

Cash	10,000,000	
Bonds Payable		10,000,000

Under IFRS, PepsiCo must split out the liability and equity component—the value of the conversion option—of the bond issue.

Thus, IFRS records separately the bond issue's debt and equity components. Many believe this provides a more faithful representation of the impact of the bond issue. However, there are concerns about reliability of the method used to estimate the liability component of the bond.

ON THE HORIZON

The FASB has been working on a standard that will likely converge to IFRS in the accounting for convertible debt. Similar to the IASB, the FASB is examining the classification of hybrid securities; the IASB is seeking comment on a discussion document similar to the FASB Preliminary Views document, *"Financial Instruments with Characteristics of Equity."* It is hoped that the Boards will develop a converged standard in this area. While U.S. GAAP and IFRS are similar as to the presentation of EPS, the Boards have been working together to resolve remaining differences related to earnings per share computations.

SUMMARY OF LEARNING OBJECTIVES

1 Describe the accounting for the issuance, conversion, and retirement of convertible securities. Convertible debt is accounted for as a compound instrument because it contains both a liability and an equity component. IFRS requires that compound instruments be separated into their liability and equity components for purposes of accounting. Companies use the with-and-without method to value compound instruments. If companies convert bonds into other securities, the principal accounting problem is to determine the amount at which to record the securities exchanged for the bonds. The book value method is considered IFRS. The retirement of convertible debt is considered a debt retirement, and the difference between the carrying amount of the retired convertible debt and the cash paid should result in a gain or loss.

2 Explain the accounting for convertible preference shares. When convertible preference shares are converted, a company uses the book value approach: It debits Share Capital—Preference, along with the related Share Premium—Conversion Equity, and credits Share Capital—Ordinary and Share Premium—Ordinary (if any excess exists).

3 Contrast the accounting for share warrants and for share warrants issued with other securities. *Share warrants:* Companies should allocate the proceeds from the sale of debt with warrants between the two securities using the with-and-without method. *Share rights:* No entry is required when a company issues rights to existing shareholders. The company needs only to make a memorandum entry to indicate the number of rights issued to existing shareholders and to ensure that the company has additional unissued shares registered for issuance in case the shareholders exercise the rights.

4 Describe the accounting for share compensation plans. Companies must use the fair value approach to account for share-based compensation. Under this approach, a company computes total compensation expense based on the fair value of the options that it expects to vest on the grant date. Companies recognize compensation expense in the periods in which the employee performs the services. Restricted-share plans follow the same general accounting principles as those for share options. Companies estimate total compensation cost at the grant date based on the fair value of the restricted share; they expense that cost over the service period.

5 Discuss the controversy involving share compensation plans. When first proposed, there was considerable opposition to the recognition provisions contained in the fair value approach. The reason: That approach could result in substantial, previously unrecognized compensation expense. Many small companies believed that the standard would place them at a competitive disadvantage with larger companies that can withstand higher compensation charges. Offsetting such opposition is the need for greater transparency in financial reporting, on which our capital markets depend.

6 Compute earnings per share in a simple capital structure. When a company has both ordinary and preference shares outstanding, it subtracts the current-year preference shares dividend from net income to arrive at income available to ordinary shareholders. The formula for computing earnings per share is net income less preference share dividends, divided by the weighted-average number of shares outstanding.

7 Compute earnings per share in a complex capital structure. A complex capital structure requires a dual presentation of earnings per share, each with equal prominence on the face of the income statement. These two presentations are referred to as basic earnings per share and diluted earnings per share. Basic earnings per share relies on the number of weighted-average ordinary shares outstanding (i.e., equivalent to EPS for a simple capital structure). Diluted earnings per share indicates the dilution of earnings per share that will occur if all potential issuances of ordinary shares that would reduce earnings per share takes place. Companies with complex capital structures should exclude antidilutive securities when computing earnings per share.

APPENDIX **16A**	ACCOUNTING FOR SHARE-APPRECIATION RIGHTS

A major disadvantage of many share-option plans is that an executive must pay income tax on the difference between the market price of the share and the option price at the **date of exercise**. This feature of share-option plans (those referred to as **non-qualified**) can be a financial hardship for an executive who wishes to keep the shares (rather than sell them immediately) because he or she would have to pay not only income tax but the option price as well. In another type of plan (an **incentive plan**), the executive pays no taxes at exercise but may need to borrow to finance the exercise price, which leads to related interest cost.

> **Objective·8**
> Explain the accounting for share-appreciation rights plans.

One solution to this problem was the creation of **share-appreciation rights (SARs)**. In this type of plan, the company gives an executive the right to receive compensation equal to the share appreciation. **Share appreciation** is the excess of the market price of the shares at the date of exercise over a pre-established price. The company may pay the share appreciation in cash, shares, or a combination of both.

The major advantage of SARs is that the executive often does not have to make a cash outlay at the date of exercise, but receives a payment for the share appreciation. Unlike shares acquired under a share-option plan, the company does not issue the shares that constitute the basis for computing the appreciation in a SARs plan. Rather, the company simply awards the executive cash or shares having a market value equivalent to the appreciation. The accounting for share-appreciation rights depends on whether the company classifies the rights as equity or as a liability.

SARS—SHARE-BASED EQUITY AWARDS

Companies classify SARs as **equity awards** if at the date of exercise, the holder receives shares from the company upon exercise. In essence, SARs are essentially equivalent to a share option. The major difference relates to the form of payment. With the share option, the holder pays the exercise price and then receives the shares. In an equity SAR, the holder receives shares in an amount equal to the **share-price appreciation** (the difference between the market price and the pre-established price). The accounting for SARs when they are equity awards follows the accounting used for share options. At the date of grant, the company determines a fair value for the SAR and then allocates this amount to compensation expense over the service period of the employees.

SARS—SHARE-BASED LIABILITY AWARDS

Companies classify SARs as liability awards if at the date of exercise, the holder receives a cash payment. In this case the holder is not receiving additional shares but a cash payment equal to the amount of share-price appreciation. The company's compensation expense therefore changes as the value of the liability changes.

A company uses the following approach to record share-based liability awards:

1. Measure the fair value of the award at the grant date and accrue compensation over the service period.
2. Remeasure the fair value each reporting period, until the award is settled; adjust the compensation cost each period for changes in fair value pro-rated for the portion of the service period completed.
3. Once the service period is completed, determine compensation expense each subsequent period by reporting the full change in market price as an adjustment to compensation expense.

For liability awards, the company estimates the fair value of the SARs, using an option-pricing model. The company then allocates this total estimated compensation cost over the service period, recording expense (or a decrease in expense if fair value declines) in each period. At the end of each period, total compensation expense reported to date should equal the percentage of the total service period that has elapsed, multiplied by the total estimated compensation cost.

For example, assume that the service period is 40 percent complete, and total estimated compensation is $100,000. The company reports cumulative compensation expense to date of $40,000 ($100,000 × .40).

The method of allocating compensation expense is called the **percentage approach**. In this method, in the first year of, say, a four-year plan, the company charges one-fourth of the estimated cost to date. In the second year, it charges off two-fourths, or 50 percent, of the estimated cost to date, less the amount already recognized in the first year. In the third year, it charges off three-fourths of the estimated cost to date, less the amount recognized previously. In the fourth year, it charges off the remaining compensation expense.

A special problem arises when the exercise date is past the service period. In the previous example, if the share-appreciation rights were not exercised at the end of four years, in the fifth year the company would have to account for the difference in the market price and the pre-established price. In this case, the company adjusts compensation expense whenever a change in the market price of the shares **occurs in subsequent reporting periods, until the rights expire or are exercised, whichever comes first**.

Increases or decreases in the fair value of the SAR between the date of grant and the exercise date, therefore, result in a change in the measure of compensation. Some periods will have credits to compensation expense if the fair value decreases from one period to the next. The credit to compensation expense, however, cannot exceed previously recognized compensation expense. In other words, **cumulative compensation expense cannot be negative**.

SHARE-APPRECIATION RIGHTS EXAMPLE

Assume that Brazil Hotels, Inc. establishes a share-appreciation rights plan on January 1, 2011. The plan entitles executives to receive cash at the date of exercise for the difference between the share's market price and the pre-established price of $10 on 10,000 SARs. The fair value of the SARs on December 31, 2011, is $3, and the service period runs for two years (2011–2012). Illustration 16A-1 indicates the amount of compensation expense to be recorded each period, assuming that the executives hold the SARs for three years, at which time they exercise the rights.

ILLUSTRATION 16A-1
Compensation Expense, Share-Appreciation Rights

SHARE-APPRECIATION RIGHTS SCHEDULE OF COMPENSATION EXPENSE							
(1)	(2)	(3)	(4)	(5)			
Date	Fair Value	Cumulative Compensation Recognizable[a]	Percentage Accrued[b]	Cumulative Compensation Accrued to Date	Expense 2011	Expense 2012	Expense 2013
12/31/11	$3	$30,000	50%	$ 15,000	$15,000		
				55,000		$55,000	
12/31/12	7	70,000	100%	70,000			
				(20,000)			$(20,000)
12/31/13	5	50,000	100%	$ 50,000			

[a]Cumulative compensation for unexercised SARs to be allocated to periods of service.
[b]The percentage accrued is based upon a two-year service period (2011–2012).

In 2011, Brazil Hotels records compensation expense of $15,000 because 50 percent of the $30,000 total compensation cost estimated at December 31, 2011, is allocable to 2011. In 2012, the fair value increased to $7 per right ($70,000 total). The company recorded additional compensation expense of $55,000 ($70,000 minus $15,000).

The executives held the SARs through 2013, during which time the fair value declined to $5 (and the obligation to the executives equals $50,000). Brazil Hotels recognizes the decrease by recording a $20,000 credit to compensation expense and a debit to Liability under Share-Appreciation Plan. Note that after the service period ends, since the rights are still outstanding, the company adjusts the rights to market at December 31, 2013. Any such credit to compensation expense cannot exceed previous charges to expense attributable to that plan.

As the company records the compensation expense each period, the corresponding credit is to a liability account, because the company will pay the share appreciation in cash. Brazil Hotels records compensation expense in the first year as follows.

Compensation Expense	15,000	
Liability under Share-Appreciation Plan		15,000

The company would credit the liability account for $55,000 again in 2012. In 2013, when it records negative compensation expense, Brazil would debit the account for $20,000. The entry to record the negative compensation expense is as follows.

Liability under Share-Appreciation Plan	20,000	
Compensation Expense		20,000

At December 31, 2013, the executives receive $50,000 (which equals the market price of the shares less the pre-established price). Brazil would remove the liability with the following entry.

Liability under Share-Appreciation Plan	50,000	
Cash		50,000

Compensation expense can increase or decrease substantially from one period to the next. The reason is that compensation expense is remeasured each year, which can lead to large swings in compensation expense.

SUMMARY OF LEARNING OBJECTIVE FOR APPENDIX 16A

KEY TERMS

percentage approach, *854*

share appreciation, *853*

share-appreciation rights (SARs), *853*

•8 **Explain the accounting for share-appreciation rights plans.** The accounting for share-appreciation rights depends on whether the rights are classified as equity- or liability-based. If equity-based, the accounting is similar to that used for share options. If liability-based, companies remeasure compensation expense each period and allocate it over the service period using the percentage approach.

APPENDIX 16B   **COMPREHENSIVE EARNINGS PER SHARE EXAMPLE**

This appendix illustrates the method of computing dilution when many securities are involved. We present the following section of the statement of financial position of Webster Corporation for analysis. Assumptions related to the capital structure follow the statement of financial position.

Objective•9
Compute earnings per share in a complex situation.

ILLUSTRATION 16B-1
Statement of Financial
Position for Comprehensive
Illustration

WEBSTER CORPORATION STATEMENT OF FINANCIAL POSITION (PARTIAL) AT DECEMBER 31, 2011	
Equity	
10% cumulative, convertible preference shares, par value $100;	
100,000 shares authorized, 25,000 shares issued and outstanding	$ 2,500,000
Share capital—ordinary, par value $1, 5,000,000 shares authorized,	
500,000 shares issued and outstanding	500,000
Share premium	2,000,000
Retained earnings	9,000,000
Total equity	$14,000,000
Long-term debt	
Notes payable, 14%	$ 1,000,000
Convertible bonds payable (Issue A)	2,500,000
Convertible bonds payable (Issue B)	2,500,000
Total long-term debt	$ 6,000,000

Notes and Assumptions
December 31, 2011

1. Options were granted in July 2009 to purchase 50,000 ordinary shares at $20 per share. The average market price of Webster's ordinary shares during 2011 was $30 per share. All options are still outstanding at the end of 2011.
2. Both convertible bonds were issued in 2010. Each convertible bond is convertible into 40 shares of ordinary shares. (Each bond has a face value of $1,000.) In 2011, interest expense of $200,000 on the liability component of convertible bonds (Issue A) is recorded, and interest expense of $250,000 is recorded on the liability component of convertible bonds (Issue B).
3. The 10 percent cumulative, convertible preference shares were issued at the beginning of 2011 at par. Each preference share is convertible into four ordinary shares.
4. The average income tax rate is 40 percent.
5. The 500,000 ordinary shares were outstanding during the entire year.
6. Preference dividends were not declared in 2011.
7. Net income was $1,750,000 in 2011.
8. No bonds or preference shares were converted during 2011.

The computation of basic earnings per share for 2011 starts with the amount based upon the weighted-average of ordinary shares outstanding, as shown in Illustration 16B-2.

ILLUSTRATION 16B-2
Computation of Earnings
per Share—Simple Capital
Structure

Net income	$1,750,000
Less: 10% cumulative, convertible preference share dividend requirements	250,000
Income applicable to ordinary shareholders	$1,500,000
Weighted-average number of ordinary shares outstanding	500,000
Earnings per ordinary share	$3.00

Note the following points concerning this calculation.

1. When preference shares are cumulative, the company subtracts the preference dividend to arrive at income applicable to ordinary shares, whether the dividend is declared or not.
2. The company must compute earnings per share of $3 as a starting point because it is the per share amount that is subject to reduction due to the existence of convertible securities and options.

DILUTED EARNINGS PER SHARE

The steps for computing diluted earnings per share are:

1. Determine, for each dilutive security, the per share effect assuming exercise/conversion.

2. Rank the results from step 1 from smallest to largest earnings effect per share. That is, rank the results from most dilutive to least dilutive.

3. Beginning with the earnings per share based upon the weighted-average of ordinary shares outstanding ($3), recalculate earnings per share by adding the smallest per share effects from step 2. If the results from this recalculation are less than $3, proceed to the next smallest per share effect and recalculate earnings per share. Continue this process so long as each recalculated earnings per share is smaller than the previous amount. The process will end either because there are no more securities to test or a particular security maintains or increases earnings per share (is antidilutive).

We'll now apply the three steps to Webster Corporation. (Note that net income and income available to ordinary shareholders are not the same if preference dividends are declared or cumulative.) Webster Corporation has four securities that could reduce EPS: options, convertible bonds (Issue A), convertible bonds (Issue B), and the convertible preference shares.

The first step in the computation of diluted earnings per share is to determine a per share effect for each potentially dilutive security. Illustrations 16B-3 through 16B-6 illustrate these computations.

Number of shares under option	50,000
Option price per share	× $20
Proceeds upon assumed exercise of options	$1,000,000
Average 2011 market price ordinary shares	$30
Treasury shares that could be acquired with proceeds ($1,000,000 ÷ $30)	33,333
Excess of shares under option over treasury shares that could be repurchased (50,000 − 33,333)	16,667

Per share effect:

$$\frac{\text{Incremental Numerator Effect}}{\text{Incremental Denominator Effect}} = \frac{\text{None}}{16{,}667 \text{ shares}} = \$0$$

ILLUSTRATION 16B-3
Per Share Effect of Options (Treasury-Share Method), Diluted Earnings per Share

Interest expense on bonds (Issue A) for year	$200,000
Income tax reduction due to interest (40% × $200,000)	80,000
Interest expense avoided (net of tax)	$120,000
Number of ordinary shares issued assuming conversion of bonds (2,500 bonds × 40 shares)	100,000

Per share effect:

$$\frac{\text{Incremental Numerator Effect}}{\text{Incremental Denominator Effect}} = \frac{\$120{,}000}{100{,}000 \text{ shares}} = \$1.20$$

ILLUSTRATION 16B-4
Per Share Effect of Issue A Bonds (If-Converted Method), Diluted Earnings per Share

Interest expense on bonds (Issue B) for year	$250,000
Income tax reduction due to interest (40% × $250,000)	100,000
Interest expense avoided (net of tax)	$150,000
Number of ordinary shares issued assuming conversion of bonds (2,500 bonds × 40 shares)	100,000

Per share effect:

$$\frac{\text{Incremental Numerator Effect}}{\text{Incremental Denominator Effect}} = \frac{\$150{,}000}{100{,}000 \text{ shares}} = \$1.50$$

ILLUSTRATION 16B-5
Per Share Effect of Issue B Bonds (If-Converted Method), Diluted Earnings per Share

ILLUSTRATION 16B-6
Per Share Effect of 10%
Convertible Preference
Shares (If-Converted
Method), Diluted
Earnings per Share

Dividend requirement on cumulative preference share (25,000 shares × $10)	$250,000
Income tax effect (dividends not a tax deduction)	none
Dividend requirement avoided	$250,000
Number of ordinary shares issued assuming conversion of preference shares (4 × 25,000 shares)	100,000
Per share effect:	
$\dfrac{\text{Incremental Numerator Effect}}{\text{Incremental Denominator Effect}} = \dfrac{\$250,000}{100,000 \text{ shares}} =$	$2.50

Illustration 16B-7 shows the ranking of all four potentially dilutive securities.

ILLUSTRATION 16B-7
Ranking of Per Share
Effects (Smallest to
Largest), Diluted Earnings
per Share

	Effect per Share
1. Options	$ 0
2. Convertible bonds (Issue A)	1.20
3. Convertible bonds (Issue B)	1.50
4. 10% convertible preferred	2.50

The next step is to determine earnings per share giving effect to the ranking in Illustration 16B-7. Starting with the earnings per share of $3 computed previously, add the incremental effects of the options to the original calculation, as follows.

ILLUSTRATION 16B-8
Recomputation of EPS
Using Incremental Effect
of Options

Options	
Income applicable to ordinary shareholders	$1,500,000
Add: Incremental numerator effect of options	none
Total	$1,500,000
Weighted-average number of ordinary shares outstanding	500,000
Add: Incremental denominator effect of options (Illustration 16B-3)	16,667
Total	516,667
Recomputed earnings per share ($1,500,000 ÷ 516,667 shares)	$2.90

Since the recomputed earnings per share is reduced (from $3 to $2.90), the effect of the options is dilutive. Again, we could have anticipated this effect because the average market price ($30) exceeded the option price ($20).

Assuming that Webster converts the bonds (Issue A), recomputed earnings per share is as shown below.

ILLUSTRATION 16B-9
Recomputation of EPS
Using Incremental Effect
of Convertible Bonds
(Issue A)

Convertible Bonds (Issue A)	
Numerator from previous calculation	$1,500,000
Add: Interest expense avoided (net of tax)	120,000
Total	$1,620,000
Denominator from previous calculation (shares)	516,667
Add: Number of ordinary shares assumed issued upon conversion of bonds	100,000
Total	616,667
Recomputed earnings per share ($1,620,000 ÷ 616,667 shares)	$2.63

Since the recomputed earnings per share is reduced (from $2.90 to $2.63), the effect of the bonds (Issue A) is dilutive.

Next, assuming Webster converts the bonds (Issue B), the company recomputes earnings per share as shown in Illustration 16B-10.

Convertible Bonds (Issue B)	
Numerator from previous calculation	$1,620,000
Add: Interest expense avoided (net of tax)	150,000
Total	$1,770,000
Denominator from previous calculation (shares)	616,667
Add: Number of ordinary shares assumed issued upon conversion of bonds	100,000
Total	716,667
Recomputed earnings per share ($1,770,000 ÷ 716,667 shares)	$2.47

ILLUSTRATION 16B-10
Recomputation of EPS Using Incremental Effect of Convertible Bonds (Issue B)

Since the recomputed earnings per share is reduced (from $2.63 to $2.47), the effect of the convertible bonds (Issue B) is dilutive.

The final step is the recomputation that includes the 10 percent preference shares. This is shown in Illustration 16B-11.

10% Convertible Preferred	
Numerator from previous calculation	$1,770,000
Add: Dividend requirement avoided	250,000
Total	$2,020,000
Denominator from previous calculation (shares)	716,667
Add: Number of ordinary shares assumed issued upon conversion of preference shares	100,000
Total	816,667
Recomputed earnings per share ($2,020,000 ÷ 816,667 shares)	$2.47

ILLUSTRATION 16B-11
Recomputation of EPS Using Incremental Effect of 10% Convertible Preference Shares

Since the recomputed earnings per share is not reduced, the effect of the 10 percent convertible preference shares are not dilutive. Diluted earnings per share is $2.47. The per share effects of the preference shares are not used in the computation.

Finally, Illustration 16B-12 shows Webster Corporation's disclosure of earnings per share on its income statement.

Net income	$1,750,000
Basic earnings per ordinary share (Note X)	$3.00
Diluted earnings per ordinary share	$2.47

ILLUSTRATION 16B-12
Income Statement Presentation, EPS

A company uses income from continuing operations (adjusted for preferred dividends) to determine whether potential ordinary shares are dilutive or antidilutive. Some refer to this measure as the **control number**. To illustrate, assume that Barton Company provides the following information.

ILLUSTRATION 16B-13
Barton Company Data

Income from continuing operations	$2,400,000
Loss from discontinued operations	3,600,000
Net loss	$1,200,000
Weighted-average shares of ordinary shares outstanding	1,000,000
Potential ordinary shares	200,000

Barton reports basic and dilutive earnings per share as follows.

ILLUSTRATION 16B-14
Basic and Diluted EPS

Basic earnings per share	
Income from continuing operations	$2.40
Loss from discontinued operations	3.60
Net loss	$1.20
Diluted earnings per share	
Income from continuing operations	$2.00
Loss from discontinued operations	3.00
Net loss	$1.00

As Illustration 16B-14 shows, basic earnings per share from continuing operations is higher than the diluted earnings per share from continuing operations. The reason: The diluted earnings per share from continuing operations includes an additional 200,000 shares of potential ordinary shares in its denominator.[20]

Companies use income from continuing operations as the control number because many of them show income from continuing operations (or a similar line item above net income if it appears on the income statement), but report a final net loss due to a loss on discontinued operations. If a company uses final net loss as the control number, basic and diluted earnings per share would be the same because the potential ordinary shares are antidilutive.[21]

KEY TERMS

control number, *859*

SUMMARY OF LEARNING OBJECTIVE FOR APPENDIX 16B

•9 **Compute earnings per share in a complex situation.** For diluted EPS, make the following computations: (1) For each potentially dilutive security, determine the per share effect assuming exercise/conversion. (2) Rank the results from most dilutive to least dilutive. (3) Recalculate EPS starting with the most dilutive, and continue adding securities until EPS does not change or becomes larger.

[20]A company that does not report a discontinued operation uses net income as the control number.

[21]If a company reports a loss from continuing operations, basic and diluted earnings per share will be the same because potential ordinary shares will be antidilutive, even if the company reports final net income. The IASB believes that comparability of EPS information will be improved by using income from continuing operations as the control number.

AUTHORITATIVE LITERATURE

Authoritative Literature References

[1] International Accounting Standard 32, *Financial Instruments: Presentation* (London, U.K.: International Accounting Standards Committee Foundation, 2003), paras. 28–32.

[2] International Accounting Standard 32, *Financial Instruments: Presentation* (London, U.K.: International Accounting Standards Committee Foundation, 2003), par. BC29.

[3] International Accounting Standard 32, *Financial Instruments: Presentation* (London, U.K.: International Accounting Standards Committee Foundation, 2003), par. AG34.

[4] International Accounting Standard 32, *Financial Instruments: Presentation* (London, U.K.: International Accounting Standards Committee Foundation, 2003), par. 36.

[5] International Financial Reporting Standard 2, *Share-Based Payment* (London, U.K.: International Accounting Standards Committee Foundation, 2004), par. 16.

[6] International Financial Reporting Standard 2, *Share-Based Payment* (London, U.K.: International Accounting Standards Committee Foundation, 2004), par. BC11.

[7] International Financial Reporting Standard 2, *Share-Based Payment* (London, U.K.: International Accounting Standards Committee Foundation, 2004), par. IN8.

[8] International Accounting Standard 33, *Earnings per Share* (London, U.K.: International Accounting Standards Committee Foundation, 2003), par. 66.

[9] International Accounting Standard 33, *Earnings per Share* (London, U.K.: International Accounting Standards Committee Foundation, 2003), par. 1.

[10] International Accounting Standard 33, *Earnings per Share* (London, U.K.: International Accounting Standards Committee Foundation, 2003), par. 39.

[11] International Accounting Standard 33, *Earnings per Share* (London, U.K.: International Accounting Standards Committee Foundation, 2003), par. 56.

[12] International Accounting Standard 33, *Earnings per Share* (London, U.K.: International Accounting Standards Committee Foundation, 2003), par. 66.

Note: All asterisked Questions, Exercises, and Problems relate to material in the appendices to the chapter.

QUESTIONS

1. What is meant by a dilutive security?

2. Briefly explain why corporations issue convertible securities.

3. Discuss the similarities between convertible debt and debt issued with share warrants.

4. Bridgewater Corp. offered holders of its 1,000 convertible bonds a premium of €160 per bond to induce conversion into ordinary shares. Upon conversion of all the bonds, Bridgewater Corp. recorded the €160,000 premium as a reduction of Share Premium—Ordinary. Comment on Bridgewater's treatment of the €160,000 "sweetener."

5. Explain how the conversion feature of convertible debt has a value (a) to the issuer and (b) to the purchaser.

6. What are the arguments for giving separate accounting recognition to the conversion feature of debentures?

7. Four years after issue, debentures with a face value of $1,000,000 and book value of $960,000 are tendered for conversion into 80,000 ordinary shares immediately after an interest payment date. At that time, the market price of the debentures is 104, and the ordinary shares are selling at $14 per share (par value $10). The company records the conversion as follows.

Bonds Payable	960,000	
Share Capital—Ordinary		800,000
Share Premium—Ordinary		160,000

Discuss the propriety of this accounting treatment.

8. On July 1, 2010, Roberts Corporation issued €3,000,000 of 9% bonds payable in 20 years. The bonds include warrants giving the bondholder the right to purchase for €30 one ordinary share of €1 par value at any time during the next 10 years. The bonds were sold for €3,000,000. The net present value of the debt at the time of issuance was €2,900,000. Prepare the journal entry to record this transaction.

9. What are share rights? How does the issuing company account for them?

10. Briefly explain the accounting requirements for share compensation plans under IFRS.

11. Cordero Corporation has an employee share-purchase plan which permits all full-time employees to purchase 10 ordinary shares on the third anniversary of their employment and an additional 15 shares on each subsequent anniversary date. The purchase price is set at the market price on the date purchased less a 10% discount. How is this discount accounted for by Cordero?

12. What date or event does the profession believe should be used in determining the value of a share option? What arguments support this position?

13. Over what period of time should compensation cost for a share-option plan be allocated?

14. How is compensation expense for a share-option plan computed using the fair value approach?

15. What are the advantages of using restricted shares to compensate employees?

16. At December 31, 2010, Reid Company had 600,000 ordinary shares issued and outstanding, 400,000 of which had been issued and outstanding throughout the year and 200,000 of which were issued on October 1, 2010. Net income for 2010 was $1,750,000, and dividends declared on preference shares were $400,000. Compute Reid's earnings per ordinary share.

17. What effect do share dividends or share splits have on the computation of the weighted-average number of shares outstanding?

18. Define the following terms.
    (a) Basic earnings per share.
    (b) Potentially dilutive security.
    (c) Diluted earnings per share.
    (d) Complex capital structure.
    (e) Potential ordinary shares.

19. What are the computational guidelines for determining whether a convertible security is to be reported as part of diluted earnings per share?

20. Discuss why options and warrants may be considered potentially dilutive common shares for the computation of diluted earnings per share.

21. Explain how convertible securities are determined to be potentially dilutive ordinary shares and how those convertible securities that are not considered to be potentially dilutive ordinary shares enter into the determination of earnings per share data.

22. Explain the treasury-share method as it applies to options and warrants in computing dilutive earnings per share data.

23. Earnings per share can affect market prices of ordinary shares. Can market prices affect earnings per share? Explain.

24. What is meant by the term antidilution? Give an example.

25. What type of earnings per share presentation is required in a complex capital structure?

26. Briefly describe some of the similarities and differences between U.S. GAAP and IFRS with respect to the accounting for share-based compensation.

27. Norman Co., a fast-growing golf equipment company, uses IFRS. It is considering the issuance of convertible bonds. The bonds mature in 10 years, have a face value of €400,000, and pay interest annually at a rate of 4%. The net present value of the liability component is €365,000. Greg Shark is curious as to the difference in accounting for these bonds if the company were to use U.S. GAAP. (a) Prepare the entry to record issuance of the bonds at par under IFRS. (b) Repeat the requirement for part (a), assuming application of U.S. GAAP to the bond issuance. (c) Which approach provides the better accounting? Explain.

*28. How is antidilution determined when multiple securities are involved?

BRIEF EXERCISES

BE16-1 Archer Company issued £4,000,000 par value, 7% convertible bonds at 99 for cash. The net present value of the debt without the conversion feature is £3,800,000. Prepare the journal entry to record the issuance of the convertible bonds.

BE16-2 Petrenko Corporation has outstanding 2,000 €1,000 bonds, each convertible into 50 shares of €10 par value ordinary shares. The bonds are converted on December 31, 2010. The bonds payable has a carrying value of €1,950,000 and conversion equity of €20,000. Record the conversion using the book value method.

•2 BE16-3 Pechstein Corporation issued 2,000 shares of $10 par value ordinary shares upon conversion of 1,000 shares of $50 par value preference shares. The preference shares were originally issued at $60 per share. The ordinary shares are trading at $26 per share at the time of conversion. Record the conversion of the convertible preference shares.

•3 BE16-4 Eisler Corporation issued 2,000 $1,000 bonds at 101. Each bond was issued with one detachable share warrant. At issuance, the net present value of the bonds without the warrants was $1,970,000. Prepare the journal entry to record the issuance of the bonds and the share warrants.

•3 BE16-5 Parsons Corporation issued 3,000 €1,000 bonds at 98. Each bond was issued with one detachable share warrant. At issuance, the net present value of the bonds without the warrants was €2,910,000. Prepare the journal entry to record the issuance of the bonds and the share warrants.

•4 BE16-6 On January 1, 2010, Barwood Corporation granted 5,000 options to executives. Each option entitles the holder to purchase one share of Barwood's $5 par value ordinary shares at $50 per share at any time during the next 5 years. The market price of the shares is $65 per share on the date of grant. The fair value of the options at the grant date is $150,000. The period of benefit is 2 years. Prepare Barwood's journal entries for January 1, 2010, and December 31, 2010 and 2011.

•4 BE16-7 Refer to the data for Barwood Corporation in BE16-6. Repeat the requirements, assuming that instead of options, Barwood granted 2,000 restricted shares.

•4 BE16-8 On January 1, 2010 (the date of grant), Lutz Corporation issues 2,000 restricted shares to its executives. The fair value of these shares is $75,000, and their par value is $10,000. The shares are forfeited if the executives do not complete 3 years of employment with the company. Prepare the journal entry (if any) on January 1, 2010, and on December 31, 2010, assuming the service period is 3 years.

•6 BE16-9 Kalin Corporation had 2010 net income of €1,000,000. During 2010, Kalin paid a dividend of €2 per share on 100,000 preference shares. During 2010, Kalin had outstanding 250,000 ordinary shares. Compute Kalin's 2010 earnings per share.

•6 BE16-10 Douglas Corporation had 120,000 ordinary shares outstanding on January 1, 2010. On May 1, 2010, Douglas issued 60,000 ordinary shares. On July 1, Douglas purchased 10,000 treasury shares, which were reissued on October 1. Compute Douglas's weighted-average number of ordinary shares outstanding for 2010.

•6 BE16-11 Tomba Corporation had 300,000 ordinary shares outstanding on January 1, 2010. On May 1, Tomba issued 30,000 ordinary shares. (a) Compute the weighted-average number of shares outstanding if the 30,000 shares were issued for cash. (b) Compute the weighted-average number of shares outstanding if the 30,000 shares were issued in a share dividend.

•7 BE16-12 Rockland Corporation earned net income of R300,000 in 2010 and had 100,000 ordinary shares outstanding throughout the year. Also outstanding all year was R800,000 of 10% bonds, which are convertible into 16,000 ordinary shares. The interest expense on the liability component of the convertible bonds was R64,000. Rockland's tax rate is 40 percent. Compute Rockland's 2010 diluted earnings per share.

•7 BE16-13 DiCenta Corporation reported net income of $270,000 in 2010 and had 50,000 ordinary shares outstanding throughout the year. Also outstanding all year were 5,000 shares of cumulative preference shares, each convertible into 2 ordinary shares. The preference shares pay an annual dividend of $5 per share. DiCenta's tax rate is 40%. Compute DiCenta's 2010 diluted earnings per share.

•7 BE16-14 Bedard Corporation reported net income of $300,000 in 2010 and had 200,000 ordinary shares outstanding throughout the year. Also outstanding all year were 45,000 options to purchase ordinary shares at $10 per share. The average market price of the shares during the year was $15. Compute diluted earnings per share.

•8 BE16-15 The 2010 income statement of Wasmeier Corporation showed net income of €480,000 and a loss from discontinued operations of €120,000. Wasmeier had 100,000 shares of ordinary shares outstanding all year. Prepare Wasmeier's income statement presentation of earnings per share.

•8 *BE16-16 Ferraro, Inc. established a share-appreciation rights (SAR) program on January 1, 2010, which entitles executives to receive cash at the date of exercise for the difference between the market price of the shares and the pre-established price of $20 on 5,000 SARs. The required service period is 2 years. The fair value of the SARs are determined to be $4 on December 31, 2010, and $9 on December 31, 2011. Compute Ferraro's compensation expense for 2010 and 2011.

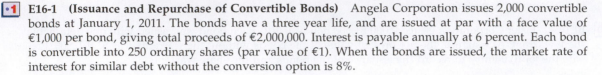

EXERCISES

•1 E16-1 (Issuance and Repurchase of Convertible Bonds) Angela Corporation issues 2,000 convertible bonds at January 1, 2011. The bonds have a three year life, and are issued at par with a face value of €1,000 per bond, giving total proceeds of €2,000,000. Interest is payable annually at 6 percent. Each bond is convertible into 250 ordinary shares (par value of €1). When the bonds are issued, the market rate of interest for similar debt without the conversion option is 8%.

Instructions

(a) Compute the liability and equity component of the convertible bond on January 1, 2011.
(b) Prepare the journal entry to record the issuance of the convertible bond on January 1, 2011.
(c) Prepare the journal entry to record the repurchase of the convertible bond for cash at January 1, 2014, its maturity date.

•1 E16-2 (Issuance and Repurchase of Convertible Bonds) Assume the same information in E16-1, except that Angela Corporation converts its convertible bonds on January 1, 2012.

Instructions

(a) Compute the carrying value of the bond payable on January 1, 2012.
(b) Prepare the journal entry to record the conversion on January 1, 2012.
(c) Assume that the bonds were repurchased on January 1, 2012, for €1,940,000 cash instead of being converted. The net present value of the liability component of the convertible bonds on January 1, 2012, is €1,900,000. Prepare the journal entry to record the repurchase on January 1, 2012.

•1 E16-3 (Issuance and Repurchase of Convertible Bonds) On January 1, 2011, Cai Company issued a 10% convertible bond at par, with a face value of ¥100,000, maturing on January 1, 2021. The bond is convertible into ordinary shares of Cai at a conversion price of ¥2,500 per share. Interest is payable semi-annually. At date of issue, Cai could have issued non-convertible debt with a 10-year term bearing an interest rate of 11%.

Instructions

(a) Prepare the journal entry to record the issuance of the convertible debt on January 1, 2011.
(b) On January 1, 2014, Cai makes a tender offer to the holder of the convertible debt to repurchase the bond for ¥112,000, which the holder accepts. At the date of repurchase, Cai could have issued non-convertible debt with a 7-year term at an effective-interest rate of 8%. Prepare the journal entry to record this repurchase on January 1, 2014.

•1 E16-4 (Issuance, Conversion, Repurchase of Convertible Bonds) On January 1, 2011, Lin Company issued a convertible bond with a par value of $50,000 in the market for $60,000. The bonds are convertible into 6,000 ordinary shares of $1 per share par value. The bond has a 5-year life and has a stated interest rate of 10% payable annually. The market interest rate for a similar non-convertible bond at January 1, 2011, is 8%. The liability component of the bond is computed to be $53,993. The following bond amortization schedule is provided for this bond.

		EFFECTIVE-INTEREST METHOD 10% BOND DISCOUNTED AT 8%		
Date	Cash Paid	Interest Expense	Premium Amortized	Carrying Amount of Bonds
1/1/11				$53,993
12/31/11	$5,000	$4,319	$681	53,312
12/31/12	5,000	4,265	735	52,577
12/31/13	5,000	4,206	794	51,783
12/31/14	5,000	4,143	857	50,926
12/31/15	5,000	4,074	926	50,000

Instructions

(a) Prepare the journal entry to record the issuance of the convertible bond on January 1, 2011.
(b) Prepare the journal entry to record the accrual of interest on December 31, 2012.
(c) Assume that the bonds were converted on December 31, 2013. The fair value of the liability component of the bond is determined to be $54,000 on December 31, 2013. Prepare the journal entry to record the conversion on December 31, 2013. Assume that the accrual of interest related to 2013 has been recorded.

(d) Assume that the convertible bonds were repurchased on December 31, 2013, for $55,500 instead of being converted. As indicated, the liability component of the bond is determined to be $54,000 on December 31, 2013. Assume that the accrual of interest related to 2013 has been recorded.

(e) Assume that the bonds matured on December 31, 2015, and Lin repurchased the bonds. Prepare the entry(ies) to record this transaction.

·1 E16-5 (Conversion of Bonds) Schuss Inc. issued €3,000,000 of 10%, 10-year convertible bonds on April 1, 2010, at 98. The bonds were dated April 1, 2010, with interest payable April 1 and October 1. Bond discount is amortized semiannually using the effective-interest method. The net present value of the bonds without the conversion feature discounted at 11% (its market rate) was €2,800,000.

On April 1, 2011, €1,000,000 of these bonds were converted into 30,000 shares of €20 par value ordinary shares. Accrued interest was paid in cash at the time of conversion.

Instructions
(a) Prepare the entry to record the issuance of the convertible bond on April 1, 2010.
(b) Prepare the entry to record the interest expense at October 1, 2010.
(c) Prepare the entry(ies) to record the conversion on April 1, 2011. (The book value method is used.)

·1 E16-6 (Conversion of Bonds) Gabel Company has bonds payable outstanding with a carrying value of $406,000. When issued, Gabel recorded $3,500 of conversion equity. Each $1,000 bond is convertible into 20 shares of preference shares with par value of $50 per share. All bonds are converted into preference shares.

Instructions
Assuming that the book value method was used, what entry would be made?

·1 ·2 ·3 E16-7 (Issuance and Conversion of Bonds) For each of the unrelated transactions described below, present the entry(ies) required to record each transaction.

1. Coyle Corp. issued €10,000,000 par value 10% convertible bonds at 99. If the bonds had not been convertible, the company's investment banker determines that they would have been sold at 95.
2. Lambert Company issued €10,000,000 par value 10% bonds at 98. One share warrant was issued with each €100 par value bond. At the time of issuance, the warrants were selling for €4. The net present value of the bonds without the warrants was €9,600,000.
3. Sepracor, Inc. called its convertible debt in 2010. Assume the following related to the transaction: The 11%, €10,000,000 par value bonds were converted into 1,000,000 shares of €1 par value ordinary shares on July 1, 2010. The carrying amount of the debt on July 1 was €9,700,000. The Share Premium—Conversion Equity account had a balance of €200,000, and the company paid an additional €75,000 to the bondholders to induce conversion of all the bonds. The company records the conversion using the book value method.

·3 E16-8 (Issuance of Bonds with Share Warrants) Sun Inc. has decided to raise additional capital by issuing HK$175,000 face value of bonds with a coupon rate of 10%. In discussions with investment bankers, it was determined that to help the sale of the bonds, share warrants should be issued at the rate of one warrant for each HK$100 bond sold. The fair value of the bonds without the warrants is HK$136,000, and the estimated value of the warrants is HK$18,000. The proceeds upon issuance of the bonds and warrants was HK$150,000.

Instructions
(a) What entry should be made at the time of the issuance of the bonds and warrants?
(b) If the warrants were non-detachable, would the entries be different? Discuss.

·3 E16-9 (Issuance of Bonds with Share Warrants) On September 1, 2010, Lin Company sold at 104 (plus accrued interest) 30,000 of its 8%, 10-year, ¥10,000 face value, non-convertible bonds with detachable share warrants. Each bond carried two detachable warrants. Each warrant was for one ordinary share at a specified option price of ¥1,500 per share. The net present value of bonds is determined to be ¥290,000,000. Interest is payable on December 1 and June 1.

Instructions
Prepare in general journal format the entry to record the issuance of the bonds.

·3 E16-10 (Issuance of Bonds with Share Warrants) On May 1, 2010, Barkley Company issued 3,000 €1,000 bonds at 102. Each bond was issued with one detachable share warrant. The fair value of the bonds on May 1, 2010, was €2,940,000.

Instructions
(a) Prepare the entry to record the issuance of the bonds and warrants.
(b) Assume the same facts as part (a), except that the warrants had an estimated fair value of €20. Prepare the entry to record the issuance of the bonds and warrants.

⁴ **E16-11** **(Issuance and Exercise of Share Options)** On November 1, 2009, Olympic Company adopted a share-option plan that granted options to key executives to purchase 40,000 shares of the company's $10 par value ordinary shares. The options were granted on January 2, 2010, and were vested 2 years after the date of grant if the grantee was still an employee of the company. The options expired 6 years from date of grant. The option price was set at $40, and the fair value option-pricing model determines the total compensation expense to be $600,000.

All of the options were exercised during the year 2012: 30,000 on January 3 when the market price was $67, and 10,000 on May 1 when the market price was $77 a share.

Instructions

Prepare journal entries relating to the share-option plan for the years 2010, 2011, and 2012. Assume that the employees perform services equally in 2010 and 2011.

⁴ **E16-12** **(Issuance, Exercise, and Forfeiture of Share Options)** On January 1, 2010, Magilla Inc. granted share options to officers and key employees for the purchase of 20,000 of the company's €10 par ordinary shares at €25 per share. The options were exercisable within a 5-year period beginning January 1, 2012, by grantees still in the employ of the company, and expiring December 31, 2016. The service period for this award is 2 years. Assume that the fair value option-pricing model determines total compensation expense to be €400,000.

On April 1, 2011, 3,000 options were forfeited when the employees resigned from the company. The market value of the ordinary shares was €35 per share on this date.

On March 31, 2012, 12,000 options were exercised when the market value of the ordinary shares was €40 per share.

Instructions

Prepare journal entries to record issuance of the share options, forfeiture of the share options, exercise of the share options, and charges to compensation expense, for the years ended December 31, 2010, 2011, and 2012.

⁴ **E16-13** **(Issuance, Exercise, and Expiration of Share Options)** On January 1, 2009, Scooby Corporation granted 10,000 options to key executives. Each option allows the executive to purchase one share of Scooby's $5 par value ordinary shares at a price of $20 per share. The options were exercisable within a 2-year period beginning January 1, 2011, if the grantee is still employed by the company at the time of the exercise. On the grant date, Scooby's shares were trading at $25 per share, and a fair value option-pricing model determines total compensation to be $450,000.

On May 1, 2011, 9,000 options were exercised when the market price of Scooby's shares were $30 per share. The remaining options lapsed in 2013 because executives decided not to exercise their options.

Instructions

Prepare the necessary journal entries related to the share-option plan for the years 2009 through 2013.

⁴ **E16-14** **(Accounting for Restricted Shares)** Derrick Company issues 4,000 restricted shares to its CFO, Dane Yaping, on January 1, 2010. The shares have a fair value of $120,000 on this date. The service period related to these restricted shares is 4 years. Vesting occurs if Yaping stays with the company for 4 years. The par value of the shares is $5. At December 31, 2011, the fair value of the shares is $145,000.

Instructions

(a) Prepare the journal entries to record the restricted shares on January 1, 2010 (the date of grant), and December 31, 2011.

(b) On March 4, 2012, Yaping leaves the company. Prepare the journal entry (if any) to account for this forfeiture.

⁴ **E16-15** **(Accounting for Restricted Shares)** Lopez Company issues 10,000 shares of restricted shares to its CFO, Juan Carlos, on January 1, 2010. The shares have a fair value of €500,000 on this date. The service period related to the restricted shares is 5 years. Vesting occurs if Carlos stays with the company for 6 years. The par value of the shares is €10. At December 31, 2010, the fair value of the shares is €450,000.

Instructions

(a) Prepare the journal entries to record the restricted shares on January 1, 2010 (the date of grant), and December 31, 2011.

(b) On January 1, 2015, Carlos leaves the company. Prepare the journal entry (if any) to account for this forfeiture.

•6 **E16-16** **(Weighted-Average Number of Shares)** Portillo Inc. uses a calendar year for financial reporting. The company is authorized to issue 9,000,000 $10 par ordinary shares. At no time has Portillo issued any potentially dilutive securities. Listed below is a summary of Portillo's ordinary share activities.

1. Number of ordinary shares issued and outstanding at December 31, 2009	2,400,000
2. Shares issued as a result of a 10% share dividend on September 30, 2010	240,000
3. Shares issued for cash on March 31, 2011	2,000,000
Number of ordinary shares issued and outstanding at December 31, 2011	4,640,000

4. A 2-for-1 share split of Portillo's ordinary shares took place on March 31, 2012.

Instructions

(a) Compute the weighted-average number of ordinary shares used in computing earnings per ordinary share for 2010 on the 2011 comparative income statement.

(b) Compute the weighted-average number of ordinary shares used in computing earnings per ordinary share for 2011 on the 2011 comparative income statement.

(c) Compute the weighted-average number of ordinary shares to be used in computing earnings per ordinary share for 2011 on the 2012 comparative income statement.

(d) Compute the weighted-average number of ordinary shares to be used in computing earnings per ordinary share for 2012 on the 2012 comparative income statement.

•6 **E16-17** **(EPS: Simple Capital Structure)** On January 1, 2010, Chang Corp. had 480,000 ordinary shares outstanding. During 2010, it had the following transactions that affected the ordinary share account.

February 1	Issued 120,000 shares
March 1	Issued a 20% share dividend
May 1	Acquired 100,000 treasury shares
June 1	Issued a 3-for-1 share split
October 1	Reissued 60,000 treasury shares

Instructions

(a) Determine the weighted-average number of shares outstanding as of December 31, 2010.

(b) Assume that Chang Corp. earned net income of ¥3,256,000,000 during 2010. In addition, it had 100,000 shares of 9%, ¥100 par non-convertible, non-cumulative preference shares outstanding for the entire year. Because of liquidity considerations, however, the company did not declare and pay a preference dividend in 2010. Compute earnings per share for 2010, using the weighted-average number of shares determined in part (a).

(c) Assume the same facts as in part (b), except that the preference shares were cumulative. Compute earnings per share for 2010.

(d) Assume the same facts as in part (b), except that net income included a loss from discontinued operations of ¥432,000,000. The loss from discontinued operations is net of applicable income taxes. Compute earnings per share for 2010.

•6 **E16-18** **(EPS: Simple Capital Structure)** Ott Company had 210,000 ordinary shares outstanding on December 31, 2010. During the year 2011, the company issued 8,000 shares on May 1 and retired 14,000 shares on October 31. For the year 2011, Ott Company reported net income of $229,690 after a loss on discontinued operations of $40,600 (net of tax).

Instructions

What earnings per share data should be reported at the bottom of its income statement?

•6 **E16-19** **(EPS: Simple Capital Structure)** Huang Company presented the following data (¥000).

Net income	¥2,200,000
Preference shares: 50,000 shares outstanding,	
¥100 par, 8% cumulative, not convertible	5,000,000
Ordinary shares: Shares outstanding 1/1	600,000
Issued for cash, 5/1	300,000
Acquired treasury shares for cash, 8/1	150,000
2-for-1 share split, 10/1	

Instructions

Compute earnings per share.

·6 **E16-20** **(EPS: Simple Capital Structure)** A portion of the statement of income and retained earnings of Pierson Inc. for the current year follows.

Income from continuing operations		$15,000,000
Loss on discontinued operations, net of applicable		
income tax (Note 1)		1,340,000
Net income		13,660,000
Retained earnings at the beginning of the year		83,250,000
		96,910,000
Dividends declared:		
On preference shares—$6.00 per share	$ 300,000	
On ordinary shares—$1.75 per share	14,875,000	15,175,000
Retained earnings at the end of the year		$81,735,000

Note 1. During the year, Pierson Inc. had a loss from discontinued operations of $1,340,000 after applicable income tax reduction of $1,200,000.

At the end of the current year, Pierson Inc. has outstanding 8,000,000 shares of $10 par ordinary shares and 50,000 shares of 6% preference shares.

On April 1 of the current year, Pierson Inc. issued 1,000,000 ordinary shares for $32 per share to help finance the loss on discontinued operations.

Instructions

Compute the earnings per share on ordinary shares for the current year as it should be reported to shareholders.

·6 **E16-21** **(EPS: Simple Capital Structure)** On January 1, 2010, Bailey Industries had shares outstanding as follows.

6% cumulative preference shares, €100 par value,	
issued and outstanding 10,000 shares	€1,000,000
Ordinary shares €10 par value, issued and	
outstanding 200,000 shares	2,000,000

To acquire the net assets of three smaller companies, Bailey authorized the issuance of an additional 170,000 ordinary shares. The acquisitions took place as shown below.

Date of Acquisition	Shares Issued
Company A: April 1, 2010	60,000
Company B: July 1, 2010	80,000
Company C: October 1, 2010	30,000

On May 14, 2010, Bailey realized a €90,000 (before taxes) gain from discontinued operations. On December 31, 2010, Bailey recorded net income of €300,000 before tax and exclusive of the gain.

Instructions

Assuming a 40% tax rate, compute the earnings per share data that should appear on the financial statements of Bailey Industries as of December 31, 2010.

·6 **E16-22** **(EPS: Simple Capital Structure)** At January 1, 2010, Cameron Company's outstanding shares included the following.

280,000 shares of $50 par value, 7% cumulative preference shares
800,000 shares of $1 par value ordinary shares

Net income for 2010 was $2,830,000. No cash dividends were declared or paid during 2010. On February 15, 2011, however, all preference dividends in arrears were paid, together with a 5% share dividend on ordinary shares. There were no dividends in arrears prior to 2010.

On April 1, 2010, 450,000 ordinary shares were sold for $10 per share, and on October 1, 2010, 110,000 ordinary shares were purchased for $20 per share and held as treasury shares.

Instructions

Compute earnings per share for 2010. Assume that financial statements for 2010 were issued in March 2011.

·7 **E16-23** **(EPS with Convertible Bonds, Various Situations)** In 2010, Buraka Enterprises issued, at par, 75 $1,000, 8% bonds, each convertible into 100 ordinary shares. The liability component of convertible bonds was $950 per bond, based on a market rate of interest of 10%. Buraka had revenues of $17,500 and expenses other than interest and taxes of $8,400 for 2011. (Assume that the tax rate is 40%.) Throughout 2011, 2,000 ordinary shares were outstanding; none of the bonds was converted or redeemed.

Instructions
- (a) Compute diluted earnings per share for 2011.
- (b) Assume the same facts as those assumed for part (a), except that the 75 bonds were issued on September 1, 2011 (rather than in 2010), and none have been converted or redeemed.
- (c) Assume the same facts as assumed for part (a), except that 25 of the 75 bonds were actually converted on July 1, 2011.

·7 E16-24 (EPS with Convertible Bonds) On June 1, 2009, Bluhm Company and Amanar Company merged to form Davenport Inc. A total of 800,000 shares were issued to complete the merger. The new corporation reports on a calendar-year basis.

On April 1, 2011, the company issued an additional 600,000 shares for cash. All 1,400,000 shares were outstanding on December 31, 2011.

Davenport Inc. also issued €600,000 of 20-year, 8% convertible bonds at par on July 1, 2011. Each €1,000 bond converts to 40 ordinary shares at any interest date. None of the bonds have been converted to date. The interest expense on the liability component of convertible bonds for 2011 was €30,000.

Davenport Inc. is preparing its annual report for the fiscal year ending December 31, 2011. The annual report will show earnings per share figures based upon a reported after-tax net income of €1,540,000. (The tax rate is 40%.)

Instructions
Determine the following for 2011.
- (a) The number of shares to be used for calculating:
  - (1) Basic earnings per share.
  - (2) Diluted earnings per share.
- (b) The earnings figures to be used for calculating:
  - (1) Basic earnings per share.
  - (2) Diluted earnings per share.

·2 ·7 E16-25 (EPS with Convertible Bonds and Preference Shares) The Ottey Corporation issued 10-year, $4,000,000 par, 7% callable convertible subordinated debentures on January 2, 2010. The bonds have a par value of $1,000, with interest payable annually. The interest expense recorded on the liability component of the convertible bond for 2010 was $320,000. The current conversion ratio is 14:1, and in 2 years it will increase to 18:1. At the date of issue, the bonds were sold at 98. Ottey's effective tax was 35%. Net income in 2010 was $7,500,000, and the company had 2,000,000 shares outstanding during the entire year.

Instructions
- (a) Prepare a schedule to compute both basic and diluted earnings per share.
- (b) Discuss how the schedule would differ if the security was convertible preference shares.

·2 ·7 E16-26 (EPS with Convertible Bonds and Preference Shares) On January 1, 2010, Lindsey Company issued 10-year, $3,000,000 face value, 6% bonds, at par. Each $1,000 bond is convertible into 15 ordinary shares of Lindsey. Lindsey's net income in 2011 was $240,000, and its tax rate was 40%. Interest expense on the liability component in 2011 was $210,000. The company had 100,000 ordinary shares outstanding throughout 2010. None of the bonds were converted in 2010.

Instructions
- (a) Compute diluted earnings per share for 2010.
- (b) Compute diluted earnings per share for 2010, assuming the same facts as above, except that $1,000,000 of 6% convertible preference shares were issued instead of the bonds. Each $100 preference share is convertible into 5 ordinary shares of Lindsey.

·7 E16-27 (EPS with Options, Various Situations) Zambrano Company's net income for 2010 is £40,000. The only potentially dilutive securities outstanding were 1,000 options issued during 2009, each exercisable for one share at £8. None has been exercised, and 10,000 ordinary shares were outstanding during 2010. The average market price of Zambrano's shares during 2010 was £20.

Instructions
- (a) Compute diluted earnings per share. (Round to two decimal places.)
- (b) Assume the same facts as those assumed for part (a), except that the 1,000 options were issued on October 1, 2010 (rather than in 2009). The average market price during the last 3 months of 2010 was £20.

•7 E16-28 (EPS with Contingent Issuance Agreement) Brooks Inc. recently purchased Donovan Corp., a large midwestern home painting corporation. One of the terms of the merger was that if Donovan's income for 2011 was $110,000 or more, 10,000 additional shares would be issued to Donovan's shareholders in 2012. Donovan's income for 2010 was $125,000.

Instructions
(a) Would the contingent shares have to be considered in Brooks's 2010 earnings per share computations?
(b) Assume the same facts, except that the 10,000 shares are contingent on Donovan's achieving a net income of $130,000 in 2011. Would the contingent shares have to be considered in Brooks's earnings per share computations for 2010?

•7 E16-29 (EPS with Warrants) Werth Corporation earned $260,000 during a period when it had an average of 100,000 ordinary shares outstanding. The ordinary shares sold at an average market price of $15 per share during the period. Also outstanding were 30,000 warrants that could be exercised to purchase one ordinary share for $10 for each warrant exercised.

Instructions
(a) Are the warrants dilutive?
(b) Compute basic earnings per share.
(c) Compute diluted earnings per share.

•8 *E16-30 (Share-Appreciation Rights) On December 31, 2007, Flessel Company issues 120,000 share-appreciation rights to its officers entitling them to receive cash for the difference between the market price of its shares and a pre-established price of $10. The fair value of the SARs is estimated to be $4 per SAR on December 31, 2008; $1 on December 31, 2009; $11 on December 31, 2010; and $9 on December 31, 2011. The service period is 4 years, and the exercise period is 7 years.

Instructions
(a) Prepare a schedule that shows the amount of compensation expense allocable to each year affected by the share-appreciation rights plan.
(b) Prepare the entry at December 31, 2011, to record compensation expense, if any, in 2011.
(c) Prepare the entry on December 31, 2011, assuming that all 120,000 SARs are exercised.

•8 *E16-31 (Share-Appreciation Rights) Derrick Company establishes a share-appreciation rights program that entitles its new president Dan Scott to receive cash for the difference between the market price of the shares and a pre-established price of $30 (also market price) on December 31, 2008, on 40,000 SARs. The date of grant is December 31, 2008, and the required employment (service) period is 4 years. President Scott exercises all of the SARs in 2014. The fair value of the SARs is estimated to be $6 per SAR on December 31, 2009; $9 on December 31, 2010; $15 on December 31, 2011; $8 on December 31, 2012; and $18 on December 31, 2013.

Instructions
(a) Prepare a 5-year (2009–2013) schedule of compensation expense pertaining to the 40,000 SARs granted to president Scott.
(b) Prepare the journal entry for compensation expense in 2009, 2012, and 2013 relative to the 40,000 SARs.

PROBLEMS

•1 •3 •4 P16-1 (Entries for Various Dilutive Securities) The equity section of Martino Inc. at the beginning of the current year appears below.

Share capital—ordinary, €10 par value, authorized 1,000,000 shares, 300,000 shares issued and outstanding	€3,000,000
Share premium—ordinary	600,000
Retained earnings	570,000

During the current year, the following transactions occurred.

1. The company issued to the shareholders 100,000 rights. Ten rights are needed to buy one share at €32. The rights were void after 30 days. The market price of the shares at this time was €34 per share.

2. The company sold to the public a €200,000, 10% bond issue at 104. The company also issued with each €100 bond one detachable share purchase warrant, which provided for the purchase of ordinary shares at €30 per share. The net present value of the bonds without the warrants was €192,000.
3. All but 5,000 of the rights issued in (1) were exercised in 30 days.
4. At the end of the year, 80% of the warrants in (2) had been exercised, and the remaining were outstanding and in good standing.
5. During the current year, the company granted share options for 10,000 ordinary shares to company executives. The company using a fair value option-pricing model determines that each option is worth €10. The option price is €30. The options were to expire at year-end and were considered compensation for the current year.
6. All but 1,000 shares related to the share-option plan were exercised by year-end. The expiration resulted because one of the executives failed to fulfill an obligation related to the employment contract.

Instructions

(a) Prepare general journal entries for the current year to record the transactions listed above.
(b) Prepare the equity section of the statement of financial position at the end of the current year. Assume that retained earnings at the end of the current year is €750,000.

P16-2 (Share-Option Plan) Berg Company adopted a share-option plan on November 30, 2009, that provided that 70,000 shares of $5 par value ordinary shares be designated as available for the granting of options to officers of the corporation at a price of $9 a share. The market value was $12 a share on November 30, 2009.

On January 2, 2010, options to purchase 28,000 shares were granted to president Tom Winter—15,000 for services to be rendered in 2010 and 13,000 for services to be rendered in 2011. Also on that date, options to purchase 14,000 shares were granted to vice president Michelle Bennett—7,000 for services to be rendered in 2010 and 7,000 for services to be rendered in 2011. The market value of the shares was $14 a share on January 2, 2010. The options were exercisable for a period of one year following the year in which the services were rendered. The fair value of the options on the grant date was $4 per option.

In 2011, neither the president nor the vice president exercised their options because the market price of the shares was below the exercise price. The market value was $8 a share on December 31, 2011, when the options for 2010 services lapsed.

On December 31, 2012, both president Winter and vice president Bennett exercised their options for 13,000 and 7,000 shares, respectively, when the market price was $16 a share.

Instructions

Prepare the necessary journal entries in 2009 when the share-option plan was adopted, in 2010 when options were granted, in 2011 when options lapsed, and in 2012 when options were exercised.

P16-3 (Share-Based Compensation) Assume that Sarazan Company has a share-option plan for top management. Each share option represents the right to purchase a $1 par value ordinary share in the future at a price equal to the fair value of the shares at the date of the grant. Sarazan has 5,000 share options outstanding, which were granted at the beginning of 2010. The following data relate to the option grant.

Exercise price for options	$40
Market price at grant date (January 1, 2010)	$40
Fair value of options at grant date (January 1, 2010)	$6
Service period	5 years

Instructions

(a) Prepare the journal entry(ies) for the first year of the share-option plan.
(b) Prepare the journal entry(ies) for the first year of the plan assuming that, rather than options, 700 shares of restricted shares were granted at the beginning of 2010.
(c) Now assume that the market price of Sarazan shares on the grant date was $45 per share. Repeat the requirements for (a) and (b).
(d) Sarazan would like to implement an employee share-purchase plan for rank-and-file employees, but it would like to avoid recording expense related to this plan. Explain how employee share-purchase plans are recorded.

P16-4 (EPS with Complex Capital Structure) Amy Dyken, controller at Fitzgerald Pharmaceutical Industries, a public company, is currently preparing the calculation for basic and diluted earnings per share and the related disclosure for Fitzgerald's financial statements. Selected financial information for the fiscal year ended June 30, 2010, is shown on the next page.

FITZGERALD PHARMACEUTICAL INDUSTRIES
SELECTED STATEMENT OF FINANCIAL POSITION INFORMATION
JUNE 30, 2010

Equity	
Share capital—preference, 6% cumulative, $50 par value,	
100,000 shares authorized, 25,000 shares issued	
and outstanding	$ 1,250,000
Share capital—ordinary, $1 par, 10,000,000 shares authorized,	
1,000,000 shares issued and outstanding	1,000,000
Share premium—ordinary	4,000,000
Retained earnings	6,000,000
Total equity	$12,250,000
Long-term debt	
Notes payable, 10%	$ 1,000,000
Convertible bonds payable	5,000,000
10% bonds payable	6,000,000
Total long-term debt	$12,000,000

The following transactions have also occurred at Fitzgerald.

1. Options were granted on July 1, 2009, to purchase 200,000 shares at $15 per share. Although no options were exercised during fiscal year 2010, the average price per ordinary share during fiscal year 2010 was $20 per share.
2. Each bond was issued at face value. The convertible bonds will convert into ordinary shares at 50 shares per $1,000 bond. It is exercisable after 5 years and was issued in 2008. The interest on the liability component of the convertible bonds payable for the fiscal year ending June 30, 2010, was $450,000.
3. The preference shares were issued in 2008.
4. There are no preference dividends in arrears; however, preference dividends were not declared in fiscal year 2010.
5. The 1,000,000 ordinary shares were outstanding for the entire 2010 fiscal year.
6. Net income for fiscal year 2010 was $1,500,000, and the average income tax rate is 40%.

Instructions

For the fiscal year ended June 30, 2010, calculate the following for Fitzgerald Pharmaceutical Industries.

(a) Basic earnings per share.
(b) Diluted earnings per share.

·6 **P16-5 (Basic EPS: Two-Year Presentation)** Melton Corporation is preparing the comparative financial statements for the annual report to its shareholders for fiscal years ended May 31, 2010, and May 31, 2011. The income from continuing operations for each year was $1,800,000 and $2,500,000, respectively. In both years, the company incurred a 10% interest expense on $2,400,000 of debt, an obligation that requires interest-only payments for 5 years. In 2011, the company experienced a loss from discontinued operations, net of tax, of $360,000. The company uses a 40% effective tax rate for income taxes.

The capital structure of Melton Corporation on June 1, 2009, consisted of 1 million ordinary shares outstanding and 20,000 shares of $50 par value, 6%, cumulative preference shares. There were no preference dividends in arrears, and the company had not issued any convertible securities, options, or warrants.

On October 1, 2009, Melton sold an additional 500,000 ordinary shares at $20 per share. Melton distributed a 20% share dividend on the ordinary shares outstanding on January 1, 2010. On December 1, 2010, Melton was able to sell an additional 800,000 ordinary shares at $22 per share. These were the only ordinary share transactions that occurred during the two fiscal years.

Instructions

(a) Identify whether the capital structure at Melton Corporation is a simple or complex capital structure, and explain why.
(b) Determine the weighted-average number of shares that Melton Corporation would use in calculating earnings per share for the fiscal year ended:
   (1) May 31, 2010.
   (2) May 31, 2011.
(c) Prepare, in good form, a comparative income statement, beginning with income from operations, for Melton Corporation for the fiscal years ended May 31, 2010, and May 31, 2011. This statement will be included in Melton's annual report and should display the appropriate earnings per share presentations.

·7 **P16-6** **(Computation of Basic and Diluted EPS)** Charles Austin of the controller's office of Thompson Corporation was given the assignment of determining the basic and diluted earnings per share values for the year ending December 31, 2011. Austin has compiled the information listed below.

1. The company is authorized to issue 8,000,000 $10 par value ordinary shares. As of December 31, 2010, 2,000,000 shares had been issued and were outstanding.
2. The per share market prices of the ordinary shares on selected dates were as follows.

	Price per Share
July 1, 2010	$20.00
January 1, 2011	21.00
April 1, 2011	25.00
July 1, 2011	11.00
August 1, 2011	10.50
November 1, 2011	9.00
December 31, 2011	10.00

3. A total of 700,000 shares of an authorized 1,200,000 shares of convertible preference shares have been issued on July 1, 2010. Each share had a par value of $25 and a cumulative dividend of $3 per share. The shares are convertible into ordinary shares at the rate of one convertible preference share for one ordinary share. The rate of conversion is to be automatically adjusted for share splits and share dividends. Dividends are paid quarterly on September 30, December 31, March 31, and June 30.
4. Thompson Corporation is subject to a 40% income tax rate.
5. The after-tax net income for the year ended December 31, 2011 was $11,550,000.

The following specific activities took place during 2011.

1. January 1—A 5% ordinary share dividend was issued. The dividend had been declared on December 1, 2010, to all shareholders of record on December 29, 2010.
2. April 1—A total of 400,000 shares of the $3 convertible preference shares were converted into ordinary shares. The company issued new ordinary shares and retired the preference shares. This was the only conversion of the preference shares during 2011.
3. July 1—A 2-for-1 split of the ordinary shares became effective on this date. The board of directors had authorized the split on June 1.
4. August 1—A total of 300,000 ordinary shares were issued to acquire a factory building.
5. November 1—A total of 24,000 ordinary shares were purchased on the open market at $9 per share. These shares were to be held as treasury shares and were still in the treasury as of December 31, 2011.
6. Ordinary share cash dividends—Cash dividends to ordinary shareholders were declared and paid as follows.
   April 15—$0.30 per share
   October 15—$0.20 per share
7. Preference share cash dividends—Cash dividends to preference shareholders were declared and paid as scheduled.

Instructions
(a) Determine the number of shares used to compute basic earnings per share for the year ended December 31, 2011.
(b) Determine the number of shares used to compute diluted earnings per share for the year ended December 31, 2011.
(c) Compute the adjusted net income to be used as the numerator in the basic earnings per share calculation for the year ended December 31, 2011.

·7 **P16-7** **(Computation of Basic and Diluted EPS)** The information below pertains to Barkley Company for 2010.

Net income for the year	$1,200,000
8% convertible bonds issued at par ($1,000 per bond). Each bond is convertible into 30 shares of ordinary shares. The liability component of the bonds is $1,800,000 based on a market rate of 9%.	2,000,000
6% convertible, cumulative preference shares, $100 par value. Each share is convertible into 3 shares of ordinary shares.	4,000,000
Ordinary shares, $10 par value	6,000,000
Tax rate for 2010	40%
Average market price of ordinary shares	$25 per share

There were no changes during 2010 in the number of ordinary shares, preference shares, or convertible bonds outstanding. There are no treasury shares. The company also has ordinary share options (granted in a prior year) to purchase 75,000 ordinary shares at $20 per share.

Instructions

(a) Compute basic earnings per share for 2010.

(b) Compute diluted earnings per share for 2010.

P16-8 (EPS with Share Dividend and Discontinued Operations) Agassi Corporation is preparing the comparative financial statements to be included in the annual report to shareholders. Agassi employs a fiscal year ending May 31.

Income before income tax for Agassi was $1,400,000 and $660,000, respectively, for fiscal years ended May 31, 2011 and 2010. Agassi experienced a loss from discontinued operations of $400,000 in March 2011. A 40% combined income tax rate pertains to any and all of Agassi Corporation's profits, gains, and losses.

Agassi's capital structure consists of preference shares and ordinary shares. The company has not issued any convertible securities or warrants and there are no outstanding share options.

Agassi issued 40,000 shares of $100 par value, 6% cumulative preference shares in 2007. All of these shares are outstanding, and no preference dividends are in arrears.

There were 1,000,000 shares of $1 par ordinary shares outstanding on June 1, 2009. On September 1, 2009, Agassi sold an additional 400,000 ordinary shares at $17 per share. Agassi distributed a 20% share dividend on the ordinary shares outstanding on December 1, 2010. These were the only ordinary share transactions during the past 2 fiscal years.

Instructions

(a) Determine the weighted-average number of ordinary shares that would be used in computing earnings per share on the current comparative income statement for:

(1) The year ended May 31, 2010.

(2) The year ended May 31, 2011.

(b) Starting with income before income tax, prepare a comparative income statement for the years ended May 31, 2011 and 2010. The statement will be part of Agassi Corporation's annual report to shareholders and should include appropriate earnings per share presentation.

(c) The capital structure of a corporation is the result of its past financing decisions. Furthermore, the earnings per share data presented on a corporation's financial statements is dependent upon the capital structure.

(1) Explain why Agassi Corporation is considered to have a simple capital structure.

(2) Describe how earnings per share data would be presented for a corporation that has a complex capital structure.

CONCEPTS FOR ANALYSIS

CA16-1 (Dilutive Securities, EPS) Two students are discussing the current chapter on dilutive securities and earnings per share. Here are some of the points raised in their discussion.

1. Is there a difference between issuing convertible debt versus issuing debt with share warrants? Also does it make a difference whether the share warrants are detachable or non-detachable?

2. Why is it that companies are not permitted to adjust compensation expense for share options when the options become worthless because the share price does not increase in value?

3. What is the rationale for using the treasury-share method in earnings per share computations?

4. Why do companies have to report compensation expense for employees share-purchase plans? After the employee receives the shares, the price can go up or down, so what is the benefit that the employee is receiving?

Instructions

Prepare a response to each of the questions asked by the students.

CA16-2 (Ethical Issues—Compensation Plan) The executive officers of Rouse Corporation have a performance-based compensation plan. The performance criteria of this plan is linked to growth in earnings per share. When annual EPS growth is 12%, the Rouse executives earn 100% of the shares; if growth is 16%, they earn 125%. If EPS growth is lower than 8%, the executives receive no additional compensation.

In 2010, Gail Devers, the controller of Rouse, reviews year-end estimates of bad debt expense and warranty expense. She calculates the EPS growth at 15%. Kurt Adkins, a member of the executive group, remarks over lunch one day that the estimate of bad debt expense might be decreased, increasing EPS growth to 16.1%. Devers is not sure she should do this because she believes that the current estimate of bad debts is sound. On the other hand, she recognizes that a great deal of subjectivity is involved in the computation.

Instructions

Answer the following questions.

(a) What, if any, is the ethical dilemma for Devers?

(b) Should Devers's knowledge of the compensation plan be a factor that influences her estimate?

(c) How should Devers respond to Adkins's request?

CA16-3 **(Share Warrants—Various Types)** For various reasons a corporation may issue warrants to purchase its ordinary shares at specified prices that, depending on the circumstances, may be less than, equal to, or greater than the current market price. For example, warrants may be issued:

1. To existing shareholders on a pro rata basis.

2. To certain key employees under an incentive share-option plan.

3. To purchasers of the corporation's bonds.

Instructions

For each of the three examples of how share warrants are used:

(a) Explain why they are used.

(b) Discuss the significance of the price (or prices) at which the warrants are issued (or granted) in relation to (1) the current market price of the company's shares, and (2) the length of time over which they can be exercised.

(c) Describe the information that should be disclosed in financial statements, or notes thereto, that are prepared when share warrants are outstanding in the hands of the three groups listed above.

CA16-4 **(Share Compensation Plans)** The following item appeared on the Internet concerning the requirement to expense share options.

"Here We Go Again!" by Jack Ciesielski (2/21/2005, http://www.accountingobserver.com/blog/2005/02/here-we-go-again) On February 17, Congressman David Dreier (R–CA), and Congresswoman Anna Eshoo (D–CA), officially entered Silicon Valley's bid to gum up the launch of honest reporting of share option compensation: They co-sponsored a bill to "preserve broad-based employee share option plans and give investors critical information they need to understand how employee share options impact the value of their shares." You know what "critical information" they mean: stuff like the share compensation for the top five officers in a company, with a rigged value set as close to zero as possible. Investors *crave* this kind of information. Other ways the good Congresspersons want to "help" investors: The bill "also requires the SEC to study the effectiveness of those disclosures over three years, during which time, no new accounting standard related to the treatment of share options could be recognized. Finally, the bill requires the Secretary of Commerce to conduct a study and report to Congress on the impact of broad-based employee share option plans on expanding employee corporate ownership, skilled worker recruitment and retention, research and innovation, economic growth, and international competitiveness."

It's the old "four corners" basketball strategy: stall, stall, stall. In the meantime, hope for regime change at your opponent, the FASB.

Instructions

(a) What are the accounting requirements related to share-based compensation?

(b) How do the provisions of IFRS in this area differ from the bill introduced by members of the U.S. Congress (Dreier and Eshoo), which would require expensing for options issued to only the top five officers in a company? Which approach do you think would result in more useful information? (Focus on comparability.)

(c) The bill in the U.S. Congress urges a standard that preserves "the ability of companies to use this innovative tool to attract talented employees." Write a response to these congresspeople explaining the importance of neutrality in financial accounting and reporting.

CA16-5 **(EPS: Preference Dividends, Options, and Convertible Debt)** "Earnings per share" (EPS) is the most featured, single financial statistic about modern corporations. Daily published quotations of share prices have recently been expanded to include for many securities a "times earnings" figure that is based on EPS. Securities analysts often focus their discussions on the EPS of the corporations they study.

Instructions

(a) Explain how dividends or dividend requirements on any class of preference shares that may be outstanding affect the computation of EPS.

(b) One of the technical procedures applicable in EPS computations is the "treasury-share method." Briefly describe the circumstances under which it might be appropriate to apply the treasury-share method.

(c) Convertible debentures are considered potentially dilutive ordinary shares. Explain how convertible debentures are handled for purposes of EPS computations.

CA16-6 (EPS Concepts and Effect of Transactions on EPS) Chorkina Corporation, a new audit client of yours, has not reported earnings per share data in its annual reports to shareholders in the past. The treasurer, Beth Botsford, requested that you furnish information about the reporting of earnings per share data in the current year's annual report in accordance with IFRS.

Instructions

(a) Define the term "earnings per share" as it applies to a corporation with a capitalization structure composed of only one class of ordinary shares. Explain how earnings per share should be computed and how the information should be disclosed in the corporation's financial statements.

(b) Discuss the treatment, if any, that should be given to each of the following items in computing earnings per share of ordinary shares for financial statement reporting.

(1) Outstanding preference shares issued at a premium with a par value liquidation right.

(2) The exercise at a price below market value but above book value of an ordinary share option issued during the current fiscal year to officers of the corporation.

(3) The replacement of a machine immediately prior to the close of the current fiscal year at a cost 20% above the original cost of the replaced machine. The new machine will perform the same function as the old machine that was sold for its book value.

(4) The declaration of current dividends on cumulative preference shares.

(5) The acquisition of some of the corporation's outstanding ordinary shares during the current fiscal year. The shares were classified as treasury shares.

(6) A 2-for-1 share split of ordinary shares during the current fiscal year.

(7) A provision created out of retained earnings for a contingent liability from a possible lawsuit.

CA16-7 (EPS, Antidilution) Brad Dolan, a shareholder of Rhode Corporation, has asked you, the firm's accountant, to explain why his share warrants were not included in diluted EPS. In order to explain this situation, you must briefly explain what dilutive securities are, why they are included in the EPS calculation, and why some securities are antidilutive and thus not included in this calculation.

Instructions

Write Mr. Dolan a 1–1.5 page letter explaining why the warrants are not included in the calculation. Use the following data to help you explain this situation.

Rhode Corporation earned $228,000 during the period, when it had an average of 100,000 ordinary shares outstanding. The ordinary shares sold at an average market price of $25 per share during the period. Also outstanding were 30,000 warrants that could be exercised to purchase one ordinary share at $30 per warrant.

USING YOUR JUDGMENT

FINANCIAL REPORTING

Financial Reporting Problem

Marks and Spencer plc (M&S)

The financial statements of M&S are presented in Appendix 5B or can be accessed at the book's companion website, **www.wiley.com/college/kiesoifrs**.

Instructions

Refer to M&S's financial statements and the accompanying notes to answer the following questions.

(a) Under M&S's share-based compensation plan, share options are granted annually to key managers and directors.

(1) How many options were granted during 2008 under the plan?

(2) How many options were exercisable at March 29, 2008?

(3) How many options were exercised in 2008, and what was the average price of those exercised?

(4) How many years from the grant date do the options expire?

(5) To what accounts are the proceeds from these option exercises credited?

(6) What was the number of outstanding options at March 29, 2008, and at what average exercise price?

(b) What number of diluted weighted-average shares outstanding was used by M&S in computing earnings per share for 2008 and 2007? What was M&S's diluted earnings per share in 2008 and 2007?

(c) What other share-based compensation plans does M&S have?

Comparative Analysis Case

Cadbury and Nestlé

Instructions

Go to the book's companion website and use information found there to answer the following questions related to **Cadbury** and **Nestlé**.

(a) What employee share-option compensation plans are offered by Cadbury and Nestlé?

(b) What are the weighted-average number of shares used by Cadbury and Nestlé in 2008 and 2007?

(c) What was the diluted net income per share for Cadbury and Nestlé for 2008 and 2007?

International Reporting Case

Sepracor, Inc., a U.S. drug company, reported the following information in a recent annual report (amounts in thousands). The company prepares its financial statements in accordance with U.S. GAAP.

Current liabilities	$ 554,114
Convertible subordinated debt	648,020
Total liabilities	1,228,313
Stockholders' equity	176,413
Net income	58,333

Analysts attempting to compare Sepracor to international drug companies may face a challenge due to differences in accounting for convertible debt under IFRS. Under *IAS 32*, "Financial Instruments," convertible bonds, at issuance, must be classified separately into their debt and equity components based on estimated fair value.

Instructions

(a) Compute the following ratios for Sepracor, Inc. (Assume that year-end balances approximate annual averages.)

(1) Return on assets.

(2) Return on shareholders' equity.

(3) Debt to assets ratio.

(b) Briefly discuss the operating performance and financial position of Sepracor. Industry averages for these ratios were: ROA 3.5%; return on equity 16%; and debt to assets 75%. Based on this analysis, would you make an investment in the company's 5% convertible bonds? Explain.

(c) Assume you want to compare Sepracor to an international company, like **Bayer** (DEU) (which prepares its financial statements in accordance with IFRS). Assuming that the fair value of the liability component of Sepracor's convertible bonds is $398,020, how would you adjust the analysis above to make valid comparisons between Sepracor and Bayer?

Accounting, Analysis, and Principles

On January 1, 2011, Garner issued 10-year $200,000 face value, 6% bonds at par. Each $1,000 bond is convertible into 30 shares of Garner $2, par value, ordinary shares. Interest on the bonds is paid annually on December 31. The market rate for Garner's non-convertible debt is 9%. The company has had 10,000 ordinary shares (and no preference shares) outstanding throughout its life. None of the bonds have been converted as of the end of 2012. (Ignore all tax effects.)

Accounting

(a) Prepare the journal entry Garner would have made on January 1, 2011, to record the issuance of the bonds and prepare an amortization table for the first three years of the bonds.

(b) Garner's net income in 2012 was $30,000 and was $27,000 in 2011. Compute basic and diluted earnings per share for Garner for 2012 and 2011.

(c) Assume that all of the holders of Garner's convertible bonds convert their bonds to shares on January 2, 2013, when Garner's shares are trading at $32 per share. Garner pays $50 per bond to induce bondholders to convert. Prepare the journal entry to record the conversion, using the book value method.

Analysis

Show how Garner Company will report income and EPS for 2012 and 2011. Briefly discuss the importance of IFRS for EPS to analysts evaluating companies based on price-earnings ratios. Consider comparisons for a company over time, as well as comparisons between companies at a point in time.

Principles

In order to converge U.S. GAAP and IFRS, U.S. standard-setters (the FASB) are considering whether the equity element of a convertible bond should be reported as equity. Describe how the journal entry you made in part (a) above would differ under U.S. GAAP. In terms of the accounting principles discussed in Chapter 2, what does IFRS for convertible debt accomplish that U.S. GAAP potentially sacrifices? What does U.S. GAAP for convertible debt accomplish that IFRS potentially sacrifices?

BRIDGE TO THE PROFESSION

I F R S

Professional Research

Richardson Company is contemplating the establishment of a share-based compensation plan to provide long-run incentives for its top management. However, members of the compensation committee of the board of directors have voiced some concerns about adopting these plans, based on news accounts related to a recent accounting standard in this area. They would like you to conduct some research on this recent standard so they can be better informed about the accounting for these plans.

Instructions

Access the IFRS authoritative literature at the IASB website (*http://eifrs.iasb.org/*). When you have accessed the documents, you can use the search tool in your Internet browser to respond to the following questions. (Provide paragraph citations.)

(a) Identify the authoritative literature that addresses the accounting for share-based payment compensation plans.

(b) Briefly discuss the objectives for the accounting for share-based compensation. What is the role of fair value measurement?

(c) The Richardson Company board is also considering an employee share-purchase plan, but the Board does not want to record expense related to the plan. What are the IFRS requirements for the accounting for an employee share-purchase plan?

Professional Simulation

In this simulation, you are asked to address questions related to the accounting for share options and earnings per share computations. Prepare responses to all parts.

KWW_Professional _Simulation

| Share Options and EPS | Time Remaining 3 hours 50 minutes | copy paste calculator sheet standards help splitter done |

| Directions | Situation | Explanation | Financial Statements | Resources |

As auditor for Banquo & Associates, you have been assigned to check Duncan Corporation's computation of earnings per share for the current year. The controller, Mac Beth, has supplied you with the following computations.

Net income	$3,374,960
Ordinary shares issued and outstanding:	
Beginning of year	1,285,000
End of year	1,200,000
Average	1,242,500
Earnings per share:	

$$\frac{\$3,374,960}{1,242,500} = \$2.72 \text{ per share}$$

You have developed the following additional information.
1. There are no other equity securities in addition to the ordinary shares.
2. There are no options or warrants outstanding to purchase ordinary shares.
3. There are no convertible debt securities.
4. Activity in ordinary shares during the year was as follows.

Outstanding, Jan. 1	1,285,000
Treasury shares acquired, Oct. 1	(250,000)
	1,035,000
Shares reissued, Dec. 1	165,000
Outstanding, Dec. 31	1,200,000

| Directions | Situation | Explanation | Financial Statements | Resources |

On the basis of the information above, do you agree with the controller's computation of earnings per share for the year? If you disagree, prepare a revised computation of earnings per share.

| Directions | Situation | Explanation | Financial Statements | Resources |

Assume the same facts as those presented above, except that options had been issued to purchase 140,000 ordinary shares at $10 per share. These options were outstanding at the beginning of the year and none had been exercised or canceled during the year. The average market price of the ordinary shares during the year was $25, and the ending market price was $35. What earnings per share amounts will be reported?

Remember to check the book's companion website to find additional resources for this chapter.

CHAPTER 17

INVESTMENTS

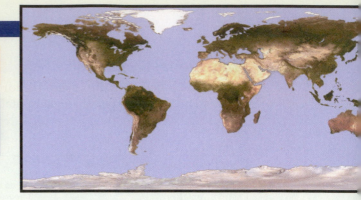

LEARNING OBJECTIVES

After studying this chapter, you should be able to:

•1 Describe the accounting framework for financial assets.

•2 Understand the accounting for debt investments at amortized cost.

•3 Understand the accounting for debt investments at fair value.

•4 Describe the accounting for the fair value option.

•5 Understand the accounting for equity investments at fair value.

•6 Explain the equity method of accounting and compare it to the fair value method for equity investments.

•7 Discuss the accounting for impairments of debt investments.

•8 Describe the accounting for transfer of investments between categories.

WHAT TO DO?

Recently, a bank reported an $87.3 million write-down on its mortgage-backed securities for the third quarter of 2008; however, the bank stated that it expected its actual losses to be only $44,000. The loss of $44,000 was equal to a modest loss on a condo foreclosure. The bank's regulator found "the accounting result absurd." However, the rest of the story is that the bank, in the third quarter of 2009, raised its credit-loss estimate by **$263.1 million**, quite a difference from its original loss estimate of **$44,000**.

The discussion above highlights the challenge of valuing financial assets such as loans, derivatives, and other debt investments. The fundamental question that arose out of the example above and, more significantly, the recent financial crisis is: Should financial instruments be valued at amortized cost, fair value, or some other measure(s)? As one writer noted, the opinion that fair value accounting weakens financial and economic stability has persisted among many regulators and politicians, mostly in Europe but also in Asia. But, some investors and others, particularly in the United States, believe that fair value is the right answer because it is more transparent information.

OK, so what to do? The IASB's response was to issue a new standard on financial assets (*IFRS 9*) that uses a mixed-attribute approach. Some of the financial assets are valued at amortized cost and others at fair value. In addition, the FASB has issued an exposure draft on how it believes financial assets should be reported. Unfortunately, at this point the two bodies do not agree as to how these instruments should be accounted for and reported.

A survey by the Chartered Financial Analysts association on *IFRS 9* contained the following question on the new standard: "Do you agree that the IASB's new standard requiring classification into amortized cost or fair value will improve the decision-usefulness of overall financial instrument accounting?" The survey results indicate that 47 percent believe the IASB's approach improves the decision-usefulness of information. This less-than-strong support for the new rules is somewhat troubling, given that the group surveyed is representative of the IASB's key constituency—investors and creditors.

Interestingly, the European Union refused to consider adopting the requirements of *IFRS 9*, arguing that it contained **too much** fair value information. Nevertheless, the standard was issued and other countries that follow IFRS will soon be implementing the new standard. At the same time, as soon as the FASB issues its new standard, the IASB has indicated that it may revisit the valuation issue once again.

Thus, the early reaction to *IFRS 9* indicates that, unfortunately, once again politics is raising its ugly head on an accounting issue. Some European regulators have suggested that the IASB's future funding may even depend on the Board putting more regulators on it. Such an intrusion could lead to the end of the convergence efforts between the IASB and the FASB.

Source: Adapted from Jonathan Weil, "Suing Wall Street Banks Never Looked So Shady," *http://www.bloomberg.com/apps/news?pid=20601039&sid=7ZeWzn42KX4* (February 28, 2010); Rachel Sanderson and Jennifer Hughes, "Carried Forward," *Financial Times Online* (April 20, 2010); and CFA Institute, *Survey on Proposed Financial Instrument Accounting Changes and International Convergence* (November 2009).

PREVIEW OF CHAPTER 17

As indicated in the opening story, the accounting for financial assets is highly controversial. How to measure, recognize, and disclose this information is now being debated and discussed extensively. In this chapter, we address the accounting for debt and equity investments. The appendices to this chapter discuss the accounting for reclassification adjustments and derivative instruments. The content and organization of the chapter are as follows.

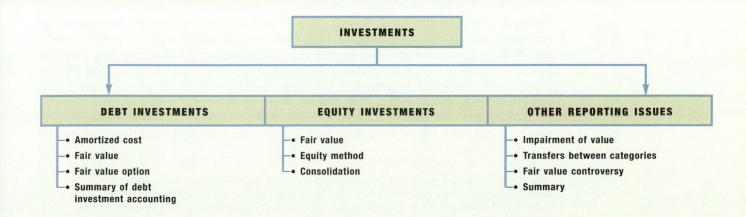

INVESTMENTS

DEBT INVESTMENTS	**EQUITY INVESTMENTS**	**OTHER REPORTING ISSUES**
• Amortized cost	• Fair value	• Impairment of value
• Fair value	• Equity method	• Transfers between categories
• Fair value option	• Consolidation	• Fair value controversy
• Summary of debt investment accounting		• Summary

ACCOUNTING FOR FINANCIAL ASSETS

Objective•1

Describe the accounting framework for financial assets.

IFRS

See the Authoritative Literature section (page 929).

A **financial asset** is cash, an equity investment of another company (e.g., ordinary or preference shares), or a contractual right to receive cash from another party (e.g., loans, receivables, and bonds). **[1]** The accounting for cash is relatively straightforward and is discussed in Chapter 7. The accounting and reporting for equity and debt investments, as discussed in the opening story, is extremely contentious, particularly in light of the credit crisis in the latter part of 2008.

Some users of financial statements support a single measurement—fair value—for all financial assets. They view fair value as more relevant than other measurements in helping investors assess the effect of current economic events on the future cash flows of the asset. In addition, they believe that the use of a single method promotes consistency in valuation and reporting on the financial asset, thereby improving the usefulness of the financial statements. Others disagree. They note that many investments are not held for sale but rather for the income they will generate over the life of the investment. They believe cost-based information (referred to as amortized cost) provides the most relevant information for predicting future cash flows in these cases. Others express concern that using fair value information to measure financial assets is unreliable when markets for the investments are not functioning in an ordinary fashion.

After much discussion, the IASB decided that reporting all financial assets at fair value is not the most appropriate approach for providing relevant information to financial statement users. **The IASB noted that both fair value and a cost-based approach can provide useful information to financial statement readers for particular types of financial assets in certain circumstances.** As a result, the IASB requires that companies classify financial assets into two measurement categories—**amortized cost and fair value**—depending on the circumstances.

Measurement Basis—A Closer Look

In general, IFRS requires that companies determine how to measure their financial assets based on two criteria:

- The company's business model for managing its financial assets; and
- The contractual cash flow characteristics of the financial asset.

If a company has (1) a business model whose objective is to hold assets in order to collect contractual cash flows and (2) the contractual terms of the financial asset provides specified dates to cash flows that are solely payments of principal and interest on the principal amount outstanding, then the company should use amortized cost. **[2]**[1]

For example, assume that **Mitsubishi** (JPN) purchases a bond investment that it intends to hold to maturity. Its business model for this type of investment is to collect interest and then principal at maturity. The payment dates for the interest rate and principal are stated on the bond. In this case, Mitsubishi accounts for the investment at amortized cost. If, on the other hand, Mitsubishi purchased the bonds as part of a trading strategy to speculate on interest rate changes (a trading investment), then the debt investment is reported at fair value. As a result, only debt investments such as receivables, loans, and bond investments that meet the two criteria above are recorded at amortized cost. All other debt investments are recorded and reported at fair value.

Equity investments are generally recorded and reported at fair value. Equity investments do not have a fixed interest or principal payment schedule and therefore cannot

---

[1]The IASB indicates that the business model should be considered first. And, that the contractual cash flow characteristics should be considered only for financial assets (e.g., debt investments) that are eligible to be measured at amortized cost. It states that both classification conditions are essential to ensure that amortized cost provides useful information about debt investments. **[3]**

be accounted for at amortized cost. In summary, companies account for investments based on the type of security, as indicated in Illustration 17-1.

Type of Investment	Assessment of Accounting Criteria	Valuation Approach
Debt (Section 1)	Meets business model (held-for-collection) and contractual cash flow tests.	Amortized cost
	Does not meet the business model test (not held-for-collection).	Fair value
Equity (Section 2)	Does not meet contractual cash flow test.	Fair value*

*For some equity investments for which the investor exercises some control over the investee, use the equity method.

ILLUSTRATION 17-1
Summary of Investment Accounting Approaches

We organize our study of investments by type of investment security; within each section, we explain how the accounting for investments in debt and equity securities varies according to how the investment is managed and the contractual cash flow characteristics of the investment.

SECTION 1 · DEBT INVESTMENTS

Debt investments are characterized by contractual payments on specified dates of principal and interest on the principal amount outstanding. Companies measure debt investments at amortized cost if the objective of the company's business model is to hold the financial asset to collect the contractual cash flows (**held-for-collection**). **Amortized cost** is the initial recognition amount of the investment minus repayments, plus or minus cumulative amortization and net of any reduction for uncollectibility. If the criteria for measurement at amortized cost are not met, then the debt investment is valued and accounted for at fair value. **Fair value** is the amount for which an asset could be exchanged between knowledgeable willing parties in an arm's length transaction. [4]

DEBT INVESTMENTS—AMORTIZED COST

Only debt investments can be measured at amortized cost. If a company like **Carrefour** (FRA) makes an investment in the bonds of **Nokia** (FIN), it will receive contractual cash flows of interest over the life of the bonds and repayment of the principal at maturity. If it is Carrefour's strategy to hold this investment in order to receive these cash flows over the life of the bond, it has a held-for-collection strategy and it will measure the investment at amortized cost.[2]

Objective•2
Understand the accounting for debt investments at amortized cost.

Example: Debt Investment at Amortized Cost

To illustrate the accounting for a debt investment at amortized cost, assume that Robinson Company purchased $100,000 of 8 percent bonds of Evermaster Corporation

[2]Classification as held-for-collection does not mean the security must be held to maturity. For example, a company may sell an investment before maturity if (1) the security does not meet the company's investment strategy (e.g., the company has a policy to invest in only AAA-rated bonds but the bond investment has a decline in its credit rating), (2) a company changes its strategy to invest only in securities within a certain maturity range, or (3) the company needs to sell a security to fund certain capital expenditures. However, if a company begins trading held-for-collection investments on a regular basis, it should assess whether such trading is consistent with the held-for-collection classification. [5]

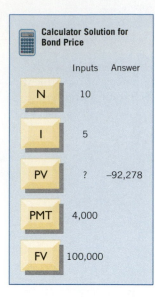

Calculator Solution for Bond Price

	Inputs	Answer
N	10	
I	5	
PV	?	−92,278
PMT	4,000	
FV	100,000	

on January 1, 2011, at a discount, paying $92,278. The bonds mature January 1, 2016, and yield 10 percent; interest is payable each July 1 and January 1. Robinson records the investment as follows.

January 1, 2011

Debt Investments	92,278	
Cash		92,278

As indicated in Chapter 14, companies must amortize premiums or discounts using the **effective-interest method**. They apply the effective-interest method to bond investments in a way similar to that for bonds payable. To compute interest revenue, companies compute the effective-interest rate or yield at the time of investment and apply that rate to the beginning carrying amount (book value) for each interest period. The investment carrying amount is increased by the amortized discount or decreased by the amortized premium in each period.

Illustration 17-2 shows the effect of the discount amortization on the interest revenue that Robinson records each period for its investment in Evermaster bonds.

ILLUSTRATION 17-2
Schedule of Interest Revenue and Bond Discount Amortization— Effective-Interest Method

				8% BONDS PURCHASED TO YIELD 10%	
Date	Cash Received	Interest Revenue	Bond Discount Amortization	Carrying Amount of Bonds
1/1/11				$ 92,278
7/1/11	$ 4,000ᵃ	$ 4,614ᵇ	$ 614ᶜ	92,892ᵈ
1/1/12	4,000	4,645	645	93,537
7/1/12	4,000	4,677	677	94,214
1/1/13	4,000	4,711	711	94,925
7/1/13	4,000	4,746	746	95,671
1/1/14	4,000	4,783	783	96,454
7/1/14	4,000	4,823	823	97,277
1/1/15	4,000	4,864	864	98,141
7/1/15	4,000	4,907	907	99,048
1/1/16	4,000	4,952	952	100,000
	$40,000	$47,722	$7,722	

ᵃ$4,000 = $100,000 × .08 × ½
ᵇ$4,614 = $92,278 × .10 × ½
ᶜ$614 = $4,614 − $4,000
ᵈ$92,892 = $92,278 + $614

Robinson records the receipt of the first semiannual interest payment on July 1, 2011 (using the data in Illustration 17-2), as follows.

July 1, 2011

Cash	4,000	
Debt Investments	614	
Interest Revenue		4,614

Because Robinson is on a calendar-year basis, it accrues interest and amortizes the discount at December 31, 2011, as follows.

December 31, 2011

Interest Receivable	4,000	
Debt Investments	645	
Interest Revenue		4,645

Again, Illustration 17-2 shows the interest and amortization amounts.

Robinson reports its investment in Evermaster bonds in its December 31, 2011, financial statements, as follows.[3]

ILLUSTRATION 17-3
Reporting of Bond
Investments at
Amortized Cost

Statement of Financial Position	
Long-term investments	
Debt investments	$93,537
Current assets	
Interest receivable	$ 4,000
Income Statement	
Other income and expense	
Interest revenue ($4,614 + $4,645)	$ 9,259

Sometimes, a company sells a bond investment before its maturity. For example, Robinson Company may sell securities as part of a change in its investment strategy to move away from five-year debt investments, like the Evermaster bonds, to invest in shorter-term bonds. Such a strategy would allow the bonds to reprice more frequently in response to interest rate changes. Let's assume that Robinson Company sells its investment in Evermaster bonds on November 1, 2013, at 99¾ plus accrued interest. The discount amortization from July 1, 2013, to November 1, 2013, is $522 (⅔ × $783). Robinson records this discount amortization as follows.

November 1, 2013

Debt Investments	522	
Interest Revenue		522

Illustration 17-4 shows the computation of the realized gain on the sale.

ILLUSTRATION 17-4
Computation of Gain on
Sale of Bonds

Selling price of bonds (exclusive of accrued interest)		$99,750
Less: Book value of bonds on November 1, 2013:		
Amortized cost, July 1, 2013	$95,671	
Add: Discount amortized for the period July 1, 2013,		
to November 1, 2013	522	96,193
Gain on sale of bonds		$ 3,557

Robinson records the sale of the bonds as:

November 1, 2013

Cash	102,417	
Interest Revenue (4/6 × $4,000)		2,667
Debt Investments		96,193
Gain on Sale of Debt Investment		3,557

The credit to Interest Revenue represents accrued interest for four months, for which the purchaser pays cash. The debit to Cash represents the selling price of the bonds plus accrued interest ($99,750 + $2,667). The credit to Debt Investments represents the book value of the bonds on the date of sale. The credit to Gain on Sale of Debt Investment represents the excess of the selling price over the book value of the bonds.

---

[3]Although the example here is based on a single investment, the IASB indicates that companies evaluate the investment strategy (or business model for managing the investments) at a higher level of aggregation than the individual security. As a result, a company may have more than one investment strategy. That is, a company may hold a portfolio of investments that is managed to collect contractual cash flows and another portfolio of investments that is managed to realize gains and losses on fair value changes. **[6]**

DEBT INVESTMENTS—FAIR VALUE

Objective•3
Understand the accounting for debt investments at fair value.

In some cases, companies both manage and evaluate investment performance on a fair value basis. In these situations, these investments are managed and evaluated based on a documented risk-management or investment strategy based on fair value information. For example, some companies often hold debt investments with the intention of selling them in a short period of time. These debt investments are often referred to as **trading investments** because companies frequently buy and sell these investments to generate profits in short-term differences in price.

Companies that account for and report debt investments at fair value follow the same accounting entries as debt investments held-for-collection during the reporting period. That is, they are recorded at amortized cost. However, **at each reporting date, companies adjust the amortized cost to fair value, with any unrealized holding gain or loss reported as part of net income** (**fair value method**). An **unrealized holding gain or loss** is the net change in the fair value of a debt investment from one period to another.

Example: Debt Investment at Fair Value (Single Security)

To illustrate the accounting for debt investments using the fair value approach, assume the same information as in our previous illustration for Robinson Company. Recall that Robinson Company purchased $100,000 of 8 percent bonds of Evermaster Corporation on January 1, 2011, at a discount, paying $92,278.[4] The bonds mature January 1, 2016, and yield 10 percent; interest is payable each July 1 and January 1.

The journal entries in 2011 are exactly the same as those for amortized cost. These entries are as follows.

January 1, 2011

Debt Investments	92,278	
Cash		92,278

July 1, 2011

Cash	4,000	
Debt Investments		614
Interest Revenue		4,614

December 31, 2011

Interest Receivable	4,000	
Debt Investments		645
Interest Revenue		4,645

Again, Illustration 17-2 shows the interest and amortization amounts. If the debt investment is held-for-collection, no further entries are necessary. To apply the fair value approach, Robinson determines that, due to a decrease in interest rates, the fair value of the debt investment increased to $95,000 at December 31, 2011. Comparing the fair value with the carrying amount of these bonds at December 31, 2011, Robinson has an unrealized holding gain of $1,463, as shown in Illustration 17-5.

ILLUSTRATION 17-5
Computation of Unrealized Gain on Fair Value Debt Investment (2011)

Fair value at December 31, 2011	$95,000
Amortized cost at December 31, 2011 (per Illustration 17-2)	93,537
Unrealized holding gain or (loss)	$ 1,463

[4]Companies may incur brokerage and transaction costs in purchasing securities. For investments accounted for at fair value (both debt and equity), IFRS requires that these costs be recorded in net income as other income and expense and not as an adjustment to the carrying value of the investment. **[7]**

Robinson therefore makes the following entry to record the adjustment of the debt investment to fair value at December 31, 2011.

Securities Fair Value Adjustment	1,463	
Unrealized Holding Gain or Loss—Income		1,463

Robinson uses a valuation account (**Securities Fair Value Adjustment**) instead of debiting Debt Investments to record the investment at fair value. The use of the Securities Fair Value Adjustment account enables Robinson to maintain a record at amortized cost in the accounts. Because the valuation account has a debit balance, in this case the fair value of Robinson's debt investment is higher than its amortized cost.

The Unrealized Holding Gain or Loss—Income account is reported in the other income and expense section of the income statement as part of net income. This account is closed to net income each period. The Securities Fair Value Adjustment account is not closed each period and is simply adjusted each period to its proper valuation. The Securities Fair Value Adjustment balance is not shown on the statement of financial position but is simply used to restate the debt investment account to fair value.

Robinson reports its investment in Evermaster bonds in its December 31, 2011, financial statements as shown in Illustration 17-6.

ILLUSTRATION 17-6
Financial Statement Presentation of Debt Investments at Fair Value

Statement of Financial Position	
Investments	
Debt investments	$95,000
Current assets	
Interest receivable	$ 4,000
Income Statement	
Other income and expense	
Interest revenue ($4,614 + $4,645)	$ 9,259
Unrealized holding gain or (loss)	1,463

Continuing with our example, at December 31, 2012, assume that the fair value of the Evermaster debt investment is $94,000. In this case, Robinson records an unrealized holding loss of $2,388, as shown in Illustration 17-7.

ILLUSTRATION 17-7
Computation of Unrealized Gain on Debt Investment (2012)

DEBT INVESTMENTS **DECEMBER 31, 2012**			
Investment	Amortized Cost	Fair Value	Unrealized Gain (Loss)
Evermaster Corporation 10% bonds	$94,925	$94,000	$ (925)
Less: Previous securities fair value adjustment balance (Dr.)			1,463
Securities fair value adjustment (Cr.)			$(2,388)

As indicated in Illustration 17-7, the fair value of the debt investment is now less than the amortized cost by $925. However, Robinson had recorded an unrealized gain in 2011. Therefore, Robinson records a loss of $2,388 ($925 + $1,463), which offsets the gain recorded in 2011, resulting in a credit in the Securities Fair Value Adjustment account of $925. Robinson makes the following journal entry.

Unrealized Holding Gain or Loss—Income	2,388	
Securities Fair Value Adjustment		2,388

A credit balance in the Securities Fair Value Adjustment account of $925 ($2,388 − $1,463) reduces the amortized cost amount to fair value. Robinson reports its investment in Evermaster bonds in its December 31, 2012, financial statements as shown in Illustration 17-8.

ILLUSTRATION 17-8
Financial Statement
Presentation of Debt
Investments at Fair
Value (2012)

Statement of Financial Position	
Investments	
Debt investments	$94,000
Current assets	
Interest receivable	$ 4,000
Income Statement	
Other income and expense	
Interest revenue ($4,677 + $4,711)	$ 9,388
Unrealized holding gain or (loss)	$ (2,388)

Assume now that Robinson sells its investment in Evermaster bonds on November 1, 2013, at 99¾ plus accrued interest, similar to our earlier illustration on page 885. All the entries and computations are the same as the amortized cost example. The only difference occurs on December 31, 2013. In that case, since the bonds are no longer owned by Robinson, the Securities Fair Value Adjustment account should now be reported at zero. Robinson makes the following entry to record the elimination of the valuation account.

Securities Fair Value Adjustment	925	
Unrealized Holding Gain or Loss—Income		925

ILLUSTRATION 17-9
Income Effects on Debt
Investment (2011–2013)

At December 31, 2013, the income related to the Evermaster bonds is as shown in Illustration 17-9.

	Amortized Cost				Fair Value			
Years	Interest	Gain on Sale	Unrealized Gain (Loss)	Total	Interest	Gain on Sale	Unrealized Gain (Loss)	Total
2011	$ 9,259	$ 0	$0	$ 9,259	$ 9,259	$ 0	$1,463	$10,722
2012	9,388	0	0	9,388	9,388	0	(2,388)	7,000
2013	7,935	3,557	0	11,492	7,935	3,557	925	12,417
Total	$26,582	$3,557	$0	$30,139	$26,582	$3,557	$ 0	$30,139

As indicated, over the life of the bond investment, interest revenue and the gain on sale are the same using either amortized cost or fair value measurement. However, under the fair value approach, an unrealized gain or loss is recorded in each year as the fair value of the investment changes; overall, the gains or losses net out to zero.

WHAT IS FAIR VALUE?

What do the numbers mean?

In the fall of 2000, Wall Street brokerage firm **Morgan Stanley** (USA) told investors that the rumor of big losses in its bond portfolio were "greatly exaggerated." As it turns out, Morgan Stanley was also exaggerating. As a result, the U.S. SEC accused Morgan Stanley of violating securities laws by overstating the value of certain bonds by $75 million. The SEC said that the overvaluations stemmed more from wishful thinking than reality, in violation of accounting standards. The SEC wrote, "In effect, Morgan Stanley valued its positions at the price at which it thought a willing buyer and seller should enter into an exchange, rather than at a price at which a willing buyer and a willing seller would enter into a **current** exchange."

Especially egregious, stated one accounting expert, were the findings that Morgan Stanley in some instances used its own more optimistic assumptions as a substitute for external pricing sources. "What that is saying is: 'Fair value is what you want the value to be. Pick a number. . . .' That's especially troublesome."

As indicated in the text, both the IASB and the FASB are assessing what is fair and what isn't when it comes to assigning valuations. Concerns over the issue caught fire after the collapses of **Enron Corp.** (USA) and other energy traders that abused the wide discretion given them under fair value accounting. Investors have expressed similar worries about some financial companies, which use internal—and subjectively designed—mathematical models to come up with valuations when market quotes aren't available.

Source: Adapted from Susanne Craig and Jonathan Weil, "SEC Targets Morgan Stanley Values," *Wall Street Journal* (November 8, 2004), p. C3. See also *http://www.iasb.org/Current+Projects/IASB+Projects/Fair+Value+Measurement/ Fair+Value+Measurement.htm* for the latest information on the IASB fair value project.

Example: Debt Investment at Fair Value (Portfolio)

To illustrate the accounting for a portfolio of debt investments, assume that Webb Corporation has two debt investments accounted for at fair value. Illustration 17-10 identifies the amortized cost, fair value, and the amount of the unrealized gain or loss.

DEBT INVESTMENT PORTFOLIO DECEMBER 31, 2011			
Investments	Amortized Cost	Fair Value	Unrealized Gain (Loss)
Watson Corporation 8% bonds	$ 93,537	$103,600	$ 10,063
Anacomp Corporation 10% bonds	200,000	180,400	(19,600)
Total of portfolio	$293,537	$284,000	(9,537)
Previous securities fair value adjustment balance			–0–
Securities fair value adjustment—Cr.			$ (9,537)

ILLUSTRATION 17-10
Computation of Securities Fair Value Adjustment—Fair Value Debt Investments (2011)

The fair value of Webb's debt investment portfolio totals $284,000. The gross unrealized gains are $10,063, and the gross unrealized losses are $19,600, resulting in a net unrealized loss of $9,537. That is, the fair value of the portfolio is $9,537 lower than its amortized cost. Webb makes an adjusting entry to the Securities Fair Value Adjustment account to record the decrease in value and to record the loss as follows.

December 31, 2011		
Unrealized Holding Gain or Loss—Income	9,537	
Securities Fair Value Adjustment		9,537

Webb reports the unrealized holding loss of $9,537 in income.

Sale of Debt Investments

If a company sells bonds carried as fair value investments before the maturity date, it must make entries to remove from the Debt Investments account the amortized cost of bonds sold. To illustrate, assume that Webb Corporation sold the Watson bonds (from

Illustration 17-10) on July 1, 2012, for $90,000, at which time it had an amortized cost of $94,214. Illustration 17-11 shows the computation of the realized loss.

ILLUSTRATION 17-11
Computation of Loss on
Sale of Bonds

Amortized cost (Watson bonds)	$94,214
Less: Selling price of bonds	90,000
Loss on sale of bonds	$ 4,214

Webb records the sale of the Watson bonds as follows.

July 1, 2012

Cash	90,000	
Loss on Sale of Debt Investment	4,214	
Debt Investments		94,214

Webb reports this realized loss in the "Other income and expense" section of the income statement. Assuming no other purchases and sales of bonds in 2012, Webb on December 31, 2012, has the information shown in Illustration 17-12.

ILLUSTRATION 17-12
Computation of Securities
Fair Value Adjustment
(2012)

DEBT INVESTMENT PORTFOLIO DECEMBER 31, 2012			
Investments	Amortized Cost	Fair Value	Unrealized Gain (Loss)
Anacomp Corporation 10% bonds (total portfolio)	$200,000	$195,000	$(5,000)
Previous securities fair value adjustment balance—Cr.			(9,537)
Securities fair value adjustment—Dr.			$ 4,537

Webb has an unrealized holding loss of $5,000. However, the Securities Fair Value Adjustment account already has a credit balance of $9,537. To reduce the adjustment account balance to $5,000, Webb debits it for $4,537, as follows.

December 31, 2012

Securities Fair Value Adjustment	4,537	
Unrealized Holding Gain or Loss—Income		4,537

Financial Statement Presentation

Webb's December 31, 2012, statement of financial position and the 2012 income statement include the following items and amounts (the Anacomp bonds are current assets because they are held for trading).

ILLUSTRATION 17-13
Reporting of Debt
Investments at Fair Value

Statement of Financial Position	
Investments	
Debt Investments, at fair value	$195,000
Current assets	
Interest receivable	$ xxx
Income Statement	
Other income and expense	
Interest revenue	$ xxx
Loss on sale of investments	4,214
Unrealized gain or loss	4,537

FAIR VALUE OPTION

In some situations, a company meets the criteria for accounting for a debt investment at amortized cost, but it would rather account for the investment at fair value, with all gains and losses related to changes in fair value reported in income. The most common reason is to address a measurement or recognition "mismatch." For example, assume that **Pirelli** (ITA) purchases debt investments that it plans to manage on a held-for-collection basis (and account for at amortized cost). Pirelli also manages and evaluates this investment in conjunction with a related liability that is measured at fair value. Pirelli has a mismatch on these related financial assets because, even though the fair value of the investment may change, no gains and losses are recognized, while gains and losses on the liability are recorded in income.

> **Objective·4**
> Describe the accounting for the fair value option.

To address this mismatch, **companies have the option to report most financial assets at fair value**. This option is applied on an instrument-by-instrument basis and is generally available only at the time a company first purchases the financial asset or incurs a financial liability. If a company chooses to use the fair value option, it measures this instrument at fair value until the company no longer has ownership. **[8]** By choosing the fair value option for the debt investment, Pirelli records gains and losses in income, which will offset the gains and losses recorded on the liability, thereby providing more relevant information about these related financial assets.

To illustrate, assume that Hardy Company purchases bonds issued by the German Central Bank. Hardy plans to hold the debt investment until it matures in five years. At December 31, 2011, the amortized cost of this investment is €100,000; its fair value at December 31, 2011, is €113,000. If Hardy chooses the fair value option to account for this investment, it makes the following entry at December 31, 2011.

Debt Investment—German Bonds	13,000	
Unrealized Holding Gain or Loss—Income		13,000

In this situation, Hardy uses an account titled Debt Investment—German Bonds to record the change in fair value at December 31. It does not use a Securities Fair Value Adjustment account because the accounting for the fair value option is on an investment-by-investment basis rather than on a portfolio basis. Because Hardy selected the fair value option, the unrealized gain or loss is recorded as part of net income even though it is managing the investment on a held-for-collection basis. Hardy must continue to use the fair value method to record this investment until it no longer has ownership of the security.

SUMMARY OF DEBT INVESTMENT ACCOUNTING

The following chart illustrates the basic accounting for debt investments.

ILLUSTRATION 17-14
Summary of Debt Investment Accounting

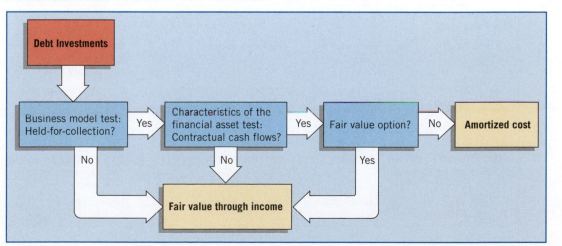

SECTION 2 • EQUITY INVESTMENTS

Objective•5
Understand the accounting for equity investments at fair value.

An **equity investment** represents ownership interest, such as ordinary, preference, or other capital shares. It also includes rights to acquire or dispose of ownership interests at an agreed-upon or determinable price, such as in warrants and rights. The cost of equity investments is measured at the purchase price of the security. Broker's commissions and other fees incidental to the purchase are recorded as expense. [9]

The degree to which one corporation (**investor**) acquires an interest in the shares of another corporation (**investee**) generally determines the accounting treatment for the investment subsequent to acquisition. The classification of such investments depends on the percentage of the investee voting shares that is held by the investor:

1. Holdings of less than 20 percent (**fair value method**)—investor has passive interest.
2. Holdings between 20 percent and 50 percent (**equity method**)—investor has significant influence.
3. Holdings of more than 50 percent (**consolidated statements**)—investor has controlling interest.

Illustration 17-15 lists these levels of interest or influence and the corresponding valuation and reporting method that companies must apply to the investment.

ILLUSTRATION 17-15
Levels of Influence Determine Accounting Methods

Percentage of Ownership	0% ⟷	20% ⟷	50% ⟷	100%
Level of Influence	Little or None	Significant	Control	
Valuation Method	Fair Value Method	Equity Method	Consolidation	

The accounting and reporting for equity investments therefore depend on the level of influence and the type of security involved, as shown in Illustration 17-16.

ILLUSTRATION 17-16
Accounting and Reporting for Equity Investments by Category

Category	Valuation	Unrealized Holding Gains or Losses	Other Income Effects
Holdings less than 20%			
1. Trading	Fair value	Recognized in net income	Dividends declared; gains and losses from sale.
2. Non-Trading	Fair value	Recognized in "Other comprehensive income" and as separate component of equity	Dividends declared; gains and losses from sale.
Holdings between 20% and 50%	Equity	Not recognized	Proportionate share of investee's net income.
Holdings more than 50%	Consolidation	Not recognized	Not applicable.

EQUITY INVESTMENTS AT FAIR VALUE

When an investor has an interest of less than 20 percent, it is presumed that the investor has little or no influence over the investee. As indicated in Illustration 17-16, there are two classifications for holdings less than 20 percent. Under IFRS, the presumption is that equity investments are held-for-trading. That is, companies hold these securities to profit from price changes. As with debt investments that are held-for-trading, the general accounting and reporting rule for these investments is to value the securities at fair value and record unrealized gains and losses in net income (**fair value method**).[5]

However, some equity investments are held for purposes other than trading. For example, a company may be required to hold an equity investment in order to sell its products in a particular area. In this situation, the recording of unrealized gains and losses in income, as is required for trading investments, is not indicative of the company's performance with respect to this investment. As a result, IFRS allows companies to classify some equity investments as non-trading. **Non-trading equity investments** are recorded at fair value on the statement of financial position, with unrealized gains and losses reported in other comprehensive income. **[11]**

Example: Equity Investment (Income)   *Trading*

Upon acquisition, companies record equity investments at fair value.[6] To illustrate, assume that on November 3, 2011, Republic Corporation purchased ordinary shares of three companies, each investment representing less than a 20 percent interest.

	Cost
Burberry	€259,700
Nestlé	317,500
St. Regis Pulp Co.	141,350
Total cost	€718,550

Republic records these investments as follows.

November 3, 2011

| Equity Investments | 718,550 | |
| Cash | | 718,550 |

On December 6, 2011, Republic receives a cash dividend of €4,200 on its investment in the ordinary shares of Nestlé. It records the cash dividend as follows.

December 6, 2011

| Cash | 4,200 | |
| Dividend Revenue | | 4,200 |

---

[5]Fair value at initial recognition is the transaction price (exclusive of brokerage and other transaction costs). Subsequent fair value measurements should be based on market prices, if available. For non-trading investments, a valuation technique based on discounted expected cash flows can be used to develop a fair value estimate. While IFRS requires that all equity investments be measured at fair value, in certain limited cases, cost may be an appropriate estimate of fair value for an equity investment. **[10]**

[6]Companies should record equity investments acquired in **exchange for non-cash consideration** (property or services) at the fair value of the consideration given, if the fair value can be measured reliably. Otherwise, the value of the exchange can be determined with reference to the fair value of the equity investment. Accounting for numerous purchases of securities requires the preservation of information regarding the cost of individual purchases, as well as the dates of purchases and sales. If **specific identification** is not possible, companies may use an **average cost** for multiple purchases of the same class of security. The **first-in, first-out** method (FIFO) of assigning costs to investments at the time of sale is also acceptable and normally employed.

All three of the investee companies reported net income for the year, but only Nestlé declared and paid a dividend to Republic. But, recall that when an investor owns less than 20 percent of the shares of another corporation, it is presumed that the investor has relatively little influence on the investee. As a result, **net income earned by the investee is not a proper basis for recognizing income from the investment by the investor**. Why? Because the increased net assets resulting from profitable operations may be permanently retained for use in the investee's business. Therefore, **the investor earns net income only when the investee declares cash dividends**.

At December 31, 2011, Republic's equity investment portfolio has the carrying value and fair value shown in Illustration 17-17.

ILLUSTRATION 17-17
Computation of Securities Fair Value Adjustment— Equity Investment Portfolio (2011)

EQUITY INVESTMENT PORTFOLIO DECEMBER 31, 2011			
Investments	Carrying Value	Fair Value	Unrealized Gain (Loss)
Burberry	€259,700	€275,000	€ 15,300
Nestlé	317,500	304,000	(13,500)
St. Regis Pulp Co.	141,350	104,000	(37,350)
Total of portfolio	€718,550	€683,000	(35,550)
Previous securities fair value adjustment balance			–0–
Securities fair value adjustment—Cr.			€(35,550)

For Republic's equity investment portfolio, the gross unrealized gains are €15,300, and the gross unrealized losses are €50,850 (€13,500 + €37,350), resulting in a net unrealized loss of €35,550. The fair value of the equity investment portfolio is below cost by €35,550.

As with **debt** investments, Republic records the net unrealized gains and losses related to changes in the fair value of **equity** investments in an Unrealized Holding Gain or Loss—Income account. Republic reports this amount as other income and expense. In this case, Republic prepares an adjusting entry debiting the Unrealized Holding Gain or Loss—Income account and crediting the Securities Fair Value Adjustment account to record the decrease in fair value and to record the loss as follows.

December 31, 2011

Unrealized Holding Gain or Loss—Income	35,550	
Securities Fair Value Adjustment		35,550

On January 23, 2012, Republic sold all of its Burberry ordinary shares, receiving €287,220. Illustration 17-18 shows the computation of the realized gain on the sale.

ILLUSTRATION 17-18
Computation of Gain on Sale of Burberry Shares

Net proceeds from sale	€287,220
Cost of Burberry shares	259,700
Gain on sale of shares	€ 27,520

Republic records the sale as follows.

January 23, 2012

Cash	287,220	
Equity Investments		259,700
Gain on Sale of Equity Investment		27,520

In addition, assume that on February 10, 2012, Republic purchased €255,000 of Continental Trucking ordinary shares (20,000 shares × €12.75 per share), plus brokerage commissions of €1,850.

Illustration 17-19 lists Republic's equity investment portfolio as of December 31, 2012.

ILLUSTRATION 17-19
Computation of Securities Fair Value Adjustment—Equity Investment Portfolio (2012)

EQUITY INVESTMENT PORTFOLIO DECEMBER 31, 2012			
Investments	Carrying Value	Fair Value	Unrealized Gain (Loss)
Continental Trucking	€255,000ª	€278,350	€ 23,350
Nestlé	317,500	362,550	45,050
St. Regis Pulp Co.	141,350	139,050	(2,300)
Total of portfolio	€713,850	€779,950	66,100
Previous securities fair value adjustment balance—Cr.			(35,550)
Securities fair value adjustment—Dr.			€101,650

ªThe brokerage commissions are expensed.

At December 31, 2012, the fair value of Republic's equity investment portfolio exceeds carrying value by €66,100 (unrealized gain). The Securities Fair Value Adjustment account had a credit balance of €35,550 at December 31, 2012. To adjust its December 31, 2012, equity investment portfolio to fair value, the company debits the Securities Fair Value Adjustment account for €101,650 (€35,550 + €66,100). Republic records this adjustment as follows.

December 31, 2012

Securities Fair Value Adjustment	101,650	
Unrealized Holding Gain or Loss—Income		101,650

Example: Equity Investments (OCI)

The accounting entries to record non-trading equity investments are the same as for trading equity investments, except for recording the unrealized holding gain or loss. For non-trading equity investments, companies **report the unrealized holding gain or loss as other comprehensive income**. Thus, the account titled Unrealized Holding Gain or Loss—Equity is used.

To illustrate, assume that on December 10, 2011, Republic Corporation purchased 1,000 ordinary shares of Hawthorne Company for €20.75 per share (total cost €20,750). The investment represents less than a 20 percent interest. Hawthorne is a distributor for Republic products in certain locales, the laws of which require a minimum level of share ownership of a company in that region. The investment in Hawthorne meets this regulatory requirement. As a result, Republic accounts for this investment at fair value, with unrealized gains and losses recorded in other comprehensive income (OCI).[7] Republic records this investment as follows.

December 10, 2011

Equity Investments	20,750	
Cash		20,750

[7]The classification of an equity investment as non-trading is irrevocable. This approach is designed to provide some discipline to the application of the non-trading classification, which allows unrealized gains and losses to bypass net income. **[12]**

On December 27, 2011, Republic receives a cash dividend of €450 on its investment in the ordinary shares of Hawthorne Company. It records the cash dividend as follows.

December 27, 2011

Cash	450	
Dividend Revenue		450

Similar to the accounting for trading investments, when an investor owns less than 20 percent of the ordinary shares of another corporation, it is presumed that the investor has relatively little influence on the investee. Therefore, **the investor earns income when the investee declares cash dividends**.

At December 31, 2011, Republic's investment in Hawthorne has the carrying value and fair value shown in Illustration 17-20.

ILLUSTRATION 17-20
Computation of Securities Fair Value Adjustment—Non-Trading Equity Investment (2011)

Non-Trading Equity Investment	Carrying Value	Fair Value	Unrealized Gain (Loss)
Hawthorne Company	€20,750	€24,000	€3,250
Previous securities fair value adjustment balance			0
Securities fair value adjustment (Dr.)			€3,250

For Republic's non-trading investment, the unrealized gain is €3,250. That is, the fair value of the Hawthorne investment exceeds cost by €3,250. Because Republic has classified this investment as non-trading, Republic records the unrealized gains and losses related to changes in the fair value of this non-trading **equity** investment in an Unrealized Holding Gain or Loss—Equity account. Republic reports this amount as **a part of other comprehensive income and as a component of other accumulated comprehensive income (reported in equity) until realized**. In this case, Republic prepares an adjusting entry crediting the Unrealized Holding Gain or Loss—Equity account and debiting the Securities Fair Value Adjustment account to record the increase in fair value and to record the gain as follows.

December 31, 2011

Securities Fair Value Adjustment	3,250	
Unrealized Holding Gain or Loss—Equity		3,250

Republic reports its equity investments in its December 31, 2011, financial statements as shown in Illustration 17-21.

ILLUSTRATION 17-21
Financial Statement Presentation of Equity Investments at Fair Value (2011)

Statement of Financial Position	
Investments	
Equity investments	€24,000
Equity	
Accumulated other comprehensive gain	€ 3,250
Statement of Comprehensive Income	
Other income and expense	
Dividend revenue	€ 450
Other comprehensive income	
Unrealized holding gain	€ 3,250

During 2012, sales of Republic products through Hawthorne as a distributor did not meet management's goals. As a result, Republic withdrew from these markets and on December 20, 2012, Republic sold all of its Hawthorne Company ordinary shares, receiving net proceeds of €22,500. Illustration 17-22 shows the computation of the realized gain on the sale.

ILLUSTRATION 17-22
Computation of Gain on Sale of Shares

Net proceeds from sale	€22,500	
Cost of Hawthorne shares	20,750	
Gain on sale of shares	€ 1,750	

Republic records the sale as follows.

December 20, 2012

Cash	22,500	
Equity Investments		20,750
Gain on Sale of Equity Investment		1,750

Because Republic no longer holds any equity investments, it makes the following entry to eliminate the Securities Fair Value Adjustment account.[8]

Unrealized Holding Gain or Loss—Equity	3,250	
Securities Fair Value Adjustment		3,250

In summary, the accounting for non-trading equity investments deviates from the general provisions for equity investments. The IASB noted that while fair value provides the most useful information about investments in equity investments, recording unrealized gains or losses in other comprehensive income is more representative for non-trading equity investments. [14]

EQUITY METHOD

An investor corporation may hold an interest of less than 50 percent in an investee corporation and thus not possess legal control. However, an investment in voting shares of less than 50 percent can still give an investor the ability to exercise significant influence over the operating and financial policies of an investee. [15] For example, **Siemens AG** (DEU) owns 34 percent of **Areva** (FRA) (which constructs power plants). Areva is very important to Siemens because the power industry is a key customer for its generators and other power-related products. Thus, Siemens has a significant (but not controlling) ownership stake in a power plant construction company, which helps Siemens push its products into the market. **Significant influence** may be indicated in several ways. Examples include representation on the board of directors, participation in policy-making processes, material intercompany transactions, interchange of managerial personnel, or technological dependency.

Another important consideration is the extent of ownership by an investor in relation to the concentration of other shareholdings. To achieve a reasonable degree of uniformity in application of the "significant influence" criterion, the profession concluded that an investment (direct or indirect) of 20 percent or more of the voting shares

Objective·6

Explain the equity method of accounting and compare it to the fair value method for equity investments.

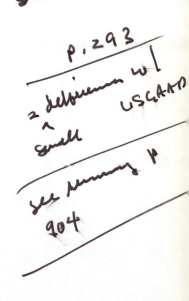

---

[8]Once non-trading equity investments are sold, companies may transfer the balance of unrealized holding gains or losses in accumulated other comprehensive income to retained earnings. Transferring the balance to retained earnings has merit, as these gains or losses would have been recorded in net income in a prior period if these securities were accounted for as trading securities. Some contend that these unrealized gains or losses should be "recycled"; that is, these amounts should be recorded in net income when a non-trading investment is sold. The IASB rejected this approach because it would increase the complexity of the accounting for these investments. [13]

of an investee should lead to a presumption that in the absence of evidence to the contrary, an investor has the ability to exercise significant influence over an investee.[9]

In instances of "significant influence" (generally an investment of 20 percent or more), the investor must account for the investment using the **equity method**.

Example: Equity Method

Under the equity method, the investor and the investee acknowledge a substantive economic relationship. The company originally records the investment at the cost of the shares acquired but subsequently adjusts the amount each period for changes in the investee's net assets. That is, **the investor's proportionate share of the earnings (losses) of the investee periodically increases (decreases) the investment's carrying amount. All dividends received by the investor from the investee also decrease the investment's carrying amount.** The equity method recognizes that investee's earnings increase investee's net assets, and that investee's losses and dividends decrease these net assets.

To illustrate the equity method and compare it with the fair value method, assume that Maxi Company purchases a 20 percent interest in Mini Company. To apply the fair value method in this example, assume that Maxi does not have the ability to exercise significant influence, and classifies the investment as trading. Where this example applies the equity method, assume that the 20 percent interest permits Maxi to exercise significant influence. Illustration 17-23 (page 899) shows the entries.

Note that under the **fair value method**, Maxi reports as revenue only the cash dividends received from Mini. **The earning of net income by Mini (the investee) is not considered a proper basis for recognition of income from the investment by Maxi (the investor).** Why? Mini may permanently retain in the business any increased net assets resulting from its profitable operation. Therefore, Maxi only earns revenue when it receives dividends from Mini.

Under the **equity method**, Maxi reports as revenue its share of the net income reported by Mini. Maxi records the cash dividends received from Mini as a decrease in the investment carrying value. As a result, Maxi records its share of the net income of Mini in the year when it is earned. With significant influence, Maxi can ensure that Mini will pay dividends, if desired, on any net asset increases resulting from net income. To wait until receiving a dividend ignores the fact that Maxi is better off if the investee has earned income.

Using dividends as a basis for recognizing income poses an additional problem. For example, assume that the investee reports a net loss. However, the investor exerts influence to force a dividend payment from the investee. In this case, the investor reports income, even though the investee is experiencing a loss. **In other words, using dividends as a basis for recognizing income fails to report properly the economics of the situation.**

For some companies, equity accounting can be a real pain to the bottom line. For example, **Amazon.com** (USA), the pioneer of Internet retailing, at one time struggled to turn a profit. Furthermore, some of Amazon's equity investments had resulted in Amazon's earnings performance going from bad to worse. In a recent year, Amazon.com

---

[9]Cases in which an investment of 20 percent or more might not enable an investor to exercise significant influence include:
 (1) The investee opposes the investor's acquisition of its shares.
 (2) The investor and investee sign an agreement under which the investor surrenders significant shareholder rights.
 (3) The investor's ownership share does not result in "significant influence" because majority ownership of the investee is concentrated among a small group of shareholders who operate the investee without regard to the views of the investor.
 (4) The investor tries and fails to obtain representation on the investee's board of directors. [16]

ENTRIES BY MAXI COMPANY

Fair Value Method		Equity Method	
On January 2, 2011, Maxi Company acquired 48,000 shares (20% of Mini Company ordinary shares) at a cost of $10 a share.			
Equity Investments	480,000	Equity Investments	480,000
Cash	480,000	Cash	480,000
For the year 2011, Mini Company reported net income of $200,000; Maxi Company's share is 20%, or $40,000.			
No entry		Equity Investments	40,000
		Revenue from Investment	40,000
At December 31, 2011, the 48,000 shares of Mini Company have a fair value (market price) of $12 a share, or $576,000.			
Securities Fair Value Adjustment	96,000	No entry	
Unrealized Holding Gain			
or Loss—Income	96,000		
On January 28, 2012, Mini Company announced and paid a cash dividend of $100,000; Maxi Company received 20%, or $20,000.			
Cash	20,000	Cash	20,000
Dividend Revenue	20,000	Equity Investments	20,000
For the year 2012, Mini reported a net loss of $50,000; Maxi Company's share is 20%, or $10,000.			
No entry		Loss on Investment	10,000
		Equity Investments	10,000
At December 31, 2012, the Mini Company 48,000 shares have a fair value (market price) of $11 a share, or $528,000.			
Unrealized Holding Gain		No entry	
or Loss—Income	48,000		
Securities Fair Value Adjustment			
($528,000 − $480,000)	48,000		

ILLUSTRATION 17-23
Comparison of Fair Value Method and Equity Method

disclosed equity stakes in such companies as **Altera International** (USA), **Basis Technology** (USA), **Drugstore.com** (USA), and **Eziba.com** (USA). These equity investees reported losses that made Amazon's already bad bottom line even worse, accounting for up to 22 percent of its reported loss in one year alone.

Investee Losses Exceed Carrying Amount

If an investor's share of the investee's losses exceeds the carrying amount of the investment, should the investor recognize additional losses? Ordinarily, the investor should discontinue applying the equity method and not recognize additional losses.

If the investor's potential loss is not limited to the amount of its original investment (by guarantee of the investee's obligations or other commitment to provide further financial support), or if imminent return to profitable operations by the investee appears to be assured, the investor should recognize additional losses. **[17]**

Underlying Concepts

A low level of ownership indicates that a company should defer the income from an investee until cash is received because such revenue may not meet recognition criteria.

CONSOLIDATION

When one corporation acquires a voting interest of more than 50 percent in another corporation, it is said to have a **controlling interest**. In such a relationship, the investor corporation is referred to as the **parent** and the investee corporation as the **subsidiary**. Companies present the investment in the ordinary shares of the subsidiary as a long-term investment on the separate financial statements of the parent.

When the parent treats the subsidiary as an investment, the parent generally prepares **consolidated financial statements**. Consolidated financial statements treat the parent and subsidiary corporations as a single economic entity. (Advanced accounting courses extensively discuss the subject of when and how to prepare consolidated financial statements.) Whether or not consolidated financial statements are prepared, the parent company generally accounts for the investment in the subsidiary **using the equity method** as explained in the previous section of this chapter.

WHO'S IN CONTROL HERE?

What do the numbers mean?

Lenovo Group (CHN) owns a significant percentage (45 percent) of the shares of Beijing Lenovo Parasaga Information Technology Co. (CHN) (which develops and distributes computer software). Beijing Lenovo is important to Lenovo because it develops and sells the software that is used with Lenovo computers. In return, Beijing Lenovo depends on Lenovo to provide the products that make its software and services valuable, as well as significant customer and market support. Indeed, it can be said that to some extent, Lenovo controls Beijing Lenovo, which would likely not exist without the support of Lenovo.

As you have learned, because Lenovo owns less than 50 percent of the shares, Lenovo does not consolidate Beijing Lenovo, but instead it accounts for its investment using the *equity method*. Under the equity method, Lenovo reports a single income item for its profits from Beijing Lenovo and only the net amount of its investment in the statement of financial position. Equity method accounting gives Lenovo a pristine statement of financial position and income statement, by separating the assets and liabilities and the profit margins of the related companies from its laptop-computer businesses.

Some are critical of equity method accounting; they argue that some investees, like Beijing Lenovo, should be consolidated. The IASB and the FASB have been working to tighten up consolidation rules, so that companies will be more likely to consolidate more of their 20 to 50 percent-owned investments. Consolidation of entities, such as for Beijing Lenovo, is warranted if Lenovo effectively controls its equity method investments. See *http://www.iasb.org/Current+Projects/IASB+Projects/Consolidation/Consolidation.htm* for more information on the consolidation project.

SECTION 3 • OTHER REPORTING ISSUES

We have identified the basic issues involved in accounting for investments in debt and equity securities. In addition, the following issues relate to the accounting for investments.

1. Impairment of value.
2. Transfers between categories.
3. Fair value controversy.

IMPAIRMENT OF VALUE

Objective·7

Discuss the accounting for impairments of debt investments.

A company should evaluate every held-for-collection investment, at each reporting date, to determine if it has suffered **impairment**—a loss in value such that the fair value of the investment is below its carrying value.[10] For example, if an investee experiences a bankruptcy or a significant liquidity crisis, the investor may

---

[10]Note that impairments tests are conducted only for debt investments that are held-for-collection (which are accounted for at amortized cost). Other debt and equity investments are measured at fair value each period; thus, an impairment test is not needed.

suffer a permanent loss. **If the company determines that an investment is impaired, it writes down the amortized cost basis of the individual security to reflect this loss in value.** The company accounts for the write-down as a realized loss, and it includes the amount in net income.

For debt investments, a company uses the impairment test to determine whether "it is probable that the investor will be unable to collect all amounts due according to the contractual terms." If an investment is impaired, the company should measure the loss due to the **impairment**. This impairment loss is calculated as the difference between the carrying amount plus accrued interest and the expected future cash flows discounted at the investment's historical effective-interest rate. **[18]**

Example: Impairment Loss

At December 31, 2010, Mayhew Company has a debt investment in Bellovary Inc., purchased at par for $200,000. The investment has a term of four years, with annual interest payments at 10 percent, paid at the end of each year (the historical effective-interest rate is 10 percent). This debt investment is classified as held-for-collection. Unfortunately, Bellovary is experiencing significant financial difficulty and indicates that it will be unable to make all payments according to the contractual terms. Mayhew uses the present value method for measuring the required impairment loss. Illustration 17-24 shows the cash flow schedule prepared for this analysis.

Dec. 31	Contractual Cash Flows	Expected Cash Flows	Loss of Cash Flows
2011	$ 20,000	$ 16,000	$ 4,000
2012	20,000	16,000	4,000
2013	20,000	16,000	4,000
2014	220,000	216,000	4,000
Total cash flows	$280,000	$264,000	$16,000

ILLUSTRATION 17-24
Investment Cash Flows

As indicated, the expected cash flows of $264,000 are less than the contractual cash flows of $280,000. The amount of the impairment to be recorded equals the difference between the recorded investment of $200,000 and the present value of the expected cash flows, as shown in Illustration 17-25.

Recorded investment		$200,000
Less: Present value of $200,000 due in 4 years at 10%		
(Table 6-2); $FV(PVF_{4,10\%})$; ($200,000 × .68301)	$136,602	
Present value of $16,000 interest receivable annually		
for 4 years at 10% (Table 6-4); $R(PVF\text{-}OA_{4,10\%})$;		
($16,000 × 3.16986)	50,718	187,312
Loss on impairment		$ 12,688

ILLUSTRATION 17-25
Computation of Impairment Loss

The loss due to the impairment is $12,688.[11] Why isn't it $16,000 ($280,000 − $264,000)? A loss of $12,688 is recorded because Mayhew must measure the loss at a present value amount, not at an undiscounted amount. Mayhew recognizes an impairment loss of $12,688 by debiting Loss on Impairment for the expected loss. At the same time, it reduces the overall value of the investment. The journal entry to record the loss is therefore as follows.

Loss on Impairment	12,688	
Debt Investments		12,688

[11]Many question this present value calculation because it uses the investment's historical effective-interest rate—not the current market rate. As a result, the present value computation does not reflect the fair value of the debt investment, and many believe the impairment loss is misstated.

Recovery of Impairment Loss

Subsequent to recording an impairment, events or economic conditions may change such that the extent of the impairment loss decreases (e.g., due to an improvement in the debtor's credit rating). In this situation, some or all of the previously recognized impairment loss shall be reversed with a debit to the Debt Investments account and crediting Recovery of Impairment Loss. Similar to the accounting for impairments of receivables shown in Chapter 7, the reversal of impairment losses shall not result in a carrying amount of the investment that exceeds the amortized cost that would have been reported had the impairment not been recognized.

TRANSFERS BETWEEN CATEGORIES

Objective·8

Describe the accounting for transfer of investments between categories.

Transferring an investment from one classification to another should occur only when the business model for managing the investment changes. The IASB expects such changes to be rare. [19] Companies account for transfers between classifications prospectively, at the beginning of the accounting period after the change in the business model.[12]

To illustrate, assume that **British Sky Broadcasting Group plc** (GBR) has a portfolio of debt investments that are classified as trading; that is, the debt investments are not held-for-collection but managed to profit from interest rate changes. As a result, it accounts for these investments at fair value. At December 31, 2010, British Sky has the following balances related to these securities.

Debt investments	£1,200,000
Securities fair value adjustment	125,000
Carrying value	£1,325,000

As part of its strategic planning process, completed in the fourth quarter of 2010, British Sky management decides to move from its prior strategy—which requires active management—to a held-for-collection strategy for these debt investments. British Sky makes the following entry to transfer these securities to the held-for-collection classification.

January 1, 2011

Debt Investments	125,000	
Securities Fair Value Adjustment		125,000

Therefore, at January 1, 2011, the debt investments are stated at fair value. However, in subsequent periods, British Sky will account for the investment at amortized cost. The effective-interest rate used in the amortized cost model is the rate used to discount the future cash flows to the fair value of British Sky's debt investment of £125,000 on January 1, 2011.

FAIR VALUE CONTROVERSY

The reporting of investments is controversial. Some favor the present approach, which reflects a mixed-attribute model based on a company's business model for managing the investment and the type of security. Under this model, some debt investments are accounted

---

[12]The Board rejected retrospective application because recasting prior periods according to the new investment model would not reflect how the investments were managed in the prior periods. The IASB indicates that a change in a company's investment business model is a significant and demonstrable event, and it is likely that this change will be disclosed when the change occurs. [20]

for at amortized cost and others at fair value. Others call for fair value measurement for all financial assets, with gains and losses recorded in income. In this section, we look at some of the major unresolved issues.

Measurement Based on Business Model

Companies value debt investments at fair value or amortized cost, depending on the business model for managing the investments. Some believe that this framework provides the most relevant information about the performance of these investments. Others disagree; they note that two identical debt investments could be reported in different ways in the financial statements. They argue that this approach increases complexity and reduces the understandability of financial statements. Furthermore, the held-for-collection classification relies on management's plans, which can change. In other words, the classifications are subjective, resulting in arbitrary and non-comparable classifications.

Gains Trading

Debt investments classified as held-for-collection are reported at amortized cost; unrealized gains and losses on these investments are not recognized in income. Similarly, the unrealized gains or losses on non-trading equity investments also bypass income. Although significant trading out of these classifications might call into question management's business model assertions with respect to these classifications, a company can engage in "gains trading" (also referred to as "cherry picking," "snacking," or "sell the best and keep the rest"). In **gains trading**, companies sell their "winners," reporting the gains in income, and hold on to the losers. Furthermore, as one IASB member noted, in the recent financial crisis some of the most significant losses were recorded on investments that qualify for accounting in which unrealized gains or losses were not reported in income. That is, fair value accounting would have provided much more timely information on these investments when the markets needed it the most.

Liabilities Not Fairly Valued

Many argue that if companies report investments at fair value, they also should report liabilities at fair value. Why? By recognizing changes in value on only one side of the statement of financial position (the asset side), a high degree of volatility can occur in the income and equity amounts. Further, financial institutions are involved in asset and liability management (not just asset management). Viewing only one side may lead managers to make uneconomic decisions as a result of the accounting. The fair value option may address this concern to some extent, but as we discussed in Chapter 14, there is debate on the usefulness of fair value estimates for liabilities.

Fair Values—Final Comment

The IASB (and the FASB) believe that fair value information for many financial assets and financial liabilities provides more useful and relevant information than a cost-based system. The Boards take this position because fair value reflects the current cash equivalent of the financial instrument rather than the cost of a past transaction. As a consequence, only fair value provides an understanding of the current worth of the investment. Under the recently issued *IFRS 9*, companies must report fair values for more types of financial assets relative to prior standards in this area. However, an exception is allowed for some debt investments. Whether this approach results in an improvement in the reporting for debt and equity investments remains to be seen.

SUMMARY OF REPORTING TREATMENT OF INVESTMENTS

Illustration 17-26 summarizes the major debt and equity investment classifications and their reporting treatment.

Classification	Valuation Approach and Reporting on the Statement of Financial Position	Income Effects
Debt Investment		
1. Meets business model (held-for-collection) and contractual cash flow tests.	Amortized cost. Current or Non-current assets.	Interest is recognized as revenue.
2. Does not meet the business model test (not held-for-collection).	Fair value. Current assets.	Interest is recognized as revenue. Unrealized holding gains and losses are included in income.
3. Fair value option	Fair value. Current or Non-current assets.	Interest is recognized as revenue. Unrealized holding gains and losses are included in income.
Equity Investment		
1. Does not meet contractual cash flow test; holdings less than 20 percent (trading).	Fair value. Current assets.	Dividends are recognized as revenue. Unrealized holding gains and losses are included in income.
2. Does not meet contractual cash flow test; holdings less than 20 percent (non-trading).	Fair value. Non-current assets.	Dividends are recognized as revenue. Unrealized holding gains and losses are not included in income but in other comprehensive income.
3. Holdings greater than 20 percent (significant influence or control).	Investments originally recorded at cost with periodic adjustment for the investor's share of the investee's income or loss, and decreased by all dividends received from the investee. Non-current assets.	Revenue is recognized to the extent of the investee's income or loss reported subsequent to the date of the investment.

ILLUSTRATION 17-26
Summary of Investment
Accounting Approaches

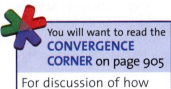

You will want to read the
**CONVERGENCE
CORNER** on page 905

For discussion of how international convergence efforts relate to the accounting for investments.

CONVERGENCE CORNER

Until recently, when the IASB issued *IFRS 9*, the accounting and reporting for investments under IFRS and U.S. GAAP were for the most part very similar. However, *IFRS 9* introduces new investment classifications and increases the situations when investments are accounted for at fair value, with gains and losses recorded in income.

RELEVANT FACTS

• U.S. GAAP classifies investments as trading, available-for-sale (both debt and equity investments), and held-to-maturity (only for debt investments). IFRS uses held-for-collection (debt investments), trading (both debt and equity investments), and non-trading equity investment classifications.

• The accounting for trading investments is the same between U.S. GAAP and IFRS. Held-to-maturity (U.S. GAAP) and held-for-collection investments are accounted for at amortized cost. Gains and losses related to available-for-sale securities (U.S. GAAP) and non-trading equity investments (IFRS) are reported in other comprehensive income.

• Both U.S. GAAP and IFRS use the same test to determine whether the equity method of accounting should be used—that is, significant influence with a general guide of over 20 percent ownership.

• The basis for consolidation under IFRS is control. Under U.S. GAAP, a bipolar approach is used, which is a risk-and-reward model (often referred to as a variable-entity approach) and a voting-interest approach. However, under both systems, for consolidation to occur, the investor company must generally own 50 percent of another company.

• U.S. GAAP and IFRS are similar in the accounting for the fair value option. That is, the option to use the fair value method must be made at initial recognition, the selection is irrevocable, and gains and losses are reported as part of income. One difference is that U.S. GAAP permits the fair value option for equity method investments.

• While measurement of impairments is similar, U.S. GAAP does not permit the reversal of an impairment charge related to available-for-sale debt and equity investments. IFRS allows reversals of impairments of held-for-collection investments.

ABOUT THE NUMBERS

The following example illustrates the accounting for investment impairments under IFRS. Belerus Company has a held-for-collection investment in the 8 percent, 10-year bonds of Wimbledon Company. The investment has a carrying value of €2,300,000 at December 31, 2011. Early in January 2012, Belerus learns that Wimbledon has lost a major customer. As a result, Belerus determines that this investment is impaired and now has a fair value of €1,500,000. Belerus makes the following entry to record the impairment.

Loss on Impairment (€2,300,000 − €1,500,000)	800,000	
Debt Investments (HFC)		800,000

Early in 2013, Wimbledon secures several new customers, and its prospects have improved considerably. Belerus determines the fair value of its investment is now €2,000,000 and makes the following entry under IFRS.

Debt Investments (HFC) (€2,000,000 − €1,500,000)	500,000	
Recovery of Investment Loss		500,000

Under U.S. GAAP, Belerus is prohibited from recording the recovery in value of the impaired investment. That is, once an investment is impaired, the impaired value becomes the new basis for the investment.

ON THE HORIZON

At one time, both the FASB and IASB have indicated that they believe that all financial instruments should be reported at fair value and that changes in fair value should be reported as part of net income. However, the recently issued IFRS indicates that the IASB believes that certain debt investments should not be reported at fair value. The IASB's decision to issue new rules on investments, earlier than the FASB has completed its deliberations on financial instrument accounting, could create obstacles for the Boards in converging the accounting in this area.

SUMMARY OF LEARNING OBJECTIVES

•1 Describe the accounting framework for financial assets. Financial assets (debt and equity investments) are accounted for either at amortized cost or fair value. If a company has (1) a business model whose objective is to hold assets in order to collect contractual cash flows and (2) the contractual terms of the financial asset give specified dates to cash flows that are solely payments of principal and interest on the principal amount outstanding, then the company should use amortized cost. Thus, only debt investments can be accounted for at amortized cost. Equity investments are generally recorded and reported at fair value. Equity investments do not have a fixed interest or principal payment schedule and therefore cannot be accounted for at amortized cost. In general, equity investments are valued at fair value, with all gains and losses reported in income.

•2 Understand the accounting for debt investments at amortized cost. Similar to bonds payable, companies should amortize discounts or premiums on debt investments using the effective-interest method. They apply the effective-interest rate or yield to the beginning carrying value of the investment for each interest period in order to compute interest revenue.

•3 Understand the accounting for debt investments at fair value. Companies that account for and report debt investments at fair value follow the same accounting entries as debt investments held-for-collection during the reporting period. That is, they are recorded at amortized cost. However, at each reporting date, companies adjust the amortized cost to fair value, with any unrealized holding gain or loss reported as part of net income.

•4 Describe the accounting for the fair value option. Companies have the option to report most financial instruments at fair value, with all gains and losses related to changes in fair value reported in the income statement. This option is applied on an instrument-by-instrument basis. The fair value option is generally available only at the time a company first purchases the financial asset or incurs a financial liability. If a company chooses to use the fair value option, it must measure this instrument at fair value until the company no longer has ownership.

•5 Understand the accounting for equity investments at fair value. For equity investment holdings less than 20 percent, it is presumed that companies hold the investment to profit from price changes. The accounting and reporting rule for these investments is to value the investments at fair value and record unrealized gains and losses in net income (the fair value method). Dividends received are recorded in income. Equity investments held for purposes other than trading are recorded at fair value on the statement of financial position, with unrealized gains and losses reported in other comprehensive income.

•6 Explain the equity method of accounting and compare it to the fair value method for equity investments. The equity method is used when an investor company acquires ordinary shares of another company (investee), such that the investor has significant influence—a holding between 20 and 50 percent. Under the equity method, the investor and the investee acknowledge a substantive economic relationship. The company originally records the investment at cost but subsequently adjusts the amount each period for changes in the net assets of the investee. That is, the investor's proportionate share of the earnings (losses) of the investee periodically increases (decreases) the investment's carrying amount. In contrast to the fair value method, all dividends received by the investor from the investee decrease the investment's carrying amount.

•7 Discuss the accounting for impairments of debt investments. Companies use the impairment test to determine whether it is probable that the investor will be unable to collect all amounts due according to the contractual terms. This impairment loss is reported in income, calculated as the difference between the carrying amount plus accrued interest and the expected future cash flows discounted at the investment's historical effective-interest rate.

·8 **Describe the accounting for transfer of investments between categories.** Transfers of securities between categories of investments occur when a company changes it business model for managing the investments. The transfers are accounted for prospectively, at the beginning of the period following the business model change.

| APPENDIX **17A** | RECLASSIFICATION ADJUSTMENTS |

As we indicated in Chapter 4, companies report changes in unrealized holding gains and losses related to non-trading equity investments as part of other comprehensive income. Companies may display the components of other comprehensive income in one of two ways: (1) in a combined statement of income and comprehensive income or (2) in a separate statement of comprehensive income that begins with net income.

> **Objective·9**
> Explain why companies report reclassification adjustments.

The reporting of changes in unrealized gains or losses in comprehensive income is straightforward unless a company sells securities during the year. In that case, double counting results when the company reports realized gains or losses as part of net income but also shows the amounts as part of other comprehensive income in the current period or in previous periods.

To ensure that gains and losses are not counted twice when a sale occurs, a **reclassification adjustment** is necessary. To illustrate, assume that Open Company has the following two non-trading equity investments at the end of 2010 (its first year of operations).

Investments	Carrying Value	Fair Value	Unrealized Holding Gain (Loss)
Lehman Inc. shares	$ 80,000	$105,000	$25,000
Choi Co. shares	120,000	135,000	15,000
Total of portfolio	$200,000	$240,000	40,000
Previous securities fair value adjustment balance			–0–
Securities fair value adjustment—Dr.			$40,000

ILLUSTRATION 17A-1
Non-Trading Equity Investment Portfolio (2010)

If Open Company reports net income in 2010 of $350,000, it presents a statement of comprehensive income as follows.

OPEN COMPANY
STATEMENT OF COMPREHENSIVE INCOME
FOR THE YEAR ENDED DECEMBER 31, 2010

Net income	$350,000
Other comprehensive income	
Holding gains arising during period	40,000
Comprehensive income	$390,000

ILLUSTRATION 17A-2
Statement of Comprehensive Income (2010)

During 2011, Open Company sold the Lehman Inc. investment for $105,000 and realized a gain on the sale of $25,000 ($105,000 − $80,000). At the end of 2011, the fair value of the Choi Co. shares increased an additional $20,000, to $155,000. Illustration 17A-3 (page 908) shows the computation of the change in the Securities Fair Value Adjustment account.

ILLUSTRATION 17A-3
Non-Trading Equity
Investment Portfolio
(2011)

Investments	Cost	Fair Value	Unrealized Holding Gain (Loss)
Choi Co. shares	$120,000	$155,000	$35,000
Previous securities fair value adjustment balance—Dr.			(40,000)
Securities fair value adjustment—Cr.			$ (5,000)

Illustration 17A-3 indicates that Open should report an unrealized holding loss of $5,000 in comprehensive income in 2011. In addition, Open realized a gain of $25,000 on the sale of the Lehman shares. **Comprehensive income includes both realized and unrealized components.** Therefore, Open recognizes a total holding gain (loss) in 2011 of $20,000, computed as follows.

ILLUSTRATION 17A-4
Computation of Total
Holding Gain (Loss)

Unrealized holding gain (loss)	$ (5,000)
Realized holding gain	25,000
Total holding gain recognized	$20,000

Open reports net income of $720,000 in 2011, which includes the realized gain on sale of the Lehman shares. Illustration 17A-5 shows a statement of comprehensive income for 2011, indicating how Open reported the components of holding gains (losses).

ILLUSTRATION 17A-5
Statement of
Comprehensive
Income (2011)

OPEN COMPANY
STATEMENT OF COMPREHENSIVE INCOME
FOR THE YEAR ENDED DECEMBER 31, 2011

Net income (includes $25,000 realized gain on Lehman shares)		$720,000
Other comprehensive income		
Total holding gains arising during period [$(5,000) + $25,000]	$20,000	
Less: Reclassification adjustment for gains included in net income	25,000	(5,000)
Comprehensive income		$715,000

In 2010, Open included the unrealized gain on the Lehman Co. shares in comprehensive income. In 2011, Open sold the shares. It reported the realized gain in net income, which increased comprehensive income again. To avoid double counting this gain, Open makes a reclassification adjustment to eliminate the realized gain from the computation of comprehensive income in 2011.

A company may display reclassification adjustments on the face of the financial statement in which it reports comprehensive income. Or it may disclose these reclassification adjustments in the notes to the financial statements.

COMPREHENSIVE EXAMPLE

To illustrate the reporting of equity investments and related gain or loss on non-trading equity investments, assume that on January 1, 2011, Hinges Co. had cash and share capital of $50,000.[13] At that date, the company had no other asset, liability, or equity balance.

---

[13]We adapted this example from Dennis R. Beresford, L. Todd Johnson, and Cheri L. Reither, "Is a Second Income Statement Needed?" *Journal of Accountancy* (April 1996), p. 71.

On January 2, Hinges purchased for cash $50,000 of equity investments classified as non-trading. On June 30, Hinges sold part of the non-trading equity investment portfolio, realizing a gain as shown in Illustration 17A-6.

Fair value of investments sold	$22,000	
Less: Cost of investments sold	20,000	
Realized gain	$ 2,000	

ILLUSTRATION 17A-6
Computation of Realized Gain

Hinges did not purchase or sell any other securities during 2011. It received $3,000 in dividends during the year. At December 31, 2011, the remaining portfolio is as shown in Illustration 17A-7.

Fair value of portfolio	$34,000	
Less: Cost of portfolio	30,000	
Unrealized holding gain	$ 4,000	

ILLUSTRATION 17A-7
Computation of Unrealized Holding Gain

Illustration 17A-8 shows the company's income statement for 2011.

HINGES CO.
INCOME STATEMENT
FOR THE YEAR ENDED DECEMBER 31, 2011

Dividend revenue	$3,000
Realized gain on investments	2,000
Net income	$5,000

ILLUSTRATION 17A-8
Income Statement

The company reports its change in the unrealized holding gain in a statement of comprehensive income as follows.

HINGES CO.
STATEMENT OF COMPREHENSIVE INCOME
FOR THE YEAR ENDED DECEMBER 31, 2011

Net income		$5,000
Other comprehensive income:		
Holding gains arising during the period ($4,000 + $2,000)	$6,000	
Less: Reclassification adjustment for gains included in net income	2,000	4,000
Comprehensive income		$9,000

ILLUSTRATION 17A-9
Statement of Comprehensive Income

Its statement of changes in equity appears in Illustration 17A-10.

HINGES CO.
STATEMENT OF CHANGES IN EQUITY
FOR THE YEAR ENDED DECEMBER 31, 2011

	Share Capital	Retained Earnings	Accumulated Other Comprehensive Income	Total
Beginning balance	$50,000	$–0–	$–0–	$50,000
Add: Net income		5,000		5,000
Other comprehensive income			4,000	4,000
Ending balance	$50,000	$5,000	$4,000	$59,000

ILLUSTRATION 17A-10
Statement of Changes in Equity

The comparative statements of financial position are shown in Illustration 17A-11.

ILLUSTRATION 17A-11
Comparative Statements
of Financial Position

HINGES CO. COMPARATIVE STATEMENTS OF FINANCIAL POSITION		
	1/1/11	12/31/11
Assets		
Equity investment		$34,000
Cash	$50,000	25,000
Total assets	$50,000	$59,000
Equity		
Share capital	$50,000	$50,000
Retained earnings		5,000
Accumulated other comprehensive income		4,000
Total equity	$50,000	$59,000

This example indicates how an unrealized gain or loss on non-trading equity investments affects all the financial statements. Note that a company must disclose the components that comprise accumulated other comprehensive income.

KEY TERM

reclassification
adjustment, *907*

SUMMARY OF LEARNING OBJECTIVE FOR APPENDIX 17A

•9 **Explain why companies report reclassification adjustments.** A company needs a reclassification adjustment when it reports realized gains or losses as part of net income but also shows the amounts as part of other comprehensive income in the current or in previous periods. Companies should report unrealized holding gains or losses related to non-trading equity investments in other comprehensive income and the aggregate balance as accumulated other comprehensive income on the statement of financial position.

APPENDIX 17B

ACCOUNTING FOR DERIVATIVE INSTRUMENTS

Until the early 1970s, most financial managers worked in a cozy, if unthrilling, world. Since then, constant change caused by volatile markets, new technology, and deregulation has increased the risks to businesses. In response, the financial community developed products to manage these risks.

These products—called **derivative financial instruments** or simply, **derivatives**—are useful for managing risk. Companies use the fair values or cash flows of these instruments to offset the changes in fair values or cash flows of the at-risk assets. The development of powerful computing and communication technology has aided the growth in derivative use. This technology provides new ways to analyze information about markets as well as the power to process high volumes of payments.

DEFINING DERIVATIVES

In order to understand derivatives, consider the following examples.

Example 1—Forward Contract. Assume that a company like **Lenovo** (CHN) believes that the price of **Google**'s (USA) shares will increase substantially in the next three months.

Unfortunately, it does not have the cash resources to purchase the shares today. Lenovo therefore enters into a contract with a broker for delivery of 10,000 Google shares in three months at the price of $110 per share.

Lenovo has entered into a **forward contract**, a type of derivative. As a result of the contract, Lenovo **has received the right** to receive 10,000 Google shares in three months. Further, it **has an obligation** to pay $110 per share at that time. What is the benefit of this derivative contract? Lenovo can buy Google shares today and take delivery in three months. If the price goes up, as it expects, Lenovo profits. If the price goes down, Lenovo loses.

Example 2—Option Contract. Now suppose that Lenovo needs two weeks to decide whether to purchase Google shares. It therefore enters into a different type of contract, one that gives it the right to purchase Google shares at its current price any time within the next two weeks. As part of the contract, the broker charges $3,000 for holding the contract open for two weeks at a set price.

Lenovo has now entered into an **option contract**, another type of derivative. As a result of this contract, **it has received the right**, **but not the obligation**, to purchase these shares. If the price of the Google shares increases in the next two weeks, Lenovo exercises its option. In this case, the cost of the shares is the price of the shares stated in the contract, plus the cost of the option contract. If the price does not increase, Lenovo does not exercise the contract but still incurs the cost for the option.

The forward contract and the option contract both involve a future delivery of shares. The value of the contract relies on the underlying asset—the Google shares. Thus, these financial instruments are known as derivatives because they **derive their value from** values of other assets (e.g., ordinary shares, bonds, or commodities). Or, put another way, their value relates to a market-determined indicator (e.g., share price, interest rates, or the London Stock Exchange composite index).

In this appendix, we discuss the accounting for three different types of derivatives:

1. Financial forwards or financial futures.
2. Options.
3. Swaps.

WHO USES DERIVATIVES, AND WHY?

Whether to protect for changes in interest rates, the weather, share prices, oil prices, or foreign currencies, derivative contracts help to smooth the fluctuations caused by various types of risks. A company that wants to ensure against certain types of business risks often uses derivative contracts to achieve this objective.[14]

> **Objective·10**
> Explain who uses derivatives and why.

Producers and Consumers

To illustrate, assume that Heartland Ag is a large producer of potatoes for the consumer market. The present price for potatoes is excellent. Unfortunately, Heartland needs two months to harvest its potatoes and deliver them to the market. Because Heartland expects the price of potatoes to drop in the coming months, it signs a forward contract. It agrees to sell its potatoes today at the current market price for delivery in two months.

Who would buy this contract? Suppose on the other side of the contract is **McDonald's Corporation** (USA). McDonald's wants to have potatoes (for French fries) in two months and believes that prices will increase. McDonald's is therefore agreeable to accepting delivery in two months at current prices. It knows that it will need potatoes in two months, and that it can make an acceptable profit at this price level.

---

[14]Derivatives are traded on many exchanges throughout the world. In addition, many derivative contracts (primarily interest rate swaps) are privately negotiated.

In this situation, if the price of potatoes increases before delivery, Heartland loses and McDonald's wins. Conversely, if the price decreases, Heartland wins and McDonald's loses. However, the objective is not to gamble on the outcome. Regardless of which way the price moves, both Heartland and McDonald's have received a price at which they obtain an acceptable profit. In this case, although Heartland is a **producer** and McDonald's is a **consumer**, both companies are **hedgers**. They both **hedge their positions** to ensure an acceptable financial result.

Commodity prices are volatile. They depend on weather, crop production, and general economic conditions. For the producer and the consumer to plan effectively, it makes good sense to lock in specific future revenues or costs in order to run their businesses successfully.

Speculators and Arbitrageurs

In some cases, instead of McDonald's taking a position in the forward contract, a speculator may purchase the contract from Heartland. The speculator bets that the price of potatoes will rise, thereby increasing the value of the forward contract. The speculator, who may be in the market for only a few hours, will then sell the forward contract to another speculator or to a company like McDonald's.

Arbitrageurs also use derivatives. These market players attempt to exploit inefficiencies in markets. They seek to lock in profits by simultaneously entering into transactions in two or more markets. For example, an arbitrageur might trade in a futures contract. At the same time, the arbitrageur will also trade in the commodity underlying the futures contract, hoping to achieve small price gains on the difference between the two. Markets rely on speculators and arbitrageurs to keep the market liquid on a daily basis.

In these illustrations, we explained why Heartland (the producer) and McDonald's (the consumer) would become involved in a derivative contract. Consider other types of situations that companies face.

1. Airlines, like **Japan Airlines** (JPN), **British Airways** (GBR), and **Delta** (USA), are affected by changes in the price of jet fuel.

2. Financial institutions, such as **Barclays** (GBR), **Bankers Trust** (USA), and **ING** (NLD), are involved in borrowing and lending funds that are affected by changes in interest rates.

3. Multinational corporations, like **Nokia** (FIN), **Coca-Cola** (USA), and **Siemens** (DEU), are subject to changes in foreign exchange rates.

In fact, most corporations are involved in some form of derivatives transactions. Companies give these reasons (in their annual reports) as to why they use derivatives:

1. **ExxonMobil** (USA) uses derivatives to hedge its exposure to fluctuations in interest rates, foreign currency exchange rates, and hydrocarbon prices.

2. **HSBC** (GBR) uses derivatives to manage foreign currency exchange rates and interest rates.

3. **GlaxoSmithKline** (GBR) uses derivatives to manage the impact of interest rate and foreign exchange rate changes on earnings and cash flows.

Many corporations use derivatives extensively and successfully. However, derivatives can be dangerous. All parties involved must understand the risks and rewards associated with these contracts.[15]

[15]There are some well-publicized examples of companies that have suffered considerable losses using derivatives. For example, companies such as **Fannie Mae** (USA), **Enron** (USA), **Showa Shell Sekiyu** (JPN), **Metallgesellschaft** (DEU), **Procter & Gamble** (USA), and **Air Products & Chemicals** (USA) incurred significant losses from investments in derivative instruments.

BASIC PRINCIPLES IN ACCOUNTING FOR DERIVATIVES

The IASB concluded that derivatives such as forwards and options are assets and liabilities. It also concluded that companies should report them in the statement of financial position **at fair value**.[16] The Board believes that fair value will provide statement users the best information about derivatives. Relying on some other basis of valuation for derivatives, such as historical cost, does not make sense. Why? Because many derivatives have a historical cost of zero. Furthermore, the markets for derivatives, and the assets upon which derivatives' values rely, are well developed. As a result, the Board believes that companies can determine reliable fair value amounts for derivatives.[17]

> **Objective•11**
> Understand the basic guidelines for accounting for derivatives.

On the income statement, a company should recognize any unrealized gain or loss in income, if it uses the derivative for speculation purposes. If using the derivative for hedging purposes, the accounting for any gain or loss depends on the type of hedge used. We discuss the accounting for hedged transactions later in the appendix.

In summary, companies follow these guidelines in accounting for derivatives.

1. Recognize derivatives in the financial statements as assets and liabilities.
2. Report derivatives at fair value.
3. Recognize gains and losses resulting from speculation in derivatives immediately in income.
4. Report gains and losses resulting from hedge transactions differently, depending on the type of hedge.

Example: Derivative Financial Instrument (Speculation)

To illustrate the measurement and reporting of a derivative for speculative purposes, we examine a derivative whose value depends on the market price of Laredo Inc. ordinary shares. A company can realize a gain from the increase in the value of the Laredo shares with the use of a derivative, such as a call option.[18] A **call option** gives the holder the right, but not the obligation, to buy shares at a preset price. This price is often referred to as the **strike price** or the **exercise price**.

> **Objective•12**
> Describe the accounting for derivative financial instruments.

For example, assume a company enters into a call option contract with Baird Investment Co., which gives it the option to purchase Laredo shares at $100 per share.[19]

---

[16]IFRS covers accounting and reporting for all derivative instruments, whether financial or not. In this appendix, we focus on derivative financial instruments because of their widespread use in practice. [21]

[17]As discussed in earlier chapters, fair value is defined as "the amount for which an asset could be exchanged or a liability settled between knowledgeable, willing parties in an arm's length transaction." Fair value is therefore a market-based measure. The IASB has also developed a fair value hierarchy, which indicates the reporting of valuation techniques to use to determine fair value. *Level 1* fair value measures are based on observable inputs that reflect quoted prices for identical assets or liabilities in active markets. *Level 2* measures are based on inputs other than quoted prices included in Level 1 but that can be corroborated with observable data. *Level 3* fair values are based on unobservable inputs (e.g., a company's own data or assumptions). Thus, Level 1 is the most reliable because it is based on quoted prices, like a closing share price in the *Financial Times*. Level 2 is the next most reliable and would rely on evaluating similar assets or liabilities in active markets. For Level 3 (the least reliable), much judgment is needed, based on the best information available, to arrive at a relevant and reliable fair value measurement. [22]

[18]Investors can use a different type of option contract—a **put option**—to realize a gain if anticipating a decline in the value of Laredo shares. A put option gives the holder the option to sell shares at a preset price. Thus, a put option **increases** in value when the underlying asset **decreases** in value.

[19]Baird Investment Co. is referred to as the **counterparty**. Counterparties frequently are investment bankers or other companies that hold inventories of financial instruments.

If the price of Laredo shares increases above $100, the company can exercise this option and purchase the shares for $100 per share. If Laredo's shares never increase above $100 per share, the call option is worthless.

Accounting Entries. To illustrate the accounting for a call option, assume that the company purchases a call option contract on January 2, 2011, when Laredo shares are trading at $100 per share. The contract gives it the option to purchase 1,000 shares (referred to as the **notional amount**) of Laredo shares at an option price of $100 per share. The option expires on April 30, 2011. The company purchases the call option for $400 and makes the following entry.

January 2, 2011

Call Option	400	
Cash		400

This payment is referred to as the **option premium**. It is generally much less than the cost of purchasing the shares directly. The option premium consists of two amounts: (1) intrinsic value and (2) time value. Illustration 17B-1 shows the formula to compute the option premium.

ILLUSTRATION 17B-1
Option Premium Formula

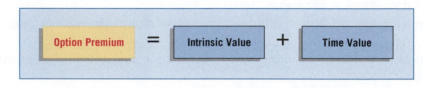

Intrinsic value is the difference between the market price and the preset strike price at any point in time. It represents the amount realized by the option holder, if exercising the option immediately. On January 2, 2011, the intrinsic value is zero because the market price equals the preset strike price.

Time value refers to the option's value over and above its intrinsic value. Time value reflects the possibility that the option has a fair value greater than zero. How? Because there is some expectation that the price of Laredo shares will increase above the strike price during the option term. As indicated, the time value for the option is $400.[20]

The following additional data are available with respect to the call option.

Date	Market Price of Laredo Shares	Time Value of Call Option
March 31, 2011	$120 per share	$100
April 16, 2011	$115 per share	$60

As indicated, on March 31, 2011, the price of Laredo shares increases to $120 per share. The intrinsic value of the call option contract is now $20,000. That is, the company can exercise the call option and purchase 1,000 shares from Baird Investment for $100 per share. It can then sell the shares in the market for $120 per share. This gives the company a gain of $20,000 ($120,000 − $100,000) on the option contract.[21] It records the increase in the intrinsic value of the option as follows.

March 31, 2011

Call Option	20,000	
Unrealized Holding Gain or Loss—Income		20,000

[20]This cost is estimated using option-pricing models, such as the Black-Scholes model. The volatility of the underlying shares, the expected life of the option, the risk-free rate of interest, and expected dividends on the underlying shares during the option term affect the Black-Scholes fair value estimate.

[21]In practice, investors generally do not have to actually buy and sell the Laredo shares to settle the option and realize the gain. This is referred to as the **net settlement** feature of option contracts.

A market appraisal indicates that the time value of the option at March 31, 2011, is $100.[22] The company records this change in value of the option as follows.

March 31, 2011

Unrealized Holding Gain or Loss—Income	300	
Call Option ($400 − $100)		300

At March 31, 2011, the company reports the call option in its statement of financial position at fair value of $20,100.[23] The unrealized holding gain increases net income for the period. The loss on the time value of the option decreases net income.

On April 16, 2011, the company settles the option before it expires. To properly record the settlement, it updates the value of the option for the decrease in the intrinsic value of $5,000 ([$20 − $15]) × 1,000) as follows.

April 16, 2011

Unrealized Holding Gain or Loss—Income	5,000	
Call Option		5,000

The decrease in the time value of the option of $40 ($100 − $60) is recorded as follows.

April 16, 2011

Unrealized Holding Gain or Loss—Income	40	
Call Option		40

Thus, at the time of the settlement, the call option's carrying value is as follows.

Call Option

January 2, 2011	400	March 31, 2011	300
March 31, 2011	20,000	April 16, 2011	5,000
		April 16, 2011	40
Balance, April 16, 2011	15,060		

The company records the settlement of the option contract with Baird as follows.

April 16, 2011

Cash	15,000	
Loss on Settlement of Call Option	60	
Call Option		15,060

Illustration 17B-2 summarizes the effects of the call option contract on net income.

Date	Transaction	Income (Loss) Effect
March 31, 2011	Net increase in value of call option ($20,000 − $300)	$19,700
April 16, 2011	Decrease in value of call option ($5,000 + $40)	(5,040)
April 16, 2011	Settle call option	(60)
	Total net income	$14,600

ILLUSTRATION 17B-2
Effect on Income—
Derivative Financial
Instrument

The accounting summarized in Illustration 17B-2 is in accord with IFRS. That is, because the call option meets the definition of an asset, the company records it in the statement of financial position on March 31, 2011. Furthermore, it reports the call option at fair value, with any gains or losses reported in income.

[22]The decline in value reflects both the decreased likelihood that the Laredo shares will continue to increase in value over the option period and the shorter time to maturity of the option contract.

[23]As indicated earlier, the total value of the option at any point in time equals the intrinsic value plus the time value.

Differences between Traditional and Derivative Financial Instruments

How does a traditional financial instrument differ from a derivative one? A derivative financial instrument has the following three basic characteristics. [23]

1. *The instrument has (1) one or more underlyings and (2) an identified payment provision.* An **underlying** is a specified interest rate, security price, commodity price, index of prices or rates, or other market-related variable. The interaction of the underlying, with the face amount or the number of units specified in the derivative contract (the notional amounts), determines payment. For example, the value of the call option increased in value when the value of the Laredo shares increased. In this case, the underlying is the share price. To arrive at the payment provision, multiply the change in the share price by the number of shares (notional amount).

2. *The instrument requires little or no investment at the inception of the contract.* To illustrate, the company paid a small premium to purchase the call option—an amount much less than if purchasing the Laredo shares as a direct investment.

3. *The instrument requires or permits net settlement.* As indicated in the call option example, the company could realize a profit on the call option without taking possession of the shares. This **net settlement** feature reduces the transaction costs associated with derivatives.

Illustration 17B-3 summarizes the differences between traditional and derivative financial instruments. Here, we use an equity investment (trading) for the traditional financial instrument and a call option as an example of a derivative one.

ILLUSTRATION 17B-3
Features of Traditional and Derivative Financial Instruments

Feature	Traditional Financial Instrument Equity Investment (Trading)	Derivative Financial Instrument (Call Option)
Payment provision	Share price times the number of shares.	Change in share price (underlying) times number of shares (notional amount).
Initial investment	Investor pays full cost.	Initial investment is much less than full cost.
Settlement	Deliver shares to receive cash.	Receive cash equivalent, based on changes in share price times the number of shares.

DERIVATIVES USED FOR HEDGING

Flexibility in use, and the low-cost features of derivatives relative to traditional financial instruments, explain the popularity of derivatives. An additional use for derivatives is in risk management. For example, companies such as **Coca-Cola** (USA), **BP** (GBR), and **Siemens** (DEU) borrow and lend substantial amounts in credit markets. In doing so, they are exposed to significant **interest rate risk**. That is, they face substantial risk that the fair values or cash flows of interest-sensitive assets or liabilities will change if interest rates increase or decrease. These same companies also have significant international operations. As such, they are also exposed to **exchange rate risk**—the risk that changes in foreign currency exchange rates will negatively impact the profitability of their international businesses.

Companies can use derivatives to offset the negative impacts of changes in interest rates or foreign currency exchange rates. This use of derivatives is referred to as **hedging**.

The IASB established accounting and reporting standards for derivative financial instruments used in hedging activities. IFRS allows special accounting for two types of hedges—fair value and cash flow hedges.[24]

As shown in the graph below, use of derivatives has grown steadily in the past several years. In fact, nearly *$500 trillion* (in notional amounts) in derivative contracts were in play at the end of 2008. The primary players in the market for derivatives are large companies and various financial institutions, which continue to find new uses for derivatives for speculation and risk management.

What do the numbers mean?

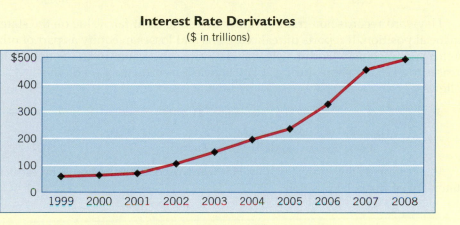

Interest Rate Derivatives
($ in trillions)

Source: International Swaps and Derivatives Association Market Survey (2008).

Financial engineers continue to develop new uses for derivatives, many times through the use of increasingly complex webs of transactions, spanning a number of markets. As new uses for derivatives appear, the financial system as a whole can be dramatically affected. As a result, some market-watchers are concerned about the risk that a crisis in one company or sector could bring the entire financial system to its knees.

This was the case recently when credit default swaps were used to facilitate the sales of mortgage-backed securities (MBS). However, when the real estate market went south, the MBS defaulted, exposing large international financial institutions, like **Barclays** (GBR), **AIG** (USA), and **Bank of America** (USA), to massive losses. The losses were so widespread that government bailouts were required to prevent international securities markets from collapsing. In response, market regulators are proposing new rules to mitigate risks to broader markets from derivatives trading.

Source: P. Eavis, "Bill on Derivatives Overhaul Is Long Overdue," *Wall Street Journal* (April 14, 2010).

Fair Value Hedge

In a **fair value hedge**, a company uses a derivative to hedge (offset) the exposure to changes in the fair value of a recognized asset or liability or of an unrecognized commitment. In a perfectly hedged position, the gain or loss on the fair value of the derivative equals and offsets that of the hedged asset or liability.

Objective·13
Explain how to account for a fair value hedge.

---

[24]IFRS also addresses the accounting for certain foreign currency hedging transactions. In general, these transactions are special cases of the two hedges we discuss here. **[24]** Understanding of foreign currency hedging transactions requires knowledge related to consolidation of multinational entities, which is beyond the scope of this textbook.

Companies commonly use several types of fair value hedges. For example, companies use interest rate swaps to hedge the risk that changes in interest rates will impact the fair value of debt obligations. Or, they use put options to hedge the risk that an equity investment will decline in value.

To illustrate a fair value hedge, assume that on April 1, 2011, Hayward Co. purchases 100 ordinary shares of Sonoma Company at a market price of $100 per share. Due to a legal requirement, Hayward does not intend to actively trade this investment. It consequently classifies the Sonoma investment as a non-trading equity investment. Hayward records this investment as follows.

April 1, 2011

Equity Investments	10,000	
Cash		10,000

Hayward records non-trading equity investments at fair value on the statement of financial position. It reports unrealized gains and losses in equity as part of other comprehensive income.[25] Fortunately for Hayward, the value of the Sonoma shares increases to $125 per share during 2011. Hayward records the gain on this investment as follows.

December 31, 2011

Security Fair Value Adjustment	2,500	
Unrealized Holding Gain or Loss—Equity		2,500

Illustration 17B-4 indicates how Hayward reports the Sonoma investment in its statement of financial position.

ILLUSTRATION 17B-4
Statement of Financial Position Presentation of Non-Trading Equity Investment

HAYWARD CO. STATEMENT OF FINANCIAL POSITION (PARTIAL) DECEMBER 31, 2011	
Assets	
Equity investment	$12,500
Equity	
Accumulated other comprehensive income	
Unrealized holding gain	$2,500

While Hayward benefits from an increase in the price of Sonoma shares, it is exposed to the risk that the price of the Sonoma shares will decline. To hedge this risk, Hayward locks in its gain on the Sonoma investment by purchasing a put option on 100 Sonoma shares.

Hayward enters into the put option contract on January 2, 2012, and designates the option as a fair value hedge of the Sonoma investment. This put option (which expires in two years) gives Hayward the option to sell Sonoma shares at a price of $125. Since the exercise price equals the current market price, no entry is necessary at inception of the put option.[26]

January 2, 2012

No entry required. A memorandum entry indicates the signing of the put option contract and its designation as a fair value hedge for the Sonoma investment.

At December 31, 2012, the price of the Sonoma shares has declined to $120 per share. Hayward records the following entry for the Sonoma investment.

---

[25]We discussed the distinction between trading and non-trading equity investments in the chapter.

[26]To simplify the example, we assume no premium is paid for the option.

December 31, 2012

Unrealized Holding Gain or Loss—Income	500	
Security Fair Value Adjustment		500

Note that upon designation of the hedge, the accounting for the non-trading equity investment changes from regular IFRS. That is, Hayward records the unrealized holding loss in income, not in equity. If Hayward had not followed this accounting, a mismatch of gains and losses in the income statement would result. Thus, special accounting for the hedged item (in this case, a non-trading equity investment) is necessary in a fair value hedge.

The following journal entry records the increase in value of the put option on Sonoma shares.

December 31, 2012

Put Option	500	
Unrealized Holding Gain or Loss—Income		500

The decline in the price of Sonoma shares results in an increase in the fair value of the put option. That is, Hayward could realize a gain on the put option by purchasing 100 shares in the open market for $120 and then exercise the put option, selling the shares for $125. This results in a gain to Hayward of $500 (100 shares × [$125 − $120]).[27]

Illustration 17B-5 indicates how Hayward reports the amounts related to the Sonoma investment and the put option.

ILLUSTRATION 17B-5
Statement of Financial Position Presentation of Fair Value Hedge

HAYWARD CO. STATEMENT OF FINANCIAL POSITION (PARTIAL) DECEMBER 31, 2012	
Assets	
Equity investment	$12,000
Put option	500

The increase in fair value on the option offsets or hedges the decline in value on Hayward's non-trading investment. The financial statements reflect the underlying substance of Hayward's net exposure to the risks of holding Sonoma shares. By using fair value accounting for both these financial instruments, the statement of financial position reports the amount that Hayward would receive on the investment and the put option contract if Hayward sold and settled them, respectively.

Illustration 17B-6 illustrates the reporting of the effects of the hedging transaction on income for the year ended December 31, 2012.

ILLUSTRATION 17B-6
Income Statement Presentation of Fair Value Hedge

HAYWARD CO. INCOME STATEMENT (PARTIAL) FOR THE YEAR ENDED DECEMBER 31, 2012	
Other income and expense	
Unrealized holding gain—put option	$ 500
Unrealized holding loss—equity investment	(500)

The income statement indicates that the gain on the put option offsets the loss on the equity investment.[28] The reporting for these financial instruments, even when they

---

[27]In practice, Hayward generally does not have to actually buy and sell the Sonoma shares to realize this gain. Rather, unless the counterparty wants to hold Hayward shares, Hayward can "close out" the contract by having the counterparty pay it $500 in cash. This is an example of the net settlement feature of derivatives.

[28]Note that the fair value changes in the option contract will not offset **increases** in the value of the Hayward investment. Should the price of Sonoma shares increase above $125 per share, Hayward would have no incentive to exercise the put option.

reflect a hedging relationship, illustrates why the IASB argued that fair value accounting provides the most relevant information about financial instruments, including derivatives.

Cash Flow Hedge

Companies use **cash flow hedges** to hedge exposures to **cash flow risk**, which results from the variability in cash flows. The IASB allows special accounting for cash flow hedges. Generally, companies measure and report derivatives at fair value on the statement of financial position. They report gains and losses directly in net income. However, companies account for derivatives used in cash flow hedges at fair value on the statement of financial position, but they **record gains or losses in equity, as part of other comprehensive income**.

To illustrate, assume that in September 2011 Allied Can Co. anticipates purchasing 1,000 metric tons of aluminum in January 2012. Concerned that prices for aluminum will increase in the next few months, Allied wants to hedge the risk that it might pay higher prices for inventory in January 2012. As a result, Allied enters into an aluminum futures contract.

A **futures contract** gives the holder the right and the obligation to purchase an asset at a preset price for a specified period of time.[29] In this case, the aluminum futures contract gives Allied the right and the obligation to purchase 1,000 metric tons of aluminum for $1,550 per ton. This contract price is good until the contract expires in January 2012. The underlying for this derivative is the price of aluminum. If the price of aluminum rises above $1,550, the value of the futures contract to Allied increases. Why? Because Allied will be able to purchase the aluminum at the lower price of $1,550 per ton.[30]

Allied enters into the futures contract on September 1, 2011. Assume that the price to be paid today for inventory to be delivered in January—the **spot price**—equals the contract price. With the two prices equal, the futures contract has no value. Therefore, no entry is necessary.

September 1, 2011

No entry required. A memorandum entry indicates
the signing of the futures contract.

At December 31, 2011, the price for January delivery of aluminum increases to $1,575 per metric ton. Allied makes the following entry to record the increase in the value of the futures contract.

December 31, 2011

Futures Contract	25,000	
Unrealized Holding Gain or Loss—Equity		
([$1,575 − $1,550] × 1,000 tons)		25,000

Allied reports the futures contract in the statement of financial position as a current asset. It reports the gain on the futures contract as part of other comprehensive income.

Since Allied has not yet purchased and sold the inventory, this gain arises from an **anticipated transaction**. In this type of transaction, a company accumulates in equity gains or losses on the futures contract as part of other comprehensive income until the period in which it sells the inventory, thereby affecting earnings.

---

[29]A **futures contract** is a firm contractual agreement between a buyer and seller for a specified asset on a fixed date in the future. The contract also has a standard specification so both parties know exactly what is being traded. A **forward** is similar but is not traded on an exchange and does not have standardized conditions.

[30]As with the earlier call option example, the actual aluminum does not have to be exchanged. Rather, the parties to the futures contract settle by paying the cash difference between the futures price and the price of aluminum on each settlement date.

In January 2012, Allied purchases 1,000 metric tons of aluminum for $1,575 and makes the following entry.[31]

January 2012

Aluminum Inventory	1,575,000	
Cash ($1,575 × 1,000 tons)		1,575,000

At the same time, Allied makes final settlement on the futures contract. It records the following entry.

January 2012

Cash	25,000	
Futures Contract ($1,575,000 − $1,550,000)		25,000

Through use of the futures contract derivative, Allied fixes the cost of its inventory. The $25,000 futures contract settlement offsets the amount paid to purchase the inventory at the prevailing market price of $1,575,000. The result: net cash outflow of $1,550 per metric ton, as desired. As Illustration 17B-7 shows, Allied has therefore effectively hedged the cash flow for the purchase of inventory.

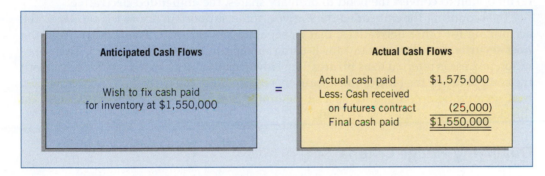

ILLUSTRATION 17B-7
Effect of Hedge on Cash Flows

There are no income effects at this point. Allied accumulates in equity the gain on the futures contract as part of other comprehensive income until the period when it sells the inventory, affecting earnings through cost of goods sold.

For example, assume that Allied processes the aluminum into finished goods (cans). The total cost of the cans (including the aluminum purchases in January 2012) is $1,700,000. Allied sells the cans in July 2012 for $2,000,000, and records this sale as follows.

July 2012

Cash	2,000,000	
Sales Revenue		2,000,000
Cost of Goods Sold	1,700,000	
Inventory (Cans)		1,700,000

Since the effect of the anticipated transaction has now affected earnings, Allied makes the following entry related to the hedging transaction.

July 2012

Unrealized Holding Gain or Loss—Equity	25,000	
Cost of Goods Sold		25,000

The gain on the futures contract, which Allied reported as part of other comprehensive income, now reduces cost of goods sold. As a result, the cost of aluminum included in the overall cost of goods sold is $1,550,000. The futures contract has worked as planned. Allied has managed the cash paid for aluminum inventory and the amount of cost of goods sold.

---

[31]In practice, futures contracts are settled on a daily basis. For our purposes, we show only one settlement for the entire amount.

OTHER REPORTING ISSUES

Objective•15

Identify special reporting issues related to derivative financial instruments that cause unique accounting problems.

The preceding examples illustrate the basic reporting issues related to the accounting for derivatives. Next, we discuss the following additional issues:

1. The accounting for embedded derivatives.
2. Qualifying hedge criteria.

Embedded Derivatives

As we indicated at the beginning of this appendix, rapid innovation in the development of complex financial instruments drove efforts toward unifying and improving the accounting standards for derivatives. In recent years, this innovation has led to the development of **hybrid securities**. These securities have characteristics of both debt and equity. They often combine traditional and derivative financial instruments.

For example, a convertible bond (discussed in Chapter 16) is a hybrid instrument. It consists of two parts: (1) a debt security, referred to as the **host security**, combined with (2) an option to convert the bond to ordinary shares, the **embedded derivative**.

In accounting for embedded derivatives, some support an approach similar to the accounting for other derivatives; that is, **separate the embedded derivative from the host security** and then account for it using the accounting for derivatives. This separation process is referred to as **bifurcation**. However, the IASB, based on concerns about the complexity of the bifurcation approach, required that the embedded derivative and host security be accounted for as a single unit.[32] The accounting followed is based on the classification of the host security.[33]

Qualifying Hedge Criteria

The IASB identified certain criteria that hedging transactions must meet before requiring the special accounting for hedges. The IASB designed these criteria to ensure the use of hedge accounting in a consistent manner across different hedge transactions. The general criteria relate to the following areas.

1. *Documentation, risk management, and designation.* At inception of the hedge, there must be formal **documentation** of the hedging relationship, the company's **risk management** objective, and the strategy for undertaking the hedge. **Designation** refers to identifying the hedging instrument, the hedged item or transaction, the nature of the risk being hedged, and how the hedging instrument will offset changes in the fair value or cash flows attributable to the hedged risk. **[25]**

The IASB decided that documentation and designation are critical to the implementation of the special accounting for hedges. Without these requirements, companies might try to apply the hedge accounting provisions retroactively, only in response to negative changes in market conditions, to offset the negative impact of a transaction on the financial statements. Allowing special hedge accounting in such a setting could mask the speculative nature of the original transaction.

2. *Effectiveness of the hedging relationship.* At inception and on an ongoing basis, the hedging relationship should be **highly effective** in achieving offsetting changes in fair value or cash flows. Companies must assess effectiveness whenever preparing financial statements. **[26]**

The general guideline for effectiveness is that the fair values or cash flows of the hedging instrument (the derivative) and the hedged item exhibit a high degree

---

[32]A company can also designate such a derivative as a hedging instrument. The company would apply the hedge accounting provisions outlined earlier in the chapter.

[33]As discussed in Chapter 16, the **issuer** of the convertible bonds would bifurcate the option component of the convertible bonds payable.

of correlation. In practice, high effectiveness is assumed when the correlation is close to one (e.g., within plus or minus .10, or that the ratio of gains to losses on the hedging transaction is in the range of .8 to 1.25). In our earlier hedging examples (put option and the futures contract on aluminum inventory), the fair values and cash flows are perfectly correlated. That is, when the cash payment for the inventory purchase increased, it offset, dollar for dollar, the cash received on the futures contract.

If the effectiveness criterion is not met, either at inception or because of changes following inception of the hedging relationship, IFRS no longer allows special hedge accounting. The company should then account for the derivative as a free-standing derivative.[34]

3. *Effect on reported earnings of changes in fair values or cash flows.* A change in the fair value of a hedged item or variation in the cash flow of a hedged forecasted transaction must have the potential to change the amount recognized in reported earnings. There is no need for special hedge accounting if a company accounts for both the hedging instrument and the hedged item at fair value under existing IFRS. In this case, earnings will properly reflect the offsetting gains and losses.[35]

For example, special accounting is not needed for a fair value hedge of a trading security, because a company accounts for both the investment and the derivative at fair value on the statement of financial position with gains or losses reported in earnings. Thus, "special" hedge accounting is necessary only when there is a mismatch of the accounting effects for the hedging instrument and the hedged item under IFRS.[36]

Summary of Derivatives Accounting

Illustration 17B-8 summarizes the accounting provisions for derivatives and hedging transactions.

Derivative Use	Accounting for Derivative	Accounting for Hedged Item	Common Example
Speculation	At fair value with unrealized holding gains and losses recorded in income.	Not applicable.	Call or put option on an equity security.
Hedging Fair value	At fair value with holding gains and losses recorded in income.	At fair value with gains and losses recorded in income.	Put option to hedge a non-trading equity investment.
Cash flow	At fair value with unrealized holding gains and losses from the hedge recorded in other comprehensive income, and reclassified in income when the hedged transaction's cash flows affect earnings.	Use other IFRS for the hedged item.	Use of a futures contract to hedge a forecasted purchase of inventory.

ILLUSTRATION 17B-8
Summary of Derivative Accounting under IFRS

[34]The accounting for the part of a derivative that is not effective in a hedge is at fair value, with gains and losses recorded in income.

[35]IFRS gives companies the option to measure most types of financial instruments—from equity investments to debt issued by the company—at fair value. Changes in fair value are recognized in net income each reporting period. Thus, IFRS provides companies with the opportunity to hedge their financial instruments without the complexity inherent in applying hedge accounting provisions. **[27]**

[36]An important criterion specific to cash flow hedges is that the forecasted transaction in a cash flow hedge "is likely to occur." A company should support this probability (defined as significantly greater than the term "more likely than not") by observable facts such as frequency of similar past transactions and its financial and operational ability to carry out the transaction.

As indicated, the general accounting for derivatives relies on fair values. IFRS also establishes special accounting guidance when companies use derivatives **for hedging purposes**. For example, when a company uses a put option to hedge price changes in a non-trading equity investment in a fair value hedge (see the Hayward example earlier), it records unrealized gains on the investment in earnings, which is not IFRS for these investments without such a hedge. This special accounting is justified in order to accurately report the nature of the hedging relationship in the statement of financial position (recording both the put option and the investment at fair value) and in the income statement (reporting offsetting gains and losses in the same period).

Special accounting also is used for cash flow hedges. Companies account for derivatives used in qualifying cash flow hedges at fair value on the statement of financial position, but record unrealized holding gains or losses in other comprehensive income until selling or settling the hedged item. In a cash flow hedge, a company continues to record the hedged item at its historical cost.

Disclosure requirements for derivatives are complex. Recent pronouncements on fair value information and financial instruments provide a helpful disclosure framework for reporting derivative instruments. In general, companies that have derivatives are required to disclose the objectives for holding or issuing those instruments (speculation or hedging), the hedging context (fair value or cash flow), and the strategies for achieving risk-management objectives.

COMPREHENSIVE HEDGE ACCOUNTING EXAMPLE

To provide a comprehensive example of hedge accounting, we examine the use of an interest rate swap. First, let's consider how swaps work and why companies use them.

Options and futures trade on organized securities exchanges. Because of this, options and futures have standardized terms. Although that standardization makes the trading easier, it limits the flexibility needed to tailor contracts to specific circumstances. In addition, most types of derivatives have relatively short time horizons, thereby excluding their use for reducing long-term risk exposure.

As a result, many corporations instead turn to the swap, a very popular type of derivative. A **swap** is a transaction between two parties in which the first party promises to make a payment to the second party. Similarly, the second party promises to make a simultaneous payment to the first party.

The most common type of swap is the **interest rate swap**. In this type, one party makes payments based on a fixed or floating rate, and the second party does just the opposite. In most cases, large money-center banks bring together the two parties. These banks handle the flow of payments between the parties, as shown in Illustration 17B-9.

ILLUSTRATION 17B-9
Swap Transaction

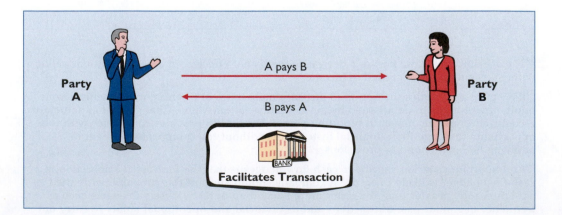

A pays B

B pays A

Party A

Party B

BANK
Facilitates Transaction

Fair Value Hedge

To illustrate the use of a swap in a fair value hedge, assume that Jones Company issues €1,000,000 of five-year, 8 percent bonds on January 2, 2011. Jones records this transaction as follows.

January 2, 2011

Cash	1,000,000	
Bonds Payable		1,000,000

Jones offered a fixed interest rate to appeal to investors. But Jones is concerned that if market interest rates decline, the fair value of the liability will increase. The company will then suffer an economic loss.[37] To protect against the risk of loss, Jones hedges the risk of a decline in interest rates by entering into a five-year interest rate swap contract. Jones agrees to the following terms:

1. Jones will receive fixed payments at 8 percent (based on the €1,000,000 amount).
2. Jones will pay variable rates, based on the market rate in effect for the life of the swap contract. The variable rate at the inception of the contract is 6.8 percent.

As Illustration 17B-10 shows, this swap allows Jones to change the interest on the bonds payable from a fixed rate to a variable rate.

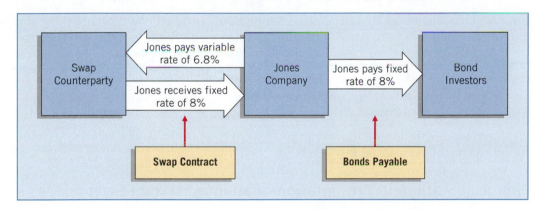

ILLUSTRATION 17B-10
Interest Rate Swap

The settlement dates for the swap correspond to the interest payment dates on the debt (December 31). On each interest payment (settlement) date, Jones and the counterparty compute the difference between current market interest rates and the fixed rate of 8 percent, and determine the value of the swap.[38] If interest rates decline, the value of the swap contract to Jones increases (Jones has a gain), while at the same time Jones's fixed-rate debt obligation increases (Jones has an economic loss).

The swap is an effective risk-management tool in this setting. Its value relates to the same underlying (interest rates) that will affect the value of the fixed-rate bond payable. Thus, if the value of the swap goes up, it offsets the loss related to the debt obligation.

Assuming that Jones enters into the swap on January 2, 2011 (the same date as the issuance of the debt), the swap at this time has no value. Therefore no entry is necessary.

January 2, 2011

No entry required. A memorandum entry indicates the signing of the swap contract.

---

[37]This economic loss arises because Jones is locked into the 8 percent interest payments even if rates decline.

[38]The underlying for an interest rate swap is some index of market interest rates. The most commonly used index is the London Interbank Offer Rate, or LIBOR. In this example, we assume the LIBOR is 6.8 percent.

At the end of 2011, Jones makes the interest payment on the bonds. It records this transaction as follows.

December 31, 2011

Interest Expense	80,000	
Cash (8% × €1,000,000)		80,000

At the end of 2011, market interest rates have declined substantially. Therefore, the value of the swap contract increases. Recall (see Illustration 17B-9) that in the swap, Jones receives a fixed rate of 8 percent, or €80,000 (€1,000,000 × 8%), and pays a variable rate (6.8%), or €68,000. Jones therefore receives €12,000 (€80,000 − €68,000) as a settlement payment on the swap contract on the first interest payment date. Jones records this transaction as follows.

December 31, 2011

Cash	12,000	
Interest Expense		12,000

In addition, a market appraisal indicates that the value of the interest rate swap has increased €40,000. Jones records this increase in value as follows.[39]

December 31, 2011

Swap Contract	40,000	
Unrealized Holding Gain or Loss—Income		40,000

Jones reports this swap contract in the statement of financial position. It reports the gain on the hedging transaction in the income statement. Because interest rates have declined, the company records a loss and a related increase in its liability as follows.

December 31, 2011

Unrealized Holding Gain or Loss—Income	40,000	
Bonds Payable		40,000

Jones reports the loss on the hedging activity in net income. It adjusts bonds payable in the statement of financial position to fair value.

Financial Statement Presentation of an Interest Rate Swap

Illustration 17B-11 indicates how Jones reports the asset and liability related to this hedging transaction on the statement of financial position.

ILLUSTRATION 17B-11
Statement of Financial Position Presentation of Fair Value Hedge

JONES COMPANY STATEMENT OF FINANCIAL POSITION (PARTIAL) DECEMBER 31, 2011	
Current assets	
Swap contract	€40,000
Non-current liabilities	
Bonds payable	€1,040,000

The effect on Jones's statement of financial position is the addition of the swap asset and an increase in the carrying value of the bonds payable. Illustration 17B-12 indicates how Jones reports the effects of this swap transaction in the income statement.

On the income statement, Jones reports interest expense of €68,000. Jones has effectively changed the debt's interest rate from fixed to variable. That is, by receiving a fixed rate and paying a variable rate on the swap, the company converts the fixed

[39]Theoretically, this fair value change reflects the present value of expected future differences in variable and fixed interest rates.

JONES COMPANY INCOME STATEMENT (PARTIAL) FOR THE YEAR ENDED DECEMBER 31, 2011		
Interest expense (€80,000 − €12,000)		€68,000
Other income and expense		
Unrealized holding gain—swap contract	€40,000	
Unrealized holding loss—bonds payable	(40,000)	
Net gain (loss)		€-0-

ILLUSTRATION 17B-12
Income Statement
Presentation of Fair
Value Hedge

rate on the bond payable to variable. This results in an effective interest rate of 6.8 percent in 2011.[40] Also, the gain on the swap offsets the loss related to the debt obligation. Therefore, the net gain or loss on the hedging activity is zero.

Illustration 17B-13 shows the overall impact of the swap transaction on the financial statements.

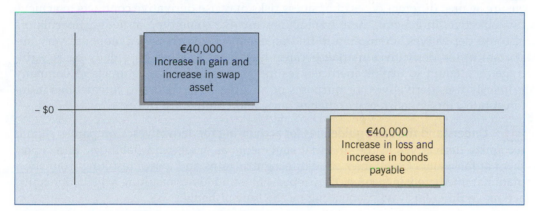

ILLUSTRATION 17B-13
Impact on Financial
Statements of Fair
Value Hedge

In summary, to account for fair value hedges (as illustrated in the Jones example) **record the derivative at its fair value in the statement of financial position, and record any gains and losses in income**. Thus, the gain on the swap offsets or hedges the loss on the bond payable, due to the decline in interest rates.

By adjusting the hedged item (the bond payable in the Jones case) to fair value, with the gain or loss recorded in earnings, the accounting for the Jones bond payable deviates from amortized cost. This special accounting is justified in order to report accurately the nature of the hedging relationship between the swap and the bond payable in the statement of financial position (both the swap and the debt obligation are recorded at fair value) and in the income statement (offsetting gains and losses are reported in the same period).[41]

CONTROVERSY AND CONCLUDING REMARKS

Companies need rules to properly measure and report derivatives in financial statements. However, some argue that reporting derivatives at fair value results in unrealized gains and losses that are difficult to interpret. Still, others raise concerns about the complexity and cost of implementing IFRS in this area.

[40]Jones will apply similar accounting and measurement at future interest payment dates. Thus, if interest rates increase, Jones will continue to receive 8 percent on the swap (records a loss) but will also be locked into the fixed payments to the bondholders at an 8 percent rate (records a gain).

[41]An interest rate swap can also be used in a cash flow hedge. A common setting is the cash flow risk inherent in having variable rate debt as part of a company's debt structure. In this situation, the variable debt issuer can hedge the cash flow risk by entering into a swap contract to receive variable rate cash flows but pay fixed rate. The cash received on the swap contract will offset the variable cash flows to be paid on the debt obligation.

However, we believe that the long-term benefits of using fair value and reporting derivatives at fair value will far outweigh any short-term implementation costs. As the volume and complexity of derivatives and hedging transactions continue to grow, so does the risk that investors and creditors will be exposed to unexpected losses arising from derivative transactions. Statement readers must have comprehensive information concerning many derivative financial instruments and the effects of hedging transactions using derivatives.

SUMMARY OF LEARNING OBJECTIVES FOR APPENDIX 17B

•10 Explain who uses derivatives and why. Any company or individual that wants to ensure against different types of business risks may use derivative contracts to achieve this objective. In general, these transactions involve some type of hedge. Speculators also use derivatives, attempting to find an enhanced return. Speculators are very important to the derivatives market because they keep it liquid on a daily basis. Arbitrageurs attempt to exploit inefficiencies in various derivative contracts. A company primarily uses derivatives for purposes of hedging its exposure to fluctuations in interest rates, foreign currency exchange rates, and commodity prices.

•11 Understand the basic guidelines for accounting for derivatives. Companies should recognize derivatives in the financial statements as assets and liabilities, and report them at fair value. Companies should recognize gains and losses resulting from speculation immediately in income. They report gains and losses resulting from hedge transactions in different ways, depending on the type of hedge.

•12 Describe the accounting for derivative financial instruments. Companies report derivative financial instruments in the statement of financial position, and record them at fair value. Except for derivatives used in hedging, companies record realized and unrealized gains and losses on derivative financial instruments in income.

•13 Explain how to account for a fair value hedge. A company records the derivative used in a qualifying fair value hedge at its fair value in the statement of financial position, recording any gains and losses in income. In addition, the company also accounts for the item being hedged with the derivative at fair value. By adjusting the hedged item to fair value, with the gain or loss recorded in earnings, the accounting for the hedged item may deviate from IFRS in the absence of a hedge relationship. This special accounting is justified in order to report accurately the nature of the hedging relationship between the derivative hedging instruments and the hedged item. A company reports both in the statement of financial position, reporting offsetting gains and losses in income in the same period.

•14 Explain how to account for a cash flow hedge. Companies account for derivatives used in qualifying cash flow hedges at fair value on the statement of financial position, but record gains or losses in equity as part of other comprehensive income. Companies accumulate these gains or losses, and reclassify them in income when the hedged transaction's cash flows affect earnings. Accounting is according to IFRS for the hedged item.

•15 Identify special reporting issues related to derivative financial instruments that cause unique accounting problems. A company should, based on the classification of the host security, account for a hybrid security containing a host security and an embedded derivative as a single unit. Special hedge accounting is allowed only for hedging relationships that meet certain criteria. The main criteria are: (1) There is formal documentation of the hedging relationship, the company's risk management objective, and the strategy for undertaking the hedge, and the company designates the derivative as either a cash flow or fair value hedge. (2) The company expects the hedging relationship to be highly effective in achieving offsetting changes in fair value or cash flows. (3) "Special" hedge accounting is necessary only when there is a mismatch of the accounting effects for the hedging instrument and the hedged item under IFRS.

AUTHORITATIVE LITERATURE

Authoritative Literature References

[1] International Accounting Standard 32, *Financial Instruments: Presentation* (London, U.K.: International Accounting Standards Committee Foundation, 2003), par. 11.

[2] International Financial Reporting Standard 9, *Financial Instruments* (London, U.K.: International Accounting Standards Committee Foundation, 2009), par. 4.1.

[3] International Financial Reporting Standard 9, *Financial Instruments* (London, U.K.: International Accounting Standards Committee Foundation, 2009), paras. BC19–21.

[4] International Accounting Standard 32, *Financial Instruments: Presentation* (London, U.K.: International Accounting Standards Committee Foundation, 2003), par. 11.

[5] International Financial Reporting Standard 9, *Financial Instruments* (London, U.K.: International Accounting Standards Committee Foundation, 2009), par. B4.3.

[6] International Financial Reporting Standard 9, *Financial Instruments* (London, U.K.: International Accounting Standards Committee Foundation, 2009), par. B4.2.

[7] International Financial Reporting Standard 9, *Financial Instruments* (London, U.K.: International Accounting Standards Committee Foundation, 2009), par. 5.1.1.

[8] International Financial Reporting Standard 9, *Financial Instruments* (London, U.K.: International Accounting Standards Committee Foundation, 2009), par. 4.5.

[9] International Financial Reporting Standard 9, *Financial Instruments* (London, U.K.: International Accounting Standards Committee Foundation, 2009), par. B5.1.1.

[10] International Financial Reporting Standard 9, *Financial Instruments* (London, U.K.: International Accounting Standards Committee Foundation, 2009), paras. B5.1–B5.6.

[11] International Financial Reporting Standard 9, *Financial Instruments* (London, U.K.: International Accounting Standards Committee Foundation, 2009), par. 5.4.4.

[12] International Financial Reporting Standard 9, *Financial Instruments* (London, U.K.: International Accounting Standards Committee Foundation, 2009), par. BC86(d).

[13] International Financial Reporting Standard 9, *Financial Instruments* (London, U.K.: International Accounting Standards Committee Foundation, 2009), par. BC86(b).

[14] International Financial Reporting Standard 9, *Financial Instruments* (London, U.K.: International Accounting Standards Committee Foundation, 2009), paras. BC83–BC84.

[15] International Accounting Standard 28, *Investments in Associates* (London, U.K.: International Accounting Standards Committee Foundation, 2003).

[16] International Accounting Standard 28, *Investments in Associates* (London, U.K.: International Accounting Standards Committee Foundation, 2003), paras. 6–10.

[17] International Accounting Standard 28, *Investments in Associates* (London, U.K.: International Accounting Standards Committee Foundation, 2003), paras. 29–30.

[18] International Accounting Standard 39, *Financial Instruments: Recognition and Measurement*, International Accounting Standards Committee Foundation, London (March 1999), paras. 58-65 and AG84–AG93.

[19] International Financial Reporting Standard 9, *Financial Instruments* (London, U.K.: International Accounting Standards Committee Foundation, 2009), paras. BC69–70.

[20] International Financial Reporting Standard 9, *Financial Instruments* (London, U.K.: International Accounting Standards Committee Foundation, 2009), paras. BC72–73.

[21] International Accounting Standard 39, *Financial Instruments: Recognition and Measurement*, International Accounting Standards Committee Foundation, London (March 1999), paras. 89–102.

[22] International Financial Reporting Standard 7, *Financial Instruments: Disclosure*, International Accounting Standards Committee Foundation, London (August 2005), paras. 27–29.

[23] International Accounting Standard 39, *Financial Instruments: Recognition and Measurement*, International Accounting Standards Committee Foundation, London (March 1999), paras. 9 and AG10–11.

[24] International Accounting Standard 39, *Financial Instruments: Recognition and Measurement*, International Accounting Standards Committee Foundation, London (March 1999).

[25] International Accounting Standard 39, *Financial Instruments: Recognition and Measurement*, International Accounting Standards Committee Foundation, London (March 1999), par. 88(a).

[26] International Accounting Standard 39, *Financial Instruments: Recognition and Measurement*, International Accounting Standards Committee Foundation, London (March 1999), paras. 88(b) and AG105.

[27] International Financial Reporting Standard 9, *Financial Instruments* (London, U.K.: International Accounting Standards Committee Foundation, 2009), par. 4.5.

Note: All asterisked Questions, Exercises, and Problems relate to material in the appendices to the chapter.

QUESTIONS

1. Describe the two criteria for determining the valuation of financial assets.

2. Which types of investments are valued at amortized cost? Explain the rationale for this accounting.

3. What is amortized cost? What is fair value?

4. Lady Gaga Co. recently made an investment in the bonds issued by Chili Peppers Inc. Lady Gaga's business model for this investment is to profit from trading in response to changes in market interest rates. How should this investment be classified by Lady Gaga? Explain.

5. Consider the bond investment by Lady Gaga in question 4. Discuss the accounting for this investment if Lady Gaga's business model is to hold the investment to collect interest while outstanding and to receive the principal at maturity.

6. On July 1, 2010, Wheeler Company purchased $4,000,000 of Duggen Company's 8% bonds, due on July 1, 2017. The bonds, which pay interest semiannually on January 1 and July 1, were purchased for $3,500,000 to yield 10%. Determine the amount of interest revenue Wheeler should report on its income statement for year ended December 31, 2010, assuming Wheeler plans to hold this investment to collect contractual cash flows.

7. If the bonds in question 6 are classified as trading and they have a fair value at December 31, 2010, of $3,604,000, prepare the journal entry (if any) at December 31, 2010, to record this transaction.

8. Indicate how unrealized holding gains and losses should be reported for investments classified as trading and held-for-collection.

9. (a) Assuming no Securities Fair Value Adjustment account balance at the beginning of the year, prepare the adjusting entry at the end of the year if Laura Company's trading bond investment has a fair value €60,000 below carrying value. (b) Assume the same information as part (a), except that Laura Company has a debit balance in its Securities Fair Value Adjustment account of €10,000 at the beginning of the year. Prepare the adjusting entry at year-end.

10. What is the fair value option? Briefly describe its application to debt investments.

11. Franklin Corp. has an investment that it has held for several years. When it purchased the investment, Franklin accounted for the investment at amortized cost. Can Franklin use the fair value option for this investment? Explain.

12. Identify and explain the different types of classifications for equity investments.

13. Why is the held-for-collection classification not applicable to equity investments?

14. Hayes Company purchased 10,000 ordinary shares of Kenyon Co., paying $26 per share plus $1,500 in broker fees. Hayes plans to actively trade this investment. Prepare the entry to record this investment.

15. Hayes Company sold 10,000 shares of Kenyon Co. that it bought in question 14 for $27.50 per share, incurring $1,770 in brokerage commissions. The carrying value of the investment is $260,000. Prepare the entry to record the sale of this investment.

16. Distinguish between the accounting treatment for nontrading equity investments and trading equity investments.

17. What constitutes "significant influence" when an investor's financial interest is below the 50% level?

18. Explain how the investment account is affected by investee activities under the equity method.

19. When the equity method is applied, what amounts relate to the investment, and where will these amounts be reported in the financial statements?

20. Hiram Co. uses the equity method to account for investments in ordinary shares. What accounting should be made for dividends received from these investments subsequent to the date of investment?

21. Raleigh Corp. has an investment with a carrying value (equity method) on its books of £170,000 representing a 30% interest in Borg Company, which suffered a £620,000 loss this year. How should Raleigh Corp. handle its proportionate share of Borg's loss?

22. Where on the asset side of the statement of financial position are amounts related to equity investments classified as trading and non-trading reported? Explain.

23. When is a debt investment considered impaired? Explain how to account for the impairment of a held-for-collection debt investment.

24. Briefly discuss how a transfer of investments from the trading category to the held-for-collection category affects the financial statements.

25. Briefly describe the unresolved issues related to fair value accounting.

26. Briefly describe some of the similarities and differences between U.S. GAAP and IFRS with respect to the accounting for investments.

27. Ramirez Company has a held-for-collection investment in the 6%, 20-year bonds of Soto Company. The investment was originally purchased for R$1,200,000 in 2009. Early in 2010, Ramirez recorded an impairment of R$300,000 on the Soto investment, due to Soto's financial distress. In 2011, Soto returned to profitability and the Soto investment was no longer impaired. What entry does Ramirez make in 2011 under (a) U.S. GAAP and (b) IFRS?

28. Discuss how recent IFRS developments in the accounting for investments might affect convergence with U.S. GAAP.

*29.** Explain why reclassification adjustments are necessary.

*30.** What is meant by the term underlying as it relates to derivative financial instruments?

*31.** What are the main distinctions between a traditional financial instrument and a derivative financial instrument?

*32.** What is the purpose of a fair value hedge?

*33.** In what situation will the unrealized holding gain or loss on a non-trading equity investment be reported in income?

*34.** Why might a company become involved in an interest rate swap contract to receive fixed interest payments and pay variable?

*35.** What is the purpose of a cash flow hedge?

*36.** Where are gains and losses related to cash flow hedges involving anticipated transactions reported?

*37.** What are hybrid securities? Give an example of a hybrid security.

BRIEF EXERCISES

BE17-1 Garfield Company made an investment in €80,000 of the 9%, 5-year bonds of Chester Corporation for €74,086, which provides an 11% return. Garfield plans to hold these bonds to collect contractual cash flows. Prepare Garfield's journal entries for (a) the purchase of the investment, and (b) the receipt of annual interest and discount amortization.

BE17-2 Use the information from BE17-1, but assume Garfield plans to actively trade the bonds to profit from market interest rates changes. Prepare Garfield's journal entries for (a) the purchase of the investment, (b) the receipt of annual interest and discount amortization, and (c) the year-end fair value adjustment. The bonds have a year-end fair value of €75,500.

BE17-3 Carow Corporation purchased, as a held-for-collection investment, €60,000 of the 8%, 5-year bonds of Harrison, Inc. for €65,118, which provides a 6% return. The bonds pay interest semiannually. Prepare Carow's journal entries for (a) the purchase of the investment, and (b) the receipt of semiannual interest and premium amortization.

BE17-4 Hendricks Corporation purchased $50,000 of bonds at par. Hendricks has an active trading business model for this investment. At December 31, Hendricks received annual interest of $2,000, and the fair value of the bonds was $47,400. Prepare Hendricks' journal entries for (a) the purchase of the investment, (b) the interest received, and (c) the fair value adjustment.

•4 **BE17-5** Refer to the information in BE17-3. Assume that, to address a measurement mismatch, Carow elects the fair value option for this debt investment. Prepare the journal entry at year-end, assuming the fair value of the bonds is €64,000.

•5 **BE17-6** Fairbanks Corporation purchased 400 ordinary shares of Sherman Inc. as a trading investment for £13,200. During the year, Sherman paid a cash dividend of £3.25 per share. At year-end, Sherman shares were selling for £34.50 per share. Prepare Fairbanks's journal entries to record (a) the purchase of the investment, (b) the dividends received, and (c) the fair value adjustment.

•5 **BE17-7** Use the information from BE17-6 but assume the shares were purchased to meet a non-trading regulatory requirement. Prepare Fairbanks's journal entries to record (a) the purchase of the investment, (b) the dividends received, and (c) the fair value adjustment.

•5 **BE17-8** Cleveland Company has a non-trading equity investment portfolio valued at $4,000. Its cost was $3,300. If the Securities Fair Value Adjustment account has a debit balance of $200, prepare the journal entry at year-end.

•6 **BE17-9** Zoop Corporation purchased for $300,000 a 30% interest in Murphy, Inc. This investment enables Zoop to exert significant influence over Murphy. During the year, Murphy earned net income of $180,000 and paid dividends of $60,000. Prepare Zoop's journal entries related to this investment.

•7 **BE17-10** Hillsborough Co. has a held-for-collection investment in the bonds of Schuyler Corp. with a carrying (and fair) value of $70,000. Hillsborough determined that due to poor economic prospects for Schuyler, Hillsborough will not be able to collect all contractual cash flows and the bonds have decreased in value to $60,000. It is determined that this is a permanent loss in value. Prepare the journal entry, if any, to record the reduction in value.

•8 **BE17-11** Cameron Company has a portfolio of debt investments that it has managed as a trading investment. At December 31, 2010, Cameron had the following balances related to this portfolio: debt investments, £250,000; securities fair value adjustment, £10,325 (Dr). Cameron management decides to change its business model for these investments to a held-for-collection strategy, beginning in January 2011. Prepare the journal entry to transfer these investments to the held-for-collection classification.

•9 ***BE17-12** The following information relates to Archibold Co. for 2011: net income €672.638 million; unrealized holding loss of €20.380 million related to a non-trading equity investment during the year; accumulated other comprehensive income of €37.273 million on October 1, 2010. Assuming no other changes in accumulated other comprehensive income, determine (a) other comprehensive income for 2011, (b) comprehensive income for 2011, and (c) accumulated other comprehensive income at September 30, 2011.

EXERCISES

•1 •3 **E17-1** **(Investment Classifications)** For the following investments, identify whether they are:

1. Debt investments at amortized cost.
2. Debt investments at fair value.
3. Trading equity investments.
4. Non-trading equity investments.

Each case is independent of the other.

(a) A bond that will mature in 4 years was bought 1 month ago when the price dropped. As soon as the value increases, which is expected next month, it will be sold.

(b) 10% of the outstanding shares of Farm-Co was purchased. The company is planning on eventually getting a total of 30% of its outstanding shares.

(c) 10-year bonds were purchased this year. The bonds mature at the first of next year, and the company plans to sell the bonds if interest rates fall.

(d) Bonds that will mature in 5 years are purchased. The company has a strategy to hold them to collect the contractual cash flows on the bond.

(e) A bond that matures in 10 years was purchased. The company is investing money set aside for an expansion project planned 10 years from now.

(f) Ordinary shares in a distributor are purchased to meet a regulatory requirement for doing business in the distributor's region. The investment will be held indefinitely.

•2 E17-2 (Debt Investments) On January 1, 2010, Jennings Company purchased at par 10% bonds having a maturity value of €300,000. They are dated January 1, 2010, and mature January 1, 2015, with interest receivable December 31 of each year. The bonds are held to collect contractual cash flows.

Instructions

(a) Prepare the journal entry at the date of the bond purchase.
(b) Prepare the journal entry to record the interest received for 2010.
(c) Prepare the journal entry to record the interest received for 2011.

•2 E17-3 (Debt Investments) On January 1, 2010, Roosevelt Company purchased 12% bonds, having a maturity value of $500,000, for $537,907.40. The bonds provide the bondholders with a 10% yield. They are dated January 1, 2010, and mature January 1, 2015, with interest receivable December 31 of each year. Roosevelt's business model is to hold these bonds to collect contractual cash flows.

Instructions

(a) Prepare the journal entry at the date of the bond purchase.
(b) Prepare a bond amortization schedule.
(c) Prepare the journal entry to record the interest received and the amortization for 2010.
(d) Prepare the journal entry to record the interest received and the amortization for 2011.

•2 E17-4 (Debt Investments) On January 1, 2010, Morgan Company acquires $300,000 of Nicklaus, Inc., 9% bonds at a price of $278,384. The interest is payable each December 31, and the bonds mature December 31, 2012. The investment will provide Morgan Company a 12% yield. The bonds are classified as held-for-collection.

Instructions

(a) Prepare a 3-year schedule of interest revenue and bond discount amortization. (Round to nearest cent.)
(b) Prepare the journal entry for the interest receipt of December 31, 2011, and the discount amortization.

•3 E17-5 (Debt Investments) Assume the same information as in E17-3 except that Roosevelt has an active trading strategy for these bonds. The fair value of the bonds at December 31 of each year-end is as follows.

2010	$534,200	2013	$517,000
2011	$515,000	2014	$500,000
2012	$513,000		

Instructions

(a) Prepare the journal entry at the date of the bond purchase.
(b) Prepare the journal entries to record the interest received and recognition of fair value for 2010.
(c) Prepare the journal entry to record the recognition of fair value for 2011.

•4 E17-6 (Fair Value Option) Refer to the information in E17-3 and assume that Roosevelt elected the fair value option for this held-for-collection investment.

Instructions

(a) Prepare any entries necessary at December 31, 2010, assuming the fair value of the bonds is $540,000.
(b) Prepare any entries necessary at December 31, 2011, assuming the fair value of the bonds is $525,000.

•4 E17-7 (Fair Value Option) Presented below is selected information related to the financial instruments of Dawson Company at December 31, 2010. This is Dawson Company's first year of operations.

	Carrying Amount	Fair Value (at December 31)
Debt investments (intent is to hold for collection)	$ 40,000	$ 41,000
Bonds payable	220,000	195,000

Instructions

(a) Dawson elects to use the fair value option whenever possible. Assuming that Dawson's net income is $100,000 in 2010 before reporting any financial instrument gains or losses, determine Dawson's net income for 2010.
(b) Record the journal entry, if any, necessary at December 31, 2010, to record the fair value option for the bonds payable.

•5 **E17-8** **(Entries for Equity Investments)** The following information is available for Kinney Company at December 31, 2010, regarding its investments.

Investments	Cost	Fair Value
3,000 ordinary shares of Petty Corporation	£40,000	£46,000
1,000 preference shares of Dowe Incorporated	25,000	22,000
	£65,000	£68,000

Instructions

(a) Prepare the adjusting entry (if any) for 2010, assuming the investments are classified as trading.

(b) Prepare the adjusting entry (if any) for 2010, assuming the investments are classified as non-trading.

(c) Discuss how the amounts reported in the financial statements are affected by the entries in (a) and (b).

•5 **E17-9** **(Equity Investments)** On December 21, 2010, Zurich Company provided you with the following information regarding its trading investments.

December 31, 2010

Investments (Trading)	Cost	Fair Value	Unrealized Gain (Loss)
Stargate Corp. shares	€20,000	€19,000	€(1,000)
Carolina Co. shares	10,000	9,000	(1,000)
Vectorman Co. shares	20,000	20,600	600
Total of portfolio	€50,000	€48,600	(1,400)
Previous securities fair value adjustment balance			–0–
Securities fair value adjustment—Cr.			€(1,400)

During 2011, Carolina Company shares were sold for €9,500. The fair value of the shares on December 31, 2011, was: Stargate Corp. shares—€19,300; Vectorman Co. shares—€20,500.

Instructions

(a) Prepare the adjusting journal entry needed on December 31, 2010.

(b) Prepare the journal entry to record the sale of the Carolina Company shares during 2011.

(c) Prepare the adjusting journal entry needed on December 31, 2011.

•5 **E17-10** **(Equity Investment Entries and Reporting)** Player Corporation makes an equity investment costing $73,000 and classifies it as non-trading. At December 31, the fair value of the investment is $67,000.

Instructions

Prepare the adjusting entry to report the investments properly. Indicate the statement presentation of the accounts in your entry.

•5 **E17-11** **(Equity Investment Entries and Financial Statement Presentation)** At December 31, 2010, the equity investment portfolio for Wenger, Inc. is as follows.

Investment	Cost	Fair Value	Unrealized Gain (Loss)
A	$17,500	$15,000	($2,500)
B	12,500	14,000	1,500
C	23,000	25,500	2,500
Total	$53,000	$54,500	1,500
Previous securities fair value adjustment balance—Dr.			200
Securities fair value adjustment—Dr.			$1,300

On January 20, 2011, Wenger, Inc. sold investment A for $15,300. The sale proceeds are net of brokerage fees.

Instructions

(a) Prepare the adjusting entry at December 31, 2010, to report the portfolio at fair value.

(b) Show the statement of financial position presentation of the investment related accounts at December 31, 2010. (Ignore notes presentation.)

(c) Prepare the journal entry for the 2011 sale of investment A.

(d) Repeat requirement (a), assuming the portfolio of investments is non-trading.

•5 **E17-12** **(Equity Investment Entries)** Capriati Corporation made the following cash investments during 2010, which is the first year in which Capriati invested in securities.

1. On January 15, purchased 9,000 ordinary shares of Gonzalez Company at $33.50 per share plus commission $1,980.

    2. On April 1, purchased 5,000 ordinary shares of Belmont Co. at $52.00 per share plus commission $3,370.

    3. On September 10, purchased 7,000 preference shares of Thep Co. at $26.50 per share plus commission $4,910.

On May 20, 2010, Capriati sold 3,000 shares of Gonzalez Company at a market price of $35 per share less brokerage commissions, taxes, and fees of $2,850. The year-end fair values per share were: Gonzalez $30, Belmont $55, and Thep $28. In addition, the chief accountant of Capriati told you that Capriati Corporation plans to actively trade these investments.

Instructions

    (a) Prepare the journal entries to record the above three investment purchases.

    (b) Prepare the journal entry for the investment sale on May 20.

    (c) Compute the unrealized gains or losses and prepare the adjusting entries for Capriati on December 31, 2010.

•5 •6 E17-13 **(Journal Entries for Fair Value and Equity Methods)** Presented below are two independent situations.

Situation 1

Hatcher Cosmetics acquired 10% of the 200,000 ordinary shares of Ramirez Fashion at a total cost of $14 per share on March 18, 2010. On June 30, Ramirez declared and paid a $75,000 cash dividend. On December 31, Ramirez reported net income of $122,000 for the year. At December 31, the market price of Ramirez Fashion was $15 per share. The investment is classified as trading.

Situation 2

Holmes, Inc. obtained significant influence over Nadal Corporation by buying 25% of Nadal's 30,000 outstanding ordinary shares at a total cost of $9 per share on January 1, 2010. On June 15, Nadal declared and paid a cash dividend of $36,000. On December 31, Nadal reported a net income of $85,000 for the year.

Instructions

Prepare all necessary journal entries in 2010 for both situations.

•6 E17-14 **(Equity Method)** Gator Co. invested $1,000,000 in Demo Co. for 25% of its outstanding shares. Demo Co. pays out 40% of net income in dividends each year.

Instructions

Use the information in the following T-account for the investment in Demo to answer the following questions.

Investment in Demo Co.

1,000,000	
130,000	
	52,000

    (a) How much was Gator Co.'s share of Demo Co.'s net income for the year?

    (b) How much was Gator Co.'s share of Demo Co.'s dividends for the year?

    (c) What was Demo Co.'s total net income for the year?

    (d) What was Demo Co.'s total dividends for the year?

•5 E17-15 **(Equity Investments—Trading)** Feiner Co. had purchased 300 shares of Guttman Co. for $40 each this year and classified the investment as a trading investment. Feiner Co. sold 100 shares for $43 each. At year-end, the price per share had dropped to $35.

Instructions

Prepare the journal entries for these transactions and any year-end adjustments.

•5 E17-16 **(Equity Investments—Trading)** Swanson Company has the following trading investment portfolio on December 31, 2010.

Investments (Trading)	Cost	Fair Value
1,500 ordinary shares of Parker, Inc.	£ 71,500	£ 69,000
5,000 ordinary shares of Beilman Corp.	180,000	175,000
400 preference shares of Duncan, Inc.	60,000	61,600
	£311,500	£305,600

All of the investments were purchased in 2010. In 2011, Swanson completed the following investment transactions.

March 1	Sold the 1,500 ordinary shares of Parker, Inc., @ £45 less fees of £1,200.
April 1	Bought 700 ordinary shares of McDowell Corp., @ £75 plus fees of £1,300.

Swanson Company's portfolio of trading investments appeared as follows on December 31, 2011.

Investments (Trading)	Cost	Fair Value
5,000 ordinary shares of Beilman Corp.	£180,000	£175,000
700 ordinary shares of McDowell Corp.	52,500	50,400
400 preference shares of Duncan, Inc.	60,000	58,000
	£292,500	£283,400

Instructions

Prepare the general journal entries for Swanson Company for:

(a) The 2010 adjusting entry.
(b) The sale of the Parker shares.
(c) The purchase of the McDowell shares.
(d) The 2011 adjusting entry for the trading portfolio.

•5 •6 E17-17 (Fair Value and Equity Method Compared) Chen Inc. acquired 20% of the outstanding ordinary shares of Cho Corp. on December 31, 2010. The purchase price was ¥125,000,000 for 50,000 shares. Cho Corp. declared and paid an ¥80 per share cash dividend on June 30 and on December 31, 2011. Cho reported net income of ¥73,000,000 for 2011. The fair value of Cho's shares was ¥2,700 per share at December 31, 2011.

Instructions

(a) Prepare the journal entries for Chen Inc. for 2010 and 2011, assuming that Chen cannot exercise significant influence over Cho. The investments should be classified as trading.
(b) Prepare the journal entries for Chen Inc. for 2010 and 2011, assuming that Chen can exercise significant influence over Cho.
(c) At what amount is the investment reported on the statement of financial position under each of these methods at December 31, 2011? What is the total net income reported in 2011 under each of these methods?

•6 E17-18 (Equity Method) On January 1, 2010, Meredith Corporation purchased 25% of the ordinary shares of Pirates Company for £200,000. During the year, Pirates earned net income of £80,000 and paid dividends of £20,000.

Instructions

Prepare the entries for Meredith to record the purchase and any additional entries related to this investment in Pirates Company in 2010.

•7 E17-19 (Impairment) Cairo Corporation has government bonds classified as held-for-collection at December 31, 2010. These bonds have a par value of $800,000, an amortized cost of $800,000, and a fair value of $740,000. In evaluating the bonds, Cairo determines the bonds have a $60,000 permanent decline in value. That is, the company believes that impairment accounting is now appropriate for these bonds.

Instructions

(a) Prepare the journal entry to recognize the impairment.
(b) What is the new cost basis of the bonds? Given that the maturity value of the bonds is $800,000, should Cairo Corporation amortize the difference between the carrying amount and the maturity value over the life of the bonds?
(c) At December 31, 2011, the fair value of the municipal bonds is $760,000. Prepare the entry (if any) to record this information.

•7 E17-20 (Impairment) Komissarov Company has a debt investment in the bonds issued by Keune Inc. The bonds were purchased at par for €400,000 and, at the end of 2010, have a remaining life of 3 years with annual interest payments at 10%, paid at the end of each year. This debt investment is classified as held-for-collection. Keune is facing a tough economic environment and informs all of its investors that it will be unable to make all payments according to the contractual terms. The controller of Komissarov has prepared the following revised expected cash flow forecast for this bond investment.

Dec. 31	Expected Cash Flows
2011	€ 35,000
2012	35,000
2013	385,000
Total cash flows	€455,000

Instructions

(a) Determine the impairment loss for Komissarov at December 31, 2010.
(b) Prepare the entry to record the impairment loss for Komissarov at December 31, 2010.
(c) On January 15, 2011, Keune receives a major capital infusion from a private equity investor. It informs Komissarov that the bonds now will be paid according to the contractual terms. Briefly describe how Komissarov would account for the bond investment in light of this new information.

•9 ***E17-21** **(Comprehensive Income Disclosure)** Assume the same information as in E17-11 (non-trading investments) and that Wenger, Inc. reports net income in 2010 of $120,000 and in 2011 of $140,000. Total holding gains (including any realized holding gain or loss) arising during 2011 total $30,000.

Instructions

(a) Prepare a statement of comprehensive income for 2010, starting with net income.
(b) Prepare a statement of comprehensive income for 2011, starting with net income.

•12 ***E17-22** **(Derivative Transaction)** On January 2, 2010, Jones Company purchases a call option for $300 on Merchant ordinary shares. The call option gives Jones the option to buy 1,000 shares of Merchant at a strike price of $50 per share. The market price of a Merchant share is $50 on January 2, 2010 (the intrinsic value is therefore $0). On March 31, 2010, the market price for Merchant shares is $53 per share, and the time value of the option is $200.

Instructions

(a) Prepare the journal entry to record the purchase of the call option on January 2, 2010.
(b) Prepare the journal entry(ies) to recognize the change in the fair value of the call option as of March 31, 2010.
(c) What was the effect on net income of entering into the derivative transaction for the period January 2 to March 31, 2010? (Ignore tax effects.)

•13 ***E17-23 (Fair Value Hedge)** On January 2, 2010, MacCloud Co. issued a 4-year, €100,000 note at 6% fixed interest, interest payable semiannually. MacCloud now wants to change the note to a variable-rate note.
   As a result, on January 2, 2010, MacCloud Co. enters into an interest rate swap where it agrees to receive 6% fixed and pay LIBOR of 5.7% for the first 6 months on €100,000. At each 6-month period, the variable rate will be reset. The variable rate is reset to 6.7% on June 30, 2010.

Instructions

(a) Compute the net interest expense to be reported for this note and related swap transaction as of June 30, 2010.
(b) Compute the net interest expense to be reported for this note and related swap transaction as of December 31, 2010.

•14 ***E17-24 (Cash Flow Hedge)** On January 2, 2010, Parton Company issues a 5-year, $10,000,000 note at LIBOR, with interest paid annually. The variable rate is reset at the end of each year. The LIBOR rate for the first year is 5.8%.
   Parton Company decides it prefers fixed-rate financing and wants to lock in a rate of 6%. As a result, Parton enters into an interest rate swap to pay 6% fixed and receive LIBOR based on $10 million. The variable rate is reset to 6.6% on January 2, 2011.

Instructions

(a) Compute the net interest expense to be reported for this note and related swap transactions as of December 31, 2010.
(b) Compute the net interest expense to be reported for this note and related swap transactions as of December 31, 2011.

•13 ***E17-25** **(Fair Value Hedge)** Sarazan Company issues a 4-year, 7.5% fixed-rate interest only, non-prepayable £1,000,000 note payable on December 31, 2010. It decides to change the interest rate from a fixed rate to variable rate and enters into a swap agreement with M&S Corp. The swap agreement specifies that Sarazan will receive a fixed rate at 7.5% and pay variable with settlement dates that match the interest payments on the debt. Assume that interest rates have declined during 2011 and that Sarazan received £13,000 as an adjustment to interest expense for the settlement at December 31, 2011. The loss related to the debt (due to interest rate changes) was £48,000. The value of the swap contract increased £48,000.

Instructions

(a) Prepare the journal entry to record the payment of interest expense on December 31, 2011.
(b) Prepare the journal entry to record the receipt of the swap settlement on December 31, 2011.

   (c) Prepare the journal entry to record the change in the fair value of the swap contract on December 31, 2011.

   (d) Prepare the journal entry to record the change in the fair value of the debt on December 31, 2011.

•12 *E17-26 (Call Option) On August 15, 2010, Outkast Co. invested idle cash by purchasing a call option on Counting Crows Inc. ordinary shares for $360. The notional value of the call option is 400 shares, and the option price is $40. (Market price of a Counting Crows share is $40.) The option expires on January 31, 2011. The following data are available with respect to the call option.

Date	Market Price of Counting Crows Shares	Time Value of Call Option
September 30, 2010	$48 per share	$180
December 31, 2010	$46 per share	65
January 15, 2011	$47 per share	30

Instructions

Prepare the journal entries for Outkast for the following dates.

   (a) Investment in call option on Counting Crows shares on August 15, 2010.

   (b) September 30, 2010—Outkast prepares financial statements.

   (c) December 31, 2010—Outkast prepares financial statements.

   (d) January 15, 2011—Outkast settles the call option on the Counting Crows shares.

•14 *E17-27 (Cash Flow Hedge) Choi Golf Co. uses titanium in the production of its specialty drivers. Choi anticipates that it will need to purchase 200 ounces of titanium in October 2010, for clubs that will be shipped in the holiday shopping season. However, if the price of titanium increases, this will increase the cost to produce the clubs, which will result in lower profit margins.

   To hedge the risk of increased titanium prices, on May 1, 2010, Choi enters into a titanium futures contract and designates this futures contract as cash flow hedge of the anticipated titanium purchase. The notional amount of the contract is 200 ounces, and the terms of the contract give Choi the right and the obligation to purchase titanium at a price of ¥50,000 per ounce. The price will be good until the contract expires on November 30, 2010.

   Assume the following data with respect to the price of the call options and the titanium inventory purchase.

Date	Spot Price for November Delivery
May 1, 2010	¥50,000 per ounce
June 30, 2010	52,000 per ounce
September 30, 2011	52,500 per ounce

Instructions

Present the journal entries for the following dates/transactions.

   (a) May 1, 2010—Inception of futures contract, no premium paid.

   (b) June 30, 2010—Choi prepares financial statements.

   (c) September 30, 2010—Choi prepares financial statements.

   (d) October 5, 2010—Choi purchases 200 ounces of titanium at ¥52,500 per ounce and settles the futures contract.

   (e) December 15, 2010—Choi sells clubs containing titanium purchased in October 2010 for ¥25,000,000. The cost of the finished goods inventory is ¥14,000,000.

   (f) Indicate the amount(s) reported in the income statement related to the futures contract and the inventory transactions on December 31, 2010.

PROBLEMS

•2 •3 P17-1 (Debt Investments) Presented below is an amortization schedule related to Spangler Company's 5-year, $100,000 bond with a 7% interest rate and a 5% yield, purchased on December 31, 2008, for $108,660.

Date	Cash Received	Interest Revenue	Bond Premium Amortization	Carrying Amount of Bonds
12/31/08				$108,660
12/31/09	$7,000	$5,433	$1,567	107,093
12/31/10	7,000	5,354	1,646	105,447
12/31/11	7,000	5,272	1,728	103,719
12/31/12	7,000	5,186	1,814	101,905
12/31/13	7,000	5,095	1,905	100,000

The following schedule presents a comparison of the amortized cost and fair value of the bonds at year-end.

	12/31/09	12/31/10	12/31/11	12/31/12	12/31/13
Amortized cost	$107,093	$105,447	$103,719	$101,905	$100,000
Fair value	$106,500	$107,500	$105,650	$103,000	$100,000

Instructions

(a) Prepare the journal entry to record the purchase of these bonds on December 31, 2008, assuming the bonds are classified as held-for-collection investments.

(b) Prepare the journal entry(ies) related to the held-for-collection bonds for 2009.

(c) Prepare the journal entry(ies) related to the held-for-collection bonds for 2011.

(d) Prepare the journal entry(ies) to record the purchase of these bonds, assuming they are classified as trading.

(e) Prepare the journal entry(ies) related to the trading bonds for 2009.

(f) Prepare the journal entry(ies) related to the trading bonds for 2011.

•2 •4 P17-2 (Debt Investments, Fair Value Option) On January 1, 2010, Novotna Company purchased €400,000, 8% bonds of Aguirre Co. for €369,114. The bonds were purchased to yield 10% interest. Interest is payable semiannually on July 1 and January 1. The bonds mature on January 1, 2015. Novotna Company plans to hold the bonds to collect contractual cash flows. On January 1, 2012, after receiving interest, Novotna Company sold the bonds for €370,726 after receiving interest to meet its liquidity needs.

Instructions

(a) Prepare the journal entry to record the purchase of bonds on January 1.

(b) Prepare the amortization schedule for the bonds.

(c) Prepare the journal entries to record the semiannual interest on July 1, 2010, and December 31, 2010.

(d) Prepare the journal entry to record the sale of the bonds on January 1, 2012.

(e) Assume that Novotna elected the fair value option for this investment. If the fair value of Aguirre bonds is €368,000 on December 31, 2010, prepare the necessary adjusting entry.

•3 •5 P17-3 (Debt and Equity Investments) Cardinal Paz Corp. carries an account in its general ledger called Investments, which contained debits for investment purchases, and no credits, with the following descriptions.

Feb. 1, 2010	Sharapova Company ordinary shares, $100 par, 200 shares	$ 37,400
April 1	Government bonds, 11%, due April 1, 2020, interest payable April 1 and October 1, 110 bonds of $1,000 par each	110,000
July 1	McGrath Company 12% bonds, par $50,000, dated March 1, 2010 purchased at 104, plus accrued interest payable annually on March 1, due March 1, 2030	54,000

Instructions

(Round all computations to the nearest dollar.)

(a) Prepare entries necessary to classify the amounts into proper accounts, assuming that Paz plans to actively manage these investments.

(b) Prepare the entry to record the accrued interest on December 31, 2010.

(c) The fair values of the investments on December 31, 2010, were:

Sharapova Company shares	$ 31,800
Government bonds	124,700
McGrath Company bonds	58,600

What entry or entries, if any, would you recommend be made?

(d) The government bonds were sold on July 1, 2011, for $119,200 plus accrued interest. Give the proper entry.

•3 P17-4 (Debt Investments) Presented below is information taken from a bond investment amortization schedule with related fair values provided. These bonds are managed to profit from changes in market interest rates.

	12/31/10	12/31/11	12/31/12
Amortized cost	$491,150	$519,442	$550,000
Fair value	$497,000	$509,000	$550,000

Instructions

(a) Indicate whether the bonds were purchased at a discount or at a premium.

(b) Prepare the adjusting entry to record the bonds at fair value at December 31, 2010. The Securities Fair Value Adjustment account has a debit balance of $1,000 prior to adjustment.

(c) Prepare the adjusting entry to record the bonds at fair value at December 31, 2011.

·5 P17-5 (Equity Investment Entries and Disclosures) Parnevik Company has the following investments in its investment portfolio on December 31, 2010 (all investments were purchased in 2010): (1) 3,000 ordinary shares of Anderson Co. which cost $58,500, (2) 10,000 ordinary shares of Munter Ltd. which cost $580,000, and (3) 6,000 preference shares of King Company which cost $255,000. The Securities Fair Value Adjustment account shows a credit of $10,100 at the end of 2010.

In 2011, Parnevik completed the following investment transactions.

1. On January 15, sold 3,000 ordinary shares of Anderson at $22 per share less fees of $2,150.
2. On April 17, purchased 1,000 ordinary shares of Castle at $33.50 per share plus fees of $1,980.

On December 31, 2011, the fair values per share of these investments were: Munter $61, King $40, and Castle $29. Parnevik classifies these investments as trading.

Instructions

(a) Prepare the entry for the sale on January 15, 2011.
(b) Prepare the journal entry to record the purchase on April 17, 2011.
(c) Compute the unrealized gains or losses and prepare the adjusting entry for Parnevik on December 31, 2011.
(d) How should the unrealized gains or losses be reported on Parnevik's financial statements?
(e) Assuming the investment in King Company preference shares is classified as non-trading, briefly describe the accounting and reporting of this investment.

·6 P17-6 (Equity Investments) McElroy Company has the following portfolio of investments at September 30, 2010, its last reporting date.

Trading Investments	Cost	Fair Value
Horton, Inc. ordinary (5,000 shares)	£215,000	£200,000
Monty, Inc. preference (3,500 shares)	133,000	140,000
Oakwood Corp. ordinary (1,000 shares)	180,000	179,000

On October 10, 2010, the Horton shares were sold at a price of £54 per share. In addition, 3,000 ordinary shares of Patriot were acquired at £54.50 per share on November 2, 2010. The December 31, 2010, fair values were: Monty £106,000, Patriot £132,000, and the Oakwood ordinary £193,000. All the investments are classified as trading.

Instructions

(a) Prepare the journal entries to record the sale, purchase, and adjusting entries related to the trading investments in the last quarter of 2010.
(b) How would the entries in part (a) change if the investments were classified as non-trading?

·2 ·3 ·4 P17-7 (Debt Investment Entries) The following information relates to the debt investments of Wildcat Company.

1. On February 1, the company purchased 10% bonds of Gibbons Co. having a par value of $300,000 at 100 plus accrued interest. Interest is payable April 1 and October 1.
2. On April 1, semiannual interest is received.
3. On July 1, 9% bonds of Sampson, Inc. were purchased. These bonds with a par value of $200,000 were purchased at 100 plus accrued interest. Interest dates are June 1 and December 1.
4. On September 1, bonds with a par value of $60,000, purchased on February 1, are sold at 99 plus accrued interest.
5. On October 1, semiannual interest is received.
6. On December 1, semiannual interest is received.
7. On December 31, the fair value of the bonds purchased February 1 and July 1 are 95 and 93, respectively.

Instructions

(a) Prepare any journal entries you consider necessary, including year-end entries (December 31), assuming these investments are managed to profit from changes in market interest rates.
(b) If Wildcat classified these as held-for-collection investments, explain how the journal entries would differ from those in part (a).
(c) Assume that Wildcat elects the fair value option for these investments under the part (b) conditions. Briefly discuss how the accounting will change.

·5 ·6 P17-8 (Fair Value and Equity Methods) Brooks Corp. is a medium-sized corporation specializing in quarrying stone for building construction. The company has long dominated the market, at one time achieving a 70% market penetration. During prosperous years, the company's profits, coupled with a conservative dividend policy, resulted in funds available for outside investment. Over the years, Brooks has had a policy of investing idle cash in equity investments. In particular, Brooks has made periodic investments in the company's principal supplier, Norton Industries. Although the firm currently owns 12% of the outstanding ordinary shares of Norton Industries, Brooks does not have significant influence over the operations of Norton Industries.

Cheryl Thomas has recently joined Brooks as assistant controller, and her first assignment is to prepare the 2010 year-end adjusting entries for the accounts that are valued by the "fair value" rule for financial reporting purposes. Thomas has gathered the following information about Brooks's pertinent accounts.

1. Brooks has trading equity investments related to Delaney Motors and Patrick Electric. During this fiscal year, Brooks purchased 100,000 shares of Delaney Motors for $1,400,000; these shares currently have a fair value of $1,600,000. Brooks' investment in Patrick Electric has not been profitable; the company acquired 50,000 shares of Patrick in April 2010 at $20 per share, a purchase that currently has a value of $720,000.
2. Prior to 2010, Brooks invested $22,500,000 in Norton Industries and has not changed its holdings this year. This investment in Norton Industries was valued at $21,500,000 on December 31, 2009. Brooks' 12% ownership of Norton Industries has a current fair value of $22,225,000.

Instructions

(a) Prepare the appropriate adjusting entries for Brooks as of December 31, 2010, to reflect the application of the "fair value" rule for both classes of investments described above.

(b) For both classes of investments presented above, describe how the results of the valuation adjustments made in (a) would be reflected in Brooks' 2010 financial statements.

(c) Prepare the entries for the Norton investment, assuming that Brooks owns 25% of Norton's shares. Norton reported income of $500,000 in 2010 and paid cash dividends of $100,000.

·5 **P17-9** **(Financial Statement Presentation of Equity Investments)** Kennedy Company has the following portfolio of trading investments at December 31, 2010.

Investment	Quantity	Percent Interest	Per Share	
			Cost	Market
Frank, Inc.	2,000 shares	8%	$11	$16
Ellis Corp.	5,000 shares	14%	23	19
Mendota Company	4,000 shares	2%	31	24

On December 31, 2011, Kennedy's portfolio of equity investments consisted of the following investments.

Investment	Quantity	Percent Interest	Per Share	
			Cost	Market
Ellis Corp.	5,000 shares	14%	$23	$28
Mendota Company	4,000 shares	2%	31	23
Mendota Company	2,000 shares	1%	25	23

At the end of year 2011, Kennedy Company changed the classification of its investment in Frank, Inc. to non-trading when the shares were selling for $8 per share.

Instructions

(a) What should be reported on Kennedy's December 31, 2010, statement of financial position relative to these equity investments?

(b) What should be reported on the face of Kennedy's December 31, 2011, statement of financial position relative to the equity investments? What should be reported to reflect the transactions above in Kennedy's 2011 income statement?

 ·5 **P17-10** **(Equity Investments)** Castleman Holdings, Inc. had the following investment portfolio at January 1, 2010.

Evers Company	1,000 shares @ £15 each	£15,000
Rogers Company	900 shares @ £20 each	18,000
Chance Company	500 shares @ £9 each	4,500
Non-trading investments @ cost		37,500
Securities fair value adjustment		(7,500)
Non-trading investments @ fair value		£30,000

During 2010, the following transactions took place.

1. On March 1, Rogers Company paid a £2 per share dividend.
2. On April 30, Castleman Holdings, Inc. sold 300 shares of Chance Company for £11 per share.
3. On May 15, Castleman Holdings, Inc. purchased 100 more shares of Evers Co. at £16 per share.
4. At December 31, 2010, the shares had the following price per share values: Evers £17, Rogers £19, and Chance £8.

During 2011, the following transactions took place.

5. On February 1, Castleman Holdings, Inc. sold the remaining Chance shares for £8 per share.
6. On March 1, Rogers Company paid a £2 per share dividend.
7. On December 21, Evers Company declared a cash dividend of £3 per share to be paid in the next month.
8. At December 31, 2011, the shares had the following price per shares values: Evers £19 and Rogers £21.

Instructions

(a) Prepare journal entries for each of the above transactions.
(b) Prepare a partial statement of financial position showing the Investments account at December 31, 2010 and 2011.
(c) Briefly describe how the accounting would change if the Evers investment was classified as trading.

P17-11 (Investments—Statement Presentation) Fernandez Corp. invested its excess cash in equity investments during 2010. The business model for these investments is to profit from trading on price changes.

Instructions

(a) As of December 31, 2010, the equity investment portfolio consisted of the following.

Investment	Quantity	Cost	Fair Value
Lindsay Jones, Inc.	1,000 shares	€ 15,000	€ 21,000
Poley Corp.	2,000 shares	40,000	42,000
Arnold Aircraft	2,000 shares	72,000	60,000
Totals		€127,000	€123,000

What should be reported on Fernandez's December 31, 2010, statement of financial position relative to these investments? What should be reported on Fernandez's 2010 income statement?

(b) During the year 2011, Fernandez Corp. sold 2,000 shares of Poley Corp. for €38,200 and purchased 2,000 more shares of Lindsay Jones, Inc. and 1,000 shares of Duff Company. On December 31, 2011, Fernandez's equity investment portfolio consisted of the following.

Investment	Quantity	Cost	Fair Value
Lindsay Jones, Inc.	1,000 shares	€ 15,000	€20,000
Lindsay Jones, Inc.	2,000 shares	33,000	40,000
Duff Company	1,000 shares	16,000	12,000
Arnold Aircraft	2,000 shares	72,000	22,000
Totals		€136,000	€94,000

What should be reported on Fernandez's December 31, 2011, statement of financial position? What should be reported on Fernandez's 2011 income statement?

(c) During the year 2012, Fernandez Corp. sold 3,000 shares of Lindsay Jones, Inc. for €39,900 and 500 shares of Duff Company at a loss of €2,700. On December 31, 2012, Fernandez's equity investment portfolio consisted of the following.

Investment	Quantity	Cost	Fair Value
Arnold Aircraft	2,000 shares	€72,000	€82,000
Duff Company	500 shares	8,000	6,000
Totals		€80,000	€88,000

What should be reported on the face of Fernandez's December 31, 2012, statement of financial position? What should be reported on Fernandez's 2012 income statement?

 *P17-12 (Gain on Sale of Investments and Comprehensive Income) On January 1, 2010, Acker Inc. had the following statement of financial position.

ACKER INC.
STATEMENT OF FINANCIAL POSITION
AS OF JANUARY 1, 2010

Assets		Equity	
Equity investments	€240,000	Share capital	€260,000
Cash	50,000	Accumulated other comprehensive income	30,000
Total	€290,000	Total	€290,000

The accumulated other comprehensive income related to unrealized holding gains on non-trading equity investments. The fair value of Acker Inc.'s investments at December 31, 2010, was €190,000; its cost was €140,000. No securities were purchased during the year. Acker Inc.'s income statement for 2010 was as follows. (Ignore income taxes.)

ACKER INC.
INCOME STATEMENT
FOR THE YEAR ENDED DECEMBER 31, 2010

Dividend revenue	€ 5,000
Gain on sale of equity investments	30,000
Net income	€35,000

Instructions

(Assume all transactions during the year were for cash.)

(a) Prepare the journal entry to record the sale of the equity investments in 2010.
(b) Prepare a statement of comprehensive income for 2010.
(c) Prepare a statement of financial position as of December 31, 2010.

•12 *P17-13 (Derivative Financial Instrument) The treasurer of Miller Co. has read on the Internet that the price of Wade Inc. ordinary shares is about to take off. In order to profit from this potential development, Miller Co. purchased a call option on Wade shares on July 7, 2010, for $240. The call option is for 200 shares (notional value), and the strike price is $70. (The market price of a Wade share on that date is $70.) The option expires on January 31, 2011. The following data are available with respect to the call option.

Date	Market Price of Wade Shares	Time Value of Call Option
September 30, 2010	$77 per share	$180
December 31, 2010	75 per share	65
January 4, 2011	76 per share	30

Instructions
Prepare the journal entries for Miller Co. for the following dates.

(a) July 7, 2010—Investment in call option on Wade shares.
(b) September 30, 2010—Miller prepares financial statements.
(c) December 31, 2010—Miller prepares financial statements.
(d) January 4, 2011—Miller settles the call option on the Wade shares.

•12 *P17-14 (Derivative Financial Instrument) Johnstone Co. purchased a put option on Ewing ordinary shares on July 7, 2010, for $240. The put option is for 200 shares, and the strike price is $70. (The market price of an ordinary share of Ewing on that date is $70.) The option expires on January 31, 2011. The following data are available with respect to the put option.

Date	Market Price of Ewing Shares	Time Value of Put Option
September 30, 2010	$77 per share	$125
December 31, 2010	75 per share	50
January 31, 2011	78 per share	0

Instructions
Prepare the journal entries for Johnstone Co. for the following dates.

(a) July 7, 2010—Investment in put option on Ewing shares.
(b) September 30, 2010—Johnstone prepares financial statements.
(c) December 31, 2010—Johnstone prepares financial statements.
(d) January 31, 2011—Put option expires.

•12 *P17-15 **(Free-Standing Derivative)** Warren Co. purchased a put option on Echo ordinary shares on January 7, 2010, for $360. The put option is for 400 shares, and the strike price is $85 (which equals the price of an Echo share on the purchase date). The option expires on July 31, 2010. The following data are available with respect to the put option.

Date	Market Price of Echo Shares	Time Value of Put Option
March 31, 2010	$80 per share	$200
June 30, 2010	82 per share	90
July 6, 2010	77 per share	25

Instructions
Prepare the journal entries for Warren Co. for the following dates.

(a) January 7, 2010—Investment in put option on Echo shares.
(b) March 31, 2010—Warren prepares financial statements.
(c) June 30, 2010—Warren prepares financial statements.
(d) July 6, 2010—Warren settles the put option on the Echo shares.

•13 *P17-16 **(Fair Value Hedge Interest Rate Swap)** On December 31, 2010, Mercantile Corp. had a $10,000,000, 8% fixed-rate note outstanding, payable in 2 years. It decides to enter into a 2-year swap with Chicago First Bank to convert the fixed-rate debt to variable-rate debt. The terms of the swap indicate that Mercantile will receive interest at a fixed rate of 8.0% and will pay a variable rate equal to the 6-month LIBOR rate, based on the $10,000,000 amount. The LIBOR rate on December 31, 2010, is 7%. The LIBOR rate will be reset every 6 months and will be used to determine the variable rate to be paid for the following 6-month period.

Mercantile Corp. designates the swap as a fair value hedge. Assume that the hedging relationship meets all the conditions necessary for hedge accounting. The 6-month LIBOR rate and the swap and debt fair values are as follows.

Date	6-Month LIBOR Rate	Swap Fair Value	Debt Fair Value
December 31, 2010	7.0%	—	$10,000,000
June 30, 2011	7.5%	(200,000)	9,800,000
December 31, 2011	6.0%	60,000	10,060,000

Instructions
(a) Present the journal entries to record the following transactions.
  (1) The entry, if any, to record the swap on December 31, 2010.
  (2) The entry to record the semiannual debt interest payment on June 30, 2011.
  (3) The entry to record the settlement of the semiannual swap amount receivables at 8%, less amount payable at LIBOR, 7%.
  (4) The entry to record the change in the fair value of the debt on June 30, 2011.
  (5) The entry to record the change in the fair value of the swap at June 30, 2011.
(b) Indicate the amount(s) reported on the statement of financial position and income statement related to the debt and swap on December 31, 2010.
(c) Indicate the amount(s) reported on the statement of financial position and income statement related to the debt and swap on June 30, 2011.
(d) Indicate the amount(s) reported on the statement of financial position and income statement related to the debt and swap on December 31, 2011.

•14 *P17-17 **(Cash Flow Hedge)** Suzuki Jewelry Co. uses gold in the manufacture of its products. Suzuki anticipates that it will need to purchase 500 ounces of gold in October 2010, for jewelry that will be shipped for the holiday shopping season. However, if the price of gold increases, Suzuki's cost to produce its jewelry will increase, which would reduce its profit margins.

To hedge the risk of increased gold prices, on April 1, 2010, Suzuki enters into a gold futures contract and designates this futures contract as a cash flow hedge of the anticipated gold purchase. The notional amount of the contract is 500 ounces, and the terms of the contract give Suzuki the right and the obligation to purchase gold at a price of ¥30,000 per ounce. The price will be good until the contract expires on October 31, 2010.

Assume the following data with respect to the price of the call options and the gold inventory purchase.

Date	Spot Price for October Delivery
April 1, 2010	¥30,000 per ounce
June 30, 2010	31,000 per ounce
September 30, 2010	31,500 per ounce

Instructions

Prepare the journal entries for the following transactions.

(a) April 1, 2010—Inception of the futures contract, no premium paid.
(b) June 30, 2010—Suzuki Co. prepares financial statements.
(c) September 30, 2010—Suzuki Co. prepares financial statements.
(d) October 10, 2010—Suzuki Co. purchases 500 ounces of gold at ¥31,500 per ounce and settles the futures contract.
(e) December 20, 2010—Suzuki sells jewelry containing gold purchased in October 2010 for ¥35,000,000. The cost of the finished goods inventory is ¥20,000,000.
(f) Indicate the amount(s) reported on the statement of financial position and income statement related to the futures contract on June 30, 2010.
(g) Indicate the amount(s) reported in the income statement related to the futures contract and the inventory transactions on December 31, 2010.

•13 *****P17-18 (Fair Value Hedge)** On November 3, 2010, Sprinkle Co. invested €200,000 in 4,000 shares of the ordinary shares of Pratt Co. Sprinkle classified this investment as non-trading equity. Sprinkle Co. is considering making a more significant investment in Pratt Co. at some point in the future but has decided to wait and see how the shares do over the next several quarters.

To hedge against potential declines in the value of Pratt shares during this period, Sprinkle also purchased a put option on the Pratt shares. Sprinkle paid an option premium of €600 for the put option, which gives Sprinkle the option to sell 4,000 Pratt shares at a strike price of €50 per share. The option expires on July 31, 2011. The following data are available with respect to the values of the Pratt shares and the put option.

Date	Market Price of Pratt Shares	Time Value of Put Option
December 31, 2010	€50 per share	€375
March 31, 2011	45 per share	175
June 30, 2011	43 per share	40

Instructions

(a) Prepare the journal entries for Sprinkle Co. for the following dates.
   (1) November 3, 2010—Investment in Pratt shares and the put option on Pratt shares.
   (2) December 31, 2011—Sprinkle Co. prepares financial statements.
   (3) March 31, 2011—Sprinkle prepares financial statements.
   (4) June 30, 2011—Sprinkle prepares financial statements.
   (5) July 1, 2011—Sprinkle settles the put option and sells the Pratt shares for €43 per share.
(b) Indicate the amount(s) reported on the statement of financial position and income statement related to the Pratt investment and the put option on December 31, 2010.
(c) Indicate the amount(s) reported on the statement of financial position and income statement related to the Pratt investment and the put option on June 30, 2011.

CONCEPTS FOR ANALYSIS

CA17-1 (Issues Raised about Investments) You have just started work for Warren Co. as part of the controller's group involved in current financial reporting problems. Jane Henshaw, controller for Warren, is interested in your accounting background because the company has experienced a series of financial reporting surprises over the last few years. Recently, the controller has learned from the company's auditors that there is authoritative literature that may apply to its debt and equity investments. She assumes that you are familiar with literature in this area and asks how the following situations should be reported in the financial statements.

Situation 1
Investments that are actively traded are reported in the current assets section and have a fair value that is $4,200 lower than cost.

Situation 2
A debt investment whose fair value is currently less than cost is transferred to the held-for-collection category.

Situation 3
A debt investment, whose fair value is currently less than cost is classified as non-current but is to be reclassified as current.

Situation 4
A company's portfolio of debt investments at fair value consists of the bonds of one company. At the end of the prior year, the fair value of the bonds was 50% of original cost, and this reduction in value was reported as an impairment. However, at the end of the current year, the fair value of the bonds had appreciated to twice the original cost.

Situation 5
The company has purchased some convertible debentures that it plans to sell if the price increases. The fair value of the convertible debentures is $7,700 below its cost.

Instructions
What is the effect upon carrying value and earnings for each of the situations above? Assume that these situations are unrelated.

CA17-2 **(Equity Investments)** Lexington Co. has the following equity investments on December 31, 2010 (its first year of operations).

	Cost	Fair Value
Greenspan Corp. Ordinary Shares	$20,000	$19,000
Summerset Company Ordinary Shares	9,500	8,800
Tinkers Company Ordinary Shares	20,000	20,600
	$49,500	$48,400

During 2011 Summerset Company shares were sold for $9,200, the difference between the $9,200 and the "fair value" of $8,800 being recorded as a "Gain on Sale of Equity Investment." The market price of the shares on December 31, 2011, was: Greenspan Corp. shares $19,900; Tinkers Company shares $20,500.

Instructions
(a) What justification is there for valuing these investments at fair value and reporting the unrealized gain or loss in income?
(b) How should Lexington Company apply this rule on December 31, 2010? Explain.
(c) Did Lexington Company properly account for the sale of the Summerset Company shares? Explain.
(d) Are there any additional entries necessary for Lexington Company at December 31, 2011, to reflect the facts on the financial statements in accordance with IFRS? Explain.

CA17-3 **(Financial Statement Effect of Investments)** Presented below are three unrelated situations involving equity investments.

Situation 1
A debt investment portfolio, whose fair value is currently less than cost, is classified as trading but is to be reclassified as held-for-collection.

Situation 2
A debt investment portfolio with an aggregate fair value in excess of cost includes one particular debt investment whose fair value has declined to less than one-half of the original cost. The decline in value is considered to be permanent.

Situation 3
The portfolio of trading equity investments has a cost in excess of fair value of $13,500. The portfolio of non-trading equity investments has a fair value in excess of cost of $28,600.

Instructions
What is the effect upon carrying value and earnings for each of the situations above?

CA17-4 **(Equity Investments)** The IASB issued accounting guidance to clarify accounting methods and procedures with respect to debt and equity investments. An important part of the statement concerns the distinction between held-for-collection debt investments, trading debt and equity investments, and non-trading equity investments.

Instructions
(a) Why does a company maintain investment portfolios for these different types of investments?
(b) What factors should be considered in determining whether investments should be classified as held-for-collection, trading, or non-trading? How do these factors affect the accounting treatment for unrealized losses?

CA17-5 **(Investment Accounted for under the Equity Method)** On July 1, 2011, Fontaine Company purchased for cash 40% of the outstanding ordinary shares of Knoblett Company. Both Fontaine Company and Knoblett Company have a December 31 year-end. Knoblett Company, whose shares are actively traded in the over-the-counter market, reported its total net income for the year to Fontaine Company and also paid cash dividends on November 15, 2011, to Fontaine Company and its other shareholders.

Instructions

How should Fontaine Company report the above facts in its December 31, 2011, statement of financial position and its income statement for the year then ended? Discuss the rationale for your answer.

 CA17-6 **(Equity Investments)** On July 1, 2010, Selig Company purchased for cash 40% of the outstanding ordinary shares of Spoor Corporation. Both Selig and Spoor have a December 31 year-end. Spoor Corporation, whose shares are actively traded on the American Stock Exchange, paid a cash dividend on November 15, 2010, to Selig Company and its other shareholders. It also reported its total net income for the year of $920,000 to Selig Company.

Instructions

Prepare a one-page memorandum of instructions on how Selig Company should report the above facts in its December 31, 2010, statement of financial position and its 2010 income statement. In your memo, identify and describe the method of valuation you recommend. Provide rationale where you can. Address your memo to the chief accountant at Selig Company.

CA17-7 **(Fair Value)** Addison Manufacturing holds a large portfolio of debt and equity investments. The fair value of the portfolio is greater than its original cost, even though some investments have decreased in value. Sam Beresford, the financial vice president, and Angie Nielson, the controller, are near year-end in the process of classifying for the first time this investment portfolio in accordance with IFRS. Beresford wants to classify those investments that have increased in value during the period as trading investments in order to increase net income this year. He wants to classify all the investments that have decreased in value as non-trading (the equity investments) and as held-for-collection (the debt investments).

Nielson disagrees. She wants to classify those investments that have decreased in value as trading and those that have increased in value as non-trading (equity) and held-for-collection (debt). She contends that the company is having a good earnings year and that recognizing the losses will help to smooth the income this year. As a result, the company will have built-in gains for future periods when the company may not be as profitable.

Instructions

Answer the following questions.

(a) Will classifying the portfolio as each proposes actually have the effect on earnings that each says it will?

(b) Is there anything unethical in what each of them proposes? Who are the stakeholders affected by their proposals?

(c) Assume that Beresford and Nielson properly classify the entire portfolio into trading, non-trading, and held-for-collection categories. But then each proposes to sell just before year-end the investments with gains or with losses, as the case may be, to accomplish their effect on earnings. Is this unethical?

USING YOUR JUDGMENT

FINANCIAL REPORTING

Financial Reporting Problem
Marks and Spencer plc (M&S)

The financial statements of **M&S** are presented in Appendix 5B or can be accessed at the book's companion website, **www.wiley.com/college/kiesoifrs**.

Instructions

Refer to M&S's financial statements and the accompanying notes to answer the following questions.

(a) What investments does M&S report in 2008, and where are these investments reported in its financial statements?

(b) How are M&S's investments valued? How does M&S determine fair value?

(c) How does M&S use derivative financial instruments?

Comparative Analysis Case

Cadbury and Nestlé

Instructions

Go to the book's companion website and use information found there to answer the following questions related to **Cadbury** and **Nestlé**.

(a) Based on the information contained in these financial statements, determine each of the following for each company.
   (1) Cash used in (for) investing activities during 2008 (from the statement of cash flows).
   (2) Cash used for acquisitions and investments in unconsolidated affiliates during 2008.
   (3) Total investment in unconsolidated affiliates (or investments and other assets) at the end of 2008.
   (4) What conclusions concerning the management of investments can be drawn from these data?

(b) (1) Briefly identify from Cadbury's December 31, 2008, statement of financial position the investments it reported as being accounted for under the equity method. (2) What is the amount of investments that Cadbury reported in its 2008 statement of financial position as "cost method investments," and what is the nature of these investments?

Financial Statement Analysis Case

Union Planters

Union Planters is a bank holding company (that is, a corporation that owns banks). Union Planters manages $32 billion in assets, the largest of which is its loan portfolio of $19 billion. In addition to its loan portfolio, however, like other banks it has significant debt investments. The nature of these investments varies from short-term in nature to long-term in nature. As a consequence, consistent with the requirements of accounting rules, Union Planters reports both the fair value and amortized cost of its investments. The following facts were found in a recent Union Planters' annual report.

(all dollars in millions)	Amortized Cost	Gross Unrealized Gains	Gross Unrealized Losses	Fair Value
Trading account assets	$ 275	—	—	$ 275
Non-trading equity investments	8,209	$108	$15	8,302
Net income				224
Net investment gains (losses)				(9)

Instructions

(a) Why do you suppose Union Planters purchases investments, rather than simply making loans? Why does it purchase investments that vary in nature both in terms of their maturities and in type (debt versus equity)?

(b) How must Union Planters account for its investments at fair value and amortized cost?

(c) In what ways does classifying investments into two different categories assist investors in evaluating the profitability of a company like Union Planters?

(d) Suppose that the management of Union Planters was not happy with its net income for the year. What step could it have taken with its investment portfolio that would have definitely increased reported profit? How much could it have increased reported profit? Why do you suppose it chose not to do this?

Accounting, Analysis, and Principles

Instar Company has several investments in other companies. The following information regarding these investments is available at December 31, 2010.

1. Instar holds bonds issued by Dorsel Corp. The bonds have an amortized cost of $320,000 (which is par value) and their fair value at December 31, 2010, is $400,000. Instar plans to hold the bonds to collect contractual cash flows until they mature on December 31, 2020. The bonds pay interest at 10%, payable annually on December 31.

2. Instar has invested idle cash in the equity investments of several publicly traded companies. Instar intends to sell these investments during the first quarter of 2011, when it will need the cash to acquire seasonal inventory. These equity investments have a cost basis of $800,000 and a fair value of $920,000 at December 31, 2010.

3. Instar has an ownership stake in one of the companies that supplies Instar with various components that Instar uses in its products. Instar owns 6% of the ordinary shares of the supplier, does not have any representation on the supplier's board of directors, does not exchange any personnel with the supplier, and does not consult with the supplier on any of the supplier's operating, financial, or strategic decisions. The cost basis of the investment in the supplier is $1,200,000, and the fair value of the investment at December 31, 2010, is $1,550,000. Instar may sell the investment if it needs cash. The supplier reported net income of $80,000 for 2010 and paid no dividends.

4. Instar owns some Forter Corp. ordinary shares. The cost basis of the investment in Forter is $200,000, and the fair value at December 31, 2010, is $187,000. Instar does not intend to trade the investment because it helps it meet regulatory requirements to sell its products in Forter's market area.

5. Instar purchased 25% of the shares of Slobbaer Co. for $900,000. Instar has significant influence over the operating activities of Slobbaer Co. During 2010, Slobbaer Co. reported net income of $300,000 and paid a dividend of $100,000.

Accounting

(a) Determine whether each of the investments described above should be classified as held-for-collection, trading, or non-trading equity.

(b) Prepare any December 31, 2010, journal entries needed for Instar relating to Instar's various investments in other companies. Assume 2010 is Instar's first year of operations.

Analysis

What is the effect on Instar's 2010 net income (as reported on Instar's income statement) of its investments in other companies?

Principles

Briefly explain the different rationales for the different accounting and reporting rules for different types of investments in other companies.

I F R S   BRIDGE TO THE PROFESSION

Professional Research

Your client, Cascade Company, is planning to invest some of its excess cash in 5-year revenue bonds issued by the county and in the shares of one of its suppliers, Teton Co. Teton's shares trade on the over-the-counter market. Cascade plans to classify these investments as trading. They would like you to conduct some research on the accounting for these investments.

Instructions

Access the IFRS authoritative literature at the IASB website (*http://eifrs.iasb.org/*). When you have accessed the documents, you can use the search tool in your Internet browser to respond to the following questions. (Provide paragraph citations.)

(a) Since the Teton shares do not trade on one of the large securities exchanges, Cascade argues that the fair value of this investment is not readily available. According to the authoritative literature, when is the fair value of a security "readily determinable"?

(b) How is an impairment of a debt investment accounted for?

(c) To avoid volatility in their financial statements due to fair value adjustments, Cascade debated whether the bond investment could be classified as held-for-collection; Cascade is pretty sure it will hold the bonds for 5 years. What criteria must be met for Cascade to classify it as held-for-collection?

Professional Simulation

In this simulation, you are asked to address questions related to investments. Provide responses to all parts.

KWW_Professional_Simulation

Investments

Time Remaining
3 hours 20 minutes

copy | paste | calculator | sheet | standards | help | splitter | done

| Directions | Situation | Journal Entries | Measurement | Explanation | Resources |

Powerpuff Corp. carries an account in its general ledger called investments, which contained the following debits for investment purchases and no credits.

Feb. 1, 2010	Blossom Company ordinary shares, $100 par, 200 shares	$ 37,400
April 1	Government bonds, 11%, due April 1, 2020, interest payable April 1 and October 1, 100 bonds of $1,000 par each	100,000
July 1	Buttercup Company 12% bonds, par $50,000, dated March 1, 2010, purchased at par plus accrued interest, interest payable annually on March 1, due March 1, 2030	52,000

| Directions | Situation | Journal Entries | Measurement | Explanation | Resources |

(a) Assuming that Powerpuff's business model is to trade these investments to profit from price changes, prepare the journal entries necessary to classify the amounts into the proper accounts.
(b) Prepare the entry to record the accrued interest on December 31, 2010.

| Directions | Situation | Journal Entries | Measurement | Explanation | Resources |

The fair values of the securities on December 31, 2010, were:

Blossom Company shares	$ 33,800 (1% interest)
Government bonds	124,700
Buttercup Company bonds	58,600

Use a computer spreadsheet to prepare a schedule indicating any fair value adjustment needed at December 31, 2010.

| Directions | Situation | Journal Entries | Measurement | Explanation | Resources |

Now assume Powerpuff's investment in Blossom Company represents 30% of Blossom's shares. In 2010, Blossom declared and paid dividends of $9,000 (on September 30) and reported net income of $30,000. Prepare a brief memorandum explaining how the accounting for the Blossom investment will change, and discuss the impact on the financial statements of Powerpuff Corp.

Remember to check the book's companion website to find additional resources for this chapter.

www.wiley.com/college/kiesoifrs

LEARNING OBJECTIVES

After studying this chapter, you should be able to:

•1 Apply the revenue recognition principle.

•2 Describe accounting issues for revenue recognition at point of sale.

•3 Apply the percentage-of-completion method for long-term contracts.

•4 Apply the cost-recovery method for long-term contracts.

•5 Identify the proper accounting for losses on long-term contracts.

•6 Describe the accounting issues for service contracts.

•7 Identify the proper accounting for multiple-deliverable arrangements.

| IT'S BACK | Revenue recognition practices are the most prevalent reasons for accounting restatements. A number of the revenue recognition issues relate to possible fraudulent behavior by company executives and employees. Consider the following situations: |

- The former co-chairman and CEO of **Qwest Communications International Inc.** (USA) and eight other former Qwest officers and employees were charged with fraud and other violations of U.S. securities laws. Three of these people fraudulently characterized non-recurring revenue from one-time sales as revenue from recurring data and Internet services. Internal correspondence likened Qwest's dependence on these transactions to fill the gap between actual and projected revenue to an addiction.

- Three former senior officers of **iGo Corp.** (USA) caused iGo to improperly recognize revenue on consignment sales and products that were not shipped or that were shipped after the end of a fiscal quarter.

- The former CEO and chairman of **Homestore Inc.** (USA) and its former executive vice president of business development were accused of engaging in a fraudulent scheme to overstate advertising and subscription revenues. The scheme involved a complex structure of "round-trip" transactions using various third-party companies that, in essence, allowed Homestore to recognize its own cash as revenue.

- **Lantronix** (USA) is alleged to have deliberately sent excessive product to distributors and granted them generous return rights and extended payment terms. In addition, as part of its alleged "channel stuffing" and to prevent product returns, Lantronix loaned funds to a third party to purchase Lantronix products from one of its distributors. The third party later returned the product. It was also asserted that Lantronix engaged in other improper revenue recognition practices, including shipping without a purchase order and recognizing revenue on a contingent sale.

Though the cases cited involved fraud and irregularity, not all revenue recognition errors are intentional. For example, in April 2005 **American Home Mortgage Investment Corp.** (USA) announced that it would reverse revenue recognized from its fourth-quarter 2004 loan securitization, and would recognize it in the first quarter of 2005 instead. As a result, American Home restated its financial results for 2004.

So, how does a company ensure that revenue transactions are recorded properly? Some answers will become apparent after you study this chapter.

Sources: Cheryl de Mesa Graziano, "Revenue Recognition: A Perennial Problem," *Financial Executive* (July 14, 2005), *www.fei.org/mag/articles/7-2005_revenue.cfm;* and S. Taub, "SEC Accuses Ex-CFO of Channel Stuffing," *CFO.com* (September 30, 2006).

PREVIEW OF CHAPTER 18

As indicated in the opening story, the issue of when revenue should be recognized is complex. The many methods of marketing products and services make it difficult to develop guidelines that will apply to all situations. This chapter provides you with general guidelines used in most business transactions. The content and organization of the chapter are as follows.

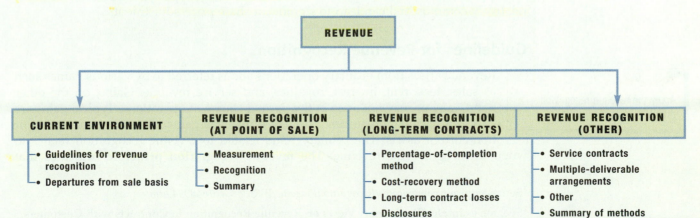

CURRENT ENVIRONMENT

Most revenue transactions pose few problems for revenue recognition. This is because, in many cases, the transaction is initiated and completed at the same time. However, not all transactions are that simple. For example, consider a customer who enters into a mobile phone contract with a company such as **Vodafone** (GBR). The customer is often provided with a package that may include a handset, free minutes of talk time, data downloads, and text messaging service. In addition, some providers will bundle that with a fixed-line broadband service. At the same time, customers may pay for these services in a variety of ways, possibly receiving a discount on the handset, then paying higher prices for connection fees, and so forth. In some cases, depending on the package purchased, the company may provide free applications in subsequent periods. How then should the various pieces of this sale be reported by Vodafone? The answer is not obvious.

It is therefore not surprising that a recent survey of financial executives noted that the revenue recognition process is increasingly more complex to manage, prone to error, and material to financial statements compared to any other area in financial reporting. The report went on to note that revenue recognition is a top fraud risk and that regardless of the accounting rules followed (IFRS or U.S. GAAP), the risk or errors and inaccuracies in revenue reporting is significant.[1]

Indeed, both the IASB and the FASB indicate that the present state of reporting for revenue is unsatisfactory. IFRS is criticized because it lacks guidance in a number of areas. For example, IFRS has one basic standard on revenue recognition—*IAS 18*—plus some limited guidance related to certain minor topics. In contrast, U.S. GAAP has numerous standards related to revenue recognition (by some counts over 100), but many believe the standards are often inconsistent with one another. Thus, the accounting for revenues provides a most fitting contrast of the principles-based (IFRS) and rules-based (U.S. GAAP) approaches. While both sides have their advocates, the IASB and FASB recognize a number of deficiencies in this area.[2]

Unfortunately, inappropriate recognition of revenue can occur in any industry. Products that are sold to distributors for resale pose different risks than products or services that are sold directly to customers. Sales in high-technology industries, where rapid product obsolescence is a significant issue, pose different risks than sales of inventory with a longer life, such as farm or construction equipment, automobiles, trucks, and appliances.[3] As a consequence, restatements for improper revenue recognition are relatively common and can lead to significant share price adjustments.

Guidelines for Revenue Recognition

Objective·1

Apply the revenue recognition principle.

Revenue arises from ordinary operations and is referred to by various names such as sales, fees, rent, interest, royalties, and service revenue. Gains, on the other hand, may or may not arise in the normal course of operations. Typical gains are gains on sales of non-current assets or unrealized gains related to investments or non-current assets. The primary issue related to revenue recognition relates to when to recognize the revenue. The **revenue recognition principle** indicates that

---

[1]See *www.prweb.com/releases/RecognitionRevenue/IFRS/prweb1648994.htm*.

[2]See, for example, "Preliminary Views on Revenue Recognition in Contracts with Customers," *IASB/FASB Discussion Paper* (December 19, 2008). Some of the problems noted are that U.S. GAAP has so many standards that at times they are inconsistent with each other in applying basic principles. In addition, even with the many standards, no guidance is provided for service transactions. Conversely, IFRS has a lack of guidance in certain fundamental areas such as multiple-deliverable arrangements, which are becoming increasingly common. In addition, there is inconsistency in applying revenue recognition principles to long-term contracts versus other elements of revenue recognition.

[3]Adapted from American Institute of Certified Public Accountants, Inc., *Audit Issues in Revenue Recognition* (New York: AICPA, 1999).

revenue is recognized when it is probable that the economic benefits will flow to the company and the benefits can be measured reliably.[4]

Four revenue transactions are recognized in accordance with this principle:

1. Companies recognize revenue from selling products at the date of sale. This date is usually interpreted to mean the date of delivery to customers.

2. Companies recognize revenue from services provided, when services have been performed and are billable.

3. Companies recognize revenue from permitting others to use enterprise assets, such as interest, rent, and royalties, as time passes or as the assets are used.

4. Companies recognize revenue from disposing of assets other than products at the date of sale.

These revenue transactions are diagrammed in Illustration 18-1.

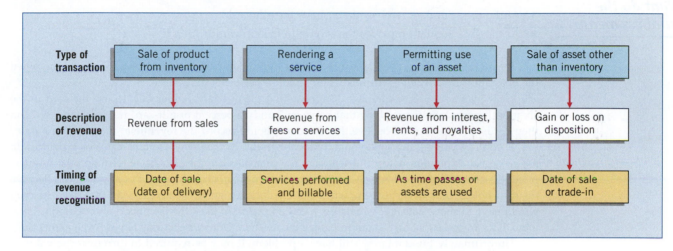

ILLUSTRATION 18-1
Revenue Recognition
Classified by Nature
of Transaction

The preceding statements are the basis of accounting for revenue transactions. In general, companies recognize revenue at the point of sale (sale basis). However, in practice there are departures from this recognition point, depending on the circumstances.[5]

Departures from the Sale Basis

Companies depart from sale-basis revenue recognition for a variety of reasons. One reason is a desire to **recognize earlier** than the time of sale the effect of earning activities. Earlier recognition is appropriate if there is a high degree of certainty about the amount of revenue earned. A second reason is a desire to **delay recognition** of revenue beyond the time of sale. Delayed recognition is appropriate if the degree of uncertainty

[4]A more formal definition of revenue is as follows: "gross inflow of economic benefits during the period arising in the ordinary activities of an entity when those inflows result in increases in equity, other than increases relating to contributions from equity participants." [1]

[5]The IASB and FASB are now involved in a joint project on revenue recognition. The purpose of this project is to develop comprehensive conceptual guidance on when to recognize revenue. Presently, the Boards are evaluating a customer-consideration model. In this model, a company accounts for the contract asset or liability that arises from the rights and performance obligations in an enforceable contract with the customer. At contract inception, the rights in the contract are measured at the amount of the promised customer payment (that is, the customer consideration). That amount is then allocated to the individual performance obligations identified within the contract in proportion to the standalone selling price of each good or service underlying the performance obligation. It is hoped that this approach (rather than using the current criteria based on probable economic benefits and reliable measurement) will lead to a better basis for revenue recognition. (See *www.fasb.org/project/ revenue_recognition.shtml*.)

I F R S

See the Authoritative Literature section (pages 989–990).

concerning the amount of either revenue or costs is sufficiently high or if the sale does not represent substantial completion of the earnings process.

This chapter focuses on four general types of revenue transactions:

1. Revenue recognition at point of sale.
2. Revenue recognition for long-term contracts (construction).
3. Revenue recognition for services.
4. Revenue recognition for multiple-deliverable arrangements.

What do the numbers mean?

LIABILITY OR REVENUE?

Suppose you purchased a gift card for spa services at Sundara Spa for $300. The gift card expires at the end of six months. When should Sundara record the revenue? Here are two choices:

1. At the time Sundara receives the cash for the gift card.
2. At the time Sundara provides the service to the gift-card holder.

If you answered number 2, you would be right. Companies should recognize revenue when the obligation is satisfied—which is when Sundara performs the service.

Now let's add a few more facts. Suppose that the gift-card holder fails to use the card in the six-month period. Statistics show that between 2 and 15 percent of gift-card holders never redeem their cards. So, do you still believe that Sundara should record the revenue at the expiration date?

If you say you are not sure, you are probably right. Here is why: Certain states or provinces do not recognize expiration dates, and therefore the customer has the right to redeem an otherwise expired gift card at any time. Let's say for the moment we are in one of these states or provinces. Because the card holder may never redeem, when can Sundara recognize the revenue? In that case, Sundara would have to show statistically that after a certain period of time, the likelihood of redemption is remote. If it can make that case, it can recognize the revenue. Otherwise, it may have to wait a long time.

Unfortunately, Sundara may still have a problem. It may be required to turn over the value of the spa service to the state or province. The treatment for unclaimed gift cards may fall under the abandoned-and-unclaimed-property laws. Most common unclaimed items are required to be remitted to the states or provinces after a five-year period. Failure to report and remit the property can result in additional fines and penalties. So if Sundara is in a jurisdiction where unclaimed property must be sent to the state or province, Sundara should report a liability on its statement of financial position.

Source: PricewaterhouseCoopers, "Issues Surrounding the Recognition of Gift Card Sales and Escheat Liabilities," *Quick Brief* (December 2004).

REVENUE RECOGNITION AT POINT OF SALE

Objective·2
Describe accounting issues for revenue recognition at point of sale.

Two issues must be addressed in the accounting for sales transactions:

- Measurement of sales revenue.
- Recognition of sales revenue.

Measurement of Sales Revenue

Revenue should be measured at the fair value of consideration received or receivable. Any trade discounts or volume rebates should reduce consideration received or receivable and the related revenue. In addition, if the payment is delayed, the seller should impute an interest rate for the difference between the cash or cash equivalent price and the deferred amount. In essence, the seller is financing the sale and should record interest revenue over the payment term. Presented on the next pages are a series of transactions that illustrate these points, beginning with Illustration 18-2.

ILLUSTRATION 18-2
Revenue Measurement—
Volume Discount

VOLUME DISCOUNT

Facts: Sansung Company has an arrangement with its customers that it will provide a 3% volume discount to its customers if they purchase at least €2 million of its product during the calendar year. On March 31, 2011, Sansung has made sales of €700,000 to Artic plc. In the previous two years, Sansung sold over €3,000,000 to Artic in the period April 1 to December 31.

Question: How much revenue should Sansung recognize for the first three months of 2011?

Solution: In this case, Sansung should reduce its revenue by €21,000 (€700,000 × 3%) because it is probable that it will provide this rebate. Revenue should therefore be reported at €679,000 (€700,000 − €21,000). To not recognize this volume discount overstates Sansung's revenue for the first three months of 2011.

In this case, Sansung makes the following entry on March 31, 2011.

Accounts Receivable	679,000	
Sales		679,000

Assuming that Sansung's customers **meet the discount threshold**, Sansung makes the following entry.

Cash	679,000	
Accounts Receivable		679,000

If Sansung's customers **fail to meet the discount threshold**, Sansung makes the following entry upon payment.

Cash	700,000	
Accounts Receivable		679,000
Sales Discounts Forfeited		21,000

As indicated in Chapter 7 (page 350), Sales Discounted Forfeited is reported in the other income and expense section of the income statement.

In some cases, companies provide cash discounts to customers for a short period of time (often referred to as prompt settlement discounts). For example, assume that terms are payment due in 60 days, but if payment is made within 5 days, a 4 percent discount is given. Given that revenue should be measured at the fair value of the consideration received or receivable, these prompt settlement discounts should reduce revenues.

When a sales transaction involves a financing arrangement, the fair value is determined by discounting the payment using an imputed interest rate. The imputed interest rate is the more clearly determinable of either (1) the prevailing rate for a similar instrument of an issuer with a similar credit rating, or (2) a rate of interest that discounts the nominal amount of the instrument to the current sales price of the goods or services. [2] This issue is addressed in Illustration 18-3.

ILLUSTRATION 18-3
Revenue Measurement—
Deferred Payment

EXTENDED PAYMENT TERMS

Facts: On July 1, 2011, SEK Company sold goods to Grant Company for €900,000 in exchange for a 4-year zero-interest-bearing note in the face amount of €1,416,163. The goods have an inventory cost on SEK's books of €590,000.

Questions: (a) How much revenue should SEK Company record on July 1, 2011? (b) How much revenue should it report related to this transaction on December 31, 2011?

> *Solution:*
> (a) SEK should record revenue of €900,000 on July 1, 2011, which is the fair value of the inventory. The general rule is to measure the revenue at the fair value of the consideration received or receivable.
> (b) SEK is also financing this purchase and records interest revenue on the note over the 4-year period. In this case, the interest rate is imputed and is determined to be 12%. SEK records interest revenue of €54,000 (12% × ½ × €900,000) at December 31, 2011.

The journal entry to record SEK's sale to Grant Company is as follows (ignoring cost of goods sold entry).

July 1, 2011

Notes Receivable	900,000	
Sales		900,000

SEK makes the following entry to record interest revenue.

December 31, 2011

Notes Receivable	54,000	
Interest Revenue (12% × ½ × €900,000)		54,000

Another issue related to the measurement of sales revenue involves **barter transactions**. In these transactions, revenues arise when a company exchanges or swaps goods or services for goods or services of another company without the use of money. For example, Internet companies may exchange rights to place advertisements on each other's websites. Or, an attorney may perform legal services for a client, and the client gives the attorney ordinary shares as payment. The issue here is to determine how to measure the revenue at the fair value of what we receive.

Under IFRS, revenue is measured at the fair value of the goods or services received, adjusted by the amount of any cash or cash equivalents received or paid. In addition, **if the goods (services) that are exchanged are dissimilar in nature, the exchange is recorded as revenue. If similar, revenue is not reported.** For example, in the case of the Internet companies swapping advertisements, it may be difficult to show that the exchange is dissimilar in nature—no revenue therefore is recognized.[6] In the attorney situation, revenues should be recognized. IFRS notes that for exchanges of inventory, such as oil or milk, where suppliers swap these items to meet demand at various locations on a timely basis, no revenue should be recognized. **[4]**

Recognition of Sales Revenue

Revenue from the sale of goods is recognized when all the following conditions are met: **[5]**

1. The company has transferred to the buyer the significant risks and rewards of ownership of the goods;
2. The company retains neither continuing managerial involvement to the degree usually associated with ownership nor effective control over the goods sold;
3. The amount of revenue can be measured reliably;

---

[6]Barter transactions for advertising services are addressed in *SIC 31*. **[3]** In the past, there were numerous situations when advertising companies made overly optimistic valuations related to bartered advertising services provided to clients. As a result, there are several specific requirements that must be met when recognizing revenue for bartered advertising services; these requirements are beyond the scope of this textbook.

4. It is probable that the economic benefits will flow to the company; and

5. The costs incurred or to be incurred can be estimated reliably.[7]

The most important of these criteria relates to the transfer of the risks and rewards of ownership. The critical event is often considered the point when these risks and rewards of ownership transfer to the buyer. The following illustrations highlight the measurement and recognition issues related to point of sale accounting.

Bill and Hold Sales

Bill and hold sales result when the buyer is not yet ready to take delivery but does take title and accept billing. Illustration 18-4 provides an example of a bill and hold arrangement.

BILL AND HOLD

Facts: Butler Company sells $450,000 of fireplaces to a local coffee shop, Baristo, which is planning to expand its locations around the city. Under the agreement, Baristo asks Butler to retain these fireplaces in its warehouses until the new coffee shops that will house the fireplaces are ready. Title passes to Baristo at the time the agreement is signed.

Question: Should Butler report the revenue from this bill and hold arrangement when the agreement is signed, or should revenue be deferred and reported when the fireplaces are delivered?

Solution: When to recognize revenue in a bill and hold situation depends on the circumstances. Butler should record the revenue at the time title passes, provided (1) it is probable that delivery will be made; (2) the item is on hand, identified, and ready for delivery at the time the sale is recognized; (3) Baristo acknowledges the deferred delivery arrangement; and (4) the usual payment terms apply. Otherwise, if all four conditions are not met, it is assumed that the risks and rewards of ownership remain with the seller even though title has passed. In this case, it appears that these conditions were probably met and therefore revenue recognition should be permitted at the time the agreement is signed.

ILLUSTRATION 18-4
Recognition—Bill and Hold

Butler makes the following entry to record the bill and hold sale.

Accounts Receivable	450,000	
Sales		450,000

If a significant period of time elapses before payment, the accounts receivable should be discounted. This is because it is likely that one of the conditions above is violated (such as the usual payment terms). In this case, the most appropriate approach for bill and hold sales is to defer revenue recognition to the point of delivery because the risks and rewards of ownership usually do not transfer until that point.

Sales Subject to Installation or Inspection

Companies often sell goods, such as technology equipment, which must be installed in the customer's building or plant. Only if installation is simple in nature, such as the

---

[7]In some cases, IFRS provides detailed criteria to use in determining when to recognize the revenue, such as bill and hold situations. In other situations, however, the abovementioned criteria are followed and considerable judgment must be exercised. In some cases, U.S. GAAP, because of its more detailed nature, may provide perspective on the accounting for point of sale accounting.

installation of a factory-tested receiver that only requires unpacking and connection of power and antennae, should revenue be recognized upon delivery. The same principle holds for inspections. Illustration 18-5 presents this situation.

ILLUSTRATION 18-5
Recognition—Installation

INSTALLATION

Facts: Cabrera Company sells complex medical scanning equipment to physicians and hospitals. Installation takes approximately three weeks and must be performed by Cabrera's skilled technicians.

Question: When should Cabrera recognize the revenue related to the medical equipment?

Solution: In this case, the risks and rewards of ownership appear to be with Cabrera until after the installation occurs. As a result, no revenue related to sale of the medical equipment should be recorded until the installation is completed. That is, it appears that the risks and rewards of ownership have not transferred until the installation is completed.

It is possible that the Cabrera sale transaction may be considered a multiple-deliverable arrangement (discussed later in the chapter), which means that some revenue may be associated with the installation and the remainder with the sale of the product.

Layaway Sales
Some companies sell goods on the installment basis. As a result, the companies hold the goods until the final payment is made. These goods are often referred to as **layaway sales** because the goods are "laid away" and are delivered only when the buyer makes the final payment. The situation in Illustration 18-6 addresses recognition when customers delay taking delivery of the goods.

ILLUSTRATION 18-6
Recognition—Layaway Sales

LAYAWAY SALES

Facts: Milano Company sells merchandise on the installment basis. As a result, it holds the goods until the final payment is made.

Question: Should Milano recognize the sale at the time of sale or when it receives its last payment?

Solution: Generally, revenue is recognized when the goods are delivered. The buyer may not make all payments and the sale will not be completed. In general, revenue may be recognized before delivery only when a significant deposit is received, provided the goods are on hand and ready for delivery to the buyer.

Sales with Right of Return
Whether cash or credit sales are involved, a special problem arises with claims for returns and allowances. Certain companies experience such a **high rate of return**—a high ratio of returned merchandise to sales—that they find it necessary to postpone recognizing sales revenue. For example, in the publishing industry, the rate of return approaches 25 percent for hardcover books and 65 percent for some magazines. Other types of companies that experience high return rates are perishable food dealers, distributors who sell to retail outlets, recording-industry companies, and some toy and sporting goods manufacturers. Returns in these industries are frequently made either through a right of contract or as a matter of practice involving "guaranteed sales" agreements or consignments.

When a right of return is present, companies must determine whether the goods have been delivered and accepted by the customer *and* the time period for returning the goods has elapsed. [6] Two possible revenue recognition methods are available when the right of return exposes the seller to continued risks of ownership: (1) not recording a sale until all return privileges have expired or (2) recording the sale, but reducing sales by an estimate of future returns. An example of a return situation is presented in Illustration 18-7.

ILLUSTRATION 18-7
Recognition—Returns

SALES WITH RETURNS

Facts: Pesido Company is in the beta-testing stage for new laser equipment that will help patients who have acid reflux problems. The product that Pesido is selling has been very successful in trials to date. As a result, Pesido has received regulatory authority to sell this equipment to various hospitals. Because of the uncertainty surrounding this product, Pesido has granted to the participating hospitals the right to return the device and receive full reimbursement for a period of 9 months.

Question: When should Pesido recognize the revenue for the sale of the new laser equipment?

Solution: Given that the hospital has the right to rescind the purchase for a reason specified in the sales contract and Pesido is uncertain about the probability of return, Pesido should not record revenue at the time of delivery. If there is uncertainty about the possibility of return, revenue is recognized when the goods have been delivered and the time period for rejection has elapsed. Only at that time have the risks and rewards of ownership transferred.

Companies may retain only an insignificant risk of ownership when a refund or right of return is provided. For example, revenue is recognized at the time of sale (even though a right of return exists or refund is permitted), provided the seller can reliably estimate future returns. In this case, the seller recognizes an allowance for returns based on previous experience and other relevant factors. [7][8]

Returning to the Pesido example, assume that Pesido sold $300,000 of laser equipment on August 1, 2011, and retains only an insignificant risk of ownership. On October 15, 2011, $10,000 in equipment was returned. In this case, Pesido makes the following entries.

August 1, 2011

Accounts Receivable	300,000	
Sales		300,000

October 15, 2011

Sales Returns and Allowances	10,000	
Accounts Receivable		10,000

At December 31, 2011, based on prior experience, Pesido estimates that returns on the remaining balance will be 4 percent. Pesido makes the following entry to record the expected returns.

December 31, 2011

Sales Returns and Allowances		
[($300,000 − $10,000) × 4%]	11,600	
Allowance for Sales Returns and Allowances		11,600

[8]Here is an example where the criteria under IFRS are very general. Although U.S. GAAP does not override the specific requirements of IFRS, companies sometimes will use the more explicit guidance in the U.S. GAAP approach to help resolve a difficult revenue recognition issue. It should be made clear that the *IAS 8* hierarchy does not require that companies refer to either U.S. GAAP or any other national standard-setter.

The Sales Returns and Allowances account is reported as contra revenue in the income statement, and Allowance for Sales Returns and Allowances is reported as a contra account to Accounts Receivable in the statement of financial position. As a result, the net revenue and net accounts receivable recognized are adjusted for the amount of the expected returns.

Sales with Buyback Agreements

If a company sells a product in one period and agrees to buy it back in the next period, has the company sold the product? As indicated in Chapter 8, legal title has transferred in this situation. However, the economic substance of this transaction is that the seller retains the risks of ownership, as indicated in the example in Illustration 18-8.

ILLUSTRATION 18-8
Recognition—Sale with Buyback

SALE WITH BUYBACK

Facts: Morgan plc, an equipment dealer, sells equipment to Lane Company for £135,000. The equipment has a cost of £115,000. Morgan agrees to repurchase the equipment at the end of 2 years at its fair value. Lane Company pays full price at the sales date, and there are no restrictions on the use of the equipment over the 2 years.

Question: How should Morgan record this transaction?

Solution: For a sale and repurchase agreement, the terms of the agreement need to be analyzed to ascertain whether, in substance, the seller has transferred the risks and rewards of ownership to the buyer. In this case, it appears that the risks and rewards of ownership are transferred to Lane Company and therefore a sale should be recorded. That is, Lane will receive fair value at the date of repurchase, which indicates Morgan has transferred risks of ownership. Furthermore, Lane has no restrictions on use of the equipment, which indicates that Morgan has transferred the rewards of ownership.

Morgan records the sale and related cost of goods sold as follows.

Cash	135,000	
Sales		135,000
Cost of Goods Sold	115,000	
Inventory		115,000

Now assume that Morgan requires Lane to sign a note with repayment to be made in 24 monthly payments. Lane is also required to maintain the equipment at a certain level. Morgan sets the payment schedule such that it receives a normal lender's rate of return on the transaction. In addition, Morgan agrees to repurchase the equipment after two years for £95,000.

In this case, this arrangement appears to be a financing transaction rather than a sale. That is, Lane is required to maintain the equipment at a certain level and Morgan agrees to repurchase at a set price, resulting in a lender's return. Thus, the risks and rewards of ownership are to a great extent still with Morgan. When the seller has retained the risks and rewards of ownership, even though legal title has been transferred, the transaction is a financing arrangement and does not give rise to revenue.[9]

Principal-Agent Relationships

In a **principal-agent relationship**, amounts collected on behalf of the principal are not revenue of the agent. Instead, revenue for the agent is the amount of the commission it receives (usually a percentage of the total revenue). An example of principal-agent relationships is an airline that sells tickets through a travel agent. For example, assume that Fly-Away Travels sells airplane tickets for **British Airways (BA)** (GBR) to

[9]In essence, Lane is renting the equipment from Morgan for two years. We discuss the accounting for such rental or lease arrangements in Chapter 21.

various customers. In this case, the principal is BA and the agent is Fly-Away Travels. BA is acting as a principal because it has exposure to the significant risks and rewards associated with the sale of its services. Fly-Away is acting as an agent because it does not have exposure to significant risks and rewards related to the tickets. Although Fly-Away collects the full airfare from the client, it then remits this amount to BA less a commission. Fly-Away therefore should not record the full amount of the fare as revenue on its books—to do so overstates its revenue. **Its revenue is the commission—not the full fare price**. The risks and rewards of ownership are not transferred to Fly-Away because it does not bear any inventory risk as it sells tickets to customers.

This distinction is very important for revenue recognition purposes. Some might argue that there is no harm in letting Fly-Away record revenue for the full price of the ticket and then charging the cost of the ticket against the revenue (often referred to as the **gross method** of recognizing revenue). Others note that this approach overstates the agent's revenue and is misleading. The revenue received is the commission for providing the travel services, not the full fare price (often referred to as the **net approach**). The profession believes the net approach is the correct method for recognizing revenue in a principal-agent relationship. As a result, the IASB has developed specific criteria to determine when a principal-agent relationship exists.[10] An important feature in deciding whether Fly-Away is acting as an agent is whether the amount it earns is predetermined, being either a fixed fee per transaction or a stated percentage of the amount billed to the customer.

GROSSED OUT

Consider Priceline.com (USA), the company made famous by William Shatner's ads about "naming your own price" for airline tickets and hotel rooms. In one quarter, Priceline reported that it earned $152 million in revenues. But, that included the full amount customers paid for tickets, hotel rooms, and rental cars. Traditional travel agencies call that amount "gross bookings," not revenues. And, much like regular travel agencies, Priceline keeps only a small portion of gross bookings—namely, the spread between the customers' accepted bids and the price it paid for the merchandise. The rest, which Priceline calls "product costs," it pays to the airlines and hotels that supply the tickets and rooms.

What do the numbers mean?

However, Priceline's product costs came to $134 million, leaving Priceline just $18 million of what it calls "gross profit" and what most other companies would call revenues. And, that's before all of Priceline's other costs—like advertising and salaries—which netted out to a loss of $102 million. The difference isn't academic: Priceline shares traded at about 23 times its reported revenues but at a mind-boggling 214 times its "gross profit." This and other aggressive recognition practices explains the stricter revenue recognition guidance, indicating that if a company performs as an agent or broker without assuming the risks and rewards of ownership of the goods, the company should report sales on a net (fee) basis.

Source: Jeremy Kahn, "Presto Chango! Sales Are Huge," *Fortune* (March 20, 2000), p. 44.

Consignments

Another common principal-agent relationship involves consignments. In these cases, manufacturers (or wholesalers) deliver goods but retain title to the goods until they are sold. This specialized method of marketing certain types of products makes use of a device known as a **consignment**. Under this arrangement, the **consignor** (manufacturer or wholesaler) ships merchandise to the **consignee** (dealer), who is to act as an agent for the consignor in selling the merchandise. Both consignor and consignee are interested in selling—the former to make a profit or develop a market, the latter to make a commission on the sale.

[10]Features indicating that a company is acting as a principal include (1) having the primary responsibility for providing the goods and services to the customer or for fulfilling the order; (2) having the inventory risk before and after the order, during shipment, or on return; (3) having the latitude to set prices (either directly or indirectly, e.g., by providing additional goods and services); and (4) bearing the customer's credit risk for sales made on credit. [8]

The consignee accepts the merchandise and agrees to exercise due diligence in caring for and selling it. The consignee remits to the consignor cash received from customers, after deducting a sales commission and any chargeable expenses.

In consignment sales, the consignor uses a modified version of the sale basis of revenue recognition. That is, the consignor recognizes revenue only after receiving notification of sale and the cash remittance from the consignee. The consignor carries the merchandise as inventory throughout the consignment, separately classified as Merchandise on Consignment. **The consignee does not record the merchandise as an asset on its books.** Upon sale of the merchandise, the consignee has **a liability for the net amount due the consignor**. The consignor periodically receives from the consignee a report called **account sales** that shows the merchandise received, merchandise sold, expenses chargeable to the consignment, and the cash remitted. Revenue is then recognized by the consignor. Analysis of a consignment arrangement is provided in Illustration 18-9.

ILLUSTRATION 18-9
Entries for Consignment
Sales

SALES ON CONSIGNMENT

Facts: Nelba Manufacturing Co. ships merchandise costing $36,000 on consignment to Best Value Stores. Nelba pays $3,750 of freight costs, and Best Value pays $2,250 for local advertising costs that are reimbursable from Nelba. By the end of the period, Best Value has sold two-thirds of the consigned merchandise for $40,000 cash. Best Value notifies Nelba of the sales, retains a 10% commission, and remits the cash due Nelba.

Question: What are the journal entries that the consignor (Nelba) and the consignee (Best Value) make to record this transaction?

Solution:

NELBA MFG. CO. (CONSIGNOR)			BEST VALUE STORES (CONSIGNEE)		
Shipment of consigned merchandise					
Inventory on Consignment	36,000		No entry (record memo of merchandise		
Finished Goods Inventory		36,000	received).		
Payment of freight costs by consignor					
Inventory on Consignment	3,750		No entry.		
Cash		3,750			
Payment of advertising by consignee					
No entry until notified.			Receivable from Consignor	2,250	
			Cash		2,250
Sales of consigned merchandise					
No entry until notified.			Cash	40,000	
			Payable to Consignor		40,000
Notification of sales and expenses and remittance of amount due					
Cash	33,750		Payable to Consignor	40,000	
Advertising Expense	2,250		Receivable from		
Commission Expense	4,000		Consignor		2,250
Revenue from			Commission Revenue		4,000
Consignment Sales		40,000	Cash		33,750
Adjustment of inventory on consignment for cost of sales					
Cost of Goods Sold	26,500		No entry.		
Inventory on Consignment		26,500			
[2/3 ($36,000 + $3,750) = $26,500]					

Under the consignment arrangement, the consignor accepts the risk that the merchandise might not sell and relieves the consignee of the need to commit part of its working capital to inventory. Companies use a variety of different systems and account titles to record consignments, but they all share the common goal of postponing the recognition of revenue until it is known that a sale to a third party has occurred.

Trade Loading and Channel Stuffing

One commentator describes **trade loading** this way: "Trade loading is a crazy, uneconomic, insidious practice through which manufacturers—trying to show sales, profits, and market share they don't actually have—induce their wholesale customers, known as the trade, to buy more product than they can promptly resell." For example, the cigarette industry appears to have exaggerated a couple years' operating profits by as much as $600 million by taking the profits from future years.

In the computer software industry, a similar practice is referred to as **channel stuffing**. When a software maker needed to make its financial results look good, it offered deep discounts to its distributors to overbuy, and then recorded revenue when the software left the loading dock. Of course, the distributors' inventories become bloated and the marketing channel gets too filled with product, but the software maker's current-period financials are improved. However, financial results in future periods will suffer, unless the company repeats the process.

Trade loading and channel stuffing distort operating results and "window dress" financial statements. In addition, similar to consignment transactions or sales with buy-back agreements, these arrangements generally do not transfer the risks and rewards of ownership. If used without an appropriate allowance for sales returns, channel stuffing is a classic example of booking tomorrow's revenue today. Business managers need to be aware of the ethical dangers of misleading the financial community by engaging in such practices to improve their financial statements.

Summary

Illustration 18-10 (page 966) provides a summary of the major issues related to revenue recognition at the point of sale.

NO TAKE-BACKS

Investors in **Lucent Technologies** (USA) were negatively affected when Lucent violated one of the fundamental criteria for revenue recognition—the "no take-back" rule. This rule holds that revenue should not be booked on inventory that is shipped if the customer can return it at some point in the future. In this particular case, Lucent agreed to take back shipped inventory from its distributors if the distributors were unable to sell the items to their customers.

What do the numbers mean?

In essence, Lucent was "stuffing the channel." By booking sales when goods were shipped, even though they most likely would get them back, Lucent was able to report continued sales growth. However, Lucent investors got a nasty surprise when distributors returned those goods and Lucent had to restate its financial results. The restatement erased $679 million in revenues, turning an operating profit into a loss. In response to this bad news, Lucent's share price declined $1.31 per share, or 8.5 percent. Lucent is not alone in this practice. **Sunbeam** (USA) got caught stuffing the sales channel with barbeque grills and other outdoor items, which contributed to its troubles when it was forced to restate its earnings.

Investors can be tipped off to potential channel stuffing by carefully reviewing a company's revenue recognition policy for generous return policies and by watching inventory and receivable levels. When sales increase along with receivables, that's one sign that customers are not paying for goods shipped on credit. And growing inventory levels are an indicator that customers have all the goods they need. Both scenarios suggest a higher likelihood of goods being returned and revenues and income being restated. So remember, no take-backs!

Source: Adapted from S. Young, "Lucent Slashes First Quarter Outlook, Erases Revenue from Latest Quarter," Wall Street Journal Online (December 22, 2000); and Tracey Byrnes, "Too Many Thin Mints: Spotting the Practice of Channel Stuffing," Wall Street Journal Online (February 7, 2002).

General Principles

1. Recognize revenue when it is probable that the economic benefits flow to the company and the benefits can be measured reliably.
2. Revenue is measured at the fair value of the consideration received or receivable.

Specific Transactions	Accounting Guidance
Sales with discounts	Trade, volume, and cash discounts reduce sales revenue.
Sales with extended payment terms	The fair value measurement of revenue is determined by discounting the future payments using an imputed interest rate.
Barter sales	If the goods (services) exchanged are dissimilar in nature, the exchange is recorded as revenue. If similar in nature, no revenue is recorded. Special rules apply to advertising services.
Bill and hold sales	Recognition depends on the circumstances. Recognize revenue when title passes if (1) it is probable that goods will be delivered; (2) the item is identified, on hand, and ready for delivery; (3) the buyer acknowledges the deferred delivery arrangement; and (4) usual payment terms apply. In practice, revenue is generally recognized at delivery because these conditions are not met.
Sales with installation (inspection)	Recognize revenue at delivery only if installation (inspection) is simple in nature; otherwise, recognize when these follow-up procedures are completed.
Layaway sales	Recognize revenue when the final payment is received, unless a significant deposit is received.
Sales with right of return	If there is uncertainty about the possibility of return, recognize revenue when the goods are delivered and the return period has lapsed. If the company can reliably estimate future returns, revenue (less estimated returns) is recognized at the point of sale.
Sales with buyback	Terms of the buyback agreement must be analyzed to determine if, in substance, the seller has transferred the risks and rewards of ownership.
Sales involving principal-agent relationship (general)	Amounts collected by the agent on behalf of the principal are not revenue of the agent. Instead, revenue to the agent is the amount of commission it receives.
Sales involving principal-agent relationship (consignments)	Consignor recognizes revenue (sales and cost of goods sold) when goods are sold by consignee. Consignee recognizes revenue for commissions received.
Trade loading and channel stuffing	Unless returns can be reliably measured, revenue should not be recognized until the goods are sold (by the distributor) to third parties.

ILLUSTRATION 18-10
Revenue Recognition at
the Point of Sale

LONG-TERM CONTRACTS (CONSTRUCTION)

For the most part, companies recognize revenue at the point of sale (delivery) because at point of sale the risks and rewards of ownership are transferred and the exchange price is known. Under certain circumstances, however, companies recognize revenue prior to completion and delivery. The most notable example is long-term construction contract accounting, which uses the percentage-of-completion method.[11]

Long-term contracts frequently provide that the seller (builder) may bill the purchaser at intervals, as it reaches various points in the project. Examples of long-term contracts are construction-type contracts, development of military and commercial aircraft, weapons-delivery systems, and space exploration hardware. When the project consists of separable units, such as a group of buildings or miles of roadway, contract provisions may provide for delivery in installments. In that case, the seller would bill the buyer and transfer title at stated stages of completion, such as the completion of each building unit or every 10 miles of road. The accounting records should record sales when installments are "delivered."

---

[11]Some service contracts are long-term; these arrangements follow the same accounting as long-term construction contracts. Service contracts are discussed later in the chapter.

Two distinctly different methods of accounting for long-term construction contracts are recognized. They are:

- **Percentage-of-completion method.** Companies recognize revenues and gross profits each period based upon the progress of the construction—that is, the percentage of completion. The company accumulates construction costs **plus gross profit earned to date** in an inventory account (Construction in Process), and it accumulates progress billings in a contra inventory account (Billings on Construction in Progress).

- **Cost-recovery (zero-profit) method.** In some cases, contract revenue is recognized only to the extent of costs incurred that are expected to be recoverable. Once all costs are recognized, profit is recognized. The company accumulates construction costs in an inventory account (Construction in Process), and it accumulates progress billings in a contra inventory account (Billings on Construction in Process).

The rationale for using percentage-of-completion accounting is that under most of these contracts, the buyer and seller have enforceable rights. The buyer has the legal right to require specific performance on the contract. The seller has the right to require progress payments that provide evidence of the buyer's ownership interest. As a result, a continuous sale occurs as the work progresses. Companies should recognize revenue according to that progression.

Companies *must* use the percentage-of-completion method when estimates of progress toward completion, revenues, and costs can be estimated reliably and **all of the following conditions** exist.

1. Total contract revenue can be measured reliably;
2. It is probable that the economic benefits associated with the contract will flow to the company;
3. Both the contract costs to complete the contract and the stage of contract completion at the end of the reporting period can be measured reliably; and
4. The contract costs attributable to the contract can be clearly identified and measured reliably so the actual contract costs incurred can be compared with prior estimates. **[9]**

Companies should use the cost-recovery method when one of the following conditions applies:

- When a company cannot meet the conditions for using the percentage-of-completion method, *or*
- When there are inherent hazards in the contract beyond the normal, recurring business risks.

The presumption is that percentage-of-completion is the better method. Therefore, companies should use the cost-recovery method only when the percentage-of-completion method is inappropriate. We discuss the two methods in more detail in the following sections.

Percentage-of-Completion Method

The **percentage-of-completion method** recognizes revenues, costs, and gross profit as a company makes progress toward completion on a long-term contract. To defer recognition of these items until completion of the entire contract is to misrepresent the efforts (costs) and accomplishments (revenues) of the accounting periods during the contract. In order to apply the percentage-of-completion

Objective·3

Apply the percentage-of-completion method for long-term contracts.

method, a company must have some basis or standard for measuring the progress toward completion at particular interim dates.

Measuring the Progress toward Completion

As one practicing accountant wrote, "The big problem in applying the percentage-of-completion method . . . has to do with the ability to make reasonably accurate estimates of completion and the final gross profit." Companies use various methods to determine the **extent of progress toward completion**. The most common are the *cost-to-cost* and *units-of-delivery* methods.

The objective of all these methods is to measure the extent of progress in terms of costs, units, or value added. The stage of completion of a contract may be determined in a variety of ways. The company should use the method that measures most reliably the work performed. Note that progress payments and advances received from customers often do not reflect the work performed.[12] Companies identify the various measures (costs incurred, labor hours worked, tons produced, floors completed, etc.) and classify them as input or output measures. **Input measures** (costs incurred, labor hours worked) are efforts devoted to a contract. **Output measures** (with units of delivery measured as tons produced, floors of a building completed, miles of a highway completed) track results. Neither are universally applicable to all long-term projects. Their use requires the exercise of judgment and careful tailoring to the circumstances.

Both input and output measures have certain disadvantages. The input measure is based on an established relationship between a unit of input and productivity. If inefficiencies cause the productivity relationship to change, inaccurate measurements result. Another potential problem is front-end loading, in which significant up-front costs result in higher estimates of completion. To avoid this problem, companies should disregard some early-stage construction costs—for example, costs of uninstalled materials or costs of subcontracts not yet performed—if they do not relate to contract performance.

Similarly, output measures can produce inaccurate results if the units used are not comparable in time, effort, or cost to complete. For example, using floors (stories) completed can be deceiving. Completing the first floor of an eight-story building may require more than one-eighth the total cost because of the substructure and foundation construction.

The most popular input measure used to determine the progress toward completion is the **cost-to-cost basis**. Under this basis, a company like **Ultra Electronics Holdings plc (UEH)** (GBR) measures the percentage of completion by comparing costs incurred to date with the most recent estimate of the total costs required to complete the contract. Illustration 18-11 shows the formula for the cost-to-cost basis.

ILLUSTRATION 18-11
Formula for Percentage-of-Completion, Cost-to-Cost Basis

$$\frac{\text{Costs incurred to date}}{\text{Most recent estimate of total costs}} = \textbf{Percent complete}$$

Once UEH knows the percentage that costs incurred bear to total estimated costs, it applies that percentage to the total revenue or the estimated total gross profit on the contract. The resulting amount is the revenue or the gross profit to be recognized to date. Illustration 18-12 shows this computation.

---

[12]*IAS 11* indicates that, depending on the nature of the contract, the methods may include (1) the proportion that contract costs incurred for work performed to date bear to the estimated total contract costs, (2) surveys of work performed, and (3) completion of a physical proportion of the contract work. **[10]**

ILLUSTRATION 18-12
Formula for Total
Revenue to Be Recognized
to Date

Percent complete	×	Estimated total revenue (or gross profit)	=	Revenue (or gross profit) to be recognized to date

To find the amounts of revenue and gross profit recognized each period, UEH subtracts total revenue or gross profit recognized in prior periods, as shown in Illustration 18-13.

ILLUSTRATION 18-13
Formula for Amount of
Current-Period Revenue,
Cost-to-Cost Basis

Revenue (or gross profit) to be recognized to date	−	Revenue (or gross profit) recognized in prior periods	=	Current-period revenue (or gross profit)

Because **the cost-to-cost method is widely used** (without excluding other bases for measuring progress toward completion), we have adopted it for use in our examples.

Example of Percentage-of-Completion Method—Cost-to-Cost Basis

To illustrate the percentage-of-completion method, assume that Hardhat Construction Company has a contract to construct a €4,500,000 bridge at an estimated cost of €4,000,000. The contract is to start in July 2010, and the bridge is to be completed in October 2012. The following data pertain to the construction period. (Note that by the end of 2011, Hardhat has revised the estimated total cost from €4,000,000 to €4,050,000.)

	2010	2011	2012
Costs to date	€1,000,000	€2,916,000	€4,050,000
Estimated costs to complete	3,000,000	1,134,000	—
Progress billings during the year	900,000	2,400,000	1,200,000
Cash collected during the year	750,000	1,750,000	2,000,000

Hardhat determines the stage of completion for the contract by calculating the proportion of contract costs incurred for work performed to date relative to the latest estimated total contract costs. As a result, Hardhat would compute the percentage complete as shown in Illustration 18-14.

ILLUSTRATION 18-14
Application of Percentage-
of-Completion Method,
Cost-to-Cost Basis

	2010	2011	2012
Contract price	€4,500,000	€4,500,000	€4,500,000
Less estimated cost:			
Costs to date	1,000,000	2,916,000	4,050,000
Estimated costs to complete	3,000,000	1,134,000	—
Estimated total costs	4,000,000	4,050,000	4,050,000
Estimated total gross profit	€ 500,000	€ 450,000	€ 450,000
Percent complete	25%	72%	100%
	$\left(\dfrac{\text{€}1{,}000{,}000}{\text{€}4{,}000{,}000}\right)$	$\left(\dfrac{\text{€}2{,}916{,}000}{\text{€}4{,}050{,}000}\right)$	$\left(\dfrac{\text{€}4{,}050{,}000}{\text{€}4{,}050{,}000}\right)$

On the basis of the data above, Hardhat would make the entries shown in Illustration 18-15 (page 970) to record (1) the costs of construction, (2) progress billings, and (3) collections. These entries appear as summaries of the many transactions that would be entered individually as they occur during the year.

ILLUSTRATION 18-15
Journal Entries—
Percentage-of-Completion
Method, Cost-to-Cost
Basis

	2010		2011		2012	
To record cost of construction:						
Construction in Process	1,000,000		1,916,000		1,134,000	
Materials, Cash,						
Payables, etc.		1,000,000		1,916,000		1,134,000
To record progress billings:						
Accounts Receivable	900,000		2,400,000		1,200,000	
Billings on Construction						
in Process		900,000		2,400,000		1,200,000
To record collections:						
Cash	750,000		1,750,000		2,000,000	
Accounts Receivable		750,000		1,750,000		2,000,000

In this example, the costs incurred to date are a measure of the extent of progress toward completion. To determine this, Hardhat evaluates the costs incurred to date as a proportion of the estimated total costs to be incurred on the project. The estimated revenue, costs, and gross profit that Hardhat will recognize for each year are calculated as shown in Illustration 18-16.

ILLUSTRATION 18-16
Percentage-of-Completion
Revenue, Costs, and Gross
Profit by Year

	To Date	Recognized in Prior Years	Recognized in Current Year
2010			
Revenues (€4,500,000 × 25%)	€1,125,000		€1,125,000
Costs	1,000,000		1,000,000
Gross profit	€ 125,000		€ 125,000
2011			
Revenues (€4,500,000 × 72%)	€3,240,000	€1,125,000	€2,115,000
Costs	2,916,000	1,000,000	1,916,000
Gross profit	€ 324,000	€ 125,000	€ 199,000
2012			
Revenues (€4,500,000 × 100%)	€4,500,000	€3,240,000	€1,260,000
Costs	4,050,000	2,916,000	1,134,000
Gross profit	€ 450,000	€ 324,000	€ 126,000

Illustration 18-17 shows Hardhat's entries to recognize revenue and gross profit each year and to record completion and final approval of the contract.

ILLUSTRATION 18-17
Journal Entries to
Recognize Revenue and
Gross Profit and to Record
Contract Completion—
Percentage-of-Completion
Method, Cost-to-Cost
Basis

	2010		2011		2012	
To recognize revenue and						
gross profit:						
Construction in Process						
(gross profit)	125,000		199,000		126,000	
Construction Expenses	1,000,000		1,916,000		1,134,000	
Revenue from Long-Term						
Contracts		1,125,000		2,115,000		1,260,000
To record completion of						
the contract:						
Billings on Construction						
in Process					4,500,000	
Construction in Process						4,500,000

Note that Hardhat debits gross profit (as computed in Illustration 18-16) to Construction in Process. Similarly, it credits Revenue from Long-Term Contracts for the amounts computed in Illustration 18-16. Hardhat then debits the difference between the amounts recognized each year for revenue and gross profit to a nominal account, Construction Expenses (similar to Cost of Goods Sold in a manufacturing company). It reports that amount in the income statement as the actual cost of construction incurred in that period. For example, Hardhat uses the actual costs of €1,000,000 to compute both the gross profit of €125,000 and the percent complete (25 percent).

Hardhat continues to accumulate costs in the Construction in Process account, in order to maintain a record of total costs incurred (plus recognized profit) to date. Although theoretically a series of "sales" takes place using the percentage-of-completion method, the selling company cannot remove the inventory cost until the construction is completed and transferred to the new owner. Hardhat's Construction in Process account for the bridge would include the following summarized entries over the term of the construction project.

Construction in Process				
2010 construction costs	€1,000,000	12/31/12	to close	
2010 recognized gross profit	125,000		completed	
2011 construction costs	1,916,000		project	€4,500,000
2011 recognized gross profit	199,000			
2012 construction costs	1,134,000			
2012 recognized gross profit	126,000			
Total	€4,500,000	Total		€4,500,000

ILLUSTRATION 18-18
Content of Construction in Process Account— Percentage-of-Completion Method

Recall that the Hardhat Construction Company example contained a **change in estimate**: In the second year, 2011, it increased the estimated total costs from €4,000,000 to €4,050,000. The change in estimate is accounted for in a **cumulative catch-up manner**. This is done by, first, adjusting the percent completed to the new estimate of total costs. Next, Hardhat deducts the amount of revenues and gross profit recognized in prior periods from revenues and gross profit computed for progress to date. That is, it accounts for the change in estimate in the period of change. That way, the statement of financial position at the end of the period of change and the accounting in subsequent periods are as they would have been if the revised estimate had been the original estimate.

Financial Statement Presentation—Percentage-of-Completion

Generally, when a company records a receivable from a sale, it reduces the Inventory account. Under the percentage-of-completion method, however, the company continues to carry both the receivable and the inventory. Subtracting the balance in the **Billings account** from Construction in Process avoids double-counting the inventory. During the life of the contract, Hardhat reports in the statement of financial position the difference between the Construction in Process and the Billings on Construction in Process accounts. If that amount is a debit, Hardhat reports it **as a current asset**; if it is a credit, it reports it **as a current liability**.

At times, the costs incurred plus the gross profit recognized to date (the balance in Construction in Process) exceed the billings. In that case, Hardhat reports this excess as a current asset entitled "Cost and recognized profit in excess of billings." Hardhat can at any time calculate the unbilled portion of revenue recognized to date by subtracting the billings to date from the revenue recognized to date, as illustrated for 2010 for Hardhat Construction in Illustration 18-19 (page 972).

ILLUSTRATION 18-19
Computation of Unbilled
Contract Price at
12/31/10

Contract revenue recognized to date: €4,500,000 × $\frac{€1,000,000}{€4,000,000}$		€1,125,000
Billings to date		900,000
Unbilled revenue *current asset*		€ 225,000

At other times, the billings exceed costs incurred and gross profit to date. In that case, Hardhat reports this excess as a current liability entitled "Billings in excess of costs and recognized profit."

It probably has occurred to you that companies often have more than one project going at a time. When a company has a number of projects, costs exceed billings on some contracts and billings exceed costs on others. In such a case, the company segregates the contracts. The asset side includes only those contracts on which costs and recognized profit exceed billings. The liability side includes only those on which billings exceed costs and recognized profit. Separate disclosures of the dollar volume of billings and costs are preferable to a summary presentation of the net difference.

Using data from the bridge example, Hardhat Construction Company would report the status and results of its long-term construction activities under the perentage-of-completion method as shown in Illustration 18-20.

ILLUSTRATION 18-20
Financial Statement
Presentation—Percentage-
of-Completion Method

HARDHAT CONSTRUCTION COMPANY

Income Statement	2010	2011	2012
Revenue from long-term contracts	€1,125,000	€2,115,000	€1,260,000
Costs of construction	1,000,000	1,916,000	1,134,000
Gross profit	€ 125,000	€ 199,000	€ 126,000

Statement of Financial Position (12/31)		2010	2011	2012
Current assets				
Inventories				
Construction in process	€1,125,000			
Less: Billings	900,000			
Costs and recognized profit in excess of billings		€ 225,000		€ –0–
Accounts receivable		150,000	€ 800,000	–0–
Current liabilities				
Billings	€3,300,000			
Less: Construction in process	3,240,000			
Billings in excess of costs and recognized profits			€ 60,000	€ –0–

Note 1. Summary of significant accounting policies.
Long-Term Construction Contracts. The company recognizes revenues and reports profits from long-term construction contracts, its principal business, under the percentage-of-completion method of accounting. These contracts generally extend for periods in excess of one year. The amounts of revenues and profits recognized each year are based on the ratio of costs incurred to the total estimated costs. Costs included in construction in process include direct materials, direct labor, and project-related overhead. Corporate general and administrative expenses are charged to the periods as incurred and are not allocated to construction contracts.

Cost-Recovery (Zero-Profit) Method

Objective·4
Apply the cost-recovery method for long-term contracts.

During the early stages of a contract, a company like **Alcatel-Lucent** (FRA) may not be able to estimate reliably the outcome of a long-term construction contract. Nevertheless, Alcatel-Lucent is confident that it will recover the contract costs incurred. In this case, Alcatel-Lucent uses the **cost-recovery method** (sometimes referred to as the zero-profit method). This method recognizes revenue only to the extent of costs incurred that are expected to be recoverable. Only after all costs are incurred is gross profit recognized.

To illustrate the cost-recovery method for the bridge project illustrated on the preceding pages, Hardhat Construction would report the following revenues and costs for 2010–2012, as shown in Illustration 18-21.

	To Date	Recognized in Prior Years	Recognized in Current Year
2010			
Revenues (costs incurred)	€1,000,000		€1,000,000
Costs	1,000,000		1,000,000
Gross profit	€ 0		€ 0
2011			
Revenues (costs incurred)	€2,916,000	€ 1,000,000	€1,916,000
Costs	2,916,000	1,000,000	1,916,000
Gross profit	€ 0	€ 0	€ 0
2012			
Revenues (€4,500,000 × 100%)	€4,500,000	€ 2,916,000	€1,584,000
Costs	4,050,000	2,916,000	1,134,000
Gross profit	€ 450,000	€ 0	€ 450,000

ILLUSTRATION 18-21
Cost-Recovery Method Revenue, Costs, and Gross Profit by Year

Illustration 18-22 shows Hardhat's entries to recognize revenue and gross profit each year and to record completion and final approval of the contract.

	2010		2011		2012	
Construction Expense	1,000,000		1,916,000			
Revenue from Long-Term Contract		1,000,000		1,916,000		
(To recognize costs and related expenses)						
Construction in Process (Gross Profit)					450,000	
Construction Expense					1,134,000	
Revenue from Long-Term Contract						1,584,000
(To recognize costs and related expenses)						
Billings on Construction in Process					4,500,000	
Construction in Process						4,500,000
(To record completion of the contract)						

ILLUSTRATION 18-22
Journal Entries—Cost-Recovery Method

As indicated, no gross profit is recognized in 2010 and 2011. In 2012, Hardhat then recognizes gross profit and closes the Billings and Construction in Process accounts.

Illustration 18-23 compares the amount of gross profit that Hardhat Construction Company would recognize for the bridge project under the two revenue recognition methods.

	Percentage-of-Completion	Cost-Recovery
2010	€125,000	€ 0
2011	199,000	0
2012	126,000	450,000

ILLUSTRATION 18-23
Comparison of Gross Profit Recognized under Different Methods

Under the cost-recovery method, Hardhat Construction would report its long-term construction activities as shown in Illustration 18-24 (page 974).

ILLUSTRATION 18-24
Financial Statement
Presentation—Cost-
Recovery Method

HARDHAT CONSTRUCTION COMPANY			
Income Statement	2010	2011	2012
Revenue from long-term contracts	€1,000,000	€1,916,000	€1,584,000
Costs of construction	1,000,000	1,916,000	1,134,000
Gross profit	€ 0	€ 0	€ 450,000

Statement of Financial Position (12/31)		2010	2011	2012
Current assets				
Inventories				
Construction in process	€1,000,000			
Less: Billings	900,000			
Costs in excess of billings		€ 100,000		€ –0–
Accounts receivable		150,000	€ 800,000	–0–
Current liabilities				
Billings	€3,300,000			
Less: Construction in process	2,916,000			
Billings in excess of costs and recognized profits			€ 384,000	€ –0–

Note 1. Summary of significant accounting policies.
Long-Term Construction Contracts. The company recognizes revenues and reports profits from long-term construction contracts, its principal business, under the cost-recovery method. These contracts generally extend for periods in excess of one year. Contract costs and billings are accumulated during the periods of construction, and revenues are recognized only to the extent of costs incurred that are expected to be recoverable. Only after all costs are incurred is net income recognized. Costs included in construction in process include direct material, direct labor, and project-related overhead. Corporate general and administrative expenses are charged to the periods as incurred.

Long-Term Contract Losses

Objective·5
Identify the proper accounting for losses on long-term contracts.

Two types of losses can become evident under long-term contracts:[13]

1. *Loss in the current period on a profitable contract.* This condition arises when, during construction, there is a significant increase in the estimated total contract costs but the increase does not eliminate all profit on the contract. Under the percentage-of-completion method only, the estimated cost increase requires a current-period adjustment of excess gross profit recognized on the project in prior periods. The company records this adjustment as a loss in the current period because it is a **change in accounting estimate** (discussed in Chapter 22).

2. *Loss on an unprofitable contract.* Cost estimates at the end of the current period may indicate that a loss will result on completion of the *entire* contract. Under both the percentage-of-completion and the cost-recovery methods, the company must recognize in the current period the entire expected contract loss.

The treatment described for unprofitable contracts is consistent with the accounting for impairments of non-current assets. That is, an asset is impaired when a company is not able to recover the asset's carrying amount either by using or selling it.

Loss in Current Period

To illustrate a loss in the current period on a contract expected to be profitable upon completion, we'll continue with the Hardhat Construction Company bridge project. Assume that on December 31, 2011, Hardhat estimates the costs to complete the bridge contract at €1,468,962 instead of €1,134,000 (refer to page 969). Assuming all other data

[13]Sak Bhamornsiri, "Losses from Construction Contracts," *The Journal of Accountancy* (April 1982), p. 26.

are the same as before, Hardhat would compute the percentage complete and recognize the loss as shown in Illustration 18-25. Compare these computations with those for 2011 in Illustration 18-14 (page 969). The "percent complete" has dropped, from 72 percent to 66½ percent, due to the increase in estimated future costs to complete the contract.

Cost to date (12/31/11)	€2,916,000
Estimated costs to complete (revised)	1,468,962
Estimated total costs	€4,384,962
Percent complete (€2,916,000 ÷ €4,384,962)	66½%
Revenue recognized in 2011	
(€4,500,000 × 66½%) − €1,125,000	€1,867,500
Costs incurred in 2011	1,916,000
Loss recognized in 2011	€ 48,500

ILLUSTRATION 18-25
Computation of Recognizable Loss, 2011—Loss in Current Period

The 2011 loss of €48,500 is a cumulative adjustment of the "excessive" gross profit recognized on the contract in 2010. Instead of restating the prior period, the company absorbs the prior period misstatement entirely in the current period. In this illustration, the adjustment was large enough to result in recognition of a loss.

Hardhat Construction would record the loss in 2011 as follows.

Construction Expenses	1,916,000	
Construction in Process (Loss)		48,500
Revenue from Long-Term Contracts		1,867,500

Hardhat will report the loss of €48,500 on the 2011 income statement as the difference between the reported revenues of €1,867,500 and the costs of €1,916,000.[14] **Under the cost-recovery method, the company does not recognize a loss in 2011.** Why not? Because the company still expects the contract **to result in a profit**, to be recognized in the year of completion.

Loss on an Unprofitable Contract

To illustrate the accounting for an **overall loss on a long-term contract**, assume that at December 31, 2011, Hardhat Construction Company estimates the costs to complete the bridge contract at €1,640,250 instead of €1,134,000. Revised estimates for the bridge contract are as follows.

	2010 Original Estimates	2011 Revised Estimates
Contract price	€4,500,000	€4,500,000
Estimated total cost	4,000,000	4,556,250*
Estimated gross profit	€ 500,000	
Estimated loss		€ (56,250)

*(€2,916,000 + €1,640,250)

Under the percentage-of-completion method, Hardhat recognized €125,000 of gross profit in 2010 (see Illustration 18-16 on page 970). This amount must be offset in 2011 because it is no longer expected to be realized. In addition, since losses must be recognized as soon as estimable, the company must recognize the total estimated loss of

[14]In 2012, Hardhat Construction will recognize the remaining 33½ percent of the revenue (€1,507,500), with costs of €1,468,962 as expected, and will report a gross profit of €38,538. The total gross profit over the three years of the contract would be €115,038 [€125,000 (2010) − €48,500 (2011) + €38,538 (2012)]. This amount is the difference between the total contract revenue of €4,500,000 and the total contract costs of €4,384,962.

€56,250 in 2011. Therefore, Hardhat must recognize a total loss of €181,250 (€125,000 + €56,250) in 2011.

Illustration 18-26 shows Hardhat's computation of the revenue to be recognized in 2011.

ILLUSTRATION 18-26
Computation of Revenue Recognizable, 2011—Unprofitable Contract

Revenue recognized in 2011:		
Contract price		€4,500,000
Percent complete		× 64%*
Revenue recognizable to date		2,880,000
Less: Revenue recognized prior to 2011		1,125,000
Revenue recognized in 2011		€1,755,000
*Cost to date (12/31/11)	€2,916,000	
Estimated cost to complete	1,640,250	
Estimated total costs	€4,556,250	
Percent complete: €2,916,000 ÷ €4,556,250 = 64%		

To compute the construction costs to be expensed in 2011, Hardhat adds the total loss to be recognized in 2011 (€125,000 + €56,250) to the revenue to be recognized in 2011. Illustration 18-27 shows this computation.

ILLUSTRATION 18-27
Computation of Construction Expense, 2011—Unprofitable Contract

Revenue recognized in 2011 (computed above)		€1,755,000
Total loss recognized in 2011:		
Reversal of 2010 gross profit	€125,000	
Total estimated loss on the contract	56,250	181,250
Construction cost expensed in 2011		€1,936,250

Hardhat Construction would record the long-term contract revenues, expenses, and loss in 2011 as follows.

Construction Expenses	1,936,250	
Construction in Process (Loss)		181,250
Revenue from Long-Term Contracts		1,755,000

At the end of 2011, Construction in Process has a balance of €2,859,750 as shown below.[15]

ILLUSTRATION 18-28
Content of Construction in Process Account at End of 2011—Unprofitable Contract

Construction in Process			
2010 Construction costs	1,000,000		
2010 Recognized gross profit	125,000		
2011 Construction costs	1,916,000	2011 Recognized loss	181,250
Balance	**2,859,750**		

Under the cost-recovery method, Hardhat also would recognize the contract loss of €56,250, through the following entries in 2011 (the year in which the loss first became evident).

Construction Expenses	1,916,000	
Revenue from Long-Term Contracts		1,916,000
Loss from Long-Term Contracts	56,250	
Construction in Process (Loss)		56,250

[15]If the costs in 2012 are €1,640,250 as projected, at the end of 2012 the Construction in Process account will have a balance of €1,640,250 + €2,859,750, or €4,500,000, equal to the contract price. When the company matches the revenue remaining to be recognized in 2012 of €1,620,000 [€4,500,000 (total contract price) − €1,125,000 (2010) − €1,755,000 (2011)] with the construction expense to be recognized in 2012 of €1,620,000 [total costs of €4,556,250 less the total costs recognized in prior years of €2,936,250 (2010, €1,000,000; 2011, €1,936,250)], a zero profit results. Thus the total loss has been recognized in 2011, the year in which it first became evident.

Just as the Billings account balance cannot exceed the contract price, neither can the balance in Construction in Process exceed the contract price. In circumstances where the **Construction in Process balance exceeds the billings**, the company can deduct the recognized loss from such accumulated costs on the statement of financial position. That is, under both the percentage-of-completion and the cost-recovery methods, the provision for the loss (the credit) may be combined with Construction in Process, thereby reducing the inventory balance. In those circumstances, however (as in the 2011 example above), where the **billings exceed the accumulated costs**, Hardhat must report separately on the statement of financial position, as a current liability, the amount of the estimated loss. That is, under both the percentage-of-completion and the cost-recovery methods, Hardhat would take the €56,250 loss, as estimated in 2011, from the Construction in Process account and report it separately as a current liability titled "Estimated liability from long-term contracts."

Disclosures in Financial Statements

Construction contractors usually make some unique financial statement disclosures in addition to those required of all businesses. Generally, these additional disclosures are made in the notes to the financial statements. For example, a construction contractor should disclose the following: revenue recognized during the period and the methods used to determine the contract revenue and stage of completion. For contracts in progress, companies should disclose the aggregate amount of costs incurred and recognized net income, amount of advances received, and amount of retentions. Any contingent assets or liabilities related to these contracts are also disclosed. [11]

OTHER REVENUE RECOGNITION ISSUES

Service Contracts

Service contracts follow the same criteria as long-term contracts. That is, to recognize revenue:

> **Objective·6**
> Describe the accounting issues for service contracts.

- It must be reliably measurable;
- Economic benefits are probable;
- Stage of completion must be reliably measurable; and
- Costs must be reliably measurable.

Examples of service-type enterprises are presented in Illustration 18-29.

Accounting	Management consulting
Advertising agencies	Medical
Architecture	Modeling agencies
Cemetery associations	Mortgage banking
Computer service organizations	Moving and storage
Correspondence schools	Perpetual care societies
Electronic security	Placement agencies
Employment agencies	Private and social clubs
Engineering firms	Public relations
Entertainment	Real estate brokerage
Equipment and office maintenance	Research and development labs
Garbage and waste removal	Retirement homes
Health spas	Transportation
Interior design or decoration	Travel agencies
Legal services	

ILLUSTRATION 18-29
Service Enterprises

Service contracts may be short-term or long-term. Many service contracts extend over multiple accounting periods, similar to long-term contracts in the construction industry. In these situations, service companies follow the same accounting approaches used earlier for construction contracts.

The general rule is that the **performance of the service is the critical event for revenue recognition.** As a result, if a service transaction consists of a single act, revenue should be recognized at the time the act takes place. For example, the single-act approach can be used by a real estate broker who records sales commissions as revenue when the real estate transaction is consummated at the closing.

When services are delivered by performing more than one act, revenue should be recognized as the various acts that make up the entire transaction occur. This method can be applied in a slightly different manner to three differing sets of circumstances:

1. *Specified number of identical or similar acts.* An equal amount of revenue is recorded for each act expected to be performed. For example, the processing of monthly mortgage payments by a mortgage banker is an appropriate application of this method.

2. *Specified number of defined but not identical acts.* Revenue is recognized on the percentage-of-completion basis using some appropriate measure, such as cost incurred to total costs to determine percentage of completion. For example, a correspondence school that provides progress evaluations, lessons, examinations, and grading might use this method.

3. *Unspecified number of identical acts or similar acts with a fixed period for performance.* Revenue is recognized on a straight-line basis over the specified period unless there is evidence that another method is more representative of the pattern of performance. A two-year membership in which the health club's facilities are available for the member's usage throughout the period is an example of appropriate application of the straight-line method.

If a company cannot estimate reliably the outcome of a transaction involving the providing of a service, it recognizes revenue only to the extent of the expenses recoverable. Examples of revenue recognition for service arrangements are presented in Illustrations 18-30, 18-31, and 18-32.

ILLUSTRATION 18-30
Research and Development (R&D) Services

R&D SERVICE CONTRACT

Facts: Jackson Bio-Tech has signed a contract to provide research and development services to Andes Company for 5 years. Andes must also use certain technology owned by Jackson. The technology may not be sold or licensed by Jackson unless the service agreement is also accepted. Under terms of the arrangement, Andes pays a non-refundable upfront technology fee of £1,000,000 on January 1, 2011. In addition, it must pay £400,000 at the end of each year for 5 years for the related R&D.

Question: How should the upfront fee of £1,000,000 be recognized and how should the £400,000 annual payment for the related R&D services be reported?

Solution: In this case, it appears that Andes is purchasing the technology and the related R&D services in a single package. For example, the technology cannot be sold separately from the R&D. Even though the initial fee is non-refundable, the upfront fee should be recognized over the life of the arrangement on a straight-line basis. The £400,000 payment related to the R&D should also be reported in each period as revenue.

Assuming R&D services are provided according to the contract in 2011, Jackson makes the following entries in 2011 to recognized revenue on the Andes contract.

January 1, 2011

Cash	1,000,000	
Unearned R&D Service Revenue		1,000,000

December 31, 2011

Cash	400,000	
Unearned R&D Service Revenue (£1,000,000 ÷ 5)	200,000	
R&D Service Revenue		600,000

Contracts of this nature often involve trade-offs between the upfront payment and subsequent payments. Thus, the key issue is whether the initial activity of "selling the technology" should be recognized in the first year or should be allocated over the five-year period.

Recognizing service revenue for an advertising arrangement is shown is Illustration 18-31.

ILLUSTRATION 18-31
Advertising Services

ADVERTISING

Facts: Garcia Company produces, publishes, and distributes telephone directories. Its revenue source arises from advertisements placed by companies and individuals selling goods and services. In many cases, the amounts paid for the advertising are received before the telephone directories are distributed.

Question: How should the advertising and the related costs associated with the production and distribution of the directories be reported?

Solution: Revenue should be recognized only when the directories are distributed to the public. If the directories are distributed over an extended period of time, the revenues should be based on a percentage of completion, using the percentage of directories delivered relative to the total directories to be distributed. Appropriate costs should be deferred in inventory and allocated to income as the revenue is recognized.

A service contract with revenue recognized in a manner similar to construction contracts is shown in Illustration 18-32.

ILLUSTRATION 18-32
Internet Services

INTERNET SERVICES

Facts: SeniorLife Company offers various services for the senior citizen market. The company delivers Internet-based content (photos, albums, memoir writing, games, and much more) to keep senior citizens involved with their family and friends. In addition, it provides ambassadors to help senior development facilities provide worthwhile activities for its members. The services provided by SeniorLife include a subscription that provides a mix of services. Recently, the company has contracted with a large senior citizen organization called Attic Angels to provide the standard service package. The fee for this arrangement is £300,000, to be paid on January 1, 2011. At this point, it is still somewhat uncertain what will be the entire level of services provided as of January 1, 2011. However, SeniorLife is able to make a reliable estimate of the level of costs that it will incur over the next 3 years of the contract. SeniorLife estimates that these costs will be £120,000. A schedule of the costs incurred and the cumulative percentages complete related to these costs is provided below.

	December 31, 2011	December 31, 2012	December 31, 2013
Costs incurred	£24,000	£42,000	£54,000
Cumulative costs to date	£24,000	£66,000	£120,000
Cumulative percentage complete	20%	55%	100%

ILLUSTRATION 18-32
(continued)

Questions: (a) How much revenue should SeniorLife record in 2011 related to the arrangement with Attic Angels? (b) How much revenue should SeniorLife record in 2012 related to the arrangement with Attic Angels?

Solution:

(a) SeniorLife should report revenue of £60,000 (£300,000 × 20%) of the total revenue based on the percentage-of-completion method in 2011. In this case, SeniorLife can use the percentage-of-completion method for this arrangement, given it can reliably estimate the percentage complete related to the costs incurred.

(b) SeniorLife should report revenue of £105,000 [(£300,000 × 55%) − £60,000] for 2012.

SeniorLife makes the following entries related to the service contract.

January 1, 2011

Cash	300,000	
Unearned Service Revenue		300,000

December 31, 2011

Unearned Service Revenue	60,000	
Service Revenue		60,000

December 31, 2012

Unearned Service Revenue	105,000	
Service Revenue		105,000

SeniorLife would also record expenses as incurred to provide these services.

Multiple-Deliverable Arrangements

Objective·7

Identify the proper accounting for multiple-deliverable arrangements.

One of the most difficult issues related to revenue recognition involves **multiple-deliverable arrangements** (MDAs). MDAs provide multiple products or services to customers as part of a single arrangement. The major accounting issues related to this type of arrangement are how to allocate the revenue to the various products and services and how to allocate the revenue to the proper period.

These issues are particularly complex in the technology area. Many devices have contracts that typically include such multiple deliverables as hardware, software, professional services, maintenance, and support—all of which are valued and accounted for differently. A classic example relates to the **Apple** (USA) iPhone and its AppleTV product. Basically, until a recent rule change, revenues and related costs were accounted for on a subscription basis over a period of years. The reason was that Apple provides future unspecified software upgrades and other features without charge. It was argued that Apple should defer a significant portion of the cash received for the iPhone and recognize it over future periods. At the same time, engineering, marketing, and warranty costs were expensed as incurred. As a result, Apple reported conservative numbers related to its iPhone revenue. However, as a result of efforts to more clearly define the various services related to an item such as the iPhone, Apple is now able to report more revenue at the point of sale.

In general, all units in a multiple-deliverable arrangement are considered separate units of accounting, provided that:

1. A delivered item has value to the customer on a standalone basis; and
2. The arrangement includes a general right of return relative to the delivered item; and
3. Delivery or performance of the undelivered item is considered probable and substantially in the control of the seller.

Once the separate units of accounting are determined, the amount paid for the arrangement is allocated among the separate units based on **relative fair value**. A company determines fair value based on what the vendor could sell the component for on a standalone basis. If this information is not available, the seller may rely on third-party evidence or if not available, the seller may use its best estimate of what the item might sell for as a standalone unit. **[12]**[16] Illustration 18-33 identifies the steps in the evaluation process.

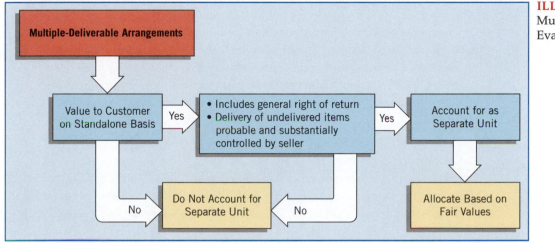

ILLUSTRATION 18-33
Multiple-Deliverable
Evaluation Process

Compare w/ US GAAP Edition.

Presented in Illustrations 18-34 and 18-35 (page 982) are two examples of the accounting for MDAs.

MULTIPLE DELIVERABLES

ILLUSTRATION 18-34
MDA—Equipment and
Maintenance

Facts: Lopez Company enters into a contract to build, run, and maintain a highly complex piece of electronic equipment for a period of 5 years, commencing upon delivery of the equipment. There is a fixed fee for each of the build, run, and maintenance deliverables, and any progress payments made are not refundable. In addition, there is a right of return in the arrangement. All the deliverables have a standalone value, and there is verifiable evidence of the selling price for the building and maintenance but not for running the equipment.

Question: **Should Lopez separate and then measure and allocate the amounts paid for the MDA?**

Solution: Assuming delivery (performance) is probable and Lopez controls any undelivered items, Lopez determines whether the components have standalone value. The components of the MDA are the equipment, maintenance of the equipment, and running the equipment; each component has a standalone value. Lopez can determine standalone values of equipment and the maintenance agreement by third-party evidence of fair values. The company then makes a best estimate of the selling price for running of the equipment. Lopez next applies the relative fair value method at the inception of the MDA to determine the proper allocation to each component. Once the allocation is performed, the company recognizes revenue independently for each component using regular revenue recognition criteria.

[16]The accounting requirements to account for MDAs under IFRS are general in nature. While IFRS requires that revenue be measured at the fair value of the consideration received or receivable for each separable component of the transaction, the standards do not dictate the method to be used in determining the fair value of each component. Similarly, IFRS does not prescribe a method for allocating revenue to the components, as long as the method selected reflects a transaction's economic substance.

ILLUSTRATION 18-35
MDA—Product,
Installation, and Service

PRODUCT, INSTALLATION, AND SERVICE

Facts: Handler Company is an experienced manufacturer of equipment used in the construction industry. Handler's products range from small to large individual pieces of automated machinery to complex systems containing numerous components. Unit selling prices range from $600,000 to $4,000,000 and are quoted inclusive of installation and training. The installation process does not involve changes to the features of the equipment and does not require proprietary information about the equipment in order for the installed equipment to perform to specifications. Handler has the following arrangement with Chai Company.

- Chai purchases equipment from Handler for a price of $2,000,000 and chooses Handler to do the installation. Handler charges the same price for the equipment irrespective of whether it does the installation or not. (Some companies do the installation themselves because they either prefer their own employees to do the work or because of relationships with other customers.) The price of the installation service is estimated to have a fair value of $20,000.

- The fair value of the training sessions is estimated at $50,000.

- Chai is obligated to pay Handler the $2,000,000 upon the delivery and installation of the equipment. Handler delivers the equipment on September 1, 2011, and completes the installation of the equipment on November 1, 2011. Training related to the equipment starts once the installation is completed and lasts for 1 year. The equipment has a useful life of 10 years.

Questions: (a) What are the standalone units for purposes of accounting for the sale of the equipment? (b) If there is more than one standalone unit, how should the fee of $2,000,000 be allocated to various components?

Solution:

(a) The first condition for separation into a standalone unit for the equipment is met. That is, the equipment, installation, and training are three separate components.

(b) The total revenue of $2,000,000 should be allocated to the three components based on their relative fair values. In this case, the fair value of the equipment should be considered $2,000,000, the installation fee is $20,000, and the training is $50,000. The total fair value to consider is $2,070,000 ($2,000,000 + $20,000 + $50,000). The allocation is as follows.

Equipment	$1,932,367	($2,000,000 ÷ $2,070,000) × $2,000,000
Installation	19,324	($20,000 ÷ $2,070,000) × $2,000,000
Training	48,309	($50,000 ÷ $2,070,000) × $2,000,000

Handler makes the following entries on November 1, 2011.

November 1, 2011

Cash	2,000,000	
Installation Revenue		19,324
Unearned Training Revenue		48,309
Sales		1,932,367

The sale of the equipment should be recognized once the installation is completed on November 1, 2011, and the installation fee also should be recognized because these services have been provided. The training revenues should be allocated on a straight-line basis starting on November 1, 2011, or $4,026 ($48,309 ÷ 12) per month for one year (unless a more appropriate method using the percentage-of-completion method is warranted). The journal entry to recognize the training revenue for two months in 2011 is as follows.

December 31, 2011

Unearned Training Revenue	8,052	
Training Revenue ($4,026 × 2)		8,052

Therefore, the total revenue recognized at December 31, 2011, is $1,959,743 ($1,932,367 + $19,324 + $8,052). Handler makes the following journal entry to recognize the training revenue in 2012.

December 31, 2012

Unearned Training Revenue	40,257	
Training Revenue ($48,309 − $8,052)		40,257

Other Revenue Situations

Interest, Royalties, and Dividends

Revenues arising from the use by others of a company's asset that yield interest, royalties, or dividends are recognized as follows.

- The recognition of interest revenue follows the traditional concept of accrual accounting. Interest revenue is recognized over the period the assets are providing service to another party and shall be recognized using the effective-interest method.
- Royalty revenue received for the use of a company's assets (e.g., patents, music copyrights, and motion picture films) are normally recognized in accordance with the substance of the agreement. In general, this means that a company will use the straight-line method to recognize revenue for a specified period of time.
- Dividends shall be recognized when the shareholder's right to receive payment is established (date of declaration). **[13]**

Accretion

As indicated in Chapter 9, a company's activities may involve production through natural growth or aging of biological assets (plant or living animal). In this case, the company earns revenue as the plant or living animal grows. This revenue recognition procedure is referred to as the **accretion approach**. Plants or living animals are reported at fair value each reporting period, which is in effect recording revenue before the product is sold. At harvest, the biological assets are reported at fair value, which becomes cost for inventory reporting purposes.

Completion-of-Production Basis

In certain cases, companies recognize revenue at the completion of **production** even though no sale has been made. Examples of such situations involve precious metals and other mineral product with assured prices. Under the **completion-of-production basis**, companies recognize revenue when these metals are mined because the sales price is reasonably assured, the units are interchangeable, and no significant costs are involved in distributing the product (see discussion in Chapter 11).

Summary of Revenue Recognition Methods

Illustration 18-36 (page 984) provides a summary of revenue recognition methods and related accounting guidance.

Langning w/ vs GAAP Edition

General Principles

1. Recognize revenue when it is probable that the economic benefits flow to the company and the benefits can be measured reliably.
2. Revenue is measured at the fair value of the consideration received or receivable.

Specific Transactions	Accounting Guidance
Point of sale	See Illustration 18-10 (page 966).
Long-Term Contracts (Construction)	
Percentage-of-completion	Use for either long-term construction or service contracts. Criteria for use includes (1) total contract revenue can be reliably measured, (2) it is probable that the economic benefits associated with the contract will flow to the company, (3) both the contract costs to complete and the stage of contract completion at the end of the reporting period can be reliably measured, and (4) the contract costs attributable to the contract can be clearly identified and reliably measured so that the actual costs incurred can be compared to prior estimates.
Cost-recovery method (zero-profit approach)	Use when the criteria for using the percentage-of-completion method are not met or when there are inherent hazards in the contract beyond normal, recurring business risks.
Other	
Service arrangements *	The performance of the service is the critical event for revenue recognition. Recognize single-act service revenue when the act occurs. For multiple acts, various approaches are followed depending on whether (1) the multiple acts are similar, (2) defined but not identical, or (3) unspecified. Accounting for long-term service contracts is similar to that used for construction contracts.
Multiple-deliverable arrangements	Apply general revenue recognition principles to each element of the arrangement that has standalone value. Once the separate units of accounting are determined, the amount paid for the arrangement is allocated among the separate units based on relative fair value.
Interest, royalties, and dividends	For interest, follow accrual accounting, using the effective-interest method; royalties are recognized in accordance with the term of the agreement, usually on a straight-line basis over the life of the arrangement; dividends are recognized on the date of declaration.
Accretion	Apply to biological assets, which increase in value due to growth and development.
Completion-of-production	Recognize at completion of production for minerals and other mining resources because the sales price is reasonably assured, the units are interchangeable, and no significant costs are involved in distributing the product.

ILLUSTRATION 18-36
Revenue Recognition
Methods

* cost-to-cost % of completion for service contracts is prohibited under US GAAP.

You will want to read the CONVERGENCE CORNER on page 985

For discussion of how international convergence efforts relate to revenue.

CONVERGENCE CORNER

REVENUE

The general concepts and principles used for revenue recognition are similar between IFRS and U.S. GAAP. Where they differ is in the detail. As indicated in the chapter, U.S. GAAP provides specific guidance related to revenue recognition for many different industries. That is not the case for IFRS.

RELEVANT FACTS

- The IASB defines revenue to include both revenues and gains. U.S. GAAP provides separate definitions for revenues and gains.

- Revenue recognition fraud is a major issue in revenue recognition. The same situation occurs in the United States as evidenced by revenue recognition breakdowns at telecom company **Global Crossing** (USA), technology company **Lucent Technologies** (USA), and utility company **Enron** (USA).

- A specific standard exists for revenue recognition under IFRS *(IAS 18)*. In general, the standard is based on the probability that the economic benefits associated with the transaction will flow to the company selling the goods, rendering the service, or receiving investment income. In addition, the revenues and costs must be capable of being measured reliably. U.S. GAAP uses concepts such as realized or realizable, and earned as a basis for revenue recognition.

- U.S. GAAP permits the use of the completed-contract method of accounting for long-term construction contracts *(IAS 11)*. Companies generally use the percentage-of-completion method. If revenues and costs are difficult to estimate, then companies recognize revenue only to the extent of the cost incurred—a zero-profit approach under IFRS.

- U.S. GAAP does not allow the percentage-of-completion method for service contracts. Under IFRS, costs can be deferred if the company is using percentage-of-completion. Under GAAP, costs are generally expensed as incurred.

- U.S. GAAP provides detailed guidance in multiple-deliverable arrangements. IFRS guidance is more general.

ABOUT THE NUMBERS

As mentioned, U.S. GAAP permits the completed-contract method of accounting for long-term construction contracts if costs or revenues cannot be reliably determined. To illustrate, assume the following facts for Radom Construction Co. for a contract to build a dam at Windswept Canyon.

- The contract price to construct the dam is $400 million.
- Estimated incurred costs are $54 million in 2010, $180 million in 2011, and $126 million in 2012.
- Radom uses U.S. GAAP but is uncertain as regards these cost numbers.

In this case, Radom does not recognize any gross profit until the contract is completed. For example, assume that Radom incurred total costs of $363 million. The presentation on its income statement would be as follows.

Radom Construction Co. Income Statement (partial) for 2012	
Revenue from long-term contracts	$400,000,000
Costs of construction	363,000,000
Gross profit	$ 37,000,000

Under U.S. GAAP, Radom recognizes no revenue in 2010 and 2011.

ON THE HORIZON

The FASB and IASB are now involved in a joint project on revenue recognition. The objective of the project is to develop coherent conceptual guidance for revenue recognition and a comprehensive statement on revenue recognition based on those concepts. Presently, the Boards are evaluating a "customer-consideration" model. It is hoped that this approach will lead to a better basis for revenue recognition. For more on this topic, see *http://www.fasb.org/project/revenue_recognition.shtml*.

SUMMARY OF LEARNING OBJECTIVES

•1 **Apply the revenue recognition principle.** The revenue recognition principle provides that a company should recognize revenue when it is probable that the economic benefits will flow to the company and the benefits can be measured reliably. Four revenue transactions are recognized in accordance with this principle. (1) Companies recognize revenue from selling products at the date of sale. This date is usually interpreted to mean the date of delivery to customers. (2) Companies recognize revenue from services provided, when services have been performed and are billable. (3) Companies recognize revenue from permitting others to use enterprise assets, such as interest, rent, and royalties, as time passes or as the assets are used. (4) Companies recognize revenue from disposing of assets other than products at the date of sale.

•2 **Describe accounting issues for revenue recognition at point of sale.** Two issues must be addressed in the accounting for sales transactions: (1) measurement of sales revenue, and (2) recognition of sales revenue. Revenue should be measured at the fair value of consideration received or receivable. Any trade discounts or volume rebates should reduce consideration received or receivable and the related revenue. In addition, if the payment is delayed, the seller should impute an interest rate for difference between the cash or cash equivalent price and the deferred amount. Recognition occurs at the critical event, which is when risks and rewards of ownership have been transferred. Illustration 18-10 provides a summary of accounting guidance for various revenue arrangements at point of sale.

•3 **Apply the percentage-of-completion method for long-term contracts.** To apply the percentage-of-completion method to long-term contracts, a company must have some basis for measuring the progress toward completion at particular interim dates. One of the most popular input measures used to determine the progress toward completion is the cost-to-cost basis. Using this basis, a company measures the percentage of completion by comparing costs incurred to date with the most recent estimate of the total costs to complete the contract. The company applies that percentage to the total revenue or the estimated total gross profit on the contract, to arrive at the amount of revenue or gross profit to be recognized to date.

•4 **Apply the cost-recovery method for long-term contracts.** Under this method, companies recognize revenue and gross profit only at point of sale—that is, when the company completes the contract. The company accumulates costs of long-term contracts in process and current billings. This method (sometimes referred to as the zero-profit method) recognizes revenue only to the extent of costs incurred that are expected to be recoverable. Only after all costs are incurred is gross profit recognized.

•5 **Identify the proper accounting for losses on long-term contracts.** Two types of losses can become evident under long-term contracts: (1) *Loss in current period on a profitable contract*: Under the percentage-of-completion method only, the estimated cost increase requires a current-period adjustment of excess gross profit recognized on the project in prior periods. The company records this adjustment as a loss in the current period because it is a change in accounting estimate. (2) *Loss on an unprofitable contract*: Under both the percentage-of-completion and the cost-recovery methods, the company must recognize the entire expected contract loss in the current period.

•6 **Describe the accounting issues for service contracts.** Service contracts follow similar criteria as those applied to other revenue arrangements. That is, to recognize revenue it must be reliably measurable, economic benefits are probable, stage of completion must be reliably measurable, and costs must be reliably measurable. The general rule is that the performance of the service is the critical event for revenue recognition. If a service transaction consists of a single act, revenue should be recognized at the time the act takes place. Service contracts that extend over multiple accounting periods are accounted for similar to long-term contracts (using percentage-of-completion or cost-recovery methods).

|·7| **Identify the proper accounting for multiple-deliverable arrangements.** Companies recognize revenue from multiple-deliverable arrangements by allocating the amounts received for various products and services. This allocation is required only if the elements of the arrangement are considered separate units of accounting, which means that (1) a delivered item has value to the customer on a standalone basis, (2) the arrangement includes a general right of return relative to the delivered item, and (3) delivery or performance of the undelivered item is considered probable and substantially in the control of the seller. Once the separate units of accounting are determined, the amount paid for the arrangement is allocated among the separate units based on relative fair value. If the criteria are not met, that arrangement is accounted for as a single unit.

APPENDIX **18A**	REVENUE RECOGNITION FOR FRANCHISE TRANSACTIONS

FRANCHISES

> **Objective·8**
> Explain revenue recognition for franchise sales.

In accounting for franchise sales, a company must analyze the transaction and, considering all the circumstances, use judgment in selecting one or more of the revenue recognition bases, and then possibly monitor the situation over a long period of time.

Franchise companies derive their revenue from one or both of two sources: (1) from the sale of initial franchises and related assets or services, and (2) from continuing fees based on the operations of franchises. Thus, franchise arrangements have features of multiple-deliverable arrangements. The **franchisor** (the party who grants business rights under the franchise) normally provides the **franchisee** (the party who operates the franchised business) with the following services.

1. Assistance in site selection: (a) analyzing location and (b) negotiating lease.
2. Evaluation of potential income.
3. Supervision of construction activity: (a) obtaining financing, (b) designing building, and (c) supervising contractor while building.
4. Assistance in the acquisition of signs, fixtures, and equipment.
5. Bookkeeping and advisory services: (a) setting up franchisee's records; (b) advising on income, real estate, and other taxes; and (c) advising on local regulations of the franchisee's business.
6. Employee and management training.
7. Quality control.
8. Advertising and promotion.[17]

At one time, it was standard practice for franchisors to recognize the entire franchise fee at the date of sale, whether the fee was received then or was collectible over a long period of time. Frequently, franchisors recorded the entire amount as revenue in the year of sale even though many of the services were yet to be performed and

---

[17]Archibald E. MacKay, "Accounting for Initial Franchise Fee Revenue," *The Journal of Accountancy* (January 1970), pp. 66–67.

uncertainty existed regarding the collection of the entire fee. (In effect, the franchisors were counting their fried chickens before they were hatched.) However, a **franchise agreement** may provide for refunds to the franchisee if certain conditions are not met, and franchise fee profit can be reduced sharply by future costs of obligations and services to be rendered by the franchisor.

Initial Franchise Fees

The **initial franchise fee** is payment for establishing the franchise relationship and providing some initial services. Franchisors record initial franchise fees as revenue only when and as they make "substantial performance" of the services they are obligated to perform and when collection of the fee is reasonably assured. **Substantial performance** occurs when the franchisor has no remaining obligation to refund any cash received or excuse any non-payment of a note and has performed all the initial services required under the contract. Commencement of operations by the franchisee shall be presumed to be the earliest point at which substantial performance has occurred, unless it can be demonstrated that substantial performance of all obligations, including services rendered voluntarily, has occurred before that time.

Example of Entries for Initial Franchise Fee

To illustrate, assume that Tum's Pizza Inc. charges an initial franchise fee of $50,000 for the right to operate as a franchisee of Tum's Pizza. Of this amount, $10,000 is payable when the franchisee signs the agreement, and the balance is payable in five annual payments of $8,000 each. In return for the initial franchise fee, Tum's will help locate the site, negotiate the lease or purchase of the site, supervise the construction activity, and provide the bookkeeping services. The credit rating of the franchisee indicates that money can be borrowed at 8 percent. The present value of an ordinary annuity of five annual receipts of $8,000 each discounted at 8 percent is $31,942. The discount of $8,058 represents the interest revenue to be accrued by the franchisor over the payment period. The following examples show the entries that Tum's Pizza Inc. would make under various conditions.

1. If there is reasonable expectation that Tum's Pizza Inc. may refund the down payment and if substantial future services remain to be performed by Tum's Pizza Inc., the entry should be:

Cash	10,000	
Notes Receivable ($40,000 − $8,058)	31,942	
Unearned Franchise Fees		41,942

2. If the probability of refunding the initial franchise fee is extremely low, the amount of future services to be provided to the franchisee is minimal, collectibility of the note is reasonably assured, and substantial performance has occurred, the entry should be:

Cash	10,000	
Notes Receivable	31,942	
Revenue from Franchise Fees		41,942

3. If the initial down payment is not refundable, represents a fair measure of the services already provided, with a significant amount of services still to be performed by Tum's Pizza in future periods, and collectibility of the note is reasonably assured, the entry should be:

Cash	10,000	
Notes Receivable	31,942	
Revenue from Franchise Fees		10,000
Unearned Franchise Fees		31,942

4. If the initial down payment is not refundable and no future services are required by the franchisor, but collection of the note is so uncertain that recognition of the note as an asset is unwarranted, the entry should be:

Cash	10,000	
Revenue from Franchise Fees		10,000

5. Under the same conditions as those listed in case 4 above, except that the down payment is refundable or substantial services are yet to be performed, the entry should be:

Cash	10,000	
Unearned Franchise Fees		10,000

In cases 4 and 5—where collection of the note is extremely uncertain—franchisors may recognize cash collections using the cost-recovery method.

Continuing Franchise Fees

Continuing franchise fees are received in return for the continuing rights granted by the franchise agreement and for providing such services as management training, advertising and promotion, legal assistance, and other support. Franchisors report continuing fees as revenue when they are earned and receivable from the franchisee, unless a portion of them has been designated for a particular purpose, such as providing a specified amount for building maintenance or local advertising. In that case, the portion deferred shall be an amount sufficient to cover the estimated cost in excess of continuing franchise fees and provide a reasonable profit on the continuing services.

SUMMARY OF LEARNING OBJECTIVE FOR APPENDIX 18A

[•8] Explain revenue recognition for franchise sales. In a franchise arrangement, the franchisor records as revenue the initial franchise fee as it makes substantial performance of the services it is obligated to perform and collection of the fee is reasonably assured. Franchisors recognize continuing franchise fees as revenue when they are earned and receivable from the franchisee.

KEY TERMS

continuing franchise fees, *989*
franchisee, *987*
franchisor, *987*
initial franchise fee, *988*
substantial performance, *988*

IFRS

AUTHORITATIVE LITERATURE

Authoritative Literature References

[1] International Accounting Standard 18, *Revenue* (London, U.K.: International Accounting Standards Committee Foundation, 2001), par. 7.

[2] International Accounting Standard 18, *Revenue* (London, U.K.: International Accounting Standards Committee Foundation, 2001), par. 11.

[3] SIC Interpretation 31, *Revenue—Barter Transactions Involving Advertising Services* (London, U.K.: International Accounting Standards Committee Foundation, 2003).

[4] International Accounting Standard 18, *Revenue* (London, U.K.: International Accounting Standards Committee Foundation, 2001), par. 12.

[5] International Accounting Standard 18, *Revenue* (London, U.K.: International Accounting Standards Committee Foundation, 2001), par. 14.

[6] International Accounting Standard 18, *Revenue* (London, U.K.: International Accounting Standards Committee Foundation, 2001), Appendix, par. 2(b).

[7] International Accounting Standard 18, *Revenue* (London, U.K.: International Accounting Standards Committee Foundation, 2001), par. 17.

[8] International Accounting Standard 18, *Revenue* (London, U.K.: International Accounting Standards Committee Foundation, 2001), par. 8 and Appendix, par. 21 (2009 amendment).

[9] International Accounting Standard 11, *Construction Contracts* (London, U.K.: International Accounting Standards Committee Foundation, 2001), par. 23.

[10] International Accounting Standard 11, *Construction Contracts* (London, U.K.: International Accounting Standards Committee Foundation, 2001), par. 30.

[11] International Accounting Standard 11, *Construction Contracts* (London, U.K.: International Accounting Standards Committee Foundation, 2001), paras. 39–45.

[12] International Accounting Standard 18, *Revenue* (London, U.K.: International Accounting Standards Committee Foundation, 2001), par. 13.

[13] International Accounting Standard 18, *Revenue* (London, U.K.: International Accounting Standards Committee Foundation, 2001), paras. 29–34.

Note: All asterisked Questions, Exercises, and Problems relate to material in the appendix to the chapter.

QUESTIONS

1. Explain the current environment regarding revenue recognition.

2. What is viewed as a major criticism of IFRS as regards revenue recognition?

3. What is the revenue recognition principle?

4. When is revenue recognized in the following situations: (a) revenue from selling products, (b) revenue from services rendered, (c) revenue from permitting others to use enterprise assets, and (d) revenue from disposing of assets other than products?

5. How should revenue be measured?

6. What is the proper accounting for volume discounts on sales of products?

7. Explain the accounting for barter transactions.

8. Explain a bill and hold sale. When is revenue recognized in these situations?

9. What is a layaway sale, and how should sales revenue be reported for these types of transactions?

10. What are the reporting issues in a sale and buyback agreement?

11. What are two accounting methods available to a seller that is exposed to continued risks of ownership through return of product?

12. Explain a principal-agent relationship and its significance to revenue recognition.

13. What is the nature of a sale on consignment? When is revenue recognized from a consignment sale?

14. What are the two basic methods of accounting for long-term construction contracts? Indicate the circumstances that determine when one or the other of these methods should be used.

15. Hawkins Construction Co. has a $60 million contract to construct a highway overpass and cloverleaf. The total estimated cost for the project is $50 million. Costs incurred in the first year of the project are $8 million. Hawkins Construction Co. appropriately uses the percentage-of-completion method. How much revenue and gross profit should Hawkins recognize in the first year of the project?

16. What methods are used in practice to determine the extent of progress toward completion? Identify some "input measures" and some "output measures" that might be used to determine the extent of progress.

17. What are the two types of losses that can become evident in accounting for long-term contracts? What is the nature of each type of loss? How is each type accounted for?

18. Under the percentage-of-completion method, how are the Construction in Process and the Billings on Construction in Process accounts reported in the statement of financial position?

19. When is revenue recognized under the cost-recovery method?

20. What are the revenue recognition criteria that should be used to record service contracts?

21. Indicate how service revenue should be recognized in the following situations: (a) specified number of similar acts, (b) specified number of defined but not identical acts, and (c) unspecified number of identical acts.

22. Explain a multiple-deliverable arrangement. What is the major accounting issue related to these arrangements?

23. Explain how multiple-deliverable arrangements are measured and reported.

24. Explain when dividend revenue is recognized.

25. What is a major difference between IFRS and U.S. GAAP as regards revenue recognition practices?

26. Under U.S. GAAP, how must companies account for long-term contracts if revenues and costs cannot be reliably measured?

27. Livesey Company has signed a long-term contract to build a new basketball arena. The total revenue related to the contract is $120 million. Estimated costs for building the arena are $40 million in the first year and $30 million in both the second and third year. The costs cannot be reliably estimated. How much revenue should Livesey Company report in the first year under U.S. GAAP using the completed-contract method of accounting?

*28. Why in franchise arrangements may it not be proper to recognize the entire franchise fee as revenue at the date of sale?

*29. How does the concept of "substantial performance" apply to accounting for franchise sales?

*30. How should a franchisor account for continuing franchise fees and routine sales of equipment and supplies to franchisees?

BRIEF EXERCISES

BE18-1 Manual Company sells goods to Nolan Company during 2010. It offers Nolan the following rebates based on total sales to Nolan. If total sales to Nolan are 10,000 units, it will grant a rebate of 2%. If it sells up to 20,000 units, it will grant a rebate of 4%. If it sells up to 30,000 units, it will grant a rebate of 6%. In the first quarter of the year, Manual sells 11,000 units to Nolan at a sales price of $110,000. Manual, based on past experience, has sold over 40,000 units to Nolan and these sales normally take place in the third quarter of the year. Prepare the journal entry to record the sale of the 11,000 units in the first quarter of the year.

BE18-2 Adani plc sells goods to Geo Company for £11,000 on January 2, 2010, with payment due in 12 months. The fair value of the goods at the date of sale is £10,000. Prepare the journal entry to record this transaction on January 2, 2010. How much total revenue should be recognized on this sale in 2010?

BE18-3 Linde Company is a retailer that offers layaway sales to its customers. Assume that Linde sells ¥100,000 of merchandise to Penrod Company on March 1, 2010, and Penrod chooses to use the layaway plan. Linde therefore retains the goods, segregating them from other goods for sale, and accepts a cash deposit for the sale of ¥30,000. Linde requires that final payment for this sale be made in 60 days. If Penrod fails to pay the remaining portion of the sales price, it forfeits its deposit. Linde is confident that Penrod will make the payment due on these sales as it considers the deposit significant. Prepare the journal entry to record the transaction on March 1, 2010.

BE18-4 Travel Inc. sells tickets for a Caribbean cruise to Carmel Company employees. The total cruise package costs Carmel €70,000 from ShipAway cruise liner. Travel Inc. receives a commission of 6% of the total price. Travel Inc. therefore remits €65,800 to ShipAway. Prepare the entry to record the revenue recognized by Travel Inc. on this transaction.

BE18-5 Aamodt Music sold CDs to retailers and recorded sales revenue of $700,000. During 2010, retailers returned CDs to Aamodt and were granted credit of $78,000. Past experience indicates that the normal return rate is 15%. Prepare Aamodt's entries to record (a) the $78,000 of returns and (b) estimated returns at December 31, 2010.

BE18-6 Jansen Corporation shipped $20,000 of merchandise on consignment to Gooch Company. Jansen paid freight costs of $2,000. Gooch Company paid $500 for local advertising, which is reimbursable from Jansen. By year-end, 60% of the merchandise had been sold for $21,500. Gooch notified Jansen, retained a 10% commission, and remitted the cash due to Jansen. Prepare Jansen's entry when the cash is received.

BE18-7 Telephone Sellers plc sells prepaid telephone cards to customers. Telephone Sellers then pays the telecommunications company, TeleExpress, for the actual use of its telephone lines. Assume that

Telephone Sellers sells £4,000 of prepaid cards in January 2010. It then pays TeleExpress based on usage, which turns out to be 50% in February, 30% in March, and 20% in April. The total payment by Telephone Sellers for TeleExpress lines over the 3 months is £3,000. Indicate how much income Telephone Sellers should recognize in January, February, March, and April.

•3 BE18-8 Turner, Inc. began work on a $7,000,000 contract in 2010 to construct an office building. During 2010, Turner, Inc. incurred costs of $1,700,000, billed their customers for $1,200,000, and collected $960,000. At December 31, 2010, the estimated future costs to complete the project total $3,300,000. Prepare Turner's 2010 journal entries using the percentage-of-completion method.

•4 BE18-9 Use the information from BE18-8, but assume Turner uses the cost-recovery method. Prepare the company's 2010 journal entries.

•3 BE18-10 O'Neil, Inc. began work on a $7,000,000 contract in 2010 to construct an office building. O'Neil uses the percentage-of-completion method. At December 31, 2010, the balances in certain accounts were Construction in Process $2,450,000; Accounts Receivable $240,000; and Billings on Construction in Process $1,400,000. Indicate how these accounts would be reported in O'Neil's December 31, 2010, statement of financial position.

•4 BE18-11 Guillen, Inc. began work on a $7,000,000 contract in 2010 to construct an office building. Guillen uses the cost-recovery method. At December 31, 2010, the balances in certain accounts were Construction in Process $1,715,000; Accounts Receivable $240,000; and Billings on Construction in Process $1,000,000. Indicate how these accounts would be reported in Guillen's December 31, 2010, statement of financial position.

•5 BE18-12 Archer Construction Company began work on a $420,000 construction contract in 2010. During 2010, Archer incurred costs of $278,000, billed its customer for $215,000, and collected $175,000. At December 31, 2010, the estimated future costs to complete the project total $162,000. Prepare Archer's journal entry to record profit or loss in 2010, if any, using (a) the percentage-of-completion method and (b) the cost-recovery method.

•8 *BE18-13 Frozen Delight, Inc. charges an initial franchise fee of $75,000 for the right to operate as a franchisee of Frozen Delight. Of this amount, $25,000 is collected immediately. The remainder is collected in 4 equal annual installments of $12,500 each. These installments have a present value of $41,402. There is reasonable expectation that the down payment may be refunded and substantial future services be performed by Frozen Delight, Inc. Prepare the journal entry required by Frozen Delight to record the franchise fee.

EXERCISES

•2 E18-1 (Revenue Recognition—Point of Sale) Jupiter Company sells goods that have a cost of €500,000 to Danone plc for €700,000, with payment due in 1 year. The cash price for these goods is €610,000, with payment due in 30 days. If Danone paid immediately upon delivery, it would receive a cash discount of €10,000.

Instructions
(a) Prepare the journal entry to record this transaction at the date of sale.
(b) How much revenue should Jupiter report for the entire year?

•2 E18-2 (Revenue Recognition—Point of Sale) Shaw Company sells goods that cost £300,000 to Ricard Company for £410,000 on January 2, 2010. The sales price includes an installation fee, which is valued at £40,000. The fair value of the goods is $370,000. The installation is expected to take 6 months.

Instructions
(a) Prepare the journal entry (if any) to record the sale on January 2, 2010.
(b) Shaw prepares an income statement for the first quarter of 2010, ending on March 31, 2010. How much revenue should Shaw recognize related to its sale to Ricard?

·2 **E18-3** **(Revenue Recognition—Point of Sale)** Presented below are three revenue recognition situations.

    (a) Grupo sells goods to MTN for ¥1,000,000, payment due at delivery.

    (b) Grupo sells goods on account to Grifols for ¥800,000, payment due in 30 days.

    (c) Grupo sells goods to Magnus for ¥500,000, payment due in two installments: the first installment payable in 6 months and the second payment due 3 months later.

Instructions

Indicate how each of these transactions is reported.

·2 **E18-4** **(Revenue Recognition—Point of Sale)** Wood-Mode Company is involved in the design, manufacture, and installation of various types of wood products for large construction projects. Wood-Mode recently completed a large contract for Stadium Inc., which consisted of building 35 different types of concession counters for a new soccer arena under construction. The terms of the contract are that upon completion of the counters, Stadium would pay €2,000,000. Unfortunately, due to the depressed economy, the completion of the new soccer arena is now delayed. Stadium has therefore asked Wood-Mode to hold the counters at its manufacturing plant until the arena is completed. Stadium acknowledges in writing that it ordered the counters and that they now have ownership. The time that Wood-Mode Company must hold the counters is totally dependent on when the arena is completed. Because Wood-Mode has not received additional progress payments for the arena due to the delay, Stadium has provided a deposit of €300,000.

Instructions

    (a) Explain this type of revenue recognition transaction.

    (b) What factors should be considered in determining when to recognize revenue in this transaction?

    (c) Prepare the journal entry(ies) that Wood-Mode should make, assuming it signed a valid sales contract to sell the counters and received at the time of sale the €300,000 payment.

·2 **E18-5** **(Right of Return)** Organic Growth Company is presently testing a number of new agricultural seeds that it has recently harvested. To stimulate interest, it has decided to grant to five of its largest customers the unconditional right of return to these products if not fully satisfied. The right of return extends for 4 months. Organic Growth sells these seeds on account for £1,500,000 on January 2, 2010. Companies are required to pay the full amount due by March 15, 2010.

Instructions

    (a) Prepare the journal entry for Organic Growth at January 2, 2010, assuming Organic Growth estimates returns of 20% based on prior experience. (Ignore cost of goods sold.)

    (b) Assume that one customer returns the crops on March 1, 2010, due to unsatisfactory performance. Prepare the journal entry to record this transaction, assuming this customer purchased £100,000 of seeds from Organic Growth.

    (c) Briefly describe the accounting for these sales, if Organic Growth is unable to reliably estimate returns.

·1 ·2 **E18-6** **(Revenue Recognition on Book Sales with High Returns)** Uddin Publishing Co. publishes college textbooks that are sold to bookstores on the following terms. Each title has a fixed wholesale price, terms f.o.b. shipping point, and payment is due 60 days after shipment. The retailer may return a maximum of 30% of an order at the retailer's expense. Sales are made only to retailers who have good credit ratings. Past experience indicates that the normal return rate is 12%, and the average collection period is 72 days.

Instructions

    (a) Identify alternative revenue recognition criteria that Uddin could employ concerning textbook sales.

    (b) Briefly discuss the reasoning for your answers in (a) above.

    (c) In late July, Uddin shipped books invoiced at $15,000,000. Prepare the journal entry to record this event that best conforms to IFRS and your answer to part (b).

    (d) In October, $2 million of the invoiced July sales were returned according to the return policy, and the remaining $13 million was paid. Prepare the entries recording the return and payment.

·1 ·2 **E18-7** **(Sales Recorded Both Gross and Net)** On June 3, Hunt Company sold to Ann Mount merchandise having a sale price of $8,000 with terms of 2/10, n/60, f.o.b. shipping point. An invoice totaling $120, terms n/30, was received by Mount on June 8 from the Olympic Transport Service for the freight cost. Upon receipt of the goods, June 5, Mount notified Hunt Company that merchandise costing $600 contained flaws that rendered it worthless. The same day, Hunt Company issued a credit memo covering the worthless merchandise and asked that it be returned at company expense. The freight on the returned merchandise was $24, paid by Hunt Company on June 7. On June 12, the company received a check for the balance due from Mount.

Instructions

(a) Prepare journal entries on Hunt Company books to record all the events noted above under each of the following bases.

    (1) Sales and receivables are entered at gross selling price.

    (2) Sales and receivables are entered net of cash discounts.

(b) Prepare the journal entry under basis 2, assuming that Ann Mount did not remit payment until August 5.

•1 •2 E18-8 (Revenue Recognition on Marina Sales with Discounts) Taylor Marina has 300 available slips that rent for $800 per season. Payments must be made in full at the start of the boating season, April 1, 2011. Slips for the next season may be reserved if paid for by December 31, 2010. Under a new policy, if payment is made by December 31, 2010, a 5% discount is allowed. The boating season ends October 31, and the marina has a December 31 year-end. To provide cash flow for major dock repairs, the marina operator is also offering a 20% discount to slip renters who pay for the 2012 season.

For the fiscal year ended December 31, 2010, all 300 slips were rented at full price. Two hundred slips were reserved and paid for for the 2011 boating season, and 60 slips were reserved and paid for for the 2012 boating season.

Instructions

(a) Prepare the appropriate journal entries for fiscal 2010.

(b) Assume the marina operator is unsophisticated in business. Explain the managerial significance of the accounting above to this person.

•2 E18-9 (Consignment Computations) On May 3, 2010, Eisler Company consigned 80 freezers, costing $500 each, to Remmers Company. The cost of shipping the freezers amounted to $840 and was paid by Eisler Company. On December 30, 2010, a report was received from the consignee, indicating that 40 freezers had been sold for $750 each. Remittance was made by the consignee for the amount due, after deducting a commission of 6%, advertising of $200, and total installation costs of $320 on the freezers sold.

Instructions

(a) Compute the inventory value of the units unsold in the hands of the consignee.

(b) Compute the profit for the consignor for the units sold.

(c) Compute the amount of cash that will be remitted by the consignee.

•3 •4 E18-10 (Recognition of Profit on Long-Term Contracts) During 2010, Nilsen Company started a construction job with a contract price of $1,600,000. The job was completed in 2012. The following information is available.

	2010	2011	2012
Costs incurred to date	$400,000	$825,000	$1,070,000
Estimated costs to complete	600,000	275,000	–0–
Billings to date	300,000	900,000	1,600,000
Collections to date	270,000	810,000	1,425,000

Instructions

(a) Compute the amount of gross profit to be recognized each year, assuming the percentage-of-completion method is used.

(b) Prepare all necessary journal entries for 2011.

(c) Compute the amount of gross profit to be recognized each year, assuming the cost-recovery method is used.

•3 E18-11 (Analysis of Percentage-of-Completion Financial Statements) In 2010, Steinrotter Construction Corp. began construction work under a 3-year contract. The contract price was $1,000,000. Steinrotter uses the percentage-of-completion method for financial accounting purposes. The income to be recognized each year is based on the proportion of cost incurred to total estimated costs for completing the contract. The financial statement presentations relating to this contract at December 31, 2010, follow.

Statement of Financial Position

Construction in progress	$65,000	
Less: Contract billings	61,500	
Cost of uncompleted contract in excess of billings		$ 3,500
Accounts receivable—construction contract billings		18,000

Income Statement

Income (before tax) on the contract recognized in 2010	$19,500

Instructions

(a) How much cash was collected in 2010 on this contract?

(b) What was the initial estimated total income before tax on this contract?

•3 **E18-12** **(Gross Profit on Uncompleted Contract)** On April 1, 2010, Dougherty Inc. entered into a cost-plus-fixed-fee contract to construct an electric generator for Altom Corporation. At the contract date, Dougherty estimated that it would take 2 years to complete the project at a cost of $2,000,000. The fixed fee stipulated in the contract is $450,000. Dougherty appropriately accounts for this contract under the percentage-of-completion method. During 2010, Dougherty incurred costs of $800,000 related to the project. The estimated cost at December 31, 2010, to complete the contract is $1,200,000. Altom was billed $600,000 under the contract.

Instructions

Prepare a schedule to compute the amount of gross profit to be recognized by Dougherty under the contract for the year ended December 31, 2010. Show supporting computations in good form.

•3 **E18-13** **(Recognition of Profit, Percentage-of-Completion)** In 2010, Gurney Construction Company agreed to construct an apartment building at a price of $1,200,000. The information relating to the costs and billings for this contract is shown below.

	2010	2011	2012
Costs incurred to date	$280,000	$600,000	$ 785,000
Estimated costs yet to be incurred	520,000	200,000	–0–
Customer billings to date	150,000	500,000	1,200,000
Collection of billings to date	120,000	320,000	940,000

Instructions

(a) Assuming that the percentage-of-completion method is used, (1) compute the amount of gross profit to be recognized in 2010 and 2011, and (2) prepare journal entries for 2011.

(b) For 2011, show how the details related to this construction contract would be disclosed on the statement of financial position and on the income statement.

•3 •4 **E18-14** **(Recognition of Revenue on Long-Term Contract and Entries)** Hamilton Construction Company uses the percentage-of-completion method of accounting. In 2010, Hamilton began work under contract #E2-D2, which provided for a contract price of $2,200,000. Other details are as follows.

	2010	2011
Costs incurred during the year	$640,000	$1,425,000
Estimated costs to complete, as of December 31	960,000	–0–
Billings during the year	420,000	1,680,000
Collections during the year	350,000	1,500,000

Instructions

(a) What portion of the total contract price would be recognized as income in 2010? In 2011?

(b) Assuming the same facts as those above except that Hamilton uses the cost-recovery method of accounting, what portion of the total contract price would be recognized as income in 2011?

(c) Prepare a complete set of journal entries for 2010 (using the percentage-of-completion method).

•3 •4 **E18-15** **(Recognition of Profit and Statement of Financial Position Amounts for Long-Term Contracts)** Yanmei Construction Company began operations January 1, 2010. During the year, Yanmei Construction entered into a contract with Lundquist Corp. to construct a manufacturing facility. At that time, Yanmei estimated that it would take 5 years to complete the facility at a total cost of $4,500,000. The total contract price for construction of the facility is $6,000,000. During the year, Yanmei incurred $1,185,800 in construction costs related to the construction project. The estimated cost to complete the contract is $4,204,200. Lundquist Corp. was billed and paid 25% of the contract price.

Instructions

Prepare schedules to compute the amount of gross profit to be recognized for the year ended December 31, 2010, and the amount to be shown as "costs and recognized profit on uncompleted contract in excess of related billings" or "billings on uncompleted contract in excess of related costs and recognized profit" at December 31, 2010, under each of the following methods.

(a) Cost-recovery method.

(b) Percentage-of-completion method.

Show supporting computations in good form.

•4 •5 **E18-16** **(Long-Term Contract Reporting)** Berstler Construction Company began operations in 2010. Construction activity for the first year is shown below. All contracts are with different customers, and any work remaining at December 31, 2010, is expected to be completed in 2011.

Project	Total Contract Price	Billings through 12/31/10	Cash Collections through 12/31/10	Contract Costs Incurred through 12/31/10	Estimated Additional Costs to Complete
1	€ 560,000	€ 360,000	€340,000	€450,000	€130,000
2	670,000	220,000	210,000	126,000	504,000
3	520,000	500,000	440,000	330,000	–0–
	€1,750,000	€1,080,000	€990,000	€906,000	€634,000

Instructions

Prepare a partial income statement and statement of financial position to indicate how the above information would be reported for financial statement purposes. Berstler Construction Company uses the cost-recovery method.

•2 •6 **E18-17** **(Barter Arrangement)** Weather Accurate Inc. provides weather updates to various television stations. In lieu of cash payments, the television stations run various advertisements for Weather Accurate. Weather Accurate estimates that this advertising has a fair value of $1,000,000 a year and therefore records revenue for this amount. The television stations often have excess capacity, and therefore their cost for providing the advertising due to lost revenue is negligible.

Instructions

(a) Explain this type of revenue recognition transaction.

(b) What factors should be considered in determining when to recognize revenue in this transaction?

(c) Prepare the journal entry that Weather Accurate should make to record revenue related to its receipt of this advertising on the television stations.

•7 **E18-18** **(Service Arrangement)** Highland Health Club charges an initiation fee of $1,800 to join the club and $250 per month in dues. During its first year of operation, it enrolled 400 members starting on January 2, 2010. It is estimated, based on past experience at its other locations, that a member will use the club approximately 18 months before resigning. The entire initiation fee is non-refundable.

Instructions

Determine the amount of revenue Highland should report in 2010 related to these members.

•7 **E18-19** **(Multiple-Deliverable Arrangement)** Appliance Center is an experienced home appliance dealer. Appliance Center also offers a number of services together with the home appliances that it sells. Assume that Appliance Center sells ovens on a standalone basis. Appliance Center also sells installation services and maintenance services for ovens. However, Appliance Center does not offer installation or maintenance services to customers who buy ovens from other vendors. Pricing for ovens is as follows.

Oven only	$ 800
Oven with installation service	850
Oven with maintenance services	975
Oven with installation and maintenance services	1,000

In each instance in which maintenance services are provided, the maintenance service is separately priced within the arrangement at $175. Additionally, the incremental amount charged by Appliance Center for installation approximates the amount charged by independent third parties. Ovens are sold subject to a general right of return. If a customer purchases an oven with installation and/or maintenance services, in the event Appliance Center does not complete the service satisfactorily, the customer is only entitled to a refund of the portion of the fee that exceeds $800.

Instructions

(a) Assume that a customer purchases an oven with both installation and maintenance services for $1,000. Based on its experience, Appliance Center believes that it is probable that the installation of the equipment will be performed satisfactorily to the customer. Assume that the maintenance services are priced separately. Explain whether the conditions for a multiple-deliverable arrangement exist in this situation.

(b) Indicate the amount of revenues that should be allocated to the oven, the installation, and to the maintenance contract.

·7 **E18-20** **(Multiple-Deliverable Arrangement)** On December 31, 2010, Grando Company sells production equipment to Fargo AG for €50,000. Grando includes a 1-year warranty service with the sale of all its equipment. The customer receives and pays for the equipment on December 31, 2010. Grando estimates the prices to be €48,800 for the equipment and €1,200 for the warranty.

Instructions
(a) Prepare the journal entry to record this transaction on December 31, 2010.
(b) Indicate how much (if any) revenue should be recognized on January 31, 2011, and for the year 2011.

·8 ***E18-21** **(Franchise Entries)** Pacific Crossburgers Inc. charges an initial franchise fee of $70,000 at the beginning of the year. Upon the signing of the agreement, a payment of $28,000 is due. Thereafter, three annual payments of $14,000 are required at the end of each year. The credit rating of the franchisee is such that it would have to pay interest at 10% to borrow money.

Instructions
Prepare the entries to record the initial franchise fee on the books of the franchisor under the following assumptions.
(a) The down payment is not refundable, no future services are required by the franchisor, and collection of the note is reasonably assured.
(b) The franchisor has substantial services to perform, the down payment is refundable, and the collection of the note is very uncertain.
(c) The down payment is not refundable, collection of the note is reasonably certain, the franchisor has yet to perform a substantial amount of services, and the down payment represents a fair measure of the services already performed.

·8 ***E18-22** **(Franchise Fee, Initial Down Payment)** On January 1, 2010, Lesley Benjamin signed an agreement to operate as a franchisee of Campbell Inc. for an initial franchise fee of $50,000. The amount of $10,000 was paid when the agreement was signed, and the balance is payable in five annual payments of $8,000 each, beginning January 1, 2011. The agreement provides that the down payment is not refundable and that no future services are required of the franchisor. Lesley Benjamin's credit rating indicates that she can borrow money at 11% for a loan of this type.

Instructions
(Round to nearest dollar.)
(a) How much should Campbell record as revenue from franchise fees on January 1, 2010? At what amount should Benjamin record the acquisition cost of the franchise on January 1, 2010?
(b) What entry would be made by Campbell on January 1, 2010, if the down payment is refundable and substantial future services remain to be performed by Campbell?
(c) How much revenue from franchise fees would be recorded by Campbell on January 1, 2010, if:
   (1) The initial down payment is not refundable, it represents a fair measure of the services already provided, a significant amount of services is still to be performed by Campbell in future periods, and collectibility of the note is reasonably assured?
   (2) The initial down payment is not refundable and no future services are required by the franchisor, but collection of the note is so uncertain that recognition of the note as an asset is unwarranted?
   (3) The initial down payment has not been earned and collection of the note is so uncertain that recognition of the note as an asset is unwarranted?

PROBLEMS

·2 ·3 ·4 **P18-1** **(Comprehensive Three-Part Revenue Recognition)** Van Hatten Industries has three operating
·6 divisions—Depp Construction Division, DeMent Publishing Division, and Ankiel Securities Division. Each
division maintains its own accounting system and method of revenue recognition.

Depp Construction Division
During the fiscal year ended November 30, 2010, Depp Construction Division had one construction project in process. A $30,000,000 contract for construction of a civic center was granted on June 19, 2010, and construction began on August 1, 2010. Estimated costs of completion at the contract date were $25,000,000 over a 2-year time period from the date of the contract. On November 30, 2010, construction costs of

$7,200,000 had been incurred and progress billings of $9,500,000 had been made. The construction costs to complete the remainder of the project were reviewed on November 30, 2010, and were estimated to amount to only $16,800,000 because of an expected decline in raw materials costs. Revenue recognition is based upon a percentage-of-completion method.

DeMent Publishing Division

The DeMent Publishing Division sells large volumes of novels to a few book distributors, which in turn sell to several national chains of bookstores. DeMent allows distributors to return up to 30% of sales, and distributors give the same terms to bookstores. While returns from individual titles fluctuate greatly, the returns from distributors have averaged 20% in each of the past 5 years. A total of $7,000,000 of paperback novel sales were made to distributors during fiscal 2010. On November 30, 2010 (the end of the fiscal year) $1,500,000 of fiscal 2010 sales were still subject to return privileges over the next 6 months. The remaining $5,500,000 of fiscal 2010 sales had actual returns of 21%. Sales from fiscal 2009 totaling $2,000,000 were collected in fiscal 2010 less 18% returns. This division records revenue according to the method referred to as revenue recognition when the right of return exists.

Ankiel Securities Division

Ankiel Securities Division works through manufacturers' agents in various cities. Orders for alarm systems and down payments are forwarded from agents, and the Division ships the goods f.o.b. factory directly to customers (usually police departments and security guard companies). Customers are billed directly for the balance due plus actual shipping costs. The company received orders for $6,000,000 of goods during the fiscal year ended November 30, 2010. Down payments of $600,000 were received, and $5,200,000 of goods were billed and shipped. Actual freight costs of $100,000 were also billed. Commissions of 10% on product price are paid to manufacturing agents after goods are shipped to customers. Such goods are warranted for 90 days after shipment, and warranty returns have been about 1% of sales. Revenue is recognized at the point of sale by this division.

Instructions

(a) There are a variety of methods of revenue recognition. Define and describe each of the following methods of revenue recognition, and indicate whether each is in accordance with IFRS.
   (1) Point of sale.
   (2) Cost-recovery.
   (3) Percentage-of-completion.
(b) Compute the revenue to be recognized in fiscal year 2010 for each of the three operating divisions of Van Hatten Industries in accordance with IFRS.

•3 •4 P18-2 (Recognition of Profit on Long-Term Contract) Shanahan Construction Company has entered into a contract beginning January 1, 2010, to build a parking complex. It has been estimated that the complex will cost £600,000 and will take 3 years to construct. The complex will be billed to the purchasing company at £900,000. The following data pertain to the construction period.

	2010	2011	2012
Costs to date	£270,000	£450,000	£610,000
Estimated costs to complete	330,000	150,000	–0–
Progress billings to date	270,000	550,000	900,000
Cash collected to date	240,000	500,000	900,000

Instructions

(a) Using the percentage-of-completion method, compute the estimated gross profit that would be recognized during each year of the construction period.
(b) Using the cost-recovery method, compute the estimated gross profit that would be recognized during each year of the construction period.

•3 •4 P18-3 (Recognition of Profit and Entries on Long-Term Contract) On March 1, 2010, Chance Company entered into a contract to build an apartment building. It is estimated that the building will cost $2,000,000 and will take 3 years to complete. The contract price was $3,000,000. The following information pertains to the construction period.

	2010	2011	2012
Costs to date	$ 600,000	$1,560,000	$2,100,000
Estimated costs to complete	1,400,000	520,000	–0–
Progress billings to date	1,050,000	2,000,000	3,000,000
Cash collected to date	950,000	1,950,000	2,850,000

Instructions
(a) Compute the amount of gross profit to be recognized each year assuming the percentage-of-completion method is used.
(b) Prepare all necessary journal entries for 2012.
(c) Prepare a partial statement of financial position for December 31, 2011, showing the balances in the receivables and inventory accounts.

·3 **P18-4 (Recognition of Profit and Statement of Financial Position Presentation, Percentage-of-Completion)** On February 1, 2010, Hewitt Construction Company obtained a contract to build an athletic stadium. The stadium was to be built at a total cost of €5,400,000 and was scheduled for completion by September 1, 2012. One clause of the contract stated that Hewitt was to deduct €15,000 from the €6,600,000 billing price for each week that completion was delayed. Completion was delayed 6 weeks, which resulted in a €90,000 penalty. Below are the data pertaining to the construction period.

	2010	2011	2012
Costs to date	€1,620,000	€3,850,000	€5,500,000
Estimated costs to complete	3,780,000	1,650,000	–0–
Progress billings to date	1,200,000	3,300,000	6,510,000
Cash collected to date	1,000,000	2,800,000	6,510,000

Instructions
(a) Using the percentage-of-completion method, compute the estimated gross profit recognized in the years 2010–2012.
(b) Prepare a partial statement of financial position for December 31, 2011, showing the balances in the receivables and inventory accounts.

·3 ·4 ·5 **P18-5 (Cost-Recovery and Percentage-of-Completion with Interim Loss)** Reynolds Custom Builders (RCB) was established in 1985 by Avery Conway and initially built high-quality customized homes under contract with specific buyers. In the 1990s, Conway's two sons joined the company and expanded RCB's activities into the high-rise apartment and industrial plant markets. Upon the retirement of RCB's long-time financial manager, Conway's sons recently hired Ed Borke as controller for RCB. Borke, a former college friend of Conway's sons, has been associated with a public accounting firm for the last 6 years.

Upon reviewing RCB's accounting practices, Borke observed that RCB followed the cost-recovery method of revenue recognition, a carryover from the years when individual home building was the majority of RCB's operations. Several years ago, the predominant portion of RCB's activities shifted to the high-rise and industrial building areas. From land acquisition to the completion of construction, most building contracts cover several years. Under the circumstances, Borke believes that RCB should follow the percentage-of-completion method of accounting. From a typical building contract, Borke developed the following data.

BLUESTEM TRACTOR PLANT
Contract price: $8,000,000

	2010	2011	2012
Estimated costs	$1,600,000	$2,880,000	$1,920,000
Progress billings	1,000,000	2,500,000	4,500,000
Cash collections	800,000	2,300,000	4,900,000

Instructions
(a) Explain the difference between cost-recovery revenue recognition and percentage-of-completion revenue recognition.
(b) Using the data provided for the Bluestem Tractor Plant and assuming the percentage-of-completion method of revenue recognition is used, calculate RCB's revenue and gross profit for 2010, 2011, and 2012, under **each** of the following circumstances.
   (1) Assume that all costs are incurred, all billings to customers are made, and all collections from customers are received within 30 days of billing, as planned.
   (2) Further assume that, as a result of unforeseen local ordinances and the fact that the building site was in a wetlands area, RCB experienced cost overruns of $800,000 in 2010 to bring the site into compliance with the ordinances and to overcome wetlands barriers to construction.
   (3) Further assume that, in addition to the cost overruns of $800,000 for this contract incurred under part (b)(2), inflationary factors over and above those anticipated in the development of the original contract cost have caused an additional cost overrun of $850,000 in 2011. It is not anticipated that any cost overruns will occur in 2012.

P18-6 **(Long-Term Contract with Interim Loss)** On March 1, 2010, Pechstein Construction Company contracted to construct a factory building for Fabrik Manufacturing Inc. for a total contract price of $8,400,000. The building was completed by October 31, 2012. The annual contract costs incurred, estimated costs to complete the contract, and accumulated billings to Fabrik for 2010, 2011, and 2012 are given below.

	2010	2011	2012
Contract costs incurred during the year	$2,880,000	$2,230,000	$2,190,000
Estimated costs to complete the contract at 12/31	3,520,000	2,190,000	–0–
Billings to Fabrik during the year	3,200,000	3,500,000	1,700,000

Instructions

(a) Using the percentage-of-completion method, prepare schedules to compute the profit or loss to be recognized as a result of this contract for the years ended December 31, 2010, 2011, and 2012. (Ignore income taxes.)

(b) Using the cost-recovery method, prepare schedules to compute the profit or loss to be recognized as a result of this contract for the years ended December 31, 2010, 2011, and 2012. (Ignore incomes taxes.)

P18-7 **(Long-Term Contract with an Overall Loss)** On July 1, 2010, Torvill Construction Company Inc. contracted to build an office building for Gumbel Corp. for a total contract price of €1,900,000. On July 1, Torvill estimated that it would take between 2 and 3 years to complete the building. On December 31, 2012, the building was deemed substantially completed. Following are accumulated contract costs incurred, estimated costs to complete the contract, and accumulated billings to Gumbel for 2010, 2011, and 2012.

	At 12/31/10	At 12/31/11	At 12/31/12
Contract costs incurred to date	€ 300,000	€1,200,000	€2,100,000
Estimated costs to complete the contract	1,200,000	800,000	–0–
Billings to Gumbel	300,000	1,100,000	1,850,000

Instructions

(a) Using the percentage-of-completion method, prepare schedules to compute the profit or loss to be recognized as a result of this contract for the years ended December 31, 2010, 2011, and 2012. (Ignore income taxes.)

(b) Using the cost-recovery method, prepare schedules to compute the profit or loss to be recognized as a result of this contract for the years ended December 31, 2010, 2011, and 2012. (Ignore income taxes.)

P18-8 **(Cost-Recovery Method)** Monat Construction Company, Inc., entered into a firm fixed-price contract with Hyatt Clinic on July 1, 2010, to construct a four-story office building. At that time, Monat estimated that it would take between 2 and 3 years to complete the project. The total contract price for construction of the building is £4,400,000. Due to reliability concerns for its estimated costs, Monat appropriately accounts for this contract under the cost-recovery method in its financial statements and for income tax reporting. The building was deemed substantially completed on December 31, 2012. Estimated percentage of completion, accumulated contract costs incurred, estimated costs to complete the contract, and accumulated billings to the Hyatt Clinic under the contract are shown below.

	At December 31, 2010	At December 31, 2011	At December 31, 2012
Percentage of completion	30%	70%	100%
Contract costs incurred	£1,140,000	£3,290,000	£4,800,000
Estimated costs to complete the contract	£2,660,000	£1,410,000	–0–
Billings to Hyatt Clinic	£1,400,000	£2,500,000	£4,300,000

Instructions

(a) Prepare schedules to compute the amount to be shown as "Cost of uncompleted contract in excess of related billings" or "Billings on uncompleted contract in excess of related costs" at December 31, 2010, 2011, and 2012. Ignore income taxes. Show supporting computations in good form.

(b) Prepare schedules to compute the profit or loss to be recognized as a result of this contract for the years ended December 31, 2010, 2011, and 2012. Ignore income taxes. Show supporting computations in good form.

P18-9 **(Revenue Recognition Methods—Comparison)** Sue's Construction is in its fourth year of business. Sue performs long-term construction projects and accounts for them using the cost-recovery method. Sue built an apartment building at a price of $1,100,000. The costs and billings for this contract for the first three years are as follows.

	2010	2011	2012
Costs incurred to date	$240,000	$600,000	$ 790,000
Estimated costs yet to be incurred	560,000	200,000	–0–
Customer billings to date	150,000	410,000	1,100,000
Collection of billings to date	120,000	340,000	950,000

Sue has contacted you, a public accountant, about the following concern. She would like to attract some investors, but she believes that in order to recognize revenue she must first "deliver" the product. Therefore, on her income statement, she did not recognize any gross profits from the above contract until 2012, when she recognized the entire $310,000. That looked good for 2012, but the preceding years looked grim by comparison. She wants to know about an alternative to this cost-recovery revenue recognition.

Instructions

Draft a letter to Sue, telling her about the percentage-of-completion method of recognizing revenue. Compare it to the cost-recovery method. Explain the idea behind the percentage-of-completion method. In addition, illustrate how much revenue she could have recognized in 2010, 2011, and 2012 if she had used this method.

 P18-10 **(Comprehensive Problem—Long-Term Contracts)** You have been engaged by Buhl Construction Company to advise it concerning the proper accounting for a series of long-term contracts. Buhl commenced doing business on January 1, 2010. Construction activities for the first year of operations are shown below. All contract costs are with different customers, and any work remaining at December 31, 2010, is expected to be completed in 2011.

Project	Total Contract Price	Billings Through 12/31/10	Cash Collections Through 12/31/10	Contract Costs Incurred Through 12/31/10	Estimated Additional Costs to Complete
A	$ 300,000	$200,000	$180,000	$248,000	$ 72,000
B	350,000	110,000	105,000	67,800	271,200
C	280,000	280,000	255,000	186,000	–0–
D	200,000	35,000	25,000	118,000	87,000
E	240,000	205,000	200,000	190,000	10,000
	$1,370,000	$830,000	$765,000	$809,800	$440,200

Instructions

(a) Prepare a schedule to compute gross profit (loss) to be reported, unbilled contract costs and recognized profit, and billings in excess of costs and recognized profit using the percentage-of-completion method.

(b) Prepare a partial income statement and statement of financial position to indicate how the information would be reported for financial statement purposes.

(c) Repeat the requirements for part (a), assuming Buhl uses the cost-recovery method.

(d) Using the responses above for illustrative purposes, prepare a brief report comparing the conceptual merits (both positive and negative) of the two revenue recognition approaches.

P18-11 **(Multiple-Deliverable Arrangement)** On December 31, 2010, Meier Company sells a television to a customer. The customer also buys a 3-year warranty from Meier. Meier normally sells the television and warranty separately for €2,000 and €400, respectively. However, as part of a year-end promotion, it sells the television and warranty separately at the reduced price of €2,300. The customer pays in full at the point of sale and takes immediate delivery of the television. When a warranty claim arises, Meier processes it and repairs or replaces the television. Its experience with that type of television suggests a 5% likelihood that a claim will be filed during the first year of warranty coverage, and a 5–10% likelihood in the second and third years, respectively.

Instructions

(a) Determine how the transaction price should be allocated between the sale of the television and the warranty.

(b) Prepare the journal entry to record this transaction on December 31, 2010.

(c) Indicate the amount of revenue that should be recorded in 2011 and 2012.

·2 ·7 **P18-12** (Revenue Recognition—Various) Consider the following independent situations. Prepare responses to each as indicated.

1. Richardson Company sells goods and offers rebates to customers based on volume purchased. For the first 10,000 units sold, it grants a rebate of 1%. If it sells up to 15,000 units, it will grant a rebate of 2%. If it sells over 25,000 units, it will grant a rebate of 3%. In the first quarter of the year, Richardson sells 12,000 units for $220,000. Based on past experience, Richardson has sold over 30,000 units, with sales normally taking place in the third quarter of the year. Prepare the journal entry to record the sale of the 12,000 units in the first quarter of the year.

2. Longnecker Company offers layaway sales to its customers. Assume that Longnecker sells €200,000 of merchandise to Perrywinkle Inc. on April 1, 2010, and Perrywinkle chooses to use the layaway plan. Longnecker therefore retains the goods, segregating them from other goods for sale, and accepts a cash deposit for the sale of €2,000. Longnecker requires that final payment be made in 60 days (if the remaining portion of the sales price is not paid, the deposit is forfeited). Longnecker is not sure that Perrywinkle will make the full payment due on these sales, because the deposit is not that large. Prepare the journal entry (if any) to record the transaction on April 1, 2010.

3. On December 31, 2010, Pico Company sells production equipment to Franco plc for £100,000. Pico includes a 1-year warranty service contract with the sale of all its equipment. The customer receives and pays for the equipment on December 31, 2010. Pico estimates the prices to be £98,000 for the equipment and £3,000 for the warranty. Prepare the entry to record the sale on December 31, 2010.

·2 ·6 **P18-13** (Revenue Recognition—Various) Consider the following independent situations. Prepare responses to each as indicated.

1. Holmes Company sells goods to Watson Corp. for £22,000 on January 2, 2010, with payment due in 12 months. The fair value of the goods at the date of sale is £20,000. Prepare the journal entry to record this transaction on January 2, 2010. How much total revenue should be recognized related to this sale in 2010?

2. Golf Package Inc. (GPI) sells tickets for golfing vacations to members of local country clubs. The total 4-day golfing package, including green fees and hotel, costs customers $3,500. GPI pays the hotels and golf courses for the services provided in each package, and GPI receives a commission of 6% of the total price. GPI sold 20 of these packages. Prepare the entry to record the revenue recognized by GPI on this transaction.

3. INET Connections Inc. sells prepaid access cards for Internet cafes located across Europe. These cards are very popular with students on international study trips. For a €25 fee, a customer gets unlimited Internet access for a 7-day period. INET then pays the Internet providers the actual Internet use. Assume that INET sells €16,000 of prepaid cards in January 2010. It then pays Inter-Express based on usage, which turns out to be 20% in February, 40% in March, and 40% in April. The total payment to InterExpress over the 3 months is €13,000. Indicate how much revenue INET should recognize in January, February, March, and April.

CONCEPTS FOR ANALYSIS

CA18-1 (Revenue Recognition—Alternative Methods) Peterson Industries has three operating divisions—Farber Mining, Enyart Paperbacks, and Glesen Protection Devices. Each division maintains its own accounting system and method of revenue recognition.

Farber Mining
Farber Mining specializes in the extraction of precious metals such as silver, gold, and platinum. During the fiscal year ended November 30, 2010, Farber entered into contracts worth $2,250,000 and shipped metals worth $2,000,000. A quarter of the shipments were made from inventories on hand at the beginning of the fiscal year, and the remainder were made from metals that were mined during the year. Mining totals for the year, valued at market prices, were: silver at $750,000, gold at $1,400,000, and platinum at $490,000. Farber uses the completion-of-production method to recognize revenue, because its operations meet the specified criteria—i.e., reasonably assured sales prices, interchangeable units, and insignificant distribution costs.

Enyart Paperbacks
Enyart Paperbacks sells large quantities of novels to a few book distributors that in turn sell to several national chains of bookstores. Enyart allows distributors to return up to 30% of sales, and distributors give the same terms to bookstores. While returns from individual titles fluctuate greatly, the returns from distributors have averaged 20% in each of the past 5 years. A total of €7,000,000 of paperback novel sales were made to distributors during the fiscal year. On November 30, 2010, €2,200,000 of fiscal 2010 sales

were still subject to return privileges over the next 6 months. The remaining €4,800,000 of fiscal 2010 sales had actual returns of 21%. Sales from fiscal 2009 totaling €2,500,000 were collected in fiscal 2010, with less than 18% of sales returned. Enyart records revenue according to the method referred to as revenue recognition when the right of return exits, because all applicable criteria for use of this method are met by Enyart's operations.

Glesen Protection Devices

Glesen Protection Devices works through manufacturers' agents in various cities. Orders for alarm systems and down payments are forwarded from agents, and Glesen ships the goods f.o.b. shipping point. Customers are billed for the balance due plus actual shipping costs. The firm received orders for $6,000,000 of goods during the fiscal year ended November 30, 2010. Down payments of $600,000 were received, and $5,000,000 of goods were billed and shipped. Actual freight costs of $100,000 were also billed. Commissions of 10% on product price were paid to manufacturers' agents after the goods were shipped to customers. Such goods are warranted for 90 days after shipment, and warranty returns have been about 1% of sales. Revenue is recognized at the point of sale by Glesen.

Instructions

(a) There are a variety of methods for revenue recognition. Define and describe each of the following methods of revenue recognition, and indicate whether each is in accordance with IFRS.

    (1) Completion-of-production method.

    (2) Percentage-of-completion method.

    (3) Cost-recovery method.

(b) Compute the revenue to be recognized in the fiscal year ended November 30, 2010, for

    (1) Farber Mining.

    (2) Enyart Paperbacks.

    (3) Glesen Protection Devices.

CA18-2 (Recognition of Revenue—Theory) Revenue is usually recognized at the point of sale. Under special circumstances, however, bases other than the point of sale are used for the timing of revenue recognition.

Instructions

(a) Why is the point of sale usually used as the basis for the timing of revenue recognition?

(b) Disregarding the special circumstances when bases other than the point of sale are used, discuss the merits of each of the following objections to the sale basis of revenue recognition:

    (1) It is too conservative because revenue is earned throughout the entire process of production.

    (2) It is not conservative enough because accounts receivable do not represent disposable funds, sales returns and allowances may be made, and collection and bad debt expenses may be incurred in a later period.

(c) Revenue may also be recognized (1) during production and (2) when all costs are incurred. For each of these two bases of timing revenue recognition, give an example of the circumstances in which it is properly used and discuss the accounting merits of its use in lieu of the sale basis.

CA18-3 (Recognition of Revenue—Theory) In some situations, revenue is recognized approximately as it is earned in the economic sense. In other situations, however, accountants have developed guidelines for recognizing revenue by other criteria, such as at the point of sale.

Instructions

(Ignore income taxes.)

(a) Explain and justify why revenue is often recognized at time of sale.

(b) Explain in what situations it would be appropriate to recognize revenue as the productive activity takes place.

(c) At what times, other than those included in (a) and (b) above, may it be appropriate to recognize revenue? Explain.

CA18-4 (Recognition of Revenue—Bonus Dollars) Griseta & Dubel Inc. was formed early this year to sell merchandise credits to merchants, who distribute the credits free to their customers. For example, customers can earn additional credits based on the dollars they spend with a merchant (e.g., airlines and hotels). Accounts for accumulating the credits and catalogs illustrating the merchandise for which the credits may be exchanged are maintained online. Centers with inventories of merchandise premiums have been established for redemption of the credits. Merchants may not return unused credits to Griseta & Dubel.

The following schedule expresses Griseta & Dubel's expectations as to percentages of a normal month's activity that will be attained. For this purpose, a "normal month's activity" is defined as the level of operations expected when expansion of activities ceases or tapers off to a stable rate. The company expects that this level will be attained in the third year and that sales of credits will average $6,000,000 per month throughout the third year.

Month	Actual Credit Sales Percent	Merchandise Premium Purchases Percent	Credit Redemptions Percent
6th	30%	40%	10%
12th	60	60	45
18th	80	80	70
24th	90	90	80
30th	100	100	95

Griseta & Dubel plans to adopt an annual closing date at the end of each 12 months of operation.

Instructions

(a) Discuss the factors to be considered in determining when revenue should be recognized in measuring the income of a business enterprise.

(b) Discuss the accounting alternatives that should be considered by Griseta & Dubel Inc. for the recognition of its revenues and related expenses.

(c) For each accounting alternative discussed in (b), give statement of financial position accounts that should be used and indicate how each should be classified.

CA18-5 (Recognition of Revenue from Subscriptions) *Cutting Edge* is a monthly magazine that has been on the market for 18 months. It currently has a circulation of 1.4 million copies. Negotiations are underway to obtain a bank loan in order to update the magazine's facilities. They are producing close to capacity and expect to grow at an average of 20% per year over the next 3 years.

After reviewing the financial statements of *Cutting Edge*, Andy Rich, the bank loan officer, had indicated that a loan could be offered to *Cutting Edge* only if it could increase its current ratio and decrease its debt to equity ratio to a specified level.

Jonathan Embry, the marketing manager of *Cutting Edge*, has devised a plan to meet these requirements. Embry indicates that an advertising campaign can be initiated to immediately increase circulation. The potential customers would be contacted after the purchase of another magazine's mailing list. The campaign would include:

1. An offer to subscribe to *Cutting Edge* at 3/4 the normal price.
2. A special offer to all new subscribers to receive the most current world atlas whenever requested at a guaranteed price of $2.
3. An unconditional guarantee that any subscriber will receive a full refund if dissatisfied with the magazine.

Although the offer of a full refund is risky, Embry claims that few people will ask for a refund after receiving half of their subscription issues. Embry notes that other magazine companies have tried this sales promotion technique and experienced great success. Their average cancellation rate was 25%. On average, each company increased its initial circulation threefold and in the long run increased circulation to twice that which existed before the promotion. In addition, 60% of the new subscribers are expected to take advantage of the atlas premium. Embry feels confident that the increased subscriptions from the advertising campaign will increase the current ratio and decrease the debt to equity ratio.

You are the controller of *Cutting Edge* and must give your opinion of the proposed plan.

Instructions

(a) When should revenue from the new subscriptions be recognized?

(b) How would you classify the estimated sales returns stemming from the unconditional guarantee?

(c) How should the atlas premium be recorded? Is the estimated premium claims a liability? Explain.

(d) Does the proposed plan achieve the goals of increasing the current ratio and decreasing the debt to equity ratio?

CA18-6 (Long-Term Contract—Percentage-of-Completion) Widjaja Company is accounting for a long-term construction contract using the percentage-of-completion method. It is a 4-year contract that is currently in its second year. The latest estimates of total contract costs indicate that the contract will be completed at a profit to Widjaja Company.

Instructions

(a) What theoretical justification is there for Widjaja Company's use of the percentage-of-completion method?

(b) How would progress billings be accounted for? Include in your discussion the classification of progress billings in Widjaja Company financial statements.

(c) How would the income recognized in the second year of the 4-year contract be determined using the cost-to-cost method of determining percentage of completion?

(d) What would be the effect on earnings per share in the second year of the 4-year contract of using the percentage-of-completion method instead of the cost-recovery method? Discuss.

CA18-7 (Revenue Recognition—Real Estate Development) Lillehammer Lakes is a new recreational real estate development which consists of 500 lake-front and lake-view lots. As a special incentive to the first 100 buyers of lake-view lots, the developer is offering 3 years of free financing on 10-year, 12% notes, no down payment, and one week at a nearby established resort—"a $1,200 value." The normal price per lot is $15,000. The cost per lake-view lot to the developer is an estimated average of $3,000. The development costs continue to be incurred; the actual average cost per lot is not known at this time. The resort promotion cost is $700 per lot. The notes are held by Harper Corp., a wholly owned subsidiary.

Instructions

(a) Discuss the revenue recognition and gross profit measurement issues raised by this situation.

(b) How would the developer's past financial and business experience influence your decision concerning the recording of these transactions?

(c) Assume 50 persons have accepted the offer, signed 10-year notes, and have stayed at the local resort. Prepare the journal entries that you believe are proper.

(d) What should be disclosed in the notes to the financial statements?

CA18-8 (Revenue Recognition) Nimble Health and Racquet Club (NHRC), which operates eight clubs in the Chicago metropolitan area, offers one-year memberships. The members may use any of the eight facilities but must reserve racquetball court time and pay a separate fee before using the court. As an incentive to new customers, NHRC advertised that any customers not satisfied for any reason could receive a refund of the remaining portion of unused membership fees. Membership fees are due at the beginning of the individual membership period. However, customers are given the option of financing the membership fee over the membership period at a 9% interest rate.

Some customers have expressed a desire to take only the regularly scheduled aerobic classes without paying for a full membership. During the current fiscal year, NHRC began selling coupon books for aerobic classes to accommodate these customers. Each book is dated and contains 50 coupons that may be redeemed for any regularly scheduled aerobics class over a 1-year period. After the 1-year period, unused coupons are no longer valid.

During 2011, NHRC expanded into the health equipment market by purchasing a local company that manufactures rowing machines and cross-country ski machines. These machines are used in NHRC's facilities and are sold through the clubs and mail order catalogs. Customers must make a 20% down payment when placing an equipment order; delivery is 60–90 days after order placement. The machines are sold with a 2-year unconditional guarantee. Based on past experience, NHRC expects the costs to repair machines under guarantee to be 4% of sales.

NHRC is in the process of preparing financial statements as of May 31, 2011, the end of its fiscal year. Marvin Bush, corporate controller, expressed concern over the company's performance for the year and decided to review the preliminary financial statements prepared by Joyce Kiley, NHRC's assistant controller. After reviewing the statements, Bush proposed that the following changes be reflected in the May 31, 2011, published financial statements.

1. Membership revenue should be recognized when the membership fee is collected.
2. Revenue from the coupon books should be recognized when the books are sold.
3. Down payments on equipment purchases and expenses associated with the guarantee on the rowing and cross-country machines should be recognized when paid.

Kiley indicated to Bush that the proposed changes are not in accordance with IFRS, but Bush insisted that the changes be made. Kiley believes that Bush wants to manage income to forestall any potential financial problems and increase his year-end bonus. At this point, Kiley is unsure what action to take.

Instructions

(a) (1) Describe when Nimble Health and Racquet Club (NHRC) should recognize revenue from membership fees, court rentals, and coupon book sales.

  (2) Describe how NHRC should account for the down payments on equipment sales, explaining when this revenue should be recognized.

  (3) Indicate when NHRC should recognize the expense associated with the guarantee of the rowing and cross-country machines.

(b) Discuss why Marvin Bush's proposed changes and his insistence that the financial statement changes be made is unethical. Structure your answer around or to include the following aspects of ethical conduct: competence, confidentiality, integrity, and/or objectivity.

(c) Identify some specific actions Joyce Kiley could take to resolve this situation.

CA18-9 (Revenue Recognition—Membership Fees) Middle-South Health Club (MHC) offers 1-year memberships. Membership fees are due in full at the beginning of the individual membership period. As an incentive to new customers, MHC advertised that any customers not satisfied for any reason could receive a refund of the remaining portion of unused membership fees. As a result of this policy, Richard Nies, corporate controller, recognized revenue ratably over the life of the membership.

MHC is in the process of preparing its year-end financial statements. Rachel Avery, MHC's treasurer, is concerned about the company's lackluster performance this year. She reviews the financial statements Nies prepared and tells Nies to recognize membership revenue when the fees are received.

Instructions

Answer the following questions.

(a) What are the ethical issues involved?

(b) What should Nies do?

*CA18-10 **(Franchise Revenue)** Amigos Burrito Inc. sells franchises to independent operators throughout the northwestern part of the United States. The contract with the franchisee includes the following provisions.

1. The franchisee is charged an initial fee of $120,000. Of this amount, $20,000 is payable when the agreement is signed, and a $20,000 non-interest-bearing note is payable at the end of each of the 5 subsequent years.

2. All of the initial franchise fee collected by Amigos is to be refunded and the remaining obligation canceled if, for any reason, the franchisee fails to open his or her franchise.

3. In return for the initial franchise fee, Amigos agrees to (a) assist the franchisee in selecting the location for the business, (b) negotiate the lease for the land, (c) obtain financing and assist with building design, (d) supervise construction, (e) establish accounting and tax records, and (f) provide expert advice over a 5-year period relating to such matters as employee and management training, quality control, and promotion.

4. In addition to the initial franchise fee, the franchisee is required to pay to Amigos a monthly fee of 2% of sales for menu planning, recipe innovations, and the privilege of purchasing ingredients from Amigos at or below prevailing market prices.

Management of Amigos Burrito estimates that the value of the services rendered to the franchisee at the time the contract is signed amounts to at least $20,000. All franchisees to date have opened their locations at the scheduled time, and none have defaulted on any of the notes receivable.

The credit ratings of all franchisees would entitle them to borrow at the current interest rate of 10%. The present value of an ordinary annuity of five annual receipts of $20,000 each discounted at 10% is $75,816.

Instructions

(a) Discuss the alternatives that Amigos Burrito Inc. might use to account for the initial franchise fees, evaluate each by applying IFRS, and give illustrative entries for each alternative.

(b) Given the nature of Amigos Burrito's agreement with its franchisees, when should revenue be recognized? Discuss the question of revenue recognition for both the initial franchise fee and the additional monthly fee of 2% of sales, and give illustrative entries for both types of revenue.

(c) Assume that Amigos Burrito sells some franchises for $100,000, which includes a charge of $20,000 for the rental of equipment for its useful life of 10 years; that $50,000 of the fee is payable immediately and the balance on non-interest-bearing notes at $10,000 per year; that no portion of the $20,000 rental payment is refundable in case the franchisee goes out of business; and that title to the equipment remains with the franchisor. Under those assumptions, what would be the preferable method of accounting for the rental portion of the initial franchise fee? Explain.

USING YOUR JUDGMENT

FINANCIAL REPORTING

Financial Reporting Problem

Marks and Spencer plc (M&S)

The financial statements of M&S are presented in Appendix 5B or can be accessed at the book's companion website, **www.wiley.com/college/kiesoifrs**.

Instructions

Refer to M&S's financial statements and the accompanying notes to answer the following questions.

(a) What were M&S's sales for 2008?

(b) What was the percentage of increase or decrease in M&S's sales from 2007 to 2008? From 2006 to 2007? From 2006 to 2008?

(c) In its notes to the financial statements, what criteria does M&S use to recognize revenue?

(d) How does M&S account for discounts and loyalty schemes? Does the accounting conform to accrual-accounting concepts? Explain.

Comparative Analysis Case

Cadbury and Nestlé

Instructions

Go to the book's companion website and use information found there to answer the following questions related to **Cadbury** and **Nestlé**.

(a) What were Cadbury's and Nestlé's net revenues (sales) for the year 2008? Which company increased its revenues more (amounts and percentage) from 2007 to 2008?

(b) Are the revenue recognition policies of Cadbury and Nestlé similar? Explain.

(c) In which foreign countries (geographic areas) did Cadbury (see Note) and Nestlé experience significant revenues in 2008? Compare the amounts of foreign revenues to revenues in their home country for both Cadbury and Nestlé.

Financial Statement Analysis Case

British Airways

The following note appears in the "Summary of Significant Accounting Policies" section of the annual report of **British Airways** (GBR).

Summary of significant accounting policies (in part)

Revenue

Passenger and cargo revenue is recognised when the transportation service is provided. Passenger tickets net of discounts are recorded as current liabilities in the 'sales in advance of carriage' account until recognised as revenue. Unused tickets are recognised as revenue using estimates regarding the timing of recognition based on the terms and conditions of the ticket and historical trends. Other revenue is recognised at the time the service is provided. Commission costs are recognised at the same time as the revenue to which they relate and are charged to operating expenditure.

Key Accounting Estimates and Judgments

Passenger revenue recognition

Passenger revenue is recognised when the transportation is provided. Ticket sales that are not expected to be used for transportation ('unused tickets') are recognised as revenue using estimates regarding the timing of recognition based on the terms and conditions of the ticket and historical trends. During the current year, changes in estimates regarding the timing of revenue recognition primarily for unused flexible tickets were made, resulting in increased revenue in the current year of £109 million. During the prior year, changes in estimates regarding the timing of revenue recognition for unused restricted tickets were made, resulting in increased revenue in the prior year of £36 million. Both the above changes reflect more accurate and timely data obtained through the increased use of electronic tickets.

Instructions

(a) Identify the revenue recognition policies used by British Airways as discussed in its note on significant accounting policies.

(b) Under what conditions are the revenue recognition methods identified in the first paragraph of British Airways' note above acceptable?

(c) From the information provided in the second paragraph of British Airways' note, identify the type of operation being described and defend the acceptability of the revenue recognition method.

Accounting, Analysis, and Principles

Diversified Products, Inc. operates in several lines of business, including the construction and building supply industries. While the majority of its revenues are recognized at point of sale, Diversified appropriately recognizes revenue on long-term construction contracts using the percentage-of-completion method. It sells some products on a consignment basis. Income data for 2010 from operations other than construction and consignment sales are as follows.

Revenues	$9,500,000
Expenses	7,750,000

1. Diversified started a construction project during 2009. The total contract price is $1,000,000, and $200,000 in costs were incurred in both 2009 and 2010. In 2009, Diversified recognized $50,000 gross profit on the project. Estimated costs to complete the project in 2011 are $400,000.

2. During this year, Diversified sold products on a consignment basis, with a total sales value of $330,000 (cost is $280,000). Diversified retains a 5% fee on each dollar of these sales and remits the balance to the consignor.

Accounting

Determine Diversified Product's 2010 net income. Ingore taxes.

Analysis

Determine free cash flow (see Chapter 5) for Diversified Products for 2010. In 2010, Diversified had depreciation expense of $175,000 and a net increase in working capital (changes in accounts receivable and accounts payable) of $250,000. In 2010, capital expenditures were $500,000; Diversified paid dividends of $120,000.

Principles

"Application of the percentage-of-completion and consignment revenue recognition approaches illustrates the trade-off between relevance and faithful representation of accounting information." Explain.

I F R S BRIDGE TO THE PROFESSION

Professional Research

Employees at your company disagree about the accounting for sales returns. The sales manager believes that granting more generous return provisions and allowing customers to order items on a bill and hold basis can give the company a competitive edge and increase sales revenue. The controller cautions that, depending on the terms granted, loose return or bill and hold provisions might lead to non-IFRS revenue recognition. The company CFO would like you to research the issue to provide an authoritative answer.

Instructions

Access the IFRS authoritative literature at the IASB website (*http://eifrs.iasb.org/*). When you have accessed the documents, you can use the search tool in your Internet browser to respond to the following questions. (Provide paragraph citations.)

(a) What is the authoritative literature addressing revenue recognition when right of return exists?

(b) What is meant by "right of return"? "Bill and hold"?

(c) When there is a right of return, what conditions must the company meet to recognize the revenue at the time of sale?

(d) What factors may impair the ability to make a reasonable estimate of future returns?

(e) When goods are sold on a bill and hold basis, what conditions must be met to recognize revenue upon receipt of the order?

Professional Simulation

In this simulation, you are asked to address questions related to revenue recognition issues. Prepare responses to all parts.

KWW_Professional _Simulation

| Revenue Recognition | Time Remaining 3 hours 00 minutes | copy | paste | calculator | sheet | standards | help | spliter | done |

| Directions | Situation | Measurement | Journal Entries | Financial Statements | Explanation | Resources |

Nomar Industries, Inc. operates in several lines of business, including the construction and real estate industries. While the majority of its revenues are recognized at point of sale, Nomar appropriately recognizes revenue on long-term construction contracts using the percentage-of-completion method. It recognizes sales of some inventory on a bill and hold basis. Income data for 2011 from operations other than construction and bill and hold sales are as follows:

Revenues	$5,500,000
Expenses	4,200,000

1. Nomar started a construction project during 2010. The total contract price is $500,000, and $100,000 in costs were incurred in 2011. Estimated costs to complete the project in 2012 are $200,000. In 2010, Nomar incurred $100,000 of costs and recognized $25,000 gross profit on this project. Total billings at the end of 2011 were $230,000, and total cash collected as of the end of 2011 was $202,500.
2. During this year, Nomar sold goods at a price of $480,000. Nomar recognizes a 40% gross profit rate when the order is received. Nomar has transferred title but is unsure when the customer will be able to take delivery of the goods.

| Directions | Situation | Measurement | Journal Entries | Financial Statements | Explanation | Resources |

Determine net income for Nomar for 2011. Ignore income taxes.

| Directions | Situation | Measurement | Journal Entries | Financial Statements | Explanation | Resources |

Prepare the journal entries to record the costs incurred and gross profit recognized in 2011 on the construction project.

| Directions | Situation | Measurement | Journal Entries | Financial Statements | Explanation | Resources |

For 2011, show how the details related to this construction contract would be reported on the statement of financial position.

| Directions | Situation | Measurement | Journal Entries | Financial Statements | Explanation | Resources |

Nomar is negotiating construction contracts with some new customers, which are more uncertain as to their ability to make all payments. Is there a more appropriate revenue recognition policy for these customers? Explain.

CHAPTER 19

ACCOUNTING FOR INCOME TAXES

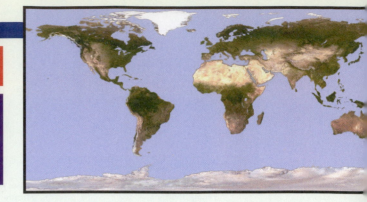

LEARNING OBJECTIVES

After studying this chapter, you should be able to:

•1 Identify differences between pretax financial income and taxable income.

•2 Describe a temporary difference that results in future taxable amounts.

•3 Describe a temporary difference that results in future deductible amounts.

•4 Explain the non-recognition of a deferred tax asset.

•5 Describe the presentation of income tax expense in the income statement.

•6 Describe various temporary and permanent differences.

•7 Explain the effect of various tax rates and tax rate changes on deferred income taxes.

•8 Apply accounting procedures for a loss carryback and a loss carryforward.

•9 Describe the presentation of income taxes in financial statements.

•10 Indicate the basic principles of the asset-liability method.

SAFE (TAX) HAVEN?

One set of costs that companies manage are those related to taxes. In fact, in today's competitive markets, managers are expected to look for places in the tax code that a company can exploit to pay less tax to various tax authorities. By paying less in taxes, companies have more cash available to fund operations, finance expansion, and create new jobs. What happens, though, when companies push the tax-saving envelope? Well, they may face a tax audit, the results of which could hurt their financial statements.

A notable example of corporate maneuvering to reduce taxable income involved **Limited Brands Inc.** (USA). It managed its tax costs downward by locating part of its business in low-tax-rate jurisdictions while operating retail outlets elsewhere. For example, by basing a subsidiary (which does nothing more than hold the trademarks for Bath and Body Works and Victoria's Secret) in a low-tax jurisdiction, it is able to transfer hundreds of millions of dollars from Limited's retail outlets in high-tax jurisdictions into a jurisdiction with a zero tax rate.

However, regulators have been increasing their scrutiny of transactions that seem done only to avoid taxes and that do not serve a legitimate business purpose. In one case, a prosecutor alleged that Limited Brands Inc. ". . . engaged in hocus pocus bookkeeping and deceptive accounting," the sole purpose of which was to reduce its tax bill. The court agreed, and Limited Inc. had to pay millions of dollars in taxes dating back to 1994.

Limited Brands shareholders likely got an unpleasant surprise when they learned the company also had a big tax obligation from its "uncertain tax position" related to off-shore locations. The same can be said for many other companies that take tax deductions that may not hold up under the scrutiny of regulators. International tax regulators are now working together to crack down on tax havens. At its recent London summit, the Group of Twenty Finance Ministers and Central Bank Governors (G20) agreed to define a blacklist for tax havens, to be segmented according to a four-tier system, which is based on compliance with an "internationally agreed tax standard." The list, drawn up by the Organisation for Economic Co-operation and Development (OECD), identifies the four tiers as:

1. Those that have substantially implemented the standard (includes countries such as Argentina, Australia, Brazil, Canada, China, Czech Republic, France, Germany, Greece, Guernsey, Hungary, Ireland, Italy, Japan, Jersey, Isle of Man, Mexico, the Netherlands, Poland, Portugal, Russia, Slovakia, South Africa, South Korea, Spain, Sweden, Turkey, United Arab Emirates, United Kingdom, and the United States);

2. Tax havens that have committed to—but not yet fully implemented—the standard (includes Andorra, the Bahamas, Cayman Islands, Gibraltar, Liechtenstein, and Monaco);

3. Financial centers that have committed to—but not yet fully implemented—the standard (includes Chile, Costa Rica, Malaysia, the Philippines, Singapore, Switzerland, Uruguay, and three EU countries—Austria, Belgium, and Luxembourg); and

4. Those that have not committed to the standard (now an empty category).

Countries in the bottom tier were classified as being "non-cooperative tax havens." Uruguay was initially classified as being uncooperative. However, upon appeal the OECD stated that Uruguay did meet tax transparency rules and thus moved it up from the bottom tier. Some countries (e.g., the Philippines) are already reported to be taking steps to be removed from the blacklist. As with convergence of international accounting standards, international agreements on tax havens should level the playing field across the globe and facilitate fair and effective tax policies.

Source: See Glenn Simpson, "A Tax Maneuver in Delaware Puts Squeeze on States," *Wall Street Journal* (August 9, 2002), p. A1, and Anonymous, "G20 Declares Door Shut on Tax Havens," *The Guardian* (April 2, 2009).

PREVIEW OF CHAPTER 19

As our opening story indicates, companies spend a considerable amount of time and effort to minimize their income tax payments. And with good reason, as income taxes are a major cost of doing business for most corporations. Yet, at the same time, companies must present financial information to the investment community that provides a clear picture of present and potential tax obligations and tax benefits. In this chapter, we discuss the basic guidelines that companies must follow in reporting income taxes. The content and organization of the chapter are as follows.

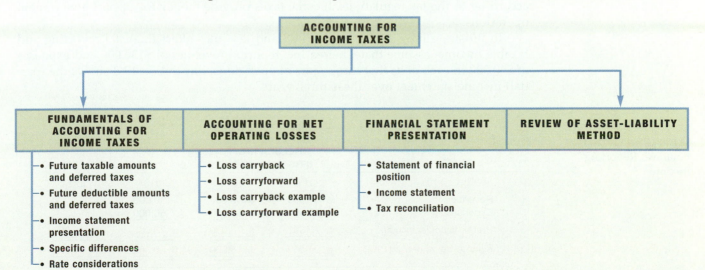

FUNDAMENTALS OF ACCOUNTING FOR INCOME TAXES

Up to this point, you have learned the basic guidelines that corporations use to report information to investors and creditors. Corporations also must file income tax returns following the guidelines developed by the appropriate taxing authority. Because IFRS and tax regulations differ in a number of ways, so frequently do pretax financial income and taxable income. Consequently, the amount that a company reports as tax expense will differ from the amount of taxes payable to the taxing authority. Illustration 19-1 highlights these differences.

ILLUSTRATION 19-1
Fundamental Differences between Financial and Tax Reporting

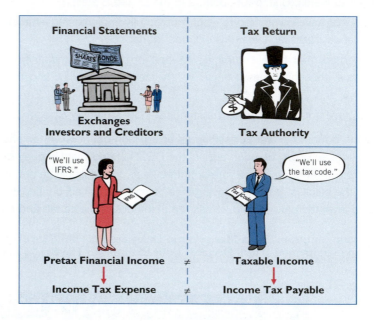

Pretax financial income is a *financial reporting* term. It also is often referred to as *income before taxes, income for financial reporting purposes*, or *income for book purposes*. Companies determine pretax financial income according to IFRS. They measure it with the objective of providing useful information to investors and creditors.

Taxable income (income for tax purposes) is a *tax accounting* term. It indicates the amount used to compute income tax payable. Companies determine taxable income according to the tax regulations. Income taxes provide money to support government operations.

To illustrate how differences in IFRS and tax rules affect financial reporting and taxable income, assume that Chelsea Inc. reported revenues of $130,000 and expenses of $60,000 in each of its first three years of operations. Illustration 19-2 shows the (partial) income statement over these three years.

ILLUSTRATION 19-2
Financial Reporting Income

CHELSEA INC. IFRS REPORTING				
	2011	2012	2013	Total
Revenues	$130,000	$130,000	$130,000	
Expenses	60,000	60,000	60,000	
Pretax financial income	$ 70,000	$ 70,000	$ 70,000	$ 210,000
Income tax expense (40%)	$ 28,000	$ 28,000	$ 28,000	$ 84,000

For tax purposes (following the tax rules), Chelsea reported the same expenses to the tax authority in each of the years. But, as Illustration 19-3 shows, Chelsea reported taxable revenues of $100,000 in 2011, $150,000 in 2012, and $140,000 in 2013.

ILLUSTRATION 19-3
Tax Reporting Income

CHELSEA INC. TAX REPORTING				
	2011	2012	2013	Total
Revenues	$100,000	$150,000	$140,000	
Expenses	60,000	60,000	60,000	
Taxable income	$ 40,000	$ 90,000	$ 80,000	$ 210,000
Income tax payable (40%)	$ 16,000	$ 36,000	$ 32,000	$ 84,000

Income tax expense and income tax payable differed over the three years, but were equal **in total**, as Illustration 19-4 shows.

ILLUSTRATION 19-4
Comparison of Income Tax Expense to Income Tax Payable

CHELSEA INC. INCOME TAX EXPENSE AND INCOME TAX PAYABLE				
	2011	2012	2013	Total
Income tax expense	$28,000	$28,000	$28,000	$84,000
Income tax payable	16,000	36,000	32,000	84,000
Difference	$12,000	$ (8,000)	$ (4,000)	$ 0

The differences between income tax expense and income tax payable in this example arise for a simple reason. For financial reporting, companies use the full accrual method to report revenues. For tax purposes, they generally use a modified cash basis. As a result, Chelsea reports pretax financial income of $70,000 and income tax expense of $28,000 for each of the three years. However, taxable income fluctuates. For example, in 2011 taxable income is only $40,000, so Chelsea owes just $16,000 to the tax authority that year. Chelsea classifies the income tax payable as a current liability on the statement of financial position.

As Illustration 19-4 indicates, for Chelsea the $12,000 ($28,000 − $16,000) difference between income tax expense and income tax payable in 2011 reflects taxes that it will pay in future periods. This $12,000 difference is often referred to as a **deferred tax amount**. In this case, it is a **deferred tax liability**. In cases where taxes will be lower in the future, Chelsea records a **deferred tax asset**. We explain the measurement and accounting for deferred tax liabilities and assets in the following two sections.[1]

Future Taxable Amounts and Deferred Taxes

The example summarized in Illustration 19-4 shows how income tax payable can differ from income tax expense. This can happen when there are temporary differences between the amounts reported for tax purposes and those reported for book purposes. A **temporary difference** is the difference between the tax basis of an asset or liability and its reported (carrying or book) amount in the financial statements, which will result in taxable amounts or deductible amounts in future

Objective·2
Describe a temporary difference that results in future taxable amounts.

[1]Determining the amount of tax to pay the tax authority is a costly exercise for both individuals and companies. For example, a recent study documented that the average person in the United States spends about $200 annually collecting, calculating, and compiling tax data. U.S. corporations had a total cost of compliance of $170 billion. This is not surprising, when you consider that **General Electric** (USA) filed a return equivalent to 24,000 printed pages. J. Abrams, "Americans Spend 27 Hours, $200," *Naples (FL) Daily News* (April 15, 2008), p. 3a.

years. **Taxable amounts** increase taxable income in future years. **Deductible amounts** decrease taxable income in future years.

In Chelsea's situation, the only difference between the book basis and tax basis of the assets and liabilities relates to accounts receivable that arose from revenue recognized for book purposes. Illustration 19-5 indicates that Chelsea reports accounts receivable at $30,000 in the December 31, 2011, IFRS-basis statement of financial position. However, the receivables have a zero tax basis.

ILLUSTRATION 19-5
Temporary Difference, Sales Revenue

Per Books	12/31/11	Per Tax Return	12/31/11
Accounts receivable	$30,000	Accounts receivable	$–0–

What will happen to the $30,000 temporary difference that originated in 2011 for Chelsea? Assuming that Chelsea expects to collect $20,000 of the receivables in 2012 and $10,000 in 2013, this collection results in future taxable amounts of $20,000 in 2012 and $10,000 in 2013. These future taxable amounts will cause taxable income to exceed pretax financial income in both 2012 and 2013.

An assumption inherent in a company's IFRS statement of financial position is that companies recover and settle the assets and liabilities at their reported amounts (carrying amounts). This assumption creates a requirement under accrual accounting to recognize *currently* the deferred tax consequences of temporary differences. That is, companies recognize the amount of income taxes that are payable (or refundable) when they recover and settle the reported amounts of the assets and liabilities, respectively. Illustration 19-6 shows the reversal of the temporary difference described in Illustration 19-5 and the resulting taxable amounts in future periods.

ILLUSTRATION 19-6
Reversal of Temporary Difference, Chelsea Inc.

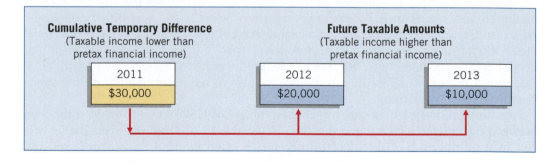

Chelsea assumes that it will collect the accounts receivable and report the $30,000 collection as taxable revenues in future tax returns. A payment of income tax in both 2012 and 2013 will occur. Chelsea should therefore record in its books in 2011 the deferred tax consequences of the revenue and related receivables reflected in the 2011 financial statements. Chelsea does this by recording a deferred tax liability.

Deferred Tax Liability

A deferred tax liability is the deferred tax consequences attributable to taxable temporary differences. In other words, **a deferred tax liability represents the increase in taxes payable in future years as a result of taxable temporary differences existing at the end of the current year.**

Recall from the Chelsea example that income tax payable is $16,000 ($40,000 × 40%) in 2011 (Illustration 19-4 on page 1013). In addition, a temporary difference exists at year-end because Chelsea reports the revenue and related accounts receivable differently for book and tax purposes. The book basis of accounts receivable is $30,000, and the tax basis is zero. Thus, the total deferred tax liability at the end of 2011 is $12,000, computed as shown in Illustration 19-7.

Book basis of accounts receivable	$30,000	
Tax basis of accounts receivable	–0–	
Cumulative temporary difference at the end of 2011	30,000	
Tax rate	× 40%	
Deferred tax liability at the end of 2011	$12,000	

ILLUSTRATION 19-7
Computation of Deferred
Tax Liability, End of 2011

Companies may also compute the deferred tax liability by preparing a schedule that indicates the future taxable amounts due to existing temporary differences. Such a schedule, as shown in Illustration 19-8, is particularly useful when the computations become more complex.

	Future Years		
	2012	**2013**	**Total**
Future taxable amounts	$20,000	$10,000	$30,000
Tax rate	× 40%	× 40%	
Deferred tax liability at the end of 2011	$ 8,000	$ 4,000	$12,000

ILLUSTRATION 19-8
Schedule of Future
Taxable Amounts

Because it is the first year of operations for Chelsea, there is no deferred tax liability at the beginning of the year. Chelsea computes the income tax expense for 2011 as shown in Illustration 19-9.

Deferred tax liability at end of 2011	$12,000	
Deferred tax liability at beginning of 2011	–0–	
Deferred tax expense for 2011	12,000	
Current tax expense for 2011 (Income tax payable)	16,000	
Income tax expense (total) for 2011	$28,000	

ILLUSTRATION 19-9
Computation of Income
Tax Expense, 2011

This computation indicates that income tax expense has two components—**current tax expense** (the amount of income tax payable for the period) and deferred tax expense. **Deferred tax expense** is the increase in the deferred tax liability balance from the beginning to the end of the accounting period.

Companies credit taxes due and payable to Income Tax Payable and credit the increase in deferred taxes to Deferred Tax Liability. They then debit the sum of those two items to Income Tax Expense. For Chelsea, it makes the following entry at the end of 2011.

Income Tax Expense	28,000	
Income Tax Payable		16,000
Deferred Tax Liability		12,000

At the end of 2012 (the second year), the difference between the book basis and the tax basis of the accounts receivable is $10,000. Chelsea multiplies this difference by the applicable tax rate to arrive at the deferred tax liability of $4,000 ($10,000 × 40%), which it reports at the end of 2012. Income tax payable for 2012 is $36,000 (Illustration 19-3 on page 1013), and the income tax expense for 2012 is as shown in Illustration 19-10.

Deferred tax liability at end of 2012	$ 4,000	
Deferred tax liability at beginning of 2012	12,000	
Deferred tax expense (benefit) for 2012	(8,000)	
Current tax expense for 2012 (Income tax payable)	36,000	
Income tax expense (total) for 2012	$28,000	

ILLUSTRATION 19-10
Computation of Income
Tax Expense, 2012

Chelsea records income tax expense, the change in the deferred tax liability, and income tax payable for 2012 as follows.

Income Tax Expense	28,000	
Deferred Tax Liability	8,000	
Income Tax Payable		36,000

The entry to record income taxes at the end of 2013 reduces the Deferred Tax Liability by $4,000. The Deferred Tax Liability account appears as follows at the end of 2013.

ILLUSTRATION 19-11
Deferred Tax Liability
Account after Reversals

Deferred Tax Liability			
2012	8,000	2011	12,000
2013	4,000		

The Deferred Tax Liability account has a zero balance at the end of 2013.

What do the numbers mean?

"REAL LIABILITIES"

Some analysts dismiss deferred tax liabilities when assessing the financial strength of a company. But the IASB indicates that the deferred tax liability meets the definition of a liability established in the IASB Framework because:

1. *It is a present obligation.* Taxable income in future periods will exceed pretax financial income as a result of this temporary difference. Thus, a present obligation exists.

2. *It results from a past transaction.* In the Chelsea example, the company performed services for customers and recognized revenue in 2011 for financial reporting purposes but deferred it for tax purposes.

3. *It represents a future outflow of resources.* Taxable income and taxes due in future periods will result from past events. The payment of these taxes when they come due is the future outflow of resources.

A study by B. Ayers indicates that the market views deferred tax assets and liabilities similarly to other assets and liabilities. Further, the study concludes that the accounting rules in this area increased the usefulness of deferred tax amounts in financial statements.

Source: B. Ayers, "Deferred Tax Accounting Under *SFAS No. 109*: An Empirical Investigation of Its Incremental Value-Relevance Relative to *APB No. 11*," *The Accounting Review* (April 1998).

Summary of Income Tax Accounting Objectives

IFRS

See the Authoritative Literature section (page 1047).

One objective of accounting for income taxes is to recognize the amount of taxes payable or refundable for the current year. In Chelsea's case, income tax payable is $16,000 for 2011.

A **second objective** is to recognize deferred tax liabilities and assets for the future tax consequences of events already recognized in the financial statements or tax returns. [1] For example, Chelsea sold services to customers that resulted in accounts receivable of $30,000 in 2011. It reported that amount on the 2011 income statement but not on the tax return as income. That amount will appear on future tax returns as income for the period **when collected**. As a result, a $30,000 temporary difference exists at the end of 2011, which will cause future taxable amounts. Chelsea reports a deferred tax liability of $12,000 on the statement of financial position at the end of 2011, which represents the increase in taxes payable in future years ($8,000 in 2012 and $4,000 in 2013) as a result of a temporary difference existing at the end of the current year. The related deferred tax liability is reduced by $8,000 at the end of 2012 and by another $4,000 at the end of 2013.

In addition to affecting the statement of financial position, deferred taxes impact income tax expense in each of the three years affected. In 2011, taxable income ($40,000) is less than pretax financial income ($70,000). Income tax payable for 2011 is therefore $16,000 (based on taxable income). Deferred tax expense of $12,000 results from the increase in the Deferred Tax Liability account on the statement of financial position. Income tax expense is then $28,000 for 2011.

In 2012 and 2013, however, taxable income will exceed pretax financial income, due to the reversal of the temporary difference ($20,000 in 2012 and $10,000 in 2013). Income tax payable will therefore exceed income tax expense in 2012 and 2013. Chelsea will debit the Deferred Tax Liability account for $8,000 in 2012 and $4,000 in 2013. It records credits for these amounts in Income Tax Expense. These credits are often referred to as a **deferred tax benefit** (which we discuss again later on).

Future Deductible Amounts and Deferred Taxes

Assume that during 2011, Cunningham Inc. estimated its warranty costs related to the sale of microwave ovens to be $500,000, paid evenly over the next two years. For book purposes, in 2011 Cunningham reported warranty expense and a related estimated liability for warranties of $500,000 in its financial statements. For tax purposes, **the warranty tax deduction is not allowed until paid**. Therefore, Cunningham recognizes no warranty liability on a tax-basis statement of financial position. Illustration 19-12 shows the statement of financial position difference at the end of 2011.

> **Objective·3**
> Describe a temporary difference that results in future deductible amounts.

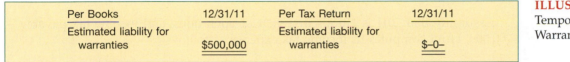

Per Books	12/31/11	Per Tax Return	12/31/11
Estimated liability for warranties	$500,000	Estimated liability for warranties	$-0-

ILLUSTRATION 19-12
Temporary Difference, Warranty Liability

When Cunningham pays the warranty liability, it reports an expense (deductible amount) for tax purposes. Because of this temporary difference, Cunningham should recognize in 2011 the tax benefits (positive tax consequences) for the tax deductions that will result from the future settlement of the liability. Cunningham reports this future tax benefit in the December 31, 2011, statement of financial position as a **deferred tax asset**.

We can think about this situation another way. Deductible amounts occur in future tax returns. These **future deductible amounts** cause taxable income to be less than pretax financial income in the future as a result of an existing temporary difference. Cunningham's temporary difference originates (arises) in one period (2011) and reverses over two periods (2012 and 2013). Illustration 19-13 diagrams this situation.

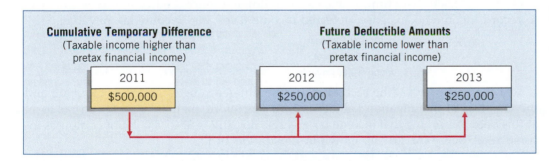

ILLUSTRATION 19-13
Reversal of Temporary Difference, Cunningham Inc.

Deferred Tax Asset (Recognition)

A deferred tax asset is the deferred tax consequence attributable to deductible temporary differences. In other words, a **deferred tax asset represents the increase in taxes refundable (or saved) in future years as a result of deductible temporary differences existing at the end of the current year**.

To illustrate, assume that Hunt Co. accrues a loss and a related liability of $50,000 in 2011 for financial reporting purposes because of pending litigation. Hunt cannot deduct this amount for tax purposes until the period it pays the liability, expected in 2012. As a result, a deductible amount will occur in 2012 when Hunt settles the liability, causing taxable income to be lower than pretax financial income. Illustration 19-14 (on page 1018) shows the computation of the deferred tax asset at the end of 2011 (assuming a 40 percent tax rate).

ILLUSTRATION 19-14
Computation of Deferred
Tax Asset, End of 2011

Book basis of litigation liability	$50,000
Tax basis of litigation liability	–0–
Cumulative temporary difference at the end of 2011	50,000
Tax rate	× 40%
Deferred tax asset at the end of 2011	$20,000

Hunt can also compute the deferred tax asset by preparing a schedule that indicates the future deductible amounts due to deductible temporary differences. Illustration 19-15 shows this schedule.

ILLUSTRATION 19-15
Schedule of Future
Deductible Amounts

	Future Years
Future deductible amounts	$50,000
Tax rate	× 40%
Deferred tax asset at the end of 2011	$20,000

Assuming that 2011 is Hunt's first year of operations, and income tax payable is $100,000, Hunt computes its income tax expense as follows.

ILLUSTRATION 19-16
Computation of Income
Tax Expense, 2011

Deferred tax asset at end of 2011	$ 20,000
Deferred tax asset at beginning of 2011	–0–
Deferred tax expense (benefit) for 2011	(20,000)
Current tax expense for 2011 (Income tax payable)	100,000
Income tax expense (total) for 2011	$ 80,000

The **deferred tax benefit** results from the increase in the deferred tax asset from the beginning to the end of the accounting period (similar to the Chelsea deferred tax liability example earlier). The deferred tax benefit is a negative component of income tax expense. The total income tax expense of $80,000 on the income statement for 2011 thus consists of two elements—current tax expense of $100,000 and a deferred tax benefit of $20,000. For Hunt, it makes the following journal entry at the end of 2011 to record income tax expense, deferred income taxes, and income tax payable.

Income Tax Expense	80,000	
Deferred Tax Asset	20,000	
Income Tax Payable		100,000

At the end of 2012 (the second year), the difference between the book value and the tax basis of the litigation liability is zero. Therefore, there is no deferred tax asset at this date. Assuming that income tax payable for 2012 is $140,000, Hunt computes income tax expense for 2012 as shown in Illustration 19-17.

ILLUSTRATION 19-17
Computation of Income
Tax Expense, 2012

Deferred tax asset at the end of 2012	$ –0–
Deferred tax asset at the beginning of 2012	20,000
Deferred tax expense (benefit) for 2012	20,000
Current tax expense for 2012 (Income tax payable)	140,000
Income tax expense (total) for 2012	$160,000

The company records income taxes for 2012 as follows.

Income Tax Expense	160,000	
Deferred Tax Asset		20,000
Income Tax Payable		140,000

The total income tax expense of $160,000 on the income statement for 2012 thus consists of two elements—current tax expense of $140,000 and deferred tax expense of $20,000. Illustration 19-18 shows the Deferred Tax Asset account at the end of 2012.

Deferred Tax Asset			
2011	20,000	2012	20,000

ILLUSTRATION 19-18
Deferred Tax Asset
Account after Reversals

"REAL ASSETS"

A key issue in accounting for income taxes is whether a company should recognize a deferred tax asset in the financial records. Based on the conceptual definition of an asset, a deferred tax asset meets the three main conditions for an item to be recognized as an asset:

What do the numbers mean?

1. *The entity controls access to the benefits.* Hunt can obtain the benefit of existing deductible temporary differences by reducing its taxes payable in the future. Hunt has the exclusive right to that benefit and can control others' access to it.

2. *It results from a past transaction.* In the Hunt example, the accrual of the loss contingency is the past event that gives rise to a future deductible temporary difference.

3. *It gives rise to a probable benefit in the future.* Taxable income exceeds pretax financial income in the current year (2011). However, in the next year the exact opposite occurs. That is, taxable income is lower than pretax financial income. Because this deductible temporary difference reduces taxes payable in the future, a probable future benefit exists at the end of the current period.

Market analysts' reactions to the **write-off** of deferred tax assets also supports their treatment as assets. When **Bethlehem Steel** (USA) reported a $1 billion charge in a recent year to write off a deferred tax asset, analysts believed that Bethlehem was signaling that it would not realize the future benefits of the tax deductions. Thus, Bethlehem should write down the asset like other assets.

Source: J. Weil and S. Liesman, "Stock Gurus Disregard Most Big Write-Offs But They Often Hold Vital Clues to Outlook," *Wall Street Journal Online* (December 31, 2001).

Deferred Tax Asset (Non-Recognition)

Companies recognize a deferred tax asset for all deductible temporary differences. However, based on available evidence, a company should reduce a deferred tax asset if it is probable that it **will not realize** some portion or all of the deferred tax asset. "Probable" means a level of likelihood of at least slightly more than 50 percent.

> **Objective·4**
> Explain the non-recognition of a deferred tax asset.

Assume that Jensen Co. has a deductible temporary difference of €1,000,000 at the end of its first year of operations. Its tax rate is 40 percent, which means it records a deferred tax asset of €400,000 (€1,000,000 × 40%). Assuming €900,000 of income taxes payable, Jensen records income tax expense, the deferred tax asset, and income tax payable as follows.

Income Tax Expense	500,000	
Deferred Tax Asset	400,000	
Income Tax Payable		900,000

After careful review of all available evidence, Jensen determines that it is probable that it will not realize €100,000 of this deferred tax asset. Jensen records this reduction in asset value as follows.

Income Tax Expense	100,000	
Deferred Tax Asset		100,000

This journal entry increases income tax expense in the current period because Jensen does not expect to realize a favorable tax benefit for a portion of the deductible temporary difference. Jensen **simultaneously recognizes a reduction in the carrying**

amount of the deferred tax asset. Jensen then reports a deferred tax asset of €300,000 in its statement of financial position.

Jensen evaluates the deferred tax asset account at the end of each accounting period. If, at the end of the next period, it expects to realize €350,000 of this deferred tax asset, Jensen makes the following entry to adjust this account.

Deferred Tax Asset (€350,000 − €300,000)	50,000	
Income Tax Expense		50,000

Jensen should consider all available evidence, both positive and negative, to determine whether, based on the weight of available evidence, it needs to adjust the deferred tax asset. For example, if Jensen has been experiencing a series of loss years, it reasonably assumes that these losses will continue. Therefore, Jensen will lose the benefit of the future deductible amounts.

Generally, sufficient taxable income arises from temporary taxable differences that will reverse in the future or from a tax-planning strategy that will generate taxable income in the future. Illustration 19-19 shows how **Ahold** (NLD) describes its reporting of deferred assets.

ILLUSTRATION 19-19
Deferred Tax Asset
Disclosure

Ahold

Note 11. Significant judgment is required in determining whether deferred tax assets are realizable. Ahold determines this on the basis of expected taxable profits arising from recognized deferred tax liabilities and on the basis of budgets, cash flow forecasts, and impairment models. Where utilization is not considered probable, deferred taxes are not recognized.

Income Statement Presentation

Objective·5
Describe the presentation of income tax expense in the income statement.

Circumstances dictate whether a company should add or subtract the change in deferred income taxes to or from income tax payable in computing income tax expense. For example, a company adds an increase in a deferred tax liability to income tax payable. On the other hand, it subtracts an increase in a deferred tax asset from income tax payable. The formula in Illustration 19-20 is used to compute income tax expense (benefit).

ILLUSTRATION 19-20
Formula to Compute
Income Tax Expense

Income Tax Payable or Refundable	±	Change in Deferred Income Taxes	=	Total Income Tax Expense or Benefit

In the income statement or in the notes to the financial statements, a company should disclose the significant components of income tax expense attributable to continuing operations. Given the information related to Chelsea on page 1013, Chelsea reports its income statement as follows.

ILLUSTRATION 19-21
Income Statement
Presentation of Income
Tax Expense

CHELSEA INC.
INCOME STATEMENT
FOR THE YEAR ENDING DECEMBER 31, 2011

Revenues		$130,000
Expenses		60,000
Income before income taxes		70,000
Income tax expense		
Current	$16,000	
Deferred	12,000	28,000
Net income		$ 42,000

As illustrated, Chelsea reports both the current portion (amount of income tax payable for the period) and the deferred portion of income tax expense. Another option is to simply report the total income tax expense on the income statement and then indicate in the notes to the financial statements the current and deferred portions. Income tax expense is often referred to as "Provision for income taxes." Using this terminology, the current provision is $16,000, and the provision for deferred taxes is $12,000.

Specific Differences

Numerous items create differences between pretax financial income and taxable income. For purposes of accounting recognition, these differences are of two types: (1) temporary, and (2) permanent.

> **Objective·6**
> Describe various temporary and permanent differences.

Temporary Differences

Taxable temporary differences are temporary differences that will result in taxable amounts in future years when the related assets are recovered. **Deductible temporary differences** are temporary differences that will result in deductible amounts in future years, when the related book liabilities are settled. Taxable temporary differences give rise to recording deferred tax liabilities. Deductible temporary differences give rise to recording deferred tax assets. Illustration 19-22 provides examples of temporary differences.

ILLUSTRATION 19-22
Examples of Temporary Differences

A. **Revenues or gains are taxable after they are recognized in financial income. (Deferred tax liability)**
An asset (e.g., accounts receivable or investment) may be recognized for revenues or gains that will result in **taxable amounts in future years** when the asset is recovered. Examples:
1. Sales accounted for on the accrual basis for financial reporting purposes and on the installment (cash) basis for tax purposes.
2. Contracts accounted for under the percentage-of-completion method for financial reporting purposes and the cost-recovery method (zero-profit method) for tax purposes.
3. Investments accounted for under the equity method for financial reporting purposes and under the cost method for tax purposes.
4. Gain on involuntary conversion of non-monetary asset which is recognized for financial reporting purposes but deferred for tax purposes.
5. Unrealized holding gains for financial reporting purposes (including use of the fair value option) but deferred for tax purposes.

B. **Expenses or losses are deductible after they are recognized in financial income. (Deferred tax asset)**
A liability (or contra asset) may be recognized for expenses or losses that will result in **deductible amounts in future years** when the liability is settled. Examples:
1. Product warranty liabilities.
2. Estimated liabilities related to discontinued operations or restructurings.
3. Litigation accruals.
4. Bad debt expense recognized using the allowance method for financial reporting purposes; direct write-off method used for tax purposes.
5. Share-based compensation expense.
6. Unrealized holding losses for financial reporting purposes (including use of the fair value option) but deferred for tax purposes.

C. **Revenues or gains are taxable before they are recognized in financial income. (Deferred tax asset)**
A liability may be recognized for an advance payment for goods or services to be provided in future years. For tax purposes, the advance payment is included in taxable income upon the receipt of cash. Future sacrifices to provide goods or services (or future refunds to those who cancel their orders) that settle the liability will result in **deductible amounts in future years**. Examples:
1. Subscriptions received in advance.
2. Advance rental receipts.
3. Sales and leasebacks for financial reporting purposes (income deferral) but reported as sales for tax purposes.
4. Prepaid contracts and royalties received in advance.

D. **Expenses or losses are deductible before they are recognized in financial income. (Deferred tax liability)**
The cost of an asset may have been deducted for tax purposes faster than it was expensed for financial reporting purposes. Amounts received upon future recovery of the amount of the asset for financial reporting (through use or sale) will exceed the remaining tax basis of the asset and thereby result in **taxable amounts in future years**. Examples:
1. Depreciable property, depletable resources, and intangibles.
2. Deductible pension funding exceeding expense.
3. Prepaid expenses that are deducted on the tax return in the period paid.
4. Development costs that are deducted on the tax return in the period paid.

Determining a company's temporary differences may prove difficult. A company should prepare a statement of financial position for tax purposes that it can compare with its IFRS statement of financial position. Many of the differences between the two statements of financial position are temporary differences.

Originating and Reversing Aspects of Temporary Differences. An **originating temporary difference** is the initial difference between the book basis and the tax basis of an asset or liability, regardless of whether the tax basis of the asset or liability exceeds or is exceeded by the book basis of the asset or liability. A **reversing difference**, on the other hand, occurs when eliminating a temporary difference that originated in prior periods and then removing the related tax effect from the deferred tax account.

For example, assume that Sharp Co. has tax depreciation in excess of book depreciation of £2,000 in 2009, 2010, and 2011. Further, it has an excess of book depreciation over tax depreciation of £3,000 in 2012 and 2013 for the same asset. Assuming a tax rate of 30 percent for all years involved, the Deferred Tax Liability account reflects the following.

ILLUSTRATION 19-23
Tax Effects of Originating and Reversing Differences

	Deferred Tax Liability			
Tax Effects	⎰2012	900	2009	600⎱	Tax Effects
of	⎱2013	900	2010	600⎰	of
Reversing Differences			2011	600⎱	Originating Differences

The originating differences for Sharp in each of the first three years are £2,000. The related tax effect of each originating difference is £600. The reversing differences in 2012 and 2013 are each £3,000. The related tax effect of each is £900.

Permanent Differences

Some differences between taxable income and pretax financial income are permanent. **Permanent differences** result from items that (1) enter into pretax financial income but **never** into taxable income, or (2) enter into taxable income but **never** into pretax financial income.

Governments enact a variety of tax law provisions to attain certain political, economic, and social objectives. Some of these provisions exclude certain revenues from taxation, limit the deductibility of certain expenses, and permit the deduction of certain other expenses in excess of costs incurred. A corporation that has tax-free income, non-deductible expenses, or allowable deductions in excess of cost, has an effective tax rate that differs from its statutory (regular) tax rate.

Since permanent differences affect only the period in which they occur, they do not give rise to future taxable or deductible amounts. As a result, **companies recognize no deferred tax consequences**. Illustration 19-24 shows examples of permanent differences, given typical country laws.

ILLUSTRATION 19-24
Examples of Permanent Differences

A. **Items are recognized for financial reporting purposes but not for tax purposes.**
   Examples:
   1. Interest received on certain types of government obligations.
   2. Expenses incurred in obtaining tax-exempt income.
   3. Fines and expenses resulting from a violation of law.
   4. Charitable donations recognized as expense but sometimes not deductible for tax purposes.
B. **Items are recognized for tax purposes but not for financial reporting purposes.**
   Examples:
   1. "Percentage depletion" of natural resources in excess of their cost.
   2. The deduction for dividends received from U.S. corporations, generally 70% or 80%.

Examples of Temporary and Permanent Differences

To illustrate the computations used when both temporary and permanent differences exist, assume that Bio-Tech Company reports pretax financial income of $200,000 in each of the years 2009, 2010, and 2011. The company is subject to a 30 percent tax rate, and has the following differences between pretax financial income and taxable income.

1. Bio-Tech reports an installment sale of $18,000 in 2009 for tax purposes over an 18-month period at a constant amount per month beginning January 1, 2010. It recognizes the entire sale for book purposes in 2009.

2. It pays life insurance premiums for its key officers of $5,000 in 2010 and 2011. Although not tax-deductible, Bio-Tech expenses the premiums for book purposes.

The installment sale is a temporary difference, whereas the life insurance premium is a permanent difference. Illustration 19-25 shows the reconciliation of Bio-Tech's pretax financial income to taxable income and the computation of income tax payable.

ILLUSTRATION 19-25
Reconciliation and Computation of Income Taxes Payable

	2009	2010	2011
Pretax financial income	$200,000	$200,000	$200,000
Permanent difference			
Non-deductible expense		5,000	5,000
Temporary difference			
Installment sale	(18,000)	12,000	6,000
Taxable income	182,000	217,000	211,000
Tax rate	× 30%	× 30%	× 30%
Income tax payable	$ 54,600	$ 65,100	$ 63,300

Note that Bio-Tech **deducts** the installment sales revenue from pretax financial income to arrive at taxable income. The reason: Pretax financial income includes the installment sales revenue; taxable income does not. Conversely, it **adds** the $5,000 insurance premium to pretax financial income to arrive at taxable income. The reason: Pretax financial income records an expense for this premium, but for tax purposes the premium is not deductible. As a result, pretax financial income is lower than taxable income. Therefore, the life insurance premium must be added back to pretax financial income to reconcile to taxable income.

Bio-Tech records income taxes for 2009, 2010, and 2011 as follows.

December 31, 2009

Income Tax Expense ($54,600 + $5,400)	60,000	
Deferred Tax Liability ($18,000 × 30%)		5,400
Income Tax Payable ($182,000 × 30%)		54,600

December 31, 2010

Income Tax Expense ($65,100 − $3,600)	61,500	
Deferred Tax Liability ($12,000 × 30%)	3,600	
Income Tax Payable ($217,000 × 30%)		65,100

December 31, 2011

Income Tax Expense ($63,300 − $1,800)	61,500	
Deferred Tax Liability ($6,000 × 30%)	1,800	
Income Tax Payable ($211,000 × 30%)		63,300

Bio-Tech has one temporary difference, which originates in 2009 and reverses in 2010 and 2011. It recognizes a deferred tax liability at the end of 2009 because the temporary difference causes future taxable amounts. As the temporary difference reverses, Bio-Tech reduces the deferred tax liability. There is no deferred tax amount associated with the difference caused by the non-deductible insurance expense because it is a permanent difference.

Although an enacted tax rate of 30 percent applies for all three years, the effective rate differs from the enacted rate in 2010 and 2011. Bio-Tech computes the **effective tax rate** by dividing total income tax expense for the period by pretax financial income. The effective rate is 30 percent for 2009 ($60,000 ÷ $200,000 = 30%) and 30.75 percent for 2010 and 2011 ($61,500 ÷ $200,000 = 30.75%).

Tax Rate Considerations

<table>
<tr><td>

Objective·7

Explain the effect of various tax rates and tax rate changes on deferred income taxes.

</td></tr>
</table>

In our previous illustrations, the enacted tax rate did not change from one year to the next. Thus, to compute the deferred income tax amount to report on the statement of financial position, a company simply multiplies the cumulative temporary difference by the current tax rate. Using Bio-Tech as an example, it multiplies the cumulative temporary difference of $18,000 by the enacted tax rate, 30 percent in this case, to arrive at a deferred tax liability of $5,400 ($18,000 × 30%) at the end of 2009.

Future Tax Rates

What happens if tax rates are expected to change in the future? In this case, a company should use the **substantially enacted tax rate** expected to apply.[2] Therefore, a company must consider presently enacted changes in the tax rate that become effective for a particular future year(s) when determining the tax rate to apply to existing temporary differences. For example, assume that Warlen Co. at the end of 2008 has the following cumulative temporary difference of $300,000, computed as shown in Illustration 19-26.

ILLUSTRATION 19-26
Computation of
Cumulative Temporary
Difference

Book basis of depreciable assets	$1,000,000
Tax basis of depreciable assets	700,000
Cumulative temporary difference	$ 300,000

Furthermore, assume that the $300,000 will reverse and result in taxable amounts in the future, with the enacted tax rates shown in Illustration 19-27.

ILLUSTRATION 19-27
Deferred Tax Liability
Based on Future Rates

	2009	2010	2011	2012	2013	Total
Future taxable amounts	$80,000	$70,000	$60,000	$50,000	$40,000	$300,000
Tax rate	× 40%	× 40%	× 35%	× 30%	× 30%	
Deferred tax liability	$32,000	$28,000	$21,000	$15,000	$12,000	$108,000

The total deferred tax liability at the end of 2008 is $108,000. Warlen may only use tax rates other than the current rate when the future tax rates have been enacted, as is the case in this example. **If new rates are not yet enacted for future years, Warlen should use the current rate.**

In some countries, the applicable tax rate depends on how the carrying amount of an asset or liability is recovered or settled. For example, a company could be operating a plant that it intends to hold for continued use. The tax rate on normal operations is 35 percent. On the other hand, if the company wishes to sell the plant and the related capital gain or loss is subject to a tax rate of 15 percent, then the applicable tax rate may change. [3]

Revision of Future Tax Rates

When a change in the tax rate is enacted, companies should record its effect on the existing deferred income tax accounts immediately. **A company reports the effect as an adjustment to income tax expense in the period of the change.**

Assume that on December 10, 2010, a new income tax act is signed into law that lowers the corporate tax rate from 40 percent to 35 percent, effective January 1, 2012.

[2]Substantially enacted generally means "virtually certain." The IASB provides guidelines as to how to interpret substantially enacted. [2] *For purposes of discussion and homework, assume that the term "enacted" is interchangeable with "substantially enacted."*

If Hostel Co. has one temporary difference at the beginning of 2010 related to $3 million of excess tax depreciation, then it has a Deferred Tax Liability account with a balance of $1,200,000 ($3,000,000 × 40%) at January 1, 2010. If taxable amounts related to this difference are scheduled to occur equally in 2011, 2012, and 2013, the deferred tax liability at the end of 2010 is $1,100,000, computed as follows.

	2011	2012	2013	Total
Future taxable amounts	$1,000,000	$1,000,000	$1,000,000	$3,000,000
Tax rate	× 40%	× 35%	× 35%	
Deferred tax liability	$ 400,000	$ 350,000	$ 350,000	$1,100,000

ILLUSTRATION 19-28
Schedule of Future Taxable Amounts and Related Tax Rates

Hostel, therefore, recognizes the decrease of $100,000 ($1,200,000 − $1,100,000) at the end of 2010 in the deferred tax liability as follows.

Deferred Tax Liability	100,000	
Income Tax Expense		100,000

Corporate tax rates do not change often. Therefore, companies usually employ the current rate. However, tax rates in some jurisdictions change more frequently, and they require adjustments in deferred income taxes accordingly.[3]

GLOBAL TAX RATES

What do the numbers mean?

If you are concerned about your tax rate and the taxes you pay, you might want to consider moving to Switzerland, which has a personal tax rate of anywhere from zero percent to 13.2 percent. You don't want to move to Denmark though. Yes, the people of Denmark are regularly voted to be the happiest people on Earth but it's uncertain how many of these polls take place at tax time. The government in Denmark charges income tax rates ranging from 38 percent to 59 percent. So, taxes are a major item to many individuals, wherever they reside.

Taxes are also a big deal to corporations. For example, the Organisation for Economic Co-operation and Development (OECD) is an international organization of 30 countries that accept the principles of a free-market economy. Most OECD members are high-income economies and are regarded as developed countries. However, companies in the OECD can be subject to significant tax levies, as indicated in the following list of the ten highest corporate income tax rates for the OECD countries.

Japan	39.54%	**Germany**	30.18%
United States	39.25	**Australia**	30.00
France	34.43	**New Zealand**	30.00
Belgium	33.99	**Spain**	30.00
Canada	33.50	**OECD Average**	26.60
Luxembourg	30.38		

On the low end of the tax rate spectrum are Iceland and Ireland, with tax rates of 15 percent and 12.5 percent, respectively. Indeed, corporate tax rates have been dropping around the world as countries attempt to spur capital investment, which in turn spurs international tax competition. However, with stagnant global economic growth, there is concern that governments will target increases in corporate tax rates as a source of revenues to address budget shortfalls. In addition, further expansion of value-added taxes (VAT) is being considered. Indirect taxes such as VAT are charged on consumption of goods and services, which is much more stable than the corporate tax.

Source: P. Toscano, "The World's Highest Tax Rates," http://www.cnbc.com/id/30727913 (May 13, 2009).

---

[3]Tax rate changes nearly always will substantially impact income numbers and the reporting of deferred income taxes on the statement of financial position. As a result, you can expect to hear an economic consequences argument every time that a legislature decides to change the tax rates. For example, when one country raised the corporate rate from 34 percent to 35 percent, companies took an additional "hit" to earnings if they were in a deferred tax liability position.

ACCOUNTING FOR NET OPERATING LOSSES

Objective·8

Apply accounting procedures for a loss carryback and a loss carryforward.

Every management hopes its company will be profitable. But hopes and profits may not materialize. For a start-up company, it is common to accumulate operating losses while expanding its customer base but before realizing economies of scale. For an established company, a major event such as a labor strike, a rapidly changing regulatory, or a competitive situation can cause expenses to exceed revenues—a net operating loss.

A **net operating loss (NOL)** occurs for tax purposes in a year when tax-deductible expenses exceed taxable revenues. An inequitable tax burden would result if companies were taxed during profitable periods without receiving any tax relief during periods of net operating losses. Under certain circumstances, therefore, tax laws permit taxpayers to use the losses of one year to offset the profits of other years.

Companies accomplish this income-averaging provision through the **carryback and carryforward of net operating losses**. Under this provision, a company pays no income taxes for a year in which it incurs a net operating loss. In addition, it may select one of the two options discussed below and on the following pages.[4]

Loss Carryback

Through use of a **loss carryback**, a company may carry the net operating loss back two years and receive refunds for income taxes paid in those years. The company must apply the loss to the earlier year first and then to the second year. It may **carry forward** any loss remaining after the two-year carryback up to 20 years to offset future taxable income. Illustration 19-29 diagrams the loss carryback procedure, assuming a loss in 2011.

ILLUSTRATION 19-29
Loss Carryback Procedure

Loss Carryforward

A company may forgo the loss carryback and use only the **loss carryforward** option, offsetting future taxable income for up to 20 years. Illustration 19-30 shows this approach.

ILLUSTRATION 19-30
Loss Carryforward Procedure

[4]Countries differ as to the years that operating losses can be carried back and forward. In our discussion, we assume that companies can carry their operating losses back two years and can carry them forward 20 years. *For homework purposes, use these periods as the basis for carrybacks and carryforwards.*

Operating losses can be substantial. For example, **Yahoo!** (USA) had net operating losses of approximately $5.4 billion in a recent year. That amount translates into tax savings of $1.4 billion if Yahoo! is able to generate taxable income before the NOLs expire.

Loss Carryback Example

To illustrate the accounting procedures for a net operating loss carryback, assume that Groh Inc. has no temporary or permanent differences. Groh experiences the following.

Year	Taxable Income or Loss	Tax Rate	Tax Paid
2007	$ 50,000	35%	$17,500
2008	100,000	30%	30,000
2009	200,000	40%	80,000
2010	(500,000)	—	–0–

In 2010, Groh incurs a net operating loss that it decides to carry back. Under the law, Groh must apply the carryback first to the **second year preceding the loss year**. Therefore, it carries the loss back first to 2008. Then, Groh carries back any unused loss to 2009. Accordingly, Groh files amended tax returns for 2008 and 2009, receiving refunds for the $110,000 ($30,000 + $80,000) of taxes paid in those years.

For accounting as well as tax purposes, the $110,000 represents the **tax effect (tax benefit)** of the loss carryback. Groh should recognize this tax effect in 2010, the loss year. Since the tax loss gives rise to a refund that is both measurable and currently realizable, Groh should recognize the associated tax benefit in this loss period.

Groh makes the following journal entry for 2010.

Income Tax Refund Receivable	110,000	
Benefit Due to Loss Carryback (Income Tax Expense)		110,000

Groh reports the account debited, **Income Tax Refund Receivable**, on the statement of financial position as a current asset at December 31, 2010. It reports the account credited on the income statement for 2010 as shown in Illustration 19-31.

GROH INC.	
INCOME STATEMENT (PARTIAL) FOR 2010	
Operating loss before income taxes	$(500,000)
Income tax benefit	
Benefit due to loss carryback	110,000
Net loss	$(390,000)

ILLUSTRATION 19-31
Recognition of Benefit of the Loss Carryback in the Loss Year

Since the $500,000 net operating loss for 2010 exceeds the $300,000 total taxable income from the two preceding years, Groh carries forward the remaining $200,000 loss.

Loss Carryforward Example

If a carryback fails to fully absorb a net operating loss or if the company decides not to carry the loss back, then it can carry forward the loss for up to 20 years. Because companies use carryforwards to offset future taxable income, the **tax effect of a loss carryforward** represents **future tax savings**. Realization of the future tax benefit depends on future earnings, an uncertain prospect.

The key accounting issue is whether there should be different requirements for recognition of a deferred tax asset for (a) deductible temporary differences, and (b) operating loss carryforwards. The IASB's position is that in substance these items are the same—both are tax-deductible amounts in future years. As a result, the Board concluded that there **should not be different requirements** for recognition of a deferred tax asset from deductible temporary differences and operating loss carryforwards.[5]

Carryforward (Recognition)

To illustrate the accounting for an operating loss carryforward, return to the Groh example from the preceding section. In 2010, the company records the tax effect of the $200,000 loss carryforward as a deferred tax asset of $80,000 ($200,000 × 40%), assuming that the enacted future tax rate is 40 percent. Groh records the benefits of the carryback and the carryforward in 2010 as follows.

To recognize benefit of loss carryback

Income Tax Refund Receivable	110,000	
Benefit Due to Loss Carryback (Income Tax Expense)		110,000

To recognize benefit of loss carryforward

Deferred Tax Asset	80,000	
Benefit Due to Loss Carryforward (Income Tax Expense)		80,000

Groh realizes the income tax refund receivable of $110,000 immediately as a refund of taxes paid in the past. It establishes a Deferred Tax Asset for the benefits of future tax savings. The two accounts credited are contra income tax expense items, which Groh presents on the 2010 income statement shown in Illustration 19-32.

ILLUSTRATION 19-32
Recognition of the Benefit of the Loss Carryback and Carryforward in the Loss Year

GROH INC.		
INCOME STATEMENT (PARTIAL) FOR 2010		
Operating loss before income taxes		$(500,000)
Income tax benefit		
Benefit due to loss carryback	$110,000	
Benefit due to loss carryforward	80,000	190,000
Net loss		$(310,000)

The **current tax benefit** of $110,000 is the income tax refundable for the year. Groh determines this amount by applying the carryback provisions of the tax law to the taxable loss for 2010. The $80,000 is the **deferred tax benefit** for the year, which results from an increase in the deferred tax asset.

For 2011, assume that Groh returns to profitable operations and has taxable income of $250,000 (prior to adjustment for the NOL carryforward), subject to a 40 percent tax rate. Groh then realizes the benefits of the carryforward for tax purposes in 2011, which it recognized for accounting purposes in 2010. Groh computes the income tax payable for 2011 as shown in Illustration 19-33.

ILLUSTRATION 19-33
Computation of Income Tax Payable with Realized Loss Carryforward

Taxable income prior to loss carryforward	$ 250,000
Loss carryforward deduction	(200,000)
Taxable income for 2011	50,000
Tax rate	× 40%
Income tax payable for 2011	$ 20,000

[5]This requirement is controversial because some believe that companies should never recognize deferred tax assets for loss carryforwards until realizing the income in the future.

Groh records income taxes in 2011 as follows.

Income Tax Expense	100,000	
Deferred Tax Asset		80,000
Income Tax Payable		20,000

The benefits of the NOL carryforward, realized in 2011, reduce the Deferred Tax Asset account to zero.

The 2011 income statement that appears in Illustration 19-34 does **not report** the tax effects of either the loss carryback or the loss carryforward, because Groh had reported both previously.

ILLUSTRATION 19-34
Presentation of the Benefit of Loss Carryforward Realized in 2011, Recognized in 2010

GROH INC.
INCOME STATEMENT (PARTIAL) FOR 2011

Income before income taxes		$250,000
Income tax expense		
Current	$20,000	
Deferred	80,000	100,000
Net income		$150,000

Carryforward (Non-Recognition)

Let us return to the Groh example. Assume that it is probable that Groh will *not* realize the entire NOL carryforward in future years. In this situation, Groh records the tax benefits of $110,000 associated with the $300,000 NOL carryback, as we previously described. It does not recognize a deferred tax asset for the loss carryforward because it is probable that it will not realize the carryforward. Groh makes the following journal entry in 2010.

To recognize benefit of loss carryback

Income Tax Refund Receivable	110,000	
Benefit Due to Loss Carryback (Income Tax Expense)		110,000

Illustration 19-35 shows Groh's 2010 income statement presentation.

ILLUSTRATION 19-35
Recognition of Benefit of Loss Carryback Only

GROH INC.
INCOME STATEMENT (PARTIAL) FOR 2010

Operating loss before income taxes	$(500,000)
Income tax benefit	
Benefit due to loss carryback	110,000
Net loss	$(390,000)

In 2011, assuming that Groh has taxable income of $250,000 (before considering the carryforward), subject to a tax rate of 40 percent, it realizes the deferred tax asset. Groh records the following entries.

To recognize deferred tax asset and loss carryforward

Deferred Tax Asset	80,000	
Benefit Due to Loss Carryforward (Income Tax Expense)		80,000

To record current and deferred income taxes

Income Tax Expense	100,000	
Deferred Tax Asset		80,000
Income Tax Payable		20,000

Groh reports the $80,000 Benefit Due to the Loss Carryforward on the 2011 income statement. The company did not recognize it in 2010 because it was probable that it would not be realized. Assuming that Groh derives the income for 2011 from continuing operations, it prepares the income statement as shown in Illustration 19-36.

ILLUSTRATION 19-36
Recognition of Benefit of Loss Carryforward When Realized

GROH INC.		
INCOME STATEMENT (PARTIAL) FOR 2011		
Income before income taxes		$250,000
Income tax expense		
Current	$ 20,000	
Deferred	80,000	
Benefit due to loss carryforward	(80,000)	20,000
Net income		$230,000

Another method is to report only one line for total income tax expense of $20,000 on the face of the income statement and disclose the components of income tax expense in the notes to the financial statements.

Non-Recognition Revisited

Whether the company will realize a deferred tax asset depends on whether sufficient taxable income exists or will exist within the carryforward period available under tax law. Illustration 19-37 shows possible sources of taxable income and related factors that companies can consider in assessing the probability that taxable income will be available against which the unused tax losses or unused tax credits can be utilized.[6]

ILLUSTRATION 19-37
Possible Sources of Taxable Income

Taxable Income Sources
a. Whether the company has sufficient taxable temporary differences relating to the same tax authority, which will result in taxable amounts against which the unused tax losses or unused tax credits can be utilized before they expire;
b. Whether it is probable that the company will have taxable profits before the unused tax losses or unused tax credits expire;
c. Whether the unused tax losses result from identifiable causes, which are unlikely to recur; and
d. Whether tax-planning opportunities are available to the company that will create taxable profit in the period in which the unused tax losses or unused tax credits can be utilized. [4]

To the extent that it is not probable that taxable profit will be available against which the unused tax losses or unused tax credits can be utilized, the deferred tax asset is not recognized.

Forming a conclusion that recognition of a loss carryforward is probable is difficult when there is negative evidence (such as cumulative losses in recent years). However, companies often cite positive evidence indicating that recognition of the carryforward is warranted.[7]

---

[6]Companies implement a tax-planning strategy to realize a tax benefit for an operating loss or tax carryforward before it expires. Companies consider tax-planning strategies when assessing the need of a deferred tax asset to recognize.

[7]**General Motors (GM)** (USA) announced that it would record a charge of $39 billion for the third quarter of 2007 related to establishing an impairment against its deferred assets in the United States, Canada, and Germany. The company noted that this large loss was taken because of the company's three-year historical loss up to the third quarter of 2007, its losses related to its mortgage business in GMAC financial services, and the challenging near-term automotive market conditions in the United States and Germany. These all indicate that it is probable that GM will not realize its deferred tax asset.

Unfortunately, the subjective nature of determining an impairment for a deferred tax asset provides a company with an opportunity to manage its earnings. As one accounting expert notes, "The 'probable' provision is perhaps the most judgmental clause in accounting." Some companies may recognize the loss carryforward immediately and then use it to increase income as needed. Others may take the income immediately to increase capital or to offset large negative charges to income.

FINANCIAL STATEMENT PRESENTATION

Statement of Financial Position

Companies classify taxes receivable or payable as current assets or current liabilities. Although current tax assets and liabilities are separately recognized and measured, they are often offset in the statement of financial position. The offset occurs because companies normally have a legally enforceable right to set off a current tax asset (Taxes Receivable) against a current tax liability (Taxes Payable) when they relate to income taxes levied by the same taxation authority. [5] Deferred tax assets and deferred tax liabilities are also separately recognized and measured but may be offset in the statement of financial position.[8] The net deferred tax asset or net deferred tax liability is reported in the non-current section of the statement of financial position.[9]

Objective•9
Describe the presentation of income taxes in financial statements.

To illustrate, assume that K. Scott Company has four deferred tax items at December 31, 2011, as shown in Illustration 19-38.

ILLUSTRATION 19-38
Classification of Temporary Differences

Temporary Difference	Resulting Deferred Tax (Asset)	Liability
1. Rent collected in advance: recognized when earned for accounting purposes and when received for tax purposes.	$(42,000)	
2. Use of straight-line depreciation for accounting purposes and accelerated depreciation for tax purposes.		$214,000
3. Recognition of profits on installment sales during period of sale for accounting purposes and during period of collection for tax purposes.		45,000
4. Warranty liabilities: recognized for accounting purposes at time of sale; for tax purposes at time paid.	(12,000)	
Totals	$(54,000)	$259,000

As indicated, K. Scott has a total deferred tax asset of $54,000 and a total deferred tax liability of $259,000. Assuming these two items can be offset, K. Scott reports a deferred tax liability of $205,000 ($259,000 − $54,000) in the non-current liability section of its statement of financial position.

To provide another illustration, **Wm Morrison Supermarkets plc** (GBR) reports its information related to income taxes on the statement of financial position and related notes as shown in Illustration 19-39 (on page 1032).

[8]Companies are permitted to offset deferred tax assets and deferred tax liabilities if, and only if: (1) the company has a legally enforceable right to set off current tax assets against current tax liabilities; and (2) the deferred tax assets and the deferred tax liabilities relate to income taxes levied by the same tax authority and for the same company. [6]

[9]Deferred tax amounts should not be discounted. The IASB apparently considers discounting to be an unnecessary complication even if the effects are material. [7]

Wm Morrison Supermarkets plc
(£m)

Statement of Financial Position
31 January 2010

Current liabilities		
Current tax liabilities		71
Non-current liabilities		
Deferred tax liabilities	(Note 20)	515

20 DEFERRED TAX

	2010 (£m)
Deferred tax liability	(563)
Deferred tax asset	48
Net deferred tax liability	(515)

IAS 12 *Income taxes* permits the offsetting of balances within the same tax jurisdiction. All of the deferred tax assets were available for offset against deferred tax liabilities.

The movements in deferred tax assets/(liabilities) during the period are shown below.

	Property, plant and equipment £m	Pensions £m	Share-based payments £m	Other short term temporary differences £m	Total £m
Current year					
At 1 February 2009	(546)	14	6	54	(472)
Charged to income statement	(17)	(29)	(3)	(33)	(82)
Credited to other comprehensive income	—	20	—	19	39
At 31 January 2010	(563)	5	3	40	(515)

The deferred income tax credited/(charged) though other comprehensive income during the period was as follows:

	2010 £m
Actuarial losses	20
Short term temporary differences	19

ILLUSTRATION 19-39
Income Tax Reporting

Note that Morrisons explains how the deferred income liability is computed as well as the composition of the net deferred income tax liability. A user of the financial statements and related notes therefore understands what comprises the net deferred tax liability of £515 million, which provides insight into the likelihood of future cash outflows related to the net deferred tax liability.

Income Statement

Companies allocate income tax expense (or benefit) to continuing operations, discontinued operations, other comprehensive income, and prior period adjustments. This approach is referred to as **intraperiod tax allocation**. In addition, the components of income tax expense (benefit) may include:

1. Current tax expense (benefit).
2. Any adjustments recognized in the period for current tax of prior periods.

3. The amount of deferred tax expense (benefit) relating to the origination and reversal of temporary differences.

4. The amount of deferred tax expense (benefit) relating to changes in tax rates or the imposition of new taxes.

5. The amount of the benefit arising from a previously unrecognized tax loss, tax credit, or temporary difference of a prior period that is used to reduce current and deferred tax expense.[10]

To illustrate, the relevant portion of the income statement of **Wm Morrison Supermarkets plc** (GBR) is presented in Illustration 19-40.

ILLUSTRATION 19-40
Income Statement and
Related Tax Note

Wm Morrison Supermarkets plc
(£m)

Income Statement (Partial)
52 weeks ended 31 January, 2010

Profit before taxation	£858
Taxation (note 6)	(260)
Profit for the period attributable to the owners of the Company	598
Other comprehensive (expense)/income:	
Actuarial loss arising in the pension scheme	(71)
Foreign exchange movements	(1)
Cash flow hedging movement	(11)
Tax in relation to components of other comprehensive (expense)/income (note 6)	22
Other comprehensive expense for the period, net of tax	£ (61)

6 TAXATION
a) Analysis of charge in the period

	2010 (£m)
Corporation tax	
- current period	205
- adjustment in respect of prior period	(27)
	178
Deferred tax	
- current period	54
- adjustment in respect of prior period	28
	82
Tax charge for the period	260

b) Tax on items (credited)/charged in other comprehensive income

	2010 £m
Actuarial loss arising in the pension scheme	(20)
Cash flow hedges	(2)
Total tax on items included in other comprehensive income	(22)
Analysis of items (credited)/charged to other comprehensive income:	
Current tax	17
Deferred tax (note 20)	(39)

[10]Other components that should be reported are the deferred tax expense arising from the write-down, or reversal of a previous write-down, of a deferred tax asset, as well as the amount of tax expense (benefit) relating to those changes in accounting policies and errors that are included in profit or loss in accordance with *IAS 8*. **[8]**

As indicated, Morrisons's income tax expense is comprised of current taxes payable, a refund from a prior period, and an increase in the deferred tax liability.

Another requirement is that companies report the current deferred tax related to equity and to each component of other comprehensive income. In addition, the tax effect related to gain or loss on discontinued operations and on the ordinary income from the discontinued operation should be disclosed. In the case of Morrisons, it had a current tax payable related to other comprehensive income of £17 million, and an increase in deferred tax assets of £39 million, for a decrease in income tax expense of £22 million.

Tax Reconciliation

Another important disclosure is the reconciliation between actual tax expense and the applicable tax rate. Companies either provide:

- A numerical reconciliation between tax expense (benefit) and the product of accounting profit multiplied by the applicable tax rate(s), disclosing also the basis on which the applicable tax rate(s) is (are) computed; or
- A numerical reconciliation between the average effective tax rate and the applicable tax rate, disclosing also the basis on which the applicable tax rate is computed.

Morrisons provides the first type of reconciliation but also notes that the effective tax rate is higher than the applicable (standard) rate, as shown in a continuation of its tax note in Illustration 19-41.

ILLUSTRATION 19-41
Tax Reconciliation
Disclosure

Wm Morrison Supermarkets plc

c) Tax reconciliation
The tax for both periods is higher than the standard rate of corporation tax in the UK of 28% (2009: 28%). The differences are explained below:

	2010 (£m)
Profit before tax	858
Profit before tax at 28%	240
Effects of:	
Expenses not deductible for tax purposes	4
Non-qualifying depreciation	24
Deferred tax on Safeway acquisition assets	(8)
Divestment profits not taxable	1
Other	(2)
Prior period adjustments	1
Tax charge for the period	260

In explaining the relationship between tax expense (benefit) and accounting income, companies use an applicable tax rate that provides the most meaningful information to the users of its financial statements.[11]

---

[11]Often, the most meaningful rate is the domestic rate of tax in the country in which the company is located, aggregating the tax rate applied for national taxes, with the rates applied for any local taxes, which are computed on a substantially similar level of taxable profit (tax loss). However, for a company operating in several jurisdictions, it may be more meaningful to aggregate separate reconciliations prepared using the domestic rate in each individual jurisdiction.

These income tax disclosures are required for several reasons:

1. *Assessing quality of earnings.* Many investors seeking to assess the quality of a company's earnings are interested in the relation between pretax financial income and taxable income. Analysts carefully examine earnings that are enhanced by a favorable tax effect, particularly if the tax effect is non-recurring. For Morrisons, it is interesting to note that its applicable tax rate is less than the effective tax rate (taxes paid divided by income before income taxes). One question that the analyst might ask is whether this is a continuing situation or if the reverse will occur in future periods.

2. *Making better predictions of future cash flows.* Examination of the deferred portion of income tax expense provides information as to whether taxes payable are likely to be higher or lower in the future. In Morrisons's case, analysts expect future taxable amounts and higher tax payments, due to lower depreciation in the future. It also appears that Morrisons is generating other deductible amounts related to pensions, share-based payments, and other short-term temporary differences. These deferred tax items indicate that actual tax payments for Morrisons will be higher than the tax expense reported on the income statement in the future.

3. *Predicting future cash flows for operating loss carryforwards.* Companies should disclose the amounts and expiration dates of any operating loss carryforwards for tax purposes. From this disclosure, analysts determine the amount of income that the company may recognize in the future on which it will pay no income tax.

   Loss carryforwards can be valuable to a potential acquirer. For example, as mentioned earlier, **Yahoo!** has a substantial net operating loss carryforward. A potential acquirer would find Yahoo more valuable as a result of these carryforwards. That is, the acquirer may be able to use these carryforwards to shield future income. However, the acquiring company has to be careful because the structure of the deal may lead to a situation where the deductions will be severely limited.[12]

REVIEW OF THE ASSET-LIABILITY METHOD

The IASB believes that the **asset-liability method** (sometimes referred to as the **liability approach**) is the most consistent method for accounting for income taxes. One objective of this approach is to recognize the amount of taxes payable or refundable for the current year. A second objective is to recognize **deferred tax liabilities and assets** for the **future tax consequences** of events that have been recognized in the financial statements or tax returns.

> **Objective·10**
> Indicate the basic principles of the asset-liability method.

To implement the objectives, companies apply some basic principles in accounting for income taxes at the date of the financial statements, as listed in Illustration 19-42.

ILLUSTRATION 19-42
Basic Principles of the Asset-Liability Method

Basic Principles
a. A current tax liability or asset is recognized for the estimated taxes payable or refundable on the tax return for the current year.
b. A deferred tax liability or asset is recognized for the estimated future tax effects attributable to temporary differences and carryforwards.
c. The measurement of current and deferred tax liabilities and assets is based on provisions of the enacted tax law; the effects of future changes in tax laws or rates are not anticipated.
d. The measurement of deferred tax assets is reduced, if necessary, by the amount of any tax benefits that, based on available evidence, are not expected to be realized.

[12]P. McConnell, J. Pegg, C. Senyak, and D. Mott, "The ABCs of NOLs," *Accounting Issues*, Bear Stearns Equity Research (June 2005). Regulators frown on acquisitions done solely to obtain operating loss carryforwards. If it determines that the merger is solely tax-motivated, the regulators generally disallow the deductions. But, because it is very difficult to determine whether a merger is or is not tax-motivated, the "purchase of operating loss carryforwards" continues.

Illustration 19-43 diagrams the procedures for implementing the asset-liability method.

ILLUSTRATION 19-43
Procedures for Computing and Reporting Deferred Income Taxes

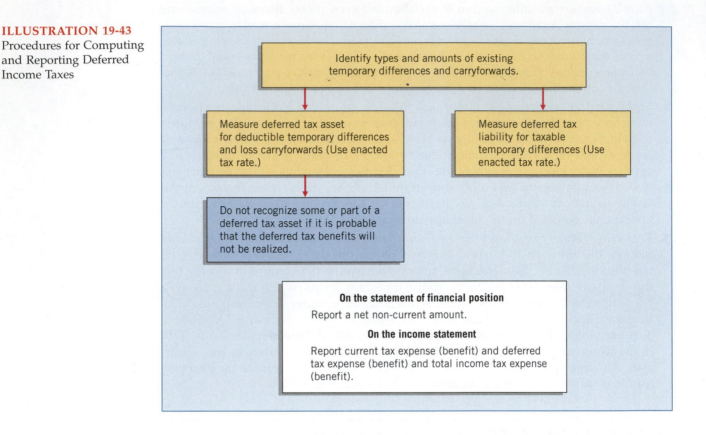

As an aid to understanding deferred income taxes, we provide the following glossary.

KEY DEFERRED INCOME TAX TERMS

CARRYBACKS. Deductions or credits that cannot be utilized on the tax return during a year and that may be carried back to reduce taxable income or taxes paid in a prior year. An **operating loss carryback** is an excess of tax deductions over gross income in a year. A **tax carryback** is the amount by which tax credits available for utilization exceed statutory limitations.

CARRYFORWARDS. Deductions or credits that cannot be utilized on the tax return during a year and that may be carried forward to reduce taxable income or taxes payable in a future year. An **operating loss carryforward** is an excess of tax deductions over gross income in a year. A **tax carryforward** is the amount by which tax credits available for utilization exceed statutory limitations.

CURRENT TAX EXPENSE (BENEFIT). The amount of income taxes paid or payable (or refundable) for a year as determined by applying the provisions of the enacted tax law to the taxable income or excess of deductions over revenues for that year.

DEDUCTIBLE TEMPORARY DIFFERENCE. Temporary differences that result in deductible amounts in future years when recovering or settling the related asset or liability, respectively.

DEFERRED TAX ASSET. The deferred tax consequences attributable to deductible temporary differences and carryforwards.

DEFERRED TAX CONSEQUENCES. The future effects on income taxes as measured by the enacted tax rate and provisions of the enacted tax law resulting from temporary differences and carryforwards at the end of the current year.

DEFERRED TAX EXPENSE (BENEFIT). The change during the year in a company's deferred tax liabilities and assets.

DEFERRED TAX LIABILITY. The deferred tax consequences attributable to taxable temporary differences.

INCOME TAXES. Domestic and foreign federal (national), state, and local (including franchise) taxes based on income.

INCOME TAXES CURRENTLY PAYABLE (REFUNDABLE). Refer to current tax expense (benefit).

INCOME TAX EXPENSE (BENEFIT). The sum of current tax expense (benefit) and deferred tax expense (benefit).

TAXABLE INCOME. The excess of taxable revenues over tax-deductible expenses and exemptions for the year as defined by the governmental taxing authority.

TAXABLE TEMPORARY DIFFERENCE. Temporary differences that result in taxable amounts in future years when recovering or settling the related asset or liability, respectively.

TAX-PLANNING STRATEGY. An action that meets certain criteria and that a company implements to realize a tax benefit for an operating loss or tax carryforward before it expires. Companies consider tax-planning strategies when assessing whether to recognize a deferred tax asset.

TEMPORARY DIFFERENCE. A difference between the tax basis of an asset or liability and its reported amount in the financial statements that will result in taxable or deductible amounts in future years when recovering or settling the reported amount of the asset or liability, respectively.

You will want to read the **CONVERGENCE CORNER** on page 1038

For discussion of how international convergence efforts relate to income taxes.

CONVERGENCE CORNER

Similar to IFRS, U.S. GAAP uses the asset and liability approach for recording deferred taxes. The differences between IFRS and U.S. GAAP involve a few exceptions to the asset-liability approach; some minor differences in the recognition, measurement, and disclosure criteria; and differences in implementation guidance.

RELEVANT FACTS

• U.S. GAAP classifies deferred taxes based on the classification of the asset or liability to which it relates. The classification of deferred taxes under IFRS is always non-current.

• U.S. GAAP uses an impairment approach for deferred tax assets. In this approach, the deferred tax asset is recognized in full. It is then reduced by a valuation account if it is more likely than not that all or a portion of the deferred tax asset will not be realized. Under IFRS, an affirmative judgment approach is used, by which a deferred tax asset is recognized up to the amount that is probable to be realized.

• For U.S. GAAP, the enacted tax rate must be used. IFRS uses the enacted tax rate or substantially enacted tax rate. ("Substantially enacted" means virtually certain.)

• The tax effects related to certain items are reported in equity under IFRS. That is not the case under U.S. GAAP, which charges or credits the tax effects to income.

• U.S. GAAP requires companies to assess the likelihood of uncertain tax positions being sustainable upon audit. Potential liabilities must be accrued and disclosed if the position is "more likely than not" to be disallowed. Under IFRS, *all potential liabilities* must be recognized. With respect to measurement, IFRS uses an expected-value approach to measure the tax liability, which differs from U.S. GAAP.

ABOUT THE NUMBERS

The following schedule taken from a recent annual report of **Glaxo-SmithKline plc** (GBR) indicates the impact of differences in IFRS and U.S. GAAP for deferred taxes.

Reconciliation to U.S. accounting principles	
(e) Deferred taxation (in part):	
Total tax expense (in millions of British pounds) IFRS:	
Current tax expense	2,710
Deferred tax (credit)/expense	(409)
Total tax expense	2,301
U.S. GAAP:	
Current tax expense	2,735
Deferred tax credit	(685)
Total tax expense	2,050
Total tax expense difference	(251)

Thus, due to the differences highlighted above, Glaxo's income tax expense under IFRS is £251 million higher than that reported under U.S. GAAP.

ON THE HORIZON

The IASB and the FASB have been working to address some of the differences in the accounting for income taxes. Some of the issues under discussion are the term "probable" under IFRS for recognition of a deferred tax asset, which might be interpreted to mean "more likely than not." If the term is changed, the reporting for impairments of deferred tax assets will be essentially the same between U.S. GAAP and IFRS. In addition, the IASB is considering adoption of the classification approach used in U.S. GAAP for deferred assets and liabilities. Also, U.S. GAAP will likely continue to use the enacted tax rate in computing deferred taxes, except in situations where the U.S. taxing jurisdiction is not involved. In that case, companies should use IFRS, which is based on enacted rates or substantially enacted tax rates. Finally, the issue of allocation of deferred income taxes to equity for certain transactions under IFRS must be addressed in order to converge with U.S. GAAP, which allocates the effects to income. At the time of this printing, deliberations on the income tax project have been suspended indefinitely.

SUMMARY OF LEARNING OBJECTIVES

[1] Identify differences between pretax financial income and taxable income. Companies compute pretax financial income (or income for book purposes) in accordance with IFRS. They compute taxable income (or income for tax purposes) in accordance with prescribed tax regulations. Because tax regulations and IFRS differ in many ways, so frequently do pretax financial income and taxable income. Differences may exist, for example, in the timing of revenue recognition and the timing of expense recognition.

[2] Describe a temporary difference that results in future taxable amounts. Revenue recognized for book purposes in the period earned but deferred and reported as revenue for tax purposes when collected results in future taxable amounts. The future taxable amounts will occur in the periods the company recovers the receivable and reports the collections as revenue for tax purposes. This results in a deferred tax liability.

[3] Describe a temporary difference that results in future deductible amounts. An accrued warranty expense that a company pays for and deducts for tax purposes, in a period later than the period in which it incurs and recognizes it for book purposes, results in future deductible amounts. The future deductible amounts will occur in the periods during which the company settles the related liability for book purposes. This results in a deferred tax asset.

[4] Explain the non-recognition of a deferred tax asset. A deferred tax asset should be reduced if it is probable that the company will not realize some portion or all of the deferred tax asset. The company should carefully consider possible sources of taxable income and related factors to assess the probability that taxable income will be available against which the unused tax losses or unused tax credits can be utilized. To the extent that it is not probable that taxable profit will be available against which the unused tax losses or unused tax credits can be utilized, the deferred tax asset is not recognized.

[5] Describe the presentation of income tax expense in the income statement. Significant components of income tax expense should be disclosed in the income statement or in the notes to the financial statements. The most commonly encountered components are the current expense (or benefit) and the deferred expense (or benefit).

[6] Describe various temporary and permanent differences. Examples of temporary differences are: (1) revenue or gains that are taxable after recognition in financial income, (2) expenses or losses that are deductible after recognition in financial income, (3) revenues or gains that are taxable before recognition in financial income, and (4) expenses or losses that are deductible before recognition in financial income. Examples of permanent differences are: (1) items recognized for financial reporting purposes but not for tax purposes, and (2) items recognized for tax purposes but not for financial reporting purposes.

[7] Explain the effect of various tax rates and tax rate changes on deferred income taxes. Companies may use tax rates other than the current rate only after enactment or substantial enactment of the future tax rates. When a change in the tax rate is enacted, a company should immediately recognize its effect on the deferred income tax accounts. The company reports the effects as an adjustment to income tax expense in the period of the change.

[8] Apply accounting procedures for a loss carryback and a loss carryforward. A company may carry a net operating loss back two years and receive refunds for income taxes paid in those years. The loss is applied to the earlier year first and then to the second year. Any loss remaining after the two-year carryback may be carried forward up to 20 years to offset future taxable income. A company may forgo the loss carryback and use the loss carryforward, offsetting future taxable income for up to 20 years.

KEY TERMS

asset-liability method, *1035*
current tax benefit (expense), *1015, 1028*
deductible amounts, *1014*
deductible temporary difference, *1021*
deferred tax asset, *1017*
deferred tax expense (benefit), *1015, 1018*
deferred tax liability, *1014*
effective tax rate, *1024*
Income Tax Refund Receivable, *1027*
intraperiod tax allocation, *1032*
loss carryback, *1026*
loss carryforward, *1026*
net operating loss (NOL), *1026*
originating temporary difference, *1022*
permanent difference, *1022*
pretax financial income, *1012*
probable, *1019*
reversing difference, *1022*
substantially enacted tax rate, *1024*
taxable amounts, *1014*
taxable income, *1012*
taxable temporary difference, *1021*
tax effect (tax benefit), *1027*
temporary difference, *1013*

·9 **Describe the presentation of income taxes in financial statements.** Companies report deferred tax accounts on the statement of financial position as assets and liabilities. Companies classify taxes receivable or payable as current assets or current liabilities, and these items may be offset in the statement of financial position. Deferred tax assets and deferred tax liabilities are also separately recognized and measured and may be offset in the statement of financial position. The net deferred tax asset or net deferred tax liability is reported in the non-current section of the statement of financial position. In the income statement, companies allocate income tax expense (or benefit) to continuing operations, discontinued operations, other comprehensive income, and prior period adjustments (intraperiod tax allocation), and indicate current tax expense (benefit) and deferred tax expense (benefit). An important disclosure is the reconciliation between actual tax expense and the applicable tax rate.

·10 **Indicate the basic principles of the asset-liability method.** Companies apply the following basic principles in accounting for income taxes at the date of the financial statements: (1) Recognize a current tax liability or asset for the estimated taxes payable or refundable on the tax return for the current year. (2) Recognize a deferred tax liability or asset for the estimated future tax effects attributable to temporary differences and carryforwards using the enacted tax rate. (3) Base the measurement of current and deferred tax liabilities and assets on provisions of the enacted (or substantially enacted) tax law. (4) Reduce the measurement of deferred tax assets, if necessary, by the amount of any tax benefits that, based on available evidence, companies do not expect to realize.

APPENDIX 19A

COMPREHENSIVE EXAMPLE OF INTERPERIOD TAX ALLOCATION

Objective·11

Understand and apply the concepts and procedures of interperiod tax allocation.

This appendix presents a comprehensive illustration of a deferred income tax problem with several temporary and permanent differences. The example follows one company through two complete years (2010 and 2011). **Study it carefully.** It should help you understand the concepts and procedures presented in the chapter.

FIRST YEAR—2010

Allman Company, which began operations at the beginning of 2010, produces various products on a contract basis. Each contract generates an income of $80,000. Some of Allman's contracts provide for the customer to pay on an installment basis. Under these contracts, Allman collects one-fifth of the contract revenue in each of the following four years. For financial reporting purposes, the company recognizes income in the year of completion (accrual basis); for tax purposes, Allman recognizes income in the year cash is collected (installment basis).

Presented below is information related to Allman's operations for 2010.

1. In 2010, the company completed seven contracts that allow for the customer to pay on an installment basis. Allman recognized the related income of $560,000 for financial reporting purposes. It reported only $112,000 of income on installment sales on the 2010 tax return. The company expects future collections on the related receivables to result in taxable amounts of $112,000 in each of the next four years.

2. At the beginning of 2010, Allman Company purchased depreciable assets with a cost of $540,000. For financial reporting purposes, Allman depreciates these assets using the straight-line method over a six-year service life. The depreciation schedules for both financial reporting and tax purposes are shown on page 1041.

Year	Depreciation for Financial Reporting Purposes	Depreciation for Tax Purposes	Difference
2010	$ 90,000	$108,000	$(18,000)
2011	90,000	172,800	(82,800)
2012	90,000	103,680	(13,680)
2013	90,000	62,208	27,792
2014	90,000	62,208	27,792
2015	90,000	31,104	58,896
	$540,000	$540,000	$ –0–

3. The company warrants its product for two years from the date of completion of a contract. During 2010, the product warranty liability accrued for financial reporting purposes was $200,000, and the amount paid for the satisfaction of warranty liability was $44,000. Allman expects to settle the remaining $156,000 by expenditures of $56,000 in 2011 and $100,000 in 2012.

4. In 2010, non-taxable governmental bond interest revenue was $28,000.

5. During 2010, non-deductible fines and penalties of $26,000 were paid.

6. Pretax financial income for 2010 amounts to $412,000.

7. Tax rates enacted before the end of 2010 were:

2010	50%
2011 and later years	40%

8. The accounting period is the calendar year.

9. The company is expected to have taxable income in all future years.

Taxable Income and Income Tax Payable—2010

The first step is to determine Allman Company's income tax payable for 2010 by calculating its taxable income. Illustration 19A-1 shows this computation.

Pretax financial income for 2010	$412,000
Permanent differences:	
Non-taxable revenue—governmental bond interest	(28,000)
Non-deductible expenses—fines and penalties	26,000
Temporary differences:	
Excess contract income per books ($560,000 − $112,000)	(448,000)
Excess depreciation per tax ($108,000 − $90,000)	(18,000)
Excess warranty expense per books ($200,000 − $44,000)	156,000
Taxable income for 2010	$100,000

ILLUSTRATION 19A-1
Computation of Taxable Income, 2010

Allman computes income tax payable on taxable income for $100,000 as follows.

Taxable income for 2010	$100,000
Tax rate	× 50%
Income tax payable (current tax expense) for 2010	$ 50,000

ILLUSTRATION 19A-2
Computation of Income Tax Payable, End of 2010

Computing Deferred Income Taxes—End of 2010

The schedule in Illustration 19A-3 (on page 1042) summarizes the temporary differences and the resulting future taxable and deductible amounts.

ILLUSTRATION 19A-3
Schedule of Future
Taxable and Deductible
Amounts, End of 2010

	Future Years					
	2011	2012	2013	2014	2015	Total
Future taxable (deductible) amounts:						
Installment sales	$112,000	$112,000	$112,000	$112,000		$448,000
Depreciation	(82,800)	(13,680)	27,792	27,792	$58,896	18,000
Warranty costs	(56,000)	(100,000)				(156,000)

Allman computes the amounts of deferred income taxes to be reported at the end of 2010 as shown in Illustration 19A-4.

ILLUSTRATION 19A-4
Computation of Deferred
Income Taxes, End of 2010

Temporary Difference	Future Taxable (Deductible) Amounts	Tax Rate	Deferred Tax (Asset)	Liability
Installment sales	$448,000	40%		$179,200
Depreciation	18,000	40%		7,200
Warranty costs	(156,000)	40%	$(62,400)	
Totals	$310,000		$(62,400)	$186,400*

*Because only a single tax rate is involved in all relevant years, these totals can be reconciled:
$310,000 × 40% = ($62,400) + $186,400.

A temporary difference is caused by the use of the accrual basis for financial reporting purposes and the installment method for tax purposes. This temporary difference will result in future taxable amounts, and hence, a deferred tax liability. Because of the installment contracts completed in 2010, a temporary difference of $448,000 originates that will reverse in equal amounts over the next four years. The company expects to have taxable income in all future years, and there is only one enacted tax rate applicable to all future years. Allman uses that rate (40 percent) to compute the entire deferred tax liability resulting from this temporary difference.

The temporary difference caused by different depreciation policies for books and for tax purposes originates over three years and then reverses over three years. This difference will cause deductible amounts in 2011 and 2012 and taxable amounts in 2013, 2014, and 2015. These amounts sum to a net future taxable amount of $18,000 (which is the cumulative temporary difference at the end of 2010). Because the company expects to have taxable income in all future years and because there is only one tax rate enacted for all of the relevant future years, Allman applies that rate to the net future taxable amount to determine the related net deferred tax liability.

The third temporary difference is caused by different methods of accounting for warranties. This difference will result in deductible amounts in each of the two future years it takes to reverse. Because the company expects to report a positive income on all future tax returns and because there is only one tax rate enacted for each of the relevant future years, Allman uses that 40 percent rate to calculate the resulting deferred tax asset.

Deferred Tax Expense (Benefit) and the Journal Entry to Record Income Taxes—2010

To determine the deferred tax expense (benefit), we need to compare the beginning and ending balances of the deferred income tax accounts. Illustration 19A-5 shows that computation.

Deferred tax asset at the end of 2010	$ 62,400	
Deferred tax asset at the beginning of 2010	–0–	
Deferred tax expense (benefit)	$ (62,400)	
Deferred tax liability at the end of 2010	$186,400	
Deferred tax liability at the beginning of 2010	–0–	
Deferred tax expense (benefit)	$186,400	

ILLUSTRATION 19A-5
Computation of Deferred Tax Expense (Benefit), 2010

The $62,400 increase in the deferred tax asset causes a deferred tax benefit to be reported in the income statement. The $186,400 increase in the deferred tax liability during 2010 results in a deferred tax expense. These two amounts **net** to a deferred tax expense of $124,000 for 2010.

Deferred tax expense (benefit)	$ (62,400)
Deferred tax expense (benefit)	186,400
Net deferred tax expense for 2010	$124,000

ILLUSTRATION 19A-6
Computation of Net Deferred Tax Expense, 2010

Allman then computes the total income tax expense as follows.

Current tax expense for 2010	$ 50,000
Deferred tax expense for 2010	124,000
Income tax expense (total) for 2010	$174,000

ILLUSTRATION 19A-7
Computation of Total Income Tax Expense, 2010

Allman records income tax payable, deferred income taxes, and income tax expense as follows.

Income Tax Expense	174,000	
Deferred Tax Asset	62,400	
Income Tax Payable		50,000
Deferred Tax Liability		186,400

Financial Statement Presentation—2010

Companies should classify deferred tax assets and liabilities as non-current on the statement of financial position. Deferred tax assets are therefore netted against deferred tax liabilities to compute a net deferred asset (liability). Illustration 19A-8 shows the classification of Allman's deferred tax accounts at the end of 2010.

Temporary Difference	Resulting Deferred Tax (Asset)	Liability
Installment sales		$179,200
Depreciation		7,200
Warranty costs	$(62,400)	
Totals	$(62,400)	$186,400

ILLUSTRATION 19A-8
Classification of Deferred Tax Accounts, End of 2010

The statement of financial position at the end of 2010 reports the following amounts.

Non-current liabilities	
Deferred tax liability ($186,400 – $62,400)	$124,000
Current liabilities	
Income tax payable	$ 50,000

ILLUSTRATION 19A-9
Statement of Financial Position Presentation of Deferred Taxes, 2010

Allman's income statement for 2010 reports the following.

ILLUSTRATION 19A-10
Income Statement
Presentation of Income
Tax Expense, 2010

Income before income taxes		$412,000
Income tax expense		
Current	$ 50,000	
Deferred	124,000	174,000
Net income		$238,000

SECOND YEAR—2011

1. During 2011, Allman collected $112,000 from customers for the receivables arising from contracts completed in 2010. The company expects recovery of the remaining receivables to result in taxable amounts of $112,000 in each of the following three years.

2. In 2011, the company completed four new contracts that allow for the customer to pay on an installment basis. These installment sales created new installment receivables. Future collections of these receivables will result in reporting income of $64,000 for tax purposes in each of the next four years.

3. During 2011, Allman continued to depreciate the assets acquired in 2010 according to the depreciation schedules appearing on page 1041. Thus, depreciation amounted to $90,000 for financial reporting purposes and $172,800 for tax purposes.

4. An analysis at the end of 2011 of the product warranty liability account showed the following details.

Balance of liability at beginning of 2011	$156,000
Expense for 2011 income statement purposes	180,000
Amount paid for contracts completed in 2010	(56,000)
Amount paid for contracts completed in 2011	(50,000)
Balance of liability at end of 2011	$230,000

The balance of the liability is expected to require expenditures in the future as follows.

$100,000 in 2012 due to 2010 contracts
$ 50,000 in 2012 due to 2011 contracts
$ 80,000 in 2013 due to 2011 contracts
$230,000

5. During 2011, non-taxable governmental bond interest revenue was $24,000.

6. Allman accrued a loss of $172,000 for financial reporting purposes because of pending litigation. This amount is not tax-deductible until the period the loss is realized, which the company estimates to be 2019.

7. Pretax financial income for 2011 amounts to $504,800.

8. The enacted tax rates still in effect are:

2010	50%
2011 and later years	40%

Taxable Income and Income Tax Payable—2011

Allman computes taxable income for 2011 as follows.

Pretax financial income for 2011	$504,800
Permanent difference:	
Non-taxable revenue—governmental bond interest	(24,000)
Reversing temporary differences:	
Collection on 2010 installment sales	112,000
Payments on warranties from 2010 contracts	(56,000)
Originating temporary differences:	
Excess contract income per books—2011 contracts	(256,000)
Excess depreciation per tax	(82,800)
Excess warranty expense per books—2011 contracts	130,000
Loss accrual per books	172,000
Taxable income for 2011	$500,000

ILLUSTRATION 19A-11
Computation of Taxable Income, 2011

Income tax payable for 2011 is as follows.

Taxable income for 2011	$500,000
Tax rate	× 40%
Income tax payable (current tax expense) for 2011	$200,000

ILLUSTRATION 19A-12
Computation of Income Tax Payable, End of 2011

Computing Deferred Income Taxes—End of 2011

ILLUSTRATION 19A-13
Schedule of Future Taxable and Deductible Amounts, End of 2011

The schedule in Illustration 19A-13 summarizes the temporary differences existing at the end of 2011 and the resulting future taxable and deductible amounts.

	Future Years						
	2012	2013	2014	2015		2019	Total
Future taxable (deductible) amounts:							
Installment sales—2010	$112,000	$112,000	$112,000				$336,000
Installment sales—2011	64,000	64,000	64,000	$64,000			256,000
Depreciation	(13,680)	27,792	27,792	58,896			100,800
Warranty costs	(150,000)	(80,000)					(230,000)
Loss accrual						$(172,000)	(172,000)

Allman computes the amounts of deferred income taxes to be reported at the end of 2011 as follows.

ILLUSTRATION 19A-14
Computation of Deferred Income Taxes, End of 2011

Temporary Difference	Future Taxable (Deductible) Amounts	Tax Rate	Deferred Tax (Asset)	Deferred Tax Liability
Installment sales	$592,000*	40%		$236,800
Depreciation	100,800	40%		40,320
Warranty costs	(230,000)	40%	$ (92,000)	
Loss accrual	(172,000)	40%	(68,800)	
Totals	$290,800		$(160,800)	$277,120**

*Cumulative temporary difference = $336,000 + $256,000
**Because of a flat tax rate, these totals can be reconciled: $290,800 × 40% = $(160,800) + $277,120

Deferred Tax Expense (Benefit) and the Journal Entry to Record Income Taxes—2011

To determine the deferred tax expense (benefit), Allman must compare the beginning and ending balances of the deferred income tax accounts, as shown in Illustration 19A-15.

ILLUSTRATION 19A-15
Computation of Deferred Tax Expense (Benefit), 2011

Deferred tax asset at the end of 2011	$160,800
Deferred tax asset at the beginning of 2011	62,400
Deferred tax expense (benefit)	$ (98,400)
Deferred tax liability at the end of 2011	$277,120
Deferred tax liability at the beginning of 2011	186,400
Deferred tax expense (benefit)	$ 90,720

The deferred tax expense (benefit) and the total income tax expense for 2011 are, therefore, as follows.

ILLUSTRATION 19A-16
Computation of Total Income Tax Expense, 2011

Deferred tax expense (benefit)	$ (98,400)
Deferred tax expense (benefit)	90,720
Deferred tax benefit for 2011	(7,680)
Current tax expense for 2011	200,000
Income tax expense (total) for 2011	$192,320

The deferred tax expense of $90,720 and the deferred tax benefit of $98,400 net to a deferred tax benefit of $7,680 for 2011.

Allman records income taxes for 2011 with the following journal entry.

Income Tax Expense	192,320	
Deferred Tax Asset	98,400	
Income Tax Payable		200,000
Deferred Tax Liability		90,720

Financial Statement Presentation—2011

Illustration 19A-17 shows the classification of Allman's deferred tax accounts at the end of 2011.

ILLUSTRATION 19A-17
Classification of Deferred Tax Accounts, End of 2011

	Resulting Deferred Tax	
Temporary Difference	(Asset)	Liability
Installment sales		$236,800
Depreciation		40,320
Warranty costs	$ (92,000)	
Loss accrual	(68,800)	
Totals	$(160,800)	$277,120

Allman's statement of financial position at the end of 2011 reports the following amounts.

ILLUSTRATION 19A-18
Statement of Financial Position Presentation of Deferred Taxes, End of 2011

Non-current liabilities	
Deferred tax liability ($277,120 − $160,800)	$116,320
Current liabilities	
Income tax payable	$200,000

The income statement for 2011 reports the following.

Income before income taxes		$504,800
Income tax expense		
Current	$200,000	
Deferred	(7,680)	192,320
Net income		$312,480

ILLUSTRATION 19A-19
Income Statement
Presentation of Income
Tax Expense, 2011

SUMMARY OF LEARNING OBJECTIVE FOR APPENDIX 19A

•11 **Understand and apply the concepts and procedures of interperiod tax allocation.** Accounting for deferred taxes involves the following steps: Calculate taxable income and income tax payable for the year. Compute deferred income taxes at the end of the year. Determine deferred tax expense (benefit) and make the journal entry to record income taxes. Classify deferred tax assets and liabilities and report a net deferred tax asset or liability.

I F R S

AUTHORITATIVE LITERATURE

Authoritative Literature References

[1] International Accounting Standard 12, *Income Taxes* (London, U.K.: International Accounting Standards Committee Foundation, 2001).

[2] International Accounting Standard 12, *Income Taxes* (London, U.K.: International Accounting Standards Committee Foundation, 2001), par. 48.

[3] International Accounting Standard 12, *Income Taxes* (London, U.K.: International Accounting Standards Committee Foundation, 2001), par. 49.

[4] International Accounting Standard 12, *Income Taxes* (London, U.K.: International Accounting Standards Committee Foundation, 2001), par. 36.

[5] International Accounting Standard 12, *Income Taxes* (London, U.K.: International Accounting Standards Committee Foundation, 2001), par. 72.

[6] International Accounting Standard 12, *Income Taxes* (London, U.K.: International Accounting Standards Committee Foundation, 2001), par. 74.

[7] International Accounting Standard 12, *Income Taxes* (London, U.K.: International Accounting Standards Committee Foundation, 2001), paras. 53–54.

[8] International Accounting Standard 12, *Income Taxes* (London, U.K.: International Accounting Standards Committee Foundation, 2001), par. 80(h).

QUESTIONS

1. Explain the difference between pretax financial income and taxable income.

2. What are the two objectives of accounting for income taxes?

3. Interest on governmental bonds is often referred to as a permanent difference when determining the proper amount to report for deferred taxes. Explain the meaning of permanent differences, and give two other examples.

4. Explain the meaning of a temporary difference as it relates to deferred tax computations, and give three examples.

5. Differentiate between an originating temporary difference and a reversing difference.

6. The book basis of depreciable assets for Erwin Co. is €900,000, and the tax basis is €700,000 at the end of 2011. The enacted tax rate is 34% for all periods. Determine the amount of deferred taxes to be reported on the statement of financial position at the end of 2011.

7. Roth Inc. has a deferred tax liability of $68,000 at the beginning of 2011. At the end of 2011, it reports accounts receivable on the books at $90,000 and the tax basis at zero (its only temporary difference). If the enacted tax rate is 34% for all periods, and income tax payable for the period is $230,000, determine the amount of total income tax expense to report for 2011.

8. What is the difference between a future taxable amount and a future deductible amount? When is it not appropriate to recognize a portion or all of a deferred tax asset?

9. Pretax financial income for Lake Inc. is $300,000, and its taxable income is $100,000 for 2011. Its only temporary difference at the end of the period relates to a $70,000 difference due to excess depreciation for tax purposes. If the tax rate is 40% for all periods, compute the amount of income tax expense to report in 2011. No deferred income taxes existed at the beginning of the year.

10. How are deferred tax assets and deferred tax liabilities reported on the statement of financial position?

11. Describe the procedure(s) involved in classifying deferred tax amounts on the statement of financial position.

12. At the end of the year, Falabella Co. has pretax financial income of $550,000. Included in the $550,000 is $70,000 interest income on governmental bonds, $25,000 fine for dumping hazardous waste, and depreciation of $60,000. Depreciation for tax purposes is $45,000. Compute income taxes payable, assuming the tax rate is 30% for all periods.

13. Addison Co. has one temporary difference at the beginning of 2010 of £500,000. The deferred tax liability established for this amount is £150,000, based on a tax rate of 30%. The temporary difference will provide the following taxable amounts: £100,000 in 2011; £200,000 in 2012; and £200,000 in 2013. If a new tax rate for 2013 of 20% is enacted into law at the end of 2010, what is the journal entry necessary in 2010 (if any) to adjust deferred taxes?

14. What are some of the reasons that the components of income tax expense should be disclosed and a reconciliation between the statutory tax rate and the effective rate be provided?

15. Differentiate between "loss carryback" and "loss carryforward." Which can be accounted for with the greater certainty when it arises? Why?

16. What are the possible treatments for tax purposes of a net operating loss? What are the circumstances that determine the option to be applied? What is the proper treatment of a net operating loss for financial reporting purposes?

17. What controversy relates to the accounting for net operating loss carryforwards?

18. Briefly describe some of the similarities and differences between IFRS and U.S. GAAP with respect to income tax accounting.

19. Describe the current convergence efforts of the IASB and FASB in the area of accounting for taxes.

BRIEF EXERCISES

•1 •2 BE19-1 In 2010, Amirante Corporation had pretax financial income of $168,000 and taxable income of $120,000. The difference is due to the use of different depreciation methods for tax and accounting purposes. The effective tax rate is 40%. Compute the amount to be reported as income taxes payable at December 31, 2010.

•1 •2 BE19-2 Oxford Corporation began operations in 2010 and reported pretax financial income of €225,000 for the year. Oxford's tax depreciation exceeded its book depreciation by €40,000. Oxford's tax rate for 2010 and years thereafter is 30%. In its December 31, 2010, statement of financial position, what amount of deferred tax liability should be reported?

•9 BE19-3 Using the information from BE19-2, assume this is the only difference between Oxford's pretax financial income and taxable income. Prepare the journal entry to record the income tax expense, deferred income taxes, and income tax payable, and show how the deferred tax liability will be classified on the December 31, 2010, statement of financial position.

•2 •5 BE19-4 At December 31, 2010, Appaloosa Corporation had a deferred tax liability of $25,000. At December 31, 2011, the deferred tax liability is $42,000. The corporation's 2011 current tax expense is $48,000. What amount should Appaloosa report as total 2011 tax expense?

·1 ·3 **BE19-5** At December 31, 2010, Suffolk Corporation had an estimated warranty liability of £105,000 for accounting purposes and £0 for tax purposes. (The warranty costs are not deductible until paid.) The effective tax rate is 40%. Compute the amount Suffolk should report as a deferred tax asset at December 31, 2010.

·3 ·5 **BE19-6** At December 31, 2010, Percheron Inc. had a deferred tax asset of $30,000. At December 31, 2011, the deferred tax asset is $59,000. The corporation's 2011 current tax expense is $61,000. What amount should Percheron report as total 2011 tax expense?

·4 **BE19-7** At December 31, 2010, Hillyard Corporation has a deferred tax asset of $200,000. After a careful review of all available evidence, it is determined that it is probable that $60,000 of this deferred tax asset will not be realized. Prepare the necessary journal entry.

·5 **BE19-8** Mitchell Corporation had income before income taxes of $195,000 in 2010. Mitchell's current income tax expense is $48,000, and deferred income tax expense is $30,000. Prepare Mitchell's 2010 income statement, beginning with income before income taxes.

·2 ·3 **BE19-9** Shetland Inc. had pretax financial income of $154,000 in 2010, in its first year of operations. Included in the computation of that amount is insurance expense of $4,000, which is not deductible for tax purposes. In addition, depreciation for tax purposes exceeds accounting depreciation by $10,000. Prepare Shetland's journal entry to record 2010 taxes, assuming a tax rate of 45%.

·2 **BE19-10** Clydesdale Corporation has a cumulative temporary difference related to depreciation of $580,000 at December 31, 2010. This difference will reverse as follows: 2011, $42,000; 2012, $244,000; and 2013, $294,000. Enacted tax rates are 34% for 2011 and 2012, and 40% for 2013. Compute the amount Clydesdale should report as a deferred tax liability at December 31, 2010.

·7 **BE19-11** At December 31, 2010, Takeshi Corporation had a deferred tax liability of ¥680,000,000 resulting from future taxable amounts of ¥2,000,000,000 and an enacted tax rate of 34%. In May 2011, a new income tax act is signed into law that raises the tax rate to 40% for 2011 and future years. Prepare the journal entry for Takeshi to adjust the deferred tax liability.

·8 **BE19-12** Conlin Corporation had the following tax information.

Year	Taxable Income	Tax Rate	Taxes Paid
2008	$300,000	35%	$105,000
2009	$325,000	30%	$ 97,500
2010	$400,000	30%	$120,000

In 2011, Conlin suffered a net operating loss of $480,000, which it elected to carry back. The 2011 enacted tax rate is 29%. Prepare Conlin's entry to record the effect of the loss carryback.

·8 **BE19-13** Rode Inc. incurred a net operating loss of €500,000 in 2010. Combined income for 2008 and 2009 was €350,000. The tax rate for all years is 40%. Rode elects the carryback option. Prepare the journal entries to record the benefits of the loss carryback and the loss carryforward.

·4 ·8 **BE19-14** Use the information for Rode Inc. given in BE19-13. Assume that it is probable that the entire net operating loss carryforward will not be realized in future years. Prepare the journal entry(ies) necessary at the end of 2010.

·9 **BE19-15** Youngman Corporation has temporary differences at December 31, 2010, that result in the following deferred taxes.

Deferred tax asset	$24,000
Deferred tax liability	$69,000

Indicate how these balances would be presented in Youngman's December 31, 2010, statement of financial position.

EXERCISES

·2 ·5 **E19-1** **(One Temporary Difference, Future Taxable Amounts, One Rate, No Beginning Deferred Taxes)** Starfleet Corporation has one temporary difference at the end of 2010 that will reverse and cause taxable amounts of $55,000 in 2011, $60,000 in 2012, and $75,000 in 2013. Starfleet's pretax financial income for 2010 is $400,000, and the tax rate is 30% for all years. There are no deferred taxes at the beginning of 2010.

Instructions

(a) Compute taxable income and income taxes payable for 2010.

(b) Prepare the journal entry to record income tax expense, deferred income taxes, and income taxes payable for 2010.

(c) Prepare the income tax expense section of the income statement for 2010, beginning with the line "Income before income taxes."

·2 E19-2 (Two Differences, No Beginning Deferred Taxes, Tracked through 2 Years) The following information is available for McKee Corporation for 2010.

1. Excess of tax depreciation over book depreciation, £40,000. This £40,000 difference will reverse equally over the years 2011–2014.
2. Deferral, for book purposes, of £25,000 of rent received in advance. The rent will be recorded as revenue in 2011.
3. Pretax financial income, £350,000.
4. Tax rate for all years, 40%.

Instructions

(a) Compute taxable income for 2010.

(b) Prepare the journal entry to record income tax expense, deferred income taxes, and income taxes payable for 2010.

(c) Prepare the journal entry to record income tax expense, deferred income taxes, and income taxes payable for 2011, assuming taxable income of £325,000.

·2 ·5 E19-3 (One Temporary Difference, Future Taxable Amounts, One Rate, Beginning Deferred Taxes)
 Brennan Corporation began 2010 with a $90,000 balance in the Deferred Tax Liability account. At the end of 2010, the related cumulative temporary difference amounts to $350,000, and it will reverse evenly over the next 2 years. Pretax accounting income for 2010 is $525,000, the tax rate for all years is 40%, and taxable income for 2010 is $400,000.

Instructions

(a) Compute income taxes payable for 2010.

(b) Prepare the journal entry to record income tax expense, deferred income taxes, and income taxes payable for 2010.

(c) Prepare the income tax expense section of the income statement for 2010, beginning with the line "Income before income taxes."

·2 ·3 ·5 E19-4 (Three Differences, Compute Taxable Income, Entry for Taxes) Havaci Company reports pre-
·6 tax financial income of €80,000 for 2010. The following items cause taxable income to be different than pretax financial income.

1. Depreciation on the tax return is greater than depreciation on the income statement by €16,000.
2. Rent collected on the tax return is greater than rent earned on the income statement by €27,000.
3. Fines for pollution appear as an expense of €11,000 on the income statement.

Havaci's tax rate is 30% for all years, and the company expects to report taxable income in all future years. There are no deferred taxes at the beginning of 2010.

Instructions

(a) Compute taxable income and income taxes payable for 2010.

(b) Prepare the journal entry to record income tax expense, deferred income taxes, and income taxes payable for 2010.

(c) Prepare the income tax expense section of the income statement for 2010, beginning with the line "Income before income taxes."

(d) Compute the effective income tax rate for 2010.

·2 ·3 ·5 E19-5 (Two Temporary Differences, One Rate, Beginning Deferred Taxes) The following facts relate to Alschuler Corporation.

1. Deferred tax liability, January 1, 2010, $40,000.
2. Deferred tax asset, January 1, 2010, $0.
3. Taxable income for 2010, $115,000.
4. Pretax financial income for 2010, $200,000.
5. Cumulative temporary difference at December 31, 2010, giving rise to future taxable amounts, $220,000.
6. Cumulative temporary difference at December 31, 2010, giving rise to future deductible amounts, $35,000.
7. Tax rate for all years, 40%.
8. The company is expected to operate profitably in the future.

Instructions

(a) Compute income taxes payable for 2010.

(b) Prepare the journal entry to record income tax expense, deferred income taxes, and income taxes payable for 2010.

(c) Prepare the income tax expense section of the income statement for 2010, beginning with the line "Income before income taxes."

·6 **E19-6** **(Identify Temporary or Permanent Differences)** Listed below are items that are commonly accounted for differently for financial reporting purposes than they are for tax purposes.

Instructions

For each item below, indicate whether it involves:

(1) A temporary difference that will result in future deductible amounts and, therefore, will usually give rise to a deferred income tax asset.

(2) A temporary difference that will result in future taxable amounts and, therefore, will usually give rise to a deferred income tax liability.

(3) A permanent difference.

Use the appropriate number to indicate your answer for each.

(a) _____ An accelerated depreciation system is used for tax purposes, and the straight-line depreciation method is used for financial reporting purposes for some plant assets.

(b) _____ A landlord collects some rents in advance. Rents received are taxable in the period when they are received.

(c) _____ Expenses are incurred in obtaining tax-exempt income.

(d) _____ Costs of guarantees and warranties are estimated and accrued for financial reporting purposes.

(e) _____ Installment sales of investments are accounted for by the accrual method for financial reporting purposes and the installment method for tax purposes.

(f) _____ Interest is received on an investment in tax-exempt governmental obligations.

(g) _____ For some assets, straight-line depreciation is used for both financial reporting purposes and tax purposes, but the assets' lives are shorter for tax purposes.

(h) _____ The tax return reports a deduction for 80% of the dividends received from various corporations. The cost method is used in accounting for the related investments for financial reporting purposes.

(i) _____ Estimated losses on pending lawsuits and claims are accrued for books. These losses are tax-deductible in the period(s) when the related liabilities are settled.

(j) _____ Expenses on share options are accrued for financial reporting purposes.

·2 ·3 ·4 **E19-7** **(Terminology, Relationships, Computations, Entries)**
·6

Instructions

Complete the following statements by filling in the blanks.

(a) In a period in which a taxable temporary difference reverses, the reversal will cause taxable income to be _____ (less than, greater than) pretax financial income.

(b) If a $68,000 balance in Deferred Tax Asset was computed by use of a 40% rate, the underlying cumulative temporary difference amounts to $_____.

(c) Deferred taxes _____ (are, are not) recorded to account for permanent differences.

(d) If a taxable temporary difference originates in 2011, it will cause taxable income for 2011 to be _____ (less than, greater than) pretax financial income for 2011.

(e) If total tax expense is $50,000 and deferred tax expense is $65,000, then the current portion of the expense computation is referred to as current tax _____ (expense, benefit) of $_____.

(f) If a corporation's tax return shows taxable income of $105,000 for Year 2 and a tax rate of 40%, how much will appear on the December 31, Year 2, statement of financial position for "Income tax payable" if the company has made estimated tax payments of $36,500 for Year 2? $_____.

(g) An increase in the Deferred Tax Liability account on the statement of financial position is recorded by a _____ (debit, credit) to the Income Tax Expense account.

(h) An income statement that reports current tax expense of $82,000 and deferred tax benefit of $23,000 will report total income tax expense of $_____.

(i) A reduction in a deferred tax asset is needed whenever it is judged to be _____ that a portion of a deferred tax asset _____ (will be, will not be) realized.

(j) If the tax return shows total taxes due for the period of $75,000 but the income statement shows total income tax expense of $55,000, the difference of $20,000 is referred to as a deferred tax _____ (expense, benefit).

E19-8 (Two Temporary Differences, One Rate, 3 Years) Jeonbuk Company has two temporary differences between its income tax expense and income taxes payable. The information is shown below.

	2010	2011	2012
Pretax financial income	₩840,000,000	₩910,000,000	₩945,000,000
Excess depreciation expense on tax return	(30,000,000)	(40,000,000)	(20,000,000)
Excess warranty expense in financial income	20,000,000	10,000,000	8,000,000
Taxable income	₩830,000,000	₩880,000,000	₩933,000,000

The income tax rate for all years is 40%.

Instructions

(a) Prepare the journal entry to record income tax expense, deferred income taxes, and income tax payable for 2010, 2011, and 2012.

(b) Assuming there were no temporary differences prior to 2010, indicate how deferred taxes will be reported on the 2012 statement of financial position. Jeonbuk's product warranty is for 12 months.

(c) Prepare the income tax expense section of the income statement for 2012, beginning with the line "Pretax financial income."

E19-9 (Carryback and Carryforward of NOL, No Temporary Differences) The pretax financial income (or loss) figures for Synergetics Company are as follows.

2006	$160,000
2007	250,000
2008	90,000
2009	(160,000)
2010	(350,000)
2011	120,000
2012	100,000

Pretax financial income (or loss) and taxable income (loss) were the same for all years involved. Assume a 45% tax rate for 2006 and 2007 and a 40% tax rate for the remaining years.

Instructions

Prepare the journal entries for the years 2008 to 2012 to record income tax expense and the effects of the net operating loss carrybacks and carryforwards, assuming Synergetics Company uses the carryback provision. All income and losses relate to normal operations. (In recording the benefits of a loss carryforward, assume that it is probable the loss carryforward will be realized.)

E19-10 (Two NOLs, No Temporary Differences, Entries and Income Statement) Lanier Corporation has pretax financial income (or loss) equal to taxable income (or loss) from 2003 through 2011 as follows.

	Income (Loss)	Tax Rate
2003	€29,000	30%
2004	40,000	30%
2005	22,000	35%
2006	48,000	50%
2007	(150,000)	40%
2008	90,000	40%
2009	30,000	40%
2010	105,000	40%
2011	(50,000)	45%

Pretax financial income (loss) and taxable income (loss) were the same for all years since Lanier has been in business. Assume the carryback provision is employed for net operating losses. In recording the benefits of a loss carryforward, assume that it is probable that the related benefits will be realized.

Instructions

(a) What entry(ies) for income taxes should be recorded for 2007?

(b) Indicate what the income tax expense portion of the income statement for 2007 should look like. Assume all income (loss) relates to continuing operations.

(c) What entry for income taxes should be recorded in 2008?

(d) How should the income tax expense section of the income statement for 2008 appear?

(e) What entry for income taxes should be recorded in 2011?

(f) How should the income tax expense section of the income statement for 2011 appear?

E19-11 (Three Differences, Classify Deferred Taxes) At December 31, 2010, Cascade Company had the following deferred tax items.

Temporary Differences	Resulting Balances in Deferred Taxes
1. Excess of tax depreciation over book depreciation	$200,000
2. Accrual, for book purposes, of estimated loss contingency from pending lawsuit that is expected to be settled in 2011. The loss will be deducted on the tax return when paid.	(50,000)
3. Accrual method used for book purposes and installment method used for tax purposes for an isolated installment sale of an investment.	300,000

In analyzing the temporary differences, you find that $30,000 of the depreciation temporary difference will reverse in 2011, and $120,000 of the temporary difference due to the installment sale will reverse in 2011. The tax rate for all years is 40%.

Instructions
Indicate the manner in which deferred taxes should be presented on Cascade Company's December 31, 2010, statement of financial position.

E19-12 (Two Temporary Differences, One Rate, Beginning Deferred Taxes, Compute Pretax Financial Income) The following facts relate to McKane Corporation.

1. Deferred tax liability, January 1, 2010, $60,000.
2. Deferred tax asset, January 1, 2010, $20,000.
3. Taxable income for 2010, $115,000.
4. Cumulative temporary difference at December 31, 2010, giving rise to future taxable amounts, $210,000.
5. Cumulative temporary difference at December 31, 2010, giving rise to future deductible amounts, $95,000.
6. Tax rate for all years, 40%. No permanent differences exist.
7. The company is expected to operate profitably in the future.

Instructions
(a) Compute the amount of pretax financial income for 2010.
(b) Prepare the journal entry to record income tax expense, deferred income taxes, and income taxes payable for 2010.
(c) Prepare the income tax expense section of the income statement for 2010, beginning with the line "Income before income taxes."
(d) Compute the effective tax rate for 2010.

E19-13 (One Difference, Multiple Rates, Effect of Beginning Balance versus No Beginning Deferred Taxes) At the end of 2010, Wasicsko Company has €180,000 of cumulative temporary differences that will result in reporting future taxable amounts as follows.

2011	€ 70,000
2012	50,000
2013	40,000
2014	20,000
	€180,000

Tax rates enacted as of the beginning of 2009 are:

2009 and 2010	40%
2011 and 2012	30%
2013 and later	25%

Wasicsko's taxable income for 2010 is €340,000. Taxable income is expected in all future years.

Instructions
(a) Prepare the journal entry for Wasicsko to record income taxes payable, deferred income taxes, and income tax expense for 2010, assuming that there were no deferred taxes at the end of 2009.
(b) Prepare the journal entry for Wasicsko to record income taxes payable, deferred income taxes, and income tax expense for 2010, assuming that there was a balance of €22,000 in a Deferred Tax Liability account at the end of 2009.

·3 ·4 **E19-14 (Deferred Tax Asset)** Callaway Corp. has a deferred tax asset account with a balance of $150,000 at the end of 2010 due to a single cumulative temporary difference of $375,000. At the end of 2011, this same temporary difference has increased to a cumulative amount of $500,000. Taxable income for 2011 is $850,000. The tax rate is 40% for all years.

Instructions

(a) Record income tax expense, deferred income taxes, and income taxes payable for 2011, assuming that it is probable that the deferred tax asset will be realized.

(b) Assuming that it is probable that $30,000 of the deferred tax asset will not be realized, prepare the journal entry at the end of 2011 to recognize this probability.

·3 ·4 ·5 **E19-15 (Deferred Tax Asset)** Assume the same information as in E19-14 for Callaway Corp.

Instructions

(a) Record income tax expense, deferred income taxes, and income taxes payable for 2011, assuming that it is probable that $20,000 of the deferred tax asset will be realized in full.

(b) Record income tax expense, deferred income taxes, and income taxes payable for 2011, assuming that it is probable that none of the deferred tax asset will be realized.

·2 ·5 ·7 ·9 **E19-16 (Deferred Tax Liability, Change in Tax Rate, Prepare Section of Income Statement)** Sharrer Inc.'s only temporary difference at the beginning and end of 2010 is caused by a $2 million deferred gain for tax purposes for an installment sale of a plant asset, and the related receivable is due in equal installments in 2011 and 2012. The related deferred tax liability at the beginning of the year is $800,000. In the third quarter of 2010, a new tax rate of 34% is enacted into law and is scheduled to become effective for 2012. Taxable income for 2010 is $5,000,000, and taxable income is expected in all future years.

Instructions

(a) Determine the amount reported as a deferred tax liability at the end of 2010. Indicate proper classification(s).

(b) Prepare the journal entry (if any) necessary to adjust the deferred tax liability when the new tax rate is enacted into law.

(c) Draft the income tax expense portion of the income statement for 2010. Begin with the line "Income before income taxes." Assume no permanent differences exist.

·2 ·3 ·7 **E19-17 (Two Temporary Differences, Tracked through 3 Years, Multiple Rates)** Taxable income and pretax financial income would be identical for Jones Co. except for its treatments of gross profit on installment sales and estimated costs of warranties. The following income computations have been prepared.

Taxable income	2010	2011	2012
Excess of revenues over expenses (excluding two temporary differences)	$160,000	$210,000	$90,000
Installment income collected	8,000	8,000	8,000
Expenditures for warranties	(5,000)	(5,000)	(5,000)
Taxable income	$163,000	$213,000	$93,000

Pretax financial income	2010	2011	2012
Excess of revenues over expenses (excluding two temporary differences)	$160,000	$210,000	$90,000
Installment gross profit earned	24,000	–0–	–0–
Estimated cost of warranties	(15,000)	–0–	–0–
Income before taxes	$169,000	$210,000	$90,000

The tax rates in effect are: 2010, 45%; 2011 and 2012, 40%. All tax rates were enacted into law on January 1, 2010. No deferred income taxes existed at the beginning of 2010. Taxable income is expected in all future years.

Instructions

Prepare the journal entry to record income tax expense, deferred income taxes, and income tax payable for 2010, 2011, and 2012.

•2 •3 •7 **E19-18** **(Three Differences, Multiple Rates, Future Taxable Income)** During 2010, Graham Co.'s first year of operations, the company reports pretax financial income of £250,000. Graham's enacted tax rate is 40% for 2010 and 35% for all later years. Graham expects to have taxable income in each of the next 5 years. The effects on future tax returns of temporary differences existing at December 31, 2010, are summarized below.

| | Future Years | | | | | |
	2011	2012	2013	2014	2015	Total
Future taxable (deductible) amounts:						
Installment sales	£ 32,000	£ 32,000	£32,000			£ 96,000
Depreciation	6,000	6,000	6,000	£6,000	£6,000	30,000
Unearned rent	(50,000)	(50,000)				(100,000)

Instructions

(a) Complete the schedule below to compute deferred taxes at December 31, 2010.
(b) Compute taxable income for 2010.
(c) Prepare the journal entry to record income tax payable, deferred taxes, and income tax expense for 2010.

| | Future Taxable | | December 31, 2010 | |
| | (Deductible) | Tax | Deferred Tax | |
Temporary Difference	Amounts	Rate	(Asset)	Liability
Installment sales	£ 96,000			
Depreciation	30,000			
Unearned rent	(100,000)			
Totals	£			

•2 •3 •9 **E19-19** **(Two Differences, One Rate, Beginning Deferred Balance, Compute Pretax Financial Income)** Luo Co. establishes a ¥90 million liability at the end of 2010 for the estimated litigation settlement for manufacturing defects. All related costs will be paid and deducted on the tax return in 2011. Also, at the end of 2010, the company has ¥50 million of temporary differences due to excess depreciation for tax purposes, ¥7 million of which will reverse in 2011.

The enacted tax rate for all years is 40%, and the company pays taxes of ¥64 million on ¥160 million of taxable income in 2010. Luo expects to have taxable income in 2011.

Instructions

(a) Determine the deferred taxes to be reported at the end of 2010.
(b) Indicate how the deferred taxes computed in (a) are to be reported on the statement of financial position.
(c) Assuming that the only deferred tax account at the beginning of 2010 was a deferred tax liability of ¥10,000,000, draft the income tax expense portion of the income statement for 2010, beginning with the line "Income before income taxes." (*Hint:* You must first compute (1) the amount of temporary difference underlying the beginning ¥10,000,000 deferred tax liability, then (2) the amount of temporary differences originating or reversing during the year, and then (3) the amount of pretax financial income.)

•2 •3 •9 **E19-20** **(Two Differences, No Beginning Deferred Taxes, Multiple Rates)** Macinski Inc., in its first year of operations, has the following differences between the book basis and tax basis of its assets and liabilities at the end of 2010.

	Book Basis	Tax Basis
Equipment (net)	$400,000	$340,000
Estimated warranty liability	$150,000	$ –0–

It is estimated that the warranty liability will be settled in 2011. The difference in equipment (net) will result in taxable amounts of $20,000 in 2011, $30,000 in 2012, and $10,000 in 2013. The company has taxable income of $550,000 in 2010. As of the beginning of 2010, the enacted tax rate is 34% for 2010–2012, and 30% for 2013. Macinski expects to report taxable income through 2013.

Instructions

(a) Prepare the journal entry to record income tax expense, deferred income taxes, and income tax payable for 2010.
(b) Indicate how deferred income taxes will be reported on the statement of financial position at the end of 2010.

E19-21 (Two Temporary Differences, Multiple Rates, Future Taxable Income) Flynn Inc. has two temporary differences at the end of 2010. The first difference stems from installment sales, and the second one results from the accrual of a loss contingency. Flynn's accounting department has developed a schedule of future taxable and deductible amounts related to these temporary differences as follows.

	2011	2012	2013	2014
Taxable amounts	$40,000	$50,000	$60,000	$90,000
Deductible amounts		(15,000)	(19,000)	
	$40,000	$35,000	$41,000	$90,000

As of the beginning of 2010, the enacted tax rate is 34% for 2010 and 2011, and 38% for 2012–2015. At the beginning of 2010, the company had no deferred income taxes on its statement of financial position. Taxable income for 2010 is $400,000. Taxable income is expected in all future years.

Instructions

(a) Prepare the journal entry to record income tax expense, deferred income taxes, and income taxes payable for 2010.

(b) Indicate how deferred income taxes would be classified on the statement of financial position at the end of 2010.

E19-22 (Two Differences, One Rate, First Year) The differences between the book basis and tax basis of the assets and liabilities of Morgan Corporation at the end of 2010 are presented below.

	Book Basis	Tax Basis
Accounts receivable	$50,000	$–0–
Litigation liability	20,000	–0–

It is estimated that the litigation liability will be settled in 2011. The difference in accounts receivable will result in taxable amounts of $30,000 in 2011 and $20,000 in 2012. The company has taxable income of $300,000 in 2010 and is expected to have taxable income in each of the following 2 years. Its enacted tax rate is 34% for all years. This is the company's first year of operations.

Instructions

(a) Prepare the journal entry to record income tax expense, deferred income taxes, and income tax payable for 2010.

(b) Indicate how deferred income taxes will be reported on the statement of financial position at the end of 2010.

E19-23 (NOL Carryback and Carryforward, Recognition versus Non-Recognition) Sondgeroth Inc. reports the following pretax income (loss) for both financial reporting purposes and tax purposes. (Assume the carryback provision is used for a net operating loss.)

Year	Pretax Income (Loss)	Tax Rate
2009	£110,000	34%
2010	90,000	34%
2011	(260,000)	38%
2012	220,000	38%

The tax rates listed were all enacted by the beginning of 2009.

Instructions

(a) Prepare the journal entries for the years 2009–2012 to record income tax expense (benefit) and income tax payable (refundable) and the tax effects of the loss carryback and carryforward, assuming that at the end of 2011 it is probable that the benefits of the loss carryforward will be realized in the future.

(b) Using the assumption in (a), prepare the income tax section of the 2011 income statement, beginning with the line "Operating loss before income taxes."

(c) Prepare the journal entries for 2011 and 2012, assuming that based on the weight of available evidence, it is probable that one-fourth of the benefits of the loss carryforward will not be realized.

(d) Using the assumption in (c), prepare the income tax section of the 2011 income statement, beginning with the line "Operating loss before income taxes."

E19-24 (NOL Carryback and Carryforward, Non-Recognition) Nielson Inc. reports the following pretax income (loss) for both book and tax purposes. (Assume the carryback provision is used where possible for a net operating loss.)

Year	Pretax Income (Loss)	Tax Rate
2009	€ 100,000	40%
2010	90,000	40%
2011	(240,000)	45%
2012	120,000	45%

The tax rates listed were all enacted by the beginning of 2009.

Instructions

(a) Prepare the journal entries for years 2009–2012 to record income tax expense (benefit) and income tax payable (refundable), and the tax effects of the loss carryback and loss carryforward, assuming that based on the weight of available evidence it is probable that one-half of the benefits of the loss carryforward will not be realized.

(b) Prepare the income tax section of the 2011 income statement, beginning with the line "Operating loss before income taxes."

(c) Prepare the income tax section of the 2012 income statement, beginning with the line "Income before income taxes."

•4 •7 •8 E19-25 (NOL Carryback and Carryforward, Non-Recognition) Hayes Co. reported the following pretax financial income (loss) for the years 2009–2013.

2009	$240,000
2010	350,000
2011	90,000
2012	(550,000)
2013	180,000

Pretax financial income (loss) and taxable income (loss) were the same for all years involved. The enacted tax rate was 34% for 2009 and 2010, and 40% for 2011–2013. Assume the carryback provision is used first for net operating losses.

Instructions

(a) Prepare the journal entries for the years 2011–2013 to record income tax expense, income tax payable (refundable), and the tax effects of the loss carryback and loss carryforward, assuming that based on the weight of available evidence it is probable that one-fifth of the benefits of the loss carryforward will not be realized.

(b) Prepare the income tax section of the 2012 income statement, beginning with the line "Income (loss) before income taxes."

PROBLEMS

•2 •3 •5 P19-1 (Three Differences, No Beginning Deferred Taxes, Multiple Rates) The following information is available for Remmers Corporation for 2010.

1. Depreciation reported on the tax return exceeded depreciation reported on the income statement by $120,000. This difference will reverse in equal amounts of $30,000 over the years 2011–2014.
2. Interest received on governmental bonds was $10,000.
3. Rent collected in advance on January 1, 2010, totaled $60,000 for a 3-year period. Of this amount, $40,000 was reported as unearned at December 31, for book purposes.
4. The tax rates are 40% for 2010 and 35% for 2011 and subsequent years.
5. Income taxes of $320,000 are due per the tax return for 2010.
6. No deferred taxes existed at the beginning of 2010.

Instructions

(a) Compute taxable income for 2010.

(b) Compute pretax financial income for 2010.

(c) Prepare the journal entries to record income tax expense, deferred income taxes, and income taxes payable for 2010 and 2011. Assume taxable income was $980,000 in 2011.

(d) Prepare the income tax expense section of the income statement for 2010, beginning with "Income before income taxes."

•3 •5 •6 P19-2 (One Temporary Difference, Tracked for 4 Years, One Permanent Difference, Change in Rate) The pretax financial income of Truttman Company differs from its taxable income throughout each of 4 years, as shown on page 1058.

Year	Pretax Financial Income	Taxable Income	Tax Rate
2010	€290,000	€180,000	35%
2011	320,000	225,000	40%
2012	350,000	260,000	40%
2013	420,000	560,000	40%

Pretax financial income for each year includes a non-deductible expense of €30,000 (never deductible for tax purposes). The remainder of the difference between pretax financial income and taxable income in each period is due to one depreciation temporary difference. No deferred income taxes existed at the beginning of 2010.

Instructions

(a) Prepare journal entries to record income taxes in all 4 years. Assume that the change in the tax rate to 40% was not enacted until the beginning of 2011.

(b) Prepare the income statement for 2011, beginning with income before income taxes.

·2·5·6 **P19-3** **(Second Year of Depreciation Difference, Two Differences, Single Rate)** The following infor-
·9 mation has been obtained for the Gocker Corporation.

1. Prior to 2010, taxable income and pretax financial income were identical.
2. Pretax financial income is $1,700,000 in 2010 and $1,400,000 in 2011.
3. On January 1, 2010, equipment costing $1,200,000 is purchased. It is to be depreciated on a straight-line basis over 5 years for tax purposes and over 8 years for financial reporting purposes. (Under applicable tax law, a half-year of tax depreciation is recorded in 2010 and 2015.)
4. Interest of $60,000 was earned on tax-exempt governmental obligations in 2011.
5. Included in 2011 pretax financial income is a gain on discontinued operations of $200,000, which is fully taxable.
6. The tax rate is 35% for all periods.
7. Taxable income is expected in all future years.

Instructions

(a) Compute taxable income and income tax payable for 2011.

(b) Prepare the journal entry to record 2011 income tax expense, income tax payable, and deferred taxes.

(c) Prepare the bottom portion of Gocker's 2011 income statement, beginning with "Income before income taxes."

(d) Indicate how deferred income taxes should be presented on the December 31, 2011, statement of financial position.

·2·3·5 **P19-4** **(Permanent and Temporary Differences, One Rate)** The accounting records of Shinault Inc. show the following data for 2010.

1. Equipment was acquired in early January for $300,000. Straight-line depreciation over a 5-year life is used, with no residual value. For tax purposes, Shinault used a 30% rate to calculate depreciation.
2. Interest revenue on governmental bonds totaled $4,000.
3. Product warranties were estimated to be $50,000 in 2010. Actual repair and labor costs related to the warranties in 2010 were $10,000. The remainder is estimated to be paid evenly in 2011 and 2012.
4. Sales on an accrual basis were $100,000. For tax purposes, $75,000 was recorded on the installment-sales method.
5. Fines incurred for pollution violations were $4,200.
6. Pretax financial income was $750,000. The tax rate is 30%.

Instructions

(a) Prepare a schedule starting with pretax financial income in 2010 and ending with taxable income in 2010.

(b) Prepare the journal entry for 2010 to record income tax payable, income tax expense, and deferred income taxes.

·5·7·8 **P19-5** **(Recognition of NOL)** Jennings Inc. reported the following pretax income (loss) and related tax
·9 rates during the years 2006–2012.

	Pretax Income (loss)	Tax Rate
2006	£ 40,000	30%
2007	25,000	30%
2008	50,000	30%
2009	80,000	40%
2010	(180,000)	45%
2011	70,000	40%
2012	100,000	35%

Pretax financial income (loss) and taxable income (loss) were the same for all years since Jennings began business. The tax rates from 2009–2012 were enacted in 2009.

Instructions

(a) Prepare the journal entries for the years 2010–2012 to record income tax payable (refundable), income tax expense (benefit), and the tax effects of the loss carryback and carryforward. Assume that Jennings elects the carryback provision where possible and it is probable that it will realize the benefits of any loss carryforward in the year that immediately follows the loss year.

(b) Indicate the effect the 2010 entry(ies) has on the December 31, 2010, statement of financial position.

(c) Prepare the portion of the income statement, starting with "Operating loss before income taxes," for 2010.

(d) Prepare the portion of the income statement, starting with "Income before income taxes," for 2011.

·2·3·9 P19-6 (Two Differences, Two Rates, Future Income Expected) Presented below are two independent situations related to future taxable and deductible amounts resulting from temporary differences existing at December 31, 2010.

1. Mooney Co. has developed the following schedule of future taxable and deductible amounts.

	2011	2012	2013	2014	2015
Taxable amounts	$300	$300	$300	$ 300	$300
Deductible amount	—	—	—	(1,600)	—

2. Roesch Co. has the following schedule of future taxable and deductible amounts.

	2011	2012	2013	2014
Taxable amounts	$300	$300	$ 300	$300
Deductible amount	—	—	(2,300)	—

Both Mooney Co. and Roesch Co. have taxable income of $4,000 in 2010 and expect to have taxable income in all future years. The tax rates enacted as of the beginning of 2010 are 30% for 2010–2013 and 35% for years thereafter.

Instructions

For each of these two situations, compute the net amount of deferred income taxes to be reported at the end of 2010, and indicate how it should be classified on the statement of financial position.

·2·5·7 P19-7 (One Temporary Difference, Tracked 3 Years, Change in Rates, Income Statement Presentation) Crosley Corp. sold an investment on an installment basis. The total gain of $60,000 was reported for financial reporting purposes in the period of sale. The company qualifies to use the installment-sales method for tax purposes. The installment period is 3 years; one-third of the sale price is collected in the period of sale. The tax rate was 40% in 2010, and 35% in 2011 and 2012. The 35% tax rate was not enacted in law until 2011. The accounting and tax data for the 3 years is shown below.

	Financial Accounting	Tax Return
2010 (40% tax rate)		
Income before temporary difference	$ 70,000	$70,000
Temporary difference	60,000	20,000
Income	$130,000	$90,000
2011 (35% tax rate)		
Income before temporary difference	$ 70,000	$70,000
Temporary difference	–0–	20,000
Income	$ 70,000	$90,000
2012 (35% tax rate)		
Income before temporary difference	$ 70,000	$70,000
Temporary difference	–0–	20,000
Income	$ 70,000	$90,000

Instructions

(a) Prepare the journal entries to record the income tax expense, deferred income taxes, and the income tax payable at the end of each year. No deferred income taxes existed at the beginning of 2010.

(b) Explain how the deferred taxes will appear on the statement of financial position at the end of each year.

(c) Draft the income tax expense section of the income statement for each year, beginning with "Income before income taxes."

·2 ·3 ·5 ·9 **P19-8** **(Two Differences, 2 Years, Compute Taxable Income and Pretax Financial Income)** The following information was disclosed during the audit of Zheng Inc.

1.

Year	Amount Due per Tax Return
2010	¥130,000,000
2011	104,000,000

2. On January 1, 2010, equipment costing ¥600,000,000 is purchased. For financial reporting purposes, the company uses straight-line depreciation over a 5-year life. For tax purposes, the company uses the double-declining balance method over 5 years.

3. In January 2011, ¥225,000,000 is collected in advance rental of a building for a 3-year period. The entire ¥225,000,000 is reported as taxable income in 2011, but ¥150,000,000 of the ¥225,000,000 is reported as unearned revenue in 2011 for financial reporting purposes. The remaining amount of unearned revenue is to be earned equally in 2012 and 2013.

4. The tax rate is 40% in 2010 and all subsequent periods. (*Hint:* To find taxable income in 2010 and 2011, the related income tax payable amounts will have to be "grossed up.")

5. No temporary differences existed at the end of 2009. Zheng expects to report taxable income in each of the next 5 years.

Instructions

(a) Determine the amount to report for deferred income taxes at the end of 2010, and indicate how it should be classified on the statement of financial position.

(b) Prepare the journal entry to record income taxes for 2010.

(c) Draft the income tax section of the income statement for 2010, beginning with "Income before income taxes." (*Hint:* You must compute taxable income and then combine that with changes in cumulative temporary differences to arrive at pretax financial income.)

(d) Determine the deferred income taxes at the end of 2011, and indicate how they should be classified on the statement of financial position.

(e) Prepare the journal entry to record income taxes for 2011.

(f) Draft the income tax section of the income statement for 2011, beginning with "Income before income taxes."

·2 ·3 ·5 ·6 ·9 **P19-9** **(Five Differences, Compute Taxable Income and Deferred Taxes, Draft Income Statement)** Wise Company began operations at the beginning of 2011. The following information pertains to this company.

1. Pretax financial income for 2011 is $100,000.

2. The tax rate enacted for 2011 and future years is 40%.

3. Differences between the 2011 income statement and tax return are listed below:

   (a) Warranty expense accrued for financial reporting purposes amounts to $7,000. Warranty deductions per the tax return amount to $2,000.

   (b) Income on construction contracts using the percentage-of-completion method per books amounts to $92,000. Income on construction contracts for tax purposes amounts to $67,000.

   (c) Depreciation of property, plant, and equipment for financial reporting purposes amounts to $60,000. Depreciation of these assets amounts to $80,000 for the tax return.

   (d) A $3,500 fine paid for violation of pollution laws was deducted in computing pretax financial income.

   (e) Interest revenue earned on an investment in tax-exempt bonds amounts to $1,500.

4. Taxable income is expected for the next few years.

Instructions

(a) Compute taxable income for 2011.

(b) Compute the deferred taxes at December 31, 2011, that relate to the temporary differences described above. Clearly label them as deferred tax asset or liability.

(c) Prepare the journal entry to record income tax expense, deferred taxes, and income taxes payable for 2011.

(d) Draft the income tax expense section of the income statement, beginning with "Income before income taxes."

CONCEPTS FOR ANALYSIS

CA19-1 (Objectives and Principles for Accounting for Income Taxes) The amount of income taxes due to the government for a period of time is rarely the amount reported on the income statement for that period as income tax expense.

Instructions

(a) Explain the objectives of accounting for income taxes in general-purpose financial statements.

(b) Explain the basic principles that are applied in accounting for income taxes at the date of the financial statements to meet the objectives discussed in (a).

(c) List the steps in the annual computation of deferred tax liabilities and assets.

CA19-2 (Basic Accounting for Temporary Differences) Dexter Company appropriately uses the asset-liability method to record deferred income taxes. Dexter reports depreciation expense for certain machinery purchased this year using an accelerated method for income tax purposes and the straight-line basis for financial reporting purposes. The tax deduction is the larger amount this year.

Dexter received rent revenues in advance this year. These revenues are included in this year's taxable income. However, for financial reporting purposes, these revenues are reported as unearned revenues, a current liability.

Instructions

(a) What are the principles of the asset-liability approach?

(b) How would Dexter account for the temporary differences?

(c) How should Dexter classify the deferred tax consequences of the temporary differences on its statement of financial position?

CA19-3 (Identify Temporary Differences and Classification Criteria) The asset-liability approach for recording deferred income taxes is an integral part of IFRS.

Instructions

(a) Indicate whether each of the following independent situations should be treated as a temporary difference or as a permanent difference, and explain why.

(1) Estimated warranty costs (covering a 3-year warranty) are expensed for financial reporting purposes at the time of sale but deducted for income tax purposes when paid.

(2) Depreciation for book and income tax purposes differs because of different bases of carrying the related property, which was acquired in a trade-in. The different bases are a result of different rules used for book and tax purposes to compute the basis of property acquired in a trade-in.

(3) A company properly uses the equity method to account for its 30% investment in another company. The investee pays dividends that are about 10% of its annual earnings.

(4) A company reports a gain on an involuntary conversion of a non-monetary asset to a monetary asset. The company elects to replace the property within the statutory period using the total proceeds so the gain is not reported on the current year's tax return.

(b) Discuss the nature of the deferred income tax accounts and possible classifications in a company's statement of financial position. Indicate the manner in which these accounts are to be reported.

CA19-4 (Accounting for Deferred Income Taxes)

This year, Gumowski Company has each of the following items in its income statement.

1. Income on installment sales.
2. Revenues on long-term construction contracts.
3. Estimated costs of product warranty contracts.
4. Interest on tax-exempt bonds.

Instructions

(a) Under what conditions would deferred income taxes need to be reported in the financial statements?

(b) Specify when deferred income taxes would need to be recognized for each of the items above, and indicate the rationale for such recognition.

CA19-5 (Explain Computation of Deferred Tax Liability for Multiple Tax Rates) At December 31, 2010, Higley Corporation has one temporary difference which will reverse and cause taxable amounts in 2011. In 2010, a new tax act set taxes equal to 45% for 2010, 40% for 2011, and 34% for 2012 and years thereafter.

Instructions

Explain what circumstances would call for Higley to compute its deferred tax liability at the end of 2010 by multiplying the cumulative temporary difference by:

(a) 45%.
(b) 40%.
(c) 34%.

CA19-6 (Explain Future Taxable and Deductible Amounts, How Carryback and Carryforward Affects Deferred Taxes) Maria Rodriquez and Lynette Kingston are discussing accounting for income taxes. They are currently studying a schedule of taxable and deductible amounts that will arise in the future as a result of existing temporary differences. The schedule is as follows.

	Current Year	Future Years			
	2010	2011	2012	2013	2014
Taxable income	€850,000				
Taxable amounts		€375,000	€375,000	€ 375,000	€375,000
Deductible amounts				(2,400,000)	
Enacted tax rate	50%	45%	40%	35%	30%

Instructions

(a) Explain the concept of future taxable amounts and future deductible amounts as illustrated in the schedule.

(b) How do the carryback and carryforward provisions affect the reporting of deferred tax assets and deferred tax liabilities?

CA19-7 (Deferred Taxes, Income Effects) Stephanie Delaney, a public accountant, is the newly hired director of corporate taxation for Acme Incorporated, which is a publicly traded corporation. Ms. Delaney's first job with Acme was the review of the company's accounting practices on deferred income taxes. In doing her review, she noted differences between tax and book depreciation methods that permitted Acme to realize a sizable deferred tax liability on its statement of financial position. As a result, Acme paid very little in income taxes at that time.

Delaney also discovered that Acme has an explicit policy of selling off plant assets before they reversed in the deferred tax liability account. This policy, coupled with the rapid expansion of its plant asset base, allowed Acme to "defer" all income taxes payable for several years, even though it always has reported positive earnings and an increasing EPS. Delaney checked with the legal department and found the policy to be legal, but she's uncomfortable with the ethics of it.

Instructions

Answer the following questions.

(a) Why would Acme have an explicit policy of selling plant assets before the temporary differences reversed in the deferred tax liability account?

(b) What are the ethical implications of Acme's "deferral" of income taxes?

(c) Who could be harmed by Acme's ability to "defer" income taxes payable for several years, despite positive earnings?

(d) In a situation such as this, what are Ms. Delaney's professional responsibilities as a public accountant?

USING YOUR JUDGMENT

FINANCIAL REPORTING

Financial Reporting Problem

Marks and Spencer plc (M&S)

The financial statements of **M&S** are presented in Appendix 5B or can be accessed at the book's companion website, **www.wiley.com/college/kiesoifrs**.

Instructions

Refer to M&S's financial statements and the accompanying notes to answer the following questions.

(a) What amounts relative to income taxes does M&S report in its:

    (1) 2008 income statement?

    (2) 29 March 2008 balance sheet?

    (3) 2008 statement of cash flows?

(b) M&S's provision for income taxes in 2007 and 2008 was computed at what effective tax rates? (See the notes to the financial statements.)

(c) How much of M&S's 2008 total provision for income taxes was current tax expense, and how much was deferred tax expense?

(d) What did M&S report as the significant components (the details) of its 29 March 2008 deferred tax assets and liabilities?

Comparative Analysis Case
Cadbury and Nestlé

Instructions

Go to the book's companion website and use information found there to answer the following questions related to **Cadbury** and **Nestlé**.

(a) What are the amounts of Cadbury's and Nestlé's provision for income taxes for the year 2008? Of each company's 2008 provision for income taxes, what portion is current expense and what portion is deferred expense?

(b) What amount of cash was paid in 2008 for income taxes by Cadbury and by Nestlé?

(c) What was the effective tax rate in 2008 for Cadbury and Nestlé? Why might their effective tax rates differ?

(d) For the year-end 2008, what amounts were reported by Cadbury and Nestlé as (1) gross deferred tax assets and (2) gross deferred tax liabilities?

(e) Do either Cadbury or Nestlé disclose any net operating loss carrybacks and/or carryforwards at year-end 2008? What are the amounts, and when do the carryforwards expire?

Financial Statement Analysis Case
Homestake Mining Company

Homestake Mining Company (USA) is a 120-year-old international gold mining company with substantial gold mining operations and exploration in the United States, Canada, and Australia. At year-end, Homestake reported the following items related to income taxes (thousands of dollars).

Total current taxes	$ 26,349
Total deferred taxes	(39,436)
Total income and mining taxes (the provision for taxes per its income statement)	(13,087)
Deferred tax liabilities	$303,050
Deferred tax assets, net of an unrecognized amount of $207,175	95,275
Net deferred tax liability	$207,775

Note 6 (partial):

Tax loss carryforwards (U.S., Canada, Australia, and Chile)	$71,151
Tax credit carryforwards	$12,007

Instructions

(a) What is the significance of Homestake's disclosure of "Current taxes" of $26,349 and "Deferred taxes" of $(39,436)?

(b) Explain the concept behind Homestake's disclosure of deferred tax liabilities (future taxable amounts) and deferred tax assets (future deductible amounts).

(c) Homestake reported tax loss carryforwards of $71,151 and tax credit carryforwards of $12,007. How do the carryback and carryforward provisions affect the reporting of deferred tax assets and deferred tax liabilities?

Accounting, Analysis, and Principles

Allman Company, which began operations at the beginning of 2009, produces various products on a contract basis. Each contract generates income of €80,000. Some of Allman's contracts provide for the customer to pay on an installment basis. Under these contracts, Allman collects one-fifth of the contract revenue in each of the following 4 years. For financial reporting purposes, the company recognizes income on an accrual basis; for tax purposes, Allman recognizes income in the year cash is collected (installment basis).

Presented below is information related to Allman's operations for 2011.

1. In 2011, the company completed seven contracts that allow for the customer to pay on an installment basis. Allman recognized the related income of €560,000 for financial reporting purposes. It reported only €112,000 of income on installment sales on the 2011 tax return. The company expects future collections on the related installment receivables to result in taxable amounts of €112,000 in each of the next 4 years.
2. Non-taxable government bond interest revenue was €28,000.
3. Non-deductible fines and penalties of €26,000 were paid.
4. Pretax financial income amounts to €500,000.
5. Tax rates (enacted before the end of 2011) are 50% for 2011 and 40% for 2012 and later.
6. The accounting period is the calendar year.
7. The company is expected to have taxable income in all future years.
8. The company had a deferred tax liability balance of €40,000 at the end of 2010.

Accounting

Prepare the journal entry to record income taxes for 2011.

Analysis

Classify deferred income taxes on the statement of financial position at December 31, 2011, and indicate, starting with income before income taxes, how income taxes are reported on the income statement. What is Allman's effective tax rate?

Principles

Explain how the IASB Framework is used as a basis for determining the proper accounting for deferred income taxes.

BRIDGE TO THE PROFESSION

Professional Research

Kleckner Company started operations in 2007, and although it has grown steadily, the company reported accumulated operating losses of $450,000 in its first four years in business. In the most recent year (2011), Kleckner appears to have turned the corner and reported modest taxable income of $30,000. In addition to a deferred tax asset related to its net operating loss, Kleckner has recorded a deferred tax asset related to product warranties and a deferred tax liability related to accelerated depreciation.

Given its past operating results, Kleckner has determined that it is not probable that it will realize any of the deferred tax assets. However, given its improved performance, Kleckner management wonders whether there are any accounting consequences for its deferred tax assets. They would like you to conduct some research on the accounting for recognition of its deferred tax asset.

Instructions

Access the IFRS authoritative literature at the IASB website (http://eifrs.iasb.org/). When you have accessed the documents, you can use the search tool in your Internet browser to respond to the following questions. (Provide paragraph citations.)

(a) Briefly explain to Kleckner management the importance of future taxable income as it relates to the recognition of deferred tax assets.
(b) What are the sources of income that may be relied upon in assessing realization of a deferred tax asset?
(c) What are tax-planning strategies? From the information provided, does it appear that Kleckner could employ a tax-planning strategy in evaluating its deferred tax asset?

Professional Simulation

In this simulation, you are asked to address questions related to the accounting for taxes. Prepare responses to all parts.

KWW_Professional_Simulation

| **Accounting for Taxes** | **Time Remaining 2 hours 40 minutes** | copy | paste | calculator | sheet | standards | help | splitter | done |

| Directions | Situation | Journal Entry | Financial Statements | Resources |

Johnny Bravo Company began operations in 2010 and has provided the following information.

1. Pretax financial income for 2010 is $100,000.
2. The tax rate enacted for 2010 and future years is 40%.
3. Differences between the 2010 income statement and tax return are listed below.
   (a) Warranty expense accrued for financial reporting purposes amounts to $5,000. Warranty deductions per the tax return amount to $2,000.
   (b) Income on construction contracts using the percentage-of-completion method for book purposes amounts to $92,000. Income on construction contracts for tax purposes amounts to $62,000.
   (c) Depreciation of property, plant, and equipment for financial reporting purposes amounts to $60,000. Depreciation of these assets amounts to $80,000 for the tax return.
   (d) A $3,500 fine paid for violation of pollution laws was deducted in computing pretax financial income.
   (e) Interest revenue earned on an investment in tax-exempt governmental bonds amounts to $1,400.
4. Taxable income is expected for the next few years.

| Directions | Situation | Journal Entry | Financial Statements | Resources |

Prepare the journal entry to record income tax expense, deferred taxes, and income taxes payable for 2010.

| Directions | Situation | Journal Entry | Financial Statements | Resources |

Draft the income tax expense section of the income statement, beginning with "Income before income taxes."

ACCOUNTING FOR PENSIONS AND POSTRETIREMENT BENEFITS

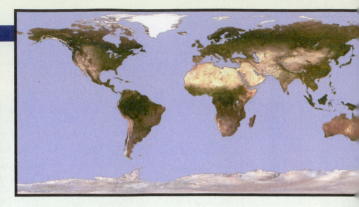

LEARNING OBJECTIVES

After studying this chapter, you should be able to:

•1 Distinguish between accounting for the employer's pension plan and accounting for the pension fund.

•2 Identify types of pension plans and their characteristics.

•3 Explain alternative measures for valuing the pension obligation.

•4 List the components of pension expense.

•5 Use a worksheet for employer's pension plan entries.

•6 Describe the amortization of past service costs.

•7 Explain the accounting for unexpected gains and losses.

•8 Explain the corridor approach to amortizing gains and losses.

•9 Describe the requirements for reporting pension plans in financial statements.

•10 Explain special issues related to postretirement benefit plans.

PENSION PERIL

The effects of the financial crisis and the resultant economic downturn continue to ripple through global markets. Pension plans, both those sponsored by governments and private companies, are now feeling the effects. Consider the following actions by private companies to deal with the effects of the financial crisis.

• Britain's largest employers **shut down pension schemes** at such a rapid rate over the past year that if the current pace continues, traditional final salary pension benefits will soon become a thing of the past, a new study has concluded. It found that total service cost—the cost of providing the current year's pension promises— had fallen by 15 percent over the past year. The drop reflects a decline in the number of workers who are earning pension benefits. At that rate, final salary pensions in the private sector will no longer be available within six years.

• **United Utilities** (GBR) has **made its defined benefit pension schemes less generous** to employees as the United Kingdom's biggest listed water company looks to cut costs in the face of a harsher regulatory regime. The utility announced that the move was backed by unions. The company said it had amended the terms of its defined benefit schemes to increase contributions made by members, while also increasing the retirement age and capping increases in pensionable salaries.

• **Marks and Spencer plc** (GBR) is planning to **increase contributions to its pension plan** (£800 million or $1.2 billion) to address a deficit in the plan assets relative to its pension obligations. The retailer insisted that it had no plans to close the final salary scheme to existing members. The clothing and food chain, which has 20,000 current members in its defined benefits scheme, said it would not be following the growing band of companies—such as **Wm Morrison Supermarkets plc** (GBR) and **Vodafone** (GBR)—which are closing their final salary schemes to existing members.

Public sector pension plans are also not immune from these pension perils.

- France, in an effort to address its growing budget shortfall, unveiled pension reforms for public employees, which will raise the legal retirement age from 60 to 62 by 2018. Since this will meet less than half the €45 billion state pension fund shortfall by 2020, civil servants' pension contributions will increase from 8.1 percent to 10.5 percent of pay.

- In Britain, the government is evaluating ways to address the pension gap between the public and private sector. More generous and much more widespread pension provisions boost public pay by a further 12 percent compared with the private sector. By requiring public sector employees to increase contributions by two percentage points, the government can raise £3 billion, or 0.2 percent of GDP. Broader reform of the system (e.g., increased retirement age) could phase in over time.

- Several state governments in the United States have cut or are considering cuts in pension benefits and requiring state employees to contribute more of the cost of their pension benefits.

Why are pension plans so vulnerable to the effects of the financial crisis? As you will learn in this chapter, pensions are a form of deferred compensation. When a pension is included in a salary and benefit package, employees may accept lower pay while working in exchange for pension benefits that will be paid in the future at retirement. Companies and governments must set aside assets to meet these future obligations. However, when economic times are tough, assets in the funds (shares and bonds) lose value, and companies and governments may not have the resources to contribute to the funds. As a result, a pension deficit arises and employees' pensions may be in peril. Given the need for good information about the impact of these continuing pension perils on companies, both the IASB and the FASB have active projects to improve the accounting for pensions and other postretirement benefit plans.

Source: Adapted from Norma Cohen, "Study Sees End for Final Salary Pensions," *Financial Times* (May 17, 2010); and J. Raife, "Time to Talk Real Public Sector Pension Costs," *Financial Times* (June 27, 2010).

PREVIEW OF CHAPTER 20

As our opening story indicates, the financial crisis has put pension plans in peril and the cost of retirement benefits is getting steep. For example, **British Airways**' (GBR) pension and healthcare costs for retirees in a recent year totaled £149 million, or approximately £4 per passenger carried. British Air and many other companies are facing substantial pension and other postretirement expenses and obligations. In this chapter, we discuss the accounting issues related to these benefit plans. The content and organization of the chapter are as follows.

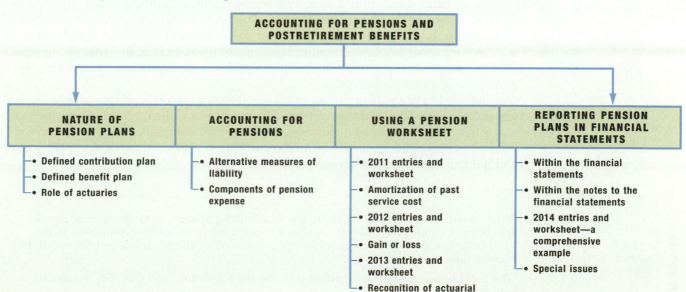

ACCOUNTING FOR PENSIONS AND POSTRETIREMENT BENEFITS			
NATURE OF PENSION PLANS	**ACCOUNTING FOR PENSIONS**	**USING A PENSION WORKSHEET**	**REPORTING PENSION PLANS IN FINANCIAL STATEMENTS**
• Defined contribution plan • Defined benefit plan • Role of actuaries	• Alternative measures of liability • Components of pension expense	• 2011 entries and worksheet • Amortization of past service cost • 2012 entries and worksheet • Gain or loss • 2013 entries and worksheet • Recognition of actuarial gains and losses	• Within the financial statements • Within the notes to the financial statements • 2014 entries and worksheet—a comprehensive example • Special issues

NATURE OF PENSION PLANS

A **pension plan** is an arrangement whereby an employer provides benefits (payments) to retired employees for services they provided in their working years. Pension accounting may be divided and separately treated as **accounting for the employer** and **accounting for the pension fund**. The *company* or *employer* is the organization sponsoring the pension plan. It incurs the cost and makes contributions to the pension fund. The *fund* or *plan* is the entity that receives the contributions from the employer, administers the pension assets, and makes the benefit payments to the retired employees (pension recipients). Illustration 20-1 shows the three entities involved in a pension plan and indicates the flow of cash among them.

ILLUSTRATION 20-1
Flow of Cash among
Pension Plan Participants

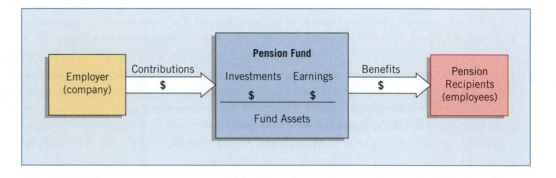

A pension plan is **funded** when the employer makes payments to a funding agency.[1] That agency accumulates the assets of the pension fund and makes payments to the recipients as the benefits come due.

Some pension plans are **contributory**. In these, the employees bear part of the cost of the stated benefits or voluntarily make payments to increase their benefits. Other plans are **non-contributory**. In these plans, the employer bears the entire cost. In some countries, companies design their pension plans so as to take advantage of certain income tax benefits. Plans that offer tax benefits are often called **qualified pension plans**. They permit **deductibility of the employer's contributions to the pension fund and tax-free status of earnings from pension fund assets**.

The pension fund should be a separate legal and accounting entity. The pension fund, as a separate entity, maintains a set of books and prepares financial statements. Maintaining records and preparing financial statements for the fund, an activity known as "accounting for employee benefit plans," is not the subject of this chapter.[2] Instead, this chapter explains the pension accounting and reporting problems **of the employer** as the sponsor of a pension plan.

The need to properly administer and account for pension funds becomes apparent when you understand the size of these funds. Listed in Illustration 20-2 are the pension fund assets and pension expenses of eight major companies. The two most common types of pension plans are **defined contribution plans** and **defined benefit plans**, and we look at each of them in the following sections.

---

[1]When used as a verb, fund means to pay to a funding agency (as to fund future pension benefits or to fund pension cost). Used as a noun, it refers to assets accumulated in the hands of a funding agency (trustee) for the purpose of meeting pension benefits when they become due.

[2]The IASB issued a separate standard covering the accounting and reporting for employee benefit plans. **[1]**

Company (in millions)	Size of Pension Fund	2008 Pension Expense	Pension Expense as % of Pretax Income (Loss)
British Airways (GBR)	£5,953	£154	−2.46%
Nokia (FIN)	€1,197	€228	4.59
Siemens (DEU)	€20,194	€239	8.93
AB InBev (BEL)	€2,783	€85	3.34
BASF (DEU)	€10,313	€288	4.82
Cathay Pacific (CHN)	$5,924	$15	−0.16
Dairy Farm International (CHN)	$123	$6	1.54
Unilever (GBR)	£11,713	£186	2.61

ILLUSTRATION 20-2
Pension Funds and Pension Expense

Defined Contribution Plan

In a **defined contribution plan**, the employer agrees to contribute to a pension trust a certain sum each period, based on a formula. This formula may consider such factors as age, length of employee service, employer's profits, and compensation level. **The plan defines only the employer's contribution.** It makes no promise regarding the ultimate benefits paid out to the employees.

Objective•2
Identify types of pension plans and their characteristics.

The size of the pension benefits that the employee finally collects under the plan depends on several factors: the amounts originally contributed to the pension trust, the income accumulated in the trust, and the treatment of forfeitures of funds caused by early terminations of other employees. A company usually turns over to an **independent third-party trustee** the amounts originally contributed. The trustee, acting on behalf of the beneficiaries (the participating employees), assumes ownership of the pension assets and is accountable for their investment and distribution. The trust is separate and distinct from the employer.

The accounting for a defined contribution plan is straightforward. The employee gets the benefit of gain (or the risk of loss) from the assets contributed to the pension plan. The employer simply contributes each year based on the formula established in the plan. As a result, the employer's annual cost (pension expense) is simply the amount that it is obligated to contribute to the pension trust. The employer reports a liability on its statement of financial position only if it does not make the contribution in full. The employer reports an asset only if it contributes more than the required amount and must disclose the amount of expense recorded for the defined contribution plan. **[2]**

Defined Benefit Plan

A **defined benefit plan** outlines the benefits that employees will receive when they retire. These benefits typically are a function of an employee's years of service and of the compensation level in the years approaching retirement.

To meet the defined benefit commitments that will arise at retirement, a company must determine what the contribution should be today (a time value of money computation). Companies may use many different contribution approaches. However, the funding method should provide enough money at retirement to meet the benefits defined by the plan.

The **employees** are the beneficiaries of a defined **contribution** trust, but the **employer** is the beneficiary of a defined **benefit** trust. Under a defined benefit plan, the trust's primary purpose is to safeguard and invest assets so that there will be enough to pay the employer's obligation to the employees. **In form**, the trust is a separate entity. **In substance**, the trust assets and liabilities belong to the employer. That is, **as long as the plan continues, the employer is responsible for the payment of the defined benefits (without regard to what happens in the trust).** The employer must make up any shortfall in the accumulated assets held by the trust. On the other hand, the employer can recapture any excess accumulated in the trust, either through reduced future funding or through a reversion of funds.

Because a defined benefit plan specifies benefits in terms of uncertain future variables, a company must establish an appropriate funding pattern to ensure the availability of funds at retirement in order to provide the benefits promised. This funding level depends on a number of factors such as turnover, mortality, length of employee service, compensation levels, and interest earnings.

Employers are at risk with defined benefit plans because they must contribute enough to meet the cost of benefits that the plan defines. The expense recognized each period is not necessarily equal to the cash contribution. Similarly, the liability is controversial because its measurement and recognition relate to unknown future variables. Thus, the accounting issues related to this type of plan are complex. **Our discussion in the following sections deals primarily with defined benefit plans.**[3]

WHICH PLAN IS RIGHT FOR YOU?

What do the numbers mean?

Defined contribution plans have become much more popular with employers than defined benefit plans. One reason is that they are cheaper. Defined contribution plans often cost no more than 3 percent of payroll, whereas defined benefit plans can cost 5 to 6 percent of payroll.

In the late 1970s, approximately 15 million individuals had defined contribution plans; today over 62 million do. The following chart reflects this significant change. It shows the percentage of companies using various types of plans, based on a survey of approximately 150 CFOs and managing corporate directors.

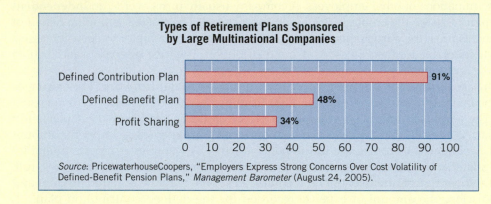

Types of Retirement Plans Sponsored by Large Multinational Companies

Plan	Percentage
Defined Contribution Plan	91%
Defined Benefit Plan	48%
Profit Sharing	34%

Source: PricewaterhouseCoopers, "Employers Express Strong Concerns Over Cost Volatility of Defined-Benefit Pension Plans," *Management Barometer* (August 24, 2005).

Although many companies are changing to defined contribution plans, over 40 million individuals still are covered under defined benefit plans.

The Role of Actuaries in Pension Accounting

The problems associated with pension plans involve complicated mathematical considerations. Therefore, companies engage **actuaries** to ensure that a pension plan is appropriate for the employee group covered.[4] Actuaries are individuals trained through a long and rigorous certification program to assign probabilities to future events and

---

[3]In many cases, companies offer a defined contribution plan in combination with a defined benefit plan.

[4]An actuary's primary purpose is to ensure that the company has established an appropriate funding pattern to meet its pension obligations. This computation involves developing a set of assumptions and continued monitoring of these assumptions to ensure their realism. IFRS encourages, but does not require, companies to use actuaries in the measurement of the pension amounts. [3] That the general public has little understanding of what an actuary does is illustrated by the following excerpt from the *Wall Street Journal*: "A polling organization once asked the general public what an actuary was, and received among its more coherent responses the opinion that it was a place where you put dead actors."

their financial effects. The insurance industry employs actuaries to assess risks and to advise on the setting of premiums and other aspects of insurance policies. Employers rely heavily on actuaries for assistance in developing, implementing, and funding pension funds.

Actuaries make predictions (called *actuarial assumptions*) of mortality rates, employee turnover, interest and earnings rates, early retirement frequency, future salaries, and any other factors necessary to operate a pension plan. They also compute the various pension measures that affect the financial statements, such as the pension obligation, the annual cost of servicing the plan, and the cost of amendments to the plan. In summary, accounting for defined benefit pension plans relies heavily upon information and measurements provided by actuaries.

ACCOUNTING FOR PENSIONS

In accounting for a company's pension plan, two questions arise: (1) What is the pension obligation that a company should report in the financial statements? (2) What is the pension expense for the period? Attempting to answer the first question has produced much controversy.

> **Objective•3**
> Explain alternative measures for valuing the pension obligation.

Alternative Measures of the Liability

Most agree that an employer's **pension obligation** is the deferred compensation obligation it has to its employees for their service under the terms of the pension plan. Measuring that obligation is not so simple, though, because there are alternative ways of measuring it.

One measure of the pension obligation is to base it only on the benefits vested to the employees. **Vested benefits** are those that the employee is entitled to receive even if he or she renders no additional services to the company. Most pension plans require a certain minimum number of years of service to the employer before an employee achieves vested benefits status. Companies compute the **vested benefit obligation** using only vested benefits, at current salary levels.

Another way to measure the obligation uses both vested and non-vested years of service. On this basis, the company computes the deferred compensation amount on all years of employees' service—**both vested and non-vested**—using current salary levels. This measurement of the pension obligation is called the **accumulated benefit obligation**.

A third measure bases the deferred compensation amount on both vested and non-vested service **using future salaries**. This measurement of the pension obligation is called the **defined benefit obligation**. Because future salaries are expected to be higher than current salaries, this approach results in the largest measurement of the pension obligation.

The choice between these measures is critical. The choice affects the amount of a company's pension liability and the annual pension expense reported. The diagram in Illustration 20-3 (page 1072) presents the differences in these three measurements.

Which of these alternative measures of the pension liability does the profession favor? **The profession adopted the defined benefit obligation—the present value of vested and non-vested benefits accrued to date, based on employees' future salary levels.**[5] Those in favor of the defined benefit obligation contend that a promise by an

---

[5]When we use the term "present value of benefits" throughout this chapter, we really mean the *actuarial* present value of benefits. **Actuarial present value** is the amount payable adjusted to reflect the time value of money *and* the probability of payment (by means of decrements for events such as death, disability, withdrawals, or retirement) between the present date and the expected date of payment. For simplicity, though, we use the term "present value" instead of "actuarial present value" in our discussion.

ILLUSTRATION 20-3
Different Measures of the
Pension Obligation

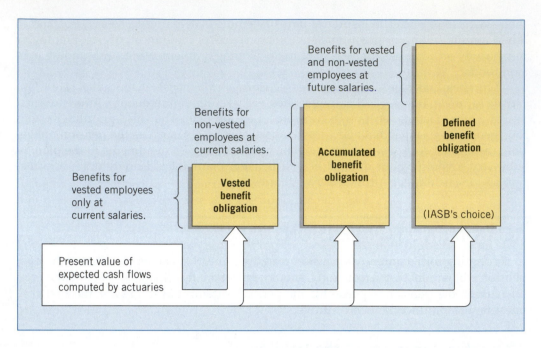

employer to pay benefits based on a percentage of the employees' future salaries
is far greater than a promise to pay a percentage of their current salary, and such
a difference should be reflected in the pension liability and pension expense.

Moreover, companies discount to present value the estimated future benefits to be paid. Minor changes in the interest rate used to discount pension benefits can dramatically affect the measurement of the employer's obligation. For
example, a 1 percent decrease in the discount rate can increase pension liabilities 15 percent. Accounting rules require that, at each measurement date, a company must determine the appropriate discount rate used to measure the pension
liability, based on current interest rates. **[4]**

Components of Pension Expense

Objective·4

List the components of pension
expense.

There is broad agreement that companies should account for pension cost on the
accrual basis.[6] The profession recognizes that **accounting for pension plans requires measurement of the cost and its identification with the appropriate time
periods**. The determination of pension cost, however, is extremely complicated
because it is a function of the following components. **[5]**

1. *Service cost.* Service cost is the expense caused by the increase in pension benefits
   payable (the **defined benefit obligation**) to employees because of their services rendered during the current year. Actuaries compute **service cost** as the present value
   of the new benefits earned by employees during the year.

2. *Interest on the liability.* Because a pension is a deferred compensation arrangement,
   there is a time value of money factor. As a result, companies record the pension
   liability on a discounted basis. **Interest expense accrues each year on the defined**

---

[6]At one time, companies applied the cash basis of accounting to pension plans by recognizing
the amount paid in a particular accounting period as the pension expense for the period.
The problem was that the amount paid or funded in a fiscal period depended on financial
management and was too often discretionary. For example, funding could depend on the
availability of cash, the level of earnings, or other factors unrelated to the requirements
of the plan. Application of the cash basis made it possible to manipulate the amount of
pension expense appearing in the income statement simply by varying the cash paid to the
pension fund.

benefit obligation just as it does on any discounted debt. The actuary helps to select the interest rate, referred to as the **discount rate**.

3. *Actual return on plan assets.* The return earned by the accumulated pension fund assets in a particular year is relevant in measuring the net cost to the employer of sponsoring an employee pension plan. Therefore, **a company should adjust annual pension expense for interest and dividends that accumulate within the fund, as well as increases and decreases in the fair value of the fund assets.**

4. *Amortization of past service cost.* Pension plan amendments (including initiation of a pension plan) often include provisions to increase benefits (or in some situations, to decrease benefits) for employee service provided in prior years. A company grants plan amendments with the expectation that it will realize economic benefits in future periods. Thus, **it allocates the cost (past service cost) of providing these retroactive benefits to pension expense in the future, specifically to the remaining service-years of the affected employees.**

5. *Gain or loss.* Volatility in pension expense can result from sudden and large changes in the fair value of plan assets and by changes in the defined benefit obligation (which changes when actuaries modify assumptions or when actual experience differs from expected experience). Two items comprise this gain or loss: (1) the difference between the actual return and the expected return on plan assets, and (2) amortization of the net gain or loss from previous periods. We will discuss this complex computation later in the chapter.

Underlying Concepts

The expense recognition principle and the definition of a liability justify accounting for pension cost on the accrual basis. This requires recording an expense when employees earn the future benefits, and recognizing an existing obligation to pay pensions later based on current services received.

Illustration 20-4 shows the **components of pension expense** and their effect on total pension expense (increase or decrease).

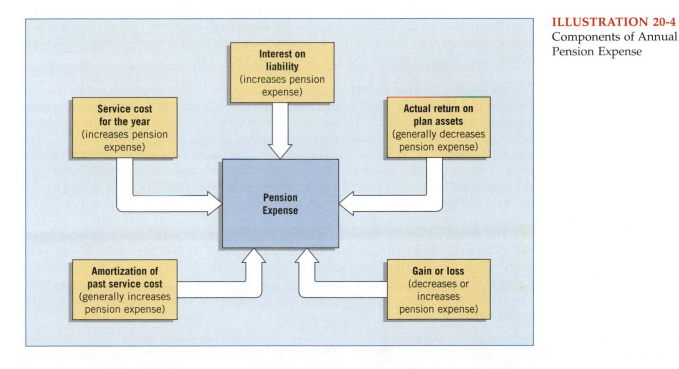

ILLUSTRATION 20-4
Components of Annual Pension Expense

Service Cost

The **service cost** is the **actuarial present value of benefits attributed by the pension benefit formula to employee service during the period.** That is, the actuary predicts the additional benefits that an employer must pay under the plan's benefit formula as a result of the employees' current year's service, and then discounts the cost of those future benefits back to their present value.

The IASB concluded that **companies must consider future compensation levels in measuring the present obligation and periodic pension expense if the plan benefit formula incorporates them**. In other words, the present obligation resulting from a promise to pay a benefit of 1 percent of an employee's **final pay** differs from the promise to pay 1 percent of **current pay**. To overlook this fact is to ignore an important aspect of pension expense. Thus, the Board adopts the **projected unit credit method** (often referred to as the **benefits/years-of-service method**), **which determines pension expense based on future salary levels**.

Some object to this determination, arguing that a company should have more freedom to select an expense recognition pattern. Others believe that incorporating future salary increases into current pension expense is accounting for events that have not yet happened. They argue that if a company terminates the plan today, it pays only liabilities for accumulated benefits. **Nevertheless, the IASB indicates that the defined benefit obligation provides a more realistic measure of the employer's obligation under the plan on a going concern basis and, therefore, companies should use it as the basis for determining service cost.**

Interest on the Liability

The second component of pension expense is **interest on the liability**, or **interest expense**. Because a company defers paying the liability until maturity, the company records it on a discounted basis. The liability then accrues interest over the life of the employee. **The interest component is the interest for the period on the defined benefit obligation outstanding during the period.** The IASB did not address the question of how often to compound the interest cost. To simplify our illustrations and problem materials, we use a simple-interest computation, applying it to the beginning-of-the-year balance of the defined benefit liability.

How do companies determine the interest rate to apply to the pension liability? The **discount rates** used should be those based on high-quality bonds of currency and term consistent with the liabilities. In countries where there is no deep market in such bonds, the yields on government bonds can be used instead. **[6]**

Actual Return on Plan Assets

Pension plan assets are usually investments in shares, bonds, other securities, and real estate that a company holds to earn a reasonable return, generally at minimum risk. Employer contributions and actual returns on pension plan assets increase pension plan assets. Benefits paid to retired employees decrease them. As we indicated, the actual return earned on these assets increases the fund balance and correspondingly reduces the employer's net cost of providing employees' pension benefits. That is, the higher the actual return on the pension plan assets, the less the employer has to contribute eventually and, therefore, the less pension expense that it needs to report.

The **actual return on the plan assets** is the increase in pension funds from interest, dividends, and realized and unrealized changes in the fair value of the plan assets. Companies compute the actual return by adjusting the change in the plan assets for the effects of contributions during the year and benefits paid out during the year. The equation in Illustration 20-5, or a variation thereof, can be used to compute the actual return.

ILLUSTRATION 20-5
Equation for Computing Actual Return

$$\text{Actual Return} = \left(\begin{array}{c} \text{Plan Assets Ending Balance} \end{array} - \begin{array}{c} \text{Plan Assets Beginning Balance} \end{array} \right) - (\text{Contributions} - \text{Benefits Paid})$$

Stated another way, the actual return on plan assets is the difference between the **fair value of the plan assets** at the beginning of the period and at the end of the period, adjusted for contributions and benefit payments. Illustration 20-6 uses the equation above to compute the actual return, using some assumed amounts.

Fair value of plan assets at end of period	€5,000,000
Deduct: Fair value of plan assets at beginning of period	4,200,000
Increase in fair value of plan assets	800,000
Deduct: Contributions to plan during period €500,000	
Less benefits paid during period 300,000	200,000
Actual return on plan assets	€ 600,000

ILLUSTRATION 20-6
Computation of Actual
Return on Plan Assets

If the actual return on the plan assets is positive (a gain) during the period, a company subtracts it when computing pension expense. If the actual return is negative (a loss) during the period, the company adds it when computing pension expense.[7]

USING A PENSION WORKSHEET

We will now illustrate the basic computation of pension expense using the first three components: (1) service cost, (2) interest on the liability, and (3) actual return on plan assets. We discuss the other pension-expense components (amortization of past service cost, and gains and losses) in later sections.

Objective•5
Use a worksheet for employer's pension plan entries.

Companies often use a worksheet to record pension-related information. As its name suggests, the worksheet is a working tool. A worksheet is **not** a permanent accounting record: It is neither a journal nor part of the general ledger. The worksheet is merely a device to make it easier to prepare entries and the financial statements.[8] Illustration 20-7 shows the format of the **pension worksheet**.

ILLUSTRATION 20-7
Basic Format of Pension Worksheet

	General Journal Entries			Memo Record	
Items	Annual Pension Expense	Cash	Pension Asset/ Liability	Defined Benefit Obligation	Plan Assets

The "General Journal Entries" columns of the worksheet (near the left side) determine the entries to record in the formal general ledger accounts. The "Memo Record" columns (on the right side) maintain balances in the defined benefit obligation and the plan assets. The difference between the defined benefit obligation and the fair value of the plan assets is the **pension asset/liability**, which is shown in the statement of financial position. If the defined benefit obligation is greater than the plan assets, a pension liability occurs. If the defined benefit obligation is less than the plan assets, a pension asset occurs.

On the first line of the worksheet, a company enters the beginning balances (if any). It then records subsequent transactions and events related to the pension plan using debits and credits, using both sets of columns as if they were one. For each transaction or event, the debits must equal the credits. **The ending balance in the Pension Asset/Liability column should equal the net balance in the memo record.**

[7]At this point, we use the actual rate of return. As we discuss later, *IAS 19* calls for use of the expected rate of return for purposes of computing pension expense. **[7]**

[8]The use of a pension entry worksheet is recommended and illustrated by Paul B. W. Miller, "The New Pension Accounting (Part 2)," *Journal of Accountancy* (February 1987), pp. 86–94.

2011 Entries and Worksheet

To illustrate the use of a worksheet and how it helps in accounting for a pension plan, assume that on January 1, 2011, Zarle Company provides the following information related to its pension plan for the year 2011.

Plan assets, January 1, 2011, are $100,000.

Defined benefit obligation, January 1, 2011, is $100,000.

Annual service cost is $9,000.

Discount rate is 10 percent.

Actual return on plan assets is $10,000.

Funding contributions are $8,000.

Benefits paid to retirees during the year are $7,000.

Using the data presented above, the worksheet in Illustration 20-8 presents the beginning balances and all of the pension entries recorded by Zarle in 2011. Zarle records the beginning balances for the defined benefit obligation and the pension plan assets on the first line of the worksheet in the memo record. Because the defined benefit obligation and the plan assets are the same at January 1, 2011, the Pension Asset/Liability account has a zero balance at January 1, 2011.

ILLUSTRATION 20-8
Pension Worksheet—2011

		General Journal Entries			**Memo Record**	
	Items	Annual Pension Expense	Cash	Pension Asset/ Liability	Defined Benefit Obligation	Plan Assets
	Balance, Jan. 1, 2011			—	100,000 Cr.	100,000 Dr.
	(a) Service cost	9,000 Dr.			9,000 Cr.	
	(b) Interest cost	10,000 Dr.			10,000 Cr.	
	(c) Actual return	10,000 Cr.				10,000 Dr.
	(d) Contributions		8,000 Cr.			8,000 Dr.
	(e) Benefits				7,000 Dr.	7,000 Cr.
	Journal entry for 2011	9,000 Dr.	8,000 Cr.	1,000 Cr.*		
	Balance, Dec. 31, 2011			1,000 Cr.**	112,000 Cr.	111,000 Dr.
	*$9,000 − $8,000 = $1,000					
	**$112,000 − $111,000 = $1.000					

Entry (a) in Illustration 20-8 records the service cost component, which increases pension expense by $9,000 and increases the liability (defined benefit obligation) by $9,000. Entry (b) accrues the interest expense component, which increases both the liability and the pension expense by $10,000 (the beginning defined benefit obligation multiplied by the discount rate of 10 percent). Entry (c) records the actual return on the plan assets, which increases the plan assets and decreases the pension expense. Entry (d) records Zarle's contribution (funding) of assets to the pension fund, thereby decreasing cash by $8,000 and increasing plan assets by $8,000. Entry (e) records the benefit payments made to retirees, which results in equal $7,000 decreases to the plan assets and the defined benefit obligation.

Zarle makes the "formal journal entry" on December 31, which records the pension expense in 2011, as follows.

2011

Pension Expense	9,000	
Cash		8,000
Pension Asset/Liability		1,000

The credit to Pension Asset/Liability for $1,000 represents the difference between the 2011 pension expense of $9,000 and the amount funded of $8,000. Pension Asset/ Liability (credit) is a liability because Zarle underfunds the plan by $1,000. The Pension Asset/Liability account balance of $1,000 also equals the net of the balances in the memo accounts. Illustration 20-9 shows that the defined benefit obligation exceeds the plan assets by $1,000, which reconciles to the pension liability reported in the statement of financial position.

Defined benefit obligation (Credit)	$(112,000)
Plan assets at fair value (Debit)	111,000
Pension asset/liability (Credit)	$ (1,000)

ILLUSTRATION 20-9
Pension Reconciliation Schedule—December 31, 2011

If the net of the memo record balances is a credit, the reconciling amount in the Pension Asset/Liability column will be a credit equal in amount. If the net of the memo record balances is a debit, the Pension Asset/Liability amount will be a debit equal in amount. The worksheet is designed to produce this reconciling feature, which is useful later in the preparation of the financial statements and required note disclosure related to pensions.

In this illustration (for 2011), the debit to Pension Expense exceeds the credit to Cash, resulting in a credit to Pension Asset/Liability—the recognition of a liability. If the credit to Cash exceeded the debit to Pension Expense, Zarle would debit Pension Asset/Liability—the recognition of an asset.[9]

Amortization of Past Service Cost (PSC)

When either initiating (adopting) or amending a defined benefit plan, a company often provides benefits to employees for years of service before the date of initiation or amendment. As a result of this **past service cost (PSC),** the defined benefit obligation is increased to recognize this additional liability. In many cases, the increase in the defined benefit obligation is substantial.

> **Objective•6**
> Describe the amortization of past service costs.

Should a company report an expense immediately for these past service costs? The IASB says it depends on when the benefits are vested. If the benefits from the amendment to the plan vest immediately, then the company should recognize the expense and related liability at the amendment date. If the benefits do not vest immediately, past service cost should be recognized as an expense on a straight-line basis over the average remaining period until the benefits become vested. **[9]**[10] The rationale for using the vesting date as the target date for recognition is that is when the liability is established.

To illustrate, assume that Hitchcock plc amends its defined pension plan on January 1, 2011, resulting in £300,000 of past service cost. The company has 300 active employees, of which 60 vest immediately (20%) and the other 240 (80%) vest in four years. The past service cost applicable to the vested employees is £60,000 and vests immediately. The unrecognized past service cost related to the unvested employees is £240,000

---

[9]The IASB in *IAS 19* limits the amount of a pension asset that is recognized, based on a recoverability test. This test, which has been further clarified in *IFRIC 14*, limits the amount of the pension asset to the sum of unrecognized actuarial gains and losses (discussed later) and amounts that will be received by the company in the form of refunds or reduction of future contributions. **[8]** *For purposes of homework, assume that a pension asset, if present, meets the criteria for full recognition.*

[10]*For purposes of homework, assume* that all past service costs are non-vested, unless stated otherwise. After initially establishing the amortization schedule for past service costs, companies do not revise the schedule (e.g., due to changes in employee service lives) unless there is a plan curtailment or settlement. **[10]** Curtailments and settlements are discussed later in the chapter.

and is amortized over four years (£60,000 per year). The amortization of the past service costs for Hitchcock for the four years is computed as shown in Illustration 20-10.

ILLUSTRATION 20-10
Computation of Past
Service Cost Amortization

Year	Beginning Balance in Unrecognized PSC	Amortization (Expense) Vested	Amortization (Expense) Unvested	Ending Balance in Unrecognized PSC
2011	£300,000	£60,000	£60,000	£180,000
2012			60,000	120,000
2013			60,000	60,000
2014			60,000	—0—

As a result, Hitchcock reports amortization of past service cost of £120,000 in 2011 and £60,000 in each of the years 2012, 2013, and 2014.

As indicated earlier, Hitchcock measures past service cost due to an increase in the liability resulting from the amendment (referred to as positive past service cost). It is also possible to decrease past service costs by decreasing the defined benefit obligation (referred to as negative past service cost). Negative past service cost arises when an entity changes the benefits attributable to past service cost so that the present value of the defined benefit obligation decreases. Both positive and negative past service cost adjustments are handled in the same manner, that is, adjust income immediately if vested and amortize the unvested amount over the average remaining period until vesting occurs. [11]

2012 Entries and Worksheet

Continuing the Zarle Company illustration into 2012, we note that the company amends the pension plan on January 1, 2012, to grant employees past service benefits with a present value of $81,600. The following additional facts apply to the pension plan for the year 2012.

Annual service cost is $9,500.

Discount rate is 10 percent.

Actual return on plan assets is $11,100.

Annual funding contributions are $20,000.

Benefits paid to retirees during the year are $8,000.

The past service cost (PSC) is not vested, and the average remaining period to vesting is three years. Amortization of PSC using the straight-line method is $27,200 ($81,600 ÷ 3).

Illustration 20-11 presents a worksheet of all the pension entries and information recorded by Zarle in 2012.

The first line of the worksheet shows the beginning balances of the Pension Asset/Liability account and the memo accounts. Entry (f) records Zarle's granting of past service cost, by adding $81,600 to the defined benefit obligation and to the new Unrecognized Past Service Cost. Entries (g), (h), (i), (k), and (l) are similar to the corresponding entries in 2011. Entry (j) records the 2012 amortization of unrecognized past service cost by debiting Pension Expense by $27,200 and crediting the Unrecognized Past Service Cost account by the same amount.

Zarle makes the following journal entry on December 31 to formally record the 2012 pension expense—the sum of the annual pension expense column.

2012

Pension Expense	44,960	
Cash		20,000
Pension Asset/Liability		24,960

Pension Worksheet—2012								
	A	B	C	D		F	G	H
1		**General Journal Entries**				**Memo Record**		
2	**Items**	Annual Pension Expense	Cash	Pension Asset/ Liability		Defined Benefit Obligation	Plan Assets	Unrecognized Past Service Cost
3	Balance, Dec. 31, 2011			1,000 Cr.		112,000 Cr.	111,000 Dr.	
4	(f) Past service cost					81,600 Cr.		81,600 Dr.
5	Balance, Jan. 1, 2012			1,000 Cr.		193,600 Cr.	111,000 Dr.	81,600 Dr.
6	(g) Service cost	9,500 Dr.				9,500 Cr.		
7	(h) Interest cost	19,360 Dr.[a]				19,360 Cr.		
8	(i) Actual return	11,100 Cr.					11,100 Dr.	
9	(j) Amortization of PSC	27,200 Dr.						27,200 Cr.
10	(k) Contributions		20,000 Cr.				20,000 Dr.	
11	(l) Benefits					8,000 Dr.	8,000 Cr.	
12								
13	Journal entry for 2012	44,960 Dr.	20,000 Cr.	24,960 Cr.				
14	Balance Dec. 31, 2012			25,960 Cr.		214,460 Cr.	134,100 Dr.	54,400 Dr.
15	[a]$19,360 = $193,600 × 10%							

Sheet1 / Sheet2 / Sheet3 /

ILLUSTRATION 20-11
Pension Worksheet—2012

Because the expense exceeds the funding, Zarle credits the Pension Asset/Liability account for the $24,960 difference. That account is a liability. In 2012, as in 2011, the balance of the Pension Asset/Liability account ($25,960) is equal to the net of the balances in the memo accounts, as shown in Illustration 20-12.

Defined benefit obligation (Credit)	$(214,460)
Plan assets at fair value (Debit)	134,100
Funded status	(80,360)
Unrecognized past service cost (Debit)	54,400
Pension asset/liability (Credit)	$ (25,960)

ILLUSTRATION 20-12
Pension Reconciliation Schedule—December 31, 2012

The reconciliation is the formula that makes the worksheet work. It relates the components of pension accounting, recorded and unrecorded, to one another.

Gain or Loss

Of great concern to companies that have pension plans are the uncontrollable and unexpected swings in pension expense that can result from (1) sudden and large changes in the fair value of plan assets, and (2) changes in actuarial assumptions that affect the amount of the defined benefit obligation. If these gains or losses impact fully the financial statements in the period of realization or incurrence, substantial fluctuations in pension expense result.

Therefore, the IASB decided to reduce the volatility associated with pension expense by using **smoothing techniques** that dampen and in some cases fully eliminate the fluctuations.

Objective·7
Explain the accounting for unexpected gains and losses.

Smoothing Unexpected Gains and Losses on Plan Assets

One component of pension expense, actual return on plan assets, reduces pension expense (assuming the actual return is positive). A large change in the actual return can substantially affect pension expense for a year. Assume a company has a 40 percent return in the securities market for the year. Should this substantial, and perhaps one-time, event affect current pension expense?

Actuaries ignore current fluctuations when they develop a funding pattern to pay expected benefits in the future. They develop an **expected rate of return** and multiply it by an asset value weighted over a reasonable period of time to arrive at an **expected return on plan assets**. They then use this return to determine a company's funding pattern.

The IASB adopted the actuary's approach to dampen wide swings that might occur in the actual return. That is, a company includes the **expected return on the plan assets as a component of pension expense, not the actual return in a given year**. To achieve this goal, the company multiplies the expected rate of return by the fair value of the plan assets.

The difference between the expected return and the actual return is referred to as the **unexpected gain or loss**; the IASB uses the term **asset gains and losses**. **Asset gains** occur when actual return exceeds expected return; **asset losses** occur when actual return is less than expected return.

What happens to unexpected gains or losses in the accounting for pensions? Companies record asset gains and asset losses in an Unrecognized Net Gain or Loss account, combining them with unrecognized gains and losses accumulated in prior years.

To illustrate the computation of an unexpected gain or loss and its related accounting, assume that in 2013 Zarle Company has an actual return on plan assets of $12,000 when the expected return in $13,410 (the expected rate of return of 10 percent on plan assets times the beginning of the year plan assets). The unexpected asset loss of $1,410 ($12,000 − $13,410) is debited to Unrecognized Net Gain or Loss and credited to Pension Expense.

Smoothing Unexpected Gains and Losses on the Pension Liability

In estimating the defined benefit obligation (the liability), actuaries make assumptions about such items as mortality rate, retirement rate, turnover rate, disability rate, and salary amounts. Any change in these actuarial assumptions affects the amount of the defined benefit obligation. Seldom does actual experience coincide exactly with actuarial predictions. These unexpected gains or losses from changes in the defined benefit obligation are called **liability gains and losses**.

Companies defer liability gains (resulting from unexpected decreases in the liability balance) and liability losses (resulting from unexpected increases). Companies combine the liability gains and losses in the same Unrecognized Net Gain or Loss account used for asset gains and losses. They accumulate the asset and liability gains and losses from year to year, off-balance-sheet, in a memo account.[11]

Corridor Amortization

> **Objective•8**
>
> Explain the corridor approach to amortizing gains and losses.

The asset gains and losses and the liability gains and losses can offset each other. As a result, the accumulated total unrecognized net gain or loss may not grow very large. But, it is possible that no offsetting will occur and that the balance in the Unrecognized Net Gain or Loss account will continue to grow.

To limit the growth of the Unrecognized Net Gain or Loss account, the IASB uses the **corridor approach** for amortizing the account's accumulated balance when it gets too large. How large is too large? The IASB set a limit of 10 percent of the larger of the beginning balances of the defined benefit obligation or the fair value of the plan assets. **Above that size, the unrecognized net gain or loss balance is considered too large and must be amortized.**

---

[11]In *IAS 19*, asset gains and losses and liability gains and losses are collectively referred to as "actuarial gains and losses." [12] IFRS permits other accounting approaches for these gains and losses. We discuss these later in the chapter.

To illustrate the corridor approach, data for Callaway Co.'s defined benefit obligation and plan assets over a period of six years are shown in Illustration 20-13.

ILLUSTRATION 20-13
Computation of the
Corridor

Beginning-of-the-Year Balances	Defined Benefit Obligation	Fair Value of Assets	Corridor* +/− 10%
2010	$1,000,000	$ 900,000	$100,000
2011	1,200,000	1,100,000	120,000
2012	1,300,000	1,700,000	170,000
2013	1,500,000	2,250,000	225,000
2014	1,700,000	1,750,000	175,000
2015	1,800,000	1,700,000	180,000

*The corridor becomes 10% of the larger (in colored type) of the defined benefit obligation or the fair value of plan assets.

How the corridor works becomes apparent when we portray the data graphically, as in Illustration 20-14.

ILLUSTRATION 20-14
Graphic Illustration of
the Corridor

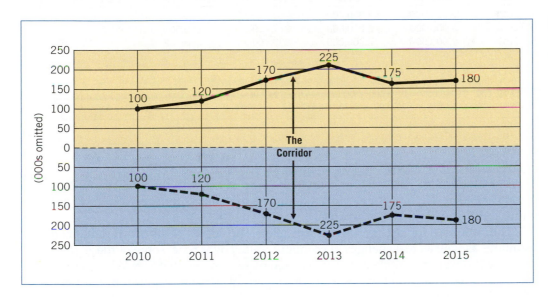

If the balance of the Unrecognized Net Gain or Loss account stays within the upper and lower limits of the corridor, no amortization is required. In that case, Callaway carries forward the unrecognized net gain or loss balance unchanged.

If amortization is required, the minimum amortization is the excess divided by the average remaining service period of active employees who are expected to receive benefits under the plan. Callaway may use any systematic method of amortization of unrecognized gains and losses in lieu of the minimum, provided it is greater than the minimum. It must use the method consistently for both gains and losses and must disclose the amortization method used.

Example of Unrecognized Gains/Losses

In applying the corridor, companies should include amortization of the excess unrecognized net gain or loss as a component of pension expense only if, at the **beginning of the year**, the unrecognized net gain or loss exceeded the corridor. That is, if no unrecognized net gain or loss exists at the beginning of the period, the company cannot recognize pension expense gains or losses in that period.

To illustrate the amortization of unrecognized net gains and losses, assume the following information for Soft-White, Inc.

	2011	2012	2013
		(beginning of the year)	
Defined benefit obligation	£2,100,000	£2,600,000	£2,900,000
Fair value of assets	2,600,000	2,800,000	2,700,000
Unrecognized net loss	–0–	400,000	300,000

If the average remaining service life of all active employees is 5.5 years, the schedule to amortize the unrecognized net loss is as shown in Illustration 20-15.

ILLUSTRATION 20-15
Corridor Test and
Gain/Loss Amortization
Schedule

Year	Defined Benefit Obligation[a]	Plan Assets[a]	Corridor[b]	Cumulative Unrecognized Net Loss[a]	Minimum Amortization of Loss (For Current Year)
2011	£2,100,000	£2,600,000	£260,000	£ –0–	£ –0–
2012	2,600,000	2,800,000	280,000	400,000	21,818[c]
2013	2,900,000	2,700,000	290,000	678,182[d]	70,579[d]

[a]All as of the beginning of the period.
[b]10% of the greater of defined benefit obligation or plan assets fair value.
[c]£400,000 − £280,000 = £120,000; £120,000 ÷ 5.5 = £21,818
[d]£400,000 − £21,818 + £300,000 = £678,182; £678,182 − £290,000 = £388,182; £388,182 ÷ 5.5 = £70,579.

As Illustration 20-15 indicates, the loss recognized in 2012 increased pension expense by £21,818. This amount is small in comparison with the total loss of £400,000. It indicates that the corridor approach dampens the effects (reduces volatility) of these gains and losses on pension expense.

The rationale for the corridor is that gains and losses result from refinements in estimates as well as real changes in economic value; over time, some of these gains and losses will offset one another. It therefore seems reasonable that Soft-White should not fully recognize gains and losses as a component of pension expense in the period in which they arise.

Summary of Calculations for Asset Gain or Loss

The difference between the actual return on plan assets and the expected return on plan assets is the **unexpected (deferred) asset gain or loss** component. This component defers the difference between the actual return and expected return on plan assets in computing current-year pension expense. Thus, after considering this component, **it is really the expected return on plan assets (not the actual return) that determines current pension expense**.

Companies determined the amortized net gain or loss by amortizing the unrecognized gain or loss at the beginning of the year subject to the corridor limitation. In other words, **if the unrecognized net gain or loss is greater than the corridor, these net gains and losses are subject to amortization**. Soft-White computed this minimum amortization by dividing the net gains or losses subject to amortization by the average remaining service period. When the current-year unexpected gain or loss is combined with the amortized net gain or loss, we determine the current-year gain or loss. Illustration 20-16 summarizes these gain and loss computations.

ILLUSTRATION 20-16
Graphic Summary of Gain
or Loss Computation

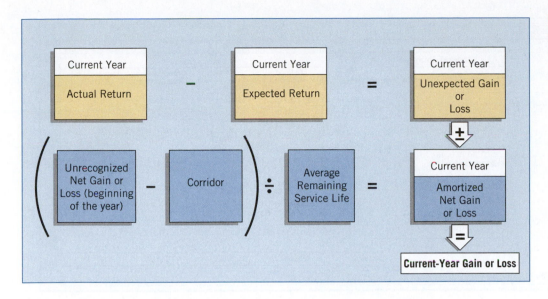

In essence, these gains and losses are subject to *triple* smoothing. That is, companies first smooth the asset gain or loss by using the expected return. Second, they do not amortize the unrecognized net gain or loss at the beginning of the year unless it is greater than the corridor. Finally, they spread the excess over the remaining service life of existing employees.[12]

2013 Entries and Worksheet

Continuing the Zarle Company illustration, the following facts apply to the pension plan for 2013.

Annual service cost is $13,000.

Discount rate is 10 percent; expected return on plan assets is 10 percent.

Actual return on plan assets is $12,000.

Amortization of past service cost (PSC) is $27,200 ($81,600 ÷ 3).

Annual funding contributions are $24,000.

Benefits paid to retirees during the year are $10,500.

Changes in actuarial assumptions establish the end-of-year defined benefit obligation at $265,000.

The worksheet in Illustration 20-17 (page 1084) presents all of Zarle's 2013 pension entries and related information. The first line of the worksheet records the beginning balances that relate to the pension plan. In this case, Zarle's beginning balances are the ending balances from its 2012 pension worksheet in Illustration 20-11 (page 1079).

Entries (m), (n), (o), (q), (r), and (s) are similar to the corresponding entries in 2011 or 2012.

Entries (o) and (p) are related. We explained the recording of the actual return in entry (o) in both 2011 and 2012; it is recorded similarly in 2013. In both 2011 and 2012,

---

[12]The IASB recently issued an exposure draft to further modify its pension standard. The proposed revisions will eliminate corridor amortization and require expanded recognition of off-balance-sheet pension amounts. For more information on this project, see *http://www.iasb.org/Current+Projects/IASB+Projects/Post-employment+Benefits+(including+Pensions)/Post-employment+Benefits+(including+pensions).htm*.

	A	B	C	D		F	G	H	I
		\multicolumn{4}{c}{Pension Worksheet—2013}					
1		\multicolumn{4}{c}{General Journal Entries}		\multicolumn{4}{c}{Memo Record}
2	Items	Annual Pension Expense	Cash	Pension Asset/ Liability		Defined Benefit Obligation	Plan Assets	Unrecognized Past Service Cost	Unrecognized Net Gain or Loss
3	Balance, Dec. 31, 2012			25,960 Cr.		214,460 Cr.	134,100 Dr.	54,400 Dr.	
4	(m) Service cost	13,000 Dr.				13,000 Cr.			
5	(n) Interest cost	21,446 Dr.				21,446 Cr.			
6	(o) Actual return	12,000 Cr.					12,000 Dr.		
7	(p) Unexpected loss	1,410 Cr.							1,410 Dr.
8	(q) Amortization of PSC	27,200 Dr.						27,200 Cr.	
9	(r) Contributions		24,000 Cr.				24,000 Dr.		
10	(s) Benefits					10,500 Dr.	10,500 Cr.		
11	(t) Liability increase					26,594 Cr.			26,594 Dr.
12									
13									
14	Journal entry for 2013	48,236 Dr.	24,000 Cr.	24,236 Cr.					
15	Balance, Dec. 31, 2013			50,196 Cr.		265,000 Cr.	159,600 Dr.	27,200 Dr.	28,004 Dr.

Sheet1 / Sheet2 / Sheet3 /

ILLUSTRATION 20-17
Pension Worksheet—2013

Zarle's actual return on plan assets was equal to the expected return on plan assets. In 2013, the expected return of $13,410 (the expected rate of return of 10 percent times the beginning-of-the-year plan assets balance of $134,100) is higher than the actual return of $12,000. To smooth pension expense, Zarle defers the unexpected loss of $1,410 ($13,410 − $12,000) by debiting the Unrecognized Net Gain or Loss account and crediting Pension Expense. **As a result of this adjustment, the expected return on the plan assets is the amount actually used to compute pension expense.**

Entry (t) records the change in the defined benefit obligation resulting from a change in actuarial assumptions. As indicated, the actuary has now computed the ending balance to be $265,000. Given that the memo record balance at December 31 is $238,406 ($214,460 + $13,000 + $21,446 − $10,500), a difference of $26,594 ($265,000 − $238,406) exists. This $26,594 increase in the employer's liability is an unexpected loss. Zarle defers that amount by debiting it to the Unrecognized Net Gain or Loss account. The journal entry on December 31 to formally record pension expense for 2013 is as follows.

2013

Pension Expense	48,236	
Cash		24,000
Pension Asset/Liability		24,236

As the 2013 worksheet indicates, the $50,196 balance of the Pension Asset/Liability account at December 31, 2013, is equal to the net of the balances in the memo accounts. Illustration 20-18 shows this computation.

ILLUSTRATION 20-18
Pension Reconciliation Schedule—December 31, 2013

Defined benefit obligation (Credit)	$(265,000)
Plan assets at fair value (Debit)	159,600
Funded status	(105,400)
Unrecognized past service cost (Debit)	27,200
Unrecognized net loss (Debit)	28,004
Pension Asset/Liability (Credit)	$ (50,196)

Immediate Recognition of Actuarial Gains and Losses

The IASB indicates that the corridor approach results in the minimum amount recognized as an actuarial gain and loss. Companies may use any systematic method that is faster than the corridor approach provided it is used for both gains and losses and is used consistently from period to period. The IASB also indicates that it favors the immediate recognition of actuarial gains and losses. **[13]**

If a company chooses the immediate recognition approach, the actuarial gain or loss can either adjust net income or other comprehensive income. To illustrate, assume that Wentworth Company has the following components of pension expense for 2011.

Service cost	€2,000
Interest on defined benefit obligation	210
Expected return on plan assets	(80)
Past service cost amortization	60
Actuarial loss recognized in full	100
Pension expense	€2,290

ILLUSTRATION 20-19
Components of Pension Expense (in thousands)

Wentworth's 2011 revenues are €100,000, and expenses for 2011 (excluding pension expense) are €70,000. If Wentworth reports the adjustment of actuarial gains and losses in net income, its income statement is as shown in Illustration 20-20.

Income Statement	
Revenues	€100,000
Expenses (excluding pension expense)	70,000
Pension expense	2,290
Net income	€ 27,710

ILLUSTRATION 20-20
Income Excluding Pension Expense

If Wentworth decides to report the adjustment of actuarial gains and losses in other comprehensive income, its statement of comprehensive income is as follows.

Statement of Comprehensive Income	
Revenues	€100,000
Expenses (excluding pension expense)	70,000
Pension expense (€2,290 − €100)	2,190
Net income	27,810
Other comprehensive income	
Actuarial loss on defined benefit plan	100
Total comprehensive income	€ 27,710

ILLUSTRATION 20-21
Comprehensive Income Reporting of Actuarial Gains and Losses

PERSONAL PENSION PLANNING

Now that you understand the operation and accounting for a pension plan by employers, what does this mean for you as you evaluate job offers and benefit packages in the not-too-distant future? To start, you should begin building *your own* retirement nest egg, rather than relying on your employer to provide postretirement income and healthcare benefits. A look at recent data on retirees' financial position, summarized in the chart on page 1086, supports a strategy to become more self-reliant.

As indicated, the average person at retirement has about $360,000 in resources to sustain him or her in the retirement years. However, Social Security and traditional pension benefits comprise a substantial share of wealth for typical near-to-retirement households—nearly two-thirds of their

What do the numbers mean?

What do the numbers mean?
(continued)

$361,000 in total wealth. This wealth snapshot highlights the extraordinary importance of Social Security, traditional pensions, and owner-occupied housing (not very liquid) for typical near-retiree households today. Together, these assets comprise nearly four-fifths of wealth of those on the verge of retirement.

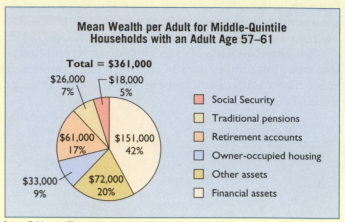

Source: G. Mermin, "Typical Wealth Held by Those at the Verge of Retirement," Urban Institute, *http://www.urban.org/url.cfm?ID=411618* (February 22, 2008).

However, as we discussed in the opening story, these sources of income are in decline and will likely continue to shrink as employers and governments wrestle with financial and other constraints discussed earlier. That means that retirement accounts, including individual retirement accounts and defined contribution pensions, will need to become a bigger piece of the pie to fill the gap left by smaller government and employer-sponsored benefits. So get started now with a personal savings strategy to ensure an adequate nest egg at your retirement.

Source: Adapted from Nanette Byrnes with David Welch, "The Benefits Trap," *BusinessWeek* (July 19, 2004), pp. 54–72.

REPORTING PENSION PLANS IN FINANCIAL STATEMENTS

Objective•9

Describe the requirements for reporting pension plans in financial statements.

As you might suspect, a phenomenon as significant and complex as pensions involves extensive reporting and disclosure requirements. We will cover these requirements in two categories: (1) those within the financial statements, and (2) those within the notes to the financial statements.

Within the Financial Statements

A company reports the pension asset/liability as an asset or a liability in the statement of financial position at the end of a reporting period. If the pension asset/liability balance is a debit, it is reported as Pension Asset. If it has a credit balance, it is reported as Pension Liability. The classification as non-current or current follows the general guidelines used for classification of other assets or liabilities.

On the income statement (or related notes), the company must report the amount of pension expense for the period. In addition, any actuarial gains or losses charged or credited to other comprehensive income should be reported in the statement of comprehensive income.

Within the Notes to the Financial Statements

Pension plans are frequently important to understanding a company's financial position, results of operations, and cash flows. In general, a company discloses the following information, either in the body of the financial statements or in the notes. **[14]**

1. A description of the plan and the accounting policy for recognizing actuarial gains and losses.
   Rationale: Helps users understand the nature of the plan and the approach the company is using to recognize actuarial gains and losses.

2. A schedule showing all the major components of pension expense.
   Rationale: Information provided about the components of pension expense helps users better understand how a company determines pension expense. It also is useful in forecasting a company's net income.

3. A reconciliation showing how the defined benefit obligation and the fair value of the plan assets changed from the beginning to the end of the period.
   Rationale: Disclosing the defined benefit obligation, the fair value of the plan assets, and changes in them should help users understand the economics underlying the obligations and resources of these plans. Explaining the changes in the defined benefit obligation and fair value of plan assets in the form of a reconciliation provides a more complete disclosure and makes the financial statements more understandable.

4. The funded status of the plan (difference between the defined benefit obligation and fair value of the plan assets) and the amounts recognized and not recognized in the financial statements.
   Rationale: Providing a reconciliation of the plan's funded status to the amount reported in the statement of financial position highlights the difference between the funded status and the statement of financial position presentation.

5. A disclosure of the rates used in measuring the benefit amounts (discount rate, expected return on plan assets, rate of compensation).
   Rationale: Disclosure of these rates permits users to determine the reasonableness of the assumptions applied in measuring the pension liability and pension expense.

6. A company's best estimate of the contributions expected to be made to the plan in the next year. A table indicating the allocation of pension plan assets by category (equity securities, debt securities, real estate, and other assets), and showing the percentage of or the amount related to the fair value to total plan assets. In addition, the actual return on the plan is disclosed, as well as information on how the expected rate of return is determined.
   Rationale: Such information helps financial statement users evaluate the pension plan's exposure to market risk and possible cash flow demands on the company. It also will help users better assess the reasonableness of the company's expected rate of return assumption in comparison to its actual return.

In summary, the disclosure requirements are extensive, and purposely so. One factor that has been a challenge for useful pension reporting has been the lack of consistent terminology. Furthermore, a substantial amount of offsetting is inherent in the measurement of pension expense and the pension liability. These disclosures are designed to address these concerns and take some of the mystery out of pension reporting.

Example of Pension Note Disclosure

In the following sections, we provide examples and explain the key pension disclosure elements.

Components of Pension Expense. The IASB requires disclosure of the individual pension expense components (derived from the information in the pension expense worksheet column): (1) service cost, (2) interest cost, (3) expected return on assets, (4) gains and losses, and (5) past service cost. The purpose of such disclosure is to clarify to more sophisticated readers how companies determine pension expense. Providing information on the components should also be useful in predicting future pension expense.

Illustration 20-22 (page 1088) presents an example of this part of the disclosure. It uses the information from the Zarle illustration, specifically the expense component information from the worksheets in Illustration 20-8 (page 1076), Illustration 20-11 (page 1079), and Illustration 20-17 (page 1084).

ILLUSTRATION 20-22
Summary of Expense
Components for Zarle
Company—2011–2013

	2011	2012	2013
Components of Net Periodic Pension Expense			
Service cost	$ 9,000	$ 9,500	$ 13,000
Interest cost	10,000	19,360	21,446
Expected return on plan assets	(10,000)	(11,100)	(13,410)*
Amortization of past service cost	–0–	27,200	27,200
Net periodic pension expense	$ 9,000	$ 44,960	$ 48,236

*Note that the expected return is $13,410, which is the actual gain ($12,000) adjusted by the unrecognized loss ($1,410).

Underlying Concepts

This represents another compromise between relevance and faithful representation. The disclosure of the unrecognized items attempts to balance these objectives.

Reconciliation and Funded Status of Plan. Having a reconciliation of the changes in the assets and liabilities from the beginning of the year to the end of the year, statement readers can better understand the underlying economics of the plan. In essence, this disclosure (reconciliation) contains the information in the pension worksheet for the defined benefit obligation and plan asset columns.

In addition, the IASB also requires a disclosure of the funded status of the plan. That is, a company must reconcile the off-balance-sheet assets, liabilities, unrecognized past service cost, and unrecognized gains and losses with the on-balance-sheet liability or asset. Many believe this is the key to understanding the accounting for pensions. Why is such a disclosure important? The delayed recognition of some pension elements may exclude the most current and the most relevant information about the pension plan from the financial statements. This disclosure, however, provides this important information.

Using the information for Zarle, the schedule in Illustration 20-23 provides an example of the reconciliation.

ILLUSTRATION 20-23
Pension Disclosure
for Zarle Company—
2011–2013

	2011	2012	2013
Change in benefit obligation			
Benefit obligation at beginning of year	$100,000	$112,000	$214,460
Service cost	9,000	9,500	13,000
Interest cost	10,000	19,360	21,446
Amendments (Past service cost)	–0–	81,600	–0–
Actuarial loss	–0–	–0–	26,594
Benefits paid	(7,000)	(8,000)	(10,500)
Benefit obligation at end of year	112,000	214,460	265,000
Change in plan assets			
Fair value of plan assets at beginning of year	100,000	111,000	134,100
Actual return on plan assets	10,000	11,100	12,000
Contributions	8,000	20,000	24,000
Benefits paid	(7,000)	(8,000)	(10,500)
Fair value of plan assets at end of year	111,000	134,100	159,600
Funded status	(1,000)	(80,360)	(105,400)
Unrecognized net actuarial loss	–0–	–0–	28,004
Unrecognized past service cost	–0–	54,400	27,200
Pension asset/liability	(1,000)	(25,960)	(50,196)

Underlying Concepts

Does it make a difference to users of financial statements whether companies recognize pension information in the financial statements or disclose it only in the notes? The IASB was unsure, so in accord with the full disclosure principle, it decided to provide extensive pension plan disclosures.

The 2011 column reveals that Zarle underfunds the defined benefit obligation by $1,000. The 2012 column reveals that Zarle reports the underfunded liability of $80,360 in the statement of financial position at $25,960, due to the unrecognized past service cost of $54,400. Finally, the 2013 column indicates that Zarle recognizes the underfunded liability of $105,400 in the statement of financial position at only $50,196 because of $27,200 in unrecognized past service costs, and $28,004 of unrecognized net loss.[13]

[13]To see a complete postretirement benefit disclosure, including asset allocations and expected cash flow information, see **Marks and Spencer**'s specimen financial statements in Appendix 5B.

2014 Entries and Worksheet—A Comprehensive Example

Incorporating the corridor computation and the required disclosures, we continue the Zarle Company pension plan accounting based on the following facts for 2014.

Service cost is $16,000.

Discount rate is 10 percent; expected return on plan assets is 10 percent.

Actual return on plan assets is $22,000.

Amortization of unrecognized past service cost is $27,200 ($81,600 ÷ 3).

Annual funding contributions are $27,000.

Benefits paid to retirees during the year are $18,000.

Average service life of all covered employees is 20 years.

Zarle prepares a worksheet to facilitate accumulation and recording of the components of pension expense and maintenance of the unrecognized amounts related to the pension plan. Illustration 20-24 shows that worksheet, which uses the basic data presented above. Beginning-of-the-year 2014 account balances are the December 31, 2013, balances from Zarle's 2013 pension worksheet in Illustration 20-17 (page 1084).

ILLUSTRATION 20-24
Comprehensive Pension Worksheet—2014

Pension Worksheet—2014

	A	B	C	D	F	G	H	I
1		**General Journal Entries**			**Memo Record**			
2	**Items**	Annual Pension Expense	Cash	Pension Asset/ Liability	Defined Benefit Obligation	Plan Assets	Unrecognized Past Service Cost	Unrecognized Net Gain or Loss
3	Balance, Dec. 31, 2013			50,196 Cr.	265,000 Cr.	159,600 Dr.	27,200 Dr.	28,004 Dr.
4	(aa) Service cost	16,000 Dr.			16,000 Cr.			
5	(bb) Interest cost	26,500 Dr.			26,500 Cr.			
6	(cc) Actual return	22,000 Cr.				22,000 Dr.		
7	(dd) Unexpected gain	6,040 Dr.						6,040 Cr.
8	(ee) Amortization of PSC	27,200 Dr.					27,200 Cr.	
9	(ff) Contributions		27,000 Cr.			27,000 Dr.		
10	(gg) Benefits				18,000 Dr.	18,000 Cr.		
11	(hh) Unrecog. loss amort.	75 Dr.						75 Cr.
12								
13								
14	Journal entry for 2014	53,815 Dr.	27,000 Cr.	26,815 Cr.				
15	Balance, Dec. 31, 2014			77,011 Cr.	289,500 Cr.	190,600 Dr.	0 Dr.	21,889 Dr.

Sheet1 / Sheet2 / Sheet3 /

Worksheet Explanations and Entries

Entries (aa) through (gg) are similar to the corresponding entries previously explained in the prior years' worksheets, with the exception of entry (dd). In 2013, the expected return on plan assets exceeded the actual return, producing an unexpected loss. In 2014, the actual return of $22,000 exceeds the expected return of $15,960 ($159,600 × 10%), resulting in an unexpected gain of $6,040, entry (dd). By netting the gain of $6,040 against the actual return of $22,000, pension expense is affected only by the expected return of $15,960.

A new entry (hh) in Zarle's worksheet results from application of the corridor test on the accumulated balance of unrecognized net gain or loss. Zarle Company begins 2014 with a balance in the Unrecognized Net Loss account of $28,004. The company applies the corridor criterion in 2014 to determine whether the balance is excessive and should be amortized. In 2014, the corridor is 10 percent of the larger of the beginning-of-the-year defined benefit obligation of $265,000 or the plan asset's $159,600 fair value. The corridor for 2014 is $26,500 ($265,000 × 10%). Because the balance in the Unrecognized Net Loss account is $28,004, the excess (outside the corridor) is $1,504 ($28,004 − $26,500). Zarle amortizes the $1,504 excess over the average remaining service life of all employees. Given an average remaining service life of 20 years, the amortization in 2014 is $75 ($1,504 ÷ 20). In the 2014 pension worksheet, Zarle debits Pension Expense for $75 and credits that amount to Unrecognized Net Loss. Illustration 20-25 shows the computation of the $75 amortization charge.

ILLUSTRATION 20-25
Computation of 2014
Amortization Charge
(Corridor Test)

2014 Corridor Test	
Unrecognized net (gain) or loss at beginning of year	$28,004
10% of larger of defined benefit obligation or fair value of plan assets	26,500
Amortizable amount	$ 1,504
Average service life of all employees	20 years
2014 amortization ($1,504 ÷ 20 years)	$75

Zarle formally records pension expense for 2014 as follows.

2014

Pension Expense	53,815	
Cash		27,000
Pension Asset/Liability		26,815

Financial Statement Presentation

Illustrations 20-26, 20-27, and 20-28 show Zarle's financial statements at December 31, 2014, relative to the company's pension plan.

ILLUSTRATION 20-26
Statement of Financial
Position Presentation of
Pension Costs—2014

ZARLE COMPANY		
STATEMENT OF FINANCIAL POSITION		
AS OF DECEMBER 31, 2014		
Assets	Liabilities	
	Non-current liabilities	
	Pension liabilities	$77,011

ILLUSTRATION 20-27
Income Statement
Presentation of Pension
Expense—2014

ZARLE COMPANY	
INCOME STATEMENT	
FOR THE YEAR ENDED DECEMBER 31, 2014	
Operating expenses	
Pension expense*	$53,815
*Pension expense is frequently reported as "Employee benefits."	

ILLUSTRATION 20-28
Statement of Cash Flows
Presentation of Pension
Liability

ZARLE COMPANY		
STATEMENT OF CASH FLOWS		
FOR THE YEAR ENDED DECEMBER 31, 2014		
Cash flows from operating activities		
Net income (assumed)		$905,000
Adjustments to reconcile net income to net		
cash provided by operating activities:		
Increase in pension liability	$26,815	

Note Disclosure

Illustration 20-29 shows the note disclosure of Zarle's pension plan for 2014.

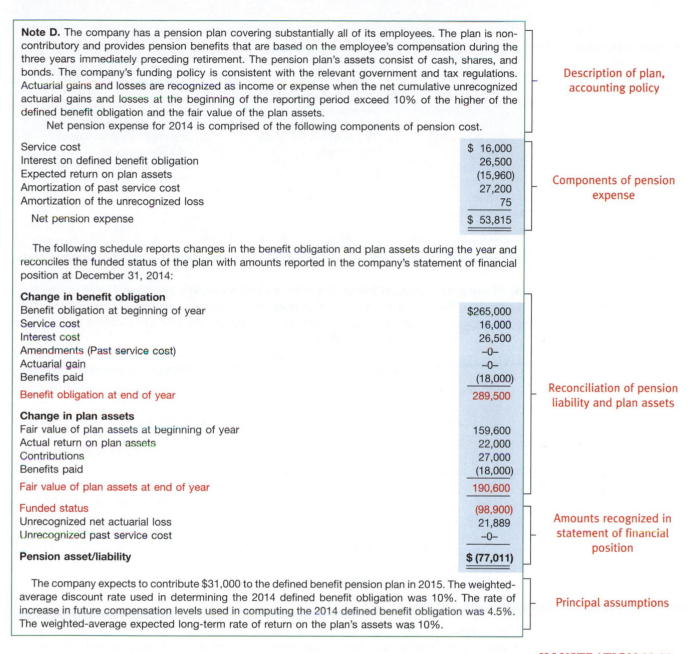

Note D. The company has a pension plan covering substantially all of its employees. The plan is non-contributory and provides pension benefits that are based on the employee's compensation during the three years immediately preceding retirement. The pension plan's assets consist of cash, shares, and bonds. The company's funding policy is consistent with the relevant government and tax regulations. Actuarial gains and losses are recognized as income or expense when the net cumulative unrecognized actuarial gains and losses at the beginning of the reporting period exceed 10% of the higher of the defined benefit obligation and the fair value of the plan assets.

Description of plan, accounting policy

Net pension expense for 2014 is comprised of the following components of pension cost.

Service cost	$ 16,000
Interest on defined benefit obligation	26,500
Expected return on plan assets	(15,960)
Amortization of past service cost	27,200
Amortization of the unrecognized loss	75
Net pension expense	$ 53,815

Components of pension expense

The following schedule reports changes in the benefit obligation and plan assets during the year and reconciles the funded status of the plan with amounts reported in the company's statement of financial position at December 31, 2014:

Change in benefit obligation	
Benefit obligation at beginning of year	$265,000
Service cost	16,000
Interest cost	26,500
Amendments (Past service cost)	–0–
Actuarial gain	–0–
Benefits paid	(18,000)
Benefit obligation at end of year	289,500
Change in plan assets	
Fair value of plan assets at beginning of year	159,600
Actual return on plan assets	22,000
Contributions	27,000
Benefits paid	(18,000)
Fair value of plan assets at end of year	190,600
Funded status	(98,900)
Unrecognized net actuarial loss	21,889
Unrecognized past service cost	–0–
Pension asset/liability	$ (77,011)

Reconciliation of pension liability and plan assets

Amounts recognized in statement of financial position

The company expects to contribute $31,000 to the defined benefit pension plan in 2015. The weighted-average discount rate used in determining the 2014 defined benefit obligation was 10%. The rate of increase in future compensation levels used in computing the 2014 defined benefit obligation was 4.5%. The weighted-average expected long-term rate of return on the plan's assets was 10%.

Principal assumptions

ILLUSTRATION 20-29
Minimum Note Disclosure of Pension Plan, Zarle Company, 2014

Although not shown in this disclosure, Zarle should indicate the major categories of plan assets. In addition, Zarle should disclose amounts for the current and previous four periods, such as the defined benefit obligation, plan assets, funded status, and adjustments for actuarial gains and losses. These additional disclosures for a real company may be observed in the **Marks and Spencer** (GBR) financial statements presented in Appendix 5B (see Note 11).

Special Issues

Other Postretirement Benefits

In addition to pensions, companies often promise other types of postretirement benefits. The benefits include life insurance outside a pension plan; medical, dental, and eye care; legal and tax services; and so on. Because healthcare benefits are the

Objective•10
Explain special issues related to postretirement benefit plans.

largest of other postretirement benefits, we provide a general description of how they differ from a traditional pension plan. Illustration 20-30 shows these differences.

ILLUSTRATION 20-30
Differences between Pensions and Postretirement Healthcare Benefits

Item	Pensions	Healthcare Benefits
Funding	Generally funded.	Generally *not* funded.
Benefit	Well-defined and level dollar amount.	Generally uncapped and great variability.
Beneficiary	Retiree (maybe some benefit to surviving spouse).	Retiree, spouse, and other dependents.
Benefit payable	Monthly.	As needed and used.
Predictability	Variables are reasonably predictable.	Utilization difficult to predict. Level of cost varies geographically and fluctuates over time.

Two of the differences in Illustration 20-30 highlight why measuring the future payments for healthcare benefit plans is so much more difficult than for pension plans.

1. *Many postretirement plans do not set a limit on healthcare benefits.* No matter how serious the illness or how long it lasts, the benefits continue to flow. (Even if the employer uses an insurance company plan, the premiums will escalate according to the increased benefits provided.)

2. *The levels of healthcare benefit use and healthcare costs are difficult to predict.* Increased longevity, unexpected illnesses (e.g., AIDS, SARS, and H1N1 flu), along with new medical technologies and cures, cause changes in healthcare utilization.

Additionally, although the fiduciary and reporting standards for employee benefit funds under government regulations generally cover healthcare benefits, the stringent minimum vesting, participation, and funding standards that apply to pensions do not apply to healthcare benefits. Nevertheless, the basic concepts of pension accounting apply to other postretirement benefits. As a result, the IASB indicates that the accounting and reporting of these other types of postretirement benefits should be the same as that used for pension plan reporting. However, companies with both pension and other postretirement benefit plans must separately disclose the plan details when the plans are subject to materially different risks. **[15]**

Curtailments and Settlements

If a company such as **Nestlé** (CHE) commits itself to substantially reduce the number of employees in a plan or to substantially reduce the benefits of an existing plan, it is often referred to as a **curtailment**. Curtailments often have a significant effect on the financial statements and often occur from an isolated event, such as the closing of a plant, discontinuance of an operation, or termination or suspension of a plan. Curtailments are often linked with a restructuring of operations.

A **settlement** occurs when a company enters into a transaction that eliminates all further obligations for part or all of the benefits provided under a defined benefit plan. For example, if **Siemens** (DEU) makes a lump-sum cash payment to participants in a defined benefit pension plan in exchange for their rights to receive specified benefits in the future, a settlement has occurred.

Companies recognize gains or losses on the curtailment or settlement of a defined benefit plan when the curtailment or settlement occurs. The gain or loss on a curtailment or settlement is comprised of the following: (1) any resulting change in the present value of the defined benefit obligation, (2) any resulting change in the fair value of the plan assets, and (3) any related actuarial gains and losses and past service cost that had not been previously been recognized.

Where a curtailment relates to only some of the employees covered by a plan, or where only part of an obligation is settled:

- The gain or loss includes a proportionate share of the previously unrecognized past service cost and actuarial gains and losses.
- The proportionate share is determined on the basis of the present value of the obligations before and after the curtailment or settlement. [16]

To illustrate, assume that Dejon Company discontinues an operating segment, and employees of the discontinued segment will earn no further benefits. Using current actuarial assumptions (including current market interest rates and other current market prices) immediately before the curtailment, Dejon has a defined benefit obligation (000 omitted) with a net present value of €1,000, plan assets with a fair value of €820, net cumulative unrecognized actuarial gains of €50, and €80 unrecognized past service costs (all unvested). The curtailment reduces the net present value of the obligation by €100 to €900. Of the previously unrecognized actuarial gains and past service costs amounts, 10 percent relates to the part of the obligation that was eliminated through the curtailment. The effect of the curtailment is summarized in Illustration 20-31.

	Before Curtailment	Gain (Loss)	After Curtailment
Defined benefit obligation (Credit)	€(1,000)	€100	€(900)
Fair value of plan assets (Debit)	820	—	820
Funded status	(180)	100	(80)
Unrecognized actuarial gains (Credit)	(50)	5*	(45)
Unrecognized past service costs (Debit)	100	(10)**	90
Pension asset/liability	**€ (130)**	**€ 95**	**€ (35)**

*10% × 50
**10% × 100

ILLUSTRATION 20-31
Computation of Gain or Loss on Curtailment

Thus, the net gain for Dejon is €95. This gain is comprised of the €100 reduction in the defined benefit obligation plus 10 percent of the unrecognized gains and losses (€5), less 10 percent of the past service costs (€10). Dejon makes the following entry to record the curtailment.

Pension Asset/Liability	95	
Gain on Curtailment		95

In the example above, Dejon has a curtailment. That is, it has reduced the number of employees in a plan or reduced the benefits of an existing plan. However, Dejon still has an obligation to employees, as indicated in the "After Curtailment" column in Illustration 20-31. If a cash payment is made to employees affected by the curtailment, such that it eliminates all further obligations for benefits provided under the plan, a gain or loss may be recorded. This is referred to as a settlement.

Concluding Observations

Hardly a day goes by without the financial press analyzing in depth some issue related to pension plans around the world. This is not surprising, since pension funds now hold trillions of dollars, euros, pounds, and yen in assets. As you have seen, the accounting issues related to pension plans are complex. Recent changes to IFRS have clarified many of these issues and should help users understand the financial implications of a company's pension plans on its financial position, results of operations, and cash flows.

You will want to read the **CONVERGENCE CORNER** on page 1094

For discussion of how international convergence efforts relate to pension accounting.

CONVERGENCE CORNER

POSTRETIREMENT BENEFITS

The underlying concepts for the accounting for postretirement benefits are similar between U.S. GAAP and IFRS—both U.S. GAAP and IFRS view pensions and other postretirement benefits as forms of deferred compensation. At present, there are significant differences in the specific accounting provisions as applied to these plans.

RELEVANT FACTS

• IFRS and U.S. GAAP separate pension plans into defined contribution plans and defined benefit plans. The accounting for defined contribution plans is similar.

• Both IFRS and U.S. GAAP compute unrecognized past service costs (PSC) (referred to as prior service cost in U.S. GAAP) in the same manner. However, IFRS recognizes any vested amounts immediately and spreads unvested amounts over the average remaining period to vesting. U.S. GAAP amortizes PSC over the remaining service lives of employees.

• Under IFRS, companies have the choice of recognizing actuarial gains and losses in income immediately (either net income or other comprehensive income) or amortizing them over the expected remaining working lives of employees. U.S. GAAP does not permit choice; actuarial gains and losses are reported in "Accumulated other comprehensive income" and amortized to income over remaining service lives.

• For defined benefit plans, U.S. GAAP recognizes a pension asset or liability as the funded status of the plan (i.e., defined benefit obligation minus the fair value of plan assets). IFRS recognizes the funded status, net of unrecognized past service cost and unrecognized net gain or loss.

• The accounting for pensions and other postretirement benefit plans is the same under IFRS. U.S. GAAP has separate standards for these types of benefits, and significant differences exist in the accounting.

ABOUT THE NUMBERS

As indicated, U.S. GAAP and IFRS differ in the amount of Pension Asset/Liability that is recognized on the statement of financial position. Consider the following reconciliation for Altidore Company.

	IFRS	U.S. GAAP	
Defined benefit obligation	€289,500	€289,500	
Fair value of assets	190,600	190,600	
Funded status	98,900	€ 98,900	Pension liability
Unrecognize past service cost	(15,500)		
Unrecognized loss	(23,000)		
	€ 60,400		Pension liability

Thus, under U.S. GAAP, Altidore reports a much higher pension liability compared to IFRS. This results because PSC and unrecognized losses are recorded in accumulated other comprehensive income, not in memo accounts (or off-balance-sheet).

ON THE HORIZON

The IASB and the FASB are working collaboratively on a postretirement benefit project. The FASB has issued GAAP rules addressing the recognition of the funded status of benefit plans in financial statements. The FASB has begun work on the second phase of the project, which will reexamine expense measurement of postretirement benefit plans. The IASB also has added a project in this area but on a different schedule. The IASB has already issued an exposure draft on expense measurement in pension plans. It is unclear whether the Boards' differences in schedule will lead to a converged standard.

SUMMARY OF LEARNING OBJECTIVES

·1 Distinguish between accounting for the employer's pension plan and accounting for the pension fund. The company or employer is the organization sponsoring the pension plan. It incurs the cost and makes contributions to the pension fund. The fund or plan is the entity that receives the contributions from the employer, administers the pension assets, and makes the benefit payments to the pension recipients (retired employees). The fund should be a separate legal and accounting entity; it maintains a set of books and prepares financial statements.

·2 Identify types of pension plans and their characteristics. The two most common types of pension arrangements are: (1) *Defined contribution plans:* The employer agrees to contribute to a pension trust a certain sum each period based on a formula. This formula may consider such factors as age, length of employee service, employer's profits, and compensation level. Only the employer's contribution is defined; no promise is made regarding the ultimate benefits paid out to the employees. (2) *Defined benefit plans:* These plans define the benefits that the employee will receive at the time of retirement. The formula typically provides for the benefits to be a function of the employee's years of service and the compensation level when he or she nears retirement.

·3 Explain alternative measures for valuing the pension obligation. One measure bases the pension obligation only on the benefits vested to the employees. Vested benefits are those that the employee is entitled to receive even if he or she renders no additional services under the plan. Companies compute the *vested benefits pension obligation* using current salary levels; this obligation includes only vested benefits. Another measure of the obligation, called the *accumulated benefit obligation,* computes the deferred compensation amount based on all years of service performed by employees under the plan—both vested and non-vested—using current salary levels. A third measure, called the *defined benefit obligation,* bases the computation of the deferred compensation amount on both vested and non-vested service using future salaries.

·4 List the components of pension expense. Pension expense is a function of the following components: (1) service cost, (2) interest on the liability, (3) return on plan assets, (4) amortization of unrecognized past service cost, and (5) gain or loss.

·5 Use a worksheet for employer's pension plan entries. Companies may use a worksheet unique to pension accounting. This worksheet records both the formal entries and the memo entries to keep track of all the employer's relevant pension plan items and components.

·6 Describe the amortization of past service costs. An actuary generally computes the amount of the past service cost. Companies record an expense for past service costs using an amortization method. If the benefits from the amendment to the plan vest immediately, then the company should recognize the expense and related liability at the amendment date. If the benefits do not vest immediately, past service cost should be recognized as an expense on a straight-line basis over the average remaining period until the benefits become vested.

·7 Explain the accounting for unexpected gains and losses. In estimating the defined benefit obligation (the liability), actuaries make assumptions about such items as mortality rate, retirement rate, turnover rate, disability rate, and salary amounts. Any change in these actuarial assumptions affects the amount of the defined benefit obligation. These unexpected gains or losses from changes in the defined benefit obligation are liability gains and losses. Liability gains result from unexpected decreases in the liability balance; liability losses result from unexpected increases. Companies may defer (do not immediately recognize) liability gains and losses. They combine liability gains and losses in the same Unrecognized Net Gain or Loss account used for asset gains and losses, and then accumulate these amounts from year to year, off-balance-sheet, in a memo record account.

·8 **Explain the corridor approach to amortizing gains and losses.** The IASB set a limit for the size of an unrecognized net gain or loss balance. That arbitrarily selected limit (called a *corridor*) is 10 percent of the larger of the beginning balances of the defined benefit obligation or the fair value of the plan assets. Beyond that limit, an unrecognized net gain or loss balance is considered too large and must be amortized. If the balance of the unrecognized net gain or loss account stays within the upper and lower limits of the corridor, no amortization is required. The corridor approach results in the minimum amount that should be recognized as an actuarial gain and loss. Companies may use any systematic method that is faster than the corridor approach, provided it is used for both gains and losses and is used consistently from period to period. If a company chooses the immediate recognition approach, the actuarial gain or loss can either adjust net income or other comprehensive income.

·9 **Describe the requirements for reporting pension plans in financial statements.** A company reports the pension asset/liability as an asset or a liability in the statement of financial position at the end of a reporting period. The classification as non-current or current follows the general guidelines used for classification of other assets or liabilities. On the income statement (or related notes), the company must report the amount of pension expense for the period. In addition, any actuarial gains or losses charged or credited to other comprehensive income should be reported in the statement of comprehensive income.

In the notes, companies must disclose the following pension plan information in their financial statements: (1) A description of the plan and the accounting policy used for recognizing actuarial gains and losses. (2) The components of net periodic pension expense for the period. (3) A schedule showing changes in the benefit obligation and plan assets during the year. (4) A schedule reconciling the funded status of the plan with amounts reported in the employer's statement of financial position. (5) The weighted-average assumed discount rate, the rate of compensation increase used to measure the defined benefit obligation, and the weighted-average expected long-term rate of return on plan assets. (6) A company's best estimate of the contributions expected to be made to the plan in the next year and a table showing the allocation of pension plan assets by category and the percentage of the fair value to total plan assets. (7) The actual return on plan assets is disclosed, as well as information on how the expected rate of return is determined.

·10 **Explain special issues related to postretirement benefit plans.** Special issues relate to (1) other postretirement benefits and (2) curtailments and settlements. Companies often provide other types of non-pension postretirement benefits, such as life insurance outside a pension plan, medical care, and legal and tax services. The accounting for these other types of postretirement benefits is the same as that used for pension plan reporting. Companies with both pension and other postretirement benefit plans must separately disclose the plan details when the plans are subject to materially different risks. Curtailments occur when a company substantially reduces the benefits of an existing plan. A settlement occurs when curtailment results in elimination of all further obligations for part or all of the benefits provided under a defined benefit plan. Companies recognize gains or losses on the curtailment or settlement of a defined benefit plan when the curtailment or settlement occurs. The gain or loss on a curtailment or settlement is comprised of the following: (1) any resulting change in the present value of the defined benefit obligation, (2) any resulting change in the fair value of the plan assets, and (3) any related actuarial gains and losses and past service cost that had not been previously recognized.

AUTHORITATIVE LITERATURE

Authoritative Literature References

[1] International Accounting Standard 26, *Accounting and Reporting by Retirement Benefit Plans* (London, U.K.: International Accounting Standards Committee Foundation, 2001).

[2] International Accounting Standard 19, *Employee Benefits* (London, U.K.: International Accounting Standards Committee Foundation, 2001), paras. 46–47.

[3] International Accounting Standard 19, *Employee Benefits* (London, U.K.: International Accounting Standards Committee Foundation, 2001), par. 57.

[4] International Accounting Standard 19, *Employee Benefits* (London, U.K.: International Accounting Standards Committee Foundation, 2001), paras. 78–82.

[5] International Accounting Standard 19, *Employee Benefits* (London, U.K.: International Accounting Standards Committee Foundation, 2001), par. 61.

[6] International Accounting Standard 19, *Employee Benefits* (London, U.K.: International Accounting Standards Committee Foundation, 2001), par. 78.

[7] International Accounting Standard 19, *Employee Benefits* (London, U.K.: International Accounting Standards Committee Foundation, 2001), par. 61(c).

[8] International Accounting Standard 19, *Employee Benefits* (London, U.K.: International Accounting Standards Committee Foundation, 2001), par. 58; and IFRIC Interpretation 14, *IAS 19—The Limit on a Defined Benefit Asset, Minimum Funding Requirements and Their Interaction* (2007).

[9] International Accounting Standard 19, *Employee Benefits* (London, U.K.: International Accounting Standards Committee Foundation, 2001), par. 96.

[10] International Accounting Standard 19, *Employee Benefits* (London, U.K.: International Accounting Standards Committee Foundation, 2001), par. 99.

[11] International Accounting Standard 19, *Employee Benefits* (London, U.K.: International Accounting Standards Committee Foundation, 2001), par. 100.

[12] International Accounting Standard 19, *Employee Benefits* (London, U.K.: International Accounting Standards Committee Foundation, 2001), par. 73.

[13] International Accounting Standard 19, *Employee Benefits* (London, U.K.: International Accounting Standards Committee Foundation, 2001), paras. 93 and BC41.

[14] International Accounting Standard 19, *Employee Benefits* (London, U.K.: International Accounting Standards Committee Foundation, 2001), par. 120.

[15] International Accounting Standard 19, *Employee Benefits* (London, U.K.: International Accounting Standards Committee Foundation, 2001), par. 122.

[16] International Accounting Standard 19, *Employee Benefits* (London, U.K.: International Accounting Standards Committee Foundation, 2001), paras. 109–115.

QUESTIONS

1. What is a private pension plan? How does a contributory pension plan differ from a non-contributory plan?

2. Differentiate between a defined contribution pension plan and a defined benefit pension plan. Explain how the employer's obligation differs between the two types of plans.

3. Differentiate between "accounting for the employer" and "accounting for the pension fund."

4. The meaning of the term "fund" depends on the context in which it is used. Explain its meaning when used as a noun. Explain its meaning when it is used as a verb.

5. What is the role of an actuary relative to pension plans? What are actuarial assumptions?

6. What factors must be considered by the actuary in measuring the amount of pension benefits under a defined benefit plan?

7. Name three approaches to measuring benefits from a pension plan and explain how they differ.

8. Explain how cash-basis accounting for pension plans differs from accrual-basis accounting for pension plans. Why is cash-basis accounting generally considered unacceptable for pension plan accounting?

9. Identify the five components of pension expense. Briefly explain the nature of each component.

10. What is service cost, and what is the basis of its measurement?

11. In computing the interest component of pension expense, what interest rates may be used?

12. Explain the difference between service cost and past service cost.

13. What is meant by "past service cost"? When is past service cost recognized as pension expense?

14. What are "liability gains and losses," and how are they accounted for?

15. If pension expense recognized in a period exceeds the current amount funded by the employer, what kind of account arises, and how should it be reported in the financial statements? If the reverse occurs—that is, current funding by the employer exceeds the amount recognized as pension expense—what kind of account arises, and how should it be reported?

16. Given the following items and amounts, compute the actual return on plan assets: fair value of plan assets at the beginning of the period $9,200,000; benefits paid during the period $1,400,000; contributions made during the period $1,000,000; and fair value of the plan assets at the end of the period $10,150,000.

17. How does an "asset gain or loss" develop in pension accounting? How does a "liability gain or loss" develop in pension accounting?

18. What is the meaning of "corridor amortization"?

19. Describe the immediate recognition approach for unrecognized actuarial gains and losses.

20. Bill Haley is learning about pension accounting. He is convinced that, regardless of the method used to recognize actuarial gains and losses, total comprehensive income will always be the same. Is Bill correct? Explain.

21. At the end of the current period, Jacob Inc. has a defined benefit obligation of €125,000 and pension plan assets with a fair value of €98,000. The amount of the vested benefits for the plan is €95,000. What amount and account(s) related to its pension plan will be reported on the company's statement of financial position?

22. At the end of the current year, Joshua Co. has a defined benefit obligation of £335,000 and pension plan assets with a fair value of £245,000. The amount of the vested benefits for the plan is £225,000. Joshua has unrecognized past service costs of £24,000 and an unrecognized actuarial gain of £8,300. What amount and account(s) related to its pension plan will be reported on the company's statement of financial position?

23. Explain the meaning of the following terms.

   (a) Contributory plan.

   (b) Vested benefits.

   (c) Retroactive benefits.

24. Of what value to the financial statement reader is the schedule reconciling the funded status of the plan with amounts reported in the employer's statement of financial position?

25. What are postretirement benefits other than pensions?

26. What are the major differences between postretirement healthcare benefits and pension benefits?

27. What is a plan curtailment? What is a plan settlement?

28. Describe the accounting for pension plan curtailments and settlements.

29. Briefly describe some of the similarities and differences between U.S. GAAP and IFRS with respect to the accounting for pensions and other postretirement benefits.

30. Briefly discuss the convergence efforts that are underway with respect to the accounting for pensions and other postretirement benefits.

BRIEF EXERCISES

BE20-1 **Cathay Pacific Airlines** (CHN) reported the following for 2009 (in millions).

Service cost	HK$316
Interest on DBO	342
Return on plan assets	371
Amortization of unrecognized net loss	30

Compute Cathay Pacific's 2009 pension expense.

•4 **BE20-2** For Becker Corporation, year-end plan assets were $2,000,000. At the beginning of the year, plan assets were $1,680,000. During the year, contributions to the pension fund were $120,000, and benefits paid were $200,000. Compute Becker's actual return on plan assets.

•5 **BE20-3** At January 1, 2010, Uddin Company had plan assets of $250,000 and a defined benefit obligation of the same amount. During 2010, service cost was $27,500, the discount rate was 10%, actual and expected return on plan assets were $25,000, contributions were $20,000, and benefits paid were $17,500. Prepare a pension worksheet for Uddin Company for 2010.

•4 **BE20-4** For 2010, **Wm Morrison Supermarkets plc** (GBR) had pension expense of £61 million and contributed £52 million to the pension fund. Prepare Morrisons's journal entry to record pension income and funding.

•6 **BE20-5** Duesbury Corporation amended its pension plan on January 1, 2010, and granted $120,000 of unrecognized past service costs to its employees. The employees have an average time to vesting of four years. Compute unrecognized past service cost amortization for 2010.

•6 **BE20-6** Villa Company has experienced tough competition, leading it to seek concessions from its employees in the company's pension plan. In exchange for promises to avoid layoffs and wage cuts, the employees agreed to receive lower pension benefits in the future. As a result, Villa amended its pension plan on January 1, 2010, and recorded negative unrecognized past service cost of €125,000. The average period to vesting for the benefits affected by this plan is 5 years. Compute unrecognized past service cost amortization for 2010. Discuss the impact of this amendment on Villa's pension expense in 2010 and 2011.

•8 **BE20-7** Hunt Corporation had a defined benefit obligation of $3,100,000 and plan assets of $2,900,000 at January 1, 2010. Hunt's unrecognized net pension loss was $475,000 at that time. The average remaining service period of Hunt's employees is 7 years. Compute Hunt's minimum amortization of pension loss.

•8 **BE20-8** Tevez Company experienced an actuarial loss of €750 in its defined benefit plan in 2010. Tevez has elected to recognize this loss immediately. For 2010, Tevez's revenues are €125,000, and expenses (excluding pension expense of €14,000, which does not include the actuarial loss) are €85,000. Prepare Tevez's statement of comprehensive income for 2010, assuming Tevez recognizes the loss in (a) net income, and (b) other comprehensive income.

•9 **BE20-9** At December 31, 2010, Conway Corporation had a defined benefit obligation of €510,000, plan assets of €322,000, and unrecognized past service cost of €127,000. Prepare a pension reconciliation schedule for Conway.

•10 **BE20-10** Caleb Corporation has the following information available concerning its postretirement medical benefit plan for 2010.

Service cost	$40,000
Interest cost	52,400
Actual and expected return on plan assets	26,900

Compute Caleb's 2010 postretirement expense.

•10 **BE20-11** For 2010, Benjamin Inc. computed its annual postretirement expense as £240,900. Benjamin's contribution to the plan during 2010 was £160,000. Prepare Benjamin's 2010 entry to record postretirement expense.

•10 **BE20-12** As a result of a discontinued operation, Wasson Company is curtailing some benefits provided in its pension plan. It has the following data related to the plan.

Defined benefit obligation (Credit)	€(1,500)
Fair value of plan assets (Debit)	1,350
Funded status	(150)
Unrecognized actuarial gains (Credit)	(30)
Unrecognized past service costs (PSC) (Debit)	80
Pension asset/liability	€ (100)

The curtailment results in a €180 reduction in the defined benefit obligation (there is no impact on the plan assets). The employees affected comprise 20% of all employees in the plan. Prepare the entry to record the curtailment for Wasson.

•10 **BE20-13** Using the information in BE20-12, prepare the journal entry for Wasson, assuming that instead of having unrecognized actuarial gains, Wasson has unrecognized losses before the curtailment of €50. Prepare the pension plan reconciliation after recording the curtailment.

EXERCISES

•4 •6 E20-1 (Pension Expense, Journal Entry) The following information is available for the pension plan of Kiley Company for the year 2010.

Actual and expected return on plan assets	$ 12,000
Benefits paid to retirees	40,000
Contributions (funding)	95,000
Interest/discount rate	10%
Past service cost amortization	8,000
Defined benefit obligation, January 1, 2010	500,000
Service cost	60,000

Instructions

(a) Compute pension expense for the year 2010.

(b) Prepare the journal entry to record pension expense and the employer's contribution to the pension plan in 2010.

•4 •6 E20-2 (Computation of Pension Expense) Rebekah Company provides the following information about its defined benefit pension plan for the year 2010.

Service cost	€ 90,000
Contribution to the plan	105,000
Past service cost amortization	10,000
Actual and expected return on plan assets	64,000
Benefits paid	40,000
Pension asset/liability at January 1, 2010	10,000
Plan assets at January 1, 2010	640,000
Defined benefit obligation at January 1, 2010	800,000
Unrecognized past service cost balance at January 1, 2010	150,000
Interest/discount rate	10%

Instructions

Compute the pension expense for the year 2010.

•5 E20-3 (Preparation of Pension Worksheet with Reconciliation) Using the information in E20-2 prepare a pension worksheet inserting January 1, 2010, balances, showing December 31, 2010, balances, the reconciliation schedule, and the journal entry recording pension expense.

•5 E20-4 (Basic Pension Worksheet) The following facts apply to the pension plan of Trudy Borke Inc. for the year 2010.

Plan assets, January 1, 2010	£490,000
Defined benefit obligation, January 1, 2010	490,000
Discount rate	8.5%
Service cost	40,000
Contributions (funding)	30,000
Actual and expected return on plan assets	49,700
Benefits paid to retirees	33,400

Instructions

Using the preceding data, compute pension expense for the year 2010. As part of your solution, prepare a pension worksheet that shows the journal entry for pension expense for 2010 and the year-end balances in the related pension accounts.

•6 E20-5 (Past Service Costs) Merkel Corporation is evaluating amendments to its pensions plans. Plan A covers its salaried employees and Plan B provides benefits to its hourly workers. On January 1, 2010, Merkel will grant employees in Plan B additional pension benefits of €318,000 based on their past service. Employees in this plan have an average period to vesting of 6 years. Plan A will be amended to reduce benefits by €160,000 (in exchange, employees will receive increased contributions to the company's defined contribution plan). Employees in this plan have an average period to vesting of 5 years. Compute total unrecognized past service cost amortization for 2010. Discuss the impact of this amendment on Merkel's pension expense in 2010 and 2011.

•4 E20-6 (Computation of Actual Return) James Paul Importers provides the following pension plan information.

Fair value of pension plan assets, January 1, 2010	$2,300,000
Fair value of pension plan assets, December 31, 2010	2,725,000
Contributions to the plan in 2010	250,000
Benefits paid retirees in 2010	350,000

Instructions

From the data above, compute the actual return on the plan assets for 2010.

•5 •6   E20-7   (Basic Pension Worksheet) The following defined pension data of Doreen Corp. apply to the year 2010.

Defined benefit obligation, 1/1/10 (before amendment)	$560,000
Plan assets, 1/1/10	546,200
Pension asset/liability	13,800 Cr.
On January 1, 2010, Doreen Corp., through plan amendment, grants past service benefits having a present value of	100,000
Discount rate	9%
Service cost	58,000
Contributions (funding)	55,000
Actual (expected) return on plan assets	52,280
Benefits paid to retirees	40,000
Past service cost amortization for 2010	17,000

Instructions

For 2010, prepare a pension worksheet for Doreen Corp. that shows the journal entry for pension expense and the year-end balances in the related pension accounts.

•8   E20-8   (Application of the Corridor Approach) Shin Corp. has beginning-of-the-year present values for its defined benefit obligation and fair values for its pension plan assets (amounts in thousands).

	Defined Benefit Obligation	Plan Assets Value
2010	¥2,000,000	¥1,900,000
2011	2,400,000	2,500,000
2012	2,900,000	2,600,000
2013	3,600,000	3,000,000

The average remaining service life per employee in 2010 and 2011 is 10 years and in 2012 and 2013 is 12 years. The unrecognized net gain or loss that occurred during each year is as follows: 2010, ¥280,000 loss; 2011, ¥90,000 loss; 2012, ¥10,000 loss; and 2013, ¥25,000 gain. (In working the solution, the unrecognized gains and losses must be aggregated to arrive at year-end balances.)

Instructions

Using the corridor approach, compute the amount of unrecognized net gain or loss amortized and charged to pension expense in each of the four years, setting up an appropriate schedule.

•9   E20-9   (Disclosures: Pension Expense and Reconciliation Schedule) Mildred Enterprises provides the following information relative to its defined benefit pension plan.

Balances or Values at December 31, 2010

Defined benefit obligation	€2,737,000
Vested benefit obligation	1,645,852
Fair value of plan assets	2,278,329
Unrecognized past service cost	205,000
Unrecognized net loss (1/1/10 balance, –0–)	45,680
Pension liability	207,991
Other pension plan data:	
Service cost for 2010	€ 94,000
Unrecognized past service cost amortization for 2010	45,000
Actual return on plan assets in 2010	130,000
Expected return on plan assets in 2010	175,680
Interest on January 1, 2010, defined benefit obligation	253,000
Contributions to plan in 2010	92,329
Benefits paid	140,000

Instructions

(a) Prepare the note disclosing the components of pension expense for the year 2010.

(b) Reconcile the funded status of the plan with the amount reported in the December 31, 2010, statement of financial position.

 E20-10 **(Pension Worksheet with Reconciliation Schedule)** Buhl Corp. sponsors a defined benefit pension plan for its employees. On January 1, 2010, the following balances relate to this plan.

Plan assets	$480,000
Defined benefit obligation	625,000
Pension asset/liability	45,000
Unrecognized past service cost	100,000

As a result of the operation of the plan during 2010, the following additional data are provided by the actuary.

Service cost for 2010	$90,000
Discount rate, 9%	
Actual return on plan assets in 2010	57,000
Amortization of past service cost	19,000
Expected return on plan assets	52,000
Unexpected loss from change in defined benefit obligation,	
due to change in actuarial predictions	76,000
Contributions in 2010	99,000
Benefits paid retirees in 2010	85,000

Instructions

(a) Using the data above, compute pension expense for Buhl Corp. for the year 2010 by preparing a pension worksheet that shows the journal entry for pension expense and the year-end balances in the related pension accounts.

(b) At December 31, 2010, prepare a schedule reconciling the funded status of the plan with the pension amount reported on the statement of financial position.

E20-11 **(Pension Expense, Journal Entry, Statement Presentation)** Griseta Company sponsors a defined benefit pension plan for its employees. The following data relate to the operation of the plan for the year 2010 in which no benefits were paid.

1. The actuarial present value of future benefits earned by employees for services rendered in 2010 amounted to $56,000.

2. The company's funding policy requires a contribution to the pension trustee amounting to $145,000 for 2010.

3. As of January 1, 2010, the company had a defined benefit obligation of $1,000,000 and an unrecognized past service cost of $400,000. The fair value of pension plan assets amounted to $600,000 at the beginning of the year. The actual and expected return on plan assets was $54,000. The discount rate was 9%. No gains or losses occurred in 2010 and no benefits were paid.

4. Amortization of unrecognized past service cost was $40,000 in 2010. Amortization of unrecognized net gain or loss was not required in 2010.

Instructions

(a) Determine the amounts of the components of pension expense that should be recognized by the company in 2010.

(b) Prepare the journal entry to record pension expense and the employer's contribution to the pension trustee in 2010.

(c) Indicate the amounts that would be reported on the income statement and the statement of financial position for the year 2010.

E20-12 **(Pension Expense, Journal Entry, Statement Presentation)** Nellie Altom Company received the following selected information from its pension plan trustee concerning the operation of the company's defined benefit pension plan for the year ended December 31, 2010.

	January 1, 2010	December 31, 2010
Defined benefit obligation	€2,000,000	€2,077,000
Fair value of plan assets	800,000	1,130,000
Actuarial (gains) losses (Unrecognized net (gain) or loss)	–0–	(200,000)

The service cost component of pension expense for employee services rendered in the current year amounted to €77,000 and the amortization of unrecognized past service cost was €115,000. The company's actual funding (contributions) of the plan in 2010 amounted to €250,000. The expected return on plan assets and the actual rate were both 10%; the interest/discount rate was 10%. No pension asset/liability existed on January 1, 2010. Assume no benefits paid in 2010.

Instructions

(a) Determine the amounts of the components of pension expense that should be recognized by the company in 2010.

(b) Prepare the journal entry to record pension expense and the employer's contribution to the pension plan in 2010.

(c) Indicate the pension-related amounts that would be reported on the income statement and the statement of financial position for Nellie Altom Company for the year 2010.

E20-13 (Computation of Actual Return, Gains and Losses, Corridor Test, Past Service Cost, Pension Expense, and Reconciliation) Linda Berstler Company sponsors a defined benefit pension plan. The corporation's actuary provides the following information about the plan.

	January 1, 2010	December 31, 2010
Vested benefit obligation	£1,500	£1,900
Defined benefit obligation	2,800	3,645
Plan assets (fair value)	1,700	2,620
Discount rate and expected rate of return		10%
Pension asset/liability	–0–	?
Unrecognized past service cost	1,100	?
Service cost for the year 2010		400
Contributions (funding in 2010)		800
Benefits paid in 2010		200

The average remaining service life per employee is 20 years. The average time to vesting past service costs is 10 years.

Instructions

(a) Compute the actual return on the plan assets in 2010.

(b) Compute the amount of the unrecognized net gain or loss as of December 31, 2010. (Assume the January 1, 2010, balance was zero.)

(c) Compute the amount of unrecognized net gain or loss amortization for 2010 (corridor approach).

(d) Compute the amount of past service cost amortization for 2010.

(e) Compute pension expense for 2010.

(f) Prepare a schedule reconciling the plan's funded status with the amounts reported in the December 31, 2010, statement of financial position.

E20-14 (Worksheet for E20-13) Using the information in E20-13 about Linda Berstler Company's defined benefit pension plan, prepare a 2010 pension worksheet with supplementary schedules of computations. Prepare the journal entries at December 31, 2010, to record pension expense. Also, prepare a schedule reconciling the plan's funded status with the pension amounts reported in the statement of financial position.

E20-15 (Pension Expense, Journal Entry) Walker Company provides the following information related to its defined benefit pension plan for 2010.

Pension asset/liability (January 1)	$515,000 Cr.
Actual and expected return on plan assets	15,000
Contributions (funding) in 2010	150,000
Fair value of plan assets (December 31)	350,000
Discount rate	10%
Defined benefit obligation (January 1)	700,000
Service cost	90,000

Instructions

(a) Compute pension expense and prepare the journal entry to record pension expense and the employer's contribution to the pension plan in 2010.

(b) Prepare the schedule reconciling the plan's funded status to amounts reported in the statement of financial position.

E20-16 **(Pension Expense, Statement Presentation)** Blum Foods Company obtained the following information from the insurance company that administers the company's employee defined benefit pension plan.

	For Year Ended December 31,		
	2010	2011	2012
Plan assets (at fair value)	€393,000	€582,300	€765,530
Defined benefit obligation	378,000	545,300	797,530
Pension expense	95,000	128,000	130,000
Employer's funding contribution	110,000	150,000	125,000

Prior to 2010, cumulative pension expense was equal to cumulative contributions.

Instructions

(a) Prepare the journal entries to record pension expense and the employer's funding contribution for the years 2010, 2011, and 2012. (Preparation of a pension worksheet is not a requirement of this exercise; insufficient information is given to prepare one.)

(b) Indicate the pension-related amounts that would be reported on the company's income statement and statement of financial position for 2010, 2011, and 2012.

E20-17 **(Reconciliation Schedule and Unrecognized Loss)** Presented below is partial information related to Jean Burr Company at December 31, 2010.

Defined benefit obligation	£930,000
Plan assets (at fair value)	700,000
Vested benefits	200,000
Past service cost not yet recognized in pension expense	120,000
Gains and losses	–0–

Instructions

(a) Present the schedule reconciling the funded status with the pension asset/liability reported on the statement of financial position. Assume no asset or liability existed at the beginning of period for pensions on Jean Burr Company's statement of financial position.

(b) Assume the same facts as in (a) except that Jean Burr Company has an unrecognized loss of $16,000 during 2010.

(c) Explain the rationale for the treatment of the unrecognized loss and the past service cost not yet recognized in pension expense.

E20-18 **(Amortization of Unrecognized Net Gain or Loss [Corridor Approach], Pension Expense Computation)** The actuary for the pension plan of Joyce Bush Inc. calculated the following net gains and losses.

Unrecognized Net Gain or Loss	
Incurred during the Year	(Gain) or Loss
2010	$ 300,000
2011	480,000
2012	(210,000)
2013	(290,000)

Other information about the company's pension obligation and plan assets is as follows.

As of January 1	Defined Benefit Obligation	Plan Assets (fair value)
2010	$4,000,000	$2,400,000
2011	4,520,000	2,200,000
2012	4,980,000	2,600,000
2013	4,250,000	3,040,000

Joyce Bush Inc. has a stable labor force of 400 employees who are expected to receive benefits under the plan. The beginning balance of unrecognized net gain or loss is zero on January 1, 2010. Use the average remaining service life per employee of 14 years as the basis for amortization.

Instructions

(Round to the nearest dollar.)

(a) Prepare a schedule that reflects the minimum amount of unrecognized net gain or loss amortized as a component of net periodic pension expense for each of the years 2010, 2011, 2012, and 2013. Apply the corridor approach in determining the amount to be amortized each year.

(b) Assume that Bush elects to recognize actuarial gains and losses immediately in other comprehensive income. Determine the effect of this accounting choice on pension expense in 2010, 2011, 2012, and 2013 in comparison to pension expense under corridor amortization.

•8 E20-19 (Amortization of Unrecognized Net Gain or Loss [Corridor Approach]) Lowell Company sponsors a defined benefit pension plan for its 600 employees. The company's actuary provided the following information about the plan.

	January 1,	December 31,	
	2010	2010	2011
Defined benefit obligation	$2,800,000	$3,650,000	$4,400,000
Plan assets (fair value)	1,700,000	2,900,000	2,100,000
Unrecognized net (gain) or loss (for purposes of the corridor calculation)	–0–	101,000	(24,000)
Discount rate	11%	8%	
Actual and expected asset return rate	10%	10%	

The average remaining service life per employee is 20 years. The service cost component of net periodic pension expense for employee services rendered amounted to $400,000 in 2010 and $475,000 in 2011. The unrecognized past service cost on January 1, 2010, was $1,155,000. The average service period to vesting is 10 years. No benefits have been paid.

Instructions
(Round to the nearest dollar.)

(a) Compute the amount of unrecognized past service cost to be amortized as a component of net periodic pension expense for each of the years 2010 and 2011.

(b) Prepare a schedule that reflects the amount of unrecognized net gain or loss to be amortized as a component of net periodic pension expense for 2010 and 2011, using the corridor approach.

(c) Determine the total amount of net periodic pension expense to be recognized by Lowell Company in 2010 and 2011.

(d) Determine pension expense, assuming Lowell chooses to immediately recognize actuarial gains and losses in net income.

•10 E20-20 (Other Postretirement Benefit Expense Computation) Marvelous Marvin Co. provides the following information about its postretirement medical benefit plan for the year 2010.

Service cost	$ 90,000
Past service cost amortization	3,000
Contribution to the plan	16,000
Actual and expected return on plan assets	62,000
Benefits paid	40,000
Plan assets at January 1, 2010	710,000
Defined benefit obligation at January 1, 2010	810,000
Unrecognized past service cost balance at January 1, 2010	100,000
Discount rate	9%

Instructions
Compute the postretirement benefit expense for 2010.

•10 E20-21 (Other Postretirement Benefit Worksheet) Using the information in E20-20, prepare a worksheet inserting January 1, 2010, balances, showing December 31, 2010, balances, and the journal entry recording postretirement benefit expense.

•10 E20-22 (Other Postretirement Benefit Reconciliation Schedule) Presented below is partial information related to Sandra Conley Co. at December 31, 2010.

Defined benefit obligation	€950,000
Plan assets (at fair value)	650,000
Past service cost not yet recognized in postretirement expense	60,000
Gain and losses	–0–

Instructions

(a) Present the schedule reconciling the funded status with the pension asset/liability reported on the statement of financial position. Assume no asset or liability existed at the beginning of the period for postretirement benefits on Sandra Conley Co.'s statement of financial position.

(b) Assume the same facts as in (a) except that Sandra Conley Co. has an unrecognized loss of €20,000. Present the reconciliation schedule, assuming (1) Conley uses corridor amortization, and (2) Conley immediately recognizes gains and losses in other comprehensive income.

PROBLEMS

·5 ·6 ·7 ·9 **P20-1** **(2-Year Worksheet and Reconciliation Schedule)** On January 1, 2010, Diana Peter Company has the following defined benefit pension plan balances.

Defined benefit obligation	€4,200,000
Fair value of plan assets	4,200,000

The discount rate applicable to the plan is 10%. On January 1, 2011, the company amends its pension agreement so that past service costs of €500,000 are created. Other data related to the pension plan are as follows.

	2010	2011
Service costs	€150,000	€180,000
Unrecognized past service costs amortization	–0–	90,000
Contributions (funding) to the plan	140,000	185,000
Benefits paid	200,000	280,000
Actual return on plan assets	252,000	260,000
Expected rate of return on assets	6%	8%

Instructions

(a) Prepare a pension worksheet for the pension plan for 2010 and 2011.

(b) As of December 31, 2011, prepare a schedule reconciling the funded status with the reported liability.

·5 ·6 ·7 ·9 **P20-2** **(3-Year Worksheet, Journal Entries, and Reconciliation Schedules)** Katie Day Company adopts *IAS 19* in accounting for its defined benefit pension plan on January 1, 2010, with the following beginning balances: plan assets $200,000; defined benefit obligation $200,000. Other data relating to 3 years' operation of the plan are as follows.

	2010	2011	2012
Annual service cost	$16,000	$ 19,000	$ 26,000
Discount rate and expected rate of return	10%	10%	10%
Actual return on plan assets	17,000	21,900	24,000
Annual funding (contributions)	16,000	40,000	48,000
Benefits paid	14,000	16,400	21,000
Unrecognized past service cost (plan amended, 1/1/11)		160,000	
Amortization of unrecognized past service cost		54,400	41,600
Change in actuarial assumptions establishes a December 31, 2012, defined benefit obligation of:			520,000

Instructions

(a) Prepare a pension worksheet presenting all 3 years' pension balances and activities.

(b) Prepare the journal entries (from the worksheet) to reflect all pension plan transactions and events at December 31 of each year.

(c) At December 31 of each year, prepare a schedule reconciling the funded status of the plan with the pension amounts reported in the financial statements.

·6 ·7 ·8 ·9 **P20-3** **(Pension Expense, Journal Entry, Amortization of Unrecognized Loss, Reconciliation Schedule)** Paul Dobson Company sponsors a defined benefit plan for its 100 employees. On January 1, 2010, the company's actuary provided the following information.

Unrecognized past service cost	£150,000
Pension plan assets (fair value)	200,000
Defined benefit obligation	350,000

The average remaining service period for the participating employees is 10.5 years. The average period to vesting of past service costs in 7.5 years. All employees are expected to receive benefits under the plan. On December 31, 2010, the actuary calculated that the present value of future benefits earned for employee services rendered in the current year amounted to £52,000; the defined benefit obligation was £452,000; and fair value of pension assets was £276,000. The expected return on plan assets and the discount rate on the defined benefit obligation were both 10%. The actual return on plan assets is £11,000. The company's current year's contribution to the pension plan amounted to £65,000. No benefits were paid during the year.

Instructions

(Round to the nearest pound.)

(a) Determine the components of pension expense that the company would recognize in 2010. (With only one year involved, you need not prepare a worksheet.)

(b) Prepare the journal entry to record the pension expense and the company's funding of the pension plan in 2010.

(c) Compute the amount of the 2010 increase/decrease in unrecognized gains or losses and the amount to be amortized in 2010 and 2011, using corridor amortization.

(d) Prepare a schedule reconciling the funded status of the plan with the pension amounts reported in the financial statements as of December 31, 2010.

·5 ·6 ·7 **P20-4** **(Pension Expense and Journal Entries for 2 Years)** Ichiro Company sponsors a defined benefit
·8 ·9 pension plan. The following information related to the pension plan is available for 2010 and 2011 (amounts in thousands).

	2010	2011
Plan assets (fair value), December 31	¥380,000	¥465,000
Defined benefit obligation, January 1	600,000	700,000
Pension asset/liability balance, January 1	40,000 Cr.	?
Unrecognized past service cost, January 1	250,000	240,000
Service cost	60,000	90,000
Actual and expected return on plan assets	24,000	30,000
Amortization of past service cost	10,000	12,000
Contributions (funding)	110,000	120,000
Discount rate	9%	9%

Instructions

(a) Compute pension expense for 2010 and 2011.

(b) Prepare the journal entries to record the pension expense and the company's funding of the pension plan for both years.

·7 ·8 **P20-5** **(Computation of Pension Expense, Amortization of Unrecognized Net Gain or Loss [Corridor Approach], and Journal Entries for 3 Years)** Dubel Toothpaste Company initiates a defined benefit pension plan for its 50 employees on January 1, 2010. The insurance company, which administers the pension plan, provided the following information for the years 2010, 2011, and 2012.

	For Year Ended December 31,		
	2010	2011	2012
Plan assets (fair value)	$50,000	$ 85,000	$170,000
Defined benefit obligation	55,000	200,000	324,000
Unrecognized net (gain) loss (for purposes of corridor calculation)	–0–	83,950	86,121
Employer's funding contribution (made at end of year)	50,000	60,000	95,000

There were no balances as of January 1, 2010, when the plan was initiated. The actual and expected return on plan assets was 10% over the 3-year period, but the rate used to discount the company's pension obligation was 13% in 2010, 11% in 2011, and 8% in 2012. The service cost component of net periodic pension expense amounted to the following: 2010, $55,000; 2011, $85,000; and 2012, $119,000. The average remaining service life per employee is 12 years. No benefits were paid in 2010, $30,000 of benefits were paid in 2011, and $18,500 of benefits were paid in 2012 (all benefits paid at end of year).

Instructions

(Round to the nearest dollar.)

(a) Calculate the amount of net periodic pension expense that the company would recognize in 2010, 2011, and 2012.

(b) Prepare the journal entries to record net periodic pension expense and employer's funding contribution for the years 2010, 2011, and 2012. Dubel uses corridor amortization for actuarial gains and losses.

(c) Repeat the requirements for part (b), assuming that Dubel immediately recognizes actuarial gains and losses in net income.

·6 ·7 ·8 **P20-6** **(Computation of Unrecognized Past Service Cost Amortization, Pension Expense, Journal Entries, Net Gain or Loss, and Reconciliation Schedule)** Widjaja Inc. has sponsored a non-contributory, defined benefit pension plan for its employees since 1990. Prior to 2010, cumulative net pension expense recognized equaled cumulative contributions to the plan. Other relevant information about the pension plan on January 1, 2010, is as follows.

1. The company has 200 employees. All these employees are expected to receive benefits under the plan. The average remaining service life per employee is 13 years. The average period to vesting past service costs is 10 years.
2. The defined benefit obligation amounted to €5,000,000 and the fair value of pension plan assets was €3,000,000. Unrecognized past service cost was €2,000,000.

On December 31, 2010, the defined benefit obligation was €4,750,000. The fair value of the pension plan assets amounted to €3,900,000 at the end of the year. A 10% discount rate and a 10% expected asset return rate were used in the actuarial present value computations in the pension plan. The present value of benefits attributed by the pension benefit formula to employee service in 2010 amounted to €200,000. The employer's contribution to the plan assets amounted to €575,000 in 2010. This problem assumes no payment of pension benefits.

Instructions

(Round all amounts to the nearest euro.)

(a) Prepare a schedule, based on the average remaining life per employee, showing the unrecognized past service cost that would be amortized as a component of pension expense for 2010, 2011, and 2012.
(b) Compute pension expense for the year 2010.
(c) Prepare the journal entries required to report the accounting for the company's pension plan for 2010.
(d) Compute the amount of the 2010 increase/decrease in unrecognized net gains or losses and the amount to be amortized in 2010 and 2011.
(e) Prepare a schedule reconciling the funded status of the plan with the pension amounts reported in the financial statements as of December 31, 2010.

·5 ·6 ·7 **P20-7** **(Pension Worksheet)** Farber Corp. sponsors a defined benefit pension plan for its employees.
·8 On January 1, 2010, the following balances related to this plan.

Plan assets	£520,000
Defined benefit obligation	725,000
Pension asset/liability	33,000 Dr.
Unrecognized past service cost	81,000
Unrecognized net gain or loss	91,000 Dr.

As a result of the operation of the plan during 2010, the actuary provided the following additional data at December 31, 2010.

Service cost for 2010	£108,000
Discount rate, 9%; expected return rate, 10%	
Actual return on plan assets in 2010	48,000
Amortization of past service cost	25,000
Contributions in 2010	138,000
Benefits paid retirees in 2010	85,000
Average remaining service life of active employees	10 years
Accumulated benefit obligation at 12/31/10	671,000

Instructions

Using the preceding data, compute pension expense for Farber Corp. for the year 2010 by preparing a pension worksheet that shows the journal entry for pension expense.

·5 ·6 ·7 **P20-8** **(Comprehensive 2-Year Worksheet)** Glesen Company sponsors a defined benefit pension plan
·8 ·9 for its employees. The following data relate to the operation of the plan for the years 2010 and 2011.

	2010	2011
Defined benefit obligation, January 1	$650,000	
Plan assets (fair value), January 1	410,000	
Pension asset/liability, January 1	80,000 Cr.	
Unrecognized past service cost, January 1	160,000	
Service cost	40,000	$ 59,000
Discount rate	10%	10%
Expected rate of return	10%	10%

	2010	2011
Actual return on plan assets	36,000	61,000
Amortization of past service cost	70,000	55,000
Annual contributions	72,000	81,000
Benefits paid retirees	31,500	54,000
Increase in defined benefit obligation due to changes in actuarial assumptions	87,000	–0–
Average service life of all employees		20 years
Vested benefit obligation at December 31		464,000

Instructions

(a) Prepare a pension worksheet presenting both years 2010 and 2011 and accompanying computations (2010 and 2011) and amortization of the unrecognized loss (2011) using the corridor approach.

(b) Prepare the journal entries (from the worksheet) to reflect all pension plan transactions and events at December 31 of each year.

(c) At December 31, 2011, prepare a schedule reconciling the funded status of the pension plan with the pension amounts reported in the financial statements.

P20-9 **(Comprehensive 2-Year Worksheet)** Mount Co. has the following defined benefit pension plan balances on January 1, 2010.

Defined benefit obligation	$4,500,000
Fair value of plan assets	4,500,000

The discount rate applicable to the plan is 10%. On January 1, 2011, the company amends its pension agreement so that past service costs of $600,000 are created. Other data related to the pension plan are:

	2010	2011
Service costs	$150,000	$170,000
Unrecognized past service costs amortization	–0–	90,000
Contributions (funding) to the plan	150,000	184,658
Benefits paid	220,000	280,000
Actual return on plan assets	252,000	250,000
Expected rate of return on assets	6%	8%

Instructions

(a) Prepare a pension worksheet for the pension plan in 2010.

(b) Prepare any journal entries related to the pension plan that would be needed at December 31, 2010.

(c) Prepare a pension worksheet for 2011 and any journal entries related to the pension plan as of December 31, 2011.

(d) As of December 31, 2011, prepare a schedule reconciling the funded status with the reported pension liability.

P20-10 **(Postretirement Benefit Worksheet with Reconciliation)** Dusty Hass Foods Inc. sponsors a postretirement medical and dental benefit plan for its employees. The following balances relate to this plan on January 1, 2010.

Plan assets	€200,000
Defined benefit obligation	200,000
No past service costs exist.	

As a result of the plan's operation during 2010, the following additional data are provided by the actuary.

Service cost for 2010 is €70,000
Discount rate is 9%
Contributions to plan in 2010 are €60,000
Expected return on plan assets is €9,000
Actual return on plan assets is €15,000
Benefits paid to employees from plan are €44,000
Average remaining service lives of employees: 20 years

Instructions

(a) Using the preceding data, compute the net periodic postretirement benefit cost for 2010 by preparing a worksheet that shows the journal entry for postretirement expense and the year-end balances in the related postretirement benefit memo accounts. (Assume that contributions and benefits are paid at the end of the year.)

(b) At December 31, 2010, prepare a schedule reconciling the funded status of the plan with the postretirement amount reported on the statement of financial position.

(c) Hass elects corridor amortization for actuarial gains and losses. Will any amortization be recorded in 2010? 2011? Explain.

CONCEPTS FOR ANALYSIS

CA20-1 (Pension Terminology and Theory) Many business organizations have been concerned with providing for the retirement of employees since the late 1800s. During recent decades, a marked increase in this concern has resulted in the establishment of private pension plans in most large companies and in many medium- and small-sized ones.

The substantial growth of these plans, both in numbers of employees covered and in amounts of retirement benefits, has increased the significance of pension cost in relation to the financial position, results of operations, and cash flows of many companies. In examining the costs of pension plans, a public accountant encounters certain terms. The components of pension costs that the terms represent must be dealt with appropriately if IFRS is to be reflected in the financial statements of entities with pension plans.

Instructions

(a) Define a private pension plan. How does a contributory pension plan differ from a non-contributory plan?

(b) Differentiate between "accounting for the employer" and "accounting for the pension fund."

(c) Explain the terms "funded" and "pension liability" as they relate to:
   (1) The pension fund.
   (2) The employer.

(d) (1) Discuss the theoretical justification for accrual recognition of pension costs.
   (2) Discuss the relative objectivity of the measurement process of accrual versus cash (pay-as-you-go) accounting for annual pension costs.

(e) Distinguish among the following as they relate to pension plans.
   (1) Service cost.
   (2) Past service costs.
   (3) Vested benefits.

CA20-2 (Pension Terminology) The following items appear on Hollingsworth Company's financial statements.

1. Under the caption Assets:
   Pension asset/liability.
2. Under the caption Liabilities:
   Pension asset/liability.
3. Under the caption Equity:
   Actuarial loss as a component of Accumulated Other Comprehensive Income.
4. On the income statement:
   Pension expense.

Instructions

Explain the significance of each of the items above on corporate financial statements. (*Note:* All items set forth above are not necessarily to be found on the statements of a single company.)

CA20-3 (Basic Terminology) In examining the costs of pension plans, Leah Hutcherson, public accountant, encounters certain terms. The components of pension costs that the terms represent must be dealt with appropriately if IFRS is to be reflected in the financial statements of entities with pension plans.

Instructions

(a) (1) Discuss the theoretical justification for accrual recognition of pension costs.

(2) Discuss the relative objectivity of the measurement process of accrual versus cash (pay-as-you-go) accounting for annual pension costs.

(b) Explain the following terms as they apply to accounting for pension plans.

(1) Fair value of pension assets.

(2) Defined benefit obligation.

(3) Corridor approach.

(c) What information should be disclosed about a company's pension plans in its financial statements and its notes?

CA20-4 (Major Pension Concepts) Lyons Corporation is a medium-sized manufacturer of paperboard containers and boxes. The corporation sponsors a non-contributory, defined benefit pension plan that covers its 250 employees. Tim Shea has recently been hired as president of Lyons Corporation. While reviewing last year's financial statements with Anita Kroll, controller, Shea expressed confusion about several of the items in the footnote to the financial statements relating to the pension plan. In part, the footnote reads as follows.

> **Note J.** The company has a defined benefit pension plan covering substantially all of its employees. The benefits are based on years of service and the employee's compensation during the last four years of employment. The company's funding policy is to contribute annually the maximum amount allowed under the tax law. Contributions are intended to provide for benefits expected to be earned in the future as well as those earned to date.

The net periodic pension expense on Lyons Corporation's comparative income statement was £72,000 in 2011 and £57,680 in 2010.

The following are selected figures from the plan's funded status and amounts recognized in the Lyons Corporation's statement of financial position at December 31, 2011 (£000 omitted).

Defined benefit obligation	£(1,200)
Plan assets at fair value	1,050
Defined benefit obligation in excess of plan assets	£ (150)

Given that Lyons Corporation's work force has been stable for the last 6 years, Shea could not understand the increase in the net periodic pension expense. Kroll explained that the net periodic pension expense consists of several elements, some of which may increase or decrease the net expense.

Instructions

(a) The determination of the net periodic pension expense is a function of five elements. List and briefly describe each of the elements.

(b) Describe the major difference and the major similarity between the vested benefit obligation and the defined benefit obligation.

(c) (1) Explain why pension gains and losses may not be recognized on the income statement in the period in which they arise.

(2) Briefly describe how pension gains and losses are recognized.

CA20-5 (Implications of *International Accounting Standard No. 19*) Ruth Moore and Carl Nies have to do a class presentation on the pension pronouncement "Employee Benefits." In developing the class presentation, they decided to provide the class with a series of questions related to pensions and then discuss the answers in class. Given that the class has all read *IAS 19*, they felt this approach would provide a lively discussion. Here are the situations:

1. In an article prior to *IAS 19*, it was reported that the discount rates used by the largest 200 companies for pension reporting ranged from 5% to 11%. How can such a situation exist, and does the pension pronouncement alleviate this problem?

2. An article indicated that when *IAS 19* was issued, it caused an increase in the liability for pensions for a significant number of companies. Why might this situation occur?

3. A recent article noted that while "smoothing" is not necessarily an accounting virtue, pension accounting has long been recognized as an exception—an area of accounting in which at least some dampening of market swings is appropriate. This is because pension funds are managed so that their performance is insulated from the extremes of short-term market swings. A pension expense that reflects the volatility of market swings might, for that reason, convey information of little relevance. Are these statements true?

4. Many companies held assets twice as large as they needed to fund their pension plans at one time. Are these assets reported on the statement of financial position of these companies per the pension pronouncement? If not, where are they reported?

5. Understanding the impact of the changes required in pension reporting requires detailed information about its pension plan(s) and an analysis of the relationship of many factors, particularly:
    (a) The type of plan(s) and any significant amendments.
    (b) The plan participants.
    (c) The funding status.
    (d) The actuarial funding method and assumptions currently used.
    What impact does each of these items have on financial statement presentation?

6. An article noted "You also need to decide whether to amortize gains and losses using the corridor method, or to use some other systematic method. Under the corridor approach, only gains and losses in excess of 10% of the greater of the defined benefit obligation or the plan assets would have to be amortized." What is the corridor method and what is its purpose?

Instructions

What answers do you believe Ruth and Carl gave to each of these questions?

CA20-6 (Unrecognized Gains and Losses, Corridor Amortization) Rachel Avery, accounting clerk in the personnel office of Clarence G. Avery Corp., has begun to compute pension expense for 2011 but is not sure whether or not she should include the amortization of unrecognized gains/losses. She is currently working with the following beginning-of-the-year present values for the defined benefit obligation and fair values for the pension plan:

	Defined Benefit Obligation	Plan Assets Value
2008	$2,200,000	$1,900,000
2009	2,400,000	2,600,000
2010	2,900,000	2,600,000
2011	3,900,000	3,000,000

The average remaining service life per employee in 2008 and 2009 is 10 years and in 2010 and 2011 is 12 years. The unrecognized net gain or loss that occurred during each year is as follows.

2008	$280,000 loss
2009	90,000 loss
2010	12,000 loss
2011	25,000 gain

(In working the solution, you must aggregate the unrecognized gains and losses to arrive at year-end balances.)

Instructions

You are the manager in charge of accounting. Write a memo to Rachel Avery, explaining:

(a) Why in some years she must amortize some of the unrecognized net gains and losses and in other years she does not need to. In order to explain this situation fully, you must compute the amount of unrecognized net gain or loss that is amortized and charged to pension expense in each of the 4 years listed above. Include an appropriate amortization schedule, referring to it whenever necessary.

(b) IFRS offers an alternative approach to corridor amortization for actuarial gains and losses. Describe this method and explain how its use affects pension expense and the pension asset/liability in the period an actuarial gain or loss arises.

CA20-7 (Non-Vested Employees—An Ethical Dilemma) Cardinal Technology recently merged with College Electronix, a computer graphics manufacturing firm. In performing a comprehensive audit of CE's accounting system, Richard Nye, internal audit manager for Cardinal Technology, discovered that the new subsidiary did not capitalize pension assets and liabilities, subject to the requirements of IFRS.

The net present value of CE's pension assets was $15.5 million, the vested benefit obligation was $12.9 million, and the defined benefit obligation was $17.4 million. Nye reported this audit finding to Renée Selma, the newly appointed controller of CE. A few days later, Selma called Nye for his advice on what to do. Selma started her conversation by asking, "Can't we eliminate the negative income effect of our pension dilemma simply by terminating the employment of non-vested employees before the end of our fiscal year?"

Instructions

How should Nye respond to Selma's remark about firing non-vested employees?

USING YOUR JUDGMENT

Financial Reporting Problem

Marks and Spencer plc (M&S)

The financial statements of **M&S** are presented in Appendix 5B or can be accessed at the book's companion website, **www.wiley.com/college/kiesoifrs**.

Instructions

Refer to M&S's financial statements and the accompanying notes to answer the following questions.

(a) What kind of pension plan does M&S provide its employees?

(b) What was M&S's pension expense for 2008 and 2007?

(c) What is the impact of M&S's pension plans for 2008 on its financial statements?

(d) What information does M&S provide on the target allocation of its pension assets? How do the allocations relate to the expected returns on these assets?

Comparative Analysis Case

Cadbury and Nestlé

Instructions

Go to the book's companion website and use information found there to answer the following questions related to **Cadbury** and **Nestlé**.

(a) What kind of pension plans do Cadbury and Nestlé provide their employees?

(b) What net periodic pension expense (cost) did Cadbury and Nestlé report in 2008?

(c) What is the year-end 2008 funded status of Cadbury's and Nestlé's plans?

(d) What relevant rates were used by Cadbury and Nestlé in computing their pension amounts?

(e) Compare the expected benefit payments and contributions for Cadbury and Nestlé.

International Reporting Case

Walgreens (USA) is the leading drug store chain in the United States. The company provided the disclosures shown on page 1114 related to its retirement benefits in its 2009 annual report.

Walgreens

14. Retirement Benefits (in past)

The principal retirement plan for employees is the Walgreen Profit-Sharing Retirement Plan, to which both the Company and the employees contribute.

The Company provides certain health insurance benefits for retired employees who meet eligibility requirements, including age, years of service and date of hire. The costs of these benefits are accrued over the period earned. The Company's postretirement health benefit plans are not funded.

Components of net periodic benefit costs (*In millions*):

	2009	2008
Service cost	$12	$14
Interest cost	26	24
Amortization of actuarial loss	4	5
Amortization of prior service cost	(6)	(4)
Special retirement benefit expense	4	—
Curtailment income	(16)	—
Total postretirement benefit cost	$24	$39

Change in benefit obligation (*In millions*):

	2009	2008
Benefit obligation at September 1	$371	$370
Service cost	12	14
Interest cost	26	24
Amendments	(106)	—
Special termination benefits	4	—
Actuarial (gain)/loss	31	(29)
Benefit payments	(13)	(11)
Participants contributions	3	3
Benefit obligation at August 31	$328	$371

Change in plan assets (*In millions*):

	2009	2008
Plan assets at fair value at September 1	$ —	$ —
Plan participants contributions	3	3
Employer contributions	10	8
Benefits paid	(13)	(11)
Plan assets at fair value at August 31	$ —	$ —

Funded status (*In millions*):

	2009	2008
Funded status	$(328)	$(371)
Unrecognized actuarial gain	—	—
Unrecognized prior service cost	—	—
Accrued benefit cost at August 31	$(328)	$(371)

Amounts recognized in the Consolidated Balance Sheets (*In millions*):

	2009	2008
Current liabilities (present value of expected 2010 net benefit payments)	$ (11)	$ (8)
Non-current liabilities	(317)	(363)
Net liability recognized at August 31	$(328)	$(371)

Amounts recognized in accumulated other comprehensive loss (*In millions*):

	2009	2008
Prior service credit	$(141)	$(57)
Net actuarial loss	104	77

The discount rate assumption used to compute the postretirement benefit obligation at year-end was 6.15% for 2009 and 7.30% for 2008. The discount rate assumption used to determine net periodic benefit cost was 7.50%, 6.50% and 6.25% for fiscal years ending 2009, 2008 and 2007, respectively.

Instructions

Use the information on Walgreens to respond to the following requirements.

(a) What are the key differences in accounting for pensions under U.S. GAAP and IFRS?

(b) Briefly explain how differences in U.S. GAAP and IFRS for pensions would affect the amounts reported in the financial statements.

(c) In light of the differences identified above, would Walgreens' income and equity be higher or lower under U.S. GAAP compared to IFRS standards? Explain.

Accounting, Analysis, and Principles

PENCOMP's statement of financial position at December 31, 2010, is as follows.

<table>
<tr><td colspan="4" align="center">**PENCOMP, INC.**
STATEMENT OF FINANCIAL POSITION
AS OF DECEMBER 31, 2010</td></tr>
<tr><td>*Assets*</td><td></td><td>*Equity*</td><td></td></tr>
<tr><td>Plant and equipment</td><td>€2,000</td><td>Share capital</td><td>€2,000</td></tr>
<tr><td>Accumulated depreciation</td><td>(240)</td><td>Retained earnings</td><td>896</td></tr>
<tr><td></td><td>1,760</td><td>**Total equity**</td><td>**2,896**</td></tr>
<tr><td>Inventory</td><td>1,800</td><td>*Liabilities*</td><td></td></tr>
<tr><td>Cash</td><td>438</td><td>Notes payable</td><td>1,000</td></tr>
<tr><td>**Total current assets**</td><td>**2,238**</td><td>Pension liability</td><td>102</td></tr>
<tr><td>**Total assets**</td><td>**€3,998**</td><td>**Total liabilities**</td><td>**1,102**</td></tr>
<tr><td></td><td></td><td>**Total equity and liabilities**</td><td>**€3,998**</td></tr>
</table>

Additional information concerning PENCOMP's defined benefit pension plan is as follows.

Defined benefit obligation at 12/31/10	€ 820.5
Plan assets (fair value) at 12/31/10	476.5
Unamortized past service cost at 12/31/10	150.0
Amortization of past service cost during 2011	15.0
Service cost for 2011	42.0
Discount rate	10%
Expected rate of return on plan assets in 2011	12%
Actual return on plan assets in 2011	10.4
Contributions to pension fund in 2011	70.0
Benefits paid during 2011	40.0
Pension liability at 12/31/10	102.0
Unamortized net **loss** due to changes in actuarial assumptions and deferred net losses on plan assets at 12/31/10	92.0
Expected remaining service life of employees	15.0
Average period to vesting of past service costs	10.0

Other information about PENCOMP is as follows.

Salary expense, all paid with cash during 2011	€ 700.0
Sales, all for cash	3,000.0
Purchases, all for cash	2,000.0
Inventory at 12/31/2011	1,800.0

Property originally cost €2,000 and is depreciated on a straight-line basis over 25 years with no residual value.

Interest on the note payable is 10% annually and is paid in cash on 12/31 of each year. Dividends declared and paid are €200 in 2011.

Accounting

Prepare an income statement for 2011 and a statement of financial position as of December 31, 2011. Also, prepare the pension expense journal entry for the year ended December 31, 2011. Round to the nearest tenth (e.g., round 2.87 to 2.9).

Analysis

Compute return on equity for PENCOMP for 2011 (assume equity is equal to year-end equity). Do you think an argument can be made for including some or even all of the past service cost and actuarial gains and losses in the numerator of return on equity? Illustrate that calculation.

Principles

Explain a rationale for why the IASB has (so far) decided to exclude from the current-period income statement the effects of pension plan amendments and gains and losses due to changes in actuarial assumptions.

I F R S BRIDGE TO THE PROFESSION

Professional Research

Jack Kelly Company has grown rapidly since its founding in 2002. To instill loyalty in its employees, Kelly is contemplating establishment of a defined benefit plan. Kelly knows that lenders and potential investors will pay close attention to the impact of the pension plan on the company's financial statements, particularly any gains or losses that develop in the plan. Kelly has asked you to conduct some research on the accounting for gains and losses in a defined benefit plan.

Instructions

Access the IFRS authoritative literature at the IASB website (*http://eifrs.iasb.org/*). When you have accessed the documents, you can use the search tool in your Internet browser to respond to the following questions. (Provide paragraph citations.)

(a) Briefly describe how pension gains and losses are accounted for.

(b) Explain the rationale behind the accounting method described in part (a).

(c) What is the related pension asset or liability that may show up on the statement of financial position? When will each of these situations occur?

Professional Simulation

In this simulation, you are asked to address questions related to the accounting for pensions. Prepare responses to all parts.

KWW_Professional _Simulation

| Accounting for Pensions | Time Remaining 2 hours 20 minutes | copy | paste | calculator | sheet | standards | help | splitter | done |

| Directions | Situation | Measurement | Journal Entry | Disclosure | Resources |

Melanie Vail Corp. sponsors a defined benefit pension plan for its employees. On January 1, 2010, the following balances relate to this plan.

Plan assets	$480,000
Defined benefit obligation	625,000
Pension asset/liability	45,000 Cr.
Unrecognized past service cost	100,000

As a result of the operation of the plan during 2010, the following additional data are provided by the actuary for 2010.

Service cost	$90,000
Discount rate	9%
Actual return on plan assets	57,000
Amortization of past service cost	19,000
Expected return on plan assets	52,000
Unexpected loss from change in defined benefit obligation, due to change in actuarial predictions	76,000
Contributions	99,000
Benefits paid retirees	85,000

| Directions | Situation | Measurement | Journal Entry | Disclosure | Resources |

(a) Use a computer spreadsheet to prepare a pension worksheet. On the pension worksheet, compute pension expense, pension asset/liability, defined benefit obligation, plan assets, unrecognized past service cost, and unrecognized net gain or loss.

(b) Compute the same items as in (a), assuming that the discount rate is now 7% and the expected rate of return is 10%.

| Directions | Situation | Measurement | Journal Entry | Disclosure | Resources |

Prepare the journal entry to record pension expense in 2010.

| Directions | Situation | Measurement | Journal Entry | Disclosure | Resources |

Prepare a schedule reconciling the funded status of the plan with the pension amount reported on the statement of financial position.

Remember to check the book's companion website to find additional resources for this chapter.

CHAPTER 21

ACCOUNTING FOR LEASES

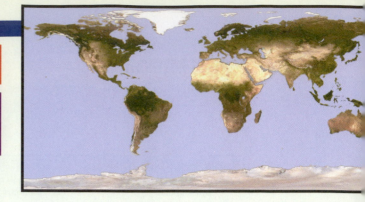

LEARNING OBJECTIVES

After studying this chapter, you should be able to:

•1 Explain the nature, economic substance, and advantages of lease transactions.

•2 Describe the accounting criteria and procedures for capitalizing leases by the lessee.

•3 Contrast the operating and capitalization methods of recording leases.

•4 Identify the classifications of leases for the lessor.

•5 Describe the lessor's accounting for direct-financing leases.

•6 Identify special features of lease arrangements that cause unique accounting problems.

•7 Describe the effect of residual values, guaranteed and unguaranteed, on lease accounting.

•8 Describe the lessor's accounting for sales-type leases.

•9 List the disclosure requirements for leases.

MORE COMPANIES ASK, "WHY BUY?"

Leasing has grown tremendously in popularity. Today, it is the fastest growing form of capital investment. Instead of borrowing money to buy an airplane, computer, nuclear core, or satellite, a company makes periodic payments to lease these assets. Even gambling casinos lease their slot machines. Companies that lease tend to be smaller, are high growth, and are in technology-oriented industries (see *www.techlease.com*).

A classic example is the airline industry. Many travelers on airlines such as **British Airways** (GBR), **Cathay Pacific** (CHN), and **Japan Airlines** (JPN) believe these airlines own the planes on which they are flying. Often, this is not the case. Airlines lease many of their airplanes due to the favorable accounting treatment they receive if they lease rather than purchase. Presented on the next page are the lease percentages for the major international airlines.

What about other companies? They are also exploiting the existing lease-accounting rules to keep assets and liabilities off the books. For example, **Krispy Kreme** (USA), a chain of 217 doughnut shops, had been showing good growth and profitability, using a relatively small bit of capital. That's an impressive feat if you care about return on capital. But, there's a hole in this doughnut. The company explained that it was building a $30 million new mixing plant and warehouse in Effingham, Illinois. Yet, the financial statements failed to disclose the investments and obligations associated with that $30 million.

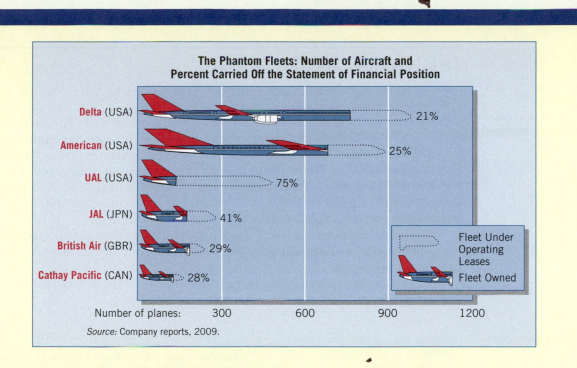

The Phantom Fleets: Number of Aircraft and Percent Carried Off the Statement of Financial Position

Delta (USA)		21%
American (USA)		25%
UAL (USA)		75%
JAL (JPN)		41%
British Air (GBR)		29%
Cathay Pacific (CAN)		28%

Number of planes: 300 600 900 1200

Fleet Under Operating Leases
Fleet Owned

Source: Company reports, 2009.

By financing through a synthetic lease, Krispy Kreme kept the investment and obligation off the books. In a synthetic lease, a financial institution like **Credit Suisse** (CHE) sets up a *special-purpose entity* (SPE) that borrows money to build the plant and then leases it to Krispy Kreme. For accounting purposes, Krispy Kreme reports only rent expense, but for tax purposes Krispy Kreme can be considered the owner of the asset and gets depreciation tax deductions.

In response to negative publicity about the use of SPEs to get favorable financial reporting and tax benefits, Krispy Kreme announced it would change its method of financing construction of its dough-making plant.

Source: Adapted from Seth Lubore and Elizabeth MacDonald, "Debt? Who, Me?" *Forbes* (February 18, 2002), p. 56.

PREVIEW OF CHAPTER 21

Our opening story indicates the increased significance and prevalence of lease arrangements. As a result, the need for uniform accounting and informative reporting of these transactions has intensified. In this chapter, we look at the accounting issues related to leasing. The content and organization of this chapter are as follows.

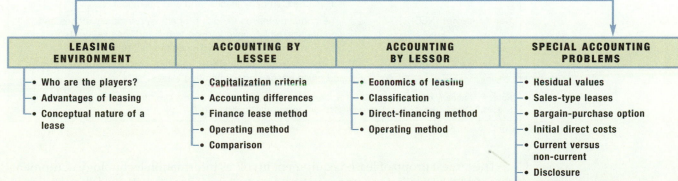

ACCOUNTING FOR LEASES

LEASING ENVIRONMENT	ACCOUNTING BY LESSEE	ACCOUNTING BY LESSOR	SPECIAL ACCOUNTING PROBLEMS
• Who are the players?	• Capitalization criteria	• Economics of leasing	• Residual values
• Advantages of leasing	• Accounting differences	• Classification	• Sales-type leases
• Conceptual nature of a lease	• Finance lease method	• Direct-financing method	• Bargain-purchase option
	• Operating method	• Operating method	• Initial direct costs
	• Comparison		• Current versus non-current
			• Disclosure
			• Unresolved problems

THE LEASING ENVIRONMENT

Objective•1

Explain the nature, economic substance, and advantages of lease transactions.

Aristotle once said, "Wealth does not lie in ownership but in the use of things"! Clearly, many companies have decided that Aristotle is right, as they have become heavily involved in leasing assets rather than owning them. For example, according to the Equipment Leasing Association (ELA), the global equipment-leasing market is a $600–$700 billion business. The ELA estimates that of the $850 billion in total fixed investment, $229 billion (27 percent) will be financed through leasing. Remember that these statistics are just for equipment leasing; add in real estate leasing, which is probably larger, and we are talking about a very large and growing business, one that is at least in part driven by the accounting.

What types of assets are being leased? As the opening story indicated, any type of equipment can be leased, such as railcars, helicopters, bulldozers, barges, CT scanners, computers, and so on.

Illustration 21-1 summarizes, in their own words, what several major companies are leasing.

ILLUSTRATION 21-1

What Do Companies Lease?

Company	Description
Carrefour (FRA)	"Stores not fully owned are rented under leasing agreements. The Group also owns shopping centres, mainly anchored by its hypermarkets and supermarkets, that are rented out."
Delhaize Group (BEL)	"Delhaize Group operates a significant number of its stores under finance and operating lease arrangements. Various properties leased are (partially or in full) subleased to third parties, where the Group is therefore acting as a lessor (see further below). Lease terms (including reasonably certain renewal options) generally range from 1 to 36 years with renewal options ranging from 3 to 30 years."
Diageo (GBR)	"The company owns or leases land and buildings throughout the world. Diageo's largest individual facility, in terms of net book value of property, is St James's Gate brewery in Dublin. Approximately 96% by value of the group's properties are owned and approximately 3% are held under leases running for 50 years or longer."
ExxonMobil Corp. (USA)	"Minimum commitments for operating leases, shown on an undiscounted basis, cover drilling equipment, tankers, service stations, and other properties."
Marks and Spencer plc (GBR)	"The Group leases various stores, offices, warehouses and equipment under non-cancellable operating lease agreements. The leases have varying terms, escalation clauses and renewal rights."
McDonald's Corp. (USA)	"The Company was the lessee at 15,235 restaurant locations through ground leases (the Company leases the land and the Company or franchisee owns the building) and through improved leases (the Company leases land and buildings)."
Reed Elsevier (NLD)	"The company leases various properties, principally offices and warehouses, which have varying terms and renewal rights that are typical to the territory in which they are located."
Starbucks Corp. (USA)	"Starbucks leases retail stores, roasting and distribution facilities, and office space under operating leases."

Source: Company reports; and D. Zion, B. Carcache, and A. Varshney, "Bring It On: Off–Balance Sheet Operating Leases," *Credit Suisse Equity Research: Accounting and Tax* (April 19, 2006).

The largest group of leased equipment involves information technology equipment, followed by assets in the transportation area (trucks, aircraft, rail), and then construction and agriculture.

Who Are the Players?

A **lease** is a contractual agreement between a lessor and a lessee. This arrangement gives the **lessee** the right to use specific property, owned by the **lessor**, for an agreed period of time. In return for the use of the property, the lessee makes rental payments over the lease term to the lessor.

Who are the lessors that own this property? They generally fall into one of three categories:

1. Banks.

2. Captive leasing companies.

3. Independents.

Banks

Banks are the largest players in the leasing business. They have low-cost funds, which give them the advantage of being able to purchase assets at less cost than their competitors. Banks also have been more aggressive in the leasing markets. They have decided that there is money to be made in leasing, and as a result they have expanded their product lines in this area. Finally, leasing transactions are now more standardized, which gives banks an advantage because they do not have to be as innovative in structuring lease arrangements. Thus banks like **Credit Suisse** (CHE), **Chase** (USA), **Barclays** (GBR), and **Deutsche Bank** (DEU) have substantial leasing subsidiaries.

Captive Leasing Companies

Captive leasing companies are subsidiaries whose primary business is to perform leasing operations for the parent company. Companies like **CNH Capital** (NLD) (for CNH Global), **BMW Financial Services** (DEU) (for BMW), and **IBM Global Financing** (USA) (for IBM) facilitate the sale of products to consumers. For example, suppose that **Ivanhoe Mines Ltd.** (CAN) wants to acquire a number of earthmovers from CNH Global. In this case, CNH Capital will offer to structure the transaction as a lease rather than as a purchase. Thus, CNH Capital provides the financing rather than an outside financial institution.

Captive leasing companies have the point-of-sale advantage in finding leasing customers. That is, as soon as CNH Global receives a possible order, its leasing subsidiary can quickly develop a lease-financing arrangement. Furthermore, the captive lessor has product knowledge that gives it an advantage when financing the parent's product.

The current trend is for captives to focus primarily on their companies' products rather than do general lease financing. For example, **Boeing Capital** (USA) and **UPS Capital** (USA) are two captives that have left the general finance business to focus exclusively on their parent companies' products.

Look at UPS vs FedEx

Independents

Independents are the final category of lessors. Independents have not done well over the last few years. Their market share has dropped fairly dramatically as banks and captive leasing companies have become more aggressive in the lease-financing area. Independents do not have point-of-sale access, nor do they have a low cost of funds advantage. What they *are* often good at is developing innovative contracts for lessees. In addition, they are starting to act as captive finance companies for some companies that do not have a leasing subsidiary.

According to recent data at *www.ficinc.com* on new business volume by lessor type, banks hold about 44 percent of the market, followed by independents at 30 percent. Captives had the remaining 26 percent of new business. Data on changes in market share show that both banks and captives have increased business at the expense of the independents. That is, banks' and captives' market shares had grown by 58 percent and 36 percent, respectively, while the independents' market share declined by 44 percent.

Advantages of Leasing

The growth in leasing indicates that it often has some genuine advantages over owning property, such as:

1. *100% financing at fixed rates.* Leases are often signed without requiring any money down from the lessee. This helps the lessee conserve scarce cash—an especially desirable feature for new and developing companies. In addition, lease payments often remain fixed, which protects the lessee against inflation and increases in the cost of money. The following comment explains why companies choose a lease instead of a conventional loan: "Our local bank finally came up to 80 percent of the purchase price but wouldn't go any higher, and they wanted a floating interest rate. We just couldn't afford the down payment, and we needed to lock in a final payment rate we knew we could live with."

2. *Protection against obsolescence.* Leasing equipment reduces risk of obsolescence to the lessee, and in many cases passes the risk of residual value to the lessor. For example, **Elan** (IRL) (a pharmaceutical maker) leases computers. Under the lease agreement, Elan may turn in an old computer for a new model at any time, canceling the old lease and writing a new one. The lessor adds the cost of the new lease to the balance due on the old lease, less the old computer's trade-in value. As one treasurer remarked, "Our instinct is to purchase." But if a new computer is likely to come along in a short time, "then leasing is just a heck of a lot more convenient than purchasing." Naturally, the lessor also protects itself by requiring the lessee to pay higher rental payments or provide additional payments if the lessee does not maintain the asset.

3. *Flexibility.* Lease agreements may contain less restrictive provisions than other debt agreements. Innovative lessors can tailor a lease agreement to the lessee's special needs. For instance, the duration of the lease—the **lease term**—may be anything from a short period of time to the entire expected economic life of the asset. The rental payments may be level from year to year, or they may increase or decrease in amount. The payment amount may be predetermined or may vary with sales, the prime interest rate, a price index, or some other factor. In most cases, the rent is set to enable the lessor to recover the cost of the asset plus a fair return over the life of the lease.

4. *Less costly financing.* Some companies find leasing cheaper than other forms of financing. For example, start-up companies in depressed industries or companies in low tax brackets may lease to claim tax benefits that they might otherwise lose. Depreciation deductions offer no benefit to companies that have little if any taxable income. Through leasing, the leasing companies or financial institutions use these tax benefits. They can then pass some of these tax benefits back to the user of the asset in the form of lower rental payments.

5. *Tax advantages.* In some cases, companies can "have their cake and eat it too" with tax advantages that leases offer. That is, for financial reporting purposes, companies do not report an asset or a liability for the lease arrangement. For tax purposes, however, companies can capitalize and depreciate the leased asset. As a result, a company takes deductions earlier rather than later and also reduces its taxes. A common vehicle for this type of transaction is a "synthetic lease" arrangement, such as that described in the opening story for **Krispy Kreme** (USA).

6. *Off–balance-sheet financing.* Certain leases do not add debt on a statement of financial position or affect financial ratios. In fact, they may add to borrowing capacity.[1] Such **off–balance-sheet financing** is critical to some companies.

---

[1] As demonstrated later in this chapter, certain types of lease arrangements are not capitalized on the statement of financial position. The liabilities section is thereby relieved of large future lease commitments that, if recorded, would adversely affect the debt to equity ratio. The reluctance to record lease obligations as liabilities is one of the primary reasons some companies resist capitalized lease accounting.

OFF–BALANCE-SHEET FINANCING

As shown in our opening story, airlines use lease arrangements extensively. This results in a great deal of off–balance-sheet financing. The following chart indicates that many airlines that lease aircraft understate debt levels by a substantial amount.

What do the numbers mean?

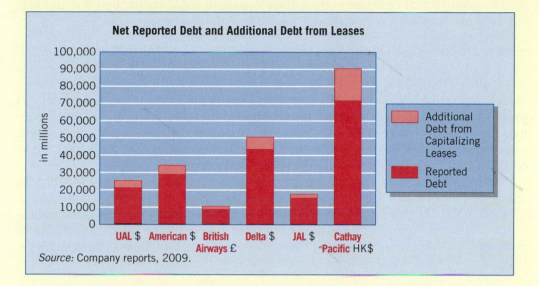

Net Reported Debt and Additional Debt from Leases

Source: Company reports, 2009.

Airlines are not the only ones playing the off–balance-sheet game. As indicated in Illustration 21-1, retailers, like Marks and Spencer plc and Carrefour, and publisher Reed Elsevier employ leases in their businesses. Thus, analysts must adjust reported debt levels for the effects of non-capitalized leases. A methodology for making this adjustment is discussed in Eugene A. Imhoff, Jr., Robert C. Lipe, and David W. Wright, "Operating Leases: Impact of Constructive Capitalization," *Accounting Horizons* (March 1991).

Conceptual Nature of a Lease

If **Air France—KLM** (FRA) borrows €47 million on a 10-year note from **UBS** (CHE) to purchase an Airbus A330 jet plane, Air France should clearly report an asset and related liability at that amount on its statement of financial position. Similarly, if Air France purchases the A330 for €47 million directly from Airbus through an installment purchase over 10 years, it should obviously report an asset and related liability (i.e., it should "capitalize" the installment transaction).

However, what if Air France **leases** the Airbus A330 for 10 years from **International Lease Finance Corp. (ILFC)** (USA)—the world's largest lessor of airplanes—through a non-cancelable lease transaction with payments of the same amount as the installment purchase transaction? In that case, opinion differs over how to report this transaction. The various views on **capitalization of leases** are as follows.

1. *Do not capitalize any leased assets.* This view considers capitalization inappropriate, because Delta does not own the property. Furthermore, a lease is an **"executory" contract** requiring continuing performance by both parties. Because companies do not currently capitalize other executory contracts (such as purchase commitments and employment contracts), they should not capitalize leases either.

2. *Capitalize leases that are similar to installment purchases.* This view holds that companies should report transactions in accordance with their economic substance. Therefore, if companies capitalize installment purchases, they should also capitalize leases that have similar characteristics. For example, Air France makes the same payments over a 10-year period for either a lease or an installment purchase. Lessees make rental payments, whereas owners make mortgage payments. Why should the financial statements not report these transactions in the same manner?

Underlying Concepts

The issue of how to report leases is the classic case of substance versus form. Although legal title does not technically pass in lease transactions, the benefits from the use of the property do transfer.

3. *Capitalize all long-term leases.* This approach requires only the long-term right to use the property in order to capitalize. This property-rights approach capitalizes all long-term leases.

4. *Capitalize non-cancelable leases where the penalty for non-performance is substantial.* A final approach advocates capitalizing only non-cancelable contractual rights and obligations. Non-cancelable means that it is unlikely to avoid performance under the lease without a severe penalty.[2]

In short, the various viewpoints range from no capitalization to capitalization of all leases. The IASB apparently agrees with the capitalization approach when the lease is similar to an installment purchase: It notes that Air France **should capitalize a lease that transfers substantially all of the benefits and risks of property ownership, provided the lease is non-cancelable**.[3] Non-cancelable means that Air France can cancel the lease contract only upon the outcome of some remote contingency, or that the cancellation provisions and penalties of the contract are so costly to Air France that cancellation probably will not occur.

This viewpoint leads to three basic conclusions: (1) Companies must identify the characteristics that indicate the transfer of substantially all of the benefits and risks of ownership. (2) The same characteristics should apply consistently to the lessee and the lessor. (3) Those leases that do **not** transfer substantially all the benefits and risks of ownership are operating leases. Companies should not capitalize operating leases. Instead, companies should account for them as rental payments and receipts.

ACCOUNTING BY THE LESSEE

Objective·2

Describe the accounting criteria and procedures for capitalizing leases by the lessee.

If Air France (the lessee) **capitalizes** a lease, it records an asset and a liability generally equal to the present value of the rental payments. ILFC (the lessor), having transferred substantially all the benefits and risks of ownership, recognizes a sale by removing the asset from the statement of financial position and replacing it with a receivable. The typical journal entries for Air France and ILFC, assuming leased and capitalized equipment, appear as shown in Illustration 21-2.

ILLUSTRATION 21-2
Journal Entries for Capitalized Lease

Air France (Lessee)			ILFC (Lessor)		
Leased Equipment	XXX		Lease Receivable	XXX	
Lease Liability		XXX	Equipment		XXX

Having capitalized the asset, Air France records depreciation on the leased asset. Both ILFC and Air France treat the lease rental payments as consisting of interest and principal.

If Air France does not capitalize the lease, it does not record an asset, nor does ILFC remove one from its books. When Air France makes a lease payment, it records rental expense; ILFC recognizes rental revenue.

---

[2]Capitalization of most leases (based on either a right of use or on non-cancelable rights and obligations) has the support of financial analysts. Peter H. Knutson, "Financial Reporting in the 1990s and Beyond," *Position Paper* (Charlottesville, Va.: AIMR, 1993); and Warren McGregor, "Accounting for Leases: A New Approach," Special Report (Norwalk, Conn.: FASB, 1996). The joint IASB/FASB project on lease accounting is based on a right of use model, which will require expanded capitalization of lease assets and liabilities (see *http://www.iasb.org/Current+Projects/IASB+Projects/Leases/Leases.htm*).

[3]Benefits may be represented by the expectation of profitable operations over the asset's economic life and from appreciation in residual value. Risks include the possibility of losses from idle capacity or technological obsolescence and variation in return because of changing economic conditions. **[1]**

IFRS
See the Authoritative Literature section (page 1163).

A lease is classified as a **finance lease** if it transfers substantially all the risks and rewards incidental to ownership. In order to record a lease as a finance lease, the lease must be non-cancelable. The IASB identifies the four criteria listed in Illustration 21-3 for assessing whether the risks and rewards have been transferred in the lease arrangement.

ILLUSTRATION 21-3
Capitalization Criteria for Lessee

Capitalization Criteria (Lessee)

1. The lease transfers ownership of the property to the lessee.
2. The lease contains a bargain-purchase option.[4]
3. The lease term is for the major part of the economic life of the asset.
4. The present value of the minimum lease payments amounts to substantially all of the fair value of the leased asset. [2]

Air France classifies and accounts for leases that **do not meet any of the four criteria** as **operating leases**. Illustration 21-4 shows that a lease meeting any one of the four criteria results in the lessee having a finance lease.[5]

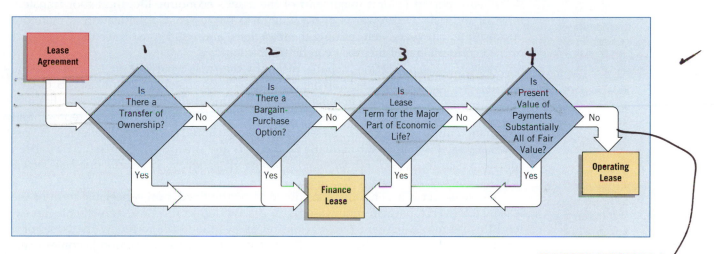

ILLUSTRATION 21-4
Diagram of Lessee's Criteria for Lease Classification

Thus, the proper classification of a lease is determined based on the substance of the lease transaction, rather than on its mere form. This determination often requires the use of professional judgment of whether the risks and rewards of ownership are transferred.

Capitalization Criteria

Three of the four **capitalization criteria** that apply to lessees are controversial and can be difficult to apply in practice. We discuss each of the criteria in detail on the following pages.

---

[4]We define a bargain-purchase option in the next section.

[5]A fifth criterion applies to the relatively less common setting in which the leased asset is of such a specialized nature that only the lessee can use it without major modifications. If a lease involves an asset with these characteristics, then the risks and rewards of ownership are likely to transfer. In addition to the determinative criteria, lessees and lessors should also consider the following indicators of situations that individually or in combination could also lead to a lease being classified as a finance lease: (1) the lessee can cancel the lease, and the lessor's losses associated with the cancellation are borne by the lessee; (2) gains or losses from the fluctuation in the fair value of the residual accrue to the lessee (e.g., in the form of a rent rebate equaling most of the sales proceeds at the end of the lease); and (3) the lessee has the ability to continue the lease for a secondary period at a rent that is substantially lower than market rent. [3]

Transfer of Ownership Test

If the lease transfers ownership of the asset to the lessee, it is a finance lease. This criterion is not controversial and easily implemented in practice.

Bargain-Purchase Option Test

A bargain-purchase option allows the lessee to purchase the leased property for a price that is **significantly lower** than the property's expected fair value at the date the option becomes exercisable. At the inception of the lease, the difference between the option price and the expected fair value must be large enough to make exercise of the option reasonably assured.

For example, assume that Brett's Delivery Service was to lease a Honda Accord for $599 per month for 40 months, with an option to purchase for $100 at the end of the 40-month period. If the estimated fair value of the Honda Accord is $3,000 at the end of the 40 months, the $100 option to purchase is clearly a bargain. Therefore, Brett must capitalize the lease. In other cases, the criterion may not be as easy to apply, and determining *now* that a certain *future* price is a bargain can be difficult.

Economic Life Test

If the lease period is for a major part of the asset's economic life, the lessor transfers most of the risks and rewards of ownership to the lessee. Capitalization is therefore appropriate. However, determining the lease term and what constitutes the major part of the economic life of the asset can be troublesome.

The IASB has not defined what is meant by the "major part" of an asset's economic life. In practice, following the IASB hierarchy, it has been customary to look to U.S. GAAP, which has a 75 percent of economic life threshold for evaluating the economic life test. While the 75 percent guideline may be a useful reference point, it does not represent an automatic cutoff point. Rather, lessees and lessors should consider all relevant factors when assessing whether substantially all the risks and rewards of ownership have been transferred in the lease.[6] *For purposes of homework, assume a 75 percent threshold for the economic life test, unless otherwise stated.*

The **lease term** is generally considered to be the fixed, non-cancelable term of the lease. However, a bargain-renewal option, if provided in the lease agreement, can extend this period. A bargain-renewal option allows the lessee to renew the lease for a rental that is lower than the expected fair rental at the date the option becomes exercisable. At the inception of the lease, the difference between the renewal rental and the expected fair rental must be great enough to make exercise of the option to renew reasonably assured. **[4]**

For example, assume that **Carrefour** (FRA) leases **Lenovo** (CHN) PCs for two years at a rental of €100 per month per computer and subsequently can lease them for €10 per month per computer for another two years. The lease clearly offers a bargain-renewal option; the lease term is considered to be four years. However, with bargain-renewal options, as with bargain-purchase options, it is sometimes difficult to determine what is a bargain.

Determining estimated economic life can also pose problems, especially if the leased item is a specialized item or has been used for a significant period of time. For example, determining the economic life of a nuclear core is extremely difficult. It is subject to much more than normal "wear and tear."

Recovery of Investment Test

If the present value of the minimum lease payments equals or exceeds substantially all of the fair value of the asset, then a lessee like Air France should capitalize the

---

[6]See KPMG, *Insights into IFRS*, Fifth Edition (Thomson Reuters: London, 2008), pp. 1011; and The International Financial Reporting Group of Ernst and Young, *International GAAP, 2009* (John Wiley and Sons: New York, 2009), p. 1356.

leased asset. Why? If the present value of the minimum lease payments is reasonably close to the fair value of the aircraft, Air France is effectively purchasing the asset.

As with the economic life test, the IASB has not defined what is meant by "substantially all" of an asset's fair value. In practice, it has been customary to look to U.S. GAAP, which has a 90 percent of fair value threshold for assessing the recovery of investment test. Again, rather than focusing on any single element of the lease classification indicators, lessees and lessors should consider all relevant factors when evaluating lease classification criteria.[7] *For purposes of homework, assume a 90 percent threshold for the recovery of investment test.*

Determining the present value of the minimum lease payments involves three important concepts: (1) minimum lease payments, (2) executory costs, and (3) discount rate.

Minimum Lease Payments. Air France is obligated to make, or expected to make, **minimum lease payments** in connection with the leased property. These payments include the following. **[5]**

1. *Minimum rental payments.* Minimum rental payments are those that Air France must make to ILFC under the lease agreement. In some cases, the minimum rental payments may equal the minimum lease payments. However, the minimum lease payments may also include a guaranteed residual value (if any), penalty for failure to renew, or a bargain-purchase option (if any), as we note below.

2. *Guaranteed residual value.* The residual value is the estimated fair value of the leased property at the end of the lease term. ILFC may transfer the risk of loss to Air France or to a third party by obtaining a guarantee of the estimated residual value. The **guaranteed residual value** is either (1) the certain or determinable amount that Air France will pay ILFC at the end of the lease to purchase the aircraft at the end of the lease, or (2) the amount Air France guarantees that ILFC will realize if the aircraft is returned. If not guaranteed in full, the **unguaranteed residual value** is the estimated residual value exclusive of any portion guaranteed.[8]

3. *Penalty for failure to renew or extend the lease.* The amount Air France must pay if the agreement specifies that it must extend or renew the lease, and it fails to do so.

4. *Bargain-purchase option.* As we indicated earlier (in item 1), an option given to Air France to purchase the aircraft at the end of the lease term at a price that is fixed sufficiently below the expected fair value, so that, at the inception of the lease, purchase is reasonably assured.

Air France excludes executory costs (defined below) from its computation of the present value of the minimum lease payments.

Executory Costs. Like most assets, leased tangible assets incur insurance, maintenance, and tax expenses—called **executory costs**—during their economic life. If ILFC retains responsibility for the payment of these "ownership-type costs," **it should exclude**, in

---

[7]*Ibid.* The 75 percent of useful life and 90 percent of fair value "bright-line" cutoffs in U.S. GAAP have been criticized. Many believe that lessees structure leases so as to just miss the 75 and 90 percent cutoffs, avoiding classifying leases as finance leases, thereby keeping leased assets and the related liabilities off the statement of financial position. See Warren McGregor, "Accounting for Leases: A New Approach," Special Report (Norwalk, Conn.: FASB, 1996).

[8]If the residual value is guaranteed by a third party, it is not included in the minimum lease payments. (Third-party guarantors are, in essence, insurers who for a fee assume the risk of deficiencies in leased asset residual value.) A lease provision requiring the lessee to make up a residual value deficiency that is attributable to damage, extraordinary wear and tear, or excessive usage is not included in the minimum lease payments. Lessees recognize such costs as period costs when incurred. As noted earlier, such a provision could be an indicator that a lease should be classified as a finance lease. **[6]**

computing the present value of the minimum lease payments, the portion of each lease payment that represents executory costs. Executory costs do not represent payment on or reduction of the obligation.

Many lease agreements specify that the lessee directly pays executory costs to the appropriate third parties. In these cases, the lessor can use the rental payment **without adjustment** in the present value computation.

Discount Rate. A lessee, like Air France, computes the present value of the minimum lease payments using the **implicit interest rate**. [7] This rate is defined as the discount rate that, at the inception of the lease, causes the aggregate present value of the minimum lease payments and the unguaranteed residual value to be equal to the fair value of the leased asset. [8]

While Air France may argue that it cannot determine the implicit rate of the lessor, in most cases Air France can approximate the implicit rate used by ILFC. In the event that it is impracticable to determine the implicit rate, Air France should use its incremental borrowing rate. The **incremental borrowing rate** is the rate of interest the lessee would have to pay on a similar lease or the rate that, at the inception of the lease, the lessee would incur to borrow over a similar term the funds necessary to purchase the asset.

If known or practicable to estimate, use of the implicit rate is preferred. This is because **the implicit rate of ILFC is generally a more realistic rate** to use in determining the amount (if any) to report as the asset and related liability for Air France. In addition, use of the implicit rate avoids use of **an artificially high incremental borrowing rate** that would cause the present value of the minimum lease payments to be lower, supporting an argument that the lease does not meet the recovery of investment test. Use of such a rate would thus make it more likely that the lessee avoids capitalization of the leased asset and related liability.

Air France may argue that it cannot determine the implicit rate of the lessor and therefore should use the higher incremental rate. However, in most cases, Air France can approximate the implicit rate used by ILFC. The determination of whether or not a reasonable estimate could be made will require judgment, particularly where the result from using the incremental borrowing rate comes close to meeting the fair value test. Because Air France **may not capitalize the leased property at more than its fair value** (as we discuss later), it cannot use an excessively low discount rate.

Asset and Liability Accounted for Differently

In a finance lease transaction, Air France uses the lease as a source of financing. ILFC finances the transaction (provides the investment capital) through the leased asset. Air France makes rent payments, which actually are installment payments. Therefore, over the life of the aircraft rented, **the rental payments to ILFC constitute a payment of principal plus interest**.

Asset and Liability Recorded
Under the finance lease method, Air France treats the lease transaction as if it purchases the aircraft in a financing transaction. That is, Air France acquires the aircraft and creates an obligation. Therefore, it records a finance lease as an asset and a liability at either (1) the present value of the minimum lease payments (excluding executory costs) or (2) the fair value of the leased asset at the inception of the lease. The rationale for this approach is that companies should not record a leased asset for more than its fair value.

Depreciation Period
One troublesome aspect of accounting for the depreciation of the capitalized leased asset relates to the period of depreciation. If the lease agreement transfers ownership of the asset to Air France (criterion 1) or contains a bargain-purchase option (criterion 2), Air France depreciates the aircraft consistent with its normal depreciation policy for other aircraft, **using the economic life of the asset**.

On the other hand, if the lease does not transfer ownership or does not contain a bargain-purchase option, then Air France depreciates it over the **term of the lease**. In this case, the aircraft reverts to ILFC after a certain period of time.

Effective-Interest Method

Throughout the term of the lease, Air France uses the **effective-interest method** to allocate each lease payment between principal and interest. This method produces a periodic interest expense equal to a constant percentage of the carrying value of the lease obligation. When applying the effective-interest method to finance leases, Air France must use the same discount rate that determines the present value of the minimum lease payments.

Depreciation Concept

Although Air France computes the amounts initially capitalized as an asset and recorded as an obligation at the same present value, the **depreciation of the aircraft and the discharge of the obligation are independent accounting processes** during the term of the lease. It should depreciate the leased asset by applying conventional depreciation methods: straight-line, sum-of-the-years'digits, declining-balance, units of production, etc.

Finance Lease Method (Lessee)

To illustrate a finance lease, assume that **CNH Capital** (NLD) (a subsidiary of CNH Global) and **Ivanhoe Mines Ltd.** (CAN) sign a lease agreement dated January 1, 2012, that calls for CNH to lease a front-end loader to Ivanhoe beginning January 1, 2012. The terms and provisions of the lease agreement, and other pertinent data, are as follows.

- The term of the lease is five years. The lease agreement is non-cancelable, requiring equal rental payments of $25,981.62 at the beginning of each year (annuity-due basis).
- The loader has a fair value at the inception of the lease of $100,000, an estimated economic life of five years, and no residual value.
- Ivanhoe pays all of the executory costs directly to third parties except for the property taxes of $2,000 per year, which is included as part of its annual payments to CNH.
- The lease contains no renewal options. The loader reverts to CNH at the termination of the lease.
- Ivanhoe's incremental borrowing rate is 11 percent per year.
- Ivanhoe depreciates similar equipment that it owns on a straight-line basis.
- CNH sets the annual rental to earn a rate of return on its investment of 10 percent per year; Ivanhoe knows this fact.

The lease meets the criteria for classification as a finance lease for the following reasons:

1. The lease term of five years, being equal to the equipment's estimated economic life of five years, satisfies the economic life test.
2. The present value of the minimum lease payments ($100,000 as computed below) equals the fair value of the loader ($100,000).

The minimum lease payments are $119,908.10 ($23,981.62 × 5). Ivanhoe computes the amount capitalized as leased assets as the present value of the minimum lease payments (excluding executory costs—property taxes of $2,000) as shown in Illustration 21-5.

Capitalized amount = ($25,981.62 − $2,000) × Present value of an annuity due of 1 for 5 periods at 10% (Table 6-5)
= $23,981.62 × 4.16986
= $100,000

ILLUSTRATION 21-5
Computation of Capitalized Lease Payments

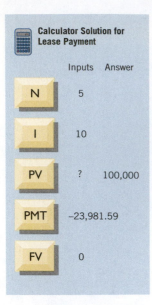

Calculator Solution for Lease Payment

	Inputs	Answer
N	5	
I	10	
PV	?	100,000
PMT	−23,981.59	
FV	0	

Ivanhoe uses CNH's implicit interest rate of 10 percent instead of its incremental borrowing rate of 11 percent because it knows about it.[9] Ivanhoe records the finance lease on its books on January 1, 2012, as:

Leased Equipment under Finance Leases	100,000	
Lease Liability		100,000

Note that the entry records the obligation at the net amount of $100,000 (the present value of the future rental payments) rather than at the gross amount of $119,908.10 ($23,981.62 × 5).

Ivanhoe records the **first lease payment on January 1, 2012**, as follows.

Property Tax Expense	2,000.00	
Lease Liability	23,981.62	
Cash		25,981.62

Each lease payment of $25,981.62 consists of three elements: (1) a reduction in the lease liability, (2) a financing cost (interest expense), and (3) executory costs (property taxes). The total financing cost (interest expense) over the term of the lease is $19,908.10. This amount is the difference between the present value of the lease payments ($100,000) and the actual cash disbursed, net of executory costs ($119,908.10). The annual interest expense, applying the effective-interest method, is a function of the outstanding liability, as Illustration 21-6 shows.

ILLUSTRATION 21-6
Lease Amortization Schedule for Lessee— Annuity-Due Basis

IVANHOE MINES
LEASE AMORTIZATION SCHEDULE
ANNUITY-DUE BASIS

Date	Annual Lease Payment	Executory Costs	Interest (10%) on Liability	Reduction of Lease Liability	Lease Liability
	(a)	(b)	(c)	(d)	(e)
1/1/12					$100,000.00
1/1/12	$ 25,981.62	$ 2,000	$ −0−	$ 23,981.62	76,018.38
1/1/13	25,981.62	2,000	7,601.84	16,379.78	59,638.60
1/1/14	25,981.62	2,000	5,963.86	18,017.76	41,620.84
1/1/15	25,981.62	2,000	4,162.08	19,819.54	21,801.30
1/1/16	25,981.62	2,000	2,180.32*	21,801.30	−0−
	$129,908.10	$10,000	$19,908.10	$100,000.00	

(a) Lease payment as required by lease.
(b) Executory costs included in rental payment.
(c) Ten percent of the preceding balance of (e) except for 1/1/12; since this is an annuity due, no time has elapsed at the date of the first payment and no interest has accrued.
(d) (a) minus (b) and (c).
(e) Preceding balance minus (d).

*Rounded by 19 cents.

At the end of its fiscal year, December 31, 2012, Ivanhoe records **accrued interest** as follows.

Interest Expense	7,601.84	
Interest Payable		7,601.84

[9]If it is impracticable for Ivanhoe to determine the implicit rate and it has an incremental borrowing rate of, say, 9 percent (lower than the 10 percent rate used by CNH), the present value computation would yield a capitalized amount of $101,675.35 ($23,981.62 × 4.23972). Thus, use of an unrealistically low discount rate could lead to a lessee recording a leased asset at an amount exceeding the fair value of the equipment, which is generally prohibited in IFRS. This explains why the implicit rate should be used to capitalize the minimum lease payments.

Depreciation of the leased equipment over its five-year lease term, applying Ivanhoe's normal depreciation policy (straight-line method), results in the following entry on December 31, 2012.

Depreciation Expense—Finance Leases	20,000	
Accumulated Depreciation—Finance Leases		20,000
($100,000 ÷ 5 years)		

At December 31, 2012, Ivanhoe separately identifies the assets recorded under finance leases on its statement of financial position. Similarly, it separately identifies the related obligations. Ivanhoe classifies the portion due within one year or the operating cycle, whichever is longer, with current liabilities, and the rest with non-current liabilities. For example, the current portion of the December 31, 2012, total obligation of $76,018.38 in Ivanhoe's amortization schedule is the amount of the reduction in the obligation in 2013, or $16,379.78. Illustration 21-7 shows the liabilities section as it relates to lease transactions at December 31, 2012.

Non-current liabilities	
Lease liability ($76,018.38 − $16,379.78)	$59,638.60
Current liabilities	
Interest payable	$ 7,601.84
Lease liability	16,379.78

ILLUSTRATION 21-7
Reporting Current and Non-Current Lease Liabilities

Ivanhoe records the lease payment of January 1, 2013, as follows.

Property Tax Expense	2,000.00	
Interest Payable	7,601.84	
Lease Liability	16,379.78	
Cash		25,981.62

Entries through 2016 would follow the pattern above. Ivanhoe records its other executory costs (insurance and maintenance) in a manner similar to how it records any other operating costs incurred on assets it owns.

Upon expiration of the lease, Ivanhoe has fully depreciated the amount capitalized as leased equipment. It also has fully discharged its lease obligation. If Ivanhoe does not purchase the loader, it returns the equipment to CNH. Ivanhoe then removes the leased equipment and related accumulated depreciation accounts from its books.

If Ivanhoe purchases the equipment at termination of the lease, at a price of $5,000 and the estimated life of the equipment changes from five to seven years, it makes the following entry.

Equipment ($100,000 + $5,000)	105,000	
Accumulated Depreciation—Finance Leases	100,000	
Leased Equipment under Finance Leases		100,000
Accumulated Depreciation—Equipment		100,000
Cash		5,000

Operating Method (Lessee)

Under the **operating method**, rent expense (and the associated liability) accrues day by day to the lessee as it uses the property. **The lessee assigns rent to the periods benefiting from the use of the asset and ignores, in the accounting, any commitments to make future payments.** The lessee makes appropriate accruals or deferrals if the accounting period ends between cash payment dates.

For example, assume that the finance lease illustrated in the previous section did not qualify as a finance lease. Ivanhoe therefore accounts for it as an operating lease.

The first-year charge to operations is now $25,981.62, the amount of the rental payment. Ivanhoe records this payment on January 1, 2012, as follows.

Rent Expense	25,981.62	
Cash		25,981.62

Ivanhoe does not report the loader, as well as any long-term liability for future rental payments, on the statement of financial position. Ivanhoe reports rent expense on the income statement. And, as discussed later in the chapter, **Ivanhoe must disclose all operating leases that have non-cancelable lease terms in excess of one year**.

Comparison of Finance Lease with Operating Lease

Objective·3

Contrast the operating and capitalization methods of recording leases.

As we indicated, if accounting for the lease as an operating lease, the first-year charge to operations is $25,981.62, the amount of the rental payment. Treating the transaction as a finance lease, however, results in a first-year charge of $29,601.84: depreciation of $20,000 (assuming straight-line), interest expense of $7,601.84 (per Illustration 21-6), and executory costs of $2,000. Illustration 21-8 shows that **while the total charges to operations are the same over the lease term whether accounting for the lease as a finance lease or as an operating lease, under the finance lease treatment the charges are higher in the earlier years and lower in the later years**.[10]

ILLUSTRATION 21-8
Comparison of Charges to Operations—Finance vs. Operating Leases

IVANHOE MINES
SCHEDULE OF CHARGES TO OPERATIONS
FINANCE LEASE VERSUS OPERATING LEASE

Year	Finance Lease				Operating Lease Charge	Difference
	Depreciation	Executory Costs	Interest	Total Charge		
2012	$ 20,000	$ 2,000	$ 7,601.84	$ 29,601.84	$ 25,981.62	$ 3,620.22
2013	20,000	2,000	5,963.86	27,963.86	25,981.62	1,982.24
2014	20,000	2,000	4,162.08	26,162.08	25,981.62	180.46
2015	20,000	2,000	2,180.32	24,180.32	25,981.62	(1,801.30)
2016	20,000	2,000	—	22,000.00	25,981.62	(3,981.62)
	$100,000	$10,000	$19,908.10	$129,908.10	$129,908.10	$ –0–

If using an accelerated method of depreciation, the differences between the amounts charged to operations under the two methods would be even larger in the earlier and later years.

In addition, using the finance lease approach results in an asset and related liability of $100,000 initially reported on the statement of financial position. The lessee would not report any asset or liability under the operating method. Therefore, the following differences occur if using a finance lease instead of an operating lease:

1. An increase in the amount of reported debt (both short-term and long-term).

2. An increase in the amount of total assets (specifically long-lived assets).

3. A lower income early in the life of the lease and, therefore, lower retained earnings.

Thus, many companies believe that finance leases negatively impact their financial position: Their debt to total equity ratio increases, and their rate of return on total assets decreases. As a result, the business community resists capitalizing leases.

---

[10]The higher charges in the early years is one reason lessees are reluctant to adopt the finance lease accounting method. Lessees (especially those of real estate) claim that it is really no more costly to operate the leased asset in the early years than in the later years. Thus, they advocate an even charge similar to that provided by the operating method.

Whether this resistance is well founded is debatable. From a cash flow point of view, the company is in the same position whether accounting for the lease as an operating or a finance lease. Managers often argue against capitalization because it can more easily lead to **violation of loan covenants**. Capitalization also can affect the **amount of compensation received by owners** (for example, a share compensation plan tied to earnings). Finally, capitalization can **lower rates of return** and **increase debt to equity relationships**, making the company less attractive to present and potential investors.[11]

ARE YOU LIABLE?

Under current accounting rules, companies can keep the obligations associated with operating leases off the statement of financial position. (For example, see the "What Do the Numbers Mean?" box on page 1123 for the effects of this approach for airlines.) This approach may change if the IASB and FASB are able to craft a new lease-accounting rule. The current plans for a new rule in this area should result in fewer operating leases on statements of financial position. Analysts are beginning to estimate the expected impact of a new rule. As shown in the table below, if the IASB and FASB issue a new rule on leases, a company like **Whole Foods** (USA) could see its liabilities jump a whopping 374 percent.

What do the numbers mean?

Ring It Up

Rule-makers are debating a change to lease accounting that would have a major impact on the financial statements of some big-name retailers:

Retailer	Estimated Off–Balance-Sheet Lease Liabilities	Jump in Liabilities If They Were on the Statement of Financial Position
Whole Foods Market (USA) Organic grocer leases all but five of its 175 stores, plus its distribution centers, "bakehouses," and administrative facilities.	$1.96 billion	374%
Walgreen (USA) Drugstore has opened 886 stores in the past two years. Of all its stores, 82% are leased, a total of $24 billion in obligations.	15.24	266
Bed Bath & Beyond (USA) Home goods retailer leases most of its 809 stores, plus 690,000 square feet of storage space, and 270,000 square feet of offices.	2.24	224
Starbucks (USA) Owns its U.S. roasting and distribution locations, but nearly all of its 6,000 retail coffee bars are leased.	2.45	172
CVS (USA) Owns approximately 3% of its 5,471 retail and specialty pharmacy drugstores and leases its mail-order sites.	11.11	160

*as of 5/22/06   *Data:* Credit Suisse Group, company reports, Bloomberg Financial Markets.

And, it is not just retailers who will be impacted. A PricewaterhouseCoopers survey of 3,000 international companies indicated the following impacts for several industries.

---

[11]One study indicates that management's behavior did change as a result of lease accounting rules. For example, many companies restructure their leases to avoid capitalization. Others increase their purchases of assets instead of leasing. Still others, faced with capitalization, postpone their debt offerings or issue shares instead. However, note that the study found no significant effect on share or bond prices as a result of capitalization of leases. A. Rashad Abdel-khalik, "The Economic Effects on Lessees of *FASB Statement No. 13,* Accounting for Leases," Research Report (Stamford, Conn.: FASB, 1981).

What do the numbers mean?

(continued)

	Average Increase in Interest- Bearing Debt	Companies with over 25% Increase	Average Increase in Leverage
Retail and Trade	213%	71%	64%
Other Services	51	35	34
Transportation and Warehousing	95	38	31
Professional Services	158	52	19
Accommodation	101	41	18
Wholesale Trade	34	28	17
Manufacturing	50	21	9
Construction	68	20	8
All companies	**58**	**24**	**13**

As indicated, the expected effects are significant, with all companies expecting a 58 percent increase in their debt levels and a 13 percent increase in leverage ratios.

This is not a pretty picture, but investors need to see it if they are to fully understand a company's lease obligations.

Source: Nanette Byrnes, "You May Be Liable for That Lease," *BusinessWeek* (June 5, 2006), p. 76; and PricewaterhouseCoopers, *The Future of Leasing: Research of Impact on Companies' Financial Ratios* (2009).

ACCOUNTING BY THE LESSOR

Earlier in this chapter, we discussed leasing's advantages to the lessee. Three important benefits are available to the lessor:

1. *Interest revenue.* Leasing is a form of financing. Banks, captives, and independent leasing companies find leasing attractive because it provides competitive interest margins.

2. *Tax incentives.* In many cases, companies that lease cannot use the tax benefit of the asset, but leasing allows them to transfer such tax benefits to another party (the lessor) in return for a lower rental rate on the leased asset. To illustrate, **Airbus** (FRA) might sell one of its Airbus 330 jet planes to a wealthy investor who needed only the tax benefit. The investor then leased the plane to a foreign airline, for whom the tax benefit was of no use. Everyone gained. Airbus sold its airplane, the investor received the tax benefit, and the foreign airline cheaply acquired a 330.[12]

3. *High residual value.* Another advantage to the lessor is the return of the property at the end of the lease term. Residual values can produce very large profits. **Citigroup** (USA) at one time assumed that the commercial aircraft it was leasing to the airline industry would have a residual value of 5 percent of their purchase price. It turned out that they were worth 150 percent of their cost—a handsome profit. At the same time, if residual values decline, lessors can suffer losses when less-valuable leased assets are returned at the conclusion of the lease. Recently, automaker **Ford** (USA) took a $2.1 billion write-down on its lease portfolio, when rising gas prices spurred dramatic declines in the resale values of leased trucks and SUVs. Such residual value losses led **Chrysler** (USA) to get out of the leasing business altogether.

[12]Some would argue that there is a loser—the tax authorities. The tax benefits enable the profitable investor to reduce or eliminate taxable income.

Economics of Leasing

A lessor, such as CNH Capital in our earlier example, determines the amount of the rental, basing it on the rate of return—the implicit rate—needed to justify leasing the front-end loader. In establishing the rate of return, CNH considers the credit standing of Ivanhoe, the length of the lease, and the status of the residual value (guaranteed versus unguaranteed).

In the CNH/Ivanhoe example on pages 1129–1131, CNH's implicit rate was 10 percent, the cost of the equipment to CNH was $100,000 (also fair value), and the estimated residual value was zero. CNH determines the amount of the lease payment as follows.

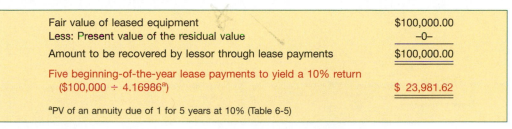

Fair value of leased equipment	$100,000.00
Less: Present value of the residual value	–0–
Amount to be recovered by lessor through lease payments	$100,000.00
Five beginning-of-the-year lease payments to yield a 10% return ($100,000 ÷ 4.16986ª)	$ 23,981.62
ªPV of an annuity due of 1 for 5 years at 10% (Table 6-5)	

ILLUSTRATION 21-9
Computation of Lease Payments

If a residual value is involved (whether guaranteed or not), CNH would not have to recover as much from the lease payments. Therefore, the lease payments would be less. (Illustration 21-16, on page 1140, shows this situation.)

Classification of Leases by the Lessor

For accounting purposes, the **lessor** also classifies leases as operating or finance leases. Finance leases may be further subdivided into direct-financing and sales-type leases.

As with lessee accounting, if the lease transfers substantially all the risks and rewards incidental to ownership, the lessor shall classify and account for the arrangement as a finance lease. Lessors evaluate the same criteria shown in Illustration 21-3 on page 1125 to make this determination.

The distinction for the lessor between a direct-financing lease and a sales-type lease is the presence or absence of a manufacturer's or dealer's profit (or loss): A sales-type lease involves a manufacturer's or dealer's profit, and a direct-financing lease does not. The profit (or loss) to the lessor is evidenced by the difference between the fair value of the leased property at the inception of the lease and the lessor's cost or carrying amount (book value).

Normally, sales-type leases arise when manufacturers or dealers use leasing as a means of marketing their products. For example, a computer manufacturer will lease its computer equipment (possibly through a captive) to businesses and institutions. Direct-financing leases generally result from arrangements with lessors that are primarily engaged in financing operations (e.g., banks).

Lessors classify and account for all leases that do not qualify as direct-financing or sales-type leases as operating leases. Illustration 21-10 (on page 1136) shows the circumstances under which a lessor classifies a lease as operating, direct-financing, or sales-type.

For purposes of comparison with the lessee's accounting, we will illustrate only the operating and direct-financing leases in the following section. We will discuss the more complex sales-type lease later in the chapter.

Objective·4

Identify the classifications of leases for the lessor.

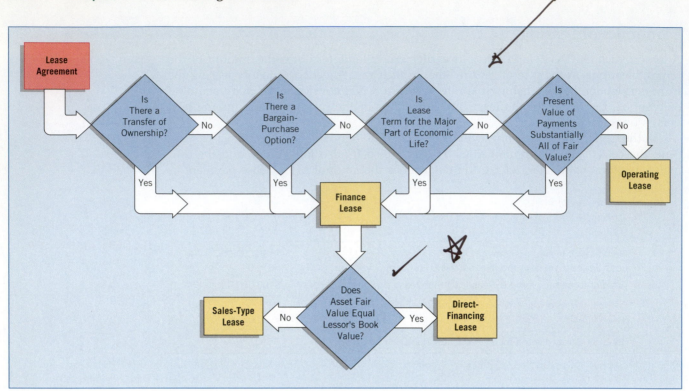

ILLUSTRATION 21-10
Diagram of Lessor's
Criteria for Lease
Classification

Objective·5

Describe the lessor's accounting
for direct-financing leases.

Direct-Financing Method (Lessor)

Direct-financing leases are in substance the financing of an asset purchase by the lessee. In this type of lease, the lessor records a **lease receivable** instead of a leased asset. The lease receivable is the present value of the minimum lease payments plus the present value of the unguaranteed residual value. Remember that "minimum lease payments" include (1) rental payments (excluding executory costs), (2) bargain-purchase option (if any), (3) guaranteed residual value (if any), and (4) penalty for failure to renew (if any).

Thus, the lessor records the residual value, whether guaranteed or not. Also, recall that if the lessor pays any executory costs, then it should reduce the rental payment by that amount in computing minimum lease payments.

The following presentation, using the data from the preceding CNH/Ivanhoe example on pages 1129–1131, illustrates the accounting treatment for a direct-financing lease. We repeat here the information relevant to CNH in accounting for this lease transaction.

1. The term of the lease is five years beginning January 1, 2012, non-cancelable, and requires equal rental payments of $25,981.62 at the beginning of each year. Payments include $2,000 of executory costs (property taxes).

2. The equipment (front-end loader) has a cost of $100,000 to CNH, a fair value at the inception of the lease of $100,000, an estimated economic life of five years, and no residual value.

3. CNH incurred no initial direct costs in negotiating and closing the lease transaction.

4. The lease contains no renewal options. The equipment reverts to CNH at the termination of the lease.

5. CNH sets the annual lease payments to ensure a rate of return of 10 percent (implicit rate) on its investment, as shown in Illustration 21-11.

As shown in the earlier analysis, the lease meets the criteria for classification as a direct-financing lease for two reasons: (1) The lease term equals the equipment's estimated economic life, and (2) the present value of the minimum lease payments equals the equipment's fair value. It is not a sales-type lease because there is no difference between the fair value ($100,000) of the loader and CNH's cost ($100,000).

Fair value of leased equipment		$100,000.00
Less: Present value of residual value		–0–
Amount to be recovered by lessor through lease payments		$100,000.00
Five beginning-of-the-year lease payments to yield a 10% return ($100,000 ÷ 4.16986ᵃ)		$ 23,981.62

ᵃPV of an annuity due of 1 for 5 years at 10% (Table 6-5).

ILLUSTRATION 21-11
Computation of Lease Payments

The Lease Receivable is the present value of the minimum lease payments (excluding executory costs which are property taxes of $2,000). CNH computes it as follows.

Lease receivable = ($25,981.62 – $2,000) × Present value of an annuity due of 1 for 5 periods at 10% (Table 6-5)

= $23,981.62 × 4.16986

= $100,000

ILLUSTRATION 21-12
Computation of Lease Receivable

CNH records the lease of the asset and the resulting receivable on January 1, 2012 (the inception of the lease), as follows.

Lease Receivable	100,000	
Equipment		100,000

Companies often **report** the lease receivable in the statement of financial position as "Net investment in finance leases." Companies classify it either as current or non-current, depending on when they recover the net investment.[13]

CNH replaces its investment (the leased front-end loader, a cost of $100,000) with a lease receivable. In a manner similar to Ivanhoe's treatment of interest, CNH applies the effective-interest method and recognizes interest revenue as a function of the lease receivable balance, as Illustration 21-13 shows.

ILLUSTRATION 21-13
Lease Amortization Schedule for Lessor—Annuity-Due Basis

CNH CAPITAL
LEASE AMORTIZATION SCHEDULE
ANNUITY-DUE BASIS

Date	Annual Lease Payment	Executory Costs	Interest (10%) on Lease Receivable	Lease Receivable Recovery	Lease Receivable
	(a)	(b)	(c)	(d)	(e)
1/1/12					$100,000.00
1/1/12	$ 25,981.62	$ 2,000.00	$ –0–	$ 23,981.62	76,018.38
1/1/13	25,981.62	2,000.00	7,601.84	16,379.78	59,638.60
1/1/14	25,981.62	2,000.00	5,963.86	18,017.76	41,620.84
1/1/15	25,981.62	2,000.00	4,162.08	19,819.54	21,801.30
1/1/16	25,981.62	2,000.00	2,180.32*	21,801.30	–0–
	$129,908.10	$10,000.00	$19,908.10	$100,000.00	

(a) Annual rental that provides a 10% return on net investment.
(b) Executory costs included in rental payment.
(c) Ten percent of the preceding balance of (e) except for 1/1/12.
(d) (a) minus (b) and (c).
(e) Preceding balance minus (d).

*Rounded by 19 cents.

On January 1, 2012, CNH records receipt of the first year's lease payment as follows.

Cash	25,981.62	
Lease Receivable		23,981.62
Property Tax Expense/Property Taxes Payable		2,000.00

[13]In the notes to the financial statements (see Illustration 21-31, page 1151), the lease receivable is reported at its gross amount (minimum lease payments plus the unguaranteed residual value). In addition, the lessor also reports total unearned interest related to the lease. As a result, some lessors record lease receivable on a gross basis and record the unearned interest in a separate account. We illustrate the net approach here because it is consistent with the accounting for the lessee.

On December 31, 2012, CNH recognizes the interest revenue earned during the first year through the following entry.

Interest Receivable	7,601.84	
Interest Revenue—Leases		7,601.84

At December 31, 2012, CNH reports the lease receivable in its statement of financial position among current assets or non-current assets, or both. It classifies the portion due within one year or the operating cycle, whichever is longer, as a current asset, and the rest with non-current assets.

Illustration 21-14 shows the assets section as it relates to lease transactions at December 31, 2012.

ILLUSTRATION 21-14
Reporting Lease
Transactions by Lessor

Non-current assets (investments)	
Lease receivable ($76,018.38 − $16,379.78)	$59,638.60
Current assets	
Interest receivable	$ 7,601.84
Lease receivable	16,379.78

The following entries record receipt of the second year's lease payment and recognition of the interest earned.

January 1, 2013

Cash	25,981.62	
Lease Receivable		16,379.78
Interest Receivable		7,601.84
Property Tax Expense/Property Taxes Payable		2,000.00

December 31, 2013

Interest Receivable	5,963.86	
Interest Revenue—Leases		5,963.86

Journal entries through 2016 follow the same pattern except that CNH records no entry in 2016 (the last year) for earned interest. Because it fully collects the receivable by January 1, 2016, no balance (investment) is outstanding during 2016. CNH recorded no depreciation. If Ivanhoe buys the loader for $5,000 upon expiration of the lease, CNH recognizes disposition of the equipment as follows.

Cash	5,000	
Gain on Sale of Leased Equipment		5,000

Operating Method (Lessor)

Under the **operating method**, the lessor records each rental receipt as rental revenue. It **depreciates the leased asset in the normal manner**, with the depreciation expense of the period matched against the rental revenue. The amount of revenue recognized in each accounting period is a level amount (straight-line basis) regardless of the lease provisions, unless another systematic and rational basis better represents the time pattern in which the lessor derives benefit from the leased asset.

In addition to the depreciation charge, the lessor expenses maintenance costs and the cost of any other services rendered under the provisions of the lease that pertain to the current accounting period. The lessor **amortizes over the life of the lease** any costs paid to independent third parties, such as appraisal fees, finder's fees, and costs of credit checks, usually on a straight-line basis.

To illustrate the operating method, assume that the direct-financing lease illustrated in the previous section does not qualify as a finance lease. Therefore, CNH accounts for it as an operating lease. It records the cash rental receipt as follows.

Cash	25,981.62	
Rental Revenue		25,981.62

CNH records depreciation as follows (assuming a straight-line method, a cost basis of $100,000, and a five-year life).

Depreciation Expense—Finance Leases	20,000	
Accumulated Depreciation—Finance Leases		20,000

If CNH pays property taxes, insurance, maintenance, and other operating costs during the year, it records them as expenses chargeable against the gross rental revenues.

If CNH owns plant assets that it uses in addition to those leased to others, the company **separately classifies the leased equipment and accompanying accumulated depreciation** as Equipment Leased to Others or Investment in Leased Property. If significant in amount or in terms of activity, CNH separates the rental revenues and accompanying expenses in the income statement from sales revenue and cost of goods sold.

SPECIAL ACCOUNTING PROBLEMS

The features of lease arrangements that cause unique accounting problems are:

> **Objective•6**
>
> Identify special features of lease arrangements that cause unique accounting problems.

1. Residual values.
2. Sales-type leases (lessor).
3. Bargain-purchase options.
4. Initial direct costs.
5. Current versus non-current classification.
6. Disclosure.

We discuss each of these features on the following pages.

Residual Values

Up to this point, in order to develop the basic accounting issues related to lessee and lessor accounting, we have generally ignored residual values. Accounting for residual values is complex and will probably provide you with the greatest challenge in understanding lease accounting.

Meaning of Residual Value

The **residual value** is the estimated fair value of the leased asset at the end of the lease term. Frequently, a significant residual value exists at the end of the lease term, especially when the economic life of the leased asset exceeds the lease term. If title does not pass automatically to the lessee (criterion 1) and a bargain-purchase option does not exist (criterion 2), the lessee returns physical custody of the asset to the lessor at the end of the lease term.

Guaranteed versus Unguaranteed

The residual value may be unguaranteed or guaranteed by the lessee. Sometimes, the lessee agrees to make up any deficiency below a stated amount that the lessor realizes in residual value at the end of the lease term. In such a case, that stated amount is the **guaranteed residual value**.

The parties to a lease use guaranteed residual value in lease arrangements for two reasons. The first is a business reason: It protects the lessor against any loss in estimated residual value, thereby ensuring the lessor of the desired rate of return on investment. The second reason is an accounting benefit that you will learn from the discussion at the end of this chapter.

Lease Payments

A guaranteed residual value—by definition—has more assurance of realization than does an unguaranteed residual value. As a result, the lessor may adjust lease payments because of the increased certainty of recovery. After the lessor establishes the payments, it makes no difference from an accounting point of view whether the residual value is guaranteed or unguaranteed. The net investment that the lessor records (once the payments are set) will be the same.

Assume the same data as in the CNH/Ivanhoe illustrations except that CNH estimates a residual value of $5,000 at the end of the five-year lease term. In addition, CNH assumes a 10 percent return on investment (ROI),[14] whether the residual value is guaranteed or unguaranteed. CNH would compute the amount of the lease payments as follows.

ILLUSTRATION 21-15
Lessor's Computation of Lease Payments

CNH'S COMPUTATION OF LEASE PAYMENTS (10% ROI) GUARANTEED OR UNGUARANTEED RESIDUAL VALUE ANNUITY-DUE BASIS, INCLUDING RESIDUAL VALUE	
Fair value of leased asset to lessor	$100,000.00
Less: Present value of residual value ($5,000 × .62092, Table 6-2)	3,104.60
Amount to be recovered by lessor through lease payments	$ 96,895.40
Five periodic lease payments ($96,895.40 ÷ 4.16986, Table 6-5)	$ 23,237.09

Contrast the foregoing lease payment amount to the lease payments of $23,981.62 as computed in Illustration 21-9 (on page 1135), where no residual value existed. In the second example, the payments are less because the present value of the residual value reduces CNH's total recoverable amount from $100,000 to $96,895.40.

Lessee Accounting for Residual Value

Objective•7

Describe the effect of residual values, guaranteed and unguaranteed, on lease accounting.

Whether the estimated residual value is guaranteed or unguaranteed has both economic and accounting consequence to the lessee. We saw the economic consequence—lower lease payments—in the preceding example. The accounting consequence is that the **minimum lease payments**, the basis for capitalization, include the guaranteed residual value but exclude the unguaranteed residual value.

Guaranteed Residual Value (Lessee Accounting). A guaranteed residual value affects the lessee's computation of minimum lease payments. Therefore, it also affects the amounts capitalized as a leased asset and a lease obligation. In effect, the guaranteed residual value **is an additional lease payment that the lessee will pay in property or cash, or both, at the end of the lease term**.

Using the rental payments as computed by the lessor in Illustration 21-15, the minimum lease payments are $121,185.45 ([$23,237.09 × 5] + $5,000). Illustration 21-16 shows the capitalized present value of the minimum lease payments (excluding executory costs) for Ivanhoe Mining.

ILLUSTRATION 21-16
Computation of Lessee's Capitalized Amount— Guaranteed Residual Value

IVANHOE'S CAPITALIZED AMOUNT (10% RATE) ANNUITY-DUE BASIS, INCLUDING **GUARANTEED** RESIDUAL VALUE	
Present value of five annual rental payments ($23,237.09 × 4.16986, Table 6-5)	$ 96,895.40
Present value of guaranteed residual value of $5,000 due five years after date of inception: ($5,000 × .62092, Table 6-2)	3,104.60
Lessee's capitalized amount	$100,000.00

Ivanhoe prepares a schedule of interest expense and amortization of the $100,000 lease liability. That schedule, shown in Illustration 21-17, is based on a $5,000 final guaranteed residual value payment at the end of five years.

[14]Technically, the rate of return CNH demands would differ depending upon whether the residual value was guaranteed or unguaranteed. To simplify the illustrations, we are ignoring this difference in subsequent sections.

IVANHOE MINING
LEASE AMORTIZATION SCHEDULE
ANNUITY-DUE BASIS, **GUARANTEED** RESIDUAL VALUE—GRV

Date	Lease Payment Plus GRV	Executory Costs	Interest (10%) on Liability	Reduction of Lease Liability	Lease Liability
	(a)	(b)	(c)	(d)	(e)
1/1/12					$100,000.00
1/1/12	$ 25,237.09	$ 2,000	–0–	$ 23,237.09	76,762.91
1/1/13	25,237.09	2,000	$ 7,676.29	15,560.80	61,202.11
1/1/14	25,237.09	2,000	6,120.21	17,116.88	44,085.23
1/1/15	25,237.09	2,000	4,408.52	18,828.57	25,256.66
1/1/16	25,237.09	2,000	2,525.67	20,711.42	4,545.24
12/31/16	5,000.00*		454.76**	4,545.24	–0–
	$131,185.45	$10,000	$21,185.45	$100,000.00	

(a) Annual lease payment as required by lease.
(b) Executory costs included in rental payment.
(c) Preceding balance of (e) × 10%, except 1/1/12.
(d) (a) minus (b) and (c).
(e) Preceding balance minus (d).

*Represents the guaranteed residual value.
**Rounded by 24 cents.

Ivanhoe records the leased asset (front-end loader) and liability, depreciation, interest, property tax, and lease payments on the basis of a guaranteed residual value. (These journal entries are shown in Illustration 21-22, on page 1143.) The format of these entries is the same as illustrated earlier, although the amounts are different because of the guaranteed residual value. Ivanhoe records the loader at $100,000 and depreciates it over five years. To compute depreciation, it subtracts the guaranteed residual value from the cost of the loader. Assuming that Ivanhoe uses the straight-line method, the depreciation expense each year is $19,000 ([$100,000 − $5,000] ÷ 5 years).

At the end of the lease term, before the lessee transfers the asset to CNH, the lease asset and liability accounts have the following balances.

Leased equipment under finance leases	$100,000.00	Interest payable	$ 454.76
Less: Accumulated depreciation—		Lease liability	4,545.24
finance leases	95,000.00		
	$ 5,000.00		$5,000.00

If, at the end of the lease, the fair value of the residual value is less than $5,000, Ivanhoe will have to record a loss. Assume that Ivanhoe depreciated the leased asset down to its residual value of $5,000 but that the fair value of the residual value at December 31, 2016, was $3,000. In this case, Ivanhoe would have to report a loss of $2,000. Assuming that it pays cash to make up the residual value deficiency, Ivanhoe would make the following journal entry.

Loss on Finance Lease	2,000.00	
Interest Expense (or Interest Payable)	454.76	
Lease Liability	4,545.24	
Accumulated Depreciation—Finance Leases	95,000.00	
Leased Equipment under Finance Leases		100,000.00
Cash		2,000.00

If the fair value *exceeds* $5,000, a gain may be recognized. CNH and Ivanhoe may apportion gains on guaranteed residual values in whatever ratio the parties initially agree.

When there is a guaranteed residual value, the lessee must be careful not to depreciate the total cost of the asset. For example, if Ivanhoe mistakenly depreciated the total cost of the loader ($100,000), a misstatement would occur. That is, the carrying amount of the asset at the end of the lease term would be zero, but Ivanhoe would show the liability under the finance lease at $5,000. In that case, if the asset was worth $5,000, Ivanhoe would end up reporting a gain of $5,000 when it transferred the asset back to CNH. As a result, Ivanhoe would overstate depreciation and would understate net income in 2012–2015; in the last year (2016), net income would be overstated.

Unguaranteed Residual Value (Lessee Accounting). From the lessee's viewpoint, an unguaranteed residual value is the same as no residual value in terms of its effect upon the lessee's method of computing the minimum lease payments and the capitalization of the leased asset and the lease liability.

Assume the same facts as those above except that the $5,000 residual value is **unguaranteed** instead of guaranteed. The amount of the annual lease payments would be the same—$23,237.09. Whether the residual value is guaranteed or unguaranteed, CNH will recover the same amount through lease rentals—that is, $96,895.40. The minimum lease payments are $116,185.45 ($23,237.09 × 5). Ivanhoe would capitalize the amount shown in Illustration 21-19.

ILLUSTRATION 21-19
Computation of Lessee's Capitalized Amount—Unguaranteed Residual Value

IVANHOE'S CAPITALIZED AMOUNT (10% RATE) ANNUITY-DUE BASIS, INCLUDING UNGUARANTEED RESIDUAL VALUE	
Present value of 5 annual rental payments of $23,237.09 × 4.16986 (Table 6-5)	$96,895.40
Unguaranteed residual value of $5,000 (not capitalized by lessee)	–0–
Lessee's capitalized amount	$96,895.40

Illustration 21-20 shows Ivanhoe's schedule of interest expense and amortization of the lease liability of $96,895.40, assuming an unguaranteed residual value of $5,000 at the end of five years.

ILLUSTRATION 21-20
Lease Amortization Schedule for Lessee—Unguaranteed Residual Value

			IVANHOE MINING LEASE AMORTIZATION SCHEDULE (10%) ANNUITY-DUE BASIS, UNGUARANTEED RESIDUAL VALUE		
Date	Annual Lease Payments	Executory Costs	Interest (10%) on Liability	Reduction of Lease Liability	Lease Liability
	(a)	(b)	(c)	(d)	(e)
1/1/12					$96,895.40
1/1/12	$ 25,237.09	$ 2,000	–0–	$23,237.09	73,658.31
1/1/13	25,237.09	2,000	$ 7,365.83	15,871.26	57,787.05
1/1/14	25,237.09	2,000	5,778.71	17,458.38	40,328.67
1/1/15	25,237.09	2,000	4,032.87	19,204.22	21,124.45
1/1/16	25,237.09	2,000	2,112.64*	21,124.45	–0–
	$126,185.45	$10,000	$19,290.05	$96,895.40	

(a) Annual lease payment as required by lease.
(b) Executory costs included in rental payment.
(c) Preceding balance of (e) × 10%.
(d) (a) minus (b) and (c).
(e) Preceding balance minus (d).

*Rounded by 19 cents.

Ivanhoe records the leased asset and liability, depreciation, interest, property tax, and lease payments on the basis of an unguaranteed residual value. (These journal entries are shown in Illustration 21-22, on page 1143.) The format of these finance lease entries is the same as illustrated earlier. Note that Ivanhoe records the leased asset at

$96,895.40 and depreciates it over five years. Assuming that it uses the straight-line method, the depreciation expense each year is $19,379.08 ($96,895.40 ÷ 5 years). At the end of the lease term, before Ivanhoe transfers the asset to CNH, the lease asset and liability accounts have the following balances.

Leased equipment under finance leases	$96,895	Lease liability	$–0–	
Less: Accumulated depreciation— finance leases	96,895			
	$ –0–			

ILLUSTRATION 21-21
Account Balances on Lessee's Books at End of Lease Term— Unguaranteed Residual Value

Assuming that Ivanhoe has fully depreciated the leased asset and has fully amortized the lease liability, no entry is required at the end of the lease term, except to remove the asset from the books.

If Ivanhoe depreciated the asset down to its unguaranteed residual value, a misstatement would occur. That is, the carrying amount of the leased asset would be $5,000 at the end of the lease, but the liability under the finance lease would be stated at zero before the transfer of the asset. Thus, Ivanhoe would end up reporting a loss of $5,000 when it transferred the asset back to CNH. Ivanhoe would understate depreciation and would overstate net income in 2012–2015; in the last year (2016), net income would be understated because of the recorded loss.

Lessee Entries Involving Residual Values. Illustration 21-22 shows, in comparative form, Ivanhoe's entries for both a guaranteed and an unguaranteed residual value.

ILLUSTRATION 21-22
Comparative Entries for Guaranteed and Unguaranteed Residual Values, Lessee Company

Guaranteed Residual Value			**Unguaranteed Residual Value**		
Capitalization of lease (January 1, 2012):					
Leased Equipment under Finance Leases	100,000.00		Leased Equipment under Finance Leases	96,895.40	
Lease Liability		100,000.00	Lease Liability		96,895.40
First payment (January 1, 2012):					
Property Tax Expense	2,000.00		Property Tax Expense	2,000.00	
Lease Liability	23,237.09		Lease Liability	23,237.09	
Cash		25,237.09	Cash		25,237.09
Adjusting entry for accrued interest (December 31, 2012):					
Interest Expense	7,676.29		Interest Expense	7,365.83	
Interest Payable		7,676.29	Interest Payable		7,365.83
Entry to record depreciation (December 31, 2012):					
Depreciation Expense— Finance Leases	19,000.00		Depreciation Expense— Finance Leases	19,379.08	
Accumulated Depreciation— Finance Leases ([$100,000 − $5,000] ÷ 5 years)		19,000.00	Accumulated Depreciation— Finance Leases ($96,895.40 ÷ 5 years)		19,379.08
Second payment (January 1, 2013):					
Property Tax Expense	2,000.00		Property Tax Expense	2,000.00	
Lease Liability	15,560.80		Lease Liability	15,871.26	
Interest Expense (or Interest Payable)	7,676.29		Interest Expense (or Interest Payable)	7,365.83	
Cash		25,237.09	Cash		25,237.09

Lessor Accounting for Residual Value

As we indicated earlier, the lessor will recover the same net investment whether the residual value is guaranteed or unguaranteed. That is, the lessor works on the assumption that it will realize **the residual value at the end of the lease term whether guaranteed or unguaranteed**. The lease payments required in order for the company to earn a certain return on investment are the same (e.g., $23,237.09 in our example) whether the residual value is guaranteed or unguaranteed.

To illustrate, we again use the CNH/Ivanhoe data and assume classification of the lease as a direct-financing lease. With a residual value (either guaranteed or unguaranteed) of $5,000, CNH determines the payments as follows.

ILLUSTRATION 21-23
Computation of Direct-Financing Lease Payments

Fair value of leased equipment	$100,000.00
Less: Present value of residual value ($5,000 × .62092, Table 6-2)	3,104.60
Amount to be recovered by lessor through lease payments	$ 96,895.40
Five beginning-of-the-year lease payments to yield a 10% return ($96,895.40 ÷ 4.16986, Table 6-5)	$ 23,237.09

The amortization schedule is the same for guaranteed or unguaranteed residual value, as Illustration 21-24 shows.

ILLUSTRATION 21-24
Lease Amortization Schedule, for Lessor—Guaranteed or Unguaranteed Residual Value

CNH CAPITAL
LEASE AMORTIZATION SCHEDULE
ANNUITY-DUE BASIS, **GUARANTEED OR UNGUARANTEED** RESIDUAL VALUE

Date	Annual Lease Payment Plus Residual Value (a)	Executory Costs (b)	Interest (10%) on Lease Receivable (c)	Lease Receivable Recovery (d)	Lease Receivable (e)
1/1/12					$100,000.00
1/1/12	$ 25,237.09	$ 2,000.00	$ –0–	$ 23,237.09	76,762.91
1/1/13	25,237.09	2,000.00	7,676.29	15,560.80	61,202.11
1/1/14	25,237.09	2,000.00	6,120.21	17,116.88	44,085.23
1/1/15	25,237.09	2,000.00	4,408.52	18,828.57	25,256.66
1/1/16	25,237.09	2,000.00	2,525.67	20,711.42	4,545.24
12/31/16	5,000.00	–0–	454.76*	4,545.24	–0–
	$131,185.45	$10,000.00	$21,185.45	$100,000.00	

(a) Annual lease payment as required by lease.
(b) Executory costs included in rental payment.
(c) Preceding balance of (e) × 10%, except 1/1/12.
(d) (a) minus (b) and (c).
(e) Preceding balance minus (d).

*Rounded by 24 cents.

Using the amounts computed above, CNH would make the entries shown in Illustration 21-25 for this direct-financing lease in the first year. Note the similarity to Ivanhoe's entries in Illustration 21-22 (on page 1143).

Sales-Type Leases (Lessor)

Objective•8
Describe the lessor's accounting for sales-type leases.

As already indicated, the primary difference between a direct-financing lease and a **sales-type lease** is the manufacturer's or dealer's gross profit (or loss). The diagram in Illustration 21-26 presents the distinctions between direct-financing and sales-type leases.

Inception of lease (January 1, 2012):		
Lease Receivable	100,000.00	
Equipment		100,000.00
First payment received (January 1, 2012):		
Cash	25,237.09	
Lease Receivable		23,237.09
Property Tax Expense/Property Taxes Payable		2,000.00
Adjusting entry for accrued interest (December 31, 2012):		
Interest Receivable	7,676.29	
Interest Revenue		7,676.29

ILLUSTRATION 21-25
Entries for Either
Guaranteed or
Unguaranteed Residual
Value, Lessor Company

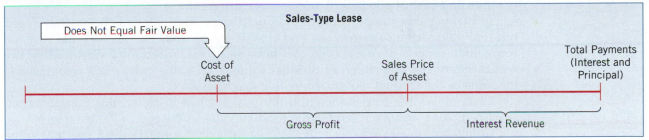

ILLUSTRATION 21-26
Direct-Financing versus
Sales-Type Leases

In a sales-type lease, the lessor records the sales price of the asset, the cost of goods sold and related inventory reduction, and the lease receivable. The information necessary to record the sales-type lease is as follows.

SALES-TYPE LEASE TERMS

LEASE RECEIVABLE (also referred to as **NET INVESTMENT**). The present value of the minimum lease payments plus the present value of any unguaranteed residual value. The lease receivable therefore includes the present value of the residual value, whether guaranteed or not.

SALES PRICE OF THE ASSET. The present value of the minimum lease payments.

COST OF GOODS SOLD. The cost of the asset to the lessor, less the present value of any unguaranteed residual value.

When recording sales revenue and cost of goods sold, there is a difference in the accounting for guaranteed and unguaranteed residual values. The guaranteed residual value can be considered part of sales revenue because the lessor knows that the entire asset has been sold. But, there is less certainty that the unguaranteed residual portion of the asset has been "sold" (i.e., will be realized). Therefore, the lessor recognizes sales and cost of goods sold only for the portion of the asset for which realization is assured. However, **the gross profit amount on the sale of the asset is the same whether a guaranteed or unguaranteed residual value is involved.**

To illustrate a sales-type lease with a guaranteed residual value and with an unguaranteed residual value, assume the same facts as in the preceding direct-financing lease situation (pages 1136–1138). The estimated residual value is $5,000 (the present value of which is $3,104.60), and the leased equipment has an $85,000 cost to the dealer, CNH. Assume that the fair value of the residual value is $3,000 at the end of the lease term.

Illustration 21-27 shows computation of the amounts relevant to a sales-type lease.

ILLUSTRATION 21-27
Computation of Lease Amounts by CNH Capital—Sales-Type Lease

	Sales-Type Lease	
	Guaranteed Residual Value	Unguaranteed Residual Value
Lease receivable	$100,000 [$23,237.09 × 4.16986 (Table 6-5) + $5,000 × .62092 (Table 6-2)]	Same
Sales price of the asset	$100,000	$96,895.40 ($100,000 − $3,104.60)
Cost of goods sold	$85,000	$81,895.40 ($85,000 − $3,104.60)
Gross profit	$15,000 ($100,000 − $85,000)	$15,000 ($96,895.40 − $81,895.40)

CNH records the same profit ($15,000) at the point of sale whether the residual value is guaranteed or unguaranteed. The difference between the two is that **the sales revenue and cost of goods sold amounts are different**.

In making this computation, we deduct the present value of the unguaranteed residual value from sales revenue and cost of goods sold. The reason—the revenue recognition criteria have not been met **because of the uncertainty surrounding the realization of the unguaranteed residual value**. That is, the gross profit recognized is the same as the amount recognized in an outright sale. **[9]**[15]

CNH makes the entries shown in Illustration 21-28 to record this transaction on January 1, 2012, and the receipt of the residual value at the end of the lease term.

Companies must periodically review the **estimated unguaranteed residual value in a sales-type lease**. If the estimate of the unguaranteed residual value declines, the company must revise the accounting for the transaction using the changed estimate. The decline represents a reduction in the lessor's lease receivable (net investment). The lessor recognizes the decline as a loss in the period in which it reduces the residual estimate. Companies do not recognize upward adjustments in estimated residual value.

Bargain-Purchase Option (Lessee)

As stated earlier, a bargain-purchase option allows the lessee to purchase the leased property for a future price that is substantially lower than the property's expected future fair value. The price is so favorable at the lease's inception that the future exercise of the option appears to be reasonably assured. If a bargain-purchase option exists, **the lessee must increase the present value of the minimum lease payments by the present value of the option price**.

For example, assume that Ivanhoe Mining in Illustration 21-17 (on page 1141) had an option to buy the leased equipment for $5,000 at the end of the five-year lease term. At that point, Ivanhoe and CNH expect the fair value to be $18,000. The significant difference between the option price and the fair value creates a bargain-purchase option, and the exercise of that option is reasonably assured.

A bargain-purchase option affects the accounting for leases in essentially the same way as a guaranteed residual value. In other words, with a guaranteed residual value, the lessee must pay the residual value at the end of the lease. Similarly, a purchase option

---

[15]Thus, in accounting for sales-type leases, lessors must also look to IFRS to apply revenue recognition guidelines. Recall (in Chapter 18) that revenue is recognized when it is probable that the economic benefits will flow to the company and the benefits can be measured reliably. **[10]**

Guaranteed Residual Value			Unguaranteed Residual Value		
To record sales-type lease at inception (January 1, 2012):					
Cost of Goods Sold	85,000.00		Cost of Goods Sold	81,895.40	
Lease Receivable	100,000.00		Lease Receivable	100,000.00	
Sales Revenue		100,000.00	Sales Revenue		96,895.40
Inventory		85,000.00	Inventory		85,000.00
To record receipt of the first lease payment (January 1, 2012):					
Cash	25,237.09		Cash	25,237.09	
Lease Receivable		23,237.09	Lease Receivable		23,237.09
Property Tax Exp./Pay.		2,000.00	Property Tax Exp./Pay.		2,000.00
To recognize interest revenue earned during the first year (December 31, 2012):					
Interest Receivable	7,676.29		Interest Receivable	7,676.29	
Interest Revenue		7,676.29	Interest Revenue		7,676.29
(See lease amortization schedule, Illustration 21-17 on page 1141.)					
To record receipt of the second lease payment (January 1, 2013):					
Cash	25,237.09		Cash	25,237.09	
Interest Receivable		7,676.29	Interest Receivable		7,676.29
Lease Receivable		15,560.80	Lease Receivable		15,560.80
Property Tax Exp./Pay.		2,000.00	Property Tax Exp./Pay.		2,000.00
To recognize interest revenue earned during the second year (December 31, 2013):					
Interest Receivable	6,120.21		Interest Receivable	6,120.21	
Interest Revenue		6,120.21	Interest Revenue		6,120.21
To record receipt of residual value at end of lease term (December 31, 2016):					
Inventory	3,000		Inventory	3,000	
Cash	2,000		Loss on Finance Lease	2,000	
Lease Receivable		5,000	Lease Receivable		5,000

ILLUSTRATION 21-28
Entries for Guaranteed and Unguaranteed Residual Values, Lessor Company—Sales-Type Lease

that is a bargain will almost certainly be paid by the lessee. Therefore, the computations, amortization schedule, and entries that would be prepared for this $5,000 bargain-purchase option are identical to those shown for the $5,000 guaranteed residual value (see Illustrations 21-15, 21-16, and 21-17 on pages 1140 and 1141).

The only difference between the accounting treatment for a bargain-purchase option and a guaranteed residual value of identical amounts and circumstances is in the **computation of the annual depreciation**. In the case of a guaranteed residual value, Ivanhoe depreciates the asset over the lease term; in the case of a bargain-purchase option, it uses the **economic life** of the asset.

Initial Direct Costs (Lessor)

Initial direct costs are of two types: incremental and internal. **Incremental direct costs** are paid to independent third parties for originating a lease arrangement. Examples include the cost of independent appraisal of collateral used to secure a lease, the cost of an outside credit check of the lessee, or a broker's fee for finding the lessee.

Internal direct costs are directly related to specified activities performed by the lessor on a given lease. Examples are evaluating the prospective lessee's financial condition; evaluating and recording guarantees, collateral, and other security arrangements; negotiating lease terms and preparing and processing lease documents; and closing the transaction. The costs directly related to an employee's time spent on a specific lease transaction are also considered initial direct costs.

However, initial direct costs should **not** include **internal indirect costs**. Such costs are related to activities the lessor performs for advertising, servicing existing leases, and establishing and monitoring credit policies. Nor should the lessor include the costs for supervision and administration or for expenses such as rent and depreciation.

The accounting for initial direct costs depends on the type of lease: [11]

- For **operating leases**, the lessor should defer initial direct costs and **allocate them over the lease term** in proportion to the recognition of rental revenue.[16]
- For **sales-type leases**, the lessor expenses the initial direct costs **in the period** in which it recognizes the profit on the sale.
- For a **direct-financing lease**, the lessor adds initial direct costs to the net investment in the lease and **amortizes them over the life of the lease as a yield adjustment**.

In a direct-financing lease, the lessor must disclose the unamortized deferred initial direct costs that are part of its investment in the direct-financing lease. For example, if the carrying value of the asset in the lease is $4,000,000 and the lessor incurs initial direct costs of $35,000, then the lease receivable (net investment in the lease) would be $4,035,000. The yield would be lower than the initial rate of return, and the lessor would adjust the yield to ensure proper amortization of the amount over the life of the lease.

XEROX TAKES ON THE SEC

What do the numbers mean?

Xerox (USA) derives much of its income from leasing equipment. Reporting such leases as sales leases, Xerox records a lease contract as a sale, therefore recognizing income immediately. One problem is that each lease receipt consists of payments for items such as supplies, services, financing, and equipment.

The U.S. SEC *accused* Xerox of inappropriately allocating lease receipts, which affects the timing of income that it reports. If Xerox applied SEC guidelines, which are similar to IFRS, it would report income in different time periods. Xerox contended that its methods were correct. It also noted that when the lease term is up, the bottom line is the same using either the SEC's recommended allocation method or its current method.

Although Xerox can refuse to change its method, the SEC has the right to prevent a company from selling shares or bonds to the public if the agency rejects filings of the company.

Apparently, being able to access public markets is very valuable to Xerox. The company agreed to change its accounting according to SEC wishes, and Xerox must pay $670 million to settle a shareholder lawsuit related to its lease transactions. Its former auditor, **KPMG LLP** (USA), must pay $80 million.

Source: Adapted from "Xerox Takes on the SEC," *Accounting Web* (January 9, 2002) (*www.account-ingweb.com*); and K. Shwiff and M. Maremont, "Xerox, KPMG Settle Shareholder Lawsuit," *Wall Street Journal Online* (March 28, 2008), p. B3.

Current versus Non-Current

Earlier in the chapter, we presented the classification of the lease liability/receivable in an annuity-due situation. Illustration 21-7 (on page 1131) indicated that Ivanhoe's current liability is the payment of $23,981.62 (excluding $2,000 of executory costs) to be made on January 1 of the next year. Similarly, as shown in Illustration 21-14 (on page 1138), CNH's current asset is the $23,981.62 (excluding $2,000 of executory costs) it will collect on January 1 of the next year. In these annuity-due instances, the statement of financial position date is December 31 and the due date of the lease payment is January 1 (less than one year), so the present value ($23,981.62) of the payment due the following January 1 is the same as the rental payment ($23,981.62).

[16]Technically, initial direct costs for operating leases are reported as an addition to the carrying amount of the leased asset. Because the deferred costs may be amortized on a different basis that used for depreciation expense, it is common for lessors to present these amounts as follows (assumed amounts).

Leased assets	€100,000
Less: Accumulated depreciation	20,000
	80,000
Deferred initial direct costs	10,000
	€ 90,000

What happens if the situation is an ordinary annuity rather than an annuity due? For example, assume that the rent is due at the **end of the year** (December 31) rather than at the beginning (January 1). Lease liabilities should be classified into current and non-current amounts. **[12]** However, IFRS does not indicate how to measure the current and non-current amounts. **A common method of measuring the current liability portion in ordinary annuity leases is the change-in-the-present-value method.**[17]

To illustrate the change-in-the-present-value method, assume an ordinary-annuity situation with the same facts as the CNH/Ivanhoe case, excluding the $2,000 of executory costs. Because Ivanhoe pays the rents at the end of the period instead of at the beginning, CNH sets the five rents at $26,379.73, to have an effective-interest rate of 10 percent. Illustration 21-29 shows the ordinary-annuity amortization schedule.

ILLUSTRATION 21-29
Lease Amortization Schedule—Ordinary-Annuity Basis

IVANHOE/CNH
LEASE AMORTIZATION SCHEDULE
ORDINARY-ANNUITY BASIS

Date	Annual Lease Payment	Interest 10%	Reduction of Lease Liability/Receivable	Balance of Lease Liability/Receivable
1/1/12				$100,000.00
12/31/12	$ 26,379.73	$10,000.00	$ 16,379.73	83,620.27
12/31/13	26,379.73	8,362.03	18,017.70	65,602.57
12/31/14	26,379.73	6,560.26	19,819.47	45,783.10
12/31/15	26,379.73	4,578.31	21,801.42	23,981.68
12/31/16	26,379.73	2,398.05*	23,981.68	–0–
	$131,898.65	$31,898.65	$100,000.00	

*Rounded by 12 cents.

The current portion of the lease liability/receivable under the **change-in-the-present-value method** as of December 31, 2012, would be $18,017.70 ($83,620.27 − $65,602.57). As of December 31, 2013, the current portion would be $19,819.47 ($65,602.57 − $45,783.10). At December 31, 2012, CNH classifies $65,602.57 of the receivable as non-current.

Thus, both the annuity-due and the ordinary-annuity situations report the reduction of principal for the next period as a current liability/current asset. In the annuity-due situation, CNH accrues interest during the year but is not paid until the next period. As a result, **a current asset arises for the receivable reduction and for the interest** that was earned in the preceding period.

In the ordinary-annuity situation, the interest accrued during the period is also paid in the same period. Consequently, the lessor shows as a current asset only the principal reduction due in the next period.

Disclosing Lease Data

Objective·9
List the disclosure requirements for leases.

In addition to the amounts reported in the financial statements related to lease assets and liabilities, the IASB requires **lessees** and **lessors** to disclose certain information about leases. These requirements vary based upon the type of lease

[17]For additional discussion on this approach and possible alternatives, see R. J. Swieringa, "When Current Is Noncurrent and Vice Versa!" *The Accounting Review* (January 1984), pp. 123–30; and A. W. Richardson, "The Measurement of the Current Portion of the Long-Term Lease Obligations—Some Evidence from Practice," *The Accounting Review* (October 1985), pp. 744–52.

(finance or operating) and whether the issuer is the lessor or lessee. These disclosure requirements provide investors with the following information:

For lessees: [13]

- A general description of material leasing arrangements.
- A reconciliation between the total of future minimum lease payments at the end of the reporting period and their present value.
- The total of future minimum lease payments at the end of the reporting period, and their present value for periods (1) not later than one year, (2) later than one year and not later than five years, and (3) later than five years.

For lessors: [14]

- A general description of material leasing arrangements.
- A reconciliation between the gross investment in the lease at the end of the reporting period, and the present value of minimum lease payments receivable at the end of the reporting period.
- Unearned finance income.
- The gross investment in the lease and the present value of minimum lease payments receivable at the end of the reporting period for periods (1) not later than one year, (2) later than one year and not later than five years, and (3) later than five years.

Illustration 21-30 presents financial statement excerpts from the 2008 annual report of **Delhaize Group** (BEL). These excerpts represent the statement and note disclosures typical of a lessee having both finance leases and operating leases.

ILLUSTRATION 21-30
Disclosure of Leases by Lessee

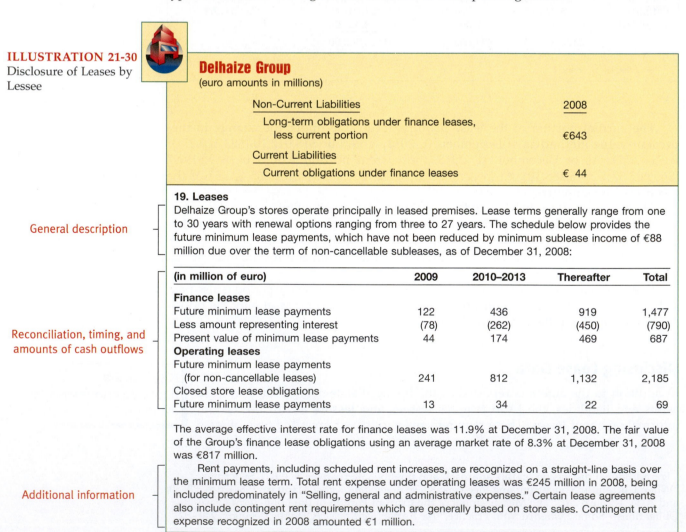

Delhaize Group
(euro amounts in millions)

Non-Current Liabilities	2008
Long-term obligations under finance leases, less current portion	€643
Current Liabilities	
Current obligations under finance leases	€ 44

19. Leases

General description — Delhaize Group's stores operate principally in leased premises. Lease terms generally range from one to 30 years with renewal options ranging from three to 27 years. The schedule below provides the future minimum lease payments, which have not been reduced by minimum sublease income of €88 million due over the term of non-cancellable subleases, as of December 31, 2008:

Reconciliation, timing, and amounts of cash outflows

(in million of euro)	2009	2010–2013	Thereafter	Total
Finance leases				
Future minimum lease payments	122	436	919	1,477
Less amount representing interest	(78)	(262)	(450)	(790)
Present value of minimum lease payments	44	174	469	687
Operating leases				
Future minimum lease payments (for non-cancellable leases)	241	812	1,132	2,185
Closed store lease obligations				
Future minimum lease payments	13	34	22	69

The average effective interest rate for finance leases was 11.9% at December 31, 2008. The fair value of the Group's finance lease obligations using an average market rate of 8.3% at December 31, 2008 was €817 million.

Additional information — Rent payments, including scheduled rent increases, are recognized on a straight-line basis over the minimum lease term. Total rent expense under operating leases was €245 million in 2008, being included predominately in "Selling, general and administrative expenses." Certain lease agreements also include contingent rent requirements which are generally based on store sales. Contingent rent expense recognized in 2008 amounted €1 million.

Illustration 21-31 presents the lease note disclosure from the 2009 annual report of **Trinity Biotech plc** (IRL). The disclosure highlights required lessor disclosures.

ILLUSTRATION 21-31
Disclosure of Leases by Lessor

Trinity Biotech
Notes to Financial Statements
(in millions)

Note 16: Trade and Other Receivables (in part)

Finance Lease Commitments

The Group leases instruments as part of its business. Future minimum finance lease receivables with non-cancellable terms are as follows:

General description

	December 31, 2009 US$'000		
	Gross Investment	Unearned Income	Minimum Payments Receivable
Less than one year	1,002	310	692
Between one and five years	1,559	453	1,106
	2,561	763	1,798

Reconciliation and timing of amounts receivable and unearned revenue

Operating Lease Commitments

The Group has leased a facility consisting of 9,000 square feet in Dublin, Ireland. This property has been sublet by the Group. The lease contains a clause to enable upward revision of the rent charge on a periodic basis. The Group also leases instruments under operating leases as part of its business. Future minimum rentals receivable under non-cancellable operating leases are as follows:

Description of leased assets

	December 31, 2009 US$'000		
	Land and Buildings	Instruments	Total
Less than one year	228	1,992	2,220
Between one and five years	911	852	1,763
More than five years	399	—	399
	1,538	2,844	4,382

Nature, timing, and amounts of future rentals

LEASE ACCOUNTING—UNRESOLVED PROBLEMS

As we indicated at the beginning of this chapter, lease accounting is subject to abuse. Companies make strenuous efforts to circumvent IFRS in this area. In practice, the strong desires of lessees to resist capitalization have rendered the accounting rules for capitalizing leases partially ineffective. Leasing generally involves large monetary amounts that, when capitalized, materially increase reported liabilities and adversely affect the debt to equity ratio. Lessees also resist lease capitalization because charges to expense made in the early years of the lease term are higher under the finance lease method than under the operating method, frequently without tax benefit. As a consequence, "let's beat the lease standard" is one of the most popular games in town.

To avoid leased asset capitalization, companies design, write, and interpret lease agreements to prevent satisfying any of the four finance lease criteria. Companies can easily devise lease agreements in such a way, by meeting the following specifications.

1. Ensure that the lease does not specify the transfer of title of the property to the lessee.
2. Do not write in a bargain-purchase option.
3. Set the lease term sufficiently below the estimated economic life of the leased property such that the economic life test is not met.
4. Arrange for the present value of the minimum lease payments to be sufficiently less than the fair value of the leased property.

The real challenge lies in disqualifying the lease as a finance lease to the lessee, while having the same lease qualify as a finance (sales or financing) lease to the lessor. Unlike lessees, lessors try to avoid having lease arrangements classified as operating leases.[18]

Avoiding the first three criteria is relatively simple, but it takes a little ingenuity to avoid the recovery of investment test for the lessee while satisfying it for the lessor. Two of the factors involved in this effort are (1) the use of the incremental borrowing rate by the lessee when it is higher than the implicit interest rate of the lessor, by making information about the implicit rate unavailable to the lessee; and (2) residual value guarantees.

The lessee's use of the higher interest rate is probably the more popular subterfuge. Lessees are knowledgeable about the fair value of the leased property and, of course, the rental payments. However, they generally are unaware of the estimated residual value used by the lessor. Therefore, the lessee who does not know exactly the lessor's implicit interest rate might use a different (higher) incremental borrowing rate.

The residual value guarantee is the other unique, yet popular, device used by lessees and lessors. In fact, a whole new industry has emerged to circumvent symmetry between the lessee and the lessor in accounting for leases. The residual value guarantee has spawned numerous companies whose principal, or even sole, function is to guarantee the residual value of leased assets.

Because the minimum lease payments include the guaranteed residual value for the lessor, this satisfies the recovery of investment test. The lease is a non-operating lease to the lessor. **But because a third-party guarantees the residual value, the minimum lease payments of the lessee exclude the guarantee.** Thus, by merely transferring some of the risk to a third party, lessees can alter substantially the accounting treatment by converting what would otherwise be finance leases to operating leases.[19]

The nature of the criteria encourages much of this circumvention, stemming from weaknesses in the basic objective of the lease-accounting guidelines to determine whether the lease qualifies as an operating or finance lease. This is often a very blurry line. The IASB has recognized that the existing lease accounting does not meet investors' needs and has proposed new rules to improve lease accounting.[20]

Based on a right of use model, the proposed rules require that all leases, regardless of their terms, be accounted for in a manner similar to how finance leases are treated today. That is, the notion of an operating lease will be eliminated. In addition, the rules call for including not only the contractual amounts due over the lease term but also the lessee's best estimate of contingent rents due over that period. The lease term is not just the term of the initial lease but includes renewal periods that are more likely than not to occur.

It is hoped that this overhaul of lease accounting will address the concerns under current rules in which no asset or liability is recorded for many operating leases. Recorded assets and liabilities under the proposal will be higher and income will be lower than under lease accounting today. As was discussed in the "What Do the Numbers Mean?" box on page 1133, the new rules are expected to have a significant impact on lessee financial statements. We believe that these new rules have the potential to

---

[18]The reason is that most lessors are banks, which are not permitted to hold these assets on their statements of financial position except for relatively short periods of time. Furthermore, the finance lease transaction from the lessor's standpoint provides higher income flows in the earlier periods of the lease life.

[19]As an aside, third-party guarantors have experienced some difficulty. **Lloyd's of London** (GBR) at one time insured the fast-growing U.S. computer-leasing industry in the amount of $2 billion against revenue losses, and losses in residual value, for canceled leases. Because of "overnight" technological improvements and the successive introductions of more efficient and less expensive computers, lessees in abundance canceled their leases. As the market for second-hand computers became flooded, residual values plummeted, and third-party guarantor Lloyd's of London projected a loss of $400 million. The lessees' and lessors' desire to circumvent accounting rules stimulated much of the third-party guarantee business.

[20]This is a joint project with the FASB. See *http://www.iasb.org/Current+Projects/IASB+Projects/Leases/Leases.htm*.

make financial statements more relevant and faithful representations of the significant leasing activity in global markets today.

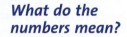

SWAP MEET

Telecommunication companies have developed one of the more innovative and controversial uses of leases. In order to provide fiber-optic service to their customers in areas where they did not have networks installed, telecommunication companies such as **Global Crossing** (USA), **Qwest Communications International** (USA), and **Cable and Wireless** (USA) entered into agreements to swap some of their unused network capacity in exchange for the use of another company's fiber-optic cables. Here's how it works:

What do the numbers mean?

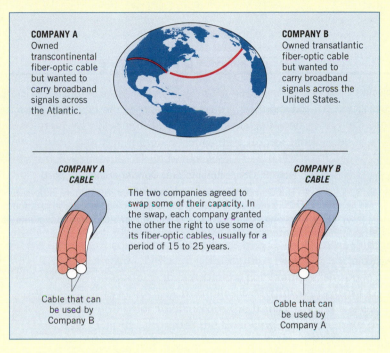

COMPANY A
Owned transcontinental fiber-optic cable but wanted to carry broadband signals across the Atlantic.

COMPANY B
Owned transatlantic fiber-optic cable but wanted to carry broadband signals across the United States.

COMPANY A CABLE

COMPANY B CABLE

The two companies agreed to swap some of their capacity. In the swap, each company granted the other the right to use some of its fiber-optic cables, usually for a period of 15 to 25 years.

Cable that can be used by Company B

Cable that can be used by Company A

Such trades seem like a good way to make efficient use of telecommunication assets. What got some telecommunications companies in trouble, though, was how they did the accounting for the swap.

The most conservative accounting for the capacity trades is to treat the swap as an exchange of assets, which does not affect the income statement. However, Global Crossing got into trouble with market regulators when it structured some of its capacity swaps as leases—the legal right to use capacity. Global Crossing was recognizing as revenue the payments received for the outgoing transfer of capacity, while payments for the incoming cable capacity were treated as capital expenditures and therefore not expensed. As a result, Global Crossing was showing strong profits from its capacity swaps. However, the company's investors got an unpleasant surprise when the market for bandwidth cooled off and there was no longer demand for its broadband capacity or its long-term leasing arrangements.

Source: Simon Romero and Seth Schiesel, "The Fiber-Optic Fantasy Slips Away," *New York Times on the Web* (February 17, 2002). By permission.

You will want to read the
CONVERGENCE CORNER on page 1154

For discussion of how international convergence efforts relate to lease accounting.

CONVERGENCE CORNER

LEASE ACCOUNTING

Leasing is a global business. Lessors and lessees enter into arrangements with one another without regard to national boundaries. Although U.S. GAAP and IFRS for leasing are similar, both the FASB and the IASB have decided that the existing accounting does not provide the most useful, transparent, and complete information about leasing transactions that should be provided in the financial statements.

RELEVANT FACTS

• Both U.S. GAAP and IFRS share the same objective of recording leases by lessees and lessors according to their economic substance—that is, according to the definitions of assets and liabilities.

• U.S. GAAP for leases uses bright-line criteria to determine if a lease arrangement transfers the risks and rewards of ownership; IFRS is more general in its provisions.

• Much of the terminology for lease accounting in IFRS and U.S. GAAP is the same. One difference is that finance leases are referred to as capital leases in U.S. GAAP.

• Under IFRS, lessees and lessors use the same lease capitalization criteria to determine if the risks and rewards of ownership have been transferred in the lease. U.S. GAAP has additional lessor criteria that payments are collectible and there are no additional costs associated with a lease.

• IFRS requires that lessees use the implicit rate to record a lease, unless it is impractical to determine the lessor's implicit rate. U.S. GAAP requires use of the incremental rate, unless the implicit rate is known by the lessee *and* the implicit rate is lower than the incremental rate.

ABOUT THE NUMBERS

Under U.S. GAAP, extensive disclosure of future non-cancelable lease payments is required for each of the next five years and the years thereafter, as shown in disclosure below by **Tasty Baking**.

Note 8: Commitments and Contingencies (in part)

The Company leases certain facilities, machinery, automotive and computer equipment under noncancelable lease agreements. The following is a schedule of future minimum lease payments as of December 29, 2007:

	Capital Leases	Noncancelable Operating Leases
2008	$ 565	$1,119
2009	503	947
2010	395	645
2011	193	467
2012	—	180
Later years	—	396
Total minimum lease payments	$1,656	$3,754
Less interest portion of payments	221	
Present value of future minimum lease payments	$1,435	

Rental expense was approximately $2,634 in 2007.*

*Although some international companies (e.g., **Nokia** (FIN)) provide a year-by-year breakout of payments due in years 1 through 5, IFRS does not require it.

ON THE HORIZON

Lease accounting is one of the areas identified in the IASB/FASB Memorandum of Understanding. The Boards have issued proposed rules based on "right of use," which requires that all leases, regardless of their terms, be accounted for in a manner similar to how finance leases are treated today. That is, the notion of an operating lease will be eliminated, which will address the concerns under current rules in which no asset or liability is recorded for many operating leases. A final standard is expected in 2011. You can follow the lease project at either the FASB (*http://www.fasb.org*) or IASB (*http://www.iasb.org*) websites.

SUMMARY OF LEARNING OBJECTIVES

•1 Explain the nature, economic substance, and advantages of lease transactions. A lease is a contractual agreement between a lessor and a lessee that conveys to the lessee the right to use specific property (real or personal), owned by the lessor, for a specified period of time. In return, the lessee periodically pays cash (rent) to the lessor. The advantages of lease transactions are (1) 100 percent financing, (2) protection against obsolescence, (3) flexibility, (4) less costly financing, (5) possible tax advantages, and (6) off–balance-sheet financing.

•2 Describe the accounting criteria and procedures for capitalizing leases by the lessee. A lease is a finance lease if it meets one or more of the following criteria: (1) The lease transfers ownership of the property to the lessee. (2) The lease contains a bargain-purchase option. (3) The lease term is for a major part of the estimated economic life of the leased property. (4) The present value of the minimum lease payments (excluding executory costs) amounts to subtantially all of the fair value of the leased property. For a finance lease, the lessee records an asset and a liability at the present value of the minimum lease payments at the inception of the lease.

•3 Contrast the operating and capitalization methods of recording leases. The total charges to operations are the same over the lease term whether accounting for the lease as a finance lease or as an operating lease. Under the finance lease treatment, the charges are higher in the earlier years and lower in the later years. If using an accelerated method of depreciation, the differences between the amounts charged to operations under the two methods would be even larger in the earlier and later years. If using a finance lease instead of an operating lease, the following occurs: (1) an increase in the amount of reported debt (both short-term and long-term), (2) an increase in the amount of total assets (specifically long-lived assets), and (3) lower income early in the life of the lease and, therefore, lower retained earnings.

•4 Identify the classifications of leases for the lessor. A lessor may classify leases for accounting purposes as follows: (1) operating leases, (2) direct-financing leases, and (3) sales-type leases. The lessor should classify and account for an arrangement as a direct-financing lease or a sales-type lease if, at the date of the lease agreement, the lease meets one or more of the lease capitalization criteria (as shown in learning objective 2 for lessees). The lessor classifies and accounts for all leases that fail to meet the criteria as operating leases.

•5 Describe the lessor's accounting for direct-financing leases. Leases that are in substance the financing of an asset purchase by a lessee require the lessor to substitute a "lease receivable" for the leased asset. "Lease receivable" is the present value of the minimum lease payments plus the present value of the unguaranteed residual value. Therefore, lessors include the residual value, whether guaranteed or unguaranteed, as part of lease receivable.

•6 Identify special features of lease arrangements that cause unique accounting problems. The features of lease arrangements that cause unique accounting problems are (1) residual values, (2) sales-type leases (lessor), (3) bargain-purchase options, (4) initial direct costs, (5) current versus non-current, and (6) disclosure.

•7 Describe the effect of residual values, guaranteed and unguaranteed, on lease accounting. Whether the estimated residual value is guaranteed or unguaranteed is of both economic and accounting consequence to the lessee. The accounting consequence is that the minimum lease payments, the basis for capitalization, include the guaranteed residual value but exclude the unguaranteed residual value. A guaranteed residual value affects the lessee's computation of minimum lease payments and the amounts

KEY TERMS

bargain-purchase
   option, *1126*
bargain-renewal
   option, *1126*
capitalization
   criteria, *1125*
capitalization of
   leases, *1123*
direct-financing
   lease, *1136*
effective-interest
   method, *1129*
executory costs, *1127*
finance lease, *1125*
guaranteed residual
   value, *1127, 1139*
implicit interest rate, *1128*
incremental borrowing
   rate, *1128*
initial direct costs, *1148*
lease, *1121*
lease receivable, *1136*
lease term, *1122, 1126*
lessee, *1121*
lessor, *1121*
manufacturer's or
   dealer's profit
   (or loss), *1135*
minimum lease
   payments, *1127*
non-cancelable, *1124*
off–balance-sheet
   financing, *1122*
operating lease, *1125*
residual value, *1139*
sales-type lease, *1144*
third-party
   guarantors, *1127 (n)*
unguaranteed residual
   value, *1142*

capitalized as a leased asset and a lease obligation. In effect, the guaranteed residual value is an additional lease payment that the lessee will pay in property or cash, or both, at the end of the lease term. An unguaranteed residual value from the lessee's viewpoint is the same as no residual value in terms of its effect upon the lessee's method of computing the minimum lease payments and the capitalization of the leased asset and the lease liability.

•8 Describe the lessor's accounting for sales-type leases. A sales-type lease recognizes interest revenue like a direct-financing lease. It also recognizes a manufacturer's or dealer's profit. In a sales-type lease, the lessor records at the inception of the lease the sales price of the asset, the cost of goods sold and related inventory reduction, and the lease receivable. Sales-type leases differ from direct-financing leases in terms of the cost and fair value of the leased asset, which results in gross profit. Lease receivable and interest revenue are the same whether a guaranteed or an unguaranteed residual value is involved. The accounting for guaranteed and for unguaranteed residual values requires recording sales revenue and cost of goods sold differently. The guaranteed residual value can be considered part of sales revenue because the lessor knows that the entire asset has been sold. There is less certainty that the unguaranteed residual portion of the asset has been "sold"; therefore, lessors recognize sales and cost of goods sold only for the portion of the asset for which realization is assured. However, the gross profit amount on the sale of the asset is the same whether a guaranteed or unguaranteed residual value is involved.

•9 List the disclosure requirements for leases. The disclosure requirements for lessees and lessors vary based upon the type of lease (finance or operating) and whether the issuer is the lessor or lessee. These disclosure requirements provide investors with the following information: (1) general description of the nature of leasing arrangements; (2) the nature, timing, and amount of cash inflows and outflows associated with leases, including payments to be paid or received in the next year, in years 2–5, and years thereafter; and (3) amounts receivable and unearned revenues under lease agreements.

APPENDIX 21A | **EXAMPLES OF LEASE ARRANGEMENTS**

Objective•10

Understand and apply lease accounting concepts to various lease arrangements.

To illustrate concepts discussed in this chapter, assume that Morgan Bakeries is involved in four different lease situations. Each of these leases is non-cancelable, and in no case does Morgan receive title to the properties leased during or at the end of the lease term. All leases start on January 1, 2012, with the first rental due at the beginning of the year. The additional information is shown in Illustration 21A-1.

EXAMPLE 1: HARMON, INC.

The following is an analysis of the Harmon, Inc. lease.

1. **Transfer of title?** No.
2. **Bargain-purchase option?** No.
3. **Economic life test.** The lease term is 20 years and the estimated economic life is 30 years. Thus, it **does not** meet the economic life test.

	Harmon, Inc.	Arden's Oven Co.	Mendota Truck Co.	Appleland Computer
Type of property	Cabinets	Oven	Truck	Computer
Yearly rental	€6,000	€15,000	€5,582.62	€3,557.25
Lease term	20 years	10 years	3 years	3 years
Estimated economic life	30 years	25 years	7 years	5 years
Purchase option	None	€75,000 at end of 10 years €4,000 at end of 15 years	None	€3,000 at end of 3 years, which approximates fair value
Renewal option	None	5-year renewal option at €15,000 per year	None	1 year at €1,500; no penalty for non-renewal; standard renewal clause
Fair value at inception of lease	€70,000	€120,000	€20,000	€10,000
Cost of asset to lessor	€70,000	€120,000	€15,000	€10,000
Residual value				
Guaranteed	–0–	–0–	€7,000	–0–
Unguaranteed	€5,000	–0–	–0–	€3,000
Incremental borrowing rate of lessee	12%	12%	12%	12%
Executory costs paid by	*Lessee* €300 per year	*Lessee* €1,000 per year	*Lessee* €500 per year	*Lessor* Estimated to be €500 per year
Present value of minimum lease payments				
Using incremental borrowing rate of lessee	€50,194.68	€115,153.35	€20,000	€8,224.16
Using implicit rate of lessor	Impracticable to determine	Impracticable to determine	Known by lessee, €20,000	Known by lessee, €8,027.45
Estimated fair value at end of lease	€5,000	€80,000 at end of 10 years €60,000 at end of 15 years	Not available	€3,000

ILLUSTRATION 21A-1
Illustrative Lease Situations, Lessors

4. **Recovery of investment test:**

Rental payments		€ 6,000
PV of annuity due for 20 years at 12%		× 8.36578
PV of rental payments		€50,194.68

Because the present value of the minimum lease payments is just 72 percent (€50,195 ÷ €70,000) of the fair value of the asset, it does not appear that this is a substantial part of the fair value of the asset. Thus, the lease does not meet the recovery of investment test.

Both Morgan and Harmon should account for this lease as an operating lease, as indicated by the January 1, 2012, entries shown in Illustration 21A-2.

ILLUSTRATION 21A-2
Comparative Entries for Operating Lease

Morgan Bakeries (Lessee)			Harmon, Inc. (Lessor)		
Rent Expense	6,000		Cash	6,000	
Cash		6,000	Rental Revenue		6,000

EXAMPLE 2: ARDEN'S OVEN CO.

The following is an analysis of the Arden's Oven Co. lease.

1. **Transfer of title?** No.
2. **Bargain-purchase option?** The €75,000 option at the end of 10 years does not appear to be sufficiently lower than the expected fair value of €80,000 to make it reasonably assured that it will be exercised. However, the €4,000 at the end of 15 years when the fair value is $60,000 does appear to be a bargain. From the information given, criterion 2 is therefore met. Note that both the guaranteed and the unguaranteed residual values are assigned zero values because the lessor does not expect to repossess the leased asset.
3. **Economic life test:** Given that a bargain-purchase option exists, the lease term is the initial lease period of 10 years plus the five-year renewal option since it precedes a bargain-purchase option. Even though the lease term is now considered to be 15 years, this test is still not met because the term of the lease is just 60 percent (15 years ÷ 25 years).
4. **Recovery of investment test:**

Rental payments	€ 15,000.00
PV of annuity due for 15 years at 12%	× 7.62817
PV of rental payments	€114,422.55

PV of bargain-purchase option: = €4,000 × (PVF$_{15,12\%}$) = €4,000 ×.18270 = €730.80

PV of rental payments	€114,422.55
PV of bargain-purchase option	730.80
PV of minimum lease payments	€115,153.35

The present value of the minimum lease payments is 96 percent (€115,153 ÷ €120,000) of the fair value of the asset. Thus, the recovery of investment test appears to be met since substantially all of the fair value of the asset will be recovered in the lease payments. Note that the incremental borrowing rate is used here because it is impracticable to determine the implicit rate of the lessor.

Morgan Bakeries should account for this as a finance lease because the lease meets both criteria 2 and 4. Assuming that Arden's implicit rate is less than Morgan's incremental borrowing rate, the following entries are made on January 1, 2012.

ILLUSTRATION 21A-3
Comparative Entries for Finance Lease—Bargain-Purchase Option

Morgan Bakeries (Lessee)			Arden's Oven Co. (Lessor)		
Leased Equipment Under			Lease Receivable	120,000	
Finance Leases	115,153.35		Asset—Oven		120,000
Lease Liability		115,153.35			

Morgan Bakeries would depreciate the leased asset over its economic life of 25 years, given the bargain-purchase option. Arden's Oven Co. does not use sales-type accounting because the fair value and the cost of the asset are the same at the inception of the lease.

EXAMPLE 3: MENDOTA TRUCK CO.

The following is an analysis of the Mendota Truck Co. lease.

1. **Transfer of title?** No.
2. **Bargain-purchase option?** No.

3. **Economic life test:** The lease term is three years and is just 43 percent of the estimated economic life of seven years. Thus, it **does not** meet the economic life test.

4. **Recovery of investment test:**

Rental payments	€ 5,582.62
PV of annuity due for 3 years at 12%	× 2.69005
PV of rental payments	€15,017.54

(Note: Adjusted for €0.01 due to rounding)

PV of guaranteed residual value: = €7,000 × (PVF$_{3,12\%}$) = €7,000 × .71178 = €4,982.46

PV of rental payments	€15,017.54
PV of guaranteed residual value	4,982.46
PV of minimum lease payments	€20,000.00

The present value of the minimum lease payments is equal to the fair value; therefore, the lease meets the recovery of investment.

Assuming that Mendota's implicit rate is the same as Morgan's incremental borrowing rate, the following entries are made on January 1, 2012.

Morgan Bakeries (Lessee)			Mendota Truck Co. (Lessor)		
Leased Equipment Under Finance Leases	20,000		Lease Receivable	20,000	
			Cost of Goods Sold	15,000	
Lease Liability		20,000	Inventory—Truck		15,000
			Sales		20,000

ILLUSTRATION 21A-4
Comparative Entries for Finance Lease

Morgan depreciates the leased asset over three years to its guaranteed residual value.

EXAMPLE 4: APPLELAND COMPUTER

The following is an analysis of the Appleland Computer lease.

1. **Transfer of title?** No.

2. **Bargain-purchase option?** No. The option to purchase at the end of three years at approximate fair value is clearly not a bargain.

3. **Economic life test:** The lease term is three years, which is just 60 percent (3 years ÷ 5 years) of the economic life of the asset, and no bargain-renewal period exists. Therefore, the economic life test **is not** met.

4. **Recovery of investment test:**

Rental payments	€3,557.25
Less executory costs	500.00
	3,057.25
PV of annuity-due factor for 3 years at 12%	× 2.69005
PV of minimum lease payments using incremental borrowing rate	€8,224.16

The present value of the minimum lease payments using the incremental borrowing rate is €8,224.16 (see Illustration 21A-1 on page 1157). However, the higher implicit rate used by the lessor is known by Morgan. Given this situation, the lessee uses the implicit rate, which results in a present value of €8,027.45. Because the present value of the minimum lease payments is just 80 percent (€8,027 ÷ €10,000) of the fair value, the lease does **not** meet the recovery of investment test.

The following entries are made on January 1, 2012, indicating an operating lease.

ILLUSTRATION 21A-5
Comparative Entries for
Operating Lease

Morgan Bakeries (Lessee)			Appleland Computer (Lessor)		
Rent Expense	3,557.25		Cash	3,557.25	
Cash		3,557.25	Rental Revenue		3,557.25

SUMMARY OF LEARNING OBJECTIVE FOR APPENDIX 21A

•10 **Understand and apply lease accounting concepts to various lease arrangements.** The classification of leases by lessees and lessors is based on criteria that assess whether the lessor has transferred to the lessee substantially all of the risks and benefits of ownership of the asset. Lessees capitalize leases that meet any of the criteria, recording a lease asset and related lease liability. For leases that are in substance a financing of an asset purchase, lessors substitute a lease receivable for the leased asset. In a sales-type lease, the fair value of the leased asset is greater than the cost, and lessors record gross profit. Leases that do not meet capitalization criteria are classified as operating leases, on which rent expense (revenue) is recognized by lessees (lessors) for lease payments.

APPENDIX **21B** SALE-LEASEBACKS

Objective•11
Describe the lessee's accounting for sale-leaseback transactions.

The term **sale-leaseback** describes a transaction in which the owner of the property (seller-lessee) sells the property to another and simultaneously leases it back from the new owner. The use of the property is generally continued without interruption.

Sale-leasebacks are common. Financial institutions (e.g., **HSBC** (GBR) and **BBVA** (ESP)) have used this technique for their administrative offices, retailers (**Liberty** (GBR)) for their stores, and hospitals (**Healthscope** (AUS)) for their facilities. The advantages of a sale-leaseback from the seller's viewpoint usually involve two primary considerations:

1. *Financing*—If the purchase of equipment has already been financed, a sale-leaseback can allow the seller to refinance at lower rates, assuming rates have dropped. In addition, a sale-leaseback can provide another source of working capital, particularly when liquidity is tight.

2. *Taxes*—At the time a company purchased equipment, it may not have known that it would be subject to certain tax laws and that ownership might increase its minimum tax liability. By selling the property, the seller-lessee may deduct the entire lease payment, which is not subject to these tax considerations.

DETERMINING ASSET USE

To the extent the **seller-lessee continues to use** the asset after the sale, the sale-leaseback is really a form of financing. Therefore, the lessor **should not recognize a gain or loss** on the transaction. In short, the seller-lessee is simply borrowing funds.

On the other hand, if the **seller-lessee gives up the right to the use** of the asset, the transaction is in substance a sale. In that case, **gain or loss recognition** is appropriate. Trying to ascertain when the lessee has given up the use of the asset is difficult, however, and the IASB has formulated complex rules to identify this situation.[21] To understand the profession's position in this area, we discuss the basic accounting for the lessee and lessor below.

> **Underlying Concepts**
>
> A sale-leaseback is similar in substance to the parking of inventories (discussed in Chapter 8). The ultimate economic benefits remain under the control of the "seller," thus satisfying the definition of an asset.

Lessee

If the lease meets one of the four criteria for treatment as a finance lease (see Illustration 21-3 on page 1125), the **seller-lessee accounts for the transaction as a sale and the lease as a finance lease**. The seller-lessee should defer any profit or loss it experiences from the sale of the assets that are leased back under a finance lease; it should **amortize that profit over the lease term** (or the economic life if either criterion 1 or 2 is satisfied) in proportion to the depreciation of the leased assets.

For example, assume **Stora Enso** (FIN) sells equipment having a book value of €580,000 and a fair value of €623,110 to **Deutsche Bank** (DEU) for €623,110 and leases the equipment back for €50,000 a year for 20 years. Stora Enso should amortize the profit of €43,110 over the 20-year period at the same rate that it depreciates the €623,110. [15] It credits the €43,110 (€623,110 − €580,000) to **Unearned Profit on Sale-Leaseback**.

If none of the finance lease criteria are satisfied, **the seller-lessee accounts for the transaction as a sale and the lease as an operating lease**. Under an operating lease, as long as the sale-leaseback transaction is established at fair value, any gain or loss is recognized immediately.[22]

Lessor

If the lease meets one of the lease capitalization criteria, the **purchaser-lessor** records the transaction as a purchase and a direct-financing lease. If the lease does not meet the criteria, the purchaser-lessor records the transaction as a purchase and an operating lease.

SALE-LEASEBACK EXAMPLE

To illustrate the accounting treatment accorded a sale-leaseback transaction, assume that **Japan Airlines (JAL)** (JPN) on January 1, 2012, sells a used Boeing 757 having a carrying amount on its books of $75,500,000 to **CitiCapital** (USA) for $80,000,000. JAL

---

[21]Sales and leasebacks of real estate are often accounted for differently. A discussion of the issues related to these transactions is beyond the scope of this textbook.

[22]If the sales price is not at fair value and the loss is compensated for by reduced future lease payments (below market rates), the loss shall be deferred and amortized in proportion to the lease payments over the period for which the asset is expected to be used. If the sales price is above fair value, the excess over fair value shall be deferred and amortized over the period for which the asset is expected to be used. [16]

immediately leases the aircraft back under the following conditions:

1. The term of the lease is 15 years, non-cancelable, and requires equal rental payments of $10,487,443 at the beginning of each year.
2. The aircraft has a fair value of $80,000,000 on January 1, 2012, and an estimated economic life of 15 years.
3. JAL pays all executory costs.
4. JAL depreciates similar aircraft that it owns on a straight-line basis over 15 years.
5. The annual payments assure the lessor a 12 percent return.
6. JAL knows the implicit rate.

This lease is a finance lease to JAL because the lease term is equal to the estimated life of the aircraft and because the present value of the lease payments is equal to the fair value of the aircraft to CitiCapital. CitiCapital should classify this lease as a direct-financing lease.

ILLUSTRATION 21B-1

Comparative Entries for Sale-Leaseback for Lessee and Lessor

Illustration 21B-1 presents the typical journal entries to record the sale-leaseback transactions for JAL and CitiCapital for the first year.

JAL (Lessee)			CitiCapital (Lessor)		
Sale of Aircraft by JAL to CitiCapital (January 1, 2012):					
Cash	80,000,000		Aircraft	80,000,000	
Aircraft		75,500,000	Cash		80,000,000
Unearned Profit on Sale-Leaseback		4,500,000	Lease Receivable	80,000,000	
Leased Aircraft under Finance Leases	80,000,000		Aircraft		80,000,000
Lease Liability		80,000,000			
First Lease Payment (January 1, 2012):					
Lease Liability	10,487,443		Cash	10,487,443	
Cash		10,487,443	Lease Receivable		10,487,443
Incurrence and Payment of Executory Costs by JAL throughout 2012:					
Insurance, Maintenance, Taxes, etc.	XXX		(No entry)		
Cash or Accounts Payable		XXX			
Depreciation Expense on the Aircraft (December 31, 2012):					
Depreciation Expense	5,333,333		(No entry)		
Accumulated Depr.—Finance Leases ($80,000,000 ÷ 15)		5,333,333			
Amortization of Profit on Sale-Leaseback by JAL (December 31, 2012):					
Unearned Profit on Sale-Leaseback	300,000		(No entry)		
Depreciation Expense ($4,500,000 ÷ 15)		300,000			
Note: A case might be made for crediting Revenue instead of Depreciation Expense.					
Interest for 2012 (December 31, 2012):					
Interest Expense	8,341,507[a]		Interest Receivable	8,341,507	
Interest Payable		8,341,507	Interest Revenue		8,341,507[a]

[a]Partial Lease Amortization Schedule:

Date	Annual Rental Payment	Interest 12%	Reduction of Balance	Balance
1/1/12				$80,000,000
1/1/12	$10,487,443	$ –0–	$10,487,443	69,512,557
1/1/13	10,487,443	8,341,507	2,145,936	67,366,621

SUMMARY OF LEARNING OBJECTIVE FOR APPENDIX 21B

•11 **Describe the lessee's accounting for sale-leaseback transactions.** If the lease meets one of the criteria for treatment as a finance lease, the seller-lessee accounts for the transaction as a sale and the lease as a finance lease. The seller-lessee defers any profit it experiences from the sale of the assets that are leased back under a finance lease. The seller-lessee amortizes any profit over the lease term (or the economic life if either criterion 1 or 2 is satisfied) in proportion to the amortization of the leased assets. If the lease satisfies none of the finance lease criteria, the seller-lessee accounts for the transaction as a sale and the lease as an operating lease. Under an operating lease, the lessee recognizes any gain or loss immediately if the sale-leaseback is at fair value.

AUTHORITATIVE LITERATURE

Authoritative Literature References

[1] International Accounting Standard 17, *Leases* (London, U.K.: International Accounting Standards Committee Foundation, 2003), par. 7.

[2] International Accounting Standard 17, *Leases* (London, U.K.: International Accounting Standards Committee Foundation, 2003), par. 10.

[3] International Accounting Standard 17, *Leases* (London, U.K.: International Accounting Standards Committee Foundation, 2003), paras. 10(e) and 11.

[4] International Accounting Standard 17, *Leases* (London, U.K.: International Accounting Standards Committee Foundation, 2003), par. 11.

[5] International Accounting Standard 17, *Leases* (London, U.K.: International Accounting Standards Committee Foundation, 2003), par. 4.

[6] International Accounting Standard 17, *Leases* (London, U.K.: International Accounting Standards Committee Foundation, 2003), par. 11(b).

[7] International Accounting Standard 17, *Leases* (London, U.K.: International Accounting Standards Committee Foundation, 2003), par. 20.

[8] International Accounting Standard 17, *Leases* (London, U.K.: International Accounting Standards Committee Foundation, 2003), par. 4.

[9] International Accounting Standard 17, *Leases* (London, U.K.: International Accounting Standards Committee Foundation, 2003), par. 44.

[10] International Accounting Standard 18, *Revenue* (London, U.K.: International Accounting Standards Committee Foundation, 2001), par. 7.

[11] International Accounting Standard 17, *Leases* (London, U.K.: International Accounting Standards Committee Foundation, 2003), paras. 38 and 52.

[12] International Accounting Standard 17, *Leases* (London, U.K.: International Accounting Standards Committee Foundation, 2003), par. 23.

[13] International Accounting Standard 17, *Leases* (London, U.K.: International Accounting Standards Committee Foundation, 2003), paras. 31 and 35.

[14] International Accounting Standard 17, *Leases* (London, U.K.: International Accounting Standards Committee Foundation, 2003), paras. 47 and 56.

[15] International Accounting Standard 17, *Leases* (London, U.K.: International Accounting Standards Committee Foundation, 2003), par. 59.

[16] International Accounting Standard 17, *Leases* (London, U.K.: International Accounting Standards Committee Foundation, 2003), par. 61.

Note: All asterisked Questions, Exercises, and Problems relate to material in the appendices to the chapter.

QUESTIONS

1. What are the major lessor groups? What advantage does a captive have in a leasing arrangement?

2. Bradley Co. is expanding its operations and is in the process of selecting the method of financing this program. After some investigation, the company determines that it may (1) issue bonds and with the proceeds purchase the needed assets or (2) lease the assets on a long-term basis. Without knowing the comparative costs involved, answer these questions:

   (a) What might be the advantages of leasing the assets instead of owning them?

   (b) What might be the disadvantages of leasing the assets instead of owning them?

   (c) In what way will the statement of financial position be differently affected by leasing the assets as opposed to issuing bonds and purchasing the assets?

3. Identify the two recognized lease-accounting methods for lessees and distinguish between them.

4. Ballard Company rents a warehouse on a month-to-month basis for the storage of its excess inventory. The company periodically must rent space whenever its production greatly exceeds actual sales. For several years, the company officials have discussed building their own storage facility, but this enthusiasm wavers when sales increase sufficiently to absorb the excess inventory. What is the nature of this type of lease arrangement, and what accounting treatment should be accorded it?

5. Distinguish between minimum rental payments and minimum lease payments, and indicate what is included in minimum lease payments.

6. Explain the distinction between a direct-financing lease and a sales-type lease for a lessor.

7. Outline the accounting procedures involved in applying the operating method by a lessee.

8. Outline the accounting procedures involved in applying the finance lease method by a lessee.

9. Identify the lease classifications for lessors and the criteria that must be met for each classification.

10. Outline the accounting procedures involved in applying the direct-financing method.

11. Outline the accounting procedures involved in applying the operating method by a lessor.

12. Walker Company is a manufacturer and lessor of computer equipment. What should be the nature of its lease arrangements with lessees if the company wishes to account for its lease transactions as sales-type leases?

13. Metheny Corporation's lease arrangements qualify as sales-type leases at the time of entering into the transactions. How should the corporation recognize revenues and costs in these situations?

14. Dr. Alice Foyle (lessee) has a non-cancelable 20-year lease with Brownback Realty, Inc. (lessor) for the use of a medical building. Taxes, insurance, and maintenance are paid by the lessee in addition to the fixed annual payments, of which the present value is equal to the fair value of the leased property. At the end of the lease period, title becomes the lessee's at a nominal price. Considering the terms of the lease described above, comment on the nature of the lease transaction and the accounting treatment that should be accorded it by the lessee.

15. The residual value is the estimated fair value of the leased property at the end of the lease term.

   (a) Of what significance is (1) an unguaranteed and (2) a guaranteed residual value in the lessee's accounting for a finance lease transaction?

   (b) Of what significance is (1) an unguaranteed and (2) a guaranteed residual value in the lessor's accounting for a direct-financing lease transaction?

16. How should changes in the estimated unguaranteed residual value be handled by the lessor?

17. Describe the effect of a "bargain-purchase option" on accounting for a finance lease transaction by a lessee.

18. What are "initial direct costs" and how are they accounted for?

19. What disclosures should be made by lessees and lessors related to future lease payments?

20. Briefly describe some of the similarities and differences between U.S. GAAP and IFRS with respect to the accounting for leases.

21. Both U.S. GAAP and IFRS require footnote disclosure of operating lease payments. Are there any differences in the information provided to statement readers in these disclosures? Explain.

22. Briefly discuss the IASB and FASB efforts to converge their accounting guidelines for leases.

*23. What is the nature of a "sale-leaseback" transaction?

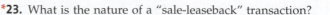

BRIEF EXERCISES

•2 BE21-1 **Mizuno Corp.** (JPN) leases telecommunication equipment. Assume the following data for equipment leased from Photon Company. The lease term is 5 years and requires equal rental payments of ¥3,100,000 at the beginning of each year. The equipment has a fair value at the inception of the lease of ¥13,800,000, an estimated useful life of 8 years, and no residual value. Mizuno pays all executory costs directly to third parties. Photon set the annual rental to earn a rate of return of 10%, and this fact is known to Mizuno. The lease does not transfer title or contain a bargain-purchase option. How should Mizuno classify this lease?

•2 BE21-2 Waterworld Company leased equipment from Costner Company. The lease term is 4 years and requires equal rental payments of $43,019 at the beginning of each year. The equipment has a fair value at the inception of the lease of $150,000, an estimated useful life of 4 years, and no residual value. Waterworld pays all executory costs directly to third parties. The appropriate interest rate is 10%. Prepare Waterworld's January 1, 2011, journal entries at the inception of the lease.

•2 BE21-3 Rick Kleckner Corporation recorded a finance lease at $300,000 on January 1, 2011. The interest rate is 12%. Kleckner Corporation made the first lease payment of $53,920 on January 1, 2011. The lease requires eight annual payments. The equipment has a useful life of 8 years with no residual value. Prepare Kleckner Corporation's December 31, 2011, adjusting entries.

•2 BE21-4 Use the information for Rick Kleckner Corporation from BE21-3. Assume that at December 31, 2011, Kleckner made an adjusting entry to accrue interest expense of $29,530 on the lease. Prepare Kleckner's January 1, 2012, journal entry to record the second lease payment of $53,920.

•3 BE21-5 Jana Kingston Corporation enters into a lease on January 1, 2011, that does not transfer ownership or contain a bargain-purchase option. It covers 3 years of the equipment's 8-year useful life, and the present value of the minimum lease payments is less than 80% of the fair value of the asset leased. Prepare Jana Kingston's journal entry to record its January 1, 2011, annual lease payment of €35,000.

•4 •5 BE21-6 Assume that **Lenovo** (CHN) leased equipment that was carried at a cost of $150,000 to Sharon Swander Company. The term of the lease is 6 years beginning January 1, 2011, with equal rental payments of $30,044 at the beginning of each year. All executory costs are paid by Swander directly to third parties. The fair value of the equipment at the inception of the lease is $150,000. The equipment has a useful life of 6 years with no residual value. The lease has an implicit interest rate of 8%, no bargain-purchase option, and no transfer of title. Prepare Lenovo's January 1, 2011, journal entries at the inception of the lease.

•4 •5 BE21-7 Use the information for Lenovo from BE21-6. Assume the direct-financing lease was recorded at a present value of $150,000. Prepare Lenovo's December 31, 2011, entry to record interest.

•4 BE21-8 Jennifer Brent Corporation owns equipment that cost €80,000 and has a useful life of 8 years with no residual value. On January 1, 2011, Jennifer Brent leases the equipment to Lopez Inc. for one year with one rental payment of €15,000 on January 1. Prepare Jennifer Brent Corporation's 2011 journal entries.

•6 •7 BE21-9 Indiana Jones Corporation enters into a 6-year lease of equipment on January 1, 2011, which requires 6 annual payments of $40,000 each, beginning January 1, 2011. In addition, Indiana Jones guarantees the lessor a residual value of $20,000 at lease-end. The equipment has a useful life of 6 years. Prepare Indiana Jones' January 1, 2011, journal entries assuming an interest rate of 10%.

•6 •7 BE21-10 Use the information for Indiana Jones Corporation from BE21-9. Assume that for Lost Ark Company, the lessor, the carrying amount of the machinery is $202,921. Prepare Lost Ark's January 1, 2011, journal entries.

•8 BE21-11 Buzz Lightyear Corporation manufactures replicators. On January 1, 2011, it leased to BoPeep Company a replicator that had cost £110,000 to manufacture. The lease agreement covers the 5-year useful life of the replicator and requires 5 equal annual rentals of £40,800 payable each January 1, beginning January 1, 2011. An interest rate of 12% is implicit in the lease agreement. Prepare Lightyear's January 1, 2011, journal entries.

•11 *BE21-12 On January 1, 2011, Iniesta Animation sold a truck to Robben Finance for €33,000 and immediately leased it back. The truck was carried on Iniesta's books at €28,000. The term of the lease is 5 years, and title transfers to Iniesta at lease-end. The lease requires five equal rental payments of €8,705 at the end of each year. The appropriate rate of interest is 10%, and the truck has a useful life of 5 years with no residual value. Prepare Iniesta's 2011 journal entries.

EXERCISES

•2 **E21-1** **(Lessee Entries, Finance Lease with Unguaranteed Residual Value)** On January 1, 2011, Adams Corporation signed a 5-year non-cancelable lease for a machine. The terms of the lease called for Adams to make annual payments of $9,968 at the beginning of each year, starting January 1, 2011. The machine has an estimated useful life of 6 years and a $5,000 unguaranteed residual value. The machine reverts back to the lessor at the end of the lease term. Adams uses the straight-line method of depreciation for all of its plant assets. Adams's incremental borrowing rate is 10%, and the lessor's implicit rate is unknown (it is impracticable to determine).

Instructions
  (a) What type of lease is this? Explain.
  (b) Compute the present value of the minimum lease payments.
  (c) Prepare all necessary journal entries for Adams for this lease through January 1, 2012.

•2 **E21-2** **(Lessee Computations and Entries, Finance Lease with Guaranteed Residual Value)** Brecker Company leases an automobile with a fair value of €10,906 from Emporia Motors, Inc., on the following terms:

  1. Non-cancelable term of 50 months.
  2. Rental of €250 per month (at end of each month). (The present value at 1% per month is €9,800.)
  3. Estimated residual value after 50 months is €1,180. (The present value at 1% per month is €715.) Brecker Company guarantees the residual value of €1,180.
  4. Estimated economic life of the automobile is 60 months.
  5. Brecker Company's incremental borrowing rate is 12% a year (1% a month). It is impracticable to determine Emporia's implicit rate.

Instructions
  (a) What is the nature of this lease to Brecker Company?
  (b) What is the present value of the minimum lease payments?
  (c) Record the lease on Brecker Company's books at the date of inception.
  (d) Record the first month's depreciation on Brecker Company's books (assume straight-line).
  (e) Record the first month's lease payment.

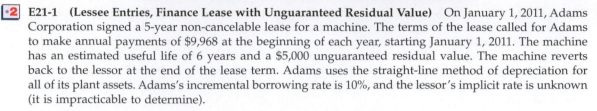

•2 •7 **E21-3** **(Lessee Entries, Finance Lease with Executory Costs and Unguaranteed Residual Value)** Assume that on January 1, 2011, **Stora Enso** (FIN) signs a 10-year non-cancelable lease agreement to lease a storage building from Balesteros Storage Company. The following information pertains to this lease agreement.

  1. The agreement requires equal rental payments of $90,000 beginning on January 1, 2011.
  2. The fair value of the building on January 1, 2011, is $550,000.
  3. The building has an estimated economic life of 12 years, with an unguaranteed residual value of $10,000. Stora Enso depreciates similar buildings on the straight-line method.
  4. The lease is non-renewable. At the termination of the lease, the building reverts to the lessor.
  5. Stora Enso's incremental borrowing rate is 12% per year. It is impracticable to determine the lessor's implicit rate.
  6. The yearly rental payment includes $3,088.14 of executory costs related to taxes on the property.

Instructions
Prepare the journal entries on the lessee's books to reflect the signing of the lease agreement and to record the payments and expenses related to this lease for the years 2011 and 2012. Stora Enso's corporate year-end is December 31.

•5 **E21-4** **(Lessor Entries, Direct-Financing Lease with Option to Purchase)** Krauss Leasing Company signs a lease agreement on January 1, 2011, to lease electronic equipment to Stewart Company. The term of the non-cancelable lease is 2 years, and payments are required at the end of each year. The following information relates to this agreement.

  1. Stewart has the option to purchase the equipment for £16,000 upon termination of the lease.
  2. The equipment has a cost and fair value of £240,000 to Krauss Leasing Company. The useful economic life is 2 years, with a residual value of £16,000.
  3. Stewart Company is required to pay £7,000 each year to the lessor for executory costs.
  4. Krauss Leasing Company desires to earn a return of 10% on its investment.

Instructions
  (a) Prepare the journal entries on the books of Krauss Leasing to reflect the payments received under the lease and to recognize income for the years 2011 and 2012.
  (b) Assuming that Stewart Company exercises its option to purchase the equipment on December 31, 2012, prepare the journal entry to reflect the sale on Krauss's books.

·2 ·3 **E21-5** **(Type of Lease, Amortization Schedule)** Jacobsen Leasing Company leases a new machine that has a cost and fair value of $75,000 to K. J. Choi Corporation on a 3-year non-cancelable contract. K. J. Choi Corporation agrees to assume all risks of normal ownership, including costs such as insurance, taxes, and maintenance. The machine has a 3-year useful life and no residual value. The lease was signed on January 1, 2011. Jacobsen Leasing Company expects to earn a 9% return on its investment. The annual rentals are payable on each December 31.

Instructions

(a) Discuss the nature of the lease arrangement and the accounting method that each party to the lease should apply.

(b) Prepare an amortization schedule that would be suitable for both the lessor and the lessee and that covers all the years involved.

·8 **E21-6** **(Lessor Entries, Sales-Type Lease)** Wadkins Company, a machinery dealer, leased a machine to Aoki Corporation on January 1, 2011. The lease is for an 8-year period and requires equal annual payments of ¥38,514,000 at the beginning of each year. The first payment is received on January 1, 2011. Wadkins had purchased the machine during 2010 for ¥170,000,000. Wadkins set the annual rental to ensure an 11% rate of return. The machine has an economic life of 8 years with no residual value and reverts to Wadkins at the termination of the lease.

Instructions

(a) Compute the amount of the lease receivable.

(b) Prepare all necessary journal entries for Wadkins for 2011.

·8 **E21-7** **(Lessee-Lessor Entries, Sales-Type Lease)** On January 1, 2011, Palmer Company leased equipment to Immelman Corporation. The following information pertains to this lease.

1. The term of the non-cancelable lease is 6 years, with no renewal option. The equipment reverts to the lessor at the termination of the lease.
2. Equal rental payments are due on January 1 of each year, beginning in 2011.
3. The fair value of the equipment on January 1, 2011, is $200,000, and its cost is $150,000.
4. The equipment has an economic life of 8 years, with an unguaranteed residual value of $10,000. Immelman depreciates all of its equipment on a straight-line basis.
5. Palmer sets the annual rental to ensure an 11% rate of return. Immelman's incremental borrowing rate is 12%, and it is impracticable for Immelman to determine the implicit rate.

Instructions

(Both the lessor and the lessee's accounting period ends on December 31.)

(a) Discuss the nature of this lease to Palmer and Immelman.

(b) Calculate the amount of the annual rental payment.

(c) Prepare all the necessary journal entries for Immelman for 2011.

(d) Prepare all the necessary journal entries for Palmer for 2011.

·6 ·7 **E21-8** **(Lessee Entries with Bargain-Purchase Option)** The following facts pertain to a non-cancelable lease agreement between Lennox Leasing Company and Gill Company, a lessee.

Inception date:	May 1, 2010
Annual lease payment due at the beginning of each year, beginning with May 1, 2010	€18,829.49
Bargain-purchase option price at end of lease term	€ 4,000.00
Lease term	5 years
Economic life of leased equipment	10 years
Lessor's cost	€65,000.00
Fair value of asset at May 1, 2010	€81,000.00
Lessor's implicit rate	10%
Lessee's incremental borrowing rate	10%

The lessee assumes responsibility for all executory costs.

Instructions

(Round all numbers to the nearest cent.)

(a) Discuss the nature of this lease to Gill Company.

(b) Discuss the nature of this lease to Lennox Company.

(c) Prepare a lease amortization schedule for Gill Company for the 5-year lease term.

(d) Prepare the journal entries on the lessee's books to reflect the signing of the lease agreement and to record the payments and expenses related to this lease for the years 2010 and 2011. Gill's annual accounting period ends on December 31. Reversing entries are used by Gill.

•8 **E21-9** **(Lessor Entries with Bargain-Purchase Option)** A lease agreement between Lennox Leasing Company and Gill Company is described in E21-8.

Instructions
Refer to the data in E21-8 and do the following for the lessor. (Round all numbers to the nearest cent.)

(a) Compute the amount of the lease receivable at the inception of the lease.
(b) Prepare a lease amortization schedule for Lennox Leasing Company for the 5-year lease term.
(c) Prepare the journal entries to reflect the signing of the lease agreement and to record the receipts and income related to this lease for the years 2010, 2011, and 2012. The lessor's accounting period ends on December 31. Reversing entries are not used by Lennox.

•5 **E21-10** **(Computation of Rental, Journal Entries for Lessor)** Fieval Leasing Company signs an agreement on January 1, 2010, to lease equipment to Reid Company. The following information relates to this agreement.

1. The term of the non-cancelable lease is 6 years with no renewal option. The equipment has an estimated economic life of 6 years.
2. The cost and fair value of the asset at January 1, 2010, is £343,000.
3. The asset will revert to the lessor at the end of the lease term, at which time the asset is expected to have a residual value of £61,071, none of which is guaranteed.
4. Reid Company assumes direct responsibility for all executory costs.
5. The agreement requires equal annual rental payments, beginning on January 1, 2010.

Instructions
(Round all numbers to the nearest cent.)

(a) Assuming the lessor desires a 10% rate of return on its investment, calculate the amount of the annual rental payment required. Round to the nearest pound.
(b) Prepare an amortization schedule that would be suitable for the lessor for the lease term.
(c) Prepare all of the journal entries for the lessor for 2010 and 2011 to record the lease agreement, the receipt of lease payments, and the recognition of income. Assume the lessor's annual accounting period ends on December 31.

•2 **E21-11 (Amortization Schedule and Journal Entries for Lessee)** Grady Leasing Company signs an agreement on January 1, 2010, to lease equipment to Azure Company. The following information relates to this agreement.

1. The term of the non-cancelable lease is 5 years with no renewal option. The equipment has an estimated economic life of 5 years.
2. The fair value of the asset at January 1, 2010, is $90,000.
3. The asset will revert to the lessor at the end of the lease term, at which time the asset is expected to have a residual value of $7,000, none of which is guaranteed.
4. Azure Company assumes direct responsibility for all executory costs, which include the following annual amounts: (1) $900 to Frontier Insurance Company for insurance and (2) $1,600 for property taxes.
5. The agreement requires equal annual rental payments of $20,541.11 to the lessor, beginning on January 1, 2010.
6. The lessee's incremental borrowing rate is 12%. The lessor's implicit rate is 10% and is known to the lessee.
7. Azure Company uses the straight-line depreciation method for all equipment.
8. Azure uses reversing entries when appropriate.

Instructions
(Round all numbers to the nearest cent.)

(a) Prepare an amortization schedule that would be suitable for the lessee for the lease term.
(b) Prepare all of the journal entries for the lessee for 2010 and 2011 to record the lease agreement, the lease payments, and all expenses related to this lease. Assume the lessee's annual accounting period ends on December 31.

•3 •4 **E21-12** **(Accounting for an Operating Lease)** On January 1, 2011, Secada Co. leased a building to Ryker Inc. The relevant information related to the lease is as follows.

1. The lease arrangement is for 10 years.
2. The leased building cost €3,600,000 and was purchased for cash on January 1, 2011.
3. The building is depreciated on a straight-line basis. Its estimated economic life is 50 years with no residual value.

4. Lease payments are €220,000 per year and are made at the end of the year.
5. Property tax expense of €85,000 and insurance expense of €10,000 on the building were incurred by Secada in the first year. Payment on these two items was made at the end of the year.
6. Both the lessor and the lessee are on a calendar-year basis.

Instructions

(a) Prepare the journal entries that Secada Co. should make in 2011.
(b) Prepare the journal entries that Ryker Inc. should make in 2011.
(c) If Secada paid €30,000 to a real estate broker on January 1, 2011, as a fee for finding the lessee, how much should be reported as an expense for this item in 2011 by Secada Co.?

•3 •4 E21-13 (Accounting for an Operating Lease) On January 1, 2011, a machine was purchased for $900,000 by Floyd Co. The machine is expected to have an 8-year life with no residual value. It is to be depreciated on a straight-line basis. The machine was leased to Crampton Inc. on January 1, 2011, at an annual rental of $180,000. Other relevant information is as follows.

1. The lease term is for 3 years.
2. Floyd Co. incurred maintenance and other executory costs of $25,000 in 2011 related to this lease.
3. The machine could have been sold by Floyd Co. for $940,000 instead of leasing it.
4. Crampton is required to pay a rent security deposit of $35,000 and to prepay the last month's rent of $15,000.

Instructions

(a) How much should Floyd Co. report as income before income tax on this lease for 2011?
(b) What amount should Crampton Inc. report for rent expense for 2011 on this lease?

•3 •4 E21-14 (Operating Lease for Lessee and Lessor) On February 20, 2011, Hooke Inc., purchased a machine for $1,200,000 for the purpose of leasing it. The machine is expected to have a 10-year life, no residual value, and will be depreciated on the straight-line basis. The machine was leased to Sage Company on March 1, 2011, for a 4-year period at a monthly rental of $15,600. There is no provision for the renewal of the lease or purchase of the machine by the lessee at the expiration of the lease term. Hooke paid $30,000 of commissions associated with negotiating the lease in February 2011.

Instructions

(a) What expense should Sage Company record as a result of the facts above for the year ended December 31, 2011? Show supporting computations in good form.
(b) What income or loss before income taxes should Hooke record as a result of the facts above for the year ended December 31, 2011? (*Hint:* Amortize commissions over the life of the lease.)

•11 *E21-15 (Sale-Leaseback) Assume that on January 1, 2011, Peking Duck Co. sells a computer system to Liquidity Finance Co. for ¥510,000 and immediately leases the computer system back. The relevant information is as follows.

1. The computer was carried on Peking's books at a value of ¥450,000.
2. The term of the non-cancelable lease is 10 years; title will transfer to Peking.
3. The lease agreement requires equal rental payments of ¥83,000.11 at the end of each year.
4. The incremental borrowing rate for Peking is 12%. Peking is aware that Liquidity Finance Co. set the annual rental to ensure a rate of return of 10%.
5. The computer has a fair value of ¥510,000 on January 1, 2011, and an estimated economic life of 10 years.
6. Peking pays executory costs of ¥9,000 per year.

Instructions

Prepare the journal entries for both the lessee and the lessor for 2011 to reflect the sale-leaseback agreement.

•11 *E21-16 (Lessee-Lessor, Sale-Leaseback) Presented below are four independent situations.

(a) On December 31, 2011, Beard Inc. sold computer equipment to Barber Co. and immediately leased it back for 10 years. The sales price of the equipment was $560,000, its carrying amount is $400,000, and its estimated remaining economic life is 12 years. Determine the amount of deferred revenue to be reported from the sale of the computer equipment on December 31, 2011.

(b) On December 31, 2011, Mikkelson Co. sold a machine to Ozaki Co. and simultaneously leased it back for one year. The sales price of the machine was $480,000, the carrying amount is $420,000, and it had an estimated remaining useful life of 14 years. The present value of the rental payments for the one year is $35,000. At December 31, 2011, how much should Mikkelson report as deferred revenue from the sale of the machine? Assume that the sale was at fair value.

(c) On January 1, 2011, Barone Corp. sold an airplane with an estimated useful life of 10 years. At the same time, Barone leased back the plane for 10 years. The sales price of the airplane was $500,000, the carrying amount $401,000, and the annual rental $73,975.22. Barone Corp. intends to depreciate the leased asset using the sum-of-the-years'-digits depreciation method. Discuss how the gain on the sale should be reported at the end of 2011 in the financial statements.

(d) On January 1, 2011, Durocher Co. sold equipment with an estimated useful life of 5 years. At the same time, Durocher leased back the equipment for 2 years under a lease classified as an operating lease. The sales price (fair value) of the equipment was $212,700, the carrying amount is $300,000, the monthly rental under the lease is $6,000, and the present value of the rental payments is $115,753. For the year ended December 31, 2011, determine which items would be reported on its income statement for the sale-leaseback transaction.

PROBLEMS

•2 •8 P21-1 (Lessee-Lessor Entries, Sales-Type Lease) Glaus Leasing Company agrees to lease machinery to Jensen Corporation on January 1, 2010. The following information relates to the lease agreement.

1. The term of the lease is 7 years with no renewal option, and the machinery has an estimated economic life of 9 years.
2. The cost of the machinery is $525,000, and the fair value of the asset on January 1, 2010, is $700,000.
3. At the end of the lease term, the asset reverts to the lessor. At the end of the lease term, the asset has a guaranteed residual value of $100,000. Jensen depreciates all of its equipment on a straight-line basis.
4. The lease agreement requires equal annual rental payments, beginning on January 1, 2010.
5. Glaus desires a 10% rate of return on its investments. Jensen's incremental borrowing rate is 11%, and it is impracticable to determine the lessor's implicit rate.

Instructions

(Assume the accounting period ends on December 31.)

(a) Discuss the nature of this lease for both the lessee and the lessor.
(b) Calculate the amount of the annual rental payment required.
(c) Compute the present value of the minimum lease payments.
(d) Prepare the journal entries Jensen would make in 2010 and 2011 related to the lease arrangement.
(e) Prepare the journal entries Glaus would make in 2010 and 2011.

•3 •4 P21-2 (Lessee-Lessor Entries, Operating Lease) Cancun Inc. leased a new crane to Abriendo Construction under a 5-year non-cancelable contract starting January 1, 2011. Terms of the lease require payments of $33,000 each January 1, starting January 1, 2011. Cancun will pay insurance, taxes, and maintenance charges on the crane, which has an estimated life of 12 years, a fair value of $240,000, and a cost to Cancun of $240,000. The estimated fair value of the crane is expected to be $45,000 at the end of the lease term. No bargain-purchase or -renewal options are included in the contract. Both Cancun and Abriendo adjust and close books annually at December 31. Abriendo's incremental borrowing rate is 10%, and Cancun's implicit interest rate of 9% is known to Abriendo.

Instructions

(a) Identify the type of lease involved and give reasons for your classification. Discuss the accounting treatment that should be applied by both the lessee and the lessor.
(b) Prepare all the entries related to the lease contract and leased asset for the year 2011 for the lessee and lessor, assuming the following amounts.
   (1) Insurance $500.
   (2) Taxes $2,000.
   (3) Maintenance $650.
   (4) Straight-line depreciation and residual value $15,000.
(c) Discuss what should be presented in the statement of financial position, the income statement, and the related notes of both the lessee and the lessor at December 31, 2011.

•2 •8 •9 P21-3 (Lessee-Lessor Entries, Financial Statement Presentation, Sales-Type Lease) Labron Industries and Ewing Inc. enter into an agreement that requires Ewing Inc. to build three diesel-electric engines to Labron's specifications. Upon completion of the engines, Labron has agreed to lease them for a period of 10 years and to assume all costs and risks of ownership. The lease is non-cancelable, becomes effective on January 1, 2011, and requires annual rental payments of $413,971 each January 1, starting January 1, 2011.

Labron's incremental borrowing rate is 10%. The implicit interest rate used by Ewing Inc. and known to Labron is 8%. The total cost of building the three engines is $2,600,000. The economic life of the engines is estimated to be 10 years, with residual value set at zero. Labron depreciates similar equipment on a straight-line basis. At the end of the lease, Labron assumes title to the engines.

Instructions

(Round all numbers to the nearest dollar.)

(a) Discuss the nature of this lease transaction from the viewpoints of both lessee and lessor.

(b) Prepare the journal entry or entries to record the transaction on January 1, 2011, on the books of Labron Industries.

(c) Prepare the journal entry or entries to record the transaction on January 1, 2011, on the books of Ewing Inc.

(d) Prepare the journal entries for both the lessee and lessor to record the first rental payment on January 1, 2011.

(e) Prepare the journal entries for both the lessee and lessor to record interest expense (revenue) at December 31, 2011. (Prepare a lease amortization schedule for 2 years.)

(f) Show the items and amounts that would be reported on the statement of financial position (not notes) at December 31, 2011, for both the lessee and the lessor.

·2·6·9 **P21-4** **(Statement of Financial Position and Income Statement Disclosure—Lessee)** The following facts pertain to a non-cancelable lease agreement between Alschuler Leasing Company and McKee Electronics, a lessee, for a computer system.

Inception date	October 1, 2010
Lease term	6 years
Economic life of leased equipment	6 years
Fair value of asset at October 1, 2010	£300,383
Residual value at end of lease term	–0–
Lessor's implicit rate	10%
Lessee's incremental borrowing rate	10%
Annual lease payment due at the beginning of each year, beginning with October 1, 2010	£62,700

The lessee assumes responsibility for all executory costs, which amount to £5,500 per year and are to be paid each October 1, beginning October 1, 2010. (This £5,500 is not included in the rental payment of £62,700.) The asset will revert to the lessor at the end of the lease term. The straight-line depreciation method is used for all equipment.

The following amortization schedule has been prepared correctly for use by both the lessor and the lessee in accounting for this lease. The lease is to be accounted for properly as a finance lease by the lessee and as a direct-financing lease by the lessor.

Date	Annual Lease Payment/ Receipt	Interest (10%) on Unpaid Liability/Receivable	Reduction of Lease Liability/Receivable	Balance of Lease Liability/Receivable
10/01/10				£300,383
10/01/10	£ 62,700		£ 62,700	237,683
10/01/11	62,700	£23,768	38,932	198,751
10/01/12	62,700	19,875	42,825	155,926
10/01/13	62,700	15,593	47,107	108,819
10/01/14	62,700	10,822	51,818	57,001
10/01/15	62,700	5,699*	57,001	–0–
	£376,200	£75,817	£300,383	

*Rounding error is £1.

Instructions

(Round all numbers to the nearest cent.)

(a) Assuming the lessee's accounting period ends on September 30, answer the following questions with respect to this lease agreement.

(1) What items and amounts will appear on the lessee's income statement for the year ending September 30, 2011?

(2) What items and amounts will appear on the lessee's statement of financial position at September 30, 2011?

   (3) What items and amounts will appear on the lessee's income statement for the year ending September 30, 2012?

   (4) What items and amounts will appear on the lessee's statement of financial position at September 30, 2012?

  (b) Assuming the lessee's accounting period ends on December 31, answer the following questions with respect to this lease agreement.

   (1) What items and amounts will appear on the lessee's income statement for the year ending December 31, 2010?

   (2) What items and amounts will appear on the lessee's statement of financial position at December 31, 2010?

   (3) What items and amounts will appear on the lessee's income statement for the year ending December 31, 2011?

   (4) What items and amounts will appear on the lessee's statement of financial position at December 31, 2011?

•5 •9 P21-5 (Statement of Financial Position and Income Statement Disclosure—Lessor) Assume the same information as in P21-4.

Instructions
(Round all numbers to the nearest cent.)

  (a) Assuming the lessor's accounting period ends on September 30, answer the following questions with respect to this lease agreement.

   (1) What items and amounts will appear on the lessor's income statement for the year ending September 30, 2011?

   (2) What items and amounts will appear on the lessor's statement of financial position at September 30, 2011?

   (3) What items and amounts will appear on the lessor's income statement for the year ending September 30, 2012?

   (4) What items and amounts will appear on the lessor's statement of financial position at September 30, 2012?

  (b) Assuming the lessor's accounting period ends on December 31, answer the following questions with respect to this lease agreement.

   (1) What items and amounts will appear on the lessor's income statement for the year ending December 31, 2010?

   (2) What items and amounts will appear on the lessor's statement of financial position at December 31, 2010?

   (3) What items and amounts will appear on the lessor's income statement for the year ending December 31, 2011?

   (4) What items and amounts will appear on the lessor's statement of financial position at December 31, 2011?

•2 •7 P21-6 (Lessee Entries with Residual Value) The following facts pertain to a non-cancelable lease agreement between Faldo Leasing Company and Shigeki Company, a lessee.

Inception date	January 1, 2010
Annual lease payment due at the beginning of each year, beginning with January 1, 2010	€124,798
Residual value of equipment at end of lease term, guaranteed by the lessee	€50,000
Lease term	6 years
Economic life of leased equipment	6 years
Fair value of asset at January 1, 2010	€600,000
Lessor's implicit rate	12%
Lessee's incremental borrowing rate	12%

The lessee assumes responsibility for all executory costs, which are expected to amount to €5,000 per year. The asset will revert to the lessor at the end of the lease term. The lessee has guaranteed the lessor a residual value of €50,000. The lessee uses the straight-line depreciation method for all equipment.

Instructions
(Round all numbers to the nearest cent.)

  (a) Prepare an amortization schedule that would be suitable for the lessee for the lease term.

  (b) Prepare all of the journal entries for the lessee for 2010 and 2011 to record the lease agreement, the lease payments, and all expenses related to this lease. Assume the lessee's annual accounting period ends on December 31 and reversing entries are used when appropriate.

P21-7 **(Lessee Entries and Statement of Financial Position Presentation, Finance Lease)** Ludwick Steel Company as lessee signed a lease agreement for equipment for 5 years, beginning December 31, 2010. Annual rental payments of $40,000 are to be made at the beginning of each lease year (December 31). The taxes, insurance, and the maintenance costs are the obligation of the lessee. The interest rate used by the lessor in setting the payment schedule is 9%; Ludwick's incremental borrowing rate is 10%. It is impracticable for Ludwick to determine the rate being used by the lessor. At the end of the lease, Ludwick has the option to buy the equipment for $1, considerably below its estimated fair value at that time. The equipment has an estimated useful life of 7 years, with no residual value. Ludwick uses the straight-line method of depreciation on similar owned equipment.

Instructions
(Round all numbers to the nearest dollar.)

(a) Prepare the journal entry or entries, with explanations, that should be recorded on December 31, 2010, by Ludwick.

(b) Prepare the journal entry or entries, with explanations, that should be recorded on December 31, 2011, by Ludwick. (Prepare the lease amortization schedule for all five payments.)

(c) Prepare the journal entry or entries, with explanations, that should be recorded on December 31, 2012, by Ludwick.

(d) What amounts would appear on Ludwick's December 31, 2012, statement of financial position relative to the lease arrangement?

P21-8 **(Lessee Entries and Statement of Financial Position Presentation, Finance Lease)** On January 1, 2011, Cage Company contracts to lease equipment for 5 years, agreeing to make a payment of $137,899 (including the executory costs of $6,000) at the beginning of each year, starting January 1, 2011. The taxes, the insurance, and the maintenance, estimated at $6,000 a year, are the obligations of the lessee. The leased equipment is to be capitalized at $550,000. The asset is to be depreciated on a double-declining-balance basis, and the obligation is to be reduced on an effective-interest basis. Cage's incremental borrowing rate is 12%, and the implicit rate in the lease is 10%, which is known by Cage. Title to the equipment transfers to Cage when the lease expires. The asset has an estimated useful life of 5 years and no residual value.

Instructions
(Round all numbers to the nearest dollar.)

(a) Explain the probable relationship of the $550,000 amount to the lease arrangement.

(b) Prepare the journal entry or entries that should be recorded on January 1, 2011, by Cage Company.

(c) Prepare the journal entry to record depreciation of the leased asset for the year 2011.

(d) Prepare the journal entry to record the interest expense for the year 2011.

(e) Prepare the journal entry to record the lease payment of January 1, 2012, assuming reversing entries are not made.

(f) What amounts will appear on the lessee's December 31, 2011, statement of financial position relative to the lease contract?

P21-9 **(Lessee Entries, Finance Lease with Monthly Payments)** Shapiro Inc. was incorporated in 2010 to operate as a computer software service firm with an accounting fiscal year ending August 31. Shapiro's primary product is a sophisticated online inventory-control system; its customers pay a fixed fee plus a usage charge for using the system.

Shapiro has leased a large, Alpha-3 computer system from the manufacturer. The lease calls for a monthly rental of €40,000 for the 144 months (12 years) of the lease term. The estimated useful life of the computer is 15 years.

Each scheduled monthly rental payment includes €3,000 for full-service maintenance on the computer to be performed by the manufacturer. All rentals are payable on the first day of the month beginning with August 1, 2011, the date the computer was installed and the lease agreement was signed. The lease is non-cancelable for its 12-year term, and it is secured only by the manufacturer's chattel lien on the Alpha-3 system.

This lease is to be accounted for as a finance lease by Shapiro, and it will be depreciated by the straight-line method with no expected residual value. Borrowed funds for this type of transaction would cost Shapiro 12% per year (1% per month). Following is a schedule of the present value of €1 for selected periods discounted at 1% per period when payments are made at the beginning of each period.

Periods (months)	Present Value of €1 per Period Discounted at 1% per Period
1	1.000
2	1.990
3	2.970
143	76.658
144	76.899

Instructions

Prepare, in general journal form, all entries Shapiro should have made in its accounting records during August 2011 relating to this lease. Give full explanations and show supporting computations for each entry. Remember, August 31, 2011, is the end of Shapiro's fiscal accounting period and it will be preparing financial statements on that date. Do not prepare closing entries.

P21-10 (Lessor Computations and Entries, Sales-Type Lease with Unguaranteed Residual Value) Moonstruck Company manufactures a reservation system with an estimated economic life of 12 years and leases it to National Airlines for a period of 10 years. The normal selling price of the equipment is $278,072, and its unguaranteed residual value at the end of the lease term is estimated to be $20,000. National will pay annual payments of $40,000 at the beginning of each year and all maintenance, insurance, and taxes. Moonstruck incurred costs of $180,000 in manufacturing the equipment and $4,000 in negotiating and closing the lease. Moonstruck has determined that the implicit interest rate is 10%.

Instructions

(Round all numbers to the nearest dollar.)

(a) Discuss the nature of this lease in relation to the lessor and compute the amount of each of the following items.
   (1) Lease receivable.
   (2) Sales price.
   (3) Cost of sales.
(b) Prepare a 10-year lease amortization schedule.
(c) Prepare all of the lessor's journal entries for the first year.

P21-11 (Lessee Computations and Entries, Finance Lease with Unguaranteed Residual Value) Assume the same data as in P21-10 with National Airlines Co. having an incremental borrowing rate of 10%.

Instructions

(Round all numbers to the nearest dollar.)

(a) Discuss the nature of this lease in relation to the lessee, and compute the amount of the initial obligation under finance leases.
(b) Prepare a 10-year lease amortization schedule.
(c) Prepare all of the lessee's journal entries for the first year.

P21-12 (Basic Lessee Accounting with Difficult PV Calculation) In 2009, Grishell Shipping Company negotiated and closed a long-term lease contract for newly constructed truck terminals and freight storage facilities. The buildings were erected to the company's specifications on land owned by the company. On January 1, 2010, Grishell Shipping Company took possession of the lease properties. On January 1, 2010 and 2011, the company made cash payments of £948,000 that were recorded as rental expenses.

Although the terminals have a composite useful life of 40 years, the non-cancelable lease runs for 20 years from January 1, 2010, with a bargain-purchase option available upon expiration of the lease.

The 20-year lease is effective for the period January 1, 2010, through December 31, 2029. Advance rental payments of £800,000 are payable to the lessor on January 1 of each of the first 10 years of the lease term. Advance rental payments of £320,000 are due on January 1 for each of the last 10 years of the lease. The company has an option to purchase all of these leased facilities for £1 on December 31, 2029. It also must make annual payments to the lessor of £125,000 for property taxes and £23,000 for insurance. The lease was negotiated to assure the lessor a 6% rate of return.

Instructions

(Round all numbers to the nearest pound.)

(a) Prepare a schedule to compute for Grishell Shipping Company the discounted present value of the terminal facilities and related obligation at January 1, 2010.
(b) Assuming that the discounted present value of terminal facilities and related obligation at January 1, 2010, was £7,600,000, prepare journal entries for Grishell Shipping Company to record the:
   (1) Cash payment to the lessor on January 1, 2012.
   (2) Amortization of the cost of the leased properties for 2012 using the straight-line method and assuming a zero residual value.
   (3) Accrual of interest expense at December 31, 2012.

Selected present value factors are as follows.

Periods	For an Ordinary Annuity of £1 at 6%	For £1 at 6%
1	.943396	.943396
2	1.833393	.889996
8	6.209794	.627412
9	6.801692	.591898
10	7.360087	.558395
19	11.158117	.330513
20	11.469921	.311805

•4 •7 •8 P21-13 (Lessor Computations and Entries, Sales-Type Lease with Guaranteed Residual Value)
Amirante Inc. manufactures an X-ray machine with an estimated life of 12 years and leases it to Chambers Medical Center for a period of 10 years. The normal selling price of the machine is $411,324, and its guaranteed residual value at the end of the non-cancelable lease term is estimated to be $15,000. The hospital will pay rents of $60,000 at the beginning of each year and all maintenance, insurance, and taxes. Amirante Inc. incurred costs of $250,000 in manufacturing the machine and $14,000 in negotiating and closing the lease. Amirante Inc. has determined that the implicit interest rate is 10%.

Instructions
(Round all numbers to the nearest dollar.)

(a) Discuss the nature of this lease in relation to the lessor and compute the amount of each of the following items.
   (1) Lease receivable at inception of the lease.
   (2) Sales price.
   (3) Cost of sales.
(b) Prepare a 10-year lease amortization schedule.
(c) Prepare all of the lessor's journal entries for the first year.

•2 •7 P21-14 (Lessee Computations and Entries, Finance Lease with Guaranteed Residual Value) Assume the same data as in P21-13 and that Chambers Medical Center has an incremental borrowing rate of 10%.

Instructions
(Round all numbers to the nearest dollar.)

(a) Discuss the nature of this lease in relation to the lessee, and compute the amount of the initial obligation under finance leases.
(b) Prepare a 10-year lease amortization schedule.
(c) Prepare all of the lessee's journal entries for the first year.

•2 •3 •7 P21-15 (Operating Lease vs. Finance Lease) You are auditing the December 31, 2011, financial statements of Hockney, Inc., manufacturer of novelties and party favors. During your inspection of the company garage, you discovered that a 2010 Shirk automobile not listed in the equipment subsidiary ledger is parked in the company garage. You ask Stacy Reeder, plant manager, about the vehicle, and she tells you that the company did not list the automobile because the company was only leasing it. The lease agreement was entered into on January 1, 2011, with Crown New and Used Cars.

You decide to review the lease agreement to ensure that the lease should be afforded operating lease treatment, and you discover the following lease terms.

1. Non-cancelable term of 4 years.
2. Rental of $3,240 per year (at the end of each year). (The present value at 8% per year is $10,731.)
3. Estimated residual value after 4 years is $1,100. (The present value at 8% per year is $809.) Hockney guarantees the residual value of $1,100.
4. Estimated economic life of the automobile is 5 years.
5. The implicit rate and Hockney's incremental borrowing rate is 8% per year.

Instructions
You are a senior auditor writing a memo to your supervisor, the audit partner in charge of this audit, to discuss the above situation. Be sure to include (a) why you inspected the lease agreement, (b) what you determined about the lease, and (c) how you advised your client to account for this lease. Explain every journal entry that you believe is necessary to record this lease properly on the client's books. (It is also necessary to include the fact that you communicated this information to your client.)

·2··4··7· P21-16 (Lessee-Lessor Accounting for Residual Values) Goring Dairy leases its milking equipment from King Finance Company under the following lease terms.

1. The lease term is 10 years, non-cancelable, and requires equal rental payments of €30,300 due at the beginning of each year starting January 1, 2011.
2. The equipment has a fair value and cost at the inception of the lease (January 1, 2011) of €220,404, an estimated economic life of 10 years, and a residual value (which is guaranteed by Goring Dairy) of €20,000.
3. The lease contains no renewable options, and the equipment reverts to King Finance Company upon termination of the lease.
4. Goring Dairy's incremental borrowing rate is 9% per year. The implicit rate is also 9%.
5. Goring Dairy depreciates similar equipment that it owns on a straight-line basis.

Instructions

(a) Evaluate the criteria for classification of the lease, and describe the nature of the lease. In general, discuss how the lessee and lessor should account for the lease transaction.

(b) Prepare the journal entries for the lessee and lessor at January 1, 2011, and December 31, 2011 (the lessee's and lessor's year-end). Assume no reversing entries.

(c) What would have been the amount capitalized by the lessee upon the inception of the lease if:
  (1) The residual value of €20,000 had been guaranteed by a third party, not the lessee?
  (2) The residual value of €20,000 had not been guaranteed at all?

(d) On the lessor's books, what would be the amount recorded as the Net Investment (Lease Receivable) at the inception of the lease, assuming:
  (1) The residual value of €20,000 had been guaranteed by a third party?
  (2) The residual value of €20,000 had not been guaranteed at all?

(e) Suppose the useful life of the milking equipment is 20 years. How large would the residual value have to be at the end of 10 years in order for the lessee to qualify for the operating method? (Assume that the residual value would be guaranteed by a third party.) (*Hint*: The lessee's annual payments will be appropriately reduced as the residual value increases.)

CONCEPTS FOR ANALYSIS

CA21-1 (Lessee Accounting and Reporting) On January 1, 2011, Evans Company entered into a non-cancelable lease for a machine to be used in its manufacturing operations. The lease transfers ownership of the machine to Evans by the end of the lease term. The term of the lease is 8 years. The minimum lease payment made by Evans on January 1, 2011, was one of eight equal annual payments. At the inception of the lease, the criteria established for classification as a finance lease by the lessee were met.

Instructions

(a) What is the theoretical basis for the accounting standard that requires certain long-term leases to be capitalized by the lessee? Do not discuss the specific criteria for classifying a specific lease as a finance lease.

(b) How should Evans account for this lease at its inception and determine the amount to be recorded?

(c) What expenses related to this lease will Evans incur during the first year of the lease, and how will they be determined?

(d) How should Evans report the lease transaction on its December 31, 2011, statement of financial position?

CA21-2 (Lessor and Lessee Accounting and Disclosure) Sylvan Inc. entered into a non-cancelable lease arrangement with Breton Leasing Corporation for a certain machine. Breton's primary business is leasing; it is not a manufacturer or dealer. Sylvan will lease the machine for a period of 3 years, which is 50% of the machine's economic life. Breton will take possession of the machine at the end of the initial 3-year lease and lease it to another, smaller company that does not need the most current version of the machine. Sylvan does not guarantee any residual value for the machine and will not purchase the machine at the end of the lease term.

Sylvan's incremental borrowing rate is 10%, and the implicit rate in the lease is 9%. Sylvan has no practicable way to determine the implicit rate used by Breton. Using either rate, the present value of the minimum lease payments is between 90% and 100% of the fair value of the machine at the date of the lease agreement.

Sylvan has agreed to pay all executory costs directly, and no allowance for these costs is included in the lease payments.

Assume that no indirect costs are involved.

Instructions

(a) With respect to Sylvan (the lessee), answer the following.
  (1) What type of lease has been entered into? Explain the reason for your answer.
  (2) How should Sylvan compute the appropriate amount to be recorded for the lease or asset acquired?
  (3) What accounts will be created or affected by this transaction, and how will the lease or asset and other costs related to the transaction be recorded in earnings?
  (4) What disclosures must Sylvan make regarding this leased asset?

(b) With respect to Breton (the lessor), answer the following.
  (1) What type of leasing arrangement has been entered into? Explain the reason for your answer.
  (2) How should this lease be recorded by Breton, and how are the appropriate amounts determined?
  (3) How should Breton determine the appropriate amount of earnings to be recognized from each lease payment?
  (4) What disclosures must Breton make regarding this lease?

CA21-3 **(Lessee Capitalization Criteria)** On January 1, Santiago Company, a lessee, entered into three non-cancelable leases for brand-new equipment, Lease L, Lease M, and Lease N. None of the three leases transfers ownership of the equipment to Santiago at the end of the lease term. For each of the three leases, the present value at the beginning of the lease term of the minimum lease payments, excluding that portion of the payments representing executory costs such as insurance, maintenance, and taxes to be paid by the lessor, is 75% of the fair value of the equipment.

The following information is peculiar to each lease.

1. Lease L does not contain a bargain-purchase option. The lease term is equal to 85% of the estimated economic life of the equipment.
2. Lease M contains a bargain-purchase option. The lease term is equal to 50% of the estimated economic life of the equipment.
3. Lease N does not contain a bargain-purchase option. The lease term is equal to 50% of the estimated economic life of the equipment.

Instructions

(a) How should Santiago Company classify each of the three leases above, and why? Discuss the rationale for your answer.
(b) What amount, if any, should Santiago record as a liability at the inception of the lease for each of the three leases above?
(c) Assuming that the minimum lease payments are made on a straight-line basis, how should Santiago record each minimum lease payment for each of the three leases above?

CA21-4 **(Comparison of Different Types of Accounting by Lessee and Lessor)**

Part 1
Finance leases and operating leases are the two classifications of leases described in IFRS from the standpoint of the **lessee**.

Instructions

(a) Describe how a finance lease would be accounted for by the lessee both at the inception of the lease and during the first year of the lease, assuming the lease transfers ownership of the property to the lessee by the end of the lease.
(b) Describe how an operating lease would be accounted for by the lessee both at the inception of the lease and during the first year of the lease, assuming equal monthly payments are made by the lessee at the beginning of each month of the lease.

Do **not** discuss the criteria for distinguishing between finance leases and operating leases.

Part 2

Sales-type leases and direct-financing leases are two of the classifications of leases described in IFRS from the standpoint of the **lessor**.

Instructions

Compare and contrast a sales-type lease with a direct-financing lease as follows.

(a) Lease receivable.
(b) Recognition of interest revenue.
(c) Manufacturer's or dealer's profit.

Do **not** discuss the criteria for distinguishing between the leases described above and operating leases.

CA21-5 (Lessee Capitalization of Bargain-Purchase Option) Albertsen Corporation is a diversified company with nationwide interests in commercial real estate developments, banking, copper mining, and metal fabrication. The company has offices and operating locations in major cities throughout the United Kingdom. Corporate headquarters for Albertsen Corporation is located in a metropolitan area of The Lake District, and executives connected with various phases of company operations travel extensively. Corporate management is currently evaluating the feasibility of acquiring a business aircraft that can be used by company executives to expedite business travel to areas not adequately served by commercial airlines. Proposals for either leasing or purchasing a suitable aircraft have been analyzed, and the leasing proposal was considered to be more desirable.

The proposed lease agreement involves a twin-engine turboprop Viking that has a fair value of £1,000,000. This plane would be leased for a period of 10 years beginning January 1, 2011. The lease agreement is cancelable only upon accidental destruction of the plane. An annual lease payment of £141,780 is due on January 1 of each year; the first payment is to be made on January 1, 2011. Maintenance operations are strictly scheduled by the lessor, and Albertsen Corporation will pay for these services as they are performed. Estimated annual maintenance costs are £6,900. The lessor will pay all insurance premiums and local property taxes, which amount to a combined total of £4,000 annually and are included in the annual lease payment of £141,780. Upon expiration of the 10-year lease, Albertsen Corporation can purchase the Viking for £44,440. The estimated useful life of the plane is 15 years, and its residual value in the used plane market is estimated to be £100,000 after 10 years. The residual value probably will never be less than £75,000 if the engines are overhauled and maintained as prescribed by the manufacturer. If the purchase option is not exercised, possession of the plane will revert to the lessor, and there is no provision for renewing the lease agreement beyond its termination on December 31, 2020.

Albertsen Corporation can borrow £1,000,000 under a 10-year term loan agreement at an annual interest rate of 12%. The lessor's implicit interest rate is not expressly stated in the lease agreement, but this rate appears to be approximately 8% based on 10 net rental payments of £137,780 per year and the initial fair value of £1,000,000 for the plane. On January 1, 2011, the present value of all net rental payments and the purchase option of £44,440 is £888,890 using the 12% interest rate. The present value of all net rental payments and the £44,440 purchase option on January 1, 2011, is £1,022,226 using the 8% interest rate implicit in the lease agreement. The financial vice president of Albertsen Corporation has established that this lease agreement is a finance lease as defined in IFRS.

Instructions

(a) What is the appropriate amount that Albertsen Corporation should recognize for the leased aircraft on its statement of financial position after the lease is signed?
(b) Without prejudice to your answer in part (a), assume that the annual lease payment is £141,780 as stated in the question, that the appropriate capitalized amount for the leased aircraft is £1,000,000 on January 1, 2011, and that the interest rate is 9%. How will the lease be reported in the December 31, 2011, statement of financial position and related income statement? (Ignore any tax implications.)

CA21-6 (Lease Capitalization, Bargain-Purchase Option) Baden Corporation entered into a lease agreement for 10 photocopy machines for its corporate headquarters. The lease agreement qualifies as an operating lease in all terms except there is a bargain-purchase option. After the 5-year lease term, the corporation can purchase each copier for $1,000, when the anticipated fair value is $2,500.

Jerry Suffolk, the financial vice president, thinks the financial statements must recognize the lease agreement as a finance lease because of the bargain-purchase agreement. The controller, Diane Buchanan, disagrees: "Although I don't know much about the copiers themselves, there is a way to avoid recording the lease liability." She argues that the corporation might claim that copier technology advances rapidly and that by the end of the lease term the machines will most likely not be worth the $1,000 bargain price.

Instructions

Answer the following questions.

    (a) What ethical issue is at stake?

    (b) Should the controller's argument be accepted if she does not really know much about copier technology? Would it make a difference if the controller were knowledgeable about the pace of change in copier technology?

    (c) What should Suffolk do?

*CA21-7 (Sale-Leaseback) On January 1, 2011, Perriman Company sold equipment for cash and leased it back. As seller-lessee, Perriman retained the right to substantially all of the remaining use of the equipment.

    The term of the lease is 8 years. There is a gain on the sale portion of the transaction. The lease portion of the transaction is classified appropriately as a finance lease.

Instructions

    (a) What is the theoretical basis for requiring lessees to capitalize certain long-term leases? **Do not discuss the specific criteria for classifying a lease as a finance lease.**

    (b) **(1)** How should Perriman account for the sale portion of the sale-leaseback transaction at January 1, 2011?

        (2) How should Perriman account for the leaseback portion of the sale-leaseback transaction at January 1, 2011?

    (c) How should Perriman account for the gain on the sale portion of the sale-leaseback transaction during the first year of the lease? Why?

*CA21-8 (Sale-Leaseback) On December 31, 2010, Shellhammer Co. sold 6-month-old equipment at fair value and leased it back. There was a loss on the sale. Shellhammer pays all insurance, maintenance, and taxes on the equipment. The lease provides for 8 equal annual payments, beginning December 31, 2011, with a present value equal to 80% of the equipment's fair value and sales price. The lease's term is 85% of the equipment's useful life. There is no provision for Shellhammer to reacquire ownership of the equipment at the end of the lease term.

Instructions

    (a) **(1)** Why is it important to compare an equipment's fair value to its lease payments' present value and its useful life to the lease term?

        (2) Evaluate Shellhammer's leaseback of the equipment in terms of each of the four criteria for determination of a finance lease.

    (b) How should Shellhammer account for the sale portion of the sale-leaseback transaction at December 31, 2010?

    (c) How should Shellhammer report the leaseback portion of the sale-leaseback transaction on its December 31, 2011, statement of financial position?

USING YOUR JUDGMENT

FINANCIAL REPORTING

Financial Reporting Problem

Marks and Spencer plc (M&S)

The financial statements of **M&S** are presented in Appendix 5B or can be accessed at the book's companion website, **www.wiley.com/college/kiesoifrs**.

Instructions

Refer to M&S's financial statements and the accompanying notes to answer the following questions.

    (a) What types of leases are used by M&S?

    (b) What amount of finance leases was reported by M&S in total and for less than one year?

    (c) What minimum annual rental commitments under all non-cancelable leases at March 29, 2008, did M&S disclose?

Comparative Analysis Case

British Airways and Air France

Instructions

Go to the **British Airways** (GBR) and **Air France** (FRA) company websites and use information found there to answer the following questions related to these airlines.

(a) What types of leases are used by Air France and on what assets are these leases primarily used?

(b) How long-term are some of Air France's leases? What are some of the characteristics or provisions of Air France's (as lessee) leases?

(c) What did Air France report in 2009 as its future minimum annual rental commitments under non-cancelable leases?

(d) At year-end 2009, what was the present value of the minimum rental payments under Air France's finance leases? How much imputed interest was deducted from the future minimum annual rental commitments to arrive at the present value?

(e) What were the amounts and details reported by Air France for rental expense in 2009 and 2008?

(f) How does British Air's use of leases compare with Air France's?

Financial Statement Analysis Case

Delhaize Group

Presented in Illustration 21-30 are the financial statement disclosures from the 2008 annual report of **Delhaize Group** (BEL).

Instructions

Answer the following questions related to these disclosures.

(a) What is the total obligation under finance leases at year-end 2008 for Delhaize?

(b) What is the total rental expense reported for leasing activity for the year ended December 31, 2008, for Delhaize?

(c) Estimate the off–balance-sheet liability due to Delhaize operating leases at fiscal year-end 2008.

Accounting, Analysis, and Principles

Salaur Company is evaluating a lease arrangement being offered by TSP Company for use of a computer system. The lease is non-cancelable, and in no case does Salaur receive title to the computers during or at the end of the lease term. The lease starts on January 1, 2011, with the first rental due at the beginning of the year. Additional information related to the lease is as follows.

Yearly rental	$3,557.25
Lease term	3 years
Estimated economic life	5 years
Purchase option	$3,000 at end of 3 years, which approximates fair value
Renewal option	1 year at $1,500; no penalty for non-renewal; standard renewal clause
Fair value at inception of lease	$10,000
Cost of asset to lessor	$10,000
Residual value	
Guaranteed	–0–
Unguaranteed	$3,000
Lessor's implicit rate (known by lessee)	12%
Executory costs paid by:	Lessee; estimated to be $500 per year
Estimated fair value at end of lease	$3,000

Accounting

Analyze the lease capitalization criteria for this lease for Salaur Company. Prepare the journal entry for Salaur on January 1, 2011.

Analysis

Briefly discuss the impact of the accounting for this lease for two common ratios: return on assets and debt to total assets.

Principles

What fundamental quality of the conceptual framework is being addressed when a company like Salaur evaluates lease capitalization criteria?

BRIDGE TO THE PROFESSION

Professional Research

Daniel Hardware Co. is considering alternative financing arrangements for equipment used in its warehouses. Besides purchasing the equipment outright, Daniel is also considering a lease. Accounting for the outright purchase is fairly straightforward, but because Daniel has not used equipment leases in the past, the accounting staff is less informed about the specific accounting rules for leases.

The staff is aware of some general lease rules related to "risks and rewards," but they are unsure about the meanings of these terms in lease accounting. Daniel has asked you to conduct some research on these items related to lease capitalization criteria.

Instructions

Access the IFRS authoritative literature at the IASB website (*http://eifrs.iasb.org/*). When you have accessed the documents, you can use the search tool in your Internet browser to respond to the following questions. (Provide paragraph citations.)

(a) What is the objective of lease classification criteria?

(b) An important element of evaluating leases is determining whether substantially all of the risks and rewards of ownership are transferred in the lease. How is "substantially all" defined in the authoritative literature?

(c) Besides the non-cancelable term of the lease, name at least three other considerations in determining the "lease term."

Professional Simulations

Simulation 1

In this simulation, you are asked to address questions related to the accounting for leases. Prepare responses to all parts.

KWW_Professional _Simulation

Accounting for Leases | Time Remaining 2 hours 00 minutes | copy | paste | calculator | sheet | standards | help | splitter | done

| Directions | Situation | Explanation | Research | Resources |

Assume that the following facts pertain to a non-cancelable lease agreement between Fifth-Third Leasing Company and Evans Farms, a lessee.

Inception date	January 1, 2010
Annual lease payment due at the beginning of each year, beginning with January 1, 2010	$81,365
Residual value of equipment at end of lease term, guaranteed by the lessee	$50,000
Lease term	6 years
Economic life of leased equipment	6 years
Fair value of asset at January 1. 2010	$400,000
Lessor's implicit rate	12%
Lessee's incremental borrowing rate	12%

The lessee assumes responsibility for all executory costs, which are expected to amount to $4,000 per year. The asset will revert to the lessor at the end of the lease term. The lessee has guaranteed the lessor a residual value of $50,000. The lessee uses the straight-line depreciation method for all equipment.

| Directions | Situation | Explanation | Research | Resources |

Use a computer spreadsheet to prepare an amortization schedule that would be suitable for the lessee for the lease term.

| Directions | Situation | Explanation | Research | Resources |

Prepare the journal entries for the lessee for 2010 and 2011 to record the lease agreement and all expenses related to the lease. Assume the lessee's annual accounting period ends on December 31 and that reversing entries are used when appropriate. (Round amounts to nearest dollar.)

Simulation 2

In this simulation, you are asked to address questions related to the accounting for leases. Prepare responses to all parts.

KWW_Professional _Simulation

| **Accounting for Leases** | **Time Remaining**
 1 hours 40 minutes | copy | paste | calculator | sheet | standards | help | splitter | done |

| Directions | Situation | Explanation | Measurement | Journal Entries | Resources |

On January 1, 2010, Dexter Labs. Inc. signed a 5-year non-cancelable lease for a machine. The terms of the lease called for Dexter to make annual payments of $8,668 at the beginning of each year, starting January 1, 2010. The machine has an estimated useful life of 6 years and a $5,000 unguaranteed residual value. The machine reverts back to the lessor at the end of the lease term. Dexter uses the straight-line method of depreciation for all of its plant assets. Dexter's incremental borrowing rate is 10%, and the lessor's implicit rate is unknown.

| Directions | Situation | Explanation | Measurement | Journal Entries | Resources |

What type of lease is this? Explain.

| Directions | Situation | Explanation | Measurement | Journal Entries | Resources |

Compute the present value of the minimum lease payments.

| Directions | Situation | Explanation | Measurement | Journal Entries | Resources |

Prepare all necessary journal entries for Dexter Labs. Inc. for this lease through January 1, 2011.

Remember to check the book's companion website to find additional resources for this chapter.

www.wiley.com/college/kiesoifrs

CHAPTER 22

ACCOUNTING CHANGES AND ERROR ANALYSIS

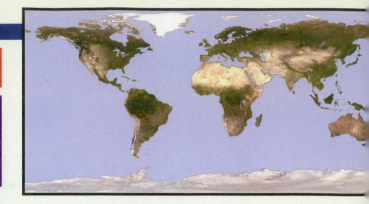

LEARNING OBJECTIVES

After studying this chapter, you should be able to:

•1 Identify the two types of accounting changes.

•2 Describe the accounting for changes in accounting policies.

•3 Understand how to account for retrospective accounting changes.

•4 Understand how to account for impracticable changes.

•5 Describe the accounting for changes in estimates.

•6 Describe the accounting for correction of errors.

•7 Identify economic motives for changing accounting policies.

•8 Analyze the effect of errors.

NEEDED: VALID COMPARISONS

The IASB's conceptual framework describes comparability (including consistency) as one of the qualitative characteristics that contribute to the usefulness of accounting information. Unfortunately, companies are finding it difficult to maintain comparability and consistency due to the numerous changes in accounting policies mandated by the IASB.

Presented below is a condensed version of the change in accounting policy note of **United Business Media (UBM)** (IRL) in a recent annual report.

Changes in accounting policies (in part)

The accounting policies adopted are consistent with those of the previous financial year except as follows:

IAS 1—Presentation of Financial Statements (revised) The Group adopted this revised standard on 1 January 2009. The revision separates owner and non-owner changes in equity. The statement of changes in equity includes only details of transactions with owners, with non-owner changes in equity presented as a single line. In addition, the standard introduces the statement of comprehensive income to be presented either as a single statement, or as two linked statements. The Group has elected to present two statements.

IAS 36—Impairment of Assets When discounted cash flows are used to estimate "fair value less costs to sell," additional disclosure is required about the discount rate, consistent with disclosures required when discounted cash flows are used to estimate "value in use." For those cash-generating units where the Group is required to compute the recoverable amount, fair value less costs to sell is used on an earnings multiples approach. Additional disclosures will be included in the future where applicable.

IFRS 7—Financial Instruments Disclosures: The Group adopted this amendment which requires increased disclosures about fair value measurements and liquidity risk. Fair value measurements related to items recorded at fair value are to be disclosed by source of inputs using a three-level fair value hierarchy, by class, for all financial instruments recognized at fair value.

IFRS 8—Operating Segments The Group adopted IFRS 8, which requires disclosure of information about the Group's operating segments and replaces the requirement to determine primary (business) and secondary (geographical) reporting segments of the Group. Adoption of this Standard did not have any effect on the financial position or performance of the Group. The Group determined that the four operating and reportable segments are Events, Data, Services and Online, Print—Magazines and Targeting, Distribution and Monitoring. Additional disclosures about each of these segments are shown in Note 3.

What these excerpts indicate is that the IASB is constantly attempting to improve financial reporting as conditions change in the financial world. In addition, a number of companies have faced restatements due to errors in their financial statements. Presented to the right is a chart that shows the total restatements per year since 2001.

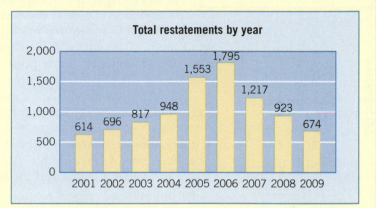

There is much good news in the chart. In 2007, restatements declined by 32.2 percent (from 1,795 to 1,217). In 2008, restatements declined another 24 percent (from 1,217 to 923). The declining trend continued in 2009. The steady decline is attributed to improved reliability of internal controls, but some observers suspect that the drop may also be due to relaxed enforcement by market regulators.

The trend in restatements is a positive development. However, when restatements and accounting changes arise, users of financial statements still need high-quality accounting information to make valid comparisons of financial performance to periods before the accounting change or restatement.

Source: 2009 Financial Restatements: A Nine Year Comparison, Audit Analytics (Feb. 10, 2010), p. 3.

PREVIEW OF CHAPTER 22

As our opening story indicates, changes in accounting policies and errors in financial information are significant. When these changes occur, companies must follow specific accounting and reporting requirements. In addition, to ensure comparability among companies, the IASB has standardized reporting of accounting changes, changes in accounting estimates, error corrections, and related earnings per share information. In this chapter, we discuss these reporting standards, which help investors better understand a company's financial condition. The content and organization of the chapter are as follows.

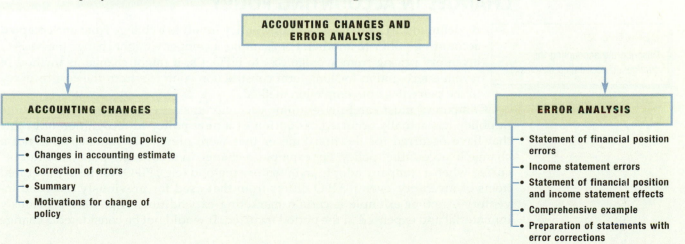

ACCOUNTING CHANGES AND ERROR ANALYSIS

ACCOUNTING CHANGES
- Changes in accounting policy
- Changes in accounting estimate
- Correction of errors
- Summary
- Motivations for change of policy

ERROR ANALYSIS
- Statement of financial position errors
- Income statement errors
- Statement of financial position and income statement effects
- Comprehensive example
- Preparation of statements with error corrections

SECTION 1 · ACCOUNTING CHANGES

Objective·1

Identify the two types of accounting changes.

I
F See the Authoritative
R Literature section
S (page 1217).

Accounting alternatives diminish the comparability of financial information between periods and between companies; they also obscure useful historical trend data. For example, if **Toyota** (JPN) revises its estimates for equipment useful lives, depreciation expense for the current year will not be comparable to depreciation expense reported by Toyota in prior years. Similarly, if **Tesco** (GBR) changes to FIFO inventory pricing while **Marks and Spencer plc** (GBR) uses the retail method, it will be difficult to compare these companies' reported results. A reporting framework helps preserve comparability when there is an accounting change.

The IASB has established a reporting framework, which involves two types of accounting changes. [1] The two types of accounting changes are:

1. *Change in accounting policy.* A change from one accepted accounting policy to another one. As an example, **Alcatel-Lucent** (FRA) changed its method of accounting for actuarial gains and losses from using the corridor approach to immediate recognition.

2. *Change in accounting estimate.* A change that occurs as the result of new information or additional experience. As an example, **Daimler AG** (DEU) revised its estimates of the useful lives of its depreciable property recently due to modifications in its productive processes.

A third category necessitates changes in accounting, though it is not classified as an accounting change.

3. *Errors in financial statements.* Errors result from mathematical mistakes, mistakes in applying accounting policies, or oversight or misuse of facts that existed when preparing the financial statements. For example, a company may incorrectly apply the retail inventory method for determining its final inventory value.

The IASB classifies changes in these categories because each category involves different methods of recognizing changes in the financial statements. In this chapter, we discuss these classifications. We also explain how to report each item in the accounts and how to disclose the information in comparative statements.

CHANGES IN ACCOUNTING POLICY

Objective·2

Describe the accounting for changes in accounting policies.

By definition, a **change in accounting policy involves a change from one accepted accounting policy to another**. For example, a company might change the basis of inventory pricing from average cost to FIFO. Or, it might change its method of revenue recognition for long-term construction contracts from the cost-recovery to the percentage-of-completion method.

Companies must carefully examine each circumstance to ensure that a change in policy has actually occurred. **Adoption of a new policy** in recognition of events that have occurred for the first time or that were previously immaterial is not a change in accounting policy. For example, a change in accounting policy has not occurred when a company adopts an inventory method (e.g., FIFO) for **newly** acquired items of inventory, even if FIFO differs from that used for **previously recorded** inventory. Another example is certain marketing expenditures that were previously immaterial and expensed in the period incurred. It would not be considered a change in accounting policy if they become material and so may be acceptably deferred and amortized.

Finally, what if a company previously followed an accounting policy that was not acceptable? Or, what if the company applied a policy incorrectly? In such cases, this type of change is **a correction of an error**. For example, a switch from the cash (income tax) basis of accounting to the accrual basis is a correction of an error. Or, if a company deducted residual value when computing double-declining depreciation on plant assets and later recomputed depreciation without deducting estimated residual value, it has corrected an error.

There are three possible approaches for reporting changes in accounting policies:

- *Report changes currently.* In this approach, companies report the cumulative effect of the change in the current year's income statement. The **cumulative effect** is the difference in prior years' income between the newly adopted and prior accounting policy. Under this approach, the effect of the change on prior years' income appears only in the current-year income statement. The company does not change **prior-year financial statements**.

   Advocates of this position argue that changing prior years' financial statements results in a loss of confidence in financial reports. How do investors react when told that the earnings computed three years ago are now entirely different? Changing prior periods, if permitted, also might upset contractual arrangements based on the old figures. For example, profit-sharing arrangements computed on the old basis might have to be recomputed and completely new distributions made, creating numerous legal problems. Many practical difficulties also exist: The cost of changing prior period financial statements may be excessive, or determining the amount of the prior period effect may be impossible on the basis of available data.

- *Report changes retrospectively.* **Retrospective application** refers to the application of a different accounting policy to recast previously issued financial statements—**as if the new policy had always been used**. In other words, the company "goes back" and adjusts **prior years' statements** on a basis consistent with the newly adopted policy. The company shows any cumulative effect of the change as an adjustment to beginning retained earnings of the earliest year presented.

   Advocates of this position argue that retrospective application ensures comparability. Think for a moment what happens if this approach is not used: The year *previous* to the change will be on the old method; the year *of the change* will report the entire cumulative adjustment; and the *following* year will present financial statements on the new basis without the cumulative effect of the change. Such lack of consistency fails to provide meaningful earnings-trend data and other financial relationships necessary to evaluate the business.

- *Report changes prospectively (in the future).* In this approach, previously reported results remain. As a result, companies do not adjust opening balances to reflect the change in policy. Advocates of this position argue that once management presents financial statements based on acceptable accounting policies, they are final; management cannot change prior periods by adopting a new policy. According to this line of reasoning, the current-period cumulative adjustment is not appropriate because that approach includes amounts that have little or no relationship to the current year's income or economic events.

Given these three possible approaches, which does the accounting profession prefer? The IASB **requires that companies use the retrospective approach**. Why? Because it provides financial statement users with more useful information than the cumulative-effect or prospective approaches. **[2]** The rationale is that changing the prior statements to be on the same basis as the newly adopted policy results in greater consistency across accounting periods. Users can then better compare results from one period to the next.

**What do the
numbers mean?**

The cumulative-effect approach results in a loss of comparability. Also, reporting the cumulative adjustment in the period of the change can significantly affect net income, resulting in a misleading income figure. For example, at one time **Chrysler Corporation** (USA) changed its inventory accounting. If Chrysler had used the cumulative-effect approach, it would have reported a $53,500,000 adjustment to net income. That adjustment would have resulted in net income of $45,900,000 instead of a net loss of $7,600,000.

A second case: In the early 1980s, the U.S. railroad industry switched from the retirement-replacement method of depreciating railroad equipment to more generally used methods such as straight-line depreciation. Using cumulative treatment, railroad companies would have made substantial adjustments to income in the period of change. Many in the industry argued that including such large cumulative-effect adjustments in the current year would distort the information and make it less useful.

Such situations lend support to retrospective application so that comparability is maintained.

Retrospective Accounting Change Approach

Objective·3

Understand how to account for retrospective accounting changes.

A presumption exists that once a company adopts an accounting policy, it should not change. That presumption is understandable, given the idea that consistent use of an accounting policy enhances the usefulness of financial statements. [3] However, the environment continually changes, and companies change in response. Recent standards, such as borrowing costs and operating segments, and proposed standards on revenue recognition and financial instruments indicate that changes in accounting policies will continue to exist.

As a consequence, the IASB permits companies to change an accounting policy if:

1. It is required by IFRS (e.g., the new IFRS on financial instruments will be subject to the proper accounting for changes in accounting policy); or

2. It results in the financial statements providing more reliable and relevant information about a company's financial position, financial performance, and cash flows. For example, a company may determine that changing from the average cost method of inventory valuation to the FIFO method provides more reliable and relevant information on the current value of its inventory.[1]

When a company changes an accounting policy, it should report the change using retrospective application. In general terms, here is what it must do:

1. It adjusts its financial statements for each prior period presented. Thus, financial statement information about prior periods is on the same basis as the new accounting policy.

2. It adjusts the carrying amounts of assets and liabilities as of the beginning of the first year presented. By doing so, these accounts reflect the cumulative effect on periods prior to those presented of the change to the new accounting policy. The company

---

[1]In some cases, a particular transaction is not specifically addressed by IFRS. In this situation, *IAS 8* sets out a hierarchy of guidance to be considered in the selection of an accounting policy. The primary requirement is that management must use judgment to develop information that is relevant and reliable. In making that judgment, it should use the following sources in descending order: (1) the requirements and guidance in IFRS dealing with similar and related issues; (2) the definitions, recognition criteria, and measurement concepts for the elements in the Framework; and (3) other materials such as standards from other countries that use a similar conceptual framework. [4]

also makes an offsetting adjustment to the opening balance of retained earnings or other appropriate component of equity or net assets as of the beginning of the first year presented.

For example, assume that **Carrefour** (FRA) decides to change its inventory valuation method in 2011 from the retail inventory method (FIFO) to the retail inventory (average cost). It provides comparative information for 2009 and 2010 based on the new method. Carrefour would adjust its assets, liabilities, and retained earnings for periods prior to 2009 and report these amounts in the 2009 financial statements, when it prepares comparative financial statements.

Retrospective Accounting Change: Long-Term Contracts

To illustrate the retrospective approach, assume that Denson Company has accounted for its income from long-term construction contracts using the cost-recovery (zero-profit) method. In 2011, the company changed to the percentage-of-completion method. Management believes this approach provides a more appropriate measure of the income earned. For tax purposes, the company uses the cost-recovery method and plans to continue doing so in the future. (We assume a 40 percent enacted tax rate.)

Illustration 22-1 shows portions of three income statements for 2009–2011—for both the cost-recovery and percentage-of-completion methods.

COST-RECOVERY METHOD
DENSON COMPANY
INCOME STATEMENT (PARTIAL)
FOR THE YEAR ENDED DECEMBER 31

	2009	2010	2011
Income before income tax	€400,000	€160,000	€190,000
Income tax (40%)	160,000	64,000	76,000
Net income	€240,000	€ 96,000	€114,000

PERCENTAGE-OF-COMPLETION METHOD
DENSON COMPANY
INCOME STATEMENT (PARTIAL)
FOR THE YEAR ENDED DECEMBER 31

	2009	2010	2011
Income before income tax	€600,000	€180,000	€200,000
Income tax (40%)	240,000	72,000	80,000
Net income	€360,000	€108,000	€120,000

ILLUSTRATION 22-1
Comparative Income Statements for Cost-Recovery versus Percentage-of-Completion Methods

To record a change from the cost-recovery to the percentage-of-completion method, we analyze the various effects, as Illustration 22-2 shows.

Year	Pretax Income from		Difference in Income		
	Percentage-of-Completion	Cost-Recovery	Difference	Tax Effect 40%	Income Effect (net of tax)
Prior to 2010	€600,000	€400,000	€200,000	€80,000	€120,000
In 2010	180,000	160,000	20,000	8,000	12,000
Total at beginning of 2011	€780,000	€560,000	€220,000	€88,000	€132,000
Total in 2011	€200,000	€190,000	€ 10,000	€ 4,000	€ 6,000

ILLUSTRATION 22-2
Data for Retrospective Change Example

The entry to record the change at the beginning of 2011 would be:

Construction in Process	220,000	
Deferred Tax Liability		88,000
Retained Earnings		132,000

The Construction in Process account increases by €220,000 (as indicated in the first column under "Difference in Income" in Illustration 22-2). The credit to Retained Earnings of €132,000 reflects the cumulative income effects prior to 2011 (third column under "Difference in Income" in Illustration 22-2). The company credits Retained Earnings because prior years' income is closed to this account each year. The credit to Deferred Tax Liability represents the adjustment to prior years' tax expense. The company now recognizes that amount, €88,000, as a tax liability for future taxable amounts. That is, in future periods, taxable income will be higher than book income as a result of current temporary differences. Therefore, Denson must report a deferred tax liability in the current year.

Reporting a Change in Policy. The disclosure of changes in accounting policies is particularly important. Users of the financial statements want consistent information from one period to the next. Such consistency ensures the usefulness of financial statements. The major disclosure requirements are as follows.

1. The nature of the change in accounting policy;
2. The reasons why applying the new accounting policy provides reliable and more relevant information;
3. For the current period and each prior period presented, to the extent practicable, the amount of the adjustment:
   (a) For each financial statement line item affected; and
   (b) Basic and diluted earnings per share.
4. The amount of the adjustment relating to periods before those presented, to the extent practicable.[2]

The disclosure here relates to a voluntary change in accounting policy, such as a change from the average cost to FIFO method of inventory measurement. The requirements for disclosure are slightly different if the change is mandated by the issuance of a new IFRS. In that case, transitional adjustments are also considered, as required by the standard.

To illustrate, Denson will prepare comparative financial statements for 2010 and 2011 using the percentage-of-completion method (the new-construction accounting method). Illustration 22-3 indicates how Denson presents this information.

As Illustration 22-3 shows, Denson Company reports net income under the newly adopted percentage-of-completion method for both 2010 and 2011. The company retrospectively adjusted the 2010 income statement to report the information on a percentage-of-completion basis. Also, the note to the financial statements indicates the nature of the change, why the company made the change, and the years affected.

In addition, companies are required to provide data on important differences between the amounts reported under percentage-of-completion versus cost-recovery. When identifying the significant differences, some companies show the *entire* financial statements and line-by-line differences between percentage-of-completion and cost-recovery. However, most companies will show only line-by-line differences. For example, Denson would show the differences in construction in process, retained earnings, gross profit,

---

[2]Financial statements of subsequent periods need not repeat these disclosures. **[5]**

and net income for 2010 and 2011 under the cost-recovery and percentage-of-completion methods.

DENSON COMPANY
INCOME STATEMENT (PARTIAL)
FOR THE YEAR ENDED

	2011	2010
		As adjusted (Note A)
Income before income tax	€200,000	€180,000
Income tax (40%)	80,000	72,000
Net income	€120,000	€108,000

Note A: Change in Method of Accounting for Long-Term Contracts. The company has accounted for revenue and costs for long-term construction contracts by the percentage-of-completion method in 2011, whereas in all prior years revenue and costs were determined by the cost-recovery method. The new method of accounting for long-term contracts was adopted to recognize . . . [state justification for change in accounting policy] . . . , and financial statements of prior years have been restated to apply the new method retrospectively. For income tax purposes, the cost-recovery method has been continued. The effect of the accounting change on income of 2011 was an increase of €6,000 net of related taxes and on income of 2010 as previously reported was an increase of €12,000 net of related taxes. The balances of retained earnings for 2010 and 2011 have been adjusted for the effect of applying retrospectively the new method of accounting. As a result of the accounting change, retained earnings as of January 1, 2010, increased by €120,000 compared to that reported using the cost-recovery method.

Retained Earnings Adjustment. As indicated earlier, one of the disclosure requirements is to show the cumulative effect of the change on retained earnings as of the beginning of the earliest period presented. For Denson Company, that date is January 1, 2010. Denson disclosed that information by means of a narrative description (see Note A in Illustration 22-3). Denson also would disclose this information in its retained earnings statement. Assuming a retained earnings balance of €1,360,000 at the beginning of 2009, Illustration 22-4 shows Denson's retained earnings statement under the cost-recovery method—that is, before giving effect to the change in accounting policy. (The income information comes from Illustration 22-1 on page 1189.)

ILLUSTRATION 22-4
Retained Earnings
Statement before
Retrospective Change

DENSON COMPANY
RETAINED EARNINGS STATEMENT
FOR THE YEAR ENDED

	2011	2010	2009
Retained earnings, January 1	€1,696,000	€1,600,000	€1,360,000
Net income	114,000	96,000	240,000
Retained earnings, December 31	€1,810,000	€1,696,000	€1,600,000

If Denson presents comparative statements for 2010 and 2011 under percentage-of-completion, then it must change the beginning balance of retained earnings at January 1, 2010. The difference between the retained earnings balances under cost-recovery and percentage of completion is computed as follows.

Retained earnings, January 1, 2010 (percentage-of-completion)	€1,720,000
Retained earnings, January 1, 2010 (cost-recovery)	1,600,000
Cumulative-effect difference	€ 120,000

The €120,000 difference is the cumulative effect. Illustration 22-5 shows a comparative retained earnings statement for 2010 and 2011, giving effect to the change in accounting policy to percentage-of-completion.

ILLUSTRATION 22-5
Retained Earnings
Statement after
Retrospective Application

DENSON COMPANY RETAINED EARNINGS STATEMENT FOR THE YEAR ENDED		
	2011	2010
Retained earnings, January 1, as reported	—	€1,600,000
Add: Adjustment for the cumulative effect on prior years of applying retrospectively the new method of accounting for construction contracts		120,000
Retained earnings, January 1, as adjusted	€1,828,000	1,720,000
Net income	120,000	108,000
Retained earnings, December 31	€1,948,000	€1,828,000

Denson adjusted the beginning balance of retained earnings on January 1, 2010, for the excess of percentage-of-completion net income over cost-recovery net income in 2009. This comparative presentation indicates the type of adjustment that a company needs to make. It follows that this adjustment would be much larger if a number of prior periods were involved.

Retrospective Accounting Change: Inventory Methods

As a second illustration of the retrospective approach, assume that Lancer Company has accounted for its inventory using the average cost method. In 2011, the company changes to the FIFO method because management believes this approach provides a more appropriate measure of its inventory costs. Illustration 22-6 provides additional information related to Lancer Company.

ILLUSTRATION 22-6
Lancer Company
Information

1. Lancer Company started its operations on January 1, 2009. At that time, shareholders invested $100,000 in the business in exchange for ordinary shares.
2. All sales, purchases, and operating expenses for the period 2009–2011 are cash transactions. Lancer's cash flows over this period are as follows.

	2009	2010	2011
Sales	$300,000	$300,000	$300,000
Purchases	90,000	110,000	125,000
Operating expenses	100,000	100,000	100,000
Cash flow from operations	$110,000	$ 90,000	$ 75,000

3. Lancer has used the average cost method for financial reporting since its inception.
4. Inventory determined under average cost and FIFO for the period 2009–2011 is as follows.

	Average Cost Method	FIFO Method	Difference
January 1, 2009	$ 0	$ 0	$ 0
December 31, 2009	10,000	12,000	2,000
December 31, 2010	20,000	25,000	5,000
December 31, 2011	32,000	39,000	7,000

5. Cost of goods sold under average cost and FIFO for the period 2009–2011 is as follows.

	Cost of Goods Sold Average Cost	Cost of Goods Sold FIFO	Difference
2009	$ 80,000	$ 78,000	$2,000
2010	100,000	97,000	3,000
2011	113,000	111,000	2,000

6. Earnings per share information is not required on the income statement.
7. All tax effects for this illustration should be ignored.

Given the information about Lancer Company, Illustration 22-7 shows its income statement, retained earnings statement, statement of financial position, and statement of cash flows for 2009–2011 under average cost.

ILLUSTRATION 22-7
Lancer Financial
Statements (Average Cost)

LANCER COMPANY
INCOME STATEMENT
FOR THE YEAR ENDED DECEMBER 31

	2009	2010	2011
Sales	$300,000	$300,000	$300,000
Cost of goods sold (average cost)	80,000	100,000	113,000
Operating expenses	100,000	100,000	100,000
Net income	$120,000	$100,000	$ 87,000

LANCER COMPANY
RETAINED EARNINGS STATEMENT
FOR THE YEAR ENDED DECEMBER 31

	2009	2010	2011
Retained earnings (beginning)	$ 0	$120,000	$220,000
Add: Net income	120,000	100,000	87,000
Retained earnings (ending)	$120,000	$220,000	$307,000

LANCER COMPANY
STATEMENT OF FINANCIAL POSITION
AT DECEMBER 31

	2009	2010	2011
Inventory (average cost)	$ 10,000	$ 20,000	$ 32,000
Cash	210,000	300,000	375,000
Total assets	$220,000	$320,000	$407,000
Share capital	$100,000	$100,000	$100,000
Retained earnings	120,000	220,000	307,000
Total equity	$220,000	$320,000	$407,000

LANCER COMPANY
STATEMENT OF CASH FLOWS
FOR THE YEAR ENDED DECEMBER 31

	2009	2010	2011
Cash flows from operating activities			
Sales	$300,000	$300,000	$300,000
Purchases	90,000	110,000	125,000
Operating expenses	100,000	100,000	100,000
Net cash provided by operating activities	110,000	90,000	75,000
Cash flows from financing activities			
Issuance of ordinary shares	100,000	—	—
Net increase in cash	210,000	90,000	75,000
Cash at beginning of year	0	210,000	300,000
Cash at end of year	$210,000	$300,000	$375,000

As Illustration 22-7 indicates, under average cost Lancer Company reports $120,000 net income in 2009, $100,000 net income in 2010, and $87,000 net income in 2011. The amount of inventory reported on Lancer's statement of financial position reflects average cost inventory accounting.

Illustration 22-8 (page 1194) shows Lancer's income statement, retained earnings statement, statement of financial position, and statement of cash flows for 2009–2011 under **FIFO**. You can see that **the cash flow statement under FIFO is the same as under average cost**. Although the net incomes are different in each period, there is no cash flow effect from these differences in net income. (If we considered income taxes, a cash flow effect would result.)

ILLUSTRATION 22-8
Lancer Financial
Statements (FIFO)

LANCER COMPANY
INCOME STATEMENT
FOR THE YEAR ENDED DECEMBER 31

	2009	2010	2011
Sales	$300,000	$300,000	$300,000
Cost of goods sold (FIFO)	78,000	97,000	111,000
Operating expenses	100,000	100,000	100,000
Net income	$122,000	$103,000	$ 89,000

LANCER COMPANY
RETAINED EARNINGS STATEMENT
FOR THE YEAR ENDED DECEMBER 31

	2009	2010	2011
Retained earnings (beginning)	$ 0	$122,000	$225,000
Add: Net income	122,000	103,000	89,000
Retained earnings (ending)	$122,000	$225,000	$314,000

LANCER COMPANY
STATEMENT OF FINANCIAL POSITION
AT DECEMBER 31

	2009	2010	2011
Inventory (FIFO)	$ 12,000	$ 25,000	$ 39,000
Cash	210,000	300,000	375,000
Total assets	$222,000	$325,000	$414,000
Share capital	$100,000	$100,000	$100,000
Retained earnings	122,000	225,000	314,000
Total equity	$222,000	$325,000	$414,000

LANCER COMPANY
STATEMENT OF CASH FLOWS
FOR THE YEAR ENDED DECEMBER 31

	2009	2010	2011
Cash flows from operating activities			
Sales	$300,000	$300,000	$300,000
Purchases	90,000	110,000	125,000
Operating expenses	100,000	100,000	100,000
Net cash provided by operating activities	110,000	90,000	75,000
Cash flows from financing activities			
Issuance of ordinary shares	100,000	—	—
Net increase in cash	210,000	90,000	75,000
Cast at beginning of year	0	210,000	300,000
Cash at end of year	$210,000	$300,000	$375,000

Compare the financial statements reported in Illustration 22-7 and Illustration 22-8. You can see that, under retrospective application, the change to FIFO inventory valuation affects reported inventories, cost of goods sold, net income, and retained earnings. In the following sections, we discuss the accounting and reporting of Lancer's accounting change from average cost to FIFO.

Given the information provided in Illustrations 22-6, 22-7, and 22-8, we now are ready to account for and report on the accounting change.

Our first step is to adjust the financial records for the change from average cost to FIFO. To do so, we perform the analysis in Illustration 22-9.

Year	Net Income Average Cost	Net Income FIFO	Difference in Income
2009	$120,000	$122,000	$2,000
2010	100,000	103,000	3,000
Total at beginning of 2011	$220,000	$225,000	$5,000
Total in 2011	$ 87,000	$ 89,000	$2,000

ILLUSTRATION 22-9
Data for Recording Change in Accounting Policy

The entry to record the change to the FIFO method at the beginning of 2011 is as follows.

Inventory	5,000	
Retained Earnings		5,000

The change increases the inventory account by $5,000. This amount represents the difference between the ending inventory at December 31, 2010, under average cost ($20,000) and the ending inventory under FIFO ($25,000). The credit to Retained Earnings indicates the amount needed to change prior-year's income, assuming that Lancer had used FIFO in previous periods.

Reporting a Change in Policy. Lancer Company will prepare comparative financial statements for 2010 and 2011 using FIFO (the new inventory method). Illustration 22-10 indicates how Lancer might present this information.

ILLUSTRATION 22-10
Comparative Information Related to Accounting Change (FIFO)

LANCER COMPANY
INCOME STATEMENT
FOR THE YEAR ENDED DECEMBER 31

	2011	2010 As adjusted (Note A)
Sales	$300,000	$300,000
Cost of goods sold	111,000	97,000
Operating expenses	100,000	100,000
Net income	$ 89,000	$103,000

Note A

Change in Method of Accounting for Inventory Valuation On January 1, 2011, Lancer Company elected to change its method of valuing its inventory to the FIFO method; in all prior years inventory was valued using the average cost method. The Company adopted the new method of accounting for inventory to better report cost of goods sold in the year incurred. Comparative financial statements of prior years have been adjusted to apply the new method retrospectively. The following financial statement line items for years 2011 and 2010 were affected by the change in accounting policy.

Nature and reason for change and description of prior period information adjusted

Statement of Financial Position	2011 Average Cost	2011 FIFO	2011 Difference	2010 Average Cost	2010 FIFO	2010 Difference
Inventory	$ 32,000	$ 39,000	$7,000	$ 20,000	$ 25,000	$5,000
Retained earnings	307,000	314,000	7,000	220,000	225,000	5,000
Income Statement						
Cost of goods sold	$113,000	$111,000	$2,000	$100,000	$ 97,000	$3,000
Net income	87,000	89,000	2,000	100,000	103,000	3,000
Statement of Cash Flows						
(no effect)						

Effect of change on each financial statement affected

As a result of the accounting change, retained earnings as of January 1, 2010, increased from $120,000, as originally reported using the average cost method, to $122,000 using the FIFO method.

Cumulative effect on retained earnings

As Illustration 22-10 shows, Lancer Company reports net income under the newly adopted FIFO method for both 2010 and 2011. The company retrospectively adjusted the 2010 income statement to report the information on a FIFO basis. In addition, the note to the financial statements indicates the nature of the change, why the company made the change, and the years affected. The note also provides data on important differences between the amounts reported under average cost versus FIFO. (When identifying the significant differences, some companies show the *entire* financial statements and line-by-line differences between average cost and FIFO.)

Retained Earnings Adjustment. As indicated earlier, one of the disclosure requirements is to show the cumulative effect of the change on retained earnings as of the beginning of the earliest period presented. For Lancer Company, that date is January 1, 2010. Lancer disclosed that information by means of a narrative description (see Note A in Illustration 22-10). Lancer also would disclose this information in its retained earnings statement. Illustration 22-11 shows Lancer's retained earnings statement under average cost—that is, before giving effect to the change in accounting policy. (This information comes from Illustration 22-7 on page 1193.)

ILLUSTRATION 22-11
Retained Earnings
Statements (Average Cost)

	2011	2010	2009
Retained earnings, January 1	$220,000	$120,000	$ 0
Net income	87,000	100,000	120,000
Retained earnings, December 31	$307,000	$220,000	$120,000

If Lancer presents comparative statements for 2010 and 2011 under FIFO, then it must change the beginning balance of retained earnings at January 1, 2010. The difference between the retained earnings balances under average cost and FIFO is computed as follows.

Retained earnings, January 1, 2010 (FIFO)	$122,000
Retained earnings, January 1, 2010 (average cost)	120,000
Cumulative effect difference	$ 2,000

The $2,000 difference is the cumulative effect. Illustration 22-12 shows a comparative retained earnings statement for 2010 and 2011, giving effect to the change in accounting policy to FIFO.

ILLUSTRATION 22-12
Retained Earnings
Statements after
Retrospective Application

	2011	2010
Retained earnings, January 1, as reported		$120,000
Add: Adjustment for the cumulative effect on prior years of applying retrospectively the new method of accounting for inventory		2,000
Retained earnings, January 1, as adjusted	$225,000	122,000
Net income	89,000	103,000
Retained earnings, December 31	$314,000	$225,000

Lancer adjusted the beginning balance of retained earnings on January 1, 2010, for the excess of FIFO net income over average cost net income in 2009. This comparative presentation indicates the type of adjustment that a company needs to make. It follows that the amount of this adjustment would be much larger if a number of prior periods were involved.

Direct and Indirect Effects of Changes

Are there other effects that a company should report when it makes a change in accounting policy? For example, what happens when a company like Lancer has a bonus plan based on net income and the prior year's net income changes when FIFO is retrospectively applied? Should Lancer also change the reported amount of bonus expense? Or, what happens if we had not ignored income taxes in the Lancer example? Should Lancer adjust net income, given that taxes will be different under average cost and FIFO in prior periods? The answers depend on whether the effects are direct or indirect.

Direct Effects. The IASB takes the position that companies should retrospectively apply the **direct effects of a change in accounting policy**. An example of a **direct effect** is an adjustment to an inventory balance as a result of a change in the inventory valuation method. For example, Lancer Company should change the inventory amounts in prior periods to indicate the change to the FIFO method of inventory valuation. Another inventory-related example would be an impairment adjustment resulting from applying the lower-of-cost-or-net realizable value test to the adjusted inventory balance. Related changes, such as deferred income tax effects of the impairment adjustment, are also considered direct effects. This entry was illustrated in the Denson example, in which the change to percentage-of-completion accounting resulted in recording a deferred tax liability.

Indirect Effects. In addition to direct effects, companies can have **indirect effects related to a change in accounting policy**. An **indirect effect** is any change to current or future cash flows of a company that result from making a change in accounting policy that is applied retrospectively. An example of an indirect effect is a change in profit-sharing or royalty payment that is based on a reported amount such as revenue or net income. The IASB is silent on what to do in this situation. U.S. GAAP (likely because its standard in this area was issued after *IAS 8*) requires that indirect effects do not change prior period amounts.

For example, let's assume that Lancer has an employee profit-sharing plan based on net income. As Illustration 22-9 (on page 1195) showed, Lancer would report higher income in 2009 and 2010 if it used the FIFO method. In addition, let's assume that the profit-sharing plan requires that Lancer pay the incremental amount due based on the FIFO income amounts. In this situation, Lancer reports this additional expense **in the current period**; it would not change prior periods for this expense. If the company prepares comparative financial statements, it follows that it does not recast the prior periods for this additional expense.[3]

If the terms of the profit-sharing plan indicate that *no payment is necessary* in the current period due to this change, then the company need not recognize additional profit-sharing expense in the current period. Neither does it change amounts reported for prior periods.

When a company recognizes the indirect effects of a change in accounting policy, it includes in the financial statements a description of the indirect effects. In doing so, it discloses the amounts recognized in the current period and related per share information.

Impracticability

It is not always possible for companies to determine how they would have reported prior periods' financial information under retrospective application of an accounting policy change. Retrospective application is considered **impracticable** if a company cannot determine the prior period effects using every reasonable effort to do so.

> **Objective•4**
> Understand how to account for impracticable changes.

---

[3]The rationale for this approach is that companies should recognize, in the period the adoption occurs (not the prior period), the effect on the cash flows that is caused by the adoption of the new accounting policy. That is, the accounting change is a necessary "past event" in the definition of an asset or liability that gives rise to the accounting recognition of the indirect effect in the current period.

Companies should not use retrospective application if one of the following conditions exists:

1. The company cannot determine the effects of the retrospective application.
2. Retrospective application requires assumptions about management's intent in a prior period.
3. Retrospective application requires significant estimates for a prior period, and the company cannot objectively verify the necessary information to develop these estimates.

If any of the above conditions exists, it is deemed impracticable to apply the retrospective approach. In this case, the company **prospectively applies** the new accounting policy as of the earliest date it is practicable to do so. **[6]**

For example, assume that Williams Company changed its accounting policy for depreciable assets so as to more fully apply component depreciation under revaluation accounting. Unfortunately, the company does not have detailed accounting records to establish a basis for the components of these assets. As a result, Williams determines it is not practicable to account for the change to full component depreciation using the retrospective application approach. It therefore applies the policy prospectively, starting at the beginning of the current year.

Williams must disclose only the effect of the change on the results of operations in the period of change. Also, the company should explain the reasons for omitting the computations of the cumulative effect for prior years. Finally, it should disclose the justification for the change to component depreciation. **[7]**

CHANGES IN ACCOUNTING ESTIMATE

To prepare financial statements, companies must estimate the effects of future conditions and events. For example, the following items require estimates.

1. Bad debts.
2. Inventory obsolescence.
3. Useful lives and residual values of assets.
4. Periods benefited by deferred costs.
5. Liabilities for warranty costs and income taxes.
6. Recoverable mineral reserves.
7. Change in depreciation methods.
8. Fair value of financial assets or financial liabilities.

A company cannot perceive future conditions and events and their effects with certainty. Therefore, estimating requires the exercise of judgment. Accounting estimates will change as new events occur, as a company acquires more experience, or as it obtains additional information.

Prospective Reporting

Companies report prospectively changes in accounting estimates. That is, companies should not adjust previously reported results for changes in estimates. Instead, they account for the effects of all changes in estimates in (1) the period of change if the change affects that period only (e.g., a change in the estimate of the amount of bad debts affects only the current period's income), or (2) the period of change and future periods if the change affects both (e.g., a change in the estimated useful life of a depreciable asset affects depreciation expense in the current and future periods). **[8]** The IASB views changes in estimates as **normal recurring corrections and adjustments**, the natural result of the accounting process. It prohibits retrospective treatment.

The circumstances related to a change in estimate differ from those for a change in accounting policy. If companies reported changes in estimates retrospectively, continual adjustments of prior years' income would occur. It seems proper to accept the view that, because new conditions or circumstances exist, the revision fits the new situation (not the old one). Companies should therefore handle such a revision in the current and future periods.

To illustrate, Underwriters Labs Inc. purchased for $300,000 a building that it originally estimated to have a useful life of 15 years and no residual value. It recorded depreciation for 5 years on a straight-line basis. On January 1, 2011, Underwriters Labs revises the estimate of the useful life. It now considers the asset to have a total life of 25 years. (Assume that the useful life for financial reporting and tax purposes and depreciation method are the same.) Illustration 22-13 shows the accounts at the beginning of the sixth year.

Building	$300,000
Less: Accumulated depreciation—building (5 × $20,000)	100,000
Book value of building	$200,000

ILLUSTRATION 22-13
Book Value after Five Years' Depreciation

Underwriters Labs records depreciation for the year 2011 as follows.

Depreciation Expense	10,000	
Accumulated Depreciation—Building		10,000

The company computes the $10,000 depreciation charge as shown in Illustration 22-14.

$$\text{Depreciation charge} = \frac{\text{Book value of asset}}{\text{Remaining service live}} = \frac{\$200,000}{25 \text{ years} - 5 \text{ years}} = \$10,000$$

ILLUSTRATION 22-14
Depreciation after Change in Estimate

Companies sometime find it difficult to differentiate between a change in estimate and a change in accounting policy. Is it a change in policy or a change in estimate when a company changes from deferring and amortizing marketing costs to expensing them as incurred because future benefits of these costs have become doubtful? **If it is impossible to determine whether a change in policy or a change in estimate has occurred, the rule is this: Consider the change as a change in estimate.**

Another example is a change in depreciation (as well as amortization or depletion) methods. Because companies change depreciation methods based on changes in estimates about future benefits from long-lived assets, it is not possible to separate the effect of the accounting policy change from that of the estimates. **As a result, companies account for a change in depreciation methods as a change in estimate.**

A similar problem occurs in differentiating between a change in estimate and a correction of an error, although here the answer is more clear-cut. How does a company determine whether it overlooked the information in earlier periods (an error), or whether it obtained new information (a change in estimate)? Proper classification is important because the accounting treatment differs for corrections of errors versus changes in estimates. The general rule is this: **Companies should consider careful estimates that later prove to be incorrect as changes in estimate.** Only when a company obviously computed the estimate incorrectly because of lack of expertise or in bad faith should it consider the adjustment an error. There is no clear demarcation line here. Companies must use good judgment in light of all the circumstances.

Disclosures

A company should disclose the nature and amount of a change in an accounting estimate that has an effect in the current period or is expected to have an effect in future periods (unless it is impracticable to estimate that effect). **[9]** Illustration 22-15 shows disclosure of a change in estimated useful lives, which appeared in the annual report of **Portugal Telecom, SGPS, S.A.** (PRT).

ILLUSTRATION 22-15
Disclosure of Change in
Estimated Useful Lives

Portugal Telecom, SGPS, S.A.

Note 4 (in Part): Changes in Accounting Policies and Estimates

The change in estimate of the useful life of the UMTS license was effective as at 30 June 2008. According to IAS 8 this change should be applicable on a prospective basis and, on an annual basis, the impact of this change will be a reduction in depreciation and amortisation costs by €26 million.

For the most part, companies need not disclose changes in accounting estimate made as part of normal operations, such as bad debt allowances or inventory obsolescence, unless such changes are material.

CORRECTION OF ERRORS

Objective•6
Describe the accounting for
correction of errors.

No business, large or small, is immune from errors. As the opening story discussed, the number of accounting errors that lead to restatement are beginning to decline. However, without accounting and disclosure guidelines for the reporting of errors, investors can be left in the dark about the effects of errors.

Certain errors, such as misclassifications of balances within a financial statement, are not as significant to investors as other errors. Significant errors would be those resulting in overstating assets or income, for example. However, investors should know the potential impact of all errors. Even "harmless" misclassifications can affect important ratios. Also, some errors could signal important weaknesses in internal controls that could lead to more significant errors.

In general, accounting errors include the following types:

1. A change from an accounting policy that is **not** generally accepted to an accounting policy that is acceptable. The rationale is that the company incorrectly presented prior periods because of the application of an improper accounting policy. For example, a company may change from the cash (income tax) basis of accounting to the accrual basis.

2. Mathematical mistakes, such as incorrectly totaling the inventory count sheets when computing the inventory value.

3. Changes in estimates that occur because a company did not prepare the estimates in good faith. For example, a company may have adopted a clearly unrealistic depreciation rate.

4. An oversight, such as the failure to accrue or defer certain expenses and revenues at the end of the period.

5. A misuse of facts, such as the failure to use residual value in computing the depreciation base for the straight-line approach.

6. The incorrect classification of a cost as an expense instead of an asset, and vice versa.

Accounting errors occur for a variety of reasons. Illustration 22-16 indicates 11 major categories of accounting errors that drive restatements.

Accounting Category	Type of Restatement
Expense recognition	Recording expenses in the incorrect period or for an incorrect amount.
Revenue recognition	Improper revenue accounting. This category includes instances in which revenue was improperly recognized, questionable revenues were recognized, or any other number of related errors that led to misreported revenue.
Misclassification	Misclassifying significant accounting items on the statement of financial position, income statement, or statement of cash flows. These include restatements due to misclassification of current or non-current accounts or those that impact cash flows from operations.
Equity—other	Improper accounting for EPS, restricted shares, warrants, and other equity instruments.
Reserves/Contingencies	Errors involving accounts receivables bad debts, inventory reserves, income tax allowances, and loss contingencies.
Long-lived assets	Asset impairments of property, plant, and equipment; goodwill; or other related items.
Taxes	Errors involving correction of tax provision, improper treatment of tax liabilities, and other tax-related items.
Equity—other comprehensive income	Improper accounting for comprehensive income equity transactions including foreign currency items, revaluations of plant assets, unrealized gains and losses on certain investments in debt, equity securities, and derivatives.
Inventory	Inventory costing valuations, quantity issues, and cost of sales adjustments.
Equity—share options	Improper accounting for employee share options.
Other	Any restatement not covered by the listed categories, including those related to improper accounting for acquisitions or mergers.

Source: T. Baldwin and D. Yoo, "Restatements—Traversing Shaky Ground," *Trend Alert*, Glass Lewis & Co. (June 2, 2005), p. 8.

ILLUSTRATION 22-16
Accounting-Error Types

As soon as a company discovers an error, it must correct the error. Companies record **corrections of errors** from prior periods as an adjustment to the beginning balance of retained earnings in the current period. Such corrections are called **prior period adjustments**.

If it presents comparative statements, a company should restate the prior statements affected, to correct for the error.[4] The company need not repeat the disclosures in the financial statements of subsequent periods.

Example of Error Correction

To illustrate, in 2012 the bookkeeper for Selectro Company discovered an error: In 2011, the company failed to record £20,000 of depreciation expense on a newly constructed building. This building is the only depreciable asset Selectro owns. The company correctly included the depreciation expense in its tax return and correctly reported its income taxes payable. Illustration 22-17 presents Selectro's income statement for 2011 (starting with income before depreciation expense) with and without the error.

ILLUSTRATION 22-17
Error Correction Comparison

SELECTRO COMPANY INCOME STATEMENT FOR THE YEAR ENDED, DECEMBER 31, 2011				
		Without Error		With Error
Income before depreciation expense		£100,000		£100,000
Depreciation expense		20,000		0
Income before income tax		80,000		100,000
Current	£32,000		£ 32,000	
Deferred	–0–	32,000	8,000	40,000
Net income		£ 48,000		£ 60,000

[4]The term **retrospective restatement** is used for the process of revising previously issued financial statements to reflect a correction of an error. This term distinguishes an error correction from a change in accounting policy, referred to as retrospective application.

Illustration 22-18 shows the entries that Selectro should have made and did make for recording depreciation expense and income taxes.

ILLUSTRATION 22-18
Error Entries

Entries Company Should Have Made (Without Error)			Entries Company Did Make (With Error)		
Depreciation Expense	20,000		No entry made for depreciation		
Accumulated					
Depreciation—Buildings		20,000			
Income Tax Expense	32,000		Income Tax Expense	40,000	
Income Tax Payable		32,000	Deferred Tax Liability		8,000
			Income Tax Payable		32,000

As Illustration 22-18 indicates, the £20,000 omission error in 2011 results in the following effects.

Income Statement Effects

Depreciation expense (2011) is understated £20,000.

Income tax expense (2011) is overstated £8,000 (£20,000 × 40%).

Net income (2011) is overstated £12,000 (£20,000 − £8,000).

Statement of Financial Position Effects

Accumulated depreciation—buildings is understated £20,000.

Deferred tax liability is overstated £8,000 (£20,000 × 40%).

To make the proper correcting entry in 2012, Selectro should recognize that net income in 2011 is overstated by £12,000, the Deferred Tax Liability is overstated by £8,000, and Accumulated Depreciation—Buildings is understated by £20,000. The entry to correct this error in 2012 is as follows.

Retained Earnings	12,000	
Deferred Tax Liability	8,000	
Accumulated Depreciation—Buildings		20,000

The debit to Retained Earnings results because net income for 2011 is overstated. The debit to the Deferred Tax Liability is made to remove this account, which was caused by the error. The credit to Accumulated Depreciation—Buildings reduces the book value of the building to its proper amount. Selectro will make the same journal entry to record the correction of the error in 2012 whether it prepares single-period (non-comparative) or comparative financial statements.

Single-Period Statements

To demonstrate how to show this information in a single-period statement, assume that Selectro Company has a beginning retained earnings balance at January 1, 2012, of £350,000. The company reports net income of £400,000 in 2012. Illustration 22-19 shows Selectro's retained earnings statement for 2012.

The statement of financial position in 2012 would not have any deferred tax liability related to the building, and Accumulated Depreciation—Buildings is now restated at a higher amount. The income statement would not be affected.

Comparative Statements

If preparing comparative financial statements, a company should make adjustments to correct the amounts for all affected accounts reported in the statements for **all periods**

ILLUSTRATION 22-19
Reporting an Error—
Single-Period Financial
Statement

SELECTRO COMPANY		
RETAINED EARNINGS STATEMENT		
FOR THE YEAR ENDED DECEMBER 31, 2012		
Retained earnings, January 1, as reported		£350,000
Correction of an error (depreciation)	£20,000	
Less: Applicable income tax reduction	8,000	(12,000)
Retained earnings, January 1, as adjusted		338,000
Add: Net income		400,000
Retained earnings, December 31		£738,000

reported. The company should restate the data to the correct basis for each year presented. It should **show any catch-up adjustment as a prior period adjustment to retained earnings for the earliest period it reported**. These requirements are essentially the same as those for reporting a change in accounting policy.

For example, in the case of Selectro, the error of omitting the depreciation of £20,000 in 2011, discovered in 2012, results in the restatement of the 2011 financial statements. Illustration 22-20 shows the accounts that Selectro restates in the 2011 financial statements.

ILLUSTRATION 22-20
Reporting an Error—
Comparative Financial
Statements

In the statement of financial position:	
Accumulated depreciation—buildings	£20,000 increase
Deferred tax liability	£ 8,000 decrease
Retained earnings, ending balance	£12,000 decrease
In the income statement:	
Depreciation expense—buildings	£20,000 increase
Income tax expense	£ 8,000 decrease
Net income	£12,000 decrease
In the retained earnings statement:	
Retained earnings, ending balance (due to lower net income for the period)	£12,000 decrease

Selectro prepares the 2012 financial statements in comparative form with those of 2011 **as if the error had not occurred**. In addition, Selectro must disclose that it has restated its previously issued financial statements, and it describes the nature of the error. Selectro also must disclose the following:

1. The effect of the correction on each financial statement line item and any per share amounts affected for each prior period presented.
2. The cumulative effect of the change on retained earnings or other appropriate components of equity or net assets in the statement of financial position, as of the beginning of the earliest period presented.

As indicated earlier, it is sometimes impracticable to adjust comparative information for one or more prior periods for changes in accounting policies. It is also sometimes impracticable to correct a prior period error through retrospective restatement. For example, the company may have made errors in computing fringe-benefit amounts in prior years but is unable to now reconstruct this information fully. As a result, any adjustment is made at the beginning of the earliest period for which retrospective application is applicable.

GUARD THE FINANCIAL STATEMENTS!

What do the numbers mean?

Restatements sometimes occur because of financial fraud. Financial frauds involve the intentional misstatement or omission of material information in the organization's financial reports. Common methods of financial fraud manipulation include recording fictitious revenues, concealing liabilities or expenses, and artificially inflating reported assets. Financial frauds made up only 5 percent of the frauds in a recent study on occupational fraud but caused a median loss of more than $4 million—by far the most costly category of fraud. Presented below is a chart that compares loss amounts for 2010 versus 2008 for financial statement fraud, corruption, and asset misappropriation.

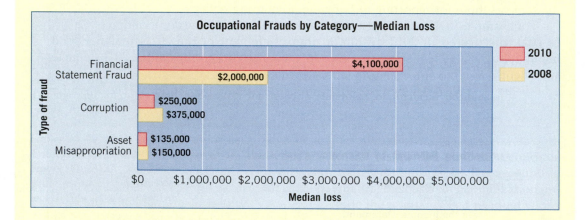

Unfortunately, the trend is going in the wrong direction (the median loss from financial statement fraud more than doubled). Therefore, companies must increase their efforts to protect their statements from the negative effects of fraud.

Source: Report to the Nations on Occupational Fraud and Abuse: 2010 Global Fraud Study, Association of Certified Fraud Examiners (2010), p. 11.

SUMMARY OF ACCOUNTING CHANGES AND CORRECTION OF ERRORS

Having guidelines for reporting accounting changes and corrections has helped resolve several significant and long-standing accounting problems. Yet, because of diversity in situations and characteristics of the items encountered in practice, use of professional judgment is of paramount importance. In applying these guidelines, the primary objective is to serve the users of the financial statements. Achieving this objective requires accuracy, full disclosure, and an absence of misleading inferences.

Illustration 22-21 summarizes the main distinctions and treatments presented in the discussion in this chapter.

Changes in accounting policy are appropriate **only** when a company demonstrates that the newly adopted generally accepted accounting policy is more reliable and relevant than the existing one. Companies and accountants determine reliability and

- **Changes in accounting policy**
  Employ the retrospective approach by:
  a. Changing the financial statements of all prior periods presented.
  b. Disclosing in the year of the change the effect on net income and earnings per share for all prior periods presented.
  c. Reporting an adjustment to the beginning retained earnings balance in the statement of retained earnings in the earliest year presented.
  If impracticable to determine the prior period effect:
  a. Do not change prior years' income.
  b. Use opening asset balance in the year the method is adopted as the base-year balance for all subsequent computations.
  c. Disclose the effect of the change on the current year, and the reasons for omitting the computation of the cumulative effect and amounts for prior years.

- **Changes in accounting estimate.**
  Employ the current and prospective approach by:
  a. Reporting current and future financial statements on the new basis.
  b. Presenting prior period financial statements as previously reported.
  c. Making no adjustments to current-period opening balances for the effects in prior periods.

- **Changes due to error.**
  Employ the restatement approach by:
  a. Correcting all prior period statements presented.
  b. Restating the beginning balance of retained earnings for the first period presented when the error effects occur in a period prior to the first period presented.

ILLUSTRATION 22-21
Summary of Guidelines for Accounting Changes and Errors

relevance on the basis of whether the new policy constitutes an **improvement in financial reporting**, not on the basis of the income tax effect alone.

But, it is not always easy to determine an improvement in financial reporting. **How does one measure preferability or improvement?** For example, a change from average cost to FIFO because the accounting system is now computerized and has scanning capabilities seems justifiable. However, a change from immediate recognition of actuarial gains and losses (which is the method preferred by the IASB) to the corridor approach does not appear to be an improvement. Determining an improved method requires some "standard" or "objective." Because no universal standard or objective is generally accepted, the problem of determining improvement continues to be difficult and requires good judgment.

MOTIVATIONS FOR CHANGE OF ACCOUNTING POLICY

Difficult as it is to determine which accounting standards have the strongest conceptual support, other complications make the process even more complex. These complications stem from the fact that managers have self-interest in how the financial statements make the company look. They naturally wish to show their financial performance in the best light. A **favorable profit picture** can influence investors, and a strong liquidity position can influence creditors. **Too favorable a profit picture**, however, can provide union negotiators and government regulators with ammunition during bargaining talks. Hence, managers might have varying motives for reporting income numbers.

Research has provided additional insight into why companies may prefer certain accounting policies.[5] Some of these reasons are as follows.

Objective·7
Identify economic motives for changing accounting policies.

[5]See Ross L. Watts and Jerold L. Zimmerman, "Positive Accounting Theory: A Ten-Year Perspective," *The Accounting Review* (January 1990) for an excellent review of research findings related to management incentives in selecting accounting policies.

1. *Political costs.* As companies become larger and more politically visible, politicians and regulators devote more attention to them. The larger the firm, the more likely it is to become subject to regulation, such as antitrust, and the more likely it is to be required to pay higher taxes. Therefore, companies that are politically visible may seek to report low income numbers, to avoid the scrutiny of regulators. In addition, other constituents, such as labor unions, may be less willing to ask for wage increases if reported income is low. Researchers have found that the larger the company, the more likely it is to adopt income-decreasing approaches in selecting accounting policies.

2. *Capital structure.* A number of studies have indicated that the capital structure of the company can affect the selection of accounting policies. For example, a company with a high debt to equity ratio is more likely to be constrained by debt covenants. The debt covenant may indicate that the company cannot pay dividends if retained earnings fall below a certain level. As a result, such a company is more likely to select accounting policies that will increase net income.

3. *Bonus payments.* Studies have found that if compensation plans tie managers' bonus payments to income, management will select accounting policies that maximize their bonus payments.

4. *Smooth earnings.* Substantial earnings increases attract the attention of politicians, regulators, and competitors. In addition, large increases in income are difficult to achieve in following years. Further, executive compensation plans would use these higher numbers as a baseline and make it difficult for managers to earn bonuses in subsequent years. Conversely, investors and competitors might view large decreases in earnings as a signal that the company is in financial trouble. Also, substantial decreases in income raise concerns on the part of shareholders, lenders, and other interested parties about the competency of management. For all these reasons, companies have an incentive to "manage" or "smooth" earnings. In general, management tends to believe that a steady 10 percent growth a year is much better than a 30 percent growth one year and a 10 percent decline the next.[6] In other words, managers usually prefer a gradually increasing income report and sometimes change accounting policies to ensure such a result.

Management pays careful attention to the accounting it follows and often changes accounting policies, not for conceptual reasons, but for economic reasons. As indicated throughout this textbook, such arguments have come to be known as **economic consequences** arguments. These arguments focus on the supposed impact of the accounting policy on the behavior of investors, creditors, competitors, governments, or managers of the reporting companies themselves.[7]

To counter these pressures, the IASB has declared, as part of its conceptual framework, that it will assess the merits of proposed standards from a position of **neutrality**. That is, the IASB evaluates the soundness of standards on the basis of conceptual soundness, not on the grounds of possible impact on behavior. It is not the IASB's place to choose standards according to the kinds of behavior it wishes to promote and the

---

[6]O. Douglas Moses, "Income Smoothing and Incentives: Empirical Tests Using Accounting Changes," *The Accounting Review* (April 1987). The findings provide evidence that earnings smoothing is associated with firm size, the existence of bonus plans, and the divergence of actual earnings from expectations.

[7]Lobbyists use economic consequences arguments—and there are many of them—to put pressure on standard-setters. We have seen examples of these arguments in the oil and gas industry about successful efforts versus full cost, and in the technology area with the issue of mandatory expensing of research costs and share options.

kinds it wishes to discourage. At the same time, it must be admitted that some standards often **will have** the effect of influencing behavior. Yet, their justification should be conceptual and not viewed in terms of their economic impact.

SECTION 2 • ERROR ANALYSIS

In this section, we show some additional types of accounting errors. Companies generally do not correct for errors that do not have a significant effect on the presentation of the financial statements. For example, should a company with a total annual payroll of $1,750,000 and net income of $940,000 correct its financial statements if it finds it failed to record accrued wages of $5,000? No—it would not consider this error significant.

> **Objective•8**
> Analyze the effect of errors.

Obviously, defining materiality is difficult, and managers and auditors must use experience and judgment to determine whether adjustment is necessary for a given error. We assume **all errors discussed in this section to be material and to require adjustment**. (Also, we ignore all tax effects in this section.)

Companies must answer three questions in error analysis:

1. What type of error is involved?
2. What entries are needed to correct for the error?
3. After discovery of the error, how are financial statements to be restated?

As indicated earlier, companies treat errors **as prior period adjustments and report them in the current year as adjustments to the beginning balance of Retained Earnings**. If a company presents comparative statements, it restates the prior affected statements to correct for the error.

STATEMENT OF FINANCIAL POSITION ERRORS

Statement of financial position errors affect only the presentation of an asset, liability, or equity account. Examples are the classification of a short-term receivable as part of the investment section, the classification of a note payable as an account payable, and the classification of plant assets as inventory.

When the error is discovered, the company reclassifies the item to its proper position. If the company prepares comparative statements that include the error year, it should correctly restate the statement of financial position for the error year.

INCOME STATEMENT ERRORS

Income statement errors involve the improper classification of revenues or expenses. Examples include recording interest revenue as part of sales, purchases as bad debt expense, and depreciation expense as interest expense. An income statement classification error has no effect on the statement of financial position and **no effect on net income**.

A company must make a reclassification entry when it discovers the error if it makes the discovery in the same year in which the error occurs. If the error occurred in prior periods, the company does not need to make a reclassification entry at the date of discovery because the accounts for the current year are correctly stated. (Remember that the company has closed the income statement accounts from the prior period to retained earnings.) If the company prepares comparative statements that include the error year, it restates the income statement for the error year.

STATEMENT OF FINANCIAL POSITION AND INCOME STATEMENT ERRORS

The third type of error involves both the statement of financial position and income statement. For example, assume that the bookkeeper overlooked accrued wages payable at the end of the accounting period. The effect of this error is to understate expenses, understate liabilities, and overstate net income for that period of time. This type of error affects both the statement of financial position and the income statement. We classify this type of error in one of two ways—counterbalancing or non-counterbalancing.

Counterbalancing errors are those that will be offset or corrected over two periods. For example, the failure to record accrued wages is a counterbalancing error because over a two-year period the error will no longer be present. In other words, the failure to record accrued wages in the previous period means (1) net income for the first period is overstated, (2) accrued wages payable (a liability) is understated, and (3) wages expense is understated. In the next period, net income is understated, accrued wages payable (a liability) is correctly stated, and wages expense is overstated. For the two **years combined** (1) net income is correct, (2) wages expense is correct, and (3) accrued wages payable at the end of the second year is correct. Most errors in accounting that affect both the statement of financial position and income statement are counterbalancing errors.

Non-counterbalancing errors are those that are not offset in the next accounting period. An example would be the failure to capitalize equipment that has a useful life of five years. If we expense this asset immediately, expenses will be overstated in the first period but understated in the next four periods. At the end of the second period, the effect of the error is not fully offset. Net income is correct in the aggregate only at the end of five years because the asset is fully depreciated at this point. Thus, **non-counterbalancing errors are those that take longer than two periods to correct themselves**.

Only in rare instances is an error never reversed. An example would be if a company initially expenses land. Because land is not depreciable, theoretically the error is never offset, unless the land is sold.

Counterbalancing Errors

We illustrate the usual types of counterbalancing errors on the following pages. In studying these illustrations, keep in mind a couple of points, discussed below.

First, determine whether the company has closed the books for the period in which the error is found:

1. **If the company has closed the books in the current year:**
   (a) If the error is already counterbalanced, no entry is necessary.
   (b) If the error is not yet counterbalanced, make an entry to adjust the present balance of retained earnings.

2. **If the company has not closed the books in the current year:**
   (a) If the error is already counterbalanced, make an entry to correct the error in the current period and to adjust the beginning balance of Retained Earnings.
   (b) If the error is not yet counterbalanced, make an entry to adjust the beginning balance of Retained Earnings.

Second, if the company presents comparative statements, it must restate the amounts for comparative purposes. **Restatement is necessary even if a correcting journal entry is not required.**

To illustrate, assume that Sanford's Cement Co. failed to accrue revenue in 2009 when earned but recorded the revenue in 2010 when received. The company discovered the error in 2012. It does not need to make an entry to correct for this error because the effects have been counterbalanced by the time Sanford discovered the error in 2012. However, if Sanford presents comparative financial statements for 2009 through 2012, it must **restate the accounts and related amounts for the years 2009 and 2010 for financial reporting purposes**.

The sections that follow demonstrate the accounting for the usual types of counterbalancing errors.

Failure to Record Accrued Wages

On December 31, 2011, Hurley Enterprises did not accrue wages in the amount of $1,500. The entry in 2012 to correct this error, assuming Hurley has not closed the books for 2012, is:

Retained Earnings	1,500	
Wages Expense		1,500

The rationale for this entry is as follows: (1) When Hurley pays the 2011 accrued wages in 2012, it makes an additional debit of $1,500 to 2012 Wages Expense. (2) Wages Expense—2012 is overstated by $1,500. (3) Because the company did not record 2011 accrued wages as Wages Expense in 2011, the net income for 2011 was overstated by $1,500. (4) Because 2011 net income is overstated by $1,500, the Retained Earnings account is overstated by $1,500 (because net income is closed to Retained Earnings).

If Hurley has closed the books for 2012, it makes no entry because the error is counterbalanced.

Failure to Record Prepaid Expenses

In January 2011, Hurley Enterprises purchased a two-year insurance policy costing $1,000. It debited Insurance Expense and credited Cash. The company made no adjusting entries at the end of 2011.

The entry on December 31, 2012, to correct this error, assuming Hurley has not closed the books for 2012, is:

Insurance Expense	500	
Retained Earnings		500

If Hurley has closed the books for 2012, it makes no entry because the error is counterbalanced.

Understatement of Unearned Revenue

On December 31, 2011, Hurley Enterprises received $50,000 as a prepayment for renting certain office space for the following year. At the time of receipt of the rent payment, the company recorded a debit to Cash and a credit to Rent Revenue. It made no adjusting entry as of December 31, 2011. The entry on December 31, 2012, to correct for this error, assuming that Hurley has not closed the books for 2012, is:

Retained Earnings	50,000	
Rent Revenue		50,000

If Hurley has closed the books for 2012, it makes no entry because the error is counterbalanced.

Overstatement of Accrued Revenue

On December 31, 2011, Hurley Enterprises accrued as interest revenue $8,000 that applied to 2012. On that date, the company recorded a debit to Interest Receivable and a credit to Interest Revenue. The entry on December 31, 2012, to correct for this error, assuming that Hurley has not closed the books for 2012, is:

Retained Earnings	8,000	
Interest Revenue		8,000

If Hurley has closed the books for 2012, it makes no entry because the error is counterbalanced.

Overstatement of Purchases

Hurley's accountant recorded a purchase of merchandise for $9,000 in 2011 that applied to 2012. The physical inventory for 2011 was correctly stated. The company uses the periodic inventory method. The entry on December 31, 2012, to correct for this error, assuming that Harley has not closed the books for 2012, is:

Purchases	9,000	
Retained Earnings		9,000

If Hurley has closed the books for 2012, it makes no entry because the error is counterbalanced.

Non-Counterbalancing Errors

The entries for non-counterbalancing errors are more complex. Companies must make correcting entries, even if they have closed the books.

Failure to Record Depreciation

Assume that on January 1, 2011, Hurley Enterprises purchased a machine for $10,000 that had an estimated useful life of five years. The accountant incorrectly expensed this machine in 2011 but discovered the error in 2012. If we assume that Hurley uses straight-line depreciation on this asset, the entry on December 31, 2012, to correct for this error, given that Hurley has not closed the books, is:

Machinery	10,000	
Depreciation Expense	2,000	
Retained Earnings		8,000*
Accumulated Depreciation (20% × $10,000 × 2)		4,000

*Computations:

Retained Earnings

Overstatement of expense in 2011	$10,000
Proper depreciation for 2011 (20% × $10,000)	(2,000)
Retained earnings understated as of Dec. 31, 2011	$ 8,000

If Hurley has closed the books for 2012, the entry is:

Machinery	10,000	
Retained Earnings		6,000*
Accumulated Depreciation		4,000

*Computations:

Retained Earnings

Retained earnings understated as of Dec. 31, 2011	$ 8,000
Proper depreciation for 2012 (20% × $10,000)	(2,000)
Retained earnings understated as of Dec. 31, 2012	$ 6,000

Failure to Adjust for Bad Debts

Companies sometimes use a specific charge-off method in accounting for bad debt expense when a percentage of sales is more appropriate. They then make adjustments to change from the specific write-off to some type of allowance method. For example, assume that Hurley Enterprises has recognized bad debt expense when it has the following uncollectible debts.

	2011	2012
From 2011 sales	$550	$690
From 2012 sales		700

Hurley estimates that it will charge off an additional $1,400 in 2013, of which $300 is applicable to 2011 sales and $1,100 to 2012 sales. The entry on December 31, 2012, assuming that Hurley **has not closed the books for 2012**, is:

Bad Debt Expense	410	
Retained Earnings	990	
Allowance for Doubtful Accounts		1,400

Allowance for doubtful accounts: Additional $300 for 2011 sales and $1,100 for 2012 sales.
Bad debts and retained earnings balance:

	2011	2012
Bad debts charged for	$1,240*	$ 700
Additional bad debts anticipated in 2013	300	1,100
Proper bad debt expense	1,540	1,800
Charges currently made to each period	(550)	(1,390)
Bad debt adjustment	$ 990	$ 410

*$550 + $690 = $1,240

If Hurley **has closed the books for 2012**, the entry is:

Retained Earnings	1,400	
Allowance for Doubtful Accounts		1,400

COMPREHENSIVE EXAMPLE: NUMEROUS ERRORS

In some circumstances, a combination of errors occurs. The company therefore prepares a worksheet to facilitate the analysis. The following problem demonstrates use of the worksheet. The mechanics of its preparation should be obvious from the solution format. The income statements of Hudson Company for the years ended December 31, 2010, 2011, and 2012, indicate the following net incomes.

2010	€17,400
2011	20,200
2012	11,300

An examination of the accounting records for these years indicates that Hudson Company made several errors in arriving at the net income amounts reported:

1. The company consistently omitted from the records wages earned by workers but not paid at December 31. The amounts omitted were:

December 31, 2010	€1,000
December 31, 2011	€1,400
December 31, 2012	€1,600

When paid in the year following that in which they were earned, Hudson recorded these amounts as expenses.

2. The company overstated merchandise inventory on December 31, 2010, by €1,900 as the result of errors made in the footings and extensions on the inventory sheets.

3. On December 31, 2011, Hudson expensed unexpired insurance of €1,200, applicable to 2012.

4. The company did not record on December 31, 2011, interest receivable in the amount of €240.

5. On January 2, 2011, Hudson sold for €1,800 a piece of equipment costing €3,900. At the date of sale, the equipment had accumulated depreciation of €2,400. The company recorded the cash received as Miscellaneous Income in 2011. In addition, the company continued to record depreciation for this equipment in both 2011 and 2012 at the rate of 10 percent of cost.

The first step in preparing the worksheet is to prepare a schedule showing the corrected net income amounts for the years ended December 31, 2010, 2011, and 2012. Each correction of the amount originally reported is clearly labeled. The next step is to indicate the statement of financial position accounts affected as of December 31, 2012. Illustration 22-22 shows the completed worksheet for Hudson Company.

HUDSON COMPANY
Worksheet to Correct Income and Statement of Financial Position Errors

	A	B	C	D	E	F	G	H
1		Worksheet Analysis of Changes in Net Income				Statement of Financial Position Correction at December 31, 2012		
2		2010	2011	2012	Totals	Debit	Credit	Account
3	Net income as reported	€17,400	€20,200	€11,300	€48,900			
4	Wages unpaid, 12/31/10	(1,000)	1,000		–0–			
5	Wages unpaid, 12/31/11		(1,400)	1,400	–0–			
6	Wages unpaid, 12/31/12			(1,600)	(1,600)		€1,600	Wages Payable
7	Inventory overstatement, 12/31/10	(1,900)	1,900		–0–			
8	Unexpired insurance, 12/31/11		1,200	(1,200)	–0–			
9	Interest receivable, 12/31/11		240	(240)	–0–			
10	Correction for entry made upon sale of equipment, 1/2/11ᵃ		(1,500)		(1,500)	€2,400	3,900	Accumulated Depreciation Machinery
11	Overcharge of depreciation, 2011		390		390	390		Accumulated Depreciation
12	Overcharge of depreciation, 2012			390	390	390		Accumulated Depreciation
13	Corrected net income	€14,500	€22,030	€10,050	€46,580			
14	ᵃCost	€3,900						
15	Accumulated depreciation	2,400						
16	Book value	1,500						
17	Proceeds from sale	1,800						
18	Gain on sale	300						
19	Income reported	(1,800)						
20	Adjustment	€(1,500)						

Sheet1 / Sheet2 / Sheet3

ILLUSTRATION 22-22
Worksheet to Correct Income and Statement of Financial Position Errors

Assuming that Hudson Company **has not closed the books**, correcting entries on December 31, 2012, are:

Retained Earnings	1,400	
Wages Expense		1,400
(To correct improper charge to Wages Expense for 2012)		
Wages Expense	1,600	
Wages Payable		1,600
(To record proper wages expense for 2012)		
Insurance Expense	1,200	
Retained Earnings		1,200
(To record proper insurance expense for 2012)		
Interest Revenue	240	
Retained Earnings		240
(To correct improper credit to Interest Revenue in 2012)		

Retained Earnings	1,500	
Accumulated Depreciation	2,400	
Machinery		3,900
(To record write-off of machinery in 2011 and adjustment of Retained Earnings)		
Accumulated Depreciation	780	
Depreciation Expense		390
Retained Earnings		390
(To correct improper charge for depreciation expense in 2011 and 2012)		

If Hudson Company has closed the books for 2012, the correcting entries are:

Retained Earnings	1,600	
Wages Payable		1,600
(To record proper wage expense for 2012)		
Retained Earnings	1,500	
Accumulated Depreciation	2,400	
Machinery		3,900
(To record write-off of machinery in 2011 and adjustment of Retained Earnings)		
Accumulated Depreciation	780	
Retained Earnings		780
(To correct improper charge for depreciation expense in 2011 and 2012)		

PREPARATION OF FINANCIAL STATEMENTS WITH ERROR CORRECTIONS

Up to now, our discussion of error analysis has focused on identifying the type of error involved and accounting for its correction in the records. We have noted that companies must present the correction of the error on comparative financial statements.

The following example illustrates how a company would restate a typical year's financial statements, given many different errors.

Dick & Wally's Outlet is a small retail outlet in the town of Holiday. Lacking expertise in accounting, the company does not keep adequate records, and numerous errors occurred in recording accounting information.

1. The bookkeeper inadvertently failed to record a cash receipt of $1,000 on the sale of merchandise in 2012.

2. Accrued wages expense at the end of 2011 was $2,500; at the end of 2012, $3,200. The company does not accrue for wages; all wages are charged to Administrative Expenses.

3. The company had not set up an allowance for estimated uncollectible receivables. Dick and Wally decided to set up such an allowance for the estimated probable losses, as of December 31, 2012, for 2011 accounts of $700, and for 2012 accounts of $1,500. They also decided to correct the charge against each year so that it shows the losses (actual and estimated) relating to that year's sales. The company has written off accounts to bad debt expense (selling expense) as follows.

	In 2011	In 2012
2011 accounts	$400	$2,000
2012 accounts		1,600

4. Unexpired insurance not recorded at the end of 2011 was $600, and at the end of 2012, $400. All insurance is charged to Administrative Expenses.

5. An account payable of $6,000 should have been a note payable.

6. During 2011, the company sold for $7,000 an asset that cost $10,000 and had a book value of $4,000. At the time of sale, Cash was debited and Miscellaneous Income was credited for $7,000.

7. As a result of the last transaction, the company overstated depreciation expense (an administrative expense) in 2011 by $800 and in 2012 by $1,200.

Illustration 22-23 presents a worksheet that begins with the unadjusted trial balance of Dick & Wally's Outlet. You can determine the correcting entries and their effect on the financial statements by examining the worksheet.

DICK & WALLY'S OUTLET
Worksheet Analysis to Adjust Financial Statements for the Year 2012

A	Trial Balance Unadjusted Debit	Credit		Adjustments Debit		Credit	Income Statement Adjusted Debit	Credit	Statement of Financial Position Adjusted Debit	Credit
Cash	3,100		(1)	1,000					4,100	
Accounts Receivable	17,600								17,600	
Notes Receivable	8,500								8,500	
Inventory	34,000								34,000	
Property, Plant, and Equipment	112,000				(6)	10,000ª			102,000	
Accumulated Depreciation		83,500	(6)	6,000ª						75,500
			(7)	2,000						
Investments	24,300								24,300	
Accounts Payable		14,500	(5)	6,000						8,500
Notes Payable		10,000			(5)	6,000				16,000
Share Capital		43,500								43,500
Retained Earnings		20,000	(3)	2,700ᵇ						
			(6)	4,000ª	(4)	600				
			(2)	2,500	(7)	800				12,200
Sales		94,000			(1)	1,000		95,000		
Cost of Goods Sold	21,000						21,000			
Selling Expenses	22,000				(3)	500ᵇ	21,500			
Administrative Expenses	23,000		(2)	700	(4)	400	22,700			
			(4)	600	(7)	1,200				
Totals	265,500	265,500								
Wages Payable					(2)	3,200				3,200
Allowance for Doubtful Accounts					(3)	2,200ᵇ				2,200
Unexpired Insurance			(4)	400					400	
Net Income							29,800			29,800
Totals				25,900		25,900	95,000	95,000	190,900	190,900

Sheet1 / Sheet2 / Sheet3

Computations:

ᵃMachinery

Proceeds from sale	$7,000
Book value of machinery	4,000
Gain on sale	3,000
Income credited	7,000
Retained earnings adjustment	$4,000

ᵇBad Debts

	2011	2012
Bad debts charged for	$2,400	$1,600
Additional bad debts anticipated	700	1,500
	3,100	3,100
Charges currently made to each year	(400)	(3,600)
Bad debt adjustment	$2,700	$ (500)

ILLUSTRATION 22-23
Worksheet to Analyze Effect of Errors in Financial Statements

You will want to read the **CONVERGENCE CORNER** on page 1215

For discussion of how international convergence efforts relate to accounting changes and errors.

CONVERGENCE CORNER

ACCOUNTING CHANGES AND ERRORS

The FASB has issued guidance on changes in accounting policies, changes in estimates, and corrections of errors, which essentially converges U.S. GAAP to *IAS 8*.

RELEVANT FACTS

- One area in which U.S. GAAP and IFRS differ is the reporting of error corrections in previously issued financial statements. While both sets of standards require restatement, U.S. GAAP is an absolute standard—that is, there is no exception to this rule.

- The accounting for changes in estimates is similar between U.S. GAAP and IFRS.

- Under U.S. GAAP and IFRS, if determining the effect of a change in accounting policy is considered impracticable, then a company should report the effect of the change in the period in which it believes it practicable to do so, which may be the current period.

- Under IFRS, the impracticality exception applies both to changes in accounting policies and to the correction of errors. Under U.S. GAAP, this exception applies only to changes in accounting policy.

- *IAS 8* does not specifically address the accounting and reporting for indirect effects of changes in accounting policies. As indicated in the chapter, U.S. GAAP has detailed guidance on the accounting and reporting of indirect effects.

ABOUT THE NUMBERS

An interesting sidelight to our discussion of accounting changes involves how companies that follow IFRS report financial information related to the equity method of accounting. Under the equity method of accounting, the investor increases its investment for the pro-rata share of the net income of the investee (often referred to as an associated company under IFRS). On the other hand, the investor reduces its investment for any dividends received from the investee. Both IFRS and U.S. GAAP follow this accounting approach.

However, there is a subtle difference between IFRS and U.S. GAAP related to how the investor evaluates the accounting policies of the investee. To illustrate, assume that Kirkland Company (the investor company) uses the FIFO inventory method, and Margo Company (the investee company) uses average cost for its inventory valuation. If Kirkland follows IFRS, Kirkland must conform the accounting policies of Margo to its own accounting policies. Therefore, Kirkland adjusts the net income of Margo so its net income is reported on the FIFO basis.

This procedure is not used under U.S. GAAP. Under U.S. GAAP, Kirkland ignores the fact that Margo uses a different method of inventory valuation. Kirkland records its pro-rata share of the net income of Margo without adjusting for the fact that Margo uses a different inventory valuation method. As a result, there is a lack of comparability in the inventory methods used to report net income for Kirkland Company under U.S. GAAP.

ON THE HORIZON

For the most part, IFRS and U.S. GAAP are similar in the area of accounting changes and reporting the effects of errors. Thus, there is no active project in this area. A related development involves the presentation of comparative data. Under IFRS, when a company prepares financial statements on a new basis, two years of comparative data are reported. U.S. GAAP requires comparative information for a three-year period. Use of the shorter comparative data period must be addressed before U.S. companies can adopt IFRS.

SUMMARY OF LEARNING OBJECTIVES

[1] **Identify the two types of accounting changes.** The two different types of accounting changes are: (1) *Change in accounting policy:* a change from one accepted accounting policy to another accepted accounting policy. (2) *Change in accounting estimate:* a change that occurs as the result of new information or as additional experience is acquired.

[2] **Describe the accounting for changes in accounting policies.** A change in accounting policy involves a change from one accepted accounting policy to another. A change in accounting policy is not considered to result from the adoption of a new policy in recognition of events that have occurred for the first time or that were previously immaterial. If the accounting policy previously followed was not acceptable or if the policy was applied incorrectly, a change to a accepted accounting policy is considered a correction of an error.

[3] **Understand how to account for retrospective accounting changes.** The general requirement for changes in accounting policy is retrospective application. Under retrospective application, companies change prior years' financial statements on a basis consistent with the newly adopted policy. They treat any part of the effect attributable to years prior to those presented as an adjustment of the earliest retained earnings presented.

[4] **Understand how to account for impracticable changes.** Retrospective application is impracticable if the prior period effect cannot be determined using every reasonable effort to do so. For example, in changing to average cost, the base-year inventory for all subsequent average cost calculations may be the opening inventory in the year the company adopts the method. There is no restatement of prior years' income because it is often too impractical to do so.

[5] **Describe the accounting for changes in estimates.** Companies report changes in estimates prospectively. That is, companies should make no changes in previously reported results. They do not adjust opening balances nor change financial statements of prior periods.

[6] **Describe the accounting for correction of errors.** Companies must correct errors as soon as they discover them, by proper entries in the accounts, and report them in the financial statements. The profession requires that a company treat corrections of errors as prior period adjustments, record them in the year in which it discovered the errors, and report them in the financial statements in the proper periods. If presenting comparative statements, a company should restate the prior statements affected to correct for the errors. The company need not repeat the disclosures in the financial statements of subsequent periods.

[7] **Identify economic motives for changing accounting policies.** Managers might have varying motives for income reporting, depending on economic times and whom they seek to impress. Some of the reasons for changing accounting policies are (1) political costs, (2) capital structure, (3) bonus payments, and (4) smoothing of earnings.

[8] **Analyze the effect of errors.** Three types of errors can occur: (1) *Statement of financial position errors,* which affect only the presentation of an asset, liability, or equity account. (2) *Income statement errors,* which affect only the presentation of revenue, expense, gain, or loss accounts in the income statement. (3) *Statement of financial position and income statement errors,* which involve both the statement of financial position and income statement. Errors are classified into two types: (1) *Counterbalancing errors* are offset or corrected over two periods. (2) *Non-counterbalancing errors* are not offset in the next accounting period and take longer than two periods to correct themselves.

As an aid to understanding accounting changes, we provide the following glossary. **[10]**

KEY TERMS RELATED TO ACCOUNTING CHANGES

ACCOUNTING POLICIES. The specific principles, bases, conventions, rules, and practices applied by an entity in preparing and presenting financial statements.

CHANGE IN ACCOUNTING ESTIMATE. An adjustment of the carrying amount of an asset or a liability, or the amount of the periodic consumption of an asset, that results from the assessment of the present status of, and expected future benefits and obligations associated with, assets and liabilities. Changes in accounting estimates result from new information or new developments and, accordingly, are not corrections of errors.

DIRECT EFFECTS OF A CHANGE IN ACCOUNTING POLICY. Those recognized changes in assets or liabilities necessary to effect a change in accounting policy.

ERRORS. Omissions from, and misstatements in, the entity's financial statements for one or more prior periods arising from a failure to use, or misuse of, reliable information that (1) was available when financial statements for those periods were authorized for issue, and (2) could reasonably be expected to have been obtained and taken into account in the preparation and presentation of those financial statements. Such errors include the effects of mathematical mistakes, mistakes in applying accounting policies, oversights or misinterpretations of facts, and fraud.

IMPRACTICABLE. Applying a requirement is impracticable when the entity cannot apply it after making every reasonable effort to do so. For a particular prior period, it is impracticable to apply a change in an accounting policy retrospectively or to make a retrospective restatement to correct an error if (1) the effects of the retrospective application or retrospective restatement are not determinable, (2) the retrospective application or retrospective restatement requires assumptions about what management's intent would have been in that period, or (3) the retrospective application or retrospective restatement requires significant estimates of amounts and it is impossible to distinguish objectively information about those estimates.

INDIRECT EFFECTS OF A CHANGE IN ACCOUNTING POLICY. Any changes to current or future cash flows of an entity that result from making a change in accounting policy that is applied retrospectively.

PROSPECTIVE APPLICATION. Change in accounting policy requires (1) applying the new accounting policy to transactions, other events, and conditions occurring after the date as at which the policy is changed; and (2) recognizing the effect of the change in the accounting estimate in the current and future periods affected by the change.

RETROSPECTIVE APPLICATION. Applying a new accounting policy to transactions, other events, and conditions as if that policy had always been applied.

RETROSPECTIVE RESTATEMENT. Correcting the recognition, measurement, and disclosure of amounts of elements of financial statements as if a prior period error had never occurred.

AUTHORITATIVE LITERATURE

Authoritative Literature References

[1] International Accounting Standard 8, *Accounting Policies, Changes in Accounting Estimates, and Errors* (London, U.K.: International Accounting Standards Committee Foundation, 2003).

[2] International Accounting Standard 8, *Accounting Policies, Changes in Accounting Estimates, and Errors* (London, U.K.: International Accounting Standards Committee Foundation, 2003), paras. 19–22.

[3] International Accounting Standard 8, *Accounting Policies, Changes in Accounting Estimates, and Errors* (London, U.K.: International Accounting Standards Committee Foundation, 2003), par. 13.

[4] International Accounting Standard 8, *Accounting Policies, Changes in Accounting Estimates, and Errors* (London, U.K.: International Accounting Standards Committee Foundation, 2003), paras. 11–12.

[5] International Accounting Standard 8, *Accounting Policies, Changes in Accounting Estimates, and Errors* (London, U.K.: International Accounting Standards Committee Foundation, 2003), par. 29.

[6] International Accounting Standard 8, *Accounting Policies, Changes in Accounting Estimates, and Errors* (London, U.K.: International Accounting Standards Committee Foundation, 2003), par. 24.

[7] International Accounting Standard 8, *Accounting Policies, Changes in Accounting Estimates, and Errors* (London, U.K.: International Accounting Standards Committee Foundation, 2003), par. 29(e).

[8] International Accounting Standard 8, *Accounting Policies, Changes in Accounting Estimates, and Errors* (London, U.K.: International Accounting Standards Committee Foundation, 2003), paras. 37–38.

[9] International Accounting Standard 8, *Accounting Policies, Changes in Accounting Estimates, and Errors* (London, U.K.: International Accounting Standards Committee Foundation, 2003), par. 39.

[10] International Accounting Standard 8, *Accounting Policies, Changes in Accounting Estimates, and Errors* (London, U.K.: International Accounting Standards Committee Foundation, 2003), par. 5.

QUESTIONS

1. In recent years, the financial press has indicated that many companies have changed their accounting policies. What are the major reasons why companies change accounting policies?

2. State how each of the following items is reflected in the financial statements.

(a) Change from FIFO to average cost method for inventory valuation purposes.

(b) Charge for failure to record depreciation in a previous period.

(c) Litigation won in current year, related to prior period.

(d) Change in the realizability of certain receivables.

(e) Write-off of receivables.

(f) Change from the percentage-of-completion to the cost-recovery method for reporting net income.

3. Discuss briefly the three approaches that have been suggested for reporting changes in accounting policies.

4. Identify and describe the approach the IASB requires for reporting changes in accounting policies.

5. What is the indirect effect of a change in accounting policy? Briefly describe the approach to reporting the indirect effects of a change in accounting policy.

6. Define a change in estimate and provide an illustration.

7. Lenexa State Bank has followed the practice of capitalizing certain marketing costs and amortizing these costs over their expected life. In the current year, the bank determined that the future benefits from these costs were doubtful. Consequently, the bank adopted the policy of expensing these costs as incurred. How should the bank report this accounting change in the comparative financial statements?

8. Indicate how the following items are recorded in the accounting records in the current year of Coronet Co.

(a) Impairment of goodwill.

(b) A change in depreciating plant assets from accelerated to the straight-line method.

(c) Large write-off of inventories because of obsolescence.

(d) Change from the cash basis to accrual basis of accounting.

(e) Change from average cost to FIFO method for inventory valuation purposes.

(f) Change in the estimate of service lives for plant assets.

9. Whittier Construction Co. had followed the practice of expensing all materials assigned to a construction job without recognizing any residual inventory. On December 31, 2010, it was determined that residual inventory should be valued at $52,000. Of this amount, $29,000 arose during the current year. How does this information affect the financial statements to be prepared at the end of 2010?

10. Parsons Inc. wishes to change from the cost-recovery to the percentage-of-completion method for financial reporting purposes. The auditor indicates that a change would be permitted only if it is to a preferable method. What difficulties develop in assessing preferability?

11. Discuss how a change in accounting policy is handled when it is impracticable to determine previous amounts.

12. What relevance do political costs have to accounting changes?

13. What are some of the key motivations that managers might have to change accounting policies?

14. Distinguish between counterbalancing and non-counter-balancing errors. Give an example of each.

15. Discuss and illustrate how a correction of an error in previously issued financial statements should be handled.

16. Prior to 2010, Heberling Inc. excluded manufacturing overhead costs from work in process and finished goods inventory. These costs have been expensed as incurred. In 2010, the company decided to change its accounting methods for manufacturing inventories to full costing by including these costs as product costs. Assuming that these costs are material, how should this change be reflected in the financial statements for 2009 and 2010?

17. Elliott Corp. failed to record accrued salaries for 2009, €2,000; 2010, €2,100; and 2011, €3,900. What is the amount of the overstatement or understatement of Retained Earnings at December 31, 2012?

18. In January 2010, installation costs of £6,000 on new machinery were charged to Repair Expense. Other costs of this machinery of £30,000 were correctly recorded and have been depreciated using the straight-line method with an estimated life of 10 years and no residual value. At December 31, 2011, it is decided that the machinery has a remaining useful life of 20 years, starting with January 1, 2011. What entry(ies) should be made in 2011 to correctly record transactions related to machinery, assuming the machinery has no residual value? The books have not been closed for 2011 and depreciation expense has not yet been recorded for 2011.

19. An entry to record Purchases and related Accounts Payable of ¥130,000 for merchandise purchased on December 23, 2011, was recorded in January 2012. This merchandise was not included in inventory at December 31, 2011. What effect does this error have on reported net income for 2011? What entry should be made to correct for this error, assuming that the books are not closed for 2011?

20. Equipment was purchased on January 2, 2010, for $24,000, but no portion of the cost has been charged to depreciation. The corporation wishes to use the straight-line method for these assets, which have been estimated to have a life of 10 years and no residual value. What effect does this error have on net income in 2010? What entry is necessary to correct for this error, assuming that the books are not closed for 2010?

21. What is the major difference in accounting for errors under IFRS versus U.S. GAAP?

22. How are direct and indirect changes in accounting policy reported under U.S. GAAP?

23. What is the difference in approach between U.S. GAAP and IFRS in regards to the equity method of accounting for the investor?

BRIEF EXERCISES

BE22-1 Wertz Construction Company decided at the beginning of 2010 to change from the cost-recovery method to the percentage-of-completion method for financial reporting purposes. The company will continue to use the cost-recovery method for tax purposes. For years prior to 2010, pretax income under the two methods was as follows: percentage-of-completion $120,000, and cost-recovery $80,000. The tax rate is 35%. Prepare Wertz's 2010 journal entry to record the change in accounting policy.

BE22-2 Refer to the accounting change by Wertz Construction Company in BE22-1. Wertz has a profit-sharing plan, which pays all employees a bonus at year-end based on 1% of pretax income. Compute the indirect effect of Wertz's change in accounting policy that will be reported in the 2010 income statement, assuming that the profit-sharing contract explicitly requires adjustment for changes in income numbers.

BE22-3 Shannon, Inc., changed from the average cost to the FIFO cost flow assumption in 2010. The increase in the prior year's income before taxes is €1,200,000. The tax rate is 40%. Prepare Shannon's 2010 journal entry to record the change in accounting policy.

BE22-4 Tedesco Company changed depreciation methods in 2010 from double-declining-balance to straight-line. Depreciation prior to 2010 under double-declining-balance was $90,000, whereas straight-line depreciation prior to 2010 would have been $50,000. Tedesco's depreciable assets had a cost of $250,000 with a $40,000 residual value, and an 8-year remaining useful life at the beginning of 2010. Prepare the 2010 journal entry, if necessary, related to Tedesco's depreciable assets.

BE22-5 Sesame Company purchased a computer system for £74,000 on January 1, 2009. It was depreciated based on a 7-year life and an £18,000 residual value. On January 1, 2011, Sesame revised these estimates to a total useful life of 4 years and a residual value of £10,000. Prepare Sesame's entry to record 2011 depreciation expense.

BE22-6 In 2010, Bailey Corporation discovered that equipment purchased on January 1, 2008, for $50,000 was expensed at that time. The equipment should have been depreciated over 5 years, with no residual value. The effective tax rate is 30%. Prepare Bailey's 2010 journal entry to correct the error.

•6 **BE22-7** At January 1, 2010, Cheng Company reported retained earnings of ¥20,000,000. In 2010, Cheng discovered that 2009 depreciation expense was understated by ¥4,000,000. In 2010, net income was ¥9,000,000 and dividends declared were ¥2,500,000. The tax rate is 40%. Prepare a 2010 retained earnings statement for Cheng Company.

•6 **BE22-8** Indicate the effect—**U**nderstate, **O**verstate, **N**o Effect—that each of the following errors has on 2010 net income and 2011 net income.

	2010	2011
(a) Equipment purchased in 2009 was expensed.	___	___
(b) Wages payable were not recorded at 12/31/10.	___	___
(c) Equipment purchased in 2010 was expensed.	___	___
(d) 2010 ending inventory was overstated.	___	___
(e) Patent amortization was not recorded in 2011.	___	___

•3 •5 **BE22-9** Roundtree Manufacturing Co. is preparing its year-end financial statements and is considering the accounting for the following items.

1. The vice president of sales had indicated that one product line has lost its customer appeal and will be phased out over the next 3 years. Therefore, a decision has been made to lower the estimated lives on related production equipment from the remaining 5 years to 3 years.
2. The Hightone Building was converted from a sales office to offices for the Accounting Department at the beginning of this year. Therefore, the expense related to this building will now appear as an administrative expense rather than a selling expense on the current year's income statement.
3. Estimating the lives of new products in the Leisure Products Division has become very difficult because of the highly competitive conditions in this market. Therefore, the practice of deferring and amortizing preproduction costs has been abandoned in favor of expensing such costs as they are incurred.

Identify and explain whether each of the above items is a change in policy, a change in estimate, or an error.

•3 •6 **BE22-10** Palmer Co. is evaluating the appropriate accounting for the following items.

1. Management has decided to switch from the FIFO inventory valuation method to the average cost inventory valuation method for all inventories.
2. When the year-end physical inventory adjustment was made for the current year, the controller discovered that the prior year's physical inventory sheets for an entire warehouse were mislaid and excluded from last year's count.
3. Palmer's Custom Division manufactures large-scale, custom-designed machinery on a contract basis. Management decided to switch from the cost-recovery method to the percentage-of-completion method of accounting for long-term contracts.

Identify and explain whether each of the above items is a change in accounting policy, a change in estimate, or an error.

EXERCISES

•3 **E22-1 (Change in Policy—Long-Term Contracts)** Cherokee Construction Company changed from the cost-recovery to the percentage-of-completion method of accounting for long-term construction contracts during 2010. For tax purposes, the company employs the cost-recovery method and will continue this approach in the future. (*Hint:* Adjust all tax consequences through the Deferred Tax Liability account.) The appropriate information related to this change is as follows.

	Pretax Income from:		
	Percentage-of-Completion	Cost-Recovery	Difference
2009	$780,000	$610,000	$170,000
2010	700,000	480,000	220,000

Instructions
(a) Assuming that the tax rate is 35%, what is the amount of net income that would be reported in 2010?
(b) What entry(ies) is necessary to adjust the accounting records for the change in accounting policy?

•3 **E22-2 (Change in Policy—Inventory Methods)** Whitman Company began operations on January 1, 2008, and uses the average cost method of pricing inventory. Management is contemplating a change in inventory methods for 2011. The following information is available for the years 2008–2010.

	Net Income Computed Using	
	Average Cost Method	FIFO Method
2008	€16,000	€19,000
2009	18,000	21,000
2010	20,000	25,000

Instructions

(Ignore all tax effects.)

(a) Prepare the journal entry necessary to record a change from the average cost method to the FIFO method in 2011.

(b) Determine net income to be reported for 2008, 2009, and 2010, after giving effect to the change in accounting policy.

•3 **E22-3 (Accounting Change)** Ramirez Co. decides at the beginning of 2010 to adopt the FIFO method of inventory valuation. Ramirez had used the average cost method for financial reporting since its inception on January 1, 2008, and had maintained records adequate to apply the FIFO method retrospectively. Ramirez concluded that FIFO is the preferable inventory method because it reflects the current cost of inventory on the statement of financial position. The table presents the effects of the change in accounting policy on inventory and cost of goods sold.

	Inventory Determined by		Cost of Goods Sold Determined by	
Date	Average Cost Method	FIFO Method	Average Cost Method	FIFO Method
January 1, 2008	$ 0	$ 0	$ 0	$ 0
December 31, 2008	100	80	800	820
December 31, 2009	200	240	1,000	940
December 31, 2010	320	390	1,130	1,100

Retained earnings reported under average cost are as follows.

	Retained Earnings Balance
December 31, 2008	$2,200
December 31, 2009	4,200
December 31, 2010	6,070

Other information:

1. For each year presented, sales are $4,000 and operating expenses are $1,000.
2. Ramirez provides two years of financial statements. Earnings per share information is not required.

Instructions

(a) Prepare income statements under average cost and FIFO for 2008, 2009, and 2010.

(b) Prepare income statements reflecting the retrospective application of the accounting change from the average cost method to the FIFO method for 2010 and 2009.

(c) Prepare the note to the financial statements describing the change in method of inventory valuation. In the note, indicate the income statement line items for 2010 and 2009 that were affected by the change in accounting policy.

(d) Prepare comparative retained earnings statements for 2009 and 2010 under FIFO.

•3 **E22-4 (Accounting Change)** Linden Company started operations on January 1, 2006, and has used the FIFO method of inventory valuation since its inception. In 2012, it decides to switch to the average cost method. You are provided with the following information.

	Net Income		Retained Earnings (ending balance)
	Under FIFO	Under Average Cost	Under FIFO
2006	£100,000	£ 92,000	£100,000
2007	70,000	65,000	160,000
2008	90,000	80,000	235,000
2009	120,000	130,000	340,000
2010	300,000	293,000	590,000
2011	305,000	310,000	780,000

Instructions

(a) What is the beginning retained earnings balance at January 1, 2008, if Linden prepares comparative financial statements starting in 2008?

(b) What is the beginning retained earnings balance at January 1, 2011, if Linden prepares comparative financial statements starting in 2011?

(c) What is the beginning retained earnings balance at January 1, 2012, if Linden prepares single-period financial statements for 2012?

(d) What is the net income reported by Linden in the 2011 income statement if it prepares comparative financial statements starting with 2009?

·3 E22-5 (Accounting Change) Presented below are income statements prepared on an average cost and FIFO basis for Carlton Company, which started operations on January 1, 2009. The company presently uses the average cost method of pricing its inventory and has decided to switch to the FIFO method in 2010. The FIFO income statement is computed in accordance with IFRS. Carlton's profit-sharing agreement with its employees indicates that the company will pay employees 5% of income before profit sharing. Income taxes are ignored.

	Average Cost Basis		FIFO Basis	
	2010	2009	2010	2009
Sales	$3,000	$3,000	$3,000	$3,000
Cost of goods sold	1,130	1,000	1,100	940
Operating expenses	1,000	1,000	1,000	1,000
Income before profit sharing	870	1,000	900	1,060
Profit-sharing expense	44	50	45	53
Net income	$ 826	$ 950	$ 855	$1,007

Instructions

Answer the following questions.

(a) If comparative income statements are prepared, what net income should Carlton report in 2009 and 2010?

(b) Explain why, under the FIFO basis, Carlton reports $50 in 2009 and $48 in 2010 for its profit-sharing expense.

(c) Assume that Carlton has a beginning balance of retained earnings at January 1, 2010, of $8,000 using the average cost method. The company declared and paid dividends of $2,500 in 2010. Prepare the retained earnings statement for 2010, assuming that Carlton has switched to the FIFO method.

·5 E22-6 (Accounting Changes—Depreciation) Robillard Inc. acquired the following assets in January 2007.

Equipment, estimated service life, 5 years; residual value, $15,000	$465,000
Building, estimated service life, 30 years; no residual value	$780,000

The equipment has been depreciated using the sum-of-the-years'-digits method for the first 3 years for financial reporting purposes. In 2010, the company decided to change the method of computing depreciation to the straight-line method for the equipment, but no change was made in the estimated service life or residual value. It was also decided to change the total estimated service life of the building from 30 years to 40 years, with no change in the estimated residual value. The building is depreciated on the straight-line method.

Instructions

(a) Prepare the journal entry to record depreciation expense for the equipment in 2010.

(b) Prepare the journal entry to record depreciation expense for the building in 2010. (Round to nearest dollar.)

·5 ·6 E22-7 (Change in Estimate and Error; Financial Statements) Presented below are the comparative income statements for Pannebecker Inc. for the years 2009 and 2010.

	2010	2009
Sales	$340,000	$270,000
Cost of sales	200,000	142,000
Gross profit	140,000	128,000
Expenses	88,000	50,000
Net income	$ 52,000	$ 78,000
Retained earnings (Jan. 1)	$125,000	$ 72,000
Net income	52,000	78,000
Dividends	(30,000)	(25,000)
Retained earnings (Dec. 31)	$147,000	$125,000

The following additional information is provided.

1. In 2010, Pannebecker Inc. decided to switch its depreciation method from sum-of-the-years'-digits to the straight-line method. The assets were purchased at the beginning of 2009 for $90,000 with

an estimated useful life of 4 years and no residual value. (The 2010 income statement contains depreciation expense of $27,000 on the assets purchased at the beginning of 2009.)

2. In 2010, the company discovered that the ending inventory for 2009 was overstated by $20,000; ending inventory for 2010 is correctly stated.

Instructions

Prepare the revised retained earnings statement for 2009 and 2010, assuming comparative statements. (Ignore income taxes.)

•3 •5 •6 E22-8 (Accounting for Accounting Changes and Errors) Listed below are various types of accounting changes and errors.

_____ 1. Change from FIFO to average cost inventory method.
_____ 2. Change due to overstatement of inventory.
_____ 3. Change from an accelerated to straight-line method of depreciation.
_____ 4. Change from average cost to FIFO inventory method.
_____ 5. Change in the rate used to compute warranty costs.
_____ 6. Change from an unacceptable accounting policy to an acceptable accounting policy.
_____ 7. Change in a patent's amortization period.
_____ 8. Change from cost-recovery to percentage-of-completion method on construction contracts.
_____ 9. Change in a plant asset's residual value.

Instructions

For each change or error, indicate how it would be accounted for using the following code letters:

(a) Accounted for prospectively.
(b) Accounted for retrospectively.
(c) Neither of the above.

•5 •6 E22-9 (Error and Change in Estimate—Depreciation) Yoon Co. purchased a machine on January 1, 2007, for ₩44,000,000. At that time, it was estimated that the machine would have a 10-year life and no residual value. On December 31, 2010, the firm's accountant found that the entry for depreciation expense had been omitted in 2008. In addition, management has informed the accountant that the company plans to switch to straight-line depreciation, starting with the year 2010. At present, the company uses the sum-of-the-years'-digits method for depreciating equipment.

Instructions

Prepare the general journal entries that should be made at December 31, 2010, to record these events. (Ignore tax effects.)

•5 E22-10 (Depreciation Changes) On January 1, 2006, McElroy Company purchased a building and equipment that have the following useful lives, residual values, and costs.

> Building, 40-year estimated useful life, £50,000 residual value, £1,200,000 cost
> Equipment, 12-year estimated useful life, £10,000 residual value, £130,000 cost

The building has been depreciated under the double-declining-balance method through 2009. In 2010, the company decided to switch to the straight-line method of depreciation. McElroy also decided to change the total useful life of the equipment to 9 years, with a residual value of £5,000 at the end of that time. The equipment is depreciated using the straight-line method.

Instructions

(a) Prepare the journal entry(ies) necessary to record the depreciation expense on the building in 2010.
(b) Compute depreciation expense on the equipment for 2010.

•5 E22-11 (Change in Estimate—Depreciation) Thurber Co. purchased equipment for $710,000 which was estimated to have a useful life of 10 years with a residual value of $10,000 at the end of that time. Depreciation has been entered for 7 years on a straight-line basis. In 2011, it is determined that the total estimated life should be 15 years with a residual value of $4,000 at the end of that time.

Instructions

(a) Prepare the entry (if any) to correct the prior years' depreciation.
(b) Prepare the entry to record depreciation for 2011.

•5 E22-12 (Change in Estimate—Depreciation) Frederick Industries changed from the double-declining-balance to the straight-line method in 2010 on all its plant assets. There was no change in the assets' residual values or useful lives. Plant assets, acquired on January 2, 2007, had an original cost of $2,400,000, with a $100,000 residual value and an 8-year estimated useful life. Income before depreciation expense was $370,000 in 2009 and $300,000 in 2010.

Instructions

(a) Prepare the journal entry(ies) to reflect the change in depreciation method in 2010.

(b) Starting with income before depreciation expense, prepare the remaining portion of the income statement for 2009 and 2010.

•3 E22-13 (Change in Policy—Long-Term Contracts) Bryant Construction Company changed from the cost-recovery to the percentage-of-completion method of accounting for long-term construction contracts during 2010. For tax purposes, the company employs the cost-recovery method and will continue this approach in the future. The information related to this change is as follows.

	Pretax Income from		
	Percentage-of-Completion	Cost-Recovery	Difference
2009	$980,000	$730,000	$250,000
2010	900,000	480,000	420,000

Instructions

(a) Assuming that the tax rate is 40%, what is the amount of net income that would be reported in 2010?

(b) What entry(ies) are necessary to adjust the accounting records for the change in accounting policy?

•3 E22-14 (Various Changes in Policy—Inventory Methods) Below is the net income of Benchley Instrument Co., a private corporation, computed under the two inventory methods using a periodic system.

	FIFO	Average Cost
2008	€26,000	€23,000
2009	30,000	25,000
2010	29,000	27,000
2011	34,000	30,000

Instructions

(Ignore tax considerations.)

(a) Assume that in 2011 Benchley decided to change from the FIFO method to the average cost method of pricing inventories. Prepare the journal entry necessary for the change that took place during 2011, and show net income reported for 2008, 2009, 2010, and 2011.

(b) Assume that in 2011 Benchley, which had been using the average cost method since incorporation in 2008, changed to the FIFO method of pricing inventories. Prepare the journal entry necessary to record the change in 2011, and show net income reported for 2008, 2009, 2010, and 2011.

•6 E22-15 (Error Correction Entries) The first audit of the books of Fenimore Company was made for the year ended December 31, 2010. In examining the books, the auditor found that certain items had been overlooked or incorrectly handled in the last 3 years. These items are:

1. At the beginning of 2008, the company purchased a machine for $510,000 (residual value of $51,000) that had a useful life of 5 years. The bookkeeper used straight-line depreciation but failed to deduct the residual value in computing the depreciation base for the 3 years.

2. At the end of 2009, the company failed to accrue sales salaries of $45,000.

3. A tax lawsuit that involved the year 2008 was settled late in 2010. It was determined that the company owed an additional $85,000 in taxes related to 2008. The company did not record a liability in 2008 or 2009 because the possibility of loss was considered remote, and debited the $85,000 to a loss account in 2010 and credited Cash for the same amount.

4. Fenimore Company purchased a copyright from another company early in 2008 for $50,000. Fenimore had not amortized the copyright because its value had not diminished. The copyright has a useful life at purchase of 20 years.

5. In 2010, the company wrote off $87,000 of inventory considered to be obsolete; this loss was charged directly to Retained Earnings and credited to Inventory.

Instructions

Prepare the journal entries necessary in 2010 to correct the books, assuming that the books have not been closed. Disregard effects of corrections on income tax.

•6 E22-16 (Error Analysis and Correcting Entry) You have been engaged to review the financial statements of Longfellow Corporation. In the course of your examination, you conclude that the bookkeeper hired during the current year is not doing a good job. You notice a number of irregularities, as follows.

1. Year-end wages payable of $3,400 were not recorded because the bookkeeper thought that "they were immaterial."

2. Accrued vacation pay for the year of $31,100 was not recorded because the bookkeeper "never heard that you had to do it."

3. Insurance for a 12-month period purchased on November 1 of this year was charged to insurance expense in the amount of $3,300 because "the amount of the check is about the same every year."
4. Reported sales revenue for the year is $1,908,000. This includes all sales taxes collected for the year. The sales tax rate is 6%. Because the sales tax is forwarded to the Department of Revenue, the Sales Tax Expense account is debited. The bookkeeper thought that "the sales tax is a selling expense." At the end of the current year, the balance in the Sales Tax Expense account is $103,400.

Instructions

Prepare the necessary correcting entries, assuming that Longfellow uses a calendar-year basis.

·6 **E22-17** **(Error Analysis and Correcting Entry)** The reported net incomes for the first 2 years of Sinclair Products, Inc., were as follows: 2010, $147,000; 2011, $185,000. Early in 2012, the following errors were discovered.

1. Depreciation of equipment for 2010 was overstated $19,000.
2. Depreciation of equipment for 2011 was understated $38,500.
3. December 31, 2010, inventory was understated $50,000.
4. December 31, 2011, inventory was overstated $14,200.

Instructions

Prepare the correcting entry necessary when these errors are discovered. Assume that the books for 2011 are closed. (Ignore income tax considerations.)

·6 ·8 **E22-18** **(Error Analysis)** Emerson Tool Company's December 31 year-end financial statements contained the following errors.

	December 31, 2009	December 31, 2010
Ending inventory	£9,600 understated	£7,100 overstated
Depreciation expense	£2,300 understated	—

An insurance premium of £60,000 was prepaid in 2009 covering the years 2009, 2010, and 2011. The entire amount was charged to expense in 2009. In addition, on December 31, 2010, fully depreciated machinery was sold for £15,000 cash, but the entry was not recorded until 2011. There were no other errors during 2009 or 2010, and no corrections have been made for any of the errors. (Ignore income tax considerations.)

Instructions

(a) Compute the total effect of the errors on 2010 net income.
(b) Compute the total effect of the errors on the amount of Emerson's working capital at December 31, 2010.
(c) Compute the total effect of the errors on the balance of Emerson's retained earnings at December 31, 2010.

·6 ·8 **E22-19** **(Error Analysis and Correcting Entries)** A partial trial balance of Dickinson Corporation is as follows on December 31, 2010.

	Dr.	Cr.
Supplies on hand	$ 2,500	
Accrued salaries and wages		$ 1,500
Interest receivable	5,100	
Prepaid insurance	90,000	
Unearned rent		–0–
Accrued interest payable		15,000

Additional adjusting data:

1. A physical count of supplies on hand on December 31, 2010, totaled $1,100.
2. Through oversight, the Accrued Salaries and Wages account was not changed during 2010. Accrued salaries and wages on December 31, 2010, amounted to $4,400.
3. The Interest Receivable account was also left unchanged during 2010. Accrued interest on investments amounts to $4,350 on December 31, 2010.
4. The unexpired portions of the insurance policies totaled $65,000 as of December 31, 2010.
5. $24,000 was received on January 1, 2010, for the rent of a building for both 2010 and 2011. The entire amount was credited to rental income.
6. Depreciation for the year was erroneously recorded as $5,000 rather than the correct figure of $50,000.
7. A further review of depreciation calculations of prior years revealed that depreciation of $7,200 was not recorded. It was decided that this oversight should be corrected by a prior period adjustment.

Instructions

(a) Assuming that the books have not been closed, what are the adjusting entries necessary at December 31, 2010? (Ignore income tax considerations.)

(b) Assuming that the books have been closed, what are the adjusting entries necessary at December 31, 2010? (Ignore income tax considerations.)

E22-20 (Error Analysis) The before-tax income for Fitzgerald Co. for 2010 was $101,000, and for 2011 was $77,400. However, the accountant noted that the following errors had been made.

1. Sales for 2010 included amounts of $38,200 which had been received in cash during 2010, but for which the related products were delivered in 2011. Title did not pass to the purchaser until 2011.
2. The inventory on December 31, 2010, was understated by $8,640.
3. The bookkeeper in recording interest expense for both 2010 and 2011 on bonds payable made the following entry on an annual basis.

Interest Expense	15,000	
Cash		15,000

The bonds have a face value of $250,000 and pay a stated interest rate of 6%. They were issued at a discount of $10,000 on January 1, 2010, to yield an effective-interest rate of 7%. (Assume that the effective-interest method should be used.)

4. Ordinary repairs to equipment had been erroneously charged to the Equipment account during 2010 and 2011. Repairs in the amount of $8,000 in 2010 and $9,400 in 2011 were so charged. The company applies a rate of 10% to the balance in the Equipment account at the end of the year in its determination of depreciation charges.

Instructions

Prepare a schedule showing the determination of corrected income before taxes for 2010 and 2011.

E22-21 (Error Analysis) When the records of Aoki Corporation were reviewed at the close of 2011, the errors listed below were discovered. For each item, indicate by a check mark in the appropriate column whether the error resulted in an overstatement, an understatement, or had no effect on net income for the years 2010 and 2011.

Item	2010			2011		
	Over-statement	Under-statement	No Effect	Over-statement	Under-statement	No Effect
1. Failure to reflect supplies on hand on statement of financial position at end of 2010.						
2. Failure to record the correct amount of ending 2010 inventory. The amount was understated because of an error in calculation.						
3. Failure to record merchandise purchased in 2010. Merchandise was also omitted from ending inventory in 2010 but was not yet sold.						
4. Failure to record accrued interest on notes payable in 2010; that amount was recorded when paid in 2011.						
5. Failure to record amortization of patent in 2011.						

PROBLEMS

•2 •5 •6 **P22-1** **(Change in Estimate and Error Correction)** Holtzman Company is in the process of preparing its financial statements for 2010. Assume that no entries for depreciation have been recorded in 2010. The following information related to depreciation of fixed assets is provided to you.

1. Holtzman purchased equipment on January 2, 2007, for $85,000. At that time, the equipment had an estimated useful life of 10 years with a $5,000 residual value. The equipment is depreciated on a straight-line basis. On January 2, 2010, as a result of additional information, the company determined that the equipment has a remaining useful life of 4 years with a $3,000 residual value.

2. During 2010, Holtzman changed from the double-declining-balance method for its building to the straight-line method. The building originally cost $300,000. It had a useful life of 10 years and a residual value of $30,000. The following computations present depreciation on both bases for 2008 and 2009.

	2009	2008
Straight-line	$27,000	$27,000
Declining-balance	48,000	60,000

3. Holtzman purchased a machine on July 1, 2008, at a cost of $120,000. The machine has a residual value of $16,000 and a useful life of 8 years. Holtzman's bookkeeper recorded straight-line depreciation in 2008 and 2009 but failed to consider the residual value.

Instructions

(a) Prepare the journal entries to record depreciation expense for 2010 and correct any errors made to date related to the information provided.

(b) Show comparative net income for 2009 and 2010. Income before depreciation expense was $300,000 in 2010, and was $310,000 in 2009. Ignore taxes.

•3 •5 •6 **P22-2** **(Comprehensive Accounting Change and Error Analysis Problem)** Botticelli Inc. was organized in late 2008 to manufacture and sell hosiery. At the end of its fourth year of operation, the company has been fairly successful, as indicated by the following reported net incomes.

2008	€140,000[a]		2010	€205,000
2009	160,000		2011	276,000

[a]Includes a €10,000 increase because of change in bad debt experience rate.

The company has decided to expand operations and has applied for a sizable bank loan. The bank officer has indicated that the records should be audited and presented in comparative statements to facilitate analysis by the bank. Botticelli Inc. therefore hired the auditing firm of Check & Doublecheck Co. and has provided the following additional information.

1. In early 2009, Botticelli Inc. changed its estimate from 2% to 1% on the amount of bad debt expense to be charged to operations. Bad debt expense for 2008, if a 1% rate had been used, would have been €10,000. The company therefore restated its net income for 2008.

2. In 2011, the auditor discovered that the company had changed its method of inventory pricing from average cost to FIFO. The effect on the income statements for the previous years is as follows.

	2008	2009	2010	2011
Net income unadjusted—average cost basis	€140,000	€160,000	€205,000	€276,000
Net income unadjusted—FIFO basis	155,000	165,000	215,000	260,000
	€ 15,000	€ 5,000	€ 10,000	(€ 16,000)

3. In 2011, the auditor discovered that:
   a. The company incorrectly overstated the ending inventory by €14,000 in 2010.
   b. A dispute developed in 2009 with the tax authorities over the deductibility of entertainment expenses. In 2008, the company was not permitted these deductions, but a tax settlement was reached in 2011 that allowed these expenses. As a result of the court's finding, tax expenses in 2011 were reduced by €60,000.

Instructions

(a) Indicate how each of these changes or corrections should be handled in the accounting records. Ignore income tax considerations.

(b) Present comparative net income numbers for the years 2008 to 2011. Ignore income tax considerations.

 P22-3 **(Error Corrections and Accounting Changes)** Penn Company is in the process of adjusting and correcting its books at the end of 2010. In reviewing its records, the following information is compiled.

1. Penn has failed to accrue sales commissions payable at the end of each of the last 2 years, as follows.

December 31, 2009	$3,500
December 31, 2010	$2,500

2. In reviewing the December 31, 2011, inventory, Penn discovered errors in its inventory-taking procedures that have caused inventories for the last 3 years to be incorrect, as follows.

December 31, 2008	Understated	$16,000
December 31, 2009	Understated	$19,000
December 31, 2010	Overstated	$ 6,700

Penn has already made an entry that established the incorrect December 31, 2010, inventory amount.

3. At December 31, 2010, Penn decided to change the depreciation method on its office equipment from double-declining-balance to straight-line. The equipment had an original cost of $100,000 when purchased on January 1, 2008. It has a 10-year useful life and no residual value. Depreciation expense recorded prior to 2010 under the double-declining-balance method was $36,000. Penn has already recorded 2010 depreciation expense of $12,800 using the double-declining-balance method.

4. Before 2010, Penn accounted for its income from long-term construction contracts on the cost-recovery basis. Early in 2010, Penn changed to the percentage-of-completion basis for accounting purposes. It continues to use the cost-recovery method for tax purposes. Income for 2010 has been recorded using the percentage-of-completion method. The following information is available.

	Pretax Income	
	Percentage-of-Completion	Cost-Recovery
Prior to 2010	$150,000	$105,000
2010	60,000	20,000

Instructions

Prepare the journal entries necessary at December 31, 2010, to record the above corrections and changes. The books are still open for 2010. The income tax rate is 40%. Penn has not yet recorded its 2010 income tax expense and payable amounts so current-year tax effects may be ignored. Prior-year tax effects must be considered in item 4.

 P22-4 **(Accounting Changes)** Aston Corporation performs year-end planning in November of each year before its calendar year ends in December. The preliminary estimated net income is £3 million. The CFO, Rita Warren, meets with the company president, J. B. Aston, to review the projected numbers. She presents the following projected information.

ASTON CORPORATION		
PROJECTED INCOME STATEMENT		
FOR THE YEAR ENDED DECEMBER 31, 2010		
Sales		£29,000,000
Cost of goods sold	£14,000,000	
Depreciation	2,600,000	
Operating expenses	6,400,000	23,000,000
Income before income tax		6,000,000
Income tax		3,000,000
Net income		£ 3,000,000

ASTON CORPORATION
SELECTED STATEMENT OF FINANCIAL POSITION INFORMATION
AT DECEMBER 31, 2010

Estimated cash balance	£ 5,000,000
Debt investments (held-for-collection)	10,000,000
Security fair value adjustment account (1/1/10)	200,000

Estimated fair value at December 31, 2010:

Investment	Cost	Estimated Fair Value
A	£ 2,000,000	£ 2,200,000
B	4,000,000	3,900,000
C	3,000,000	3,000,000
D	1,000,000	1,800,000
Total	£10,000,000	£10,900,000

Other information at December 31, 2010:

Equipment	£3,000,000
Accumulated depreciation (5-year SL)	1,200,000
New robotic equipment (purchased 1/1/10)	5,000,000
Accumulated depreciation (5-year DDB)	2,000,000

The corporation has never used robotic equipment before, and Warren assumed an accelerated method because of the rapidly changing technology in robotic equipment. The company normally uses straight-line depreciation for production equipment.

Aston explains to Warren that it is important for the corporation to show a £7,000,000 income before taxes because Aston receives a £1,000,000 bonus if the income before taxes and bonus reaches £7,000,000. Aston also does not want the company to pay more than £3,000,000 in income taxes to the government.

Instructions

(a) What can Warren do within IFRS to accommodate the president's wishes to achieve £7,000,000 in income before taxes and bonus? Present the revised income statement based on your decision.

(b) Are the actions ethical? Who are the stakeholders in this decision, and what effect do Warren's actions have on their interests?

·3 **P22-5 (Change in Policy—Inventory—Periodic)** The management of Utrillo Instrument Company had concluded, with the concurrence of its independent auditors, that results of operations would be more fairly presented if Utrillo changed its method of pricing inventory from FIFO to average cost in 2010. Given below is the 5-year summary of income under FIFO and a schedule of what the inventories would be if stated on the average cost method (amounts in millions, except earnings per share).

UTRILLO INSTRUMENT COMPANY
STATEMENT OF INCOME AND RETAINED EARNINGS
FOR THE YEARS ENDED MAY 31

	2006	2007	2008	2009	2010
Sales—net	¥13,964	¥15,506	¥16,673	¥18,221	¥18,898
Cost of goods sold					
Beginning inventory	1,000	1,100	1,000	1,115	1,237
Purchases	13,000	13,900	15,000	15,900	17,100
Ending inventory	(1,100)	(1,000)	(1,115)	(1,237)	(1,369)
Total	12,900	14,000	14,885	15,778	16,968
Gross profit	1,064	1,506	1,788	2,443	1,930
Administrative expenses	700	763	832	907	989
Income before taxes	364	743	956	1,536	941
Income taxes (50%)	182	372	478	768	471
Net income	182	371	478	768	470
Retained earnings—beginning	1,206	1,388	1,759	2,237	3,005
Retained earnings—ending	¥ 1,388	¥ 1,759	¥ 2,237	¥ 3,005	¥ 3,475
Earnings per share	¥1.82	¥3.71	¥4.78	¥7.68	¥4.70

SCHEDULE OF INVENTORY BALANCES USING AVERAGE COST METHOD FOR THE YEAR ENDED MAY 31					
2005	2006	2007	2008	2009	2010
¥1,010	¥1,124	¥1,101	¥1,270	¥1,500	¥1,720

Instructions

Prepare comparative statements for the 5 years, assuming that Utrillo changed its method of inventory pricing to average cost. Indicate the effects on net income and earnings per share for the years involved. Utrillo Instruments started business in 2005. (All amounts except EPS are rounded up to the nearest yen.)

 P22-6 **(Accounting Change and Error Analysis)** On December 31, 2010, before the books were closed, the management and accountants of Madrasa Inc. made the following determinations about three depreciable assets.

1. Depreciable asset A was purchased January 2, 2007. It originally cost $540,000 and, for depreciation purposes, the straight-line method was originally chosen. The asset was originally expected to be useful for 10 years and have a zero residual value. In 2010, the decision was made to change the depreciation method from straight-line to sum-of-the-years'-digits, and the estimates relating to useful life and residual value remained unchanged.
2. Depreciable asset B was purchased January 3, 2006. It originally cost $180,000 and, for depreciation purposes, the straight-line method was chosen. The asset was originally expected to be useful for 15 years and have a zero residual value. In 2010, the decision was made to shorten the total life of this asset to 9 years and to estimate the residual value at $3,000.
3. Depreciable asset C was purchased January 5, 2006. The asset's original cost was $160,000, and this amount was entirely expensed in 2006. This particular asset has a 10-year useful life and no residual value. The straight-line method was chosen for depreciation purposes.

Additional data:

1. Income in 2010 before depreciation expense amounted to $400,000.
2. Depreciation expense on assets other than A, B, and C totaled $55,000 in 2010.
3. Income in 2009 was reported at $370,000.
4. Ignore all income tax effects.
5. 100,000 ordinary shares were outstanding in 2009 and 2010.

Instructions

(a) Prepare all necessary entries in 2010 to record these determinations.
(b) Prepare comparative retained earnings statements for Madrasa Inc. for 2009 and 2010. The company had retained earnings of $200,000 at December 31, 2008.

 P22-7 **(Error Corrections)** You have been assigned to examine the financial statements of Zarle Company for the year ended December 31, 2010. You discover the following situations.

1. Depreciation of $3,200 for 2010 on delivery vehicles was not recorded.
2. The physical inventory count on December 31, 2009, improperly excluded merchandise costing $19,000 that had been temporarily stored in a public warehouse. Zarle uses a periodic inventory system.
3. A collection of $5,600 on account from a customer received on December 31, 2010, was not recorded until January 2, 2011.
4. In 2010, the company sold for $3,700 fully depreciated equipment that originally cost $25,000. The company credited the proceeds from the sale to the Equipment account.
5. During November 2010, a competitor company filed a patent-infringement suit against Zarle claiming damages of $220,000. The company's legal counsel has indicated that an unfavorable verdict is probable and a reasonable estimate of the court's award to the competitor is $125,000. The company has not reflected or disclosed this situation in the financial statements.
6. Zarle has a portfolio of investments that it manages to profit from short-term price changes. No entry has been made to adjust to fair value. Information on cost and fair value is as follows.

	Cost	Fair Value
December 31, 2009	$95,000	$95,000
December 31, 2010	$84,000	$82,000

7. At December 31, 2010, an analysis of payroll information shows accrued salaries of $12,200. The Accrued Salaries Payable account had a balance of $16,000 at December 31, 2010, which was unchanged from its balance at December 31, 2009.

8. A large piece of equipment was purchased on January 3, 2010, for $40,000 and was charged to Repairs Expense. The equipment is estimated to have a service life of 8 years and no residual value. Zarle normally uses the straight-line depreciation method for this type of equipment.

9. A $12,000 insurance premium paid on July 1, 2009, for a policy that expires on June 30, 2012, was charged to insurance expense.

10. A trademark was acquired at the beginning of 2009 for $50,000. No amortization has been recorded since its acquisition. The maximum allowable amortization period is 10 years.

Instructions

Assume the trial balance has been prepared but the books have not been closed for 2010. Assuming all amounts are material, prepare journal entries showing the adjustments that are required. (Ignore income tax considerations.)

 P22-8 (Comprehensive Error Analysis) On March 5, 2011, you were hired by Hemingway Inc., a closely held company, as a staff member of its newly created internal auditing department. While reviewing the company's records for 2009 and 2010, you discover that no adjustments have yet been made for the items listed below.

Items

1. Interest income of $14,100 was not accrued at the end of 2009. It was recorded when received in February 2010.

2. A computer costing $4,000 was expensed when purchased on July 1, 2009. It is expected to have a 4-year life with no residual value. The company typically uses straight-line depreciation for all fixed assets.

3. Research costs of $33,000 were incurred early in 2009. They were capitalized and were to be amortized over a 3-year period. Amortization of $11,000 was recorded for 2009 and $11,000 for 2010.

4. On January 2, 2009, Hemingway leased a building for 5 years at a monthly rental of $8,000. On that date, the company paid the following amounts, which were expensed when paid.

Security deposit	$20,000
First month's rent	8,000
Last month's rent	8,000
	$36,000

5. The company received $36,000 from a customer at the beginning of 2009 for services that it is to perform evenly over a 3-year period beginning in 2009. None of the amount received was reported as unearned revenue at the end of 2009.

6. Merchandise inventory costing $18,200 was in the warehouse at December 31, 2009, but was incorrectly omitted from the physical count at that date. The company uses the periodic inventory method.

Instructions

Indicate the effect of any errors on the net income figure reported on the income statement for the year ending December 31, 2009, and the retained earnings figure reported on the statement of financial position at December 31, 2010. Assume all amounts are material and ignore income tax effects. Using the following format, enter the appropriate dollar amounts in the appropriate columns. Consider each item independent of the other items. It is not necessary to total the columns on the grid.

	Net Income for 2009		Retained Earnings at 12/31/10	
Item	Understated	Overstated	Understated	Overstated

 P22-9 (Error Analysis) Lowell Corporation has used the accrual basis of accounting for several years. A review of the records, however, indicates that some expenses and revenues have been handled on a cash basis because of errors made by an inexperienced bookkeeper. Income statements prepared by the bookkeeper reported €29,000 net income for 2009 and €37,000 net income for 2010. Further examination of the records reveals that the following items were handled improperly.

1. Rent was received from a tenant in December 2009. The amount, €1,000, was recorded as income at that time even though the rental pertained to 2010.

2. Wages payable on December 31 have been consistently omitted from the records of that date and have been entered as expenses when paid in the following year. The amounts of the accruals recorded in this manner were:

December 31, 2008	€1,100
December 31, 2009	1,200
December 31, 2010	940

3. Invoices for office supplies purchased have been charged to expense accounts when received. Inventories of supplies on hand at the end of each year have been ignored, and no entry has been made for them.

December 31, 2008	€1,300
December 31, 2009	940
December 31, 2010	1,420

Instructions

Prepare a schedule that will show the corrected net income for the years 2009 and 2010. All items listed should be labeled clearly. (Ignore income tax considerations.)

•6 •8 P22-10 (Error Analysis and Correcting Entries) You have been asked by a client to review the records of Roberts Company, a small manufacturer of precision tools and machines. Your client is interested in buying the business, and arrangements have been made for you to review the accounting records. Your examination reveals the following information.

1. Roberts Company commenced business on April 1, 2008, and has been reporting on a fiscal year ending March 31. The company has never been audited, but the annual statements prepared by the bookkeeper reflect the following income before closing and before deducting income taxes.

Year Ended March 31	Income Before Taxes
2009	$ 71,600
2010	111,400
2011	103,580

2. A relatively small number of machines have been shipped on consignment. These transactions have been recorded as ordinary sales and billed as such. On March 31 of each year, machines billed and in the hands of consignees amounted to:

2009	$6,500
2010	none
2011	5,590

Sales price was determined by adding 25% to cost. Assume that the consigned machines are sold the following year.

3. On March 30, 2010, two machines were shipped to a customer on a C.O.D. basis. The sale was not entered until April 5, 2010, when cash was received for $6,100. The machines were not included in the inventory at March 31, 2010. (Title passed on March 30, 2010.)

4. All machines are sold subject to a 5-year warranty. It is estimated that the expense ultimately to be incurred in connection with the warranty will amount to ½ of 1% of sales. The company has charged an expense account for warranty costs incurred.

Sales per books and warranty costs were as follows.

Year Ended March 31	Sales	Warranty Expense for Sales Made in 2009	2010	2011	Total
2009	$ 940,000	$760			$ 760
2010	1,010,000	360	$1,310		1,670
2011	1,795,000	320	1,620	$1,910	3,850

5. Bad debts have been recorded on a direct write-off basis. Experience of similar enterprises indicates that losses will approximate ¼ of 1% of sales. Bad debts written off were:

	Bad Debts Incurred on Sales Made in 2009	2010	2011	Total
2009	$750			$ 750
2010	800	$ 520		1,320
2011	350	1,800	$1,700	3,850

6. The bank deducts 6% on all contracts financed. Of this amount, ½% is placed in a reserve to the credit of Roberts Company, which is refunded to Roberts as finance contracts are paid in full. The reserve established by the bank has not been reflected in the books of Roberts. The excess of credits over debits (net increase) to the Dealer Fund Reserve account with Roberts on the books of the bank for each fiscal year were as follows.

2009	$ 3,000
2010	3,900
2011	5,100
	$12,000

7. Commissions on sales have been entered when paid. Commissions payable on March 31 of each year were as follows.

2009	$1,400
2010	900
2011	1,120

8. A review of the corporate minutes reveals the manager is entitled to a bonus of 1% of the income before deducting income taxes and the bonus. The bonuses have never been recorded or paid.

Instructions

(a) Present a schedule showing the revised income before income taxes for each of the years ended March 31, 2009, 2010, and 2011. Make computations to the nearest whole dollar.

(b) Prepare the journal entry or entries you would give the bookkeeper to correct the books. Assume the books have not yet been closed for the fiscal year ended March 31, 2011. Disregard correction of income taxes.

CONCEPTS FOR ANALYSIS

CA22-1 (Analysis of Various Accounting Changes and Errors) Joblonsky Inc. has recently hired a new independent auditor, Karen Ogleby, who says she wants "to get everything straightened out." Consequently, she has proposed the following accounting changes in connection with Joblonsky Inc.'s 2010 financial statements.

1. At December 31, 2009, the client had a receivable of $820,000 from Hendricks Inc. on its statement of financial position. Hendricks Inc. has gone bankrupt, and no recovery is expected. The client proposes to write off the receivable as a prior period item.

2. The client proposes the following changes in depreciation policies.
   (a) For office furniture and fixtures, it proposes to change from a 10-year useful life to an 8-year life. If this change had been made in prior years, retained earnings at December 31, 2009, would have been $250,000 less. The effect of the change on 2010 income alone is a reduction of $60,000.
   (b) For its equipment in the leasing division, the client proposes to adopt the sum-of-the-years'-digits depreciation method. The client had never used SYD before. The first year the client operated a leasing division was 2010. If straight-line depreciation were used, 2010 income would be $110,000 greater.

3. In preparing its 2009 statements, one of the client's bookkeepers overstated ending inventory by $235,000 because of a mathematical error. The client proposes to treat this item as a prior period adjustment.

4. In the past, the client has spread preproduction costs in its furniture division over 5 years. Because its latest furniture is of the "fad" type, it appears that the largest volume of sales will occur during the first 2 years after introduction. Consequently, the client proposes to amortize preproduction costs on a per-unit basis, which will result in expensing most of such costs during the first 2 years after the furniture's introduction. If the new accounting method had been used prior to 2010, retained earnings at December 31, 2009, would have been $375,000 less.

5. For the nursery division, the client proposes to switch from FIFO to average cost inventories because it believes that average cost will provide a better matching of current costs with revenues. The effect of making this change on 2010 earnings will be an increase of $320,000. The client says that the effect of the change on December 31, 2009, retained earnings cannot be determined.

6. To achieve a better matching of revenues and expenses in its building construction division, the client proposes to switch from the cost-recovery method of accounting to the percentage-of-completion method. Had the percentage-of-completion method been employed in all prior years, retained earnings at December 31, 2009, would have been $1,075,000 greater.

Instructions

(a) For each of the changes described above, decide whether:
  (1) The change involves an accounting policy, accounting estimate, or correction of an error.
  (2) Restatement of opening retained earnings is required.
(b) What would be the proper adjustment to the December 31, 2009, retained earnings?

CA22-2 (Analysis of Various Accounting Changes and Errors) Various types of accounting changes can affect the financial statements of a business differently. Assume that the following list describes changes that have a material effect on the financial statements for the current year of your business.

1. A change from the cost-recovery method to the percentage-of-completion method of accounting for long-term construction-type contracts.
2. A change in the estimated useful life of previously recorded fixed assets as a result of newly acquired information.
3. A change from deferring and amortizing preproduction costs to recording such costs as an expense when incurred because future benefits of the costs have become doubtful. The new accounting method was adopted in recognition of the change in estimated future benefits.
4. A change from including the employer share of taxes with payroll tax expenses to including it with "Retirement benefits" on the income statement.
5. Correction of a mathematical error in inventory pricing made in a prior period.
6. A change in the method of accounting for leases for tax purposes to conform with the financial accounting method. As a result, both deferred and current taxes payable changed substantially.
7. A change from the FIFO method of inventory pricing to the average cost method of inventory pricing.

Instructions

Identify the type of change that is described in each item above and indicate whether the prior year's financial statements should be retrospectively applied or restated when presented in comparative form with the current year's financial statements.

CA22-3 (Analysis of Three Accounting Changes and Errors) Listed below are three independent, unrelated sets of facts relating to accounting changes.

Situation 1

Sanford Company is in the process of having its first audit. The company has used the cash basis of accounting for revenue recognition. Sanford president, B. J. Jimenez, is willing to change to the accrual method of revenue recognition.

Situation 2

Hopkins Co. decides in January 2011 to change from FIFO to weighted-average pricing for its inventories.

Situation 3

Marshall Co. determined that the depreciable lives of its fixed assets are too long at present to fairly match the cost of the fixed assets with the revenue produced. The company decided at the beginning of the current year to reduce the depreciable lives of all of its existing fixed assets by 5 years.

Instructions

For each of the situations described, provide the information indicated below.

(a) Type of accounting change.
(b) Manner of reporting the change under IFRS, including a discussion, where applicable, of how amounts are computed.
(c) Effect of the change on the statement of financial position and income statement.

CA22-4 (Analysis of Various Accounting Changes and Errors) Katherine Irving, controller of Lotan Corp., is aware that a pronouncement on accounting changes has been issued. After reading the pronouncement, she is confused about what action should be taken on the following items related to Lotan Corp. for the year 2010.

1. In 2010, Lotan decided to change its policy on accounting for certain marketing costs. Previously, the company had chosen to defer and amortize all marketing costs over at least 5 years because Lotan believed that a return on these expenditures did not occur immediately. Recently, however, the time differential has considerably shortened, and Lotan is now expensing the marketing costs as incurred.

2. In 2010, the company examined its entire policy relating to the depreciation of plant equipment. Plant equipment had normally been depreciated over a 15-year period, but recent experience has indicated that the company was using too short a period in its estimates and that the assets should be depreciated over a 20-year period.

3. One division of Lotan Corp., Hawthorne Co., has consistently shown an increasing net income from period to period. On closer examination of its operating statement, it is noted that bad debt expense and inventory obsolescence charges are much lower than in other divisions. In discussing this with the controller of this division, it has been learned that the controller has increased his net income each period by knowingly making low estimates related to the write-off of receivables and inventory.

4. In 2010, the company purchased new machinery that should increase production dramatically. The company has decided to depreciate this machinery on an accelerated basis, even though other machinery is depreciated on a straight-line basis.

5. All equipment sold by Lotan is subject to a 3-year warranty. It has been estimated that the expense ultimately to be incurred on these machines is 1% of sales. In 2010, because of a production break-through, it is now estimated that $\frac{1}{2}$ of 1% of sales is sufficient. In 2008 and 2009, warranty expense was computed as $64,000 and $70,000, respectively. The company now believes that these warranty costs should be reduced by 50%.

6. In 2010, the company decided to change its method of inventory pricing from average cost to the FIFO method. The effect of this change on prior years is to increase 2008 income by $65,000 and increase 2009 income by $20,000.

Instructions

Katherine Irving has come to you, as her accountant, for advice about the situations above. Prepare a report, indicating the appropriate accounting treatment that should be given each of these situations.

CA22-5 **(Change in Policy, Estimate)** As a public accountant, you have been contacted by Joe Davison, CEO of Sports-Pro Athletics, Inc., a manufacturer of a variety of athletic equipment. He has asked you how to account for the following changes.

1. Sports-Pro appropriately changed its depreciation method for its production machinery from the double-declining-balance method to the production method effective January 1, 2010.

2. Effective January 1, 2010, Sports-Pro appropriately changed the residual values used in computing depreciation for its office equipment.

Instructions

Write a 1–1.5 page letter to Joe Davison, explaining how each of the above changes should be presented in the December 31, 2010, financial statements.

CA22-6 **(Change in Estimate)** Mike Crane, audit senior of a large public accounting firm, has just been assigned to the Frost Corporation's annual audit engagement. Frost has been a client of Crane's firm for many years. Frost is a fast-growing business in the commercial construction industry. In reviewing the fixed asset ledger, Crane discovered a series of unusual accounting changes, in which the useful lives of assets, depreciated using the straight-line method, were substantially lowered near the midpoint of the original estimate. For example, the useful life of one dump truck was changed from 10 to 6 years during its fifth year of service. Upon further investigation, Mike was told by Kevin James, Frost's accounting manager, "I don't really see your problem. After all, it's perfectly legal to change an accounting estimate. Besides, our CEO likes to see big earnings!"

Instructions

Answer the following questions.

(a) What are the ethical issues concerning Frost's practice of changing the useful lives of fixed assets?

(b) Who could be harmed by Frost's unusual accounting changes?

(c) What should Crane do in this situation?

USING YOUR JUDGMENT

FINANCIAL REPORTING

Financial Reporting Problem

Marks and Spencer plc (M&S)

The financial statements of **M&S** are presented in Appendix 5B or can be accessed at the book's companion website, **www.wiley.com/college/kiesoifrs**.

Instructions

Refer to M&S's financial statements and the accompanying notes to answer the following questions.

(a) Were there changes in accounting policies reported by M&S during the two years covered by its income statements (2007–2008)? If so, describe the nature of the change and the year of change.

(b) What types of estimates did M&S discuss in 2008?

Comparative Analysis Case

Cadbury and Nestlé

Instructions

Go to the book's companion website and use information found there to answer the following questions related to **Cadbury** and **Nestlé**.

(a) Identify the changes in accounting policies reported by Cadbury during the 2 years covered by its income statements (2007–2008). Describe the nature of the change and the year of change.

(b) Identify the changes in accounting policies reported by Nestlé during the 2 years covered by its income statements (2007–2008). Describe the nature of the change and the year of change.

(c) For each change in accounting policy by Cadbury and Nestlé, identify, if possible, the cumulative effect of each change on prior years and the effect on operating results in the year of change.

Accounting, Analysis, and Principles

In preparation for significant international operations, ABC Co. has adopted a plan to gradually shift to the same accounting policies as used by its international competitors. Part of this plan includes a switch from average cost inventory accounting to FIFO. ABC decides to make the switch to FIFO at January 1, 2011. The following data pertains to ABC's 2011 financial statements.

Sales	$550
Inventory purchases	350
12/31/11 inventory (using FIFO)	580
Compensation expense	17

All sales and purchases were with cash as were all of 2011's compensation expense (ignore taxes). ABC's plant, property, and equipment cost $400 and has an estimated useful life of 10 years with no residual value.

ABC Co. reported the following for fiscal 2010 (amounts are in millions).

ABC CO.
STATEMENT OF FINANCIAL POSITION
AT DECEMBER 31, 2010

	2010	2009		2010	2009
Plant, property, and equipment	$ 400	$ 400	Retained earnings	$ 685	$ 540
Accumulated depreciation	(80)	(40)	Share capital	500	500
Inventory	500	480			
Cash	365	200			
Total assets	$1,185	$1,040	Total equity	$1,185	$1,040

ABC CO.
INCOME STATEMENT
FOR THE YEAR ENDED DECEMBER 31, 2010

	2010
Sales	$ 500
Cost of goods sold	(300)
Depreciation expense	(40)
Compensation expense	(15)
Net income	$ 145

Summary of Significant Accounting Policies
Inventory: The company accounts for inventory by the average cost method. The current cost of the company's inventory, which approximates FIFO, was $60 and $50 higher at the end of fiscal 2010 and 2009, respectively, than those reported in the statement of financial position.

Accounting

Prepare ABC's December 31, 2011, statement of financial position and an income statement for the year ended December 31, 2011. In columns beside 2011's numbers, include 2010's numbers *as they would appear in the 2011 financial statements* for comparative purposes.

Analysis

Compute ABC's inventory turnover for 2010 under both average cost and FIFO. Assume averages are equal to year-end balances where necessary. What causes the differences in this ratio between average cost and FIFO?

Principles

Briefly explain, in terms of the policies discussed in Chapter 22, why IFRS requires that companies that change accounting policies present restated prior year's financial statement data.

BRIDGE TO THE PROFESSION

Professional Research

As part of the year-end accounting process and review of operating policies, Cullen Co. is considering a change in the accounting for its equipment from the straight-line method to an accelerated method. Your supervisor wonders how the company will report this change in accounting. It has been few years since he took intermediate accounting, and he cannot remember whether this change would be treated in a retrospective or prospective manner. Your supervisor wants you to research the authoritative guidance on a change in accounting policy related to depreciation methods.

Instructions

Access the IFRS authoritative literature at the IASB website (*http://eifrs.iasb.org/*). When you have accessed the documents, you can use the search tool in your Internet browser to respond to the following questions. (Provide paragraph citations.)

(a) What are the accounting and reporting guidelines for a change in accounting policy related to depreciation methods?

(b) What are the conditions that justify a change in depreciation method, as contemplated by Cullen Co.?

Professional Simulation

In this simulation, you are asked questions about changes in accounting policy. Prepare responses to all parts.

KWW_Professional _Simulation

| Changes in Accounting Policy | Time Remaining 1 hours 20 minutes | copy | paste | calculator | sheet | standards | help | splitter | done |

| Directions | Situation | Journal Entries | Financial Statements | Resources |

Garner Company began operations on January 1, 2008, and uses the average cost method of pricing inventory. Management is contemplating a change in inventory methods for 2011. The following information is available for the years 2008–2010.

| | Net Income Computed Using | |
	Average Cost Method	FIFO Method
2008	$15,000	$20,000
2009	18,000	24,000
2010	20,000	27,000

On January 1, 2010, Garner issued 10-year, $200,000 face value, 6% bonds, at par. Each $1,000 bond is convertible into 30 Garner ordinary shares. The company has had 10,000 ordinary shares outstanding throughout its life. None of the bonds have been exercised as of the end of 2011. (Ignore tax effects.)

| Directions | Situation | Journal Entries | Financial Statements | Resources |

Prepare the journal entry necessary to record a change from the average cost method to the FIFO method in 2011.

| Directions | Situation | Journal Entries | Financial Statements | Resources |

Assuming Garner had the accounting change described above, Garner's income in 2011 was $30,000. Compute basic and diluted earnings per share for Garner Company for 2011. Show how income and EPS will be reported for 2011 and 2010.

Remember to check the book's companion website to find additional resources for this chapter.

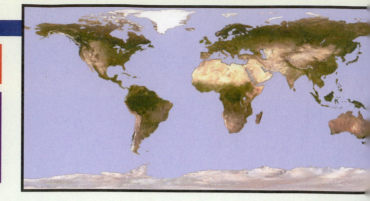

LEARNING OBJECTIVES

After studying this chapter, you should be able to:

•1 Describe the purpose of the statement of cash flows.

•2 Identify the major classifications of cash flows.

•3 Differentiate between net income and net cash flow from operating activities.

•4 Contrast the direct and indirect methods of calculating net cash flow from operating activities.

•5 Determine net cash flows from investing and financing activities.

•6 Prepare a statement of cash flows.

•7 Identify sources of information for a statement of cash flows.

•8 Discuss special problems in preparing a statement of cash flows.

•9 Explain the use of a worksheet in preparing a statement of cash flows.

DON'T TAKE CASH FLOWS FOR GRANTED

Investors usually look to net income as a key indicator of a company's financial health and future prospects. The following graph shows the net income of one company over a seven-year period.

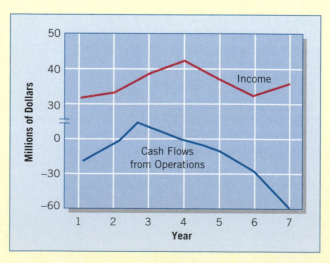

The company showed a pattern of consistent profitability and even some periods of income growth. Between years 1 and 4, net income for this company grew by 32 percent, from $31 million to $41 million. Would you expect its profitability to continue? The company had consistently paid dividends and interest. Would you expect it to continue to do so? Investors answered "yes" to these questions, by buying the company's shares. Eighteen months later, this company—**W. T. Grant** (USA)—filed for bankruptcy, in what was then the largest bankruptcy filing in the United States.

How could this happen? As indicated by the second line in the graph, the company had experienced several years of negative cash flows from its operations even though it reported profits. How can a company have negative cash flows while reporting profits? The answer lay partly in the fact that W. T. Grant was having trouble collecting the receivables from its credit sales, causing cash flows to be less than the net income. Investors who analyzed the cash flows would have been likely to find an early warning signal of W. T. Grant's operating problems.

Source: Adapted from James A. Largay III and Clyde P. Stickney, "Cash Flows, Ratio Analysis, and the W. T. Grant Company Bankruptcy," *Financial Analysts Journal* (July–August 1980), p. 51.

PREVIEW OF CHAPTER 23

As the opening story indicates, examination of **W. T. Grant**'s cash flows from operations would have shown the financial inflexibility that eventually caused the company's bankruptcy. This chapter explains the main components of a statement of cash flows and the types of information it provides. The content and organization of the chapter are as follows.

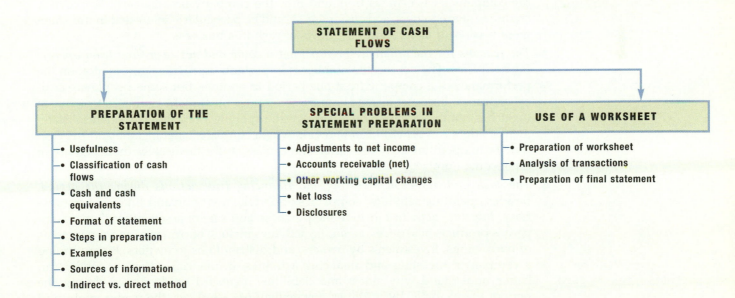

STATEMENT OF CASH FLOWS

PREPARATION OF THE STATEMENT	SPECIAL PROBLEMS IN STATEMENT PREPARATION	USE OF A WORKSHEET
• Usefulness	• Adjustments to net income	• Preparation of worksheet
• Classification of cash flows	• Accounts receivable (net)	• Analysis of transactions
• Cash and cash equivalents	• Other working capital changes	• Preparation of final statement
• Format of statement	• Net loss	
• Steps in preparation	• Disclosures	
• Examples		
• Sources of information		
• Indirect vs. direct method		

Objective·1

Describe the purpose of the statement of cash flows.

The primary purpose of the **statement of cash flows** is to provide information about a company's cash receipts and cash payments during a period. A secondary objective is to provide cash-basis information about the company's operating, investing, and financing activities. [1] The statement of cash flows therefore reports cash receipts, cash payments, and net change in cash resulting from a company's operating, investing, and financing activities during a period. Its format reconciles the beginning and ending cash balances for the period.

IFRS

See the Authoritative Literature section (page 1284).

USEFULNESS OF THE STATEMENT OF CASH FLOWS

The statement of cash flows provides information to help investors, creditors, and others assess the following:

1. *The entity's ability to generate future cash flows.* A primary objective of financial reporting is to provide information with which to predict the amounts, timing, and uncertainty of future cash flows. By examining relationships between items such as sales and net cash flow from operating activities, or net cash flow from operating activities and increases or decreases in cash, it is possible to better predict the future cash flows than is possible using accrual-basis data alone.

2. *The entity's ability to pay dividends and meet obligations.* Simply put, cash is essential. Without adequate cash, a company cannot pay employees, settle debts, pay out dividends, or acquire equipment. A statement of cash flows indicates where the company's cash comes from and how the company uses its cash. Employees, creditors, shareholders, and customers should be particularly interested in this statement because it alone shows the flows of cash in a business.

3. *The reasons for the difference between net income and net cash flow from operating activities.* The net income number is important: It provides information on the performance of a company from one period to another. But some people are critical of accrual-basis net income because companies must make estimates to arrive at it. Such is not the case with cash. Thus, as the opening story showed, financial statement readers can benefit from knowing why a company's net income and net cash flow from operating activities differ, and can assess for themselves the reliability of the income number.

4. *The cash and non-cash investing and financing transactions during the period.* Besides operating activities, companies undertake investing and financing transactions. *Investing* activities include the purchase and sale of assets other than a company's products or services. *Financing* activities include borrowings and repayments of borrowings, investments by owners, and distributions to owners. By examining a company's investing and financing activities, a financial statement reader can better understand why assets and liabilities increased or decreased during the period. For example, by reading the statement of cash flows, the reader might find answers to following questions:

Why did cash decrease for **Aixtron Aktiengesellschaft** (DEU) when it reported net income for the year?

How much did **Telefónica, S.A.** (ESP) spend on property, plant, and equipment, and intangible assets last year?

Did dividends paid by **BP plc** (GBR) increase last year?

How much money did **Coca-Cola** (USA) borrow last year?

How much cash did **Delhaize Group** (BEL) use to repurchase ordinary shares?

CLASSIFICATION OF CASH FLOWS

The statement of cash flows classifies cash receipts and cash payments by operating, investing, and financing activities. Transactions and other events characteristic of each kind of activity is as follows. **[2]**

> **Objective·2**
> Identify the major classifications of cash flows.

1. **Operating activities** involve the cash effects of transactions that enter into the determination of net income, such as cash receipts from sales of goods and services, and cash payments to suppliers and employees for acquisitions of inventory and expenses. The amount of cash flows arising from operating activities is a key indicator of the extent to which the operations of the entity have generated sufficient cash flows to repay loans, maintain the operating capability of the entity, pay dividends, and make new investments without recourse to external sources of financing.

2. **Investing activities** generally involve non-current assets and include (a) making and collecting loans, and (b) acquiring and disposing of investments and productive long-lived assets. The separate disclosure of cash flows arising from investing activities is important because the cash flows represent the extent to which expenditures have been made for resources intended to generate future income and cash flows.

3. **Financing activities** involve liability and equity items and include (a) obtaining cash from creditors and repaying the amounts borrowed, and (b) obtaining capital from owners and providing them with a return on, and a return of, their investment. The separate disclosure of cash flows arising from financing activities is important because it is useful in predicting claims on future cash flows by providers of capital to a company.

Illustration 23-1 (page 1244) classifies the typical cash receipts and payments of a company according to operating, investing, and financing activities. The operating activities category is the most important. It shows the cash provided by company operations. This source of cash is generally considered to be the best measure of a company's ability to generate enough cash to continue as a going concern.

Note the following general guidelines about the classification of cash flows.

1. Operating activities involve income statement items.

2. Investing activities involve cash flows resulting from changes in investments and other non-current asset items.

3. Financing activities involve cash flows resulting from changes in equity and non-current liability items.

IFRS allows some flexibility regarding the classification of certain items. Interest and dividends paid can be classified as either operating or financing, depending on what treatment the company thinks is most appropriate. Similarly, interest and dividends received can be classified as either operating or investing. Taxes paid are classified as operating except in circumstances where they can be identified with specific investing or financing activities. In order to limit the complexity of our presentation and to avoid ambiguity in assignment material, in Illustration 23-1 we have identified specific

ILLUSTRATION 23-1
Classification of Typical
Cash Inflows and
Outflows

Operating Activities—Income Statement Items
Cash inflows
From sales of goods or services.
From returns on loans (interest) and on equity
securities (dividends).
Cash outflows
To suppliers for inventory.
To employees for services.
To government for taxes.
To lenders for interest.
To others for expenses.

Investing Activities—Generally Non-Current Asset Items
Cash inflows
From sale of property, plant, and equipment, and intangibles.
From sale of debt or equity securities of other entities.
From collection of principal on loans to other entities.
Cash outflows
To purchase property, plant, and equipment, and intangibles.
To purchase debt or equity securities of other entities.
To make loans to other entities.

Financing Activities—Generally Equity and Non-Current Liabilities
Cash inflows
From sale of equity securities.
From issuance of debt (bonds and notes).
Cash outflows
To shareholders as dividends.
To redeem long-term debt or reacquire share capital.

treatment for each of these items rather than allowing choices. *All assignment material is based on this treatment.*[1]

Also, companies classify some cash flows relating to operating activities as investing or financing activities. For example, a company classifies the total cash received from the sale of property, plant, and equipment as an investing activity. Therefore, sales of those assets are not considered operating activities. Because of this (as is discussed more fully below), companies must eliminate any gains or losses arising from the disposal of these assets to arrive at net cash flow from operating activities. Likewise, the payment to extinguish debt is a financing cash flow and should be classified as such. Any gain or loss related to the extinguishment is eliminated from net cash provided by operating activities.

CASH AND CASH EQUIVALENTS

The basis recommended by the IASB for the statement of cash flows is actually "cash and cash equivalents." **Cash equivalents** are short-term, highly liquid investments that are both:

- Readily convertible to known amounts of cash, and
- So near their maturity that they present insignificant risk of changes in value (e.g., due to changes in interest rates).

Generally, only investments with original maturities of three months or less qualify under this definition. Examples of cash equivalents are Treasury bills, commercial paper, and money market funds purchased with cash that is in excess of immediate needs. Equity investments are excluded from cash equivalents unless they are, in substance,

[1]*IFRS Accounting Trends and Techniques—2010* indicates that most companies surveyed report income taxes paid or received, interest received and paid, and dividends received as operating activities. However, most companies show dividends paid as a financing activity. These results are consistent with how this information is reported in Illustration 23-1.

cash equivalents. Although we use the term "cash" throughout our discussion and illustrations, we mean cash and cash equivalents when reporting the cash flows and the net increase or decrease in cash. **[3]**

HOW'S MY CASH FLOW?

To evaluate overall cash flows, it is useful to understand where in the product life cycle a company is. Generally, companies move through several stages of development, which have implications for cash flows. As the graph below shows, the pattern of cash flows from operating, financing, and investing activities will vary depending on the stage of the product life cycle.

What do the numbers mean?

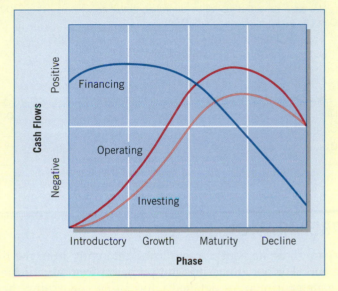

In the introductory phase, the product is likely not generating much revenue (net operating cash flow is negative). Because the company is making heavy investments to get a product off the ground, cash flow from investment is negative, and financing cash flows are positive.

As the product moves to the growth and maturity phases, these cash flow relationships reverse. The product generates more cash flows from operations, which can be used to cover investments needed to support the product, and less cash is needed from financing. So are negative operating cash flows bad? Not always. It depends on the product life cycle.

Source: Adapted from Paul D. Kimmel, Jerry J. Weygandt, and Donald E. Kieso, *Financial Accounting: Tools for Business Decision Making*, 5th ed. (New York: John Wiley & Sons, 2009), p. 606.

FORMAT OF THE STATEMENT OF CASH FLOWS

The three activities we discussed above constitute the general format of the statement of cash flows. The operating activities section always appears first. It is followed by the investing activities section and then the financing activities section.

A company reports the individual inflows and outflows from investing and financing activities separately. That is, a company reports them gross, not netted against one another. Thus, a cash outflow from the purchase of property is reported separately from the cash inflow from the sale of property. Similarly, a cash inflow from the issuance of debt is reported separately from the cash outflow from its retirement.

The net increase or decrease in cash reported during the period should reconcile the beginning and ending cash balances as reported in the comparative statements of financial position. The general format of the statement of cash flows presents the results of the three activities discussed previously—operating, investing, and financing. Illustration 23-2 shows a widely used form of the statement of cash flows.

ILLUSTRATION 23-2
Format of the Statement
of Cash Flows

COMPANY NAME
STATEMENT OF CASH FLOWS
PERIOD COVERED

Cash flows from operating activities		
Net income		XXX
Adjustments to reconcile net income to net		
cash provided (used) by operating activities:		
(List of individual items)	XX	XX
Net cash provided (used) by operating activities		XXX
Cash flows from investing activities		
(List of individual inflows and outflows)	XX	
Net cash provided (used) by investing activities		XXX
Cash flows from financing activities		
(List of individual inflows and outflows)	XX	
Net cash provided (used) by financing activities		XXX
Net increase (decrease) in cash		XXX
Cash at beginning of period		XXX
Cash at end of period		XXX

STEPS IN PREPARATION

Companies prepare the statement of cash flows differently from the three other basic financial statements. For one thing, it is not prepared from an adjusted trial balance. The cash flow statement requires detailed information concerning the changes in account balances that occurred between two points in time. An adjusted trial balance will not provide the necessary data. Second, the statement of cash flows deals with cash receipts and payments. As a result, the company must adjust the effects of the use of accrual accounting to determine cash flows. The information to prepare this statement usually comes from three sources:

1. **Comparative statements of financial position** provide the amount of the changes in assets, liabilities, and equities from the beginning to the end of the period.
2. **Current income statement** data help determine the amount of cash provided by or used by operations during the period.
3. **Selected transaction data** from the general ledger provide additional detailed information needed to determine how the company provided or used cash during the period.

Preparing the statement of cash flow from the data sources above involves three major steps:

Step 1. *Determine the change in cash.* This procedure is straightforward. A company can easily compute the difference between the beginning and the ending cash balance from examining its comparative statements of financial position.

Step 2. *Determine the net cash flow from operating activities.* This procedure is complex. It involves analyzing not only the current year's income statement but also comparative statements of financial position as well as selected transaction data.

Step 3. *Determine net cash flows from investing and financing activities.* A company must analyze all other changes in the statement of financial position accounts to determine their effects on cash.

On the following pages, we work through these three steps in the process of preparing the statement of cash flows for Tax Consultants Inc. over several years.

FIRST EXAMPLE—2010

To illustrate a statement of cash flows, we use the **first year of operations** for Tax Consultants Inc. The company started on January 1, 2010, when it issued 60,000 ordinary shares of $1 par value for $60,000 cash. The company rented its office space, furniture, and equipment, and performed tax consulting services throughout the first year. The comparative statements of financial position at the beginning and end of the year 2010 appear in Illustration 23-3.

ILLUSTRATION 23-3
Comparative Statements of Financial Position, Tax Consultants Inc., Year 1

TAX CONSULTANTS INC. COMPARATIVE STATEMENTS OF FINANCIAL POSITION			
Assets	Dec. 31, 2010	Jan. 1, 2010	Change Increase/Decrease
Accounts receivable	$36,000	$–0–	$36,000 Increase
Cash	49,000	–0–	49,000 Increase
Total	$85,000	$–0–	
Equity and Liabilities			
Ordinary shares ($1 par)	$60,000	$–0–	$60,000 Increase
Retained earnings	20,000	–0–	20,000 Increase
Accounts payable	5,000	–0–	5,000 Increase
Total	$85,000	$–0–	

Illustration 23-4 shows the income statement and additional information for Tax Consultants.

ILLUSTRATION 23-4
Income Statement, Tax Consultants Inc., Year 1

TAX CONSULTANTS INC. INCOME STATEMENT FOR THE YEAR ENDED DECEMBER 31, 2010	
Revenues	$125,000
Operating expenses	85,000
Income before income taxes	40,000
Income tax expense	6,000
Net income	$ 34,000

Additional Information:
Examination of selected data indicates that a dividend of $14,000 was declared and paid during the year.

Step 1: Determine the Change in Cash

To prepare a statement of cash flows, the first step is to **determine the change in cash**. This is a simple computation. Tax Consultants had no cash on hand at the beginning of the year 2010. It had $49,000 on hand at the end of 2010. Thus, cash changed (increased) in 2010 by $49,000.

Step 2: Determine Net Cash Flow from Operating Activities

Objective•3

Differentiate between net income and net cash flow from operating activities.

To determine net cash flow from operating activities,[2] companies adjust net income in numerous ways. A useful starting point is to understand why net income must be converted to net cash provided by operating activities.

Under IFRS, most companies use the accrual basis of accounting. As you have learned, this basis requires that companies record revenue when it is probable that the economic benefits will flow to the company and record expenses when incurred. Revenues may include credit sales for which the company has not yet collected cash. Expenses incurred may include some items that the company has not yet paid in cash. Thus, under the accrual basis of accounting, net income is not the same as net cash flow from operating activities.

To arrive at net cash flow from operating activities, a company must determine revenues and expenses on a **cash basis**. It does this by eliminating the effects of income statement transactions that do not result in an increase or decrease in cash. Illustration 23-5 shows the relationship between net income and net cash flow from operating activities.

ILLUSTRATION 23-5
Net Income versus
Net Cash Flow from
Operating Activities

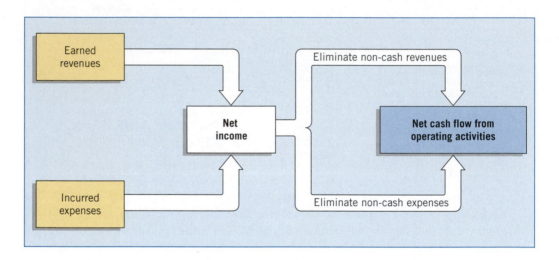

In this chapter, we use the term net income to refer to accrual-based net income. A company may convert net income to net cash flow from operating activities through either a direct method or an indirect method. We explain both methods in the following sections. The advantages and disadvantages of these two methods are discussed later in the chapter.

Direct Method

Objective•4

Contrast the direct and indirect methods of calculating net cash flow from operating activities.

The **direct method** (also called the **income statement method**) reports cash receipts and cash disbursements from operating activities. The difference between these two amounts is the net cash flow from operating activities. In other words, the direct method deducts operating cash disbursements from operating cash receipts. The direct method results in the presentation of a condensed cash receipts and cash disbursements statement.

As indicated from the accrual-based income statement, Tax Consultants reported revenues of $125,000. However, because the company's accounts receivable increased during 2010 by $36,000, the company collected only $89,000 ($125,000 − $36,000) in cash from these revenues. Similarly, Tax Consultants reported operating expenses of

---

[2]"Net cash flow from operating activities" is a generic phrase, replaced in the statement of cash flows with either "Net cash provided by operating activities" if operations increase cash, or "Net cash used by operating activities" if operations decrease cash.

$85,000. However, accounts payable increased during the period by $5,000. Assuming that these payables relate to operating expenses, cash operating expenses were $80,000 ($85,000 − $5,000). Because no taxes payable exist at the end of the year, the company must have paid $6,000 income tax expense for 2010 in cash during the year. Tax Consultants computes net cash flow from operating activities as shown in Illustration 23-6.

Cash collected from revenues	$89,000
Cash payments for expenses	80,000
Income before income taxes	9,000
Cash payments for income taxes	6,000
Net cash provided by operating activities	$ 3,000

ILLUSTRATION 23-6
Computation of Net Cash Flow from Operating Activities, Year 1—Direct Method

"Net cash provided by operating activities" is the equivalent of cash-basis net income. ("Net cash used by operating activities" is equivalent to cash-basis net loss.)

Indirect Method

The **indirect method** (or **reconciliation method**) starts with net income and converts it to net cash flow from operating activities. In other words, **the indirect method adjusts net income for items that affected reported net income but did not affect cash**. To compute net cash flow from operating activities, a company adds back non-cash charges in the income statement to net income and deducts non-cash credits. We explain the two adjustments to net income for Tax Consultants, namely, the increases in accounts receivable and accounts payable, as follows.

Increase in Accounts Receivable—Indirect Method. Tax Consultant's accounts receivable increased by $36,000 (from $0 to $36,000) during the year. For Tax Consultants, this means that cash receipts were $36,000 lower than revenues. The Accounts Receivable account in Illustration 23-7 shows that Tax Consultants had $125,000 in revenues (as reported on the income statement), but it collected only $89,000 in cash.

	Accounts Receivable			
1/1/10	Balance	–0–	Receipts from customer	89,000
	Revenues	125,000		
12/31/10	Balance	36,000		

ILLUSTRATION 23-7
Analysis of Accounts Receivable

As shown in Illustration 23-8 (on page 1250), to adjust net income to net cash provided by operating activities, Tax Consultants must deduct the increase of $36,000 in accounts receivable from net income. When the Accounts Receivable balance *decreases*, cash receipts are higher than revenue earned under the accrual basis. Therefore, the company adds to net income the amount of the decrease in accounts receivable to arrive at net cash provided by operating activities.

Increase in Accounts Payable—Indirect Method. When accounts payable increase during the year, expenses on an accrual basis exceed those on a cash basis. Why? Because Tax Consultants incurred expenses, but some of the expenses are not yet paid. To convert net income to net cash flow from operating activities, Tax Consultants must add back the increase of $5,000 in accounts payable to net income.

As a result of the accounts receivable and accounts payable adjustments, Tax Consultants determines net cash provided by operating activities is $3,000 for the year 2010. Illustration 23-8 shows this computation.

ILLUSTRATION 23-8
Computation of Net Cash Flow from Operating Activities, Year 1—Indirect Method

Net income		$34,000
Adjustments to reconcile net income to net cash provided by operating activities:		
Increase in accounts receivable	$(36,000)	
Increase in accounts payable	5,000	(31,000)
Net cash provided by operating activities		$ 3,000

Note that net cash provided by operating activities is the same whether using the direct (Illustration 23-6) or the indirect method (Illustration 23-8).

PUMPING UP CASH

What do the numbers mean?

Due to recent concerns about a decline in the quality of earnings, some investors have been focusing on cash flow. Management has an incentive to make operating cash flow look good because Wall Street has paid a premium for companies that generate a lot of cash from operations, rather than through borrowings. However, similar to earnings, companies have ways to pump up net cash flow from operations.

One way that companies can boost their operating cash flow is by "securitizing" receivables. That is, companies can speed up cash collections by selling their receivables. For example, **Federated Department Stores** (USA) reported a $2.2 billion increase in net cash flow from operations. This seems impressive until you read the fine print, which indicates that a big part of the increase was due to the sale of receivables. As discussed in this section, decreases in accounts receivable increase cash flow from operations. So while it appeared that Federated's core operations had improved, the company really did little more than accelerate collections of its receivables. In fact, the cash flow from the securitizations represented more than half of Federated's operating cash flow. Thus, just like earnings, cash flows can be of high or low quality.

Source: Adapted from Ann Tergesen, "Cash Flow Hocus Pocus," *Business Week* (July 16, 2002), pp. 130–131. *See also* Bear Stearns Equity Research, *Accounting Issues: Cash Flow Metrics* (June 2006).

Step 3: Determine Net Cash Flows from Investing and Financing Activities

Objective·5

Determine net cash flows from investing and financing activities.

After Tax Consultants has computed the net cash provided by operating activities, the next step is to determine whether any other changes in the statement of financial position accounts caused an increase or decrease in cash.

For example, an examination of the remaining statement of financial position accounts for Tax Consultants shows increases in both ordinary shares and retained earnings. The Share Capital—Ordinary increase of $60,000 resulted from the issuance of ordinary shares for cash. The issuance of ordinary shares is reported in the statement of cash flows as a receipt of cash from a financing activity.

Two items caused the retained earnings increase of $20,000:

1. Net income of $34,000 increased retained earnings.
2. Declaration of $14,000 of dividends decreased retained earnings.

Tax Consultants has converted net income into net cash flow from operating activities, as explained earlier. The additional data indicate that it paid the dividend. Thus, the company reports the dividend payment as a cash outflow, classified as a financing activity.

Statement of Cash Flows—2010

We are now ready to prepare the statement of cash flows. The statement starts with the operating activities section. Tax Consultants may use either the direct or indirect method to report net cash flow from operating activities.

> **Objective·6**
> Prepare a statement of cash flows.

The IASB **encourages** the use of the direct method over the indirect method. If a company uses the indirect method, it can either report the reconciliation within the statement of cash flows or can provide it in a separate schedule, with the statement of cash flows reporting only the **net** cash flow from operating activities. Throughout this chapter, we use the indirect method, which is also used more extensively in practice.[3] *In doing homework assignments, you should follow instructions for use of either the direct or indirect method.*

Illustration 23-9 shows the statement of cash flows for Tax Consultants Inc., for year 1 (2010).

TAX CONSULTANTS INC.
STATEMENT OF CASH FLOWS
FOR THE YEAR ENDED DECEMBER 31, 2010
INCREASE (DECREASE) IN CASH

Cash flows from operating activities		
Net income		$34,000
Adjustments to reconcile net income to net cash provided by operating activities:		
Increase in accounts receivable	$(36,000)	
Increase in accounts payable	5,000	(31,000)
Net cash provided by operating activities		3,000
Cash flows from financing activities		
Issuance of ordinary shares	60,000	
Payment of cash dividends	(14,000)	
Net cash provided by financing activities		46,000
Net increase in cash		49,000
Cash, January 1, 2010		–0–
Cash, December 31, 2010		$49,000

ILLUSTRATION 23-9
Statement of Cash Flows, Tax Consultants Inc., Year 1

As indicated, the $60,000 increase in ordinary shares results in a financing-activity cash inflow. The payment of $14,000 in cash dividends is a financing-activity outflow of cash. The $49,000 increase in cash reported in the statement of cash flows agrees with the increase of $49,000 shown in the comparative statements of financial position (in Illustration 23-3 on page 1247) as the change in the Cash account.

SECOND EXAMPLE—2011

Tax Consultants Inc. continued to grow and prosper in its second year of operations. The company purchased land, building, and equipment, and revenues and net income increased substantially over the first year. Illustrations 23-10 and 23-11 (on page 1252) present information related to the second year of operations for Tax Consultants Inc.

---

[3]*Accounting Trends and Techniques—2010* reports that out of its 100 surveyed companies, 91 used the indirect method and 9 used the direct method.

ILLUSTRATION 23-10
Comparative Statements of Financial Position, Tax Consultants Inc., Year 2

TAX CONSULTANTS INC.
COMPARATIVE STATEMENTS OF FINANCIAL POSITION
AS OF DECEMBER 31

Assets	2011	2010	Change Increase/Decrease
Land	$ 70,000	$ –0–	$ 70,000 Increase
Buildings	200,000	–0–	200,000 Increase
Accumulated depreciation—buildings	(11,000)	–0–	11,000 Increase
Equipment	68,000	–0–	68,000 Increase
Accumulated depreciation—equipment	(10,000)	–0–	10,000 Increase
Accounts receivable	26,000	36,000	10,000 Decrease
Prepaid expenses	6,000	–0–	6,000 Increase
Cash	37,000	49,000	12,000 Decrease
Total	$386,000	$85,000	
Equity and Liabilities			
Share capital—ordinary ($1 par)	$ 60,000	$60,000	$ –0–
Retained earnings	136,000	20,000	116,000 Increase
Bonds payable	150,000	–0–	150,000 Increase
Accounts payable	40,000	5,000	35,000 Increase
Total	$386,000	$85,000	

ILLUSTRATION 23-11
Income Statement, Tax Consultants Inc., Year 2

TAX CONSULTANTS INC.
INCOME STATEMENT
FOR THE YEAR ENDED DECEMBER 31, 2011

Revenues		$492,000
Operating expenses (excluding depreciation)	$269,000	
Depreciation expense	21,000	290,000
Income from operations		202,000
Income tax expense		68,000
Net income		$134,000

Additional Information
(a) The company declared and paid an $18,000 cash dividend.
(b) The company obtained $150,000 cash through the issuance of long-term bonds.
(c) Land, building, and equipment were acquired for cash.

Step 1: Determine the Change in Cash

To prepare a statement of cash flows from the available information, the first step is to determine the change in cash. As indicated from the information presented, cash decreased $12,000 ($49,000 − $37,000).

Step 2: Determine Net Cash Flow from Operating Activities—Indirect Method

Using the indirect method, we adjust net income of $134,000 on an accrual basis to arrive at net cash flow from operating activities. Explanations for the adjustments to net income follow.

Decrease in Accounts Receivable. Accounts receivable decreased during the period because cash receipts (cash-basis revenues) are higher than revenues reported on an accrual basis. To convert net income to net cash flow from operating activities, the decrease of $10,000 in accounts receivable must be added to net income.

Increase in Prepaid Expenses. When prepaid expenses (assets) increase during a period, expenses on an accrual-basis income statement are lower than they are on a cash-basis income statement. The reason: Tax Consultants has made cash payments in the current period, but expenses (as charges to the income statement) have been deferred to future periods. To convert net income to net cash flow from operating activities, the company must deduct from net income the increase of $6,000 in prepaid expenses. An increase in prepaid expenses results in a decrease in cash during the period.

Increase in Accounts Payable. Like the increase in 2010, Tax Consultants must add the 2011 increase of $35,000 in accounts payable to net income, to convert to net cash flow from operating activities. The company incurred a greater amount of expense than the amount of cash it disbursed.

Depreciation Expense (Increase in Accumulated Depreciation). The purchase of depreciable assets is a use of cash, shown in the investing section in the year of acquisition. Tax Consultant's depreciation expense of $21,000 (also represented by the increase in accumulated depreciation) is a non-cash charge; the company adds it back to net income, to arrive at net cash flow from operating activities. The $21,000 is the sum of the $11,000 depreciation on the building plus the $10,000 depreciation on the equipment.

Certain other periodic charges to expense do not require the use of cash. Examples are the amortization of intangible assets and depletion expense. Such charges are treated in the same manner as depreciation. Companies frequently list depreciation and similar non-cash charges as the first adjustments to net income in the statement of cash flows.

As a result of the foregoing items, net cash provided by operating activities is $194,000, as shown in Illustration 23-12.

Net income		$134,000
Adjustments to reconcile net income to		
net cash provided by operating activities:		
Depreciation expense	$21,000	
Decrease in accounts receivable	10,000	
Increase in prepaid expenses	(6,000)	
Increase in accounts payable	35,000	60,000
Net cash provided by operating activities		$194,000

ILLUSTRATION 23-12
Computation of Net Cash Flow from Operating Activities, Year 2—Indirect Method

Step 3: Determine Net Cash Flows from Investing and Financing Activities

After you have determined the items affecting net cash provided by operating activities, the next step involves analyzing the remaining changes in the statement of financial position accounts. Tax Consultants Inc. analyzed the following accounts.

Increase in Land. As indicated from the change in the Land account, the company purchased land of $70,000 during the period. This transaction is an investing activity, reported as a use of cash.

Increase in Buildings and Related Accumulated Depreciation. As indicated in the additional data, and from the change in the Buildings account, Tax Consultants acquired an office building using $200,000 cash. This transaction is a cash outflow, reported in the investing section. The $11,000 increase in accumulated depreciation results from recording depreciation expense on the building. As indicated earlier, the reported depreciation expense has no effect on the amount of cash.

Increase in Equipment and Related Accumulated Depreciation. An increase in equipment of $68,000 resulted because the company used cash to purchase equipment. This transaction is an outflow of cash from an investing activity. The depreciation expense entry for the period explains the increase in Accumulated Depreciation—Equipment.

Increase in Bonds Payable. The Bonds Payable account increased $150,000. Cash received from the issuance of these bonds represents an inflow of cash from a financing activity.

Increase in Retained Earnings. Retained earnings increased $116,000 during the year. Two factors explain this increase: (1) Net income of $134,000 increased retained earnings, and (2) dividends of $18,000 decreased retained earnings. As indicated earlier, the company adjusts net income to net cash provided by operating activities in the operating activities section. Payment of the dividends is a financing activity that involves a cash outflow.

Statement of Cash Flows—2011

Combining the foregoing items, we get a statement of cash flows for 2011 for Tax Consultants Inc., using the indirect method to compute net cash flow from operating activities.

ILLUSTRATION 23-13
Statement of Cash Flows, Tax Consultants Inc., Year 2

TAX CONSULTANTS INC. STATEMENT OF CASH FLOWS FOR THE YEAR ENDED DECEMBER 31, 2011 INCREASE (DECREASE) IN CASH		
Cash flows from operating activities		
Net income		$134,000
Adjustments to reconcile net income to		
net cash provided by operating activities:		
Depreciation expense	$ 21,000	
Decrease in accounts receivable	10,000	
Increase in prepaid expenses	(6,000)	
Increase in accounts payable	35,000	60,000
Net cash provided by operating activities		194,000
Cash flows from investing activities		
Purchase of land	(70,000)	
Purchase of building	(200,000)	
Purchase of equipment	(68,000)	
Net cash used by investing activities		(338,000)
Cash flows from financing activities		
Issuance of bonds	150,000	
Payment of cash dividends	(18,000)	
Net cash provided by financing activities		132,000
Net decrease in cash		(12,000)
Cash, January 1, 2011		49,000
Cash, December 31, 2011		$ 37,000

THIRD EXAMPLE—2012

Our third example, covering the 2012 operations of Tax Consultants Inc., is more complex. It again uses the indirect method to compute and present net cash flow from operating activities.

Tax Consultants Inc. experienced continued success in 2012 and expanded its operations to include the sale of computer software used in tax-return preparation and tax planning. Thus, inventory is a new asset appearing in the company's December 31, 2012, statement of financial position. Illustrations 23-14 and 23-15 show the comparative statements of financial position, income statements, and selected data for 2012.

Step 1: Determine the Change in Cash

The first step in the preparation of the statement of cash flows is to determine the change in cash. As the comparative statements of financial position show, cash increased $17,000 in 2012.

ILLUSTRATION 23-14
Comparative Statements
of Financial Position, Tax
Consultants Inc., Year 3

TAX CONSULTANTS INC.
COMPARATIVE STATEMENTS OF FINANCIAL POSITION
AS OF DECEMBER 31

Assets	2012	2011	Change Increase/Decrease
Land	$ 45,000	$ 70,000	$ 25,000 Decrease
Buildings	200,000	200,000	–0–
Accumulated depreciation—buildings	(21,000)	(11,000)	10,000 Increase
Equipment	193,000	68,000	125,000 Increase
Accumulated depreciation—equipment	(28,000)	(10,000)	18,000 Increase
Inventories	54,000	–0–	54,000 Increase
Accounts receivable	68,000	26,000	42,000 Increase
Prepaid expenses	4,000	6,000	2,000 Decrease
Cash	54,000	37,000	17,000 Increase
Totals	$569,000	$386,000	

Equity and Liabilities			
Share capital—ordinary ($1 par)	$220,000	$ 60,000	$160,000 Increase
Retained earnings	206,000	136,000	70,000 Increase
Bonds payable	110,000	150,000	40,000 Decrease
Accounts payable	33,000	40,000	7,000 Decrease
Totals	$569,000	$386,000	

ILLUSTRATION 23-15
Income Statement, Tax
Consultants Inc., Year 3

TAX CONSULTANTS INC.
INCOME STATEMENT
FOR THE YEAR ENDED DECEMBER 31, 2012

Revenues		$890,000
Cost of goods sold	$465,000	
Operating expenses	221,000	
Interest expense	12,000	
Loss on sale of equipment	2,000	700,000
Income from operations		190,000
Income tax expense		65,000
Net income		$125,000

Additional Information
(a) Operating expenses include depreciation expense of $33,000 and expiration of prepaid expenses of $2,000.
(b) Land was sold at its book value for cash.
(c) Cash dividends of $55,000 were declared and paid.
(d) Interest expense of $12,000 was paid in cash.
(e) Equipment with a cost of $166,000 was purchased for cash. Equipment with a cost of $41,000 and a book value of $36,000 was sold for $34,000 cash.
(f) Bonds were redeemed at their book value for cash.
(g) Ordinary shares ($1 par) were issued for cash.

Step 2: Determine Net Cash Flow from Operating Activities—Indirect Method

We explain the adjustments to net income of $125,000 as follows.

Increase in Accounts Receivable. The increase in accounts receivable of $42,000 represents recorded accrual-basis revenues in excess of cash collections in 2012. The company deducts this increase from net income to convert from the accrual basis to the cash basis.

Increase in Inventories. The $54,000 increase in inventories represents an operating use of cash, not an expense. Tax Consultants therefore deducts this amount from net income, to arrive at net cash flow from operations. In other words, when inventory purchased exceeds inventory sold during a period, cost of goods sold on an accrual basis is lower than on a cash basis.

Decrease in Prepaid Expenses. The $2,000 decrease in prepaid expenses represents a charge to the income statement for which Tax Consultants made no cash payment in the current period. The company adds back the decrease to net income, to arrive at net cash flow from operating activities.

Decrease in Accounts Payable. When accounts payable decrease during the year, cost of goods sold and expenses on a cash basis are higher than they are on an accrual basis. To convert net income to net cash flow from operating activities, the company must deduct the $7,000 in accounts payable from net income.

Depreciation Expense (Increase in Accumulated Depreciation). Accumulated Depreciation—Buildings increased $10,000 ($21,000 − $11,000). The Buildings account did not change during the period, which means that Tax Consultants recorded depreciation expense of $10,000 in 2012.

Accumulated Depreciation—Equipment increased by $18,000 ($28,000 − $10,000) during the year. But Accumulated Depreciation—Equipment decreased by $5,000 as a result of the sale during the year. Thus, depreciation for the year was $23,000. The company reconciled Accumulated Depreciation—Equipment as follows.

Beginning balance	$10,000
Add: Depreciation for 2012	23,000
	33,000
Deduct: Sale of equipment	5,000
Ending balance	$28,000

The company must add back to net income the total depreciation of $33,000 ($10,000 + $23,000) charged to the income statement, to determine net cash flow from operating activities.

Loss on Sale of Equipment. Tax Consultants Inc. sold for $34,000 equipment that cost $41,000 and had a book value of $36,000. As a result, the company reported a loss of $2,000 on its sale. To arrive at net cash flow from operating activities, it must add back to net income the loss on the sale of the equipment. The reason is that the loss is a non-cash charge to the income statement. The loss did not reduce cash, but it did reduce net income.

From the foregoing items, the company prepares the operating activities section of the statement of cash flows, as shown in Illustration 23-16.

ILLUSTRATION 23-16
Operating Activities Section of Cash Flow Statement

Cash flows from operating activities		
Net income		$125,000
Adjustments to reconcile net income to		
net cash provided by operating activities:		
Depreciation expense	$33,000	
Loss on sale of equipment	2,000	
Increase in accounts receivable	(42,000)	
Increase in inventories	(54,000)	
Decrease in prepaid expenses	2,000	
Decrease in accounts payable	(7,000)	(66,000)
Net cash provided by operating activities		59,000

Step 3: Determine Net Cash Flows from Investing and Financing Activities

By analyzing the remaining changes in the statement of financial position accounts, Tax Consultants identifies cash flows from investing and financing activities.

Land. Land decreased $25,000 during the period. As indicated from the information presented, the company sold land for cash at its book value. This transaction is an investing activity, reported as a $25,000 source of cash.

Equipment. An analysis of the Equipment account indicates the following.

Beginning balance	$ 68,000
Purchase of equipment	166,000
	234,000
Sale of equipment	41,000
Ending balance	$193,000

The company used cash to purchase equipment with a fair value of $166,000—an investing transaction reported as a cash outflow. The sale of the equipment for $34,000 is also an investing activity, but one that generates a cash inflow.

Bonds Payable. Bonds payable decreased $40,000 during the year. As indicated from the additional information, the company redeemed the bonds at their book value. This financing transaction used $40,000 of cash.

Share Capital—Ordinary. The Share Capital—Ordinary account increased $160,000 during the year. As indicated from the additional information, Tax Consultants issued ordinary shares of $160,000 at par. This financing transaction provided cash of $160,000.

Retained Earnings. Retained earnings changed $70,000 ($206,000 − $136,000) during the year. The $70,000 change in retained earnings results from net income of $125,000 from operations and the financing activity of paying cash dividends of $55,000.

Statement of Cash Flows—2012

Tax Consultants Inc. combines the foregoing items to prepare the statement of cash flows shown in Illustration 23-17.

ILLUSTRATION 23-17
Statement of Cash Flows, Tax Consultants Inc., Year 3

TAX CONSULTANTS INC.
STATEMENT OF CASH FLOWS
FOR THE YEAR ENDED DECEMBER 31, 2012
INCREASE (DECREASE) IN CASH

Cash flows from operating activities		
Net income		$125,000
Adjustments to reconcile net income to net cash provided by operating activities:		
Depreciation expense	$ 33,000	
Loss on sale of equipment	2,000	
Increase in accounts receivable	(42,000)	
Increase in inventories	(54,000)	
Decrease in prepaid expenses	2,000	
Decrease in accounts payable	(7,000)	(66,000)
Net cash provided by operating activities		59,000
Cash flows from investing activities		
Sale of land	25,000	
Sale of equipment	34,000	
Purchase of equipment	(166,000)	
Net cash used by investing activities		(107,000)
Cash flows from financing activities		
Redemption of bonds	(40,000)	
Sale of ordinary shares	160,000	
Payment of dividends	(55,000)	
Net cash provided by financing activities		65,000
Net increase in cash		17,000
Cash, January 1, 2012		37,000
Cash, December 31, 2012		$ 54,000

SOURCES OF INFORMATION FOR THE STATEMENT OF CASH FLOWS

Objective•7
Identify sources of information for a statement of cash flows.

Important points to remember in the preparation of the statement of cash flows are these:

1. Comparative statements of financial position provide the basic information from which to prepare the report. Additional information obtained from analyses of specific accounts is also included.

2. An analysis of the Retained Earnings account is necessary. The net increase or decrease in Retained Earnings without any explanation is a meaningless amount in the statement. Without explanation, it might represent the effect of net income, dividends declared, or prior period adjustments.

3. The statement includes all changes that have passed through cash or have resulted in an increase or decrease in cash.

4. Write-downs, amortization charges, and similar "book" entries, such as depreciation of plant assets, represent neither inflows nor outflows of cash because they have no effect on cash. To the extent that they have entered into the determination of net income, however, the company must add them back to or subtract them from net income, to arrive at net cash provided (used) by operating activities.

NET CASH FLOW FROM OPERATING ACTIVITIES—INDIRECT VERSUS DIRECT METHOD

As we discussed previously, the two different methods available to adjust income from operations on an accrual basis to net cash flow from operating activities are the indirect (reconciliation) method and the direct (income statement) method. The IASB encourages use of the direct method and permits use of the indirect method. [4]

Indirect Method

For consistency and comparability and because it is the most widely used method in practice, we used the indirect method in the examples just presented. We determined net cash flow from operating activities by adding back to or deducting from net income those items that had no effect on cash. Illustration 23-18 presents more completely

ILLUSTRATION 23-18
Adjustments Needed to Determine Net Cash Flow from Operating Activities—Indirect Method

Net Income	
Additions	**Deductions**
Depreciation expense	Amortization of bond premium
Amortization of intangibles	Decrease in deferred income tax liability
Amortization of bond discount	Income on investment in ordinary shares using equity method
Increase in deferred income tax liability	Gain on sale of plant assets
Loss on investment in ordinary shares using equity method	Increase in receivables
Loss on sale of plant assets	Increase in inventories
Loss on impairment of assets	Increase in prepaid expense
Decrease in receivables	Decrease in accounts payable
Decrease in inventories	Decrease in accrued liabilities
Decrease in prepaid expense	
Increase in accounts payable	
Increase in accrued liabilities	

Net Cash Flow from Operating Activities

the common types of adjustments that companies make to net income to arrive at net cash flow from operating activities.

The additions and deductions in Illustration 23-18 reconcile net income to net cash flow from operating activities, illustrating why the indirect method is also called the reconciliation method.

Direct Method—An Example

Under the direct method the statement of cash flows reports net cash flow from operating activities as major classes of *operating cash receipts* (e.g., cash collected from customers and cash received from interest and dividends) and *cash disbursements* (e.g., cash paid to suppliers for goods, to employees for services, to creditors for interest, and to government authorities for taxes).

We illustrate the direct method here in more detail to help you understand the difference between accrual-based income and net cash flow from operating activities. This example also illustrates the data needed to apply the direct method. Drogba Company, which began business on January 1, 2011, has the following selected statement of financial position information.

	December 31, 2011	January 1, 2011
Property, plant, and equipment (net)	€ 90,000	€–0–
Inventory	160,000	–0–
Accounts payable	60,000	–0–
Accrued expenses payable	20,000	–0–
Accounts receivable	15,000	–0–
Prepaid expenses	8,000	–0–
Cash	159,000	–0–

ILLUSTRATION 23-19
Statement of Financial Position Accounts, Drogba Co.

Drogba Company's December 31, 2011, income statement and additional information are as follows.

Revenues from sales		€780,000
Cost of goods sold		450,000
Gross profit		330,000
Operating expenses	€160,000	
Depreciation	10,000	170,000
Income before income taxes		160,000
Income tax expense		48,000
Net income		€112,000

Additional Information
(a) Dividends of €70,000 were declared and paid in cash.
(b) The accounts payable increase resulted from the purchase of merchandise.
(c) Prepaid expenses and accrued expenses payable relate to operating expenses.

ILLUSTRATION 23-20
Income Statement, Drogba Co.

Under the **direct method**, companies compute net cash provided by operating activities by **adjusting each item in the income statement** from the accrual basis to the cash basis. To simplify and condense the operating activities section, only major classes of operating cash receipts and cash payments are reported. As Illustration 23-21 (on page 1260) shows, the difference between these major classes of cash receipts and cash payments is the net cash provided by operating activities.

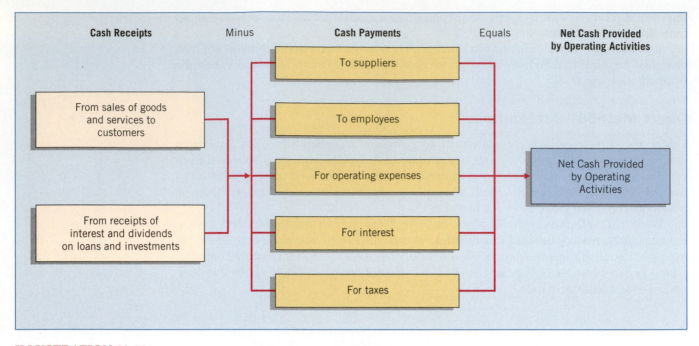

ILLUSTRATION 23-21
Major Classes of Cash
Receipts and Payments

An efficient way to apply the direct method is to analyze the revenues and expenses reported in the income statement in the order in which they are listed. The company then determines cash receipts and cash payments related to these revenues and expenses. In the following sections, we present the direct method adjustments for Drogba Company in 2011, to determine net cash provided by operating activities.

Cash Receipts from Customers. The income statement for Drogba Company reported revenues from customers of €780,000. To determine cash receipts from customers, the company considers the change in accounts receivable during the year.

When accounts receivable increase during the year, revenues on an accrual basis are higher than cash receipts from customers. In other words, operations led to increased revenues, but not all of these revenues resulted in cash receipts. To determine the amount of increase in cash receipts, deduct the amount of the increase in accounts receivable from the total sales revenues. Conversely, a decrease in accounts receivable is added to sales revenues because cash receipts from customers then exceed sales revenues.

For Drogba Company, accounts receivable increased €15,000. Thus, cash receipts from customers were €765,000, computed as follows.

Revenues from sales	€780,000
Deduct: Increase in accounts receivable	15,000
Cash receipts from customers	€765,000

Drogba could also determine cash receipts from customers by analyzing the Accounts Receivable account, as shown below.

Accounts Receivable				
1/1/11	Balance	–0–	Receipts from customers	765,000
	Revenue from sales	780,000		
12/31/11	Balance	15,000		

Illustration 23-22 shows the relationships between cash receipts from customers, revenues from sales, and changes in accounts receivable.

Cash receipts from customers	=	Revenues from sales	{	+ Decrease in accounts receivable or − Increase in accounts receivable

ILLUSTRATION 23-22
Formula to Compute Cash Receipts from Customers

Cash Payments to Suppliers. Drogba Company reported cost of goods sold on its income statement of €450,000. To determine cash payments to suppliers, the company first finds purchases for the year, by adjusting cost of goods sold for the change in inventory. When inventory increases during the year, purchases this year exceed cost of goods sold. As a result, the company adds the increase in inventory to cost of goods sold, to arrive at purchases.

In 2011, Drogba Company's inventory increased €160,000. The company computes purchases as follows.

Cost of goods sold	€450,000
Add: Increase in inventory	160,000
Purchases	€610,000

After computing purchases, Drogba determines cash payments to suppliers by adjusting purchases for the change in accounts payable. When accounts payable increase during the year, purchases on an accrual basis are higher than they are on a cash basis. As a result, it deducts from purchases the increase in accounts payable to arrive at cash payments to suppliers. Conversely, if cash payments to suppliers exceed purchases, Drogba adds to purchases the decrease in accounts payable. Cash payments to suppliers were €550,000, computed as follows.

Purchases	€610,000
Deduct: Increase in accounts payable	60,000
Cash payments to suppliers	€550,000

Drogba also can determine cash payments to suppliers by analyzing Accounts Payable, as shown below.

Accounts Payable				
Payments to suppliers	550,000	1/1/11	Balance	–0–
			Purchases	610,000
		12/31/11	Balance	60,000

Illustration 23-23 shows the relationships between cash payments to suppliers, cost of goods sold, changes in inventory, and changes in accounts payable.

Cash payments to suppliers	=	Cost of goods sold	{	+ Increase in inventory or − Decrease in inventory	{	+ Decrease in accounts payable or − Increase in accounts payable

ILLUSTRATION 23-23
Formula to Compute Cash Payments to Suppliers

Cash Payments for Operating Expenses. Drogba reported operating expenses of €160,000 on its income statement. To determine the cash paid for operating expenses, it must adjust this amount for any changes in prepaid expenses and accrued expenses payable.

For example, when prepaid expenses increased €8,000 during the year, cash paid for operating expenses was €8,000 higher than operating expenses reported on the income statement. To convert operating expenses to cash payments for operating expenses, the company adds to operating expenses the increase of €8,000. Conversely, if prepaid expenses decrease during the year, it deducts from operating expenses the amount of the decrease.

Drogba also must adjust operating expenses for changes in accrued expenses payable. When accrued expenses payable increase during the year, operating expenses on an accrual basis are higher than they are on a cash basis. As a result, the company deducts from operating expenses an increase in accrued expenses payable, to arrive at cash payments for operating expenses. Conversely, it adds to operating expenses a decrease in accrued expenses payable, because cash payments exceed operating expenses.

Drogba Company's cash payments for operating expenses were €148,000, computed as follows.

Operating expenses	€160,000
Add: Increase in prepaid expenses	8,000
Deduct: Increase in accrued expenses payable	20,000
Cash payments for operating expenses	€148,000

The relationships among cash payments for operating expenses, changes in prepaid expenses, and changes in accrued expenses payable are shown in Illustration 23-24.

ILLUSTRATION 23-24
Formula to Compute Cash Payments for Operating Expenses

Cash payments for operating expenses	=	Operating expenses	+ Increase in prepaid expense or − Decrease in prepaid expense	+ Decrease in accrued expenses payable or − Increase in accrued expenses payable

Note that the company did not consider depreciation expense because it is a non-cash charge.

Cash Payments for Income Taxes. The income statement for Drogba shows income tax expense of €48,000. This amount equals the cash paid. How do we know that? Because the comparative statement of financial position indicated no income taxes payable at either the beginning or end of the year.

Summary of Net Cash Flow from Operating Activities—Direct Method
The following schedule summarizes the computations illustrated above.

ILLUSTRATION 23-25
Accrual Basis to Cash Basis

Accrual Basis		Adjustment	Add (Subtract)	Cash Basis
Revenues from sales	€780,000 −	Increase in accounts receivable	€ (15,000)	€765,000
Cost of goods sold	450,000 +	Increase in inventory	160,000	
	−	Increase in accounts payable	(60,000)	550,000
Operating expenses	160,000 +	Increase in prepaid expenses	8,000	
	−	Increase in accrued expenses payable	(20,000)	148,000
Depreciation expense	10,000 −	Depreciation expense	(10,000)	–0–
Income tax expense	48,000			48,000
Total expense	668,000			746,000
Net income	€112,000	Net cash provided by operating activities		€ 19,000

Illustration 23-26 shows the presentation of the direct method for reporting net cash flow from operating activities for the Drogba Company illustration.

DROGBA COMPANY		
STATEMENT OF CASH FLOWS (PARTIAL)		
Cash flows from operating activities		
Cash received from customers		€765,000
Cash payments:		
To suppliers	€550,000	
For operating expenses	148,000	
For income taxes	48,000	746,000
Net cash provided by operating activities		€ 19,000

ILLUSTRATION 23-26
Operating Activities
Section—Direct
Method, 2011

If Drogba Company uses the direct method to present the net cash flow from operating activities, it may provide in a separate schedule the reconciliation of net income to net cash provided by operating activities. The reconciliation assumes the identical form and content of the indirect method of presentation, as shown below.

DROGBA COMPANY		
RECONCILIATION		
Net income		€112,000
Adjustments to reconcile net income to net cash provided by operating activities:		
Depreciation expense	€ 10,000	
Increase in accounts receivable	(15,000)	
Increase in inventory	(160,000)	
Increase in prepaid expenses	(8,000)	
Increase in accounts payable	60,000	
Increase in accrued expense payable	20,000	(93,000)
Net cash provided by operating activities		€ 19,000

ILLUSTRATION 23-27
Reconciliation of Net
Income to Net Cash
Provided by Operating
Activities, 2011

Direct versus Indirect Controversy

The most contentious decision that the IASB faced related to cash flow reporting was choosing between the direct method and the indirect method of determining net cash flow from operating activities. Companies lobbied *against* the direct method, urging adoption of the indirect method. Commercial lending officers expressed to the IASB a strong preference in favor of the direct method. In the next two sections, we consider the arguments in favor of each of the methods.

In Favor of the Direct Method

The principal advantage of the direct method is that **it shows operating cash receipts and payments**. Thus, it is more consistent with the objective of a statement of cash flows—to provide information about cash receipts and cash payments—than the indirect method, which does not report operating cash receipts and payments.

Supporters of the direct method contend that knowledge of the specific sources of operating cash receipts and the purposes for which operating cash payments were made in past periods is useful in estimating future operating cash flows. Furthermore, information about amounts of major classes of operating cash receipts and payments is more useful than information only about their arithmetic sum (the net cash flow from operating activities). Such information is more revealing of a company's ability (1) to generate sufficient cash from operating activities to pay its debts, (2) to reinvest in its operations, and (3) to make distributions to its owners.

Many companies indicate that they do not currently collect information in a manner that allows them to determine amounts, such as cash received from customers or cash paid to suppliers directly, from their accounting systems. But supporters of the direct method contend that the incremental cost of determining operating cash receipts and payments is not significant.

In Favor of the Indirect Method

The principal advantage of the indirect method is that **it focuses on the differences between net income and net cash flow from operating activities**. That is, it provides a useful link between the statement of cash flows and the income statement and the statement of financial position.

Many companies contend that it is less costly to adjust net income to net cash flow from operating activities (indirect) than it is to report gross operating cash receipts and payments (direct). Supporters of the indirect method also state that the direct method, which effectively reports income statement information on a cash rather than an accrual basis, may erroneously suggest that net cash flow from operating activities are as good as, or better than, net income as a measure of performance.

NOT WHAT IT SEEMS

What do the numbers mean?

The controversy over direct and indirect methods highlights the importance that the market attributes to operating cash flows. By showing an improving cash flow, a company can give a favorable impression of its ongoing operations. For example, **WorldCom** (USA) concealed declines in its operations by capitalizing certain operating expenses—to the tune of $3.8 billion! This practice not only "juiced up" income but also made it possible to report the cash payments in the investing section of the cash flow statement rather than as a deduction from operating cash flows.

The U.S. SEC recently addressed a similar cash flow classification issue with automakers like **Ford** (USA), **GM** (USA), and **Chrysler** (USA). For years, automakers classified lease receivables and other dealer-financing arrangements as investment cash flows. Thus, they reported an increase in lease or loan receivables from cars sold as a use of cash in the investing section of the statement of cash flows. The SEC objected and now requires automakers to report these receivables as operating cash flows, since the leases and loans are used to facilitate car sales. At GM, these reclassifications reduced its operating cash flows from $7.6 billion to $3 billion in the year before the change. So while the overall cash flows—from operations, investing, and financing—remained the same, operating cash flows at these companies looked better than they really were.

Source: Peter Elstrom, "How to Hide $3.8 Billion in Expenses," *BusinessWeek Online* (July 8, 2002); and Judith Burns, "SEC Tells US Automakers to Retool Cash-Flow Accounting," *Wall Street Journal Online* (February 28, 2005).

SECTION 2 • SPECIAL PROBLEMS IN STATEMENT PREPARATION

Objective•8

Discuss special problems in preparing a statement of cash flows.

We discussed some of the special problems related to preparing the statement of cash flows in connection with the preceding illustrations. Other problems that arise with some frequency in the preparation of this statement include the following.

1. Adjustments to net income.
2. Accounts receivable (net).
3. Other working capital changes.
4. Net loss.
5. Disclosures.

ADJUSTMENTS TO NET INCOME

Depreciation and Amortization

Depreciation expense is the most common adjustment to net income that companies make to arrive at net cash flow from operating activities. But there are numerous other non-cash expense or revenue items. Examples of expense items that companies must add back to net income are the **amortization of limited-life intangible assets**, such as patents, and **depletion of mineral resources**. These charges to expense involve expenditures made in prior periods that a company amortizes currently. These charges reduce net income without affecting cash in the current period.

Also, **amortization of bond discount or premium** on long-term bonds payable affects the amount of interest expense. However, neither changes cash. As a result, a company should add back discount amortization and subtract premium amortization from net income to arrive at net cash flow from operating activities.

Postretirement Benefit Costs

If a company has postretirement costs such as an employee pension plan, chances are that the pension expense recorded during a period will either be higher or lower than the cash funded. It will be higher when there is an unfunded liability and will be lower when there is a prepaid pension cost. When the expense is higher or lower than the cash paid, **the company must adjust net income by the difference between cash paid and the expense reported** in computing net cash flow from operating activities.

Change in Deferred Income Taxes

Changes in deferred income taxes affect net income but have no effect on cash. For example, **Delta Airlines** (USA) reported an increase in its liability for deferred taxes of approximately $1.2 billion. This change in the liability increased tax expense and decreased net income, but did not affect cash. Therefore, Delta added back $1.2 billion to net income on its statement of cash flows.

Equity Method of Accounting

Another common adjustment to net income is **a change related to an investment in ordinary shares** when recording income or loss under the equity method. Recall that under the equity method, the investor (1) debits the investment account and credits revenue for its share of the investee's net income, and (2) credits dividends received to the investment account. Therefore, the net increase in the investment account does not affect cash flows. A company must deduct the net increase from net income to arrive at net cash flow from operating activities.

Assume that Victor Co. owns 40 percent of Milo Inc. During the year, Milo reports net income of $100,000 and pays a cash dividend of $30,000. Victor reports this in its statement of cash flows as a deduction from net income in the following manner— Equity in earnings of Milo, net of dividends, $28,000 [($100,000 − $30,000) × 40%].

Losses and Gains

Realized Losses and Gains

In the illustration for Tax Consultants, the company experienced a loss of $2,000 from the sale of equipment. The company added this loss to net income to compute net cash flow from operating activities because **the loss is a non-cash charge in the income statement.**

If Tax Consultants experiences a **gain** from a sale of equipment, it too requires an adjustment to net income. Because a company reports the gain in the statement of cash flows as part of the cash proceeds from the sale of equipment under investing activities, **it deducts the gain from net income to avoid double-counting**—once as part of net income and again as part of the cash proceeds from the sale.

To illustrate, assume that Tax Consultants had land with a carrying value of $200,000, which was condemned by the provincial government for a highway project. The condemnation proceeds received were $205,000, resulting in a gain of $5,000. In the statement of cash flows (indirect method), the company would deduct the $5,000 gain from net income in the operating activities section. It would report the $205,000 cash inflow from the condemnation as an investing activity, as follows.

Cash flows from investing activities	
Condemnation of land	$205,000

Unrealized Losses and Gains

Unrealized losses and gains generally occur for debt investments not held for collection and for equity investments. For example, assume that **InBev** (BEL) purchases the following two security investments on January 10, 2011.

1. Debt investment for €1 million that it does not intend to hold for collection. During 2011, the debt investment has an unrealized holding gain of €110,000 (recorded in net income).

2. Equity investment for €600,000 that is non-trading in nature. During 2011, the non-trading equity investment has an unrealized holding loss of €50,000 (recorded in other comprehensive income).

On the statement of cash flows, InBev reports the investments in the debt and equity investments as follows.

Cash flows from investing activities	
Purchase of debt investment	€1,000,000
Purchase of equity investment	600,000

For InBev, the unrealized holding gain of €110,000 on the debt investment increases net income but does not increase net cash flow from operating activities. As a result, the unrealized holding gain of €110,000 is deducted from net income to compute net cash flow from operating activities.

On the other hand, the unrealized holding loss of €50,000 that InBev incurs on the non-trading equity investment does not affect net income or cash flows—this loss is reported in the other comprehensive income section. As a result, no adjustment to net income is necessary in computing net cash flow from operating activities.

Thus, the general rule is that unrealized holding gains or losses that affect net income must be adjusted to determine net cash flow from operating activities. Conversely, unrealized holding gains or losses that do not affect net income are not adjusted to determine net cash flow from operating activities.[4]

Share-Based Compensation

Recall for share-based compensation plans that companies are required to use the fair value method to determine total compensation cost. The compensation cost is then recognized as an expense in the periods in which the employee provides services. When Compensation Expense is debited, Share Premium—Options is often credited. Cash is not affected by recording the expense. **Therefore, the company must increase net income by the amount of compensation expense from share options in computing net cash flow from operating activities.**

[4]Other unrealized holding gains or losses, such as revaluations on property, plant, and equipment, or intangible assets, are also reported as part of other comprehensive income. As a result, net income is not adjusted in computing cash flows from operating activities for any type of unrealized holding gains or losses that are reported in other comprehensive income.

To illustrate how this information should be reported on a statement of cash flows, assume that First Wave Inc. grants 5,000 options to its CEO, Ann Johnson. Each option entitles Johnson to purchase one share of First Wave's $1 par value ordinary shares at $50 per share at any time in the next two years (the service period). The fair value of the options is $200,000. First Wave records compensation expense in the first year as follows.

Compensation Expense ($200,000 ÷ 2)	100,000	
Share Premium—Options		100,000

In addition, if we assume that First Wave has a 35 percent tax rate, it would recognize a deferred tax asset of $35,000 ($100,000 × 35%) in the first year, as follows.

Deferred Tax Asset	35,000	
Income Tax Expense		35,000

Therefore, on the statement of cash flows for the first year, First Wave reports the following (assuming a net income of $600,000).

Net income	$600,000
Adjustments to reconcile net income to net cash provided by operating activities:	
Share-based compensation expense	100,000
Increase in deferred tax asset	(35,000)

As shown in First Wave's statement of cash flows, it adds the share-based compensation expense to net income because it is a non-cash expense. The increase in the deferred tax asset and the related reduction in income tax expense increase net income. Although the negative income tax expense increases net income, it does not increase cash. Therefore, it should be deducted. Subsequently, if Ann Johnson exercises her options, Third Wave reports "Cash provided by exercise of share options" in the financing section of the statement of cash flows.[5]

ACCOUNTS RECEIVABLE (NET)

Up to this point, we assumed no allowance for doubtful accounts—a contra account—to offset accounts receivable. However, if a company needs an allowance for doubtful accounts, how does that allowance affect the company's determination of net cash flow from operating activities? For example, assume that Redmark Co. reports net income of $40,000. It has the accounts receivable balances, as shown in Illustration 23-28.

ILLUSTRATION 23-28
Accounts Receivable Balances, Redmark Co.

	2011	2010	Change Increase/Decrease
Accounts receivable	$105,000	$90,000	$15,000 Increase
Allowance for doubtful accounts	(10,000)	(4,000)	6,000 Increase
Accounts receivable (net)	$ 95,000	$86,000	9,000 Increase

[5]In some countries, companies receive a tax deduction related to share-based compensation plans at the time employees exercise their options. The amount of the deduction is equal to the difference between the market price of the share and the exercise price at the date the employee purchases the shares, which in most cases is much larger than the total compensation expense recorded. When the tax deduction exceeds the total compensation recorded, this provides an additional cash inflow to the company. For example, in a recent year Cisco Systems (USA) reported additional cash inflow related to its share-option plans equal to $537 million. Under IFRS, this tax-related cash inflow should be reported in the financing section of the statement of cash flows. [5]

Indirect Method

Because an increase in Allowance for Doubtful Accounts results from a charge to bad debt expense, a company should add back an increase in Allowance for Doubtful Accounts to net income to arrive at net cash flow from operating activities. Illustration 23-29 shows one method for presenting this information in a statement of cash flows.

ILLUSTRATION 23-29
Presentation of Allowance for Doubtful Accounts—Indirect Method

REDMARK CO.		
STATEMENT OF CASH FLOWS (PARTIAL)		
FOR THE YEAR 2011		
Cash flows from operating activities		
Net income		$40,000
Adjustments to reconcile net income to net		
cash provided by operating activities:		
Increase in accounts receivable	$(15,000)	
Increase in allowance for doubtful accounts	6,000	(9,000)
		$31,000

As we indicated, the increase in the Allowance for Doubtful Accounts balance results from a charge to bad debt expense for the year. Because bad debt expense is a non-cash charge, a company must add it back to net income in arriving at net cash flow from operating activities.

Instead of separately analyzing the allowance account, a short-cut approach is to net the allowance balance against the receivable balance and compare the change in accounts receivable on a net basis. Illustration 23-30 shows this presentation.

ILLUSTRATION 23-30
Net Approach to Allowance for Doubtful Accounts—Indirect Method

REDMARK CO.	
STATEMENT OF CASH FLOWS (PARTIAL)	
FOR THE YEAR 2011	
Cash flows from operating activities	
Net income	$40,000
Adjustments to reconcile net income to	
net cash provided by operating activities:	
Increase in accounts receivable (net)	(9,000)
	$31,000

This short-cut procedure works also if the change in the allowance account results from a write-off of accounts receivable. This reduces both Accounts Receivable and Allowance for Doubtful Accounts. No effect on cash flows occurs. Because of its simplicity, *use the net approach for your homework assignments.*

Direct Method

If using the direct method, a company **should not net** Allowance for Doubtful Accounts against Accounts Receivable. To illustrate, assume that Redmark Co.'s net income of $40,000 consisted of the following items.

ILLUSTRATION 23-31
Income Statement, Redmark Co.

REDMARK CO.		
INCOME STATEMENT		
FOR THE YEAR 2011		
Sales		$100,000
Expenses		
Salaries	$46,000	
Utilities	8,000	
Bad debts	6,000	60,000
Net income		$ 40,000

If Redmark deducts the $9,000 increase in accounts receivable (net) from sales for the year, it would report cash sales at $91,000 ($100,000 − $9,000) and cash payments for operating expenses at $60,000. Both items would be misstated: Cash sales should be reported at $85,000 ($100,000 − $15,000), and total cash payments for operating expenses should be reported at $54,000 ($60,000 − $6,000). Illustration 23-32 shows the proper presentation.

ILLUSTRATION 23-32
Bad Debts—Direct Method

REDMARK CO. STATEMENT OF CASH FLOWS (PARTIAL) FOR THE YEAR 2011		
Cash flows from operating activities		
Cash received from customers		$85,000
Salaries paid	$46,000	
Utilities paid	8,000	54,000
Net cash provided by operating activities		$31,000

An added complication develops when a company writes off accounts receivable. Simply adjusting sales for the change in accounts receivable will not provide the proper amount of cash sales. The reason is that the write-off of the accounts receivable is not a cash collection. Thus, an additional adjustment is necessary.

OTHER WORKING CAPITAL CHANGES

Up to this point, we showed how companies handled all of the changes in working capital items (current asset and current liability items) as adjustments to net income in determining net cash flow from operating activities. You must be careful, however, because **some changes in working capital**, **although they affect cash**, **do not affect net income**. Generally, these are investing or financing activities of a current nature.

One activity is the purchase of **short-term non-trading equity investments**. For example, the purchase of short-term non-trading equity investments for $50,000 cash has no effect on net income, but it does cause a $50,000 decrease in cash. A company reports this transaction as a cash flow from investing activities as follows.

Cash flows from investing activities	
Purchase of short-term non-trading equity investments	$(50,000)

Another example is the issuance of a **short-term non-trade note payable** for cash. This change in a working capital item has no effect on income from operations, but it increases cash by the amount of the note payable. For example, a company reports the issuance of a $10,000 short-term, non-trade note payable for cash in the statement of cash flows as follows.

Cash flows from financing activities	
Issuance of short-term note	$10,000

Another change in a working capital item that has no effect on income from operations or on cash is a **cash dividend payable**. Although a company will report the cash dividends when paid as a financing activity, it does not report the declared but unpaid dividend on the statement of cash flows.

NET LOSS

If a company reports a net loss instead of a net income, it must adjust the net loss for those items that do not result in a cash inflow or outflow. The net loss, after adjusting for the charges or credits not affecting cash, may result in a negative or a positive cash flow from operating activities.

For example, if the net loss is $50,000 and the total amount of charges to add back is $60,000, then net cash provided by operating activities is $10,000. Illustration 23-33 shows this computation.

ILLUSTRATION 23-33
Computation of Net Cash Flow from Operating Activities—Cash Inflow

Net loss		$(50,000)
Adjustments to reconcile net income to net cash provided by operating activities:		
Depreciation of plant assets	$55,000	
Amortization of patents	5,000	60,000
Net cash provided by operating activities		$ 10,000

If the company experiences a net loss of $80,000 and the total amount of the charges to add back is $25,000, the presentation appears as follows.

ILLUSTRATION 23-34
Computation of Net Cash Flow from Operating Activities—Cash Outflow

Net loss	$(80,000)
Adjustments to reconcile net income to net cash used by operating activities:	
Depreciation of plant assets	25,000
Net cash used by operating activities	$(55,000)

Although not illustrated in this chapter, a negative cash flow may result even if the company reports a net income.

DISCLOSURES

Significant Non-Cash Transactions

Because the statement of cash flows reports only the effects of operating, investing, and financing activities in terms of cash flows, it omits some **significant non-cash transactions** and other events that are investing or financing activities. Among the more common of these non-cash transactions that a company should report or disclose in some manner are the following.

1. Acquisition of assets by assuming liabilities (including finance lease obligations) or by issuing equity securities.
2. Exchanges of non-monetary assets.
3. Refinancing of long-term debt.
4. Conversion of debt or preference shares to ordinary shares.
5. Issuance of equity securities to retire debt.

Investing and financing transactions that do not require the use of cash are excluded from the statement of cash flows. [6] If material in amount, these disclosures may be either narrative or summarized in a separate schedule. This schedule may appear in a separate note or supplementary schedule to the financial statements.[6] Illustration 23-35 shows the presentation of these significant non-cash transactions or other events in a separate schedule in the notes to the financial statements.

---

[6]Some non-cash investing and financing activities are part cash and part non-cash. Companies should report only the cash portion on the statement of cash flows. The non-cash component should be reported in a separate note.

ILLUSTRATION 23-35
Note Presentation of
Non-Cash Investing and
Financing Activities

Note G: Significant non-cash transactions. During the year, the company engaged in the following significant non-cash investing and financing transactions:	
Issued 250,000 ordinary shares to purchase land and building	$1,750,000
Exchanged land in Steadfast, New York, for land in Bedford, Pennsylvania	$2,000,000
Converted 12% bonds to 50,000 ordinary shares	$ 500,000

Companies do not generally report certain other significant non-cash transactions or other events in conjunction with the statement of cash flows. Examples of these types of transactions are **share dividends, share splits, and restrictions on retained earnings**. Companies generally report these items, neither financing nor investing activities, in conjunction with the statement of changes in equity or schedules and notes pertaining to changes in equity accounts.

Special Disclosures

IAS 7 indicates that cash flows related to interest received and paid, and dividends received and paid, should be separately disclosed in the statement of cash flows. [7] Each item should be classified in a consistent manner from period to period as operating, investing, or financing cash flows. As indicated earlier, *for homework purposes classify interest received and paid and dividends received as part of cash flows from operating activities and dividends paid as cash flows from financing activities.* The justification for reporting the first three items in cash flows from operating activities is that each item affects net income. Dividends paid, however, do not affect net income and are often considered a cost of financing.

Companies should also disclose income taxes paid separately in the cash flows from operating activities unless they can be separately identified as part of investing or financing activities. While tax expense may be readily identifiable with investing or financing activities, the related tax cash flows are often impracticable to identify and may arise in a different period from the cash flows of the underlying transaction. Therefore, taxes paid are usually classified as cash flows from operating activities. IFRS requires that the cash paid for taxes, as well as cash flows from interest and dividends received and paid, be disclosed. The category (operating, investing, or financing) that each item was included in must be disclosed as well.

An example of such a disclosure from the notes to **Daimler**'s (DEU) financial statement is provided in Illustration 23-36.

ILLUSTRATION 23-36
Note Disclosure of
Interest, Taxes, and
Dividends

Daimler

Cash provided by operating activities includes the following cash flows:

(in millions of €)	2009	2008	2007
Interest paid	(894)	(651)	(1,541)
Interest received	471	765	977
Income taxes paid, net	(358)	(898)	(1,020)
Dividends received	109	67	69

Other companies choose to report these items directly in the statement of cash flows. In many cases, companies start with income before income taxes and then show income taxes paid as a separate item. In addition, they often add back interest expense on an accrual basis and then subtract interest paid. Reporting these items in the operating activites section is shown for Mermel Company in Illustration 23-37 (on page 1272).

ILLUSTRATION 23-37
Reporting of Interest, Taxes, and Dividends in the Operating Section

MERMEL COMPANY STATEMENT OF CASH FLOWS (¥000,000) (OPERATING ACTIVITIES SECTION ONLY)		
Income before income tax		¥4,000	
Adjustments to reconcile income before income tax to net cash provided by operating activities			
Depreciation expense	¥1,000	
Interest expense	500	
Investment revenue	(650)	
Decrease in inventories	1,050	
Increase in trade receivables	(310)	1,590
Cash generated from operations		5,590
Interest paid	(300)	
Income taxes paid	(760)	(1,060)
Net cash provided by operating activities		¥ 4,530

Companies often provide a separate section to identify interest and income taxes paid.

CASH FLOW TOOL

What do the numbers mean?

By understanding the relationship between cash flows and income measures, analysts can gain better insights into company performance. Because earnings altered through creative accounting practices generally do not change operating cash flows, analysts can use the relationship between earnings and operating cash flows to detect suspicious accounting practices. Also, by monitoring the ratio between cash flows from operations and operating income, they can get a clearer picture of developing problems in a company.

For example, the chart below plots the ratio of operating cash flows to earnings for **Xerox Corp.** (USA) in the years leading up to the U.S. SEC singling it out in 2000 for aggressive revenue recognition practices on its leases.

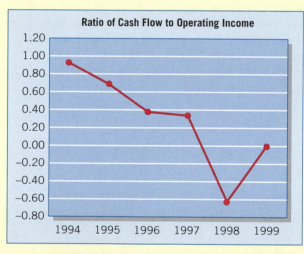

Similar to **W. T. Grant** (USA) in the chapter opening story, Xerox was reporting earnings growth in the years leading up to its financial breakdown in 2000 but teetering near bankruptcy in 2001. However, Xerox's ratio of cash flow to operating income showed a declining trend and became negative well before its revenue recognition practices were revealed. The trend revealed in the graph should have given any analyst reason to investigate Xerox further. As one analyst noted, "Earnings growth that exceeds the growth in operating cash flow cannot continue for extended periods and should be investigated."

Source: Adapted from Charles Mulford and Eugene Comiskey, *The Financial Numbers Game: Detecting Creative Accounting Practices* (New York: John Wiley & Sons, 2002), Chapter 11, by permission.

SECTION 3 · USE OF A WORKSHEET

When numerous adjustments are necessary or other complicating factors are present, companies often use **a worksheet to assemble and classify the data that will appear on the statement of cash flows**. The worksheet (a **spreadsheet** when using computer software) is merely a device that aids in the preparation of the statement. Its use is optional. Illustration 23-38 shows the skeleton format of the worksheet for preparation of the statement of cash flows using the indirect method.

Objective·9

Explain the use of a worksheet in preparing a statement of cash flows.

XYZ COMPANY
Statement of Cash Flows For the Year Ended...

	A	B	C	D	E
	Statement of Financial Position Accounts	End of Prior Year Balances	Reconciling Items Debits	Reconciling Items Credits	End of Current Year Balances
1					
2	Debit balance accounts	XX	XX	XX	XX
3		XX	XX	XX	XX
4	Totals	XXX			XXX
5	Credit balance accounts	XX	XX	XX	XX
6		XX	XX	XX	XX
7	Totals	XXX			XXX
8	Statement of Cash Flows Effects				
9	Operating activities				
10	Net income		XX		
11	Adjustments		XX	XX	
12	Investing activities				
13	Receipts and payments		XX	XX	
14	Financing activities				
15	Receipts and payments		XX	XX	
16	Totals		XXX	XXX	
17	Increase (decrease) in cash		(XX)	XX	
18	Totals		XXX	XXX	

Sheet1 / Sheet2 / Sheet3 /

ILLUSTRATION 23-38
Format of Worksheet for Preparation of Statement of Cash Flows

The following guidelines are important in using a worksheet.

1. In the statement of financial position accounts section, **list accounts with debit balances separately from those with credit balances**. This means, for example, that Accumulated Depreciation is listed under credit balances and not as a contra account under debit balances. Enter the beginning and ending balances of each account in the appropriate columns. Then, enter the transactions that caused the change in the account balance during the year as reconciling items in the two middle columns.

   After all reconciling items have been entered, each line pertaining to a statement of financial position account should foot across. That is, the beginning balance plus or minus the reconciling item(s) must equal the ending balance. When this agreement exists for all statement of financial position accounts, all changes in account balances have been reconciled.

2. The bottom portion of the worksheet consists of the operating, investing, and financing activities sections. Accordingly, it provides the information necessary to

prepare the formal statement of cash flows. **Enter inflows of cash as debits in the reconciling columns, and outflows of cash as credits in the reconciling columns.** Thus, in this section, a company would enter the sale of equipment for cash at book value as a debit under inflows of cash from investing activities. Similarly, it would enter the purchase of land for cash as a credit under outflows of cash from investing activities.

3. **Do not enter in any journal or post to any account the reconciling items shown in the worksheet.** These items do not represent either adjustments or corrections of the statement of financial position accounts. They are used only to facilitate the preparation of the statement of cash flows.

PREPARATION OF THE WORKSHEET

The preparation of a worksheet involves the following steps.

Step 1. Enter the statement of financial position accounts and their beginning and ending balances in the statement of financial position accounts section.

Step 2. Enter the data that explain the changes in the statement of financial position accounts (other than cash) and their effects on the statement of cash flows in the reconciling columns of the worksheet.

Step 3. Enter the increase or decrease in cash on the cash line and at the bottom of the worksheet. This entry should enable the totals of the reconciling columns to be in agreement.

To illustrate the preparation and use of a worksheet and to illustrate the reporting of some of the special problems discussed in the prior section, we present a comprehensive example for Satellite Corporation. Again, the indirect method serves as the basis for the computation of net cash provided by operating activities. Illustrations 23-39 and 23-40 (on page 1276) present the statement of financial position, combined statement of income and retained earnings, and additional information for Satellite Corporation. The discussion that follows these financial statements provides additional explanations related to the preparation of the worksheet.

ANALYSIS OF TRANSACTIONS

The following discussion explains the individual adjustments that appear on the worksheet in Illustration 23-41 (page 1280). Because cash is the basis for the analysis, Satellite reconciles the cash account last. Because income is the first item that appears on the statement of cash flows, it is handled first.

Change in Retained Earnings

Net income for the period is $117,000. The entry for it on the worksheet is as follows.

(1)

Operating—Net Income	117,000	
Retained Earnings		117,000

Satellite reports net income on the bottom section of the worksheet. This **is the starting point for preparation of the statement of cash flows (under the indirect method).**

A share dividend and a cash dividend also affected retained earnings. The retained earnings statement reports a share dividend of $15,000. The worksheet entry for this transaction is as follows.

	A	B	C	D	
	SATELLITE CORPORATION Comparative Statement of Financial Position–December 31, 2011 and 2010				
1		2011	2010	Increase or (Decrease)	
2	**Assets**				
3	Equity investment in Porter Co. (equity method)	$ 18,500	$ 15,000	$ 3,500	
4	Land	131,500	82,000	49,500	
5	Equipment	198,000	142,000	56,000	
6	Accumulated depreciation—equipment	(40,000)	(31,000)	9,000	
7	Buildings	262,000	262,000	—	
8	Accumulated depreciation—buildings	(74,100)	(71,000)	3,100	
9	Trademark	7,600	10,000	(2,400)	
10	Inventories	493,000	341,000	152,000	
11	Prepaid expenses	16,500	17,000	(500)	
12	Accounts receivable (net)	104,000	51,000	53,000	
13	Cash	59,000	66,000	(7,000)	
14	Total assets	$1,176,000	$884,000		
15	**Equity**				
16	Share capital—ordinary ($1 par)	$ 60,000	$ 50,000	$ 10,000	
17	Share premium—ordinary	187,000	38,000	149,000	
18	Retained earnings	592,000	496,000	96,000	
19	Treasury shares	(17,000)	—	17,000	
20	Total equity	822,000	584,000		
21	**Liabilities**				
22	Notes payable (long-term)	60,000	—	60,000	
23	Bonds payable	107,000	108,000	(1,000)	
24	Deferred tax liability (long-term)	9,000	6,000	3,000	
25	Accounts payable	132,000	131,000	1,000	
26	Accrued liabilities	43,000	39,000	4,000	
27	Income tax payable	3,000	16,000	(13,000)	
28	Total liabilities	354,000	300,000		
29	Total equity and liabilities	$1,176,000	$884,000		

Sheet1 / Sheet2 / Sheet3

ILLUSTRATION 23-39
Comparative Statement of Financial Position, Satellite Corporation

(2)

Retained Earnings	15,000	
Share Capital—Ordinary		1,000
Share Premium—Ordinary		14,000

The issuance of share dividends is not a cash operating, investing, or financing item. Therefore, **although the company enters this transaction on the worksheet for reconciling purposes, it does not report it in the statement of cash flows**.

The $6,000 cash dividend paid represents a financing activity cash outflow. Satellite makes the following worksheet entry:

(3)

Retained Earnings	6,000	
Financing—Cash Dividends		6,000

The company reconciles the beginning and ending balances of retained earnings by entry of the three items above.

Retained Earnings			
(2)	15,000	Bal.	496,000
(3)	6,000	(1)	117,000
		Bal.	592,000

ILLUSTRATION 23-40
Income and Retained
Earnings Statements,
Satellite Corporation

SATELLITE CORPORATION
COMBINED STATEMENT OF INCOME AND RETAINED EARNINGS
FOR THE YEAR ENDED DECEMBER 31, 2011

Net sales		$526,500
Other revenue		3,500
Total revenues		530,000
Expense		
Cost of goods sold		310,000
Selling and administrative expenses		47,000
Other income and expense		4,000
Total expenses		361,000
Income before income tax		169,000
Income tax		
Current	$49,000	
Deferred	3,000	52,000
Net income		117,000
Retained earnings, January 1		496,000
Less:		
Cash dividends	6,000	
Share dividend	15,000	21,000
Retained earnings, December 31		$592,000
Per share:		
Net income		$2.13

Additional Information

(a) Other income of $3,500 represents Satellite's equity share in the net income of Porter Co., an equity investee. Satellite owns 22% of Porter Co.

(b) An analysis of the Equipment account and related Accumulated Depreciation—Equipment account indicates the following.

	Equipment Dr./(Cr.)	Accum. Dep. Dr./(Cr.)	Gain or (Loss)
Balance at end of 2010	$142,000	$(31,000)	
Purchases of equipment	53,000		
Sale of equipment	(8,000)	2,500	$(1,500)
Depreciation for the period		(11,500)	
Major repair charged to equipment	11,000		
Balance at end of 2011	$198,000	$(40,000)	

(c) Land in the amount of $60,000 was purchased through the issuance of a long-term note; in addition, certain parcels of land costing $10,500 were condemned. The government paid Satellite $18,500, resulting in an $8,000 gain.

(d) The change in the Accumulated Depreciation—Buildings, Trademark, and Bonds Payable accounts resulted from depreciation and amortization entries.

(e) An analysis of the share capital and premium accounts in equity discloses the following:

	Share Capital— Ordinary	Share Premium— Ordinary
Balance at end of 2010	$50,000	$ 38,000
Issuance of 2% share dividend	1,000	14,000
Sale of shares for cash	9,000	135,000
Balance at end of 2011	$60,000	$187,000

(f) Interest paid is $9,000; income taxes paid is $62,000.

Accounts Receivable (Net)

The increase in accounts receivable (net) of $53,000 represents adjustments that did not result in cash inflows during 2011. As a result, the company would deduct from net income the increase of $53,000. Satellite makes the following worksheet entry.

(4)

Accounts Receivable (net)	53,000	
Operating—Increase in Accounts Receivable (net)		53,000

Inventories

The increase in inventories of $152,000 represents an operating use of cash. The incremental investment in inventories during the year reduces cash without increasing the cost of goods sold. Satellite makes the following worksheet entry.

(5)

Inventories	152,000	
Operating—Increase in Inventories		152,000

Prepaid Expense

The decrease in prepaid expenses of $500 represents a charge in the income statement for which there was no cash outflow in the current period. Satellite should add that amount back to net income through the following entry.

(6)

Operating—Decrease in Prepaid Expenses	500	
Prepaid Expenses		500

Equity Investment in Porter Co. (Equity Method)

Satellite's investment in the shares of Porter Co. increased $3,500. This amount reflects Satellite's share of net income earned by Porter (its equity investee) during the current year. Although Satellite's revenue, and therefore its net income, increased $3,500 by recording Satellite's share of Porter Co.'s net income, no cash (dividend) was provided. Satellite makes the following worksheet entry.

(7)

Equity Investment in Porter Co.	3,500	
Operating—Equity in Earnings of Porter Co.		3,500

Land

Satellite purchased land in the amount of $60,000 through the issuance of a long-term note payable. This transaction did not affect cash. It is a significant non-cash investing/financing transaction that the company would disclose in the accompanying notes. Satellite makes the following entry to reconcile the worksheet.

(8)

Land	60,000	
Notes Payable		60,000

In addition to the non-cash transaction involving the issuance of a note to purchase land, the Land account was decreased by the condemnation proceedings. The following worksheet entry records the receipt of $18,500 for land having a book value of $10,500.

Land			
Bal.	82,000	(9)	10,500
(8)	60,000		
Bal.	131,500		

(9)

Investing—Proceeds from Condemnation of Land	18,500	
Land		10,500
Operating—Gain on Condemnation of Land		8,000

In reconciling net income to net cash flow from operating activities, Satellite deducts from net income the gain of $8,000. The reason is that the transaction that gave rise to the gain is an item whose cash effect is already classified as an investing cash inflow. The Land account is now reconciled.

Equipment and Accumulated Depreciation—Equipment

An analysis of Equipment and Accumulated Depreciation—Equipment shows that a number of transactions have affected these accounts. The company purchased equipment in the amount of $53,000 during the year. Satellite records this transaction on the worksheet as follows.

(10)

Equipment	53,000	
Investing—Purchase of Equipment		53,000

In addition, Satellite sold at a loss of $1,500 equipment with a book value of $5,500. It records this transaction as follows.

(11)

Investing—Sale of Equipment	4,000	
Operating—Loss on Sale of Equipment	1,500	
Accumulated Depreciation—Equipment	2,500	
Equipment		8,000

The proceeds from the sale of the equipment provided cash of $4,000. In addition, the loss on the sale of the equipment has reduced net income but did not affect cash. Therefore, the company adds back to net income the amount of the loss, in order to accurately report cash provided by operating activities.

Satellite reported depreciation on the equipment at $11,500 and recorded it on the worksheet as follows.

(12)

Operating—Depreciation Expense—Equipment	11,500	
Accumulated Depreciation—Equipment		11,500

The company adds depreciation expense back to net income because that expense reduced income but did not affect cash.

Finally, the company made a major repair to the equipment. It charged this expenditure, in the amount of $11,000, to the Equipment account. This expenditure required cash, and so Satellite makes the following worksheet entry.

(13)

Equipment	11,000	
Investing—Major Repairs of Equipment		11,000

After adjusting for the foregoing items, Satellite has reconciled the balances in the Equipment and related Accumulated Depreciation accounts.

Building Depreciation and Amortization of Trademark

Depreciation expense on the buildings of $3,100 and amortization of trademark of $2,400 are both expenses in the income statement that reduced net income but did not require cash outflows in the current period. Satellite makes the following worksheet entry.

(14)

Operating—Depreciation Expense—Buildings	3,100	
Operating—Amortization of Trademark	2,400	
Accumulated Depreciation—Buildings		3,100
Trademark		2,400

Equipment

Bal.	142,000	(11)	8,000
(10)	53,000		
(13)	11,000		
Bal.	198,000		

Accumulated Depreciation— Equipment

(11)	2,500	Bal.	31,000
		(12)	11,500
		Bal.	40,000

Other Non-Cash Charges or Credits

Analysis of the remaining accounts indicates that changes in the Accounts Payable, Accrued Liabilities, Income Tax Payable, Bonds Payable, and Deferred Tax Liability balances resulted from charges or credits to net income that did not affect cash. The company should individually analyze each of these items and enter them in the worksheet. The following compound entry summarizes these non-cash, income-related items.

(15)

Income Tax Payable	13,000	
Bonds Payable	1,000	
Operating—Increase in Accounts Payable	1,000	
Operating—Increase in Accrued Liabilities	4,000	
Operating—Increase in Deferred Tax Liability	3,000	
Operating—Decrease in Income Tax Payable		13,000
Operating—Amortization of Bond Premium		1,000
Accounts Payable		1,000
Accrued Liabilities		4,000
Deferred Tax Liability		3,000

Share Capital—Ordinary and Related Accounts

Comparison of the Share Capital—Ordinary balances and the Share Premium—Ordinary balances shows that transactions during the year affected these accounts. First, Satellite issues a share dividend of 2 percent to shareholders. As the discussion of worksheet entry (2) indicated, no cash was provided or used by the share dividend transaction. In addition to the shares issued via the share dividend, Satellite sold ordinary shares at $16 per share. The company records this transaction as follows.

Share Capital—Ordinary		
	Bal.	50,000
	(2)	1,000
	(16)	9,000
	Bal.	60,000

Share Premium—Ordinary		
	Bal.	38,000
	(2)	14,000
	(16)	135,000
	Bal.	187,000

(16)

Financing—Sale of Ordinary Shares	144,000	
Share Capital—Ordinary		9,000
Share Premium—Ordinary		135,000

Also, the company purchased its ordinary shares in the amount of $17,000. It records this transaction on the worksheet as follows.

(17)

Treasury Shares	17,000	
Financing—Purchase of Treasury Shares		17,000

Final Reconciling Entry

The final entry to reconcile the change in cash and to balance the worksheet is shown below. The $7,000 amount is the difference between the beginning and ending cash balance.

(18)

Decrease in Cash	7,000	
Cash		7,000

Once the company has determined that the differences between the beginning and ending balances per the worksheet columns have been accounted for, it can total the reconciling transactions columns, and they should balance. Satellite can prepare the statement of cash flows entirely from the items and amounts that appear at the bottom of the worksheet under "Statement of Cash Flows Effects," as shown in Illustration 23-41 (on page 1280).

ILLUSTRATION 23-41
Completed Worksheet for Preparation of Statement of Cash Flows, Satellite Corporation

SATELLITE CORPORATION
Worksheet for Preparation of Statement of Cash Flows For the Year Ended December 31, 2011

	A	B	C	D	E	F	G
		Balance 12/31/10		Reconciling Items–2011			Balance 12/31/11
1				Debits		Credits	
2	Debits						
3	Cash	$ 66,000			(18)	7,000	$ 59,000
4	Accounts receivable (net)	51,000	(4)	$ 53,000			104,000
5	Inventories	341,000	(5)	152,000			493,000
6	Prepaid expenses	17,000			(6)	500	16,500
7	Investment (equity method)	15,000	(7)	3,500			18,500
8	Land	82,000	(8)	60,000	(9)	10,500	131,500
9	Equipment	142,000	(10)	53,000	(11)	8,000	198,000
10			(13)	11,000			
11	Building	262,000					262,000
12	Trademark	10,000			(14)	2,400	7,600
13	Treasury shares		(17)	17,000			17,000
14	Total debits	$986,000					$1,307,100
15	Credits						
16	Accum. depr.–equipment	$ 31,000	(11)	2,500	(12)	11,500	$ 40,000
17	Accum. depr.–building	71,000			(14)	3,100	74,100
18	Accounts payable	131,000			(15)	1,000	132,000
19	Accrued liabilities	39,000			(15)	4,000	43,000
20	Income tax payable	16,000	(15)	13,000			3,000
21	Notes payable	-0-			(8)	60,000	60,000
22	Bonds payable	108,000	(15)	1,000			107,000
23	Deferred tax liability	6,000			(15)	3,000	9,000
24	Share capital—ordinary	50,000			(2)	1,000	
25					(16)	9,000	60,000
26	Share premium—ordinary	38,000			(2)	14,000	
27					(16)	135,000	187,000
28	Retained earnings	496,000	(2)	15,000	(1)	117,000	
29			(3)	6,000			592,000
30	Total credits	$986,000					$1,307,100
31	Statement of Cash Flows Effects						
32	Operating activities						
33	Net income		(1)	117,000			
34	Increase in accounts receivable (net)				(4)	53,000	
35	Increase in inventories				(5)	152,000	
36	Decrease in prepaid expenses		(6)	500			
37	Equity in earnings of Porter Co.				(7)	3,500	
38	Gain on condemnation of land				(9)	8,000	
39	Loss on sale of equipment		(11)	1,500			
40	Depr. expense–equipment		(12)	11,500			
41	Depr. expense–building		(14)	3,100			
42	Amortization of trademark		(14)	2,400			
43	Increase in accounts payable		(15)	1,000			
44	Increase in accrued liabilities		(15)	4,000			
45	Increase in deferred tax liability		(15)	3,000			
46	Decrease in income tax payable				(15)	13,000	
47	Amortization of bond premium				(15)	1,000	
48	Investing activities						
49	Proceeds from condemnation of land		(9)	18,500			
50	Purchase of equipment				(10)	53,000	
51	Sale of equipment		(11)	4,000			
52	Major repairs of equipment				(13)	11,000	
53	Financing activities						
54	Payment of cash dividend				(3)	6,000	
55	Issuance of ordinary shares		(16)	144,000			
56	Purchase of treasury shares				(17)	17,000	
57	Totals			697,500		704,500	
58	Decrease in cash		(18)	7,000			
59	Totals			$704,500		$704,500	

Sheet1 / Sheet2 / Sheet3 /

PREPARATION OF FINAL STATEMENT

Illustration 23-42 presents a formal statement of cash flows prepared from the data compiled in the lower portion of the worksheet.

SATELLITE CORPORATION
STATEMENT OF CASH FLOWS
FOR THE YEAR ENDED DECEMBER 31, 2011
INCREASE (DECREASE) IN CASH

Cash flows from operating activities		
Net income		$117,000
Adjustments to reconcile net income to net		
cash used by operating activities:		
Depreciation expense	$ 14,600	
Amortization of trademark	2,400	
Amortization of bond premium	(1,000)	
Equity in earnings of Porter Co.	(3,500)	
Gain on condemnation of land	(8,000)	
Loss on sale of equipment	1,500	
Increase in deferred tax liability	3,000	
Increase in accounts receivable (net)	(53,000)	
Increase in inventories	(152,000)	
Decrease in prepaid expenses	500	
Increase in accounts payable	1,000	
Increase in accrued liabilities	4,000	
Decrease in income tax payable	(13,000)	(203,500)
Net cash used by operating activities		(86,500)
Cash flows from investing activities		
Proceeds from condemnation of land	18,500	
Purchase of equipment	(53,000)	
Sale of equipment	4,000	
Major repairs of equipment	(11,000)	
Net cash used by investing activities		(41,500)
Cash flows from financing activities		
Payment of cash dividend	(6,000)	
Issuance of ordinary shares	144,000	
Purchase of treasury shares	(17,000)	
Net cash provided by financing activities		121,000
Net decrease in cash		(7,000)
Cash, January 1, 2011		66,000
Cash, December 31, 2011		$ 59,000

ILLUSTRATION 23-42
Statement of Cash Flows, Satellite Corporation

In addition, a supplemental note of Non-Cash Investing and Financing Activities is as follows.

Supplemental Note of Non-Cash Investing and Financing Activities
Purchase of land for $60,000 in exchange for a $60,000 long-term note.

You will want to read the
CONVERGENCE CORNER on page 1282

For discussion of how international convergence efforts relate to the statement of cash flows.

CONVERGENCE CORNER

STATEMENT OF CASH FLOWS

As in IFRS, the statement of cash flows is a required statement for U.S. GAAP. In addition, the content and presentation of a U.S. statement of cash flows is similar to one used for IFRS. However, the disclosure requirements related to the statement of cash flows are more extensive under U.S. GAAP.

RELEVANT FACTS

- Companies preparing financial statements under U.S. GAAP must prepare a statement of cash flows as an integral part of the financial statements.

- Both IFRS and U.S. GAAP require that the statement of cash flows should have three major sections—operating, investing, and financing—along with changes in cash and cash equivalents.

- Similar to IFRS, the cash flow statement can be prepared using either the indirect or direct method under U.S. GAAP. For both IFRS and U.S. GAAP, companies choose for the most part to use the indirect method for reporting net cash flow from operating activities.

- U.S. GAAP encourages companies to disclose the aggregate amount of cash flows that are attributable to the increase in operating capacity separately from those cash flows that are required to maintain operating capacity.

- The definition of cash equivalents used in IFRS is similar to that used in U.S. GAAP. A major difference is that in certain situations, bank overdrafts are considered part of cash and cash equivalents under IFRS (which is not the case in U.S. GAAP). Under U.S. GAAP, bank overdrafts are classified as financing activities.

- IFRS requires that non-cash investing and financing activities be excluded from the statement of cash flows. Instead, these non-cash activities should be reported elsewhere. This requirement is interpreted to mean that non-cash investing and financing activities should be disclosed in the notes to the financial statements instead of in the financial statements. Under U.S. GAAP, companies may present this information in the cash flow statement.

ABOUT THE NUMBERS

One area where there can be substantive differences between IFRS and U.S. GAAP relates to the classification of interest, dividends, and taxes. The following table indicates the differences between the two approaches.

Item	IFRS	U.S. GAAP
Interest paid	Operating or financing	Operating
Interest received	Operating or investing	Operating
Dividends paid	Operating or financing	Financing
Dividends received	Operating or investing	Operating
Taxes paid	Operating—unless specific identification with financing or investing	Operating[1, 2]

[1] U.S. GAAP has additional disclosure rules
[2] U.S. GAAP has specific rules regarding the classification of the benefit associated with share-based compensation arrangements and the classification of derivatives that contain a financing element

Source: PricewaterhouseCoopers, *Similarities and Difference–A Comparison of IFRS and U.S. GAAP* (October 2007).

As indicated, the major difference is that IFRS provides more alternatives for disclosing certain items.

ON THE HORIZON

Presently, the IASB and the FASB are involved in a joint project on the presentation and organization of information in the financial statements. With respect to the cash flow statement specifically, the notion of *cash equivalents* will probably not be retained. The definition of cash in the existing literature would be retained, and the statement of cash flows would present information on changes in cash only. In addition, the IASB and FASB favor presentation of operating cash flows using the direct method only.

SUMMARY OF LEARNING OBJECTIVES

•1 Describe the purpose of the statement of cash flows. The primary purpose of the statement of cash flows is to provide information about cash receipts and cash payments of an entity during a period. A secondary objective is to report the entity's operating, investing, and financing activities during the period.

•2 Identify the major classifications of cash flows. Companies classify cash flows as: (1) *Operating activities*—transactions that result in the revenues, expenses, gains, and losses that determine net income. (2) *Investing activities*—lending money and collecting on those loans, and acquiring and disposing of investments, plant assets, and intangible assets. (3) *Financing activities*—obtaining cash from creditors and repaying loans, issuing and reacquiring share capital, and paying cash dividends.

•3 Differentiate between net income and net cash flow from operating activities. Companies must adjust net income on an accrual basis to determine net cash flow from operating activities because some expenses and losses do not cause cash outflows, and some revenues and gains do not provide cash inflows.

•4 Contrast the direct and indirect methods of calculating net cash flow from operating activities. Under the direct approach, companies calculate the major classes of operating cash receipts and cash disbursements. Presentation of the direct approach of reporting net cash flow from operating activities takes the form of a condensed cash-basis income statement. The indirect method adds back to net income the non-cash expenses and losses and subtracts the non-cash revenues and gains.

•5 Determine net cash flows from investing and financing activities. Once a company has computed the net cash flow from operating activities, the next step is to determine whether any other changes in statement of financial position accounts caused an increase or decrease in cash. Net cash flows from investing and financing activities can be determined by examining the changes in non-current statement of financial position accounts.

•6 Prepare a statement of cash flows. Preparing the statement involves three major steps: (1) *Determine the change in cash*. This is the difference between the beginning and the ending cash balance shown on the comparative statements of financial position. (2) *Determine the net cash flow from operating activities*. This procedure is complex; it involves analyzing not only the current year's income statement but also the comparative statements of financial position and the selected transaction data. (3) *Determine cash flows from investing and financing activities*. Analyze all other changes in the statement of financial position accounts to determine the effects on cash.

•7 Identify sources of information for a statement of cash flows. The information to prepare the statement usually comes from three sources: (1) *Comparative statements of financial position*. Information in these statements indicates the amount of the changes in assets, liabilities, and equities during the period. (2) *Current income statement*. Information in this statement is used in determining the cash provided by operations during the period. (3) *Selected transaction data*. These data from the general ledger provide additional detailed information needed to determine how cash was provided or used during the period.

•8 Discuss special problems in preparing a statement of cash flows. These special problems are (1) adjustments to net income; (2) accounts receivable (net); (3) other working capital changes; (4) net loss; and (5) disclosures.

•9 Explain the use of a worksheet in preparing a statement of cash flows. When numerous adjustments are necessary, or other complicating factors are present, companies often use a worksheet to assemble and classify the data that will appear on the statement of cash flows. The worksheet is merely a device that aids in the preparation of the statement. Its use is optional.

AUTHORITATIVE LITERATURE

Authoritative Literature References

[1] International Accounting Standard 7, *Statement of Cash Flows* (London, U.K.: International Accounting Standards Committee Foundation, 2001).

[2] International Accounting Standard 7, *Statement of Cash Flows* (London, U.K.: International Accounting Standards Committee Foundation, 2001), paras. 13–17.

[3] International Accounting Standard 7, *Statement of Cash Flows* (London, U.K.: International Accounting Standards Committee Foundation, 2001), par. 7.

[4] International Accounting Standard 7, *Statement of Cash Flows* (London, U.K.: International Accounting Standards Committee Foundation, 2001), par. 19.

[5] International Accounting Standard 7, *Statement of Cash Flows* (London, U.K.: International Accounting Standards Committee Foundation, 2001), par. 36.

[6] International Accounting Standard 7, *Statement of Cash Flows* (London, U.K.: International Accounting Standards Committee Foundation, 2001), par. 43.

[7] International Accounting Standard 7, *Statement of Cash Flows* (London, U.K.: International Accounting Standards Committee Foundation, 2001), par. 31.

QUESTIONS

1. What is the purpose of the statement of cash flows? What information does it provide?

2. Of what use is the statement of cash flows?

3. Differentiate between investing activities, financing activities, and operating activities.

4. What are the major sources of cash (inflows) in a statement of cash flows? What are the major uses (outflows) of cash?

5. Identify and explain the major steps involved in preparing the statement of cash flows.

6. Identify the following items as (1) operating, (2) investing, or (3) financing activities: purchase of land; payment of dividends; cash sales; and purchase of treasury shares.

7. Unlike the other major financial statements, the statement of cash flows is not prepared from the adjusted trial balance. From what sources does the information to prepare this statement come, and what information does each source provide?

8. Why is it necessary to convert accrual-based net income to a cash basis when preparing a statement of cash flows?

9. Differentiate between the direct method and the indirect method by discussing each method.

10. Broussard Company reported net income of $3.5 million in 2010. Depreciation for the year was $520,000; accounts receivable increased $500,000; and accounts payable increased $300,000. Compute net cash flow from operating activities using the indirect method.

11. Collinsworth Co. reported sales on an accrual basis of £100,000. If accounts receivable increased £30,000, and the allowance for doubtful accounts increased £9,000 after a write-off of £2,000, compute cash sales.

12. Your roommate is puzzled. During the last year, the company in which she is a shareholder reported a net loss of $675,000, yet its cash increased $321,000 during the same period of time. Explain to your roommate how this situation could occur.

13. The board of directors of Gifford Corp. declared cash dividends of $260,000 during the current year. If dividends payable was $85,000 at the beginning of the year and $90,000 at the end of the year, how much cash was paid in dividends during the year?

14. Explain how the amount of cash payments to suppliers is computed under the direct method.

15. The net income for Letterman Company for 2010 was €320,000. During 2010, depreciation on plant assets was

€124,000, amortization of patent was €40,000, and the company incurred a loss on sale of plant assets of €21,000. Compute net cash flow from operating activities.

16. Each of the following items must be considered in preparing a statement of cash flows for Blackwell Inc. for the year ended December 31, 2010. Indicate how each item is to be shown in the statement, if at all.

  (a) Plant assets that had cost $18,000 6½ years before and were being depreciated on a straight-line basis over 10 years with no estimated residual value were sold for $4,000.

  (b) During the year, 10,000 ordinary shares with a stated value of $20 a share were issued for $41 a share.

  (c) Uncollectible accounts receivable in the amount of $22,000 were written off against Allowance for Doubtful Accounts.

  (d) The company sustained a net loss for the year of $50,000. Depreciation amounted to $22,000, and a gain of $9,000 was realized on the sale of non-trading equity investments for $38,000 cash.

17. Classify the following items as (1) operating, (2) investing, (3) financing, or (4) significant non-cash investing and financing activities, using the direct method.

  (a) Cash payments to employees.

  (b) Redemption of bonds payable.

  (c) Sale of building at book value.

  (d) Cash payments to suppliers.

  (e) Exchange of equipment for furniture.

  (f) Issuance of preference shares.

  (g) Cash received from customers.

  (h) Purchase of treasury shares.

  (i) Issuance of bonds for land.

  (j) Payment of dividends.

  (k) Purchase of equipment.

  (l) Cash payments for operating expenses.

18. Stan Conner and Mark Stein were discussing the statement of cash flows of Bombeck Co. In the notes to the statement of cash flows was a schedule entitled "Non-cash investing and financing activities." Give three examples of significant non-cash transactions that would be reported in this schedule.

19. During 2010, Simms Company redeemed $2,000,000 of bonds payable for $1,880,000 cash. Indicate how this transaction would be reported on a statement of cash flows, if at all.

20. What are some of the arguments in favor of using the indirect (reconciliation) method as opposed to the direct method for reporting a statement of cash flows?

21. Why is it desirable to use a worksheet when preparing a statement of cash flows? Is a worksheet required to prepare a statement of cash flows?

22. Briefly describe some of the similarities and differences between IFRS and U.S. GAAP with respect to cash flow reporting.

23. Explain how the accounting for interest received and paid in a statement of cash flows may differ between IFRS and U.S. GAAP.

24. What are some of the key obstacles for the IASB and FASB in their convergence project for the statement of cash flows?

BRIEF EXERCISES

WILEY PLUS

•5 **BE23-1** Wainwright Corporation had the following activities in 2010.

  1. Sale of land $180,000
  2. Purchase of inventory $845,000
  3. Purchase of treasury shares $72,000
  4. Purchase of equipment $415,000
  5. Issuance of ordinary shares $320,000
  6. Purchase of investments—equity $59,000

Compute the amount Wainwright should report as net cash provided (used) by investing activities in its statement of cash flows.

•5 **BE23-2** Stansfield Corporation had the following activities in 2010.

  1. Payment of accounts payable €770,000
  2. Issuance of ordinary shares €250,000
  3. Payment of dividends €350,000
  4. Collection of note receivable €100,000
  5. Issuance of bonds payable €510,000
  6. Purchase of treasury shares €46,000

Compute the amount Stansfield should report as net cash provided (used) by financing activities in its 2010 statement of cash flows.

•2 **BE23-3** Novak Corporation is preparing its 2010 statement of cash flows, using the indirect method. Presented on page 1286 is a list of items that may affect the statement. Using the code letters provided, indicate how each item will affect Novak's 2010 statement of cash flows.

Code Letter	Effect
A	Added to net income in the operating section
D	Deducted from net income in the operating section
R-I	Cash receipt in investing section
P-I	Cash payment in investing section
R-F	Cash receipt in financing section
P-F	Cash payment in financing section
N	Non-cash investing and/or financing activity in notes

Items

____ (a) Purchase of land and building.
____ (b) Decrease in accounts receivable.
____ (c) Issuance of shares.
____ (d) Depreciation expense.
____ (e) Sale of land at book value.
____ (f) Sale of land at a gain.
____ (g) Payment of dividends.
____ (h) Increase in accounts receivable.
____ (i) Purchase of an equity investment.

____ (j) Increase in accounts payable.
____ (k) Decrease in accounts payable.
____ (l) Loan from bank by signing note.
____ (m) Purchase of equipment using a note.
____ (n) Increase in inventory.
____ (o) Issuance of bonds.
____ (p) Retirement of bonds payable.
____ (q) Sale of equipment at a loss.
____ (r) Purchase of treasury shares.

•3 •4 **BE23-4** Bloom Corporation had the following 2010 income statement.

Sales	€200,000
Cost of goods sold	120,000
Gross profit	80,000
Operating expenses (includes depreciation of €21,000)	50,000
Net income	€ 30,000

The following accounts increased during 2010: accounts receivable €12,000; inventory €11,000; and accounts payable €13,000. Prepare the cash flows from operating activities section of Bloom's 2010 statement of cash flows using the direct method.

•3 •4 **BE23-5** Use the information from BE23-4 for Bloom Corporation. Prepare the cash flows from operating activities section of Bloom's 2010 statement of cash flows using the indirect method.

•4 **BE23-6** At January 1, 2010, Eikenberry Inc. had accounts receivable of $72,000. At December 31, 2010, accounts receivable is $54,000. Sales for 2010 total $420,000. Compute Eikenberry's 2010 cash receipts from customers.

•4 **BE23-7** Moxley Corporation had January 1 and December 31 balances as follows.

	1/1/10	12/31/10
Inventory	€95,000	€113,000
Accounts payable	61,000	69,000

For 2010, cost of goods sold was €500,000. Compute Moxley's 2010 cash payments to suppliers.

•6 **BE23-8** In 2010, Elbert Corporation had net cash provided by operating activities of £531,000; net cash used by investing activities of £963,000; and net cash provided by financing activities of £585,000. At January 1, 2010, the cash balance was £333,000. Compute December 31, 2010, cash.

•3 •4 **BE23-9** Loveless Corporation had the following 2010 income statement.

Revenues	$100,000
Expenses	60,000
	$ 40,000

In 2010, Loveless had the following activity in selected accounts.

Accounts Receivable				Allowance for Doubtful Accounts			
1/1/10	20,000					1,200	1/1/10
Revenues	100,000	1,000	Write-offs	Write-offs	1,000	1,840	Bad debt expense
		90,000	Collections				
12/31/10	29,000					2,040	12/31/10

Prepare Loveless's cash flows from operating activities section of the statement of cash flows using (a) the direct method and (b) the indirect method.

•3 **BE23-10** Hendrickson Corporation reported net income of $50,000 in 2010. Depreciation expense was $17,000. The following working capital accounts changed.

Accounts receivable	$11,000 increase
Non-trading equity investment	16,000 increase
Inventory	7,400 increase
Non-trade note payable	15,000 decrease
Accounts payable	12,300 increase

Compute net cash provided by operating activities.

•3 **BE23-11** In 2010, Shaw Corporation reported a net loss of $70,000. Shaw's only net income adjustments were depreciation expense $81,000, and increase in accounts receivable $8,100. Compute Shaw's net cash provided (used) by operating activities.

•8 **BE23-12** In 2010, Leppard Inc. issued 1,000 ordinary shares of $10 par value for land worth $40,000.

(a) Prepare Leppard's journal entry to record the transaction.
(b) Indicate the effect the transaction has on cash.
(c) Indicate how the transaction is reported on the statement of cash flows.

•9 **BE23-13** Indicate in general journal form how the items below would be entered in a worksheet for the preparation of the statement of cash flows.

(a) Net income is ¥317,000,000.
(b) Cash dividends declared and paid totaled ¥120,000,000.
(c) Equipment was purchased for ¥114,000,000.
(d) Equipment that originally cost ¥40,000,000 and had accumulated depreciation of ¥32,000,000 was sold for ¥10,000,000.

EXERCISES

•2 **E23-1** **(Classification of Transactions)** Springsteen Co. had the following activity in its most recent year of operations.

(a) Pension expense exceeds amount funded.
(b) Redemption of bonds payable.
(c) Sale of building at book value.
(d) Depreciation.
(e) Exchange of equipment for furniture.
(f) Issuance of ordinary shares.
(g) Amortization of intangible assets.
(h) Purchase of treasury shares.
(i) Issuance of bonds for land.
(j) Payment of dividends.
(k) Increase in interest receivable on notes receivable.
(l) Purchase of equipment.

Instructions

Classify the items as (1) operating—add to net income; (2) operating—deduct from net income; (3) investing; (4) financing; or (5) significant non-cash investing and financing activities. Use the indirect method.

•2 •3 **E23-2** **(Statement Presentation of Transactions—Indirect Method)** Each of the following items must be considered in preparing a statement of cash flows (indirect method) for Granderson Inc. for the year ended December 31, 2010.

(a) Plant assets that had cost €25,000 6 years before and were being depreciated on a straight-line basis over 10 years with no estimated residual value were sold at the beginning of the year for €5,300.
(b) During the year, 10,000 ordinary shares with a stated value of €10 a share were issued for €33 a share.
(c) Uncollectible accounts receivable in the amount of €27,000 were written off against Allowance for Doubtful Accounts.

(d) The company sustained a net loss for the year of €50,000. Depreciation amounted to €22,000, and a gain of €9,000 was realized on the sale of land for €39,000 cash.

(e) A 3-month certificate of deposit was purchased for €100,000. The company uses a cash and cash-equivalent basis for its cash flow statement.

(f) Patent amortization for the year was €20,000.

(g) The company exchanged ordinary shares for a 70% interest in Plumlee Co. for €900,000.

(h) During the year, treasury shares costing €47,000 were purchased.

(i) The company recognized an unrealized holding gain on a debt investment not held for collection.

Instructions

State where each item is to be shown in the statement of cash flows, if at all.

E23-3 **(Preparation of Operating Activities Section—Indirect Method, Periodic Inventory)** The income statement of Rodriquez Company is shown below.

RODRIQUEZ COMPANY
INCOME STATEMENT
FOR THE YEAR ENDED DECEMBER 31, 2010

Sales		$6,900,000
Cost of goods sold		
Beginning inventory	$1,900,000	
Purchases	4,400,000	
Goods available for sale	6,300,000	
Ending inventory	1,600,000	
Cost of goods sold		4,700,000
Gross profit		2,200,000
Operating expenses		
Selling expenses	450,000	
Administrative expenses	700,000	1,150,000
Net income		$1,050,000

Additional information:

1. Accounts receivable decreased $310,000 during the year.
2. Prepaid expenses increased $170,000 during the year.
3. Accounts payable to suppliers of merchandise decreased $275,000 during the year.
4. Accrued expenses payable decreased $120,000 during the year.
5. Administrative expenses include depreciation expense of $60,000.

Instructions

Prepare the operating activities section of the statement of cash flows for the year ended December 31, 2010, for Rodriquez Company, using the indirect method.

E23-4 **(Preparation of Operating Activities Section—Direct Method)** Data for the Rodriquez Company are presented in E23-3.

Instructions

Prepare the operating activities section of the statement of cash flows using the direct method.

E23-5 **(Preparation of Operating Activities Section—Direct Method)** Norman Company's income statement for the year ended December 31, 2010, contained the following condensed information.

Revenue from fees		€840,000
Operating expenses (excluding depreciation)	€624,000	
Depreciation expense	60,000	
Loss on sale of equipment	26,000	710,000
Income before income taxes		130,000
Income tax expense		40,000
Net income		€ 90,000

Norman's statement of financial position contained the following comparative data at December 31.

	2010	2009
Accounts receivable	€37,000	€59,000
Accounts payable	46,000	31,000
Income taxes payable	4,000	8,500

(Accounts payable pertains to operating expenses.)

Instructions

Prepare the operating activities section of the statement of cash flows using the direct method.

•3 •4 E23-6 (Preparation of Operating Activities Section—Indirect Method) Data for Norman Company are presented in E23-5.

Instructions

Prepare the operating activities section of the statement of cash flows using the indirect method.

•3 •4 E23-7 (Computation of Operating Activities—Direct Method) Presented below are two independent situations.

Situation A:

Chenowith Co. reports revenues of $200,000 and operating expenses of $110,000 in its first year of operations, 2010. Accounts receivable and accounts payable at year-end were $71,000 and $39,000, respectively. Assume that the accounts payable related to operating expenses. Ignore income taxes.

Instructions

Using the direct method, compute net cash provided (used) by operating activities.

Situation B:

The income statement for Edgebrook Company shows cost of goods sold $310,000 and operating expenses (exclusive of depreciation) $230,000. The comparative statements of financial position for the year show that inventory increased $21,000, prepaid expenses decreased $8,000, accounts payable (related to merchandise) decreased $17,000, and accrued expenses payable increased $11,000.

Instructions

Compute (a) cash payments to suppliers and (b) cash payments for operating expenses.

•3 •4 E23-8 (Schedule of Net Cash Flow from Operating Activities—Indirect Method) Messner Co. reported $145,000 of net income for 2010. The accountant, in preparing the statement of cash flows, noted several items occurring during 2010 that might affect cash flows from operating activities. These items are listed below.

1. Messner purchased 100 treasury shares at a cost of $20 per share. These shares were then resold at $25 per share.
2. Messner sold 100 ordinary shares of Nokia at $200 per share. The acquisition cost of these shares was $165 per share. This investment was shown on Messner's December 31, 2009, statement of financial position as a non-trading equity investment.
3. Messner revised its estimate for bad debts. Before 2010, Messner's bad debt expense was 1% of its net sales. In 2010, this percentage was increased to 2%. Net sales for 2010 were $500,000, and net accounts receivable decreased by $12,000 during 2010.
4. Messner issued 500 ordinary shares with a $10 par value for a patent. The fair value of the shares on the date of the transaction was $23 per share.
5. Depreciation expense is $39,000.
6. Messner Co. holds 30% of the Sanchez Company's ordinary shares as a long-term investment. Sanchez Company reported $27,000 of net income for 2010.
7. Sanchez Company paid a total of $2,000 of cash dividends to all investees in 2010.
8. Messner declared a 10% share dividend. One thousand ordinary shares with a $10 par value were distributed. The market price at date of issuance was $20 per share.

Instructions

Prepare a schedule that shows the net cash flow from operating activities using the indirect method. Assume no items other than those listed above affected the computation of 2010 net cash flow from operating activities.

•6 E23-9 (SCF—Direct Method) Waubansee Corp. uses the direct method to prepare its statement of cash flows. Waubansee's trial balances at December 31, 2010 and 2009, are shown on page 1290.

	December 31	
	2010	2009
Debits		
Cash	$ 35,000	$ 32,000
Accounts receivable	33,000	30,000
Inventory	31,000	47,000
Property, plant, & equipment	100,000	95,000
Cost of goods sold	250,000	380,000
Selling expenses	141,500	172,000
General and administrative expenses	137,000	151,300
Interest expense	4,300	2,600
Income tax expense	20,400	61,200
	$752,200	$971,100
Credits		
Allowance for doubtful accounts	$ 1,300	$ 1,100
Accumulated depreciation	16,500	13,500
Trade accounts payable	25,000	17,000
Income taxes payable	21,000	29,100
Deferred income taxes	5,300	4,600
8% callable bonds payable	40,500	15,000
Share capital—ordinary	50,000	40,000
Share premium—ordinary	9,100	7,500
Retained earnings	44,700	64,600
Sales	538,800	778,700
	$752,200	$971,100

Additional information:

1. Waubansee purchased $5,000 in equipment during 2010.
2. Waubansee allocated one-third of its depreciation expense to selling expenses and the remainder to general and administrative expenses.
3. Bad debt expense for 2010 was $5,000, and write-offs of uncollectible accounts totaled $3,800.
4. Interest expense includes $500 of discount amortization.

Instructions

Determine what amounts Waubansee should report in its statement of cash flows for the year ended December 31, 2010, for the following items.

(a) Cash collected from customers.   (d) Cash paid for income taxes.
(b) Cash paid to suppliers.   (e) Cash paid for selling expenses.
(c) Cash paid for interest.

·2 ·8 **E23-10 (Classification of Transactions)** Following are selected statement of financial position accounts of Sander Bros. Corp. at December 31, 2010 and 2009, and the increases or decreases in each account from 2009 to 2010. Also presented is selected income statement information for the year ended December 31, 2010, and additional information.

Selected statement of financial position accounts	2010	2009	Increase (Decrease)
Assets			
Property, plant, and equipment	$ 277,000	$ 247,000	$ 30,000
Accumulated depreciation	(178,000)	(167,000)	(11,000)
Accounts receivable	34,000	24,000	10,000
Equity and liabilities			
Share capital—ordinary, $1 par	$ 22,000	$ 19,000	$ 3,000
Share premium—ordinary	9,000	3,000	6,000
Retained earnings	104,000	91,000	13,000
Bonds payable	49,000	46,000	3,000
Dividends payable	8,000	5,000	3,000

Selected income statement information for the year ended December 31, 2010

Sales revenue	$ 155,000
Depreciation	38,000
Gain on sale of equipment	14,500
Net income	31,000

Additional information:

1. During 2010, equipment costing $45,000 was sold for cash.
2. Accounts receivable relate to sales of merchandise.
3. During 2010, $25,000 of bonds payable were issued in exchange for property, plant, and equipment. There was no amortization of bond discount or premium.

Instructions

Determine the category (operating, investing, or financing) and the amount that should be reported in the statement of cash flows for the following items.

(a) Payments for purchase of property, plant, and equipment.
(b) Proceeds from the sale of equipment.
(c) Cash dividends paid.
(d) Redemption of bonds payable.

•6 E23-11 (SCF—Indirect Method) Condensed financial data of Fairchild Company for 2010 and 2009 are presented below.

FAIRCHILD COMPANY
COMPARATIVE STATEMENTS OF FINANCIAL POSITION
AS OF DECEMBER 31, 2010 AND 2009

	2010	2009
Plant assets	€ 1,900	€ 1,700
Accumulated depreciation	(1,200)	(1,170)
Debt investments (held-for-collection)	1,300	1,470
Inventory	1,600	1,900
Receivables	1,750	1,300
Cash	1,800	1,100
	€ 7,150	€ 6,300
Share capital—ordinary	€ 1,900	€ 1,700
Retained earnings	2,450	1,900
Bonds payable	1,400	1,650
Accounts payable	1,200	800
Accrued liabilities	200	250
	€ 7,150	€ 6,300

FAIRCHILD COMPANY
INCOME STATEMENT
FOR THE YEAR ENDED DECEMBER 31, 2010

Sales	€6,900
Cost of goods sold	4,700
Gross margin	2,200
Selling and administrative expense	930
Income from operations	1,270
Other income and expense	
Gain on sale of investments	80
Income before tax	1,350
Income tax expense	540
Net income	€ 810

Additional information:

During the year, €70 of ordinary shares were issued in exchange for plant assets. No plant assets were sold in 2010. Cash dividends were €260.

Instructions

Prepare a statement of cash flows using the indirect method.

•6 E23-12 (SCF—Direct Method) Data for Fairchild Company are presented in E23-11.

Instructions

Prepare a statement of cash flows using the direct method.

E23-13 (SCF—Direct Method) Andrews Inc., a greeting card company, had the following statements prepared as of December 31, 2010.

ANDREWS INC.
COMPARATIVE STATEMENT OF FINANCIAL POSITION
AS OF DECEMBER 31, 2010 AND 2009

	12/31/10	12/31/09
Printing equipment	€154,000	€130,000
Accumulated depr.—equipment	(35,000)	(25,000)
Copyrights	46,000	50,000
Inventories	40,000	60,000
Short-term investments (non-trading)	35,000	18,000
Prepaid rent	5,000	4,000
Accounts receivable	62,000	49,000
Cash	6,000	9,000
Total assets	€313,000	€295,000
Share capital—ordinary, €10 par	€100,000	€100,000
Share premium—ordinary	30,000	30,000
Retained earnings	57,000	36,000
Long-term loans payable	60,000	67,000
Accounts payable	46,000	42,000
Income taxes payable	4,000	6,000
Wages payable	8,000	4,000
Short-term loans payable	8,000	10,000
Total equity and liabilities	€313,000	€295,000

ANDREWS INC.
INCOME STATEMENT
FOR THE YEAR ENDING DECEMBER 31, 2010

Sales		€338,150
Cost of goods sold		175,000
Gross margin		163,150
Operating expenses		120,000
Operating income		43,150
Interest expense	€11,400	
Gain on sale of equipment	2,000	9,400
Income before tax		33,750
Income tax expense		6,750
Net income		€ 27,000

Additional information:

1. Dividends in the amount of €6,000 were declared and paid during 2010.
2. Depreciation expense and amortization expense are included in operating expenses.
3. No unrealized gains or losses have occurred on the investments during the year.
4. Equipment that had a cost of €30,000 and was 70% depreciated was sold during 2010.

Instructions
Prepare a statement of cash flows using the direct method.

 E23-14 (SCF—Indirect Method) Data for Andrews Inc. are presented in E23-13.

Instructions
Prepare a statement of cash flows using the indirect method.

 E23-15 (SCF—Indirect Method) Presented on page 1293 are data taken from the records of Morganstern Company.

	December 31, 2010	December 31, 2009
Cash	$ 15,000	$ 10,000
Current assets other than cash	85,000	58,000
Long-term investments	10,000	53,000
Plant assets	335,000	215,000
	$445,000	$336,000
Accumulated depreciation	$ 20,000	$ 40,000
Current liabilities	40,000	22,000
Bonds payable	75,000	–0–
Share capital—ordinary	254,000	254,000
Retained earnings	56,000	20,000
	$445,000	$336,000

Additional information:

1. Held-for-collection investments carried at a cost of $43,000 on December 31, 2009, were sold in 2010 for $34,000. The loss was incorrectly charged directly to Retained Earnings.
2. Plant assets that cost $60,000 and were 80% depreciated were sold during 2010 for $8,000. The loss was incorrectly charged directly to Retained Earnings.
3. Net income as reported on the income statement for the year was $59,000.
4. Dividends paid amounted to $10,000.
5. Depreciation charged for the year was $28,000.

Instructions
Prepare a statement of cash flows for the year 2010 using the indirect method.

·2 ·3 ·5 E23-16 (Cash Provided by Operating, Investing, and Financing Activities) The statement of financial position data of Wyeth Company at the end of 2010 and 2009 follow.

	2010	2009
Equipment	$ 90,000	$ 75,000
Accumulated depreciation—equipment	(18,000)	(8,000)
Land	70,000	40,000
Merchandise inventory	65,000	45,000
Accounts receivable (net)	55,000	45,000
Prepaid expenses	15,000	25,000
Cash	30,000	35,000
	$307,000	$257,000
Share capital—ordinary, $10 par	$189,000	$159,000
Retained earnings	8,000	5,000
Notes payable—bank, long-term	–0–	23,000
Bonds payable	30,000	–0–
Accounts payable	65,000	52,000
Accrued expenses	15,000	18,000
	$307,000	$257,000

Land was acquired for $30,000 in exchange for ordinary shares, par $30,000, during the year; all equipment purchased was for cash. Equipment costing $13,000 was sold for $3,000; book value of the equipment was $6,000. Cash dividends of $9,000 were declared and paid during the year.

Instructions
Compute net cash provided (used) by:

(a) Operating activities.
(b) Investing activities.
(c) Financing activities.

·6 E23-17 (SCF—Indirect Method and Statement of Financial Position) Ochoa Inc., had the condensed statement of financial position, shown on page 1294, at the end of operations for 2009.

OCHOA INC.
STATEMENT OF FINANCIAL POSITION
DECEMBER 31, 2009

Investments	$ 20,000	Share capital—ordinary	$ 75,000
Plant assets (net)	67,500	Retained earnings	24,500
Land	40,000	Long-term notes payable	25,500
Current assets other than cash	29,000	Bonds payable	25,000
Cash	8,500	Current liabilities	15,000
	$165,000		$165,000

During 2010, the following occurred.

1. A tract of land was purchased for $11,000.
2. Bonds payable in the amount of $20,000 were retired at par.
3. An additional $10,000 in ordinary shares were issued at par.
4. Dividends totaling $9,375 were paid to shareholders.
5. Net income was $30,250 after deducting depreciation of $13,500.
6. Land was purchased through the issuance of $22,500 in bonds.
7. Ochoa Inc. sold part of its investment portfolio for $12,875. This transaction resulted in a gain of $2,000 for the company. The company classifies them as non-trading equity investments.
8. Both current assets (other than cash) and current liabilities remained at the same amount.

Instructions

(a) Prepare a statement of cash flows for 2010 using the indirect method.
(b) Prepare the condensed statement of financial position for Ochoa Inc. as it would appear at December 31, 2010.

•6 •8 E23-18 (Partial SCF—Indirect Method) The accounts below appear in the ledger of Popovich Company.

Retained Earnings		Dr.	Cr.	Bal.
Jan. 1, 2010	Credit Balance			€ 42,000
Aug. 15	Dividends (cash)	€15,000		27,000
Dec. 31	Net Income for 2010		€50,000	77,000

Machinery		Dr.	Cr.	Bal.
Jan. 1, 2010	Debit Balance			€140,000
Apr. 8	Major Repairs	€21,000		161,000
Aug. 3	Purchase of Machinery	62,000		223,000
Sept. 10	Cost of Machinery Constructed	48,000		271,000
Nov. 15	Machinery Sold		€66,000	205,000

Accumulated Depreciation—Machinery		Dr.	Cr.	Bal.
Jan. 1, 2010	Credit Balance			€ 84,000
Nov. 15	Accum. Depreciation on Machinery Sold	€25,200		58,800
Dec. 31	Depreciation for 2010		€16,800	85,600

Instructions

From the postings in the accounts above, indicate how the information is reported on a statement of cash flows by preparing a partial statement of cash flows using the indirect method. The loss on sale of equipment (November 15) was €5,800.

•9 E23-19 (Worksheet Analysis of Selected Accounts) Data for Popovich Company are presented in E23-18.

Instructions

Prepare entries in journal form for all adjustments that should be made on a worksheet for a statement of cash flows.

•9 **E23-20** **(Worksheet Analysis of Selected Transactions)** The transactions below took place during the year 2010.

1. Convertible bonds payable with a par value of $300,000 were exchanged for unissued ordinary shares with a par value of $300,000. The market price of both types of securities was par.
2. The net income for the year was $360,000.
3. Depreciation expense for the building was $90,000.
4. Some old office equipment was traded in on the purchase of some newer office equipment and the following entry was made. (The exchange has commercial substance.)

Office Equipment	45,000	
Accum. Depreciation—Office Equipment	30,000	
Office Equipment		40,000
Cash		34,000
Gain on Disposal of Plant Assets		1,000

The Gain on Disposal of Plant Assets was credited to current operations as ordinary income.

5. Dividends in the amount of $123,000 were declared. They are payable in January of next year.

Instructions
Show by journal entries the adjustments that would be made on a worksheet for a statement of cash flows.

•9 **E23-21** **(Worksheet Preparation)** Below are the comparative statements of financial position for Lowenstein Corporation.

	Dec. 31, 2010	Dec. 31, 2009
Land	$ 50,000	$ 50,000
Buildings	125,000	78,500
Accumulated depreciation—buildings	(30,000)	(23,000)
Equipment	53,000	46,000
Accumulated depreciation—equipment	(19,000)	(15,500)
Delivery equipment	39,000	39,000
Accumulated depreciation—delivery equipment	(22,000)	(20,500)
Patents	15,000	–0–
Inventories	81,500	57,000
Equity investments	25,000	19,000
Prepaid expenses	4,200	2,500
Accounts receivable	43,000	45,000
Allowance for doubtful accounts	(1,800)	(2,000)
Cash	16,500	24,000
	$379,400	$300,000
Share capital—ordinary	$140,000	$102,000
Share premium—ordinary	10,000	4,000
Retained earnings	73,400	51,500
Mortgage payable	73,000	53,400
Bonds payable	50,000	62,500
Accounts payable	26,000	16,000
Short-term notes payable (trade)	4,000	6,000
Accrued payables	3,000	4,600
	$379,400	$300,000

Dividends in the amount of $10,000 were declared and paid in 2010.

Instructions
From this information, prepare a worksheet for a statement of cash flows. Make reasonable assumptions as appropriate. The equity investments are considered non-trading, and no unrealized gains or losses have occurred on these securities.

PROBLEMS

 P23-1 (SCF—Indirect Method) The following is Sullivan Corp.'s comparative statement of financial position accounts at December 31, 2010 and 2009, with a column showing the increase (decrease) from 2009 to 2010.

COMPARATIVE STATEMENTS OF FINANCIAL POSITION

	2010	2009	Increase (Decrease)
Property, plant and equipment	$3,307,000	$2,967,000	$340,000
Accumulated depreciation	(1,165,000)	(1,040,000)	(125,000)
Equity investment (Myers Co.)	310,000	275,000	35,000
Debt investment	250,000	—	250,000
Inventories	1,850,000	1,715,000	135,000
Accounts receivable	1,128,000	1,168,000	(40,000)
Cash	815,000	700,000	115,000
Total assets	$6,495,000	$5,785,000	$710,000
Share capital—ordinary, $1 par	$ 500,000	$ 500,000	—
Share premium—ordinary	1,500,000	1,500,000	—
Retained earnings	2,970,000	2,680,000	$290,000
Finance lease obligation	400,000	—	400,000
Accounts payable	1,015,000	955,000	60,000
Income taxes payable	30,000	50,000	(20,000)
Dividends payable	80,000	100,000	(20,000)
Total equity and liabilities	$6,495,000	$5,785,000	$710,000

Additional information:

1. On December 31, 2009, Sullivan acquired 25% of Myers Co.'s ordinary shares for $275,000. On that date, the carrying value of Myers's assets and liabilities, which approximated their fair values, was $1,100,000. Myers reported income of $140,000 for the year ended December 31, 2010. No dividend was paid on Myers's ordinary shares during the year.
2. During 2010, Sullivan loaned $300,000 to TLC Co., an unrelated company. TLC made the first semi-annual principal repayment of $50,000, plus interest at 10%, on December 31, 2010.
3. On January 2, 2010, Sullivan sold equipment costing $60,000, with a carrying amount of $38,000, for $40,000 cash.
4. On December 31, 2010, Sullivan entered into a finance lease for an office building. The present value of the annual rental payments is $400,000, which equals the fair value of the building. Sullivan made the first rental payment of $60,000 when due on January 2, 2011.
5. Net income for 2010 was $370,000.
6. Sullivan declared and paid cash dividends for 2010 and 2009 as shown below.

	2010	2009
Declared	December 15, 2010	December 15, 2009
Paid	February 28, 2011	February 28, 2010
Amount	$80,000	$100,000

Instructions

Prepare a statement of cash flows for Sullivan Corp. for the year ended December 31, 2010, using the indirect method.

 P23-2 (SCF—Indirect Method) The comparative statements of financial position for Hinckley Corporation show the following information.

	December 31	
	2010	2009
Investments	$ –0–	$ 3,000
Building	–0–	29,750
Equipment	45,000	20,000
Patent	5,000	6,250
Inventory	12,000	9,000
Accounts receivable	12,250	10,000
Cash	33,500	13,000
	$107,750	$91,000
Share capital—ordinary	$ 43,000	$33,000
Retained earnings	20,750	6,000
Allowance for doubtful accounts	3,000	4,500
Accumulated depreciation on equipment	2,000	4,500
Accumulated depreciation on building	–0–	6,000
Accounts payable	5,000	3,000
Dividends payable	–0–	5,000
Long-term notes payable	31,000	25,000
Notes payable, short-term (non-trade)	3,000	4,000
	$107,750	$91,000

Additional data related to 2010 are as follows.

1. Equipment that had cost $11,000 and was 40% depreciated at time of disposal was sold for $2,500.
2. $10,000 of the long-term note payable was paid by issuing ordinary shares.
3. Cash dividends paid were $5,000.
4. On January 1, 2010, the building was completely destroyed by a flood. Insurance proceeds on the building were $32,000.
5. Equity investments (non-trading) were sold at $1,700 above their cost.
6. Cash was paid for the acquisition of equipment.
7. A long-term note for $16,000 was issued for the acquisition of equipment.
8. Interest of $2,000 and income taxes of $6,500 were paid in cash.

Instructions
Prepare a statement of cash flows using the indirect method.

•6 P23-3 (SCF—Direct Method) Mortonson Company has not yet prepared a formal statement of cash flows for the 2010 fiscal year. Comparative statements of financial position as of December 31, 2009 and 2010, and a statement of income and retained earnings for the year ended December 31, 2010, are presented below and on page 1298.

MORTONSON COMPANY
STATEMENT OF INCOME AND RETAINED EARNINGS
FOR THE YEAR ENDED DECEMBER 31, 2010
($000 OMITTED)

Sales		$3,800
Expenses		
Cost of goods sold	$1,200	
Salaries and benefits	725	
Heat, light, and power	75	
Depreciation	80	
Property taxes	19	
Patent amortization	25	
Miscellaneous expenses	10	
Interest	30	2,164
Income before income taxes		1,636
Income taxes		818
Net income		818
Retained earnings—Jan. 1, 2010		310
		1,128
Share dividend declared and issued		600
Retained earnings—Dec. 31, 2010		$ 528

MORTONSON COMPANY
COMPARATIVE STATEMENTS OF FINANCIAL POSITION
AS OF DECEMBER 31
($000 OMITTED)

Assets	2010	2009
Land	$ 150	$ 70
Buildings and equipment	910	600
Accumulated depreciation	(200)	(120)
Patents (less amortization)	105	130
Inventory	720	560
Equity investments (non-trading)	10	50
Accounts receivable	780	500
Cash	333	100
Total assets	$2,808	$1,890
Equity and Liabilities		
Share capital—ordinary	$1,300	$ 700
Retained earnings	528	310
Total equity	1,828	1,010
Long-term notes payable—due 2012	200	200
Accounts payable	420	330
Income taxes payable	40	30
Notes payable	320	320
Total liabilities	980	880
Total equity and liabilities	$2,808	$1,890

Instructions

Prepare a statement of cash flows using the direct method. Changes in accounts receivable and accounts payable relate to sales and cost of goods sold.

•6 •7 •8 **P23-4 (SCF—Direct Method)** Michaels Company had available at the end of 2010 the information below and on page 1299.

MICHAELS COMPANY
COMPARATIVE STATEMENTS OF FINANCIAL POSITION
AS OF DECEMBER 31, 2010 AND 2009

	2010	2009
Land	$125,000	$175,000
Building	350,000	350,000
Accumulated depreciation	(105,000)	(87,500)
Equipment	525,000	400,000
Accumulated depreciation	(130,000)	(112,000)
Patent	45,000	50,000
Inventory	42,000	35,000
Prepaid rent	3,000	12,000
Prepaid insurance	2,100	900
Office supplies	1,000	750
Short-term equity investments	22,000	30,000
Accounts receivable	20,500	12,950
Cash	10,000	4,000
Total assets	$910,600	$871,100
Share capital—ordinary	$240,000	$220,000
Share premium—ordinary	25,000	17,500
Retained earnings	123,297	88,747
Long-term notes payable	60,000	70,000
Bonds payable	420,303	425,853
Accounts payable	22,000	32,000
Income taxes payable	5,000	4,000
Wages payable	5,000	3,000
Short-term notes payable	10,000	10,000
Total equity and liabilities	$910,600	$871,100

MICHAELS COMPANY
INCOME STATEMENT
FOR THE YEAR ENDED DECEMBER 31, 2010

Sales revenue		$1,160,000
Cost of goods sold		(748,000)
		412,000
Gross margin		
Operating expenses		
Selling expenses	$ 79,200	
Administrative expenses	156,700	
Depreciation/amortization expense	40,500	
Total operating expenses		(276,400)
Income from operations		135,600
Other income and expense		
Gain on sale of land	8,000	
Gain on sale of short-term investment	4,000	
Dividend revenue	2,400	
Interest expense	(51,750)	(37,350)
Income before taxes		98,250
Income tax expense		(39,400)
Net income		58,850
Dividends to ordinary shareholders		(24,300)
To retained earnings		$ 34,550

Instructions

Prepare a statement of cash flows for Michaels Company using the direct method. Assume the short-term investments are non-trading. Bond premium amortized was $5,550.

·3·4·6·8 **P23-5** **(SCF—Indirect Method, and Net Cash Flow from Operating Activities, Direct Method)** Comparative statement of financial position accounts of Marcus Inc. are presented below.

MARCUS INC.
COMPARATIVE STATEMENT OF FINANCIAL POSITION ACCOUNTS
AS OF DECEMBER 31, 2010 AND 2009

	December 31	
Debit Accounts	2010	2009
Cash	$ 42,000	$ 33,750
Accounts Receivable	70,500	60,000
Merchandise Inventory	30,000	24,000
Equity Investments (non-trading)	22,250	38,500
Machinery	30,000	18,750
Buildings	67,500	56,250
Land	7,500	7,500
	$269,750	$238,750
Credit Accounts		
Allowance for Doubtful Accounts	$ 2,250	$ 1,500
Accumulated Depreciation—Machinery	5,625	2,250
Accumulated Depreciation—Buildings	13,500	9,000
Accounts Payable	35,000	24,750
Accrued Payables	3,375	2,625
Long-Term Note Payable	21,000	31,000
Share Capital—Ordinary, no par	150,000	125,000
Retained Earnings	39,000	42,625
	$269,750	$238,750

Additional data (ignoring taxes):

1. Net income for the year was $42,500.
2. Cash dividends declared and paid during the year were $21,125.
3. A 20% share dividend was declared during the year. $25,000 of retained earnings was capitalized.
4. Equity investments that cost $25,000 were sold during the year for $28,750.
5. Machinery that cost $3,750, on which $750 of depreciation had accumulated, was sold for $2,200.

Marcus's 2010 income statement follows (ignoring taxes).

Sales		$540,000
Less: Cost of goods sold		380,000
Gross margin		160,000
Less: Operating expenses (includes $8,625 depreciation and $5,400 bad debts)		120,450
Income from operations		39,550
Other: Gain on sale of equity investments (non-trading)	$3,750	
Loss on sale of machinery	(800)	2,950
Net income		$ 42,500

Instructions

(a) Compute net cash flow from operating activities using the direct method.
(b) Prepare a statement of cash flows using the indirect method.

•3 •4 •6 •8 **P23-6 (SCF—Direct and Indirect Methods from Comparative Financial Statements)** Chapman Company, a major retailer of bicycles and accessories, operates several stores and is a publicly traded company. The comparative statement of financial position and income statement for Chapman as of May 31, 2010, are shown below and on the next page. The company is preparing its statement of cash flows.

CHAPMAN COMPANY
COMPARATIVE STATEMENTS OF FINANCIAL POSITION
AS OF MAY 31

	2010	2009
Plant assets		
Plant assets	$600,000	$502,000
Less: Accumulated depreciation	150,000	125,000
Net plant assets	450,000	377,000
Current assets		
Merchandise inventory	220,000	250,000
Prepaid expenses	9,000	7,000
Accounts receivable	75,000	58,000
Cash	28,250	20,000
Total current assets	332,250	335,000
Total assets	$782,250	$712,000
Equity		
Share capital—ordinary, $10 par	$370,000	$280,000
Retained earnings	145,000	120,000
Total equity	515,000	400,000
Long-term debt		
Bonds payable	70,000	100,000
Current liabilities		
Accounts payable	123,000	115,000
Salaries payable	47,250	72,000
Interest payable	27,000	25,000
Total current liabilities	197,250	212,000
Total liabilities	267,250	312,000
Total equity and liabilities	$782,250	$712,000

CHAPMAN COMPANY
INCOME STATEMENT
FOR THE YEAR ENDED MAY 31, 2010

Sales	$1,255,250
Cost of merchandise sold	722,000
Gross profit	533,250
Expenses	
Salary expense	252,100
Interest expense	75,000
Other expenses	8,150
Depreciation expense	25,000
Total expenses	360,250
Operating income	173,000
Income tax expense	43,000
Net income	$ 130,000

The following is additional information concerning Chapman's transactions during the year ended May 31, 2010.

1. All sales during the year were made on account.
2. All merchandise was purchased on account, comprising the total accounts payable account.
3. Plant assets costing $98,000 were purchased by paying $28,000 in cash and issuing 7,000 ordinary shares.
4. The "other expenses" are related to prepaid items.
5. All income taxes incurred during the year were paid during the year.
6. In order to supplement its cash, Chapman issued 2,000 ordinary shares at par value.
7. There were no penalties assessed for the retirement of bonds.
8. Cash dividends of $105,000 were declared and paid at the end of the fiscal year.

Instructions

(a) Compare and contrast the direct method and the indirect method for reporting cash flows from operating activities.

(b) Prepare a statement of cash flows for Chapman Company for the year ended May 31, 2010, using the direct method. Be sure to support the statement with appropriate calculations.

(c) Using the indirect method, calculate only the net cash flow from operating activities for Chapman Company for the year ended May 31, 2010.

·6·7·8 **P23-7** (**SCF—Direct and Indirect Methods**) Comparative statement of financial position accounts of Sharpe Company are presented below.

SHARPE COMPANY
COMPARATIVE STATEMENT OF FINANCIAL POSITION ACCOUNTS
AS OF DECEMBER 31

Debit Balances	2010	2009
Cash	$ 70,000	$ 51,000
Accounts Receivable	155,000	130,000
Merchandise Inventory	75,000	61,000
Equity Investments (non-trading)	55,000	85,000
Equipment	70,000	48,000
Buildings	145,000	145,000
Land	40,000	25,000
Totals	$610,000	$545,000
Credit Balances		
Allowance for Doubtful Accounts	$ 10,000	$ 8,000
Accumulated Depreciation—Equipment	21,000	14,000
Accumulated Depreciation—Building	37,000	28,000
Accounts Payable	66,000	60,000
Income Taxes Payable	12,000	10,000
Long-Term Notes Payable	62,000	70,000
Share Capital—Ordinary	310,000	260,000
Retained Earnings	92,000	95,000
Totals	$610,000	$545,000

Additional data:

1. Equipment that cost $10,000 and was 60% depreciated was sold in 2010.
2. Cash dividends were declared and paid during the year.
3. Ordinary shares were issued in exchange for land.
4. Equity investments that cost $35,000 were sold during the year.
5. There were no write-offs of uncollectible accounts during the year.

Sharpe's 2010 income statement is as follows.

Sales		$950,000
Less: Cost of goods sold		600,000
Gross profit		350,000
Less: Operating expenses (includes depreciation expense and bad debt expense)		250,000
Income from operations		100,000
Other income and expense		
Gain on sale of investments	$15,000	
Loss on sale of equipment	(3,000)	12,000
Income before taxes		112,000
Income taxes		45,000
Net income		$ 67,000

Instructions

(a) Compute net cash provided by operating activities under the direct method.
(b) Prepare a statement of cash flows using the indirect method.

·6 ·7 ·8 P23-8 (Indirect SCF) Dingel Corporation has contracted with you to prepare a statement of cash flows. The controller has provided the following information.

	December 31	
	2010	2009
Cash	$ 38,500	$13,000
Accounts receivable	12,250	10,000
Inventory	12,000	10,000
Equity investments (non-trading)	–0–	3,000
Building	–0–	29,750
Equipment	40,000	20,000
Copyright	5,000	5,250
Totals	$107,750	$91,000

Allowance for doubtful accounts	$ 3,000	$ 4,500
Accumulated depreciation on equipment	2,000	4,500
Accumulated depreciation on building	–0–	6,000
Accounts payable	5,000	4,000
Dividends payable	–0–	5,000
Notes payable, short-term (non-trade)	3,000	4,000
Long-term notes payable	36,000	25,000
Share capital—ordinary	38,000	33,000
Retained earnings	20,750	5,000
	$107,750	$91,000

Additional data related to 2010 are as follows.

1. Equipment that had cost $11,000 and was 30% depreciated at time of disposal was sold for $2,500.
2. $5,000 of the long-term note payable was paid by issuing ordinary shares.
3. Cash dividends paid were $5,000.
4. On January 1, 2010, the building was completely destroyed by a flood. Insurance proceeds on the building were $33,000 (net of $4,000 taxes).
5. Equity investments (non-trading) were sold at $1,500 above their cost. The company has made similar sales and investments in the past.

6. Cash and a long-term note for $16,000 were given for the acquisition of equipment.
7. Interest of $2,000 and income taxes of $5,000 were paid in cash.

Instructions

(a) Use the indirect method to analyze the above information and prepare a statement of cash flows for Dingel.

(b) What would you expect to observe in the operating, investing, and financing sections of a statement of cash flows of:

(1) A severely financially troubled firm?

(2) A recently formed firm that is experiencing rapid growth?

CONCEPTS FOR ANALYSIS

CA23-1 (Analysis of Improper SCF) The following statement was prepared by Maloney Corporation's accountant.

MALONEY CORPORATION
STATEMENT OF SOURCES AND USES OF CASH
FOR THE YEAR ENDED SEPTEMBER 30, 2010

Sources of cash	
Net income	$111,000
Depreciation and depletion	70,000
Increase in long-term debt	179,000
Changes in current receivables and inventories, less current	
liabilities (excluding current maturities of long-term debt)	14,000
	$374,000
Application of cash	
Cash dividends	$ 60,000
Expenditure for property, plant, and equipment	214,000
Investments and other uses	20,000
Change in cash	80,000
	$374,000

The following additional information relating to Maloney Corporation is available for the year ended September 30, 2010.

1. Wage and salary expense attributable to share-option plans was $25,000 for the year.
2. Expenditures for property, plant, and equipment $250,000
   Proceeds from retirements of property, plant, and equipment   36,000
   Net expenditures $214,000

3. A share dividend of 10,000 Maloney Corporation ordinary shares was distributed to ordinary shareholders on April 1, 2010, when the per share market price was $7 and par value was $1.
4. On July 1, 2010, when its market price was $6 per share, 16,000 of Maloney Corporation ordinary shares were issued in exchange for 4,000 preference shares.
5. Depreciation expense $ 65,000
   Depletion expense   5,000
   $ 70,000

6. Increase in long-term debt $620,000
   Retirement of debt   441,000
   Net increase $179,000

Instructions

(a) In general, what are the objectives of a statement of the type shown above for Maloney Corporation? Explain.

(b) Identify the weaknesses in the form and format of Maloney Corporation's statement of cash flows without reference to the additional information. (Assume adoption of the indirect method.)

(c) For each of the six items of additional information for the statement of cash flows, indicate the preferable treatment and explain why the suggested treatment is preferable.

CA23-2 (SCF Theory and Analysis of Improper SCF) Teresa Ramirez and Lenny Traylor are examining the following statement of cash flows for Pacific Clothing Store's first year of operations.

PACIFIC CLOTHING STORE STATEMENT OF CASH FLOWS FOR THE YEAR ENDED JANUARY 31, 2010	
Sources of cash	
From sales of merchandise	€ 382,000
From sale of ordinary shares	380,000
From sale of debt investment	120,000
From depreciation	80,000
From issuance of note for truck	30,000
From interest on investments	8,000
Total sources of cash	1,000,000
Uses of cash	
For purchase of fixtures and equipment	330,000
For merchandise purchased for resale	253,000
For operating expenses (including depreciation)	170,000
For purchase of investment	95,000
For purchase of truck by issuance of note	30,000
For purchase of treasury shares	10,000
For interest on note	3,000
Total uses of cash	891,000
Net increase in cash	€ 109,000

Teresa claims that Pacific's statement of cash flows is an excellent portrayal of a superb first year, with cash increasing €109,000. Lenny replies that it was not a superb first year—that the year was an operating failure, the statement was incorrectly presented, and €109,000 is not the actual increase in cash.

Instructions

(a) With whom do you agree, Teresa or Lenny? Explain your position.

(b) Using the data provided, prepare a statement of cash flows in proper indirect method form. The only non-cash items in income are depreciation and the gain from the sale of the investment (purchase and sale are related).

CA23-3 (SCF Theory and Analysis of Transactions) Ashley Company is a young and growing producer of electronic measuring instruments and technical equipment. You have been retained by Ashley to advise it in the preparation of a statement of cash flows using the indirect method. For the fiscal year ended October 31, 2010, you have obtained the following information concerning certain events and transactions of Ashley.

1. The amount of reported earnings for the fiscal year was $700,000, which included a deduction for a loss of $110,000 (see item 5 below).

2. Depreciation expense of $315,000 was included in the income statement.

3. Uncollectible accounts receivable of $40,000 were written off against the allowance for doubtful accounts. Also, $51,000 of bad debt expense was included in determining income for the fiscal year, and the same amount was added to the allowance for doubtful accounts.

4. A gain of $6,000 was realized on the sale of a machine. It originally cost $75,000, of which $30,000 was undepreciated on the date of sale.

5. On April 1, 2010, lightning caused an uninsured building loss of $110,000 ($180,000 loss, less reduction in income taxes of $70,000). This loss was included in determining income as indicated in 1 above.

6. On July 3, 2010, building and land were purchased for $700,000. Ashley gave in payment $75,000 cash, $200,000 fair value of its unissued ordinary shares, and signed a $425,000 mortgage note payable.
7. On August 3, 2010, $800,000 face value of Ashley's 10% convertible preference shares was converted into $150,000 par value of its ordinary shares.

Instructions

Explain whether each of the seven numbered items above is a source or use of cash, and explain how each should be disclosed in Ashley's statement of cash flows for the fiscal year ended October 31, 2010. If any item is neither a source nor a use of cash, explain why it is not, and indicate the disclosure, if any, that should be made of the item for the fiscal year ended October 31, 2010.

CA23-4 (Analysis of Transactions' Effect on SCF) Each of the following items must be considered in preparing a statement of cash flows for Cruz Fashions Inc. for the year ended December 31, 2010.

1. Fixed assets that had cost R20,000 6½ years before and were being depreciated on a 10-year basis, with no estimated residual value, were sold for R4,750.
2. During the year, goodwill of R15,000 was considered impaired and was completely written off to expense.
3. During the year, 500 ordinary shares with a stated value of R25 a share were issued for R32 a share.
4. The company sustained a net loss for the year of R2,100. Depreciation amounted to R2,000 and patent amortization was R400.
5. Uncollectible accounts receivable in the amount of R2,000 were written off against Allowance for Doubtful Accounts.
6. Equity investments (non-trading) that cost R12,000 when purchased 4 years earlier were sold for R10,600.
7. Bonds payable with a par value of R24,000 on which there was an unamortized bond premium of R2,000 were redeemed at 101.

Instructions

For each item, state where it is to be shown in the statement and then how you would present the necessary information, including the amount. Consider each item to be independent of the others. Assume that correct entries were made for all transactions as they took place.

CA23-5 (Purpose and Elements of SCF) IFRS requires the statement of cash flows be presented when financial statements are prepared.

Instructions

(a) Explain the purposes of the statement of cash flows.
(b) List and describe the three categories of activities that must be reported in the statement of cash flows.
(c) Identify and describe the two methods that are allowed for reporting cash flows from operations.
(d) Describe the presentation of non-cash investing and financing transactions. Include in your description an example of a non-cash investing and financing transaction.

CA23-6 (Cash Flow Reporting) Brockman Guitar Company is in the business of manufacturing top-quality, steel-string folk guitars. In recent years, the company has experienced working capital problems resulting from the procurement of factory equipment, the unanticipated buildup of receivables and inventories, and the payoff of a balloon mortgage on a new manufacturing facility. The founder and president of the company, Barbara Brockman, has attempted to raise cash from various financial institutions, but to no avail because of the company's poor performance in recent years. In particular, the company's lead bank, First Financial, is especially concerned about Brockman's inability to maintain a positive cash position. The commercial loan officer from First Financial told Barbara, "I can't even consider your request for capital financing unless I see that your company is able to generate positive cash flows from operations."

Thinking about the banker's comment, Barbara came up with what she believes is a good plan: With a more attractive statement of cash flows, the bank might be willing to provide long-term financing. To "window dress" cash flows, the company can sell its accounts receivables to factors and liquidate its raw materials inventories. These rather costly transactions would generate lots of cash. As the chief accountant for Brockman Guitar, it is your job to tell Barbara what you think of her plan.

Instructions

Answer the following questions.

(a) What are the ethical issues related to Barbara Brockman's idea?
(b) What would you tell Barbara Brockman?

USING YOUR JUDGMENT

FINANCIAL REPORTING

Financial Reporting Problem
Marks and Spencer plc (M&S)

The financial statements of **M&S** are presented in Appendix 5B or can be accessed at the book's companion website, **www.wiley.com/college/kiesoifrs**.

Instructions

Refer to M&S's financial statements and the accompanying notes to answer the following questions.

(a) Which method of computing net cash provided by operating activities does M&S use? What were the amounts of net cash provided by operating activities for the years 2007 and 2008? Which two items were most responsible for the increase in net cash provided by operating activities in 2008?

(b) What was the most significant item in the cash flows used for investing activities section in 2008? What was the most significant item in the cash flows used for financing activities section in 2008?

(c) Where is "deferred income taxes" reported in M&S's statement of cash flows? Why does it appear in that section of the statement of cash flows?

(d) Where is depreciation reported in M&S's statement of cash flows? Why is depreciation added to net income in the statement of cash flows?

Comparative Analysis Case
Cadbury and Nestlé

Instructions

Go to the book's companion website and use information found there to answer the following questions related to **Cadbury** and **Nestlé**.

(a) What method of computing net cash provided by operating activities does Cadbury use? What method does Nestlé use? What were the amounts of cash provided by operating activities reported by Cadbury and Nestlé in 2008?

(b) What was the most significant item reported by Cadbury and Nestlé in 2008 in their investing activities sections? What is the most significant item reported by Cadbury and Nestlé in 2008 in their financing activities sections?

(c) What were these two companies' trends in net cash provided by operating activities over the period 2006 to 2008?

(d) Where is "depreciation and amortization" reported by Cadbury and Nestlé in their statements of cash flows? What is the amount and why does it appear in that section of the statement of cash flows?

(e) Based on the information contained in Cadbury's and Nestlé's financial statements, compute the following 2008 ratios for each company. These ratios require the use of statement of cash flows data. (These ratios were covered in Chapter 5.)

  (1) Current cash debt coverage ratio.

  (2) Cash debt coverage ratio.

(f) What conclusions concerning the management of cash can be drawn from the ratios computed in (e)?

Financial Statement Analysis Case

On the facing page is the consolidated statement of cash flows for **Telefónica, S.A.** (ESP) for the year ended December 31, 2008 and 2009.

(Millions of euros)	2009	2008
Cash flows from operating activities		
Cash received from customers	67,358	69,060
Cash paid to suppliers and employees	(46,198)	(48,500)
Dividends received	100	113
Net interest and other financial expenses paid	(2,170)	(2,894)
Taxes paid	(2,942)	(1,413)
Net cash from operating activities	16,148	16,366
Cash flows from investing activities		
Proceeds on disposals of property, plant, and equipment and intangible assets	242	276
Payments on investments in property, plant and equipment and intangible assets	(7,593)	(7,889)
Proceeds on disposals of companies, net of cash and cash equivalents disposed	34	686
Payments on investments in companies, net of cash and cash equivalents acquired	(48)	(2,178)
Proceeds on financial investments not included under cash equivalents	6	31
Payments made on financial investments not included under cash equivalents	(1,411)	(114)
Interest (paid) received on cash surpluses not included under cash equivalents	(548)	76
Government grants received	18	11
Net cash used in investing activities	(9,300)	(9,101)
Cash flows from financing activities		
Dividends paid	(4,838)	(4,440)
Transactions with equity holders	(947)	(2,241)
Proceeds on issue of debentures and bonds	8,617	1,317
Proceeds on loans, borrowings and promissory notes	2,330	3,693
Cancellation of debentures and bonds	(1,949)	(1,167)
Repayments of loans, borrowings and promissory notes	(5,494)	(4,927)
Net cash flow used in financing activities	(2,281)	(7,765)
Effect of foreign exchange rate changes on collections and payments	269	(302)
Effect of changes in consolidation methods and other non-monetary effects	—	14
Net increase (decrease) in cash and cash equivalents during the period	4,836	(788)
Cash and cash equivalents at January 1	4,277	5,065
Cash and cash equivalents at December 31	9,113	4,277

Instructions

(a) What method does Telefónica use to prepare the operating cash flows section of its statement of cash flows? Briefly discuss how you can determine this.

(b) Telefónica reported net income of €7,937 in 2009 and €7,826 in 2008 (in millions). Briefly discuss some of the adjustments that would explain such a difference in its income and operating cash flows.

(c) IFRS requires disclosure of interest, taxes, and dividends. Briefly describe how Telefónica has complied with these requirements. What other approach could a company take to comply with the reporting requirement?

International Reporting Case

Vermont Teddy Bear Co.

Founded in the early 1980s, the **Vermont Teddy Bear Co.** (USA) designs and manufactures American-made teddy bears and markets them primarily as gifts called Bear-Grams or Teddy Bear-Grams. Bear-Grams are personalized teddy bears delivered directly to the recipient for special occasions such as birthdays and anniversaries. The Shelburne, Vermont, company's primary markets are New York, Boston, and Chicago. Sales have jumped dramatically in recent years. Such dramatic growth has significant implications for cash flows. Provided below are the cash flow statements for two recent years for the company.

	Current Year	Prior Year
Cash flows from operating activities:		
Net income	$ 17,523	$ 838,955
Adjustments to reconcile net income to net cash provided by operating activities		
Deferred income taxes	(69,524)	(146,590)
Depreciation and amortization	316,416	181,348
Changes in assets and liabilities:		
Accounts receivable, trade	(38,267)	(25,947)
Inventories	(1,599,014)	(1,289,293)
Prepaid and other current assets	(444,794)	(113,205)
Deposits and other assets	(24,240)	(83,044)
Accounts payable	2,017,059	(284,567)
Accrued expenses	61,321	170,755
Accrued interest payable, debentures	—	(58,219)
Other	—	(8,960)
Income taxes payable	—	117,810
Net cash provided by (used for) operating activities	236,480	(700,957)
Net cash used for investing activities	(2,102,892)	(4,422,953)
Net cash (used for) provided by financing activities	(315,353)	9,685,435
Net change in cash and cash equivalents	(2,181,765)	4,561,525

Other information:

	Current Year	Prior Year
Current liabilities	$ 4,055,465	$ 1,995,600
Total liabilities	4,620,085	2,184,386
Net sales	20,560,566	17,025,856

Instructions

(a) Briefly describe any similarities or differences in Vermont's U.S. GAAP-based statement of cash flows compared to the requirements of IFRS.

(b) Note that net income in the current year was only $17,523 compared to prior-year income of $838,955, but cash flows from operations was $236,480 in the current year and a negative $700,957 in the prior year. Explain the causes of this apparent paradox.

(c) Evaluate Vermont Teddy Bear's liquidity, solvency, and profitability for the current year using cash flow-based ratios (as covered in Chapter 5).

Accounting, Analysis, and Principles

The income statement for the year ended December 31, 2010, for Laskowski Manufacturing Company contains the following condensed information.

LASKOWSKI CO. INCOME STATEMENT		
Revenues		€6,583,000
Operating expenses (excluding depreciation)	€4,920,000	
Depreciation expense	880,000	5,800,000
Income before income tax		783,000
Income tax expense		353,000
Net income		€ 430,000

Included in operating expenses is a €24,000 loss resulting from the sale of machinery for €270,000 cash. The company purchased machinery at a cost of €750,000.

Laskowski reports the following balances on its comparative statements of financial position at December 31.

LASKOWSKI CO. COMPARATIVE STATEMENTS OF FINANCIAL POSITION (PARTIAL)		
	2010	**2009**
Inventories	€834,000	€867,000
Accounts receivable	775,000	610,000
Cash	672,000	130,000
Accounts payable	521,000	501,000

Income tax expense of €353,000 represents the amount paid in 2010. Dividends declared and paid in 2010 totaled €200,000.

Accounting

Prepare the statement of cash flows using the indirect method.

Analysis

Laskowski has an aggressive growth plan, which will require significant investments in plant and equipment over the next several years. Preliminary plans call for an investment of over €500,000 in the next year. Compute Laskowski's free cash flow and use it to evaluate the investment plans with the use of only internally generated funds.

Principles

How does the statement of cash flows contribute to achieving the objective of financial reporting?

I F R S BRIDGE TO THE PROFESSION

Professional Research

As part of the year-end accounting process for your company, you are preparing the statement of cash flows according to IFRS. One of your team, a finance major, believes the statement should be prepared to report the change in working capital because analysts many times use working capital in ratio analysis. Your supervisor would like research conducted to verify the basis for preparing the statement of cash flows.

Instructions

Access the IFRS authoritative literature at the IASB website (*http://eifrs.iasb.org/*). When you have accessed the documents, you can use the search tool in your Internet browser to respond to the following questions. (Provide paragraph citations.)

(a) What is the primary objective for the statement of cash flows? Is working capital the basis for meeting this objective?

(b) What information is provided in a statement of cash flows?

(c) List some of the typical cash inflows and outflows from operations.

Professional Simulation

The professional simulation for this chapter asks you to address questions related to the accounting for the statement of cash flows.

KWW_Professional _Simulation

| Statement of Cash Flows | Time Remaining 1 hour 00 minutes | copy | paste | calculator | sheet | standards | help | spliter | done |

| Directions | Situation | Financial Statements | Explanation | Resources |

Ellwood House, Inc. had the following condensed statement of financial position at the end of 2010.

ELLWOOD HOUSE, INC.
Statement of Financial Position
December 31, 2010

Land	$ 38,500	Share capital—ordinary	$ 80,000
Plant assets	57,500	Retained earnings	23,500
Investments	40,000	Long-term notes payable	30,000
Current assets (non-cash)	34,000	Bonds payable	32,000
Cash	10,000	Current liabilities	14,500
	$180,000		$180,000

During 2011, the following occurred.
1. Ellwood House, Inc., sold part of its investment portfolio, which was classified as non-trading equity, for $15,500, resulting in a gain of $500 for the firm.
2. Dividends totaling $19,000 were paid to shareholders.
3. A parcel of land was purchased for $5,500.
4. $20,000 of ordinary shares were issued at par.
5. $10,000 of bonds payable were retired at par.
6. Heavy equipment was purchased through the issuance of $32,000 of bonds.
7. Net income for 2011 was $42,000 after allowing depreciation of $13,550.
8. Both current assets (other than cash) and current liabilities remained at the same amount.

| Directions | Situation | Financial Statements | Explanation | Resources |

Prepare a statement of cash flows for 2011, using the indirect method.

| Directions | Situation | Financial Statements | Explanation | Resources |

Draft a one-page letter to Gerald Brauer, president of Ellwood House, Inc., briefly explaining the changes within each major cash flow category. Refer to your cash flow statement whenever necessary.

Remember to check the book's companion website to find additional resources for this chapter.

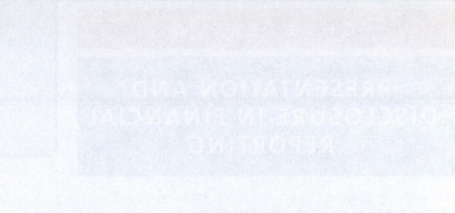

CHAPTER 24

PRESENTATION AND DISCLOSURE IN FINANCIAL REPORTING

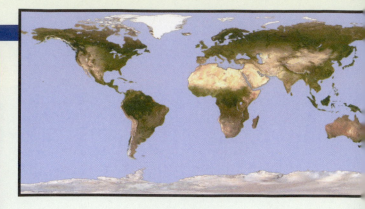

LEARNING OBJECTIVES

After studying this chapter, you should be able to:

•1 Review the full disclosure principle and describe implementation problems.

•2 Explain the use of notes in financial statement preparation.

•3 Discuss the disclosure requirements for major business segments.

•4 Describe the accounting problems associated with interim reporting.

•5 Identify the major disclosures in the auditor's report.

•6 Understand management's responsibilities for financials.

•7 Identify issues related to financial forecasts and projections.

•8 Describe the profession's response to fraudulent financial reporting.

HIGH-QUALITY FINANCIAL REPORTING—ALWAYS IN FASHION

As you have learned in your study of this text, financial statements contain a wealth of useful information to help investors and creditors assess the amounts, timing, and uncertainty of future cash flows. In addition, the usefulness of accounting reports is enhanced when companies provide note disclosures to help statement readers understand how IFRS was applied to transactions. These additional disclosures help readers understand both the judgments that management made and how those judgments affected the amount reported in the financial statements. Some users, however, feel we need to go even further.

A recent proposal to accounting standard-setters involves development of a disclosure framework for all significant financial statement items. Such a framework is needed to provide investors a transparent picture of the potential future impact on earnings and cash flows from financial transactions. Here is an example of a disclosure, when applied to compensation:

Note X. Compensation

General. Describes significant accounting policies underpinning a particular financial statement's account or line item. For example, for an account that includes benefits/deferred compensation, it should describe the accounting policies for pensions, share-based compensation arrangements, and other incentive compensation calculations.

Composition. Includes the account composition and what comprises this line item. For example, as it relates to benefits/deferred compensation, it may include:

Pension liabilities	XXX	
Pension assets	(XXX)	
Pension obligations, net		XXX
Deferred compensation:		
Restricted shares		XXX
Long-term incentive pay		XXX
Total benefits/deferred compensation		XXX

This section will also include roll-forwards for assets and liabilities in a manner similar to that required by IFRS.

Assumption and Uncertainties. Provides a discussion of main assumptions and estimates in a manner similar to what is required by IFRS for postretirement and for share-based compensation, coupled with information on measurement attributes (e.g., application of fair value guidelines) as well as additional disclosures on future cash flows and sensitivities (some of which may currently be required).

Some have commented that a disclosure framework is not needed. Why? IFRS already requires sufficient disclosures, like those proposed. Others disagree. While there are numerous disclosure requirements in IFRS, in many cases the content and format of the disclosures are inconsistent. This reduces the transparency and therefore the quality of the overall financial reporting package.

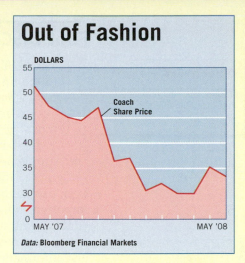

Out of Fashion

The case of **Coach, Inc.** (USA) illustrates the consequences of less transparent reporting. In a recent quarter, Coach stopped reporting as separate items sales from regular stores (full price) and factory outlets. As a result, readers of its financial statements have a hard time determining the source of Coach's sales growth. Analysts are especially concerned that the less-transparent reporting may obscure slowing sales at its regular stores, as consumers cut down on luxury goods in the sluggish economy. Did Coach's share price suffer as a result of this lower-quality reporting? You bet, as shown in the price graph on the right.

Since the change in reporting in 2007, Coach's share price has been down 34 percent. As one analyst noted, "It's never a good sign when you reduce transparency . . . It's a sign of weakness." In short, the above illustrates why high-quality reporting is always in fashion—for companies, investors, and the capital markets. And, as the Coach example illustrates, full disclosure is at the heart of high-quality reporting.

Sources: The Investors Technical Advisory Committee, "Proposal for a Project to Develop a Disclosure Framework" (December 11, 2007). See *www.fasb.org/cs/ContentServer?c=Document_C&pagename=FASB%2FDocument_C%2FDocumentPage&cid=1175801635556*. See also J. Porter, "As Belts Tighten, Coach Feels the Pinch," *BusinessWeek* (May 29, 2008), p. 66.

PREVIEW OF CHAPTER 24

As the opening story indicates, investors and other interested parties need to read and understand all aspects of financial reporting—the financial statements, the notes, the president's letter, and management commentary. In this chapter, we cover the full disclosure principle in more detail and examine disclosures that must accompany financial statements so that they are not misleading. The content and organization of this chapter are as follows.

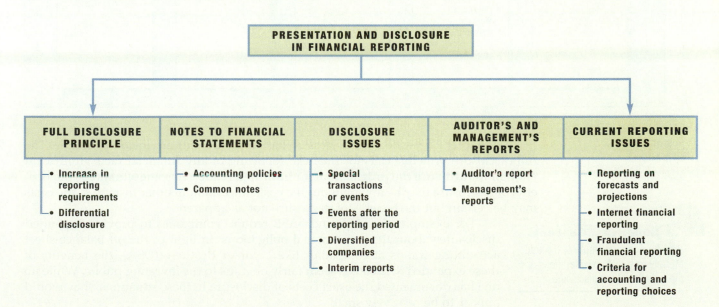

PRESENTATION AND DISCLOSURE IN FINANCIAL REPORTING

FULL DISCLOSURE PRINCIPLE	NOTES TO FINANCIAL STATEMENTS	DISCLOSURE ISSUES	AUDITOR'S AND MANAGEMENT'S REPORTS	CURRENT REPORTING ISSUES
• Increase in reporting requirements • Differential disclosure	• Accounting policies • Common notes	• Special transactions or events • Events after the reporting period • Diversified companies • Interim reports	• Auditor's report • Management's reports	• Reporting on forecasts and projections • Internet financial reporting • Fraudulent financial reporting • Criteria for accounting and reporting choices

FULL DISCLOSURE PRINCIPLE

The IASB Framework notes that while some useful information is best provided in the financial statements, some is best provided by other means. For example, net income and cash flows are readily available in financial statements, but investors might do better to look at comparisons to other companies in the same industry, found in news articles or brokerage house reports.

IASB rules directly affect financial statements, notes to the financial statements, and supplementary information. These accounting standards provide guidance on recognition and measurement of amounts reported in the financial statements. However, due to the many judgments involved in applying IFRS, note disclosures provide important information about the application of IFRS. Supplementary information includes items such as disclosures about the risks and uncertainties, resources and obligations not recognized in the statement of financial position (such as mineral reserves), and information about geographical and industry segments. Other types of information found in the annual report, such as management commentary and the letters to shareholders, are not subject to IASB rules. [1] Illustration 24-1 indicates the various types of financial information.

I F R S

See the Authoritative Literature section (page 1363).

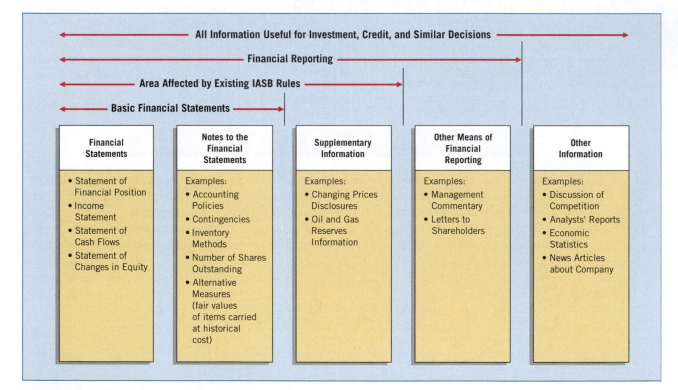

Financial Statements	Notes to the Financial Statements	Supplementary Information	Other Means of Financial Reporting	Other Information
• Statement of Financial Position • Income Statement • Statement of Cash Flows • Statement of Changes in Equity	Examples: • Accounting Policies • Contingencies • Inventory Methods • Number of Shares Outstanding • Alternative Measures (fair values of items carried at historical cost)	Examples: • Changing Prices Disclosures • Oil and Gas Reserves Information	Examples: • Management Commentary • Letters to Shareholders	Examples: • Discussion of Competition • Analysts' Reports • Economic Statistics • News Articles about Company

ILLUSTRATION 24-1
Types of Financial Information

As Chapter 2 indicated, the profession has adopted a **full disclosure principle**. The full disclosure principle calls for financial reporting of **any financial facts significant enough to influence the judgment of an informed reader**. In some situations, the benefits of disclosure may be apparent but the costs uncertain. In other instances, the costs may be certain but the benefits of disclosure not as apparent.

For example, the IASB and FASB require companies to provide expanded disclosures about their contractual obligations. In light of the off-balance-sheet accounting frauds at companies like **Lehman Brothers** (USA), the benefits of these expanded disclosures seem fairly obvious to the investing public. While no one has documented the exact costs of disclosure in these situations, they would appear to be relatively small.

On the other hand, the cost of disclosure can be substantial in some cases and the benefits difficult to assess. For example, at one time the financial press reported that if segment reporting were adopted, a company like **Fruehauf** (USA) would have had to increase its accounting staff 50 percent, from 300 to 450 individuals. In this case, the cost of disclosure can be measured, but the benefits are less well defined.

Some even argue that the reporting requirements are so detailed and substantial that users have a difficult time absorbing the information. These critics charge the profession with engaging in **information overload**.

Financial disasters at **Parmalat** (ITA), **Mahindra Satyam** (IND), **Société Générale** (FRA), and **AIG** (USA) highlight the difficulty of implementing the full disclosure principle. They raise the issue of why investors were not aware of potential problems: Was the information these companies presented not comprehensible? Was it buried? Was it too technical? Was it properly presented and fully disclosed as of the financial statement date, but the situation later deteriorated? Or was it simply not there? In the following sections, we describe the elements of high-quality disclosure that will enable companies to avoid these disclosure pitfalls.

Increase in Reporting Requirements

Disclosure requirements have increased substantially. One survey showed that the size of many companies' annual reports is growing in response to demands for increased transparency. For example, annual report page counts ranged from 92 pages for **Wm Morrison Supermarkets plc** (GBR) up to a whopping 268 pages in **Telefónica**'s (ESP) annual report. This result is not surprising; as illustrated throughout this textbook, the IASB has issued many pronouncements in the last 10 years that have substantial disclosure provisions.

The reasons for this increase in disclosure requirements are varied. Some of them are:

Complexity of the business environment. The increasing complexity of business operations magnifies the difficulty of distilling economic events into summarized reports. Areas such as derivatives, leasing, business combinations, pensions, financing arrangements, revenue recognition, and deferred taxes are complex. As a result, companies extensively use **notes to the financial statements** to explain these transactions and their future effects.

Necessity for timely information. Today, more than ever before, users are demanding information that is current and predictive. For example, users want more complete **interim data**.

Accounting as a control and monitoring device. Regulators have recently sought public disclosure of such phenomena as management compensation, off-balance-sheet financing arrangements, and related-party transactions. Many of these newer disclosure requirements enlist accountants and auditors as the agents to assist in controlling and monitoring these concerns.

> **Underlying Concepts**
>
> Surveys of users indicate that to meet users' changing needs, business reporting must (1) provide more forward-looking information; (2) focus more on the factors that create longer-term value, including non-financial measures; and (3) better align information reported externally with the information reported internally.

Differential Disclosure

A trend toward **differential disclosure** is also occurring.[1] The IASB has developed IFRS for small- and medium-sized entities (SMEs). SMEs are entities that publish general-purpose financial statements for external users but do not issue shares or other securities in a public market. Many believe a simplified set of standards makes sense for these companies because they do not have the resources to implement full IFRS.

---

[1]The IASB is evaluating disclosure issues such as those related to fair value measurements and management commentary. However, as noted by one standard-setter, the usefulness of expanded required disclosure also depends on users' ability to distinguish between disclosed versus recognized items in financial statements. Research to date is inconclusive on this matter. See Katherine Schipper, "Required Disclosures in Financial Reports," Presidential Address to the American Accounting Association Annual Meeting (San Francisco, Calif.: August 2005).

Simplified IFRS for SMEs is a single standard of fewer than 230 pages. It is designed to meet the needs and capabilities of SMEs, which are estimated to account for over 95 percent of all companies around the world. Compared with full IFRS (and many national accounting standards), simplified IFRS for SMEs is less complex in a number of ways:

- Topics not relevant for SMEs are omitted. Examples are earnings per share, interim financial reporting, and segment reporting.

- Simplified IFRS for SMEs allows fewer accounting policy choices. Examples are no option to revalue property, equipment, or intangibles, and no corridor approach for actuarial gains and losses.

- Many principles for recognizing and measuring assets, liabilities, revenue, and expenses are simplified. For example, goodwill is amortized (as a result, there is no annual impairment test) and all borrowing and R&D costs are expensed.

- Significantly fewer disclosures are required (roughly 300 versus 3,000).

- To further reduce standard overload, revisions to the IFRS for SMEs will be limited to once every three years.

Thus, the option of using simplified IFRS helps SMEs meet the needs of their financial statement users while balancing the costs and benefits from a preparer perspective. [2][2]

"THE HEART OF THE MATTER"

What do the numbers mean?

As we discussed in the opening story, a good disclosure framework can contribute to high-quality reporting. In fact, a recent study of disclosure and other mechanisms (such as civil lawsuits and criminal sanctions) found that good disclosure is the most important contributor to a vibrant market.

The study, which compared disclosure and other legal and regulatory elements across 49 countries, found that countries with the best disclosure laws have the biggest securities markets. Countries with more successful market environments also tend to have regulations that make it relatively easy for private investors to sue corporations that provide bad information. That is, while criminal sanctions can be effective in some circumstances, disclosure and other legal and regulatory elements encouraging good disclosure are the most important determinants of highly liquid and deep securities markets.

These findings hold for nations in all stages of economic development, with particular importance for nations that are in the early stages of securities regulation. The lesson: Disclosure is good for your market.

Source: Rebecca Christie, "Study: Disclosure at Heart of Effective Securities Laws," *Wall Street Journal Online* (August 11, 2003).

NOTES TO THE FINANCIAL STATEMENTS

Objective·2

Explain the use of notes in financial statement preparation.

As you know from your study of this textbook, notes are an integral part of the financial statements of a business enterprise. However, readers of financial statements often overlook them because they are highly technical and often appear in small print. **Notes are the means of amplifying or explaining the items presented**

---

[2]In the United States, there has been a preference for one set of GAAP except in unusual situations. With the advent of simplified IFRS for SMEs, this position is under review. Both the FASB and the AICPA are studying the big GAAP/little GAAP issue to ensure that any kind of differential reporting is conceptually sound and meets the needs of users. The FASB has formed a Private Company Financial Reporting Committee, whose primary objectives are to provide recommendations on FASB standard-setting for privately held enterprises (see *http://www.pcfr.org/*).

in the main body of the statements. They can explain in qualitative terms information pertinent to specific financial statement items. In addition, they can provide supplementary data of a quantitative nature to expand the information in the financial statements. Notes also can explain restrictions imposed by financial arrangements or basic contractual agreements. Although notes may be technical and difficult to understand, they provide meaningful information for the user of the financial statements.

Accounting Policies

Accounting policies are the specific principles, bases, conventions, rules, and practices applied by a company in preparing and presenting financial statements. IFRS states that information about the accounting policies adopted by a reporting entity is essential for financial statement users in making economic decisions. It recommended that companies should present **as an integral part of the financial statements a statement identifying the accounting policies adopted and followed by the reporting entity**. Companies should present the disclosure as the first note or in a separate Summary of Significant Accounting Policies section preceding the notes to the financial statements.

The Summary of Significant Accounting Policies answers such questions as: What method of depreciation is used on plant assets? What valuation method is employed on inventories? What amortization policy is followed in regard to intangible assets? How are marketing costs handled for financial reporting purposes?

Refer to Appendix 5B, pages 223–261, for an illustration of note disclosure of accounting policies (Note 1) and other notes accompanying the audited financial statements of **Marks and Spencer plc** (GBR). Illustration 24-2 shows another example, from **Wm Morrison Supermarkets plc** (GBR).

ILLUSTRATION 24-2
Note Disclosure of
Accounting Policies

Wm Morrison Supermarkets plc

Group accounting policies (in part)

Significant accounting policies
The Directors consider the following to be significant accounting policies in the context of the Group's operations:

Revenue recognition
Revenue is recognised when significant risks and rewards of ownership have been transferred to the buyer, there is reasonable certainty of recovery of the consideration and the amount of revenue, associated costs and possible return of goods can be estimated reliably.

Other operating income
Other operating income primarily consists of income not directly related to the operating of supermarkets and mainly comprises rental income from investment properties and income generated from recycling of packaging. Rental income arising from operating leases on investment properties is accounted for on a straight-line basis over the lease term.

Cost of sales
Cost of sales consists of all costs to the point of sale including manufacturing, warehouse and transportation costs. Store depreciation, store overheads and store based employee costs are also allocated to cost of sales.

Supplier income
Supplier incentives, rebates and discounts are collectively referred to as supplier income in the retail industry. Supplier income is recognised as a deduction from cost of sales on an accruals basis based on the expected entitlement which has been earned up to the balance sheet date for each relevant supplier contract. The accrued incentives, rebates and discounts receivable at year end are included within prepayments and accrued income. Where amounts received are in the expectation of future business, these are recognised in line with that future business.

Deferred and current tax
Current tax payable is based on the taxable profit for the period, using tax rates enacted at the balance sheet date and any adjustments to tax payable in respect of previous periods. Taxable profit differs from the profit as reported in the income statement as it is adjusted both for items that will never be taxable or deductible and temporary differences. Current tax is charged in the income statement, except when it relates to items charged or credited directly in equity in which case the current tax is reflected in equity....

Accruals for tax contingencies require management to make judgements and estimates of ultimate exposures in relation to tax compliance issues. All accruals are included in current liabilities.

Retirement benefits
The Group operates defined benefit and defined contribution schemes. A defined contribution scheme is a pension scheme under which the Group pays fixed contributions into a separate entity. A defined benefit scheme is one that is not a defined contribution scheme. Pension benefits under defined benefit schemes are defined on retirement based on age at date of retirement, years of service and a formula using either the employee's compensation package or career average revalued earnings....

Actuarial gains and losses are recognised immediately in other comprehensive income.

Share-based payments

The Group issues equity settled share-based payments to certain employees in exchange for services rendered by them. The fair value of the share-based award is calculated at the date of grant and is expensed on a straight line basis over the vesting period with a corresponding increase in equity. This is based on the Group's estimate of share options that will eventually vest. This takes into account movement of non-market conditions, being service conditions and financial performance, if relevant.

Fair value is measured by use of a binomial stochastic model. The expected life used in the model has been adjusted, based on management's best estimate, for effects of non-transferability, exercise restrictions and behavioural considerations.

Financial instruments

Financial assets and liabilities are recognised on the Group's balance sheet when the Group becomes a party to the contractual provisions of the instrument.

a) Financial assets

i) Trade and other debtors
Trade and other debtors are carried at the lower of their original invoiced value and recoverable amount. Provision is made when there is objective evidence that the Group will not be able to recover balances in full, with the charge being recognised in administrative expenses in the income statement. Balances are written off when the probability of recovery is assessed as being remote.

ii) Cash and cash equivalents
Cash and cash equivalents for cash flow purposes includes cash-in-hand, cash-at-bank and bank overdrafts together with short term, highly-liquid investments that are readily convertible into known amounts of cash, with an insignificant risk of a change in value, within three months from the date of acquisition. In the balance sheet bank overdrafts are presented within current liabilities.

ii) Cash and cash equivalents
Cash and cash equivalents for cash flow purposes includes cash-in-hand, cash-at-bank and bank overdrafts together with short term, highly-liquid investments that are readily convertible into known amounts of cash, with an insignificant risk of a change in value, within three months from the date of acquisition. In the balance sheet bank overdrafts are presented within current liabilities.

b) Financial liabilities

i) Trade and other creditors
Trade and other creditors are stated at cost.

ii) Borrowings
Interest-bearing bank loans and overdrafts are initially recorded at fair value, net of attributable transaction costs. Subsequent to initial recognition, any difference between the redemption value and the initial carrying amount is recognised in the income statement over the period of the borrowings on an effective interest rate basis.

c) Derivative financial instruments and hedge accounting

Derivative financial instruments are initially measured at fair value, which normally equates to cost, and are remeasured at fair value through profit or loss.

Derivative financial instruments are classified as cash flow hedges when they hedge the Group's exposure to variability in cash flows that are either attributable to a particular risk associated with a recognised asset or liability, or a highly probable forecasted transaction.

Net debt

Net debt is cash and cash equivalents, long term cash on deposit, bank and other current loans, bonds and derivative financial instruments (stated at current fair value).

Share capital

Ordinary shares are classified as equity. Incremental costs directly attributable to the issue of new shares or options are shown in equity as a deduction, net of tax, from the proceeds.

Business combinations and goodwill

All business combinations are accounted for by applying the purchase method.

The assets, liabilities and contingent liabilities of subsidiaries are measured at their fair values at the date of acquisition. Any excess of the cost of acquisition over the fair values of the identifiable net assets acquired is recognised as goodwill.

Property, plant and equipment

a) **Property, plant and equipment** are stated at cost less accumulated depreciation and accumulated impairment losses. Costs include directly attributable costs. Annual reviews are made of estimated useful lives and material residual values.

b) **Depreciation rates** used to write off cost less residual value on a straight line basis are:

Freehold land	0%
Freehold buildings	2.5%
Leasehold buildings	Over the shorter of lease period and 2.5%
Plant, equipment, fixtures and vehicles	14-33%
Assets under construction	0%

Impairment of non-financial assets

Property, plant and equipment and investment property are annually reviewed for indications of impairment, or when events or changes in circumstances indicate that the carrying amount may not be recoverable....

An asset impaired is written down to its recoverable amount which is the higher of value in use or its fair value less costs to sell. In assessing value in use, the estimated future cash flows are discounted to their present value using a pre-tax discount rate that reflects current market assessments of the time value of money and the risks specific to the asset.

Stocks

Stocks are measured at the lower of cost and net realisable value. Cost is calculated on a weighted average basis and comprises purchase price, import duties and other non-recoverable taxes less rebates. Stocks represent goods for resale.

Net realisable value is the estimated selling price in the ordinary course of business, less the estimated costs necessary to make the sale.

Leases

Leases in which substantially all the risks and rewards of ownership are retained by the lessor are classified as operating leases; all other leases are classified as finance leases. The Group does not lease any assets on a finance lease basis either as lessor or lessee.

Provisions

Provisions are created where the Group has a present obligation as a result of a past event, where it is probable that it will result in an outflow of economic benefits to settle the obligation from the Group, and where it can be reliably measured. Provisions are made in respect of individual properties where there are obligations for onerous contracts, dilapidations and certain decommissioning obligations for petrol filling stations.

Analysts examine carefully the summary of accounting policies to determine whether a company is taking a conservative or a liberal approach to accounting practices. For example, depreciating plant assets over an unusually long period of time is considered liberal. Using weighted-average inventory valuation in a period of inflation is generally viewed as conservative.

In addition to disclosure of significant accounting policies, companies must:

1. Identify the judgments that management made in the process of applying the accounting policies and that have the most significant effect on the amounts recognized in the financial statements, and

2. Disclose information about the assumptions they make about the future, and other major sources of estimation uncertainty at the end of the reporting period, that have a significant risk of resulting in a material adjustment to the carrying amounts of assets and liabilities within the next financial year. In respect of those assets and liabilities, the notes shall include details of (a) their nature and (b) their carrying amount as at the end of the reporting period.

These disclosures are many times presented with the accounting policy note or may be provided in a specific policy note. The disclosures should identify the estimates that require management's most difficult, subjective, or complex judgments. **[3]** An example of this disclosure is presented in Illustration 24-3 for **British Airways** (GBR).

ILLUSTRATION 24-3
Accounting Estimate and Judgment Disclosure

British Airways

Key accounting estimates and judgements (in part)
The preparation of financial statements requires management to make judgements, estimates and assumptions that affect the application of policies and reported amounts of assets and liabilities, income and expenses. These estimates and associated assumptions are based on historical experience and various other factors believed to be reasonable under the circumstances. Actual results could differ from these estimates. These underlying assumptions are reviewed on an ongoing basis. Revisions to accounting estimates are recognised in the period in which the estimate is revised if the revision affects only that period, or in the period of the revision and future periods if these are also affected. The estimates and assumptions that have a significant risk of causing a material adjustment to the carrying amounts of assets and liabilities within the next financial year are discussed below.

a Impairment of non-financial assets
The Group assesses whether there are any indicators of impairment for all non-financial assets at each reporting date. Goodwill and intangible assets with indefinite economic lives are tested for impairment annually and at other times when such indicators exist. The recoverable amounts of cash-generating units have been determined based on value-in-use calculations. These calculations require the use of estimates as disclosed in note 18.

Other non-financial assets are tested for impairment when there are indicators that the carrying amounts may not be recoverable.

e Passenger revenue recognition
Passenger revenue is recognised when the transportation is provided. Ticket sales that are not expected to be used for transportation (unused tickets) are recognised as revenue using estimates regarding the timing of recognition based on the terms and conditions of the ticket and historical trends.

During the prior year, changes in estimates regarding the timing of revenue recognition primarily for unused flexible tickets were made, resulting in increased revenue in the prior year of £109 million. The change in estimate reflected more accurate and timely data obtained through the increased use of electronic tickets.

Collectively, these disclosures help statement readers evaluate the quality of a company's accounting policies in providing information in the financial statements for assessing future cash flows. Companies that fail to adopt high-quality reporting policies may be heavily penalized by the market. For example, when **Isoft** (GBR) disclosed that it would restate prior-year results due to use of aggressive revenue recognition policies, its share price dropped over 39 percent in one day. Investors viewed Isoft's quality of earnings as low.

Common Notes

We have discussed many of the **notes to the financial statements** throughout this textbook and will discuss others more fully in this chapter. The more common are as follows.

MAJOR DISCLOSURES

INVENTORY. Companies should report the basis upon which inventory amounts are stated (lower-of-cost-or-net realizable value) and the method used in determining cost (FIFO, average cost, etc.). Manufacturers should report, either in the statement of financial position or in a separate schedule in the notes, the inventory composition (finished goods, work in process, raw materials). Unusual or significant financing arrangements relating to inventories that may require disclosure include transactions with related parties, product financing arrangements, firm purchase commitments, and pledging of inventories as collateral. Chapter 9 (pages 487–489) illustrates these disclosures.

PROPERTY, PLANT, AND EQUIPMENT. Companies should state the basis of valuation for property, plant, and equipment (e.g., revaluation or historical cost). It is usually historical cost. Companies also should disclose pledges, liens, and other commitments related to these assets. In the presentation of depreciation, companies should disclose the following in the financial statements or in the notes: (1) depreciation expense for the period; (2) balances of major classes of depreciable assets, by nature and function, at the statement date; (3) accumulated depreciation, either by major classes of depreciable assets or in total, at the statement date; and (4) a general description of the method or methods used in computing depreciation with respect to major classes of depreciable assets. Finally, companies should explain any major impairments. Chapter 11 (pages 583–585) illustrates these disclosures.

CREDITOR CLAIMS. Investors normally find it extremely useful to understand the nature and cost of creditor claims. However, the liabilities section in the statement of financial position can provide the major types of liabilities only in the aggregate. Note schedules regarding such obligations provide additional information about how a company is financing its operations, the costs that it will bear in future periods, and the timing of future cash outflows. Financial statements must disclose for each of the five years following the date of the statements the aggregate amount of maturities and sinking fund requirements for all long-term borrowings. Chapter 14 (pages 745–746) illustrates these disclosures.

EQUITY HOLDERS' CLAIMS. Many companies present in the body of the statement of financial position information about equity securities: the number of shares authorized, issued, and outstanding and the par value for each type of security. Or, companies may present such data in a note. Beyond that, a common equity note disclosure relates to contracts and senior securities outstanding that might affect the various claims of the residual equity holders. An example would be the existence of outstanding share options, outstanding convertible debt, redeemable preference shares, and convertible preference shares. In addition, it is necessary to disclose certain types of restrictions currently in force. Generally, these types of restrictions involve the amount of earnings available for dividend distribution. Examples of these types of disclosures are illustrated in Chapter 15 (pages 792–793) and Chapter 16 (page 837).

CONTINGENCIES AND COMMITMENTS. A company may have gain or loss contingencies that are not disclosed in the body of the financial statements. These contingencies include litigation, debt and other guarantees, possible tax assessments, renegotiation of government contracts, and sales of receivables with recourse. In addition, companies should disclose in the notes commitments that relate to dividend restrictions, purchase agreements (through-put and take-or-pay), hedge contracts, and employment contracts. Disclosures of such items are illustrated in Chapter 7 (pages 368–369), Chapter 9 (pages 487–489), and Chapter 13 (pages 690, 692–693).

FAIR VALUES. Companies that have assets or liabilities measured at fair value generally disclose both the cost and the fair value in the notes to the financial statements. Fair value measurements may be used for many financial assets and liabilities; investments; revaluations for property, plant, and equipment; impairments of long-lived assets; and some contingencies. Companies also provide disclosure of information that enables users to determine the extent of usage of fair value and the inputs used to implement fair value measurement. This fair value hierarchy identifies three broad levels related to the measurement of fair values (Levels 1, 2, and 3). The levels indicate the reliability of the measurement of fair value information.

DEFERRED TAXES, PENSIONS, AND LEASES. The IASB also requires extensive disclosure in the areas of deferred taxes, pensions, and leases. Chapter 19 (pages 1032–1035), Chapter 20 (page 1091), and Chapter 21 (pages 1150–1151) discuss in detail each of these disclosures. Users of financial statements should carefully read notes to the financial statements for information about off-balance-sheet commitments, future financing needs, and the quality of a company's earnings.

CHANGES IN ACCOUNTING POLICIES. The profession defines various types of accounting changes and establishes guides for reporting each type. Companies discuss, either in the summary of significant accounting policies or in the other notes, changes in accounting policies (as well as material changes in estimates and corrections of errors). See Chapter 22 (pages 1195 and 1200).

In earlier chapters, we discussed the disclosures listed above. The following sections of this chapter illustrate four additional disclosures of significance—special transactions or events, subsequent events, segment reporting, and interim reporting.

FOOTNOTE SECRETS

Often, note disclosures are needed to give a complete picture of a company's financial position. A good example of such disclosures is the required disclosure of debt triggers that may be buried in financing arrangements. These triggers can require a company to pay off a loan immediately if the debt rating collapses; they are one of the reasons Enron (USA) crumbled so quickly. But few Enron shareholders knew about the debt triggers until the gun had gone off. Companies are also disclosing more about their bank credit lines, liquidity, and any special-purpose entities. (The latter were major villains in the Enron drama.)

What do the numbers mean?

How can you get better informed about note disclosures that may contain important information related to your investments? Beyond your study in this class, a good web resource for understanding the contents of note disclosures is *http://www.footnoted.org/*. This site highlights "the things companies bury" in their annual reports. It notes that company reports are more complete of late, but only the largest companies are preparing documents that are readable. As the editor of the site noted, "[some companies] are being dragged kicking and screaming into plain English."

Source: Gretchen Morgenson, "Annual Reports: More Pages, but Better?" *New York Times* (March 17, 2002), and D. Stead, "The Secrets in SEC Filings," *BusinessWeek* (August 25, 2008), p. 12.

DISCLOSURE ISSUES

Disclosure of Special Transactions or Events

Related-party transactions, errors, and fraud pose especially sensitive and difficult problems. The accountant/auditor who has responsibility for reporting on these types of transactions must take care to properly balance the rights of the reporting company and the needs of users of the financial statements.

Related-party transactions arise when a company engages in transactions in which one of the parties has the ability to significantly influence the policies of the other. They may also occur when a non-transacting party has the ability to influence the policies of the two transacting parties.[3] Competitive, free-market dealings may not exist in related-party transactions, and so an "arm's-length" basis cannot be assumed. Transactions such as borrowing or lending money at abnormally low or high interest rates, real estate sales at amounts that differ significantly from appraised value, exchanges of non-monetary assets, and transactions involving companies that have no economic substance ("shell corporations") suggest that related parties may be involved.

In order to make adequate disclosure, companies should report the economic substance, rather than the legal form, of these transactions. IFRS requires the following minimum disclosures of material related-party transactions. **[5]**

1. The nature of the related-party relationship;
2. The amount of the transactions and the amount of outstanding balances, including commitments, the nature of consideration, and details of any guarantees given or received;
3. Provisions for doubtful debts related to the amount of outstanding balances; and
4. The expense recognized during the period in respect of bad or doubtful debts due from related parties.

Illustration 24-4, from the annual report of **Volvo Group** (SWE), shows disclosure of related-party transactions.

ILLUSTRATION 24-4
Disclosure of Related-Party Transactions

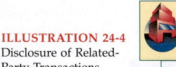

Volvo Group

Note 32. Transactions with related parties

The Volvo Group has transactions with some of its associated companies. The transactions consist mainly of sales of vehicles to dealers. Commercial terms and market prices apply for the supply of goods and services to/from associated companies.

	2008	2009
Sales to associated companies	1,222	529
Purchase from associated companies	116	91
Receivables from associated companies, Dec 31	273	297
Liabilities to associated companies, Dec 31	63	8

Group holdings of shares in associated companies are presented in note 15, Shares and participations.

The Volvo Group also has transactions with Renault s.a.s. and its subsidiaries. Sales to and purchases from Renault s.a.s. amounted to 85 and 2,110. Amounts due from and due to Renault s.a.s. amounted to 20 and 457 at December 31, 2009. The sales were mainly from Renault Trucks to Renault s.a.s. and consisted of components and spare parts. The purchases were mainly made by Renault Trucks from Renault s.a.s. and consisted mainly of light trucks. Renault Trucks has a license from Renault s.a.s. for the use of the trademark Renault.

Many companies are involved in related-party transactions. Errors and fraud (sometimes referred to as irregularities), however, are the exception rather than the rule. Accounting **errors** are **unintentional** mistakes, whereas **fraud** (misappropriation of

---

[3]Examples of related-party transactions include transactions between (a) a parent company and its subsidiaries, (b) subsidiaries of a common parent, (c) a company and trusts for the benefit of employees (controlled or managed by the enterprise), and (d) a company and its principal owners, management, or members of immediate families, and affiliates. **[4]**

assets and fraudulent financial reporting) involves **intentional** distortions of financial statements.[4] As indicated earlier, companies should correct the financial statements when they discover errors. The same treatment should be given fraud. The discovery of fraud, however, gives rise to a different set of procedures and responsibilities for the accountant/auditor.

Disclosure plays a very important role in these types of transactions because the events are more qualitative than quantitative and involve more subjective than objective evaluation. Users of the financial statements need some indication of the existence and nature of these transactions, through disclosures, modifications in the auditor's report, or reports of changes in auditors.

Events after the Reporting Period (Subsequent Events)

Notes to the financial statements should explain any significant financial events that took place after the formal statement of financial position date, but before the statements are authorized for issuance (hereafter referred to as the authorization date). These events are referred to as **events after the reporting date**, or **subsequent events**. Illustration 24-5 shows a time diagram of the subsequent events period.

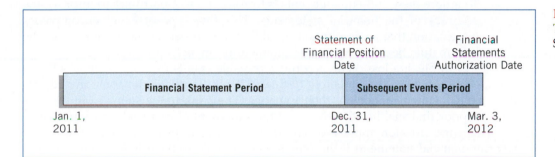

ILLUSTRATION 24-5
Time Periods for
Subsequent Events

A period of several weeks, and sometimes months, may elapse after the end of the fiscal year but before the management or the board of directors authorizes issuance of the financial statements.[5] Various activities involved in closing the books for the period and issuing the statements all take time: taking and pricing the inventory, reconciling subsidiary ledgers with controlling accounts, preparing necessary adjusting

---

[4]International Standard on Auditing 240, "The Auditor's Responsibilities Related to Fraud in an Audit of Financial Statements," *Handbook of International Quality Control, Auditing, Review, Other Assurance, and Other Related Services Pronouncements* (New York: International Federation of Accountants (IFAC), April 2010). We have an expanded discussion of fraud later in this chapter. Requirements for company audits vary according to the jurisdiction and market listing. Most public international companies outside the United States comply with the international auditing standards issued by the International Auditing and Assurance Standards Board (IAASB).

[5]In many jurisdictions, management is required to issue its financial statements to a supervisory board (made up solely of non-executives) for approval. In such cases, the financial statements are authorized for issue—the end of the subsequent events period—when the management authorizes them for issue to the supervisory board. In other jurisdictions, companies are required to submit the financial statements to its shareholders for approval after the financial statements have been made public. In such cases, the subsequent events period ends on the date of issue, not the date when shareholders approve the financial statements. [6]

entries, ensuring that all transactions for the period have been entered, obtaining an audit of the financial statements by independent certified public accountants, and printing the annual report. During the period between the statement of financial position date and its authorization date, important transactions or other events may occur that materially affect the company's financial position or operating situation.

Many who read a statement of financial position believe the financial condition is constant, and they project it into the future. However, readers must be told if the company has experienced a significant change—e.g., sold one of its plants, acquired a subsidiary, suffered unusual losses, settled significant litigation, or experienced any other important event in the post-statement of financial position period. Without an explanation in a note, the reader might be misled and draw inappropriate conclusions.

Two types of events or transactions occurring after the statement of financial position date may have a material effect on the financial statements or may need disclosure so that readers interpret these statements accurately:

Underlying Concepts

The periodicity or time period assumption implies that economic activities of an enterprise can be divided into artificial time periods for purpose of analysis.

1. Events that provide additional evidence about conditions **that existed** at the statement of financial position date, including the estimates inherent in the process of preparing financial statements. These events are referred to as **adjusted subsequent events** and require adjustments to the financial statements. All information available prior to the authorization date of the financial statements helps investors and creditors evaluate estimates previously made. To ignore these subsequent events is to pass up an opportunity to improve the accuracy of the financial statements. This first type of event encompasses information that an accountant would have recorded in the accounts had the information been known at the statement of financial position date.

For example, if a loss on an account receivable results from a customer's bankruptcy subsequent to the statement of financial position date, the company adjusts the financial statements before their issuance. The bankruptcy stems from the customer's poor financial health existing at the statement of financial position date.

The same criterion applies to settlements of litigation. The company must adjust the financial statements if the events that gave rise to the litigation, such as personal injury or patent infringement, took place prior to the statement of financial position date.

2. Events that provide evidence about conditions that **did not exist** at the statement of financial position date but arise subsequent to that date. These events are referred as **non-adjusted subsequent events** and do not require adjustment of the financial statements. To illustrate, a loss resulting from a customer's fire or flood *after* the statement of financial position date does not reflect conditions existing at that date. Thus, adjustment of the financial statements is not necessary. A company should not recognize subsequent events that provide evidence about conditions that did not exist at the date of the statement of financial position but that arose after the statement of financial position date.

The following are examples of non-adjusted subsequent events:

- A major business combination after the reporting period or disposing of a major subsidiary.
- Announcing a plan to discontinue an operation or commencing the implementation of a major restructuring.
- Major purchases of assets, other disposals of assets, or expropriation of major assets by government.
- The destruction of a major production plant or inventories by a fire or natural disaster after the reporting period.
- Major ordinary share transactions and potential ordinary share transactions after the reporting period.

- Abnormally large changes after the reporting period in asset prices, foreign exchange rates, or taxes.
- Entering into significant commitments or contingent liabilities, for example, by issuing significant guarantees after the statement date. **[7]**[6]

Some non-adjusted subsequent events may have to be disclosed to keep the financial statements from being misleading. For such events, a company discloses the nature of the event and an estimate of its financial effect.

Illustration 24-6 presents an example of subsequent events disclosure, excerpted from the annual report of **Cadbury plc** (GBR).

Underlying Concepts

A company also should consider supplementing the historical financial statements with pro forma financial data. Occasionally, a non-adjusted subsequent event may be so significant that disclosure can best be made by means of pro forma financial data.

Cadbury plc

Note 38. Events After the Balance Sheet Date

On 23 January 2009, the Group obtained committed credit facilities totalling £300 million. This facility expires at the earlier of the disposal of Australia Beverages, capital market debt or equity issuance or 28 February 2010.

On 4 March 2009, the Group issued a £300 million bond that matures in 2014. On issuance of the bond the £300 million committed credit facilities expired.

The Group announced that it had entered into a conditional agreement with Asahi Breweries, Ltd ("Asahi") on 24 December 2008 to sell the Australia Beverages business and, as a result of this agreement, Australia Beverages was treated as a discontinued operation in the presentation of the results for 2008.

Subsequent to the balance sheet date, on 12 March 2009, the Group entered into a definitive sale and purchase agreement for the sale of the Australia Beverages business to Asahi for a total consideration in cash of approximately £550m (AUDI, 185m). The agreement with Asahi is subject to normal closing conditions, which do not include financing or competition authority clearance conditions, and the Group expects that the pre-conditions to closing will have been satisfied by 30 April 2009.

ILLUSTRATION 24-6
Disclosure of Subsequent Events

Many subsequent events or developments do not require adjustment of or disclosure in the financial statements. Typically, these are non-accounting events or conditions that management normally communicates by other means. These events include legislation, product changes, management changes, strikes, unionization, marketing agreements, and loss of important customers.

Reporting for Diversified (Conglomerate) Companies

In certain business climates, companies have a tendency to diversify their operations. Take the case of **Siemens AG** (DEU), whose products include energy technologies, consumer products, and financial services. When businesses are so diversified, investors and investment analysts want more information about the details behind conglomerate financial statements. Particularly, they want income statement, statement of financial position, and cash flow information on the **individual segments** that compose the total income figure.

Illustration 24-7 (page 1326) shows **segmented** (disaggregated) financial information of an office equipment and auto parts company.

Objective•3

Discuss the disclosure requirements for major business segments.

---

[6]The effects from natural disasters, like the eruption of the Icelandic volcano, which occurred after the year-end for companies with March fiscal years, require disclosure in order to keep the statements from being misleading. Some companies may have to consider whether these disasters affect their ability to continue as going concerns.

ILLUSTRATION 24-7
Segmented Income
Statement

OFFICE EQUIPMENT AND AUTO PARTS COMPANY INCOME STATEMENT DATA (IN MILLIONS)			
	Consolidated	Office Equipment	Auto Parts
Net sales	$78.8	$18.0	$60.8
Manufacturing costs			
Inventories, beginning	12.3	4.0	8.3
Materials and services	38.9	10.8	28.1
Wages	12.9	3.8	9.1
Inventories, ending	(13.3)	(3.9)	(9.4)
	50.8	14.7	36.1
Selling and administrative expenses	12.1	1.6	10.5
Total operating expenses	62.9	16.3	46.6
Income before taxes	15.9	1.7	14.2
Income taxes	(9.3)	(1.0)	(8.3)
Net income	$ 6.6	$ 0.7	$ 5.9

Much information is hidden in the aggregated totals. If the analyst has only the consolidated figures, he/she cannot tell the extent to which the differing product lines **contribute to the company's profitability, risk, and growth potential**. For example, in Illustration 24-7, the office equipment segment looks like a risky venture. Segmented reporting would provide useful information about the two business segments and would be useful for making an informed investment decision regarding the whole company.

In addition to the example of **Coach, Inc.** (USA) in the opening story, a classic situation that demonstrates the need for segmented data involved **Caterpillar, Inc.** (USA). Market regulators cited Caterpillar because it failed to tell investors that nearly a quarter of its income in one year came from a Brazilian unit and was non-recurring in nature. The company knew that different economic policies in the next year would probably greatly affect earnings of the Brazilian unit. But, Caterpillar presented its financial results on a consolidated basis, not disclosing the Brazilian operations. Caterpillar's failure to include information about Brazil left investors with an incomplete picture of the company's financial results and denied investors the opportunity to see the company "through the eyes of management."

Companies have always been somewhat hesitant to disclose segmented data for various reasons:

1. Without a thorough knowledge of the business and an understanding of such important factors as the competitive environment and capital investment requirements, the investor may find the segmented information meaningless or may even draw improper conclusions about the reported earnings of the segments.

2. Additional disclosure may be helpful to competitors, labor unions, suppliers, and certain government regulatory agencies, and thus harm the reporting company.

3. Additional disclosure may discourage management from taking intelligent business risks because segments reporting losses or unsatisfactory earnings may cause shareholder dissatisfaction with management.

4. The wide variation among companies in the choice of segments, cost allocation, and other accounting problems limits the usefulness of segmented information.

5. The investor is investing in the company as a whole and not in the particular segments, and it should not matter how any single segment is performing if the overall performance is satisfactory.

6. Certain technical problems, such as classification of segments and allocation of segment revenues and costs (especially "common costs"), are formidable.

On the other hand, the advocates of segmented disclosures offer these reasons in support of the practice:

1. Investors need segmented information to make an intelligent investment decision regarding a diversified company.
   (a) Sales and earnings of individual segments enable investors to evaluate the differences between segments in growth rate, risk, and profitability, and to forecast consolidated profits.
   (b) Segmented reports help investors evaluate the company's investment worth by disclosing the nature of a company's businesses and the relative size of the components.
2. The absence of segmented reporting by a diversified company may put its unsegmented, single product-line competitors at a competitive disadvantage because the conglomerate may obscure information that its competitors must disclose.

The advocates of segmented disclosures appear to have a much stronger case. Many users indicate that segmented data are the most useful financial information provided, aside from the basic financial statements. As a result, the IASB has issued extensive reporting guidelines in this area.

Objective of Reporting Segmented Information

The objective of reporting segmented financial data is to provide information about the **different types of business activities** in which an enterprise engages and the **different economic environments** in which it operates. Meeting this objective will help users of financial statements do the following.

(a) Better understand the enterprise's performance.
(b) Better assess its prospects for future net cash flows.
(c) Make more informed judgments about the enterprise as a whole.

Basic Principles

Financial statements can be disaggregated in several ways. For example, they can be disaggregated by products or services, by geography, by legal entity, or by type of customer. However, it is not feasible to provide all of that information in every set of financial statements. IFRS requires that general-purpose financial statements include selected information on a single basis of segmentation. Thus, a company can meet the segmented reporting objective by providing financial statements segmented based on how the company's operations are managed. The method chosen is referred to as the management approach. **[8]** **The management approach reflects how management segments the company for making operating decisions.** The segments are evident from the components of the company's organization structure. These components are called **operating segments**.

Identifying Operating Segments

An **operating segment** is a component of an enterprise:

(a) That engages in business activities from which it earns revenues and incurs expenses.
(b) Whose operating results are regularly reviewed by the company's chief operating decision maker to assess segment performance and allocate resources to the segment.
(c) For which discrete financial information is available that is generated by or based on the internal financial reporting system.

Companies may aggregate information about two or more operating segments only if the segments have the same basic characteristics in each of the following areas.

(a) The nature of the products and services provided.
(b) The nature of the production process.
(c) The type or class of customer.
(d) The methods of product or service distribution.
(e) If applicable, the nature of the regulatory environment.

After the company decides on the possible segments for disclosure, it makes a quantitative materiality test. This test determines whether the segment is significant enough to warrant actual disclosure. An operating segment is deemed significant, and therefore a reportable segment, if it satisfies **one or more** of the following quantitative thresholds.

1. Its **revenue** (including both sales to external customers and intersegment sales or transfers) is 10 percent or more of the combined revenue of all the company's operating segments.
2. The absolute amount of its **profit or loss** is 10 percent or more of the greater, in absolute amount, of **(a)** the combined operating profit of all operating segments that did not incur a loss, or **(b)** the combined loss of all operating segments that did report a loss.
3. Its **identifiable assets** are 10 percent or more of the combined assets of all operating segments.

In applying these tests, the company must consider two additional factors. First, segment data must explain a significant portion of the company's business. Specifically, the segmented results must equal or exceed 75 percent of the combined sales to unaffiliated customers for the entire company. This test prevents a company from providing limited information on only a few segments and lumping all the rest into one category.

Second, the profession recognizes that reporting too many segments may overwhelm users with detailed information. The IASB decided that 10 is a reasonable upper limit for the number of segments that a company must disclose. **[9]**

To illustrate these requirements, assume a company has identified six possible reporting segments, as shown in Illustration 24-8 (000s omitted).

ILLUSTRATION 24-8
Data for Different Possible Reporting Segments

Segments	Total Revenue (Unaffiliated)	Operating Profit (Loss)	Identifiable Assets
A	€ 100	€10	€ 60
B	50	2	30
C	700	40	390
D	300	20	160
E	900	18	280
F	100	(5)	50
	€2,150	€85	€970

The company would apply the respective tests as follows:

Revenue test: 10% × €2,150 = €215; C, D, and E meet this test.
Operating profit (loss) test: 10% × €90 = €9 (note that the €5 loss is ignored, because the test is based on non-loss segments); A, C, D, and E meet this test.
Identifiable assets tests: 10% × €970 = €97; C, D, and E meet this test.

The reporting segments are therefore A, C, D, and E, assuming that these four segments have enough sales to meet the 75 percent of combined sales test. The 75 percent test is computed as follows.

75% of combined sales test: 75% × €2,150 = €1,612.50. The sales of A, C, D, and E total €2,000 (€100 + €700 + €300 + €900); therefore, the 75 percent test is met.

Measurement Principles

The accounting principles that companies use for segment disclosure need not be the same as the principles they use to prepare the consolidated statements. This flexibility may at first appear inconsistent. But, preparing segment information in accordance with IFRS would be difficult because some IFRS are not expected to apply at a segment level. Examples are accounting for the cost of company-wide employee benefit plans and accounting for income taxes in a company that files a consolidated tax return with segments in different tax jurisdictions.

The IASB does not require allocations of joint, common, or company-wide costs solely for external reporting purposes. **Common costs** are those incurred for the benefit of more than one segment and whose interrelated nature prevents a completely objective division of costs among segments. For example, the company president's salary is difficult to allocate to various segments. Allocations of common costs are inherently arbitrary and may not be meaningful. There is a presumption that if companies allocate common costs to segments, these allocations are either directly attributable or reasonably allocable to the segments.

Segmented Information Reported

The IASB requires that an enterprise report the following.

1. *General information about its operating segments.* This includes factors that management considers most significant in determining the company's operating segments, and the types of products and services from which each operating segment derives its revenues.

2. *Segment profit and loss and related information.* Specifically, companies must report the following information about each operating segment if the amounts are included in determining segment profit or loss.
   (a) Revenues from transactions with external customers.
   (b) Revenues from transactions with other operating segments of the same enterprise.
   (c) Interest revenue.
   (d) Interest expense.
   (e) Depreciation and amortization expense.
   (f) Unusual items.
   (g) Equity in the net income of investees accounted for by the equity method.
   (h) Income tax expense or benefit.
   (i) Significant non-cash items other than depreciation, depletion, and amortization expense.

3. *Segment assets and liabilities.* A company must report each operating segment's total assets and liabilities.

4. *Reconciliations.* A company must provide a reconciliation of the total of the segments' revenues to total revenues, a reconciliation of the total of the operating segments' profits and losses to its income before income taxes, and a reconciliation of the total of the operating segments' assets and liabilities to total assets and liabilities.

5. *Information about products and services and geographic areas.* For each operating segment not based on geography, the company must report (unless it is impracticable): (1) revenues from external customers, (2) long-lived assets, and (3) expenditures

during the period for long-lived assets. This information, if material, must be reported (a) in the enterprise's country of domicile and (b) in each other country.

6. *Major customers.* If 10 percent or more of company revenue is derived from a single customer, the company must disclose the total amount of revenue from each such customer by segment.

ILLUSTRATION 24-9
Segment Disclosure

Illustration of Disaggregated Information

Illustration 24-9 shows the segment disclosure for **Statoil** (NOR).

Statoil

Note 5. Segments (in part)
Segment data for the years ended 31 December, 2009 and 2008 is presented below:

(in NOK million)	Exploration and Production Norway	International Exploration and Production	Natural Gas	Manufacturing and Marketing	Other	Eliminations	Total
Year ended 31 December 2009							
Revenues third party and Other income	4,153	12,301	96,973	348,941	1,287	0	463,655
Revenues inter-segment	154,431	28,459	1,241	2,014	2,295	(188,440)	0
Net income from associated companies	79	1,075	399	280	(55)	0	1,778
Total revenues and other income	158,663	41,835	98,613	351,235	3,527	(188,440)	465,433
Net operating income	104,318	2,599	18,488	(541)	(1,146)	(2,078)	121,640
Significant non-cash items recognised in segment profit or loss							
- Depreciation and amortisation	25,653	16,231	1,778	2,390	687	0	46,739
- Impairment losses	0	873	1,001	5,369	74	0	7,317
- Inventory valuation	0	0	(24)	(5,171)	0	1,377	(3,818)
- Commodity based derivatives	(1,781)	0	(2,814)	1,072	(122)	0	(3,645)
- Exploration expenditure written off	1,177	5,821	0	0	0	0	6,998
Investments in associated companies	214	4,962	2,829	917	1,134	0	10,056
Other segment non-current assets	175,998	152,678	34,797	28,587	3,028	0	395,088
Non-current assets, not allocated to segments*							41,312
Total non-current assets							446,456
Additions to PP&E and intangible assets**	34,875	39,354	2,528	7,618	1,340	0	85,715

*Deferred tax assets, post employment benefit assets and non-current financial instruments are not allocated to segments.
**Excluding movements due to changes in abandonment and removal obligations.

Interim Reports

Objective•4
Describe the accounting problems associated with interim reporting.

Another source of information for the investor is interim reports. As noted earlier, **interim reports** cover periods of less than one year. The securities exchanges, market regulators, and the accounting profession have an active interest in the presentation of interim information.

Because of the short-term nature of the information in these reports, there is considerable controversy as to the general approach companies should employ. One group, which favors the **discrete approach**, believes that companies should treat each interim period as a separate accounting period. Using that treatment, companies would follow the principles for deferrals and accruals used for annual reports. In this view, companies should report accounting transactions as they occur, and expense recognition should not change with the period of time covered.

Underlying Concepts

For information to be relevant, it must be available to decision-makers before it loses its capacity to influence their decisions (timeliness). Interim reporting is an excellent example of this concept.

Another group, which favors the **integral approach**, believes that the interim report is an integral part of the annual report and that deferrals and accruals should take into consideration what will happen for the entire year. In this approach, companies should assign estimated expenses to parts of a year on the basis of sales volume or some other activity base. In general, IFRS requires companies to follow the discrete approach. [10]

Interim Reporting Requirements
Generally, companies should use the same accounting policies for interim reports and for annual reports. They should recognize revenues in interim periods on the same basis as they are for annual periods. For example, if Cedars Corp. uses the percentage-of-completion method as the basis for recognizing revenue on an annual basis, then it should use the percentage-of-completion method for interim reports as well. Also, Cedars should treat costs directly associated with revenues (product costs, such as materials, labor and related fringe benefits, and manufacturing overhead) in the same manner for interim reports as for annual reports.

Companies should use the same inventory pricing methods (FIFO, average cost, etc.) for interim reports and for annual reports. However, companies may use the gross profit method for interim inventory pricing. But, they must disclose the method and adjustments to reconcile with annual inventory.

Discrete Approach. Following the discrete approach, companies record in interim reports revenues and expenses according to the revenue and expense recognition principles. This includes costs and expenses other than product costs (often referred to as period costs). No accruals or deferrals in anticipation of future events during the year should be reported. For example, the cost of a planned major periodic maintenance or overhaul for a company like **Airbus** (FRA) or other seasonal expenditure that is expected to occur late in the year is not anticipated for interim reporting purposes. The mere intention or necessity to incur expenditure related to the future is not sufficient to give rise to an obligation.

Or, a company like **Carrefour** (FRA) may budget certain costs expected to be incurred irregularly during the financial year, such as advertising and employee training costs. Those costs generally are discretionary even though they are planned and tend to recur from year to year. However, recognizing an obligation at the end of an interim financial reporting period for such costs that have not yet been incurred generally is not consistent with the definition of a liability.

While year-to-date measurements may involve changes in estimates of amounts reported in prior interim periods of the current financial year, the principles for recognizing assets, liabilities, income, and expenses for interim periods are the same as in annual financial statements. For example, **Wm Morrison Supermarkets plc** (GBR) records losses from inventory write-downs, restructurings, or impairments in an interim period similar to how it would treat these items in the annual financial statements (when incurred). However, if an estimate from a prior interim period changes in a subsequent interim period of that year, the original estimate is adjusted in the subsequent interim period.

Interim Disclosures. IFRS does not require a complete set of financial statements at the interim reporting date. Rather, companies may comply with the requirements by providing condensed financial statements and selected explanatory notes. Because users of interim financial reports also have access to the most recent annual financial report, companies only need provide explanation of significant events and transactions since the end of the last annual reporting period. Companies should report the following interim data at a minimum.

1. Statement that the same accounting policies and methods of computation are followed in the interim financial statements as compared with the most recent annual financial statements or, if those policies or methods have been changed, a description of the nature and effect of the change.

2. Explanatory comments about the seasonality or cyclicality of interim operations.

3. The nature and amount of items affecting assets, liabilities, equity, net income, or cash flows that are unusual because of their nature, size, or incidence.

4. The nature and amount of changes in accounting policies and estimates of amounts previously reported.

5. Issuances, repurchases, and repayments of debt and equity securities.

6. Dividends paid (aggregate or per share) separately for ordinary shares and other shares.

7. Segment information, as required by *IFRS 8*, "Operating Segments."

8. Changes in contingent liabilities or contingent assets since the end of the last annual reporting period.

9. Effect of changes in the composition of the company during the interim period, such as business combinations, obtaining or losing control of subsidiaries and long-term investments, restructurings, and discontinued operations.

10. Other material events subsequent to the end of the interim period that have not been reflected in the financial statements for the interim period.

If a complete set of financial statements is provided in the interim report, companies comply with the provisions of *IAS 1*, "Presentation of Financial Statements."

Unique Problems of Interim Reporting

IFRS reflects a preference for the discrete approach. However, within this broad guideline, a number of unique reporting problems develop related to the following items.

Income Taxes. Not every dollar of corporate taxable income may be taxed at the same rate if the tax rate is progressive. This aspect of business income taxes poses a problem in preparing interim financial statements. Should the company use the **annualized approach**, which is to annualize income to date and accrue the proportionate income tax for the period to date? Or should it follow the **marginal principle approach**, which is to apply the lower rate of tax to the first amount of income earned? At one time, companies generally followed the latter approach and accrued the tax applicable to each additional dollar of income.

IFRS requires use of the annualized approach. Income tax expense is recognized in each interim period based on the best estimate of the weighted-average annual income tax rate expected for the full financial year. This approach is consistent with applying the same principles in interim reports as applied to annual report; that is, income taxes are assessed on an annual basis. However, amounts accrued for income tax expense in one interim period may have to be adjusted in a subsequent interim period of that financial year if the estimate of the annual income tax rate changes. **[11]**[7]

Seasonality. Seasonality occurs when most of a company's sales occur in one short period of the year, while certain costs are fairly evenly spread throughout the year. For example, the natural gas industry has its heavy sales in the winter months. In contrast, the beverage industry has its heavy sales in the summer months.

The problem of seasonality is related to the expense recognition principle in accounting. Generally, expenses are associated with the revenues they create. In a seasonal business, wide fluctuations in profits occur because off-season sales do not absorb the company's fixed costs (for example, manufacturing, selling, and administrative costs that tend to remain fairly constant regardless of sales or production).

To illustrate why seasonality is a problem, assume the following information.

ILLUSTRATION 24-10
Data for Seasonality Example

Selling price per unit	$1
Annual sales for the period (projected and actual)	
100,000 units @ $1	$100,000
Manufacturing costs	
Variable	10¢ per unit
Fixed	20¢ per unit or $20,000 for the year
Non-manufacturing costs	
Variable	10¢ per unit
Fixed	30¢ per unit or $30,000 for the year

[7]The estimated annual effective tax rate should reflect anticipated tax credits, foreign tax rates, percentage depletion, capital gains rates, and other available tax-planning alternatives.

Sales for four quarters and the year (projected and actual) were:

ILLUSTRATION 24-11
Sales Data for Seasonality Example

		Percent of Sales
1st Quarter	$ 20,000	20%
2nd Quarter	5,000	5
3rd Quarter	10,000	10
4th Quarter	65,000	65
Total for the year	$100,000	100%

Under the present accounting framework, the income statements for the quarters might be as shown in Illustration 24-12.

ILLUSTRATION 24-12
Interim Net Income for Seasonal Business—Discrete Approach

	1st Qtr	2nd Qtr	3rd Qtr	4th Qtr	Year
Sales	$20,000	$ 5,000	$10,000	$65,000	$100,000
Manufacturing costs					
Variable	(2,000)	(500)	(1,000)	(6,500)	(10,000)
Fixed[a]	(4,000)	(1,000)	(2,000)	(13,000)	(20,000)
	14,000	3,500	7,000	45,500	70,000
Non-manufacturing costs					
Variable	(2,000)	(500)	(1,000)	(6,500)	(10,000)
Fixed[b]	(7,500)	(7,500)	(7,500)	(7,500)	(30,000)
Net income	$ 4,500	$(4,500)	$ (1,500)	$31,500	$ 30,000

[a]The fixed manufacturing costs are inventoried, so that equal amounts of fixed costs do not appear during each quarter.
[b]The fixed non-manufacturing costs are not inventoried, so equal amounts of fixed costs appear during each quarter.

An investor who uses the first quarter's results might be misled. If the first quarter's earnings are $4,500, should this figure be multiplied by four to predict annual earnings of $18,000? Or, if first-quarter sales of $20,000 are 20 percent of the predicted sales for the year, would the net income for the year be $22,500 ($4,500 × 5)? Both figures are obviously wrong, and after the second quarter's results occur, the investor may become even more confused.

The problem with the conventional approach is that the fixed non-manufacturing costs are not charged in proportion to sales. Some enterprises have adopted a way of avoiding this problem by making all fixed non-manufacturing costs follow the sales pattern, as shown in Illustration 24-13.

ILLUSTRATION 24-13
Interim Net Income for Seasonal Business—Integral Approach

	1st Qtr	2nd Qtr	3rd Qtr	4th Qtr	Year
Sales	$20,000	$ 5,000	$10,000	$65,000	$100,000
Manufacturing costs					
Variable	(2,000)	(500)	(1,000)	(6,500)	(10,000)
Fixed	(4,000)	(1,000)	(2,000)	(13,000)	(20,000)
	14,000	3,500	7,000	45,500	70,000
Non-manufacturing costs					
Variable	(2,000)	(500)	(1,000)	(6,500)	(10,000)
Fixed	(6,000)	(1,500)	(3,000)	(19,500)	(30,000)
Net income	$ 6,000	$ 1,500	$ 3,000	$19,500	$ 30,000

This approach solves some of the problems of interim reporting: Sales in the first quarter are 20 percent of total sales for the year, and net income in the first quarter is 20 percent of total income. In this case, as in the previous example, the investor cannot rely on multiplying any given quarter by four but can use comparative data or rely on some estimate of sales in relation to income for a given period.

The greater the degree of seasonality experienced by a company, the greater the possibility of distortion. Because there are no definitive guidelines for handling such items as the fixed non-manufacturing costs, variability in income can be substantial. To alleviate this problem, IFRS requires companies subject to material seasonal variations to disclose the seasonal nature of their business and consider supplementing their interim reports with information for 12-month periods ended at the interim date for the current and preceding years.

The two illustrations highlight the difference between the **discrete** and **integral** approaches. Illustration 24-12 represents the discrete approach, in which the fixed non-manufacturing expenses are expensed as incurred. Illustration 24-13 shows the integral approach, in which expenses are charged to expense on the basis of some measure of activity.

Continuing Controversy. While IFRS has developed some rules for interim reporting, additional issues remain. For example, there is continuing debate on the independent auditor's involvement in interim reports. Many auditors are reluctant to express an opinion on interim financial information, arguing that the data are too tentative and subjective. On the other hand, more people are advocating some examination of interim reports. Generally, auditors perform a review of interim financial information. Such a review, which is much more limited in its procedures than the annual audit, provides some assurance that the interim information appears to be in accord with IFRS.[8]

Analysts and investors want financial information as soon as possible, before it's old news. We may not be far from a continuous database system in which corporate financial records can be accessed via the Internet. Investors might be able to access a company's financial records whenever they wish and put the information in the format they need. Thus, they could learn about sales slippage, cost increases, or earnings changes as they happen, rather than waiting until after the quarter has ended.

A steady stream of information from the company to the investor could be very positive because it might alleviate management's continual concern with short-run interim numbers. Today, many contend that management is too oriented to the short-term. The truth of this statement is echoed by the words of the president of a large company who decided to retire early: "I wanted to look forward to a year made up of four seasons rather than four quarters."

DISCLOSURE OVERLOAD?

What do the numbers mean?

As we discussed in Chapter 1 and throughout the text, IFRS is gaining popularity around the world. And in 2011, the U.S. Securities and Exchange Commission decides whether publicly traded companies in the United States will be required to adopt IFRS. There is some debate on U.S. readiness to make the switch. For example, there are several areas in which the FASB and the IASB must iron out a number of technical accounting issues before they reach a substantially converged set of accounting standards. Here is a list of six important areas yet to be converged.

1. *Error correction.* According to *IAS 8*, it's not always necessary to retrospectively restate financial results when a company corrects errors, especially if the adjustment is impractical or too costly. U.S. GAAP, on the other hand, requires restatements in many error-correction cases.

2. *Death of LIFO.* Last-in, first-out inventory (LIFO) accounting is prohibited under *IAS 2*, so any U.S. company using the method will have to abandon it (and the tax benefits) and move to another methodology. Although LIFO is permitted under U.S. GAAP, the repeal of LIFO for tax purposes is an ongoing debate.

---

[8]These are referred to as review engagements, which are less extensive than an audit. See International Standards on Review Engagements (ISRE) 2410, "Review of Interim Financial Information Performed by the Independent Auditor of the Entity," *Handbook of International Quality Control, Auditing, Review, Other Assurance, and Other Related Services Pronouncements* (April 2010).

3. *Reversal of impairments.* IAS 36 permits companies to reverse impairment losses up to the amount of the original impairment when the reason for the charge decreases or no longer exists. However, U.S. GAAP bans reversal.

4. *PP&E valuation.* IAS 16 allows for the revaluation of property, plant, and equipment, but the entire asset class must be revalued. That means a company can choose to use the revaluation model if the asset class's fair value can be measured reliably. But, it must choose to use one model or the other; both cannot be used at the same time. U.S. GAAP does not allow revaluation.

5. *Component depreciation.* Also under IAS 16, companies must recognize and depreciate equipment components separately if the components can be physically separated from the asset and have different useful life spans. In practical terms, that means controllers will have to rely on the operations side of the business to help assess equipment components. U.S. GAAP allows component depreciation, but it is not required.

6. *Development costs.* Based on IAS 38, companies are permitted to capitalize development costs as long as they meet six criteria. However, research costs are still expensed. U.S. GAAP requires that all R&D costs be charged to expense when incurred.

What do the numbers mean?
(continued)

Some are already debating what will happen if and when U.S. companies adopt these new standards. It is almost certain that expanded disclosure will be needed to help users navigate accounting reports upon adoption of IFRS. As one accounting analyst remarked, "get ready for an avalanche of footnotes." Since using IFRS requires more judgment than using U.S. GAAP, two to three times as many footnotes will be needed to explain the rationales for accounting approaches. So while principles-based standards should promote more comparability, they require investors to dig into the disclosures in the footnotes.

Source: Marie Leone, "GAAP and IFRS: Six Degrees of Separation," *CFO.com* (June 30, 2010).

AUDITOR'S AND MANAGEMENT'S REPORTS

Auditor's Report

Another important source of information, which is often overlooked, is the **auditor's report**. An **auditor** is an accounting professional who conducts an independent examination of a company's accounting data.

Objective·5
Identify the major disclosures in the auditor's report.

If satisfied that the financial statements present the financial position, results of operations, and cash flows fairly in accordance with IFRS, the auditor expresses an **unmodified opinion**. An example is shown in Illustration 24-14 (page 1336).[9]

In preparing the report, the auditor follows these reporting standards.

1. The report states whether the financial statements are in accordance with the financial reporting framework (IFRS) and describes the responsibilities of the directors and auditors with respect to the financial statements.

2. The report identifies those circumstances in which the company has not consistently observed such policies in the current period in relation to the preceding period.

3. Users are to regard the informative disclosures in the financial statements as reasonably adequate unless the report states otherwise.

[9]This auditor's report and the following discussion are consistent with international auditing standards. See International Standard on Auditing 700, "Forming an Opinion and Reporting on Financial Statements" and International Standard on Auditing 705, "Modifications to the Opinion in the Independent Auditor's Report," *Handbook of International Quality Control, Auditing, Review, Other Assurance, and Other Related Services Pronouncements* (New York: International Federation of Accountants (IFAC), April 2010). They are also similar to the specifications for U.S. auditors contained in "Reports on Audited Financial Statements," *Statement on Auditing Standards No. 58* (New York: AICPA, 1988). U.S. standards differ due to the required audit opinion on the company's internal controls, as required by the SEC.

Wm Morrison Supermarkets plc

Independent auditors' report to the members of Wm Morrison Supermarkets plc

We have audited the financial statements of Wm Morrison Supermarkets plc for the 52 weeks ended 31 January 2010 set out on pages 45 to 85. The financial reporting framework that has been applied in the preparation of the Group financial statements is applicable law and International Financial Reporting Standards (IFRS) as adopted by the EU. The financial reporting framework that has been applied in the preparation of the Parent Company financial statements is applicable law and UK Accounting Standards (UK Generally Accepted Accounting Practice).

This report is made solely to the Company's members, as a body, in accordance with chapter 3 of part 16 of the Companies Act 2006. Our audit work has been undertaken so that we might state to the Company's members those matters we are required to state to them in an auditors' report and for no other purpose. To the fullest extent permitted by law, we do not accept or assume responsibility to anyone other than the Company and the Company's members, as a body, for our audit work, for this report, or for the opinions we have formed.

Respective responsibilities of directors and auditors
As explained more fully in the Directors' Responsibilities Statement set out on page 43, the Directors are responsible for the preparation of the financial statements and for being satisfied that they give a true and fair view. Our responsibility is to audit the financial statements in accordance with applicable law and International Standards on Auditing (UK and Ireland). Those standards require us to comply with the Auditing Practices Board's (APB) Ethical Standards for Auditors.

Scope of the audit of the financial statements
A description of the scope of an audit of financial statements is provided on the APB's website at www.frc.org.uk/apb/scope/UKP

Opinion on financial statements
In our opinion:

- The financial statements give a true and fair view of the state of the Group's and of the Parent Company's affairs as at 31 January 2010 and of the Group's profit for the year then ended;
- The Group financial statements have been properly prepared in accordance with IFRS as adopted by the EU;
- The Parent Company financial statements have been properly prepared in accordance with UK Generally Accepted Accounting Practice; and
- The financial statements have been prepared in accordance with the requirements of the Companies Act 2006; and, as

regards the Group financial statements, Article 4 of the IAS Regulation.

Opinion on other matters prescribed by the companies Act 2006
In our opinion:

- The part of the Directors' remuneration report to be audited has been properly prepared in accordance with the Companies Act 2006; and
- The information given in the Directors' report for the financial year for which the financial statements are prepared is consistent with the financial statements.

Matters on which we are required to report by exception
We have nothing to report in respect of the following:

Under the Companies Act 2006 we are required to report to you if, in our opinion:

- Adequate accounting records have not been kept by the Parent Company, or returns adequate for our audit have not been received from branches not visited by us; or
- The Parent Company financial statements and the part of the Directors' remuneration report to be audited are not in agreement with the accounting records and returns; or
- Certain disclosures of Directors' remuneration specified by law are not made; or
- We have not received all the information and explanations we require for our audit.

Under the Listing Rules we are required to review:

- The Directors' statement, set out on page 42, in relation to going concern; and
- The part of the Corporate governance statement relating to the Company's compliance with the nine provisions of the June 2008 Combined Code specified for our review.

Chris Hearld
(Senior Statutory Auditor)
for and on behalf of KPMG Audit Plc, Statutory Auditor

Chartered Accountants
1 The Embankment
Neville Street
Leeds
L51 4DW
10 March 2010

ILLUSTRATION 24-14
Auditor's Report

4. The report contains either an expression of opinion regarding the financial statements taken as a whole or an assertion to the effect that an opinion cannot be expressed. When the auditor cannot express an overall opinion, the report should state the reasons. In all cases where an auditor's name is associated with financial statements, the report should contain a clear-cut indication of the character of the auditor's examination, if any, and the degree of responsibility being taken.

In most cases, the auditor issues a standard **unmodified** or **clean opinion**, as shown in Illustration 24-14. That is, the auditor expresses the opinion that the financial statements present fairly, in all material respects, the financial position, results of operations, and cash flows of the entity in conformity with accepted accounting principles.

Certain circumstances, although they do not affect the auditor's unmodified opinion, may require the auditor to add an explanatory paragraph to the audit report. Some of the more important circumstances are as follows.

1. *Going concern.* The auditor must evaluate whether there is substantial doubt about the entity's **ability to continue as a going concern** for a reasonable period of time, taking into consideration all available information about the future. (Generally, the future is at least, but not limited to, 12 months from the end of the reporting period.) If substantial doubt exists about the company continuing as a going concern, the auditor adds to the report an explanatory note describing the potential problem.

2. *Lack of consistency.* If a company has changed accounting policies or the method of their application in a way that has a material effect on the comparability of its financial statements, the auditor should refer to the change in an explanatory paragraph of the report. Such an explanatory paragraph should identify the nature of the change and refer readers to the note in the financial statements that discusses the change in detail. The auditor's concurrence with a change is implicit unless the auditor takes exception to the change in expressing an opinion as to fair presentation in conformity with accepted accounting principles (IFRS).

3. *Emphasis of a matter.* The auditor may wish to emphasize a matter regarding the financial statements but nevertheless intends to express an unqualified opinion. For example, the auditor may wish to emphasize that the entity is a component of a larger business enterprise or that it has had significant transactions with related parties. The auditor presents such explanatory information in a separate paragraph of the report.

In some situations, however, the auditor expresses a **modified opinion**. A modified opinion can be either (1) a **qualified** opinion or (2) an **adverse** opinion, or (3) a **disclaimed** opinion.

A **qualified opinion** contains an exception to the standard opinion. Ordinarily, the exception is not of sufficient magnitude to invalidate the statements as a whole; if it were, an adverse opinion would be rendered. The usual circumstances in which the auditor may deviate from the standard unqualified report on financial statements are as follows.

1. The scope of the examination is limited or affected by conditions or restrictions.

2. The statements do not fairly present financial position or results of operations because of:

    (a) Lack of conformity with accepted accounting principles and standards.

    (b) Inadequate disclosure.

If confronted with one of the situations noted above, the auditor must offer a qualified opinion. A qualified opinion states that, except for the effects of the matter to which the qualification relates, the financial statements present fairly, in all material respects, the financial position, results of operations, and cash flows in conformity with accepted accounting principles.

Illustration 24-15 (page 1338) shows an example of an auditor's report with a modified opinion—in this case, a qualified opinion of **Helio Company** (USA). The auditor modified the opinion because the company used an accounting policy at variance with accepted accounting principles.

An **adverse opinion** is required in any report in which the exceptions to fair presentation are so material that in the independent auditor's judgment, a qualified opinion is not justified. In such a case, the financial statements taken as a whole are not presented in accordance with IFRS. Adverse opinions are rare, because most companies change their accounting to conform with IFRS. Market regulators will not permit a company listed on an exchange to have an adverse opinion.

A **disclaimer of an opinion** is appropriate when the auditor has gathered so little information on the financial statements that no opinion can be expressed.

ILLUSTRATION 24-15
Auditor's Report with
Adverse Opinion

Helio Company

Independent Auditor's Report

(Same first and second paragraphs as the standard report)

Helio Company has excluded, from property and debt in the accompanying balance sheets, certain lease obligations that, in our opinion, should be capitalized in order to conform with accepted accounting principles. If these lease obligations were capitalized, property would be increased by $1,500,000 and $1,300,000, long-term debt by $1,400,000 and $1,200,000, and retained earnings by $100,000 and $50,000 as of December 31, in the current and prior year, respectively. Additionally, net income would be decreased by $40,000 and $30,000 and earnings per share would be decreased by $.06 and $.04, respectively, for the years then ended.

In our opinion, except for the effects of not capitalizing certain lease obligations as discussed in the preceding paragraph, the financial statements referred to above present fairly, in all material respects, the financial position of Helio Company, and the results of its operations and its cash flows for the years then ended in conformity with accepted accounting principles.

The audit report should provide useful information to the investor. One investment banker noted, "Probably the first item to check is the auditor's opinion to see whether or not it is a clean one—'in conformity with accepted accounting principles'—or is qualified in regard to differences between the auditor and company management in the accounting treatment of some major item, or in the outcome of some major litigation."

Management's Reports

Management Commentary

Management commentary helps in the interpretation of the financial position, financial performance, and cash flows of a company. For example, a company like **Delhaize Group** (BEL) may present, outside the financial statements, a financial review by management that describes and explains the main features of the company's financial performance and financial position, and the principal uncertainties it faces. Such a report may include a review of:

- The main factors and influences determining financial performance, including changes in the environment in which the entity operates, the entity's response to those changes and their effect, and the company's policy for investment to maintain and enhance financial performance, including its dividend policy;
- The company's sources of funding and its targeted ratio of liabilities to equity; and
- The company's resources not recognized in the statement of financial position in accordance with IFRS.

Such commentary also provides an opportunity to understand management's objectives and its strategies for achieving those objectives. Users of financial reports, in their capacity as capital providers, routinely use the type of information provided in management commentary as a tool for evaluating an entity's prospects and its general risks, as well as the success of management's strategies for achieving its stated objectives.

For many companies, management commentary is already an important element of their communication with the capital markets, supplementing as well as complementing the financial statements. Management commentary encompasses reporting that is described in various jurisdictions as management's discussion and analysis (MD&A), operating and financial review (OFR), or management's report.

Illustration 24-16 presents an excerpt from the MD&A section of **Lectra**'s (FRA) annual report.

Lectra

ILLUSTRATION 24-16
Management's Discussion
and Analysis

Management Discussion and Analysis (in part)

4. RISK FACTORS—MANAGEMENT OF RISKS

This chapter describes the main risks facing the company having regard to the specific characteristics of its business, its structure and organization. It further describes how the company manages and prevents these risks, depending on their nature.

Identification of Risks

For internal controls to be effective, the company needs to identify and assess the risks to which it is subject. These risks are identified by means of a continuous process of analyzing the Group's external environment together with the organizational changes rendered necessary by the evolving nature of its markets. This process is overseen by the Finance division and the Legal Affairs division, with input from all Group operating and corporate divisions. The key risks that could prevent the Group from achieving its objectives are described below.

Economic Risks Specific to the Company's Business

Lectra designs, produces and markets full-line technological solutions, comprising software, CAD/CAM equipment and related services dedicated to a broad array of major global markets: fashion (apparel, accessories, and footwear), automotive (car seats and interiors, airbags), and furniture as well as a wide variety of other industries, such as the aeronautical and marine industries, wind power, personal protective equipment, etc. This activity demands continuous creativity and a relentless search for innovation, and the company consequently invests heavily in research and development. The corresponding expenditures are fully expensed in the year.

As a corollary of this policy, the company must ensure both that its innovations are not copied and that its products do not infringe third parties' intellectual property. It therefore has a dedicated team of intellectual property specialists that takes both offensive and defensive measures with regard to patents. A substantial portion of the manufacturing of the equipment the company markets is subcontracted, with Lectra providing only the R&D, final assembly and testing. . . .

Inventory valuation risk is minimized by means of just-in-time supply and manufacturing methods. Where software is concerned, the main risk lies in the revenue recognition criteria of this intangible revenue source. This risk is covered by the internal control procedures relative to the quality of accounting and financial information.

Macroeconomic Environment Risk

The solutions marketed by Group sometimes represent a major investment for clients. Part of the decision to make these investments depends on the general macroeconomic environment and on the state of the sector of activity in which the client operates. Group clients generally tend to scale back or defer their investment decisions when global economic growth slows or when a particular sector suffers a downturn or is in crisis. The current global economic and financial crisis is an additional risk factor. Its unprecedented scale is expected to lead to further deterioration in the situation of both countries and individual firms, in all sectors and in all parts of the world. The resulting sharp slowdown in activity among Group clients, their deteriorating financial performance, their uncertain outlook, and reduced access to credit are making it hard for them to finance their investments. Most companies have therefore taken drastic steps to reduce their costs, cut back or temporarily halt production, and to close plants. These situations impact Group revenues and financial results.

Underlying Concepts

The IASB Framework notes that management knows more about the company than users and therefore can increase the usefulness of financial information by identifying significant transactions that affect the company and by explaining their financial impact.

Some companies use the management commentary section of the annual report to disclose company efforts in the area of sustainability. An excerpt from the annual report of **Marks and Spencer plc** (GBR) is presented in Illustration 24-17 (page 1340).

Additional reporting on sustainability is important because it indicates the company's social responsibility and can provide insights about potential obligations that are reported in the financial statements.

While there are no formal IFRS requirements for management commentary, the IASB has initiated a project that offers a non-binding framework and limited guidance on its application, which could be adapted to the legal and economic circumstances of individual jurisdictions. While the proposal is focused on publicly traded entities, to

ILLUSTRATION 24-17
Sustainability Reporting

Marks and Spencer plc

3 more green success stories to build on . . .

1. We recycled 75% of all construction waste in 2007/08, and aim to achieve 85% in 2008/09.
2. How we design, procure and build our stores is now clearly laid out in our Sustainable Construction Manual produced in conjunction with the Building Research Establishment (BRE).
3. Like-for-like store energy usage is down by 4%.

A greener way to shop . . .

In September 2007, we opened the first of our new 'eco stores'. Located in Bournemouth, we deliberately decided to modernise one of our older stores, to find out how eco-friendly we could make it. Rising to the challenge, we incorporated a wide range of eco-features—from a green roof to capture airborne pollutants and escalators running at reduced voltage, to more efficient heating, lighting and refrigeration systems. In this way, we hope to achieve energy savings of up to 55%.

Following Bournemouth, we opened a further two green stores: at Silverburn in Pollok and a new Simply Food in Galashiels. As we continue to introduce more 'eco stores', we'll be testing a number of cutting edge techniques, such as using hempcrete—which uses hemp plant fibers as the aggregate—instead of concrete. We'll continue to trial many further innovations to ensure that as our property portfolio grows larger it also grows greener.

the extent that the framework is deemed applicable, it may be a useful tool for non-exchange traded entities, for example, privately held and state-owned enterprises.[10]

Management's Responsibilities for Financial Statements

Objective·6
Understand management's responsibilities for financials.

Management is responsible for preparing the financial statements and establishing and maintaining an effective system of internal controls. The auditor provides an independent assessment of whether the financial statements are prepared in accordance with IFRS, and for public companies, whether the internal controls are effective (see the audit opinion in Illustration 24-14 on page 1336). An example of the type of disclosure that public companies are now making is shown in Illustration 24-18.

Wm Morrison Supermarkets plc

Statement of Directors' responsibilities in respect of the Annual report and financial statements

The Directors are responsible for preparing the Annual report and the Group and Parent Company financial statements in accordance with applicable law and regulations.

Company law requires the Directors to prepare Group and Parent Company financial statements for each financial year. Under that law they are required to prepare the Group financial statements in accordance with IFRS as adopted by the EU and applicable law and have elected to prepare the Parent Company financial statements in accordance with UK Accounting Standards and applicable law (UK Generally Accepted Accounting Practice).

Under company law the Directors must not approve the financial statements unless they are satisfied that they give a true and fair view of the state of affairs of the Group and Parent Company and of their profit or loss for that period. In

preparing each of the Group and Parent Company financial statements, the Directors are required to:

- select suitable accounting policies and then apply them consistently:
- make judgements and estimates that are reasonable and prudent:
- for the Group financial statements, state whether they have been prepared in accordance with IFRS as adopted by the EU:
- for the Parent Company financial statements, state whether applicable UK Accounting Standards have been followed, subject to any material departures disclosed and explained in the Parent Company financial statements; and
- prepare the financial statements on the going concern basis unless it is inappropriate to presume that the Group and the Parent Company will continue in business.

ILLUSTRATION 24-18
Report on Management's
Responsibilities

[10]See *http://www.ifrs.org/Current+Projects/IASB+Projects/Management+Commentary/ Management+Commentary.htm.* The proposal will not result in an IFRS. Accordingly, it would not be a requirement for an entity to comply with the framework for the preparation and presentation of management commentary as a condition for asserting compliance with IFRS.

The Directors are responsible for keeping adequate accounting records that are sufficient to show and explain the Parent Company's transactions and disclose with reasonable accuracy at any time the financial positions of the Parent Company and enable them to ensure that its financial statements comply with the Companies Act 2006. They have general responsibility for taking such steps as are reasonably open to them to safeguard the assets of the Group and to prevent and detect fraud and other irregularities.

Under applicable law and regulations, the Directors are also responsible for preparing a Directors' report, Directors' remuneration report and Corporate governance statement that complies with that law and those regulations.

The Directors are responsible for the maintenance and integrity of the corporate and financial information included on the company's website. Legislation in the UK governing the preparation and dissemination of financial statements may differ from legislation in other jurisdictions.

Responsibility statement   We confirm that to the best of our knowledge:

- the financial statements, prepared in accordance with the applicable set of accounting standards, give a true and fair review of the assets, liabilities, financial position and profit or loss of the Company and its subsidiaries included in the consolidation as a whole; and
- the Directors' report includes a fair review of the development of the business and the position of the

Company and its subsidiaries included in the consolidation taken as a whole, together with a description of the principal risks and uncertainties that they face.

By order of the Board
10 March 2010

CURRENT REPORTING ISSUES

Reporting on Financial Forecasts and Projections

In recent years, the investing public's demand for more and better information has focused on disclosure of corporate expectations for the future.[11] These disclosures take one of two forms:[12]

> **Objective·7**
> Identify issues related to financial forecasts and projections.

Financial forecasts. A **financial forecast** is a set of prospective financial statements that present, to the best of the responsible party's knowledge and belief, a company's expected financial position, results of operations, and cash flows. The responsible party bases a financial forecast on conditions it expects to exist and the course of action it expects to take.

Financial projections. **Financial projections** are prospective financial statements that present, to the best of the responsible party's knowledge and belief, given one or more *hypothetical assumptions*, an entity's expected financial position, results of operations, and cash flows. The responsible party bases a financial projection on conditions it expects *would* exist and the course of action it expects *would* be taken, given one or more hypothetical assumptions.

The difference between a financial forecast and a financial projection is clear-cut: A forecast provides information on what is **expected** to happen, whereas a projection provides information on what **might** take place but is not necessarily expected to happen.

---

[11]Some areas in which companies are using financial information about the future are equipment lease-versus-buy analysis, analysis of a company's ability to successfully enter new markets, and examination of merger and acquisition opportunities. In addition, companies also prepare forecasts and projections for use by third parties in public offering documents (requiring financial forecasts), tax-oriented investments, and financial feasibility studies. Use of forward-looking data has been enhanced by the increased capability of computers to analyze, compare, and manipulate large quantities of data.

[12]There is not a specific international standard in this area. In the United States, see "Financial Forecasts and Projections" and "Guide for Prospective Financial Information," *Codification of Statements on Standards for Attestation Engagements* (New York: AICPA 2006), paras. 3.04 and 3.05.

Whether companies should be required to provide financial forecasts is the subject of intensive discussion with journalists, corporate executives, market regulators, financial analysts, accountants, and others. Predictably, there are strong arguments on either side. Listed below are some of the arguments.

Arguments for requiring published forecasts:

1. Investment decisions are based on future expectations. Therefore, information about the future facilitates better decisions.

2. Companies already circulate forecasts informally. This situation should be regulated to ensure that the forecasts are available to all investors.

3. Circumstances now change so rapidly that historical information is no longer adequate for prediction.

Arguments against requiring published forecasts:

1. No one can foretell the future. Therefore, forecasts will inevitably be wrong. Worse, they may mislead if they convey an impression of precision about the future.

2. Companies may strive only to meet their published forecasts, thereby failing to produce results that are in the shareholders' best interest.

3. If forecasts prove inaccurate, there will be recriminations and probably legal actions.[13]

4. Disclosure of forecasts will be detrimental to organizations, because forecasts will inform competitors (foreign and domestic), as well as investors.

Auditing standards establish guidelines for the preparation and presentation of financial forecasts and projections.[14] They require accountants to provide (1) a summary of significant assumptions used in the forecast or projection and (2) guidelines for minimum presentation.

To encourage management to disclose prospective financial information, market regulators have established a **safe harbor rule**. It provides protection to a company that presents an erroneous forecast, as long as the company prepared the forecast on a reasonable basis and disclosed it in good faith.[15] However, many companies note that the safe harbor rule does not work in practice, since it does not cover oral statements, nor has it kept them from investor lawsuits.

Experience in Great Britain

Great Britain permits financial forecasts, and the results have been fairly successful. Some significant differences do exist between the British and other countries' business and legal environments.[16] But, such differences probably could be overcome if influential interests in various other countries cooperated to produce an atmosphere conducive to

---

[13]The issue is serious. Over a recent three-year period, 8 percent of the companies on the New York Stock Exchange (NYSE) were sued because of an alleged lack of financial disclosure. Companies complain that they are subject to lawsuits whenever the share price drops. And as one executive noted, "You can even be sued if the share price goes up—because you did not disclose the good news fast enough."

[14]Op cit., par. 1.02.

[15]For example, the U.S. SEC Issued "Safe-Harbor Rule for Projections," *Release No. 5993* (Washington: SEC, 1979). The U.S. Private Securities Litigation Reform Act of 1995 recognizes that some information that is useful to investors is inherently subject to less certainty or reliability than other information. By providing safe harbor for forward-looking statements, this should facilitate access to this information by investors.

[16]The British system, for example, does not permit litigation on forecasted information, and the solicitor (lawyer) is not permitted to work on a contingent fee basis. See "A Case for Forecasting—The British Have Tried It and Find That It Works," *World* (New York: Peat, Marwick, Mitchell & Co., Autumn 1978), pp. 10–13.

quality forecasting. A typical British forecast adapted from a construction company's report to support a public offering of shares is as follows.

> Profits have grown substantially over the past 10 years and directors are confident of being able to continue this expansion. . . . While the rate of expansion will be dependent on the level of economic activity in Ireland and England, the group is well structured to avail itself of opportunities as they arise, particularly in the field of property development, which is expected to play an increasingly important role in the group's future expansion.
>
> Profits before taxation for the half year ended 30th June were 402,000 pounds. On the basis of trading experiences since that date and the present level of sales and completions, the directors expect that in the absence of unforeseen circumstances, the group's profits before taxation for the year to 31st December will be not less than 960,000 pounds.
>
> No dividends will be paid in respect of the current year. In a full financial year, on the basis of above forecasts (not including full year profits) it would be the intention of the board, assuming current rates of tax, to recommend dividends totaling 40% (of after-tax profits), which will be payable in the next two years.

ILLUSTRATION 24-19
Financial Forecast of a British Company

A general narrative-type forecast might appear as follows.

> On the basis of promotions planned by the company for the second half of the fiscal year, net earnings for that period are expected to be approximately the same as those for the first half of the fiscal year, with net earnings for the third quarter expected to make the predominant contribution to net earnings for the second half of the year.

ILLUSTRATION 24-20
Financial Forecast for a U.S. Company

Questions of Liability

What happens if a company does not meet its forecasts? Can the company and the auditor be sued? If a company, for example, projects an earnings increase of 15 percent and achieves only 5 percent, should shareholders be permitted to have some judicial recourse against the company?

One court case involving **Monsanto Chemical Corporation** (USA) set a precedent. In this case, Monsanto predicted that sales would increase 8 to 9 percent and that earnings would rise 4 to 5 percent. In the last part of the year, the demand for Monsanto's products dropped as a result of a business turndown. Instead of increasing, the company's earnings declined. Investors sued the company because the projected earnings figure was erroneous, but a judge dismissed the suit because the forecasts were the best estimates of qualified people whose intents were honest.

As indicated earlier, safe harbor rules are intended to protect companies that provide good-faith projections. However, much concern exists as to how market regulators and the courts will interpret such terms as "good faith" and "reasonable assumptions" when erroneous forecasts mislead users of this information.

Internet Financial Reporting

Most companies now use the power and reach of the Internet to provide more useful information to financial statement readers. All large companies have Internet sites, and a large proportion of companies' websites contain links to their financial statements and other disclosures. The popularity of such reporting is not surprising, since companies can reduce the costs of printing and disseminating paper reports with the use of Internet reporting.

Does Internet financial reporting improve the usefulness of a company's financial reports? Yes, in several ways: First, dissemination of reports via the Web allows firms **to communicate more easily and quickly with users** than do traditional paper reports.

In addition, **Internet reporting allows users to take advantage of tools** such as search engines and hyperlinks to quickly find information about the firm and, sometimes, to download the information for analysis, perhaps in computer spreadsheets. Finally, **Internet reporting can help make financial reports more relevant** by allowing companies to report expanded disaggregated data and more timely data than is possible through paper-based reporting. For example, some companies voluntarily report weekly sales data and segment operating data on their websites.

Given the widespread use of the Internet by investors and creditors, it is not surprising that organizations are developing new technologies and standards to further enable Internet financial reporting. An example is the increasing use of Extensible Business Reporting Language (XBRL). **XBRL** is a computer language adapted from the code of the Internet. It "tags" accounting data to correspond to financial reporting items that are reported in the statement of financial position, income statement, and the cash flow statement. Once tagged, any company's XBRL data can be easily processed using spreadsheets and other computer programs. In fact, XBRL is a global language with common tags across countries. As more companies prepare their financial reports using XBRL, users will be able to easily search a company's reports, extract and analyze data, and perform financial comparisons within industries and across countries.[17]

NEW FORMATS, NEW DISCLOSURE

What do the numbers mean?

As indicated earlier in the Convergence Corner discussions, the IASB and the FASB are exploring better ways to present information in the financial statements. Recently, these two standard-setters have issued a discussion paper that requests input on a proposed reformatting of the financial statements. The table below provides a "snapshot" of the proposed changes (go to *http://www.fasb.org/ project/financial_statement_presentation.shtml* to learn more about this joint international project).

Statement of Financial Position	Statement of Comprehensive Income	Statement of Cash Flows
Business	Business	Business
• Operating assets and liabilities	• Operating income and expenses	• Operating cash flows
• Investing assets and liabilities	• Investing income and expenses	• Investing cash flows
Financing	Financing	Financing
• Financing assets	• Financing asset income	• Financing asset cash flows
• Financing liabilities	• Financing liability expenses	• Financing liability cash flows
Income Taxes	Income Taxes	Income Taxes

As indicated, each statement will use the same format. While the proposed changes will not affect the measurement of individual financial statement elements, the use of a consistent format (e.g., Business, Financing, Income Taxes), will help users understand the interrelationships in the financial statements. In addition, a new schedule reconciling cash flows to comprehensive income will be provided. As part of this schedule, changes in fair value will be included. It is a good thing the timeline for the project is lengthy, as these changes in presentation are significant.

Fraudulent Financial Reporting

Objective·8
Describe the profession's response to fraudulent financial reporting.

Economic crime is on the rise around the world. A recent global survey of over 3,000 executives from 54 countries documented the types of economic crimes, as shown in Illustration 24-21.[18]

---

[17]C. Twarowski, "Financial Data 'on Steroids'," *Washington Post* (August 19, 2008), p. D01. Also, see *www.xbrl.org/us/us/BusinessCaseForXBRL.pdf* for additional information on XBRL. The IASB and the FASB are collaborating to implement XBRL with their standards. See *http://www.ifrs.org/XBRL/XBRL/htm*.

[18]PricewaterhouseCoopers, *The Global Economic Crime Survey: Economic Crime in a Downturn*, (November 2009).

ILLUSTRATION 24-21
Types of Economic Crime

As indicated, a wide range of economic crimes are reported, and unfortunately for the top three areas, the trend is not good. As shown in Illustration 24-22, there has been a steady upward trend of economic crime.

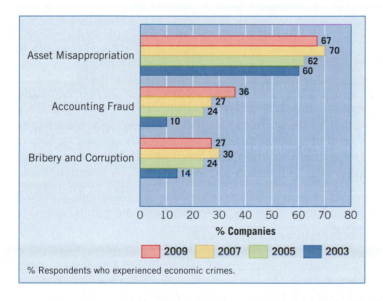

ILLUSTRATION 24-22
Trends in Reported Frauds

Important and troubling for our study are the statistics for accounting frauds, which have more than tripled since 2003.

Fraudulent financial reporting is defined as "intentional or reckless conduct, whether act or omission, that results in materially misleading financial statements."[19] Fraudulent reporting can involve gross and deliberate distortion of corporate records (such as inventory count tags), or misapplication of accounting policies (failure to

---

[19]"Report of the National Commission on Fraudulent Financial Reporting" (Washington, D.C., 1987), page 2. Unintentional errors as well as corporate improprieties (such as tax fraud, employee embezzlements, and so on) which do not cause the financial statements to be misleading are excluded from the definition of fraudulent financial reporting.

disclose material transactions). The frauds reported above and recent events involving such well-known companies as **Parmalat** (ITA), **Mahindra Satyam** (IND), and **Société Générale** (FRA) indicate that more must be done to address this issue.

Causes of Fraudulent Financial Reporting

Fraudulent financial reporting usually occurs because of conditions in a company's internal or external environment. Influences in the **internal environment** relate to poor internal control systems, management's poor attitude toward ethics, or perhaps a company's liquidity or profitability. Those in the **external environment** may relate to industry conditions, overall business environment, or legal and regulatory considerations.

General incentives for fraudulent financial reporting vary. Common ones are the desire to obtain a higher share price, to avoid default on a loan covenant, or to make a personal gain of some type (additional compensation, promotion). Situational pressures on the company or an individual manager also may lead to fraudulent financial reporting. Examples of these situational pressures include the following.

- *Sudden decreases in revenue or market share* for a single company or an entire industry.
- *Unrealistic budget pressures* may occur when headquarters arbitrarily determines profit objectives (particularly for short-term results) and budgets without taking actual conditions into account.
- *Financial pressure resulting from bonus plans* that depend on short-term economic performance. This pressure is particularly acute when the bonus is a significant component of the individual's total compensation.

Opportunities for fraudulent financial reporting are present in circumstances when the fraud is easy to commit and when detection is difficult. Frequently these opportunities arise from:

1. *The absence of a board of directors or audit committee* that vigilantly oversees the financial reporting process.
2. *Weak or non-existent internal accounting controls.* This situation can occur, for example, when a company's revenue system is overloaded as a result of a rapid expansion of sales, an acquisition of a new division, or the entry into a new, unfamiliar line of business.
3. *Unusual or complex transactions* such as the consolidation of two companies, the divestiture or closing of a specific operation, and the purchase and sale of derivative instruments.
4. *Accounting estimates requiring significant subjective judgment* by company management, such as the allowance for loan losses and the estimated liability for warranty expense.
5. *Ineffective internal audit staffs* resulting from inadequate staff size and severely limited audit scope.

A weak corporate ethical climate contributes to these situations. Opportunities for fraudulent financial reporting also increase dramatically when the accounting policies followed in reporting transactions are non-existent, evolving, or subject to varying interpretations.[20]

---

[20]The discussion in this section is based on the Report of the National Commission on Fraudulent Financial Reporting, pp. 23–24. See "2004 and 2010 Reports to the Nation on Occupational Fraud and Abuse, Association of Certified Fraud Examiners" (*www.cfenet.com/ pdfs/2004RttN.pdf* and *http//butest.acfe.com/rttn/rttn-2010.pdf*) for fraudulent financial reporting causes and consequences.

As discussed earlier, auditing regulators have issued numerous auditing standards in response to concerns of the accounting profession, the media, and the public.[21] For example, the recent standard on fraudulent financial reporting "raises the bar" on the performance of financial statement audits by explicitly requiring auditors to assess the risk of material financial misstatement due to fraud.[22]

Criteria for Making Accounting and Reporting Choices

Throughout this textbook, we have stressed the need to provide information that is useful to predict the amounts, timing, and uncertainty of future cash flows. To achieve this objective, companies must make judicious choices between alternative accounting concepts, methods, and means of disclosure. You are probably surprised by the large number of choices that exist among acceptable alternatives.

You should recognize, however, as indicated in Chapter 1, that accounting is greatly influenced by its environment. It does not exist in a vacuum. Therefore, it is unrealistic to assume that the profession can entirely eliminate alternative presentations of certain transactions and events. Nevertheless, we are hopeful that the profession, by adhering to the conceptual framework, will be able to focus on the needs of financial statement users and eliminate diversity where appropriate. The IASB's focus on principles-based standards are directed at these very issues. It seeks to develop guidance that will result in accounting and financial reporting that reflects the economic substance of the transactions, not the desired financial result of management. The profession must continue its efforts to develop a sound foundation upon which to build financial standards and practice. As Aristotle said, "The correct beginning is more than half the whole."

> **Underlying Concepts**
> The IASB statements on the objective of financial reporting, elements of financial statements, and qualitative characteristics of accounting information are important steps in the right direction.

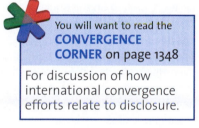

You will want to read the **CONVERGENCE CORNER** on page 1348

For discussion of how international convergence efforts relate to disclosure.

---

[21]Because the profession believes that the role of the auditor is not well understood outside the profession, much attention has been focused on the expectation gap. The **expectation gap** is the gap between (1) the expectation of financial statement users concerning the level of assurance they believe the independent auditor provides, and (2) the assurance that the independent auditor actually does provide under generally accepted auditing standards.

[22] See International Standard on Auditing 240, "The Auditor's Responsibilities Relating to Fraud in an Audit of Financial Statements," *Handbook of International Quality Control, Auditing, Review, Other Assurance, and Other Related Services Pronouncements* (April 2010).

CONVERGENCE CORNER

IFRS and U.S. GAAP disclosure requirements are similar in many regards. The IFRS addressing various disclosure issues are *IAS 24* ("Related Party Disclosures"), disclosure and recognition of post-statement of financial position events in *IAS 10* ("Events after the Balance Sheet Date"), segment reporting IFRS provisions in *IFRS 8* ("Operating Segments"), and interim reporting requirements in *IAS 34* ("Interim Financial Reporting").

RELEVANT FACTS

• Due to the broader range of judgments allowed in more principles-based IFRS, note disclosures generally are more expansive under IFRS compared to U.S. GAAP.

• U.S. GAAP and IFRS have similar standards on post-statement of financial position (subsequent) events. That is, under both sets of standards, events that occurred after the statement of financial position date that provide additional evidence of conditions that existed at the statement of financial position date are recognized in the financial statements.

• Subsequent events under IFRS are evaluated through the date that financial instruments are "authorized for issue." U.S. GAAP uses the date when financial statements are "issued." Also, for share dividends and splits in the subsequent period, IFRS does not adjust but U.S. GAAP does.

• Like IFRS, U.S. GAAP requires that for transactions with related parties, companies disclose the amounts involved in a transaction, the amount, terms and nature of the outstanding balances, and any doubtful amounts related to those outstanding balances for each major category of related parties. There is no specific requirement to disclose the name of the related party.

• Following the recent issuance of *IFRS 8*, "Operating Segments," the requirements under IFRS and U.S. GAAP are very similar. That is, both standards use the management approach to identify reportable segments, and similar segment disclosures are required.

ABOUT THE NUMBERS

Because IFRS and U.S. GAAP are quite similar in their disclosure provisions, we provide some observations on the application of IFRS by foreign companies listing securities in the United States. Recently, the staff of the U.S. SEC reviewed the financial statements filed with the SEC by 100 foreign issuers, prepared for the first time using IFRS. The staff did not make any statements regarding the overall *quality* of the reports but did identify areas where additional questions might be asked. Here are some of the items that warranted staff comment:

1. Revenue recognition, especially where a company provided generic policy disclosure but did not provide disclosure specific to its circumstances.
2. Intangible assets and goodwill, including the factors that led a company to recognize them in a business combination.
3. Companies' policies for identifying and evaluating impairment, the circumstances resulting in impairment recognition, or the circumstances surrounding impairment reversals of long-lived assets including goodwill.
4. Leases, including their terms and the future minimum payments under operating and financial leases.
5. Contingent liabilities, including their nature and estimated financial effects.
6. The significant terms of financial instruments, including derivatives, their effects on future cash flow, and the recognition and measurement criteria the company applied in accounting for financial instruments.
7. Additional issues related to income statement and cash flow statement formats and related notes.

ON THE HORIZON

Sir David Tweedie, chair of the IASB, recently stated, "By 2011–2012, U.S. and international accounting should be pretty much the same." There is no question that IFRS and U.S. GAAP are converging quickly. We have provided the Convergence Corner discussions to help you understand the issues surrounding convergence as they relate to intermediate accounting. After reading these discussions, you should realize that IFRS and U.S. GAAP are very similar in many areas, with differences in those areas revolving around some minor technical points. In other situations, the differences are major; for example, IFRS does not permit LIFO inventory accounting. Our hope is that the FASB and IASB can quickly complete their convergence efforts, resulting in a single set of high-quality accounting standards for use by companies around the world.

SUMMARY OF LEARNING OBJECTIVES

`•1` **Review the full disclosure principle and describe implementation problems.** The full disclosure principle calls for financial reporting of any financial facts significant enough to influence the judgment of an informed reader. Implementing the full disclosure principle is difficult, because the cost of disclosure can be substantial and the benefits difficult to assess. Disclosure requirements have increased because of (1) the growing complexity of the business environment, (2) the necessity for timely information, and (3) the use of accounting as a control and monitoring device.

`•2` **Explain the use of notes in financial statement preparation.** Notes are the accountant's means of amplifying or explaining the items presented in the main body of the statements. Notes can explain in qualitative terms information pertinent to specific financial statement items, and can provide supplementary data of a quantitative nature. Common note disclosures relate to such items as accounting policies; inventories; property, plant, and equipment; creditor claims; contingencies and commitments; and subsequent events.

`•3` **Discuss the disclosure requirements for major business segments.** Aggregated figures hide much information about the composition of these consolidated figures. There is no way to tell from the consolidated data the extent to which the differing product lines contribute to the company's profitability, risk, and growth potential. As a result, the profession requires segment information in certain situations.

`•4` **Describe the accounting problems associated with interim reporting.** Interim reports cover periods of less than one year. Two viewpoints exist regarding interim reports. The discrete approach holds that each interim period should be treated as a separate accounting period. The integral approach is that the interim report is an integral part of the annual report and that deferrals and accruals should take into consideration what will happen for the entire year. IFRS requires use of the discrete approach.

Companies should use the same accounting policies for interim reports that they use for annual reports. A number of unique reporting problems develop related to the following items: (1) income taxes and (2) seasonality.

`•5` **Identify the major disclosures in the auditor's report.** The auditor expresses an unmodified or clean opinion if satisfied that the financial statements present the financial position, results of operations, and cash flows fairly in accordance with IFRS. A qualified opinion contains an exception to the standard opinion; ordinarily the exception is not of sufficient magnitude to invalidate the statements as a whole.

An adverse opinion is required when the exceptions to fair presentation are so material that a qualified opinion is not justified. A disclaimer of an opinion is appropriate when the auditor has so little information on the financial statements that no opinion can be expressed.

`•6` **Understand management's responsibilities for financials.** Management commentary gives management an opportunity to complement information reported in the financial statements. This commentary frequently discusses financial aspects of an enterprise's business, such as liquidity, capital resources, results of operations, important risks, and sustainability. Management's responsibility for the financial statements is often indicated in a letter to shareholders in the annual report.

`•7` **Identify issues related to financial forecasts and projections.** Companies are permitted (not required) to include profit forecasts in their reports. To encourage management to disclose such information, market regulators have issued a safe harbor rule. The rule provides protection to a company that presents an erroneous forecast, as long as it prepared the projection on a reasonable basis and disclosed it in good faith. However, the safe harbor rule has not worked well in practice.

KEY TERMS

accounting policies, *1317*
adjusted subsequent events, *1324*
adverse opinion, *1337*
auditor, *1335*
auditor's report, *1335*
common costs, *1329*
differential disclosure, *1315*
disclaimer of an opinion, *1337*
discrete approach, *1330*
errors, *1322*
events after the reporting date, *1323*
financial forecast, *1341*
financial projection, *1341*
fraud, *1322*
fraudulent financial reporting, *1345*
full disclosure principle, *1314*
integral approach, *1330*
interim reports, *1330*
management approach, *1327*
management commentary, *1338*
modified opinion, *1337*
non-adjusted subsequent events, *1324*
notes to financial statements, *1319*
operating segment, *1327*
qualified opinion, *1337*
related-party transactions, *1322*
safe harbor rule, *1342*
seasonality, *1332*
subsequent events, *1323*
unmodified or clean opinion, *1336*
XBRL, *1344*

·8 **Describe the profession's response to fraudulent financial reporting.** Fraudulent financial reporting is intentional or reckless conduct, whether through act or omission, that results in materially misleading financial statements. Fraudulent financial reporting usually occurs because of poor internal control, management's poor attitude toward ethics, poor performance, and so on.

APPENDIX **24A** **BASIC FINANCIAL STATEMENT ANALYSIS**

What would be important to you in studying a company's financial statements? The answer depends on your particular interest—whether you are a creditor, shareholder, potential investor, manager, government agency, or labor leader. For example, **short-term creditors** such as banks are primarily interested in the ability of the firm to pay its currently maturing obligations. In that case, you would examine the current assets and their relation to short-term liabilities to evaluate the short-run solvency of the firm.

Bondholders, on the other hand, look more to long-term indicators, such as the enterprise's capital structure, past and projected earnings, and changes in financial position. **Shareholders**, present or prospective, also are interested in many of the features considered by a long-term creditor. As a shareholder, you would focus on the earnings picture, because changes in it greatly affect the market price of your investment. You also would be concerned with the financial position of the company because it affects indirectly the stability of earnings.

The **managers** of a company are concerned about the composition of its capital structure and about the changes and trends in earnings. This financial information has a direct influence on the type, amount, and cost of external financing that the company can obtain. In addition, the company managers find financial information useful on a day-to-day operating basis in such areas as capital budgeting, breakeven analysis, variance analysis, gross margin analysis, and for internal control purposes.

PERSPECTIVE ON FINANCIAL STATEMENT ANALYSIS

Objective·9
Understand the approach to financial statement analysis.

Readers of financial statements can gather information by examining relationships between items on the statements and identifying trends in these relationships. The relationships are expressed numerically in ratios and percentages, and trends are identified through comparative analysis.

A problem with learning how to analyze statements is that the means may become an end in itself. Analysts could identify and calculate thousands of possible relationships and trends. If one knows only how to calculate ratios and trends without understanding how such information can be used, little is accomplished. Therefore, a logical approach to financial statement analysis is necessary, consisting of the following steps.

Underlying Concepts

Because financial statements report on the past, they emphasize the *qualitative characteristic of feedback value.* This feedback value is useful because it can be used to better achieve the *qualitative characteristic of predictive value.*

1. *Know the questions for which you want to find answers.* As indicated earlier, various groups have different types of interest in a company.
2. *Know the questions that particular ratios and comparisons are able to help answer.* These will be discussed in this appendix.
3. *Match 1 and 2 above.* By such a matching, the statement analysis will have a logical direction and purpose.

Several caveats must be mentioned. **Financial statements report on the past.** Thus, analysis of these data is an examination of the past. When using such information in a decision-making (future-oriented) process, analysts assume that the past is a reasonable basis for predicting the future. This is usually a reasonable approach, but its limitations should be recognized.

Also, ratio and trend analyses will help identify a company's present strengths and weaknesses. They may serve as "red flags" indicating problem areas. In many cases, however, such analyses will not reveal **why** things are as they are. Finding answers about "why" usually requires an in-depth analysis and an awareness of many factors about a company that are not reported in the financial statements.

Another caveat is that a **single ratio by itself is not likely to be very useful**. For example, analysts may generally view a current ratio of 2 to 1 (current assets are twice current liabilities) as satisfactory. However, if the industry average is 3 to 1, such a conclusion may be invalid. Even given this industry average, one may conclude that the particular company is doing well if one knows the previous year's ratio was 1.5 to 1. Consequently, to derive meaning from ratios, analysts need some standard against which to compare them. Such a standard may come from industry averages, past years' amounts, a particular competitor, or planned levels.

Finally, **awareness of the limitations of accounting numbers used in an analysis** is important. We will discuss some of these limitations and their consequences later in this appendix.

RATIO ANALYSIS

In analyzing financial statement data, analysts use various devices to bring out the comparative and relative significance of the financial information presented. These devices include ratio analysis, comparative analysis, percentage analysis, and examination of related data. No one device is more useful than another. Every situation is different, and analysts often obtain the needed answers only upon close examination of the interrelationships among all the data provided. Ratio analysis is the starting point. Ratios can be classified as follows.

> **Objective·10**
> Identify major analytic ratios and describe their calculation.

MAJOR TYPES OF RATIOS

LIQUIDITY RATIOS. Measures of the company's short-run ability to pay its maturing obligations.

ACTIVITY RATIOS. Measures of how effectively the company is using the assets employed.

PROFITABILITY RATIOS. Measures of the degree of success or failure of a given company or division for a given period of time.

COVERAGE RATIOS. Measures of the degree of protection for long-term creditors and investors.[23]

We have integrated discussions and illustrations about the computation and use of these financial ratios throughout this book. Illustration 24A-1 (page 1352) summarizes all of the ratios presented in the book and identifies the specific chapters that presented that material.

---

[23]Some analysts use other terms to categorize these ratios. For example, liquidity ratios are sometimes referred to as *solvency* ratios; activity ratios as *turnover* or *efficiency* ratios; and coverage ratios as *leverage* or *capital structure* ratios.

SUMMARY OF RATIOS PRESENTED IN EARLIER CHAPTERS		
Ratio	Formula for Computation	Reference
I. Liquidity		
1. **Current ratio**	$\dfrac{\text{Current assets}}{\text{Current liabilities}}$	Chapter 13, p. 693
2. **Quick or acid-test ratio**	$\dfrac{\text{Cash, short-term investments, and net receivables}}{\text{Current liabilities}}$	Chapter 13, p. 694
3. **Current cash debt coverage ratio**	$\dfrac{\text{Net cash provided by operating activities}}{\text{Average current liabilities}}$	Chapter 5, p. 211
II. Activity		
4. **Receivables turnover**	$\dfrac{\text{Net sales}}{\text{Average trade receivables (net)}}$	Chapter 7, p. 370
5. **Inventory turnover**	$\dfrac{\text{Cost of goods sold}}{\text{Average inventory}}$	Chapter 9, p. 490
6. **Asset turnover**	$\dfrac{\text{Net sales}}{\text{Average total assets}}$	Chapter 11, p. 586
III. Profitability		
7. **Profit margin on sales**	$\dfrac{\text{Net income}}{\text{Net sales}}$	Chapter 11, p. 586
8. **Rate of return on assets**	$\dfrac{\text{Net income}}{\text{Average total assets}}$	Chapter 11, p. 586
9. **Rate of return on share capital— equity**	$\dfrac{\text{Net income minus preference dividends}}{\text{Average ordinary shareholders' equity}}$	Chapter 15, p. 794
10. **Earnings per share**	$\dfrac{\text{Net income minus preference dividends}}{\text{Weighted shares outstanding}}$	Chapter 16, p. 839
11. **Payout ratio**	$\dfrac{\text{Cash dividends}}{\text{Net income—preference dividends}}$	Chapter 15, p. 795
IV. Coverage		
12. **Debt to total assets ratio**	$\dfrac{\text{Debt}}{\text{Total assets}}$	Chapter 14, p. 747
13. **Times interest earned**	$\dfrac{\text{Income before interest expense and taxes}}{\text{Interest expense}}$	Chapter 14, p. 747
14. **Cash debt coverage ratio**	$\dfrac{\text{Net cash provided by operating activities}}{\text{Average total liabilities}}$	Chapter 5, p. 211
15. **Book value per share**	$\dfrac{\text{Ordinary shareholders' equity}}{\text{Outstanding shares}}$	Chapter 15, p. 795

You can find additional coverage of these ratios, accompanied by assignment material, at the book's companion website, at **www.wiley.com/college/kieso**. This supplemental coverage takes the form of a comprehensive case adapted from the annual report of a large international chemical company that we have disguised under the name of Anetek Chemical Corporation.

Objective·11
Explain the limitations of ratio analysis.

Limitations of Ratio Analysis

The reader of financial statements must understand the basic limitations associated with ratio analysis. As analytical tools, ratios are attractive because they are simple and convenient. But too frequently, decision-makers base their decisions on only these simple computations. The ratios are only as good as the data upon which they are based and the information with which they are compared.

One important limitation of ratios is that they generally are **based on historical cost, which can lead to distortions in measuring performance**. Inaccurate assessments of the enterprise's financial condition and performance can result from failing to incorporate fair value information.

Also, investors must remember that **where estimated items (such as depreciation and amortization) are significant, income ratios lose some of their credibility**. For example, income recognized before the termination of a company's life is an approximation. In analyzing the income statement, users should be aware of the uncertainty surrounding the computation of net income. As one writer aptly noted, "The physicist has long since conceded that the location of an electron is best expressed by a probability curve. Surely an abstraction like earnings per share is even more subject to the rules of probability and risk."[24]

Probably the greatest limitation of ratio analysis is the **difficult problem of achieving comparability among firms in a given industry**. Achieving comparability requires that the analyst (1) identify basic differences in companies' accounting policies and procedures, and (2) adjust the balances to achieve comparability. Basic differences in accounting usually involve one of the following areas.

> **Underlying Concepts**
>
> Consistency and comparability are important concepts for financial statement analysis. If the principles and assumptions used to prepare the financial statements are continually changing, accurate assessments of a company's progress become difficult.

1. Inventory valuation (FIFO, average cost).
2. Depreciation methods, particularly the use of straight-line versus accelerated depreciation.
3. Capitalization versus expensing of certain costs.
4. Capitalization of leases versus non-capitalization.
5. Investments in ordinary shares carried under the equity method versus fair value.
6. Differing treatments of postretirement benefit costs.
7. Questionable practices of defining discontinued operations, impairments, and unusual items.

The use of these different alternatives can make a significant difference in the ratios computed. For example, at one time **Anheuser-Busch** (now **InBev** (BEL)) (USA) noted that if it had used a different inventory method, inventories would have increased approximately $33,000,000. Such an increase would have a substantive impact on the current ratio. Several studies have analyzed the impact of different accounting methods on financial statement analysis. The differences in income that can develop are staggering in some cases. Investors must be aware of the potential pitfalls if they are to be able to make the proper adjustments.[25]

Finally, analysts should recognize that a **substantial amount of important information** is not included in a company's financial statements. Events involving such things as industry changes, management changes, competitors' actions, technological developments, government actions, and union activities are often critical to a company's successful operation. These events occur continuously, and information about them must come from careful analysis of financial reports in the media and other sources. Indeed many argue, in what is known as the **efficient-market hypothesis**, that financial statements contain "no surprises" to those engaged in market activities. They contend that the effect of these events is known in the marketplace—and the price of the company's shares adjusts accordingly—well before the issuance of such reports.

---

[24]Richard E. Cheney, "How Dependable Is the Bottom Line?" *The Financial Executive* (January 1971), p. 12.

[25]See for example, Eugene A. Imhoff, Jr., Robert C. Lipe, and David W. Wright, "Operating Leases: Impact of Constructive Capitalization," *Accounting Horizons* (March 1991).

COMPARATIVE ANALYSIS

Comparative analysis presents the same information for two or more different dates or periods, so that like items may be compared. Ratio analysis provides only a single snapshot, for one given point or period in time. In a comparative analysis, an investment analyst can concentrate on a given item and determine whether it appears to be growing or diminishing year by year and the proportion of such change to related items. Generally, companies present comparative financial statements. They typically include two years of statement of financial position information and three years of income statement information.

In addition, many companies include in their annual reports five- or ten-year summaries of pertinent data that permit readers to examine and analyze trends. As indicated in IFRS, "the presentation of comparative financial statements in annual and other reports enhances the usefulness of such reports and brings out more clearly the nature and trends of current changes affecting the enterprise." Illustration 24A-2 presents a five-year condensed statement, with additional supporting data, of Anetek Chemical Corporation.

ILLUSTRATION 24A-2
Condensed Comparative
Financial Information

ANETEK CHEMICAL CORPORATION
CONDENSED COMPARATIVE STATEMENTS
(000,000 OMITTED)

	2011	2010	2009	2008	2007	10 Years Ago 2001	20 Years Ago 1991
Sales and other revenue:							
Net sales	$1,600.0	$1,350.0	$1,309.7	$1,176.2	$1,077.5	$636.2	$170.7
Other revenue	75.0	50.0	39.4	34.1	24.6	9.0	3.7
Total	1,675.0	1,400.0	1,349.1	1,210.3	1,102.1	645.2	174.4
Costs and other charges:							
Cost of sales	1,000.0	850.0	827.4	737.6	684.2	386.8	111.0
Depreciation and amortization	150.0	150.0	122.6	115.6	98.7	82.4	14.2
Selling and administrative expenses	225.0	150.0	144.2	133.7	126.7	66.7	10.7
Interest expense	50.0	25.0	28.5	20.7	9.4	8.9	1.8
Income taxes	100.0	75.0	79.5	73.5	68.3	42.4	12.4
Total	1,525.0	1,250.0	1,202.2	1,081.1	987.3	587.2	150.1
Net income for the year	$ 150.0	$ 150.0	$ 146.9	$ 129.2	$ 114.8	$ 58.0	$ 24.3
Other Statistics							
Earnings per share on ordinary shares (in dollars)[a]	$ 5.00	$ 5.00	$ 4.90	$ 3.58	$ 3.11	$ 1.66	$ 1.06
Cash dividends per share on ordinary shares (in dollars)[a]	2.25	2.15	1.95	1.79	1.71	1.11	0.25
Cash dividends declared on ordinary shares	67.5	64.5	58.5	64.6	63.1	38.8	5.7
Share dividend at approximate market value				46.8		27.3	
Taxes (major)	144.5	125.9	116.5	105.6	97.8	59.8	17.0
Wages paid	389.3	325.6	302.1	279.6	263.2	183.2	48.6
Cost of employee benefits	50.8	36.2	32.9	28.7	27.2	18.4	4.4
Number of employees at year end (thousands)	47.4	36.4	35.0	33.8	33.2	26.6	14.6
Additions to property	306.3	192.3	241.5	248.3	166.1	185.0	49.0

[a]Adjusted for share splits and share dividends.

PERCENTAGE (COMMON-SIZE) ANALYSIS

Analysts also use percentage analysis to help them evaluate and compare companies. **Percentage analysis** consists of reducing a series of related amounts to a series of percentages of a given base. For example, analysts frequently express all items in an income statement as a percentage of sales or sometimes as a percentage of cost of goods sold. They may analyze a statement of financial position on the basis of total assets. Percentage analysis facilitates comparison and is helpful in evaluating the relative size of items or the relative change in items. A conversion of absolute dollar amounts to percentages may also facilitate comparison between companies of different size.

Objective•13
Describe techniques of percentage analysis.

Illustration 24A-3 shows a comparative analysis of the expense section of Anetek for the last two years.

ILLUSTRATION 24A-3
Horizontal Percentage Analysis

ANETEK CHEMICAL CORPORATION HORIZONTAL COMPARATIVE ANALYSIS (000,000 OMITTED)				
	2011	2010	Difference	% Change Inc. (Dec.)
Cost of sales	$1,000.0	$850.0	$150.0	17.6%
Depreciation and amortization	150.0	150.0	0	0
Selling and administrative expenses	225.0	150.0	75.0	50.0
Interest expense	50.0	25.0	25.0	100.0
Income taxes	100.0	75.0	25.0	33.3

This approach, normally called **horizontal analysis**, indicates the proportionate change over a period of time. It is especially useful in evaluating trends, because absolute changes are often deceiving.

Another comparative approach, called **vertical analysis**, is the proportional expression of each financial statement item in a given period to a base figure. For example, Anetek Chemical's income statement using this approach appears in Illustration 24A-4.

ILLUSTRATION 24A-4
Vertical Percentage Analysis

ANETEK CHEMICAL CORPORATION INCOME STATEMENT (000,000 OMITTED)		
	Amount	Percentage of Total Revenue
Net sales	$1,600.0	96%
Other revenue	75.0	4
Total revenue	1,675.0	100
Less:		
Cost of sales	1,000.0	60
Depreciation and amortization	150.0	9
Selling and administrative expenses	225.0	13
Interest expense	50.0	3
Income taxes	100.0	6
Total expenses	1,525.0	91
Net income	$ 150.0	9%

Vertical analysis is frequently called **common-size analysis** because it reduces all of the statement items to a "common size." That is, all of the elements within each statement are expressed in percentages of some common number and always add up to 100 percent. Common-size (percentage) analysis reveals the composition of each of the financial statements.

In the analysis of the statement of financial position, common-size analysis answers such questions as: What percentage of the capital structure is equity, current liabilities, and long-term debt? What is the mix of assets (percentage-wise) with which the company has chosen to conduct business? What percentage of current assets is in inventory, receivables, and so forth?

Common-size analysis of the income statement typically relates each item to sales. It is instructive to know what proportion of each sales dollar is absorbed by various costs and expenses incurred by the enterprise.

Analysts may use common-size statements to compare one company's statements from different years, to detect trends not evident from comparing absolute amounts. Also, common-size statements provide intercompany comparisons regardless of size because they recast financial statements into a comparable common-size format.

KEY TERMS

acid-test ratio, *1352*

activity ratios, *1351*

asset turnover, *1352*

book value per share, *1352*

cash debt coverage ratio, *1352*

common-size analysis, *1355*

comparative analysis, *1354*

coverage ratios, *1351*

current cash debt coverage ratio, *1352*

current ratio, *1352*

debt to total assets ratio, *1352*

earnings per share, *1352*

horizontal analysis, *1355*

inventory turnover, *1352*

liquidity ratios, *1351*

payout ratio, *1352*

percentage analysis, *1355*

profit margin on sales, *1352*

profitability ratios, *1351*

quick ratio, *1352*

rate of return on assets, *1352*

rate of return on share capital—equity, *1352*

receivables turnover, *1352*

times interest earned, *1352*

vertical analysis, *1355*

SUMMARY OF LEARNING OBJECTIVES FOR APPENDIX 24A

•9 **Understand the approach to financial statement analysis.** Basic financial statement analysis involves examining relationships between items on the statements (ratio and percentage analysis) and identifying trends in these relationships (comparative analysis). Analysis is used to predict the future, but ratio analysis is limited because the data are from the past. Also, ratio analysis identifies present strengths and weaknesses of a company, but it may not reveal *why* they are as they are. Although single ratios are helpful, they are not conclusive; for maximum usefulness, analysts must compare them with industry averages, past years, planned amounts, and the like.

•10 **Identify major analytic ratios and describe their calculation.** Ratios are classified as liquidity ratios, activity ratios, profitability ratios, and coverage ratios. (1) *Liquidity ratio analysis* measures the short-run ability of a company to pay its currently maturing obligations. (2) *Activity ratio analysis* measures how effectively a company is using its assets. (3) *Profitability ratio analysis* measures the degree of success or failure of a company to generate revenues adequate to cover its costs of operation and provide a return to the owners. (4) *Coverage ratio analysis* measures the degree of protection afforded long-term creditors and investors.

•11 **Explain the limitations of ratio analysis.** Ratios are based on historical cost, which can lead to distortions in measuring performance. Also, where estimated items are significant, income ratios lose some of their credibility. In addition, comparability problems exist because companies use different accounting policies and procedures. Finally, analysts must recognize that a substantial amount of important information is not included in a company's financial statements.

•12 **Describe techniques of comparative analysis.** Companies present comparative data, which generally includes two years of statement of financial position information and three years of income statement information. In addition, many companies include in their annual reports five- to ten-year summaries of pertinent data that permit the reader to analyze trends.

•13 **Describe techniques of percentage analysis.** Percentage analysis consists of reducing a series of related amounts to a series of percentages of a given base. Analysts use two approaches: *Horizontal analysis* indicates the proportionate change in financial statement items over a period of time; such analysis is most helpful in evaluating trends. *Vertical analysis* (common-size analysis) is a proportional expression of each item on the financial statements in a given period to a base amount. It analyzes the composition of each of the financial statements from different years (a) to detect trends not evident from the comparison of absolute amounts and (b) to make intercompany comparisons of different-sized enterprises.

| APPENDIX **24B** | **FIRST-TIME ADOPTION OF IFRS** |

As discussed in Chapter 1, IFRS is growing in acceptance around the world. For example, recent statistics indicate 40 percent of the Global Fortune 500 companies use IFRS. And the chair of the IASB predicts that IFRS adoption will grow from its current level of 115 countries to nearly 150 countries in the near future.

> **Objective•14**
> Describe the guidelines for first-time adoption of IFRS.

When countries accept IFRS for use as accepted accounting policies, companies need guidance to ensure that their first IFRS financial statements contain high-quality information. Specifically, *IFRS 1* requires that information in a company's first IFRS statements (1) be transparent, (2) provide a suitable starting point, and (3) have a cost that does not exceed the benefits. **[12]**

The overriding principle in converting from national GAAP to IFRS (the conversion process) is full retrospective application of all IFRS. Retrospective application—recasting prior financial statements on the basis of IFRS—provides financial statement users with comparable information. However, the IASB recognizes that full retrospective application may be difficult in some situations, particularly when information related to past periods is not readily available. In response, the IASB has established guidelines to ensure that financial statement users have high-quality comparable information while balancing the costs and benefits of providing comparable data.

GENERAL GUIDELINES

The objective of the conversion process is to present a set of IFRS financial statements as if the company always reported on IFRS. To achieve this objective, a company must:

1. Identify the timing for its first IFRS statements.
2. Prepare an opening statement of financial position at the date of transition to IFRS.
3. Select accounting policies that comply with IFRS, and apply these policies retrospectively.
4. Consider whether to apply any optional exemptions and apply mandatory exceptions.
5. Make extensive disclosure to explain the transition to IFRS.

Relevant Dates

Once a company decides to convert to IFRS, it must decide on the following dates—the transition date and the reporting date. The **transition date** is the beginning of the earliest period for which full comparative IFRS information is presented. The **reporting date** is the closing statement of financial position date for the first IFRS financial statements.

To illustrate, assume that FirstChoice Company plans to provide its first IFRS statements for the year ended December 31, 2014. FirstChoice decides to present comparative information for one year only. Therefore, its date of transition to IFRS is January 1, 2013, and its reporting date is December 31, 2014. The timeline for first-time adoption is presented in Illustration 24B-1 (page 1358).

Illustration 24B-1 shows the following.

1. The **opening IFRS statement of financial position** for FirstChoice on January 1, 2013, serves as the starting point (date of transition) for the company's accounting under IFRS.
2. The first full IFRS statements are shown for FirstChoice for December 31, 2014. In other words, a minimum of two years of IFRS statements must be presented before

ILLUSTRATION 24B-1
First-Time Adoption
Timeline

a conversion to IFRS occurs. As a result, FirstChoice must prepare at least one year of comparative financial statements (for 2013) using IFRS.

3. FirstChoice presents financial statements in accordance with its national GAAP annually to December 31, 2013.

Following this conversion process, FirstChoice provides users of the financial statements with comparable IFRS statements for 2013 and 2014.

IMPLEMENTATION STEPS

Opening IFRS Statement of Financial Position

> **Objective•15**
>
> Describe the implementation steps for preparing the opening IFRS statement of financial position.

As indicated, to start the conversion process, companies first prepare an opening IFRS statement of financial position. This process involves the following steps.

1. Include all assets and liabilities that IFRS requires.
2. Exclude any assets and liabilities that IFRS does not permit.
3. Classify all assets, liabilities, and equity in accordance with IFRS.
4. Measure all assets and liabilities according to IFRS. **[13]**

Completing this process requires knowledge of both the prior GAAP used and IFRS (which you have obtained by your study of this text). To illustrate, the following facts for NewWorld Company are presented in Illustration 24B-2.

ILLUSTRATION 24B-2
Policy Changes—Opening
Statement of Financial
Position

OPENING STATEMENT OF FINANCIAL POSITION

Facts: NewWorld Company is preparing to adopt IFRS. It is preparing its opening statement of financial position on January 1, 2012. NewWorld identified the following accounting policy differences between IFRS and the national GAAP it currently uses. Under national GAAP, NewWorld:

1. Expenses development costs of €500,000 on a project that had met economic viability.
2. Does not make a provision for a warranty of €100,000 because the concept of a "constructive obligation" was not recognized.
3. Does not capitalize design fees of €150,000 into the cost of machinery that was put into service at the beginning of 2010, even though those costs were necessary to bring the asset to its working condition. The machinery has a 5-year life, no residual value, and NewWorld uses straight-line depreciation.

Question: How should NewWorld account for these items in its opening IFRS statement of financial position?

Solution:

1. IFRS allows the deferral of development costs in this case (see Chapter 12), and NewWorld should capitalize these costs.
2. IFRS requires recognition of a warranty provision (see Chapter 13), so a liability should be recorded.
3. Under IFRS, all costs incurred in bringing an asset to its place and condition for its intended use are capitalized into the cost of the asset.

Adjustments as a result of applying IFRS for the first time are generally recorded in retained earnings. NewWorld makes the following entries on January 1, 2012, to adjust the accounts to IFRS treatment.

Development Costs (or related intangible asset)	500,000	
Retained Earnings		500,000
(To capitalize development costs)		
Retained Earnings	100,000	
Warranty Liability		100,000
(To recognize warranty liability)		
Equipment	150,000	
Accumulated Depreciation—Equipment		30,000
Retained Earnings		120,000
(To recognized cost of machinery)		

In each of these situations, NewWorld adjusts retained earnings for the differences between IFRS and national GAAP to ensure that the opening statement of financial position is reported in accordance with IFRS.

After recording these adjustments, NewWorld prepares its opening IFRS statement of financial position. The January 1, 2012, statement of financial position is the starting point (the date of transition). Subsequently, in 2012 and 2013 NewWorld prepares IFRS financial statements internally. At December 31, 2013, it will formally adopt IFRS.[26]

Exemptions from Retrospective Treatment

In some cases, adjustments relating to prior periods cannot be reasonably determined. In other cases, it is "impracticable" to provide comparable information because the cost of generating the information exceeds the benefits. The IASB therefore targeted exemptions from the general retrospective treatment where it appeared appropriate. Two types of exemptions are provided—required and elective.

> **Objective·16**
>
> Describe the exemptions to retrospective application in first-time adoption of IFRS.

Required Exemptions

The Board identified three areas in which companies are prohibited from retrospective application in first-time adoption of IFRS:

1. Estimates.
2. Hedge accounting.
3. Non-controlling interests.

---

[26]To maintain comparisons in the transition year, companies may present comparative information in accordance with previous GAAP as well as the comparative information required by IFRS. Companies must (a) label the previous GAAP information prominently as not being prepared in accordance with IFRS, and (b) disclose the nature of the main adjustments that would make it comply with IFRS. Companies need not quantify those adjustments. **[14]**

These required exemptions are imposed because implementation of retrospective application in these areas generally requires companies to obtain information that may not be readily available. In these cases, companies may have to re-create information about past transactions with the benefit of hindsight. [15] For example, retrospective application with respect to non-controlling interests requires information about conditions and estimates made at the time of a business combination—an often difficult task. In addition, this exception provides relief for companies that otherwise might have to determine the allocation of transactions between owners and non-controlling interests in periods prior to the transition period.

Elective Exemptions

In addition to the required exemptions for retrospective treatment, the **IASB identified specific additional areas in which companies may elect exemption from retrospective treatment.** These exemptions provide companies some relief from full retrospective application. This simplifies the preparation of the first-time IFRS statements. Areas addressed in *Intermediate Accounting* are presented in Illustration 24B-3.[27]

ILLUSTRATION 24B-3
Elective Exemption from Retrospective Treatment

Companies may elect an exemption from retrospective application for one or more of the following areas.

(a) Share-based payment transactions.

(b) Fair value or revaluation as deemed cost.

(c) Leases.

(d) Employee benefits.

(e) Compound financial instruments.

(f) Fair value measurement of financial assets or financial liabilities at initial recognition.

(g) Decommissioning liabilities included in the cost of property, plant, and equipment.

(h) Borrowing costs.

Optional exemption from retrospective treatment is understandable for certain situations. The accounting for the areas identified above generally requires a number of estimates and assumptions at initial recognition and in subsequent accounting. Depending on the accounting under previous GAAP, the information necessary for retrospective application may not be available, or may be obtained only at a high cost. We discuss two examples.[28]

Exemption Example: Compound Securities. As discussed in Chapter 16, IFRS requires splitting the debt and equity components of convertible debt, using the "with and without" approach. The subsequent accounting for the debt element reflects effective-interest amortization on the estimated debt component. However, if the liability component is no longer outstanding at the date of first-time adoption, retrospective application involves separating two portions of equity. The first portion is in retained earnings and represents the cumulative interest accreted on the liability component. The other portion represents the original equity component. Since the company would not have records on the debt once it is no longer outstanding, it would be costly to re-create that information for retrospective application. As a result, a first-time adopter need not separate these two portions if the liability component is no longer outstanding at the date of transition to IFRS.

Exemption Example: Fair Value or Revaluation as Deemed Cost. Companies can elect to measure property, plant, and equipment at fair value at the transition date and use

---

[27]Other areas subject to the option are (1) business combinations; (2) insurance contracts; (3) investments in subsidiaries, jointly controlled entities, and associates; (4) designation of previously recognized financial instruments; (5) financial assets or intangible assets accounted for as Service Concession Arrangements; and (6) transfers of assets from customers. [16]

[28]Specific implementation guidance for other areas is provided in *IFRS 1*. [17]

that fair value as their **deemed cost** in accounting for those assets subsequent to the adoption of IFRS. This exemption may also be applied to intangible assets in certain situations. By using the exemption, companies avoid re-creating depreciation records for property, plant, and equipment, which is a costly exercise for many companies. In fact, in providing this exemption, the IASB noted that reconstructed cost data might be less relevant to users, and less reliable, than current fair value data. The Board therefore concluded that it would allow companies to use fair value as deemed cost. A company that applies the fair value as deemed cost exemption is not required to revalue the assets subsequent to first-time adoption. **[18]**[29]

Presentation and Disclosure

Upon first-time adoption of IFRS, a company must present at least one year of comparative information under IFRS. **[19]** To comply with *IAS 1*, an entity's first IFRS financial statements shall include at least three statements of financial position, two statements of comprehensive income, two separate income statements (if presented), two statements of cash flows, and two statements of changes in equity and related notes, including comparative information. Companies must explain how the transition from previous GAAP to IFRS affected its reported financial position, financial performance, and cash flows.

> **Objective·17**
> Describe the presentation and disclosure requirements for first-time adoption of IFRS.

A company's first IFRS financial statements shall include reconciliations of:

- Its equity reported in accordance with previous GAAP to its equity in accordance with IFRS at the transition date.
- Its total comprehensive income in accordance with IFRS to total comprehensive income in accordance with previous GAAP for the same period. The reconciliation should be prepared for latest period in the company's most recent annual financial statements under the previous GAAP. **[20]**

For example, Jones plc first adopted IFRS in 2012, with a date of transition to IFRS January 1, 2011. Its last financial statements in accordance with previous GAAP were for the year ended December 31, 2011. An example of Jones plc's reconciliations for first-time adoption is provided in Illustration 24B-4 for the non-current asset section of the statement of financial position.

ILLUSTRATION 24B-4
Reconciliation of Equity for 2011

Jones plc
(amounts in £000)

The first IFRS financial statements include the reconciliations and related notes shown below.

Reconciliation of equity at January 1, 2011 (date of transition to IFRS)

Note		Previous GAAP	Effect of Transition to IFRS	IFRS
1	Property, plant, and equipment	£ 8,299	£100	£ 8,399
2	Goodwill	1,220	150	1,370
2	Intangible assets	208	(150)	58
3	Financial assets	3,471	420	3,891
	Total non-current assets	£13,198	£520	£13,718

[29]In addition, IFRS does not restrict the use of fair value as deemed cost to an entire class of assets, as is done for revaluation accounting (see discussion in Chapter 11). For example, a company can use fair value for deemed cost for some buildings and not for others. However, if a company uses fair value as deemed cost for assets whose fair value is above cost, it cannot ignore indications that the recoverable amount of other assets may have fallen below their carrying amount. Thus, an impairment may need to be recorded.

ILLUSTRATION 24B-4
(*Continued*)

Notes to the reconciliation at January 1, 2011:
1. Depreciation was influenced by tax requirements in accordance with previous GAAP, but in accordance with IFRS reflects the useful life of the assets. The cumulative adjustment increased the carrying amount of property, plant, and equipment by £100.
2. Intangible assets in accordance with previous GAAP included £150 for items that are transferred to goodwill because they do not qualify for recognition as intangible assets in accordance with IFRS.
3. Financial assets are all classified as non-trading equity investments in accordance with IFRS and are carried at their fair value of £3,891. They were carried at cost of £3,471 in accordance with previous GAAP. The resulting gains of £294 (£420, less related deferred tax of £126) are included in the accumulated other comprehensive income.

Through this reconciliation, statement users are provided information to evaluate the impact of the adoption of IFRS on the statement of financial position. In practice, it may be helpful to include cross-references to accounting policies and supporting analyses that give further explanation of the adjustments shown in the reconciliations.

The reconciliation for total comprehensive income for Jones with respect to the gross profit section of the income statement is presented in Illustration 24B-5.

ILLUSTRATION 24B-5
Reconciliation of Total Comprehensive Income for 2011

Jones plc
(amounts in £000)

Note		Previous GAAP	Effect of Transition to IFRS	IFRS
	Revenue	£20,910	£ 0	£20,910
1, 2, 3	Cost of sales	(15,283)	(97)	(15,380)
	Gross profit	£ 5,627	£(97)	£ 5,530

Notes to the reconciliation of total comprehensive income for 20X4:
1. A pension liability is recognized in accordance with IFRS but was not recognized in accordance with previous GAAP. The pension liability increased by £130 during 2011, which caused increases in cost of sales (£50), distribution costs (£30), and administrative expenses (£50).
2. Cost of sales is higher by £47 in accordance with IFRS because inventories include fixed and variable production overhead in accordance with IFRS but not in accordance with previous GAAP.
3. Depreciation was influenced by tax requirements in accordance with previous GAAP but reflects the useful life of the assets in accordance with IFRS. The effect on the profit for 2011 was not material.

Explanation of material adjustments to the statement of cash flows for 2011:
Income taxes of £133 paid during 2011 are classified as operating cash flows in accordance with IFRS but were included in a separate category of tax cash flows in accordance with previous GAAP. There are no other material differences between the statement of cash flows presented in accordance with IFRS and the statement of cash flows presented in accordance with previous GAAP.

SUMMARY

When companies adopt IFRS, they must ensure that financial statement users receive high-quality information in order to compare financial statements prepared under IFRS and previous GAAP. IFRS guidelines are designed to ensure that upon first-time adoption, financial statements are comparable and that the costs and benefits of first-time adoption are effectively managed.

SUMMARY OF LEARNING OBJECTIVES FOR APPENDIX 24B

KEY TERMS

deemed cost, *1361*
opening IFRS statement
  of financial
  position, *1357*
reporting date, *1357*
transition date, *1357*

•14 **Describe the guidelines for first-time adoption of IFRS.** Upon first-time adoption of IFRS, a company must (1) prepare and present an opening IFRS statement of financial position at the date of transition to IFRS. This is the starting point for its accounting in accordance with IFRS. The general rule for first-time adoption of IFRS is retrospective application. That is, recast prior financial statements on the basis of IFRS and using the same accounting policies in its opening IFRS statement of financial position and throughout all periods presented in its first IFRS financial statements. Those accounting policies shall comply with each IFRS effective at the end of its first IFRS reporting period. Companies provide at least one year of comparative statements prepared in accordance with IFRS.

•15 **Describe the implementation steps for preparing the opening IFRS statement of financial position.** Companies must first prepare the opening IFRS statement of financial position by including all assets and liabilities that IFRS requires; (2) excluding any assets and liabilities that IFRS does not permit; (3) classifying all assets, liabilities, and equity in accordance with IFRS; and (4) measuring all assets and liabilities according to IFRS. Companies must make entries through retrospective application. After recording these adjustments, an opening IFRS statement of financial position is prepared, which will reflect application of the same policies that will be applied in the first IFRS financial statements.

•16 **Describe the exemptions to retrospective application in first-time adoption of IFRS.** Given the range of changes that might be required for first-time adoption, the Board considered the cost-benefit of retrospective application and developed targeted exemptions from retrospective treatment when the amount of the adjustment relating to prior periods cannot be reasonably determined and when it is "impracticable" to provide comparable information. These exemptions are classified as required (in which a company is prohibited from retrospective application) and optional.

•17 **Describe the presentation and disclosure requirements for first-time adoption of IFRS.** Upon first-time adoption of IFRS, a company presents at least one year of comparative information under IFRS. A company's first IFRS financial statements shall include at least three statements of financial position, two statements of comprehensive income, two separate income statements (if presented), two statements of cash flows, and two statements of changes in equity and related notes, including comparative information. Companies also must explain how the transition from previous GAAP to IFRS affected its reported financial position, financial performance, and cash flows. A company's first IFRS financial statements shall include reconciliations of its equity and total comprehensive income in accordance with previous GAAP to its equity and comprehensive income in accordance with IFRS.

AUTHORITATIVE LITERATURE

Authoritative Literature References

[1] "Framework for the Preparation and Presentation of Financial Statements" (London, U.K.: IASB, 2001), par. 21.

[2] *International Financial Reporting Standard for Small and Medium-sized Entities (IFRS for SMEs)* (London, U.K.: IASB, 2009).

[3] International Accounting Standard 1, *Presentation of Financial Statements* (London, U.K.: International Accounting Standards Committee Foundation, 2007).

[4] International Accounting Standard 24, *Related Party Disclosures* (London, U.K.: International Accounting Standards Committee Foundation, 2009), par. 9.

[5] International Accounting Standard 24, *Related Party Disclosures* (London, U.K.: International Accounting Standards Committee Foundation, 2009), par. 17.

[6] International Accounting Standard 10, *Events after the Reporting Period* (London, U.K.: International Accounting Standards Committee Foundation, 2007).

[7] International Accounting Standard 10, *Events after the Reporting Period* (London, U.K.: International Accounting Standards Committee Foundation, 2007), par. 22.

[8] International Financial Reporting Standard 8, *Operating Segments* (London, U.K.: International Accounting Standards Committee Foundation, 2006), par. BC15.

[9] International Financial Reporting Standard 8, *Operating Segments* (London, U.K.: International Accounting Standards Committee Foundation, 2006), par. 19.

[10] International Accounting Standard 34, *Interim Financial Reporting* (London, U.K.: International Accounting Standards Committee Foundation, 2001).

[11] International Accounting Standard 34, *Interim Financial Reporting* (London, U.K.: International Accounting Standards Committee Foundation, 2001), paras. B12–B19.

[12] International Financial Reporting Standard 1, *First-time Adoption of International Financial Reporting Standards* (London, U.K.: IASB, 2003), par. 1.

[13] International Financial Reporting Standard 1, *First-time Adoption of International Financial Reporting Standards* (London, U.K.: IASB, 2003), par. 10.

[14] International Financial Reporting Standard 1, *First-time Adoption of International Financial Reporting Standards* (London, U.K.: IASB, 2003), par. 22.

[15] International Financial Reporting Standard 1, *First-time Adoption of International Financial Reporting Standards* (London, U.K.: IASB, 2003), par. BC 22B.

[16] International Financial Reporting Standard 1, *First-time Adoption of International Financial Reporting Standards* (London, U.K.: IASB, 2003), App. C and D.

[17] International Financial Reporting Standard 1, *First-time Adoption of International Financial Reporting Standards* (London, U.K.: IASB, 2003), App. B–E.

[18] International Financial Reporting Standard 1, *First-time Adoption of International Financial Reporting Standards* (London, U.K.: IASB, 2003), paras. D5–D8 and BC41–BC47.

[19] International Financial Reporting Standard 1, *First-time Adoption of International Financial Reporting Standards* (London, U.K.: IASB, 2003), par. 19.

[20] International Financial Reporting Standard 1, *First-time Adoption of International Financial Reporting Standards* (London, U.K.: IASB, 2003), par. 24.

Note: All asterisked Questions, Exercises, and Problems relate to material in the appendices to the chapter.

QUESTIONS

1. What are the major advantages of notes to the financial statements? What types of items are usually reported in notes?

2. What is the full disclosure principle in accounting? Why has disclosure increased substantially in the last 10 years?

3. The IASB requires a reconciliation between the effective tax rate and the government's statutory rate. Of what benefit is such a disclosure requirement?

4. What type of disclosure or accounting do you believe is necessary for the following items?

   (a) Because of a general increase in the number of labor disputes and strikes, both within and outside the industry, there is an increased likelihood that a company will suffer a costly strike in the near future.

(b) A company reports a loss on a discontinued operation (net of tax) correctly on the income statement. No other mention is made of this item in the annual report.

(c) A company expects to recover a substantial amount in connection with a pending refund claim for a prior year's taxes. Although the claim is being contested, counsel for the company has confirmed the client's expectation of recovery.

5. The following information was described in a note of Canon Packing Co.

"During August, Holland Products Corporation purchased 311,003 ordinary shares of the Company, which constitutes approximately 35% of the shares outstanding. Holland has since obtained representation on the Board of Directors."

"An affiliate of Holland Products Corporation acts as a food broker for Canon Packing in the greater Amsterdam marketing area. The commissions for such services after August amounted to approximately €20,000." Why is this information disclosed?

6. What are the major types of subsequent events? Indicate how each of the following "subsequent events" would be reported.

(a) Collection of a note written off in a prior period.

(b) Issuance of a large preference share offering.

(c) Acquisition of a company in a different industry.

(d) Destruction of a major plant in a flood.

(e) Death of the company's chief executive officer (CEO).

(f) Additional wage costs associated with settlement of a four-week strike.

(g) Settlement of an income tax case at considerably more tax than anticipated at year-end.

(h) Change in the product mix from consumer goods to industrial goods.

7. What are diversified companies? What accounting problems are related to diversified companies?

8. What quantitative materiality test is applied to determine whether a segment is significant enough to warrant separate disclosure?

9. Identify the segment information that is required to be disclosed by IFRS.

10. What is an operating segment, and when can information about two operating segments be aggregated?

11. The controller for Lafayette Inc. recently commented, "If I have to disclose our segments individually, the only people who will gain are our competitors and the only people that will lose are our present shareholders." Evaluate this comment.

12. What are interim reports? Why is a complete set of financial statements often not provided with interim data?

13. What are the accounting problems related to the presentation of interim data?

14. Dierdorf Inc., a closely held corporation, has decided to go public. The controller, Ed Floyd, is concerned with presenting interim data when an inventory write-down is recorded. What problems are encountered with inventories when quarterly data are presented?

15. What approaches have been suggested to overcome the seasonality problem related to interim reporting?

16. An article in the financial press entitled "Important Information in Annual Reports This Year" noted that annual reports include a management commentary section. What would this section contain?

17. "The financial statements of a company are management's, not the accountant's." Discuss the implications of this statement.

18. Olga Conrad, a financial writer, noted recently, "There are substantial arguments for including earnings projections in annual reports and the like. The most compelling is that it would give anyone interested something now available to only a relatively select few—like large shareholders, creditors, and attentive bartenders." Identify some arguments against providing earnings projections.

19. The following comment appeared in the financial press: "Inadequate financial disclosure, particularly with respect to how management views the future and its role in the marketplace, has always been a stone in the shoe. After all, if you don't know how a company views the future, how can you judge the worth of its corporate strategy?" What are some arguments for reporting earnings forecasts?

20. What is the difference between an auditor's unmodified opinion or "clean" opinion and a modified one?

21. Jane Ellerby and Sam Callison are discussing the recent fraud that occurred at LowRental Leasing, Inc. The fraud involved the improper reporting of revenue to ensure that the company would have income in excess of $1 million. What is fraudulent financial reporting, and how does it differ from an embezzlement of company funds?

22. Briefly describe some of the similarities and differences between disclosure rules under U.S. GAAP and IFRS.

23. Bill Novak is working on an audit of a U.S. GAAP client. In his review of the client's interim reports, he notes that the reports are prepared on an integral basis. That is, each interim report is viewed as a part of the annual period. Is this acceptable under U.S. GAAP? If so, explain how that treatment could affect comparisons to an IFRS company.

*24. "The significance of financial statement data is not in the amount alone." Discuss the meaning of this statement.

*25. A close friend of yours, who is a history major and who has not had any college courses or any experience in business, is receiving the financial statements from companies in which he has minor investments (acquired for him by his now-deceased father). He asks you what he needs to know to interpret and to evaluate the financial statement data that he is receiving. What would you tell him?

*26. Distinguish between ratio analysis and percentage analysis relative to the interpretation of financial statements. What is the value of these two types of analyses?

*27. In calculating inventory turnover, why is cost of goods sold used as the numerator? As the inventory turnover increases, what increasing risk does the business assume?

*28. What is the relationship of the asset turnover ratio to the rate of return on assets?

*29. Explain the meaning of the following terms: (a) common-size analysis, (b) vertical analysis, (c) horizontal analysis, and (d) percentage analysis.

*30. Briefly explain the need for an IFRS on first-time adoption of IFRS.

*31. How is the date of transition and the date of reporting determined in first-time adoption of IFRS?

*32. What are the characteristics of high-quality information in a company's first IFRS financial statements?

*33. What are the steps to be completed in preparing the opening IFRS statement of financial position?

*34. What is the rationale for exemptions to retrospective application at first-time adoption of IFRS?

*35. Briefly describe the required exemptions to retrospective application at first-time adoption of IFRS.

*36. What are three elective exemptions to retrospective application at first-time adoption of IFRS?

*37. Briefly describe the deemed cost exemption to retrospective application at first-time adoption of IFRS.

*38. If a company elects the deemed cost exemption, must it continue to use revaluation accounting subsequent to first-time adoption? Explain.

*39. Briefly describe the presentation and disclosure requirements for first-time adoption of IFRS.

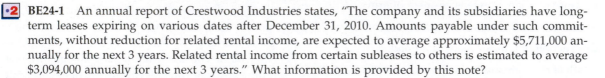

BRIEF EXERCISES

•2 BE24-1 An annual report of Crestwood Industries states, "The company and its subsidiaries have long-term leases expiring on various dates after December 31, 2010. Amounts payable under such commitments, without reduction for related rental income, are expected to average approximately $5,711,000 annually for the next 3 years. Related rental income from certain subleases to others is estimated to average $3,094,000 annually for the next 3 years." What information is provided by this note?

•2 BE24-2 An annual report of Barclays Company states, "Net income a share is computed based upon the average number of shares of all classes outstanding. Additional shares of ordinary shares may be issued or delivered in the future on conversion of outstanding convertible debentures, exercise of outstanding employee share options, and for payment of defined supplemental compensation. Had such additional shares been outstanding, net income a share would have been reduced by 10¢ in the current year and 3¢ in the previous year. . . . As a result of share transactions by the company during the current year (primarily the purchase of Class A shares from Barclay Foundation), net income a share was increased by 6¢." What information is provided by this note?

•2 BE24-3 Morlan Corporation is preparing its December 31, 2010, financial statements. Two events that occurred between December 31, 2010, and March 10, 2011, when the statements were issued, are described below.

1. A liability, estimated at €160,000 at December 31, 2010, was settled on February 26, 2011, at €170,000.
2. A flood loss of €80,000 occurred on March 1, 2011.

What effect do these subsequent events have on 2010 net income?

•3 BE24-4 Tina Bailey, a student of intermediate accounting, was heard to remark after a class discussion on segment reporting, "All this is very confusing to me. First we are told that there is merit in presenting the consolidated results, and now we are told that it is better to show segmental results. I wish they would make up their minds." Evaluate this comment.

•3 BE24-5 Foley Corporation has seven operating segments with total revenues as follows (in 000,000).

Penley	¥600	Cheng	¥225
Konami	650	Takuhi	200
KSC	250	Molina	700
Red Moon	275		

Based only on the revenues test, which operating segments are reportable?

•3 **BE24-6** Operating profits and losses for the seven operating segments of Foley Corporation are (in 000,000):

Penley	¥90	Cheng	¥ (20)
Konami	(40)	Takuhi	34
KSC	25	Molina	150
Red Moon	50		

Based only on the operating profit (loss) test, which industry segments are reportable?

•3 **BE24-7** Identifiable assets for the seven industry segments of Foley Corporation are (in 000,000):

Penley	¥500	Cheng	¥200
Konami	550	Takuhi	150
KSC	250	Molina	475
Red Moon	400		

Based only on the identifiable assets test, which industry segments are reportable?

•10 ***BE24-8** Answer each of the questions in the following unrelated situations.

(a) The current ratio of a company is 5:1 and its acid-test ratio is 1:1. If the inventories and prepaid items amount to $500,000, what is the amount of current liabilities?

(b) A company had an average inventory last year of $200,000 and its inventory turnover was 5. If sales volume and unit cost remain the same this year as last and inventory turnover is 8 this year, what will average inventory have to be during the current year?

(c) A company has current assets of $90,000 (of which $40,000 is inventory and prepaid items) and current liabilities of $40,000. What is the current ratio? What is the acid-test ratio? If the company borrows $15,000 cash from a bank on a 120-day loan, what will its current ratio be? What will the acid-test ratio be?

(d) A company has current assets of $600,000 and current liabilities of $240,000. The board of directors declares a cash dividend of $180,000. What is the current ratio after the declaration but before payment? What is the current ratio after the payment of the dividend?

•10 ***BE24-9** Heartland Company's budgeted sales and budgeted cost of goods sold for the coming year are £144,000,000 and £99,000,000, respectively. Short-term interest rates are expected to average 10%. If Heartland can increase inventory turnover from its present level of 9 times a year to a level of 12 times per year, compute its expected cost savings for the coming year.

•15 ***BE24-10** Becker Ltd. is planning to adopt IFRS and prepare its first IFRS financial statements at December 31, 2013. What is the date of Becker's opening statement of financial position, assuming one year of comparative information? What periods will be covered in Becker's first IFRS financial statements?

•15 ***BE24-11** Bohmann Company is preparing its opening IFRS statement of financial position on January 1, 2012. Under its previous GAAP, Bohmann had capitalized all development costs of $50,000. Under IFRS, only $10,000 of the costs related to a patent were incurred after the project met economic viability thresholds. Prepare the entry (if any) needed to record this adjustment at the date of transition.

•15 ***BE24-12** Stengel plc is preparing its opening IFRS statement of financial position on January 1, 2012. Under its previous GAAP, Stengel used the LIFO inventory method. Under LIFO, its inventory is reported at £250,000; under FIFO, which Stengel will use upon adoption of IFRS, the inventory is valued at £265,000. Prepare the entry (if any) needed to record this adjustment at the date of issuance.

•15 ***BE24-13** Latta Inc. is preparing its opening IFRS statement of financial position on January 1, 2012. Under its previous GAAP, Latta had deferred certain advertising costs amounting to $37,000. Prepare the entry (if any) needed to record this adjustment at the date of issuance

•15 ***BE24-14** Smitz Company is preparing its opening IFRS statement of financial position on January 1, 2012. Under its previous GAAP, Smitz did not record a provision for litigation in the amount of €85,000 that would be recognized under IFRS. Prepare the entry (if any) needed to record this adjustment at the date of issuance.

•16 ***BE24-15** Porter Company is evaluating the following assets to determine whether it can use fair value as deemed cost in first-time adoption of IFRS.

1. Biological assets related to agricultural activity for which there is *no* active market.
2. Intangible assets for which there is *no* active market.
3. Any individual item of property, plant, and equipment.
4. Financial liabilities that are *not* held for trading.

For each asset type, indicate if the deemed cost exemption can be used.

EXERCISES

•2 **E24-1** **(Subsequent Events)** Keystone Corporation issued its financial statements for the year ended December 31, 2010, on March 10, 2011. The following events took place early in 2011.

(a) On January 10, 10,000 ordinary shares of $5 par value were issued at $66 per share.
(b) On March 1, Keystone determined after negotiations with the taxing authorities that income taxes payable for 2010 should be $1,320,000. At December 31, 2010, income taxes payable were recorded at $1,100,000.

Instructions
Discuss how the preceding subsequent events should be reflected in the 2010 financial statements.

•2 **E24-2** **(Subsequent Events)** For each of the following subsequent events, indicate whether a company should (a) adjust the financial statements, (b) disclose in notes to the financial statements, or (c) neither adjust nor disclose.

_____ 1. Settlement of a tax case at a cost considerably in excess of the amount expected at year-end.
_____ 2. Introduction of a new product line.
_____ 3. Loss of assembly plant due to fire.
_____ 4. Sale of a significant portion of the company's assets.
_____ 5. Retirement of the company president.
_____ 6. Issuance of a significant number of ordinary shares.
_____ 7. Loss of a significant customer.
_____ 8. Prolonged employee strike.
_____ 9. Material loss on a year-end receivable because of a customer's bankruptcy.
_____ 10. Hiring of a new president.
_____ 11. Settlement of prior year's litigation against the company.
_____ 12. Merger with another company of comparable size.

•3 **E24-3** **(Segmented Reporting)** LaGreca Company is involved in four separate industries. The following information is available for each of the four industries.

Operating Segment	Total Revenue	Operating Profit (Loss)	Identifiable Assets
W	€ 60,000	€15,000	€167,000
X	10,000	1,500	83,000
Y	23,000	(2,000)	21,000
Z	9,000	1,000	19,000
	€102,000	€15,500	€290,000

Instructions
Determine which of the operating segments are reportable based on the:

(a) Revenue test.
(b) Operating profit (loss) test.
(c) Identifiable assets test.

•10 ***E24-4** **(Ratio Computation and Analysis; Liquidity)** As loan analyst for Madison Bank, you have been presented the following information.

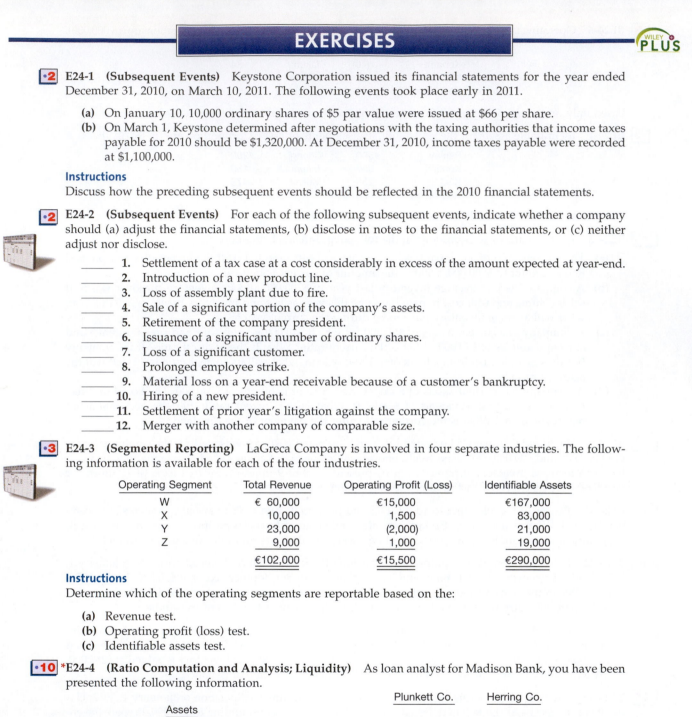

	Plunkett Co.	Herring Co.
Assets		
Other assets	$ 500,000	$ 612,000
Current assets		
Inventories	570,000	518,000
Receivables	220,000	302,000
Cash	120,000	320,000
Total current assets	910,000	1,140,000
Total assets	$1,410,000	$1,752,000
Equity and Liabilities		
Share capital and retained earnings	$ 710,000	$ 902,000
Non-current liabilities	400,000	500,000
Current liabilities	300,000	350,000
Total equity and liabilities	$1,410,000	$1,752,000
Annual sales	$ 930,000	$1,500,000
Rate of gross profit on sales	30%	40%

Each of these companies has requested a loan of $50,000 for 6 months with no collateral offered. Inasmuch as your bank has reached its quota for loans of this type, only one of these requests is to be granted.

Instructions

Which of the two companies, as judged by the information given above, would you recommend as the better risk and why? Assume that the ending account balances are representative of the entire year.

•10 *E24-5 (Analysis of Given Ratios) Robbins Company is a wholesale distributor of professional equipment and supplies. The company's sales have averaged about $900,000 annually for the 3-year period 2009–2011. The firm's total assets at the end of 2011 amounted to $850,000.

The president of Robbins Company has asked the controller to prepare a report that summarizes the financial aspects of the company's operations for the past 3 years. This report will be presented to the board of directors at their next meeting.

In addition to comparative financial statements, the controller has decided to present a number of relevant financial ratios which can assist in the identification and interpretation of trends. At the request of the controller, the accounting staff has calculated the following ratios for the 3-year period 2009–2011.

	2009	2010	2011
Current ratio	1.80	1.89	1.96
Acid-test (quick) ratio	1.04	0.99	0.87
Accounts receivable turnover	8.75	7.71	6.42
Inventory turnover	4.91	4.32	3.72
Total debt to total assets	51.0%	46.0%	41.0%
Long-term debt to total assets	31.0%	27.0%	24.0%
Sales to fixed assets (fixed asset turnover)	1.58	1.69	1.79
Sales as a percent of 2009 sales	1.00	1.03	1.05
Gross margin percentage	36.0%	35.1%	34.6%
Net income to sales	6.9%	7.0%	7.2%
Return on total assets	7.7%	7.7%	7.8%
Return on equity	13.6%	13.1%	12.7%

In preparation of the report, the controller has decided first to examine the financial ratios independent of any other data to determine if the ratios themselves reveal any significant trends over the 3-year period.

Instructions

(a) The current ratio is increasing while the acid-test (quick) ratio is decreasing. Using the ratios provided, identify and explain the contributing factor(s) for this apparently divergent trend.

(b) In terms of the ratios provided, what conclusion(s) can be drawn regarding the company's use of financial leverage during the 2009–2011 period?

(c) Using the ratios provided, what conclusion(s) can be drawn regarding the company's net investment in plant and equipment?

•10 *E24-6 (Ratio Analysis) Howser Inc. is a manufacturer of electronic components and accessories with total assets of £20,000,000. Selected financial ratios for Howser and the industry averages for firms of similar size are presented below.

	Howser			2011 Industry Average
	2009	2010	2011	
Current ratio	2.09	2.27	2.51	2.24
Quick ratio	1.15	1.12	1.19	1.22
Inventory turnover	2.40	2.18	2.02	3.50
Net sales to equity	2.75	2.00	2.05	2.85
Net income to equity	0.14	0.15	0.17	0.11
Total liabilities to equity	1.41	1.37	1.44	0.95

Howser is being reviewed by several entities whose interests vary, and the company's financial ratios are a part of the data being considered. Each of the parties listed below must recommend an action based on its evaluation of Howser's financial position.

Citizens National Bank. The bank is processing Howser's application for a new 5-year term note. Citizens National has been Howser's banker for several years but must reevaluate the company's financial position for each major transaction.

Charleston Company. Charleston is a new supplier to Howser and must decide on the appropriate credit terms to extend to the company.

Shannon Financial. A brokerage firm specializing in the shares of electronics firms that are sold over-the-counter, Shannon Financial must decide if it will include Howser in a new fund being established for sale to Shannon Financial's clients.

Working Capital Management Committee. This is a committee of Howser's management personnel chaired by the chief operating officer. The committee is charged with the responsibility of periodically reviewing the company's working capital position, comparing actual data against budgets, and recommending changes in strategy as needed.

Instructions

(a) Describe the analytical use of each of the six ratios presented above.

(b) For each of the four entities described above, identify two financial ratios, from those ratios presented in Illustration 24A-1 (on page 1353), that would be most valuable as a basis for its decision regarding Howser.

(c) Discuss what the financial ratios presented in the question reveal about Howser. Support your answer by citing specific ratio levels and trends as well as the interrelationships between these ratios.

•15 •16 *E24-7 **(Opening Statement of Financial Position)** Goodman Company is preparing to adopt IFRS. In preparing its opening statement of financial position on January 1, 2012, Goodman identified the following accounting policy differences between IFRS and its previous GAAP.

1. Under its previous GAAP, Goodman classified proposed dividends of €45,000 as a current liability.
2. Goodman had deferred advertising costs of €500,000.

Instructions

(a) Prepare the journal entries (if any) needed before preparation of Goodman's opening statement of financial position.

(b) Determine the net change in equity from these adjustments.

•15 •16 •17 *E24-8 **(Opening Statement of Financial Position, Disclosure)** Lombardo Group is preparing to adopt IFRS. It is preparing its opening statement of financial position on January 1, 2012. Lombardo identified the following accounting policy differences between IFRS and its previous GAAP.

1. Lombardo had not made a provision for a warranty of €75,000 under previous GAAP because the concept of a "constructive obligation" was not recognized.
2. Under previous GAAP, €60,000 paid for certain architect fees was not capitalized into the cost of a building that was put into service at the beginning of 2011, even though those costs were necessary to bring the asset to its working condition. The building has a 40-year life, no residual value, and Lombardo uses straight-line depreciation.

Instructions

(a) Prepare the journal entries (if any) needed before preparation of Lombardo's opening statement of financial position.

(b) Determine the net change in equity from these adjustments.

(c) Brief describe the disclosures that Lombardo will make related to the adjustments in it first IFRS financial statements.

PROBLEMS

•2 P24-1 **(Subsequent Events)** Your firm has been engaged to examine the financial statements of Almaden Corporation for the year 2010. The bookkeeper who maintains the financial records has prepared all the unaudited financial statements for the corporation since its organization on January 2, 2005. The client provides you with the information below.

ALMADEN CORPORATION
STATEMENT OF FINANCIAL POSITION
DECEMBER 31, 2010

Assets		Liabilities	
		Equity	$4,650,600
Other assets	$5,171,400	Non-current liabilities	1,439,500
Current assets	1,881,100	Current liabilities	962,400
	$7,052,500		$7,052,500

Current assets include:

Cash (restricted in the amount of $300,000 for plant expansion)	$ 571,000
Investments in land	185,000
Accounts receivable less allowance of $30,000	480,000
Inventories (weighted-average)	645,100
	$1,881,100

Other assets include:

Prepaid expenses	$ 62,400
Plant and equipment less accumulated depreciation of $1,430,000	4,130,000
Notes receivable (short-term)	162,300
Goodwill	252,000
Land	564,700
	$5,171,400

Current liabilities include:

Accounts payable	$ 510,000
Notes payable (due 2013)	157,400
Estimated income taxes payable	145,000
Share premium—ordinary	150,000
	$ 962,400

Non-current liabilities include:

Unearned revenue	$ 489,500
Dividends payable (cash)	200,000
8% bonds payable (due May 1, 2015)	750,000
	$1,439,500

Equity includes:

Retained earnings	$2,810,600
Share capital—ordinary, par value $10; authorized 200,000 shares, 184,000 shares issued	1,840,000
	$4,650,600

The supplementary information below is also provided.

1. On May 1, 2010, the corporation issued at par $750,000 of bonds to finance plant expansion. The long-term bond agreement provided for the annual payment of interest every May 1. The existing plant was pledged as security for the loan.
2. The bookkeeper made the following mistakes.
    (a) In 2008, the ending inventory was overstated by $183,000. The ending inventories for 2009 and 2010 were correctly computed.
    (b) In 2010, accrued wages in the amount of $225,000 were omitted from the statement of financial position, and these expenses were not charged on the income statement.
    (c) In 2010, a gain of $175,000 (net of tax) on the sale of certain plant assets was credited directly to retained earnings.
3. A major competitor has introduced a line of products that will compete directly with Almaden's primary line, now being produced in a specially designed new plant. Because of manufacturing innovations, the competitor's line will be of comparable quality but priced 50% below Almaden's line. The competitor announced its new line on January 14, 2011. Almaden indicates that the company will meet the lower prices that are high enough to cover variable manufacturing and selling expenses, but permit recovery of only a portion of fixed costs.
4. You learned on January 28, 2011, prior to completion of the audit, of heavy damage because of a recent fire to one of Almaden's two plants; the loss will not be reimbursed by insurance. The newspapers described the event in detail.

Instructions

Analyze the above information to prepare a corrected statement of financial position for Almaden in accordance with proper accounting and reporting policies. Prepare a description of any notes that might need to be prepared. The books are closed and adjustments to income are to be made through retained earnings.

•3 **P24-2** **(Segmented Reporting)** Cineplex Corporation is a diversified company that operates in five different industries: A, B, C, D, and E. The following information relating to each segment is available for 2011.

	A	B	C	D	E
Sales	$40,000	$ 75,000	$580,000	$35,000	$55,000
Cost of goods sold	19,000	50,000	270,000	19,000	30,000
Operating expenses	10,000	40,000	235,000	12,000	18,000
Total expenses	29,000	90,000	505,000	31,000	48,000
Operating profit (loss)	$11,000	$(15,000)	$ 75,000	$ 4,000	$ 7,000
Identifiable assets	$35,000	$ 80,000	$500,000	$65,000	$50,000

Sales of segments B and C included intersegment sales of $20,000 and $100,000, respectively.

Instructions

(a) Determine which of the segments are reportable based on the:
   (1) Revenue test.
   (2) Operating profit (loss) test.
   (3) Identifiable assets test.
(b) Prepare the necessary disclosures required by IFRS.

•10 •12 ***P24-3** **(Ratio Computations and Additional Analysis)** Bradburn Corporation was formed 5 years ago through a public subscription of ordinary shares. Daniel Brown, who owns 15% of the ordinary shares, was one of the organizers of Bradburn and is its current president. The company has been successful, but it currently is experiencing a shortage of funds. On June 10, Daniel Brown approached the Hibernia Bank, asking for a 24-month extension on two $35,000 notes, which are due on June 30, 2011, and September 30, 2011. Another note of $6,000 is due on March 31, 2012, but he expects no difficulty in paying this note on its due date. Brown explained that Bradburn's cash flow problems are due primarily to the company's desire to finance a $300,000 plant expansion over the next 2 fiscal years through internally generated funds.

The commercial loan officer of Hibernia Bank requested financial reports for the last 2 fiscal years. These reports are reproduced below.

BRADBURN CORPORATION
STATEMENT OF FINANCIAL POSITION
MARCH 31

Assets	2011	2010
Plant and equipment (net of depreciation)	$1,449,000	$1,420,500
Inventories (at cost)	105,000	50,000
Accounts receivable (net)	131,800	125,500
Notes receivable	148,000	132,000
Cash	18,200	12,500
Total assets	$1,852,000	$1,740,500

Equity and Liabilities		
Share capital—ordinary (130,000 shares, $10 par)	$1,300,000	$1,300,000
Retained earnings[a]	388,000	282,000
Accrued liabilities	9,000	6,000
Notes payable	76,000	61,500
Accounts payable	79,000	91,000
Total equity and liabilities	$1,852,000	$1,740,500

[a]Cash dividends were paid at the rate of $1 per share in fiscal year 2010 and $2 per share in fiscal year 2011.

BRADBURN CORPORATION
INCOME STATEMENT
FOR THE FISCAL YEARS ENDED MARCH 31

	2011	2010
Sales	$3,000,000	$2,700,000
Cost of goods sold[a]	1,530,000	1,425,000
Gross margin	$1,470,000	$1,275,000
Operating expenses	860,000	780,000
Income before income taxes	$ 610,000	$ 495,000
Income taxes (40%)	244,000	198,000
Net income	$ 366,000	$ 297,000

[a]Depreciation charges on the plant and equipment of $100,000 and $102,500 for fiscal years ended March 31, 2010 and 2011, respectively, are included in cost of goods sold.

Instructions

(a) Compute the following items for Bradburn Corporation.
  (1) Current ratio for fiscal years 2010 and 2011.
  (2) Acid-test (quick) ratio for fiscal years 2010 and 2011.
  (3) Inventory turnover for fiscal year 2011.
  (4) Return on assets for fiscal years 2010 and 2011. (Assume total assets were $1,688,500 at 3/31/09.)
  (5) Percentage change in sales, cost of goods sold, gross margin, and net income after taxes from fiscal year 2010 to 2011.
(b) Identify and explain what other financial reports and/or financial analyses might be helpful to the commercial loan officer of Hibernia Bank in evaluating Daniel Brown's request for a time extension on Bradburn's notes.
(c) Assume that the percentage changes experienced in fiscal year 2011 as compared with fiscal year 2010 for sales and cost of goods sold will be repeated in each of the next 2 years. Is Bradburn's desire to finance the plant expansion from internally generated funds realistic? Discuss.
(d) Should Hibernia Bank grant the extension on Bradburn's notes considering Daniel Brown's statement about financing the plant expansion through internally generated funds? Discuss.

·13 ***P24-4 (Horizontal and Vertical Analysis)** Presented below are comparative statements of financial position for the Gilmour Company.

GILMOUR COMPANY
COMPARATIVE STATEMENTS OF FINANCIAL POSITION
AS OF DECEMBER 31, 2011 AND 2010

	December 31	
	2011	2010
Assets		
Fixed assets	$2,585,000	$1,950,000
Accumulated depreciation	(1,000,000)	(750,000)
Prepaid expenses	25,000	25,000
Inventories	1,060,000	980,000
Accounts receivable (net)	220,000	155,000
Short-term investments	270,000	150,000
Cash	180,000	275,000
	$3,340,000	$2,785,000
Equity and Liabilities		
Share capital—ordinary	$2,100,000	$1,770,000
Retained earnings	570,000	550,000
Bonds payable	450,000	190,000
Accrued expenses	170,000	200,000
Accounts payable	50,000	75,000
	$3,340,000	$2,785,000

Instructions

(Round to two decimal places.)

(a) Prepare a comparative statement of financial position of Gilmour Company showing the percent each item is of the total assets or total liabilities and equity.

(b) Prepare a comparative statement of financial position of Gilmour Company showing the dollar change and the percent change for each item.

(c) Of what value is the additional information provided in part (a)?

(d) Of what value is the additional information provided in part (b)?

•10 *P24-5 (Dividend Policy Analysis)** Matheny Inc. went public 3 years ago. The board of directors will be meeting shortly after the end of the year to decide on a dividend policy. In the past, growth has been financed primarily through the retention of earnings. A share or a cash dividend has never been declared. Presented below is a brief financial summary of Matheny Inc. operations.

	2011	2010	2009	2008	2007
	(€000 omitted)				
Sales	€20,000	€16,000	€14,000	€6,000	€4,000
Net income	2,400	1,400	800	700	250
Average total assets	22,000	19,000	11,500	4,200	3,000
Current assets	8,000	6,000	3,000	1,200	1,000
Working capital	3,600	3,200	1,200	500	400
Ordinary shares:					
Number of shares outstanding (000)	2,000	2,000	2,000	20	20
Average market price	€9	€6	€4	—	—

Instructions

(a) Suggest factors to be considered by the board of directors in establishing a dividend policy.

(b) Compute the rate of return on assets, profit margin on sales, earnings per share, price-earnings ratio, and current ratio for each of the 5 years for Matheny Inc.

(c) Comment on the appropriateness of declaring a cash dividend at this time, using the ratios computed in part (b) as a major factor in your analysis.

CONCEPTS FOR ANALYSIS

CA24-1 (General Disclosures; Inventories; Property, Plant, and Equipment) Koch Corporation is in the process of preparing its annual financial statements for the fiscal year ended April 30, 2011. The company manufactures plastic, glass, and paper containers for sale to food and drink manufacturers and distributors.

Koch Corporation maintains separate control accounts for its raw materials, work in process, and finished goods inventories for each of the three types of containers. The inventories are valued at the lower-of-cost-or-net realizable value.

The company's property, plant, and equipment are classified in the following major categories: land, office buildings, furniture and fixtures, manufacturing facilities, manufacturing equipment, and leasehold improvements. All fixed assets are carried at cost. The depreciation methods employed depend on the type of asset (its classification) and when it was acquired.

Koch Corporation plans to present the inventory and fixed asset amounts in its April 30, 2011, statement of financial position as shown below.

Inventories	$4,814,200
Property, plant, and equipment (net of depreciation)	6,310,000

Instructions

What information regarding inventories and property, plant, and equipment must be disclosed by Koch Corporation in the audited financial statements issued to shareholders, either in the body or the notes, for the 2010–2011 fiscal year?

CA24-2 (Disclosures Required in Various Situations) Ace Inc. produces electronic components for sale to manufacturers of radios, television sets, and digital sound systems. In connection with her examination of Ace's financial statements for the year ended December 31, 2011, Gloria Rodd completed field work 2 weeks ago. Ms. Rodd now is evaluating the significance of the following items prior to preparing her auditor's report. Except as noted, none of these items have been disclosed in the financial statements or notes.

Item 1

A 10-year loan agreement, which the company entered into 3 years ago, provides that dividend payments may not exceed net income earned after taxes subsequent to the date of the agreement. The balance of retained earnings at the date of the loan agreement was €420,000. From that date through December 31, 2011, net income after taxes has totaled €570,000 and cash dividends have totaled €320,000. On the basis of these data, the staff auditor assigned to this review concluded that there was no retained earnings restriction at December 31, 2011.

Item 2

Recently Ace interrupted its policy of paying cash dividends quarterly to its shareholders. Dividends were paid regularly through 2010, discontinued for all of 2011 to finance purchase of equipment for the company's new plant, and resumed in the first quarter of 2012. In the annual report, dividend policy is to be discussed in the president's letter to shareholders.

Item 3

A major electronics firm has introduced a line of products that will compete directly with Ace's primary line, now being produced in the specially designed new plant. Because of manufacturing innovations, the competitor's line will be of comparable quality but priced 50% below Ace's line. The competitor announced its new line during the week following completion of field work (but before the financial statement authorization date). Ms. Rodd read the announcement in the newspaper and discussed the situation by telephone with Ace executives. Ace will meet the lower prices that are high enough to cover variable manufacturing and selling expenses but will permit recovery of only a portion of fixed costs.

Item 4

The company's new manufacturing plant building, which cost €2,400,000 and has an estimated life of 25 years, is leased from Wichita National Bank at an annual rental of €600,000. The company is obligated to pay property taxes, insurance, and maintenance. At the conclusion of its 10-year non-cancelable lease, the company has the option of purchasing the property for €1. In Ace's income statement, the rental payment is reported on a separate line.

Instructions

For each of the items, discuss any additional disclosures in the financial statements and notes that the auditor should recommend to her client. (The cumulative effect of the four items should not be considered.)

CA24-3 **(Disclosures, Conditional and Contingent Liabilities)** Presented below are three independent situations.

Situation 1

A company offers a one-year warranty for the product that it manufactures. A history of warranty claims has been compiled, and the probable amounts of claims related to sales for a given period can be determined.

Situation 2

Subsequent to the date of a set of financial statements, but prior to the authorization of issuance of the financial statements, a company enters into a contract that will probably result in a significant loss to the company. The amount of the loss can be reasonably estimated.

Situation 3

A company has adopted a policy of recording self-insurance for any possible losses resulting from injury to others by the company's vehicles. The premium for an insurance policy for the same risk from an independent insurance company would have an annual cost of £4,000. During the period covered by the financial statements, there were no accidents involving the company's vehicles that resulted in injury to others.

Instructions

Discuss the accrual or type of disclosure necessary (if any) and the reason(s) why such disclosure is appropriate for each of the three independent sets of facts above.

CA24-4 **(Subsequent Events)** At December 31, 2010, Coburn Corp. has assets of $10,000,000, liabilities of $6,000,000, share capital of $2,000,000 (representing 2,000,000 ordinary shares at $1 par), and retained

earnings of $2,000,000. Net sales for the year 2010 were $18,000,000, and net income was $800,000. You are making a review of subsequent events on February 13, 2011, and you find the following.

1. On February 3, 2011, one of Coburn's customers declared bankruptcy. At December 31, 2010, this company owed Coburn $300,000, of which $60,000 was paid in January 2011.
2. On January 18, 2011, one of the three major plants of the client burned.
3. On January 23, 2011, a strike was called at one of Coburn's largest plants, which halted 30% of its production. As of today (February 13), the strike has not been settled.
4. A major electronics enterprise has introduced a line of products that would compete directly with Coburn's primary line, now being produced in a specially designed new plant. Because of manufacturing innovations, the competitor has been able to achieve quality similar to that of Coburn's products, but at a price 50% lower. Coburn officials say they will meet the lower prices, which are high enough to cover variable manufacturing and selling costs but which permit recovery of only a portion of fixed costs.
5. Merchandise traded in the open market is recorded in the company's records at $1.40 per unit on December 31, 2010. This price had prevailed for 2 weeks, after release of an official market report that predicted vastly enlarged supplies; however, no purchases were made at $1.40. The price throughout the preceding year had been about $2, which was the level experienced over several years. On January 18, 2011, the price returned to $2, after public disclosure of an error in the official calculations of the prior December, correction of which destroyed the expectations of excessive supplies. Inventory at December 31, 2010, was on a lower-of-cost-or-net realizable value basis.
6. On February 1, 2011, the board of directors adopted a resolution accepting the offer of an investment banker to guarantee the marketing of $1,200,000 of preference shares.

Instructions

State in each case how the 2010 financial statements would be affected, if at all.

CA24-5 (Segment Reporting) You are compiling the consolidated financial statements for Winsor Corporation International (WCI). The corporation's accountant, Anthony Reese, has provided you with the segment information shown below.

Note 7: Major Segments of Business

WCI conducts funeral service and cemetery operations in the United States and Canada. Substantially all revenues of WCI's major segments of business are from unaffiliated customers. Segment information for fiscal 2011, 2010, and 2009 follows.

	Funeral	Floral	Cemetery	(thousands) Real Estate	Dried Whey	Limousine	Consolidated
Revenues							
2011	$302,000	$10,000	$ 73,000	$ 2,000	$7,000	$12,000	$406,000
2010	245,000	6,000	61,000	4,000	4,000	4,000	324,000
2009	208,000	3,000	42,000	3,000	1,000	3,000	260,000
Operating Income							
2011	74,000	1,500	18,000	(36,000)	500	2,000	60,000
2010	64,000	200	12,000	(28,000)	200	400	48,800
2009	54,000	150	6,000	(21,000)	100	350	39,600
Capital Expenditures							
2011	26,000	1,000	9,000	400	300	1,000	37,700
2010	28,000	2,000	60,000	1,500	100	700	92,300
2009	14,000	25	8,000	600	25	50	22,700
Depreciation and Amortization							
2011	13,000	100	2,400	1,400	100	200	17,200
2010	10,000	50	1,400	700	50	100	12,300
2009	8,000	25	1,000	600	25	50	9,700
Identifiable Assets							
2011	334,000	1,500	162,000	114,000	500	8,000	620,000
2010	322,000	1,000	144,000	52,000	1,000	6,000	526,000
2009	223,000	500	78,000	34,000	500	3,500	339,500

Instructions

Determine which of the above segments must be reported separately and which can be combined under the category "Other." Then, write a one-page memo to the company's accountant, Anthony Reese, explaining the following.

(a) What segments must be reported separately and what segments can be combined.
(b) What criteria you used to determine reportable segments.
(c) What major items for each must be disclosed.

CA24-6 (Segment Reporting—Theory) The following article appeared in the *Wall Street Journal*.

WASHINGTON—The Securities and Exchange Commission staff issued guidelines for companies grappling with the problem of dividing up their business into industry segments for their annual reports.

An industry segment is defined by accounting standards as a part of an enterprise engaged in providing a product or service or a group of related products or services primarily to unaffiliated customers for a profit.

Although conceding that the process is a "subjective task" that "to a considerable extent, depends on the judgment of management," the SEC staff said companies should consider . . . various factors . . . to determine whether products and services should be grouped together or reported as segments.

Instructions

(a) What does financial reporting for segments of a business enterprise involve?
(b) Identify the reasons for requiring financial data to be reported by segments.
(c) Identify the possible disadvantages of requiring financial data to be reported by segments.
(d) Identify the accounting difficulties inherent in segment reporting.

CA24-7 (Interim Reporting) Snider Corporation, a publicly traded company, is preparing the interim financial data which it will issue to its shareholders at the end of the first quarter of the 2010–2011 fiscal year. Snider's financial accounting department has compiled the following summarized revenue and expense data for the first quarter of the year.

Sales	$60,000,000
Cost of goods sold	36,000,000
Variable selling expenses	1,000,000
Fixed selling expenses	3,000,000

Included in the fixed selling expenses was the single lump-sum payment of $2,000,000 for television advertisements for the entire year.

Instructions

(a) Snider Corporation must issue its quarterly financial statements in accordance with IFRS regarding interim financial reporting.
  (1) Explain whether Snider should report its operating results for the quarter as if the quarter were a separate reporting period in and of itself, or as if the quarter were an integral part of the annual reporting period.
  (2) State how the sales, cost of goods sold, and fixed selling expenses would be reflected in Snider Corporation's quarterly report prepared for the first quarter of the 2010–2011 fiscal year. Briefly justify your presentation.
(b) What financial information, as a minimum, must Snider Corporation disclose to its shareholders in its quarterly reports?

CA24-8 (Treatment of Various Interim Reporting Situations) Listed below are six independent cases on how accounting facts might be reported on an individual company's interim financial reports.

Instructions

For each of these cases, state whether the method proposed to be used for interim reporting would be acceptable under IFRS applicable to interim financial data. Support each answer with a brief explanation.

(a) J. D. Long Company takes a physical inventory at year-end for annual financial statement purposes. Inventory and cost of sales reported in the interim quarterly statements are based on estimated gross profit rates, because a physical inventory would result in a cessation of operations. Long Company does have reliable perpetual inventory records.

(b) Rockford Company is planning to report one-fourth of its pension expense each quarter.

(c) Republic Company wrote inventory down to reflect lower-of-cost-or-net realizable value in the first quarter. At year-end, the net realizable value exceeds the original acquisition cost of this inventory. Consequently, management plans to write the inventory back up to its original cost as a year-end adjustment.

(d) Gansner Company realized a large gain on the sale of investments at the beginning of the second quarter. The company wants to report one-third of the gain in each of the remaining quarters.

(e) Fredonia Company has estimated its annual audit fee. It plans to pro rate this expense equally over all four quarters.

(f) LaBrava Company was reasonably certain it would have an employee strike in the third quarter. As a result, it shipped heavily during the second quarter but plans to defer the recognition of the sales in excess of the normal sales volume. The deferred sales will be recognized as sales in the third quarter when the strike is in progress. LaBrava Company management thinks this is more representative of normal second- and third-quarter operations.

CA24-9 (Financial Forecasts) An article in *Barron's* noted the following.

Okay. Last fall, someone with a long memory and an even longer arm reached into that bureau drawer and came out with a moldy cheese sandwich and the equally moldy notion of corporate forecasts. However, the forecast proposal was dusted off, polished up and found quite serviceable. The U.S. SEC, indeed, lost no time in running it up the old flagpole—but no one was very eager to salute. Even after some of the more objectionable features—compulsory corrections and detailed explanations of why the estimates went awry—were peeled off the original proposal.

Seemingly, despite the Commission's smiles and sweet talk, those craven corporations were still afraid that an honest mistake would lead them down the primrose path to consent decrees and class action suits. To lay to rest such qualms, the Commission last week approved a "Safe Harbor" rule that, providing the forecasts were made on a reasonable basis and in good faith, protected corporations from litigation should the projections prove wide of the mark (as only about 99% are apt to do).

Instructions

(a) What are the arguments for preparing profit forecasts?

(b) What is the purpose of the "safe harbor" rule?

(c) Why are corporations concerned about presenting profit forecasts?

CA24-10 (Disclosure of Estimates) Nancy Tercek, the financial vice president, and Margaret Lilly, the controller, of Romine Manufacturing Company are reviewing the financial ratios of the company for the years 2010 and 2011. The financial vice president notes that the profit margin on sales ratio has increased from 6% to 12%, a hefty gain for the 2-year period. Tercek is in the process of issuing a media release that emphasizes the efficiency of Romine Manufacturing in controlling costs. Margaret Lilly knows that the difference in ratios is due primarily to an earlier company decision to reduce the estimates of warranty and bad debt expense for 2011. The controller, not sure of her supervisor's motives, hesitates to suggest to Tercek that the company's improvement is unrelated to efficiency in controlling costs. To complicate matters, the media release is scheduled in a few days.

Instructions

(a) What, if any, is the ethical dilemma in this situation?

(b) Should Lilly, the controller, remain silent? Give reasons.

(c) What stakeholders might be affected by Tercek's media release?

(d) Give your opinion on the following statement and cite reasons: "Because Tercek, the vice president, is most directly responsible for the media release, Lilly has no real responsibility in this matter."

CA24-11 (Reporting of Subsequent Events) In June 2010, the board of directors for McElroy Enterprises Inc. authorized the sale of £10,000,000 of corporate bonds. Jennifer Grayson, treasurer for McElroy Enterprises Inc., is concerned about the date when the bonds are issued. The company really needs the cash, but she is worried that if the bonds are issued before the company's year-end (December 31, 2010) the additional liability will have an adverse effect on a number of important ratios. In July, she explains to company president, William McElroy, that if they delay issuing the bonds until after December 31, the bonds will not affect the ratios until December 31, 2011. They will have to report the issuance as a subsequent event which requires only footnote disclosure. Grayson expects that with expected improved financial performance in 2011 ratios should be better.

Instructions

(a) What are the ethical issues involved?

(b) Should McElroy agree to the delay?

*CA24-12 (Effect of Transactions on Financial Statements and Ratios) The transactions listed below relate to Wainwright Inc. You are to assume that on the date on which each of the transactions occurred, the corporation's accounts showed only ordinary shares ($100 par) outstanding, a current ratio of 2.7:1, and a substantial net income for the year to date (before giving effect to the transaction concerned). On that date, the book value per share was $151.53.

Each numbered transaction is to be considered completely independent of the others, and its related answer should be based on the effect(s) of that transaction alone. Assume that all numbered transactions occurred during 2011 and that the amount involved in each case is sufficiently material to distort reported net income if improperly included in the determination of net income. Assume further that each transaction was recorded in accordance with IFRS and, where applicable, in conformity with the all-inclusive concept of the income statement.

For each of the numbered transactions you are to decide whether it:

a. Increased the corporation's 2011 net income.
b. Decreased the corporation's 2011 net income.
c. Increased the corporation's total retained earnings directly (i.e., not via net income).
d. Decreased the corporation's total retained earnings directly.
e. Increased the corporation's current ratio.
f. Decreased the corporation's current ratio.
g. Increased each shareholder's proportionate share of total equity.
h. Decreased each shareholder's proportionate share of total equity.
i. Increased each shareholder's equity per share (book value).
j. Decreased each shareholder's equity per share (book value).
k. Had none of the foregoing effects.

Instructions

List the numbers 1 through 9. Select as many letters as you deem appropriate to reflect the effect(s) of each transaction as of the date of the transaction by printing beside the transaction number the letter(s) that identifies that transaction's effect(s).

Transactions

___ 1. In January, the board directed the write-off of certain patent rights that had suddenly and unexpectedly become worthless.

___ 2. The corporation sold at a profit land and a building that had been idle for some time. Under the terms of the sale, the corporation received a portion of the sales price in cash immediately, the balance maturing at 6-month intervals.

___ 3. Treasury shares originally repurchased and carried at $127 per share was sold for cash at $153 per share.

___ 4. The corporation wrote off all of the unamortized discount and issue expense applicable to bonds that it refinanced in 2011.

___ 5. The corporation called in all its outstanding ordinary shares and exchanged them for new shares on a 2-for-1 basis, reducing the par value at the same time to $50 per share.

___ 6. The corporation paid a cash dividend that had been recorded in the accounts at time of declaration.

___ 7. Litigation involving Wainwright Inc. as defendant was settled in the corporation's favor, with the plaintiff paying all court costs and legal fees. In 2008, the corporation had appropriately established a special contingency for this court action. (Indicate the effect of reversing the contingency only.)

___ 8. The corporation received a check for the proceeds of an insurance policy from the company with which it is insured against theft of trucks. No entries concerning the theft had been made previously, and the proceeds reduce but do not cover completely the loss.

___ 9. Treasury shares, which had been repurchased at and carried at $127 per share, was issued as a share dividend. In connection with this distribution, the board of directors of Wainwright Inc. had authorized a transfer from retained earnings to permanent share capital of an amount equal to the aggregate market value ($153 per share) of the shares issued. No entries relating to this dividend had been made previously.

USING YOUR JUDGMENT

FINANCIAL REPORTING

Financial Reporting Problem

Marks and Spencer plc (M&S)

As stated in the chapter, notes to the financial statements are the means of explaining the items presented in the main body of the statements. Common note disclosures relate to such items as accounting policies, segmented information, and interim reporting. The financial statements of **M&S** are presented in Appendix 5B or can be accessed at the book's companion website, **www.wiley.com/college/kiesoifrs**.

Instructions

Refer to M&S's financial statements and the accompanying notes to answer the following questions.

(a) What specific items does M&S discuss in its Note 1—Summary of Significant Accounting Policies? (List the headings only.)

(b) For what segments did M&S report segmented information? Which segment is the largest? Who is M&S's largest customer?

(c) What interim information was reported by M&S?

Comparative Analysis Case

Cadbury and Nestlé

Instructions

Go to the book's companion website and use information found there to answer the following questions related to **Cadbury** and **Nestlé**.

(a) **(1)** What specific items does Cadbury discuss in its **Note 1—Accounting Policies**? (Prepare a list of the headings only.)

(2) What specific items does Nestlé discuss in its **Note 2—Our Summary of Significant Accounting Policies**? (Prepare a list of the headings only.)

(b) For what lines of business or segments do Cadbury and Nestlé present segmented information?

(c) Note and comment on the similarities and differences between the auditors' reports submitted by the independent auditors of Cadbury and Nestlé for the year 2008.

*Financial Statement Analysis Case

RNA Inc. manufactures a variety of consumer products. The company's founders have run the company for 30 years and are now interested in retiring. Consequently, they are seeking a purchaser who will continue its operations, and a group of investors, Morgan Inc., is looking into the acquisition of RNA. To evaluate its financial stability and operating efficiency, RNA was requested to provide the latest financial statements and selected financial ratios. Summary information provided by RNA is presented below and on the next page.

RNA
INCOME STATEMENT
FOR THE YEAR ENDED NOVEMBER 30, 2011
(IN THOUSANDS)

Sales (net)	$30,500
Interest income	500
Total revenue	31,000
Costs and expenses	
Cost of goods sold	17,600
Selling and administrative expenses	3,550
Depreciation and amortization expense	1,890
Interest expense	900
Total costs and expenses	23,940
Income before taxes	7,060
Income taxes	2,800
Net income	$ 4,260

RNA
STATEMENT OF FINANCIAL POSITION
AS OF NOVEMBER 30
(IN THOUSANDS)

	2011	2010
Property, plant, & equipment (net)	$ 7,100	$ 7,000
Inventory	6,000	5,400
Accounts receivable (net)	3,200	2,900
Marketable securities (at cost)	300	200
Cash	400	500
Total current assets	9,900	9,000
Total assets	$17,000	$16,000
Share capital—ordinary ($1 par value)	$ 2,700	$ 2,700
Share premium—ordinary	1,000	1,000
Retained earnings	5,000	4,900
Total equity	8,700	8,600
Long-term debt	2,000	1,800
Accrued expenses	1,700	1,400
Income taxes payable	900	800
Accounts payable	3,700	3,400
Total current liabilities	6,300	5,600
Total equity and liabilities	$17,000	$16,000

SELECTED FINANCIAL RATIOS

	RNA		Current Industry
	2010	2009	Average
Current ratio	1.61	1.62	1.63
Acid-test ratio	.64	.63	.68
Times interest earned	8.55	8.50	8.45
Profit margin on sales	13.2%	12.1%	13.0%
Asset turnover	1.84	1.83	1.84
Inventory turnover	3.17	3.21	3.18

Instructions

(a) Calculate a new set of ratios for the fiscal year 2011 for RNA based on the financial statements presented.

(b) Explain the analytical use of each of the six ratios presented, describing what the investors can learn about RNA's financial stability and operating efficiency.

(c) Identify two limitations of ratio analysis.

Accounting, Analysis, and Principles

Savannah, Inc. is a manufacturing company that manufactures and sells a single product. Unit sales for each of the four quarters of 2011 are projected as follows.

Quarter	Units
First	80,000
Second	150,000
Third	550,000
Fourth	120,000
Annual Total	900,000

Savannah incurs variable manufacturing costs of $0.40 per unit and variable non-manufacturing costs of $0.35 per unit. Savannah will incur fixed manufacturing costs of $720,000 and fixed non-manufacturing costs of $1,080,000. Savannah will sell its product for $4.00 per unit.

Accounting

Determine the amount of net income Savannah will report in each of the four quarters of 2011, assuming actual sales are as projected and employing (a) the integral approach to interim financial reporting and (b) the discrete approach to interim financial reporting. Ignore income taxes.

Analysis

Compute Savannah's profit margin on sales for each of the four quarters of 2011. What effect does employing the integral approach instead of the discrete approach have on the degree to which Savannah's profit margin on sales varies from quarter to quarter?

Principles

Should Savannah implement the integral or discrete approach under IFRS? Do you agree? That is, explain the conceptual rationale behind the integral approach to interim financial reporting.

I F R S BRIDGE TO THE PROFESSION

Professional Research

As part of the year-end audit, you are discussing the disclosure checklist with your client. The checklist identifies the items that must be disclosed in a set of IFRS financial statements. The client is surprised by the disclosure item related to accounting policies. Specifically, since the audit report will attest to the statements being prepared in accordance with IFRS, the client questions the accounting policy checklist item. The client has asked you to conduct some research to verify the accounting policy disclosures.

Instructions

Access the IFRS authoritative literature at the IASB website (*http://eifrs.iasb.org/*). When you have accessed the documents, you can use the search tool in your Internet browser to respond to the following questions. (Provide paragraph citations.)

(a) In general, what should disclosures of accounting policies encompass?

(b) List some examples of the most commonly required disclosures.

*Professional Simulation

In this simulation, you are asked to evaluate a company's solvency and going-concern potential by analyzing a set of ratios. You also are asked to indicate possible limitations of ratio analysis. Prepare responses to all parts.

KWW_Professional _Simulation

| Financial Ratio Analysis | Time Remaining 0 hours 40 minutes | copy paste calculator sheet standards help splitter done |

| Directions | Situation | Analysis | Explanation | Resources |

As the accountant for Packard Clipper, Inc. you have been requested to develop some key ratios from the comparative financial statements. This information is to be used to convince creditors that Packard Clipper, Inc. is solvent and to support the use of going-concern valuation procedures in the financial statements.

The data requested and the computations developed from the financial statements follow.

	2010	2009
Current ratio	2.6 times	2.1 times
Acid-test ratio	.8 times	1.3 times
Property, plant and equipment to equity	2.5 times	2.2 times
Sales to equity	2.4 times	2.7 times
Net income	Up 32%	Down 9%
Earnings per share	$3.30	$2.50
Book value per share	Up 6%	Up 9%

| Directions | Situation | Analysis | Explanation | Resources |

Packard Clipper asks you to prepare a list of brief comments stating how each of these items supports the solvency and going-concern potential of the business. The company wishes to use these comments to support its presentation of data to its creditors. You are to prepare the comments as requested, giving the implications and the limitations of each item separately, and then the collective interence that may be drawn from them about Packard Clipper's solvency and going-concern potential.

| Directions | Situation | Analysis | Explanation | Resources |

Having done as the client requested in the Analysis section above, prepare a brief listing of additional ratio-analysis-type data for this client which you think its creditors are going to ask for to supplement the analytical data you provided. Explain why you think the additional data will be helpful to these creditors in evaluating the client's solvency. What warnings should you offer these creditors about the limitations or ratio analysis for the purposes stated here?

Remember to check the book's companion website to find additional resources for this chapter.